Twentieth-Century Literary Criticism

Guide to Gale Literary Criticism Series

When you need to review criticism of literary works, these are the Gale series to use:

If the author's death date is: **You should turn to:**

After Dec. 31, 1959   ***CONTEMPORARY LITERARY CRITICISM***
(or author is still living)
                               for example: Jorge Luis Borges, Anthony Burgess,
                                          Ernest Hemingway, Iris Murdoch

1900 through 1959   ***TWENTIETH-CENTURY LITERARY CRITICISM***

                               for example: Willa Cather, F. Scott Fitzgerald,
                                          Henry James, Mark Twain, Virginia Woolf

1800 through 1899   ***NINETEENTH-CENTURY LITERATURE CRITICISM***

                               for example: Fyodor Dostoevsky, Nathaniel Hawthorne,
                                          George Sand, William Wordsworth

1400 through 1799   ***LITERATURE CRITICISM FROM 1400 TO 1800***
                               (excluding Shakespeare)

                               for example: Anne Bradstreet, Alexander Pope,
                                          François Rabelais, Phillis Wheatley

                               SHAKESPEAREAN CRITICISM

                                          Shakespeare's plays and poetry

Antiquity through 1399   ***CLASSICAL AND MEDIEVAL LITERATURE CRITICISM***

                               for example: Dante, Homer, Plato, Sophocles, Vergil

Gale also publishes related criticism series:

CHILDREN'S LITERATURE REVIEW

This series covers authors of all eras who have written for the preschool through high school audience.

SHORT STORY CRITICISM

This series covers the major short fiction writers of all nationalities and periods of literary history.

POETRY CRITICISM

This series covers poets of all nationalities, movements, and periods of literary history.

DRAMA CRITICISM

This series covers playwrights of all nationalities and periods of literary history.

BLACK LITERATURE CRITICISM

This three-volume set presents criticism of works by major black writers of the past two hundred years.

WORLD LITERATURE CRITICISM, 1500 TO THE PRESENT

This six-volume set provides excerpts from criticism on 225 authors from the Renaissance to the present.

ISSN 0276-8178

R

Volume 47

Twentieth-Century Literary Criticism

**Excerpts from Criticism of the
Works of Novelists, Poets, Playwrights,
Short Story Writers, and Other Creative Writers
Who Lived between 1900 and 1960,
from the First Published Critical
Appraisals to Current Evaluations**

**Laurie DiMauro
Editor**

**Tina Grant
Elizabeth Henry
Jelena Krstović
Marie Lazzari
Thomas Ligotti
Kyung-Sun Lim
Sean René Pollack
David Segal
Robyn V. Young
Associate Editors**

 Gale Research Inc. • *DETROIT* • *WASHINGTON, D.C.* • *LONDON*

STAFF

Laurie DiMauro, *Editor*

Tina Grant, Elizabeth Henry, Jelena Krstović, Marie Lazzari, Thomas Ligotti, Kyung-Sun Lim, Sean René Pollack, David Segal, Robyn V. Young, *Associate Editors*

Paul Buczkowski, James A. Edwards, Jennifer Gariepy, Ian A. Goodhall, Kathryn Horste, Michael Magoulias, Dale Miller, Alexander Sweda, *Assistant Editors*

Jeanne A. Gough, *Permissions & Production Manager*

Linda M. Pugliese, *Production Supervisor*

Paul Lewon, Maureen Puhl, Camille Robinson,
Jennifer VanSickle, *Editorial Associates*

Donna Craft, Rosita D'Souza, Sheila Walencewicz, *Editorial Assistants*

Sandra C. Davis, *Permissions Supervisor (Text)*

Maria L. Franklin, Josephine M. Keene, Michele Lonoconus, Denise M. Singleton, Kimberly F. Smilay,
Permissions Associates

Brandy C. Merritt, Shalice Shah, *Permissions Assistants*

Margaret A. Chamberlain, *Permissions Supervisor (Pictures)*

Pamela A. Hayes, *Permissions Associate*

Karla Kulkis, Nancy Rattenbury, Keith Reed, *Permissions Assistants*

Victoria B. Cariappa, *Research Manager*

Maureen Richards, *Research Supervisor*

Robert S. Lazich, Mary Beth McElmeel, Tamara C. Nott, *Editorial Associates*

Andrea B. Ghorai, Daniel J. Jankowski, Julie K. Karmazin, Donna Melnychenko, *Editorial Assistants*

Mary Beth Trimper, *Production Director*

Catherine Kemp, *Production Assistant*

Cynthia Baldwin, *Art Director*

Nicholas Jakubiak, C. J. Jonik, *Keyliners*

Since this page cannot legibly accommodate all copyright notices, the acknowledgments constitute an extension of the copyright notice.

While every effort has been made to ensure the reliability of the information presented in this publication, Gale Research Inc. neither guarantees the accuracy of the data contained herein nor assumes any responsibility for errors, omissions, or discrepancies. Gale accepts no payment for listing; and inclusion in the publication of any organization, agency, institution, publication, service, or individual does not imply endorsement of the editors or publisher. Errors brought to the attention of the publisher and verified to the satisfaction of the publisher will be corrected in future editions.

The paper used in this publication meets the minimum requirements of American National Standard for Information Sciences—Permanence Paper for Printed Library Materials, ANSI Z39.48-1984. ∞™

Copyright © 1993
Gale Research Inc.
835 Penobscot Building
Detroit, MI 48226-4094

Library of Congress Catalog Card Number 76-46132
ISBN 0-8103-8912-6 (set)
ISBN 0-8103-7972-4 (main volume)
ISBN 0-8103-8911-8 (index)
ISSN 0276-8178

Printed in the United States of America

Published simultaneously in the United Kingdom
by Gale Research International Limited
(An affiliated company of Gale Research Inc.)

Contents

Preface   vii

Acknowledgments   xi

Ray Stannard Baker (1870-1946) 1
  American journalist and biographer

Maurice Barrès (1862-1923) 34
  French novelist and essayist

George Gissing (1857-1903) 101
  English novelist; entry devoted to New Grub Street

Henry James (1843-1916) 147
  American novelist and short story writer

Franz Kafka (1883-1924) 210
  Austro-Czech novelist; entry devoted to Das Schloss (The Castle)

Frigyes Karinthy (1887-1938) 265
  Hungarian humorist

Edwin Markham (1852-1940) 274
  American poet

Rafael Sabatini (1875-1950) 298
  English novelist and playwright

Frank R. Stockton (1834-1902) 310
  American short story writer and novelist

August Strindberg (1849-1912) 334
  Swedish dramatist; entry devoted to Fröken Julie (Miss Julie)

Yokomitsu Riichi (1898-1947) 385
  Japanese novelist and short story writer

Literary Criticism Series Cumulative Author Index   403

Literary Criticism Series Cumulative Topic Index   469

TCLC Cumulative Nationality Index   475

Preface

Since its inception more than ten years ago, *Twentieth-Century Literary Criticism* has been purchased and used by nearly 10,000 school, public, and college or university libraries. *TCLC* has covered more than 500 authors, representing 58 nationalities, and over 25,000 titles. No other reference source has surveyed the critical response to twentieth-century authors and literature as thoroughly as *TCLC*. In the words of one reviewer, "there is nothing comparable available." *TCLC* "is a gold mine of information—dates, pseudonyms, biographical information, and criticism from books and periodicals—which many libraries would have difficulty assembling on their own."

Scope of the Series

TCLC is designed to serve as an introduction to authors who died between 1900 and 1960 and to the most significant interpretations of these authors' works. The great poets, novelists, short story writers, playwrights, and philosophers of this period are frequently studied in high school and college literature courses. In organizing and excerpting the vast amount of critical material written on these authors, *TCLC* helps students develop valuable insight into literary history, promotes a better understanding of the texts, and sparks ideas for papers and assignments. Each entry in *TCLC* presents a comprehensive survey of an author's career or an individual work of literature and provides the user with a multiplicity of interpretations and assessments. Such variety allows students to pursue their own interests; furthermore, it fosters an awareness that literature is dynamic and responsive to many different opinions.

Every fourth volume of *TCLC* is devoted to literary topics that cannot be covered under the author approach used in the rest of the series. Such topics include literary movements, prominent themes in twentieth-century literature, literary reaction to political and historical events, significant eras in literary history, prominent literary anniversaries, and the literatures of cultures that are often overlooked by English-speaking readers.

TCLC is designed as a companion series to Gale's *Contemporary Literary Criticism,* which reprints commentary on authors now living or who have died since 1960. Because of the different periods under consideration, there is no duplication of material between *CLC* and *TCLC*. For additional information about *CLC* and Gale's other criticism titles, users should consult the Guide to Gale Literary Criticism Series preceding the title page in this volume.

Coverage

Each volume of *TCLC* is carefully compiled to present:

- criticism of authors, or literary topics, representing a variety of genres and nationalities

- both major and lesser-known writers and literary works of the period

- 10-15 authors or 4-6 topics per volume

- individual entries that survey critical response to each author's work or each topic in literary history, including early criticism to reflect initial reactions; later criticism to represent any rise or decline in reputation; and current retrospective analyses.

Organization of This Book

An author entry consists of the following elements: author heading, biographical and critical introduction, list of principal works, excerpts of criticism (each preceded by an annotation and followed by a bibliographic citation), and a bibliography of further reading.

- The **author heading** consists of the name under which the author most commonly wrote, followed by birth and death dates. If an author wrote consistently under a pseudonym, the pseudonym will be listed in the author heading and the real name given in parentheses on the first line of the biographical and critical introduction. Also located at the beginning of the introduction to the author entry are any name variations under which an author wrote, including transliterated forms for authors whose languages use nonroman alphabets.

• The **biographical and critical introduction** outlines the author's life and career, as well as the critical issues surrounding his or her work. References to past volumes of *TCLC* are provided at the beginning of the introduction. Additional sources of information in other biographical and critical reference series published by Gale, including *Children's Literature Review, Contemporary Authors, Dictionary of Literary Biography, Short Story Criticism,* and *Something about the Author,* are listed in a box at the end of the entry.

• Most *TCLC* entries include **portraits** of the author. Many entries also contain reproductions of materials pertinent to an author's career, including manuscript pages, title pages, dust jackets, letters, and drawings, as well as photographs of important people, places, and events in an author's life.

• The **list of principal works** is chronological by date of first book publication and identifies the genre of each work. In the case of foreign authors with both foreign-language publications and English translations, the title and date of the first English-language edition are given in brackets. Unless otherwise indicated, dramas are dated by first performance, not first publication.

• **Criticism** is arranged chronologically in each author entry to provide a perspective on changes in critical evaluation over the years. All titles of works by the author featured in the entry are printed in boldface type to enable the user to easily locate discussion of particular works. Also for purposes of easier identification, the critic's name and the publication date of the essay are given at the beginning of each piece of criticism. Unsigned criticism is preceded by the title of the journal in which it appeared. Publication information (such as publisher names and book prices) and parenthetical numerical references (such as footnotes or page and line references to specific editions of works) have been deleted at the editors' discretion to provide smoother reading of the text.

• Critical excerpts are prefaced by **annotations** providing the reader with information about both the critic and the criticism that follows. Included are the critic's reputation, individual approach to literary criticism, and particular expertise in an author's works. Also noted are the relative importance of a work of criticism, the scope of the excerpt, and the growth of critical controversy or changes in critical trends regarding an author. In some cases, these annotations cross-reference excerpts by critics who discuss each other's commentary.

• A complete **bibliographic citation** designed to facilitate location of the original essay or book follows each piece of criticism.

• An annotated list of **further reading** appearing at the end of each author entry suggests secondary sources on the author. In some cases it includes essays for which the editors could not obtain reprint rights.

Cumulative Indexes

• Each volume of *TCLC* contains a cumulative **author index** listing all authors who have appeared in Gale's Literary Criticism Series, along with cross-references to such biographical series as *Contemporary Authors* and *Dictionary of Literary Biography.* For readers' convenience, a complete list of Gale titles included appears on the first page of the author index. Useful for locating authors within the various series, this index is particularly valuable for those authors who are identified by a certain period but who, because of their death dates, are placed in another, or for those authors whose careers span two periods. For example, F. Scott Fitzgerald is found in *TCLC,* yet a writer often associated with him, Ernest Hemingway, is found in *CLC.*

• Each *TCLC* volume includes a cumulative **nationality index** which lists all authors who have appeared in *TCLC* volumes, arranged alphabetically under their respective nationalities, as well as Topics volume entries devoted to particular national literatures.

• Each new volume in Gale's Literary Criticism Series includes a cumulative **topic index,** which lists all literary topics treated in *Nineteenth-Century Literature Criticism, TCLC, Literature Criticism from 1400-1800,* and the *CLC* Yearbook.

• Each new volume of *TCLC,* with the exception of the Topics volumes, contains a **title index** listing the titles of all literary works discussed in the volume. In response to numerous suggestions from librarians, Gale has also produced a **special paperbound edition** of the *TCLC* title index. This annual cumulation lists all titles discussed in the series since its inception and is issued with the first volume of *TCLC* published each year. Additional copies of the index are available on request. Librarians and patrons have welcomed this separate index: it saves shelf space, is easy to use, and is recyclable upon receipt of the following year's cumulation. Titles discussed in the Topics volume entries are not included in the *TCLC* cumulative index.

A Note to the Reader

When writing papers, students who quote directly from any volume in Gale's Literary Criticism Series may use the following general forms to footnote reprinted criticism. The first example pertains to material drawn from periodicals, the second to material reprinted from books.

[1] T. S. Eliot, "John Donne," *The Nation and the Athenaeum,* 33 (9 June 1923), 321-32; excerpted and reprinted in *Literature Criticism from 1400 to 1800,* Vol. 10, ed. James E. Person, Jr. (Detroit: Gale Research, 1989), pp. 28-9.

[2] Clara G. Stillman, *Samuel Butler: A Mid-Victorian Modern* (Viking Press, 1932); excerpted and reprinted in *Twentieth-Century Literary Criticism,* Vol. 33, ed. Paula Kepos (Detroit: Gale Research, 1989), pp. 43-5.

Suggestions Are Welcome

In response to suggestions, several features have been added to *TCLC* since the series began, including annotations to excerpted criticism, a cumulative index to authors in all Gale literary criticism series, entries devoted to criticism on a single work by a major author, more extensive illustrations, and a title index listing all literary works discussed in the series since its inception.

Readers who wish to suggest authors or topics to appear in future volumes, or who have other suggestions, are cordially invited to write the editors.

Acknowledgments

The editors wish to thank the copyright holders of the excerpted criticism included in this volume, the permissions managers of many book and magazine publishing companies for assisting us in securing reprint rights, and Anthony Bogucki for assistance with copyright research. We are also grateful to the staffs of the Detroit Public Library, Wayne State University Purdy/Kresge Library Complex, and the University of Michigan Libraries for making their resources available to us. Following is a list of the copyright holders who have granted us permission to reprint material in the volume of *TCLC*. Every effort has been made to trace copyright, but if omissions have been made, please let us know.

COPYRIGHTED EXCERPTS IN *TCLC*, VOLUME 47, WERE REPRINTED FROM THE FOLLOWING PERIODICALS:

The Antioch Review, v. XXIII, Winter, 1963-64. Copyright © 1964 by the Antioch Review Inc. Reprinted by permission of the Editors.—*Boston University Journal,* v. XXIII, 1975 for "Dada and the 'Trial' of Maurice Barrès" by Frederick Busi. Copyright 1975 by the Trustees of Boston University. Reprinted by permission of the author.— *Cahiers Victoriens & Edouardiens,* n. 24, October, 1986. All rights reserved. Reprinted by permission of the publisher.—*The Central States Speech Journal,* v. XXI, Summer, 1970. Copyright 1970 by the Central States Speech Association. Reprinted by permission of the publisher.—*The Drama Review,* Winter, 1968, for "Strindberg and the Greater Naturalism" by Evert Sprinchorn. Copyright © 1968, *The Drama Review*. Reprinted by permission of The MIT Press, Cambridge, MA, and the author.—*The Explicator,* v. 48, Spring, 1990. Copyright 1990 by Helen Dwight Reid Educational Foundation./ v. 42, Spring, 1984; v. 45, Fall, 1986. Copyright 1984, 1986 by Helen Dwight Reid Educational Foundation. Both reprinted with permission of the Helen Dwight Reid Educational Foundation, published by Heldref Publications, 1319 18th Street, NW, Washington, DC 20036-1802.—*Forum for Modern Language Studies,* v. IV, October, 1968 for "Sartre and Barrès: Some Notes on 'La Nausée' " by Dennis J. Fletcher. Copyright © 1968 by *Forum for Modern Language Studies* and the author. Reprinted by permission of the publisher and the author.—*The Gissing Newsletter,* v. 21, January, 1985 for "Authorial Intrusion in Gissing's 'New Grub Street' " by Eugene M. Baer. Reprinted by permission of the publisher and the author./ July, 1978. Reprinted by permission of the publisher.—*The Henry James Review,* v. 8, Spring, 1982. © 1983 The Henry James Society. All rights reserved. Reprinted by permission of the publisher./ v. 11, Fall, 1990. © 1990 by The Johns Hopkins University Press. Reprinted by permission of the publisher.—*The Hudson Review,* v. XL, Autumn, 1987. Copyright © 1987 by The Hudson Review, Inc. Reprinted by permission of the publisher.—*Journal of European Studies,* v. 2, March, 1972 for "The Undiscover'd Country: The Death Motif in Kafka's 'Castle' " by W. G. Sebald. Copyright © 1972 Seminar Press Limited. Reprinted by permission of the author.—*Journal of Modern Literature,* v. 6, September, 1977. © Temple University 1977. Reprinted by permission of the publisher.—*Journalism History,* v. 9, Autumn-Winter, 1982 for "The Muckrakers and Lynching: A Case Study in Racism" by Maurine Beasley. Copyright © 1982 by CSUN Foundation. All rights reserved. Reprinted by permission of the author.—*The Lion and the Unicorn,* v. 12, December, 1988. Copyright © 1988 *The Lion and the Unicorn*. Reprinted by permission of the publisher.— *The Midwest Quarterly,* v. XXXIII, Autumn, 1991. Copyright 1991, by *The Midwest Quarterly,* Pittsburg State University. Reprinted by permission of the publisher.—*Modern Drama,* v. XXVI, September, 1983. Copyright 1983 *Modern Drama,* University of Toronto. Reprinted by permission of the publisher.—*The Modern Language Review,* v. 64, July, 1969. © Modern Humanities Association 1969. Reprinted by permission of the publisher.—*The Nation,* New York, v. CLXXXII, March 10, 1956. Copyright 1956 *The Nation* magazine/ The Nation Company, Inc. Reprinted by permission of the publisher.—*Neophilologus,* v. LXXIV, January, 1990. © 1990 by Wolters-Noordhoff bv. Reprinted by permission of the publisher.—*New Literary History,* v. XV, Autumn, 1983. Copyright © 1983 by *New Literary History*. Reprinted by permission of the publisher.—*The New York Review of Books,* v. XXX, January 19, 1984 for "Return to 'The Golden Bowl' " by Gore Vidal. Copyright © 1984 Gore Vidal. Reprinted with permission from *The New York Review of Books./* v. XXXVIII, April 25, 1991 for "A Fine Romance" by Alison Lurie. Copyright © 1991 by Alison Lurie. Used by permission of Melanie Jackson Agency./ v. XXXVIII, October 10, 1991. Copyright © 1991 Nyrev, Inc. Reprinted with permission from *The New York Review of Books.*— *Nineteenth-Century Fiction,* v. 25, September, 1970 for " 'The Valley of Books': Alienation in Gissing's 'New Grub Street' " by Robert L. Selig. © 1970 by the Regents of the University of California. Reprinted by permission of The Regents and the author.—*Nineteenth-Century French Studies,* v. XIII, Summer, 1985. © 1985 by T. H. Goetz. Reprinted by permission of the publisher.—*Nottingham French Studies,* v. 21, October, 1982. Reprinted by permission of the publisher.—*Scandinavian Studies,* v. 60, Winter, 1988 for "Rereading 'Fröken Julie': Undercurrents in Strindberg's Naturalistic Intent" by John Eric Bellquist. Reprinted by permission of the publisher and the author.—*South Atlantic Quarterly,* v. 78, Spring, 1979. Copyright © 1979 by Duke University Press, Durham, NC. Reprinted by permission of the publisher.—*Southwest Review,* v. 74, Spring, 1989 for "Henry James and the Battle of the Sexes" by Wendy Lesser. © 1989 Wendy Lesser. Reprinted by permission of the author.—*Studies in American Fiction,* v. 15, Autumn, 1988. Copyright © 1988 Northeastern University. Reprinted by permission of the publisher.—*Theatre Journal,* v. 42, December, 1990. © 1990, University and College Theatre Association of the American Theatre Association. Reprinted by permission of the publisher.

COPYRIGHTED EXCERPTS IN *TCLC,* VOLUME 47, WERE REPRINTED FROM THE FOLLOWING BOOKS:

Baker, Ray Stannard. From *American Chronicle: The Autobiography of Ray Stannard Baker [David Grayson.]* Charles Scribner's Sons, 1945. Copyright, 1945, by Ray Stannard Baker. Renewed 1972 by Rachel Baker Napier. All rights reserved. Reprinted with the permission of Charles Scribner's Sons, an imprint of Macmillan Publishing Company.—Bannister, Robert C., Jr. From *Ray Stannard Baker: The Mind and Thought of a Progressive.* Yale University Press, 1966. Copyright © 1966 by Yale University. All rights reserved. Reprinted by permission of the publisher.—Bayley, John. From an introduction to *The Wings of the Dove.* By Henry James, edited by John Bayley. Penguin Books, 1986. Introduction copyright © John Bayley, 1986. All rights reserved. Reproduced by permission of Penguin Books Ltd.—Bernheimer, Charles. From "Symbolic Bond and Textual Play: Structure of 'The Castle'," in *The Kafka Debate: New Perspectives for Our Time.* Edited by Angel Flores. Gordian Press, 1977. Copyright © 1977 Angel Flores. All rights reserved. Reprinted by permission of the publisher.—Brustein, Robert. From *The Theatre of Revolt: An Approach to the Modern Drama.* Little, Brown and Company, 1964. Copyright © 1962, 1963, 1964 by Robert Brustein. All rights reserved. Reprinted by permission of the author.—Buckley, Jerome H. From "A World of Literature: Gissing's 'New Grub Street'," in *The Worlds of Victorian Fiction.* Edited by Jerome H. Buckley. Cambridge, Mass.: Harvard University Press, 1975. Copyright © 1975 by the President and Fellows of Harvard College. All rights reserved. Excerpted by permission of the publisher.—Filler, Louis. From *The Muckrakers.* Revised edition. Pennsylvania State University Press, 1976. New and Enlarged copyright © 1976 by Louis Filler. Reprinted by permission of the author.—Gissing, George. From a letter in *The Letters of George Gissing to Eduard Bertz, 1887-1903.* Edited by Arthur C. Young. Rutgers University Press, 1961. Copyright © 1961 by Rutgers, The State University. All rights reserved. Reprinted by permission of the publisher.—Golemba, Henry L. From *Frank R. Stockton.* Twayne, 1981. Copyright © 1981 by G. K. Hall & Co. All rights reserved. Reprinted with permission of Twayne Publishers, an imprint of Macmillan Publishing Company.—Grantham, Dewey W. From an introduction to *Following the Color Line: American Negro Citizenship in the Progressive Era.* By Ray Stannard Baker. Harper and Row, 1964. Introduction to the Torchbook edition copyright © 1964 by Dewey W. Grantham, Jr. Reprinted by permission of HarperCollins Publishers, Inc.—Greenberg, Martin. From *The Terror of Art: Kafka and Modern Literature.* Basic Books, 1968. © 1965, 1966, 1968 by Martin Greenberg. Reprinted by permission of Basic Books, a division of HarperCollins Publishers, Inc.—Grylls, David. From *The Paradox of Gissing.* Allen & Unwin, 1986. © David Grylls, 1986. All rights reserved. Reprinted by permission of the publisher.—Heller, Erich. From *Franz Kafka.* The Viking Press, 1975. Copyright © 1974 by Erich Heller. All rights reserved. Used by permission of Viking Penguin, a division of Penguin Books USA Inc. In Canada by the Literary Estate of Erich Heller.—Hughson, Lois. From *From Biography to History: The Historical Imagination and American Fiction, 1880-1940.* University Press of Virginia, 1988. Copyright © 1988 by the Rector and Visitors of the University of Virginia. Reprinted by permission of the publisher.—James, Henry. From a letter in *Henry James: The Critical Heritage.* Edited by Roger Gard. Routledge & Kegan Paul Limited, 1968. © Roger Gard 1968. Reprinted by permission of the publisher.—James, William. From a letter in *Henry James: The Critical Heritage.* Edited by Roger Gard. Routledge & Kegan Paul Limited, 1968. © Roger Gard 1968. Reprinted by permission of the publisher.—Keating, P. J. From *George Gissing: "New Grub Street."* Edward Arnold (Publishers) Ltd., 1968. © P. J. Keating, 1968. Reprinted by permission of the publisher.—Keene, Dennis. From an introduction to *"Love" and Other Stories of Yokomitsu Riichi.* Translated by Dennis Keene. University of Tokyo Press, 1974. English translation © 1974 The Japan Foundation. All rights reserved. Reprinted by permission of The Japan Foundation, Dennis Keene, and Shozo Yokomitsu.—Keene, Donald. From *Dawn to the West, Japanese Literature of the Modern Era: Fiction, Vol. 1.* Holt, Rinehart and Winston, 1984. Copyright © 1984 by Donald Keene. All rights reserved. Reprinted by permission of Henry Holt and Company, Inc.—Kidd, Bill. From *Vichy France and the Resistance: Culture & Ideology.* Edited by Roderick Kedward and Roger Austin. Croom Helm, 1985. © 1985 Roderick Kedward and Roger Austin. Reprinted by permission of the publisher.—Krog, Jacob. From *George Gissing: A Critical Biography.* University of Washington Press, 1963. Copyright © 1963 by the University of Washington Press. Reprinted by permission of the publisher.—Lamm, Martin. From *August Strindberg.* Edited and translated by Harry G. Carlson. Blom, 1971. © 1971 by Benjamin Blom, Inc., New York, N.Y. 10025. All rights reserved. Reprinted by permission of the translator.—Lippit, Noriko Mizuta. From *Reality and Fiction in Modern Japanese Literature.* Sharpe, 1980. Copyright © 1980 by M. E. Sharpe, Inc. All rights reserved. Reprinted by permission of the publisher.—Mailloux, Peter. From *A Hesitation before Birth: The Life of Franz Kafka.* University of Delaware Press, 1989. © 1989 by Associated University Presses, Inc. Reprinted by permission of the publisher.—Michaux, Jean-Pierre. From "Names in 'New Grub Street'," in *George Gissing: Critical Essays.* Edited by Jean-Pierre Michaux. London: Vision Press, 1981. © 1981 by Vision Press Ltd. All rights reserved. Reprinted by permis-

PHOTOGRAPHS AND ILLUSTRATIONS APPEARING IN *TCLC,* VOLUME 47, WERE RECEIVED FROM THE FOLLOWING SOURCES:

Ray Stannard Baker

1870-1946

(Also wrote under the pseudonym David Grayson) American journalist, biographer, novelist, and autobiographer.

INTRODUCTION

Baker was one of the most prominent journalists of the early twentieth-century muckraking movement, which popularized investigations of allegedly unethical conduct in business, government, and organized labor. Baker also wrote the official biography of Woodrow Wilson and, under the pseudonym David Grayson, enjoyed great popular success as the author of sketches on the virtues of country living, hard work, and appreciation of nature. Among his contemporaries, according to Louis Filler, Baker "was known as the greatest reporter in America."

Baker was born in Lansing, Michigan, and raised in St. Croix Falls, Wisconsin. He graduated from Michigan State College (now Michigan State University) in 1889 and pursued graduate studies in law and literature at the University of Michigan. From 1892 to 1897 Baker worked as a reporter for the Chicago *Record,* where he began writing about social and economic issues after witnessing the labor unrest and unemployment occasioned by a national economic depression. During this time he accompanied and reported on Coxey's Army, a group of four hundred unemployed laborers who marched from Ohio to Washington, D.C., to petition the government to fund public works projects. He also covered the Pullman Palace Car Company workers' strike, during which he was present in a crowd of demonstrators who were fired upon by federal troops. In 1898 Baker was hired to write for the New York–based *McClure's Magazine,* to which he contributed articles over the next eight years, becoming well-known for his investigations of civic and corporate wrongdoing. In the January 1903 issue of *McClure's,* an editorial by publisher S. S. McClure on the subject of "American contempt of law" introduced articles by Baker ("The Right to Work"), Ida Tarbell (an installment of *The History of the Standard Oil Company*), and Lincoln Steffens ("The Shame of Minneapolis"), marking what is widely regarded as the beginning of the muckraking era. Baker's work brought him to the attention of President Theodore Roosevelt, who invited him to Washington to discuss corruption in government-sponsored public works programs, beginning a friendship and correspondence that lasted for many years.

In 1906 Baker, Tarbell, and other members of the *McClure's* staff purchased the *American Magazine,* and over the next decade Baker traveled extensively in his dual role as editor and contributor. During this time he continued to explore social and political issues, producing articles on race relations that he later published as *Following the*

Color Line. He also wrote a series of sketches in the persona of a farmer named David Grayson, which were published serially in the *American* and collected in the volume *Adventures in Contentment.* The sketches were a popular success, and Baker published nine Grayson books between 1907 and 1942. In 1919 Baker was selected to serve as President Woodrow Wilson's director of the press bureau for the Paris Peace Conference at which the settlement of World War I was negotiated; he wrote two books, *What Wilson Did at Paris* and *Woodrow Wilson and World Settlement,* documenting the proceedings. Subsequently Wilson chose Baker to be his official biographer. The researching and writing of the eight-volume *Woodrow Wilson: Life and Letters* occupied fourteen years of Baker's career, and he was awarded the Pulitzer Prize for biography in 1940. During the last seven years of his life, Baker wrote the autobiographies *Native American: The Book of My Youth* and *American Chronicle.* He died of a heart attack in Amherst, Massachusetts, in 1946.

Criticism of Baker's works may be divided into discussions of the David Grayson fiction and analyses of the journalistic works. Familiar in tone and optimistic in outlook, Baker's fictional sketches feature the ruminations of

David Grayson, a former city dweller who has moved to a farm where he learns to appreciate nature and the common people he encounters. For years Baker's authorship of the series was kept a secret, and when in 1916 he publicly acknowledged it as his work, critics and readers expressed surprise that a journalist generally known for covering urban and industrial problems had produced the emotional reflections on rural life found in the Grayson sketches. As Robert C. Bannister Jr. has noted, these works "had a phenomenal ability to reach the reader and provoke his response"; many readers felt a personal friendship with the Grayson persona and some formed social clubs dedicated to upholding Grayson's beliefs. While many early critics responded favorably as well, some found his depiction of the joys of country life to be unrealistic. Since that time, critics have compared Baker's nonfiction with his Grayson works, typically approaching Grayson as Baker's alter ego.

Examinations of Baker's nonfiction generally focus on his presentation of fact and opinion. Baker referred to his journalistic work as "fact articles," and critics have regarded them as detailed and comprehensive. Baker's muckraking journalism has been praised for its relatively moderate approach to political and economic issues and its avoidance of oversimplifications and generalizations. Of "The Right to Work," in which he examined an instance of union and business leaders acting in concert to the economic disadvantage of consumers and nonunion labor, Baker wrote that he "did not wish to be making ammunition for mere stupid opposition to all labor organizations, or even all strikes." However, like most muckrakers, Baker was criticized for failing to propose solutions to the political and economic problems that he addressed. In *Following the Color Line* Baker examined the growing separation of the races in America in essays describing everyday life in black communities and incidents of racially motivated violence. Contemporary African-American leaders, including Booker T. Washington and W. E. B. DuBois, admired this work for its documentation of discrimination in both the North and the South, and Baker was made an honorary member of the NAACP in 1915. Some recent critics, however, have cited stereotypical racial characterizations throughout the work and have charged that Baker's commentary on incidents of lynching fails to sufficiently condemn those responsible. Nonetheless, most have praised it as an important and insightful treatment of race relations, agreeing with Maurine Beasley that "It would be unfair to judge Baker a bigot for failing to transcend the assumptions of his era." While Baker's works on the Paris Peace Conference and his biography of Wilson were praised for their careful documentation, critics generally agree that his strong admiration for Wilson resulted in a loss of objectivity and an idealization of the Wilson presidency. Overall, Baker's nonfiction is considered valuable for its documentation of an era of American history that was characterized by public interest in the reform of social, political, and economic institutions.

PRINCIPAL WORKS

Our New Prosperity (nonfiction) 1900

Seen in Germany (travel essay) 1901
Adventures in Contentment [as David Grayson] (sketches) 1907
Following the Color Line: An Account of Negro Citizenship in American Democracy (nonfiction) 1908
New Ideals in Healing (nonfiction) 1909
Adventures in Friendship [as David Grayson] (sketches) 1910
The Spiritual Unrest (nonfiction) 1910
The Friendly Road: New Adventures in Contentment [as David Grayson] (sketches) 1913
Hempfield [as David Grayson] (novel) 1915
Great Possessions [as David Grayson] (sketches) 1917
What Wilson Did At Paris (journalism) 1919
The New Industrial Unrest (nonfiction) 1920
Woodrow Wilson and World Settlement. 3 vols. (journalism) 1922
Adventures in Understanding [as David Grayson] (sketches) 1925
An American Pioneer in Science: The Life and Service of William James Beal [with Jessie Beal Baker] (biography) 1925
Woodrow Wilson: Life and Letters. 8 vols. (biography) 1927-39
Adventures in Solitude [as David Grayson] (sketches) 1931
The Countryman's Year [as David Grayson] (sketches) 1936
Native American: The Book of My Youth (autobiography) 1941
Under My Elm [as David Grayson] (sketches) 1942
American Chronicle (autobiography) 1945

CRITICISM

Mary S. Watts   (essay date 1908)

[*In the following review of* Adventures in Contentment, *a work that Baker wrote under the pseudonym David Grayson, Watts regards Baker's depiction of country life as simplistic.*]

Adventures in Contentment might be described as a sort of literary grandchild of *Prue and I,* recalling the older book by a vague elusive resemblance in style, and leaving the reader with the same strong impression of its author's character, kind, temperate, cheerful, serenely humorous and most humane. Few people, of late years at any rate, have read *Prue and I* twice—few people, it may be, have read it even once; yet an American library would hardly be complete without it. It poses on the shelf with something of the genteel charm of a daguerreotype; it runs a chance of one day being taken down and reread; and *Adventures in Contentment* will probably occupy, as time goes on, exactly the same position. That it has an expectation of being read again in five or ten years is much to say of any book, now; it goes near to claiming immortality. We shall remember *Adventures in Contentment,* as we remember the other, not for a single seizing word or phrase, for of neither book, even upon a recent reading, can we recall one; but for the singular pleasure we had in making the acquaintance of the writer.

This little volume purports to be a record, entered at random, of the experience of a jaded city-dweller, out of health and unsuccessful, who escaped to the country, bought a farm, settled down, and rediscovered life. But, indeed, so sweet-tempered and wholesome is Mr. Grayson himself, so much the most interesting thing about his book, that we feel sure he must have got the best out of life anywhere, and could have adventured quite as contentedly in a three-room flat a folding-bed and a fire-escape. If, instead of the Scotch Preacher, the Doctor, and the other characters whom he introduces with a capital letter, he had chosen to interest himself in the Janitor, the Bellboy and the Groceryman, he would have produced just as entertaining and helpful a book, from which we would have learned just as much. There is a kind of superstition that the physical horizon viewed from a farm house window, being so much wider than that in sight from the hall bedroom of a city boarding house, must influence the mental outlook to a greater breadth, too. Yet there are probably as many cramped and narrow-minded people in the country as are to be found in town; and it seems to be a question of temperament whether delving with a hoe and spade is more ennobling, spiritually, than delving with a pen and a column of figures. Mr. Grayson thinks it so and preaches, with unmistakable sincerity, the gospel of life outdoors. But we should like to ask him, which did he enjoy the most: writing these winning little studies of nature, and his neighbors, and this simple country environment, or digging potatoes? Correcting the proofs of his book, or milking the cow? If he had the choice of doing one or the other the rest of his life, which would he choose?

These questions are asked in no spirit of levity. We want to get at the root of the matter. There is something pathetic in man's perennially recurrent hallucination that the way to be healthy, happy, and wise is to go out and sit under a tree; that in bodily inconvenience and manual labor is to be found surcease from care. The pastoral feeling (so to call it) travels in cycles with a sweeping inundation of pastoral literature, and a man who shall have lived to forty years must have witnessed at least one such deluge. Of all the trades that men pursue, the agricultural excites the most envy, and moves poets oftenest to verse. The activities of commerce somehow affront the muse.

> Rather, my people, let thy youths parade
> Their woolly flocks before the rising sun—

exclaims a forgotten sonneteer, and goes on to rail against what he calls with more poetry than truth, "Hell's minion, Trade," in good set iambics:

> If jarring interests and the greed of gold—
> The corn-rick's envy of the minéd hill,

> The steamer's grudge against the spindle's
>   skill—
> If things so mean our country's fate can mold,
> O let me hear again the shepherds trill
> Their reedy music to the drowsing fold!

This is very charming reading—but the farmer, in his way, is just as commercial as the insurance agent. Nobody spares a couplet to the latter; whereas if all the rhymes addressed to plowboys were strung together after the fashion of those ingenious statisticians who make a specialty of such calculations, they might girdle the globe or reach from here to the moon. The thing is unjust; the shepherd and the cowherd, by virtue of their antique, gracious employment, figure in a thousand poems; let the cowherd become the milkman, and, although he is engaged upon absolutely the same business, who so poor to do him reverence?

The fact is, comparisons are odious, and, what is more, profitless. When Mr. Grayson begins to exalt the country at the expense of the town, his gentle enthusiasm beclouds his view. "It would be impossible to imagine Abraham Lincoln brought up in a street of tenements," he says. It would be possible to imagine Abraham Lincoln brought up anywhere, for not the least quality of a great man is his superiority to surroundings, and not the least of his achievements his victory over circumstance. "Industry, patience, perseverance are qualities inherent in the very atmosphere of country life." Industry, patience, perseverance are qualities inherent in no atmosphere on this round earth; there are good communities and bad communities as there are good and bad individuals, and these exist indifferently in town and country alike. "After my experience in the country, if I were to be cross-examined as to the requisites of a farm, I should say the chief thing to be desired in any sort of agriculture is"—is what? Let the reader prepare himself for wisdom—"the chief thing to be desired in any sort of agriculture is good health in the farmer!" Good health is a tolerably desirable thing for everybody, everywhere, in every trade; for editors and chiropodists and carpenters and kings: we hardly need the information. "While on the subject of simplicity it may be well to observe that simplicity does not necessarily, as some of those who escape from the city seem to think, consist in doing without things, but rather in the proper use of them. One cannot return, unless with affection, to the crudities of a former existence. Do you not think the good Lord has given us the telephone (that we may better reach that elbow-rub of brotherhood which is the highest of human ideals) and the railroad (that we may widen our human knowledge and sympathy) and even the motorcar?—I do not go back. I neglect no tool of progress."

Mr. Grayson, presumably, does not want to convert people to his way of life; he only extols it. But these sentences set forth a certain theory, and there would be a mental and moral indolence in not following it up to its conclusion. "One cannot return to the crudities of a former existence." But, by your leave, you must return to the crudities of a former existence, or you are convicted of a glaring inconsistency in your pastoralism. This prattle about the good Lord having given us the telephone and the railroad and all the rest of it is very pretty and very nice and very appreciative, but consider: for every telephone, for every foot of railroad track, for every magazine on Mr. Grayson's table, for every newspaper in the tin box at the end of his lane, scores of men sweat at foundry hammers, scores of men slogged in countingrooms. They give their lives to the same hard, hurried, narrowing slavery of toil from which he is released. Suffer them to "escape from the city," too— and what would become of those gifts of the Almighty, the telephone and the railroad? It being manifestly impracticable and, on his own showing, undesirable that they should follow his example, we are reduced to the question, for whom is his book intended? Will he find for himself a virtue and a philosophy in living on a farm for less than $500 a year (with all the conveniences!) and addressing his illuminating remarks about widening our human knowledge and sympathy to a select circle who, he is perfectly confident, will not widen it at the cost of his telephone and daily mail service? And "while on the subject of simplicity it may be well to observe" that we do not understand what Mr. Grayson means by the reflections thus introduced; what is the "proper use of things" such as the railroad and the telephone? What the improper? Does anybody ever go on a wild orgy of telephoning? And who are those who use the railroad to indecent excess? Commuters?

No, the only way to be pastoral is to be pastoral—live like Abraham, parade your woolly flocks before the rising sun, and be beholden to no man's labor for your comforts and conveniences. Mr. Grayson, sitting sub tegmine fagi, penning his eclogues and telling us how happy he is, makes an infinitely picturesque and agreeable figure; but he should be satisfied with example, for the moment he enters upon precept, he is likely to land himself in a bottomless bog of contradictions and absurdities. The lurking trouble with his pastoralizing is a trouble peculiar to modern pastoral writing, and distinctly American; Mark Twain, alluding to schoolgirls' compositions, has defined it as the "inevitable sermon that wags its crippled tail" at the end of all of them. But that tail wags elsewhere, equally vehement and impotent. We say it at the risk of offence, yet with no irreverence, it seems to us a mistake to lug in "the good Lord," and couple that phrase with innocent platitudes about modern conveniences and the march of improvement; and if Mr. Grayson did not mean to be taken literally, none the less he errs against good taste. If he had said "the good Lord gave us sanitary plumbing and false teeth," we should have been conscious of a kind of shocked amusement; yet the argument is precisely the same. If telephones, why not cork legs? If railroads, why not enamel sinks? But no man nowadays can take his pen in hand, and start out to write about nature, without a number of side-excursions into theology; he is beset with the determination to find sermons in stones. Mr. Grayson and the Professor discover a flower in a fence row—and straightway launch into a discussion of the Eternal Purpose. What would Virgil or Herrick have said? Without being one-half so earnest for our good, they would have contrived to say something we could remember forever, with a species of poignant pleasure; and next year, next week, to-morrow we shall have forgot all of Mr. Grayson's honest and well-meant commonplaces. If we would be truly pastoral, we should be somewhat pagan; we should go to the classic authors, consider their ways and be wise.

They may have sacrificed the opportunity to sermonize to a desire for academic perfection of style; but they were vigorous, they were direct, they were simple (overworked word,) and they achieved an effect incomparably noble.

Mary S. Watts, "Stop and Examine 'The Simple Life'," in The New York Times Book Review, *January 4, 1908, p. 7.*

Mary White Ovington   (essay date 1909)

[In the following excerpt, Ovington examines Baker's presentation of race relations in Following the Color Line.*]*

Readers of the *American Magazine* have followed the color line for a year; but the gathering together of these articles in a book [*Following the Color Line*] and their further editing show with increasing clearness the author's careful effort to depict the conditions under which the Negroes live in the United States. This is done from the point of view of the reporter who travels rapidly from place to place, interviewing his neighbors whenever he sees that he can get an intelligent answer, carefully weighing evidence, and studying the physical environment of those about him. He thus gives us a collection of facts and opinions.

Mr. Baker's pictures of the Negro tenants in the South, working their land under the crop mortgage system, with a white overseer who dictates the planting of the crops and uses a hickory stick when he thinks it needed, show a tenant system "that is much nearer the condition that prevailed in slavery time than it is to the present northern tenant system." It is a form of feudalism. "If the master or lord is 'good' the Negro prospers; if he is harsh, grasping, unkind, the Negro suffers bitterly." To escape these feudal relations the ambitious colored men buy land or migrate to the city where the wage system prevails. But here, since men are thrown more closely together, the color line is continually drawn, and friction becomes intense, culminating, perhaps, in a riot. The story of the Atlanta riot is told in detail, and a chapter is given to lynchings, North and South, a tale of horror that Americans should read, recognizing their responsibility for such barbarity.

Mr. Baker gives full credit to the educated Negro for his progress. He describes farmers who cultivate their own land, preachers, doctors, and men of business. But he finds the white man in full control of the South, politically, socially, and industrially, and the Negro his helpless ward.

In the North the author believes color prejudice to be increasing, but he notes a growing sense of responsibility on the part of the whites for Negro conditions, and the development of philanthropic and religious work. The lack of economic opportunity is shown to be great, when even in Boston, unless he is able to conduct an enterprise of his own, the colored man has little chance to do anything but menial work. Many northerners will doubtless be chagrined at the amount of race feeling revealed to them in their part of the country; and they are told that they must not even rest in the assurance that their Negroes are enfranchised for

the North in spirit has disfranchised its lower

classes. It does it by the purchase at elections in one form or another of its 'poor whites' and its Negroes. While the South is disfranchising by legislation, the North is doing it by cash. What else is the meaning of Tammany Hall and the boss and machine system in other cities?

But the North may rightly take issue at this parallel. Government concerns itself not only with matters of state, but with the protection of individual life and property; and a disfranchised group surrounded by men of a different race who hold all political power is far more helpless, far more likely to meet with personal injustice, than any henchman of Tammany Hall.

But that part of the book that will prove of the greatest interest is the fascinating and continual play of opinion that enters into every chapter. We learn what an unsolved problem this is, and in what different ways men and women look upon it. There is the chapter telling of the division of opinion among the Negroes themselves, the schools of Du Bois and Washington, the agitators and the opportunists, there is the story of the rise to power of the middle class in the South, the Tillmans and the Vardamans, and their method of making political capital out of race prejudice, and of men like Flemming of Georgia, and Manning of Alabama who declares for the cessation of "lily-white nonsense." And lastly, there are the new educators in whom Mr. Baker finds the hope of the South,—Alderman, Dillard, Murphy, Speer, and Washington among the Negroes,—men who are working for the education and the material advancement of their section of the country. "Let us stop talking, forget the race problem, and get to work," is the dictum of these new leaders, and their doctrine has found expression in a remarkable growth of industrial activities, and in a new enthusiasm for education, "not only education of the old classical sort, but for industrial and agricultural education,—the training of workers." And after showing us these many opinions, Mr. Baker ends with a chapter of opinions of his own, giving a few kindly conclusions as to What to Do About the Negro.

Having covered so large a field, it is, perhaps, ungracious to suggest that the author should have written more; but there is a conspicuous absence of any discussion of the attitude of white organized labor in the South toward colored labor. We learn nothing of the thousands of Negroes working in the coal mines in Alabama, who last summer fought their "lost cause" side by side with their white fellow laborers. On the levees, upon the scaffolds of buildings, above and underground, an education is going on of white and colored that makes the education of the few thousand graduates of all the industrial schools of the South insignificant. More important perhaps, than the attitude of the white employer toward his servant, or the kindly educator toward the public, is the attitude of the white and colored workmen toward one another. But Mr. Baker tells us nothing on this subject. (pp. 348-50)

Mary White Ovington, "Two Books on American Race Problems," in The Survey, *Vol. XXII, April-October, 1909, pp. 348-52.*

Louis Filler   (essay date 1939)

[*Filler is a Russian-born American historian, biographer, and critic. In the following excerpt, he examines Baker's contribution to* McClure's *magazine.*]

[It] was not merely because it gave the facts that *McClure's* was read with approval by conservatives, used as a text by Harvard professors, and became the standard organ of exposure in popular esteem. McClure, whether or not he admitted it, did have a point of view, and his point of view was more acceptable to the respectable than that of other muckraking organs which were no less earnest and no less careful to print the truth. It was the point of view which made *McClure's,* and the most consistent exponent of that point of view was, not Steffens, not Tarbell—though they loomed largest in the popular mind—but Ray Stannard Baker.

Baker, born in Lansing, Michigan, in 1870, studied at Michigan State College and then took courses in law and literature at the University of Michigan. After that he entered upon a career in journalism. When he came to New York he was already practiced and mature. He was a quizzical, studious-looking man with a high earnestness regarding the meaning and purpose of his work. If he lacked something, it was on the side of humor, but he tried seriously to understand the motives and ideas of the men and events which he reported. He had, for example, traveled with Coxey's army on its march to Washington, and though he considered it a harum-scarum adventure from every point of view, he gave as honestly as he could the composition and purpose of the marchers. Surely he was infinitely fairer than Harry Thurston Peck, who in his *Twenty Years of the Republic* labeled them a band of criminals and marauders.

Baker had the gift of absorbing himself in his subject. For this reason he was able to give fascinating accounts of a wide variety of events, people, institutions and places: the casting of a great lens, Joel Chandler Harris, salmon fisheries, Mormonism, Yellowstone Park. His articles had character. During his best years as a journalist he was known as the greatest reporter in America.

He was very much like McClure himself, in the way he kept traveling about this country and going to Germany, Turkey, and other lands, sending back his excellent reports of men and things. Muckraking, however, asked more of a writer than deftness; it asked a philosophy, and Baker was not without one. He was perfectly aware of the economic and political problems that troubled the land. When he was yet in college, he had read Henry George and been stimulated to further study. He was acquainted with radical ideas of every kind.

In 1899 Baker published ***Our New Prosperity,*** a book that summed up the boom days which followed the Spanish-American War and the Klondike gold rush. It was written with a disarming simplicity that hardly revealed the vast amount of data and personal investigation that had gone into it. It was a book to warm his editor's heart. It expounded the conviction that "hard times" were but passing phases of the American way and that they were due to human greed and recklessness. The book contained

Cover for the issue of McClure's Magazine *that included Baker's "The Right to Work."*

facts in profusion. Yet it showed that Baker had his blind spot. Where was any mention of the labor unions, the excesses of the trusts, and the shame of Southern Negro policy, subjects with which Baker was soon to deal? These were facts, too; but Baker was not anxious to have his faith in American institutions troubled. Masking unpleasant facts with generalizations, he busied himself with a survey that could not but win the approval of respectable folk.

The labor question caught up with him, not he with it; it caught up with McClure, who sent Baker off to report it. And in the eight articles which Baker contributed to *McClure's* on the question, he gave the first authentic picture of labor racketeering that had appeared in print. He composed the picture confidently, with a wealth of detail and personal observation. He made sure not to make it appear the entire fault of labor: capital, he averred, was as much to blame as labor for the damage inflicted upon the "citizen" and the "consumer." He drew the picture of Chicago, caught between the racketeers of the Coal Teamsters' Union and the Owners' Association; of anarchy in Colorado as fostered by the Western Federation of Miners; of San Francisco, ruled by the "labor boss" Schmitz. Invariably both sides of the issue were presented, for Baker was by

no means anti-labor. Yet he did betray that he was more deeply worried by the rise of the unions than by the ever-tightening grip of the monopolies.

Labor racketeering was undoubtedly a growing phenomenon. It troubled labor as much as it troubled Baker. Baker, however, dared not consider the efforts labor itself was making to keep its ranks clean. That way lay Socialism! Baker was, in a word, desperately holding on to the middle ground of that Americanism which suited him; and in his first really serious effort to state his position he complained of the menace of labor.

This was a difficult position for an honest man to be in. Leroy Scott's novel *The Walking Delegate,* published in 1905, exhibited more peace of mind regarding labor and labor racketeering than did Baker's articles. But Scott was a radical in politics, a Socialist. Baker was constrained to follow a difficult course of logic until he developed that strange fantasy which enabled him at last to escape from what was apparently an inescapable dilemma. (pp. 86-8)

> Louis Filler, "The McClure Idea," in his Cru-
> saders for American Liberalism, 1939. Re-
> print by The Antioch Press, 1950, pp. 80-9.

Ray Stannard Baker   (essay date 1945)

[*In the following excerpt from the autobiography* American Chronicle, *Baker recounts his experiences as a reporter and comments on the purpose of his work.*]

My purpose all along had been to present the explosive new economic and social and perhaps political forces that affected American life. It may be recalled that I had begun in Scott's seminars at Ann Arbor to read and write about strikes and lockouts which then (in 1892) were ominous forerunners of the coming economic crisis. When I went to Chicago I found myself in the midst of the storm and later, as I have recounted, I marched with Coxey's Army of the unemployed, and "covered" the great strikes at Pullman, and the so-called "Debs rebellion." Afterward, when I joined the staff of *McClure's Magazine,* I found that if I really went on with the novel I had planned I needed a much more extensive knowledge of American economic and business conditions than I then possessed. So I made as thorough a study as I could of the economic situation in the country as it then existed (1899) and published a book about it, called *Our New Prosperity* (1900).

I kept on, as I could, enlarging my background of knowledge—even though I could not always persuade the editors at *McClure's* to publish my articles on these subjects. They did use a biographical account I wrote of J. P. Morgan (October, 1901), and another on **"What the U. S. Steel Corporation Really Is and How It Works"** (November, 1901). I also wrote an article on the great struggle between the titans of finance for the control of the Northern Pacific Railroad, which *McClure's* did not care to publish—but it came out in *Collier's Weekly* (November 30, 1901). I was especially interested in this last because it opened to me the business and financial side of the railroad situation in the Northwest—of which, during the Debs strike of 1894, I had come to see and know the workers' side. I had met Debs and many other labor leaders personally; I not only felt them as strong and able human beings, but I knew, or thought I knew, the powerful incentives for organization behind their movements, and their demands for more wages and more freedom.

It was because I needed a similar close acquaintanceship with the leaders on the other side of the battle line that I had gone with fear and trembling to see J. P. Morgan—the giant of them all. I also met other leaders, among them Charles M. Schwab of Steel and Hill of the Great Northern Railroad (but I could not get to Harriman). I worked hard and long to try to understand, thoroughly and honestly, what they were trying to do and why; what things looked real to them.

Yet I had not gone far with my novel there in my sunny room when I began to find that I was still not as clear as I had supposed upon certain of the inside arrangements and relationships, either of labor or of capital. While I had made first-hand studies of several great strikes, and had read everything I could get hold of relating to labor problems, including Sidney Webb's great book on the British labor movement, *Industrial Democracy,* I felt that I needed to know a great deal more regarding the actual practices and policies of labor organization in America.

Accordingly I dropped my work and dashed off to New York and Chicago and elsewhere to see the leaders themselves. I met Samuel Gompers for the first time in Washington, and found him a very different type from Debs. He was a determined, indefatigable, cool-headed organizer, contrasted with Debs, the ardent, idealistic, emotional evangelist. I made careful memoranda of all I heard and saw for use in my novel.

I turned part of my material into a kind of basic explanatory article which I hoped *McClure's* would publish, thus helping to relieve, somewhat, my obligations to them. It was called **"How Labor Is Organized."**

At that time American opinion, so largely based upon the convictions of an earlier preponderant individualistic agricultural life, was generally hostile to labor unionism. It did not care to understand the underlying forces that were driving labor to organize. I considered that my articles was *news* (though it was not in itself a very good article), but the editors at *McClure's* thought it too general. I took it over to Walter H. Page, the brilliant and forward-looking editor, indeed the creator, of the new *World's Work*—and he was glad to publish it (August, 1902).

At that time I never thought of these articles, either on the capitalistic or the labor side of the new problems, as "revolutionary" or "crusading." They were fact articles on conditions which keenly interested me personally, and when published they also interested a great many other people—judging by editorial comment and by letters received. They were in no way essentially different from the articles later blasted by the highest possible authority—President Theodore Roosevelt—as being the work of "muckrakers."

During that fall, while I was busily at work on my novel, a great strike was under way in the Pennsylvania coal fields.

So I went in October to Wilkes-Barre and met John Mitchell, the able leader of the miners. He was not at all the man commonly presented in the newspapers I saw—the "wild-eyed radical," the "disturber of the peace." He seemed to me a singularly steady-headed man, with some of the qualities of both Gompers and Debs.

I met quite a group of writers and students, to say nothing of radical leaders in other fields, who sensed the historic importance of what was happening there. Two men who were there were well known in liberal gatherings, Henry D. Lloyd, whose *Wealth and Commonwealth* was one of the earliest contributions to the real "literature of exposure," and Clarence Darrow of Chicago, even then the champion of the underdogs of the world—often without bothering to inquire whether the over-dogs had any case at all. I recall gatherings in dingy hotel bedrooms filled with tobacco smoke, in which the issues were discussed with a passionate certitude not warranted, as it seemed to me, by any real or deep knowledge of the facts.

I used the same methods, as a reporter, that had proved so successful at the time of the Pullman strike in Chicago. I tramped out to the miners' homes, I went down into the mines where the men worked, I sat in at several of their long-winded meetings, and listened to their bitter discussions. I found the newly organized miners not only at war with the powerful owners of the mining properties, but even more angrily with the large numbers of their fellow workers who would not "come out" and support the strike. They hated these "scabs" to the point of murder.

I have always liked, best of all, to study minorities. Majorities may have power; minorities often have understanding. Majorities are commonly interested in property; minorities in ideas.

It was easy enough to see the glaring injustices of the coal fields—low wages, company houses, company stores, poor schools, wretched living conditions: these had not only been widely publicized by the leaders of the strike, they were generally admitted. I did not need, at first anyway, to study these aspects of the situation. But why, if all these things were true, should 17,000 of the men in the anthracite fields, a sizable proportion of all the miners, doggedly refuse to support the strike? Why should they prefer to go on working in danger to their lives?

What men I met during those fiery weeks! What stories they told me: what dramas of human suffering, human loyalty, and human fear I saw: all brilliantly lighted against the scorched and dusty background of the Pennsylvania hills.

My article was a vivid series of case histories. It neither offered conclusions nor suggested remedies. I was unprepared for the enthusiasm with which it was received by the editors in New York. S. S. McClure wired me, "Your article tremendous," and even came down to Scranton to see me and to plan for vivid photographic portraits of the men whose stories I had told—remarkably find looking men they were. He afterward sent down my old friend of the German trip, George Varian, to make pictures of the miners' homes. And finally we had earnest discussions there and later in New York as to an introduction to the article which we had decided to call **"The Right to Work."** I was strong in my opinion that it should be clearly stated that I had treated only one aspect of a highly complex problem. It was true only as far as it went; I did not wish to be making ammunition for mere stupid opposition to all labor organization, or even all strikes.

After completing my article, I hurried back to my home in Michigan quite on fire with the wealth of new material, new characters and, above all, new understandings of the human elements in the vast problem I was interested in. I had written to my wife that I intended to remain at home and "write gloriously all winter long." I went at my work with enthusiasm, and a month later I was telling my father:

"I am deep in the writing of my novel." Even as late as February, 1903, I was still holding my own.

"The Right to Work" was published in January, 1903, and I soon began to receive editorial clippings regarding it and letters from all over the country. S. S. McClure himself wrote to me on January 23: "Everything has borne out the truthfulness and value of the article you wrote, and I am sorry we could not get the whole thing into one issue. I hear a great deal from the article."

That January number of *McClure's* also contained two other memorable articles, one by Lincoln Steffens on "The Shame of Minneapolis" and the other by Ida M. Tarbell, the third in her great *History of the Standard Oil Company.* Until the magazine was in "dummy" form it never seemed to have occurred to the editors that three of the articles it contained had a notable resemblance and were actually discussing the same general subject—a subject that was just then beginning to disturb the consciousness of the American people. One of the best proofs, of course, of the value of these articles was the extraordinary demand for the magazine on the newsstands and the sudden increase of subscriptions. Mr. McClure wrote me on January 13: "From all I can hear your article and the other two articles in the January magazine have been the greatest success we have ever had."

This reception of the three articles, as well as the forethought that had gone into each one of them separately, resulted in an extraordinary stroke of editorial perception. I think it was the restless, but eagerly intuitive mind of S. S. McClure that made the discovery that these articles rested upon a heretofore unrecognized groundswell of public interest. At the last moment an unusual semi-editorial was inserted on the final page of the magazine commenting, for the first time I think, on what was later to be known politely as the "literature of exposure," impolitely as "muckraking." It began:

> How many of those who have read through this number of the magazine noticed that it contains three articles on one subject? We did not plan it so, it is a coincidence that the January *McClure's* is such an arraignment of American character as should make every one of us stop and think. How many noticed that?
>
> The leading article, "The Shame of Minneapolis," might have been called "The American

Contempt of Law." That title could well have served for the current chapter of Miss Tarbell's *History of Standard Oil Company.* And it would have fitted perfectly Mr. Baker's **"The Right to Work."** All together, these articles come pretty near showing how universal is this dangerous trait of ours. Miss Tarbell has our capitalists conspiring among themselves, deliberately, shrewdly, upon legal advice, to break the law so far as it restrained them, and to misuse it to restrain others who were in their way. Mr. Baker shows labor, the ancient enemy of capital, and the chief complainant of the trusts' unlawful acts, itself committing and excusing crimes. And in "The Shame of Minneapolis" we see the administration of a city employing criminals to commit crimes for the profit of elected officials, while the citizens—Americans of good stock and more than average culture, and honest, healthy Scandinavians—stood by complacent and not alarmed.

The public response to these articles, by any test, was astonishing. I doubt whether any other magazine published in America ever achieved such sudden and overwhelming recognition. Partly by chance, partly by a new technique of reporting which demanded thoroughness of preparation and sincerity of purpose—and gave the writer the time and the freedom to cultivate those virtues—we had put our fingers upon the sorest spots in American life. (pp. 164-69)

> *Ray Stannard Baker, in his* American Chronicle: The Autobiography of Ray Stannard Baker [David Grayson], *Charles Scribner's Sons, 1945, 531 p.*

Edmund Wilson   (essay date 1952)

[*Wilson was an American reviewer, creative writer, and social and literary critic whose widely read reviews and essays introduced the best works of modern literature to the reading public. In the following excerpt, he comments on Baker's strengths and weaknesses as Woodrow Wilson's biographer.*]

The first two volumes of **Woodrow Wilson: Life and Letters,** by Ray Stannard Baker, are now before the public. The first of these deals with Woodrow Wilson's early life up to the time of his going to Princeton as a professor, and the second takes him up to his resignation as president of the University. Mr. Baker has both the vices and the advantages of an official biographer—the vices of a loquacious admiration which cannot refrain from continually exclaiming over the utterances and deeds of his hero instead of allowing them to speak for themselves, and a bias which, from beginning to end, prevents him from permitting his subject to appear for a moment as anything but a perfect gentle knight. The result is that, with the copious documentation of a history, his biography moves in something of the miraculous atmosphere of a saint's legend. You would never find out from this record that Woodrow Wilson was, among other things, a resourceful politician: he is invariably represented as carrying all before him by some divine irresistible authority. But Mr. Baker's advantage lies in the fact that he does have the documents; and it may be said that, allowing for his bias, he seems to use them conscientiously and carefully. His book is not very vivid and not very well-written: it has something of the monotony of vocabulary, the lulling repetitiousness and the dilution of ideas of Woodrow Wilson himself. Thus, after quoting from some one of Wilson's utterances in which the weakness of the latter's thought and style are already sufficiently evident, Mr. Baker will add some such comment as: "The sheer eloquence of the man!" or "The sheer fighting spirit of the man!" or something of the sort, using "sheer" in exactly the way that Wilson was in the habit of doing, with the intention of reënforcing some statement, but with the effect of rendering it feebler. It cannot, therefore, be denied that Mr. Baker has been guilty of some insipidity. On the other hand, the material of his biography has been most scrupulously and clearly arranged: his book is extremely well-ordered. He neglects none of Wilson's activities—political, academic, domestic or recreational—and he tells about everything in its place, proceeding deliberately, step by step, indicating exactly the order of events and patiently going back, when necessary, to fill in some aspect of his subject which, for fear of complicating his main narrative, he has been hitherto obliged to neglect. As a result, we have what is undoubtedly the most valuable work on Wilson which has yet appeared. Mr. Baker has thrust into the shadow some of the angles and colors of his subject, but most of Wilson's character is there: it is quite plain in his acts and in his letters. We do not feel any longer, after reading Mr. Baker's first volume—which deals with that part of his life about which least has been written—that there is anything enigmatical about Wilson. (pp. 298-99)

Edmund Wilson, "Woodrow Wilson at Princeton," in his The Shores of Light: A Literary Chronicle of the Twenties and Thirties, *Farrar, Straus and Giroux, 1952, pp. 298-324.*

David Mark Chalmers   (essay date 1958)

[*Chalmers is an American critic and historian who has written, edited, and contributed to several studies of the muckrakers and their era. In the following essay, he traces the development of Baker's social, political, and spiritual ideas as reflected in Baker's journals and letters.*]

In democratic societies where major policies are shaped by an interaction of public opinion and official programs, the press has a vital rôle in keeping the two in continuous communication. Seldom has the press—and perhaps never have the magazines—been so influential in creating and expressing public feeling as during the era of the muckrakers. One of the earliest and most prominent of this new breed of crusading journalists was Ray Stannard Baker. As an editor of *McClure's* and, then, as co-owner (with Ida Tarbell, Lincoln Steffens, Finley Peter Dunne and William Allen White) of the *American Magazine,* Ray Stannard Baker in search for moral leadership and economic reform went through most of the political alternatives of the Progressive Era. Beginning as a firm believer in individualism and the economic health of the nation, Baker moved steadily in the direction of collectivism. He had a brief though intense affair of the heart with the Socialist Party and came to believe that government ownership was the only solution to the problem of the trusts. In his public writings and his private journals he recorded the impact on his own ideas of the society which he sought to remake. Writing on the Negro and on religion, as well as on labor, capital, the railroads and politics, he both stimulated and mirrored the growing middle-class concern for social responsibility in all phases of national life.

Baker's changing ideas carried him successively into the camps of Theodore Roosevelt, Robert M. La Follette, and Woodrow Wilson. To each of these leaders he became a trusted friend and advisor, and to Wilson he eventually dedicated nearly three decades of his life. The wartime president sent him as a special envoy to report on the growing social unrest among the peoples of the Allied Powers. Baker then stood at Wilson's side at Versailles and first created the position of presidential press secretary during the Conference. In the two decades which followed the war, Baker poured out eighteen volumes on Woodrow Wilson, including the authorized edition of the public papers of the President and the eight volumes of life and letters for which he received the Pulitzer Prize in 1940.

At the beginning of the twentieth century, Baker painted a picture of national prosperity, progress, and strength. Writing for *McClure's* in 1900, he dismissed protestors like Coxey's army and the silver agitators of 1896 as people overwhelmed by a distress which had become the one reality in their lives but was not typical of the country as a whole. Such movements were unsound, he wrote: "All of this irrational and yet human turning to the Government for help, a tendency that began in the reign of the

Baker (at right) with President Wilson at the 1919 Paris Peace Conference.

first king and has descended to the last republic, was accompanied by a great outcry against capital and monied combinations of every kind—the old, old writhing of the debtor under the crowding of the creditor." People failed to realize that this was the necessary result of the health and vigor of a growing nation. The individual ought not to protest, but rather should raise and better himself through initiative and self-control. When he wrote of industry, whether in the United States or Germany, Baker saw only its organized efficiency.

Within a few years he changed his tune. He found industrial warfare and lawlessness, starving miners, anti-scab violence, labor bosses, and conspiracy between the unions and the trusts. The two giants squeezed the public which was powerless to do other than pay the bill for corruption and monopoly. Writing from the characteristic middle-class orientation of the muckrakers, he found that capital and organized labor were not very different. As one of those in the middle, he feared too great an aggregation of power on either side. Both operated to crush all competition. If there was any disparity of power, he realized, it would be abused by the more powerful. Although monopolies contributed to the corruption of dishonest working-men's organizations, he felt that the responsibility was that of the individual members.

Bossism in labor as in all other fields was but a symptom of civic laziness:

> It all comes back . . . to you and to me . . . individually. If *you* want to be rid of the Boss in your city, *you* have to go to the primaries and election booth and protest and vote and protest again. If *you,* as a working-man, want honest and efficient unionism, *you* have got to go to the union meetings and make things right, and if *you* as a stockholder, want to see common business honesty in *your* trusts and in *your* corporations, you have got to look after the thing yourself.

No matter what the evil was, Baker always came back to the same solution that "if this republic is saved it must be saved by *individual effort.*"

The response to these articles was extremely favorable, and Theodore Roosevelt called his account of lawlessness in Colorado "absolutely correct and fair." Of another of the articles, the President reported that he was most impressed by the lesson of personal responsibility which had been presented. "How emphatically this revelation emphasizes the need of drawing the line on conduct, among politicians, and among private individuals alike," he wrote.

Baker felt that he had uncovered a field in which he could do much useful work and with a strong sense of service characteristic of the muckrakers he wrote to his father early in 1904 that "it seems almost as though I had a mission to perform—to talk straight out on a difficult subject." Shortly afterwards, he credited the articles, which he, Ida Tarbell, and Lincoln Steffens were contributing, for the fact that *McClure's* was "doing more for stirring up the American people than any other publication ever did before," adding, "I think we have struck the right Grail."

But Baker soon was writing on a variety of problems. Corruption was far too broad and he was unwilling to bury himself in the study of only one corner of it. He turned to an examination of the excesses of capital which he discovered behind those of labor. At the source of the problem he found that the greatest renunciation of individual responsibility was in the corporation. The utility of such organizations was that they enabled reputable people to enjoy the profits from disreputable enterprises without disturbing their moral complacency.

Why did such unhealthy activities persist? In his notebooks, where he tested his ideas, Baker attempted a diagnosis. The disease was due to legislative lag. Despite enormous industrial development the country still operated under laws passed fifty to seventy-five years before. These statutes were based on the principle of laissez-faire which held that business would regulate itself by the self-adjusting mechanism of competition which he had come to believe was no longer operative. Once a notion penetrated the mind of the public, at least forty years were necessary to change it. In America the citizens are sovereign, he wrote, "and we have not as a people recognized the new economic principle involved in trust and railroad organization." Talking about law enforcement as the solution to such problems was like saying "be good" to a railroad engineer whose engine was about to blow up. "The real remedy is," he continued, " . . . *economic facts* and the dose is to be applied to the people not to the legislators." Again and again in his notebooks Baker swore fealty to this task. "My job is illumination," he wrote, chanting, "educate, educate, educate."

In 1905 Baker began to 'educate' the public as to the nature of the railroad power in the United States. Its grants of favoritism were, he felt, the chief cause of the trusts. Transportation was an essential tool of industry and a necessary foundation for the growth of population. Manipulations of rates could drastically affect both of these developments, he maintained, writing that "it is no exaggeration to say that the railroads . . . have infinitely more to do with the happiness and success of the people than the United States Government itself." The barons of Wall Street unfairly taxed the consumers and stretched out from their vast transportation systems to take over other industries.

When he began his study, Baker called for a public body which would discover the principles of rate making and set fares impartially. Describing the railroads' gigantic system of publicity, pressure, and misinformation, he showed how the carriers influenced newspapers to prevent criticism, and how when necessary they turned to the bosses and the corruption of legislatures. By the time he had finished, Baker had come to believe that unless a really good regulatory bill was passed, public pressure in the direction of government ownership might become irresistible. He replied to the loud cries against such 'confiscatory' action by asking if it was right for the railroads to take the people's property by unfair levies. Was there no one, he questioned, greater than transport magnates and able to prevent injustice and discrimination?

Baker's study drew the applause from railroad experts.

President Roosevelt wrote: "I haven't a criticism to suggest. . . . You have given me two or three thoughts for my own message. It seems to me that one of the lessons you teach is that these railroad men are not to be treated as exceptional villains but merely ordinary Americans who under given conditions are by the mere force of events forced into doing much of which we complain." In return he sent the galleys of the message which he was preparing for Congress, but failed to accept Baker's suggestions as to the need to close all avenues of rate manipulation.

Yet Baker had already progressed beyond the belief that the control of rates would cure the railroad problem. In February 1906 he visited the President and discussed the Hepburn bill. "Suddenly he asked me," Baker recorded, " 'If this is only a first step where do you think we are going?' 'You may not agree with me, Mr. President,' I said, 'but I believe we cannot stop short of governmental ownership of the railroads.' " Baker had moved a long way in the three short years since 1903, when in writing of the labor boss, he had stated that the problems of the nation would not be solved by such nostrums as municipal Socialism and the 'single tax' but through individual responsibility and obeying the laws.

In January 1906 he wrote to his father that, "this crusade against special privilege in high places is a real war, a real revolution. We may not have to go as far as you did, when you fought out the slavery question . . . but ink may serve the purpose. I pity the country. Signs everywhere shows a great moral awakening, the cleaning out of rotten business and still more rotten politics. But we've only begun!" For the next three years he pondered how this would be done, moving reluctantly all the time toward socialism. This was the clearest in the evolution of his conception of 'individualism.' The socialists now seemed its best practitioners for they demanded duty and responsibility from each citizen. "Socialism may be wrong," he reflected, "in its ultimate program—in the artificial state upon which it has fixed its vision but somehow I feel that I am going by the same road, that I am hoping the same hopes." Must we not have more socialism to get more individualism, he asked? Competition no longer had any place in his questioning. Through his reading Baker had become convinced that man was not a victim of the merciless law of natural selection but was able to control such forces through his consciousness and power to modify the workings of nature. This belief combined with the growth of monopoly served to wean him away from seeking reform through the mechanism of increased competition.

During 1906 Baker continually reflected on the merits and faults of socialism. It failed to recognize the individual and placed undue emphasis on the material environment and the abolition of private property. Once we reach that point, he maintained, socialism will not be necessary because man will have been completely made over. However, socialism was an unselfish, enthusiastic force and presented a positive program, much of which was good.

By the spring of 1907, however, Baker felt more closely committed to socialism. Two kinds of men were inclined toward it, he opined, the dreamer and those who

are backing toward socialism, repelled by the excesses of individualism. They see in socialism a handy weapon . . . and when the abuses from which they shrink are cured, they will part company straightway with the extremists. Of this latter class I consider myself a member. . . . And yet I admire the high & unselfish ideals of many socialists: it is a fine thing to see men working for the very great good for all the people that they can dream of—while most men are moved only by impulses of selfish individual good.

As a matter of fact there is or should be no difference in the ideals of Socialists & individualists. . . . What is best, in the largest sense, for society is best for the individual, & what is best for the individual is best for society.

In the spring of 1908, Baker's doctrinal yearnings were coming to a head. He was depressed by racial antagonism and disappointed by Roosevelt's economic conservatism. He felt that this was the most trying period of his life. Two libel suits, arising out of his railroad articles, had come to court, and he lamented that, although what he had written "*was* and *is* essentially true," the cases went against him because of legal confusion and technicalities. "How can justice be expected," he asked in anguish, "when so many of our judges are defenders of railroad corporations & trusts? They hold back every sort of economic & social reform by strict interpretations of ancient law. They stand for individualism, they deify competition & the doctrine of laissez-faire, they see nothing of the great new movements."

In his home in East Lansing, Michigan, he had been engaged in unsuccessful attempts to improve the school system and the state civil service. However, what weighed most heavily was his strong feeling of the social failure of organized religion. He had been concerned with the building of a new church, and that led him to brood continually about the shortcomings of religion. The factor of brotherhood was left out. "The Socialists have a community spirit of service," Baker wrote, for he had come to believe that they offered "brotherhood nearer than anything I know to the *real church*. There are men there who have given *everything* for a community good."

"From this time on," he asserted, "I am going to pursue this subject: I *must join something*. I shall look deeply into the subject of Socialism—I mean upon its organization side." With this, he began to work even harder to dispel the doubts that remained. "Intellectual individuality & freedom must not be confused with economic individualism," he wrote. "Intellectual individualism is quite compatible with economic Socialism." He felt that the muckrakers were not going far enough; the socialists were the only ones whose activities were basically religions.

But Baker's striving to find a movement of which he might become a part was doomed to failure, for no one had the spiritual panacea he sought. Others operated on a material level:

> If it were not for the socialists, I should be a Socialist. Sitting at home, reading and thinking, dreaming of the ideal human state, I see that So-

cialism is, ultimately, the only way out. But when I attend Socialist meetings and hear the intemperate clamor of half ignorant men (themselves not prepared to exercise the self-restraint so necessary to socialism, themselves not willing to become servants) I am afraid! How necessary is education, *education!* How great must be the patience of all leaders and idealists, that they do not lead too fast.

Once he made up his mind, however, Baker felt enormous relief, and socialism seemed to have lost most of its attraction for him. His disillusionment marked the passing of a definite stage. Although he continued to think about the Party, he did so with growing distaste. As he summed it up, "Socialism is *not religious* but *economic.* The great body of Socialists are not looking for . . . opportunity to *serve society;* but for a better *distribution of wealth* . . . they have not got beyond property-worship!" With a final renunciation, "No, Socialism does not go far enough for me. I demand not only a better system: but a higher *individual character,*" Baker ceased the flirtation.

Yet while he rejected socialism, his deliberations had done much to crystallize his ideas. Although he did not accept the party of Karl Marx, he retained many of its tools. The two main developments in his approach which were the outcome of this period were his collectivist concept of social action and his class analysis of historical movement. Both were clear in his answer to the criticism which Theodore Roosevelt had made of his articles on the Negro. Baker wrote the President, "I wish as much as you do that we had reached the stage of our civilization where we could avoid the hatred and demagogy of ignorance and class strife: where men could and would think in national or world terms, not in terms of class, party, union or family. But *class action is a condition now existent.*" Even movements led by such demagogues as Pitchfork Ben Tillman were useful to democracy. The important fact was that class was the dynamic factor of change and Baker ascribed the President's political success to the leadership of just such an upheaval:

> The essence of your letter is in a single sentence . . . [which] says: "Most of our fighting for betterment has to do not at all with a conflict between the Few and the Many, but with the improvement of man as man." Here you define clearly the divergence of view between the socialistic trend of thought (I don't mean socialism) and the individualistic trend: and take your stand with the latter group (although, curiously, you have *acted* in response to the impetus of the other group).
>
> You underestimate the necessity and usefulness (in our present stage) of class action and class feeling, although, in your books you defend and approve of party action, which, if it has any vitality, is always, more or less, a class action. If this were not the time of loosened party lines and of readjustment, in which there are few earnest divisions on policies, in which personality for the moment rises superior to platform, such a leader as you are, Mr. President, would be an impossibility.

The reason why people in this country, as in every part of the world, are tending toward socialism, is because they have for years been overemphasizing personal goodness, just as you do, and have found that it does not necessarily result in social justice or social morality. A man has to be more than "hard-working, thrifty, energetic, a good husband and father": he must develop also a *social conscience* and this comes, gradually, as all growths do, by a succession of larger and larger social-consciousnesses . . . his labor union (or corporation), his national federation (or trust), his *class,* and finally his country—and after that, perhaps, dimly in the future, the dream of the poet: the brotherhood of man.

As he had begun his probing of the socialist promise in 1906, Baker stressed the rôle of government action in directing the economic life of the nation. However, in his articles he cautiously steered away from any espousal of socialism, using it rather as a bogey to advance more moderate steps. Nevertheless the development of his social philosophy was mirrored in a series of articles on the Negro for *McClure's* and the *American.* Although infinitely complicated by racial animosity, the problem of the Negro was part and parcel of the big issue which beset the age. Slavery had been abolished, he maintained, because it was undemocratic. The same feudal spirit lay behind the institution of white supremacy. The ferment of the Negro, then, was but one part of a world-wide struggle. "The underman will not keep his place," Baker explained. "He is restless, ambitious, he wants civil, political, and industrial equality. Thus we see the growth of labour organizations, the spread of populists and socialists, who demand new rights and a greater share in the products of labour."

It was natural that Baker considered racial conflict a spiritual as well as a social and economic problem. One of his continued preoccupations was with the state of religion. His search for individual and national reform was a moral quest more than anything else, and he himself continued to feel a strong need to find a spiritual movement to which he might belong. His David Grayson stories of rural contentment were in part a response to this need as was his flirtation with the Socialist Party. His disillusionment with the latter stemmed from his realization that it lacked the unselfishness and community spirit which had originally been the main attraction. "How I am driven back again & again upon Jesus Christ," he reflected during the trying spring of 1908. "The more I think of human ills and social remedies, the more I see that the teaching of Jesus Christ is the only solution. Far, far beyond socialism (which is a mechanism of social force: not spiritual) stands the unreached Christ in love & serenity."

The result was a series of articles in which he attempted to show the turmoil and upset as the nation sought to readjust itself to new needs and conditions and a more complete democracy. The theme was the failure of the institutional church. In treating the disintegration of organized religion, he wrote: "every human institution has one supreme function: to serve the people in one way or another. . . . A church is not a religion: it is a mere human agency for fostering religion." Baker felt that through their ministrations to the wealthy, the Protestant churches had lost their spiritual leadership and no longer had any message for common people. There was a growing stratification and class division even in the temples of God, but the greatest separation seemed to be that those with money were inside and the poor were outside. The church must do two things: inspire the individual with a belief in divine power, and draw all men together in a democratic relationship. In the slum missions there was a degree of hope, for they took part in and provided for the life of the common people. The institutional church, he reported, was learning but slowly. Essentially it had to get at the causes of poverty and degradation if it wanted to reach out to the poor. There was a highly religious quality in dedicating one's self to the abolition of poverty. This vision and the power of faith that sustained it were the socialist's source of strength. The best chance of a similar movement within organized religion came from the 'New Christianity' of Walter Rauschenbusch and the leaders of the social gospel philosophy. In an address at Amherst College Baker summed up the message of faith that ran through *The Spiritual Unrest.* The great American accomplishment had been production, but it had come at great cost to children, families, immigrants, workers, and the Negro. The real test of national strength, he believed, was not to be found in material achievement, but in how we treated the weak. The ideal of service was Christian as well as democratic.

The groundwork of Baker's muckraking articles had been the various social ferments at work in national life. Impending change was his clearest theme. It continually appeared in the titles as well as in the text of his reports: **"Railroads and the Popular Unrest," "An Ostracised Race in Ferment," "The Western Spirit of Restlessness,' "The Spiritual Unrest,"** and **"Is the Republican Party Breaking Up?"** In the midst of this turmoil he continually sought to find a full and meaningful rôle which he could play.

Realizing that sooner or later in a democracy everything was carried into the political arena, he began to show a growing interest in local politics and party organization. At the same time his attitude toward Theodore Roosevelt was changing. For many years T. R. had symbolized political action to Baker. While he always praised the Chief Executive publicly, Baker wrote to the President what was in his mind. In these letters he was often frankly critical, while in the privacy of his notebooks, his exasperation grew. The apparent explanation of this seeming multiplicity of attitudes was that he warmly admired Roosevelt, and, recognizing the good that the strenuous Teddy had accomplished in the past and might yet do in the future, sought to win him to a deeper understanding of the 'true' forces of the times.

In 1908, in an unsigned article [in the *American*] Baker wrote that T. R.'s great contribution was that he had been instrumental in a quiet revolution when conditions were mounting to what might have caused a social explosion. In 1910 he was still writing that where the muckrakers had been the witness of the people, Roosevelt had been their attorney. Certain that the ex-president would run again in 1912, Baker for the first time publicly questioned

whether T. R. would undertake the new struggle against the forces of property.

Within months the writer openly moved from warm support of Roosevelt to doubt of his ability to handle the important problems of trusts. The Rough-rider did not realize that it was not the result but the very existence of monopoly that was wrong. After two visits to Oyster Bay during which he attempted to persuade the popular leader to take a 'more enlightened' view on national issues, particularly the tariff, Baker at last despaired. T. R. had served his purpose, he recorded in his notebook, but the old type of politics was gone and the Rough-rider had to go with it.

What had happened, Baker wrote, was that traditional party lines had broken down and historic conflicts had been removed. The concentration of corporate wealth and the alignment of political forces representing it created a vast moral restlessness among the mass of citizens which the bosses could not understand. This "aggression of capitalism" had reached the oppressive stage and the public was willing to struggle against it. The old party lines had become meaningless as everything polarized around the big issue. In the fields in which competition had been replaced by monopoly, the government must either regulate or take possession. His sympathies were all in the latter direction, as he wrote that

> however benevolent Mr. Rockefeller may show himself to be, however cheap and pure his oil, however "good" and "legal" his trust, the principle under which he holds the power of taxing the daily subsistence of men will never be accepted by this American people. We will not be bribed with cheap oil . . . nor will we be blinded by the gifts of gorgeous universities and innumerable libraries. The principle is wrong and can lead only to greater wrongs. There are no "good" monopolies in private hands.

If the old parties would not take up the new moral struggle, then a new one would surely arise. The key to this realignment seemed to be found in the rise of the insurgent forces led by Senator Robert M. La Follette of Wisconsin. Here was an upheaval drawing its primary strength from the West which Baker so loved [the critic adds in a footnote that "Baker believed that the West was more democratic because of the greater individualism and restlessness of the people, and a closer relationship with the land"], yet reaching throughout the nation, dedicating itself to the advancement of democracy. Here at last Baker momentarily found a cause and an organization of which he could be part, which appeared to offer the spiritual values for which he had so longed. In his articles of 1910 he summed up the progress of the insurgents as "a new moral force . . . abroad in the land."

During 1910 and 1911 Baker recorded his growing involvement in the movement, and he speculated on the possibility of capturing the Republican Party for the forthcoming election. He undertook the founding of an Insurgents' Club, and wrote to Theodore Roosevelt of the enthusiasm engendered by La Follette. Baker edited La Follette's autobiography, and became one of the circle of advisers that gathered about the insurgent leader.

In an article explaining **"The Meaning of Insurgency,"** Baker wrote that there had been three waves which had kept the desire for democracy alive in the nation. They were the Greenbackers, the Populists, and the growing insurgent movement. The journalists of exposure served the vital rôle of educating the public to the concrete nature of the menace of concentrated wealth and monopoly.

> They were unpalatable facts which the muckrakers presented, but they were facts; proof was piled upon proof, certainty was added to certainty, so that even the prosperous and naturally conservative jury of the whole people were thoroughly convinced. And now we are in the midst of a third great wave of political insurgency; and this wave, please God, is going over the ramparts; something will be done.

The insurgent movement and a peaceful national revolution seemed the logical outcome of the era of the muckrakers.

Despite this expression of enthusiasm, Baker retained some doubts about La Follette's statesmanship. A moral revolution had taken place, but a new world was still to be built. For that, "light & leading" were necessary. "What we need is a leader," Baker confided to his journals, "who will lay down fundamental principles, and then tell us how we should meet immediate problems." The actions of the insurgents in opposing Taft's reciprocity treaty with Canada during the special session of Congress in 1911 led him to continue asking whether the Wisconsin lawmaker was the best man.

By January 1912, with Roosevelt's hat all but in the ring, La Follette's hopes of becoming president were disappearing. Recording his reaction to a conference with the Senator, Baker wrote that the insurgent leader had "small chance of being nominated—& of course knows it perfectly well." In what direction, then, could Baker turn. The logical transfer of support to Roosevelt did not appeal to him, and he stuck to this view despite all of the charm which the ex-president hurled at him during a private luncheon given by Ida Tarbell at the Colony Club.

This distaste for Theodore Roosevelt kept Baker out of the Bull Moose Party. He felt that the third party's position on the central question of the trusts was correct. The Party was stronger than he had expected; its platform was excellent; it drew many high-minded idealists. Yet he believed that the movement was an instrument for the personal glorification of a Roosevelt "not great enough to forget himself!" Baker could not see how a permanent political force could be based primarily on a feeling for the ex-president and was not surprised when the campaign centered on personalities, not issues.

Despite his demand for 'issues instead of men,' Baker was reacting against Roosevelt rather than the principle of leadership. The image of the statesman was one which coursed through Baker's thoughts and his support of Woodrow Wilson was a clearcut victory of man over platform:

> As for me . . . I shall vote for Wilson. I distrust the old party behind him. . . . But I have great confidence in the man and in the faction of the party (The progressive-Bryan faction) which he represents. And I like his clear, calm way of putting things. It seems to me the country needs just such a steady mind on its problems.

As he analyzed each of the parties, he found little to say in behalf of the Democrats. The Bull Moose and Socialist Parties impressed him far more favorably. How then could Baker vote for a Democratic Party which he labeled as basically conservative? How could he support Woodrow Wilson who believed in individualism and the return to competition, a point of view which Baker had been attacking for many years? He sought to console himself with the belief that when regulation failed, Brandeis and the Wilsonians would accept state ownership of monopolies as the only alternative. Nevertheless, Baker seemed hardly convinced by his own arguments.

He had admired Wilson since meeting him at Princeton several years before. He had followed Wilson's career and read his books, from which he jotted down excerpts, usually on the rôle of leadership, in his notebooks. But this was not quite enough and Baker had to struggle with himself to keep up his enthusiasm. However, the greatest ally in this endeavor was Theodore Roosevelt. The Bull Moosers, Baker recorded, were idealists and enthusiasts who "feel more deeply than they think," and all of this was T. R.'s fault. Impressed by an editorial on the subject Baker finally sublimated his doubts:

> I've got to take a hand in this campaign and I've got to take it against T. R. I believe that he is a dangerous man who makes men feel intensely without making them think clearly.

Baker on reform:

If only people would stop and look, and think!—and not jump at conclusions, nor accept shibboleths and slogans, nor wind themselves up in organizations and parties for trying to do wholesale what can only be done a little at a time. For I have never been a reformer, nor desired to be. I have never accepted any cut-and-dried program for social reorganization. I have never been a Socialist, nor a Communist, nor a Single Taxer. I have never belonged to a political party, nor, since my boyhood, to any church. I am suspicious of those who would change institutions without changing the understandings upon which they rest. What I have wished most, if it can be expressed in a phrase, was to be an introducer of human beings to one another, to be a maker of understandings—those deep understandings which must underlie any social change that is effective and permanent. When men come really to understand one another—if that time ever comes—war will end, poverty will end, tyranny will end, and this under almost any sort of government, almost any economic system.

Ray Stannard Baker, in his Native American: The Book of My Youth, *Charles Scribner's Sons, 1941.*

Ray Stannard Baker, the Wilsonian, had backed on to the scene. (pp. 422-34)

David Mark Chalmers, "Ray Stannard Baker's Search for Reform," in Journal of the History of Ideas, *Vol. XIX, No. 3, June, 1958, pp. 422-34.*

Dewey W. Grantham (essay date 1964)

[*Grantham is an American historian who specializes in the political history of the South. In the following excerpt from an essay originally written in 1964, he discusses* Following the Color Line, *praising the work as one of the first comprehensive studies of race relations.*]

[Baker's articles on race relations for the *American Magazine*] were an immediate success and interest in them increased as they were published. The February and March 1908 numbers of the *American* were completely sold out. Newspaper comment was generally favorable, especially in the North, and the author observed to one correspondent that while some southern journals had given him "the anticipated fits," others had been "unexpectedly appreciative." Southern liberals and moderates applauded the series. Alexander J. McKelway, a North Carolina progressive, described the articles as "eminently fair." A northern liberal, Oswald Garrison Villard, who was later to be one of the founders of the National Association for the Advancement of Colored People, termed the first article "very successful indeed." Booker T. Washington and W. E. B. Du Bois were both complimentary in their evaluation of the series, although Du Bois had reservations about a few of Baker's points. There were a few astringent notes: some of the more militant black spokesmen were critical of an interpretation that seemed to stress the duty of Negroes to the neglect of their rights.

While the magazine articles were still appearing, Baker reached an agreement with Walter Hines Page to have them brought out as a book. . . . The articles were arranged in *Following the Color Line* in the order of their appearance in the *American Magazine,* except for the inclusion of the two articles on lynching from *McClure's,* which were combined as chapter 9 of the book. Few revisions were made in the articles for book publication. As a book the work is somewhat episodic and lacks clear unity. Yet it is a comprehensive account, possessing a balance and objectivity unusual for its time. The style is characteristically readable and lively, and the narrative reveals Baker's insatiable curiosity about the human condition. The book's publication evoked the enthusiasm of scholarly as well as popular critics. The reviewer for the *American Journal of Sociology* [July 1909], for example, described it as "remarkable for its objectivity and psychological insight." It was, students of Ray Stannard Baker agree, the most significant of his publications prior to his biography of Woodrow Wilson.

Baker, as he said, was trying "to get at the *facts,*" trying to picture conditions as they actually existed during the first decade of the twentieth century. He was an indefatigable and a talented newspaperman—keen, observant, and imaginative. He took pains to express all views on the question and his frequent use of the phrase "South or North" provides a clue to his determined search for balance. Although he eschewed the role of sociologist or historian, his constant effort to understand the data he had collected and the observations of his own eyes gave his essays a dimension lacking in most journalism. These qualities were most important, perhaps, in making his account authentic and comprehensible to the average reader. The work does not always probe deeply, but it has much to commend it: the analysis of race relations in a national context, the description of concrete social situations from which racial strife arose, the graphic portrayal of the lynching mob in action, the appraisal of Negro migration, the realistic account of Negro town life, the interpretation of the opposing parties among black leaders, the recognition of the "wide and deep" chasm developing between the best elements of the two races, and the insight into the nature of racial prejudice and discrimination in South and North.

Following the Color Line was a moderate and in many respects even a conservative appraisal of the problem it surveyed. To some extent this was a tactical decision of the *American Magazine.* As John S. Phillips, one of the magazine's editors, reminded Baker in April 1907: "For the sake of effect we must keep the interest and friendliness of Southern readers. After all, they are the people whom we wish to reach and enlighten." One observer suggested that Baker was "rubbing it in" just enough to make Southerners "face the situation." Yet, fundamentally, the journalist expressed his honest convictions. They were not essentially radical in character. Baker's associations in the South tended to be with well-meaning moderates, men who joined with northern philanthropists in the annual Conferences for Southern Education during this period, and his interpretation reflects the paternalism and optimism associated with the current vogue of the Booker T. Washington school.

Southern white readers of whatever disposition on the race question could find much to please them in Baker's book. His interpretation of Reconstruction as a time of chaos and corruption was favorable to the southern white leaders. He agreed that for the time being some segregation was necessary, and he frankly said that Negroes "as a class are to-day far inferior in education, intelligence, and efficiency to the white people as a class." While he asserted that both the approach of Booker T. Washington and that of W. E. B. Du Bois were valuable, he obviously preferred the Tuskegee idea of education for service over Du Bois' more aggressive program. As a backward race Negroes would have to go forward primarily under the tutelage of white men. Genuine progress would come only with "time, growth, education, religion, thought." Baker also held other assumptions that were common during the period of his investigation. At times he fell into the familiar southern habit of characterizing blacks as a race in various particulars. When he used the word "Southerner," he meant *white* Southerner; he did not include the Negro. It was this assumption, accepted naturally and perhaps even unconsciously by Baker, that led Du Bois to remark to him in April 1907:

> Of course, as I have said to you personally, the great trouble with anyone coming from the outside to study the Negro problem is that they do not know the Negro as a human being, as a feeling, thinking man; that they do know the Southerners, have met them in their homes and have been intimate with them and the result is that while they speak of the Southerner in the second person, they continually regard the Negro as in the third person, a sort of outside and unknown personality.

Although Ray Stannard Baker thought of himself as an objective reporter, he was intensely interested in educating his readers, in being a "maker of understandings." "The best thing," he wrote a few months before beginning his exploration of the color line, "seems to be more publicity, more information, more preaching in the wilderness." Like many other progressives, Baker had a profound faith in the possibility of awakening and regenerating the individual citizen, "his intelligence, his unselfishness, his social responsibility." Yet during the years he was working on *Following the Color Line* Baker was becoming increasingly convinced of the necessity of a collectivist approach to social action, and his book presented a class analysis of historical movements. Clearly there was some contradiction in the journalist's acceptance of a Washingtonian philosophy of improvement by individual effort and his class interpretation of history. The contradiction is never reconciled in *Following the Color Line.* But in answering Theodore Roosevelt's vigorous criticism of his division of society into the "Few" and the "Many" and of his thesis that the Negro problem was really part of a larger struggle for democracy, Baker insisted that the political revolution in the South offered proof that *"class action is a condition now existent."*

Although Baker contended that the Vardamans and Jeff Davises represented "a genuine movement for a more democratic government in the South," his interpretation was scarcely an endorsement of southern conditions. He criticized the old aristocratic leadership in the region as being selfish and undemocratic, but he also realized that the new "men of the people" like Vardaman would exploit the passions and prejudices of the white masses. Yet he was hopeful. He found democracy at work in the overthrow of the old leadership and believed that it would not stop at the color line: "once its ferment begins to work in a nation it does not stop until it reaches and animates the uttermost man." In this sense Baker's work was anything but prosouthern. In fact, a note of impending political change runs strongly through the book. And despite his darker fears, he thought the South was ready for change and that the ferment of democracy would soon bring the Negro into more active participation in American society.

If Baker subscribed to many of the conservative ideas about race so commonplace in his day, he was nevertheless able to transcend much of the racism of his contemporaries. His genuine concern over the distressing conditions of American blacks, his sympathy for the downtrodden, his ardor for justice, and his basic optimism were inseparable from the argument of *Following the Color Line.* His broad humanity embraced the Negro, and he considered racial conflict a spiritual as well as a social and economic problem. His very inconsistencies revealed as much. Thus it was impossible for him to reconcile his emphasis on the growing separation of the two races, into which he tried to read hopeful signs, with his belief in democracy and brotherhood. It was this confusion, this dilemma, that gave his chapter on the mulatto in America—the man caught in between—rare sensitiveness and pathos. The prophetic quality of *Following the Color Line* cannot compare with such a volume as Du Bois' *The Souls of Black Folk* (1903), but its very ambivalence makes it one of the most revealing documents of the progressive era. Baker had no ready solution for the American Dilemma; he could only suggest "a gradual substitution of understanding and sympathy for blind repulsion and hatred." But he was convinced that "the white man as well as the black is being tried by fire." And throughout his book he demonstrated a conviction that "the man farthest down" could be helped only if all Americans expressed a democratic spirit.

In the decade following the publication of *Following the Color Line* Baker retained his interest in the problem of the Negro in the United States, writing and speaking on the subject and stressing his conviction that the problem was basically one of democracy. For a time his optimism about an ultimate solution mounted. Thus in 1913 he predicted the early break up of the Solid South, the entrance of many blacks and poor whites into politics, and a rejuvenated southern political life in which basic issues could be attacked and solved. But events soon pricked the bubble of his optimism. In the fall of 1914 he conceded that in its patronage and segregation policies the Wilson administration had "surrendered a stronghold of democracy in the treatment of the Negro & given new territory to the occupation of the idea of caste in America." In 1916 he expressed alarm over the growing economic competition between the races in the South, the increasing migration of blacks to northern cities, the growing resort to Jim Crow measures in South and North, and the mounting bitterness of Negroes because of the discriminatory treatment they suffered.

In investigating such great national problems as the role of organized labor and the most effective way for democracy to deal with powerful business aggregations, Ray Stannard Baker had shown remarkable capacity to enlarge his understanding and to grow in sympathetic appreciation of the human beings involved. This was also true of his experience in following the color line. Puzzled by the hostile response of the more aggressive black leaders to what he had written, he reexamined some of the opinions he had expressed in his book. With the passage of time he moved closer to Du Bois' philosophy of active agitation for Negro equality and in 1915 even accepted an honorary vice-presidency of the NAACP. By that time he had begun to wonder "if social equality is not, after all, the crux of the whole problem?" He continued to have faith in the promise of progress through education, economic improvement, and humanitarianism. But as the signs of danger grew during the next few years, he became appalled at "the contemptuous indifference of a large part of white

America to what is going on in the depths of the volcano just below."

Following the Color Line was a pioneer work in the study of race relations in the United States. Baker's careful reporting and revealing insight make it a singularly useful account for the period it treats. Gunnar Myrdal and his associates used it as a major source in the preparation of *An American Dilemma* (1944), quoting from it more than two dozen times. In many respects it is superior to most southern travel accounts of the era, including Albert Bushnell Hart's *The Southern South* (1910), William Archer's *Through Afro-America* (1910), and Maurice S. Evans' *Black and White in the Southern States* (1915). Rupert B. Vance has described it as "the best account of race relations in the South during the period—one that reads like field notes for the future historian." In its description of conditions and attitudes in the South the book often goes beyond race relations, and although not the work of a social scientist, it contributed to the conviction that the South invited disciplined sociological investigation.

Baker's volume is also significant as the most substantial contribution by any muckraker and progressive to the literature on the American Negro. It is not, strictly speaking, a muckraking book, but it does recapture some of the muckraking spirit. More important, it reflects in a superb way the assumptions and aspirations of the progressive mind which Baker typified so well. The journalist understood that the problem he was discussing was ineluctably involved in the deeper currents of American democracy, and he attempted to treat it from that perspective. He had hoped, like a good muckraker, that publicity and education would stimulate the American people to take action and gradually to set their democracy in order. But like many progressives Baker would go only so far toward greater equality. The tragedy is that even the limited reconstruction he envisaged in 1908 was largely neglected, and the progressive movement failed to come to grips with the problem.

Baker was one of the first white writers in modern America to discuss the race issue comprehensively and in a spirit of fairness. His work contributed in some measure to the forces that eventually brought the question of the Negro's status in the United States to its rightful place as a compelling national issue. But *Following the Color Line*'s greatest value is as a reliable and revealing source for those interested in the course of race relations in recent American history. (pp. 110-16)

> *Dewey W. Grantham, "Ray Stannard Baker's Report on American Negro Citizenship in the Progressive Era," in his* The Regional Imagination: The South and Recent American History, *Vanderbilt University Press, 1979, pp. 107-16.*

Robert C. Bannister, Jr. (essay date 1966)

[*Bannister is an American educator, critic, and the author of the biography* Ray Stannard Baker: The Mind and Thought of a Progressive. *In the following excerpt from that book, he examines ways in which Baker's beliefs compare with those of his character David Grayson.*]

[While Baker and others were making plans to take over the *American Magazine*], John Phillips, who was to serve as editor, urged each member of the staff to search for material among half-finished articles and stories. Baker at first considered **"The Water Lord"** and another novel of life in the desert, but the theme no longer attracted him. After several soul-searching days, he destroyed both manuscripts. Then he remembered his journals, in particular some sketches of country life he had penned late in 1904 and early 1905. By early June he had sent off the first installments of the adventures of his "unlimited farmer" as he called his hero. By the end of July his editor had the entire series, which Baker now titled *Adventures in Contentment.* The first appeared in the November issue; and with it "David Grayson," as the new author was known to all but a few, made his literary debut.

Although a total of nine volumes of these adventures appeared in the next thirty-five years, the stories remained much the same, in content as simple as Grayson's bucolic existence. By profession a farmer, but by choice a wanderer, David lived with his sister Harriet in some undetermined spot within the broad bounds of the New England band of culture extending from the Vermont of Baker's ancestors to his childhood home in St. Croix Falls. The characters he encountered on his travels had usually a single dimension, and often embodied values which Baker had questioned but never entirely rejected: Harriet "the Accumulated and Personified Customs, Morals and Institutions of the Ages," who generally disapproved of her brother's adventures but never seriously interfered with them; the Scotch Preacher, a Rock of the Presbyterian Faith, who was David's closest companion; and Horace, a real farmer who consistently provided a "practical" view of things. An assortment of minor characters, often without names, then paraded with allegorical precision the complexities that confronted the modern pilgrim: the Millionaire, the Tramp, the Town Infidel, the Drunkard, the Unwed Mother, and the Celebrity, to mention only a few.

For inspiration and form, the sketches owed a number of literary debts. The wandering adventurer was an acknowledged descendant of the picaresque heroes of Sterne, Smollett, and Fielding, and of another Englishman, William Cobbett, whose *Rural Rides* (1830) Baker greatly enjoyed. Among American wanderers, Grayson most resembled Johnny Appleseed, whose story Baker had earlier planned to tell. The contented author-farmer also recalled Donald G. Mitchell ("Ik Marvel"), whose books young Baker had devoured, and was a kindred spirit to John Muir and Joel Chandler Harris, whose contented lives the reporter had already described in the *Outlook*. As the author of popular pastorals, Grayson joined Parson Charles Wagner, an honored visitor at *McClure's* and the author of the best-selling *Simple Life* (1901); the less famous Martha McCulloc Williams, whose *Next to the Ground* (1902) Baker also knew; and the host of essayists who were filling the magazines with similar "chronicles of the countryside."

Baker with the staff of the American Magazine.

More immediately, however, Grayson was the child of the *American* and, as its editors claimed, faithfully captured the "spirit" that lay at the heart of their new venture. This spirit they defined in clear terms. "We shall not only make this new *American Magazine* interesting and important in a public way, but we shall make it the most stirring and delightful monthly book of fiction, humor, sentiment, and joyous reading that is anywhere published," they proclaimed in a brochure announcing their enterprise. "It will reflect a happy, struggling, fighting world, in which, as we believe, good people are coming out on top . . . Our magazine will be wholesome, hopeful, stimulating, uplifting, and above all it will have a human interest on every page." Baker repeated the point when he wrote to Gifford Pinchot in July that their aim was "to get into the magazine just as much of the spirit of this American life as we possibly can—*all* of it, not politics or reformers alone, but every human interest." There was no explicit plan to drop muckraking, or even to make a magazine very different from *McClure's* (which after all had its share of stirring sentiment). But the *American* would definitely look for what Baker had once called "hopeful signs in our life." With Grayson as their guide, this band of muckrakers would counter Roosevelt's charge and, like the gentle David at the close of his first series of adventures, stand

at last "on the hill Clear" and look to "the gates of the celestial city."

John Phillips became Grayson's special guardian, and cautioned him if he strayed from *American* principles. He was most concerned when David went "highbrow." "After all," he warned at one point when Baker had interjected a reference to one of his favorite authors, "Maeterlinck is a thing for the sophisticated, and it gives the whole thing a literary air." When Grayson proposed solutions to the world's problems, Phillips repeated the advice he had earlier given the muckraker: "Yes we want facts, we want human nature, but as a journal of present day life, we want things relating to this life, not going too far beyond, not too much of a forecast, not too much of a solution—facts that tend to thinking in the right direction." "I doubt," he added, "if it would be a good plan to have a firmly settled plan." The Chicago *Record, McClure's,* and now the *American:* Baker once again owed a great debt to his associates.

Grayson's success was immediate. Lincoln Steffens commended his "sense of beauty . . . philosophic wisdom, and most wonderful of all,—serenity." Albert A. Boyden, who had come from *McClure's* as business manager, predicted that the "farmer stuff" was "not only great stuff, but it is going to be great stuff for us." Even [Theodore Roosevelt] had kind words, although he would soon discover how little he and Grayson had in common. When the first adventures were finished, the editors demanded more. Hundreds of readers conveyed their appreciation in letters, and in a few years "David Grayson clubs" arose spontaneously in several parts of the country. Even the unscrupulous paid a tribute of sorts when men calling themselves Grayson appeared in various places, often leaving behind them unpaid board bills. In Denver a fraudulent Grayson reportedly won himself a bride on the strength of his literary achievement.

No reviewer called the adventures a masterpiece, but over the years a number said kind words. The basis of judgment was most often the ideas they presented, rather than their literary qualities. Those reviewers who liked optimism and the traditional culture naturally praised, while those who dissented inevitably criticized. Many recognized Grayson's sources of inspiration and promptly set the books in historical perspective. One thought a particular story ranked with Stevenson's *Travels with a Donkey* (another old favorite of Baker), and a number commented on the similarity to the tales of Donald Mitchell, especially his *Wet Days at Edgewood* (1865). In the most perceptive and witty review Grayson ever received, the young poet Vachel Lindsay accurately described him as "Ik Marvel Afoot."

Although Lindsay also shrewdly guessed in 1914 that Grayson was Baker, the well-kept secret was not revealed until two years later, in an article in the *Bookman*. A few readers were shocked and dismayed. "Please tell me it is not true!" wrote one lady from Atlanta. "Why I feel as tho I'd lost my *best* friend." But in later years Grayson continued to win friends. Among them was Christopher Morley, who at the start of his own literary career saluted the older author in a parody called *Parnassus on Wheels* (1918), which he billed as an "adventure in discontentment." After the war Grayson's fame spread even further when his stories began to appear in anthologies in schoolrooms all over America. "The beauty of the thing," remarked Walter Hines Page of Doubleday and Page soon after he had published the first series, "is it steadiness." In the end the "unlimited farmer" truly earned his name by selling some two million copies in America and the British Commonwealth and in several foreign language translations.

Although the "reflex of Baker," as he once described himself, Grayson not only had roots deep in Baker's past but, in his several characteristics, summarized his creator's intellectual development. A country dweller, he realized also that the isolation of farm life often led to dreary "provincialism" and an excessive and destructive individualism. The idealistic "Noble," he had a new sympathy for the woes of the ambitious and harassed "Cartwright," a second figure who had also appeared in Baker's journal in the nineties. ("Noble" and "Cartwright" were in this sense the direct forerunners of Grayson and Baker.) A skeptical and hardheaded Yankee, he recalled in his semimystical moods the young Baker whose generation thrilled to the mental feats of Svengali or gathered in dark rooms themselves to confront the occult. ("Anything dealing with the latent and little known or understood powers of the human soul commands my deepest interest," wrote Ray's cousin Arthur after reading *Peter Ibbetson*.) Moreover, it was to be Grayson's genius to reconcile each of these extremes.

He began by describing the Good Life. He had moved to the country to escape not only the city but the relentless pressures of the life there. Yet this was not another trip to the desert. Although Grayson was "a ruddy vigorous out-of-door person," he approached nature more in the spirit of a John Muir. He felt, as he explained in a well-chosen image, "like one sore-wounded creeping from the field of Battle." Baker's own life, he wrote his wife, had become "too confounded strenuous." These new "adventures" would yield only "contentment," "friendship," and "understanding."

Although Grayson explicitly rejected the city, especially in the earlier adventures, he would not give up the benefits of urban civilization. Praising the simple life, he looked to technology to help men attain it. He welcomed rural mail delivery, the telephone, and even country trolleys, because they brought the farmer "well within the stimulating currents of world thought." He would not "return to the old, crude, time consuming ways of our ancestors." Although he sometimes spoke of planting and harvesting at nature's call, the M.A.C. graduate was quick to advise the unsuccessful farmer to write the state experiment station for information. (At these times Grayson echoed the advice of Roosevelt's Country Life Commission, headed by Liberty Hyde Bailey, his former teacher, and aided by Kenyon Butterfield, Baker's former classmate and good friend.) The balance he demanded was a delicate one. A town should be "not too far off (and yet not too near)" a railroad, "convenient (though not so near that the whistling of the engines reaches you)." But with a characteristic optimism, Grayson believed that an "agricultural course to ruralize the towns and a mechanical course to urbanize the country" would achieve the desired result.

The people who best embodied Grayson's ideal were neither real farmers nor city folk but "enthusiastic gardeners" like "Mr. and Mrs. Veddar" in *The Friendly Road.* A wealthy middle-aged couple, the Veddars had moved from a large house to the caretaker's cottage on the edge of their estate where David found them rocking contentedly on a lilac shaded porch. A lovely garden was their greatest joy, and Grayson soon learned that they shared his enthusiasm for Andrew J. Downing's *Rural Essays* (1853), "the Bible of the Gardener." Quoting from Downing, Mr. Veddar explained the philosophy behind their move: "It has always been agreed that these plantations should make amends for living at a distance from what would be [a] more congenial and agreeable dwelling place—in the midst of nature, free and unrestrained." Grayson agreed: "that's it, a garden excuses civilization."

In his rejection of the strenuous life and his praise for the Veddars, Grayson was a beacon for his time, and his image of the Good Life was curiously close to the enthusiastic blueprints for suburban living that filled the popular magazines during the progressive era. As Vachel Lindsay suggested in his review of one series of adventures, Grayson's "reaction against strenuosity" represented a new and "balanced American mood." Lindsay himself was cynical. He was tired, that poet wrote, of hearing "pie-faced, mutton headed businessmen . . . tell me they like David Grayson; tell me with a little-Eva-going-to-heaven look in their eyes; tell me, presuming it establishes a deep soulful understanding between us." "The fidgety automobile-mad upper classes" saw in the stories their ideal, he charged, but the hardworking bourgeois also recognized from Tom Fogarty's curly-headed illustrations that the dream was not to be taken too seriously, that he might be "in theory a bucolic, tho he does not leave the office or the automobile yet." But Grayson's many friends testified in their letters that there was something more, as they thanked him for giving their life new meaning, or even for inspiring new undertakings.

Baker's own life suggested that there was some truth in both judgments. By no coincidence the same year Grayson reportedly bought his farm (1898), Baker had sought the cool quiet of suburban Bronxville. It was also Grayson who returned from the Southwest to a new home in East Lansing in 1902, and settled finally in Amherst, Massachusetts, in 1910. There he worked to exhaustion in the mornings, gardened and tramped all afternoon, and sometimes even took a spin in his automobile.

Life in this new paradise would be happy, graceful, and, above all, tolerant. Freed from the past, Grayson would judge everything anew. Unhampered by custom or tradition, he was, as he boasted, "neither old nor rich nor married." A member of no church, no lodge or political party, he was not "tagged with tags." Therefore, he noted, "I think whatever I please upon any subject, and what I think I have the indiscretion to write down without apology." He would travel the "open road," he explained further, in a figure that dominated the second series of adventures. "I have no preconceived impressions, or beliefs, or opinions. My lane fence is the end of the known earth . . . I have no idea what discoveries I shall make."

On moral issues he had apparently learned with Baker that most questions were usually "grey" not "black or white." "It had become with Noble, not a choice between right and wrong, but a choice of wrongs," Baker wrote in his journal, explaining the change that had occurred in his thinking since the nineties. "From such a point of view there is no intrinsic right, only an opportunity to choose the lesser wrong." In his stories Grayson thus consistently condemned the moralizer who judged without inquiring into the circumstances. In a story of a **"Drunkard,"** he befriended an amiable alcoholic, despite the protests of his sister Harriet, who reasoned much as Baker had done as a youth. In **"Anna"** he helped a young unwed mother whose family had driven her out. Sometimes David's open mind disturbed even his editors. Boyden wrote that he liked the **"Drunkard"** but asked Grayson to "put in a little of the other side—showing how *dearly he paid*—this makes drunkenness a little too attractive and heaven's knows it is attractive enough." "After all," he pleaded, "you can get as bigoted about the value of the open mind as anything else—and David is essentially not a bigot."

Yet, despite appearances, Grayson did not really accept the moral relativism implicit in Baker's earlier discoveries. Although he examined circumstances and cautioned his readers against the traditional pieties, he did not explain away any wrongs. He would embrace the sinners, not because conditions made all judgments relative but because like Walt Whitman he would reject nothing. "I saw that the sun still shone on her as to me," he wrote of **"Anna."** "Why then if God still smiles, should I in my pride be less than kind." In the story of the **"Drunkard"** he again observed: "The sun shone too on the Drunkard, and the leaves did not turn aside from him as he passed." "Is it not," he asked, "just this at-one-ment with life which sweetens and saves us all."

A stern God who exacted obedience through fear—such as Baker had demanded as late as 1902—also found no place in Grayson's world. On this one point he agreed with the Village Infidel: "If a man has to be scared into religion, his religion ain't much good." But in his love for nature he did not reject God altogether. His friend the Botanist sparked his conversion in the first series of **Adventures.** "When I was a boy I believed implicitly in God . . . having a vision of him—a person—before my eyes," explained the old gentleman, who was clearly modeled after Dr. Beal. "As I grew older I concluded there was no God . . . [but] now—it seems to me—there is nothing but God." God to Grayson henceforth seemed "An Immanent Presence." As Baker explained the position in his journal:

> Each age must worship its own thought of God. The God of the capitalistic time peculiarly a personal god, a god approving of individual and personal virtues, a religion of predestination and foreordination—immediate rewards for thrift and decency. What then will be the idea of God in the coming era? A god of brotherhood, of love, of cooperation.

"Do we not often make the mistake of thinking of God as apart from matter?" he asked. "He is that too: that too is a part of *Him.*" "There is no end to God," he concluded. "There is no end to the growth and achievement of a man who loses himself in that greatest of unities."

As in the case of the urbanized countryside, Grayson on each of these questions reconciled the extremes at least to his own satisfaction. When he discussed other issues, the pattern was substantially the same. The beauty of his position was that one might have the best of all worlds—of conviction and of tolerance, of faith and of reason, of Nature and of God. Although David embarked on many "adventures" and often scandalized Harriet with his associates, there was always something eminently safe about the entire operation. As Malcolm Cowley has said of his own prewar illusions, Grayson's rambles on the "open road" were the sort "on which you set out to God knows where and get back in time for dinner."

In his role as a philosopher, Grayson explained the source of his success. His aim was to close the gap that had long plagued Baker, and to achieve "that equilibrium between the spiritual and the material . . . which is the ideal of life." His attack proceeded on two fronts. Against the claims of scientific materialism he urged the reality of spirit. The "true scientist," Grayson insisted, went to nature "humbly," aware of the limitations of his approach. "The chief teaching [of all the great prophets, poets and sages] . . . has been that the life of man is spiritual, not material," Baker wrote, explaining Grayson's position; "the true realities are not the things we see, feel, hear, touch, but those greater things of life that we recognize through the spirit, the imagination, or by faith." Grayson was "no materialist." "What I mean by reality, is not what you mean," he wrote, adding: "what I mean by reality may, to you, be dreams."

Although Grayson thus bordered on philosophical idealism, he insisted as strongly that he was no idealist. "It might be dimly beatific to float continually in a cloud of fine ideas but such an atmosphere is too rare for the growth of the human soul. Always there must be a return to the earth." Comparing himself to the mythical Anteus, Grayson "drew his strength from the ground." A man of the soil, he knew "how surely, soundly, deeply the physical underlies the spiritual." Others might be tempted by Christian Science (his cousin Arthur Baker, for example) or the mysteries of the New Thought, each of which emphasized the primacy of mind. But Grayson would remain the "unlimited farmer." He preferred, as he said, "to meet life (the dual life) with eyes wide open."

The several sources of his philosophy added up to a recognizable pattern. The idea of the unlimited farmer came most directly from some lines from Emerson which he had copied in 1905:

> Know he who tills this lovely field
> To reap its scanty corn
> What mystic fruits his acres yield
> At midnight and at morn.

And the others were, roughly speaking, in the same tradition. William Penn's *Fruits of Solitude,* Carlyle's essay "Characteristics," Wordsworth's poems, and the writings of Thoreau all became Baker's favorites in the Grayson years. John Burroughs' study of Whitman revealed to him new dimensions in both authors. Emerson and Whitman he repeated countless times were the "two greatest American writers."

From each he learned that, in William Penn's words, "The world is certainly a great and stately volume of natural things; and may not be improperly styled the Hieroglyphickes of a better." Grayson's reality was "dreams," not because matter did not exist, but because the natural world was a symbol for another "hidden except for the inner eye which sees not symbols but reality." Each also taught him that the world was essentially one. In the nineties Baker had pasted in his journal the lines from Emerson's "Brahma":

> If the Red Slayer thinks he slays,
> Or if the slain thinks he is slain,
> They know not well the subtle ways
> I keep and pass and turn again.

In 1905 he rediscovered this truth with fresh excitement as he read Sir Edwin Arnold's translation of the "Bhagavad Gita":

> He who should say "Lo! I have slain a man,"
> He who shall think, "Lo I am slain!" These both
> Know nought! Life cannot slay. Life is not slain.

So inspired, Grayson found Unity where Baker had found only a fierce struggle:

> I do not worship nature, but what nature typifies or suggests. In my moods of 'yea' the world pleases me: I shout in my joy. I am happy. In my moods of 'nay' the world crushes me. I am disturbed by its injustices, its inharmonies, the heedless chance by which it seems to dominate life. Cold fear touches my heart. And then I reflect that all this is but shadow, unreal, symbols which, in trying to understand bring us nearer to that power which controls us all.

"We may read *Sartor Resartus* and think we understand it," Ray's cousin had written to him in 1893. "But each one alone must fight his way through the 'everlasting yea.' " With Grayson's help Baker had reread Carlyle and, it seemed, at last understood.

In 1906 Baker did not reflect very much upon his philosophical debts nor try to place Grayson in any intellectual tradition. When one critic years later would suggest that Grayson was "the last of the transcendentalists" he would stubbornly resist the label. Yet his debt to Emerson and the other "dreamers of dreams," as Holbrook Jackson has called them, was unmistakable. Nor was it a coincidence that in their day most of these authors were also seeking refuge from the winds of change, from the unsettling consequences of a scientific, technological and commercial revolution which they both admired and feared. Like his forerunners, it would also be Grayson's job to salvage what he could in a world which seemed to be moving awfully fast.

Baker had used *noms de plume* before ("Lloyd Barrington" in letters to the editor of the *Record,* and "Sturgis B. Rand" in early *McClure's* articles) but "Grayson" clearly meant more to him, and he insisted vigorously that the secret be kept. Although one factor was his fear that public knowledge of his new work would harm his reputation as a reporter, his feeling also concealed a genuine ambivalence toward his alter ego. Sometimes the reporter clearly envied the philosopher. "One of these days I'm going to revolt at this sort of life exactly as Grayson did and raise cows or turnips," Baker wrote his wife in November 1906. Two years later he had almost given up: "I wish I had Grayson's unity and contentment but I am destined all my life, I suppose, to the rages of impatience, unsatisfied longing, inferiority to the ideal I have for myself." But the dream continued to attract him.

Yet there also remained a lingering distrust. The radical Baker periodically charged that Grayson's "contentment" was only the warm afterglow of a full stomach, while, paradoxically the convention-bound and respectable Baker often shared Harriet's misgivings at her brother's own brand of radicalism. On the everyday level, the industrious Yankee was always uneasy when Grayson wandered at harvest time, while, intellectually, his common sense distrusted both Grayson's idealism and his constant glorification of the smells, tastes, and colors of a sensuous world that had always frightened New Englanders.

Although Baker and Grayson would debate a number of issues, the prospects of a fruitful exchange were thus not bright from the start, and would grow dimmer as the two personalities inevitably blurred into one. Grayson represented Baker's imaginative side, but the rational empiricist consistently checked the free flight of Grayson's imagination. The simplest explanation of Baker's failures at novel writing was a lack of talent, but in an extremely perceptive analysis he later suggested that his shortcomings were also intellectually significant:

> I consider, with a sense of the unmutterable mystery of life, the deception of appearance, wherein nothing is itself but a symbol of something else. If I proceed from this to a still higher mood, I begin to see these concrete images of life, called metaphors, which give me a blinding, if momentary, understanding of the abstract and illusive realities of life. But metaphors are soap bubbles, the irredescent surfaces of which, having reflected the universe, dissolve swiftly into their original elements. How know that a minute drop of water should become the sign of all things? How know the ultimate magic of a single word?

How "know," that is, when "know" means to reduce experience to the manageable logic of scientific discourse. How follow imagination, in other words, when imagination is somehow suspect? Baker's desire to escape the confines of rational intellect was strong, and his models—Emerson and Whitman—well chosen. Yet, like the Hamilton Mabies of the Genteel Tradition, he borrowed their rhetoric but could never follow their example. If John Burroughs was, as Henry James said, "a sort of reduced, but also more humorous, more available, and more sociable Thoreau," Grayson accomplished much less than either. His "truths" were familiar, and his phrases "heartwarming," and neither a substitute for wisdom and art. Although Baker tried several times to write his Great American Novel after 1906, the results were unfinished manuscripts, and a string of Grayson stories which, in the end, found their best audience in the *Reader's Digest.*

If the loss of the Great American Novel was a questionable one, Grayson's effect on Baker's proven abilities as a reporter was more serious. Restless under the distinctions between literature and journalism which had earlier sustained him, Baker during 1905 and 1906 began to blur his definitions. "Do not be mistaken," he wrote: "The best journalism is truly art." He saw that "of all callings that of the journalist is and should be nearest that of the poet." "Journalism," he noted again in November 1906, "may be compared to poetry which deals in emotions and arrives by inspiration." Sometimes as he spoke of his work it almost seemed as if nothing would change: "chief purpose of a magazine then, by giving us views of other sorts of life, [is] to awaken our lazy imaginations, to reconstruct for us the lives of others, thereby waking us to sympathy." But the future would tell how important these definitions were. More than any external pressures, they marked the end of Baker's muckraking. Although the reporter had

hoped "never [to] lose sensitiveness to the new fact," the philosopher who saw "everything . . . in anything" believed that, strictly speaking, there were no new facts. As several observers would note, it became in later years increasingly difficult to tell a Baker report from a Grayson idyll.

Grayson's contribution to Baker's education lay less in conclusions than in a method, and therein was its danger. This transcendental method, as Santayana observed a few years later, might easily yield to transcendental myth when, for a strict subjectivism, one substituted a philosophical system woven only of those perceptions the individual consciousness cared to honor. The tatters of tradition would thereby receive new status, and a dogma best described as "genteel," establish itself in the guise of a free and inquiring intellect. For the middle-class reformer like Baker, who feared the very changes he demanded, the attractions of this method were many. In Grayson's world one could have everything at once—institutions and spontaneity, individual and group, rich and poor, inflation and the middle class, permanence and change—one half of each the red slayer, the other half slain, and no one hurt after all.

Unhappily, much turned on verbal tricks. As one of Grayson's companions on the **Friendly Road** remarked: "Say, you're just like a preacher I used to know when I was a kid. He was always sayin' things that meant something else and when you found out what he was drivin' at you always felt kind of queer in your insides." "Reason," "science," "radicalism," "democracy," and a dozen other key terms meant quite different things to Baker and Grayson. As the reporter turned in late 1906 to explore America's many problems, there was a real question whether he would be able to keep the definitions straight. (pp. 110-25)

> *Robert C. Bannister, Jr., in his* Ray Stannard Baker: The Mind and Thought of a Progressive, *Yale University Press, 1966, 335 p.*

Baker on his pseudonym:

I kept secret all my early [creative writing] endeavors and whenever I sent out a story or verses which I considered the "real thing" I used pseudonyms, and sometimes took the most absurd precautions not to have the correspondence come in my own name—as though any one in the world was in the least interested! Even fifteen years later when I entrusted to the editor some of the little essays and stories that made up **Adventures in Contentment,** I hid behind what I hoped would prove an impenetrable nom-de-plume—David Grayson. This was not because what I had to say was shocking or revolutionary but because I was afraid to expose my deepest and truest thoughts and feelings, which I considered—I saw afterward how mistakenly—to be wholly different from what other people felt or thought.

Ray Stannard Baker, in his Native American: The Book of My Youth, *Charles Scribner's Sons, 1941.*

John E. Semonche (essay date 1969)

[*Semonche is an American historian, lawyer, critic, and author of* Ray Stannard Baker: A Quest for Democracy in Modern America, 1870-1918. *In the following excerpt from that book, he offers an in-depth characterization of David Grayson, whom he describes as Baker's alter ego, and discusses the popular appeal of the Grayson works.*]

Nine Grayson volumes were published during the period from 1907 to 1943. There is a clear division between the first six books and the last three. In the first six volumes Grayson is maintained as a character separate from Ray Stannard Baker, even though Grayson shares many of the thoughts of his creator and though he liberally draws upon elements in Baker's youth as his own. The latter three volumes, beginning with *Adventures in Solitude* in 1931, though still constructed around the impressions of Grayson, are in reality autobiographical accounts of parts of Baker's life; in these books Grayson and Baker are one. . . . The characterization of Grayson that follows is based upon an analysis of the first six volumes. The books are drawn on freely without regard to the date of their composition, for in the twenty-year period Grayson seems neither to age nor to change his basic attitude toward life or living.

Except for the Grayson novel *Hempfield,* which is only a partial departure from the original form, the books consist of a series of impressions and studies unified through the narrator, David Grayson. The books are all written in the first person, a technique Baker believed enhanced reality. In these six volumes Grayson is drawn as a fairly consistent character, but he is not simply a farmer, nor is he intended to be. He is an educated man with impressive literary knowledge, who, when we meet him in 1906, is happily settled on a small farm. Eight years earlier he had left the fast-paced life of the city; the common quest for material success had left him depressed in spirit and broken in health. On the farm, which he now owns, he regains his physical vigor and cultivates his spirit along with his fields. He has become an "unlimited farmer," one who farms "with the plow of a perennial admiration and inquisitiveness, all the world. . . ." Intolerance he sees as the great enemy, and he has resolved to accept all, to the extent that he says he could be accused of being "bigoted about the value of the open mind. . . ." He realizes the human tendency to shape the people we meet into a certain image, but he has resolved that he will accept people as they are and seek to understand them rather than to change them. He considers the inquiring mind—one that questions all traditions, institutions, and beliefs—as essential in keeping a man "young and useful!"

Grayson's library is rather large and impressive, and when he is not revelling in the joys of outdoor life, he is enjoying his books. In *Adventures in Contentment* he pays his tribute to literature:

> What a convenient and delightful world is this world of books!—if you bring to it not the obligations of the student, or look upon it as an opiate for idleness, but enter it rather with the enthusiasm of the adventurer! It has the vast advantages over the ordinary world of daylight, of barter and trade, of work and worry. In this world every man is his own King—the sort of King one loves to imagine, not concerned in such petty matters as wars and parliaments and taxes, but a mellow and moderate despot who is a true patron of genius—a mild old chap who has in his court the greatest men and women in the world—and all of them vying to please the most vagrant of his moods! Invite any one of them to talk, and if your highness is not pleased with him you have only to put him back in his corner—and bring some jester to sharpen the laughter of your highness, or some poet to set your faintest emotion to music!

In the home, he feels, all books can find a place, but only certain books can make the transition from fireside to open country. There he prefers books like William Penn's *Some of the Fruits of Solitude,* which may be dipped into leisurely and comfortably under the open skies. Montaigne, one of his favorites, he finds too sophisticated and urbanized for outdoor reading; the pages of his volumes make better fuel for a fire than for the mind of the traveler, he says.

Being an educated man, Grayson liberally draws upon literature in his musings. At times he had to be restrained so that he would not move beyond the ken of his readers, but generally his predilection for literary allusions seems compatible with his character. One careful student of the Grayson books has counted approximately 650 literary references in the nine volumes. The Bible is referred to more than ninety times and Shakespeare more than thirty. Marcus Aurelius, Montaigne, Goethe, Emerson, Whitman, and Cervantes are quoted more than a dozen times each. Grayson writes for much the same reason Baker did: he enjoys the experience and he feels that he has something worth saying. His writing style is relaxed and appealing, and many contemporary critics saw genuine literary merit in it.

Grayson is a bachelor, presumably middle-aged, who in his free and expansive way enjoys his contacts with people. At times he seems to learn from his personal encounters, as from the Negro stringing telephone lines or from Bill Hahn, the socialist, but these exchanges are really less a learning experience than a matter of Baker's putting into the mouths of a few others the views of Grayson. Much more often Grayson teaches those he meets, either by seeking to expand their views beyond their limited occupational or social horizons or by demonstrating how truly fortunate they are. Grayson often appears somewhat smug in such encounters, and he seems to toy with the people he meets. On one occasion the farmer sees himself as a Socrates who by asking questions can open new doors for others. In this particular encounter with a "Shabby Man," Grayson, even as Socrates, is unsuccessful, but more often his influence is indelibly impressed upon the person with whom he comes in contact, whether he is a farmer, roadworker, millionaire, or peddler. In one of his prefaces Grayson slyly says that he is bound to emerge victorious from the many personal contests in which he engages, for it is he who is telling the story.

In the early "adventures" Grayson uses his neighbor Horace and his sister Harriet as foils. These characters do not succumb to Grayson's charm and are utilized to provide some balance. Horace, the practical New England farmer, who sees nearly everything in terms of dollars and cents, cannot help regarding Grayson as rather strange and impractical. Harriet gives Grayson a home with its attendant comforts without Baker's having to come to grips with the man-wife relationship. She is often shocked by her brother's ideas and actions. Her forte is her cooking, which again and again Grayson celebrates in his prose. She is homey and helpful to those in need, but she often appears reticent and skeptical in spite of her warmheartedness. In these characteristics Harriet resembles Jessie Baker, but she is never fully developed and can be at best only a partial reflection.

Though Grayson acknowledges that a farm, even his farm, cannot guarantee contentment, he pays homage to the joys of a rural existence. Happiness he sees as a dividend one receives from the hard physical work associated with the farming life. He seems to feel that hard work is not only a cure for a sick body but for an impoverished spirit as well; in a bit of personal confession, he says that he knows that the fields and hills can heal a man's soul. Grayson prescribes the farmer's life as the best way to escape from falseness and materialism, for on a farm "a man may yield himself most nearly to the quiet and orderly processes of nature. He may attain most nearly to that equilibrium between the material and spiritual, with time for the exactions of the first, and leisure for the growth of the second, which is the ideal of life." The farmer, he continues, "is like an oak, his roots strike deep in the soil, he draws a sufficiency of food from the earth itself, he breathes the free air around him, his thirst is quenched by heaven itself—and there is no tax on sunshine." He feels that those who come into contact with the soil come "to beat in consonance with the pulse of the earth." And the virtues of industry, patience, and perseverance, he says, are nowhere better taught than "in the very atmosphere of country life."

Grayson has little sympathy with the charge that the farmer is isolated and therefore tends to be provincial. On the contrary, he feels that in time the whole world passes the farmer's way. He embraces the scientific and technological developments of the industrial civilization and accepts their application to rural life. To a dispirited farmer he recommends consulting the state agricultural experimental station for advice. He cites improvements such as rural delivery, machinery, the telephone, motor car, and trolley as vehicles of communication that have shortened the physical and psychological distances between the farm and the city. He also sees the proliferation of books and magazines as bringing the farmer into intimate contact with what are commonly regarded as the "finer things in life." Here Baker ran into difficulty with the Grayson creation, for though Grayson, with his open mind, cannot help recognizing and accepting such improvements in rural life, he perfers to live in a somewhat timeless world in which he tends to accentuate the evils of urban life. He would rather remain oblivious to the larger concerns of his society. This decision seems strangely artificial, and in no other area of the Grayson characterization is it so apparent that the creation is expressive of only a part of Baker's personality.

Ray Stannard Baker could not live without the stimulation of the city, but into Grayson's mouth he put all the arguments against an urban existence. In *Adventures in Understanding,* for some unexplained reason Grayson leaves his farm and settles in the city to lend his pen to the service of the war effort. With his countrified air and his open and friendly manner, nurtured by almost two decades in rural America, he finds in the city many interesting people that lead him to the same type of "adventures" he had celebrated earlier. But this relocation of Grayson is temporary, and by the end of the volume he has returned to the solace of his farm. As a farmer, he feels that the city has little respect for man. The city, he says, tends to view man as a machine, and it demands the order, regularity, and consistency expected of machinery. In the country Grayson sees a place for the diversity and individualism that the city seems to suffocate. His travels on *The Friendly Road* take him to a city he calls Kilburn where he experiences the sensation of "a strange, deep, spiritual shrinking." He says the city shrinks men and squeezes out of them their distinctiveness and originality; it is "a poor place for reflection and contemplation." In the country he has discerned "a kind of beauty and honor" associated with old age and death, but in the city, he says, both life and death "grow cheap and shallow." For a brief moment in the streets of Kilburn Grayson believes that all he has to do is preach his message of rural rejuvenation and "all this crowded poverty would dissolve and disappear, and they would all come to the country and be as happy as I was. . . . The great point of advantage in the life of the country is that if a man is in reality simple, if he love true contentment, it is the place of all places where he can live his life most freely and fully, where he can *grow.* The city affords no such opportunity; indeed, it often destroys, by the seductiveness with which it flaunts its carnal graces, the desire for the higher life which animates every good man."

Grayson realizes that he tends to idealize the life of the farmer by minimizing its burdens and accentuating its joys, and he cautions his readers against hasty action. In one passage Grayson places his stamp of approval on the personal solution of Ray Stannard Baker: "It is easy also for many men who are engaged in professional work to live where they can get their hands into the soil for part of the time at least: and this may be as real an experience as far as it goes as though they owned wider acres and devoted their whole time to the work." This was more than the creation deferring to its creator, for in his travels Grayson finds no farmers like himself. Most farmers he seems to see in the image of Horace. His low-keyed heroes are people like the Vedders, who have moved out of their mansion to take up residence in the caretaker's cottage where they will be better able to cultivate their interest in gardening, or like Mr. Jensen, who, even in the city, manages to find a small area of land in which to grow flowers and vegetables. This was no celebration of the gentleman farmer but rather of the the man who dirtied his hands through work in the soil.

Through his Grayson writings, Ray Stannard Baker was reflecting a growing American desire, especially present in urban areas, to get back to the soil. In the early twentieth century, the advantages of suburban living were just beginning to be acclaimed, and Baker's personal rejection of the city as a place to live and raise a family was shared by many Americans. In discussing the Grayson sketches with a reporter, Baker once said that they "were written to express that reaction, that feeling of retreat and restfulness, that realization of the truly worth while things in life that one feels in the country." The busy journalist moving in a world of excitement continued to look upon his experiences in the country as "better than anything else" he experienced. And the great appeal of the Grayson writings was felt not by the rural denizens of the United States but rather by those who had been alienated from the soil and who identified with Grayson in his desire for renewed contact with it.

There was more to Grayson than his celebration of the joys of country life. Baker talked more and more of the need to improve the individual, with Grayson as his model. It was not so much Grayson the farmer that appealed to many readers, but rather Grayson the man. Grayson himself sees his farm in terms of a tool to cultivate "with diligence all the greater fields of life. . . ." His call is for all men to move beyond the limitations of their occupation, political party, or social group, so that they, too, might see themselves as "unlimited" men. The literary farmer says each man is like a magnet, and unhindered, he will draw the iron filings of his world to him in a harmonious pattern; the problem is that too many men are used by others and too many obstacles are artificially placed in the way of their exploration of their own magnetic fields. Be sincere, open-minded, and accepting, Grayson advises; the greatest gift anyone can possibly give his fellow men is his understanding.

Grayson himself desires to be a "maker of understandings," a man who can be the agent for introducing people of supposedly diverse interests to each other. Real democracy, he believes, can come only with "elbow-knowledge, that close neighborhood sympathy, that conscious surrender of little personal goods for bigger public ones. . . ." Men, he continues, are bound together in thousands of ways; in their souls they all share the same "instincts, hopes, joys, sorrows," and they need each other. Grayson's attempt to be an "introducer" fails when he tries to bring together Socialist strikers and management representatives in Kilburn; his hope is that as they come to know and respect each other as men their differences can be easily worked out. He has a friend on each side of the struggle and both are sympathetic to Grayson's suggestion of meeting as individuals rather than as contestants, but within their respective groups the old suspicions reassert themselves and both sides refuse the offer. This failure seems to convince Grayson that he should confine his attempts as a peacemaker to a smaller field where he may expect smaller but more gratifying results.

Though at times Grayson enjoys his large and satisfying library or his unaccompanied walks through the wilds, he more often seeks out human companionship. His free and easy manner inspires a certain confidence which enables him to quickly win the interest of his associates. He delights in free and uninhibited conversation, which he said "brings to birth so many half-realized thoughts of our own—besides sowing the seed of innumerable other thought-plants." Grayson sees a world filled with fine people, "if you scratch 'em deep enough." To him nothing seems to thaw the ice between strangers more than a joke shared in common, and humor he calls the "world's Esperanto." He believes and acts upon the premise that the most satisfying of all discoveries comes with the understanding of how "a man has come to be what he is." To Grayson friendship is neither a formality nor a mode, but rather a way of life.

Grayson firmly believes that non-essentials are primarily responsible for man's alienation from his fellow man. He seeks to implant a social spirit in man by demonstrating how very much he is dependent upon his society. One of the obstacles to this regeneration is the concept of the ownership of property. Early in his new life Grayson realizes how close he has come to letting his farm possess him, and he resolves to escape its grasp. When he has achieved a larger perspective he finds his possessions multiplying, for "real possession is not a thing of inheritance or of documents, but of the spirit; and passes by vision and imagination." He has a number of lively discussions on the subject with his practical friend Horace. When he tries to convince his neighbor that through his appreciation of the wild beauty of some of the acres adjoining his land he has acquired a property interest in them, Horace cannot understand what he means. Meeting Horace more on his own terms, Grayson then tells him that he has sold an essay based upon his impressions of the land for a sum of money that far exceeds that which Horace has gained from the sale of his crops. The farmer-philosopher insists that he is not interested in the ownership of property, but rather in the "independence of it," saying that some day men will hold property in common. He feels that man too often flounders "in possession as in a dark and suffocating bog, wasting . . . [his] energies not upon life but upon *things.*" He assures his readers that the truly valuable possessions are to be had for the taking.

Grayson seems to feel that through a cultivation of his senses man can possess whatever he wants. In ***Great Possessions*** he makes his strongest appeal to man's sensual nature. "It is a sad thing," he says, "to reflect that in a world so overflowing with the goodness of smell, of fine sights and sweet sounds, we pass by hastily and take so little of them." In the hope of conveying to his readers some of the sensual delight to be found in an extremely common experience, he describes his reaction on biting into a Bellflower apple: "So I bit into it, a big, liberal mouthful, which came away with a rending sound such as one hears sometimes in a winter's ice-pond. The flesh within, all dewy with moisture, was like new cream, except a rim near the surface where the skin had been broken; here it was of a clear, deep yellow." He often seeks to convey his impressions of the natural world to his readers. Though spring is the season that seems to quicken Grayson's pulse and sharpen his impressions, he also finds beauty in the lonely winter:

> This perfect morning a faint purplish haze is upon all the hills, with bright sunshine and still, cold air through which the chimney smoke rises straight upward. Hungry crows flap across the fields, or with unaccustomed daring settle close in upon the manure heaps around the barns. All the hillsides glisten and sparkle like cloth of gold, each glass knob on the telephone poles is like a resplendent jewel, and the long morning shadows of the trees lie blue upon the snow. Horses' feet crunch upon the road as the early farmers go by with milk for the creamery—the frosty breath of each driver fluttering aside like a white scarf. Through the still air ordinary voices cut sharply and clearly, and a laugh bounds out across the open country with a kind of superabundance of joy.

The contentment David Grayson communicates to his readers is "a quality not of place or of time, but of the spirit." At times he finds a spiritual wholeness in his communion with the world of nature. With all his literary allusions he does not identify with the pantheistic strain in English romantic poetry. He quotes Wordsworth a few times, but his worshipful attitude grows out of his experience and is perhaps too clearly and personally felt to require literary allusion. In nature Grayson finds a much more appropriate church than the buildings that bear the name. Though he often refers to the Bible and once calls it "the sure tallisman," he finds his God in the open fields and rolling hills. "I rarely walk in my garden or upon the hills . . ." Grayson says, "without thinking of God. It is in my garden that all things become clearer to me, even that miracle whereby one who has offended may still see God; and this I think is a wonderful thing."

Still both in religion and in his self-cultivation Grayson sees a need for a social dimension. One of the characters expresses the belief that religion should not be locked within the church but instead should widen its horizons and minister to the practical needs of society. Just as Baker would come to do more and more in his later work, Grayson preaches service and brotherhood. Democracy, he says, grows strong with the voluntary surrender of the private for the public good. Each man is heavily indebted to his society, says Grayson, and as man accepts "a feeling of immeasurable obligation" he is infused with new life and joy. On one occasion he expresses his feeling that contentment is produced by "the feeling of being necessary, of being desired. . . ."

On one of his rare ventures into the city Grayson meets Bill Hahn, a Socialist. He admires Hahn's faith and likes him as a man. Seeing the Socialists' insistence upon human brotherhood as a stimulus to progress, he says that society will have to follow the lead of the Socialists and forge new social relationships. Such changes, he says, will bring with them "a renewed and more wonderful sense of the worth of the individual soul." He pays Hahn the unique tribute of calling him the better man, reflecting that the man "who can regard himself as a function, not an end of creation, has arrived."

Such excursions into the areas of the social gospel and socialism were not common in the Grayson books. Baker felt that his creation was most effective when he focused his attention on everyday life and remained oblivious to the more serious problems of his society. The injection of concepts such as socialism and of personages such as Theodore Roosevelt into the Grayson sketches is testimony to their importance in the life of Baker, who, even when transported by the Grayson mood, could not completely escape the larger concerns of his time.

Grayson's approach to life is grounded on a deep faith in human nature and in the value of friendship. It is not a philosophy that Grayson communicates but rather a feeling, as the following passage illustrates: "I have learned that happiness is not to be had for the seeking, but comes quietly to him who pauses at his difficult task and looks upward. I have learned that friendship is very simple, and more than all else, I have learned the lesson of being quiet, of looking out across the meadows and hills, and of trusting a little to God." It was this peace of mind that so appealed to the many Grayson readers; in a world in fast motion Grayson seemed to capture a calmness and serenity that many men sought but so very few found.

Many characters weave their way through the Grayson sketches, but few are fully developed. Often they seem to be presented as types—the Scottish preacher, the country doctor, the drunkard, the shabby man, the iceman, an old maid, the millionaire, and so on. At times such character portrayals are romanticized and stereotyped, but Grayson seems to use labels less to explain a type than to indicate society's tendency to categorize people. Grayson resists the use of labels, demonstrating how little help they are in understanding people. Behind each type he discovers a man or woman worth knowing.

The character studies with which Grayson is most successful are those based upon men Baker had known as a youth. In an interview, Baker once described them as "thinly veiled portraits" of people he had known and liked. In these "portraits" Grayson seems best able to express his outlook on life, for here it is more properly clothed. In describing a local gunsmith, he says

> The more I think of it the more I think that our gunsmith possesses many of the qualities of true greatness. He has the serenity, and the humor, and the humility of greatness. He has a real faith in God. He works, he accepts what comes. He thinks there is no more honourable calling than that of gunsmith, and that the town he lives in is the best of all towns, and the people he knows the best people.

At a time of increasing urbanization, Grayson's glorification of the "common man" was welcomed by many Americans. His readers were reassured by his belief that no sincere man was really simple, that the rich were far more in need of cheer than the poor, that celebrities could not survive without the common people, and that the great man was distinguished from the rest primarily by a quality of intensity. Baker, in the guise of Grayson, celebrated the simple and common folk, and they returned his affection.

This affection was reflected in the fact that though the Grayson volumes were not "best-sellers" there was an amazing consistency in their sale. A reader newly introduced to a Grayson volume would feel compelled to order the books that had escaped his earlier attention. The first three volumes sold the best both in the United States and throughout the world, and it has been estimated that a total of about two million Grayson volumes, many in foreign translations, have been sold. Of further interest is the fact that the appeal of the Grayson work continued through a number of changing national moods. In 1927, the student body at Wellesley College included David Grayson in its list of the six most popular authors, and many of the sketches were selected by editors for inclusion in schoolroom anthologies.

The Grayson books had a phenomenal ability to reach the reader and provoke his response. In 1916 the editors of the *Bookman* commented that it would be difficult to overestimate their influence. Their appeal was not to one's intellect but to one's inner self. Baker never described the physical appearance of Grayson, and the illustrations by Thomas Fogarty that accompanied the sketches in magazine and book form through the first six volumes were rather vague. Though some readers wanted a picture of Grayson, the vast majority were satisfied to bask in the warmth of his personality. Why his readers responded as they did was in part explained by one very literate housewife, who scolded *Collier's Weekly* in 1916 for an editorial attack upon a Baker article: "Thousands and thousands of us," she said, "have changed, mentally, miraculously, even as Ray Stannard Baker changed—from muckraker to philosopher . . . thousands took to his books because his philosophy had already boiled up in their hearts and all they needed was to have somebody put it into words for them." A British literary critic acknowledged that the Grayson books were not literature of the first rank, nor the work of great intellect or talent, but then he added that Grayson had won his friendship and affection.

Grayson's confidences were shared with his readers, and they responded in kind. In *The Friendly Road,* Grayson tells them, "I shall open a little door in my heart and let you look in. . . ." And in the last chapter of *Adventures in Friendship,* he says, "I am still relishing the joy of our meeting, and . . . I part unwillingly." To thousands Grayson was neither a literary creation nor an author but a man whom they felt they knew personally. The tens of thousands of letters to Grayson, now housed in the David Grayson Room of the Jones Library in Amherst, Massachusetts, constitute a bulky testament to the power of the Grayson books. Every region of the country was represented in the letters, and though they vary greatly in content, most are quite intimate and filled with praise for the man Grayson and his writing. Students, soldiers, nostalgic elderly people, invalids, lovesick women, city dwellers, even a convict poured out their feelings and thoughts to their new-found, understanding friend. At times Baker despaired that so many of his correspondents seemed to feel that he was writing more about his farm than life itself, but many readers were well aware of Grayson's real message. Many expressed the feeling that Grayson had opened a new door for them—a door to a greater and more healthy appreciation of life.

Baker felt that these letters demonstrated that what man most desired in his world was "a working agreement" with himself. When Frank Prentice Rand wrote that the appeal of the books was "so obvious as to be profound," Baker felt that his friend and kindred soul had captured the reason for the success of the Grayson work. "Almost the whole of life is absorbed with 'real but commonplace experiences,' " he said.

> If a man has not learned to live with them comfortably, to enjoy them, he simply has not learned to live. He has no technique of joy. He must rush to other places, seek noise, confusion, sensation. He must get out of books at second hand what he cannot find in his own dooryard. His life soon becomes thin, weak, superficial; he has dissipated his strength in feeding upon the husks of a far country, when there were boundless riches at home.
>
> (pp. 165-78)

Another manifestation of the influence of the Grayson volumes was the appearance of Graysonian Clubs, the first being organized in Sarasota, Florida, in 1915. The clubs sought to follow their mentor's advice and seek enjoyment in the observation of nature and adventure in the everyday aspects of life. There is no evidence on how widespread and sustained the club idea was, and it is apparent that most readers preferred to cultivate their own personal relationship with Grayson independent of any organization.

Along with this popular effusion came a good deal of critical acclaim. The first three volumes, **Adventures in Contentment, Adventures in Friendship,** and **The Friendly Road,** were almost unanimously praised. "The volume," one critic said, referring to the first book, "is full of the poetry of rural life, mingled with much sound and sane philosophy." Hundreds of reviewers agreed, as they warmed to David Grayson in much the same way the personal correspondents had. Grayson's optimism was less in fashion when **Hempfield** and **Great Possessions** appeared in 1915 and 1917 respectively. Though by this time David Grayson had become an institution among the faithful, a few of the critics had tired of Grayson's "complacency and insistent optimism."

The more self-conscious literary critics who prided themselves on their sophistication and "high-brow" discernment seem at first to have disdainfully ignored the Grayson books. But as Grayson's following grew, they could not resist tossing a few barbs in the farmer's direction. Though he saw Grayson's "reaction against strenuosity" as a reflection of a new, "balanced American mood," Vachel Lindsay criticized the many adherents of Grayson who had established a kinship with him in a sort of dream world that had little to do with the demands of a materialistic society. The most vitriolic of all such critics was H. L. Mencken, who, in the pages of *The Smart Set,* demolished Grayson to the satisfaction of his readers. "Mr. Grayson's sentimentality," he wrote, "often descends to the maudlin. . . . I fail to respond to his enthusiasm for yokels, his long botanical catalogues, his artful forgetfulness that the country is dull, dirty and uncomfortable, and that countrymen, in overwhelming main, are stupid and rascally." As Grayson had rejected the stimulation of urban America, Mencken rejected Grayson.

Though there were a few shrewd guesses concerning who hid behind the Grayson pseudonym, Baker was fairly successful in keeping his authorship a secret until 1916. The reporter was finally brought out of hiding not because of any desire to bask publicly in Grayson's glory, but rather to expose a growing number of imposters who were trading on the farmer's reputation. Making their way to Baker's home were unpaid bills and letters describing visits he had never made. One spurious David Grayson had almost succeeded in winning the hand of a woman who had fallen in love with the Baker creation. In the March, 1916, issue of the *Bookman* Baker revealed the secret. But before the issue appeared the *Boston Post* headlined the solution to the literary mystery. Other newspapers quickly picked up the story, expressing amazement that the "pastoral prose-poet" was in actuality a muckraker in disguise. Almost all seemed to agree that Baker was quite a remarkable writer to be able to master such a different form of expression. Baker continued to maintain the Grayson pseudonym and many of the readers of the country-life sketches never seemed to know or at least to care who wrote them. Others were inevitably drawn to fit David Grayson into the life of his creator.

One such ready explanation of the relationship was that David Grayson was in reality Ray Stannard Baker at home, especially on his ten acres in Amherst, Massachusetts, which he acquired in 1912. This misinterpretation of Grayson was fostered by Baker himself, who once commented that Grayson "is myself alone." At times he longed to be Grayson, for he admired his creation's frankness, complete honesty, lack of inhibition, and out-going nature, but such was not his lot.

At times in the Grayson sketches, he made a direct personal appeal to his readers. "If you should ever come by my farm," he said in **Adventures in Friendship,** "you, whoever you are—take care lest I board you, hoist my pirate flag, and sail you away to the Enchanted Isle where I make my rendezvous." The response to such direct appeals was more than Baker bargained for. A few of his women admirers asked him to leave his sister Harriet and venture out with them on the open road, and some of the faithful surmounted all obstacles in finding their way to 118 Sunset Avenue in Amherst. Almost all such unsolicited visits were distressing to Baker. Instead of the serene, expansive, casual, homey bachelor farmer his visitors expected, they found a restless, nonplussed, often fastidiously dressed family man. The character of Grayson was exhausted in the writings; there was nothing left to give to those who knocked on Baker's door.

Walter A. Dyer, a friend of Baker's, came closest to the essence of the Baker-Grayson relationship when he commented that the reporter had released a part of himself and given it a name. Baker generally had little respect for literary critics, many of whom he felt praised too generously as a result of too little thought, but one critic hit upon an interpretation that struck him as valid: he said that David Grayson represented a particular mood. Baker picked up the concept and felt that it accurately captured his relationship with his creation. As a mood, Grayson could be exploited by Baker's mind and imagination in literary

form, but he would not and could not be represented in Baker's life. A man is the product of many moods, and though one particular mood can be artificially isolated for a particular purpose, life is a composite of his many moods. (pp. 178-81)

David Grayson failed to satisfy Baker's dreams of significant literary expression. Still thinking in terms of a novel, the reporter considered the possibility of a novel executed within the Grayson framework. The early attempts ended up where most of his partially finished novels did—in the wastebasket. Finally, with Phillips' encouragement, the reporter agreed to do a novel for serial publication; in this manner he would be forced to complete the work. Starting off with his customary enthusiasm, the aspiring novelist planned to people his story with interesting characters who would be primarily concerned with the "little things" of life, which, he said, often became the big things. Unlike the relatively free and easy composition of the sketches, the novel turned out to be a difficult form which required hard and plodding work. Unable to face his artistic limitations, Baker found many excuses for his difficulty. The requirement of monthly installments exerted a pressure upon him, which, he felt, shackled his talents. With the outbreak of war in Europe he turned upon Grayson, who had found his truth in Hempfield. "I cannot even bear to read the stuff," he wrote, "when it comes in the magazine! How can a man remain smugly contented, and bear to write such pretty things, when all the guarantees of civilization & Christianity have gone overboard." With such rationalizations he sought to explain his inherent inability to handle the intricacies of plot and his tendency to promise in the early installments far more than he could deliver in the later ones.

Hempfield, the story of the trials and tribulations of a country weekly newspaper and the people associated with it, is a failure as a novel. The faithful Grayson readers found enough of their hero in its pages to sustain their interest, but on its own terms it is an ill-conceived and ill-executed novel. Though Grayson is still the narrator, he is less in control of the situation. The book must rest upon the strength of the narrative and the appeal of the characters, and this is where it fails: it lacks substance, its plot is flimsy, and the characters come out Graysonized. Even the fundamental clash between Ed Smith and Norton Carr is never resolved, and rather than preside over the dismissal of Smith, Baker keeps the two uneasily hitched to the *Hempfield Star.* The reader tends to become bored by the recitation of the trivial aspects of life which Baker tries to pass off as drama.

The book was advertised and partially accepted as a real American story at a time when Americanism was becoming a distinct virtue. A number of people saw dramatic possibilities in the story, among them, Russell Janey, a theatrical producer. Baker and others worked on the script, and finally a version by Charlotte Thompson was produced in Milwaukee, Wisconsin, in July, 1918. But even the Russell Janey players, considered the finest repertorial group in the country, could not breathe sufficient life into what one critic evaluated as "a play of the slenderest dramatic pretensions," and it never got any closer to

Broadway. In later years a number of motion picture producers expressed an interest in the book, but Baker rejected the one definite offer he received. Perhaps he realized that any motion picture that might be made would contain his basic idea but little more.

Baker realized that the Grayson creation was limited as a literary device, but he failed to realize that with the publication of the Grayson books he had fully tapped his literary resources. He seemed to feel that if he could recognize the obstacles that stood between him and the creation of literature his ambition and hard work would carry him to that goal. He felt that only when he realized his total personality in fiction would he be able to produce literature. The artist, he said, had to maintain a firm control of his characters, and with some perception he asserted that the main failure inherent in the Grayson work was that the main character assumed too much control. Though he admitted that he had not experienced that "great inner impulse out of which . . . the true novel must be born," he continued to experiment with fictional ideas independent of the Grayson framework. His desire to produce fine literature was a reflection of his desire to be a great man. As he said, "Where there is a man who can convey a *sense of life,* can stimulate us to high thoughts & noble actions, that man is great." Significant literary creation, he wrote, was no less than the key to happiness, and what he meant was his happiness. His aims were high, for his hope of writing a book children could read for adventure and adults for wisdom could have been fulfilled by nothing less than a *Huckleberry Finn.*

Feeling that he knew much about the world, and that ultimately he would be judged by his ability to tell the truth, Baker searched for a medium by which he could transmit his knowledge. He considered a series of special nonfiction studies, or a mammoth autobiography, or a series of novels based on his own varied experiences, but he finally concluded that the truth he wished to communicate could be most nearly expressed within the fictional mode.

Baker possessed a predilection for martyrdom but not the temperament. His ideal was the "man who says in public exactly what he believes—and then tries to live according to his belief." But this is a rather somber portrait of a man who had his moments of humor, even concerning the truth. Commenting upon a friend's use of the term, "naked truth," he wrote: "I have myself always wanted to see truth naked: but have never yet been able to surprise her when she was not wearing a fig-leaf at least."

In a self-reproaching mood at the age of forty-four Baker concluded that he had accomplished nothing of literary merit. But he would not give up his dream, and he gained new determination from the fact that Cervantes, Milton, Swift, Mark Twain, and the great Russian authors had all done their best work during their later years. As late as 1922, the journalist still felt "committed to write that better & deeper book." Hoping to find within himself that greater work, he was encouraged by Phillips, who felt that beneath Grayson there was an "even richer and deeper" layer yet to be mined. Another colleague on the *American* staff dissented; John M. Siddall advised Baker that he was making a mistake in attempting to transcend his remark-

able talent for reporting. "It makes me sick to think of you giving up this sort of thing and turning to fiction," Siddall said. "You can help along this democracy by these reports more than you can possibly imagine. You know Caruso, the great singer, has no vanity except over his ability as a cartoonist. You are a little bit in his boat. But believe me, Caruso can do real business with his voice, but no where near as big business as the Honourable Ray Stannard Baker can do with his pen, reporting to millions of readers that which they cannot get any other way."

Baker failed in his quest for literary achievement because he lacked sufficient creative powers. Alternating between periods of accepting his literary shortcomings and of dreaming of significant accomplishment, he agonized over his lack of self-control, feeling that the ability to concentrate and work at a single task was truly the greatest gift. Throughout the notebooks Baker scattered hundreds of plot ideas, but when he tried to carry out the ideas his thoughts flowed into trite channels. He attempted to compensate for this deficiency by saying that once he got a firm grasp upon his characters the narrative would flow of itself. Here, too, he fell short of his goal. His characters were never fully conceived and developed as physical entities; they are rather artificially confined to a limited spiritual orbit. Baker said that "every character must be autobiographical." Certainly any writer of fiction draws heavily upon his own experience, but he must also be able to surpass its limitations and at least apply that experience within new conceptual frameworks. This Baker could not do; he simply could not give substance to something much beyond his immediate experience; he was too faithful a reporter who realized only slowly how very different literary work was from journalism.

Another stumbling block, more specific in nature, was Baker's inability to understand and portray women. The journalist believed that a man's generalizations about women were most often based upon contact with a single woman. Since he had not really known his mother, his wife provided him with his picture of womanhood. Jessie was more intellectual than physical; she was shy and somewhat uncomfortable socially; she was often physically and mentally depressed; and she lacked a spirit of adventure and wonder. In the Grayson books, Baker affords the reader some insight into his view of the opposite sex. The following passage from ***Hempfield*** reveals the insecurity of Grayson's creator:

> . . . all my life, whenever I have met a woman—I have been much alone—I have had a curious sense of being with someone a little higher or better than I am, to whom I should bow, or to whom I should present something, or with whom I should joke. With whom I should not, after all, be quite natural! I wonder if this is at all an ordinary experience with men? I wonder if any one will understand me when I say that there has always seemed to me something not quite proper in talking to a woman directly, seriously, without reservation, as to a man?

Dismissing the lure of womanly charms, Grayson said that men's souls were stirred more by the universal and human qualities of bravery, simplicity, or nobility.

With this insight into Baker's attitude toward women, his lack of success in portraying women is not difficult to comprehend. The great majority of the Grayson characters were men, and when a woman is pictured the focal point is her soul or spirit, areas in which the differentiation between the sexes is minimized. Baker had considerable difficulty in depicting a creditable man-woman love relationship. His own relationship with his wife seems to be characterized more aptly in terms of mutual respect than by any deep love. In **Hempfield** Baker tried to picture Anthy, the young woman owner of the *Star,* but by concentrating upon her inner qualities he fails to create a real person. A woman is, after all, a physical being, and Baker's lopsided picture lacks vitality. The love relationship between Anthy and Norton Carr, as a result, could only be wooden and artificial.

That Grayson was more of a conscious literary creation than Baker admitted is revealed in his literary preferences and opinions and in a developing literary consciousness. Though the reporter never belonged to a literary circle, he became a member of the National Arts Institute and he counted many writers among his friends, including Hamlin Garland, Irving Bacheller, and Ernest Poole. "The quality of the best art," Baker wrote, "inspires the reader to go back to nature." His literary preferences reflected this feeling. He read widely in the classics and in contemporary fiction and nonfiction. On each journalistic assignment he accumulated many volumes on his subject in order to introduce himself to the new area. But in his quiet moments he returned to authors like Emerson, Whitman, Marcus Aurelius, William Penn, Ben Jonson, and Cervantes, men whom he said "renewed and stimulated" him. Baker had reservations about the one writer with whom one might have expected him to identify—Thoreau. The journalist said that he could take the man of Walden Pond only in small doses, concluding that Thoreau did not accept nature "either gladly or greatly." Tolstoy was Baker's favorite novelist, a choice that conformed to his yearning for spiritual and emotional contentment. But for him even a literary preference was never unqualified, and Baker criticized the Russian novelist's reliance on outer authority. On other occasions he concluded that the world's greatest stories were stories of adventure and stories of character and its interaction with the environment. As Baker grew older, his dream of significant literary work dimmed; he lost interest in the novel as he took a greater interest in reading autobiographies, diaries, and letters.

Though he reviewed numerous books during his lifetime, he never published any literary criticism; his remarks on the state of American literature were confined to his notebooks. He felt that American authors had to proceed beyond Walt Whitman, whose genius, he said, was spent in a grand acceptance of democracy which was now the fundamental inheritance of all American writers. The duty of the present-day American literary artist, then, was to "exhibit the new principle, the vital spark of Americanism, in *action.*" Of the American realists, he wrote: "A lot of little men with a glimmer of the new light are whining around already." Though Baker said that he did not care whether a writer's work was classified as romantic or realistic, his sympathy was not with the new literary movement.

"Realistic fiction," he wrote, was so "terribly man-made"; it lacked sympathy, understanding, faith, and courage. This new literary school, along with education in general, he felt, was over-educating the intellect and undereducating the heart and will of man. In Baker's judgment, the novelist failed in his task if he depicted a dying order without some hope for the new. He further argued that the writer's sympathy should be with his age and to this extent he had to be at least part journalist. Frank Norris and Theodore Dreiser were deserving of praise, he thought, but their work lacked color, illusion, and reserve and tended to be more of an observation than a criticism of life. To Baker, the great artist had to be more than a literary technician; he had to be a great man. "Do not our artists fail," he asked, "because they cannot & do not feel the common emotions, & cherish in their own souls the great common faith of their age? Their approach is critical and intellectual, not emotional & spiritual." In such a state, he concluded, modern literature was in much the same intellectual condition as science: "It accumulates facts, it has good powers of observation, but wants penetration and understanding."

Though Baker was not oblivious to the merits and vigor of this realistic movement in American literature, he saw its shortcomings, not its achievements. He identified with none of the contemporary writers; his heroes were the literary giants of the past. Perhaps this literature was too reportorial to suit the tastes of Baker, who saw a clear division between creative reporting and literature.

The writing of fiction appealed to the journalist because he felt that in no other medium was the writer freer to express himself. This complete expression of self was what Baker saw as the prime characteristic of the best novels. Though he thought the novelist should not be obtrusive, he believed his work should reflect both his mind and his spirit. In part the David Grayson creation was spawned by such ideas, and in part the continued emphasis upon them helped justify the Grayson work. But Baker was never under any illusions concerning the literary substance of his country-life sketches; essentially he saw in them only a pale reflection of the total being he yearned to express in fiction.

Although the David Grayson writings failed to satisfy Baker's dreams of literary accomplishment, the sketches were widely read and applauded, financially successful, and at times even personally satisfying to their author. At the time of Grayson's birth, they not only filled space but also fitted well into the more general plans of John S. Phillips, who had the primary responsibility for charting the course of the new *American Magazine.* (pp. 186-93)

John E. Semonche, in his Ray Stannard Baker: A Quest for Democracy in Modern America, 1870-1918, *The University of North Carolina Press, 1969, 350 p.*

Maurine Beasley   (essay date 1982)

[*Beasley is an American journalist and educator. In the following excerpt, she examines implicit prejudice in Baker's muckraking articles on lynching.*]

The high point of the muckraker's interest in lynching came in 1905 when Ray Stannard Baker, a leading journalist who had exposed wrongdoing by both railroad magnets and labor union leaders, turned his attention to the crime. Baker published two articles on lynching in *McClure's,* the leading muckraking magazine, produced by the profitable partnership of S. S. McClure, an Irish immigrant, and John S. Phillips, a Middle Westerner educated at Harvard. Started in 1893, *McClure's* launched the muckraking phenomenon in 1902 with publication of Ida M. Tarbell's "History of the Standard Oil Company," which depicted the evils of monopoly. It also serialized Lincoln Steffen's expose of municipal corruption. "The Shame of the Cities," beginning in 1903.

A former Chicago newspaperman whose home was in East Lansing, Michigan, Baker outlined his purpose in the introduction to the first article on lynching. He wrote:

> I have just been visiting a number of 'lynching towns' in this country, both in the South and in the North. I went primarily to formulate, if I could, a clear idea of what 150 lynchings a year (the average in the U.S. for the last 22 years) might really signify, to discover in what way a lynching town is different from my town or your town, what classes of citizens constitute the mobs and what is the underlying cause of such murderous outbreaks.

The first article described two lynchings in the South: The one at Statesboro, Georgia, and one at Huntsville, Alabama. In the Statesboro incident, two illiterate turpentine workers, Paul Reed and Will Cato, were burned alive after being found guilty of murdering a well-to-do farm family. Baker told how a mob gathered round the courthouse where the prisoners were confined, broke through a squad of militia allegedly called to guard the prisoners but ordered not to load their rifles, dragged the Negroes from the building, bound them to a stump, placed fagots around them, drenched them in oil, and rejoiced in watching them die. He included sensational details as in this passage describing how the mob fought for souvenirs: "Pieces of the stump were hacked off, and finally one young man . . . gathered up a few charred remnants of bone, carried them uptown, and actually tried to give them to the judge who presided at the trial . . . "

Baker was appalled both by the murder of the farm family and by the lynching. He called Reed and Cato examples of "the floating, worthless Negro" and pronounced Black criminals generally more savage than white criminals: " . . . under stress of passion, he (the Negro) seems to revert wholly to savagery." He condemned mob violence, contending it "releases that which is ugly, violent, revengeful in the community as in the individual human heart." Still he rationalized lynching on the grounds justice often miscarried and murderers escaped punishment through the technicalities of the law. As he put it, " . . . I was astounded by the extraordinary prevalence in all these lynching counties, North as well as South, of crimes of violence, especially homicide, accompanied in every case by a poor enforcement of the law."

The journalist attributed the lynching at Huntsville, where a mob hung a Black murder suspect and shot him full of holes, to "poor white trash," who hated Blacks in part because they provided competition for employment. He praised officials for indicting 10 members of the mob even though jurors acquitted them because "a large majority felt that a white man should not be punished for lynching a Negro."

Examining the contention that lynching was "absolutely necessary" to prevent Blacks from wholesale rape of white women, Baker concluded, "The mob spirit . . . once invoked . . . spreads and spreads, until today lynching for rape forms only a very small proportion of the total number of mob hangings. It spreads until a Negro is lynched for chicken stealing, or for mere 'obnoxiousness.' " He quoted statistics that reported out of 104 lynchings in 1903 only 11 were for rape and 10 for attempted rape, while 47 were for murder, 15 for complicity in murderous assaults, four for arson, five for undefined 'race prejudice,' two for insults to whites, one for making threats, five for unknown offenses, one for refusing to give information, and three due to mistaken identity.

In his article on the North, Baker examined a lynching in Springfield, Ohio, that occurred when a mob broke into a jail and hung a Black who had killed a police officer trying to prevent the murderer from shooting his girl friend. Baker blamed this episode on "underlying conditions in Springfield: Corrupt politics, vile saloons, the law paralyzed by non-enforcement against vice, a large venal Negro vote (sold to the highest bidder), lax courts of justice." Contrasting the Springfield incident with an attempted lynching at Danville, Illinois, that failed to materialize because of vigilant law enforcement, Baker wrote, "Lynching is not so much a disease in itself as it is the symptom of a disease. It is a symptom of lawlessness, of the failure of justice, of political corruption."

Following publication of these articles in *McClure's,* Baker along with a group of other leading staff members became disenchanted with the magazine's management. Together they purchased *The American Magazine* to convert into a muckraking organ. Searching for fresh material that would make the venture an "assured success," Baker continued to explore racial issues. In 1907 and 1908 he published in *The American* an exhaustive series of articles on racial questions that also appeared as a book, ***Following the Color Line,*** in 1908. Apart from the two articles for *McClure's* which were reprinted in the book, Baker did not deal with lynching, turning instead to subjects such as the "tragic mulatto." Disturbed by social unrest, Baker endorsed Jim Crow laws on grounds it was necessary to separate the lower classes of both races, at least for the time being. (p. 88)

Of muckraking journalists Baker alone undertook a comprehensive report on lynchings and other problems besetting Blacks. While he did not defend lynching, neither did he picture it for what it was—a racist way of keeping

Blacks in "their place." Instead he depicted it as the reflection of an evil political system arisen in response to failure of "good citizens" to ensure that courts moved swiftly against criminal offenders. As Baker's biographer, Robert C. Bannister, expressed it: "There was . . . 'negative bigotry' in his insistence that the entire problem was but another 'symptom of lawlessness, of the failure of justice, of political corruption.' Offending phrases now seem to leap from every page: 'The animal-like ferocity' of the Negro criminal, the 'black and stolid' victim of the lynching. . . ."

It seems hard to understand why Baker subscribed to the judicial leniency theory since judges and juries did not hesitate to mete out capital punishment, both in the North and South, and Blacks, along with poor whites, were sold into peonage on the slightest pretense in the deep South. Baker obviously accepted the rationale offered by "good people" as an excuse for lynching, writing his father from Statesboro, Georgia, " . . . I must say that such crimes as these Negroes commit against white women are almost worthy of lynching." In his "negative bigotry" can be seen traces of the strictly racial argument that legal capital punishment was "too good" for Negroes.

In addition, Baker, like the other muckrakers, addressed a general audience composed of both Northerners and Southerners. Even if he had wished to, he would have been unable to move far ahead of his readers in terms of general attitudes. As has been pointed out, the muckrakers continually tested the winds of public opinion. Public opinion was important to the muckrakers on ideological grounds because they wanted to prompt action by a concerned citizenry to realize the Progressive ideal of democracy. It was important on practical grounds because they made their living writing for commercial publications.

It would be unfair to judge Baker a bigot for failing to transcend the assumptions of his era. Even in his endorsement of segregation, as a temporary measure to quiet racial strife, Baker continued to advocate first-class citizenship for Blacks as a long-range goal. Liberal by the standards of its day, Baker's reporting helped alert Americans to the issues of race as a national concern. It formed part of the documentation of the Black's condition used as a basis for the formation of the first major national groups for social defense—the National Association for the Advancement of Colored People and the Urban League. While preparing *Following the Color Line,* Baker consulted the leading Negro spokesmen, W. E. B. DeBois and Booker T. Washington, both of whom applauded his efforts. Praising his work, DuBois wrote to Baker, " . . . I am afraid, however, that you may not find as cordial a welcome from the white brothers the next time you come South."

In one sense, Baker's reports on lynching demonstrated the defects of muckraking in general. Baker maintained by telling the "truth" about a social problem it could be solved. One scholar contends this "abstract faith in the ability of truth to solve problems was about all the muckrakers had to offer." In the case of Baker's articles on lynching it proved insufficient. The articles did not lead to an end to lynching or to a decline. Because of the prevail-

ing racism Baker was unable to structure "facts" into truth leading to effective action, although he believed he took great pains to gather all available evidence. When there was little popular consensus on "facts" or an inclination to ignore them, the muckraker failed to accomplish the mission of stimulating reform. . . . (pp. 89-90)

Maurine Beasley, "The Muckrakers and Lynching: A Case Study in Racism," in Journalism History, *Vol. 9, Nos. 3-4, Autumn-Winter, 1982, pp. 86-91.*

FURTHER READING

Biography

Dyer, Walter A. "The Real David Grayson: His Home, His Work, and His Story—Told by His Friend and Neighbor." *Mentor* 13, No. 9 (October 1925): 1-18.

  Offers well-illustrated personal reflections on Baker, suggesting that "Ray Stannard Baker is other things, and excellent things, besides David Grayson, but that the whole of Grayson resides in him. . . ."

Rand, Frank Prentice. *The Story of David Grayson.* Amherst, Massachusetts: The Jones Library, 1963, 160 p.

  Offers a biographical treatment of the David Grayson persona and includes three previously unpublished Grayson essays.

Criticisim

Burnett, R. G. "A Distinguished American." *The London Quarterly and Holborn Review* 171 (October 1946): 345-46.

  Obituary tribute claiming that in his Grayson books Baker "broke the bread of life for troubled souls with hands experienced in the sacrament of living."

Davis, Norman H. "*Woodrow Wilson and World Settlement.*" *The Literary Digest International Book Review* 1, No. 1 (December 1922): 26, 84-5.

  Reviews *Woodrow Wilson and World Settlement,* praising Baker's documentation of the 1919 Paris Peace Conference.

Huddleston, Eugene. "Ray Stannard Baker and Daryl F. Zanuck's *Wilson.*" *Midwestern Miscellany* VI (1978): 1-6.

  Compares *Woodrow Wilson: Life and Letters* with another biography of Wilson by Arthur Link, contending that Baker's perspective of Woodrow Wilson was biased by "the confines of his Populist and genteel Midwestern intellectual milieu" and suggesting that Baker's work as a consultant for Zanuck's 1944 film *Wilson* produced a similarly biased account.

Jones, Bartlett C. "Ray Stannard Baker and the Progressive Dilemma." *The Emory University Quarterly* XVII, No. 3 (Fall 1961): 169-75.

  Traces the development of Baker's views on the issue of individual versus legislative responsibility for addressing the social, political, and economic problems of his time.

Mencken, H. L. "Three Americans." *The American Mercury* XIII, No. 50 (February 1928): 251-52.
> Reviews the first two volumes of *Woodrow Wilson: Life and Letters,* countering Baker's views with a harsher assessment of Wilson.

Metcalfe, Cranstoun. "David Grayson." *The Bookman,* London LXVII, No. 402 (March 1925): 287-89.
> Focuses on Baker's David Grayson works as constituting "a wholly good moral influence."

Moore, Frederick. "The President's Methods at the Peace Conference." *The Review* 1, No. 32 (20 December 1919): 684-85.
> Suggests that Baker's admiration of Woodrow Wilson led to a misrepresentation of the events of the Paris Peace Conference in *What Wilson Did at Paris.*

Morris, Lloyd. "Raising the Tone of Democracy." In his *Postscript to Yesterday: America—The Last Fifty Years,* pp. 267-318. New York: Random House, 1947.
> Features a section on the muckrakers that discusses Baker's work at *McClure's* and the *American.*

Review of *Hempfield,* by David Grayson. *The New York Times Review of Books* (17 October 1915): 389-90.
> Comments on the "distinctively American" aspects of Baker's novel.

Additional coverage of Baker's life and career is contained in the following source published by Gale Research: *Contemporary Authors,* Vol. 118.

Maurice Barrès

1862-1923

French novelist, essayist, journalist, biographer, short story writer, and politician.

INTRODUCTION

Barrès was one of the most prominent French novelists of the late nineteenth and early twentieth centuries. Characteristics of his novels are a lyrical prose style, didactic character types, and political themes. While celebrated as a statesman as well as a distinguished author during his lifetime, Barrès's intense nationalism and admiration for authoritarian political figures has led to a decline in his reputation.

Barrès was born at Charmes-sur-Moselle in Lorraine. He studied law at nearby Nancy, then moved at the age of nineteen to Paris. He soon began writing for such literary magazines as *Le jeune france* and in 1884 founded his own monthly gazette, *Taches d'encre.* The articles, stories, and essays contained in Barrès's newspaper were instrumental in the development of his literary reputation. Early in his career Barrès became involved in politics. In 1889 he was elected to the Chamber of Deputies (the lower house of the national legislature), as a representative from Nancy, later representing Paris until his death in 1923. Barrès was also among the first sponsors of the long-running right-wing newspaper, *Revue de l'action francaise,* founded in 1898. During the notorious military scandal known as the "Dreyfus Affair" (1897-1902), Barrès was the leading French intellectual to voice anti-Semitic and reactionary sentiments against the accused, Captain Alfred Dreyfus, who was tried and condemned for treason. Because of his celebration of the French ancestral and national past, when Barrès died he was regarded as one of his country's great patriots and honored with a state funeral.

The publication of his trilogy "Le culte du moi"—*Sous l'oeil des barbares, Un homme libre,* and *Le jardin de Bérénice*—established Barrès's literary reputation, and these novels together declare his manifesto of individualism, self-development, and cultivation of the will. Equally important, they pronounce the superiority of the emotions over the intellect. *Sous l'oeil des barbares* and *Un homme libre* chronicle a young intellectual's search for self, impeded, as he imagines, by cultural "barbarians" whose social and moral conventions inhibit his intellectual and spiritual development. *Le jardin de Bérénice,* in contrast, features a wholly uncomplicated heroine, a woman who is ruled by her unconscious impulses and is the virtuous embodiment of a primitive life force. The contrast between these two characters is a metaphor, in Barrès's novels, for the vitality that the highly cultivated classes of modern society seek but cannot attain in their own lives. This vitali-

ty, on the other hand, is shown as a natural possession of the peasantry who draw their living from the land.

In Barrès's mature novels, the preoccupation with the self is replaced by a celebration of "rootedness" in the region of one's birth and ancestry. Barrès's concept of "rootedness" is central to his second trilogy, "Le roman de l'énergie nationale" ("The Novel of National Energy"). Apart from the theme of "rootedness," the three novels of this trilogy are linked by certain main characters who reappear in each book. *Les déracinés,* the first novel in the trilogy, has as its theme the intellectual and social corruption of youth by an admired teacher. The novel tells the story of seven young men from Lorraine who travel to Paris in pursuit of knowledge and education. In Paris they fall under the influence of a charismatic teacher who encourages a contempt for authority and ethics in his students. Barrès shows the majority of the Lorraine youths later failing in life because they have exiled themselves from their native region. In the second novel of the trilogy, *L'appel au soldat,* a historical account of the rise to power of Georges Boulanger, is integrated with fictional characters introduced by Barrès in *Les déracinés.* A general in the French army, Boulanger was the leading figure of a political movement that threatened to overturn the French government. Boulanger's rise to popularity was crucial in solidifying Barrès's politics and his philosophy of National Energy. Especially important to Barrès was Boulanger's vow to take back for France the Alsace-Lorraine, the region of Barrès's birth, which had been seized by Germany during his childhood. The final volume of Barrès's National Energy trilogy, *Leurs figures,* like *L'appel au soldat,* also treats historical events in a fictional guise. The factual context for the novel is the Panama Canal scandal of 1889, in which the French treasury lost enormous sums in the misdirected and abortive campaign to construct a canal through the isthmus some twenty-five years before the successful American project was launched.

Although contemporary critics are largely unsympathetic to Barrès's social and political views, his novels are nevertheless esteemed for their powerful imagery, psychological depth, and the insights they provide into the origins of French cultural and ancestral beliefs. Through symbol and allegory Barrès's works celebrate traditional, even archaic, cultural values of the French nation and its distinct regions. In his active life as a politician, these native cultural values became the rationale for Barrès to support the exclusion of foreign ideas and influences from France. Many modern critics, in fact, believe that Barrès's novels, where they exhibit xenophobia, racial animosity, and an exaggerated nationalism, belong to that component of French culture and politics that was sympathetic to the rise of fascism in Europe in the 1930s and 1940s.

PRINCIPAL WORKS

"M. le générale Boulanger et la nouvelle génération" (essay) 1888; published in *La revue indépendante*
Huit jours chez M. Renan (imaginary conversations) 1888
*Un homme libre (novel) 1889
*Le jardin de Bérénice (novel) 1891
*Sous l'oeil des barbares (novel) 1892
L'ennemi des lois (novel) 1893
"The Panama Scandal" (essay) 1894; published in *The Cosmopolitan*
Du sang, de la volupté et de la mort (short stories and essays) 1894
†Les déracinés (novel) 1897
†L'appel au soldat (novel) 1900
†Leurs figures (novel) 1902
Amori et dolori sacrum (short stories and essays) 1903
Le voyage de Sparte (novel) 1906
L'angoisse de Pascal (biography) 1910
Colette Baudoche (novel) 1911
  [*Colette Baudoche,* 1918]
Le Greco, ou le secret de Tolède (essays) 1912
La grande pitié des églises de France (speeches) 1914
Un jardin sur l'Oronte (novel) 1922
La colline inspirée (novel) 1929
  [*The Sacred Hill,* 1929]
Mes cahiers. 7 vols. (journals) 1929-57

*These novels comprise the trilogy *Le culte du moi.*

†These novels comprise the trilogy *Le roman de l'énergie nationale.*

CRITICISM

Anatole France   (essay date ca. 1892)

[*France is one of the most conspicuous instances of an author who achieved the summit of literary acclaim in his own time but who has since lost much of his eminence to the shifting values of posterity. He embodied what are traditionally regarded as the intellectual and artistic virtues of French writing: clarity, control, perceptive judgment of worldly matters, and the virtues of tolerance and justice. While a persistent tone of irony is often considered the dominant trait of France's writing, in the following excerpt he employs nothing of that critical device. Instead his analysis of Barrès's early novel,* Le jardin de Bérénice, *brings out the elusive qualities of Barrès's literary style, as he calls Barrès "a rare spirit."*]

You are of course acquainted with Dante's *Vita nuova.* It is a little allegorical romance, in which we are conscious of the slender nudity, the fine spareness of early Florentine art. Beneath the dry and, as it were, acid outlines of the figures are hidden a number of complicated symbols. This *Vita nuova* may, strictly speaking, at least by its subtlety, give some idea of the manner of M. Maurice Barrès, who in literature is a Pre-Raphaelite. And it is doubtless thanks to this style and this cast of mind that he has charmed M. Paul Bourget and many more of our most refined writers.

The expressive inertia of the figures, the slightly awkward stiffness of the scenes, which are not linked together, the exquisite little landscapes, hung like tapestries—it is this that I call Pre-Raphaelite and Florentine in M. Barrès' art. But I must not be too insistent. **Le Jardin de Bérénice** is as far removed from the ingenuous symmetry of the *Vita nuova* as M. Barrès' metaphysics from the scholastic philosophy of the thirteenth century. Far from being arranged with exactitude and deduced according to the rules of the syllogism, the new volume is vague and indeterminate. It is an amorphous book. And the indecision of the whole makes a curious contrast with the precise sobriety of the details.

Our young contemporary's works betray, as did Penelope's web of old, a mysterious dread of the completed thing. M. Barrès does not undo his day's work at night. But he is always introducing the unfinished and the unfinishable. For he knows that this gives his work a charm, and he is fertile in artifices. His two first books, **Sous l'œil des barbares** and **Un Homme libre,** were conceived in this manner. Unfortunately they were full of complicated and difficult symbolism; and they were appreciated only by the young. . . . The **Jardin de Bérénice,** which is a sequel to these two volumes, and as it were the third panel of the triptych, seems greatly superior to the others in fineness of its tone and grace of feeling. Still, I warn those austere persons who would read this little book that they run the risk of being shocked in various ways. For in it many of the opinions which are reckoned respectable by human society are gently derided, and M. Barrès is incomparable for his polite manner of offending our sense of decency; I regard him as a rare spirit and an able writer, but I do not by any means stand surety for him as against the chaste reader. (pp. 211-12)

Never did writer sin more calmly, with more elegance, more industry and interest, more out of sheer malice, than the author of the *Jardin de Bérénice.*

He has no instincts, no passions. He is wholly intellectual, a perverse idealist.

Modifying a famous saying of Théophile Gautier's, he has said of himself: "I am a man for whom the outer world does not exist." This must be understood in the metaphysical sense, and if we remind him that here and there he has drawn some very pretty landscapes, he will reply that he has seen them in himself and that they mark the states of his soul. He has further said: "External beauty never really moves me." This is a confession of intellectual perversity. For there is malice in refusing to love visible things and in living exempt from all tenderness toward Nature, all noble idolatry in the face of the splendour of the world. M. Barrès replies once more. "There is no reality for me save pure thought. Souls alone are interesting." Is he then a spiritualist, an exalted mystic, this disdainful young man who despises instinct and feeling? What philosophy or what religion opens the dwellings of men's souls to him? No religion, no philosophy. He neither believes nor hopes. He enters the spiritual kingdom without moral support. Here again is perversity. His youthful master, M. Paul Bourget, who tries to catechize him a little, said to him lately: "Caring only for the things of the soul, you do not accept faith, which alone gives an ample and profound interpretation of the things of the soul." (pp. 213-14)

However, it must not be supposed that M. Barrès wanders through the corridors of psychology absolutely without a rule and without a guide. This inquiring person is not altogether impious, although he is very largely so. I said he has no religion. I was wrong. He has a religion, the religion of the Ego, the cult of the intimate self, the contemplation of self, the divine egotism. He regards his own life with wonder and admiration; he is a literary and political Buddha of incomparable distinction. He teaches us worldly wisdom and an elegant detachment from things. He teaches us to seek in ourselves alone for "the inward consolation" and to guard our ego as a treasure. And he wishes this to be regarded as asceticism; he will have it that there is virtue in defending the ego with jealous care against the enterprises of Nature. . . . [M. Barrès] warns us that we should protect ourselves, should belong to ourselves, should remain stable in the flux of things, should realize ourselves persistently amid the diversity of phenomena, and sell nothing, not even a vain shadow, to God, or the devil, or women. (pp. 214-15)

[M. Barrès's] ego has a peculiar tendency to diffuse itself into the infinite. It is an exquisite ego, but it is delicate, subtle and vague in the extreme. It is made up of subsi-

dences, perturbations and hesitations, and is so complicated that it is an heroic task to keep it under restraint. A perpetual irony subtilizes it and consumes it. It is a fluid but delightful ego, of a disturbing temerity. This thinking ego has the radiance of a nebula, and reminds one of those fragile stars, those comets for which the solicitude of the astronomers constantly fears some terrible celestial adventure. And these are not idle fears. Several of these subtle bodies have been lost in their hyperbolic orbits, and others have been cut in two. There are now two egos, which cannot come together again.

In order to avert such a disaster, M. Barrès has recourse to various expedients. He does not content himself with concentrating his ego in elegant, psychological novels such as *Un Homme Libre* and *Le Jardin de Bérénice.* He acts; he makes experiments. I do not think I shall annoy him if I say that his successful candidature for the Chamber of Deputies was one of these experiments in practical scepticism, and that the deputy for Nancy is an experimentalist in action. (pp. 215-16)

M. Maurice Barrès has more than once caused serious persons to knit their brows. But over young men he has exercised a sort of fascination. There is no need to be surprised by this. His mind, so unquiet, so unhealthy, so perverted, and spoilt, as we have already noted, by what the theologians call malice, is assuredly not without grace and wealth. He has represented artistically a real moral distress. And this has won for him the sympathy of many of our young men; it has procured for him a sort of tender, tearful admiration. A poet of his own period, who has written a very delightful book of critical essays, M. Le Goffic, verifies M. Barrès' profound influence and explains it in simple terms: "The truth is," he says, "that these books, with their unhealthy art and passion, exhibit in the strongest light the moral habits of a youth which is extremely civilized, habits thinly dispersed among the crowd, it is true, but which, if one were to unite the scattered members, would appear more compact than is imagined."

And, lastly (no man of letters will make a mistake in this respect), M. Barrès possesses the dangerous and penetrating weapon of style. His supple language, at once precise and elusive, has wonderful resources at its disposal. Many a landscape in the *Jardin de Bérénice,* with its rapidly drawn outlines and its infinite perspective, is unforgettable. (pp. 217-18)

> *Anatole France, "Maurice Barrès's 'Les jardin de Bérénice',"* in On Life and Letters, *fourth series, translated by Bernard Miall, Dodd, Mead and Company, 1924, pp. 211-18.*

Hannah Lynch   (essay date 1900)

[*The following excerpt discusses two leaders whose politics were important in the definition of Barrès's French nationalism: General Mercier, Minister of War during the Dreyfus Affair, and General Boulanger, a military commander who enjoyed a brief political ascendancy in the 1880s as the hero of a popular left-wing movement. Lynch dismisses Boulanger as a political fraud and cen-*

sures Barrès's literary style, as well as his characters, in a venomous response to Barrès's early political novels.]

Pending the hour when [General] Mercier's honoured ashes will be carried in triumph to the hall of heroes—the Pantheon—his admirers are busy compiling a Nationalist literature. Its lights are many, but none of such an opaque luminosity, such an aggressive dullness, such repellent modernity as M. Maurice Barrès, whose *Appel au Soldat* has just appeared. It is the second interminable volume of a trilogy in honour of national energy. The first was the unreadable and extraordinary *Déracinés*. Has an author the right to give such a misleading title as "novel" to books like *Déracinés* and *Appel au Soldat?*

Déracinés was a pretentious and uninteresting history of the development of seven Lorraine youths of different rank, who are in a kind of Dumasesque conspiracy (without any of Dumas' wit and high-spirited charm) to conquer Paris. The writer's object is to expose to us the evils of uprooting from the soil of provincial souls. . . . There is not a generous, a noble, a disinterested trait among the seven; and, considering their youth and the purpose which brings them to Paris, we cannot accept, as Mr. Barrès does, that mere contact with the capital has so speedily vulgarised and degraded them. Noble and studious and disinterested provincials live all their lives in Paris around us, and die undegraded and undiminished by years spent upon the banks of the lovely Seine. But vulgar-minded, voracious young wolves who come to devour or be devoured will naturally follow the path of M. Barrès' seven Lorraine youths.

The *Appel au Soldat* carries us into the famous and trivial Boulanger conspiracy. M. Barrès is a passionate Boulangist, ever waiting and watching for a second Boulanger. It is an open secret that he is his hero of predilection, François Sturel, the ardent follower of Boulanger. The difference between the *Appel au Soldat* and the ordinary *roman à clef* is that no key here is needed. M. Barrès gives the names in full. Cornelius Herz, Baron Reinach, the unhappy Joseph Reinach, Paul Déroulède, Dillon, Boulanger, Mme. de Bonnemains, all political and journalistic Paris, is here named in full. We see the fantastic Déroulède in his different ineffectual and rather silly dramatic scenes with that ineffable humbug, the hero of *café chantants*, General Boulanger. We are spared no cough of the unfortunate Marguerite [de Bonnemains]. Boulanger, as painted by his fervent follower, is an appalling specimen of a political mountebank. One never realised more terribly than in these deadly dull pages the truth of General de Gallifet's words in the Chamber the other day—the fool had not even the makings of a criminal in him. . . . In the hands of a writer of some dramatic instinct, with only a modest share of the novelist's art, with a large and luminous style, and a creative as well as an analytic gift, the amazing story of Boulanger's rise and fall, his inexplicable popularity—based on good looks of a very common kind, and a black charger—his instant desertion and melodramatic end, might have made an excellent subject of a novel. But M. Barrès writes a deplorable and exasperating French, and his novels resemble the lives of his seven Lorraine youths. They are not illuminated by a single ray of sunshine, by a smile, by a witty or humorous phrase, by

a vivid description, by a pleasing sentence. Style so dense, figures so inanimate, speech so dull and vulgar, scenes so purposeless, so unrevealing, so lacking in all the attributes of dramatic art, it would be impossible to match elsewhere. If you were to patch together a series of newspaper articles upon persons and public events during a certain set of years, the result would be a book much resembling *Appel au Soldat.* Only the chances are, it would be a great deal more readable, for few newspaper editors would tolerate a style so inarticulate, so stupidly impenetrable, meaning so little in an idle pretentiousness of envelope as that of M. Maurice Barrès. And certainly no editor out of Bedlam would print the terrible chapter "La Vallée de la Moselle," recording the wanderings of two of our Lorraines in search of their national roots in about 150 pages. The Prussians in this period of the awakening of national energy are handled as in the subsequent period the Anglo-Saxons may expect to be handled. In the valley of the Moselle we are told that "these excellent folk have all the distinction of old towns, apply themselves all the more to the practice of courtesy and urbanity in reprobation of that Teutonic heaviness which will always seem blackguardism to French sensibilities." It would be curious to learn what aspect "French sensibilities" have for the German mind. As revealed by the eminent Maurice Barrès, the word *goujaterie* would not be altogether inappropriate. The author, under the thin disguise of François Sturel, comports himself with complacent grossness and ineptitude. His envenomed hatred of his old master Bouteiller is scarcely more unintelligent than his deification of a cheap idol like Boulanger. And his relations with Mme. de Nelles, his accomplice in the inevitable tale of adultery, are displayed with a hideous cynicism, an absence of heart, or even passion, which leave us abashed by the thought that there are men and women who can find their pleasure in sinking for so little. As the heroine is merely a name for us, without character or features or any physical, moral or mental trait to enable us to take the faintest interest in her fortunes, it does not excite our indignation to find her falling into the arms of a lover without even the saving excuse of persecution and overmastering temptation. Her fall, like her personality, is described by words that have no actual significance for us. . . . And just so indifferent are we to Mme. de Nelles, so unmoved are we by her love, which is silly and unclean, and by her suffering in neglect, which is shallow and vain. As for her lover, we are stupefied by his fatuity and vulgarity. An animal could not possibly put less heart and brains into its loves than this mediocre partisan, who, not at all offered us as a type of political adventurer, exclaims brutally on learning of his chief's defeat: "Boulanger is but an accident. We'll find other Boulangisms." This, we know, is the gallant Paul Déroulède's theory, who stoutly professes himself to be a Boulangist waiting for a second, a third, a fourth Boulanger.

There is one little sentence in these dull 550 pages that has a touch of humanity, of feeling, a faint whiff of delicate sentiment. Writing of Boulanger's desperate solitude after the death of Mme. de Bonnemains, he says: "In these funereal soliloquies his whole being, once a little vulgar, optimist and sociable, was transformed under the beneficent influence of sorrow." The last line is "death to traitors and robbers." Here is prophecy of a future war-cry. (pp. 413-14)

> Hannah Lynch, in an originally unsigned essay titled, "A French Apostle of National Energy," in The Academy, Vol. 58, No. 1461, 1900, pp. 413-14.

A. Marinoni   (essay date 1911)

[*In the following excerpt, Marinoni takes exception to the critical formula of Abel-François Villemain, who maintained that "genius consists in reclothing a banal idea in a definitive form." Though he does not find Barrès's novel,* Colette Baudoche, *to be highly original or imaginatively plotted, Marinoni praises its engaging simplicity, human emotion, and spiritual atmosphere.*]

The novel that Maurice Barrès has recently published under the title of **Colette Baudoche** is not only a noteworthy contribution to fiction, but also a historical and social study of unusual interest.

The action of the story is laid in Metz, the city in Lorraine where the fate of the colossal struggle of 1870 was practically closed in favor of Germany. The theme of the narrative is the conflict in the heart of an Alsatian girl between love for a German Professor and her noble ideal of loyalty to France. Colette Baudoche, the heroine, is a representative of the type of girl who is proud of asserting her French ancestry and sympathy on German soil. She lives with her grandmother in a modest dwelling. As their resources are meagre, the two women, after a long hesitation, become reconciled to the idea of renting a room of their apartment to a young Professor of Königsberg, Frédéric Asmus. This young German is one of the army of peaceful invaders which since 1870 has been flowing into Alsace. He is gradually inspired by the surroundings and the noble atmosphere of Metz; he travels over the country and mingles with the people; he admires their easy, graceful bearing and good manners, the clearness and the harmony of their speech. While his taste is thus captivated by the outward forms and intrinsic worth of French civilization, his heart is fascinated by the winning charm of Colette, who represents to his eye a living expression of French spirit and grace. He soon thinks of marrying her, and after careful consideration discloses his intention to her and Mme. Baudoche. The two women are naturally perplexed, for they fully appreciate the sterling character of the Professor, and the grandmother especially is well aware that a marriage would mean an assured future to her beloved Colette. Unfortunately, however, he is German. They decide to defer a decision and give a final answer to the Professor when the latter returns from a journey to Königsberg, where lives the sweetheart he has decided to forsake for the beautiful Colette. The irresolution of the two women before the situation thrust upon them is finally overcome after a most impressive ceremony in the Cathedral of Metz—a ceremony performed each year in memory of the French soldiers who fell under the walls of the city in the battles of 1870. Colette decides that everything must be sacrificed, even the happiness of a lifetime, to what she believes to be an ideal and lofty sentiment of honor. She tells the Professor that she cannot become his wife, that she has

valued highly and always will value his friendship, but that she must answer the call of a greater obligation to the sacred memories of her country . . . . Such is in outline the plot of the story.

One can easily see that the structure of the novel is exceedingly simple and therefore lacking in those elements of excitement or complication or surprise that bind the attention and the interest of the average reader. It is a novel that will appeal particularly to those who delight in the artistic representation of real life and in the conflict of human emotions, rather than in the elaborate charm of fanciful deeds and situations. In this last work, Barrès has again aimed at the same austerity and simplicity that characterized his previous novel, **Au Service de l'Allemagné.** He has again shown a praiseworthy eagerness to keep aloof from the trend of present taste and to avoid all such common means as might have won for his book a larger audience. In **Colette Baudoche** the highly colored style, the sumptuous images, and the haughty display of a poignant individualism impatient of social discipline,—qualities that have made Barrès inimitable in his earlier works—no longer appear. The whole atmosphere in which events occur and characters move is here spiritualized no less than are thought and style, sensation and sentiment.

This accounts for the fact that the narrative, simple in content and unpretentious in form, is quite capable of making a lasting impression, an impression that is due in large measure to the enthusiastic genius of the writer, which seems to animate and enhance with affectionate sympathy the life of the characters he portrays, and charge with symbolic meaning the things and places he describes. Whatever be the excellence of Barrès' style in this work, one easily feels that it is intimately associated with and dependent upon the constant inspiration of patriotic sentiment. For here it is not a style reflecting such æsthetic qualities as may characterize mere force of intellect, nor is any effort made toward a search for that technical perfection which is only too often an indication of penury of thought. The charm of the style consists solely in its great force of suggestion. Its appeal is binding because it springs from an intimate fusion of thought and expression, from a correspondence highly convincing between the writer's *état d'âme* and outward nature in all its manifestations. It is a style thoroughly imbued with that enlightened sincerity of effort which never fails to command admiration and often finds an echo in the human heart. There is, above all, in his style the elusive harmony of poetic emotion, for all his characters and landscapes have long dwelt in his heart before they found literary expression. The writer infuses into his subject-matter the living and suggestive force of a delicate feeling and reverence. He seems to have lived in constant and spiritual intimacy not only with the men but with all objects of historic interest and natural beauty in Alsace and Lorraine, and so he feels and communicates life to what appears to be deprived of life. For example, the monuments themselves, whether it be the lofty cathedral of Metz or the modest tombs of war victims scattered in the neighboring country, appear to him as powerful symbols of undying memories conveying the silent message of the past to the present. *Nihil sine voce est.* And this ideal communion with eternal things is not in the literary fashion of the symbolistic school but rather in accord with the human sentiment of the Virgilian *sunt lacrimae rerum.*

There is somewhere in the novel a passage which indicates clearly the attitude of the author throughout the book. "Il est impossible d'aimer," says Barrès, "voire de comprendre aucun objet si nous n'avons pas mêlé nos songes à sa réalité, établi un lien entre lui et notre vie. C'est peu d'avoir conscientieusement tourné autour d'une belle chose; l'essentiel c'est de sentir sa qualité morale et de participer du principe d'où elle est née. Il faut devenir le frère d'une beauté pour bien commencer à l'aimer."

These words explain the secret of his art in *Colette Baudoche.* And it is after all natural that he should have felt so keenly the fascination of the country around the Vosges where he was born and where his early education progressed in the midst of the trying calamities visited by war upon his people and his own family. These early and poignant remembrances, somewhat softened by age, seem to form in the novel a spiritual background upon which are reflected in sympathetic atmosphere the cold and dreary realities of life. The immediate result of this earnest love for the complex life that his affectionate imagination far more than his art has fixed in *Colette Baudoche,* is one of unmistakable and convincing appeal—a fact that is the more significant in that the leading characteristic of Barrès as a stylist has nearly always been one of too conscious effort and not unfrequently of studied and deliberate affectation. The stylistic element is indeed of such importance that it can hardly be overestimated in this work of Maurice Barrès, for it is undoubtedly by virtue of its magic charm and simplicity that the narrative assumes a well-defined meaning even in its smallest details.

Yet beyond its excellence of form this new book of Barrès' must have other unusual qualities, else we should be at a loss to account for its great success and the spontaneous admiration it has elicited from all quarters. One may here venture to say that in works of art the subject-matter is a question of minor concern; that the manner and form in which a thought is developed and expressed is the preëminent factor; that, as Villemain puts it: "le génie consiste à revêtir une idée banale d'une forme définitive." Fortunately, in the case of *Colette Baudoche,* one needs not apply the questionable truth of Villemain's definition, for while it is evident that scarcely any effort is made toward originality, yet both in thought and language *Colette Baudoche* is free from all banality; it is characterized by that severe and inspiring simplicity of which, at its best, style is only a powerful adjunct.

It is hardly in place here to inquire into the relative merits of *Colette Baudoche* as compared with the numerous other contributions of Barrès. Such a task would be difficult and unsatisfying, for the simple reason that the literary production of this French writer is far too complex in nature and varied in scope. But whatever may be the work that will insure for its author the recognition of time, many will nevertheless feel that of all Barrès' books this latest one will be most likely to survive, for it was not meant to be merely an interesting novel of the day, nor a psychological study of character. It is rather a dramatic portrayal of the attempted reconstruction of two different

civilizations, or of two national spirits which force of events has brought together and which with the lapse of time have so far failed to blend into harmony. It depicts the drama without *dénouement* which, since the close of the terrible war of 1870, two peoples with opposing traditions and tendencies have been enacting in Alsace and Lorraine.

Though the frame of the book is thus historical, we can hardly call the work a historical novel. The author has not proposed to revive a *genre* which has had its day and which artistic fashion has perhaps too hastily discarded; nor has Barrès intended, in accordance with a certain aristocratic turn of his intellect, to surround with a halo of glory the leaders who have always engaged upon the soil of Alsace in the futile attempt to bend the stubborn and unyielding attitude of the conquerors, or in the task even more futile of securing for the oppressed the same rights and privileges that other German provinces enjoy. His aim is rather the historical reconstruction of the humble, the sympathetic revelation of hidden forces each striving to keep kindled in the heart the hope of warm patriotism and to preserve unchanged in the whirl of trying vicissitudes a personality formed and strengthened through a costly process of social and national development. His is not only an evocation but a true apotheosis of the commonplace, and in this Maurice Barrès has once more shown that real literary greatness may be simple. (pp. 400-04)

On the other hand, it is equally evident that the intention of the writer is not to develop a thesis that would in any way influence him to sacrifice or modify the varied evidence of reality for the sake of proving any *a priori* contention. He thus felt it his duty, not only as a writer but also as a man, to avoid the least misrepresentation that might have marred true impartiality of observation and of judgment whenever there was involved the evaluation of the opposite forces in the drama that still goes on in Alsace. In this respect the veracity of the novelist is thoroughly convincing. Both sides of the tragic controversy that is so poignantly typified in Colette Baudoche and Professor Asmus are presented in the book with unerring accuracy, with an appreciation both naïve and austere, entirely unhampered by resentment. Conscious of the important mission that he proposed to fulfil, Maurice Barrès understood that the dispassionate reader would not excuse any faltering expression or condone any superficial impression through possible sympathy for the cause he upholds. He realized that he could not place directly the right or the wrong on either side, since the solution of a problem that has confronted both adversaries for over forty years seems in fact scarcely attainable. Indeed, one may here and there see that Barrès' attitude is wellnigh one of admiration for the conqueror. He intimates that such a rôle cannot and must not be his, for the Germans have more than one way in which to show their legitimate pride. He naturally loves the conquered in that the latter show a heroic, almost incredible power of resistance. And Barrès has happily presented in his book the tragic situation arising from a cruel misunderstanding that forces irreconcilable enemies to live in perennial association. (p. 405)

The logical inference we draw is that two distinct nationalities come into daily contact on the soil of Alsace, but in spite of this coëxistence based on a community of varied relationships, their spiritual and intellectual life keeps them as widely apart as they were when the theoretical process of fusing them began. Obviously the great purpose Barrès had in mind when he wrote *Colette Baudoche* was, through the tangible example of daily life in Alsace, to prove that a national personality which is but the accumulated development of the character of previous generations cannot be overcome by a mere reorganization of racial affinities; that the sentiment of a common country from which the Alsatians were rudely disrupted cannot be easily effaced from their hearts, because, while we wait for a broader ideal than patriotism to dawn upon the world, true love for one's country will continue to be shown and perpetuated in deeds of heroic abnegation and oblivion of one's self even to the surrender of life.

The impression one gathers in reading the book is that in the attempt at an objective treatment of the soul of Alsace, Maurice Barrès appears to better advantage as a portrait-ist than as a novelist. *Colette Baudoche* is only incidentally a novel, and thus the types the author represents are not idealized nor are they in any way modified by his artistic temperament, they may live in Metz or Strasbourg, in Colmar or Mülhausen, in any of the villages of Alsace and Lorraine, wherever there is shown a constancy of determination not to accept voluntarily from the conquerors anything that would offend the dignity of partiotic sentiment. Indeed, the fact that *Colette Baudoche* is only incidentally a work of fiction is one of great importance, since here a question arises that comes fairly within the scope of the present review and deserves to be mentioned at length.

It appears that the decision of Colette not to marry Professor Asmus has met with objections at the hands of some critics. For this connection it may be interesting to know that the great poet Mistral, and Jaurès, the well-known leader of the socialist party in France, both expressed to the author of *Colette Baudoche* their disappointment at what they call the unexpected and unreasonable foolishness of the young Colette. These two distinguished men would have much preferred a happy close for the book. (pp. 406-07)

Jaurès' view is such as we should naturally expect a man to express whose attitude is largely determined by political and social preconceptions. That of the Provençal poet is but the effusion of an optimistic nature with an unbounded faith in the victorious mission of the civilization of his own people. So intense is his humanity that it makes him regretful that two creatures are thus made to suffer. But, although the novelist recognizes the admirable sentiments that underlie these criticisms, yet his own life has made him far more familiar with actual conditions at Metz; and he knows only too well that the optimism of both Mistral and Jaurès may prove entirely baseless. At the close of the book he hints clearly his fear as to the ultimate fate of the Alsatians: "Nous, cependant, acceptons-nous qu'une vive image de Metz subisse les *constantes atteintes qui doivent, à la longue, l'effacer?*" So the novelist was not hampered by sentimental limitations, and has preferred to see in the action of Colette the triumph of will over the obstacles

that oppose it, the indifference to all that brings personal satisfaction, so that the sentiment of the heroine may be purified through hardship and thus she may share worthily the common sorrow of her people.

It could not have been otherwise, if the book was to be to the very end a faithful portrayal of actual life in Lorraine. If Barrès had intended to write a book of pure fiction, a close such as Mistral and Jaurès suggested might have been possible, though it is questionable if it would enhance the artistic effect of the book. But, as we have already remarked, *Colette Baudoche* is only incidentally a novel, and so any effort toward a close *à effet* would have violated its purpose. (pp. 408-09)

Now, the fact that Maurice Barrès is a member of the French Academy and unquestionably in the front rank of living French writers may partially account for the eagerness with which each succeeding production of his is received both in and out of France. In the case of *Colette Baudoche,* however, we feel that Barrès has given us a book scarcely surpassed by any of his previous ones. If we may rightly judge by the universal admiration that the book has already won, its place among the few French novels of recent years that are likely to live is securely fixed. And it is not surprising. Whatever the opinion of critics may be with reference to the qualities of form and content whereby the excellence of a novel is measured, or however the taste in literary appreciation may differ, there is always a common ground where ultimately intellectual dissension ceases and a great book emerges to stand solely on those qualities that are eminently human and that no changing fashion of art can affect. In the long run, enduring admiration is more readily bestowed upon the book in which are expressed the higher ideals of man, even though these ideals may lack the characteristics of universality and be accordingly confined to a certain people or epoch. Of such ideals the humble no less than the great may be formative factors. This latest novel by Maurice Barrès is a successful endeavor to this very end, as we see in it artistically reflected a part of the ever-changing horizon within which is laboring the ascending evolution of a people.

A prophecy as to whether the present obstinate effort of Alsace and Lorraine to preserve intact their national individuality will save them permanently from the all-powerful mould of German influence is here irrelevant. In *Colette Baudoche* the author may, indeed, openly intimate that the problem of Alsace is far from settled and that the violence perpetrated in the treaty of Frankfort against the natural rights of the annexed provinces is not yet atoned. But we cannot be very deeply concerned in this, although, through a superior sense of justice we may feel inclined to admire this ideal assertion of a patriot. For us, the lasting impression of the book rests upon elements of greater importance: upon the stubborn resistance which, forty years after France withdrew, is still shown against the preponderant political and cultural expansion of Germany in Alsace; a resistance that time has not yet impaired and that difficulties and persecutions have failed to subdue; upon the successful zeal that urges a people to affirm a sacred inheritance of thought, of taste, of pride, and of independence, received from France; upon the determination of

Alsace to cling to an ideal which, to a people conscious of its dignity, is, after all, the only goal worth striving for. Such is the message of *Colette Baudoche,* a message that will long linger in our memory, for even though the future may leave unanswered the call which closes the book and in which is echoed the aggressive sentiment of the author, the appeal of the novel will remain unchanged, and the book will always be admired as a true and powerful representation of humble effort toward a sublime ideal. (pp. 409-11)

> *A. Marinoni, in a review of "Colette Baudoche," in* The Sewanee Review, *Vol. XIX, No. 4, Autumn, 1911, pp. 400-11.*

Albert Léon Guérard   (essay date 1916)

[*In the following excerpt, Guérard examines Barrés's early trilogy,* Le culte du moi. *He describes Barrès's philosophy of the "Culte du Moi" as a cultivation or development of the self in its capacity as pure will, and above all as an enrichment of the emotions in preference to reason.*]

Maurice Barrès, . . . is the poet rather than the theorist of those subconscious influences, ancestral and local, which create in men's souls a sense of their nationality. French "Nationalism," as a political party, has proved a failure; as a sentiment, its potency at the present day can hardly be exaggerated. In last analysis, the problem around which the Great War is raging is this: "What is a nation?" And because this problem is the keynote of Barrès's works, they assume for us a tragic significance. (p. 216)

. . . . .

The Novels of Maurice Barrès.

In 1888—he was then twenty-six—the young Lorrainer Maurice Barrès astonished Paris as the high priest of a new cult—"le culte du Moi" (Ego-worship). Such is the collective title of his first three novels, *Under the Eyes of the Barbarians, A Free Man, The Garden of Berenice.* Novels? It is impossible to tag any label on these strange concoctions, which the author himself calls "ideologies." A minimum of fact, a certain element of psycho-picturesque description, symbols, reflections, meditations—a farrago of Ignatius de Loyola, Stendhal, Heine, and not a few others: the result is wilful, absurd, exasperating to a degree, yet with undeniable powers of fascination. It belongs to that esoteric literature which is so dear to very young people. The element of conscious mystification is not lacking either—as in the symbolic poetry of Mallarmé, the Rosicrucian revival of Sâr Joséphin Péladan, or, in more recent years, Post-Impressionist Art. Maurice Barrès became a power among a widening circle of initiated. But there was sense and energy in the man, in spite of his affectations. His "culte du Moi" is no passive worship: it implies the cultivation as well as the adoration of the Ego. And, different in this respect from certain developments of Nietzscheism, it is made ethically palatable through its respect for other individualities. It is corrected by the Kantian reverence for human personality, or sim-

ply by the golden rule. When translated into a language understood by the people, there is nothing unacceptable in the anarchism of his pamphlet *Toute licence sauf contre l'Amour.* This flamboyant title might be rendered: . . . *"In non-essentials, liberty; in all things, Charity."*

The three principles of Ego-worship are quite typical, not merely of Barrès, but of a great part of French literature. "(1) We are never so happy as when we are in a state of exaltation; (2) The pleasure of exaltation is greatly increased through analysis; (3) Consequently, we must feel as much as possible whilst analyzing as much as possible." Most of us, I am sure, would demur at the minor premise. Analysis seems to imply the destruction rather than the intensification of feeling. To be consciously, wilfully, analytically passionate seems to us a contradiction in terms. This was one of the lessons that we thought we could accept at the hands of that arch-analyst, Bourget. But need this always be so? Why should analysis destroy sentiment, if the sentiment be genuine and the analysis accurate? . . . [In] the third part of his trilogy, *The Garden of Berenice,* Barrès pulls down much of his own logical scaffolding. Berenice is a simple soul, primitive and pure, in spite of degrading experiences, close to nature, bathed in the unconscious. The poet recognizes in her a force, a virtue, that his conscious analysis, unaided, cannot attain.

Before Barrès found his final way, his Ego-worship tempted him into the dangerous path of Baudelaire. To feel as intensely as possible, yet with a clear, analytical brain; to consider the world and your own soul as instruments upon which to perform the most subtle symphonies of sensation and sentiment—why, that leads straight to the cold-blooded perversities of *The Flowers of Evil.* And Barrès's book, *Blood, Pleasure, and Death,* is essentially, in title and in treatment, a product of the Baudelairian spirit. That strain has never been wholly eliminated from the thought of Maurice Barrès. In 1903, after an active political life, and half a dozen volumes which, in the main, were strong and wholesome, he went back, in *Amori and Dolori Sacrum,* to the depraved romanticism of *Blood, Pleasure, and Death.* The first and most important part of the book is devoted to Venice. But what Barrès loves in that incomparable city is the subtle fever, the morbidity, the decay, the delicate corruption, which fill his soul with complicated, and all the more delicious, melancholy. The Barrès of Venice is first cousin to Des Esseintes, the grotesque hero of Huysmans' *A Rebours,* for whom incipient putrefaction and deliquescence had irresistible charms. There are people, we are told, who like their Roquefort green and their venison high. We understand that, after being so nearly engulfed in the morass of Baudelairianism, Barrès should have felt the need of a support, of a discipline from without. His "nationalism," after all, made a man of him.

In 1889, Barrès was a candidate for Parliament under the auspices of General Boulanger. (pp. 216-21)

The demagogic agitation led by [the] General was a mixture of all primitive instincts—democracy, *revanche,* thirst for glory, hero-worship. Barrès sought in it more than an exciting game. As he told us in *Berenice,* he was aware of the limitations of his cultured and analytical self: he wanted then to enrich it by a plunge into the unconscious, by communion with the primitive soul of the people, that soul which Boulanger embodied for a moment. . . . We owe to Barrès's political experience two books which unfortunately purport to be novels, *The Appeal to the Soldier* and *Their Faces*—the latter a description of the Panama scandals. The fictitious elements—the thin veil covering the autobiographical passages, and a totally irrelevant love affair—could profitably be removed, and then we would have the most picturesque and passionate memoirs in the French language since the days of Saint-Simon. The superficial charm and the hopeless frivolity of Boulanger, his scruples and his weaknesses, the melancholy of his failure, the electric atmosphere of Parliament, the tragedies of corruption, hatred, and fear, and especially the epic description of Parisian crowds, heaving, tossing, and foaming in their changing moods have inspired Barrès with pages that neither history nor literature can well afford to forget. It is an authentic chronicle of our own drab Yesterday, but intense and vivid to a degree rarely equalled by the best historical romances. Barrès has remained almost constantly in active politics since the time of Boulanger's venture. . . . [He] was one of the leaders of the Anti-Dreyfusists, one of the strongest opponents of the religious policy of the radicals, one of the protagonists in the bellicose revival of the last decade. Some of his political books, like *Scenes and Doctrines of Nationalism,* or *The Great Distress of the Churches of France,* contain pages as perfect as the best in his purely literary works.

The Appeal to the Soldier and *Their Faces* are the second and third parts of a trilogy under the collective title: *The Romance of National Energy.* The first novel of the series, *The Uprooted,* has proved to be one of the influential books published within the last twenty years. The "Uprooted" (déracinés) are those young men estranged from their natural surroundings by moving to Paris; and, worse still, estranged from the culture of their race by the cosmopolitan ideal of such denationalized dreamers as Kant. They are young trees that will bear bitter fruit or none at all, in an uncongenial soil. The moral of the book is: "Back to your province, which has moulded your ancestors and yourselves; where you feel the close kinship of field, wood, and river; of church, castle, and cottage; where you are in line with an immemorial tradition! Root yourselves again into your native ground."

The author claims that this doctrine is a natural development of Ego-worship. He had sought self-realization in cultured anarchy, and found it wanting: his Ego could not develop in a vacuum. He had tried to commune with the popular soul: but without a principle to guide him, he found it vague and shifting. His Self is not isolated and autonomous. It is a part of a larger whole. It is determined, as Taine had taught, by "race, surroundings, and time." To recognize these limitations implies no abdication. On the contrary, you are never more completely yourself than when you bring to consciousness the obscure forces at work within you. By so doing, you follow the cardinal precept of Ego-worship: to feel as much as possible whilst analyzing as much as possible. To feel as much as possible: this you achieve through communion with like-minded people and in the most favourable surroundings. Deep is the sombre joy of spiritual isolation, enhanced by the

physical presence of a hostile crowd; deeper still, and more lasting, is the consciousness of harmony, of fellowship in time and space. Why do we congregate to pray according to ancient rituals, whilst the question is to save our own individual soul? Enlightened individualism must transcend Self. Thus Ego-worship leads to Nationalism, and Nationalism is defined as "the acceptation of a determinism, the two principal terms of which are 'la terre et les morts' (the soil and the dead)."

We may doubt the cogency of Barrès's arguments: we cannot deny the tonic effect that his "nationalism" has had on his life and on his art. Let us be thankful that he did rise from the esoteric subtleties of *Under the Eyes of the Barbarians* and the decaying romanticism of *Blood, Pleasure, and Death,* to the classic purity and strength of *The Eastern Bastions.*

The Eastern Bastions of French culture are Alsace and Lorraine. Barrès studies the problems of the two annexed provinces in those admirable novels: *In the German Service* and *Colette Baudoche.* . . . Ehrich is a young Strasbourg burgher; he might, like so many of his cousins, have crossed the frontier and served in the French Army. But he feels that his duty to Alsace and to French culture is to remain at home, a rock of resistance against German encroachments. And, in the German Army, his duty as an Alsatian is to be a good soldier, to compel the respect of his officers and comrades, whilst making it plain that, under the yoke, he remains unconquered. . . . *Colette Baudoche* is a humble young girl of Metz. A Prussian Doctor of Philosophy and High School teacher rents a room in her home. He is kindly, although pedantic and somewhat uncouth. He falls in love with the French girl, so refined in her simplicity. He breaks for her sake his engagement with the superb Brunhild who is waiting for him in far-off Koenigsberg. Colette respects him and likes him—not without a touch of amusement. But she attends a Mass for the Dead at the Cathedral—the great ceremony through which the French element expresses its loyalty to its past. She cannot break with her people and her tradition. She refuses the German Professor.

Both novels are composed and written with classical simplicity. They are absolutely free from sentimental claptrap. The author recognizes frankly that Alsace-Lorraine prospered under the efficient rule of Germany. The conquerors are not uniformly presented as vulgarians, gluttons, pedants, and swashbucklers. The problem is ethical, unaffected by material considerations. (pp. 222-29)

Barrès's art in these two books is seen at his best, like his thought. Although the characters are symbolical, they are also simply and profoundly human. There is an austere restraint in plot and style, which might repel the casual reader. *Colette Baudoche* in particular is quiet, unobtrusive, almost colourless, like a landscape of Lorraine, or like the eyes of the heroine. To the initiated, this simplicity recalls the tragedies of Racine, whilst the spirit is that of Corneille.

The last book of Barrès in narrative form—it can hardly be called a novel—*The Inspired Hill,* is one of the strangest and most fascinating in modern French literature. It tells the true story of three brothers, the Baillards, who all became Catholic priests. The eldest, Leopold, was a man of boundless ambition and devouring energy. He revived an ancient pilgrimage on the "sacred hill" of Lorraine, the Abbey of Sion-Vaudémont. He extended his influence to Ste.-Odile in Alsace. But his undertakings came to grief; his superiors had never fully approved of his spirit and methods even in the hour of success; when he failed, he was severely censured and reduced to the small parish of Saxon, near Sion. The proud man and his small band of fanatics cannot accept their downfall. We are in 1850: France is still feverish with wild Messianic dreams. The Baillards, estranged at heart from the Roman Church, as Lamennais had been in the preceding generation, fall under the influence of a mystagogue, one of the innumerable prophets of those stormy days, Vintras. They start a small Church of the new Christianity on the hill of Sion. Devotion they have, enough and to spare; and, in their madness, some indelible traces of peasant common sense. Their prestige is still great in that countryside, where they have been spiritual leaders, creators of prosperity, almost feudal lords. Yet they cannot defy the forces of Universal Rome. The new government, the Second Empire, is for the first few years of its history a repressive autocracy, closely allied with the Church. The Baillards are defeated once more. The little band is driven from its stronghold, dispersed; the heroes of that strange episode live on, obscurely, for many years—Leopold as late as 1883. To all outward appearances, they are harmless and commonplace enough: at heart, they are seers still, burning with prophetic flames. On his death-bed, Leopold is at last reconciled with the Church. (pp. 230-32)

As a study of the unbalanced and millennarian "generation of '48," [*The Inspired Hill*] is of surpassing interest. Never had Barrès shown greater qualities of minute realism, shot through with poetry. The humble life of the little community at Sion, with all its petty material difficulties, and yet with a door ever open on the mysterious Beyond; the local and historical atmosphere; the subtle differences between the characters, their interaction, their evolution: all that is rendered with a wealth of sympathy and humour wellnigh unique among recent productions. Most important of all is the symbolism of the book, the great problem which it represents to the mind of a "nationalist." Sion-Vaudémont is a natural place of worship. It antedates Lorraine, France, Gaul, and perhaps Christianity itself. . . . Countless generations have prayed at Sion-Vaudémont. But to whom? Spontaneous religion is both vaguely universal and intensely local. The spirit of Sion-Vaudémont is not Roman Catholic. The Baillards, who yield to its influence, are slowly driven to a schism, to the creation of an autonomous sanctuary. Barrès, the nationalist, the prophet of "the soil and the dead," cannot conceal his sympathy for them. How could he defend a Church which is based on Jewish traditions, Greek theology, Roman imperialism—a Church catholic in scope, and governed by Italians? Thorough-going Germanists have advocated a return to Odin-worship: this is the logical outcome of nationalism. Catholicism claims to rise superior to "race, surroundings, and time"; to borrow Barrès's phraseology, Catholicism is the great uprooter. (pp. 232-34)

* * * * *

The Doctrine of Nationalism in Maurice Barrès.

We may now consider the theory defended in *The Romance of National Energy* and in *The Eastern Bastions*—the doctrine of nationalism. It were idle to deny that this doctrine is attractive, and, within certain limits, convincing. The influence of "the soil," as Barrès calls it, of the early and ancestral surroundings, may easily be exaggerated; but, great or small, that influence is a fact. However, such as it is, it serves as a justification for local patriotism, for provincialism, rather than for nationalism. The best pages perhaps of Maurice Barrès have been inspired by the valley of the Moselle. That valley is half-German, half-French. A man from Metz, moulded by its landscape, its climate, its economic conditions, would naturally be akin to a man of Trèves: but "the soil" does not make him the brother of a Basque, a Breton or a Provençal. You will not have to scratch the nationalism of Barrès very deep before you find regionalism pure and simple—devotion to Lorraine rather than to France: this is visible in his anti-Southern pamphlet, *Cracks in the House.* We have no objection to regionalism: it is a legitimate and an inspiring sentiment. But patriots and cosmopolitans agree that regionalism, in case of conflict, should yield to the wider allegiance—national or universal. It is certainly not for regionalism, for the defence of the small province in which they were born, that the sons of Canada and Australasia are fighting in Flanders or in the Eastern Mediterranean. The true basis of nationalism cannot therefore be geographical: it must be cultural. And, fortunately, the culture of Maurice Barrès is not provincial. (pp. 234-35)

Nationalism, "the acceptation of a determinism," "obedience to our guides, the soil and the dead," is, in the mind of Barrès, not a doctrine of pride, but a doctrine of modesty. (p. 238)

Like all other masterpieces, be they the work of nature or of art, French culture, in order to be fully appreciated, must be looked at from a definite point of view, whence all its elements are seen in their right perspective and with their true proportions. This exact point is what the Barrèsians call "French Truth." Whoso fails to reach it remains an alien, a barbarian. In the same spirit, Barrès and his friends, at the time of the Dreyfus case, elaborated the theory of "French Justice." From the point of view of abstract justice, if universal principles alone were considered, Dreyfus may have been innocent. But we have outgrown the shallow cosmopolitanism of the eighteenth century. From the point of view of "French Justice" (*i.e.* Nationalism), Dreyfus was guilty. The humanitarians, the "intellectuals," the judges who reversed the verdict, were un-French, anti-French. (pp. 239-40)

For the sake of argument, I have accepted Barrès's contention that there is a French type, a French tradition, a French truth. But this is open to question. At present, it is understood that "integral nationalism," or French truth in its fulness, implies three terms—classicism, monarchy, catholicism. This we were told dogmatically by Charles Maurras and *L'Action Française*. Paul Bourget followed suit; so did Jules Lemaître. Maurice Barrès, it must be said, is much broader than his friends. Although converted to classicism, he wants romanticism to rally the main column, "flying still its own glorious banners." He embraces in his sympathy the France of Joan of Arc, the France of Louis XIV., the France of Danton, the France of Bonaparte. At the death-bed of Jaurès, he confessed that he loved the great Internationalist whom he had so long and so bitterly combated. Yet "traditionalism" would have no meaning if it did not denote a definite set of traditions. And, on the whole, Barrès accepts two terms at least of the nationalistic trinity—classicism and catholicism. [The critic adds in a footnote: "(Barrès) preserves towards the Royalists an attitude of 'benevolent neutrality.' For his religious opinions *cf.* **For our Churches** and **The Great Distress of the Churches in France.** He is not a Christian."]

Classicism and catholicism! A strange conception of traditionalism that would rule out of the French tradition Voltaire and Victor Hugo! The precarious harmony between classicism, absolute monarchy, and catholicism was attained about 1660, and preserved for less than half a century. The eighteenth century was classical, and increasingly anticatholic. The Revolution was intensely classical in taste and spirit. The Romanticists were all Catholics and Monarchists. Where is your single, harmonious, compelling tradition? (pp. 242-43)

We believe that "the soil and the dead" form an insufficient basis for nationalism. . . . *Tradition*—the love for our fathers' home, for their language, their faith, and even the form of their faith, for the heroes of a certain history—this is another bond of union, fully as real, fully as strong as the first, but of a totally different nature. . . . A third bond of union, nobler than cohabitation, nobler even than common traditions, is the possession of a common *Ideal.* (pp. 245-47)

And it is because Barrès has sought to narrow down the ideal of France from the service of mankind to the cult of an incomplete and local tradition that his work, on the whole, is not good. A Lorrainer, hypnotized by the tragic memories of 1870, he has mutilated his soul. Let us hope that after this war France will abandon the bypath of Barrèsian nationalism for the high road of humanitarianism, a road on which she will meet her sister, the Germany of Kant. (pp. 247-48)

> Albert Léon Guérard, "Maurice Barrès," in his Five Masters of French Romance: Anatole France, Pierre Loti, Paul Bourget, Maurice Barrès, Romain Rolland, *Charles Scribner's Sons, 1916, pp. 215-48.*

Theodore Stanton (essay date 1917)

[*In the following excerpt, Stanton analyzes Barrès's literary style and examines those novels in which the author articulates his ideology of French nationalism.*]

M. Maurice Barrès is a man of such varied interest that he might well be studied from more than one point of view. I shall concentrate my attention, however, particularly to that side of his character shown in his activities as a writer, with a brief glance at those as politician and patriot.

As a writer M. Barrès stands unquestionably in the front rank of living French authors. His ability for marshalling facts is unexcelled, while his style of expression has seldom been equalled. At times his ideas may not coincide with ours, but we can never fail to recognize the skill and charm with which they are presented. The following pages seem to me to reflect, even in translation, his choice diction and the masterly arrangement of his material. Indeed his gifts of style have been considered remarkable by the best critics of France. M. Paul Desjardins spoke of him in the late twenties as "that youth endowed with remarkable diction," M. Charles Maurras writes of "the music of Barrès's prose," while M. Henri Bremond, in what is to me the finest critical study of Barrès written up to ten years ago, the preface to *Vingt-cinq Années de Vie Littéraire*, devotes a section to "Barrès's rhythm." M. Anatole France, reviewing one of M. Barrès's books, says: "His language is supple and at the same time precise; it has wonderful resources."

It is interesting to note what Barrès himself says on the same subject. "The art of writing must satisfy these two requirements—it must be musical and meet the demand for mathematical precision, which exists among the French in every well-regulated soul."

As a British journalist and author, the Hon. Maurice Baring, points out, M. Barrès's "early books are written in an elaborate style and are often obscure." As he advanced in life and experience, however, his style became less involved and the obscurity disappeared completely. . . . In this respect he reverses the course of one of his admirers, Henry James, who began his literary career with a clear style and clear thought and ended with both bathed in ambiguity.

Hero-worship also stands out prominently in M. Maurice Barrès's writings. To him all "exceptional men" are heroes. He is very catholic in his choice of them, numbering in his earlier books those as varied as Napoleon, Renan and Taine. Later Boulanger and Déroulède became his chief worthies. With the coming of the war M. Barrès attains the climax of his reverence for exceptional men, for it is at the shrine of the martyr soldier boys of France that he worships, as we shall see in the pages that follow. Here, as in the matter of style, his taste mellows with age.

Considering Barrès as a patriot and politician, we are almost tempted to pronounce him the [Theodore] Roosevelt of France. There are indeed marks of resemblance between these two "exceptional men," in their character, ideas, books and activities. For Barrès, like Roosevelt, is an ardent disciple of the doctrine of "the strenuous life." Thus, in the preface to *L'Ennemi des Lois,* we read: "It is not systems which we lack, but energy,—the energy to conform our habits to our way of thinking." His **Déracinés** has been called by him "a novel of national energy."

Barrès's excessive patriotism is also Rooseveltan in many respects. He was born in Lorraine in 1862 and was consequently but a child when the Provinces were torn from France in 1871. His native region is ever in his mind and heart, and stands out conspicuously in all his writings. In the preface to **Au Service de l'Allemagne,** he says: "The author being a French Lorrainer necessarily judges everything from the standpoint of Lorraine and France." Note how he puts Lorraine even before France. It appears in his very first book. In his latest volume, **Les Diverses Familles Spirituelles de la France,** Lorraine is not forgotten. In his most recent essay, that in the July *Atlantic Monthly,* it is continually appearing, nor is it absent from the oration which follows.

I recall the presence of Barrès at Rennes during the famous Dreyfus trial of 1899. He represented a Paris daily to which he sent, nightly, long telegrams, and I performed a like duty for an American cable syndicate. But we were in opposite camps and did not speak. I still see his sparse figure of medium height and not yet touched with the *embonpoint* of the forties, leaning over the back of the bench in front of him, his swarthy face crowned with heavy dark hair which shaded his deep-set piercing eyes, following attentively every word, and intonation, and phrase of those heart-moving depositions.

Of late M. Barrès has frequently expressed the hope that the *"union sacrée"* created by the present war, would continue after the peace. "Is it possible," he asks, "that the same forces which, only yesterday, precipitated us, one against the other, but which the mobilization checked,—is it possible that this is all to begin again? Yes, but this time not for the purpose of dividing us or with any aim of exclusion; this time will be founded on our diversity the finest and most active amity. . . . The only diversities which now exist are those which spring from our nature and history. . . . To-day France is unified and purified." (pp. v-x)

During the past year or two, M. Barrès has made the home letters of the young French heroes at the front his special contribution to the literature of the war. Besides the splendid ones given in the pages which follow, similar ones may be found in the *Atlantic* article already referred to, and in **Les Diverses Familles Spirituelles de la France,** where they form the woof and warp of the text, while others are scattered through the pages of the half dozen volumes made up of his remarkable articles contributed to the Paris daily, *L'Echo de Paris,* and brought together under the collective title, **L'Ame Française et la Guerre.** Still others appear in some of the many prefaces which M. Barrès has added to the war books of his friends.

Some surprise may be occasioned in the minds of those of a skeptical turn of thought at the apparently inexhaustible stock of these letters. Whence does M. Barrès get all these epistles *d'outre tombe?* In **Les Diverses Familles Spirituelles de la France,** M. Barrès himself answers this question when he speaks of "the millions of sublime letters, which, for the past two years, have furnished France her spiritual food, . . . these innumerable letters, perhaps a million a day." (pp. xi-xii)

> *Theodore Stanton, in a foreword to* The Undying Spirit of France *by Maurice Barrès, translated by Margaret W. B. Corwin, Yale University Press, 1917, pp. v-xv.*

D. C. Cabeen   (essay date 1929)

[*The following excerpt surveys Barrès's diverse writings for small literary magazines published in Paris in the 1880s.*]

Maurice Barrès, at the age of 19, left Nancy, where he was studying law, to continue, nominally at least, this same work in Paris. But his real interest was in literature, and he was fired with a passionate desire to make his mark in the world of letters. His ambition received prompt recognition, and the very year of his début in Paris, 1881, he had two articles accepted in *La Jeune France,* a "young" review, then in its fourth year, but with a brilliant list of contributing editors which included: Alphonse Daudet, Anatole France, Leconte de Lisle, Paul Bourget, Baudelaire and Faguet. About one-third of each issue of this review was devoted to publishing the work of young and unknown writers who showed promise.

Barrès's first article, which appeared in May, 1881, is a favorable analysis of the plays of Auguste Vacquerie and shows, along with certain crudities of style, a naïvely youthful enthusiasm which we will not often find in the writer, but also an almost fanatical devotion to the highest literary ideals, which will be, of course, a constant trait in all his later work. The second article is upon the occasion of the 10th anniversary of the death of Charles Hugo, elder son of the poet. Barrès writes with a keen sympathy, and as yet little trace of the dry irony or the austere disdain which are to characterize his early and middle twenties, the period of "le culte du moi." These articles drew to Barrès the attention of Leconte de Lisle, and the famous poet brought the young writer to the favorable notice of a number of illustrious literary men, among them Bourget and Anatole France.

A year later, in the same periodical Barrès has a story which is worth brief mention because it is so unlike anything else from his pen. The story, called **"Le Chemin de l'Institut,"** is, in brief: Jean Boursaulx reads his novel "Mes débuts" to his friend Karl Ferraz who admires it immensely and secures permission to take it to his room. Boursaulx is stricken with paralysis. Ferraz publishes the novel as his own and becomes famous. Boursaulx learns this, but dies forgiving. Many years later Ferraz, covered with literary honors, is buried in the shadow of the Institute. The romantic pathos of the tale strongly suggests Alphonse Daudet, and the savage irony of the ending reminds us more of the Anatole France of *Penguin Island* than of anything the latter had published up to this time.

In 1883 *La Jeune France* printed a 20-page article by Barrès on *Le Crime de Sylvestre Bonnard* which shows a fine understanding and a deep admiration for its author. Jérôme Tharaud tells us that France was the first literary man whom Barrès visited when he came to Paris, and that the younger man admired France intensely at this time. A remarkable article on Banville shows Barrès as already in possession of a rich and colorful vocabulary, which needs only moderating to become a fine instrument of expression.

Next comes the famous *Taches d'Encre,* a monthly gazette founded, as Barrès frankly tells his readers, to make him better known. The paper had only four numbers, from the 5th of November, 1884 to the 5th of February, 1885. (pp. 532-33)

The first 26 pages of the first number are taken up with a serious and capable discussion of Baudelaire and the origins of Satanism. In the second article Barrès denounces a certain Victor Tissot who has attained considerable notoriety by writing insulting and even scurrilous books about Germany. In this connection Barrès expressed his own distaste for the war songs of Déroulède and the latter's *Lique des Patriotes,* but observes that at least no one doubts Déroulède's sincerity. Three nations, continues Barrès, guide civilization in the 19th century, France, England, and Germany, and it would be an irreparable loss if one of them were to disappear. Barrès holds up to the scorn of the younger generation such vulgar "agents provocateurs" as Tissot. He continues: "The special task which we young men have before us is to retake the captured land and to reconstitute the French ideal, in which is included the Protestant genius of Strasbourg as well as the brilliant facility of the Midi. Let us teach the people of France that they are a great nation, and that by the *élan* of its individual efforts, this people will maintain itself, for the service of the human mind, at the head of the peoples of Europe. Then, when the drum beats, we will show of what is capable a nation which esteems itself highly enough to esteem its adversary." These words of the young Barrès already give the measure of Barrès the patriot. From his earliest manhood the interior life and the need of and aptitude for action are seen to exist side by side in him. The young intellectual is also a man who wishes to serve his country, but it is the interior life of the artist which raises the public man to the dignity of being able to respect a worthy enemy.

Among the interesting indications which the student of Barrès may select from the *Gazette du Mois* of the review is the prediction that in about twenty years he (Barrès) will hold out his arms "à quelque Catholicisme un peu modifié." Under the head of *Moralités* he says "Cest le fait d'un parvenu d'insulter aux maîtres par qui se fait l'education des races."

In the last number of *Les Taches d'Encre* we find the first indication of the implacable hatred and scorn which Barrès is always to show towards the professional politician. The future deputy maintains that the governing classes nourish a jealous hatred towards the intellectual and attack him, when possible, on grounds of conventional morality.

In spite of the rare talent which they show, *Les Taches d'Encre* were a financial failure, and Barrès was forced to discontinue their publication after the fourth number.

An interesting venture was *Les Chroniques,* a monthly review founded by Barrès and Charles Le Goffic. It ran from December 1, 1886 to an October-November number in 1887. Besides the founders, contributors of distinction were few, but include Lemaître, Bourget and Verlaine (all three with sonnets) and André Bellessort. Each number opens with a **"Chronique de Paris"** by Barrès. In an article on a certain playwright named Doucet, who occupied

Vigny's chair in the Academy, Barrès writes: "Sa bouche semble fatiguée de porter son sourire." In this article, terrible in its purposely faint praise, Barrès ridicules Doucet, who seems to have been merely a sort of administrative politician, for presuming to occupy the place of a man of genius. Still, at this time, in this publication at least, Barrès shows no signs of an interest in political questions. In a powerful analysis of Leconte de Lisle, Barrès comments somberly and bitterly on the futility of the intelligence and of life itself in a manner to rival the attitude of the Parnassian leader himself. He concludes: "L'ennui baille sur ce monde décoloré par les savants." When Le Goffic passed his "agrégation" in the fall of 1887, and entered "l'Université," the review came to an abrupt end.

Among noteworthy contributions of Barrès to *La Revue Illustrée* (1885) is an article on Saint-Saens which shows that its young author has a sound grasp of the aesthetic elements and values in music. Barrès shows himself equally at home in dramatic criticism in an excellent discussion of Bernhardt's rendering of *Marion Delorme.* Discussing literary taste in general and foreign influences in particular, Barrès characterizes "Edgard Poë" as "le plus vide et le moins ingénieux des feuilletonistes."

In 1888 Barrès began contributing to *La Revue indépendante,* a small monthly, but one which commanded an illustrious list of collaborators including Moréas, Verlaine, Paul Adam, George Moore, Hérédia, Richepin, Verhaeren, Mallarmé and Hervieu. In his first article Barrès discusses General Boulanger. The article should be particularly interesting to students of the career of Barrès, as it supplies an explanation of the puzzling question as to how this mediocre soldier, this theatrical poseur, could have aroused and held the allegiance of such men as Barrès and the group of superior intelligences who followed him. The author of *L'Appel au Soldat* describes his idol as being the man "elected by the popular instinct." Barrès says that, stifled as he himself is by the barbarians, he feels the need of a savior. He writes, he says, only for a small public, but "un public divin d'ailleurs; les princes de la jeunesse." Boulanger, it seems, had shown an especial interest in this élite, because he knows that from the thousands of these young intellectuals will emerge the hundred or so who will dominate their epoch.

In an article in this same review in September, 1888, Barrès says that he was drawn to a certain Simon, because they had in common: "des préjugés, un vocabulaire, et des dédains." They are congenial because they analyse themselves and each other "avec minutie," and hold their intelligence in high esteem, but place no value at all upon the element of character. In this article we find an early appearance of the famous Barrésian formula "Il faut sentir le plus possible, en analysant le plus possible."

In 1892 Barrès has an article in *La Revue Blanche* devoted to a discussion of one of his favorite themes, the *moi* and whether or not the exterior world exists. From now on, says the author of **Un Homme Libre** he will renounce trying to convert his readers entirely to his way of thinking, but will attempt, using their preconceived notions, to convert them to the realization of the fact that there is only one value worth developing, and that is "l'exaltation du moi et sa culture." Readers of Tharaud's *Mes Années Chez Barrès* will remember that it was in *La Revue Blanche*, in 1887, that an important article appeared, in which a representative of a certain group of young intellectuals, followers of Barrès, renounced allegiance to him because of his attitude on the Dreyfus Affair.

What is probably the last important contribution of Barrès to a "young" review appears in *L'Aube* for June, 1896. In this issue he has an article on Baudelaire which, says Barrès, he had intended to include in **Un Homme Libre.** Among the illuminating ideas which appear in it is this: that the poet, the priest, and the soldier are alone among mortals worthy of being called great. In fact, the poet is really a soldier, in that he sacrifices himself in order to beautify his conception of the universe. (pp. 534-37)

Paul Bourget, as well as most of the other critics and biographers of Barrès whom I have read believe that the formulas which most completely summarize the Barrès of the "young" reviews are the highly complicated filament of principles which went to make up the famous "culte du moi." Abbé Brémond has found definite traces of the ideas contained in *Les Taches d'Encre* in almost all of the later works of Barrès.

It seems to me that if some of the writers who have so laboriously commented upon and explained the evolution and apparent contradictions in the later work of Barrès had given somewhat more study to the early articles of their subject, they would have seen that he is already expressed, completely, though in the germ, as it were, in the remarkable articles of his literary *débuts*.

The *Taches d'Encre* reveal one of the most characteristic aspects of Barrès and one not usually emphasized, namely, his gift for a haughty yet whimsical irony, his power of scornful disdain, his ability to inject a note of urbanity even into his most deadly sarcasm—these qualities which were later to be of incalculable value to him in his polemical work as a writer and public man. Barrès arms himself with this irony from the very beginning of his career. Not because he cares to inflict suffering, but in order the better to defend his ideal, his convictions, in brief, his personality, which he summed up and unified into his *Culte du Moi*, against disdain, incomprehension and stupidity—the weapons of the *Barbares*. (p. 537)

> *D. C. Cabeen, "Maurice Barrès and the 'Young' Reviews," in* Modern Language Notes, *Vol. XLIV, No. 8, December, 1929, pp. 532-37.*

Flora Emma Ross   (essay date 1937)

[*In the following excerpt, Ross examines Barrès's evolving relationship with the work of Johann Wolfgang von Goethe. She finds Barrès's earliest allusions to Goethe's worldview in the French writer's affirmation of creative energy or action in* Le jardin de Bérénice. *The critic shows Goethe's* Faust *and* Iphigenie *to have been important inspirations for Barrès's mature works, such as* La terre et les morts *and* La colline inspirée.]

Il est là, cet adolescent de génie, tel qu'on le vit

en 1770, à la Faculté de droit française de Strasbourg, content de lui et des autres, si gentiment petit-maître avec un fond de prétention allemande, ardent à la conquête. . . .

(p. 16)

What is more fitting, while tracing the development of Goethean consciousness with Maurice Barrès, than to recall the early and enduring inspiration which the German poet received from France? It is Barrès himself who thus evokes the picture of the bronze statue representing the young Goethe, in front of the University of Strasbourg, a statue which aroused pleasant reflections in the young Barrès, on his visits to the University. It is this "adolescent de génie" who particularly captivated the French author and whom he loved, while at the same time it was the mature Goethe and his wisdom which brought him most inspiration.

"Le Goetheisme de M. Barrès, c'est une plante qui, peu à peu, se développe et s'épanouit, qui arrive, par une évolution lente, à sa fleur." Almost every critical article on Maurice Barrès mentions or comments on this Goethe-cult, while some, like Duhourcau, go so far as to call him the "French Goethe." This is due, not to similarity of style, thoughts, or artistic production, but rather to a constant preoccupation with the German poet, his philosophy of life, his ideas, and his works. There are of course striking similarities, conscious or unconscious, here and there, but most of the French author's reactions to life and art are distinctly Barrèsian first, with a certain undeniable Goethean tinge in many phases.

> Des précédents goethéens, dans la vie générale des idées, . . . ont été pour l'auteur de la **Colline inspirée** une déterminante à peu près continue, et c'est de cet angle qu'il est peut-être le plus légitime d'envisager toute sa ligne de vie. Des premières suggestions émanées d'une haute personnalité voisine, . . . à l'intérêt suprême qu'il prenait, peu de jours avant sa mort, à la *Correspondance* de Goethe avec Schiller, le poète allemand n'a guère cessé d'occuper sa pensée et d'appeler son émulation. [The critic adds in a footnote that the quotation is from Fernand Baldensperger.]

A study such as this one brings out in startling relief both the originality of Barrès, in his own peculiar sensitiveness to Goethe, and the versatility of Goethe, through the manifold interpretations of his great genius and art, reflected here. (pp. 16-17)

Among the articles which discuss various phases of Barrès' Goetheism, the best, without doubt, is by Fernand Baldensperger, called "L'Appel goethéen chez Maurice Barrès," in the *Revue Comparée*, 1925. Baldensperger was a close friend and Goethean adviser of Barrès, and the article is written from a rather personal viewpoint. It is in a larger sense an attempt to show certain contacts, conceptions, and experiences which reveal a Goethean consciousness in Barrès. It is also, perhaps, a sympathetic effort on the part of one French patriot to soften certain nationalistic tendencies in another. Part of the discussion is definitely devoted to Barrès' patriotism, his humanitarian services during the war and in the Rhine district, and a comparison of these with Goethe's experiences. . . . Certain developments are extremely stimulating and suggestive, and naturally various phases of this work will help to enrich the present study, especially in the earlier Goethean manifestations. The following investigation, however, besides being much more detailed and almost exhaustive, as regards the traces of Goetheism in the life and works of Barrès, is also much more specific, concrete, and objective, with the emphasis and development in an entirely different direction.

In a direct line with the above article, and in a certain sense an elaboration of it, is a study on *Maurice Barrès; la pensée allemande et le problème du Rhin,* by Sylvia M. King. . . . Miss King's interest is primarily in Barrès and a much larger sphere of German thought than just that of Goethe. Though she devotes about ten pages in both sections of her work to the tangible evidences of Goethe's philosophy and works in the evolution of Barrès, yet her treatment is much like Baldensperger's, more general and summarizing than detailed and complete. Goethe's name is very frequently linked with other influences, Heine, Nietzsche, Hegel, Byron, Pascal, Rousseau, and the like, and one gathers an excellent idea of how complicated is the whole question. Since both Miss King and the author of this investigation acknowledge much indebtedness to Baldensperger, there must perforce be in some instances certain similar developments, and in others certain differences in interpretation and emphasis, notably in the matter of religion and nationalism. As these latter are in the main the same as those of Baldensperger and other critics whose works were available to both authors, they will not be incorporated separately in the main body of the discussion.

Another work which draws a number of convincing analogies between Goethe and Barrès is *La Voix intérieure,* by Duhourcau. This book is a study of the **Cahiers** which Barrès kept during his lifetime, and from these Duhourcau builds up a kind of spiritual biography of the author. We shall have occasion to quote from this book from time to time, as some of the sources which Duhourcau examines were not available for this study.

Ernst Robert Curtius, in his *Maurice Barrès und die geistigen Grundlagen des französischen Nationalismus,* also treats with more than casual mention the Goethean consciousness of the latter. In connection with various theories, and especially in the last chapter, Curtius sketches briefly the determining power of the German poet, as teacher and leader, for the French author. Curtius makes a certain statement and insists upon it, which one cannot ignore, however true or false it may be. As Barrès "becomes poisoned with nationalism," affirms Curtius, so does he lose proportionately his ability to approach Goethe's "Höhenwelt"; *Le Voyage de Sparte* is the last witness not only of homage, but also of the desire to understand: "In den späteren Jahren taucht Goethe kaum mehr in Barrès Büchern auf, und wenn es geschieht, so zeigt sich ein durch die Vorurteile nationalistischer Ästhetik verzerrtes Goethebild, wie in Colette Baudoche. . . ." [The critic adds in a footnote that the quotation is from E. R. Curtius, *Maurice Barrès und die geistigen Grundlagen.*]

We shall return to this opinion later. In general, the book contains, among other things, a penetrating analysis of certain "geistige Grundlagen" which Barrès received from Goethe. . . . (pp. 17-19)

There is great danger in attempting to reduce to any logical sequence or predetermined plan such a lifelong preoccupation with a revered author, as Barrès with Goethe. Since the former, however, in his **Cahiers,** various prefaces, and throughout his works, calls repeatedly upon Goethe's name and example in every conceivable connection, there is certainly much justification and rich material for a fairly complete picture under a general Goethean title. The present study develops the following tangible expressions of Goetheism in more or less chronological order: a gradual evolution of Goethean consciousness; analogies in Weltanschauung and ideas; favorite theses of Barrès, in which the German poet's sanction or example is called upon for support; esthetic and religious theories, with similarities and divergences; Barrès' use and conception of Goethe's works; finally, isolated and interesting evocations, not previously cited, to show how constant was his preoccupation with Goethe.

Gradual Evolution of Goethean Consciousness

In view of the continual reappearance of Goethean principles with Barrès, it is remarkable how little he really possessed of definite knowledge of Goethe in the beginning. Ed. Rod's "Essai sur Goethe," as Baldensperger points out, was more unfavorable than not. Most of the French author's knowledge, after his lycée days, came through translations, though not of all of Goethe's works; through articles, such as Michel Arnauld's, "La Sagesse de Goethe," in *L'Ermitage;* and, finally, through divination. From time to time, Baldensperger tells us, he came to him for information or explanation. Of the actual works of Goethe which Barrès mentions, discusses, or quotes, the following reappear most frequently: *Faust, Iphigenie, Gespräche* by Eckermann, *Briefe, Hermann und Dorothea, Kampagne in Frankreich, Dichtung und Wahrheit, Wilhelm Meister, Metamorphose der Pflanzen,* and *Italienische Reise.*

Baldensperger relates that Stanislas de Guaita, warm friend of Barrès from lycée days on, brought him in a certain intimate contact with the German poet. This Stanislas was only two generations removed from the patrician Guaitas of Frankfort, intimates of Goethe's friends, the Brentanos. This family had settled in the Rhineland and Goethe had had relations with them in 1814 and 1815. No doubt Stanislas, a later representative of this Alsatian branch, was proud to claim a distant friendship with Goethe. It was he also who inspired the young Barrès to become "intoxicated" with poetry; the two of them used to read together in "la chambre de Guaita où deux cents poètes pressés sur une table ronde . . . voilà un tableau bien simple; et pourtant rien . . . n'a pénétré aussi profondément mon être." [The critic adds in a footnote, from Barrès's **Amori et Dolori Sacrum,** p. 129] Assuredly the greatest German poet must have been among those two hundred!

What interpretation of Goethe was to be found in Paris

in 1883, the time when the young Barrès, aged twenty, arrived there? Baldensperger reminds us that Louis Ménard and Jules Soury represented the Goethean tradition of this period. From the former, Barrès assimilated a conception of Hellenic polytheism; from the latter, certain aspects of the natural philosophy of Goethe. Neither of these theories however appears in Barrès' work till later. From Soury he inherited a scorn for naturalistic determinism and "scientific" literature, and Goethe at this period is indicted as "le maître de cet art." (pp. 19-21)

"Le Culte du Moi," that much-discussed manifestation of the young literary Barrès, was not at all connected in its earlier phases with Goethe. It was begun at the age of ten, on entering the "Collège." "Le culte du moi," he wrote in his **Cahiers,** "je m'y acheminai le jour où mes parents me laissèrent . . . dans la cour d'honneur de la Malgrange . . . dans cette misère . . . je me suis mis à me replier sur moi-même *et à m'encourager à vivre quand même.*" Gradually through his school years, to save himself from absolute pessimism, Barrès clung to one single certainty, his "moi." Arrived at Paris, aged twenty, it was still his only preoccupation: "L'important, c'est soi. . . . Tout est vain, tout est futile, hors ce qui touche à notre moi." In **L'Appel au Soldat,** Barrès pictures himself at this age in Sturel: "Mais Sturel, aux lieux mêmes où Goethe apprit d'un mouton les procédés de la nature, ne sait pas écouter ce génie qui le soumettrait aux lois naturelles. Il s'enivre, au contraire, de Byron qui, sur ce sable, passa d'innombrables heures à faire galoper ses chevaux." Not Goethe, but Byron, or even Rousseau, " . . . mon cher Rousseau . . . vous, l'homme du monde que j'ai le plus aimé . . . vous, un autre moi-même," was his model.

Not only was Barrès not conscious of lessons from Goethe, but rather the picture of the calm "Olympian sage" irritated the young "dandy." He even praises other seekers of cerebral discipline, like Sainte-Beuve and B. Constant, for not stooping to "cette habileté, ces calculs, toute cette politique à la façon de Goethe," or for not joining those who, to expose their privacy to the public, "installent d'office auprès d'eux un reporter comme Eckermann." . . . (pp. 21-2)

The earliest manifestation in his literary works of this Ego-culture is in the novels which Barrès himself entitles: "Romans idéologiques du culte du moi," 1888-1891. Though these represent only a youthful stage in his development, there are some perhaps unconscious Goethean analogies here that arrest our attention. We shall not attempt any exposition of these strange "ideologies" except as they touch our theme. In the first, **Sous l'Œil des Barbares,** the young man at length attains the consciousness of his inner being, and from his tower he looks down on those opposed to his soi, the "Barbares." Then he exults: "J'existe . . . je forme et déforme l'univers. . . . Je me désintéresse de tout ce qui sort de moi. . . . Ma tâche . . . est de me conserver intact. Je m'en tiens à dégager mon Moi des alluvions qu'y rejette sans cesse le fleuve immonde des Barbares." This begins to savor a little of the "Ehrfurcht vor sich" which was one of the guiding principles of Goethe's individualism.

In an "Examen," added to a later edition to explain the

general idea of this evidently misunderstood youthful effusion, as well as that of the series, Barrès is far more explicit than in the novel itself. He tells us that he has attempted "la monographie des cinq ou six années d'apprentissage d'un jeune Français intellectuel. . . . Le culte du Moi n'est pas de s'accepter tout entier. Cette éthique . . . réclame de ses servants un constant effort . . . nous avons d'abord à épurer notre Moi de toutes les parcelles étrangères que la vie continuellement y introduit, et puis à lui ajouter." To develop himself without ceasing, to keep his inner self pure, to add to his inner experiences—thus one may translate the above into Goethean terminology. In this first novel of the series, the "Moi" is already rejected for its insufficiency, it cannot give itself and also keep itself intact: "Ce pas du dandysme intellectuel, si piquant par l'extrême simplicité des moyens, ne saurait satisfaire pleinement une double vie d'action et de pensée."

Concerning the second of this series, **Un Homme Libre,** Barrès explains in the same "Examen":

> Ce Moi, qui tout à l'heure ne savait même pas s'il pouvait exister, voici qu'il se perfectionne et s'augmente. Ce second volume est le détail des expériences que Phillipe institua. . . . A interroger son Moi dans son accord avec des groupes, Phillipe en prit le vrai sens. Il l'aperçut comme l'effort de l'instinct pour se réaliser.
>
> J'écrivais pour mettre de l'ordre en moi-même et pour me délivrer, car on ne pense, ce qui s'appelle penser, que la plume à la main. . . . je cherchais une raison de vivre et une discipline.

Here again we find a conscious effort toward self-development, and also an inner necessity for self-expression, "pour me délivrer." Of course, in these early novels, there is so much of youthful exaltation and so little of any complete system of ethics, that it is perhaps even futile to regard them. However, Barrès himself says of **Un Homme Libre:** "à vingt-quatre ans j'y indiquais tout ce que j'ai développé depuis. . . . Je me suis étendu, mais il demeure mon expression centrale." Without drawing exact parallels here with Goethe, might we not consider these expressions a kind of unconscious affinity?

A precocious inspiration it was perhaps, but an inspiration which becomes more conscious and bolder in **Le Jardin de Bérénice,** "fantaisie d'idéologue," which completes the cycle of the *Culte du Moi.* Here are mingled ideology and sensibility with an audacity of which only the young Barrès, still in formation, was capable. Like Faust, he was still groping toward experience: "je cherche ma formule à travers toutes les expériences." Several times in this book Barrès evokes Goethe's name or example. In the first chapter he excuses his interest in political affairs on the grounds of curiosity, symbolized by the name "Touchatout." "Touchatout plane pardessus le monde. Touchatout, c'est Goethe, c'est Léonard de Vinci. . . ."

One can understand better certain of Barrès' ideas in this novel if one recalls the reactions of the so-called "decadent period." In the years after the deaths of Taine and Renan, after 1890, questions had begun to arise which the philosophies of these masters could not answer. Energies and wills were left without direction, public life weakened, restoration and revenge unrealized. In a vain quest for orientation, the interests of this generation were directed toward anything vaguely moral, religious, humanitarian, or social. It was the time when "la solidarité de l'humanité" was discovered, at least in their philosophies. We find an echo of this in *Le Jardin de Bérénice,* linked with other conceptions. Through contact with the world, Philippe arrives at a new revelation, consciousness of himself as a part of humanity, perhaps a kind of social collectivity:

> Sans doute, à étudier l'âme lorraine, puis le développement de la civilisation vénitienne, je compris quel moment je représentais dans le développement de ma race, je vis que je n'étais qu'un instant d'une longue culture. . . . Seules, les masses m'ont fait toucher les assises de l'humanité.
>
> Je n'avais pas su dans l'étude de mon moi pénétrer plus loin que mes qualités; le peuple m'a révélé la substance humaine, et mieux que cela, l'énergie créatrice, la sève du monde, l'inconscient.

"L'énergie créatrice"—here is perhaps the germ of the main development in the "Culte du Moi": the discovery that a sane realization of interior reality is impossible without action. The purpose of this episode in his evolution, Barrès again explains in the "Examen":

> Lassé pourtant de cette solitude, de ce dilettantisme contemplatif et de tant d'expériences menues, aux dernières pages d'*Un Homme Libre,* Philippe est prêt pour l'action. *Le Jardin de Bérénice* raconte une campagne électorale.

Although this is not a major part of the book, nevertheless it is significant that at this early date the idea of activity should be added to the development of a complete inner consciousness. "Dieweil ich bin, muss ich auch tätig sein." How often, in his maxims and conversations, in his own life and greatest works, did the author of *Faust* repeat and exemplify these familiar words of the Homunculus!

It is Berenice, simple child of nature, through whom the laws of the universe become intelligible to Phillipe, a Goethe-Spinozian conception revealed to Barrès through Taine: Berenice, "l'image la plus complète que nous puissions concevoir des forces de la nature . . . chacun des mouvements de ton âme me révèle le sens de la nature et ses lois." This more profound penetration into knowledge of the universe, Barrès relates directly to Goethe:

> L'unité! voilà le rêve universel, l'aspiration des esprits réfléchis. . . . Elle satisfait les besoins moraux et les désirs des contemplatifs, mais elle est aussi la santé et le bien-être de nos corps: en sorte que la religion goethienne, vivre en harmonie avec les lois de la nature, n'est que la formule la plus élevée de l'hygiène.

By applying this "Goethean religion" in his peculiar clairvoyant manner to his intensive Ego-culture, Barrès arrives finally at

> la puissance infinie, l'indomptable énergie de l'âme de l'univers. . . . J'atteignais enfin, pour quelques secondes, au sublime égoïsme qui embrasse tout, qui fait l'unité par omnipotence

et vers lequel mon moi s'efforça toujours d'atteindre. . . .

Allied to this consciousness of universal laws is the corollary: " 'C'est nous qui créons l'univers.' . . . Le Moi découvre une harmonie universelle à mesure qu'il prend du monde une conscience plus large et plus sincère." Thus there is a progressive development in "le Culte du Moi": in the first volume, "le Moi" is conscious only of its own existence; in this one, of the universe and the world about: "Avant que le Moi créât l'univers, il lui fallait exister: ses duretés, ses négations, c'était effort pour briser la coquille, pour être." What is all this but a methodical curiosity, a passion for comprehending, and an ardent sympathy for everything that represents a manifestation of activity and of life? Is it not like Goethe, who strove constantly to enrich his own perceptions, to distinguish the whole truth, and to establish the harmony of the universe? This is what the young men of Barrès' generation revered so passionately in Goethe, young men with curious, reflective minds, who, through contemplation and meditation, were attempting to embrace all, and to penetrate the secret of things.

In this same oft-quoted "Examen," Barrès outlines his whole program for his "culture du moi" in the following manner. The items are numbered for the purpose of clarity later:

> (1) Attachons-nous à notre Moi, protégeons-le contre les étrangers, contre les Barbares.
>
> (2) Mais ce n'est pas assez qu'il existe; comme il est vivant, il faut le cultiver, agir sur lui mécaniquement (étude, curiosité, voyages).
>
> (3) S'il a faim encore, donne-lui l'action (recherche de la gloire, politique, industrie, finances).
>
> (4) Et s'il sent trop de sécheresse, rentre dans l'instinct, aime les humbles, les misérables, ceux qui font effort pour croître.

This program, so carefully outlined, but only vaguely and sketchily executed in the three "romans idéologiques," appears almost as if the "Examen," written later than the series, were a conscious attempt on the author's part to ally his own "Culte du Moi" with Goethe's Weltanschauung. It was at first an instinctive approach, for the young Barrès did not know the details of Goethe's biography, and could envision only some of the ulterior phases of his careful Ego-culture. But after he had become better acquainted with this "Lebensidee," he might easily have incorporated the above four items under the following Goethean principles: (1) Ehrfurcht vor sich; (2) Äussere Erlebnisse zu inneren verwandelt; (3) Tätigkeit; (4) Humanitätsideal. Then, finally, as if to link his ideas definitely with those of the great Master of Weimar, Barrès confesses, in the last paragraph of an important Note at the end of *Le Jardin de Bérénice:*

> Un nom plus affiché encore est mêlé à cet ouvrage, et chacun comprendra que je ne puis l'écrire qu'avec un profond sentiment. . . . Tout est vrai là-dedans, rien n'y est exact. Voilà les imaginations que je me faisais, tandis que les circonstances me pliaient à ceci et à cela. Goethe, écri-

vant ses relations avec son époque, les intitule: *Réalité et Poésie.*

In these early reactions, as we have seen, Barrès was groping about for a philosophy of life that could not only rescue himself from "le néant de la vie," but also the younger men about him, who were beginning to look upon him as their leader. It was around 1894 that the public began to mark a change in Barrès from the youthful dilettantism which was a kind of resignation to destiny, to the affirmation of a more vital philosophy. In the beginning this was still related to his "Culte du Moi," later it became merged into a larger vision, "la religion des ancêtres et de la Patrie," or more familiarly known as "La Terre et les Morts." (pp. 22-6)

Barrès' Conception and Use of Goethe's Works

With regard to Goethe's first world-renowned work, Barrès seems to make use of the accepted interpretation of *Werther,* both the novel and the hero. In **Colette Baudoche,** for example, Dr. Asmus, in his growing love for Colette, "sent la nature à la mode d'un Werther." At one time the novel is called "le chef-d'oeuvre panthéiste." *Werther* is mentioned at any length in only two original and interesting applications. The first is in **Mes Cahiers,** where Barrès discusses various troublesome problems, among them the question as to whether our schools and the instruction, from which we expect so much, do not really kill the race. Here the author is reminded of *Werther,* and the application suggested has a distinctly original if not ironical flavor:

> "Si je me sens agité, disait Werther, tout ce tumulte s'apaise à la vue d'une créature comme celle-là qui parcourt dans une heureuse tranquillité le cercle étroit de son existence, se tire d'affaire au jour le jour et voit tomber toutes les feuilles sans que cela lui dise autre chose sinon que l'hiver approche."

> Il s'agit de discipliner l'homme, de mater son animalité et quand on y est arrivé, on a tout détruit: La France (ce gentilhomme) et puis toute l'Europe.

Under the heading, "L'Appel au Soldat," in the **Cahiers,** we find a curious and interesting analogy made between the culmination of the Boulanger affair and Werther. Barrès recalls the familiar incident concerning *Werther:* Herder had criticized the use of a second motive for the suicide of Werther, and the author, in the edition of 1786, omitted it, or at least diminished its importance. Napoleon, who had certainly not heard this criticism and read only the original edition, made the same objection to Goethe. The latter admired the critical force of the great general. The whole anecdote Barrès applies as follows: "Cependant en réfléchissant sur le cas de Boulanger, j'ai préféré Goethe de 1774 . . . à Goethe convaincu par Herder et par Napoléon." This comment is exemplified in Chapter XX of **L'Appel au Soldat,** which is entitled, "Épuisement nerveux chez le général Boulanger," and has many similarities with the description of Werther's suicide and its motives. Here there is also a double motive: despair in love, for his sweetheart had died, and political failure and disappointment.

Hermann und Dorothea, besides the examples already discussed, reappears now and then under Barrès' pen. On a journey through Alsace he is impressed several times with Oberbronn and records whimsically: " . . . Quand je serai devenu tout à fait raisonnable, je me retirerai à Oberbronn, où tous les habitants sont fous. C'est, disent les Goethe d'Alsace, le paysage d'Hermann et Dorothée; ces jardins qui descendent." At another time, during the war, the young refugees of Verdun call forth this comment:

> Où donc les avons-nous déjà vus, ces femmes, ces jeunes filles, ces enfants de Verdun? Dans le récit de la *Campagne de France,* par Goethe. Quand l'écrivain allemand vint en France, par Longwy et Verdun, avec les envahisseurs de 1792, et prit des notes en cheminant sur ces éternelles routes de guerre, il recueillit les images qui composent, dans *Hermann et Dorothée,* le tableau des campagnards chassés par l'ennemi.

Of all the works of Goethe, *Faust* and *Iphigenie* are the two which fascinate and dominate most the mind of the Frenchman. As a young man, like many of his compatriots and others, he was unable to appreciate Goethe's masterpiece except as an intellectual work of a genius. In **Trois Stations de Psychothérapie,** Barrès characterizes Faust as: "Rien qui appartienne plus purement au domaine de l'intelligence." In an effort to find the meaning of the conflict which Leonardo da Vinci has so mysteriously painted on the faces of his women, Barrès imagines what one of them might say, and compares it to his own impressions of *Faust,* at that time:

> . . . c'est un plaisir parfait que d'être perpetuellement curieux avec méthode. . . . Mais nous sourions de voir la peine que tu prends pour deviner ce qui m'intéresse.

> Voilà ce que dit, je l'ai bien entendu, le sourire de Léonard. Goethe le répétera plus tard. C'est avec des différences sans nombre de siècle et de race, une des impressions que nous laissent les deux Faust.

How could Taine speak of Epicurean, licentious thoughts? " . . . chez Léonard, comme chez Goethe, ces dangereuses aspirations demeurent intellectuelles. . . ." Part of this reaction approaches somewhat Goethe's own idea of *Faust* as "incommensurable." In **Le Voyage de Sparte,** the author recalls his earlier impressions and links them with his inability to understand Greece in the beginning: "Et le docteur Faust, encore, que m'était-il avant que j'approchasse du temps où, trop tard, je me dirai: 'Quand j'étais jeune, plutôt que de tant étudier, j'aurais dû jouir de la vie?' " . . . (pp. 68-70)

It is very natural that the memories of *Faust* should be vividly present in the visit to Sparta, particularly those of Helen and the medieval château. Barrès relates his impressions in his own picturesque manner:

> Après qu'Hélène eut couru le monde, Goethe l'a saisie dans ses bras, et sur l'horizon de Sparte le vieux prophète a voulu la repatrier. Il n'a pas dit expressément qu'il situait son sublime épisode dans le château des Villehardouin, mais nul ne s'y trompera: ce burg doré, à l'occident de la

plaine, sur les contreforts du Taygète, c'est le poème de Goethe, dominant comme une couronne les ruines de Mistra.

The whole charm of the Mistra is intensified by the firm conviction that he is recognizing here the scenery from *Faust II*, Act III:

> . . . voici le château suscité par la magie auprès du palais de Ménélas, pour abriter les amours d'Hélène et de Faust.
>
> En gravissant les pentes du Castro, je reconnais les décors du second *Faust*. . . .
>
> C'est ici, nulle part ailleurs, que Faust put posséder Hélène . . . chez le guerrier gothique.

As he climbs the hill himself, Barrès is reminded of the symbolic union of Helen and Faust: "L'enfant né de leurs amours, Euphorion, sur les décombres, devant moi, bondit et danse: 'Toujours plus haut! Je dois monter! Toujours plus loin . . . !' "

Finally, in the country of Helen, the lessons of antiquity are more easily understood by a fundamentally romantic temperament:

> C'est un mariage de tous mes sens avec le sommeil d'Hélène . . .
>
> Ignorant, je ne puis comprendre, aux froids couloirs de nos musées, les leçons de l'arbre hellénique. Mais qu'il m'apparaisse, cet arbre, comme un buisson de flammes, au centre des jardins de Sparte, je désire et je trouve un juste accord avec l'antique. . . .

The inspiration of *Faust* and Goethe is very near to Barrès as he writes *La Colline inspirée;* in the very first paragraphs and the epilogue, as well as at other times, certain ideas from *Faust* clarify or vivify the narrative. "La colline inspirée," in Lorraine, is one of those places, bathed in mystery, which have always been the source of religious emotion; but

> . . . la superstition . . . la sorcellerie apparaissent aussitôt, et des places désignées pour être des lieux de perfectionnement par la prière deviennent des lieux de sabbat. C'est ce qu'indique le profond Goethe, lorsque son Méphistophélès entraîne Faust sur la montagne du Hartz, sacrée par le génie germanique, pour y instaurer la liturgie sacrilège du *Walpurgisnachtstraum*.

On this hill is breathed forth a magic force: "Ici ne peut planer Méphistophélès, l'esprit qui nie: la lumiére l'absorberait et le grand courant d'air lui briserait les ailes." The miraculous conversion of Leopold rather naturally recalls that of *Faust:* "La conversion de Léopold était une tentative qui dépassait les moyens humains; le pacte qui liait ce malheureux à Satan ne pouvait être rompu que par le pacte supérieur d'une âme sainte avec Dieu." In this case, it was the death of the saintly Père Aubry which released the devil's power.

In the Epilogue, under the influence of the inspired hill, the great figures of literature, who, like Leopold, have rebelled against the laws of life as imposed upon them and have sought to fathom its mysteries, pass in review before us:

> . . . c'est, par un jour semblable, quand les ruisseaux avaient rompu leurs prisons de glace au souffle du printemps et quand les cloches de Pâques sonnaient, que le docteur Faust s'insurgea contre les limites de l'intelligence et ne vit plus qu'une duperie dans son long esprit de sacrifice à la science. . . . Faust, Manfred, Prospero! éternelle race d'Hamlet, qui sait qu'il y a plus de choses sur la terre et dans le ciel qu'il n'en est rêvé dans notre philosophie, et qui s'en va chercher le secret de la vie dans les songeries de la solitude!

Shall they teach us the engima of the universe? Leopold did not accomplish his purpose in life; and the others?

> Le laboratoire de Faust, le burg de Manfred, l'île de Prospero brillent dans les nuages empourprés de l'horizon, mais ces fameux édifices . . . ne diffèrent pas tant de la pauvre masure mystique des Baillard. . . . Ce sont des châteaux de feu, des châteaux de musique, autant d'artifices qui se résolvent en baguettes brulées dans la nuit.

To what extent Goethe's experience and example, particularly in *Faust*, may have inspired the famous dialogue between the Prairie and the Chapel, at the end of *La Colline inspirée*, it is difficult even to suggest. This conversation is frequently interpreted as symbolizing the ideal toward which Barrès strove, the harmony between two opposing forces, romantic exaltation and liberty, and classic order and discipline. In its extremely beautiful and picturesque language one may recognize not only the author's ideal, but also the one modern poet by whom this ideal was most perfectly attained:

> "Je suis, dit la prairie, l'esprit de la terre et des ancêtres les plus lointaines, la liberté, l'inspiration."
>
> Et la chapelle répond:
>
> "Je suis la règle, l'autorité, le lien; je suis un corps de pensées fixes et la cité ordonnée des âmes. . . ."
>
> "Je suis un lien primitif, une source éternelle."
>
> Mais la chapelle nous dit:
>
> "Visiteurs de la prairie, apportez-moi vos rêves pour que je les épure, vos élans pour que je les oriente. C'est moi que vous cherchez, que vous voulez à votre insu. . . . Je prolonge la prairie, même quand elle me nie. J'ai été construite, à force d'y avoir rêvé. . . . Je t'accorderai avec la vie. Ta liberté, dis-tu? . . . Je suis la pierre qui dure, l'expérience des siècles, le dépôt du trésor de ta race . . . je suis conforme à tes tendances profondes . . . le verbe mystérieux, élaboré pour toi quand tu n'étais pas. Viens à moi si tu veux trouver la pierre de solidité. . . ."

(pp. 71-3)

What an inexhaustible source of inspiration *Faust* is for Barrès! . . . In *L'Appel au Soldat*, after reading the famous act of the Walpurgis, " . . . où Goethe a utilisé les vieilles traditions de la sorcellerie du seizième siècle," the German students interpreted Goethe thus: "Mes compagnons affirmèrent que l'Allemagne représente l'Esprit universel l'Idée absolue et la Puissance absolue . . . ils célébraient le Pangermanisme." Roemerspacher, who did not wish to interrupt in such a classic place their patriotic delirium, left them. Later he rejoined them, and to show his approval of their drinking to Paris, he relates: " . . . je levai mon verre au génie de Goethe, 'qui comprit la France et que la France comprend.' " (pp. 73-4)

Even in a speech before the Chamber of Deputies, Faust makes his appearance in connection with the profound need of the human soul for something which reason or rationalism cannot satisfy:

> C'est l'aventure de Faust, l'aventure de tous les Faust, des plus hautes et plus savantes intelligences. . . .
>
> Sans doute, le cours de la vie, la médiocrité et la fatigue des besognes quotidiennes nous empêchent, et nos chétives aventures sont moins fécondes en réflexions que la magnifique détresse de Faust et de Pascal.

Mephistopheles also makes his appearance before the Chamber of Deputies, in the form of Clemenceau who had said, "Je suis le diable." Barrès in his **"Journal de la Chambre"** relates how Jaurès seizes and develops this idea of "Clemenceau Méphistophélique" by showing how the latter has been opposed to everything, except himself. Barrès adds his own comment: "J'ajouterais Clemenceau qui se nie lui-même."

One is not surprised to note that Mephisto is used by Barrès to describe a certain group of the enemy, the "intellectuels": "Ces éternels pédants aiment à jouer les démons. Ils ont fait de Méphisto un des types sur lesquels ils se modèlent." It is however unusual to find a comparison between the magic power of Mephisto and the mystic inspiration of the Psalms:

> Dans la taverne de Faust, Méphisto fait couler d'une même table tous les vins dont s'enivrent les grossiers étudiants. Ce sont ici les tables de Dieu d'où le vin des forts découle.

And then Barrès explains that these "tables de Dieu," the Psalms, have sustained and nourished innumerable souls throughout the ages. . . . (pp. 74-5)

Iphigenie, even more than *Faust,* seems to have captivated the mind of Barrès, due no doubt to the fact that in its major theses, as at first interpreted by him, there appeared to be a warm affinity with his own cherished theories. Under the title, **La Terre et les Morts,** for example, he associates this doctrine definitely with the classic maid:

> Mes dieux, c'est-à-dire ma race, comment les entendre.
>
> On m'objectera comme faisait Thoas:
>
> "Ce n'est pas un dieu qui te parle, c'est ta propre cœur."
>
> Je réponds avec Iphigénie:

> "C'est par notre cœur seulement que les dieux nous parlent."
>
> (pp. 75-6)

[*Le Voyage de Sparte*] not only crystallized Barrès' views on *Faust,* and especially classic art as revealed to him by Helen, it also brought him a very different conception of *Iphigenie.* Wishing to give a vital significance to this pilgrimage, as was his habit, Barrès quite naturally turned to Goethe and *Iphigenie.* There are several developments in his train of thought here, in the chapter called "Je quitte Mycènes," which deserve a somewhat detailed exposition. It is the nearest approach to a rather long critical evaluation of any of Goethe's works. Sometimes the accepted and usual interpretation appears, more often a typically Barrésian one. The memory of Goethe's heroine is first evoked in the plains of Argos and the cliffs of Sebastopol; but she has left this region:

> Iphigénie n'est plus en Tauride. Goethe l'a prise par la main pour la conduire au cœur de la Germanie et, sous un tel précepteur, celle qu'Eschyle compare à une chienne, devient une sorte de chanoinesse élevée dans l'admiration de Marc-Aurèle et des philosophes stoïciens.

Barrès recalls that, on encountering "la Grecque costumée en jeune dame allemande," whom Taine had introduced into "nos roches druidiques," he had thought her a classic figure: "Je crus qu'Iphigénie, type classique ranimé avec nos pensées rhénanes, m'attendait à Sainte-Odile, pour me donner le sens profond de mon pays." But "la noble jeune dame un peu lourde de la cour de Weimar" was not in accord with the heroines of Racine and Corneille. Therefore, concludes the critic, "Je ne puis pas dire 'ma soeur' à l'Iphigénie." One recognizes an echo here of Goethe as a classic poet, "Germanized." In spite of his disappointment, the descendant of Racine and Corneille is not insensible to certain charms of the heroine: " . . . j'aime admirer sa belle stature, sa démarche sans trouble, sa vertu de jeune Hercule féminin." . . . "j'aime la Grecque germanisée."

Step by step Barrès then follows Iphigenia in her voyage of love with Goethe. What was the author's inner life at that time? The influence of Frau von Stein is here necessarily associated with his heroine:

> Mme. de Stein est Iphigénie, et Goethe s'est exprimé dans Thoas . . . Et pour comprendre la principale beauté de cette tragédie, c'est-à-dire sa plénitude et sa solidité, que l'on médite le sentiment de Goethe pour son amie: "La gentillesse, la grâce, l'amabilité des dames que je vois, jusqu'à leurs goûts apparents, portent la marque de la fragilité; toi seule, sur ce sol mobile, as ce qui dure." . . .
>
> (pp. 76-7)

The so-called "classicism" of *Iphigenie* is linked by Barrès very closely with the natural sciences, disciplining the individual and leading him to a submission to natural laws. Thus it becomes "une pièce civilisatrice," from which "sort une puissance capable de faire des philosophes stoïciens" . . .

> *L'Iphigénie,* œuvre d'un homme que disciplinai-

ent, par ailleurs, ses études d'histoire naturelle, ramène à la soumission nécessaire de puissantes intelligences enivrées de leur supêriorité.

(pp. 77-8)

Iphigenia, of the family of Agamemnon and Clytemnestra, cannot rebel against "les ordres des tombeaux":

> Goethe et la Grèce ont voulu nier ces fatalités. Sur les sommets de l'œuvre goethienne, on respire la confiance dans la vie. Le poète veut nous persuader d'une conception optimiste de l'univers, parce qu'elle favorise l'activité.

True, the artists are obliged to purify the passions which they place before our eyes in order to arouse our sympathy:

> Mais je pense que pour y atteindre, il est plus loyal de nous faire voir comment ces passions . . . rentrent dans un ordre universel. Et nul plus large plan où faire rentrer les faits que ce déterminisme auquel l'*Iphigénie* essaye de contredire.

For the same reason, it is more agreeable to know that Orestes is cured: "Mais que faire si je vois nettement l'absurdité de ces hypothèses optimistes?"

Perhaps in his native Lorraine Barrès might still have accepted this illusion,—

> Mais sur les tombeaux de Mycènes, rien ne s'interpose entre nous et les faits.

> Nous sommes asservis aux transmissions du passé; nos morts nous donnent leurs ordres auxquels il nous faut obéir; nous ne sommes pas libres de choisir. Ils ne sont pas nos morts, ils sont notre activité vivante.

> Ces sombres vérités demeurent les vues les plus certaines de notre raison. L'humanité, qui les avait déposées dans les grands mythes primitifs, les a transbordées dans ses lois scientifiques.

This a most characteristic conclusion, in which ideas not necessarily original with the writer are summed up in a typically Barrésian manner. More than any other example, this criticism of *Iphigenie* gives an excellent picture of the close association of ideas, of the adaptation of Goethean conceptions, and the inevitable relation of the whole to the dominating principle of Barrès. (pp. 78-9)

> *Flora Emma Ross, "Maurice Barrès and Goethe," in her* Goethe in Modern France, *The University of Illinois, 1937, pp. 16-85.*

Ronald Hilton   (essay date 1939)

[*In the excerpt below, Hilton describes the best known of Barrès's writings on Spain,* Le Greco, ou le secret de Tolède, *as derivative and historically inaccurate.*]

Our dilettante Hispanist [Maurice Barrès] began his writing in a period when a new spirit of cosmopolitanism, skilfully analyzed by Ernst Robert Curtius, was taking hold of France; in the *fin de siècle* period, when artistic Frenchmen were trying to stimulate their jaded nerves with doses of potent exoticism, extracts of anything from Tahiti to Spain.

Maurice Barrès found the largest amount of stimulant in the Iberian peninsula. René Doumic has well described his attitude to, or rather his use of Spain: "L'Espagne est le pays d'élection de M. Barrès. Il la célèbre avec une belle ferveur d'enthousiasme . . . ce qu'il goûte dans les sentiments et dans les sensations qui naissent du sol d'Espagne, c'est leur violence. Ici tout est fait pour exciter les nerfs, réveiller l'âme assoupie, rendre au tempérament sa vigueur. . . . L'histoire, les arts, la littérature, les mœurs témoignent de cette exaspération de tout l'être."

This "exaspération de tout l'être" has been the cause of the tragedy of Spanish history, and the immediate stimulus to the present Civil War. Any idealization of this characteristic proceeds from incomprehension, if not ignorance, of Spanish history and Spanish sociological development. M. René Doumic, who, as one brought up in the traditions of "la raison française," constantly opposed Barrès' glorification of force, criticizes very severely the eulogy of the brutal aspect of Spain in *Du sang, de la volupté, et de la mort,* and ends his article thus: "Nous demandons ce qu'on peut attendre d'une société qui serait fondée sur le triomphe de l'impulsion naturelle et sur la glorification de l'énergie." Had René Doumic been writing in the year, not alas of grace, 1938, the answer would have been obvious.

Maurice Barrès, who later was to become a reactionary nationalist, was, in his early days, a renegade; his ill-founded admiration for Spain was accompanied by an almost complete denial of French culture and civilization. He tells us quite plainly: "La France ne m'a rien appris: Florence m'a donné le goût de l'art. C'est en Espagne que j'ai compris la vie: la hardiesse et la liberté sèche."

As the nationalist spirit began slowly to invade his unstable intellect, he repented somewhat of his spiritual prodigalities in Spain, and returned with increasing frequency to his father's household. "De temps en temps, il m'arrivait de trop céder à ma passion orientale, à mon goût malsain pour l'Espagne et de laisser prendre en moi le dessus à des éléments négateurs de la vie moderne et de ses principes moraux. Alors je devais me rappeler que je suis Français."

A little later, he made a similar, but even more significant confession: "Bonne discipline qu'est pour moi la Lorraine. . . . Je ne dominais pas ces Espagne, ces Venise que j'ai caressées non sans bonheur. Je ne les comprenais pas dans leur formation. Elles m'étaient une ivresse." Barrès here admits that his love of Spain was a kind of drunkenness, which popular wisdom rightly describes as blind. He confesses that he understands nothing of the growth and development of Spain. Here indeed we see the grave danger of "literary" travelers such as Barrès, in whom "inspiration" is held to be more than sufficient compensation for lack of knowledge of their subject. In judging the civilization of a country, their only criterion is the reactions of their own psychological make-up.

Barrès never went to the extreme of saying to Spain: "Get thee behind me, Satan." While his enthusiasm for the Spanish fury slowly waned, he still held dear all the catholic elements in Spanish history, and, above all, as his nationalism increased, he became obsessed with the political idea of buttressing the back of France on the solid rock of Spain, so that the waves of Germanic barbarity might hurl themselves in vain against the northern dyke of France.

This political ambition is understandable in a son of Lorraine. It is curious to note how strategic interest can draw together two apparently unrelated parts of the earth. Moreover it must not be forgotten that Barrès was never a disinterested Hispanist, but first and foremost a politician. From 1889 on, when he was elected deputy for Nancy, Barrès was always in the middle of the fray. Victor Giraud has provided us with a convenient summary of Barrès' political activity. Besides his articles on public questions, Barrès has left us some literary descriptions of political life, in particular **Leurs Figures** (the third book of the trilogy *Le Roman de l'énergie nationale*), which deals chiefly with the tumultuous months of 1892 and the Panama crisis. He has also written a *comédie de mœurs* in three acts entitled **Une Journée parlementaire.**

Spain and politics were both obsessions in Barrès, and such is their hold on him that he interweaves them in a most curious fashion. The story **"La Haine emporte tout,"** which is one of his Spanish narratives, was, he says, inspired by the quarrels on the Panama question in the Chambre des Députés. Inversely, in **Le Greco ou le secret de Tolède** he mentions his experiences in the Chambre, and makes a strained comparison with El Greco.

Barrès' love of Spain, which at first was a spontaneous psychological reaction, slowly developed into a political calculation in favor of the international prestige of France. He hated Germany, and, despite manifestations of warm gratitude during the World War, was fundamentally indifferent to England. He hoped for a kind of union of the Latin world. In particular, he thought that a politically weak country like Spain would make an easy yet valuable partner in an alliance. He therefore encouraged the French Government to strengthen ties with Spain. His attitude is made clear in some notes intended for a speech he was to make in the Chamber; he died before doing so, but fortunately the *Revue des Deux Mondes* has published the notes under the title of **"Les Liens spirituels de la France et de l'Espagne."**

A year before the death of Barrès, M. Paul Guinard, directeur de l'Institut Français en Espagne, paid him a visit at Toledo. M. Guinard relates: "Il me disait son espoir d'orienter les nations vers l'Espagne, la Méditérranée, l'Orient; il ne voyait pas de meilleure sauvegarde contre tout excès de 'germanisme intellectuel.' "

Barrès grandfather had been in Spain as an officer in Napoleon's army. Thus Barrès, like Hugo, had a kind of family interest in the Peninsula. In 1922 he published the memoirs of his grandfather under the title **Souvenirs d'un Officier de la Grande Armée,** the background of the narrative being chiefly Spain. In connection with the publication of the **Souvenirs,** Barrès said about Spain: "Je suis Français, petit-fils d'un soldat de la Grande Armée. C'est dans ce sentiment que je suis parti pour ce pèlerinage." So Barrès' idea of a Franco-Spanish union is at bottom more

or less the Napoleonic one! That Spaniards should have appreciated Barrès' political interest in them is strange, and can only be explained by the probable fact that they had not scrutinized his ideas carefully.

Only a writer possessed of what the public calls inspiration can dare to write authoritatively about a country without adequate preparation. One whom Apollo scorns would feel the necessity of appealing to Minerva and, before writing a dogmatic book about the soul of Spain, of reading extensively in Spanish literature. As Barrès was a very busy man, Apollo exempted him from this duty. He seems to have known nothing of Spanish literature apart from a few manifestations of the more impassioned aspects of the Spanish genius, and he has imprudently concluded: *ab uno discite omnes!* . . . Barrès had also a superficial knowledge of the Spanish mystics, in particular of Santa Teresa. His admiration for the saint of Avila is best expressed, though duly bowdlerized for the occasion, in the preface he wrote for the translation made by the Conde de Premio Real of the Commentary on the Song of Songs.

Barrès' scanty knowledge of Spanish literature was inevitable in view of his meager acquaintance with the language. The Spanish phrases he introduces into **Du sang, de la volupté, et de la mort** are mostly grotesque. . . . As the years went on, Barrès' knowledge of Spanish improved, and by the time we reach **Le Greco ou le secret de Tolède** (1909), he could risk a quotation in Spanish with a good hope of correctness. Nevertheless, certain of his remarks suggest that he has no intimate knowledge of Spanish usage. (pp. 280-84)

Barrès' attitude to life in general and more precisely to that of southern Europe derived largely from Stendhal's. His interest was turned from Italy to Spain partly by Victor Hugo, whom he occasionally mentions, but infinitely more by Théophile Gautier. In **Le Greco ou le secret de Tolède,** Barrès admits implicitly that he is a disciple of that other dilettante Hispanist. He speaks of: "le charmant Théophile Gautier, de qui le souvenir invinciblement mélancolique apparaît sur le fond de tous nos plaisirs espagnols." Moreover, various details in the life of Barrès bear witness to his cult of Gautier. Francisco Garcia Calderón relates that when he visited Barrès, the latter showed him a manuscript of Gautier which he had just bought.

It is therefore not surprising if all Barrès' writings on Spain, even **Le Greco ou le secret de Tolède,** are characterized by patches of bad taste, tawdry jewels inherited from *le bas romantisme.* Thus for example does he describe the daughter whom he gratuitously attributes to El Greco: "On connaît les beaux yeux, l'ovale pur, le teint mat de la fille du Greco, mais de sa voix et des sentiments de cette émouvante fiévreuse, rien ne nous est parvenu. Il est assez décent que chez le peintre de la profonde Tolède micatholique, mi-arabe, la fille de la maison soit voilée." A worse example of bad taste is to be found in Barrès' description of the mass he heard in the Toledo cathedral: "Nous sommes une centaine qui regardons, à travers les grilles dorées, le prêtre dire sa messe, et j'appuie ma main sur la balustrade de jaspe, précieuse au toucher comme un beau corps de femme".

Had Barrès been inoculated with a good knowledge of Spanish language and literature, he would have been immune against Romantic Hispanism; as it was, Gautier's disease broke out all over the epidermis of his writings.

The inadequacy, indeed the distortion of this preparation for Hispanism might have been counteracted by a long stay in Spain. Unfortunately Barrès, like other amateur Hispanists, made only a series of rapid visits to the Peninsula, so that the sensation of novelty never wore off. The following trips to Spain are recorded in the "Notices biographiques" which precede each volume of *Mes Cahiers.*

> 1892—Premier voyage en Espagne.
> (1894—*Du sang, de la volupté, et de la mort*)
> 17 août 1900—A Saint-Sébastien auprès de Déroulède en exil.
> 23 février 1901—Nouveau séjour à Saint-Sébastien auprès de Déroulède.
> 8 au 19 octobre 1902—Séjour à Tolède, avec le peintre espagnol Beruete.
> Barrès retrouve M. Enrique Larreta, le futur auteur de *la Gloire de Don Ramire,* avec qui il se lie d'amitié.
> (mai 1903—Maurice Barrès fait partie du comité du monument Cervantès)
> (fin juin 1904—Barrès termine *Le Greco*)
> (janvier 1908—Préparation du *Greco ou le secret de Tolède* qui paraîtra en 1911)

[The critic adds in a footnote: There seems to be some contradiction between these last two entries. In *Le Greco,* Barrès says, "Par trois fois j'accourus entendre la chanson de l'Espagne." This means either that he is not counting one of the trips to San Sebastian, or else that he is not counting either of them, the third trip being one right into Spain, but not mentioned in the "Notices biographiques". . . .] These are the only relevant entries in the detailed "Notices biographiques," which take us up to November 1909. Although we know that Barrès visited Spain again after this date, it would seem that the "Notices" have omitted no visit previous to 1909, so crowded are the engagements and journeys recorded. It would therefore appear that Barrès wrote *Du sang, de la volupté, et de la mort* on the strength of one journey to Spain, and his book *Le Greco* with the help of three more flying visits. Comments would be superfluous.

Of all Barrès' writings on Spain, the best known is *Le Greco ou le secret de Tolède.* The vogue of this book is but one more proof of the lack of critical spirit in the reading public. A careful examination reveals that all Barrès' knowledge of El Greco is second-hand, and that if he attempts to be original, he falls into elementary mistakes. When Barrès visited Toledo, he had Aureliano de Beruete as a personal guide, and from this competent art critic he acquired a good deal of information. But it was chiefly from Cossío's masterly book on El Greco that Barrès drew the substance for his own study. Cossìo's book appeared in 1908, a year before the *Revue Bleue* published Barrès' work. The Frenchman casually admitted that he was merely reproducing the discoveries of the Spaniard: "Ainsi, des jours et des œuvres submergés par les ténèbres, tel est le sort de Greco. Il double d'un personnage énigmatique le mystère de son art. C'est seulement dans ces der-

niers mois qu'un érudit espagnol, Manuel B. Cossío, a réussi à nous fournir quelques précisions. Essayons de saisir les points brillants qu'il est, tant bien que mal, parvenu à dégager."

Barrès' work is therefore merely one of popularizing. And he made numerous mistakes, easily identified. Even Barrès' apologist, M. Paul Guinard, admits that they exist, although he upholds that only two have any importance: (1) mistaking for the Conde de Orgaz the bare figure symmetrical with that of the Virgin in the upper part of the *Entierro;* it is really Saint John the Baptist; (2) attributing to El Greco a daughter he never had.

A critic less friendly to Barrès would not pass over other unsatisfactory remarks, such as this: "Philippe II venait de fixer la vie administrative à Madrid et dans son Escurial. Mais la très noble, la très loyale, impériale Tolède, sur son âpre côte, au milieu de ses ruines romaines, de ses basiliques visigothes, de ses mosquées arabes, de ses églises et de ses palais, demeurait l'âme de l'Espagne." . . . But how can Toledo be described as "la très loyale" after all the Comuneros risings, and Philip II's decision that Toledo was unworthy of his confidence? Is it not moreover a complete misrepresentation to depict Toledo, even in El Greco's time, as full of Roman ruins, visigothic basilicas, and Arab mosques?

Other statements in *Le Greco* are merely quite uncritical. Speaking of Toledo cathedral, he says: "Sous ces nefs d'une hauteur prodigieuse, j'accepte d'être submergé." In reality, the nave of Toledo cathedral is low and seems even lower; in contrast with the great area of the building (it is as large as Cologne cathedral and larger than York), the central nave (the loftiest one) is only 100 feet high. The churches of northern France are generally smaller yet normally higher; Amiens cathedral, the largest church in France, has a nave 139 feet high, while Beauvais, the area of which is small, had a nave 153 feet high. If, then, the height of Toledo cathedral is "prodigious," what adjective would Barrès suggest to describe the churches of his own country? Or again, in his enthusiasm for Toledo cathedral (he loved to haunt and idealize Spanish churches), he says: "Où que se portent mes yeux, des raretés, des audaces m'assaillent, et jamais une médiocrité. Toute chose a du poids, porte la patine des siècles, a trouvé sa place immuable et s'harmonise avec l'ensemble." . . . It would seem that we must have little confidence in the artistic taste of Barrès, or in his knowledge of the history of art.

At the time of its appearance, art critics quickly saw the shortcomings of Barrès' book, and gave it a very cold reception. They described it scornfully as "literature," but even many literary critics were unprepared to defend it. Ernst Robert Curtius describes it politely as "ein etwas enttäuschendes Buch." M. Paul Guinard, a very able historian of art, felt himself obliged, for a series of reasons which it is not necessary to analyze here, to defend Barrès against these criticisms. He says, in the aforementioned article: "Des gens qui se croient 'avertis' prononcent volontiers cette excommunication: 'il n'y a là que belle littérature.' . . . Nous protesterons si l'on prétend que ces cadences sonnent creux."

It is now clear that Barrès' Hispanism is a troubled stream of passion incapable of bearing any intellectual trade. We must not be surprised if it breaks up into a fantastic series of waterfalls, theories about Spain which are picturesque and may even provide a lot of energy, but which are even more unsuited to the commerce of ideas. We must content ourselves with showing the course of his thoughts, and scarcely attempt to introduce into them the quiet limpidity of truth.

Barrès maintains that the genius of Spain can be expressed in the one word "passion." In **Du sang, de la volupté, et de la mort,** Delrio, the protagonist of "Un Amateur d'âmes" who lives in a *cigarral* opposite Toledo with his sister, la Pia, is dissatisfied with her spiritual development and decides to reveal to her the soul of Spain, its essentially passionate nature: "Il pense la développer, lui donner le dernier coup de pouce en lui montrant l'Espagne, qui est le pays le plus effréné du monde." For this reason, they leave their *cigarral* and undertake a tour of Spain.

It is this wildly passionate nature which is represented as distinguishing Spain from the rest of Europe, even at the present day. Spanish passion was naturally yet stronger before the influence of modern civilization began to make itself felt in the Peninsula. Barrès loves the violent Spain of the *Romancero,* with all its unbridled energy. In this he is following the pure romantic tradition of Victor Hugo.

At a later period he found the same spirit in the *Conquistadores.* As Francisco García Calderón says: "Il connaissait plusieurs aspects de notre histoire, il admirait beaucoup les Conquistadores, leur farouche énergie, le culte barbare du moi chez ces êtres fanatiques. Il lisait souvent la biographie de Cortés par Bernal Díaz dans la traduction de Hérédia. . . . Le romantisme, la violence, l'individualisme, la vie dangereuse des Espagnols d'Amérique le passionaient." It is interesting to note that it was to the chair of J. M. de Hérédia in the Académie Française that Barrès was elected on 18 January 1906. (pp. 285-89)

He contemplated with disgust the process of "europeanization" of Spain. He felt in particular that the introduction of industrialism was robbing Spain of its energy. Talking of the once picturesque *barrio de Triana* at Seville, Barrès says: "Une faïencerie, installée là par des capitalistes anglais, désireux de profiter de l'incroyable bon marché de la main d'œuvre, me révolta: dégradation d'un peuple contraint de chauffer les fours par cette terrible température à une heure que, de père en fils, ils consacraient à la sieste."

Nevertheless, despite this debilitating process, Spain still remains for Barrès the land of passion, where Europeans, dulled by the monotonous life of their industrial civilization, can take an emotional shower-bath. "Pour rompre l'atonie, l'Espagne est une grande resource. Je ne sais pas de pays où la vie ait autant de saveur. Elle réveille l'homme le mieux maté par l'administration moderne. Là, enfin, on entrevoit que la sensibilité humaine n'est pas limitée à ces deux ou trois sensations fortes (l'amour, le duel, la cour d'assises) qui, seules, subsistent dans notre civilisation parisienne. C'est une Afrique: elle met dans l'âme une sorte de fureur aussi prompte qu'un piment dans la bouche."

Stendhal made the mistake, according to Barrès, of seeking, and believing that he found, passion in Italy, which is, in comparison with Spain, a quite unimpassioned country. Thus, for Barrès, Spain is far superior: "C'est un pays pour sauvage qui ne sait rien, ou pour philosophe qui de tout est blasé, sauf d'énergie. [Despite his hostility to German intellectualism, there is an undoubted influence of Nietzsche on Barrès.] L'Italie est moins simple, plus composée; dans sa douceur tu peux sommeiller; ici tout est brusque et d'un accent qui mord." (pp. 289-90)

The human construction which best expresses the ascetic spirit of Castile is, according to Barrès, the Escurial, and in this he is in agreement with many Spanish writers, especially Unamuno. It is to the Escurial that Delrio, the protagonist of "**Un Amateur d'âmes,**" first takes his sister on their tour around Spain in quest of the country's soul. "Ce fut d'abord l'Escurial qu'il lui montra, comme le lieu de l'ascétisme et la traduction en granit de la discipline castillane issue d'une conception catholique de la mort. Monté sur un rocher de cette sombre sierra où fut imposé l'énorme monastère, quel voyageur n'a subi le despotisme de ce paysage et d'une régularité si douleureuse dans cet horizon convulsé! Mais la plupart, réagissant contre la contraction de leur âme, retournent très vite à la misérable auberge, en bouffonnant sur l'humeur mélancolique des maçons de Philippe II. Vains efforts pour tenier le tremblement de leur être sous la prise du génie castillan." Delrio's sister, la Pia, is terrified by this melancholy solitude, and when they get outside she bursts out crying. Then, "prise d'une sorte de folie du gouffre," she wishes to stay and enjoy the painful sensation. But Delrio, following his preconceived scheme, takes her straightway to Granada, so that she may feel the contrast between Castile and Andalusia.

Although the Escurial is, according to Barrès, the most typical monument of Castile, the primitive violence of Northern Spain is best felt in the Basques, who gave free vent to their instincts in the Carlist wars. This is illustrated with daring realism in the story "**La Haine emporte tout.**" A young widow of Seville, rich and well born, travels from Andalusia to the Carlist stronghold Estella, where she wishes to join the faction of Don Carlos, whom she has idealized. Her noble loyalty and her sacrifice are poorly repaid. She is taken to an inn and raped by each of a crowd of soldiers. Don Carlos himself displays the same mentality as his troops.

Barrès loves to talk of three Andalusian cities dear to the Romantics: Granada, Córdoba, and Seville. (pp. 291-92)

Barrès proceeds to relate, in a romantic way, the story of the fall of Granada, due chiefly to King Boabdil's having succumbed to Granadan sensuousness, which, at the present day, can best be appreciated in the *gitanas,* and even in gipsy children. This picture of Granada is one-sided in comparison with Barrès' usual depiction of Andalusia, of its dual spirit of sensuousness and ascetic violence.

Equally unilateral is the description which Barrès gives us of Córdoba in "Sur la volupté de Cordoue." Its quality may be judged by a remark such as this: "Cordoue . . . où toute femme nous assassine d'un regard et d'un tour de hanche sarrasins." Barrès' romantic conception of Córdoba is also expressed in the story "La Musulmane courageuse," unsuccessfully hyper-poetic.

Barrès' descriptions of Seville are likewise tawdry. He shows that he belongs to the commonplace romantic tradition by indulging in a gaudy description of the Sevillian tobacco-factory which Carmen had made notorious. Here is a typical passage of this sketch entitled "Les Bijoux perdus": "Cinq mille Sévillanes! qui, dans ces ateliers, perpétuellement rafraîchis d'eau et semés d'une excitante poussière de tabac, sont mi-dévêtues et font voir (sans plus de gêne que leurs yeux incomparables, leurs beaux cheveux et leurs petites mains brunes) des bras ronds, des seins dorés, toute leur gorge, leurs mollets, et par-ci par-là ces jolis bijoux de noms trop peu gracieux pour que je veuille en dégrader le tableau." Elsewhere he indulges in an ultra-modernistic description of Sevillian evenings: "Le soir, Séville est jeune, amoureuse et cambrée; elle est douce et bruyante comme une salle de bal où l'orangeade est vraiment glacée, où l'on ne souffre pas de lumière dans les yeux."

All Andalusian cities have one thing in common:—passion. Andalusian passion is exemplified in Violante, the heroine of **"Un Amour de Thulé"** (in *Du sang, de la volupté, et de la mort*), a Sevillian who travels around Europe in the company of her French husband. "Elle trouvait l'Italie un peu fade auprès de son âpre Espagne, détestait l'Angleterre, et dans l'Europe centrale, ne gardait de sentiment que pour les soirs d'été aux restaurants de Carlsbad, où chantent les gitanes sous le nom de *lothars*." (pp. 292-93)

The southern Spaniard drinks so deeply in the cup of the senses that he learns quicker than others that lasting satisfaction cannot be found in it. Yet he is wise enough not to reject the humble drink. This attitude is best expressed by Seneca, for whom Barrès had a cult. He shared it with his dear friend, Jules Tellier, as he explains in **"Sur la mort du sang, de la volupté, et de la mort."** In it Barrès says:

> Nous rendions en commun un culte à Sénèque, qui fut peut-être le thème le plus fréquent de nos entretiens. La constitution délicate, l'inquiétude et l'indulgence de ce grand calomnié nous enchantaient. Bien supérieur aux stoïciens dont il se réclamait, Sénèque accepta la vie de son siècle sans rien en bouder; seulement toutes ses relations avec les choses et avec les hommes étaient commandées par le sentiment intense qu'll faudra mourir et que nous vivons au milieu de choses qui doivent périr. L'ascétisme très réel de Sénèque n'est pas de se priver, mais de mésestimer ce dont il use.

Yet Barrès understands and appreciates in Andalusia an even more radical attitude, a passionate rejection of the passions, such as that which Don Juan of a sudden professed. He idealizes this traditional figure in **"Une Visite à Don Juan,"** for which he used the investigations of M. Raoul Colonna de'Cesari. He sings not the sensuous galant, but Don Juan repentant, whose bitter disillusionment is illustrated in the famous picture of Valdés Leal, "The Two Corpses," painted at the request of Don Juan, and

now in the Hospital de la Caridad, at Seville. Barrès appreciates this almost sadistic rejection of pleasure.

A similar sadism is the source of the pleasure produced by bull-fights, which the *leyenda negra* has indicted very loudly, but which aroused in Barrès untiring enthusiasm. The following is perhaps the most fundamental eulogy of bull-fights which Barrès has penned: "Le large cri que jette au ciel chaque petite ville assemblée dans son cirque, quand tombe le taureau, c'est le signe le plus véhément de la sensibilité espagnole, de cette belle fureur rendue encore plus saisissante par les formes diverses et contrastées qu'elle prend." . . . It is evident that Barrès is not interested in the skill and agility which are the essential attraction of the sport, but only in the thrill of the final bloodshed. He is in this much more Spanish than most Spaniards . . . .(pp. 293-94)

Barrès at first stressed the catholicism of Spain because of its almost psychopathic attraction, and later because he saw in it an ally for the catholic nationalism he was preaching in France. These motives led him to depict a Spain obsessed with catholicism. In *Le Greco,* he says: "Les dogmes catholiques sont la pensée constante de l'Espagne. On retrouve leur influence sur les domaines les plus imprévus. Les auto-sacramentales (sic), pièces en un acte destinées à célébrer le Saint-Sacrement, ont leur analogue en peinture. Tous les modèles du Greco psalmodient la louange de l'Immaculée Conception et de la Présence réelle." Barrès seems never to have suspected that there is in Spanish culture a strong non-catholic and even anti-catholic element, and that, while no one can deny the great importance of catholicism in Spanish history, Don Manuel Azaña was at least partially correct as far as modern times are concerned when in 1931 he said "España ha dejado de ser católica."

Of all Spanish writers, Barrès was most attracted by Santa Teresa. She is a parallel to El Greco—so inspired that she has been judged mad. Even within orthodox catholicism, Barrès loved and sought the passion, the ecstacy which he considered to be the radiant essence of Spain. In his preface to the translation which the Conde de Premio Real made of the Commentary of the Songs of Songs, he says: "Sainte Thérèse est une inspirée. Comment le nier si l'on relit sa vie. Nous connaissons ses exercises dont elle sortait transportée et ne se reconnaissait plus elle-même. . . . Fi des commentateurs que disent qu'elle avait été malade dans sa jeunesse et qui tentent de trouver là une explication."

The purely exotic charm of Andalusia at first sent a thrill of passion through Barrès, but he slowly came to prefer the more subtle and complex appeal of Toledo. Besides the pages he has devoted to the city of the Tagus in *Du sang, de la volupté, et de la mort,* and more especially in *Le Greco ou le secret de Tolède,* Barrès has written a number of now-forgotten articles on Toledo. With regard to the problem of Barrès' visits to Spain, already discussed, it seems probable that these articles, which all appeared in 1909, were the result of a visit to Spain. It is likely that Barrès went to Toledo to perfect his book on El Greco.

Toledo lies, according to Barrès, on the line of division

which he has drawn between northern and southern Spain, and partakes of both the asceticism of Castile and the sensuousness of Andalusia. Hence its subtle and complex charm. It is the only city in which the dual spirit of Spain can be felt in all its completeness. Barrès never deviated from this theory, which he thus expresses in *Du sang, de la volupté, et de la mort:* "Apreté de Castille où passe un long soupir d'Andalousie! Sur cette ville à la fois maure et catholique, les parfums qui montent de la *Sierra* se marient à l'odeur des cierges échappée des èglises. Les sensations de l'Escurial et de l'Alhambra gonflaient à la fois le sein de la Pia, et de leur mélange équivoque, loin de s'affaiblir, elles prenaient la puissance, la tristesse des passions combattues." This contrast is evident in the Cathedral, "qui est le lieu du monde le plus somptueusement meublé." On the other hand, it contains the tomb with the famous inscription "Hic jacet pulvis, cinis et nihil," which, says Barrès, "fit battre mon cœur plus qu'aucune phrase des poètes." Lucien, to whom Delrio has confided his sister during his absence from Toledo, and who has taken her to visit the Cathedral, is so moved that he suddenly kisses her within the sacred precincts, and thus provokes in her a serious illness. This episode is decidedly grotesque. While she is ill, la Pia commits suicide. After her death, Delrio sells his *cigarral* for a curious motive: "il vendit la villa sous condition expresse qu'on en fit un hôtel, afin que ce lieu, étant profané par n'importe qui, par tout le monde, les souvenirs, restitués à l'universel, n'en fussent possédés par personne." To avoid this story's being ridiculous, it is necessary to give it a symbolical meaning; it remains, none the less, unsatisfactory.

The same theme of Toledo's dual character recurs as a leitmotiv in *Le Greco ou le secret de Tolède.* "Par trois fois j'accourus entendre la chanson de l'Espagne. Dès la frontière elle m'attendait, cette chanson qui s'en va éveiller la tristesse pour lui dire de se résigner. Elle était tapie, je m'en souviens bien, dans le coin d'une petite gare. Par Burgos, si froide et gothique, par Valadolid où gisent toutes les poupées de sacristie, par la sainte Avila, cette faible chanson, de jour en jour s'amplifiait, se chargeait de sens. A Tolède, je fus rejoint par un air qui vient du midi. Comme d'autres au fond des terres, tresaillent s'ils ont senti la brise salée de l'Océan, j'avais respiré l'Orient."

This interpretation is interesting and partially true. Nevertheless, the divisions which Barrès makes are much too definite, and give to Toledo a unique character which in reality it does not possess. The same dual nature is to be found in many other towns, particularly Saragossa, Ciudad Real, and Badajoz. Barrès does not mention these cities, which he does not seem to have visited. It is very common for one with a rudimentary knowledge of a subject to make an arbitrary classification. Moreover Barrès, having made this division, quickly forgets it. Obsessed by El Greco, he neglects the sensuous side of Toledo, and expatiates on its mystical life. M. Paul Guinard rightly suggests that, blinded by the cult of El Greco, Barrès has misunderstood the spirit of Toledo, which has a definitely materialistic character; real mysticism must be sought in Burgos, Segovia, and, above all, Avila.

Du sang, de la volupté, et de la mort was given a mixed reception in France. Even modernists did not find this motley work very satisfactory, and the well-established critics, such as René Doumic, steeped in the traditions of French moderation and *bon sens,* were, as we have seen, extremely hostile. As Barrès veered towards reaction in politics, adapting the theories of energy to this new standpoint, conservative critics became more favorable towards him. In particular, M. Maurice Legendre metes out warm praise to him. This is no cause for surprise, for besides holding more or less the same political views, they were personal friends. Moreover, M. Legendre's criticism is seldom destructively critical. In an article devoted to our dilettante Hispanist, he says: "M. Barrès n'a pas cessé de rendre hommage à l'Espagne. Il y a un progrès évident vers le cœur de l'Espagne des premières notes si fines, si justes, si enthousiastes, enregistrées au livre *Du sang, de la volupté, et de la mort,* aux pages si pleines qui désormais révèlent à quiconque sait lire le français, le secret de Tolède et de la vieille Espagne impérissable." The last remark sounds like bathos.

The Barrès of *Du sang, de la volupté, et de la mort* perplexed and dismayed those Spaniards who were striving to introduce things European into Spain; Barrès lauded all those characteristics of the Peninsula which they despised. When he came to Spain for the first time in 1892, Barrès met Doña Emilia Pardo Bazán in Madrid, and had a long conversation with her. *San Francisco de Asís* (1882), which had been a best-seller, had won for Doña Emilia a reputation as an authority on mysticism; it was no doubt for this reason that Barrès questioned her at length about the Spanish mystics—Santa Teresa, San Juan de la Cruz, Malón de Chaide—and about the atmosphere of Avila and Medina. He spoke to her with great enthusiasm of "San Ignacio de Loyola, cuyos ejercicios le parecen 'la más curiosa maquinaria psicológica que ha visto en su vida.' " This interest in Spanish catholicism should have won for Barrès the sympathy of catholic Pardo Bazán. On the contrary, in the article she devotes to him, she expresses open contempt for an art which is so obscure that, while she admits that she cannot understand it, nevertheless seems to her bluff. She protests against the obscurantism of Barrès and the French writers of his school . . . As for the ideas of Barrès, it is, says Doña Emilia, incomprehensible that he should sing such fanatical eulogies of Spanish energy, when all serious Spaniards realize, only too well, that their country is suffering from "abulia."

The world-wide success of *Le Greco ou le secret de Tolède* was an excellent advertisement for Toledo and for Spain. That the civic authorities, municipal and national, should be grateful, is natural. In Toledo, on the occasion of Maurice Barrès' death, the former Calle del Barco, running from the south of the cathedral to the Tagus, was renamed the Calle Maurice Barrès at a public ceremony. . . . This was the result of a petition made to the Toledan city-council. . . . It is significant that in this petition, special stress is laid upon the propagandist value of Barrès' work. In general it would seem that the time has come to submit Barrès' Hispanomania to careful scrutiny. This is naturally no reflexion upon the value of the rest of his work. (pp. 295-99)

Ronald Hilton, "Maurice Barrès and Spain," in The Romanic Review, *Vol. XXX, No. 3, October, 1939, pp. 280-99.*

Denis Saurat   (essay date 1946)

[*In the excerpt below, Saurat argues that Barrès's early novel,* Le jardin de Bérénice, *compares to some of the first novels of Anatole France, Barrès's older contemporary. In his analysis of one of Barrès's major novels,* La colline inspirée, *Saurat propounds an idea central to modern literary criticism—that reading demands a process of collaboration between writer and reader.*]

Barrès was a Lorrainer by birth, and at first an egotist: secondarily he became a politician, deputy for Nancy from 1889. Behind the self that he at first cultivated exclusively he discovered his country, and perhaps at the end of his life he discovered mankind. He died too early at sixty-one; his *Journals* and his last books show that the wealth of his soul was as yet far from exhausted. Both his art and his thought would probably have risen higher and struck deeper had he lived to the age of Anatole France or Victor Hugo. A peculiar kind of nobility which the reader feels and respects leads Barrès pretty often into impossible situations, and his sharp intellect then opens his soul to the waters of bitterness. So, much of his work is bitter; and he was on the wrong side in many quarrels, because he wanted heroes to worship where there were no heroes. Thus his nobility led to bitterness, but his passionate love for France and the lasting elements of French culture kept a kind of deeper serenity behind his vagaries. His work has been exploited by parties who do not deserve to have him in their ranks. Perhaps he died too early because he was exhausted and wanted to escape

> D'un monde où l'action n'est pas la sœur du rêve.

He had tried to harmonize action and dreaming; he had not failed, but the world had failed him. The key to his tragedy is possibly in the fact that he could not really accept the Catholic faith, which was the basis of his life.

Of Barrès's first period, perhaps *Le Jardin de Bérénice* is the most pleasurable novel. It is not so different from Anatole France in his first period, *Le Lys rouge,* but Anatole France does it better. Yet it is so good that the reader is only too pleased to find that it can be done also by Barrès. Perhaps Barrès has remained truer to his youth than Anatole France: whereas France's *Révolte des anges* belongs to a different world from *Le Lys rouge* (in spite of some resemblances), Barrès's *Jardin sur l'Oronte* in 1922 is a return to the mentality of 1890 in both, before politics were politics. And those readers who truly liked that kind of tale—legitimately—might maintain that Barrès after all is the true Anatole France, and that *Un Jardin sur l'Oronte* is a Francean book—a Francean masterpiece written by Barrès when France had been laid to rest.

Subtlety, a delicate romantic flavour, a true epicureanism, a detachment, a great sensitiveness to all outside impressions, a somewhat cynical abandon to all impulses from the inside—and excellent French. Such is the early recipe, for Barrès as for France. But one cannot help feeling—in spite of all the pleasure they give us—that they are not yet quite grown up.

Some temperaments have to go through a serious illness before they get their strength and mature. Politics was this illness for both France and Barrès. Why insist on the illness? I hold that the middle period books from *Les Déracinés* (1897) to *Colette Baudoche* (1909) are better left unread. The racial ideas are crude, and indeed resemble overmuch other crude ideas that properly belong on the other side of the Rhine. No doubt the bitter satire of French political life in *Leurs Figures* is only too true, but one reads the malevolent pages with no joy, and literary pleasure is absent. A powerful journalist is at work—and Barrès remained to the end a powerful journalist. Those that read his daily articles against Caillaux at the end of the first world war will not forget the feelings that were aroused then. **"En regardant au fond des crevasses"** was the title, and strange monsters curled appalling tentacles deep down in the crevices of the soil of France.

But what are politics? Clemenceau is a sinister figure in Barrès's semi-historical novels of 1900; he has to be a hero for Barrès in 1918. The fact perhaps proves that no literature can hallow politics.

Barrès's most durable book is *La Colline inspirée* (1909). It is the story of a pre-Celtic sacred hill in the Lorraine region, and of some peasant prophets who felt the old spirit rise in them in the nineteenth century. This time all that was good in Barrès's patriotism and love of the ancient race came into full legitimate play. And there is no idealization of the brute peasant either; for the true peasant is not far above the animal, and animals also can be good or bad. But the rising of the religious spirit out of the sympathy between the peasant and the earth is a powerful impulse: both below the animal life really, and yet above the spiritual level of people who live in towns. This tremendous subject has never been dealt with on that level anywhere else, though several attempts have been made in the less successful regions of English literature, by writers like Buchan, for instance. Barrès has the genius of his subject, and genius is not too strong a word.

Barrès was ill at ease in his politics, and in the religion that had to go with his politics. Being above all intelligent, he knew only too well that the men he had to support were no better than those he had to attack. He knew very well that the religious party he had to side with was only a party; it was not even really the Catholic Church; besides which, he was not a Catholic. He was a rationalist trying to find in the past, in the earth, in the people, roots that should be strong enough to weather the storms. He was a rationalist who looked deeper than reason. All this had been hampering him in his *Énergie nationale* novels. Barrès was not really a salesman for patriotism: in his soul he was an artist. When he turned to the land and to the religious peasant, he found his full scope, and he drew a picture of a part of the true soul of France. Of course, his prophets had to be failures—what else was possible in our time, or so near it? But in the tale of their disaster he wove the description of their strength, and spread the mystic relationship of man and earth in the spiritual world. Not pretending to know what that spiritual world of the woods and fields is, or can be, being totally undogmatic, he therefore caught the true literary angle.

And yet *La Colline inspirée* is hard reading. All Barrès's virtuosity of style, all his profound knowledge of French, is needed, and yet the reader also has to collaborate and understand. Both the writer and the reader have to do their utmost, and the subject remains all the time slightly beyond them both. That impression of something great moving and living just beyond the phrase and the page is one of the creations of the highest literary art. A strenuous but successful masterpiece.

And in his old age, just as though to show that he could yet relax and play, play with the acquired and dearly bought wisdom of maturity, he wrote in 1922 *Un Jardin sur l'Oronte*. A simple and wicked tale of the Crusaders, of a western lord who falls in love with an eastern lady, and how he comes to his death, and how perfect destiny is. A strange book after all the great efforts. But again a masterpiece: as though the dumb Middle Ages had become intelligent and bad, and had added to their effectiveness and *naïveté* the *ruse* and the viciousness supposed to belong to our later ages. (pp. 53-6)

> *Denis Saurat, "Maurice Barrès: 1862-1923," in his* Modern French Literature: 1870-1940, *J. M. Dent & Sons Ltd., London, 1946, pp. 53-6.*

Reino Virtanen   (essay date 1947)

[*In the excerpt below, Virtanen enunciates certain common viewpoints shared by Barrès with the seventeenth-century French thinker Blaise Pascal, within the context of Barrès's philosophy of the "Culte du Moi."*]

Reading *Mes Cahiers,* one is struck by the large share accorded to Pascal in the meditations of Maurice Barrès, a share which does not always appear reflected in Barrès's finished work. Barrès tells us that, at twenty, his favorite writers included Rousseau, Chateaubriand, Lamartine, Goethe, Cervantes, and Pascal. But is was not until some time later that Pascal came to be the lode-star of the middle decades of his life. There were readers who linked his *Culte du Moi* with Pascal's analysis of the self, but such readers did not come until after this *Culte du Moi* could be retrospectively interpreted in relation to his nationalism and to his increasing impulsion toward Catholicism. It was inevitable that the skeptic and individualist should have been impressed by Pascal as a hero of independent thought. Added to this was the interest naturally felt by the artist and patriot for one of the unchallenged glories of French literature. And when the Lorrainer began to delve among the roots of the Auvergne side of his family, he would not have been the exponent of "la Terre et les Morts," if his imagination had not been stirred by the fact that Pascal too, was from Auvergne.

There had to be stronger reasons, however, for Barrès's preoccupation with Pascal than his prestige and the sentimental association with Auvergne. Barrès tells us that while the thinking of his generation was in agreement with Pascal's skepticism, the distinguishing fact about him was

his vision of life against the background of death. Another reason, certainly, was the primacy given by him to intuition and feeling, as against intellect, a primacy Barrès was disposed to emphasize even more than Pascal. Through all his changes, this interest in the unconscious was a constant element in his thought, and it is this which he found epitomized in Pascal: "Pascal. . . . Comment vous mener à l'inexprimable, à ces profondes réserves de l'âme qui seules, à bien voir, agissent." How deep, how genuine, was the effect on Barrès of Pascal's impassioned analysis of the enigma of life and death? This cannot be finally measured without a study of the whole curve of Barrès's development. My discussion of Pascal's significance for him will be plotted along this curve, taking in the egoist, the nationalist, and the later Barrès. Thus the first topic to be considered is the influence which Pascal may have exerted in the elaboration of the *Culte du Moi*.

Le Culte du Moi.

If he is not explicitly mentioned among the "intercesseurs" of *Un Homme libre,*—his name would have been somewhat incongruous in this company of "haut dilettantisme"—there is more than one passage in which his life and work are suggested. First of all, there is the parallel between their conceptions of the parts played by intelligence and instinct in human life. The impotence of reason, the powers of the heart, were favorite themes of Barrès. . . . Even in passages which show how different his conception was from the notion of instinct in Pascal—with all the difference that German metaphysics could supply—we can discern echoes of the phraseology of the *Pensées*. Declaring his dissatisfaction with the "intercesseurs" of *Un Homme libre* who only instructed him on the excesses of his "sensibilité," he writes: "Je n'avais pas su dans l'étude de mon moi pénétrer plus loin que mes qualités; le peuple m'a révélé la substance humaine . . . l'inconscient." Pascal had written in the paragraph entitled "Qu'est-ce que le *moi?*": ". . . je puis perdre ces qualités sans me perdre moi-même. . . . Où donc est ce *moi*, . . . et comment aimer le corps ou l'âme sinon pour ces qualités, qui ne sont point ce qui fait le *moi*, puisqu'elles sont périssables? Car aimerait-on la substance de l'âme d'une personne abstraitement . . .?" In Barrès's chapter on Benjamin Constant, something reminiscent of Pascal's *abêtissement* is applied in the service of the self: ". . . ceux qui par orgueil de leur vrai Moi qu'ils ne parviennent pas à dégager, meurtrissent, souillent et renient sans trêve ce qui est en eux de commun avec la masse des hommes. Quand ils humilient ce qui est en eux de commun avec Royer-Collard, . . . je les félicite." These echoes of Pascal, of course, are given the stamp of Barrès's own *sensibilité* and ideas. Thus, expressing his emotion at his discovery of the unconscious as the basic substance of life, Barrès exclaims: "Melancolie ou plutôt stupeur! devant cet abîme de l'inconscient qui s'ouvrait à l'infini devant moi."

Barrès found in Pascal an exemplar of his ideal: "l'alliance de l'intelligence la plus haute à l'émotivité la plus intense." This formulation can be linked with a later note in the *Cahiers:* "Voir tout le beau raisonnement autour de ce mot de Pascal: 'A mesure que l'on a plus d'esprit, les passions sont plus grandes.' Et surtout: 'La netteté d'esprit cause la netteté de la passion'." [The critic adds in a footnote: The citation is from Pascal's *Discours sur les Passions de l'amour*]. It is one of the lessons which the too sober Roemerspacher is made to learn in **Leurs Figures:** "La production de toute grande découverte, de toute haute et forte pensée s'accompagne toujours d'une émotivité extraordinaire." But in the *Culte du Moi*, this lesson is applied only in the interest of a dilettantism that would be "clairvoyant et fiévreux."

In Barrès's program of cultivation of the self, it was natural that Pascal could not attain the ascendancy exercised by Goethe or even the more short-lived dominion of Wagner. But some trace of certain aphorisms on the formation of character and the control of the passions is not absent from Barrès's "mechanics" of the self. The "conversation intérieure" by means of which Barrès tried to mold himself resembles that of Pascal in more than the name, if their goals are utterly unlike.

> 'Tiens en mains toutes les forces que tu as, afin que tu puisses par des commandements rapides prendre soudain toutes les figures en face des circonstances.' . . . je me replongeais dans l'étude des moyens pour posséder les ressorts de mon âme, comme un capitaine possède sa compagnie.

Though his method is avowedly based on Loyola and Cabanis, this passage has a parallel in the following from the *Pensées:*

> . . . il se sert [de ses passions] comme maître, en disant à l'une: 'Va,' et à l'autre: 'Viens' . . . . Il faut s'en servir comme d'esclaves, et, leur laissant leur aliment, empêcher que l'âme n'y en prenne; car quand les passions sont les maîtresses, elles sont vices. . . .

Like André Gide's ideal of *disponibilité*, Barrès's goal was the enjoyment of all possible emotions as a master who could choose and withdraw at will. There is a parallel, also, between the *mnémotechnie* he prescribed in **Un Homme libre** and the significance he was to find in Pascal's *mémorial* in **L'Angoisse de Pascal:**

> Que si la grâce nous est donnée de ressentir une émotion profonde, assurons-nous de la retrouver au premier appel. Et pour ce, rattachons-la, fût-elle de l'ordre métaphysique le plus haut, à quelque object matériel que nous puissions toucher jusque dans nos pires dénuements.

Pascal's conception of the self as a force tending to dominate by its very nature provides a basis, *avant la lettre*, for Barrès's *Culte du Moi*. But the *Culte du Moi* was a contemplative and cerebral enterprise that involved only studied sorties into the realm of action. This relatively innocent form of domination is exceeded, to be sure, in **Un Amateur d'âmes** in which Delrio, in his treatment of La Pia, carries the *Culte du Moi* to a point where dilettantism and tyranny coincide.

What Pascal offers the Barrès of **Un Amateur d'âmes** is the example of a peculiarly intense reaction to the fact of death. In this macabre tale, Pascal appears less in the role

of "intercesseur" than as a spectacle for the dilettante of strange emotions,—emotions, however, which the view of Toledo can evoke as well:

> Cette exaltante Tolède, voilà la complémentaire désignée pour un être dégoûté au point que, dans les arts, seuls l'eussent éveillé les violents raccourcis de Pascal et de Michel-Ange, qui eurent l'âme solitaire et tendue.

Perhaps even more suspect is his comparison between Pascal and Don Juan:

> . . . ce plâtre si grave, quand je le contemplais à la Caridad, soudain m'évoqua les traits mêmes de Pascal. Ce Don Juan, qui n'écrivit pas les *Provinciales,* mais qui argumentait passionnément et qui, lui aussi, pour se convertir, établit sa foi sur son effroi de la mort et sur son désenchantement, ne me déconcerte pas quand ses traits, ennoblis par l'agonie, prennent un air de famille avec ce fiévreux Pascal.

The Escurial is to Delrio an expression in stone of Pascal's fragment: "La grandeur de l'homme est grande en ce qu'il se connaît misérable." Pascal's feeling before his abyss is but one in a gamut of emotions to which Delrio gives himself: "Penché sur l'immense Escurial que d'un tertre il dominait, Delrio s'abandonnait au vertige du gouffre ascétique; il cédait à l'empire catholique de la douleur. . . . Ce paysage anarchique . . . lui semblait exactement la *composition de lieu* que présenterait à son imagination, pour la fixer, un Pascal qui médite." If more is needed to demonstrate that Barrès's interest in Pascal up to 1893 was that of a dilettante, we may cite the avowal: "Peu m'importe le fond des doctrines! C'est l'élan que je goûte." Barrès, so far, had not gone beyond "le goût du brisement du coeur."

The figure of Pascal was involved in the transition through which the cult of the self gave way to the cult of Lorraine. Barrès appropriated something of Pascal's dialectic of humility and hope for this key passage in the transition:

> ' . . . Lorraine, . . . tu m'as montré que j'appartenais à une race incapable de se réaliser . . .' Alors la Lorraine me répondit: 'Il est un instinct en moi qui a abouti; . . . c'est le sentiment du devoir. . . . Quand tu t'abaisses, je veux te vanter comme le favori de tes vieux parents, car tu es la conscience de notre race. . . . Pourquoi toujours te complaire dans tes humiliations.

But, as in instances cited above, the borrowings enrich his rhetoric rather than his substance. Barrès does not fully appreciate the dialectic of Pascal. His presentation nowhere reflects the intensity of the contrast between the "sovereign judge of all things" and the "sink of uncertainty and error," for he was only too ready to surrender the dignity of thought in favor of the unconscious. The elegant *Weltschmerz* of **Sous l'Oeil des Barbares,** the ironic disenchantment of **Un Homme libre,** lack of gravity of Pascal. The difference is that between the nostalgia voiced frequently in his books and the sense of cosmic exile of the *Pensées*.

Nationalism.

When, in 1901, Barrès added Pascal to the list of the Comtes and Bonalds who could be drawn into service as teachers of *nationalisme,* he did not offer a clear exposition of his idea. The difficulty of the demonstration is suggested two years later in the **Cahiers:** "Pascal nationaliste. Je n'ai pas osé publier cette thèse bizarre." It was that moment in the history of their doctrine when the nationalists were seeking among writers of the past authority for their attack upon democracy. The eagerness displayed by these men in bending to their purpose writers like Balzac, Sainte-Beuve, Renan, and Taine, gives us an idea of the enthusiasm which might have greeted a convincing adaptation of Pascal.

There are elements in Pascal's thought which could lend support to extreme conservatism in politics, if the relevance of his work for a full-blown nationalism proved, as even Barrès learned, somewhat tenuous. Pascal's political theory places him in the same camp with the "realist" Machiavelli and the authoritarian Hobbes. Fearful of civic disorder such as threatened in the Fronde, yet possessed of a sharp insight into the real forces that govern society, Pascal was a supporter of authority who saw through the illusions disposing the masses to accept authority while he affirmed the necessity of such illusions. Such a "sophisticated" defense of tradition was well-suited to the author of *L'ennemi des lois* now engaged in combatting democracy. (pp. 802-07)

Intent upon humbling reason and the order built upon "concupiscence" so as to throw into relief the superiority of the saintly order based upon charity, Pascal was following to the limit the injunction to render unto Caesar the things that are Caesar's. In this spirit, he submitted to all the forms through which deference to authority is expressed, and ridiculed the half-educated who presume to question conventions. "Ceux-là troublent le monde. . . ." He was apprehensive of those who jeopardize the peace of the world by impertinent appeals to reason. "C'est un jeu sûr pour tout perdre." With his *Discours sur la condition des grands,* as in numerous passages of the *Pensées,* he sought to moderate the evils he could not cure, writing of politics—"comme pour régler un hôpital de fous." The political counsels he proffers are for the benevolent monarch: "Le propre de la puissance est de protéger." But the kingdom of this world, however well governed, is still the kingdom of "concupiscence."

Such are the main tenets of the Pascalian political theory which Barrès's rightist friend Bourget extolled as moral realism. The anticipatory critique of Rousseau's *Contrat social,* the rejection of reason as an instrument of social betterment, the relativity of customs which could serve as point of departure for regionalism and nationalism, the submission to convention and authority with that concession to skepticism represented by the "pensée de derrière la tête"—all this part of Pascal's thought could supply chapter and verse for a nationalist interpretation.

There remains one point which Barrès made much of, though perhaps applying it in a sense not intended by Pascal. This is the aphorism on the chastity and intemperance of Alexander which describes great men as standing on the same ground as lesser men though reaching higher: "On

tient à eux par le bout par où ils tiennent au peuple. . . . Ils ne sont pas suspendus en l'air, tout abstraits de notre société." Starting with this thought, Barrès was to go on to a social determinism so complete as to have little affinity with the highly contingent political world of Pascal, which is no less subject to vary in time than it is in space.

Les Déracinés can be regarded as a development of this idea as Barrès saw it. What are these "déracinés" if not "suspended in the air, abstracted from the society" in which they could find fulfillment? . . . The danger, as Barrès saw it is that they are susceptible to influences which may corrupt them. And here one can detect in Barrès's psychology the impress of Pascal's aphorism, 502: ". . . car quand les passions sont les maîtresses, elles sont vices, et alors elles donnent à l'âme de leur aliment, et l'âme s'en nourrit et s'en empoisonne." "Avec qu'elle énergie," he writes, "ces jeunes Lorrains utilisent pour se nourrir, on pour s'empoisonner, les éléments que le milieu leur offre!" Influenced by Taine, Barrès bent in the direction of social determinism that other idea from the *Pensées:* ". . . on ne voit rien de juste ou d'injuste qui ne change de qualité en changeant de climat. . . .". Pascal was enrolled, along with Taine and Goethe, in the struggle Barrès carried on against the universalism of Kant. Roemerspacher tells Taine: "Saint-Phlin . . . oppose à Kant la constatation de Pascal: 'Vérité en deça des Pyrénées, erreur au delà' que vous avez pour nous mille fois contrôlée. Les hommes, de siècle en siècle, comme de pays en pays, conçoivent des morales diverses qui, selon les époques et les climats, sont nécessaires et partant justes. Elles sont la vérité tant qu'elles sont nécessaires." The categorical imperative receives its refutation in the maxim of Pascal, the most general of all: "que chacun suive les moeurs de son pays."

Pascal's conception of the ego is reflected in **Les Déracinés** and its sequels. Bouteiller unconsciously clothes his ambitions in the Kantian formulae on duty. "M. Bouteiller, forme son âme de domination en déformant des âmes lorraines." Bouteiller's teaching, since it "uproots" them and yet fails to impose his Kantian doctrines on them, threatens to convert his students into pure nihilists:

> Soudain [il] communiquait à ces jeunes garçons le plus aigu sentiment du néant, d'où l'on ne peut se dégager . . . qu'en s'interdisant d'y songer et par la multitude des petits soucis d'une action. . . . Il leur proposait toutes les antinomies, toutes les insupportables difficultés reconnues par une longue suite d'esprits infiniment subtils qui voulant atteindre une certitude, ne découvrirent partout que le cercle de leurs épaisses ténèbres. Ces lointains parfums orientaux de la mort, filtrés par le réseau des penseurs allemands, ne vont-ils pas troubler ces novices? La dose trop forte pourrait jeter chacun d'eux dans une affirmation désespérée de soimême; ils se composeraient une sorte de nihilisme cruel.

The affinity with Pascal may be discerned in this passage, not only in the function of *divertissement,* in the accent placed on "néant" and on "épaisses ténèbres," but also in the notion of egoism. Pascal had stated it in these terms:

> Le *moi* a deux qualités: il est injuste en soi, en

ce qu'il se fait centre de tout; il est incommode aux autres, en ce qu'il les veut asservir: car chaque *moi* est l'ennemi et voudrait êtree le tyran de tous les autres.

In the lecture delivered in the interval between his crime and punishment, Racadot pronounces his credo, which carries Sturel's Napoleon cult and Roemerspacher's "realism" to the extreme limit of amoral egoism, in a kind of caricature of Nietzsche. This credo is a desperate affirmation of the right of each individual to "Caesarize": "Chacun se comporte comme si sa propre durée était l'unique objet de la vie universelle." The difference is that Pascal was describing the state of man without grace, while for Barrès, Racadot is only a horrible example of the *déraciné.*

Racadot could have been saved by returning in time to Lorraine, to take root again, as Saint-Phlin did, to live in accordance with the "truths" of the Lorraine community. Barrès combined Pascal's relativity of customs with the notion of the social organism impressed upon him by such writers as Taine and Jules Soury, to produce the regional, national, and racial "verities" he was now endeavoring to promote. In *L'Appel au soldat,* Sturel and Saint-Phlin visit the annexed areas of the Moselle and study the conflict of national ideologies. They are moved by the innkeeper's reply to his little son into whose mind the German schoolmaster has inculcated ideas which belittle France: "Oublie tout ce qu'il t'enseigne, le maître. Il n'y a de vérité qu'en français." And the young men draw the lesson which refutes the universalism of Bouteiller:

> En l'absence d'une vérité absolue sur laquelle des membres d'espèces différentes se puissent accorder, les fonctionnaires chargés de l'enseignement doivent s'inspirer du salut publique. Ce n'est pas une vérité nationale, celle qui dénationalise les cerveaux.

Leurs Figures presents motifs from Pascal which play a significant part in the development. Saint-Phlin who had earlier returned to the land is now completely "enraciné" again. He is striving to realize in life the thesis he had derived from Pascal in *Les Déracinés.* Speaking of Suret-Lefort, now grown into a second but more opportunistic Bouteiller, he declares:

> Ce brave Suret-Lefort ne distingue pas qu'il y a des vérités lorraines, des vérités provençales, des vérités bretonnes dont l'accord ménagé par les siècles constitue ce qui . . . est vrai en France. . . . Contre toutes les singularités qu'on lui propose, qui peuvent être des vérités ailleurs et qui par là sont soutenables dans l'abstrait, il ne se ménage point de refuge dans son innéité.

Assuming the role of *raisonneur,* Saint-Phlin weaves the Pascalian theme into the fabric of Barrès's deterministic philosophy of "la Terre et les Morts."

Saint-Phlin cites Mme. Périer's *Vie de Pascal* on reproaching the Boulangist Sturel for his ambitions. . . . Roemerspacher is made to voice the same criticism.

> Le voilà toujours ton individualisme. Tu veux qui ton sentiment du juste vaille contre la paix

de la société. Tu es en rébellion contre la loi. Que ces parlementaires soient des voleurs et des êtres bas, . . . cela n'est point douteux. Mais ils sont la force, et la société est intéressée à ne pas disjoindre d'eux l'idée de justice, tant qu'elle n'a pas un autre personnel aussi fort, entre les mains de qui transporter la justice.

This counsel taken from Pascal is one of prudence in tactics, not a counsel of resignation. Roemerspacher thus expresses his author's apprehension that the ideal of justice might inspire a revolt more fundamental than that against parliamentarism sought by Boulanger and Déroulède. This is evident in Sturel's attitude toward the anarchist Fanfournot:

> Fanfournot prit la mine la plus fière et la plus méprisante. Mais précisément cette fierté, ce mépris, quelle basse confiance en soi! Sturel se répentit d'avoir contribué à exalter chez cet enfant le sentiment de la justice.

The writing of the trilogy of "national energy" overlapped the Dreyfus Case. In the conflict between traditionalism and democracy which had its focus in the *Affaire,* we might expect to see some utilization of Pascal's aphorisms on justice. Men like Maurras and Bourget, for example, drew what support they could from Goethe: "Better an injustice than disorder." In his *Morale de Nietzsche,* Pierre Lasserre called this more recent thinker into service against the belief in abstract justice. Barrès's part in the anti-Dreyfusard polemic owed something not only to Pascal's critique of justice but also the Pascalian critique of the intellect. The provenience of the concept of the relativity of justice is, to be sure, too complex to be explained only in terms of Pascal. Nevertheless the prestige and influence of Pascal were of major importance in the case of Barrès. He envisaged Pascal as an ally against the "intellectuels" like Zola whose slogan was justice. He echoed the observations on the middle level between "ignorance naturelle" and "ignorance savante:" "Une demi-culture détruit l'instinct sans lui substituer une conscience." It is such considerations which he had in mind when he wrote: "Pascal connaît toutes nos difficultes (religieuses, sociales, . . .), et il les tranche contre l'intellectuel par le traditionnalisme, mais en s'assurant l'assentiment du 'digne' intellectuel."

Even when the Dreyfus Case was becoming past history, Barrès continued to ply the critical weapons of the political "realist" against abstract justice. Assailing the "revolutionary religion" of socialism and its aim of establishing a heaven of justice on earth, he made common cause with Maurras with his statement: "J'aime dans la religion catholique une religion qui accepte 'qui ne va pas jusqu' au bout de la justice'." The affinity with the political ideas of Pascal is clear. Yet one salient point of difference remained. Pascal conceived of the world as corrupt, of reason as tangled in paradox, of man as torn by contradictions. This was the world to which Hobbes' *homo homini lupus* applied. But he was not, like Hobbes or Machiavelli, satisfied to draft a scheme of *Realpolitik.* His *Apologie* was intended to prove that redemption could only be found in Christian faith,—and that it had to be found. Barrès, on the other hand, does not reveal this need for redemption.

The corollary to Pascal's discussion on Force and Justice was that man cannot find justice in this world. Pascal's dilemma was for Barrès not so much a spur to seek justice in another world, as it was a weapon against those who looked for it in this one.

But Barrès, who as Boulangist had called for justice, and as anti-Dreyfusard had denied it, was to change his attitude once more. Years afterward, he was to invoke Pascal again. But now, in his endeavor to reconcile all Frenchmen in the "Union Sacrée," he no longer attacked justice as a Utopian abstraction, as he did when it was the *mot d'ordre* of his political opponents, but exalted it as an ideal uncorroded by the acids of relativism and untarnished by partisanship. "Pascal a donné sa loi à la pensée française: 'La force sans la justice est tyrannique. Que ce qui est fort soit juste'." He was abandoning the deeper meaning of Pascal, just as his celebration of the feudalist maxim: "Le propre de la puissance est de protéger," involved slurring over the more penetrating theses on egoism and concupiscence.

Barrès was tempted by the project of setting Pascal in the frame of "nationalist determinism." "En Pascal, la race auvergnate se pense." This is in harmony with the theory of history of *Scènes et doctrines du nationalisme.* The notion of truth bounded by racial frontiers appears in the *Voyage de Sparte.* He thought the relativists Renan and Taine inconsistent in celebrating the universality of Greek culture. The Acropolis left Barrès more convinced of his own particularity as a Frenchman and Lorrainer: "Je crois sentir que l'interprétation classique ne pourra pas être la mienne. A mon avis, Pallas Athéné n'est pas la raison universelle, mais une raison municipale, en opposition avec tous les peuples. . . ." He liked to think of Pascal as representing French culture in contradistinction to the Hellenic:

> Ce grand art de l'Acropole soulève les plus graves problèmes intellectuels; il nous fournit d'admirables représentations d'une verité qui était efficace au cinquième siècle et qui est encore une des deux grandes vérités humaines. Cependant le Parthénon n'éveille pas en moi une musique indéfinie comme fait, par exemple, un Pascal. . . . Entre le Parthénon et nous, il y a dixneur siècles de christianisme. J'ai dans le sang un idéal différent et même ennemi.

He was attracted by the fancy that some deep racial and regional bond existed between Pascal and himself. Those like Brunschvieg who do not spring from the racial and religious ground common to Pascal and Barrès narrowly miss being excluded from the circle of genuine "pascalisants." Even Pascal the inventor provides a theme for nationalist speculation: He was a practical genius, "qui ne se perd pas en théories à l'allemande."

Pascal's thoughts on *members* offered Barrès a parallel for his progression from the anarchistic cult of the self to the community of Lorraine and France:

> Le membre séparé, . . . croit être un tout, et ne se voyant point de corps dont il dépend, il croit ne dépendre que de soi, et veut se faire centre et corps lui-même. Mais n'ayant point en soi de

principe de vie, il ne fait que s'égarer. . . . Enfin, quand il vient à se connaître, il est comme revenu chez soi.

But Barrès diverted the application from the community of "members of Christ" to membership in a deified national group:

> L'homme monstre et chaos, l'homme incapable de connaître la vérité par suite de sa corruption et de sa décomposition morale, . . . je lui propose la révélation lorraine. . . .

He tried to raise this "revelation" to the level of the reasons of the heart. He found, as he thought, the same immediacy and self-evident character in love of country and respect for family which Pascal found in religion and in the three dimensions of space. The vogue being enjoyed by the irrationalism and worship of intuition led by Bergson doubtless made this kind of confusion easier for him, a confusion of the sanctions of custom with the reasons of the heart. He supposed that Pascal's self-analysis was like his own culture of the self, which had become a search for the traditional heritage of creed and custom he had been brought up in. But Pascal was seeking a religious truth which had to be absolute and universal. Barrès, on the other hand, thought that *sensibilité,* which he hardly distinguished from intuition, varies from race to race. Pascal's conception of the reasons of the heart was not, in fact, a point that he grasped even to his own satisfaction. (pp. 807-15)

To impose order and meaning on . . . chaos, he looked to nationalism: "La France a construit une tradition qu'il faut maintenir et développer, et ce soin suffirait presque à donner un sens à notre activité. . . ." Pascal would undoubtedly have regarded the nationalist discipline as a form of *divertissement* which evades the dilemma without resolving it.

Religion.

During the decade following the Dreyfus Case, the *Cahiers* show how Barrès's reflections revolved around the notion of Pascal as an exemplar of western thought. As he approached the time when he was to write: "Je sens que je glisse du nationalisme au catholicisme," there was a corresponding change in the themes which Pascal suggested to him. Now he contemplated Pascal as a high representative of the occidental world, an anti-pantheist standing against those, like Nietzsche, who are resigned to dissolution of the human personality in death. Dom Pastourel encouraged Barrès to think of himself in the lineage of Pascal, as upholding a truly French and Catholic conception of the absolute value of the personality. Inspired by Pastourel to make a formulation which he repeated without substantially enriching it, he did not present a convincing embodiment of it in the writings cited in this connection: **"La Mort de Venise", "Les Amitiés françaises", "Le 2 novembre en Lorraine."** Pascal's superiority to Nietzsche consists, he thought, in these points: "Le héros tel que le conçoit Nietzsche est antipathique, *inhumain*. En outre, ce héros, si fort qu'il affirme sa personnalité, accepte de s'anéantir, de disparaître, de se dissoudre dans la grande nature." Yet Barrès himself drew more consolation from the "immortality" of race than he seems to have derived from a belief in personal survival.

Where the author does not entangle his discussion in nebulous considerations of racial or national *Weltanschauungen,* his conception of Pascal has more validity. Yet one remains unconvinced by assertions of some writers that his meditations brought him close to the height of religious feeling attained by Pascal. His notion that he might become a convert, "peut-être par la crise Pascal" suggests how far he actually was from conversion. It is significant that whereas the first decade of the century saw several writers predict it, François Mauriac, after two decades, could think that only his death prevented him from reaching this consummation. From 1897 when he wrote that his generation was in accord with Pascal's skepticism, through 1904 when he defined his religion as that of a "catholique-athée," to 1911 when he declared that he could acknowledge the truth of religion without being able to live in accordance with it, the development is clearly toward a more and more complete acceptance.

J. S. McClelland on the relativity of moral standards in Barrès:

What is right [for Bouteiller, the esteemed teacher in "Le culte du moi"] is a universal moral standard, rationally determinable. Barrès sets his face against this. There is no 'right', only a relative 'right'. What I do is not subject to a self-consciously deduced system of moral precept. Such a conceit is not only erroneous but absurd. Thought is not free, but a result of a particular kind of determinism. This determinism is national. Each nation has a particular past and a particular present. The nation is real, and is to be found in those provincial graveyards which exerted such an unhealthy fascination on Barrès. Communion with your dead ancestors is as near to a feeling for the true France as you can possibly get. Judgment, moral or political, lies close to such a feeling. One does not ask whether a particular action, say the breaking of Dreyfus, is right. That for Barrès has literally no meaning. How can it have when there is no universal moral standard by which a proposition could be judged true or false? The question to be asked must be, "In what degree is such an action in accordance with the interests and wishes of France?" This question is anti-rational.

J. S. McClelland, in The French Right (from De Maistre to Maurras), *Harper & Row, Publishers, New York, 1970.*

In this development, the rôle of Pascal is inseparably intertwined, but often it seems to be his prestige, rather than his ideas *per se,* which impressed Barrès. His *ignoramus* was uttered with a melancholy resignation quite different from the spirit of Pascal. And it is romantic melancholy which dominates his variations on the theme of the personality "face to face with the infinite." "Quand le rossignol prélude," we read in *La Colline inspirée,* "on n'entend pas . . . un chant, mais une immense espérance. . . . Et puis soudain, ce grand sentiment, cette immortelle espérance, voilà qu'ils sont engloutis dans la mort . . . une sensation indéfinissable d'angoisse nous remplit. . . . Regarde là-haut les étoiles avec qui nous

sommes accordés: l'infini les sépare de notre destin." Lacking in this passage is that vertiginous sense of the abyss which is suggested in the apostrophe to the funeral bell in **"Les Amitiés françaises":** "Ne te tais pas, glas de terreur! Après toi commencera l'affreux silence. . . . Sur cette mer d'anéantissement, tout le salut, c'est un petit garçon, s'il porte dans son coeur l'essentiel que je lui propose." This product of his nationalist phase shows him approaching Pascal's sense of the transiency of life in a way he was never to do again: " . . . cependant que je mesure le néant de mes possessions, je me brûle des feux où je sais ne pouvoir atteindre." Later the author himself set the question of his affinity with Pascal in broader perspective:

> Serait-il vrai que dans ma vie ce que je préfère, c'est ma tombe. Je ne travaille que pour la construire. . . . Serait-ce pour ne pas me dissoudre. Serait-ce que je m'accorde avec le texte de Pascal: 'C'est une chose horrible de sentir s'écouler tout ce qu'on possède.' Vue imparfaite. Je vis pour construire mon poème de la vie, une vue chaque jour plus complète, plus riche de l'univers.

Of the numerous figures in Barrès's Pantheon, two— Goethe and Pascal—are given special places of honor:

> Ce sont deux adversaires ou plus exactement guidés par eux nous connaissons tout le terrain sur lequel les gens de notre race peuvent bâtir, nous connaissons notre conscience entière. . . . Goethe s'éloigne de Pascal jusqu'à paraître l'ennemi de la Croix. Mais par ailleurs il glorifie la Croix. . . .

Despite Pastourel, one must agree that Goethe prevailed over Pascal in certain important respects. Pantheism, so alien to Pascal, is indicated in Barrès's words on Goethe: "Dieu nous parle par cette fleur, par ce papillon." And Barrès's choice of self-development, rather than self-abnegation, is asserted in the passage above, on his "poem of life." He venerated Pascal, but he imitated Goethe. As he wrote of the former: "On veille non loin de lui, sans oser l'approcher, sur une sorte de Mont des Oliviers."

L'Angoisse de Pascal, in which this antithesis is developed, presents Pascal as one who rejected the blandishments of pleasure and facility: "Il est le modèle achevé de ceux qui résistent à tous les assuts par lesquels la nature, avant de nous anéantir, essaye, chaque jour, de nous entamer." He strove to withstand the universal flux: "Il veut . . . résister à l'univers, ne pas se dissoudre, durer." We are reminded of Astiné Aravian's debilitating influence on Sturel in *Les Déracinés.* Years later, the author is to offer a repetition of this latter theme in *Un Jardin sur l'Oronte.* But Pascal's asceticism went beyond the rejection of pleasure: "Pour un Goethe, un homme peut se perfectionner en jouissant de tout ce qu'il y a de noble dans la vie. Pour un Pascal, non." It is the drama of Pascal's repudiation of these more elevated values, science and the God of the philosophers, which is Barrès's main concern in *L'Angoisse de Pascal.*

Barrès finds that the very rigor and intensity of thought which Pascal applied to insoluble problems of human destiny contributed to his suffering . . . He examines Pascal's life in the light of the *pensée:* " . . . la maladie principale de l'homme est la curiosité inquiète des choses qu'il ne peut savoir." He dwells on the practicality of Pascal's genius which is in such strong contrast to the abstract intellectualism that Barrès opposed. "Pour lui rien ne demeure un problème abstrait et chacune de ses songeries tourne droit sur une réalité. Que sera-ce donc s'il aborde une médiation qui intéresse notre salut? A la poursuite de la vérité suprême, c'est un ébranlement de tout son être." Disillusioned with physical science and mathematics, Pascal had renounced these studies which taught him nothing about man. Barrès is struck by the dramatic aspect of that moment discussed in the **Cahiers:** " . . . à un instant il a sacrifié sa préoccupation principale, la scientifique que je ne puis pas apprécier . . . à das pensées religieuses que je ne puis pas repenser." He reduces Pascal's problem to a purely internal and individual one. Denying with justification that lack of money or rank was behind Pascal's crisis, he overlooks the deeper connection with the state of society which the aphorisms on justice disclose. His study of the *mémorial* brings out its crucial importance in the life of Pascal:

> Ce papier c'est évidemment l'attestation de la lumière que Pascal a reçue, le mémorial de la réponse accordée à son cri d'angoisse, le bulletin de sa victoire sur les ténèbres, son action de grâce et son acte de ferme propos.

His effort to penetrate the secret of religious inspiration was continued in **La Colline inspirée, Une Enquête aux Pays du Levant, Les Enfances Pascal,** and **Le Mystère en pleine lumière.** There were basic contradictions in his utilization of Pascal. He recognized Pascal to be a better guide than Chateaubriand, yet his appreciation of religion, like that of Chateaubriand, tends to be essentially esthetic, where it is not political like that of Joseph de Maistre. At one time he invoked Pascal's aid in a discussion with his Rosicrucian friend Stanislas de Guaita . . . In opposing the misty occultism of de Guaita, he was able to see that Pascal was far from repudiating reason and analysis. Yet he was later to cite Pascal on belief in sorcerors, gleaning encouragement for the vagrant religiosity which imbues his pieces on Joan of Arc and the Sibyl of Auxerre, [in **Le Mystère en pleine lumière**] as well as the cult of the sacred hill in his novel on the Baillards. A page in the **Cahiers** shows him going even farther toward making of Pascal an apostle of "free inspiration" and of the cultivation of religious emotions in those areas of the spirit left "fallow" by conventional religion. The controversy of the Jansenists with institutional Catholicism was not entirely unconnected in his mind with the struggle of the Baillards:

> La sensation de vertige devant un insondable abîme;—ces instants de connaissance par l'émotion, ces pages de Pascal toutes tremblantes de l'émotion d'une vue sur l'infini— . . . a toujours eu à lutter contre les gouvernements et les églises. . . . Les églises, parce qu'elles sont malgré tout des institutions d'un caractère temporel et social, doivent condamner et anathématiser l'inspiration libre, la vue directe des choses par l'esprit.

The contrast between the two attitudes is expressed in the dialogue between the Meadow and the Chapel, symbols, respectively, of religious enthusiasm and discipline. But he never clearly formulated the relation of Pascal to the problem. The advocate of social conformity that he saw in Pascal was at the same time almost a dissident in religion. Was he really a Jansenist at heart? Was he an individualist in religion? Barrès's answers to such questions vary without probing deeply into the subject.

The difference is great between the religious inspiration of Leopold Baillard and that of the writer of the *Pensées.* The spaces of the world were not silent for the Baillards, but echoed with the voices of meadow and hill. A romantic pantheism is evident in Barrès which sets him apart from Pascal. He found a subjective validity in a variety of religions where Pascal had been passionately concerned with establishing objective validity for one. In this respect **Le Mystère en pleine lumière** continues **La Colline inspirée,** with exotic elements suggested by his **Enquête aux pays du Levant.** His interest in the varieties of religious experience encompasses nymph, sibyl, and priestess alike; he does not even scorn the spiritualist, despite his reply to Stanislas de Guaita.

He writes of the Sibyl of Auxerre: "Sa seule présence aiderait-elle à résoudre le mystérieux problème de l'inspiration, le problème des rapports de certains êtres avec l'Esprit." He explains her powers in terms of the intuition of Pascal: " . . . elle rompt les barrières des temps et de l'espace, et par intuition connaît ce que ses sens et sa raison ignorent." But though his avowed intention is to elucidate these mysteries, his approach is impressionistic rather than critical. The essay **"Le Testament d'Eugène Delacroix"** deals with artistic inspiration in much the same way. The vague contours of his thought provide little distinction between mysticism and art. Barrès's earlier dilettantism is not entirely left behind in the period which produced **Un Jardin sur l'Oronte** and **Le Mystère en pleine Lumière.** Religious emotions play a more dominant rôle, but the same love of emotion for its own sake is in evidence.

In his preoccupation with the celestial minute which cannot be perpetuated, one may see a juncture of the contrasting influences of Goethe and Pascal. The vanity of this world did not dispose him to reject it, but rather to work the more ardently on his own monument. It can be added, however, that Pascalian asceticism might have assumed a greater importance in his "poem of life," had he lived longer. Certainly he seemed more interested in the sanctity of Pascal, becoming, indeed, an advocate of his canonization. **Le Pauvre de Monsieur Pascal** had long been developing in his mind. (pp. 815-22)

Les Enfances Pascal provides a summation of his characteristic doctrines which Barrès is happy to illustrate with one of the leading figures of his Pantheon. Like his study of Claude Lorrain, it is an attempt to describe the native ground in which his genius grew. "Pascal serait-il une pierre noire tombée du ciel . . . ? Non, c'est un quartier de nos basaltes d'Auvergne." He dwells on the affinities between Blaise and his father and sister: "Ces Pascal sont des gens chez qui la vie intellectuelle et la vie sensible concourent à une même exaltation." The lecture brings together the polemics of the Dreyfus period. **"La Terre et les Morts,"** and the main topic of *Le Mystère en pleine lumière:*

> Cette grande figure de Pascal, . . . peut encore nous apprendre ce que c'est que le véritable individualisme, d'autant plus fort, solide et sûr que nous tâchons de ramener à la surface de notre être, pour les enflammer au feu mystérieux que le ciel nous prête, les sentiments accumulés dans les longues préparations de notre race.

The passage closes with the Barrésien conclusion that brings us back to the thesis of **"Le 2 novembre en Lorraine"**:" . . . ce coeur . . . est antérieur à notre existence individuelle. C'est un coeur hérité, un coeur filial."

In the continual meditation on French writers, Pascal, Rousseau, Hugo, Taine, Renan, which his whole work reveals and which his *Cahiers* demonstrate, it is perhaps Pascal more than any other whose thought eluded his grasp, and yet it is Pascal who received his most steady and sincere veneration. He made a remark in the *Cahiers* more significant than he may have realized: "Qui n'a rêve dans les marges de Pascal? Il y convient." Much of his reflection on Pascal could be called marginal. In his movement from the *Culte du Moi* through nationalism and to Catholicism, he considered that Pascal continued to be his guide. He had sought in Pascal a forerunner of nationalism, and he did find in him a compound of individualism and traditionalism to support these two tendencies in himself. His attempt to make Pascal the one representative thinker of the "Western World" involved many ambiguities which were no doubt inevitable, both because of his own fascination with the "East" and because the issue he raised between East and West was a false one. He read in Pascal's analysis of custom as second nature, with nature as perhaps only "une première coutume," a justification for traditions *per se.* But Pascal's position was not so simple, for he had also written: " 'C'est parce que vous y êtes né,' dira-t-on. Tant s'en faut; je me roidis contre, pour cette raison-là même, de peur que cette prévention ne me suborne." It was over-simplification, too, which made it possible for Barrès to include among the "raisons du coeur," nationalist sentiment and filial piety. His interpretation of Pascal exaggerated instinct at the expense of reason, overlooking the dialectic character of his thought on reason and the heart, blurring the complexity of his insights. Thus his conception of Pascal involved distortions which reflected inadequacies and excesses in his own philosophy and attitudes. (pp. 822-23)

> *Reino Virtanen, "Barrès and Pascal," in* PMLA, *Vol. LXII, No. 3, September, 1947, pp. 802-23.*

André Gide   (essay date 1959)

[*Gide is one of France's most influential thinkers and writers of the twentieth century. In the following excerpt from articles originally published in the journal* L'ermitage *in 1897 and 1903, Gide vehemently opposes the mystical regionalism of Barrès, maintaining that a displacement from one's native soil (Barrès's "uprootedness") can be a strengthening experience. In his fiction*

and criticism, Gide stressed autobiographical honesty, unity of subject and style, modern experimental techniques, and sincere confrontation of moral issues. He is consequently disturbed by an alleged sophistry that he detects in Barrès's writing.]

[It] was while traveling that I read your book [*Les Déracines*]. It is not surprising, then, if to my great admiration I am impelled to join some criticism: forgive me this preamble; it exists only to show how obviously I am designated to be your critic, for those designated to praise you are legion.

Yet I should like to begin by saying how much I admire your book. It is true that your earlier works gave us reason to expect from you the most exquisite subtleties, and many pages dated from Spain or Italy were hardly inferior to the marvelous narrative of Mme Aravian; we knew the sharpness of your eye, the clarity of your judgments, your valor, your prudence, the excellence of your advice. Despite all that, *Les Déracinés* surprised even your warmest admirers; there is maintained untroubled within it (if perhaps not sufficiently concentrated) so serious a work, so authoritative an assertion, that respect for you follows as a matter of course, and even your most stubborn opponents are now compelled to esteem you. Under names as frightful as those of *L'Education sentimentale,* you have created types; they are painful, but they are unforgettable. You have done more; you have grouped them, graded them, established their hierarchy, or, even better, you have shown the inevitability of this hierarchy, as a professor of physics demonstrates the "vase of the four elements." The establishment of the newspaper, its harsh existence, the manner in which Sturel makes his way, all that, weighty, is of a remarkable consistency, a complete absence of fantasy. Why did you feel the need of swelling inartistically this fine plan with an electoral thesis, certainly interesting in itself (quite apart from its rightness or wrongness), but which stiffens almost all the pages and drags upon the slightest action? If you haggle over every point, and by dint of argument, attach it to your general thesis, can it be that these events were not sufficiently eloquent in themselves? Can it be that you feared others might not think of them all that you think; can it be, perhaps, that had you left the reader's mind free, he would have reached a different conclusion? And the result of your oratorical skill is that the events you recount, after you have spoken about them, seem, taken outside the book, less eloquent than you yourself were, or are less persuasive than you would wish them. For after all, Suret-Lefort, Renaudin, Sturel, Roemerspacher [the protagonists of Barrès's novel] are successful; if he had more money, it is likely that Racadot would succeed, too. Besides I grant that, *if* Racadot had never left Lorraine, he would never have killed; but then he would no longer interest me at all. While, thanks to the strange circumstances which force him into a corner, it is upon him, you know, that the dramatic interest of the book is focused; so that your book, concerned also with psychological truth, as though despite you, seems to prove nothing so much as this: "In a situation in which it often finds itself and which for many is the same, the organism acts in a banal way; in a situation which is presented to it for the first time, it will give proof of originality, if it cannot avoid doing so." *Uprooting constraining Racadot to originality:* it might be said, half-seriously, that this is the subject of your book.

For your insistent assertion inspires in us the desire to contradict, the desire to assert this: uprooting can be a school of virtue. It is only after a significant increase in external novelty than an organism, in order to lessen its suffering, is provoked into discovering an appropriate modification permitting a more assured assimilation. (pp. 75-7)

Education, displacement, uprooting—they should be utilized according to the strength of the individual. There is danger as soon as there is no longer benefit; and *Les Déracinés* shows us that the weak succumb in the process. But to preserve the weak from harm, are we to close our eyes to the gain for the strong? And it is not shown in *Les Déracinés* that the strong are strengthened by uprooting, or at least it is shown only involuntarily.

For this dilemma confronted you then: either to favor your thesis and show the danger of uprooting, to depict characters so weak and mediocre that we should have exclaimed: good riddance; or to favor the novel, to depict characters strong enough not to suffer from a new situation, characters important enough to invalidate your thesis. (pp. 79-80)

What is certain is that if the seven Lorrainers whose story you tell had not come to Paris you would not have written *Les Déracinés;* you would not have written this book if you yourself had not come to Paris. And that would have been most regrettable, for because of its very preoccupations, this weighty book of an excessive but admirable tension restores to their mediocre place very many unimportant novels with which, for lack of anything better, we were in danger of concerning ourselves. (pp. 80-1)

. . . . .

Maurice Barrès

My dear Angèle:

On the appearance of Thibaudet's book on Maurice Barrès, I bring out for you, from the bottom of a drawer, these few notes made before the war. Most of them are very old (I trust you will not find them dated). I wrote each following a reading—shortly after the publication of the book in question.

Discours à L'Académie

"If these books have any value, it is due to their logic, to the consistency of thought that for five years I have maintained in them. As for the art that readers or indulgent critics find therein, that is but a passing fad" (Barrès, letter to *La Plume*, 1 April 1891).

On the contrary, the "passing fad" is your opinions, your ideas. Moreover, what you call here your "logic" seems to me most often only a clinging to theories contradicted by the logic of God or, if you prefer, the logic of "natural history." And what we like best in you are those inconsistencies in which the man of instinct steps ahead of the dogmatist and inspires in you, a nationalist, the most exquisite

praise for Heredia, Chénier, and Moréas, your three best-loved poets: a Cuban and two Greeks. . . . And it is because of this art, which fortunately you repudiate only verbally, that your best writing will outlive your theories.

Les Déracinés

Could Barrès really have believed, could he have supposed for a moment, that his theories apparently so opportune (and I take the word in its most urgent sense), so therapeutic for our ruined country, so calculated to galvanize the middling intelligences of numerous elderly adolescents, would still find, these theories of his, an audience for as much as thirty years? And does he not understand that his theories atrophy in the very act of restoring vigor to France? For it is not appropriate to a healthy people, or to a robust mind, to remain with eyes rooted to the ground, intent only on seeing tombs there; it may well be, and I want to so believe, that the medicine will save the country; but, once saved, the country will be revolted by it.

Les Amitiés Françaises

Fortunately for him, in his books Barrès does not supply answers as much as others do for him. The unresolved question persists in his writings, and it is the best thing in them. Woe unto works that draw conclusions; they first satisfy the public most, but after twenty years the conclusion crushes the book.

There are "circumstantial thoughts" that are the equivalent of "circumstantial laws." Rousseau's writings owed their initial success neither to their style, nor to their essential pathos, nor to their psychological novelty, but precisely to what was most specious and false in their theories: excellence of the instinct, return to nature, superiority of Italian music, etc., and even to certain practical recommendations (nursing of children by the mothers, etc.), which the dullest minds could grasp readily. I sense in Barrès's books, alongside a most noble will and a keen common sense, a great clutter of sophistries. For twenty readers capable of appreciating the real qualities of the writer, there are a hundred or a thousand capable of taking his sophistries for truths; Barrès owes the major part of his fame today to these very sophistries and not to the great talent that will permit his survival.

He maintains that the animal or the plant flourishes nowhere so well as in its place of origin; that may appear "logical," but it is false; as it is false to say, conversely, that on each soil must flourish especially the species native to that soil.

Bérénice "who died through having placed her confidence in the adversary . . ." Unquestionably that should have been the *subject* of the book; but it is just *this* that the book does not demonstrate.

Would it not also have been interesting—indispensable, indeed, to destroy the doctrine of a Bouteiller—that the doctrine ("to act in such a way, always, that I can wish my action to serve as a universal rule") be the direct cause of his ruin? Nothing of the sort. On the contrary, it is following an infraction of this rule of conduct that Bouteiller is disgraced and perishes. (pp. 212-14)

[*Scènes et Doctrines du Nationalisme*]

Barrès makes the basis of his ethics what the great Arnauld notes and deplores; Barrès thinks that we must not seek to judge things by what they are in themselves, indeed, that we cannot judge them except in their relation to us. From that point to confusing the concept of truth and the concept of usefulness is but a step—a step that expediency readily takes—and the whole reasoning is falsified.

In the interest of greater usefulness Barrès depicts as Kantian and German, or Protestant and un-French, and consequently to be shunned, a form of thought that is properly Jansenist and on the contrary more profoundly French than the Jesuitical and Barrèsian form, to which it has always been opposed.

Au Service de L'Allemagne

The gesture that supports his writings is a defensive one and has no reason for existence except before the enemy. Once the danger is gone I doubt that our successors will understand the eloquence of the gesture. His emphases and repetitions will weary as soon as they are no longer timely. Even *Au Service de l'Allemagne,* an excellent little book, but of a very restricted interest, will be less interesting than, say, the narrative of Astiné Aravian, *La Mort de Venise, Les Deux Femmes du bourgeois de Bruges,* or *L'Amateur d'âmes*—these will doubtless inspire the thought that of all the "dissolvent" minds against which Barrès protests he would have been the best and most subtle, had he been more natural.

Pascal

Barrès will perhaps some day become a Catholic; I came close to writing: Barrès will surely become a Catholic; but there is no fear that he will ever turn to Jansenism. I grant that the figure of Pascal impresses him; but, by temperament, he remains nonetheless closer to Sanchez and Loyola. At the very beginning of his lecture (on Pascal) a word, an exclamation, alerts us: "Gentlemen, our object is to place you on Pascal's path, to permit you, not to accompany him (Good Heavens, that is not our concern) . . ." (pp. 215-16)

Anguish, true anguish; Pascal, the true Pascal—the anguish of Pascal: that is no subject for a fashionable lecture. Barrès is aware of that: "Here is a state of mind," he says speaking of *the state of mind* of Pascal, "of which you and I, gentlemen, can have no exact sense." And we share Barrès's awareness.

L'Appel au Soldat

Barrès furnishes a criterion, a new yardstick with which to measure minds and things of the mind. Hence the grati-

tude of young minds whose indolence he thus encourages. One judges by . . . or according to . . . such and such is recognized as good or bad, because . . . Barrès does not so much appeal to reason as to principles; the principles are there so that reason may be idle. It is forgotten that the originator sought the principles to aid in the development of his personality; the particular situation that brought them forth is forgotten; at a distance, they are attributed an absolute quality. (pp. 216-17)

> *André Gide, "The Barrès Problem" and "Notes to Angèle" in his* Pretext: Reflections on Literature and Morality, *edited by Justin O'Brien, Meridian Books, Inc., 1959, pp. 74-87, 194-217.*

Dennis J. Fletcher   (essay date 1968)

[*As the preeminent writer and thinker of the French left in the twentieth century, Jean-Paul Sartre was a scathing critic of what he considered to be Barrès's reactionary patriotism. In the following excerpt, Fletcher argues that Sartre's grim image of a denatured chestnut tree in his novel* Le nausée *is the philosopher's means of mocking Barrès's own image of the plane-tree as a symbol of beauty and power in* Les déracinés.]

One of the elements of Sartre's first novel *La Nausée* which contributes towards its predominantly destructive tone is the author's determined attempt to puncture what he obviously considers the inflated reputations of a number of well-established novelists. This attack upon the positions of certain writers entrenched in popular favour forms part of a larger campaign against the conventions and values of respectable bourgeois society which is waged throughout the novel, and it has not altogether escaped critical attention. Much of this attention, however, has been devoted to what can only be described as oblique attempts at undermining the basis of a literary reputation whilst more obvious examples of direct assault upon a selected target have been neglected. Perhaps the most explicit instance of an object of Sartre's antipathy being lampooned in this way is the treatment accorded in the novel to Maurice Barrès. Barrès more than once receives dishonourable mention and can justly be considered as one of the more prominent *bêtes noires* in the Sartrean bestiary.

The entry in Antoine Roquentin's diary for *mardi gras* begins quite arrestingly: "J'ai fessé Maurice Barrès." What follows is an account of a dream in which the violence perpetually simmering in Roquentin's subconscious has erupted at the expense of Barrès, who is subjected by him and two other soldiers to the indignity of being debagged, flagellated and having the image of his fellow right-wing Nationalist Paul Déroulède imprinted on his posterior in violet petals. This picturesque detail adequately expresses the force of Roquentin's loathing of jingoistic patriotism. Another detail, the red cardinal's robe which comes to light with surrealistic plausibility in the debagging process, indicates that respect for traditional values fostered by the Catholic Church which was another feature of Barrès' nationalism calculated to inspire disgust in the violently anti-social anti-hero of *La Nausée.*

Some of Sartre's most savage thrusts at the provincial bourgeoisie are made when Roquentin visits the municipal art-gallery, where the assembled host of portraits of past leaders of Bouville society offers abundant material for his ruminations upon the nauseating character of the mentality of the French middle-classes. After an instructive Saturday afternoon spent in the company of *les chefs,* infallible instruments of a supposedly divine will to impose authority and order upon society, imperturbable in their consciousness of their God-given right to govern, impermeable to the doubts and anxieties felt by those outside their own self-constituted élite, Roquentin takes his leave of them: "Adieu beaux lis tout en finesse dans vos petits sanctuaires peints, adieu beaux lis, notre orgueil et notre raison d'être. Adieu. Salauds." Among the *salauds* who had particularly captured his attention was Olivier Blévigne, about whom we are told that "son visage olivâtre ressemblait un peu à celui de Maurice Barrès." Sartre does not confine himself to this well-worn technique of implicit moral denigration through the unflattering description of physical characteristics to besmirch Barrès. We are told specifically that he and his fellow-*député* Blévigne belonged to the same political group in the Palais-Bourbon. Blévigne lacked the master's blandness, however: ". . . le député de Bouville n'avait pas la nonchalance du Président de la ligue des Patriotes." Sartre, in fact, seems to be presenting Barrès as a sort of super-*salaud*. Another erstwhile worthy of Bouville, Jean Pacôme, is shown by the portraitist standing before a book-case; this leads Roquentin to speculate upon his *maîtres à penser,* among whom he includes Bourget and Barrès. Both of these writers had, in fact, been exercised by the problem of the writer's role as an educator of his readers (especially the younger ones) and had portrayed the master-disciple relationship in their works. This idea of the writer as a *directeur de conscience* for young people is repugnant to Sartre, who has been at pains to avoid having this role thrust upon him. This aversion is evident in the devastatingly ironical portrait of Rémy Parrotin, professor at the *École de Médecine de Paris.* Parrotin (*le Maître, le Patron*) had won himself a reputation for cooling the ardour of rebellious young spirits and guiding the steps of those who were going astray back into the fold of the socially-acquiescent by dint of long and understanding chats. . . . Parrotin's influence, devoid of socially disruptive effects, cannot be compared, therefore, with that exercised by the philosopher Adrien Sixte upon the eponymous hero of Bourget's *Le Disciple.* It does, however, find a fairly close parallel in Barrès' novel **Les Déracinés,** where the evolution of one of the young, uprooted Lorrainers, Roemerspacher, is influenced decisively by an encounter with the philosopher Hippolyte Taine (who was taken by many, incidentally, to have been the model for Bourget's Adrien Sixte)

The arguments which Taine puts forward in the homily which he addresses to Roemerspacher are illustrated by extensive reference to a plane-tree which has, we are told, become charged with symbolical significance for the philosopher and provides him with a constant source of comforting analogies with human life. It is interesting to note that "l'arbre de M. Taine" (as the chapter dealing with Roemerspacher's interview is entitled) plays roughly the same rôle in the young *déraciné*'s spiritual and intellectual evolution as the chestnut-tree in *La Nausée* which provides the vehicle for the revelation experienced by Roquentin in the park at Bouville, which convinces him of the utter contingency of existence and shows him that in artistic creation lies the only forlorn hope of transcending the gratuitousness of life. (pp. 330-32)

A more detailed examination of **L'Arbre de M. Taine** and the crucial episode of *le marronier* in *La Nausée* will bring to light the way in which Sartre has written (whether deliberately or fortuitously is a matter for conjecture) what could almost be taken as the *contre-partie* of Barrès' chapter in **Les Déracinés.**

Sartre, in the episode in the park (as elsewhere), is concerned with debunking all "poetic" representations of nature, and especially those which exalt that *élan vital* which, it is claimed, manifests itself particularly in the spring-time. Roquentin is not touched by the vernal aspect of things; his reaction is one of disgust: "Ces arbres, ces grands corps gauches . . . Je me mis à rire parce que je pensais tout d'un coup aux printemps formidables qu'on décrit dans les livres, pleins de craquements, d'éclatements, d'éclosions géantes. Il y avait des imbéciles qui venaient vous parler de volonté, de puissance et de lutte pour la vie. Ils n'avaient donc jamais regardé une bête ni un arbre? Ce platane avec ses plaques de pelade, ce chêne à moitié pourri, on aurait voulu me les faire prendre pour de jeunes forces âpres qui jaillissent vers le ciel. . . ." Barrès, in his treatment of Taine's plane-tree, can be taken as a typical representative of the *imbéciles* to whom Roquentin here refers. The tree presents a picture of beauty and power; Taine looks lovingly upon this "bel être luisant de pluie", calls Roemerspacher's attention to "le grain serré de son tronc, ses nœuds vigoureux", and voices admiration of "son ensemble puissant". It is a constant reminder of the strength and vigour of natural processes: "sans cesse elle [la jeune force créatrice] se meut en lui". "Voyez, qu'il est d'une santé pure", exclaims the philosopher ecstatically, Roquentin, for his part, fixes his jaundiced eye upon the chestnut-tree, "cette masse noire et noueuse entièrement brute," Being-in-Itself in microcosm, and is repelled by what he sees. The sight of the trunk evokes only images of deterioration: "Une rouille verte le couvrait jusqu'à mi-hauteur; l'écorce, noire et boursouflée, semblait de cuir bouilli." The glistening bark, far from taking on an appealing air appears to have the oily look of seal-skin and therefore shares the nausea-inducing properties of all slimy objects. Wherever Roquentin looks, nature droops; the trees are limp, they display nothing of the quality of phallic symbols of creative power: "Un jaillissement vers le ciel? Un affalement plutôt; à chaque instant je m'attendais à voir les troncs se rider comme des verges lasses, se recroqueviller et choir sur le sol en un tas noir et mou avec des plis." Death and decay in all around he sees, and words like "morne", "souffreteux", "moisissure", abound in the text. For Taine, the plane-tree evokes the idea of death, but this idea is surrounded with the tranquillity of resignation. The tree offers him a lesson in determinism: "Cette masse puissante de verdure obéit à une raison secrète, à la plus sublime philosophie qui est l'acceptation des nécessités de la vie. . . . Et maintenant cet arbre qui, chaque jour avec confiance, accroissait le trésor de ses énergies, il va disparaître parce qu'il a atteint sa perfection. L'activité de la nature, sans cesser de soutenir l'espèce ne veut pas en faire davantage pour cet individu. Mon beau platane aura vécu. Sa destinée est ainsi bornée par les mêmes lois qui, ayant assuré sa naissance, amèneront sa mort." The idea of death presented in this way acts as a spur to action as far as Roemerspacher and his companions are concerned: "Cette idée de la mort et de leur animalité . . . met dans leur sang comme un aphrodisiaque, la hâte, la frénésie de vivre." Quite different is Roquentin's reaction to the spectacle of nature: "Je rêvais vaguement de me supprimer," he confides tersely to his diary. The image M. Taine's plane-tree, this "fédération bruissante", conjures up for Roemerspacher a vision of a neatly-ordered universe, a Great Chain of Being, in which each link was bound to the next through the operation of an ineluctable necessity which governed all things. For Roquentin, on the other hand, necessity is not of this world, it belongs to the realm of geometry and music, to "le monde des explications et des raisons". The rather cosy universe of Roemerspacher's dreams, with everything in its due place, fulfilling its due function and everybody nobly striving after perfection, is replaced by a world of chaos and absurdity, peopled by irremediably flawed beings: "Tout existant naît sans raison, se prolonge par faiblesse et meurt par rencontre." Seated before the chestnut-tree, Roquentin feels life as a sickening plenitude from which man could not escape even if he could muster enough energy to do so: "l'existence est un plein que l'homme ne peut quitter."

The impossibility of ordering one's existence, of introducing the rigour of Art into the messiness of Life, is demonstrated in _La nausée_ by the failure of Roquentin's mistress, Anny, to make certain phases of her life conform to a prearranged pattern, and by Roquentin's own failure to achieve what he calls _le sentiment de l'aventure_ ("Le sentiment de l'aventure", he explains, "serait, tout simplement, celui de l'irréversibilité du temps").

Anny's theories show a great similarity to those propounded in **Les Déracinés** by Sturel, Roemerspacher's closest friend, who is endowed, we are told, with an extremely fine, almost feminine sensibility. Anny's aim had been to control the events of her life in such a way as to contrive what she called "des moments parfaits", but more often than not this aim had been frustrated by Roquentin's clumsily masculine attempts to help her. She is eventually reduced to abandoning the task of fashioning the intractable raw material of the passing moments of her existence for the easier one of moulding her past experience so that it takes on satisfying forms. She confesses to her ex-lover, Roquentin: "Toute notre histoire est assez belle. Je lui donne quelques coups de pouce et ça fait une suite de moments parfaits". Her quite invaluable guide in all this, she says, has been the _Spiritual Exercises_ of Ignatius Loyola. This work of Loyola's was also Sturel's vademecum in his _culte du moi._ His succinct exposition of the master's method sums up Anny's attitude to life, as well as his own: "La méthode de Loyola, c'est l'art d'éveiller en soi des émotions, de perfectionner ses impulsions, de cultiver ses aptitudes, de nous organiser enfin une vie cérébrale telle que nous incorporions l'idéal que nous sommes proposé". The rather unlikely figure of the founder of the Society of Jesus, therefore, provides another _point de rencontre_ between the novels of Sartre and Barrès and lends colour to the view that the latter's importance as one of the literary targets chosen by the author of _La Nausée_ has not hitherto been sufficiently realized. (pp. 332-34)

Dennis J. Fletcher, "Sartre and Barrès: Some Notes on 'La nausée'," in Forum for Modern Language Studies, _Vol. IV, No. 4, October, 1968, pp. 330-34._

M. Grover (essay date 1969)

[_In the excerpt below, Grover defines the debt owed by modernists, such as Louis Aragon and André Gide, to the youthful work of Barrès and analyzes the triumphs and declines of Barrès's literary reputation as political fashions have changed._]

In one's own time it is difficult to sense what in literature and art is central and what is peripheral, what moves and what is inert, what is capable of evolution and what is lifeless. The Barresian family, the Barresian style, the Barresian myth exist: anyone deeply immersed in contemporary French literature feels it. But neither Barrès the man nor Barrès the literary-political-social phenomenon is easily accessible to most of us, particularly to English-speaking readers; we need his heirs to serve as translators and interpreters.

It is paradoxical that an author with such distinguished literary descendants should be little read today, even in France. It is François Mauriac who has been the most articulate about his indebtedness to Barrès as well as about the general influence exercised by Barrès on French youth for a quarter of a century. In 1965, Mauriac wrote:

> Barrès demeurait pour nous le maître. Que des écrivains aussi différents que Montherlant, Aragon, Malraux, moi-même, nous ne l'ayons jamais renié (Drieu la Rochelle, Roger Nimier étaient ses fils eux aussi), et que tous nous consentions à cette filiation, c'est ce qui m'a longtemps fait espérer qu'une source commune à trois générations finirait par jaillir de nouveau et que nos enfants la redécouvriraient.

The common image that the word Barrès is likely to evoke for the uninitiated is that of a political rather than a literary figure. Thus Barrès is usually identified with conservatism, traditionalism, and nationalism. In a recent book in English on French politics, _Three against the Republic,_ Barrès is presented as one of the chief representatives of anti-parliamentarism along with Charles Maurras and Georges Sorel. As Barrès' name is also associated with the founding of the _Action Française_ in 1898, most people are still convinced—wrongly—that he was, like Maurras, a monarchist.

The reader who lacks a direct acquaintance with a writer's works is likely to rely on the judgement of those respected, widely-read authors who seem to speak for their generation. In France the authors who have successively played that pontifical role for two generations since Barrès' death—André Gide and Jean-Paul Sartre—give a decidedly unfavourable impression of Barrès.

J. P. Sartre caricatured Barrès by identifying him in *La Nausée* with the stuffy, preachy bourgeois of Bouville, imbued with his own importance and the rights of his class. He makes of Barrès the archetype of the 'salaud'. The introduction of Barrès in this 1938 novel is all the more remarkable in that he is the only historical character to appear in its pages. Barrès is exploited as a convenient symbol and a butt for satire in whom are summed up all the ridiculous hypocrisies of a bygone age.

Sartre's frankly farcical handling of the Barrès legend is reminiscent of the surrealist attitude toward the representatives of tradition. For Sartre, Barrès, who is forty-three years his senior, is a grandfather figure; he is only adding the finishing touches to the image of Barrès as it was handed on to him and his generation. Gide, however, never treated Barrès with a lack of seriousness. His attacks were more subtly perfidious: Barrès was a great man in Gide's lifetime who represented something entirely different for his whole generation than for that of Sartre.

Gide is twenty when he reads, in the winter of 1889, *Un homme libre.* On 18 March 1890, he notes his impression:

> ***Un Homme Libre*** de Maurice Barrès. Lu depuis La Roque et médité tous ces derniers mois. Je reste convaincu, malgré les révoltes de Pierre [Louys] que c'est là une oeuvre maîtresse, une oeuvre type de la génération intermédiaire qui s'en va, un jalon de l'histoire littéraire. Il y aurait trop à dire. En le relisant, peut-être écrirai-je un article.

Two years later he meets Barrès who, at twenty-nine, is not only a literary lion (he has been proclaimed 'the prince of youth' by his near contemporaries of the Latin Quarter): he enjoys the prestige of political success as well (at twenty-seven Barrès was elected député for Nancy). Eight years after Barrès, Gide writes his own version of *Un homme libre,* i.e. *Les Nourritures terrestres* (1897). By this time, however, Barrès is no longer the youthful anarchistic individualist of his first books: he has emerged as the romantic nationalist of *Le Roman de l'Energie nationale.* Henceforth, André Gide is going to establish his originality by being anti-Barrès. The older writer's career and works entirely occupy the limelight, as numerous entries in Gide's *Journals* testify. The continuous interest Gide manifested in an envied rival and in all his books are clearly documented in the Journal. It would be absurd to suggest that Gide would not have become Gide without Barrès, but it is equally absurd to ignore the role that Barrès played in his formation.

When Gide chose the texts for his *Morceaux Choisis* in 1921, the first section of the volume as he constructed it was made up of articles on nationalism which developed mainly from his polemics with the Barresian thesis as exemplified in *Les Déracinés* (1897). *The Counterfeiters* (1925) is his belated response to Barrès most famous novel: in its form as well as in its content it is an anti-Déracinés. In 1948, Gide explains in a lecture (reproduced in *Feuillets d'automne*) why he broke with Barrès after the publication of *Les Déracinés.*

In the early 1920s, Gide felt rightly that many of the most gifted writers of the younger generation of that time were under Barrès influence and that this influence was in conflict with his own. He did not forget that between 1894 and 1914, Barrès had been more than a prince—he was a kind of idol of French youth.

It is difficult for us today to imagine to what extent Barrès was venerated by the young. This is how Louis Aragon describes some forty years later his first reaction on reading Barrès:

> L'année de ma première communion, j'avais onze ans, mon professeur de français à l'école Saint-Pierre de Neuilly me fit donner comme prix de narration française les ***Vingt-Cinq années de vie littéraire*** de Maurice Barrès, pages choisies avec une introduction d'Henri Brémond. La lecture de ce livre fut pour moi un grand coup de soleil, et il n'est pas exagéré de dire qu'elle décida de l'orientation de ma vie.

Aragon then sums up his emotions in one sentence: 'Egalerai-je jamais le génie de Barrès?' In the same way, Victor Hugo had been the guiding light for Barrès and the young Victor Hugo in turn had found his vocation after reading Chateaubriand: 'Etre Chateaubriand ou rien.'

Aragon's enthusiasm was not an isolated case: ' . . . ce rôle, Barrès l'a tenu pour bien d'autres enfants, d'autres adolescents . . . il a été le maître de la sensibilité de plusieurs générations: c'est là un fait impossible à négliger, même si ces enfants, ces adolescents devenus hommes . . . préfèrent aujourd'hui nier les exaltations de leur jeunesse', he concludes reproachfully.

The élite of the young men called to arms in 1914 were nourished on Barrès. But many among this élite were killed, including 'Barresiens' who might have continued the master's tradition and enhanced his reputation. The 'Barresiens' who survived had experienced French warfare while Barrès had merely written about it. They felt that, in this domain at least, action spoke louder than words. A certain romanticism of action (to which Barrès' work contributed) was born. The sentimental patriotism of Barrès' war propaganda aroused their ironic contempt. The difference between propaganda literature and 'Littérature engagée' appeared obvious to them. From then on, any committed literature that was not authenticated by a parallel commitment in life would be suspect.

Barrès himself, who was too old to fight (he was fifty-two in 1914), decided to serve as a writer. He contributed a daily article to the *Echo de Paris.* He did his best to maintain contact with the fighting soldiers by visiting the front lines as often as he could. He shared the anxiety of many parents when his son Philippe became a volunteer at eighteen.

A letter written by a young soldier of twenty-two on 24 April 1915, to one of his contemporaries allows us to follow in a concrete way the subtle evolution of feelings toward Barrès:

> Oui, Barrès a accaparé tout le mysticisme de cette guerre où est la pierre de touche de notre grandeur. Entre elle et nos cœurs il avait mis le

réseau obsédant de ses phrases. Mais, depuis
août 1914, nous avons vécu, la lettre est morte
pour nous, remplacée par l'acte divin. Tout
l'actif de la pensée de Barrès est passé dans nos
faits de soldat et le reste est resté enclos dans les
livres où nous ne le chercherons plus.

The books had served their purpose: they had provided
the impulse to act. But now war feats proved a greater
source of exaltation. This testimony of Pierre Drieu la Rochelle, who had participated in the war right from the beginning and had already been wounded twice when he
wrote these lines is characteristic:

Mais quelle vie magnifique cet homme aura connue! C'est un Chateaubriand fortuné. D'abord
anarchiste, dans ses débuts angoissés à Paris,
comme le René de *l'Essai sur les Révolutions*
dans son agonie de Londres. Mais affirmant déjà
cet orgueil qu'il n'avait besoin que d'agrandir
pour en faire son nationalisme. Puis restaurant
le génie du patriotisme et du catholicisme,
n'évitant pas l'écueil de l'Académie, mais du
moins celui du ministère. . . . Barrès restera la
preuve patente d'un des sursauts de la nation
française. . . .

In spite of his admiration for Barrès, Drieu writes about
him in his letter as if he were already a man of the past
whose career and usefulness are finished. Barrès was, however, capable of renewing his inspiration and of broadening his nationalist point of view as evidenced in his posthumous works and in his intimate notebooks.

His sudden death at the age of sixty-two, on 4 December
1923, prevented this metamorphosis and deprived us of his
"Memoirs" which, if the few pages he wrote in the last
weeks of his life are any indication, might have been his
masterpiece. Proust had died the previous year, Loti died
the same year. Anatole France died at eighty the next
year. Claudel, Gide, and Valéry, who were respectively
six, seven and nine years younger than Barrès, were to realize—rather late—the culmination of their careers and to
dominate the French literary scene for the next twenty
years.

The patriotic role that Barrès had played during the First
World War was extended beyond 1918 by his involvement
with the war sequel: official visits to the reconquered provinces; long and difficult negotiations for the peace treaties;
polemics over the question of the Rhine; the political victory of the Bloc National (1921) in which Barrès occupied
an eminent position. Thus the last image of Barrès is of a
man who is more and more absorbed in the transient political scene. This image did not appeal to those who were
too young to have read his works before the war. They
were reading Gide and Mauriac, Montherlant and Aragon, Drieu la Rochelle and, soon, Malraux—not suspecting that these younger authors derived from a common
master.

Those who knew Barrès as the patriotic speech-maker
must have been puzzled by the entirely different figure
Jean Cocteau evoked in the obituary article he contributed
to the special issue of the *Nouvelles Littéraires* after Barrès'
death: 'quel collégien que ce maître! quel complice que ce

juge! Il nous enseigne l'hommage irrespectueux. . . . ,
Derrière sa mort, il nous fait signe de ne pas y croire.' In
the same issue, Drieu la Rochelle defines Barrès' place in
French letters as follows:

Maurice Barrès a été encore plus français que les
meilleurs Français de notre temps: . . . plus
large qu'Anatole France, plus ferme qu'André
Gide, plus prudent que Paul Claudel, plus direct
que Charles Péguy, plus humain qu'Elémir
Bourges . . . Derrière lui, je vous présente ses
héritiers, Louis Aragon, Henry de Montherlant.

In an obituary article, 'Barrès Begins His Posthumous
Role', published in the same issue Montherlant salutes his
spiritual father: he sees in the tears he has just shed over
the greatness of Barrès dead a tie stronger than blood.
Now Barrès enters into his own; a second Barrès, the Barrès of his books, detaches himself from a frail body and
begins an immortal adventure: 'From now on it is up to
us to resurrect him.' For Montherlant, Barrès is the supreme example of 'the genius of conciliation':

Il chercha à sauvegarder la libre-pensée à
l'intérieur du déisme, tous les mouvements ro-
mantiques à l'intérieur d'une discipline; il fut
lyrique et cependant d'une lucidité adorable; la
corde résonnante sur laquelle joue l'invisible, et
cependant jamais ne fut dupe et jamais ne put
sentir ceux qui l'étaient . . . Ayant voulu la conciliation en lui-même, il la voulut ensuite entre
une grande personne morale et lui. C'est sa première leçon, celle de ce 'fameux individualiste'
qui sent le besoin de s'accrocher à quelque chose
qui le dépasse et qui demeure: servir, c'est se ré-
fugier dans ce qu'on sert.

(pp. 529-32)

In 1923, Montherlant seems quite anxious to claim Barrès
as his spiritual father; he is establishing his right as a literary heir in an almost official manner. In 1925, in an article
published in the same *Nouvelles Littéraires,* he seems
equally anxious to reject this paternity. 'Barrès s'éloigne'
is the title of his article. The tone of light-hearted cynicism
he adopts now is in perfect contrast to the solemn grandiloquence of the former respectful disciple. The contrast is
quite deliberate but it is too extreme not to raise questions
about the sincerity of both attitudes. After playing the dutiful son, Montherlant plays the role of the adolescent in
full revolt: 'Si après deux ans je pense toujours que Barrès
est notre plus grand écrivain dans ce premier quart de siècle, je me satisfais moins aujourd'hui de sa vie publique.'
Montherlant accuses Barrès of not having been 'un
homme libre', as a result of the artificial obligations he had
created for himself as a political person—such an intelligent man ('the most intelligent man I have ever known',
says Montherlant), cannot have believed in the politics he
preached. Why did he pretend until the end that he was
faithful to his 'party'? Why did he remain the prisoner of
his companions? Why did he claim—against all evidence—that his war literature was what mattered most to
him in the whole of his work? He should have 'spilled the
beans' (*mangé le morceau*), confessed his secret doubts
about the rightness of his cause, admitted that he might
just as well have espoused the opposite cause. Instead he

followed the advice given in one of his books: 'Let us wear our prejudices; they keep us warm.'

This article was published two years later in a volume *Aux fontaines du désir*. It was accompanied this time by a stronger, almost insulting, attack on Barrès: 'Du sang, de la volupté et de la mort (pour rire).' In this longer essay, Montherlant does not limit accusation of insincerity to Barrès' political role but extends it to the rest of his work. He pokes fun at the famous title, 'About Blood, Voluptuousness and Death': 'De tout cela, qu'a-t-il vu de près, ce Barrès? Le sang? la mort? Où? Quand? La volupté? Je ne sais quoi me souffle qu'il ne l'a guère connue. Son "roman d'amour" (ainsi la bande du *Jardin sur l'Oronte* nommait-elle drôlement cette trop élégante turquerie) est le seul de ses livres qui frôle l'insignifiance.' His speciality has always been 'to miss the boat', remain on the shore. . . . His voluptuousness has been only that of the spectator. And he could not always stand even the spectacle: he had to leave a bull-fight in a near-faint after the death of the first bull. Barrès' crime in the eyes of this thirty-year-old war veteran, toreador, and soccer player is to have believed only in art and never to have tried to transpose some of his dreams into real life.

This article may have been written partly as a 'pastiche' of Barrès (who had himself not been tender towards his own master Renan in *Huit jours chez M. Renan*). It thus provided an indirect homage although it is mainly an effort to exorcise too strong an influence. As a matter of fact, at the end of the book in which the two essays on Barrès appear, in a later essay dated 1927, Montherlant reversed his position after relating his own vain efforts to introduce poetry into his life and wrote: 'Barrès and those of his kind were right, I was wrong. Of course, it is people without dreams who try to realize their dreams: for a creator, that is superfluous.'

Most readers, however, misunderstood Montherlant's subtle game and accepted this ridiculous picture of Barrès at face value. The half truths it contained were enough to lend it credibility; the almost official status of its author as the heir of Barrès enhanced its authority. We will see that fifteen years later, the young Albert Camus, still under the influence of Montherlant, held very similar views of Barrès.

Drieu's position toward Barrès is not much different from that of Montherlant at the time, even though it is expressed more moderately:

> Chaque année je relis quelques livres de Barrès et plus je vais, plus j'admire l'écrivain et moins le penseur me satisfait. C'est sans doute que nous avons entièrement assimilé ce qu'il pouvait y avoir de nourrissant en lui. . . . Mais qui, depuis un demi-siècle, a porté avec des mains plus robustes la tradition de la langue? Comme il convient d'opposer son abondance à la pauvreté d'Anatole France!

At the surrealist trial organized against Barrès in 1923, Drieu's testimony for the defence was rather ambiguous: when asked by the presiding judge, André Breton, whether he knew the accused personally, he replied in a non-committal fashion: 'J'ai été le voir comme un des représen-

tants de la pensée contemporaine', a statement which he promptly corrected: 'Non! J'ai été le voir comme un des représentants de la . . . sensibilité contemporaine.' At the end, Breton tried to force Drieu to take sides by asking him: 'Do you know anybody in Barrès' generation whom you prefer to him?':

> 'Non, mais je préfère tous ceux de la génération suivante . . . Péguy parce qu'il était d'âge mobilisable et qu'il a détruit son génie sans précautions; D'Annunzio qui est un beau militaire. Je voudrais citer Romain Rolland qui a failli avoir une belle attitude, mais qui manque trop de force dans ses gestes et dans ses écrits. J'ajoute que je crois que nous ne sommes plus du tout sur le même terrain.'

> 'Barrès vous est-il antipathique ou sympathique?'

> 'Je ne sais', répond Drieu, 'mais j'ai le sens du respect.'

The most influential literary group at that time was the *Nouvelle Revue Française*. In that group the most influential man was André Gide who had always been anti-Barrès. Neither Roger Martin Du Gard nor Claudel, nor Jean Schlumberger—other influential literary men in that group—were favourable to Barrès. After a youthful enthusiasm for Barrès, Jacques Rivière, who was the director of the review *N.R.F.* from 1919 to 1925, turned critical. Jean Paulhan, who succeeded him, always disliked Barrès. In 1928 Marcel Arland published a study on Barrès which, while appearing to be an impartial assessment of Barrès' place in French letters five years after his death, was a devastating attack. Like Drieu and Montherlant, Arland praised Barrès' style or, as he called it, his 'voice'.

Arland feels a mixture of both gratitude and distrust for the teachings he discovered in Barrès' works at eighteen. The gratitude is short-lived, the distrust lasting: the lesson of pride and lucidity to be learned from *Un Homme Libre* may strengthen the need for grandeur and heroism, natural to a young man, but it may also serve to isolate him from the world, hide from him or make him despise half of life. By its over-calculating deliberateness the Barresian creed may fix the young man in a narrow sterilizing narcissism and inspire in him a taste for grandiose attitudes and for declamation: '. . . one looks for a man, one finds most of the time only an artist.' Barrès thinks constantly of his public image, writes in order to justify himself and constantly offers himself as an example. His early nihilism cannot be taken seriously by young men who grew up among images of war and revolution. Can he be taken more seriously when he defends a country, a civilization, a church, a system of ethics? This dilettante has utilized every theme to make his own music with it. Such is the narrow utilitarian's point of departure of all his doctrines. The only sympathetic aspect of Barrès, Arland finds, is the secret disturbance that one senses beneath the solid bourgeois convictions, which emerges occasionally to threaten the beautifully constructed doctrines. Thus he sees the key to Barrès' work in Barrès' unceasing battle against the inner forces of voluptuousness and self-destruction.

Arland cannot resist comparing Barrès and Gide to the

latter's advantage. Gide must have been gratified by Arland's study in which Barrès is judged by Gidian criteria. It represents a turning of the tide. (pp. 533-35)

In 1931, reading the third volume of Barrès' notebooks, Gide commented: 'Je me retiens pour ne pas avaler le journal de Barrès tout d'un trait. Je trouve profit à ne m'en accorder chaque jour que quelques pages. Il y en a parfois de très belles et que je lis avec ravissement.' In spite of this avid interest he felt a basic incompatibility of tastes between himself and Barrès:

> Intéressantes pages sur Hugo. A part quoi, quelle barbe, ces *Cahiers* de Barrès! Ce qu'il aime, ce qui l'intéresse, ce qu'il admire . . . rien de plus loin de moi . . . Mais l'on ne peut ne pas être touché par une probité si constante. Il y a même, dans ce rattachement à la Lorraine, une sorte de 'comme cela du moins je suis sûr de ne pas me tromper' pathétique.

Elsewhere, Gide complains that Barrès employs 'poetic' phrases: a truly great artist does not change the colours of his palette in an effort to be 'arty'. This is more like the art of the confectioner: 'C'est décidément le Barrès de *Leurs Figures* que je préfère, incisif et montrant les dents. Je ne l'aime pas quand il se parfume, asiatique et déhanché.' The exaggeration of this last statement reminds us that Gide belonged to that category of homosexuals who are allergic to anything effeminate and who are apt to react violently to the least trace of effeminacy.

Gide must admit that he is unfavourably disposed towards Barrès and that his reading is coloured by his prejudices:

> Je voudrais bien pourtant n'apporter point à la lecture de ces *Cahiers* de Barrès cette *indisposition* de l'esprit qui ne me laisse plus sensible qu'aux tares. Dans ce XIᶜ cahier les beautés abondent. La connaissance et l'acceptation de ses limites, de ses manques, de ses faiblesses (souvent il se les exagère) donnent à ces pages un accent qui saisit le coeur. Et comment ne point admirer l'expression, presque toujours parfaite, d'une volonté si constamment appliquée à obtenir de soi le meilleur, quelle sincérité dans ces aveux!

Reading these first Notebooks which were written at the same time as the books against which he had reacted so violently, helps Gide to realize how much he has orientated himself in opposition to Barrès; he picks out a quotation which sums up most strikingly this opposition: 'Qu'est-ce donc que j'aime dans le passé? Sa tristesse, son silence et surtout sa fixité. Ce qui bouge me gêne.' 'Peut-on imaginer aveu plus grave?', asks Gide:

> Et comme si tout le futur ne devait pas devenir, à son tour, du passé! L'idée d'un progrès possible de l'humanité n'effleure même pas sa pensée. Au contact de ces pages, je comprends mieux combien cette idée de progrès s'est emparée de moi, me possède. L'influence (néfaste) à la fois de Taine et de Renan à quel point sensible!

The quotations from Gide's *Journal* on the subject of Barrès could be multiplied: they would merely repeat, with variations, the same basic reactions. Gide epitomizes the strange fascination exercised by Barrès on minds and sensibilities that are opposed to everything that Barrès represents, that would like to reject or ignore him, that, in this very rejection testify to his presence.

François Mauriac, fifteen years younger than Gide and twenty-three years younger than Barrès, admires them both. He owes more to Barrès whose books were the companions of his adolescence. He is particularly grateful to Barrès for having praised his first book '*Les Mains Jointes*' (1909) in an article in l'*Echo de Paris.*

Mauriac's first novel, l'*Enfant chargé de chaînes* (1913) which is autobiographical, is full of references to Barrès and especially to the two books which marked the young Mauriac most strongly: *Sous l'oeil des Barbares* and *Un homme libre.* Those two books helped Mauriac to liberate himself from his milieu. He entirely identified with their hero who was obliged to fight against everybody to assert his own personality and to find his own destiny. In Barrès' trilogy of the *Culte du Moi,* he found sustenance and support in his desire for a literary vocation. Literature would be for Mauriac what it had been for the young hero of *Le Culte du Moi:* a revenge against the tyrants of his childhood, a compensation for all the humiliations inflicted by thick-skinned, self-satisfied, well-adjusted little brutes at school. He would show them one day his real superiority.

Mauriac discovered an admirable ambition in *Sous l'oeil des Barbares,* as well as an exemplary non-conformism. Paradoxically the conformism which Mauriac had to fight around 1900 in the fearful, provincial, catholic, nationalist, bourgeoisie of his milieu was nourished by the same ideology which had led Barrès to join the conservatives in the camp of the 'anti-Dreyfusards'.

Thus, from the beginning, Mauriac's attitude toward the master who had exercised the greatest influence on him was bound to be ambiguous. He identifies with him as with a spiritual father but he cannot accept the basic political choices of Barrès because they are the same as those of the abhorred bourgeois Right into which Mauriac was born. He expresses anxious doubts about Barrès' chances of passing on to posterity or, as he puts it, about whether a dialogue will still be possible between Barrès and the young men of twenty of future generations. Perhaps he thought that if Barrès failed to re-establish contact with younger generations, his literary heirs might maintain the Barresian presence. He knew himself to be one of these heirs. He showed the greatest clairvoyance in recognizing other members of the Barresian family. In 1940, probably fearing that the conservatives might try to annex Barrès, he anticipated that move, by nominating Barrès' 'true' heirs in an article in the *Figaro.* The list appeared at that time paradoxical and even scandalous: Malraux, Montherlant, Aragon, Drieu la Rochelle. In the article which appeared on 23 March he wrote that he did not see any successors to Barrès or rather that his true heirs, as named above, would probably be disowned by him. Since then, Mauriac has elaborated on the nature of the basic family ties uniting these writers. On 8 March 1960, commenting on Montherlant's style, he wrote:

> Montherlant, c'est pour moi un écrivain, le type même de l'écrivain francais d'une certaine fa-

mille (Chateaubriand, Barrès), à laquelle je me flatte d'appartenir aussi [. . .] Il existe un trait commun aux écrivains de cette famille, parmi lesquels figurent des cousins ennemis comme Aragon et Malraux. Je serais tenté de dire—qu'on me le pardonne, puisque je me considère comme l'un de ces messieurs—que ce trait tient dans une certaine imposture.

(pp. 535-37)

Back in 1940, Mauriac's article in the *Figaro* could not fail to provoke heated reactions: the newspapers of the moderate Right (*Le Matin*) and of the extremist Right (*L'Action Française*) protested against Mauriac's nominations of Barrès' heirs. They conceded that Drieu la Rochelle might qualify as one but denounced as pure heresy the claim of Barresian inheritance for Montherlant (aggressively apolitical), Malraux (then a Stalinist), and Aragon (a Communist Party member).

One of the most interesting results of this literary and political 'quarrel' was an article by an unknown journalist of twenty-seven, Albert Camus, in a leftist publication, *La Lumière* (5 April 1940). Camus had already published in Algiers *L'Envers et l'Endroit* and *Noces*. The lyrical style of those early essays showed the influence of both Gide and Barrès, which was not surprising for Camus' respected master, both at the lycée and at the university, was Jean Grenier who was a great admirer of Barrès and an author of essays in the Barresian tradition. The two younger writers Camus admired most, along with Gide, were Montherlant and Malraux: these three represented different aspects of Barrès' sensibility filtered through their own originality. Much of Camus' nihilism, his philosophy of the absurd, a certain 'espagnolisme' so characteristic of his early period, were akin to the mood of Montherlant in *Aux Fontaines du Désir* (1927) and in *Service Inutile* (1935). The admiring reference in this 1940 article to the more recent *Equinoxe de Septembre* is evidence of the lasting influence of Montherlant on the young Camus. The lyrical form adopted by Camus in his first books, indicates a literary kinship which, through Montherlant, goes back to the Barrès of ***Du sang, de la volupté et de la mort***. Albert Camus was therefore in a privileged position to give his opinion on the quarrel provoked by François Mauriac's article.

Camus' main point in his article is that Barrès' most obvious literary heirs have been the ones to turn most violently against him. He refers to Montherlant to demonstrate this point: 'Ce qu'on a dit de plus profond, de plus juste et de plus dur sur Barrès, c'est Montherlant qui l'a formulé.'

Obviously Camus has in mind 'Barrès' éloigne' and 'Du sang de la volupté et de la mort (pour rire)'. He develops the same themes as in Montherlant's article: i.e. between Barrès and his creation there is always a gap; he created an imaginary world of nostalgia which was quite distinct from the world of his lived experience; Barrès, according to Camus, was unable to become the hero he had conceived in his works.

Although he is adopting Montherlant's position, Camus does not use the flexible form of a lyrical essay which provided at the same time a parody of Barrès' flippant mood.

The uncertain logic of his article is marked by a facade of apparently rigorous demonstration. Camus tends to speak as a moral judge in possession of eternal truth; he uses the dogmatic tone of a pseudo-philosopher which was to irritate J. P. Sartre so much when he read *L'Homme révolté* a few years later.

As an ungrateful son denying that he owes anything to his progenitor Camus appears much more contradictory in his article than Montherlant because the apparently rational form contradicts the emotional content of the article. Camus' reasoning is that Barrès' true literary heirs disown Barrès in the name of Barrès' own literary creation! Barrès' sin is, for Camus, that his imagination was more exalted than his temperament: 'Son paradis perdu, c'était cet univers de sang, de volupté et de mort, ce monde brûlant et solitaire dont il ne fut jamais l'un des princes, quoi qu'il en eût. Le rêve chez lui n'était pas le frère de l'action . . . Il avait plus d'esprit que d'âme.' Thus, those he influenced 'having first loved the image of the solitary hero of royal lineage' later 'blamed the creator for not resembling enough this spiritual son'.

In Camus' eyes, Barrès' heirs, especially the two he knows best, Malraux and Montherlant, are superior to their master. They are superior as persons. The reason, he says, that Montherlant was most critical of Barrès is that among those of his generation he was one of the best prepared 'to live this life of prince of body and mind' for which Barrès only longed. They are also superior as writers. Camus invites us to measure the 'essential' difference which separates the two authors by comparing their patriotism as expressed in Montherlant's *Equinoxe de Septembre* and Barrès' harangues of the First World War.

Two observations are pertinent. Camus, blinded by his juvenile admiration for Montherlant, tends to identify him with the rather empty rhetoric of his beautiful style. Second, Camus still shares the romantic notion that there are heroes who lead in reality the lives of imaginary heroes in fiction. A third deduction can be made: only those authors are to be admired who live the adventures of their books; the quality of the work corresponds directly to the quality of the author as a person. 'C'est pourquoi on peut dire sans doute qu'entre Barrès, Montherlant et Malraux la filiation est sensible. Mais il n'y a aucune commune mesure entre leurs oeuvres respectives.' Here, Camus introduces a rather obvious but vague element to separate the two generations 'the whole past'. 'Et il y a tout le passé qui sépare l'écriture artiste du vrai style, l'écrivain de l'homme et, comme dirait MacOrlan, l'aventurier passif de l'aventurier actif.' This mysterious 'whole past' is probably a reference to the First World War which divided those who fought from those who were too old to participate actively. One can perceive here a distant echo of Drieu's statement: 'We have made history: it is better than reading it.' For the World War veterans, only those who risk their lives in war or revolution are entitled to write about danger and courage. Montherlant can write about bull fights because he was himself a torero. (pp. 537-39)

Whether Barrès lacked 'character', as Camus judges a little too peremptorily in his 1940 article, or whether he came at the wrong moment in French political life, as

Mauriac has argued, there is no doubt that if Barrès was excluded from a position of political power it was not for lack of desiring that power. He would have preferred to be a minister rather than a writer. He would have liked to emulate not only Chateaubriand's style but his political career. He admired in Victor Hugo not only the poet but the national hero. He said to Drieu la Rochelle after the First World War: 'Si la cause que j'avais choisie avait triomphé et si j'avais été ministre, j'aurais volontiers cessé d'écrire.'

François Mauriac's views on Barrès' career confirms this:

> Ce qui a échappé au choix du jeune vainqueur, ce fut ce moment de la vie politique française où il entra dans la carrière, et qui, après l'échec boulangiste et la déconfiture nationaliste, devait l'exclure à jamais du pouvoir.
>
> N'empêche que le Chateaubriand dont il est jaloux, c'est le ministre des Affaires étrangères, le représentant de la France au Congrès de Vérone. Barrès est resté sur sa soif la plus ardente et la plus cachée; et il ne l'aura étanchée que dans sa postérité: lorsque le général de Gaulle fait d'André Malraux un ministre, il contente enfin une ambition déçue de Barrès. . . .
>
> (p. 539)

Between 1940 and 1948 (the twenty-fifth anniversary of Barrès' death in 1948 provided the occasion for an evaluation of what had survived in his work) political considerations continued to obscure the Barrès problem. The German occupation and the Vichy régime did nothing for Barrès' reputation although Charles Maurras and Charles Péguy enjoyed a revival of influence and popularity. After the liberation, the existentialist wave swept over France. Sartre and Camus were anti-Barresians. André Gide, reinstated in a dominant position in French letters, did nothing, of course, to resurrect Barrès. However, a few manifestations here and there of interest in Barrès indicated that some serious work toward a dispassionate reevaluation was under way and showed that Camus had assumed a little too hastily that Montherlant, Malraux, Drieu, and Aragon were entirely averse to everything that Barrès represented.

The very next year—1941—Montherlant complained that a systematic silence was being maintained about Barrès and his work while an inordinate amount of critical interest was organized around much lesser figures such as Péguy, for example. He did not mention any names but implied that 'a literary chapel' had been especially intent on 'sinking' Barrès since his death and that now a 'whole fraction' of the nation, which had become extremely influential since the defeat, held Barrès in suspicion. He claimed for Barrès' the 'royal place' he deserved, and strongly denounced the scandalous near-banishment of a writer 'who is head and shoulders' above the greatest among those who came after him. In a note at the end of the book, Montherlant says that someone had pointed out to him that an important part of Barrès' work is directed against Germany and that, of course, it would be most untimely to draw attention to such an author during the German occupation. Montherlant then notes that it was revelatory that he had forgotten this whole aspect of Barrès'

work: 'le fait que je puisse penser à lui sans penser jamais à ce rameau de son oeuvre, montre que celui-ci, malgré tout, pourrait en être détaché sans gêne.' Although he admits that this anti-German element in Barrès' work explains some of the conspiracy of silence, he maintains his charge against the other anti-Barresian influences he had denounced.

More secretly, Drieu la Rochelle in his unpublished *Journal* began to weigh Barrès' chances of emerging from the threat of oblivion. Drieu noted on 1 March 1944:

> J'ai relu tout d'un coup du Barrès après des années. Aucun livre que je n'aie lu autant qu' *Un Homme Libre,* si ce n'est telle ou telle chose de Nietzsche. D'abord, je lis *La Colline Inspirée* [. . .]
>
> Je relis ensuite *L'Ennemi des Lois* et *Huit Jours Chez M. Renan* avec la suite: *Trois Stations, Toute Licence.* Comme tout cela est mince, étroit, d'une élégance sûre mais maniérée.
>
> Comme le premier Barrès est bien parent du premier Gide et du premier Valéry! Seul, Claudel a une grosse voix dans cette génération. Décidément, c'est bien inférieur à Gide et à Valéry. [. . .] Toutefois, si je relisais *Le Culte du Moi* tout entier, n'est-ce pas là un ensemble achevé, accompli qui vaut bien les premiers écrits de Valéry et de Gide?
>
> Mais pourquoi instituer un concours? C'est que Barrès est attaqué d'oubli. Ils se ressemblent comme trois frères. Sans doute se lisaient-ils, se surveillaient-ils? Barrès n'a-t-il pas eu l'inconvénient de leur montrer le chemin?
>
> (pp. 540-41)

In the same year, 1948, nationalism was going to be vindicated by another former internationalist, Louis Aragon. The occasion was a defence of Barrès which constituted a complete denial of Camus' statement of a few years before. Aragon defiantly entitled his article 'Actualité de Maurice Barrès' and he demonstrated the relevance of Barrès' thought to a renovated French nationalism in the Europe of the cold war and of the Marshall plan:

> J'ai le regret d'avoir à dire que, pour étroit qu'il soit, le nationalisme de Barrès est plus proche de ce que je ressens, et sans doute de ce que ressent aujourd'hui l'avantgarde ouvrière dans notre pays, que l'internationalisme, disons de M. Guéhenno: car, comme Barrès, les hommes de notre peuple ne sont pas disposés à sacrifier ce qui est national, à une Europe, par exemple, fabriquée par M M. Blum et Churchill et financée par M. Marshall.

The renewal of patriotism associated with all the resistance movements in Europe had given the communists and the leftist parties who had played a major role in the Resistance a nationalist appeal. The nationalists, on the contrary, were discredited in the public opinion for having not only tolerated the occupation but for having called on foreign intervention and sometimes collaborated with the occupants. In 1904, Barrès had predicted with remarkable accuracy in his notebooks this reversal of positions:

> Ce seront les conservateurs qui accepteront, ap-
> pelleront l'étranger. Oui, ceux qui sont au-
> jourd'hui les patriotes, les hommes fiers, las de
> vivre une France amoindrie et une vie humiliée,
> appelleront une annexion, si c'est en Lorraine,
> ou une domination, une intervention de
> l'étranger qui leur donne enfin la joie de parti-
> ciper à une grande vie collective—et nous ver-
> rons, au contraire, la résistance à l'étranger per-
> sonnifiée par la démagogie janséniste.

This type of neo-nationalism in the French Communist Party allows Aragon, *as a communist,* to praise Barrès in 1948. We can measure the change that has taken place in the French political climate since 1940 if we remember Camus' timid dismissal of the whole of Barrès. However, Aragon's personal courage in assuming the title of 'Barrè-sien' in 1948 should not be minimized. He must have hugely enjoyed the astonishment his statement caused among the French intelligentsia both of the left and of the right. But the value of his article extends much beyond its dramatic effect of surprise and even of shock. For the first time since Barrès' death an author who could not be suspected of ideological sympathy with Barrès deals squarely with the problem of Barrès' ideological positions and tries to understand rather than condemn them, refuses in any case to let them obscure the main issue: what is the lasting contribution of Barrès to French letters? With the authority that twenty years of loyal service to the Communist Party have earned him, Aragon can afford to give a lesson of broad-minded, common-sense criticism to more recent communist converts who are ready to perpetuate the old ritual of attacking Barrès because he is fair game.

Yes, Barrès was a bourgeois, says Aragon, he was the master of the sensibility of the bourgeoisie of a certain period of French history, he shared the limitations of that bourgeoisie. We may adopt today a broader perspective on Barrès' narrow nationalism. Even if we can't endorse his 'boulangisme', even if we are revolted by his attitude in the Dreyfus case, we must make the effort to put him back into the frame of reference of a bourgeois of his time, and into his historical situation. Barrès has been the master of the sensibility of several generations as Aragon can testify from his own experience; this is incontrovertible.

The importance of Barrès in the history of the French language is equally incontrovertible. Aragon utilizes all the resources of his own style to demonstrate that the style of this extraordinary craftsman of French prose is far superior to that of any of his contemporaries including Proust, Valéry, and Gide.

He accuses the *N.R.F.* group of having denied Barrès his eminent place as a prose-writer because they were anxious to occupy that place:

> La critique sans mesure de Barrès n'a fait place
> nette qu'au Nathanaël des *Nourritures terrestres,*
> que Gide n'aurait jamais enfanté tout seul, et qui
> a vilainement renié ce qu'il devait à son véritable
> père, Barrès. Mais enfin, de Barrès à Gide,
> l'homme ne monte pas: il descend [. . .] Un
> jour viendra où l'on relira Barrès, en faisant à ces
> idées aussi peu de place que l'on en donne à cel-

> les de Saint-Simon, quand on va chez ce grand
> seigneur chercher des leçons de langage.

Aragon is convinced that future writers will discover in Barrès secrets of the craft that cannot be learned without taking into account the Barresian science of sentence structure, the Barresian sense of the musical value of words'.

The political content of *Le Roman de l'Energie Nationale* has long kept critics from recognizing that Barrès invented a new literary form: '*Les Déracinés, L'Appel au Soldat, Leurs Figures* constituent les premiers exemples en France du roman politique moderne', which marks an essential phase in the evolution of the novel both inside and outside of France. The reason for Barrès' success, according to Aragon, is the very fact for which he is usually criticized: he has been openly a 'partisan'. He has given a more vivid picture of his time than any other writer 'because he gave politics the dominant place it has in the modern world, because for all practical purposes, he rejected the notion of "fictional distance", he wrote about the event, using for material the very event in which he had been personally involved.' The content of this political chronicle of the Third Republic may be reactionary; its technique is avant-garde. Barrès' technique is still far ahead of many left-wing novelists who are pouring their progressivist opinions into old moulds. We are therefore perfectly entitled, concludes Aragon, to claim Barrès as our master.

Barrès' materialism, being non-dialectical, may appear primitive and somewhat crude to a Marxist, but in spite of its limitations, is preferable to the illusions of idealism; there is no shame for a communist in claiming kinship with an author who thinks that 'the brain secretes thought'. Aragon can therefore pick up the gauntlet.

'Who would dare, today, say that he is Barresian?' had asked Etienne Borne in *L'Aurore,* twenty-five years after Barrès' death. Aragon breaks the silence which followed and provides the answer in the last sentence of his article:

> Au delà des enthousiasmes de ma jeunesse, pour
> toutes les raisons que je viens de dire, abandon
> fait de dix livres illisibles, au moins, dans la me-
> sure exacte où il faut prendre parti pour ou con-
> tre, quand on vient à avoir à choisir entre le
> roman politique ou la haine du roman politique,
> entre la reconnaissance de la vérité nationale et
> sa négation pure et simple, entre, non pas le
> matérialisme mécaniste et le matérialisme dia-
> lectique, mais le matérialisme quel qu'il soit et
> la condamnation théologique du matérialisme,
> et cetera, eh bien, oui, décidément, en ce sens, je
> me considère comme barrésien.

It would be interesting to know what would be the 'ten books, at least' which Aragon considers no longer readable. They would probably not be very different from those referred to by Montherlant as 'the out-dated part of Barrès' work (without mentioning the dead part inherent to the work of any writer)'.

This outdated part of Barrès' work consists of the articles he wrote and the speeches he made to please others or to conform to a certain public image of himself. This dichotomy is in Barrès himself and in Barrès' work. It cannot be denied. It explains how in his own lifetime he could be admired simultaneously by 'Dreyfusards' and 'anti-Dreyfusards'—they did not admire him for the same reasons. The ideology of a writer is likely to date fast, especially when, as in Barrès' case, the artist is far greater than the thinker. Those who admired in Barrès the theoretician of social conservatism viewed askance the artist. The artists are likely to understand better the contradictions of another artist because they know that this dramatic tension is at the very source of literary creation.

Marcel Proust, who is probably the writer of that period we rank highest now, saw the originality of the Barresian combination of politics and art. In 1911, when he was in the process of creating the figure of Bergotte, he wrote to Barrès:

> Il est arrivé qu'étant ce grand écrivain que vous êtes, et d'autre part ayant cet amour de la Lorraine et de ses morts, ces deux choses-là se sont tout à coup combinées dans l'esprit du peuple. Et ce que des velléités politiques n'eussent pu atteindre, voilà que vous êtes devenu ce que personne peut-être n'a jamais été à aucun degré, un grand écrivain qui est en même temps reconnu et obéi comme le chef le plus haut, par sa patrie, par l'unanimité du peuple. [. . .] Je me disais que c'est vraiment unique et sublime de penser qu'il y a une symétrie involontaire, la seule parfaite, celle de la vie d'une croissance végétale entre les fruits que vous portez sur les branches de l'action et ceux que vous portez sur les branches de l'art.

Aragon's article in 1948 marks the turning point in Barrès criticism and in Barrès' posthumous career. For the first time an artist, and an artist of the left, takes Barrès' defence publicly: he adopts the aesthetic point of view but at the same time he does not dismiss or ignore half or more of the work because it is political. Until then Barrès had been 'defended' by people like Henri Massis or Henry Bordeaux who could not wholly understand him: they emphasized the most dated part of his work, reduced him to their own size by considering him in his narrow, lesser aspect. They constituted the petty tradition of Barrès; they did their best to present a castrated hero; they turned the tree into a bare pole. Those who could understand him expanded his inheritance instead of impoverishing it: Mauriac, Drieu la Rochelle, Montherlant, Aragon, Malraux.

We cannot perhaps love and venerate Barrès' work as these Barresians do. But they can aid us to establish contact with him. Aragon's article, twenty-five years after Barrès' death, marked the decisive moment in the posthumous life of his work; his purgatory was ended. The conjunction of de Gaulle and Malraux, ten years later in 1958, showed that France was ready to live its Barresian hour. The next twenty years should be rich in studies of Barrès; his reputation can only gain from a genuine critical reassessment of his works. (pp. 542-45)

> *M. Grover, "The Inheritors of Maurice Barrès," in* The Modern Language Review, *Vol. 64, No. 3, July, 1969, pp. 529-45.*

Robert Soucy   (essay date 1972)

[*In the following excerpt, Soucy proposes sources for Barrès's anti-Semitism in the writer's ideology of French nationalism, defined in Barrès's novels as a championing of cultural rootedness associated with the ethnic and linguistic regions of France.*]

Henri Clouard in his study of *La Cocarde,* the newspaper Barrès edited between 1894 and 1895, concludes that in his social and historical thought during this period Barrès looked to Rousseau for sensibility and to Hegel for dialectic. Claude Digeon goes even further: "Whether it be in the domain of metaphysics or in the study of social problems, it is German philosophy which dominates Barrès's thinking. He is an outstanding example of the impact of German Idealism (on France) which he himself exposed and denounced." Barrès came to cultural nationalism long after Prussian troops invaded his native village in 1870—and to racism even later still.

If boyhood anti-Germanism was not the source of Barrès's later racism, what was? Clearly, the Dreyfus Affair was an important, if not decisive, factor. It was during the height of the affair, between 1899 and 1902, that Barrès went from rootedness to racism—or rather, combined the two. With the outbreak of the Affair, racism—anti-Semitic racism—quickly became popular in the nationalist camp, perhaps more popular than Barrès realized at first. In 1898, the year Zola published *"J'accuse!,"* Barrès campaigned for election in Nancy, and learned the hazards of not being anti-Semitic enough, of not traveling the full road to racism. His major opponent, Gervaise, another nationalist, accused Barrès of "surface anti-Semitism" and won the election. Whereas Barrès had only advocated that Jews be barred from important government positions and be deprived of voting rights until they were fully assimilated, Gervaise had been more blunt. "Death to the Jews!" he had cried. Described by Gervaise as being too "feeble" in his anti-Semitism, Barrès eventually scrapped his last reservations, if not his last scruples, and adopted a harder line. Defeated consistently since 1893 in the electoral campaigns he waged, he was anxious to find a winning formula. In 1898 Gervaise seemed to have had one such formula. And yet, for all Barrès's tendency toward pragmatism in such matters, the shift might have been more difficult had Barrès not already been ripe for racism. Perhaps equally important in his conversion to racism were other, less obvious, factors.

One such factor, surely, was his previous commitment to cultural traditionalism. The leap from roots to race was a short one, both intellectually and emotionally. Barrès's belief that the Jew was like an uprooted plant unable to grow, as he put it, in "our old French garden" was easily fused with the idea that the Jew was alien on account of race as well. Barrès's mastery of horticultural principles may have been weak (many plants, after all, *are* successfully transplanted), but his animosity toward Dreyfus was not. Only a thin line separated cultural anti-Semitism from racial anti-Semitism, and Barrès had little difficulty crossing it. The two eventually became subtly interwoven in his thought, as if one were the natural extension of the other. In 1902 Barrès wrote:

The Jews do not have a country in the sense that we understand it. For us, *la patrie* is our soil and our ancestors, the land of the dead. For them, it is the place where their self-interest is best pursued. Their intellectuals thus arrive at their famous definition: *"La patrie, it is an idea."* . . . You will not deny that the Jew is a different kind of being. . . . The more my sense of honor expresses itself, the more I feel revolted at the idea that the law is not the law of my race.

Perhaps also important, especially in light of Barrès's chief intellectual preoccupations, was the simple fact that race and blood were physical qualities, that they had a reality about them, a concreteness, which gratified Barrès's desire to relate himself to something tangible and corporeal—and thus which made him feel less alienated from the world in which he lived. Racism, in other words, offered him a certain epistemological and psychological security. This, in turn, was bolstered by his admiration for the vital energy of the masses, the masses that exemplified cultural as well as physical truth. With his belief in outward signs of inward grace, cultural rootedness and philosophical realism, Barrès already had a good deal in common with racist thought before his conversion.

His friendship with Jules Soury, the racist theoretician, increased this bond. Jules Soury (1842-1915), twenty years Barrès's senior, was from 1896 onward something of a mentor to Barrès. In his diary Barrès devoted whole passages to recording Soury's comments—some of which later found their way into Barrès's own writings. Many of Barrès's ideas on rootedness, racism, and science were first enunciated to him by Soury, an academic philosopher and historian. Although Soury had adopted a racist approach to history as early as 1877, Barrès seems to have resisted this side of his thought until the Dreyfus Affair. Barrès then weakened. Visiting Barrès at the second Dreyfus trial at Rennes in 1899, Soury underlined the importance of the racial issue to his younger friend—and noted in passing how much they had come to agree in this regard:

I have arrived at the same point that you had when you told me: "I no longer believe in anything but tradition and that there is order and dignity only in the army. . . ." We must fight for France and for the Aryan race. France is lost, but what does that matter to we who believe in an ideal. . . . Here at Rennes is a magnificent field of battle. Neither Russia nor Germany has found the right field of battle; it is here. *For you have said it well yourself, that it is not a question of a poor little Jewish captain but a question of the eternal struggle between Semitism and Aryanism. . . .*

I believe that the Jews are a race, even more, a species. . . . I truly believe that the Jew is born of a special anthropoid like the black race, the yellow race, the red-skin. . . . Today they are too dangerous to tolerate. [Italics are the critic's]

In recording this conversation in his diary, Barrès did not deny the remarks Soury attributed to him. Once Barrès had adopted a racist vision of Jews, he found it a simple matter to extend it later to Germans. That Germans might be considered fellow Aryans by some racists apparently did not trouble Barrès. His racism remained rooted and nationalistic, anti-German as well as anti-Jewish.

Whatever its causes, there should be no soft-pedaling of the racist philosophy that Barrès espoused from 1902 onward in such works as *Their Faces* (1902), *Scenes and Doctrines of Nationalism* (1902), *French Friendships* (1903), *Amori et Dolori sacrum* (1903), *Voyage to Sparta* (1906), *Colette Baudoche* (1909), and *El Greco or the Secret of Toledo* (1911). The claim by one biographer that Barrès always stopped short of racism, that when he used the word "race" he "never sought to make [it] precise and certainly never gave it a physiological meaning," is simply untenable. It is true of the early Barrès, not of the later Barrès. Barrès's denial that he was a racist at the beginning of *Scenes and Doctrines of Nationalism* ("we are not a race but a nation") did not prevent him, in the same work, from describing Jews as a different "species" and as "a race opposed to mine." In 1903 he wrote of the "very ancient *physiological* [italics are the critic's] predispositions" that had long ago determined how he would think and feel, and he paid homage to "the voice of the blood and the instinct of the soil" that had revealed to him the source of his most "profound energies." One result of his conversion to racism was to make his view of culture even more rigid and parochial than before. In *Voyage to Sparta* he told how he would never be able to respond to the architectural treasures of Greece because "the blood of the valleys of the Rhine" not that of the Hellenes flowed through his veins. Race, he wrote in 1903, was a cardinal fact of life and blood was "stronger than the decrees of politics and the commandments of religion."

Those who associate Barrès's name with Catholicism, that is, with an internationalist, antiracist creed, because of Barrès's defense of the Church in *The Great Pity of the Churches of France,* would do well to read this work carefully. It is, at best, ambivalent, an attempt to reconcile French nationalism with Roman Catholicism. . . . [Barrès] ended by calling for "the reconciliation of vanquished gods and [Catholic] saints," for an "alliance of Catholic religious feeling with the spirit of the earth [*l'esprit de la terre*]. . . ." (pp. 138-43)

Barrès's novel, *The Inspired Hill* (1913), taught the same lesson. The story of two brothers in Lorraine who seek to reestablish a cult of Celtic nature worship (similar to Barrès's own cult of blood and soil in many respects) and who eventually clash with a Catholic priest who represents the Church of Rome, the novel ends with the two religions finally reconciled. The inspired earth submits to the discipline of Rome. Or does it? According to Barrès, the Church finally says to its Celtic brethren: "I am the rock which endures, the experience of centuries." But then it adds that it is also "the repository of the treasure of your race." Had *la terre et les morts* of France yielded to the Church of Rome or had the Church of Rome yielded to *la terre et les morts* of France?

As is often the case with Barrès, it is difficult to tell whether he was being sincere or merely pragmatic. Had he really abandoned his previous belief that blood was "stronger than the decrees of politics and the commandments of religion" or was he trying to make Catholicism into a handmaiden of French nationalism? As a schoolboy Barrès had bitterly rebelled against Catholicism, remarking in a preface to **Under the Eyes of Barbarians** that he had neither "the unction nor the authority of ecclesiastics who speak in fortifying terms about humiliations of the soul. In 1892 he had written with similar irreverence that "God alone, Messieurs, has the right to be a misanthrope; still this notion is only acceptable if one admits that for a long time He had not involved Himself in human affairs." In 1897 he had recorded in his diary: "We reject revealed religions, because of what they contain and in which we cannot believe." As late as 1902 he described himself as an agnostic who rejected Taine's idea that "there were two absolutely different levels of reality" and expressed doubts about the "Semitic" elements in Christianity:

> Semitism and Semitism alone is monotheistic. Christianity is something else altogether. It is an Aryan conception. Aryans have always been polytheists; indeed atheists (Buddhism). But it is quite certain that within Christianity there is a good deal of the religion of Israel. But modified with such rapidity, since first it worships the son of the single God. Then the Virgin. Then the local saints. That is polytheism.

During the Dreyfus Affair, Barrès refused to make Catholicism a prerequisite for French nationalism:

> I am firmly opposed to the error, the betrayal, of confounding religion and nationalism. There is a place among us [nationalists] for even atheism. Catholicism was the religion of my predecessors; it remains available to my son if he should have a religious temperament and to myself if I should undergo a mystical crisis. The nourishment that it provides should not be degraded; I may have need of it. But it has no right to ask me for my ticket of confession; it must not try to associate my name with sacristy campaigns against free thinkers. Long live the sacristy when it fights the pharmacy of Homais whose customers are Dreyfusards. But if the sacristy speaks to me of other things, I will yawn, smile and depart."

Later during the Nationalist Revival that preceded the First World War, in an effort to reconcile clericalism and anti-clericalism for the good of French unity, Barrès emphasized not the truth of Catholicism but its social utility. It was only near the end of his life, in such works as **No Matter Where Beyond the World,** that he clearly turned back to Christianity, or at least to Christian mysticism, concluding that nationalism lacked "the infinite." (pp. 143-45)

During the First World War, Barrès underlined the harmony that existed between religion and the French military effort. "The French are fighting in a state of religious exaltation," he wrote in 1916. "They were the first to invent the idea of the holy war." His pragmatism was sometimes all too transparent: "Wars in behalf of glory and honor may succeed, sometimes! But in order to arouse the nation unanimously, it is necessary that it see itself as the champion of God." In 1917 Barrès paid homage to young soldiers of France who were convinced of "the righteousness of this war" and of a "great Presence" at their side.

He was especially pleased by the war diary of one lad which had reconciled the spirit of the soil with the spirit of God. . . . Barrès also spoke highly of another soldier, a "young Calvinist" who had no fear of death because he believed that his life was only a "rough sketch" of the one to follow, that after death "men will continue to act." Although Barrès himself found this vision "charmingly inadequate," he approvingly noted "how complete has been the victory, in these young hearts, of war-time discipline over the seething anarchy in which we found so much beauty only yesterday. What a wild yearning toward group-life!" He noticed, too, how French soldiers in their diaries spoke repeatedly of God and how they often prayed in the trenches before launching an attack. When one major had complained to a Catholic captain that that was no time for such things, that he would do better to attend to his orders at such a moment, the captain had replied that prayer did not prevent him from following orders and that he felt stronger for it. Barrès concluded, with the detachment of an outsider, that prayer had the same effect on scores of French soldiers. . . . He now agreed with a Captain Hassler who had written to him that "one cannot close one's eyes to the fact that many men are sustained by the idea of a superior being to whose care they entrust themselves." Barrès bowed to the power, or at least to the usefulness, of religion in war. (pp. 145-47)

In **Scenes and Doctrines of Nationalism,** a summary of Barrès's political thought at midcareer, racism was far more predominant than religion. In an essay on the Dreyfus Affair, Barrès maintained that the fact that Dreyfus was a Jew was itself proof of his guilt. "I need no one to tell me why Dreyfus committed treason," he wrote. "From the point of view of psychology, it suffices me to know that he is capable of treason . . . in order to know that he has committed treason. . . . That Dreyfus is capable of treason, I conclude from his race." Not only was Dreyfus traitorous by nature, he was subhuman as well, a creature whose capacity for emotion was well below that of normal human beings. Viewing Dreyfus at close quarters at the trial in Rennes (a Dreyfus who had just recently returned from four years incarceration on Devil's Island), Barrès concluded: "I think I can tell that his range of sentiments is quite limited. He is probably what naturalists call a monster, in the category of 'monsters by default.' He is lacking in a certain number of emotions without which we cannot conceive humanity." Barrès compared Dreyfus to a dog in a trap, to a creature who "howls" instead of talks. Barrès remembered the extreme pleasure he had felt in 1894 when, following Dreyfus's condemnation by a military tribunal, he had witnessed Dreyfus stripped of his grade in the courtyard of the *École militaire*. Barrès had shared the crowd's antipathy for this "Judas" with the "visage of a foreign race" and its anger at others of his race who were disloyal to France. He reported that he had made inquiries in Alsace about the Dreyfus family and had learned that the father was interested only in money and that the son was known to lack the most elementary sense of honor. Barrès claimed that Dreyfus himself was aware of what separated him from true Frenchmen: "He himself has a sense of this irreducible difference: he recognizes himself that he is of another species."

The ethical ramifications of Barrès's racism were often quite brutal. In *Their Faces* he attacked Jews involved in the Panama Scandal with the self-righteous callousness that characterizes those who are convinced that they are dealing with a race that is inferior yet dangerous. Of Baron de Reinach, the Jewish financier who committed suicide during the scandal, Barrès had this to say: "Baron Jacques de Reinach reminds one of those large rats which, having swallowed a pill, go behind the woodwork to die, whereupon their decomposing cadavers proceed to poison their poisoners. . . . The smell of this cadaver disgusts the whole of France." That racism had much to do with such enmity is underscored later in the novel when Sturel comes face to face with another Jew disgraced by the scandal, Cornelius Herz, a man broken both in spirit and in health. Sturel, proud of the fact that he is a product of the "soil of France and of an honest family line," refuses to give way to pity: "[Sturel] did not look at all upon the sick man, surrounded by his wife and children, with humanity, but rather with that cold indifference, easy to transform into hatred, which separates the representatives of two natural species." It is no wonder that Barrès dedicated *Their Faces* to France's leading anti-Semite, Edouard Drumont.

François Mauriac on Barrès's judgment of younger writers:

We [young writers] try to persuade ourselves that it is serving France to maintain her in the first ranks of the nations who know man best—to whom no conflicts of the human being are unknown.

Would Barrès have condemned us? I recall him at the burial of Marcel Proust of whom he had been very fond without recognizing his greatness. I believe that at that time, he was beginning to perceive it. But let us not doubt it: one defect in that work, and one that could be found in many other works today, would always have discouraged him: is that he would have found nothing in it which could serve what he considered the only necessity: the education of the soul.

François Mauriac, in his Men I Hold Great, *Philosophical Library, New York, 1951.*

After the Dreyfus Affair, Barrès toned down his anti-Semitism. As part of his campaign to bring an end to factional conflict and to restore French unity, he made certain gestures toward healing old wounds, even those inflicted on Jews. In *Colette Baudoche* he implied that French Jews could also be good patriots, pointing out their presence at a public ceremony in behalf of French nationalism at Metz. In *The Diverse Spiritual Families of France,* Barrès recognized the contribution that Jewish soldiers had made to the French war effort and honored those who had fallen at the front. The very title of the book, joined with a chapter devoted to French Jews, suggested that he now regarded the Jewish community as an integral part of France's pluralistic heritage, as one of the "diverse spiritual families of France." But the rhetoric was misleading. Barrès's previous anti-Semitism was only

muted not eclipsed. Even as he paid tribute to Jewish soldiers who had chosen to fight and die for France, he observed that their commitment to France was cerebral rather than instinctual—a fundamental difference in Barrès's scheme of things.

> These are the Israelites newly arrived among us and with whom the unreasoned, quasi-animal element that is present in our love for our country (as in our attachment for our mothers) does not exist. Their patriotism is all spiritual, an act of will, decision, an intellectual choice. They prefer France. They think of the nation as an association to which one freely consents.

In other words, they lacked the physical rootedness of true Frenchmen, that deep visceral, irrational attachment to the Motherland that was a matter of determinism not choice. Hence, a Jew's patriotism was less profound than that of other citizens and the Jew himself less than an authentic Frenchman. Barrès's anti-Semitism died hard, or not at all.

Those who later characterized Barrès, the middle-aged Barrès, as the great conciliator of feuding French political camps before the First World War, failed to point out that he had shifted the focus of nationalism, and of his racism, from a domestic to a foreign enemy, from the Jew to the German. With the passing of the Dreyfus Affair, Barrès turned his attention from the conflict between political opponents in the Chamber of Deputies to the conflict between "races" in Alsace-Lorraine. . . . (pp. 147-49)

In retrospect, despite Barrès's propaganda against Germany, one is struck by the remarkable similarity between Barrès's pseudo-Darwinian vision of racial struggle in Alsace-Lorraine, a vision projected well before the First World War, and later Nazi doctrines under the Third Reich. To be sure, in the Barrèsian account the races are reversed: it is the French not the Germans who are the superior race. But otherwise, the premises are much the same: races struggle against one another in a process equivalent to natural selection in the animal world; the superior race will eventually emerge triumphant; racial pollution must be avoided at all costs lest the fit be made unfit; and the only law that applies to a nation in such a situation is the law of the jungle. The most significant different between Barrèsian and Hitlerian nationalism at this point was that Barrès viewed the struggle as being restricted principally to Alsace-Lorraine. (p. 150)

In his efforts to keep alive the "dream of revenge" where Alsace-Lorraine was concerned, Barrès applied the same kind of dehumanizing racial typology to the Germans which he had previously applied to the Jews. The basic formula was much the same. Just as Dreyfus at the Rennes trial was "lacking in a certain number of emotions without which we cannot conceive humanity," so too were the Germans. In *In German Military Service* and *Colette Baudoche,* the German is portrayed as a banal, vulgar, ignoble being, incapable of truly understanding reality because of his lack of emotional depth. It was the fictional elaboration of a stereotype Barrès had presented in an article in 1902:

> The German student has no personal idea, no

view of the whole, no perception of the intimate sense of things. He does not *feel* beauty, *he learns by rote* the rules and regulations of its elements. Facts, dates, laws, formulas, scaffolding, never the life of things livingly felt. An immense scholarly apparatus, but his heart, his imagination does not vibrate.

In *Colette Baudoche,* Frederick Asmus, the German university professor, is such a person. Presented as an embodiment of German national character, Asmus is a pedantic rationalist, insensitive to the deep emotional realities that guide Colette's existence. (pp. 150-51)

If Barrès tended to portray Asmus as more of a ridiculous oaf than an evil monster, the message was nevertheless clear: the German was an inferior being. If Asmus is a "peaceable" young man, too dull-witted to detect the irony in Colette's remarks to him, more an object of scorn than of hatred, he is also, as Dreyfus had been, a creature with little human dignity, lacking in elementary sensibility, a member of a lower species. Inasmuch as Barrès taught that a human being's basic worth depended upon his capacity for responding to the deep emotional realities of life, Asmus, like Dreyfus, was subhuman. In *French Friendships* Barrès maintained that Germans unlike Frenchmen had no souls. The moral implications of this kind of racial typology are all too clear today: if the inferior race is ugly in behavior and subhuman in nature, why not treat it accordingly? If Barrès himself was no SS man, such premises nevertheless allowed him to move easily from contempt to hatred when circumstances warranted. During the First World War, he expressed admiration for the "superb words" that he was told French soldiers sometimes uttered as they girded themselves for an attack upon the enemy: "We will rush the Boches and drive our bayonets into their stomachs to the cry of the Eternal!" Barrès's stereotype had already reduced the German to the status of an object; revanchist nationalism reduced him to the status of a *hated* object. (pp. 152-53)

In *In German Military Service* Barrès presents an even harsher stereotype of the German than in *Colette Baudoche.* Ehrmann, an inhabitant of Strasbourg required to undergo military training in the German army, finds the Germans in his unit are an inferior lot. Their fundamental barbarism is only partly allayed by their heavy drinking: "the beer puts them to sleep without changing their brutal natures, natures lacking in innate politeness and hereditary culture." On the drill field, they are obsequious toward their superiors and arrogant toward their subordinates. German officers treat their men with extreme cruelty. Ehrmann sees one officer pull the ear of a recruit until, amidst the victim's screams, the blood begins to flow. Barrès notes that "constant brutalities are traditional in the German army due to the servility of the [German] lower classes. Where one cannot resort to honor, one necessarily resorts to the baton." Germans also lack the nonchalant grace of French soldiers; their movements are stiff and mechanical, like robots. If the German soldier has bigger muscles, the French soldier has greater physical agility. As for German civilians in Strasbourg, they are petty, spiteful, legalistic souls who constantly inform upon one another. Lacking French *gentillesse* ("kindness"), they are more concerned with rules and regulations than with human feelings. In one episode in the novel, a German law student, spying a fellow German smoking at a café concert, hastens to report him to the police. Another German informs upon a young woman in his neighborhood who, after great distress, had killed her illegitimate child. Despite her pleas for mercy, the letter of the law has to be rigidly upheld. Since the Germans have no generosity in such matters, they are astounded when Ehrmann behaves differently. When he comes upon two German soldiers drunk and asleep in the camp stable in violation of army regulations, he awakens them and sends them on their way instead of reporting them—an act of kindness that leaves them stupefied. "If I had applied the principles of the Prussian jurist," Ehrmann thinks to himself, "I would have done nothing more than what these brutes expected." After other incidents of this sort, the Germans in Ehrmann's unit bow in admiration before *"la gentillesse française."* As one of them puts it, "the French have more humanity than others."

There is a curious ambivalence between Barrès's praise of French gentillesse and generosity in *In German Military Service* and *Colette Baudoche* and the cult of Darwinian struggle for survival and tough-minded realism which he advances in both his earlier and later works. The discrepancy is less puzzling, however, if one keeps in mind the function that the former served in Barrès's anti-German crusade. Barrès's praise of French gentillesse made the Germans' alleged lack of this quality all the more glaring. The obverse of French virtue was German vice. Ehrmann's benevolence underscored German malevolence, Colette's refinement German boorishness, French nobility German ignobility. Such parallelisms were calculated to make the reader feel not more kindly toward the Germans but less—as is borne out by the revanchist conclusions of both novels. Stories of French gentillesse were additional proof of German inferiority. Although Barrès was indulging in the same kind of propaganda that he had condemned twenty years earlier in Tissot as reflecting "the ignorance and bluster of our worst traveling salesmen of yesterday," it was nonetheless propaganda with a powerful psychological appeal: one could wish a war of revenge upon the Germans while retaining a sense of moral superiority at the same time.

However *gentil* Ehrmann is in his private morality, as a loyal son of France he thirsts for war against the "Boche." He sees himself as a "modest fighter" in the struggle to liberate his homeland from the Germans, as one of the "innumerable irregulars" who have stayed behind to resist the enemy after the main troops have withdrawn, awaiting the "day of anger" to come. He is a true French hero, "a man filled with a sense of his soil and his race, who, freely, in joyous sacrifice, ranges himself with his predestination." Like other Barrèsian heroes, he is willing to employ harsh methods to achieve French ends. For despite the romantic threads in Barrès's political thought and despite his talk of French gentillesse, the heroes of his essays and novels from *The Uprooted* onward are tough-minded realists who believe that the ends justify the means and that life is a struggle for survival in which the strong ultimately triumph over the weak. (pp. 154-56)

Robert Soucy, in his Fascism in France: The Case of Maurice Barrès, *University of California Press, 1972, 350 p.*

Frederick Busi   (essay date 1975)

[*In the excerpt below, Busi chronicles the outrageous mock trial of Barrès that was staged in Paris in 1921 by Dadaists.*]

In the dim memory of the general public the chief recollection of the Dada movement is perhaps the series of outrageous performances staged in order to *épater*—or more accurately—to *emmerder le bourgeois*. From its beginning in Zurich to its flowering and demise in Paris Dada promoted several public spectacles of esthetic highjinx, the most significant of which was the so-called trial of Maurice Barrès. (p. 63)

What has become known as "the Trial of Maurice Barrès" represents the watershed of Dada, the point after which Breton and close followers went their own way, which led to Surrealism. But before reviewing the circumstances of this significant meeting, others questions must be answered. Why Barrès? It may seem difficult to imagine today, fifty years after Barrès' death, why a writer of his sort had been singled out for vilification.

In one sense posterity and taste have not been kind to the reputation of Barrès, and yet in an indirect way his moth-eaten chauvinism and xenophobia left their imprint on millions of his countrymen. Throughout most of his enormously successful career Barrès described himself as a national socialist, was rabidly anti-Semitic and anti-Dreyfusard and was largely responsible for keeping alive the dreams of reconquering Alsace-Lorraine. His position in society was not unlike that of Voltaire, Hugo, Zola, and, today, Sartre, except that they were libertarians whereas Barrès was firmly authoritarian. He was the writer-philosopher whose views on every conceivable subject were solemnly debated and often accepted. But not by all. Despite his elegant style—which captivated many Dadaists during their youth—Barrès was really a bit of a bluffer. He preached a cult of blood and war, but could not stand the sight of blood.

At the very beginning of the *Littérature* number devoted to the trial of Barrès, Breton sketches the origins of the affair: "One evening some of us assembled in a café on the Boulevard Montparnasse, were speaking about the accidents, thefts and crimes of the week. Abruptly a very lively discussion started up on the subject of Barrès. No one was in agreement. At that moment we decided to expand the discussion and to form a tribunal." Ribemont-Dessaignes writes: "For my part I couldn't be bothered with Barrès for whom I had an instinctive horror and who literally disgusted me." The deepest reservations were held by Tzara. Personally, he resented his lessened authority and philosophically he felt Dada had no business engaging in partisan activities. Up till then Dada gleefully hurled invective and accusations at everyone including itself. To single out one man, however detestable, was a breach with its own tradition of irreverence.

Barrès had been summoned to appear at his "trial"; to no one's surprise he failed to comply. He left Paris suddenly and the Dadaists naturally preferred to believe that they were responsible. The trial took place, as announced, on Friday, May 13, in the Salle des Sociétés Savantes. The presiding judge was Breton, who was assisted by Fraenkel and Deval. Ribemont-Dessaignes was the public prosecutor in a role that suited him perfectly. For the defense, Aragon, aided by Soupault, offered his services. All were dressed in judicial garb to lend a mock-serious air to the proceedings. Because of the accused's absence, Barrès was represented in the form of a store dummy seated in a chair.

The documentary record of this trial is incomplete. Of the two issues of *Littérature* devoted to it, number twenty—the last of the first series—was published and number twenty-one got only as far as the galley proofs. Breton opened the court session by reading the curious bill of indictment:

> Dada, deeming it is time for it to place an executive power at the service of its spirit and deciding above all to exercise it against those who risk impeding its dictatorship, takes from this day forth measures in order to destroy their resistance.
>
> Considering that a particular man, being in a particular period of solving certain problems, is guilty if
>
> either by desire for tranquility
>
> either by need for exterior action
>
> either by self-kleptomania
>
> either by moral reason,
>
> he renounces what there may be unique in him; if he gives cause to those who claim that without the experience and consciousness of responsibilities there can be no human proposition, that there is not without it any true possession of oneself;
>
> and if, in regard to what may have revolutionary power, he upsets the activity of those who would be tempted to draw inspiration from his early teaching,
>
> accuses Maurice Barrès of a crime against the security of the mind.

When Breton mentions "self-kleptomania" he harks back to a notion dear to early Dadaists. Theft from oneself stands out here as the most original indictment and it goes straight to the heart not only of Barrès' philosophy but also to the basis of the social contract. Like Rousseau, Tzara believed each individual possessed unique talents which were stifled by society's standards. By extended analogy Barrès would stand guilty of the same crime which led millions of young men to give up their minds and lives in the nationalist cause.

Most of Barrès' career was devoted to extolling the debt of the living to the dead. The dead weight of a glorious past took precedence over the concerns of the present. This was a far cry from the young author who wrote *Un Homme Libre* in 1889. The only hope and joy Barrès could find in subsequent works would be through some sort of service to the fatherland: castigating financiers, exposing the inferiority of non-French cultures, and matching French against German imperialism.

In reading the indictment, Breton acknowledged his generation's debt to the writer whose "reputation as a man of genius protects him from any profound scrutiny." He also called Barrès one who "satisfies the most vulgar appetites." Pursuing the list of charges, Breton contrasted the exemplary nomadic life of Rimbaud with the respectable author "who has been seduced by honors." Instead of the usual Dada buffoonery Breton drew up a pompous, philosophical, humorless list of grievances subdivided into eight sections. Presumably, after reviewing Barrès' literary talents, Breton was forced to accept the view of the *poète maudit,* Lautréamont, that "the masterpieces of the French language are the speeches for the distribution of prizes at lycées." Considering its own development, Dada could find no quarrel with Barrès for his contradictions; the change of opinions might constitute a sign of vitality. Instead, with the notion of "self-kleptomania" still in mind, Breton concluded: "No, Barrès has never been a free man."

The only comic relief in the proceedings was provided by Tzara. Breton had rightly feared his presence for the simple reason that he refused to play Breton's game, to be trapped by his humorless Gallic logic:

> Q. "Do you know why you've been asked to testify?"
>
> A. "Naturally because I'm Tristan Tzara. Although I'm not completely convinced."
>
> Q. "What is Tristan Tzara?"
>
> A. "It's the opposite of Maurice Barrès."
>
> Q. "The defense, convinced that the witness envies the fate of the accused, asks whether the witness dares to admit it."
>
> A. "The witness says shit on the defense . . ."

To conclude his testimony Tzara sang a little Dada song, to the consternation of Breton. On that discordant note the trial as reported in *Littérature* seems to come to an end. Then the public prosecutor began by painting a general portrait of Barrès, emphasizing his reputation, and then proceeded to a wild attack:

> Maurice Barrès likes to walk on maggots so long as he gets his kicks on the flag. He's a champion of civilization. To be civilized is to plant spinach in a cemetery . . . Barrès, you've lied. And you who've followed him, you're idiots. Barrès, poor miserable crook, so where's your free man? . . . Maurice Barrès, great cultivator and undertaker's assistant, I accuse you of having, with an obscure lyricism, an exalted confusion, passing off your lack of grandeur for strength; of having destroyed the energy of your little friends by a deceptive verbalism, and now of smashing them in the mouth with your bicycle . . . Gentlemen, I hand over to you the filthy remains of this dead monk (*cette sale défroque*). It's up to you to

judge whether he's fit for the executioner, a prison guard or a pimp.

Apparently capital punishment was avoided and Barrès was condemned to twenty years at hard labor. Those in the audience who supported Barrès could not let this affront pass. When Mme Rachilde jumped onto the stage to berate both Barrès' accusers and defenders, the latter responded by letting loose a barrage of dried beans from the balcony. Then, as Sanouillet relates, "about thirty patriots sang the *Marseillaise* and marched onto the stage, the curtain of which was quickly drawn." Picabia, the anarchist, who was watching the spectacle, left in disgust. And when Aragon rose to plead the "defense," half the audience got up and left.

The trial of Maurice Barrès did not enjoy the success of the Salle Gaveau but neither was it the last Dada show in Paris. It is chiefly remembered as the catalyst that precipitated the breakup of Dada. (pp. 66-9)

> *Frederick Busi, "Dada and the 'Trial' of Maurice Barrès," in* Boston University Journal, *Vol. XXIII, No. 2, 1975, pp. 63-71.*

Gordon Shenton (essay date 1979)

[*In the following excerpt, Shenton examines a complex aspect of Barrès's "Culte du Moi," the relationship between body, intelligence, emotions, and the will, as Barrès defined them in his early novels* Sous l'oeil des barbares *and* Un homme libre. *The critic shows how Barrès's theory of self allows for a positive view of physical illness as an agent of intense feeling.*]

What value should be attributed to the body in *Le Culte du Moi*? The insistence on the superiority of instinct over intelligence might lead one to expect some glorification of it; but Barrès is no D. H. Lawrence, praising the fullness of life in the surge of the blood or seeking authenticity in genital activity and virile strength. On the contrary, the body is a puny thing, sickly and unexercised, as we might expect of a young man who had spent his life among his books or in the cafés of the city. The intelligence has been developed at the expense of the physical functions and, far from glorifying the body, Barrès treats it with a self-deprecatory irony, dwelling on its puniness and calling attention to the ills that beset it. In *Sous l'œil des barbares,* he exclaims almost derisively, "Qu'importe mon corps!" He dismisses it as a mere "plaything," infinitely inferior to that inner Self which is the object of his cult. He is in no way responsible for this "mediocre product" with which he was supplied at birth. However, his attitude is not simply one of contempt for the body, for it is not altogether dismissed as an unworthy material receptacle for the mind it sustains. Certainly it is not a case of stoic disregard for the physical element of existence.

Barrès is one of many writers in the second half of the 19th Century who reflect in different ways a general preoccupation with psycho-physiological thinking. The passages in *Sous l'œil des barbares* and *Un Homme libre* which refer to the body and its functions have to be read in the context of the physiological realism which had been in vogue during the naturalist years if their full "ideological" and ironic force is to be felt. Barrès takes full advantage of the fact that his subject (the relation of the Self to the World) is a crossroads at which not only philosophy, but also its related discipline, psychology, converge on certain themes of current sensibility. In the latter part of the 19th Century, men were quite accustomed to a mixture of philosophical and psychological speculation, and he was able to make use at one and the same time of a somewhat transcendental, idealist way of talking about the Self and a view of the human being as a psycho-physiological mechanism. Idealism and materialism are strangely mixed in *Le Culte du moi.*

In its thinking about the nature of psychic phenomena, positive science in the 19th century developed the materialist orientation of 18th century philosophy. That is to say, there was a tendency to view mental phenomena as an extension of physiology and to reduce psychic activity to manifestations of organic conditions. (pp. 74-5)

In a typically ironic and high-handed manner, Barrès reverses this whole way of thinking in one simple stroke. And he does this without attempting to refute the current ideas on psychology or to reaffirm idealistic notions of the independence of the human personality. He is quite prepared to see the body and its psychic adjunct, the soul, as a mechanical system, but he certainly does not intend to be determined by it. On the contrary, he turns this physiological reduction of the personality to his own advantage in asserting his principles of total freedom and self-creation. Since the physical constitution and the complex of impulses and feelings which derive from it produce mechanical responses to the situations in which the individual finds himself, then it is up to the individual to take over conscious control of his own mechanism. Having established a fundamental discontinuity between the inner Self (the seat of consciousness and will) and the material, existential Self, the egotist is in a position to manipulate and direct the functioning of the machine by careful selection and dosing of the stimuli.

It is to religious psychology that he turns for a model upon which to base this method. The spiritual exercises of Loyola, which are designed to stimulate and direct the imaginative process around the object of their choice, provide him with a perfect analogy for his constructive meditations. Thus, in his determination to appropriate any idea that can serve his purpose, Barrès brings about a curious convergence of religious and positive psychology upon the idea that psychic processes are mechanical and that they can be manipulated. In a sense which is quite different from what the naturalists understood by the term, but with its roots in the same pseudo-medical view of human behavior, *Un Homme libre* can be said to be an "experimental" novel. Once again, then, we see that his egotism is a carefully calculated mixture of sabotage and assimilation in which irony goes hand in hand with high adolescent seriousness.

Philippe's objective in *Un Homme libre* is to perfect his "mechanical method" so as to generate emotional enthusiasm whenever he wishes—*à volonté* ("at will") is a frequent expression in the book. Thus he will become an "admirable machine"; his soul will be a mechanical organ which will play him the most varied tunes when he presses the appropriate button; and he will be able to hold his "mechanized soul" in his hands ready to provide the rarest emotions. He describes himself holding his soul in hand like a horse on a rein:

> On connaît ma méthode: je tiens en main mon âme pour qu'elle ne butte pas, comme un vieux cheval qui sommeille en trottant, et je m'ingénie à lui procurer chaque jour de nouveaux frissons. On m'accordera que j'excelle à la ramener dès qu'elle se dérobe.

The image is ironically self-deprecatory. There is a deliberate deflating contrast between the decadent overrefinement of the "nouveau frisson" and the vision of the old horse.

Barrès' view of emotion as something mechanically generated serves as a means of undercutting his flights of romantic sensibility, of bringing himself down to earth, and of reminding himself of the modest, even mediocre foundations upon which his sentimental "universe" is built. But he is not just proposing a therapy for the Romantic Agony; his purpose is to transform romantic enthusiasm into a manageable source of spiritual energy. And, of course, it is also true that the more Philippe belittles his material Self through this kind of reduction, the more he exalts the godlike independence of his will.

Philippe's program, therefore, demands a knowledge of the laws by which his mental processes are governed. The psychological method of Loyola teaches him how to cultivate his emotions mechanically, but it is to Georges Cabanis that he turns for a physiological understanding of his temperament. In his *Rapports du physique et du moral de l'homme,* Cabanis had set out to demonstrate the dependence of mental activity upon the functioning of the other organs of the body. He shows that the brain is merely an organ among others and governed by the same laws of interdependence and reciprocal influence that can be observed in the lesser organs. The moral personality is a mechanism, determined by the interaction of the organs of the body and the reactions of these organs to the sensations which affect them. Thus ideas, instinctive inclinations, conscious desires, and affections: everything which constitutes the individual character, are mechanically produced. This devaluation of the personality in Cabanis' system was in complete accord with Barrès' own idea that individual character is an accidental phenomenon quite different from the deep Self. He also finds support in Cabanis' work for his belief that it is possible to control the functioning of this mechanism. He concludes that a little practice should enable the egotist to generate the "rarest states of the human soul," simply by applying some vigorous hygienic and pharmaceutical measures.

Another similarity in the ideas of the two men is their interpretation of the Self. For Cabanis, as for Destutt de Tracy, the Self resides not in the personality but in the will, and the will is the manifestation of the unique principle of the universe, of that primary force which he calls "spontaneity":

> Cette force n'est autre chose que le principe gén-

éral du mouvement, la puissance active. . . . Je l'appelle spontanée, non que je prétende exprimer par là sa nature, mais parce que ce mot me paraît rendre l'impression qu'en reçoit l'intelligence bornée de l'homme, en voyant cette force agir sans relâche, avec une activité toujours nouvelle.

Cabanis thought that it was impossible to know this force in its essence but that it could be apprehended in its effects in the phenomenal world. It is through his will that man participates directly in this universal force.

The belief that the activity of the brain was a mechanical function like that of any other organ of the body led, of course, to a downgrading of intelligence, and in this Barrès is representative of a marked tendency among his contemporaries. Jules Soury, whom he knew personally, held views about the brain and the nature of intelligence which were very much a continuation of Cabanis' approach to psychology. Psychic activity was rigorously determined by the physical mechanism of the organs, the intelligence was functional, and consciousness was to be seen not so much as a spiritual entity as an effect, an epiphenomenon.

Soury even believed, in agreement with the ideas of Alexandre Herzen, that consciousness was a state of imperfect organic development and that cerebral activity might in time become a subconscious automatism. Without going so far, Barrès was quite prepared to belittle the intelligence or hear it decried, since his belief that the authentic Self resided in a spontaneous and at times unconscious will effectively bypassed intelligence. The yardstick of man's true nature was no longer his intelligence, but rather the instinctive force within him.

It would be a mistake, however, to think that Barrès was systematically contemptuous of intelligence. He was well aware that he was an "intellectual" whose experience of life had been formed by books and ideas. Intelligence, for him, was a tool and not an end in itself. It could not provide truth, but it could devise the method for finding it. Thus he is contemptuous of intelligence when it is divorced from the profound sources of creative energy within the Self; when, as in the Temple of Wisdom in *Sous l'œil des barbares,* it is just a sterile activity turning upon itself. He defines the essential characteristic of man—that which separates him from other animals—as the ability to "set his sensations intelligently in order." When Barrès places himself before his own feelings, before a landscape, or before a work of art, it is not to abandon himself to any intellectual surrender. On the contrary, by reflection and analysis, he attempts to uncover the real significance of the phenomenon. But the truth itself is not a logical, rational proposition. It engages the whole man, not just his head; it is rooted in the psycho-physiological totality of the human animal. Thus the truth is embodied, in Barrès' universe, by creatures (women and animals) whose intelligence is least developed, whose grasp on life and awareness of that truth are instinctive and physical.

However much he may seem to downgrade intelligence and to celebrate the Unconscious, he never attempts to give his readers any direct apprehension of the spontaneous life force. The mystery of Bérénice is decomposed and

rearranged into a thematic spectrum through the lucid prism of Philippe's mind. His books are a bringing to consciousness of intuitively experienced underlying truths. Intelligence has been dethroned, but intensity of consciousness remains a major value. In his comments on the rank of intelligence in the hierarchy of human values, Barrès adopts a position which is close in some ways to that of Proust and Gide after him. These three writers can only be classed as intellectuals; they are the product of a highly refined culture and their thought and style always bear the marks of a great subtlety of mind, but all of them in their different ways assert the primacy of sensation and immediacy. (pp. 75-82)

Sickness has several thematic functions in *Le Culte du moi*. It provides a kind of analogy with other major themes, so that, although presented literally as something from which Philippe actually suffers, its function is really metaphoric. Sickness can be related to the notion of romantic sickness, to spiritual disgust, and to depression. Romantic sickness, which is an affliction of the mind, is literalized by its association with real, physical disorders. The very notion of sickness to characterize the romantic imagination is itself metaphoric to some extent, and this metaphoric element is treated literally by Barrès. This tendency is, of course, related to the theories of psychophysiology which aim at reducing moral phenomena to their physical origins. It is not irrelevant, in this context, to remember that decadence was taken literally by some in this period. Thinkers believed in a real physical decline among the overcivilized peoples, of which decadent art was only one symptom. Historical thinking had, in its increasing pessimism, taken over the current scientific interest in degeneration.

The idea of cultural sickness was thus taken literally towards the end of the 19th Century, by Barrès and others. There was a preoccupation with hygiene which affected personal, social, and political life. Colonialism, physical action, adventure, the boy-scout movement, nationalist and racial doctrine to name a few, were manifestations of a desire to purify and reinvigorate what was felt as a diseased civilization. The romantic legacy of hypersensitivity is treated as a physical disorder by Barrès, to be remedied by appropriate hygienic measures. Thus in *Sous l'œil des barbares:*

> Silencieux et affaissé, il cachait le plus possible ses sentiments, mais la meilleure réfutation qu'il leur connût consistait en un long bain vers dix heures du soir et une préparation de chloral.
>
> (p. 83)

It is in Baudelaire's *Journaux intimes* once again that the theme of hygiene may have its origin: the second part of this work is called "Hygiène." Feeling himself threatened by insanity, Baudelaire lists the steps he takes in a program of moral and physical hygiene. Like Barrès' hero [in *Sous l'œil des Barbares*], he resorts to medicaments and remedial baths: "Poisson, bains, froids, douches, lichen, pastilles occasionnellement; d'ailleurs suppression de tout excitant." A striking similarity between "Hygiène" and *Un Homme libre* is the association of bodily hygiene and religious discipline, especially, prayer, in a wider hygiene of the soul. Of the three provisions in Baudelaire's program, only work is absent from Barrès' novel. Like Philippe, Baudelaire establishes a series of rules to govern the course of his life:

> Je me jure à moi-même de prendre désormais les règles suivantes pour règles éternelles de ma vie: Faire tous les matins ma prière à Dieu, réservoir de toute force et de toute justice, à mon père, à Mariette et à Poe, comme intercesseurs.

Even the notion of method, which is so important in *Un Homme libre,* occurs in the *Journaux intimes:* two of the sub-sections in "Hygiène" are entitled "Hygiène, Conduite, Méthode."

The complaints from which Philippe suffers are minor, symptomatic of a poor general condition. They affect the stomach and the nervous system for the most part: poor digestion, biliousness, colic, anemia, neuralgia, insomnia, migraine. These afflictions are appropriate because in most people's experience (particularly in France where nervousness and digestive problems are almost traits of national character) they do reveal a certain interdependence of the moral and physical states. Barrès always presents himself to his reader as a sickly man, with an extremely capricious gastric system which serves as a physical indicator of his emotional state. Extreme nervousness lies on the borderline between a real, physical deficiency of the nervous system and the temperamental constitution of the moral character. It partakes of both and serves as a link between the physical and the moral elements.

The feeling of depression is usually accompanied by these physical afflictions. As is true in the works of Huysmans, the obsession with food, digestion, and remedies parallels the sense of horror which life inspires in the sensitive man. In *Sous l'œil des barbares,* the young man suffers an attack of neuralgia as his emotional anguish reaches a peak. He feels himself literally poisoned by the "vulgar universe," menaced by biliousness and "coliques hépatiques"; he is troubled by rheumatism; and threatened by anemia. On the train for Saint-Germain, Philippe remarks: "Malgré que l'odeur de la houille et les visages des voyageurs toujours me bouleversent l'estomac, l'avenir me paraissait désirable." The rhetorical linking of two causes of quite a different order reduces moral revulsion to the level of physical nausea.

These details concerning the body have no fictional relevance; they do not contribute to the unfolding of any story or to the exploration of character. They are given such prominence because they function metaphorically within the total thematic complex. Of course, actual metaphors or comparisons often emerge from this relationship:

> Ces querelles émoussées, ces compliments, ces réclamations m'étaient une chose de dégoût, comme l'idée fixe dans l'anémie cérébrale, ou, dans l'indigestion, le fumet des viandes qui la causèrent.

But whether the symptoms are literally experienced by the egotist or are simply evoked to say what his feelings were like, the effect is the same. In this kind of non-realist novel, story motifs function on the axis of metaphorical significance and not on the plane of fictional illusions.

It is often the case in Barrès' writing that his images are subordinated to the thematic organization in this way, growing out of a previously established analogy or identification. The religious images emerge in *Un Homme libre* out of the essential thematic association of the cult of the Self with the adoration of a God. Similarly, the numerous images of mechanism develop from the notion of mechanical and artificial stimulation of feeling. Since the processes of the mind are interpreted as a biological mechanism, the relation between tenor and vehicle is more than just one of suggestiveness: there is a material similarity. This tendency to literalization has the effect of blurring the distinction between the literal and the figurative and, at the same time, of reducing moral phenomena to their physical equivalents.

Elsewhere we find the young egotist in such a state of feverish hypersensitivity that he experiences tingling sensations all over his body—"an intolerable acuity." In the course of his experiment with the "Object" in Chapter Eleven, Philippe's nervous anxiety attains a paroxysm of physical tension in which he feels like kicking the furniture or smashing plates and which gives an idea of what it is to be an epileptic. This feverishness is one of Barrès' most characteristic conditions, and its value is ambivalent in *Le Culte du moi.* Sickness and fever may be the symptoms of unhappiness, depression, and emotional instability, but they are also the origin of his exaltations. Periods of intense feeling are associated with sickness and good health with reduced awareness and a flat commonplace vision of the world. He is only truly himself in these hours of unhealthy excitement. Barrès is typical of his generation in preferring the superior realm of the anxious spirit, however diseased his analysis may show it to be, to the mediocrity of bourgeois normality.

At the beginning of *Un Homme libre,* Philippe declares: "Le paradis c'est d'être clairvoyant et fiévreux." A little earlier, he had explained to Simon:

> Notre vertu la moins contestable, c'est d'être clairvoyants, et nous sommes en même temps ardents avec délire. Chez nous, l'apaisement n'est que débilité; il a toute la tristesse du malade qui tourne la tête contre le mur.

The desired state of ardor is thus equated with fever, but the delirium which accompanies it is something that increases the lucidity of the mind. It is by no means a blurring of consciousness; there is no invasion of hallucinatory dreams. On the contrary, feverishness is an excitement of the brain which emotionally charges the lucid and coldly analytic vision. It usually has a positive value. . . . The image of acute unhappiness as a physical sensation akin to a high fever reinforces the idea, so essential to Barrès' work, that thought and sensation are equivalent. By abandoning himself, almost voluptuously, to his solitary misery, he experiences a joy in the self-indulgent intensification of his feelings. Feverishness and exaltation are almost identical in that they overcome the sterility which threatens the abstract intelligence. The image of the sick man turning his face to the wall translates the emptiness of resignation. Sickness should intensify the responses of the mind and of the body. It is defeat when it leads to a dulling of the senses. Among the sins which the egotists proscribe in their cult of the Self is "lack of fever," associated with everything that is gray and tepid. Fever, of course, is often used simply to mean "passion" or "violent enthusiasm," the equivalent of "ardor" in its Gidian sense, but its thematic association with literal sickness confers a double resonance upon the term. Sickness appears, then, in *Le Culte du moi* as a value, as something to be cultivated for the heightened sensibility which accompanies it. The hypersensitivity of his nerves is a guarantee of emotional intensity, by carrying to the extreme all his sensations, even the most unpleasant, so that they take on the stature of noble passions. Feverishness leads him back to emotional fullness by exacerbating his despair.

As Barrès writes in the Preface to **Un Homme libre:** "Souvent leurs maladies préparent leur santé," similarly Philippe defines his project as "la culture de [ses] inquiétudes." He underlines the relation between his sickness and the method which will lead to the creation of his universe. His feeling of disgust, that delicate reaction which makes him recoil from the vulgarity of the world around him, has a function within the framework of his method. It acts as a preventive remedy (he speaks of his "dégoût préventif") against the loss of the Self among the temptations that surround it. Furthermore the egotist intends to utilize the afflictions of his mind and body in the creation of his embellished universe. On the one hand they are a guarantee of authenticity because they are truly his own and not borrowed attitudes, and on the other the possibility of a cure can be hoped for in the deliberate cultivation of these weaknesses. The descent into the Self is a therapeutic probe which does not seek to remove the disease so much as to bring it into the light of consciousness so that the symptoms can be assimilated into a new total health.

The entire Cult of the Self can be seen, then, as a form of therapy, as a "hygiene of the soul" similar to that perfected by the religious orders. Thus when the young man exclaims at the end of **Sous l'œil des barbares:** "Maître qui guérirait de la sécheresse," the verb *guérir* is to be taken almost literally in its physical sense. Bérénice's obscure solidarity with her race and the world around her is a "strong medication" for Philippe. Her function is to incarnate many of the diseased aspects of his sensibility (melancholy, love of solitude, nostalgic dreaming), but in such a way that they are transformed into creative values.

The creation of a personal "Lorraine" is thus ultimately a "hygienic" construction in which the egotist finds health by merging himself with an organic entity of which he is a living part, but which is greater than the Self. If individualism is felt as unhealthy, it is by a conscious exaggeration of it that a cure may be effected. It serves as the basis for self-discovery. (pp. 85-90)

The same literalization can be observed in Barrès' treatment of the words *goûter* and *appétit.* His starting point is the common usage of the word appetite to mean spiritual hunger or desire. Since desire is the most authentic expression of our innermost being, appetite, suggesting the basic instinctual urge, is an appropriate term for it within

Barrès' system. The same is true of the verb *goûter,* a word which occurs with great frequency in his writing as an important element in the vocabulary of egotism. The enjoyment of emotion is reduced to the level of sensation, by association with the literal meaning of the word. As Philippe begins to meditate upon the Lorraine of his ancestors, he says: "Je me découvrais une sensibilité nouvelle et profonde qui me parut savoureuse." This revival of the metaphorical significance of *goûter* is carried even further in the following text where Barrès explains why André was fascinated by Marina: "Elle était un ragoût extrêmement savoureux et bien fait pour saisir l'imagination d'un homme exigeant et hautain dans ses désirs." André finds her quite literally "to his taste." (p. 90)

Another illustration of how Barrès attains his effects by playing on the literal and figurative meanings of *appétit* and *goûter* is a passage from Chapter Four of **L'Ennemi des lois.** In their search for the conditions of a complete mental reform by which the theories of social transformation could be assimilated to the modern sensibility, André and Claire go to Germany. André finds that German socialism is essentially the political expression of the basic needs of the masses. Socialism, he reflects, has reduced the more widely ambitious doctrines of the French *Idéologues* to a purely material, economic doctrine: "le socialisme a paru réduire le parti des idéologues au parti du ventre." (p. 91)

A basic idea in **L'Ennemi des lois** is that material appetite has an underlying spiritual value. In several anecdotes, Barrès describes the gluttony of the little girls in the convent school where Marina has been a boarder. On one occasion during the Christmas celebrations, when the big girls, the teachers, and the supervisors are at midnight Mass, the very little ones, who are supposed to be in bed, get up and, pooling their provisions of holiday delicacies, proceed to have a feast. Their selfish greed may be in shocking contrast to the solemnity of the Mass, but Barrès concludes that their ecstasy, although purely physical, is just as much to be valued as any mystical one. In a typical Barresian reduction, mystical exaltation is equated with intense physical pleasure. It is the intensity of the feeling which constitutes its value, and not its absolute merits as compared with other more or less "noble" emotions. The little girls' self-indulgent joy is exemplary because it is sincere and unreflecting. André sees an analogy between the charming sensuality of Marina and her schoolfriends and the mentality of the German people. In both the gluttony of the little girls and the socialist demands of the masses, he finds the same "naive sensibility, composed of material appetites and free instincts," and the same qualities of spontaneous self-assertion. (pp. 92-3)

Thus he establishes an interplay between the literal and figurative meanings of food and eating, linking the ideological debate to the characters and underlining their exemplary role as sources of analogies and illustrations for abstractions. We have an example of the tapestry-like composition, the intricate give and take between the literal fictional level and the intellectual content, the themes repeated and developed in complex formal patterns the result of which is that stylized reduction of reality where abstract notions are transformed into immediate moral values that can be apprehended by the senses. . . . By reducing moral entities to their physical equivalents, whether it be in his treatment of the diseased romantic sensibility and the accompanying sense of moral revulsion or in his treatment of the nature of desire, he is searching for the guarantee of authenticity which can only found in the most basic instinctual responses of the senses to the world. The physical demands of the body are a legitimate defense of the Self. Since the egotist has rejected all intellectual and moral guidelines, he must reduce his vision of the world to its basic essentials. He must rediscover the bedrock of authentic self-assertion and build from there. There is certainly in Barrès' reductions and in his willingness to utilize the most banal and even puerile experiences a deliberate attempt to break away from the impotence and oversophistication of an intellectually exhausted era.

On the stylistic level—and of course style and ideology are intimately interrelated—these reductions conform to the principle which Philippe announced in *Un Homme libre:* "Réduisons l'abstrait en images sensibles." The abstract content of socialist ideology is reduced to the most concrete terms by the literalization of the notion of appetite in the particularized anecdotes from Marina's past. The gap between the two may seem enormous, but Barrès is deliberately cultivating it. The trivial sentimentality of the anecdotes in connection with political ideology is intended to surprise, even to annoy, the reader, but it brings home his main point, which is that intellectual commitment is insufficient. To act effectively for social reform, the individual must sympathize with his whole being with the ends to be attained. For these general goals to become real to the individual, he must reduce them to particular experiences which are relevant and authentic for him. (pp. 93-4)

> *Gordon Shenton, "The Body," in his* Fictions of the Self: The Early Works of Maurice Barrès, *University of North Carolina Press, 1979, pp. 74-95.*

Trevor Field   (essay date 1982)

[*In the following excerpt, Field attributes the contemporary eclipse of Barrès's reputation to his embrace of Boulangism and his anti-Semitism, both of which estranged Barrès's writings from the post–World War II generation, particularly its youth.*]

The trough into which writers' reputations fall after their death is a well-known phenomenon: whether they later emerge safely above the waves or sink into a more inaccessible environment depends on a number of factors, including prevailing attitudes at the time and the zeal of their supporters. In reviewing critical attitudes towards Maurice Barrès since the Second World War, I have been struck by the frequent use of the image of Purgatory to evoke the writer's situation, and would suggest that the treatment of this particular image enables us both to interpret and to formulate opinions about the evolution of Barrès's reputation during this period. Without becoming too involved in theological arguments we can point out at

once that connotations will be seen to vary from one critic to another, so that while purgatory represents for some a place where those who have died in a state of grace expiate their venial sins, for others it is merely a temporary state before an eternal resting-place is chosen. The overall meaning of the image is clear enough, however, and on the basis of these various allusions, which have usually been connected with some notable Barresian anniversary, it seems appropriate to venture a comment on Barrès's long-term standing.

The close connection between the growth of this image and anniversary re-evaluations is nowhere better illustrated than in its very origin. Thus, one notes that it did not occur to the authors of three articles on Barrès in the August 1947 number of *La Nef* to use the word—even though his reputation was clearly debatable at the time, for while Robert Kanters' title delicately alluded to 'Barrès invisible et présent', there was no doubting Michel Braspart's feelings on the subject: 'Je n'écrirai pas: Présence de Barrès. Car Barrès, car Barrès est absent'. Summarizing these articles a year later, in the Dutch review *Glanes,* Pierre Descaves chose Kanters' article as a good reflection of the very complexity which meant that 'Barrès est . . . présent', a phrase he repeated in concluding that Barrès was 'injustement oublié', but it seems fair to point out that Kanters' stress on Barrès's invisible presence indicates rather well the quasi-religious faith that was already needed to justify one's support.

We cannot know when Descaves's article was written, but it appeared at the very time that the *word* 'purgatoire' made its initial impact, on the twenty-fifth anniversary of Barrès's death. Jean Cocteau would seem to have been responsible for its adoption: in a brief evaluation in *La Table ronde* (November 1948) he suggested that Barrès's damaged reputation was a result of extreme political commitment, which had cancelled out his good qualities. Cocteau therefore concluded that the 'Purgatoire' was self-inflicted. As a result of this verdict, together with a contemporary observation by Mauriac on Pierre Loti, Jean-Michel Bernardin immediately organized an inquiry in *La Gazette des Lettres:* having asked seventeen literary figures what they thought of three writers who had all died roughly thirty years earlier, he published the replies in '(Les Ecrivains au Purgatoire). Enquête sur Barrès, Loti et France'. One is struck by the overall agreement among the contributors that if all three are generally unreadable, Barrès is clearly the best while Loti is worthless. If one or two reject Barrès out of hand on political grounds, most, like Claude Roy, admit that 'il nous concerne encore, avec son génie et sa sottise', and the same ambivalence underlies even Thierry Maulnier's belief that Barrès will return ('il irrite parfois, mais il existe'). But amidst such guarded evaluations, one fierce attack immediately overshadowed all the other replies: for Claude-Edmonde Magny (perhaps because her job as a lecturer at Cambridge meant that she *had* to study Barrès and France, though, not, I feel, because Barrès was not a woman's writer, as one critic later suggested), the works of all three writers should be consigned to 'le néant dont il est regrettable qu'elles soient sorties'.

This vigorous demolition work on Barrès's reputation provoked a storm of protest from defenders of the Barresian faith, and Albert Dauzat notably suggested that Mme Magny was unworthy to be a government appointee at a great foreign university. But she was by no means alone: Edmond Humeau, in 'Barrès aux limbes', claimed that nothing had happened since 1923 to indicate that Barrès should be raised from his present resting-place, and a week later Etienne Borne was prompted by Bernardin's 'Enquête' to repeat Montherlant's affirmation of 1925 that 'Barrès s'éloigne'. Under this provocative title, Borne forecast that Barrès's decline into purgatory would continue into hell, not to salvation. Condemning him for his fundamental lack of seriousness, Borne developed the basic image more than other critics by suggesting that whereas one requires poetry and truth to escape from the Underworld, Barrès is an Orpheus endowed with music but no thought, so that his 'chant funèbre' echoes the death of his work. It is clear that a new hard-headed approach was affecting critical attitudes in the aftermath of the war, and Borne was able to develop Montherlant's criticism of Barrès as a mere 'voyeur' of action: although the word is not used, the ideal of 'engagement' infuses Borne's criticism, and whether one thinks of Barrès's caricatures of clumsy, misguided Prussians (far removed from the soldiers of the Third Reich and the reality of the Occupation) or of the lyrical escapism of his literature after 1912 (with its themes of love, death and religiosity) the rigours of war would seem to have made him even more of a lightweight than had been suggested by Montherlant's jibes at his second-hand involvement in real action.

The debate, of course, was not entirely one-sided: in 1948 André Rousseau responded to Magny's criticism by claiming that Barrès's 'éloignement' was not permanent, and—rather unwisely, in view of their respective records in terms of action—associated him with Malraux, a figure whom Borne had explicitly used as a contrasting opposite. 'Non, Barrès ne s'éloigne pas', opined Jean Soulairol at the very outset of his 'Barrès toujours présent' in March 1949, but the rather desperate nature of this affirmation seems merely to reinforce the ambiguous tone of an article entitled 'Le Tombeau de Barrès' in the monarchist *Aspects de la France*. Here Pierre Boutang attacked Cocteau's evaluation and rejected any use of Montherlant's harsh judgement, but his own final words—'Barrès ne s'éloigne pas, et Maurras est vivant'—symbolise the way in which the article loses sight of Barrès, to offer merely negative reasons for supporting him. Barrès, we note, has become not a model, but a name tacked on to conservative arguments in order to gain prestige by association. In this rearguard action the case for the defence tended always to sound hopeful rather than confident, even when argued by men whom Barrès had greatly influenced. The journalist Robert de Traz, for example, commenting on the famous 'Ecrivains au Purgatoire', admitted that Barrès, France and Loti had had defects, even though he believed they had been too harshly judged and might well return to favour one day, while Mauriac had also seen both sides of the argument in his contribution to the 1948 inquiry. If he soon came down in favour of Barrès in the wider debate it seems more of a reaction against unfair critics than a positive endorsement, and he seems almost to try to post-

pone the debate by envisaging a better critical response in another twenty-five years. Not that the outlook was bright: 'en 1973, pour accueillir sa chère Ombre, subsistera-t-il encore des mains pieuses pour écarter, sur cette pierre où les plus grands noms s'effacent, l'herbe épaisse de l'oubli?'

The question mark with which Mauriac ended his article provoked little response in the years that followed: it was almost as if critics had decided to wait until 1973 before replying. The appearance in 1952 of Pierre de Boisdeffre's *Barrès parmi nous,* with a section on his 'Purgatoire', led to some varied comment, but generally speaking the answer to titles like 'Barrès revient-il?' was that 'Barrès s'est éloigné'. The 50% reply-rate to an 'enquête' by the *Nouvelles littéraires* on Barrès's reputation and influence among young writers confirmed this attitude in 1953: indifference and hostility were both more pronounced than in the 1948 survey. Attempts to ensure Barrès's reemergence to the light of critical day either appealed to a small audience or exaggerated their claims, or both: thus Boisdeffre's opinion that Barrès seemed to be rescued from the 'purgatoire' of recent years was given in a special number of *Médecine de France* devoted to medicine and art in Lorraine, while a desperate attempt by Georges Tronquart to rescue him from an allegedly tragic and excessive 'purgatoire' was based on highly inflated praise, not unrelated to the fact that it originally occurred in a speech at Saint-Dié on the thirtieth anniversary of the writer's death.

While Tronquart could quite amazingly put Barrès on a par with Socrates in order to stress his value as an intellectual figure, mainstream criticism paid little attention to him, and all in all there seemed little justification for a claim in 1956 that Barrès was emerging for good from 'le purgatoire de la gloire'. Indeed, the subject might have received no further treatment had it not been for the centenary of his birth, in 1962: clearly, there is nothing like a good anniversary to prompt reappraisals. As early as January Maurice Chapelan was basing praise for the one-volume edition of **Mes Cahiers** on the idea that 'l'heure du retour de Barrès est proche', and Boisdeffre was again prominent in the movement: in an article drawn largely from his *Barrès parmi nous* he pieced together various evaluations (starting with Thibaudet's description of the writer's corpse and ending with his own affirmation that Barrès cannot be totally dead) in the obvious aim of showing that Cocteau was right to forecast that Barrès would emerge from purgatory.

This optimistic interpretation both of Barrès's fate and of Cocteau's words was shared by André Thérive, whose 'Survie de Maurice Barrès' represents a very fair evaluation, spoiled only by the illogical claim that Barrès's spell in purgatory should end now that so many official organizations had reconsidered him in 1962. Yet it was in that same year of 'Trois anniversaires: Pascal, Rousseau, Barrès' that a monarchist writer had affirmed that Barrès 's'éloign[ait]' with a one-way ticket to oblivion despite the piety of his supporters, while in 1964, not content with opening 'Le Purgatoire de "L'Homme libre" de Maurice Barrès' with Montherlant's famous jibe, the American Will L. McLendon claimed that 'Barrès a disparu'. The thesis here is that the hero's introspection in **Un Homme libre** creates his own purgatory, from which neither he nor the author can escape, and if the details of the argument are debatable the main point is quite clear: Barrès is rejected as a mere dilettante, and the very prominence in his *oeuvre* of a novel in which a smug and wealthy young bourgeois withdraws from life to enter a state of oddly materialistic grace marks him out as a nineteenth-century relic. (One is reminded here of Claude-Edmonde Magny's indignation at 'la grandiloquence efféminée de l'écriture et le dilettantisme satisfait des attitudes'.) (pp. 49-52).

However, there were still plenty of academic critics in France to express a positive interest in Barrès's work, and in 1963 the publication of the *Actes* of the centennial colloquium at Nancy University offered a wide range of topics. Reviewing this work, Liano Petroni expressed his confidence that 'dopo un non breve periodo di "purgatorio"' Barrès was now ready to feature once again on French University reading lists, a wish that was perhaps partially fulfilled by the inclusion of a part of **La Colline inspirée** in Pierre Curnier's *Pages commentées d'auteurs contemporains*. Curnier rejected Montherlant's original formula to proclaim that in 1967 'Barrès revient', and used Aragon's support (given in 1948 as a reaction to Borne) as a symbol of the new attitude; but this rather dated and unconvincing evidence only gives extra validity, one feels, to Paul Guth's wittily irreverent account of Barrès's declining reputation in the 1960s. If Guth opens his description by apparently endorsing the doubt about Barrès's standing ('Il n'est pas encore sorti de son purgatoire') his final attitude is conveyed rather better by the amusing image of a team of disciples and Academicians regularly trying to pull him 'du fond des gouffres du Léthé . . . mais il est trop loin.' The publication of the twenty-volume *Œuvre* is seen as the most recent rescue attempt—'Repêchera-t-on l'illustre noyé?'—but Guth's ultimately pessimistic answer is summed up in the opposition between Barrès's outdated literary success and his involvement in bad political causes: 'les bonnes intentions de l'actualité ne résistent pas, littérairement, à la postérité'. Guth was surely right to see the effects of a generation gap in the changed attitude to the ex-prince of youth, and this analysis receives support from an otherwise pointless article in which a young writer named Jean-Didier Wolfromm dismissed Barrès in January 1968: having spent a month reading the first nine volumes of the *Œuvre,* Wolfromm too felt that Barrès would seem to be in purgatory for the foreseeable future.

Boisdeffre, of course, would not agree, as an enlarged edition of *Barrès parmi nous* was soon to prove. Extracts from the questionnaire he addressed to various writers about Barrès's influence were published in 1968 under the title 'Barrès au purgatoire?', with views both for and against, though the re-ordered replies show a clear movement towards the idea that Barrès has had a raw deal from critics, and two notably pessimistic replies are omitted. The question in the article's title thus seems to refer more to whether Barrès ought to be in purgatory than to whether he was in fact there. No one, after all, could seriously doubt that he was: both Emilien Carassus, in the third and final chapter of a critical anthology, and Boisdeffre himself, in *Métamorphose de la litérature,* chose the title 'Le Purgatoire' for a major section of their work. Despite his forced optimism, Carassus opens his final paragraph with three questions about Barrès's worth, followed rather defensively by a 'du moins' and a 'tout de même', while Boisdeffre admits quite openly in 1973 that Barrès is 'aujourd'hui au Purgatoire'. At this point readers who recall Mauriac's question, a quarter of a century earlier, about Barrès's eventual fate might well become impatient with the apparent abulia which causes Boisdeffre to argue that his subject is both 'trop proche et trop loin' for a clear opinion to be possible. Surely the time has now come for a decision to be made? Even Philippe de Saint-Robert, the author of one of the more critical evaluations omitted from 'Barrès au purgatoire?', was able to write, in 1974, of a 'purgatoire indéfini', caused by the fact that Barrès had been abandoned by his own side but not yet accepted by the other.

Not yet . . . Here one is reminded of the cautious response to the 1948-9 debate offered by Michel Carrouges, who, deliberately refusing to take sides, noted that despite 'le retour de Barrès' young people (like C.-E. Magny) were still wary of him, so that he remained an ambiguous figure, 'le veau d'or des uns et le bouc émissaire des autres'. But can we really go on affirming, like Emile Henriot in 1973, that posterity will see the real value of Barrès? For what, or who, is posterity? It is made up of younger people in the future, and just as we have already seen that young writers of our modern age are hardly likely to embrace 'le prince de la jeunesse' because of the qualities which appealed to his contemporaries, so the title of Henriot's article, by its allusion to Barrès the 'Prince du Nationalisme', marks him off from a post-1945 movement towards international cooperation and cultural exchange. Barrès currently exists as a writer remembered and read by academics, with two clear sides to his activity emerging. First, thanks to such patient and indeed brilliant criticism as Jean Foyard's research on stylistic qualities and Philip Ouston's revelations of the depth of Barrès's imagination, the musicality of his style and the complexity of his thought have been revealed in more than the standard vague terms; yet however much we may admire the skill with which Barrès constructs sentences, arranges images or disguises alexandrines, the result tends to be more of an exhumation than a resurrection. Meanwhile, in political terms, a range of scholars (for the most part foreigners) have become interested in Barrès as a witness of political events and trends; but although specialists may gain much from such excellent works as Zeev Sternhell's *Le Nationalisme de Maurice Barrès,* his long-term reputation as a writer is damaged to the point of his being remembered, somewhat like Edmond de Goncourt, more as a spectator than as a novelist. Significantly, a polemical work published in 1965 by one of France's more radical political commentators referred to **Leurs Figures** as 'le plus grand pamphlet antiparlementaire qui ait jamais été écrit'. No doubt Jean-François Revel's more informed readers would know that it is also a novel. . . .

If there is a case for the permanent limbo suggested by Saint-Robert, it would be based on the fair-minded critic's objection to any automatic and total dismissal of Barrès as a man or as a writer: this argument, however, would hold for any bad or flawed artist and hardly justifies the permanent postponement of a decision. Similarly, it has often been claimed that Barrès's dual involvement in literature and politics makes a final decision difficult, but quite apart from his own desire to be judged on both forms of activity together, it is clear that in the modern world his politics could never retrieve his literary reputation if the latter were in danger of being lost. However much one may explain or justify Barrès's misguided choices in politics (Boulangism; the Dreyfus affair; women's suffrage) or literature (his dismissal of Proust) the fact remains that such errors of judgement reduce his contemporary relevance. Even after the publication in the *Livre de Poche* series of several of his novels a long-standing supporter like André Dulière can these days complain that *Colette Baudoche* is a 'niaiserie', and *L'Appel au soldat* a 'roman nationaliste dépassé'. But does he really believe that *Amori et dolori sacrum,* an alleged 'chef d'œuvre', is any more likely to attract the modern public? Rather, it seems to me that the lack of popularity of works like *La Colline inspirée,* for years held up as Barrès's masterpiece, has now prompted yet another attempt to blame his poor reputation on anything or anyone other than himself. And so it is that, at the risk of re-starting a controversy which spanned twenty-five years but, with no anniversaries in sight, now seems . . . dead, I would like to suggest that for all his qualities (which I myself have stressed in other contexts) Barrès can no longer be said to stand ahead of France and Loti, and—with the disappearance of those who knew him in their youth—must ultimately be seen as a second-class writer. (pp. 52-5)

Trevor Field, "The Critical Purgatory of Maurice Barrès," in Nottingham French Studies, *Vol. 21, No. 2, October, 1982, pp. 49-56.*

Arthur B. Bateman on Barrès and the conflict of intellect and action:

. . . with Barrès the aim is to reach a foundation upon which the moral purposes of life can rest. In the earlier psychological romance there was evinced a complete distaste for action, or moral initiative arising from a supposed antipathy between thought and action. Intellectual supremacy was necessarily opposed to the energetic prosecution of external aim and purposes, the sphere of ideas to the world of action. This imaginary conflict paralysed the age preceding Barrès, but, in a way that astonished his older contemporaries, instead of submitting to the enervation of his egoism he founded upon it a system of vitalism. His later work is a singular refutation of the words of [Hippolyte] Taine: "That young Monsieur Barrès will never amount to anything, because he is impelled by two absolutely contradictory tendencies, the liking for meditation and the desire for action."

Arthur B. Bateman, in The London Quarterly Review, *Vol. 141, No. 282, April 1924.*

Jonathan Fishbane   (essay date 1985)

[*In the excerpt below, Fishbane expands upon the issue of Barrès's advocacy of Boulangism, which the critic relates to Barrès's program to "recover the ancient virtues of France."*]

Near the end of his life, Maurice Barrès recalled that the period after the Franco-Prussian War represented a low point in French "energy." It was, he reflected: "une époque de profonde dépression. Cela commandait mon rôle." To restore *élan* to French life, this therapist of the French soul prescribed the cure of integral nationalism. His medicine entailed a profound rejection of those values which he associated with bourgeois society: positivism, progress, materialism and democracy. For him, the bourgeois Third Republic was morally and socially *déraciné.* And its rationalist ideological foundations were destroying the vital instincts of the nation. In its place, Barrès envisioned the creation of a new folk community whose values would be rooted in the mystical soil of the fatherland and its heroic ancestors; a community that would be racially closed, authoritarian, and protectionist.

Yet, what makes Barrès' vision so interesting is that it did not evolve from a carefully thought out intellectual system. It evolved from an aesthetic narcissism that is readily traceable to his early writings. Indeed, his politics emerged directly out of his decadent and symbolist poetic preoccupations of the 1880's. Like Huysmans and Mallarmé, Barrès sought to substitute a vision of reality for reality itself; to replace the world as it is with one that was aesthetically more pleasing. And this artificial world offered him a means to overcome his own obsessive introspection, his own low point in energy, and led him into the world of action. Barrès the nationalist was really Barrès the aesthete transfigured.

But what were some of the major themes and concerns of the decadent and symbolist poets that played such a prominent role in Barrès' odyssey from aesthete to nationalist? The aesthetic movement of the 1880's was characterized by a profound rejection of the value-system of bourgeois society. (p. 266)

[The poets of the 1880s] believed that the only antidote to bourgeois materialism and "the muddle of liberal democracy" was a closed intellectual elite that would survive by means of its own inner resources within an ivory tower world of its own invention. According to the code of this aesthetic caste, the artist was superior to the mass of society. And he had to stay away from it to avoid contamination, and to build a new image of reality: including a new national literature. (p. 267)

This transformation will be mirrored in Barrès' alter-ego, Philippe, as he moves from his ivory tower haven to the symbolically fertile soil of Lorraine, and ultimately to an intuitive determination as to who belongs to the "real" France.

Barrès' predisposition toward aesthetic narcissism cannot be dissociated from his biography. Born in the town of Charmes in Lorraine in 1862, he was only eight years old when he witnessed German troops take his father and grandfather hostage to prevent civilians from firing on

German troop trains. His Franco-Prussian War experience, he believed, formed a powerful subconscious current that flowed into his mature vision.

Yet, equally instructive for understanding Barrès' ideas were his humiliating boarding school experiences. Mocked for his small size and frailty, the young Barrès felt a pervasive sense of inferiority with respect to his peers. He felt like an outsider, remaining aloof from students and teachers alike. Increasingly, he concluded that the institution of the French boarding school stifled individual expression. Indeed, it encouraged intellectual and social conformity; an attitude that will provide ammunition for his assault upon the uprooting nature of the Republican educational system at the beginning of *Les Déracinés.*

Barrès recorded the trauma of his school days in the *Culte du Moi* trilogy. In *Sous l'œil des Barbares,* the main character Philippe is described as a sickly boy who suffered humiliation daily. To lessen his pain, he turned to Baudelaire for solace, spending each day alone in the library "devouring audacious doctrines." Barrès thus compensated for his inability to compete physically in the Darwinistic world of boarding school by falling back upon his own resources. He learned the value of constructing ideal worlds in which to retreat in order to find shelter and comfort. As he would reflect in *Un Homme libre:* "Ce qui importe uniquement, c'est mon moi du dedans! le Dieu que je construis. Mon royaume n'est pas de ce monde; . . . c'est un rêve plus certain que la réalité, et je m'y réfugie. . . . "

In 1882, the future apostle of rootedness left for Paris. To live in Paris meant the realization of a cherished dream. It also meant an escape from the drudgery of the Nancy Lycée. He came to the capitol, he confessed, "in search of glory and a mistress." In 1884, he founded the monthly gazette *Taches d'encre* which failed after four issues. Two years later he tried his hand at another short-lived journal—*Les Chroniques.* His thus far moribund search for aesthetic notoriety now took a new turn. He was ready to write the *Culte du Moi.*

Sous l'œil des Barbares first appeared in early 1888. In April, Paul Bourget reviewed it favorably for the *Journal des débats.* Soon after, it enjoyed a considerable popularity, electrifying the students and aesthetes of the Left Bank especially. In November, the young Charles Maurras confessed that he had been profoundly moved by the book. And when the second volume of the trilogy appeared in 1889, he announced: "Voici que vient d'éclore un culte original absolument . . . un culte neuf, prêché par un jeune prophète, au nom d'un Dieu presque nouveau, Ce Dieu, c'est le Moi; Ce culte, c'est l'Égotisme; Ce prophète n'est autre que Maurice Barrès."

Sous l'œil des Barbares describes the anguish of a young aesthete (Philippe) who felt that he was part of a dying race of enlightened men and surrounded by barbarians who delighted in sensualism and materialism. The barbarian is symbolized by old Monsieur X, whose name suggests the facelessness of the crowd. Monsieur X tells Philippe that too much contemplation in the search for truth will lead to self-torment and neurasthenia. In a world where it is difficult to recognize the relationship between our ideas and our actions, we must rely upon the resources of the ego. But this idea does not lead one toward a search for truth. Rather, for Monsieur X, attachment to the self will lead one to the conclusion that to avoid pain inflicted by the external world, he must seek notoriety and reputation. He tells Philippe: "Ayez de l'argent et soyez considéré." Recognizing one's own possibilities in others, one must never be afraid to drink to those who succeed. Philippe was repelled by this advice. It epitomized a bourgeois value-system predicated upon money and political opportunism. In his rage, he smashed Monsieur X with his cane.

Philippe's encounter with Monsieur X reinforces his belief that understanding must begin with himself. Yet, this also meant that he must avoid contact with "le fleuve immonde des Barbares." He must resist anything that is related to the materialism of the barbarian world. In this regard, his sexual encounter with a young woman leaves him deeply anxious. He senses that he has betrayed his goal of becoming pure in spirit by indulging in an unclean act. He feels like a barbarian. Barrès notes: "Il comprit qu'il était sali parce qu'il s'était abaissé à penser à autrui." In place of loving a real woman, he seeks to commune with his idea of the feminine. He wants to love the idea of love, "aimer sans objet." But within such a goal lies the danger of sterility. In fact, Philippe's longing may have been linked to doubts about his own potency. It is no accident that he shudders at the thought of descending among the barbarians. They possess the very power and vitality that he lacks. As old Monsieur X had hinted, a life of pure thought may be mental and physical suicide.

Barrès suggests this to us in Philippe's dream about the last hours of the ancient world. As the barbarians begin to flood Rome, the noble Athena addresses the statues of Homer and Plato. She has learned from them "une belle pensée est préférable même à une belle action . . . Le corps est beau, mais il vaut mieux qu'il souffre que l'esprit." In the course of her meditation, she is killed by the barbarian hordes. The classical flame is extinguished. Barrès writes: "Ainsi mourut pour ses illusions, sous l'œil des Barbares, . . . la dernière des Hellènes." Philippe cannot help admiring her martyrdom. Yet, locked in an ivory-tower world himself, he cannot help but wonder whether "her mode of existence had not doomed her from the start." At the end of *Sous l'œil des Barbares,* his relentless introspection forces him to admit: "Je n'ai plus d'énergie . . . Et ce n'est pas de conseils mais de force et de fécondité spirituelle que j'ai besoin." He is fearful of ending up like Athena. At times paralyzed by the enormous demands placed on him by the self, he longs to be rescued by some master, a religion, axiom, or prince of men. And he longs for the vitality of the barbarians he detests.

Although Barrès recognizes, at the end of *Sous l'œil des Barbares,* that his deepest wish is for force and the ability to act, he continues to believe that contact with the barbarians will contaminate him. Moreover, his aestheticism convinces him that he must create his own psychological and poetic well-springs independently of the external world. In this way, he hopes to arrive at his own dynamic spiritual principle that will end his suffering. Accordingly, he leaves Paris for Jersey with his friend Simon.

Philippe discovers there a new set of "meditative principles" that establish feeling as a precondition for thought. In syllogistic fashion he enumerates: "PREMIER PRINCIPE: Nous ne sommes jamais si heureux que dans l'exaltation. DEUXIEME PRINCIPE: Ce qui augmente beaucoup le plaisir de l'exaltation, c'est de l'analyser. CONSEQUENCE: Il faut sentir le plus possible en analysant le plus possible." In this way, even the most humiliating emotions may be transformed into something positive. With this insight, Philippe believes that he has now taken the first genuine step toward becoming *un homme libre*. These meditative principles are the means to unify the intellectual self and the emotional self. They symbolize wholeness and are thus therapeutically regenerative.

After this experience in Jersey, Philippe and Simon depart for Lorraine. In Nancy, Philippe secludes himself in the town library to read Ignatius Loyola's *Spiritual Exercises*. For him, Loyola represents spiritual honesty and self-discipline. And under the influence of the great Jesuit writer, Philippe decides to retreat to an old medieval cloister to try to practice Loyola's teachings. Philippe refers to his enactment of Loyola's teachings as a "Prière-programme." The rigid asceticism that characterizes this exercise borders on a decadent form of sensation seeking. Through Loyola, Philippe hopes to realize his long sought-after "hygiène de l'âme," an intellectual step on the road to the hygiene of the race.

Philippe's meditations on Loyola teach him to be an emotional machine. "Mon âme mécanisée est tout en ma main, prête à me fournir les plus rares émotions. Ainsi je deviens vraiment un homme libre." This freedom emerges from the intuition that he can control himself and his environment completely. He learns that he is the source of his own moods and actions. Accordingly, he now feels less threatened by the barbarians. (pp. 267-71)

Philippe's journey toward a new self-discipline also begins a movement away from a decadent self-centeredness. He grows bored with his companion Simon and secretly admits that he would like to separate himself from him. He longs for fresh cultural models with which he can receive new spiritual nourishment. His odyssey takes him to Saint-Germain where he spends the winter "avec les morts qui m'ont toujours plu. Et je m'attachai spécialement à quelques-uns, au détour d'un feuillet . . . me conduisent . . . à des coins nouveaux de mon âme."

Moreover, Philippe is drawn increasingly to Benjamin Constant. Constant represents one who is able to participate in the active world of politics as well as in the quiet world of the mind. This desire for compromise between the worlds in and outside of the self sharpens the dilemma he had begun to experience in *Sous l'œil des Barbares.* Philippe now perceives two options for himself; either a life devoted to "les affaires publiques dans un grand centre, ou la solitude." But he has grown tired of meditation and solitude. Indeed, "les douleurs sans but de la société sont insupportables . . . A dire vrai, dans la solitude je me désespérais." However, still fearful of abandoning the aes-

thetic ideal of a life devoted to the self, he finds a compromise. Philippe declares: "Servons la bonne cause et servons-nous nous-mêmes." This intensified need to reconcile his introspective tendencies with his repressed desires for notoriety represents Barrès' own fatigue with aestheticism. It is also the bridge to politics.

As his inner changes subtly unfold, Philippe discovers "une sensibilité nouvelle et profonde." Wandering outdoors, he marvels at the extraordinary beauty of the Lorraine skies and countryside. The landscape fills him with an indescribable peace that dissolves his feelings of aloneness. Feeling the most possible while analyzing the most possible, he reflects that there is an eternal quality to Lorraine that commands his attention. "Ainsi, quoique jamais je n'aie servi la terre lorraine, j'entrevois au fond de moi des traits singuliers qui me viennent de vieux laboureurs." Attachment to Lorraine thus provides an escape from the paralysis of introspection. Philippe notes:

> Lassé de ne recueillir de mes intercesseurs que des notions sur ma sensibilité, sans arriver jamais à l'améliorer, j'ai recherché en Lorraine la loi de mon développement.

Visiting the local churchyards he hears sounds on the flagstones that evoke the lost voices of the dead, and the ancient language and culture of Lorraine. Communing with the dead makes Philippe feel one with all of history. And the anxieties of the self vanish into the eternalness of the race. A new path to becoming pure spirit opens before him. Whereas previously his search led to the decadent borders of solipsism, narcissism, and sterility, the new path leads to a kind of self-extinction as a preliminary to rebirth through immersion into the historical waters of racial development. Racial politics becomes the key to health and a release from the fatigue of aestheticist introspection.

Philippe's discovery entails the identification of the history of his ego with the history of Lorraine. Reading into her history, he finds that like himself, she too had been victimized by outsiders, and threatened with extinction by foreign forces. Under the Dukes, a national soul emerged. But Lorraine allowed herself to decay culturally through the slow influx of outside barbarian elements and the subsequent exit of her great native artists. "Faute de s'être affirmée spirituellement, elle s'était condamnée à la stérilité, danger qui menaçait aussi Barrès, timide et incertain de ses forces." Hence Lorraine emerges as a symbol, an objective correlative to Barrès' interior landscape:

> Or, tous ces morts qui m'ont bâti ma sensibilité bientôt rompirent le silence. Vous comprenez comment cela fit: c'est une conversation intérieure que j'avais avec moi-même; les vertus diverses dont je suis le son total me donnaient le conseil de chacun de ceux qui m'ont créé à travers les âges.

He no longer feels finite. Lorraine allows him to participate in something infinite.

Lorraine also provides Barrès with a resolution to the decadent problem of feeling threatened by the barbarian. Peasants, laborers, indeed the entire folk community of

Lorraine are now viewed as his brothers. This perception represents a complete transformation of how Barrès originally perceived the world. Even the spiteful schoolboys who had made him so miserable are part of this kingdom of innocents. Lorraine has become that vital something to which he can now devote his life. It is only a matter of time before he attaches himself to the even greater destiny of France. However, Barrès is still too much of an elitist aesthete to mingle with the unwashed and the uneducated. He admires his new family from a distance. In fact, the new folk community exists as a function of how the poet wants to see it. It is a symbolic projection of a subjective wish to escape into an idealized landscape where pain and uncertainty have been eliminated. As Barrès reflects in his *Cahiers:* "Je ne cesse pas de construire avec ces beaux éléments une idée dont j'étais à la fois l'auteur et le disciple . . . Je n'ai pas cessé de cultiver, d'inventer, de créer en moi cette Lorraine intérieure . . . "

In spite of lingering aestheticist elements, Barrès has chosen to leave his past behind through political action. Philippe informs us:

> J'ai renoncé à la solitude; je me suis décidé à bâtir au milieu du siècle, parce qu'il y a un certain nombre d'appétits qui ne peuvent se satisfaire que dans la vie active . . . La partie basse de mon être, mécontente de son action, troublait parfois le meilleur de moi-même. Parmi des hommes je lui ai trouvé des joujoux, afin qu'elle me laisse la paix.

Although he would not care to admit it, Philippe has thus accepted many of Monsieur X's conclusions. Aesthetic individualism was a dead end. A new path was needed. Through politics he could find the notoriety he coveted.

What inclined Barrès to leave subjective idealism for collectivism and rootedness was Boulangism. His own leap into politics surprised many who knew him. For example, the poet Jules Lemaître expressed complete shock by it. Barrès' decision was no doubt born of the conflict between his longings for both solitude and action. The perceptive Taine noticed this indecision when he met Barrès in the 1880's. He told Paul Bourget: "Ce jeune Monsieur Barrès n'arrivera à rien car il est sollicité par deux tendances absolument inconciliables, le goût de la méditation et le désir de l'action." Boulangism was a means to overcome his self-torment by plunging headlong into a political movement. Political action offered the antidote to the paralysis of aestheticist introspection. But implicit in this odyssey was the psychological danger that a narcissistic egoism has itself not been confronted. Hence, the leap into politics from the murky waters of poetic decadence may translate self-torture into the torture of others. The freedom Barrès finds in political action is a variant of the decadent urge to self-indulgence.

In Boulangism, Barrès felt that he had found "de quoi nourrir . . . mon âme." He added: "Je goûtai profondément le plaisir instinctif d'être dans un troupeau." Boulangism symbolized energy and vitality. Moreover, it seemed to be a genuine movement to recover the ancient virtues of France. Boulanger represented action whereas the politicians of the Third Republic represented mediocrity and cheap-talk. In the late 1880's Barrès wrote: "The General is the only person capable of expelling the chatterers who deafen us from the Palais Bourbon." (pp. 271-73)

On September 22, 1889, Barrès declared himself a Boulangist candidate for public office from Nancy. On October 6, he was elected. Barrès entered the Chamber of Deputies on a program of "Nationalism, Socialism, and Protectionism." In the February 2, 1890 edition of *Le Figaro* he wrote: "Boulangism is a socialist program, a general movement against the omnipotence of capitalism favoring national reconciliation and love of the disinherited." Barrès was once one of those disinherited. He had simply dismantled the barriers that had protected his *moi* and set them up again around the innocent people who were threatened by the materialistic ruling class. Moreover, in his national-socialistic program, the barbarian who threatened the ego of the aesthete, is translated into the foreigner who threatens the purity of the fatherland. Long before the Dreyfus Affair he had formed anti-Jewish attitudes. In fact, Michael Curtis points out that in the Nancy election program, Barrès linked the "Jewish Question" to the national one. With their money, international contacts, and excessive numbers in the government, army and judiciary, the Jews were threats to "real" Frenchmen. His solution to this state of affairs was to make the naturalization laws more stringent. By 1889, Barrès already knew who was the *pays légal* and who was the *pays réel*.

The final volume of the *Culte du Moi* trilogy, **Le Jardin de Bérénice,** is essentially an epilogue to Barrès Boulangist experience. It is also an introduction to **Les Déracinés.** In *Le Jardin,* he symbolically expresses the elements of his nationalist doctrine through his character Bérénice. Bérénice represents the race, the popular soul, and the *élan vital.* Philippe's contact with her represents the completion of his conversion to rootedness. At the beginning of the novel, Barrès writes: "C'est ici le commentaire des efforts que tenta Philippe pour concilier les pratiques de la vie intérieure avec les nécessités de la vie active."

Philippe meets Bérénice during his own election campaign. Together they study the history of the region. He learns that he is only an instant in the long cultural development of his race. More than in **Un Homme libre,** the Philippe of **Le Jardin de Bérénice** acknowledges the importance of the *Volk.* He states:

> Je n'avais pas su dans l'étude de mon moi pénétrer plus loin que mes qualités; le peuple m'a révélé la substance humaine, et mieux que cela, l'énergie créatrice, la sève du monde, l'inconscient.

National rootedness means potency and action.

The significance of rootedness is conveyed by Bérénice's life experiences. As a young child, she was taken by her parents to live in Paris. Life in the congested capital torments her and she longs for the countryside of Lorraine. Her stay in Paris affects her physically. Worried about her declining health, Bérénice's parents bring her back to Lorraine where she recovers.

What is operative here is the theme that dominates **Les Déracinés.** The uprootedness of the individual from his natural environment leads to trauma. Lost in the city of Paris, the uprooted Lorraine students feel lost until they visit Napoleon's tomb. There they find a symbol of rootedness that gives meaning to their lives. Napoleon represents French power. Moreover, in the case of the poet Sturel, the funeral procession for Victor Hugo overwhelms him with the sense of what it means to have roots in the soil of France. What separates him from Philippe is the fact that whereas Philippe discovers his rootedness in Lorraine, Sturel, himself a Lorrainer, discovers that rootedness encompasses all of France. But the distance separating the two is very small indeed. Sturel's feelings for France are linked to his roots in Lorraine.

Philippe's awareness that he is but a small segment in the greater development of his race draws upon Taine's environmental determinism. He has accepted the notion that what is essential to understanding human beings is their relationship to their racial environment through time. The unconscious racial *milieu* is the life-source. This is precisely what Bérénice symbolizes. After her untimely death, due to her excessive contact with the oppressive Charles Martin, she returns to Philippe in ghostly fashion.

> Où je ne suis pas, c'est la mort; j'accompagne partout la vie. C'est moi que tu aimais en toi, avant même que tu me connusses, quand tu refusais de te façonner aux conditions de l'existence parmi les barbares . . . Personne ne peut agir que selon la force que je mets en lui.

This is also the message that Taine brings to Roemerspacher in *Les Déracinés.* He teaches him that acceptance of determinism is a precondition for understanding oneself and the world. *Le Jardin de Bérénice* is thus a natural bridge to *Les Déracinés.* The lesson that Philippe learns in his spiritual journey through the *Culte du Moi* is essential to the nationalism that Barrès conveys in *Les Déracinés.* The ego cannot develop in a vacuum. It is tied to a particular race, milieu, and moment. Indeed, "the self is not autonomous but part of a larger whole." Uprootedness leads to spiritual malaise. In Barrès' *Les Trois Stations de psychothérapie,* the charming cosmopolite Marie Bashkirtseff will never be satisfied. "Cette cosmopolite qui n'a ni son ciel, ni sa terre, ni sa société, c'est une déracinée." For Barrès, she is the embodiment of the modern sensibility. She is a symbol of modern adriftness and accordingly is called *Notre-Dame du Sleeping-Car.* But given his doctrine, is it not ironic that Barrès lived in Paris, that den of iniquity, far away from his childhood roots, and constructed Lorraine's pastoral landscape from there?

Barrès' quest for truth was "the quest of one who had withdrawn from the real world, the world of the barbarians, but who following a period of exile wished to return." His return meant ignoring the pain he suffered at the hands of those who tormented him as a child in Lorraine. In some way, he probably always longed to be one of them. Collectivist nationalism provided the means to resolve this inner tension. Micheline Tison-Braun has written:

> Il a . . . besoin d'appartenir à un groupe humain, de forme maternelle—patrie, famille— ayant une histoire, des légendes; un groupe qui le dépasse, qui lui survive et lui dicte des règles de conduite. Il a besoin d'aimer pour obéir et il a besoin d'obéir pour se sentir en paix avec le monde.

France and Lorraine, the soil and the dead, gave him something solid with which to identify. He hoped to end his alienation through collectivism, and provide the warmth of the herd for those who were also alienated. For Barrès, there was a mystical quality to the belief in the soil and the dead. Indeed, there was a magical quality to it. "The earth and the dead are the definitive substantive powers which no one can avoid. Being untrue to them was the source of France's defeat. Through them she will be renewed." (pp. 274-76)

[Barrès] sought to provide himself and others with a symbol of something infinite and eternal. . . . It is no accident that toward the end of his life he would painfully confess, "I have felt for several months that I have been slipping from nationalism to Catholicism. It is because nationalism lacks the infinite." (p. 277)

> Jonathan Fishbane, "From Decadence to Nationalism in the Early Writings of Maurice Barrès," in Nineteenth-Century French Studies, *Vol. XIII, No. 4, Summer, 1985, pp. 266-78.*

Bill Kidd   (essay date 1985)

[*In the following excerpt, Kidd summarizes those nationalistic and right-wing positions held by the mature Barrès, as enumerated by Ramon Fernandez, a critic sympathetic to Barrès's politics. Fernandez provides new avenues to the meaning of Barrès's novels by introducing Freudian concepts to explore such important antitheses as motherland-fatherland, emotion-intellect, and classical-romantic in Barrès's worldview.*]

The subject of this short chapter is not Ramon Fernandez's critical theories, nor his political career, both of which I have dealt with elsewhere. My aim in the space available is to show, very briefly, how Fernandez presented Barrès to the reading public of the 1930s as a right-wing nationalist figure, and after 1940 as a symbol of Franco-German reconciliation. . . . [We] are dealing with literature, or the critical reaction to it, as a vehicle for ideological manipulation and, some would say, of propaganda.

Like Péguy before him, but without the aureole of martyrdom, Barrès's reputation declined considerably between 1918 and his death in 1923. 'La revanche' was no longer an issue, and the 'lost provinces' had been recovered, although at what cost. Moreover, the writer had been too closely associated with wartime 'bourrage de crâne' for his moral and esthetic values not to appear old-fashioned and doctrinaire beside those of his more subtly emancipated contemporaries, Proust and Gide, while younger figures upon whom he had a discernible, indeed acknowledged influence, evolved towards fascism (Drieu la Rochelle) or surrealism followed by communism (Aragon), respectively. Even Montherlant affirmed: 'Barrès s'éloigne'. The 1920s were a most un-Barrèsian decade. In 1929, however, the posthumous publication of *Mes Cahiers* (11 vols. by

1938) and a new study by François Duhourcau, began a process of rediscovery which events accelerated. The 6 February 1934, the remilitarisation of the Rhineland, the electoral victory of Léon Blum's Popular Front, the Spanish Civil War, and finally, in 1938, Munich, put writers like Barrès and Péguy back on the literary-political map, as figures to be enlisted by different groups, a traditionally French phenomenon whose ambiguities were well summed-up in René Lalou's phrase: 'un guide ou un otage?'

Ramon Fernandez, highly sensitive to the changing ideological temper of his times, reflects this process. His earliest 'maîtres à penser' were Proust, Bergson and Gide, the latter a major touchstone for his political position until 1933-4. The few references to Barrès in Fernandez's writings before then were generally unfavourable; he sided with Gide, for example, in dismissing the idea of 'enracinement' as botanically and psychologically unsound, and attacked his thought as a 'sophistique et stérile construction'. But reviewing two of the 'Cahiers' prompted a reappraisal: like Duhourcau, he found Barrès more intimate, more poetic and more ideologically complex than he had remembered in the immediate post-war years. And when after a period of militancy on the left, Fernandez moved to the right, joining Doriot's PPF (Parti Populaire Français) in 1937, he produced a series of major articles on Barrès which, with minimal editorial amendment, were incorporated into the book published in February 1944. The evolution in emphasis which occurred between these dates is a measure of Fernandez's growing involvement in the subject, and of the changed ideological context in which he was writing. Comparison of the pre- and post-armistice view reveals how the very elements which made Barrès a traditional right-wing nationalist reference contained an alternative, collaborationist interpretation. Summarised very schematically, the pre-1939 Barrès is presented as follows:

1. With his cult of the dead ancestors, and his successive immersion in family, province and nation, the author of *Les Déracinés* was driven to seek emotional no less than ideological completion behind 'des murs de plus en plus espacés, mais de plus en plus solides.' As such, he was an archetypal nationalist reference, available to different shades of right-wing opinion including some, it should be said, who after 1940 supported Vichy ('le chêne du maréchal' is a Barrésian symbol), or the Resistance (Jean Touchard has identified Barrésian material in Malraux's work).

2. The Barrès of *Leurs Figures* was an anti-parliamentary but still republican reference, as was the catholic Péguy, and hence a useful banner for Doriotism which, while seeking a more authoritarian and ultimately totalitarian political system, still professed attachment to certain republican, indeed 'revolutionary' ideals. To this extent, Barrès marked off the republican right from the monarchist Maurras, although the latter's influence, perhaps because of some loss of doctrinal specificity, was extremely pervasive, and extended to members of the PPF, including Fernandez himself.

3. Finally, in spite of the contradictions revealed in the

French right by Munich, the author of *Colette Baudoche* and the 'Watch on the Rhine' remained a fundamentally anti-German reference for those whose patriotism was 'tourne' vers l'Est.' Barrès, as Fernandez would later remind us, had experienced as a child of eight 'le trauma de 1870,' had been forced as a 'lycéen' to ingest the alien philosophy of Kant, and in 1914, seen France nearly succumb once more.

In extrapolating and contextualising these points, I have of necessity simplified Fernandez's analysis very considerably. Mention must be made of the fact that the critic already saw in Barrès's 'virile' nationalism a precursor of fascism, and gave a Freudian dimension to his analysis in suggesting that the writer was driven unconsciously to closer identification with the mother in order to be reconciled with the father. Both of these factors are germane to the manner in which he arrived at the subsequent supranationalist, totalitarian and collaborationist position, which may be schematised once again, as follows:

1. Thibaudet (whose death in 1936 placed him above suspicion of 'collaborationist' sympathies), had pointed out as early as 1921 that the creator of Bouteiller had misunderstood Kantism; nor indeed did that particular antipathy neutralise the more favourable impression left by other German thinkers such as Hartmann, Fichte or Schelling. His underlying attitude was not hostile but fundamentally, ambivalent: Germany was 'à la fois un pôle d'attraction et un pôle de répulsion.' There were not only 'bad' Germanies but 'good' ones; and within the emotional geo-politics which equated the Wilhelmine Reich with 'le mal prussien' (militarists, professors of philosophy), the Moselle and Rhineland-Palatinate represented a more meridional civilisation, amenable to French influence and perhaps capable, so Barrès seems to have imagined in his last years, of achieving autonomy.

2. Barrès's mother's family originated in the Palatinate (his father was 'auvergnat'); mixed ancestry made of him 'un homme-frontière.' And since frontiers unite as well as divide, the affective, psychological and cultural divide within Barrès was the meeting place and symbol of certain Franco-German antitheses—rational/sentimental, classical/romantic, paternal/maternal—which his work was an attempt to overcome. By amalgamating pre- and post-armistice ideas in this way, and giving greater prominence to 'traumatic' influences on the author's personality, Fernandez comes close to suggesting, without stating outright, that Barrès's developing preoccupation with Germany may also have derived from oedipal dynamics.

3. Finally, Barrès himself had claimed before 1914 that the trilogy of family-province-nation might ultimately lead him to catholicism as the spiritual terminus of the progression, a kind of supranational transcendence. For critics of Fernandez's ideological persuasion, there existed a supranationalism which remained firmly terrestrial and indeed territorial: the 'New Europe' being created from the Franco-German collaboration implicit in the writer's own heredity. It was but a short step to make of 'l'homme-frontière' a kindred spirit of Charlemagne and Goethe, Kleist and Novalis, whose inspiration had presided over

Joan of Arc, that other 'Lorraine' so assiduously cultivated by the PPF, he had little to offer those whose principal motivation was hatred of 'l'Albion perfide'. Nor did Fernandez exploit as one might have expected the anti-Semitism of the caricaturist of **Leurs Figures** and the opponent of Dreyfus. In fact, although he endorsed his party's wartime 'aryanism', his eulogistic obituary of Bergson in 1941, and a major study of Proust in 1943, which angered Céline and others of like mind, reveal an ambivalence which may say something about the critic himself, and ultimately about the ambiguous nature of literary activity during the occupation as a whole. (pp. 255-58)

> *Bill Kidd, "Collaboration and Literary Criticism: Ramon Fernandez's 'Barrès'," in* Vichy France and the Resistance: Culture & Ideology, *edited by Roderick Kedward and Roger Austin, Croom Helm, 1985, pp. 255-59.*

FURTHER READING

Bateman, Arthur B. "Maurice Barrès." *The London Quarterly Review* CXLI, No. 282 (April 1924): 158-66.

Explores many of Barrès's major themes—emotion and sensation, the primacy of the ego, the conflict of ideas and action—chiefly as represented in his trilogy, *Le culte du moi.*

Frohock, W. M. "Maurice Barrès's Collaboration with the Action Française." *The Romanic Review* XXIX, No. 2 (April 1938): 167-69.

Briefly recounts the history of Barrès's part in sponsoring the right-wing Parisian newspaper, *Le revue de l'action française.*

Greaves, Anthony A. *Maurice Barrès.* Boston: Twayne Publishers, 1978 p.

Concise thematic treatment of Barrès's life and works.

Lynch, Hannah. "A Political Writer of France." *The Contemporary Review* LXXVIII (September 1900): 381-88.

Highly negative review of Barrès's novel, *L'appel au soldat,* in which the critic treats Barrès's devotion to Boulangism.

McClelland, J. S. "Introduction." In his *The French Right: From De Maistre to Maurras,* pp. 13-36. New York: Harper & Row, Publishers, 1970.

Provides insights into the politics of Barrès and other contemporary French writers, with particular focus on the Dreyfus Affair.

Mauriac, François. *Men I Hold Great.* New York: Philosophical Library, 1951, 130 p.

Mauriac, a disciple of Barrès, briefly discusses the role that politics played in Barrès's life and examines the critical reception of his work in 1949, twenty-five years after his death.

Suleiman, Susan Rubin. "The Constraints of the Real: Barrès' 'Le Roman de l'énergie nationale'." In her *Authoritarian Fictions: The Ideological Novel as a Literary Genre,* pp. 118-32. New York: Columbia University Press, 1983.

Explores how Barrès's "Le roman de l'énergie nationale" trilogy diverges from the ideal model of the narrative "novel of ideas." Suleiman argues that the historical and political events around which Barrès based his narrative—the Boulangist movement and the Dreyfus Affair—hindered him from attaining the fictional and mythical modes he sought.

George Gissing

New Grub Street

(Full name George Robert Gissing) English novelist, short story writer, critic, essayist, and travel writer.

The following entry presents criticism of Gissing's novel *New Grub Street* (1891). For further information on Gissing's complete career, see *TCLC,* Volumes 3 and 24.

INTRODUCTION

Gissing's best-known novel, *New Grub Street* is highly regarded for its realistic examination of the profession of writing. The story of an artistic young novelist whose aesthetic principles and idealistic belief in marriage render him incapable of enduring the demands of a competitive literary marketplace, *New Grub Street* denounces the profit-making mentality of a society that devalues literature and personal relationships. Critics generally attribute the strength of Gissing's narrative to his first-hand experience of the circumstances in which indigent, unknown authors lived.

New Grub Street contrasts the careers of two writers, Edwin Reardon and Jasper Milvain, who possess conflicting literary standards. A young provincial man schooled in the classics, Reardon comes to London to work as a hospital clerk. He leaves the position after writing a well-received first novel and marries Amy Yule, a middle-class woman who is delighted at the prospect of becoming the wife of a successful novelist. The pressures of supporting himself and his wife through literary output severely undermine his ability to write. Reardon, refusing to compromise his artistic standards by writing solely for profit, tells his wife that he intends to return to his former employer and write part-time, after which she leaves him.

Reardon's failure is set against the success of his friend Jasper Milvain, who accepts the fact that writing has become an industry; without any concerns about the artistic value of his work, he is able to earn a living by producing reviews and essays. Unlike Reardon, who depends on his wife for emotional support, Milvain possesses a strongly individualistic nature and views marriage as a means of acquiring wealth. He proposes to Amy's cousin Marian Yule, who has inherited a large sum of money, but he jilts her when she receives only a fraction of her bequest. Reardon, now living in a state of poverty because he sends half his income to Amy, becomes ill yet remains separated from his wife, who has received a ten-thousand-dollar legacy from her deceased uncle. He finally reconciles with Amy but dies from his illness. Milvain, seeing an opportunity to acquire wealth, marries Amy. The final scene of *New Grub Street* depicts Milvain and Amy in the comfort of their middle-class home, celebrating his appointment to the coveted position as editor of a literary magazine.

Critics have viewed *New Grub Street* as one of the greatest portrayals of the conflict between materialism and art. The need for money adversely effects the artist's ability to create, and it is with a feeling of awe and longing that Reardon contemplates a passage of Homer's *Odyssey,* concluding that it certainly "was not written at so many pages a day, with a workhouse clock clanging its admonition at the ear."

In addition to examining the conflict between materialism and culture, much criticism on *New Grub Street* focuses on the autobiographical aspect of the novel. Although many critics agree that the success of *New Grub Street* lies in Gissing's representation of events he directly encountered and opinions he formed, some believe that this autobiographical basis is damaging to the novel, especially to its portrayal of Edwin Reardon, who is viewed as losing his vitality as a character in order to serve as Gissing's mouthpiece. Also present in *New Grub Street* is Gissing's belief of the diminished marriage prospects of literary men, demonstrated in the failure of Edwin Reardon's marriage to his middle-class wife.

New Grub Street was greeted with mixed reactions by reviewers, who objected to its attack on the literary establishment; nevertheless, the emotional impact and realism of the narrative, as well as the strength of its characters, were recognized and generally praised in the reviews. *New Grub Street* became Gissing's best-selling novel and established Gissing as an important writer. Gissing's reputation as a novelist, however, declined after his death in 1903, and although such eminent authors of the first half of the century as Virginia Woolf and George Orwell praised Gissing's works, critics did not take a renewed interest in him until the early 1960s. P. J. Keating echoed the opinion of many critics when he wrote: "The main issues examined by Gissing have all become commonplaces of twentieth-century critical thought and discussion. The alienation of the artist from society; the development of a new kind of popular press; an increasingly centralized society dominated by London; the new concept of the art of fiction; and the conscious acceptance by everyone involved of the intellectual, commercial and cultural division of English life. . . . It is the forces making for this change that Gissing sets out to analyze and in doing so brilliantly captures a crucial moment in a period of cultural crisis."

CRITICISM

George Gissing   (letter date 1891)

[*One of Gissing's most intimate friends was Eduard Bertz, a German socialist author in exile whom Gissing met in January 1879. Upon Bertz's return to Germany in 1884, Gissing and Bertz corresponded for nineteen years until Gissing's death. In the following excerpt, taken from a letter dated April 26, 1891, Gissing discusses the historical place of Grub Street in English literature.*]

Well now, it is unnecessary for me to say how your remarks on *New Grub Street* rejoice me. As all my acquaintances agree in loud praise of the book, I suppose it is not bad. I wrote it in utter prostration of spirit; no book of mine was regarded so hopelessly in the production. This experience encourages me; if I could write tolerably *then,* I am pretty sure to be able to produce under any circumstances likely to befall me.

Your objection to the consensus among my characters on the subject of money is quite just. The fault arises from my own bitterness. As for the truth or untruth of the point of view itself, I know decidedly that a man has to be of much native strength if he can arrive at anything like development of his powers in the shadow of poverty. Happily, the strength is sometimes given.

Grub Street actually existed in London some hundred and fifty years ago. In Pope and his contemporaries the name has become synonymous for wretched-authordom. In Hogarth's "Distressed Author" there is "Grub Street" somewhere inscribed. Poverty and meanness of spirit being naturally associated, the street came to denote an abode, not merely of poor, but of insignificant, writers. That it could

be confined to the sense of poverty is, however, proved by one of the most humorous passages in Sam Johnson's Dictionary. He defines "GRUB STREET: Originally the name of a street near Moorfields in London, much inhabited by writers of small histories, dictionaries, and temporary poems; whence any mean production is called *grub-street.*" Then he adds the quotation:

Χαιρ Ιθακη μετ αεθλα μετ αλγεα πικρα
Ασπασιωδ πον ουδαδ ικαγομαι

["Hail, O Ithaca! Amidst joys and bitter pains,
   I gladly come to thy earth."]

Is not this delicious? Poor old Sam, rejoicing to have got so far in his Dictionary, and greeting the name "Grub Street" as that of his native land! (I have never seen this joke alluded to, though several others which the Dictionary contains are commonly mentioned.)

At present the word is used contemptuously. You know that I do not altogether mean that in the title of my book.

The reviews, as usual, I do not see. But I notice that they are spending much more money than usual in advertisements. By the bye, it is good to have my book[s] advertized all together at the end of Vol I. (pp. 121-22)

> *George Gissing, in a letter to Eduard Bertz on April 26, 1891, in* The Letters of George Gissing to Eduard Bertz, 1887-1903, *edited by Arthur C. Young, Rutgers University Press, 1961, pp. 121-23.*

The Saturday Review (essay date 1891)

[*In the review excerpted below, the anonymous critic argues that Gissing's bleak, cheerless depiction of life on Grub Street is grossly exaggerated.*]

Old Grub Street was poverty-stricken, but it was neither hopeless nor joyless. The children of this stony-hearted stepmother were merry enough, no doubt, in spite of Mr. Pope, for their quarrel with him made them conspicuous, and they must have known that there was not in all their quivers so leaden a shaft but it pierced Pope's mail, and rankled in his vanity. Great men have sojourned in Grub Street; they have admitted that it was grubby; but even Dr. Johnson does not say that it was permanently gloomy. This chief of literary hacks did his work, which was usually job-work, and took his pay, and grumbled not, but consistently spoke well of the booksellers. In brief, of old time Grub Street was a section of human life on a low level, but the sun shone into the garrets. (p. 524)

New Grub Street, according to Mr. Gissing, in his novel of that name, is a very much worse, much more miserable, place than Grub Street the old. The borders and marches of this quarter of the town are ill defined, but perhaps we may describe Grub Street as the territory inhabited by the men and women whose pens win their bread. If that be topographically correct, Carlyle and Thackeray, Leigh Hunt and Dickens, were all of the parish where Mr. Gissing's characters take their fortunes in such sorry cheer. It is, perhaps, a modern virtue to see everything in black, to abstain from wit, from humour, from gaiety, as strictly as many people abstain from alcoholic drinks. But this was not the manner of the great men whom we have named, nor of the small men in these old days. Like Philip Firmin's friend, they sang—

> And for this reason,
> And for a season,
> Let us be merry before we go!

It is a common belief that even modern Grub Street knows this carol and is not always of a sombre mood. Are there no cakes nor ale, nor any midnight chimes in Grub Street the new? Is life one unbroken and embittered pursuit of the five-pound note? Are there no men poor, but young and light of heart, in the literary parish? We cannot believe that all the parishioners are gloomy failures, conscientious *ratés*. Nay, many of us have tarried by the tables of Grub Street, and have been content with its cowheel and its porter. The entire population does not consist of worthy "realistic" novelists, underpaid and overworked on one side, and of meanly selfish and treacherous, but successful, hacks on the other. If we understand Mr. Gissing's theory of the literary life among the rank and file, he thinks that genius, or even conscientious talent, is in a way repressed, is driven into work of a low kind for the sake of bread-and-butter, while the hodmen of letters who do their hodmen's duties successfully and with acceptance are persons destitute of soul. But may we not argue that what these worthies perform is what nature has fitted them to perform; and that, though they would give ten years of their lives to possess genius and employ it, still they admire, and do not envy, its possessors? Nature has not made it possible for us all to be pessimistic novelists, however greatly we may desire it. As Dr. Johnson's friend said, he who had tried to be a philosopher, "somehow cheerfulness would break in," and that is fatal. Then the others, the noble laborious failures—it is possible that they are not all men of genius. They may have miscalculated their strength, and vanity may have had much to do with their discomfiture. On the whole, we do not feel convinced by Mr. Gissing that Grub Street is such a very ill habitation. The natives can forget their woes, and are not for ever brooding over unfavourable reviews, and on ways of hitting back at their adversaries—usually at the wrong man. They think of many things, they talk of many things, besides "shop"; indeed, if Grub Street is restricted to its profession, there is not matter enough in it to found a novel on. It is like trying to write a novel of University life. The field is too narrow; the fiction is starved. Reviews, cheques, accepted articles, rejected articles, padding, hack-work in general, is not good "stock" for a novel, and gives an ill flavour to men's loves and lives. But Mr. Gissing, we think, has made this flavour much too strong. Even in Grub Street the fog sometimes lifts, and in the window gardens of the natives you may see blossoming the herb Pantagruelion. But it never blossoms in the windows of those who are unlucky enough to think that they are neglected and underestimated. This is the besetting sorrow or besetting sin of artists of all kinds in and out of Grub Street. From this embittering error that we may all be delivered, *Beate Francisce, ora pro nobis!* (pp. 524-25)

A review of "New Grub Street," in The Satur-

day Review, *London, Vol. 71, No. 1853, May 2, 1891, pp. 524-25.*

The Athenaeum   (essay date 1891)

[*In the following unsigned review of* New Grub Street, *the critic praises Gissing for his well-portrayed characters.*]

Mr. Gissing may be generally depended on for something modern in the way of a novel. His matter is of the moment, and his treatment and touch distinctly realistic. **New Grub Street** is no exception. It deals with the pains and pleasures—particularly the pains—of "lower middle class" writing-folk. There is a great deal about the new journalism; its aims and ambitions and other and kindred topics are set forth in dialogue and suggestion. He touches, in fact, on several interesting points, and presents us with sundry fresh-looking types of men and women. Remembering **Demos** and **The Nether World** we are not prepared to say that **New Grub Street** is an advance on former work. He still, it is true, sees life through the medium of a strong and keen individuality, and there is a perceptible lightening of touch, a greater diffusiveness, not bringing with them, however, visible improvement in style. All the same the book is decidedly forcible, and to a great extent the result of experience. There are some carefully considered studies of people that strike one as very good—Jasper Milvain, at first especially, is one of them. The lower walk of "letters" may not, perhaps, smile on the reader, nor be the path he would wish to follow—it is dreary, a little grimy even; but there is undeniable interest and strength in Mr. Gissing's presentation of it. Life in **New Grub Street** may be sad enough, with few redeeming features—many go under, few rise above the surface—there is privation, disappointment, meanness; still, day by day more plunge into it. It has its fascinating times, its hours of glamour; but of these Mr. Gissing shows few or none. There is a good deal of sketchiness yet of concentration in his method; the result is a book of somewhat uneven balance, but much cleverness. Now and again we find episodes, and especially dialogue, that seem rather obviously introduced to force the "note," as it were. A good deal might have been dispensed with to the advantage of the story, or so it seems to us. Marian and her father are good, very sober in hue, and very veracious-looking. Reardon—sensitive, imaginative, low in vitality—is carefully elaborated, yet does not stand out so well as he should. There is much in his career that is painfully real; his literary failure and his agonized struggles at literary composition are drawn with some poignancy. There is also a plentiful sprinkling of average people, whose mediocrity is well and cleverly conveyed.

A review of "New Grub Street," in The Athenaeum, *No. 3315, May 9, 1891, p. 601.*

Harry Hansen   (essay date 1926)

[*Hansen was an American publishing executive, literary critic, novelist, and nonfiction writer who served as literary editor to the* Chicago Daily News, New York World, *and* New York World-Telegram. *In the excerpt*

below, drawn from his introduction to a 1926 edition of
New Grub Street, *Hansen analyzes the historical and
literary milieu which shaped Gissing's novel.*]

Gissing on the critical reception of *New Grub Street:*

New Grub Street seems to be more like a literary success
than any other of my books. There is a mad East-end parson
(an avowed atheist, by the bye,) whose acquaintance I made
some time ago; he persists in notifying to me in frequent letters all reviews of importance. Not only am I well reviewed,
but positive articles are devoted to the book. There was one
occupying a whole column the other day in the *Illustrated
London News.* Then, I have just been casually referred to in
a *leader* in the *Daily News*—which means a good deal. We
shall see whether all this has any financial results—to the
publishers. Dash it all! I ought to get more than £150 for
my next book.

George Gissing, in his The Letters of George Gissing to
Eduard Bertz, 1887-1903, *Rutgers University Press, 1961.*

New Grub Street, by George Gissing, came into the world
in 1891, at the very beginning of that auspicious decade
which showed us a new way to view old vistas. Its relation
to that aspiring age is ironic. More than anything else it
was the despairing cry of the classical scholar who finds
himself crowded into obscurity by the man of little learning. Despite its author's fidelity to form it drew no inspiration from Gautier's dictum and had nothing in common
with the glamorous search of the Beardsley group for a
new æsthetic formula. It dealt with the lower middle class
because Gissing was interested in that stratum, and not because the French naturalists had urged the claims of unattractive realism. The world that it brought to book for all
time was the world as seen through the eyes of George
Gissing, and none else.

Think of what a motley array of wares was laid before the
British public in the year 1891! In that year Arthur Symons climbed to an upper room of the Cheshire Cheese
and beheld Ernest Dowson reciting his verses and pleading a forlorn hopelessness about the world. *The Light That
Failed,* by Rudyard Kipling, slipped quietly into the libraries and distressed readers with its unhappy ending,
whereas *Peter Ibbetson,* first-born of a man whose name
was soon to command all ears, brought sighs and longing.
The quiet fascination of *The Little Minister* began to hold
readers and *The Adventures of Sherlock Holmes* burst into
full popularity, carrying on the career of the hero of Baker
Street, who had made his bow several years before. Of an
entirely different genre was *Tess of the D'Urbervilles,* also
of this year, but to a public eager for charm it proved a
bitter salad. Where one praised it a dozen cast down their
eyes and murmured "Blasphemy!" George Gissing stands
apart from all this talent, a strange, solitary figure, fashioning his sentences with meticulous precision, despairing
of anyone's recognizing the classic pattern under its crude,
English cloak.

So **New Grub Street** arrived. It was ushered into the light
in three volumes, for the benefit of that very circulating

library system which it attacks so vigorously. In fact each
of the three volumes that lie before me . . . , bears on its
inside cover the stamp of Lawrence's Subscription Library
of Rugby, with the advice that "novels are issued to and
received from subscribers in sets only." It went into one
edition and then lingered on the shelves; a cheap reprint
found its way to a few more curious readers; an American
house presented it to a nation that was engaged in genu-
flexions before Richard Harding Davis, and then, like a
disembodied spirit, it was spoken of now and then at the
tables of seminars, and in old rooms where men talked of
unworldly and highly unprofitable things. Whatever its
author received from it is problematical—hardly the one
hundred pounds that went to poor Edwin Reardon for the
novel that he wrote with his heart's blood. It is called back
to life to-day because of the insistent determination of a
new age to regard George Gissing as a capable stylist, a
keen analyst of motives and an extraordinary literary figure whose inexplicable hardships and distressing failure
stir the imagination of an age surfeited with material
things.

And opening this book, what do we find? A story of unattractive and unimaginative people that seems likely to reflect with minuteness the boredom of the commonplace,
but that moves forward with a disarming evenness until
we begin to suspect an intensive artistry behind its ease;
a knowledge of motives singularly clear, finally an unobtrusive irony. And as we turn its pages we may guess, with
so many others, that much of the author's life-blood has
gone into this work, that he has known these characters
through the intimacy of suffering shared and defeats experienced or understood; in short, that in **New Grub Street**
we have another chapter of George Gissing's book of the
heart.

The London literary panorama had an earnest and unwavering observer in George Gissing. He, too, had his pride
in Tibullus and his longing for the Ionian Sea, and he
viewed the changing world of New Grub Street as the
prophets saw the cities of the plain. Here he set down the
evil fruits of that exploitation of talent and that "popularization" which has reached its farthest development in our
own generation. In Jasper Milvain he epitomized for all
time the smooth-talking, adaptable exploiter who "gives
the public what it wants." The reader will agree that Gissing has done him full justice. If Jasper is detestable he is
also human; if his egotism causes him to talk spaciously
of his accomplishments, he is also practical enough to
admit his shortcomings—Gissing has drawn a full-length
portrait; complete, ineradicable, and you who read this
book will ever after find Jasper Milvains all about you, will
suspect their glib pretense of turning brass into gold, and
know their kind for their undisguised undervaluation of
the public and their highly successful familiarity with the
market and its wares.

Against Jasper Milvain Gissing placed Edwin Reardon,
"the old type of unpractical artist," a forlorn and frustrated novelist, whom lack of mental and physical nourishment had brought to such a pass that he no longer had the
vitality to do creative work of a high character, while his

temperament made any adaptation to the needs of his times impossible. Is there irony in Gissing's description of Reardon's style, so reminiscent of charges made against Gissing himself? "His books dealt with no particular class of society (unless one makes a distinct class of people who have brains) and they lacked local colour. Their interest was almost purely psychological. It was clear that the author had no faculty for constructing a story. . . . But strong characterisation was within his scope and an intellectual fervour, appetising to a small section of refined readers, marked all his best pages."

It is Jasper Milvain who voices the opinion that to succeed one must enthrone the vulgar, that the market must be supplied, that concessions must be made to the public demand and that therein lies prosperity for the writer. Just a year before *New Grub Street* appeared, in 1890, Thomas Hardy had published in *The New Review* a warning against the threatened popularization: "The object of the magazine and the circulating library is not upward advance but lateral advance—to suit themselves to household reading. As a consequence the magazine in particular and the circulating library in general do not foster the growth of the novel which reflects and reveals life."

If Gissing felt in his heart that Edwin Reardon represented to a slight degree his own self frustrated in his best designs by the low taste and demands of his age, then he must have drawn Jasper Milvain with a deep and abiding hatred. . . . It is easy to detest Jasper for such conduct as his caddish treatment of Miss Yule, which is done without subtlety, but also for his views, which, for the most part, are stated without comment. To-day Jasper is merely the literary carpenter who flourishes by the hundred, but in Gissing's day he was a newcomer and a rare specimen. Jasper believes that it is better to live than to starve with the garreteers in the Tottenham Court road district; hence he is ready to give his audience what it wants. He does not overestimate his abilities but seeks the place where his talents will be employed profitably. His views have the self-satisfied approval of mediocrity: "I maintain that we people of brains are justified in supplying the mob with the food it likes. We are not geniuses and if we sit down in a spirit of long-eared gravity we shall produce only commonplace stuff. Let us use our wits to earn money and make the best we can of our lives." What an abiding and oft-repeated confession of mediocrity! Jasper knows that it takes skill to write down to the herd: "To please the vulgar you must, one way or another, incarnate vulgarity,"—a copybook maxim for our complacent and bloated novelists of the commonplace. He knows the trick of writing for those who delude themselves into thinking they have wit and cleverness—"the upper middle-class of intellect." In one clear passage Gissing has packed the whole argument of the practical craftsman: "Literature nowadays is a trade. Putting aside men of genius, who may succeed by mere cosmic force, your successful man of letters is your skilful tradesman. He thinks first and foremost of the markets; when one kind of goods begins to go off slackly, he is ready with something new and appetising. He knows perfectly well all the sources of income." And in discussing Reardon's failure he continues: "I should have gone shrewdly to work with magazines and newspapers

and foreign publishers, and—all sorts of people." He knows the inhabitants of the new Grub Street are "men of business, however seedy." And his aim is direct and low: "I speak only of good, coarse, marketable stuff for the world's vulgar." How far Gissing was removed from such views is clear when we recall his conviction that all literature is poetry in its widest sense.

The point of view is not always held in *New Grub Street.* Gissing was not always successful in letting his characters speak for him. In introducing Harold Biffen's tragedy he indulges in an outburst against the successful merchant. "The chances are that you have neither understanding nor sympathy for men such as Edwin Reardon and Harold Biffen," he says to the reader. "They merely provoke you. They seem to you inert, flabby, weakly envious, foolishly obstinate, impiously mutinous and many other things. You are made angrily contemptuous by their failure to get on—why don't they bestir themselves?" Then he asks for consideration of the qualities that have no relation to the world's labor market. "These two were richly endowed with the kindly and imaginative virtues; if fate threw them amid incongruous circumstances is their endowment of less value?" He is aware that "the sum of their faults is their inability to earn money." He follows with an affecting picture of how Biffen starved to be able to write his novel of the ignobly decent—"Mr. Bailey, Grocer," remarking bitterly: "It was very weak of Harold Biffen to come so near perishing of hunger as he did in the days when he was completing his novel." There follows an affecting story of Biffen's poverty, his striving to buy bread, and finally his fight to save his manuscript from the fire. (pp. v-x)

Like Ernest Dowson, who sang his best lyrics when most despondent, Gissing saw the world through blue glasses and judged himself born out of his time. If we accept Edwin Reardon as a self-portrait, we have abundant proof of Gissing's self-pity and self-accusation. The anomaly is that no one who reads *New Grub Street* will suspect that the time it describes was one of the most fecund in English writing, and that, despite the growth of an audience without critical acumen and the coming of authors without classical standards, it was a time when books displayed both vitality and beauty and when writers became free to be as natural and individual as they pleased. (xi-xii)

> *Harry Hansen, in an introduction to* New Grub Street *by George Gissing, The Modern Library, 1926, pp. v-xii.*

Jacob Korg   (essay date 1963)

[*Korg is an American educator and critic who has edited several of Gissing's works. In the following excerpt, Korg presents an overview of* New Grub Street, *outlining its major characters and themes.*]

[Around Edwin Reardon, this tragic central figure of *New Grub Street,*] Gissing ranged a large gallery of smooth opportunists, picturesque pedants, ineffectual bookworms, and fierce quill-drivers, giving a rich panoramic picture of their world. It is a world blighted by the same forces that dehumanize the society of which it is a part: commercialism, competition, and greed. The educational reforms that had increased literacy without cultivating a taste for learning had created a mass market for amusing and superficial reading matter, especially in periodical form. This sort of literature became a valuable commodity, particularly when used in conjunction with illustrations, and numerous magazines like *The Sketch* and *Tit-Bits* depended on it. Thus the customs, standards, and practices of mass production were introduced into literature. Where it is important to command a mass market of "quarter-educated" readers, originality, individuality, or profundity are unwelcome. A flair for notoriety is the best gift for succeeding in this environment. One must apply the principles of trade to writing, try to "hit" the taste of a wide public, make friends among editors and reviewers, and curry favor where it will do the most good. It was a dangerous atmosphere that required astute maneuvering, for irrational animosities filled the air, and the fate of a book or an editorship could be determined by the operation of far-flung alliances.

The conqueror of this literary battlefield is Jasper Milvain, an acquaintance of Reardon's who begins his career as a humble and diligent journalist, confident that a creditable apprenticeship in writing articles (he is not imaginative enough for fiction) will lead him to wealth. The doctrine that literature is a trade is his, and he acts upon it unfailingly. He has no objection to the work of Dante or Shakespeare, but he feels that he is engaged in the entirely different activity of producing material that will attract readers and cause some stir, though it may be of only ephemeral interest. Milvain's success grows as Reardon's ineffectual efforts drag him to disaster, until at the end, after Reardon's death, Milvain achieves wealth by winning an editorship and marrying Reardon's widow.

A contrast to the good-natured optimist, Milvain, is the sour and defeated Alfred Yule, "a battered man of letters," whose lifetime spent in doing odd jobs of writing has taught him nothing so well as envy and hate. Ill-tempered, pedantic, hypercritical, he lives through the arid medium of print. He knows how to punish an enemy through a covert thrust in an article, and how to repay a flattering allusion in a footnote with a pleasant review. Nothing gives him so much pleasure as the misfortune of a rival whose journal has published contradictory reviews of the same book. His friends are writers, his conversation is the gossip of the editorial back stairs, his natural habitat is the reading room of the British Museum. Quaint, bookish mannerisms and turns of speech give this character a convincing individuality. Graspingly ambitious, he tries to induce his daughter to invest some money she has inherited in a journal which he will edit, but he fails in this as in all else, and ends in pathetic blindness.

Another and younger failure is Whelpdale. After suffering through some adventures in America patterned after Gissing's own, he returns to England, and, finding that he cannot sell any of his work, conceives the idea of giving instruction in fiction writing to neophytes. His plans include writing about the middle class and dealing with such topics as boating and riding. Later he writes for a periodical named *Chat;* he plans to improve it by changing its name to *Chit-Chat* and filling it with a potpourri of small items that can be read without effort by the semiliterate products of the democratic educational system. "Everything must be very short," he says, "two inches at the utmost; their attention can't sustain itself beyond two inches. Even chat is too solid for them; they want chit-chat."

Reardon's friend Biffen is a penniless scholar who shares his enthusiasm for Greek poetry and is capable of making fine metrical distinctions, but can do nothing more effective toward earning a living than occasional tutoring. He lives in picturesque squalor, wearing his overcoat indoors to disguise the fact that he has no coat over his shirt sleeves, and eating his bread-and-dripping with a knife and fork to make it seem more filling. He is at work on a new kind of novel, a photographically faithful account of the daily life of a grocer. (pp. 161-63)

Biffen carries out this project with the devotion of a Flaubert, spending infinite time, patience, and discrimination on the prose style of his drab tale. The masterpiece of tedium is nearly lost when his lodginghouse burns down, but he risks his life to save the manuscript from the flames, thus exhibiting in a dramatic action the courage that enabled him to continue his work through the hardships of his life. *Mr. Bailey, Grocer* actually achieves publication, and Biffen is paid fifteen pounds for it; he does not mind the hostility of the reviewers or the indifference of the public, for he is satisfied with it. But his heroism as an artist and a man turns out to be futile; he cannot escape the habit of isolation developed through years of work, and suffers from being deprived of a woman's love, particularly that of Reardon's widow. Ultimately, he lapses into a state of lonely depression which ends in suicide. His perfectionism asserts itself for the last time as he straightens a book on its shelf and the blotting pad on his desk before going out to poison himself.

The background of the novel swarms with minor literary artisans. There are Milvain's sisters, who find that they can make a living by writing children's books, Quarmby and Hinks, superannuated hacks who haunt the British Museum reading room like shabby ghosts, and Marian Yule, who helps her father as a kind of literary slave, doing research for his articles, copying them when they are completed, and sometimes even writing them herself.

In *New Grub Street* Gissing gives a surprisingly accurate report of the social transition described by Mr. David Riesman in *The Lonely Crowd.* It was natural that he should first sense the emergence of "other-direction" in his own profession. Milvain, Whelpdale, and the crowd of journalists they move with expect to succeed by pleasing the public; they have no abstract convictions about their work, except that it must sell and win approval. They consider it essential that a writer be able to change with the winds of trade and be ready for any sort of an assignment; when Whelpdale says that he has been hired to write a column for a journal, Milvain asks, "Cosmetics? Fashions? Cookery?" and Whelpdale regrets that he is not so versatile. They are less concerned with the instrinsic qualities of their work than with people's opinion of it, and most of their conversations are devoted to gauging the climate of opinion in editorial quarters.

Reardon, on the other hand, is an example of Mr. Riesman's "inner-directed" type, who belongs to an earlier stage of social organization. He is not entirely indifferent to general opinion, but he gives precedence to his own convictions. The easy versatility of men like Milvain seems to him to be simple insincerity. He is attached to one style of writing and one way of conducting himself, and cannot adjust, as Milvain would, to changing conditions. Popularity, Milvain's only motive for writing, means nothing to him, and when he cannot satisfy his own standards he feels no desire to write. In thinking over the actions that have driven Amy from his side, he at first wonders what her relations will say about him, but he then consults moral standards, which he considers absolute, by framing such questions as, "Had he done well? Had he done wisely?" Reardon is caught in a kind of landslide of social standards, for, while he embraces an old moral code in considering it a virtue to be true to his own modest talents, the new concept of success in writing calls for conformity, popularity, and response to public demand.

New Grub Street was a success built with the materials of failure. Gissing's early novels are marred by the tendency toward self-justification apparent in the portrayals of Arthur Golding and Osmond Waymark, and by a resentment that sometimes rendered his depiction of social evils more appropriate to melodrama than to critical realism. Because he had suffered himself, he considered suffering a requirement for merit; according to Roberts, his criticism of any writer who might be mentioned was, "He never starved." He contemplated failure with perverse pleasure because it proved "the native malignity of matter," the injustice of the scheme of things. But after twelve years of writing novels without either gaining popularity or satisfying his own aspirations, he was ready to stake the painful truth of his private deficiencies on an attempt to achieve an ultimate realism. As a result, Reardon is portrayed in *New Grub Street* not as a noble heretic but as a hesitant weakling who is bewildered by the problems of his profession; at the same time the evils of the system that destroys him are incisively analyzed. If *New Grub Street* is more authentic, more cogent, and clearer in construction than Gissing's earlier novels, it is because he had at last learned, through a discipline of self-abnegation, to balance his passionate indignation with the objectivity necessary for genuine realism. (pp. 163-65)

> *Jacob Korg, in his* George Gissing: A Critical Biography, *University of Washington Press, 1963, 311 p.*

P. J. Keating   (essay date 1968)

[*In the following excerpt, Keating discusses Edwin Reardon's plight and argues that Reardon's persona becomes flawed due to authorial intrusion.*]

In Chapter III [of *New Grub Street*] Milvain, returning from his country walk with Marian, stops to gaze at a horse: 'a poor worn-out beast, all skin and bone, which had presumably been sent here in the hope that a little more labour might still be exacted from it if it were suffered to repose for a few weeks. There were sores upon its back and legs; it stood in a fixed attitude of despondency, just flicking away troublesome flies with its grizzled tail.' The horse represents Reardon who although he does not actually appear until the fourth chapter has been a frequent subject of conversation in the preceding three. Like the horse Reardon wears himself out in ceaseless and thankless work, and his separation from Amy is to be finally brought about because of her plan for him to spend a brief, solitary holiday, from which he is to return freshened for further toil until death.

Reardon typifies the most common, and in many ways the most disturbing, kind of New Grub Street victim. According to Milvain's categories he is neither genius nor practical man. Nor is he a theorist like Biffen. Perhaps the most significant description of his work is given by Old John Yule:

> Just for curiosity I had a look at one of his books; it was called "The Optimist". Of all the morbid trash I ever saw, that beat everything. I thought of writing him a letter, advising a couple of antibilious pills before bedtime for a few weeks.

This is intended as a common late Victorian, philistine, critical judgement and means much the same as Milvain's remark that Reardon's work is 'glaringly distinct from the ordinary circulating novel'. Biffen, as usual, is more precise when he describes his friend as 'a psychological realist in the sphere of culture'. If Reardon is no genius he clearly possesses an unusual talent which he attempts to bring to fruition by conscientious workmanship. It is his tragedy that he must try to make a living from literature in an age which has adopted public applause as the only possible form of patronage. In Chapter IV he makes this point himself:

> What an insane thing it is to make literature one's only means of support! When the most trivial accident may at any time prove fatal to one's power of work for weeks or months. No, that is the unpardonable sin! To make a trade of an art! I am rightly served for attempting such a brutal folly.

He goes on to make a further important point:

> I am no uncompromising artistic pedant; I am quite willing to try and do the kind of work that will sell; under the circumstances it would be a kind of insanity if I refused. But power doesn't answer to the will.

He accepts totally the view that if a book is popular then it must by definition be of poor quality, and likewise that a book which has considerable artistic value can never be a commercial success. When Amy argues that 'good work succeeds—now and then', he answers, 'I speak of the common kind of success, which is never due to literary merit.' Because he has a wife and child to support he cannot fight against the market; he must try to make concessions, and that means artistic suicide.

By nature he is a scholar who turns to fiction writing only after he fails to get his 'essays on literary subjects' published. In Chapter V where his early career is outlined it is shown that he was inspired to write novels by a glimpse of the luxurious home of a well-known author. At that moment he believed that literary or artistic success would bring financial and social rewards, and his marriage to Amy is his first step on the road to wealth and fame: 'He had always regarded the winning of a beautiful and intellectual wife as the crown of a successful literary career, but he had not dared to hope that such a triumph would be his.' It is, in fact, the only successful achievement of his career, just as it is also the ultimate cause of his destruction. He has been married just over a year when the novel opens and from this moment on the reputation he can already claim and his hopes for the future steadily decline.

In certain respects then, Reardon is not unlike Milvain. Where he differs is in his refusal to adjust his own literary standards according to the dictates of the market. He wants public acclamation but it must be on his own terms. It is an impossible demand and his dilemma is expressed in the traditional vocabulary of romantic agony: 'Often he fell into a fit of absence, and gazed at vacancy with wide, miserable eyes'; 'feverish determination to work'; 'racking his fagged brain'; 'torments of nightmare'; 'at times he was on the border-land of imbecility; his mind looked into a cloudy chaos, a shapeless whirl of nothings'. Such moments bring about a breakdown of the one quality which to his mind matters above all others—a good prose style:

> He would write a sentence beginning thus: 'She took a book with a look of—;' or thus: 'A revision of this decision would have made him an object of derision.' Or, if the period were otherwise inoffensive, it ran in a rhythmic gallop which was torment to the ear.

For such a person even the willingness to adapt his idealism to suit the market is useless. *Margaret Home,* his skimped three-volume novel, is acknowledged by everyone to be of poor quality; and his attempt at a one volume 'sensational' tale, written on Milvain's advice, is rejected by the publisher. Worse still, by writing novels which are inferior to his earlier work he knows full well that he will lose the small group of sympathetic readers he has acquired. His ideal society is that of *old* Grub Street where aristocratic patronage would, so he reasons, have given him the necessary security to publish only what he was not ashamed to acknowledge. In *new* Grub Street there is only one criterion by which literature is judged: 'The world has no pity on a man who can't do or produce something it thinks worth money. You may be a divine poet, and if some good fellow doesn't take pity on you you will starve by the roadside. Society is as blind and brutal as fate.' There is a further reason why Reardon looks back to *old* Grub Street as to a golden age. It was a time when the essayist, educated in the classics, was highly valued, and this is the part that Reardon could fill to perfection. He writes novels because this is the only type of literature which sells; it is the literary form to which everyone in **New Grub Street** turns at one time or another. Reardon himself makes the obvious comparison: 'A man who can't journalise, yet must earn his bread by literature, nowadays inevitably turns to fiction, as the Elizabethan men turned to the drama.' One of the most important reasons for Reardon's failure is that he really has no aptitude for or indeed love of fiction. Amy fully realises that novel writing is the only

way to attain literary fame and that if Reardon was financially independent 'he would lapse into a life of scholarly self-indulgence, such as he had often told her was his ideal'. Money spent in this way, she reasons, would be money wasted. Even when Reardon does write essays there is little chance of selling them, for *Milvain* is the typical late Victorian essayist. He is the man of his day, and is thus fitted to note that Reardon 'sells a manuscript as if he lived in Sam Johnson's Grub Street'.

Remembering that his best novels were written in his free time while working as a hospital clerk, Reardon comes to believe that part-time writing is the modern equivalent of aristocratic patronage, and it is his determination to return to this system that brings his unhappy marriage to the breaking point:

> Coleridge wouldn't so easily meet with his Gillman nowadays. Well, I am not a Coleridge, and I don't ask to be lodged under any man's roof; but if I could earn money enough to leave me good long evenings unspoilt by fear of the workhouse—

It is because of what Amy sneeringly calls his 'morbid conscientiousness' that he refuses to allow Milvain to help him with introductions and publicity. As much as he desires public recognition and entry into society life his pride will not allow him to attain these ends while his work is of an inferior quality. His tirades against the market are not symptomatic of an intellectual attitude but grow out of his disillusionment with his own ability. In Chapter XII when Amy urges him to model himself on Milvain, he answers: 'You lament that I can't write in that attractive way. Well, I lament it myself—for your sake. I wish I had Milvain's peculiar talent, so that I could get reputation and money. But I haven't, and there's an end of it.' The words 'for your sake' are only a way of getting back at Amy, for Reardon really does wish he was practical. The chapter heading of his death scene, *Reardon becomes Practical,* is ambiguous. He becomes practical at last by swallowing his pride and accepting Amy together with her new-found wealth; but it also indicates that his personality is such that death alone can stop his self-inflicted torture.

The destruction of Reardon is finally brought about not so much by his character, which is totally unfitted for the new style literary life, but by his marriage to Amy who is the mouthpiece of Milvain's theories. She is a traitor in much the same way as Whelpdale, and the various stages of her moral corruption are organised so as to emphasise this point. Reardon bitterly reminds her that during the early days of their marriage she was proud of him 'because my work wasn't altogether common, and because I had never written a line that was meant to attract the vulgar'. Her intellectual snobbery is merely a form of social distinction and she soon drops entirely her concern with literature as such and develops a new interest:

> She talked of questions such as international copyright, was anxious to get an insight into the practical conduct of journals and magazines, liked to know who 'read' for the publishing-houses. To an impartial observer it might have

appeared that her intellect was growing more active and mature.

When she learns that her particular brand of intellectual snobbery can only be sustained by living perpetually on the edge of financial disaster, her whole attitude begins to change. Milvain, whom she had earlier treated with condescension—the natural feeling for the wife of an artist looking at a tradesman—now becomes to her the archetype of the literary man. His ideas she takes over wholesale, adding to them her own particular brand of venom: 'If I had to choose between a glorious reputation with poverty and a contemptible popularity with wealth, I should choose the latter.' It is the very choice which Reardon is incapable of making. His return to being a part-time author is for him the 'practical' way, while she is unable to recognise this use of the word. It is socially acceptable, she argues, for a literary man to have been poor, indeed it is expected of him, but to acknowledge that one can no longer make a full time living from literature is to confess to 'intellectual' decline. This point is further stressed in Chapter XXVI when Amy, now separated from Reardon, says to Mrs. Carter: 'My life is being wasted. I ought to have a place in the society of clever people. I was never meant to live quietly in the background.' Like Milvain she calls herself an intellectual because she recognises the practical way through life. Gissing underlines this point by referring to her 'noticeable maturing of intellect', since she has been living alone, which manifests itself in a passion for anything that savours 'of newness and boldness in philosophic thought.' At the same moment Reardon is declaring to Biffen that he can at last see that Amy was not a 'fit intellectual companion' for him. Amy's eventual marriage to Milvain is inevitable. From scorning him as the journeyman friend of her superior husband, she has progressed sufficiently to become his pupil, helped to destroy her husband, and on the way has become an 'intellectual' herself—she is his natural partner. It is the ironic theme of every success story in **New Grub Street** that intellectual pretension always accompanies moral corruption, and that to fall into poverty is to suffer both moral and intellectual degradation. Every character, except Biffen, would agree with Reardon on this subject:

> I have no sympathy with the stoical point of view; between wealth and poverty is just the difference between the whole man and the maimed. If my lower limbs are paralysed I may still be able to think, but then there is such a thing in life as walking. As a poor devil I may live nobly; but one happens to be made with faculties of enjoyment, and those have to fall into atrophy. To be sure, most rich people don't understand their happiness; if they did, they would move and talk like gods—which indeed they are.

Reardon's decline, after his wife has left him, is far from convincing. From the beginning there has been a rather incongruous element of the romantic artist stereotype about him which has tended to weaken his representative role in the novel—that of the conscientious craftsman out of tune with the society in which he lives. In the early parts of the novel there are several aspects of this incongruity. One is the romantic terminology used to describe his struggle to write. Another is the way that his social failure

induces in him extravagant bouts of self-pity. In Chapter IV, for instance, the self-pitying tone is apparent not merely in his own bursts of self-analysis, but in the detail which Gissing builds up around him: 'In the flat immediately beneath resided a successful musician, whose carriage and pair came at a regular hour each afternoon to take him and his wife for a most respectable drive.' Or, as he looks out of his window on to the backs of the houses opposite: 'in one room a man was discoverable dressing for dinner, he had not thought it worthwhile to lower the blind; in another, some people were playing billiards'. Or a more crude example in Chapter XVII when the insensitive Mr. Carter chats amiably to the impoverished Reardon about holidays in Scotland and Norway. Many similar instances could be listed. They are intended to emphasis the gap that exists between, on the one hand, Reardon's personality and the life he is forced to lead; and on the other, Reardon's extreme sensitivity and the increasing coarseness of society as a whole. They lead up to the moment in Chapter XXVII when Reardon makes his explicit statement on the finest end to which man can direct his life—the contemplation of beautiful things:

> I am only maintaining that it is the best, and infinitely preferable to sexual emotion. It leaves, no doubt, no bitterness of any kind. Poverty can't rob me of those memories. I have lived in an ideal world that was not deceitful, a world which seems to me, when I recall it, beyond the human sphere, bathed in diviner light.

But is is difficult to understand what good such moments have done him. They exist solely in the mind; embalmed, as it were, in a vacuum. They have certainly not helped calm his envy or jealousy. Indeed the memories of his visit to Greece are used to reinforce his self-pity.

The most disconcerting aspect of the characterisation of Reardon is the extremely crude symbolism that is used to heighten his outcast state. Left alone he decides to sell his furniture before moving to a new lodging: 'These stripped rooms were symbolical of his life; losing money, he had lost everything.' From this moment he is slowly stripped of everything *save* his now regular earnings. He haunts out of the way places, and in the streets he mutters snatches of poetry out loud so that onlookers take him for a lunatic. The dual life which as we have seen is his equivalent of patronage becomes merely a pose:

> He kept one suit of clothes for his hours of attendance at the hospital; it was still decent, and with much care would remain so for a long time. That which he wore at home and in his street wanderings declared poverty at every point; it had been discarded before he left the old abode. In his present state of mind he cared nothing how disreputable he looked to passers-by. These seedy habiliments were the token of his degradation, and at times he regarded them (happening to see himself in a shop mirror) with pleasurable contempt.

While working at the hospital he asks a girl patient her occupation. She answers, 'I'm unfortunate, sir', and Reardon can barely resist the temptation to leap to his feet and shake her by the hand. Although he is now comparatively wealthy, free of ties, and has plenty of spare time, he comes to realise that Reardon the author is already dead, and Reardon the man wallows in the chance to suffer: 'An extraordinary arrogance now and then possessed him; he stood amid his poor surroundings with the sensations of an outraged exile, and laughed aloud in furious contempt of all who censured or pitied him.' In the two long sections in which Gissing speaks directly to the reader (the beginnings of Chapters XXV and XXI) it is made plain that Reardon's character *is* weak, that he does seek refuge in 'the passion of self-pity', but such confessions merely emphasise the flaw in this part of the book. It is a failure to convince that reaches its lowest point when first Reardon and then Biffen quote, at the moment of death, Prospero's lines from *The Tempest:* 'We are such stuff as dreams are made on, and our—'

Too often, in the characterisation of Reardon, it is obvious that Gissing is talking of himself and of his own position in New Grub Street. The bitterness and the loathing of society descends at times into an intolerable whine, which upsets the Milvain/Whelpdale/Reardon/Biffen balance. The reader soon becomes aware that certain character details given to Reardon, while they sometimes possess a relevance to the central themes of the book, are not integrated into the total pattern. One could instance such details as Reardon's pathological dread of hearing the workhouse bell; his pedantry over classical literature; his pleasure, when he moves to the slum, in 'contemplating the little collection of sterling books that alone remained to him from his library'; and his anti-democratic sentiments. The great strength of **New Grub Street** lies in the fact that it is a personal interpretation of the changing nature of literary culture in society; a personal vision which is artistically controlled and organised. It is because of this that excessive personal involvement with the feelings of one character constitutes a serious weakness in the novel. (pp. 30-7)

> *P. J. Keating, in his* George Gissing: "New Grub Street," *Edward Arnold (Publishers) Ltd., 1968, 62 p.*

Robert L. Selig   (essay date 1970)

[*In the following essay, Selig analyzes the theme of alienation in* New Grub Street.]

Gissing's **New Grub Street** (1891) records the estrangement of the writer from the society for which he writes. Pathetically personal and deeply moving though the book is, its broader fascination lies in its vivid account of the profession of letters at a given time. In late-Victorian England marketable goods were more and more produced by machine, leaving the writer a somewhat old-fashioned figure, still creating in the slow way of the past. His isolation from his time was increased by the very nature of his craft, which immersed him in the timeless world of silent print. Perhaps most importantly of all, his transcendental belief in the value of written words estranged him from a world of commerce that tried to reduce all human effort to cash. . . .

Although Gissing succeeds, at least partly, in rendering his own estrangement and that of fellow writers in terms

of art, the novel also retains undeniable elements of case history. These may lessen its literary distinction, yet they enhance the book's value for cultural historians. What Gissing said by conscious intent about alienation is illuminating. What he revealed unintentionally, as a deeply involved recorder of writers' lives, illuminates still more. To do justice to this second aspect of his novel, one must combine textual analysis with historical perspectives unavailable to Gissing himself.

If all of Gissing's writers live in a late-Victorian world of large-scale industry and machines, only Milvain, the "Man of his Day," is really enthusiastic about modernity. Two arresting symbols that catch his attention early in the novel reflect the revolution in technology from the eighteenth to the nineteenth century. The novel's "grizzled" exponent of eighteenth-century literature, hard-working Alfred Yule, is juxtaposed symbolically in Milvain's mind with a "grizzled" horse, the chief form of eighteenth-century transportation: "a poor worn-out beast, all skin and bone, which had presumably been sent here in the hope that a little more labour might still be exacted from it if it were suffered to repose for a few weeks. There were sores upon its back and legs; it stood in a fixed attitude of despondency, just flicking away troublesome flies with its grizzled tail." The symbol of the worn-out horse is partic-

Sketch of Gissing by Sir William Rothenstein.

ularly appropriate for the hack writer, as *hack* is, of course, derived from hackney horses. Significantly, too, the horse appears to Milvain just two pages after he has consciously identified with a newer form of transportation, an express train to London:

> The front of the engine blackened nearer and nearer, coming on with dread force and speed. A blinding rush, and there burst against the bridge a great volley of sunlit steam. Milvain and his companion ran to the opposite parapet, but already the whole train had emerged, and in a few seconds it had disappeared round a sharp curve. The leafy branches that grew out over the line swayed violently backwards and forwards in the perturbed air.

> "If I were ten years younger," said Jasper, laughing, "I should say that was jolly! It enspirits me. It makes me feel eager to go back and plunge into the fight again."

The London train is an apt symbol for aggressively ambitious Milvain, a writer from the provinces who achieves success in London by a cynical exploitation of contemporary markets. By the second half of the nineteenth century, not only was the railroad bringing would-be writers to England's commercial and literary capital, but it had to a great extent replaced the horse-drawn post as a means of shipping literature back to the provinces. In a larger sense, then, the London express symbolizes the revolution in the technology of communication which, as Milvain himself notes in chapter 1, has helped to make "our Grub Street of to-day . . . a different place" from "Sam Johnson's Grub Street".

Yet whatever the attitude of Gissing's writers toward technological change, each must still create his own literary wares by the same slow and laborious method used for centuries. Like Reardon in chapter 4, each must shape his ideas within his private mind and then, in a process often lasting months, must transform them by hand into hundreds of written sheets. Even Milvain, the would-be "steam engine", finds that, under unusual pressures, he must labor "with unwonted effort to produce about a page". Alfred Yule's daughter, Marian, is so oppressed by literary work that she dreams ironically of a mechanical author to replace the labors of the writer:

> A few days ago her startled eye had caught an advertisement in the newspaper, headed "Literary Machine"; had it then been invented at last, some automaton to supply the place of such poor creatures as herself, to turn out books and articles? Alas! the machine was only one for holding volumes conveniently, that the work of literary manufacture might be physically lightened. But surely before long some Edison would make the true automaton; the problem must be comparatively such a simple one. Only to throw in a given number of old books, and have them reduced, blended, modernised into a single one for to-day's consumption.

Marian's vision of a literary machine suggests a basic difference between old and new Grub Street. The writer's trade, which is partly a handicraft, coexisted in Dr. John-

son's time with hundreds of more common handicrafts at all levels of commerce. And if, at the end of his life, Johnson himself witnessed the early stages of industrial revolution, he still wrote for an industry virtually unchanged since Caxton. If the eighteenth-century author wrote his sheets by hand, his fellow craftsmen in printing and publishing cut letter punches by hand, struck them by hand into blank matrices, cast type, composed it, and printed the final pages all entirely by hand. By the time of **New Grub Street,** however, even the printing industry had at last adjusted to machines. From the appearance in 1814 of the first steam-printed newspaper to the multiple rotary presses of the late-Victorian period, the printing of newspapers was speeded up nearly a hundredfold. Book publishers adopted machinery more slowly, but they too gradually mechanized their procedures. Other processes besides printing itself were taken over by machine; machinery was developed, for example, for punch-cutting, typecasting, and composing. But no Edison had yet developed a mechanized author. The human author, who still supplied to publishers their basic raw material, the written word, was changed, in effect, from a craftsman among craftsmen to an isolated anomaly among industrial employees.

Among the many writers in the novel who are struggling to produce, none, significantly, are poets. There are no poets in the book, even though Gissing, as he wrote his early drafts, had been reading Bell's *Lives of the Poets*. Poetry appears only as a regretted absence, as something that cannot be created within the deadening confines of Grub Street. "Yes, yes," thinks Reardon of Homer's *Odyssey*, "*that* was not written at so many pages a day, with a workhouse clock clanging its admonition at the poet's ear. How it freshened the soul! How the eyes grew dim with a rare joy in the sounding of those nobly sweet hexameters!" This late-Victorian prose writer looks yearningly back to the Homeric bard, whose poetry was an expression of the whole man rather than a mere literary commodity.

The classical world of Greece and Rome becomes, for Gissing's writers, a lost yet cherished Eden. In the past, Reardon had planned to take his wife to Greece and Rome as the crowning experience of marriage. Later he insists that his trip there as a bachelor was a deeper and more spiritual pleasure than the highest sexual love. To the almost starving Biffen, Reardon holds out the hope of a voyage to Greece. In ironic juxtaposition in the very next chapter, Whelpdale tells of nearly having starved to death in the unhomeric modern town of Troy, New York. The dying classicist Reardon has deliriums of being in Greece but, in a final flash of lucidity, declares pathetically that he shall never see it again.

The classical world is exalted by Reardon as the land where the muses were heard. Throughout the novel, the cadence and sound of classical verse are emphasized. Its singing metres bring relief from Grub Street's silent hackwork. Reardon and Biffen discuss "Greek metres as if they lived in a world where the only hunger known could be satisfied by grand or sweet cadences". Biffen needs no excuse at all for "murmuring to himself a Greek iambic line". The two writer friends are so absorbed in Euripides that they argue about his metrics even on the public streets. Into the company of the Greek singing school, Reardon is willing to admit a few more recent classics. He refreshes himself from his own belabored writing with a canto a day from *The Divine Comedy*. But late-Victorian London is no singing school. When Reardon happens to say out loud a few lines from Shakespeare, he is stared at on the street like "a strayed lunatic".

This intuitive contrast between the ancient bards and the mute, inglorious writers of modern Grub Street seems more understandable in the light of recent studies by Havelock, Ong, and others. Reardon's beloved Homer was an oral poet, united with his non-literate audience in an intensely immediate form of communication that precluded objectivity and detachment. *New Grub Street*'s prose writers work in silent detachment for an audience of silent readers, whom they never meet. Immersing themselves in the writings of others as well as their own, these bookish men of the late-nineteenth century absorb and create silently, in mental isolation.

New Grub Street's central symbol for the alienation of the writer is the British Museum Reading-room. In an early draft the opening scene was actually set in the library. In the final version it serves as the central axis around which the characters revolve. It is where they earn a living, all these drudges, surrounded in turn by other solitary drudges. H. J. Chaytor has explained why such a place, where hundreds of readers sit elbow to elbow in silent isolation, could not have existed before print and simplified prose made silent reading a widespread custom: "The reading-room of the British Museum is not divided into sound-proof compartments. The habit of silent reading has made such an arrangement unnecessary; but fill the reading-room with medieval readers and the buzz of whispering and muttering would be intolerable."

Because of its effect of alienation, the Reading-room is jokingly described by Milvain and others as "the valley of the shadow of books". It is described less jokingly by Marian as a desolate limbo for lost souls:

> The fog grew thicker; she looked up at the windows beneath the dome and saw that they were a dusky yellow. Then her eye discerned an official walking along the upper gallery, and in pursuance of her grotesque humour, her mocking misery, she likened him to a black, lost soul, doomed to wander in an eternity of vain research along endless shelves. Or again, the readers who sat here at these radiating lines of desks, what were they but hapless flies caught in a huge web, its nucleus the great circle of the Catalogue? Darker, darker. From the towering wall of volumes seemed to emanate visible motes, intensifying the obscurity; in a moment the book-lined circumference of the room would be but a featureless prison-limit.

The Museum resembles a prison of lost souls because it puts its readers behind an invisible wall of silence, in mental and spiritual isolation. If Reardon, for one, likes the Reading-room, his acquired taste for it is part of his mental withdrawal: "The Reading-room was his true home; its warmth enwrapped him kindly; the peculiar odour of its atmosphere—at first a cause of headache—grew dear and delightful to him. . . . He was a recluse in the midst of millions". In the silent library even man's most basic drives must be kept quiet and held in check. Thus, although Milvain has seen Marian many times in "the valley of the shadow of books" and has felt her sexual attraction, it is not until he meets her outside that he finds it possible to speak. Human beings are usually not talked to by other human beings in this peculiar "valley." They are reached in silence, largely by the dead, through inanimate words on a page. And whatever thoughts each reader draws from the printed word will probably stay within his own mind until he can transfer them to pages of his own making. In Marian's mocking words, each isolated visitor to the library will, in good time, "make new books out of those already existing, that yet newer books might in turn be made out of theirs".

The invisible wall of silence extends outward to envelop the lives of these library-goers even when they are away. Marian is forced to return, day after day, from the British Museum to a home which her father runs like a branch-office library. Even the eating of dinner, a time for family talk, occurs among the Yules in library-like silence. Until the moment of being called to eat, Alfred Yule stands "on the hearthrug reading an evening paper". His frequent custom at the meal itself is to switch from papers to books. In the very act of eating, he reaches for a volume and proceeds, in front of his masticating wife and daughter, to read silently. Jasper and Dora Milvain, in their household, also partake of the same silent literary meals: "Each had an open book on the table; throughout the meal they exchanged only a few words". Perhaps most revealing of all is Reardon's retreat into print after his final loud quarrel with his departing wife: "He sat reading a torn portion of a newspaper, and became quite interested in the report of a commercial meeting in the City, a thing he would never have glanced at under ordinary circumstances". Reardon's somnambulistic escape into newsprint parallels his earlier retreat into the enveloping quiet of the Reading-room. For Reardon by choice, for Marian against her will, the human voice is screened out by print.

In spite of all her efforts to break out into a world of live human voices, poor Marian is condemned to remain within silent walls. At the end of the novel she has been forced, against her deepest desires, to become an assistant in a provincial library. For the still more lonely and isolated Biffen, the Reading-room is not only a place of alienation—it is quite literally "the valley of the shadow of death." When his frustrated desire for a woman's love becomes too much for him, it is from the Reading-room that Biffen gets the recipe for the very efficient poison that will kill him. Even as he goes into the open air to commit suicide, first straightening out the books in his room, he remains in silent isolation, for, like the well-trained library-goer that he is, he takes his poison in a deserted park so that he will not disturb the other people who are trying to concentrate in the vast library of the world.

Even when characters do speak in the novel, their words deal very largely with silent print. Their talk tends to be of literature, magazines, and the press. The keynote is sounded in the novel's very first pages with a conversation based on a newspaper story: a criminal is being hanged in London at the moment that Milvain discusses his death. Milvain, who lives and works in the realm of print, can regard a printed description of another's execution as a mere matter of words, to be viewed with detachment. Milvain's remarks about the hanged man lead, in fact, to a discussion of Reardon's professional troubles, his own plans as a writer, and the problems of writers in general. The implied connection is bitterly ironic: getting hanged is an easier way of breaking into print than writing. A similar thought occurs later to Biffen when he is nearly burned to death rescuing his manuscript: "The *Daily Telegraph* would have made a leader out of me. 'This poor man was so strangely deluded as to the value of a novel in manuscript which it appears he had just completed, that he positively sacrificed his life in the endeavour to rescue it from the flames.' And the *Saturday* would have had a column of sneering jocosity on the irrepressibly sanguine temperament of authors. At all events, I should have had my day of fame". For print-oriented men, not only human words but human actions themselves, even those of the most dramatic kind, have no lasting value unless they are translated into the realm of print. In the words of that bookish Renaissance man Samuel Daniel, "What good is like to this, / To do worthy the writing, and to write / Worthy the reading, and the world's delight?"

If Gissing's characters tend to refer everything back to the printed word, they tend, with equal insistence, to refer all human actions back to the concept of money. The novel's opening conversation, dealing with the hanging, leads to a discussion of the printed word but also of its cash value. Few other novels, in fact, devote so many passages to money. Out of the book's 956 pages, money is directly mentioned on almost half!

Gissing is bitterly aware that the writer's favorite symbol, the printed word, must take a distant second place to society's favorite symbol. If men of letters care most for print, that silent and objectified preserver of human experience, most men prefer cash, that preserver of human labor in silent, objectified coin and bills. "Blessed money! root of all good, until the world invent some saner economy". The average man works in order to earn money with which he may buy the necessities of life. Gissing's high-minded men of letters take "no thought of whether . . . [their] toil would be recompensed in coin of the realm", yet discover, to their dismay, that man cannot live by words alone. Prose will bring them bread only by being transformed into money. In this necessity, writers are no different from civilization's other craftsmen, such as smiths, barbers, or shoemakers. They differ in believing that the product of their labor is sublimely transcendent in value apart from the cash it earns. Yet "what the devil," asks Milvain, "is there in typography to make everything it deals with sacred?" Behind the literary differences of Reardon's psychological realism, Biffen's naturalism, Whelpdale's "chit-chat", Yule's pedantic criticism, the Milvain sisters' hackwork for children, and Milvain's own cynical journalism, Jasper, the account keeper, is able to see the single essence of money.

Most of the writers in Gissing's novel are just as obsessed by money as by literature. Those on their way to success, such as Milvain, are preoccupied with their earnings, and those on their way to failure, such as Yule, are equally preoccupied with what they cannot earn. Money controls the plot of the novel quite as much as literature does. The book's central event is the bequest, through the will of a minor character, of ten thousand pounds to Reardon's wife, five thousand pounds to Marian, and not a pound to Marian's father. The news of the inheritance is so important that it comes three times in the novel to three separate sets of characters. Until the bequest, things have gone badly for most of Gissing's writers. Reardon's marriage has collapsed through lack of money; the somewhat poor Milvain has hesitated to marry an even poorer Marian; and Alfred Yule has yearned in vain for capital to start a literary magazine. The sudden appearance of unearned cash deflects this flow of events. Reardon's wife is saved from poverty, though too late to help her soon-to-die husband. Poor Marian is treated with respect for the first time and even fought over by Milvain and her father, who see her human value hugely enhanced by her five thousand pounds. But when Marian's creditors default on the will, this unexpected second swerve of capital alters once again the lives of all the characters. Milvain breaks his engagement to the disinherited Marian and takes Reardon's widow instead, conveniently wealthy now. Marian is left to support her blind father and wholly dependent mother on a mere fraction of the former legacy. At the novel's end, Marian, her father, Reardon, and even Biffen have been undone by lack of money, but Milvain, Amy, Dora, Maud, and Whelpdale have been rescued by its golden presence.

Of all of Gissing's men of letters, Reardon and Biffen alone are not obsessed by money. They fail, of course, as writers largely through their innocence of all financial realities. A tough-minded attitude toward money undoubtedly helps a writer's career. Yet a mercenary state of mind may conflict, even more than bookishness, with a writer's personal relationships. Such is the case with the cynical Milvain. Although Jasper, unlike Reardon and Biffen, lives more for money than for print, the result is a similar alienation, a debilitating isolation from full human contact. "He, too, was weak," Gissing declares of Milvain, "but with quite another kind of weakness than Reardon's". The contrast seems to lie in the very different ways that each expresses a similar inadequacy. Reardon withdraws from fellow human beings. Milvain uses them for his own material gain with a cold detachment that leaves him, in effect, as isolated among people as Reardon in solitude. Even when he falls in love with Marian, Milvain cannot put his feelings into speech. "She had looked forward with trembling eagerness to some sudden revelation; but it seemed as if he knew no word of the language which would have called such joyous response from her expectant soul". "It was with a sense of relief that Jasper had passed from dithyrambs to conversation on practical points". "She hid her face against him, and whispered the words that would have enraptured her had they but come from his lips. The young man found it pleasant enough to be worshipped, but he could not reply as she desired. A few phrases of tenderness, and his love-vocabulary was exhausted". More, in fact, than Gissing's other writers, Milvain, the man of pounds and shillings, finds it hard to use the spoken word for anything but superficial talk.

There is, perhaps surprisingly, a strong similarity between the supposedly opposite mentalities of literary and economic man. If one wishes to translate everything into print, the other translates everything into money. Both abstractions place human value in frozen, inanimate objects rather than in men. A commonplace figure in nineteenth-century fiction, in Dickens and many others, is the miserly businessman who views all human relationships in terms of mere cash and thus converts even himself into cash both in his own and in others' eyes. Such unlikeminded writers in Gissing's novel as Milvain and Yule accept the creed of the worshipper of cash: a man with money is valued for his money; a man without money is not valued at all. This ironic connection of literary and economic man is underscored by Amy Reardon's shift from one abstract belief to the other. Her first reason for ceasing to love her husband is his failure to produce great books. Later, as she "matures," her chief complaint becomes his failure to earn enough money. Both failures justify, in her view, a total withdrawal of her love. In other words, both economic and literary man, in their extreme forms, are deadening abstractions, which are analogous, mutually illuminating, and even interchangeable. Gissing, in **New Grub Street**, has journeyed not only into the shadow of books but also into the shadow of money. Out of this double vision of desolation, self-indulgent or not, comes perhaps the finest study in late-Victorian literature of alienation among the people of the book. (pp. 188-98)

> Robert L. Selig, " 'The Valley of the Shadow of Books': Alienation in Gissing's 'New Grub Street'," in Nineteenth-Century Fiction, Vol. 25, No. 2, September, 1970, pp. 188-98.

Adrian Poole   (essay date 1975)

[*In the following excerpt, Poole concentrates on human relationships, the mass commercialization of literature, and the quest for money in* New Grub Street.]

The most important single point about Gissing's portrayal of the literary world in [**New Grub Street**] is his subtle intimation of power changing hands. The literary world itself is viewed from an entirely oblique angle, through the comment and gossip of a few figures hovering uneasily around its fringe, or in Jasper Milvain's case, aspiring to gain entrance. But the key aspects of this sense of transition are clearly marked. The newness and contemporaneity of the situation are hammered home by those recurrent words, 'now', 'new', 'modern', 'to-day'.

There is nothing especially new in itself about the centralisation of this literary world in London. But London is not just any big city now. It is at the heart of a communications industry, that with the advent of the telegraph and linotype, and the backing of increasing concentrations of capital, is expanding and co-ordinating the resources of the written word to cover the globe. London, as Jasper understands perfectly, is now a world-city, a focal point not just for world trade and finance, but for world news, fashions and cultural attitudes. The age of publicity is dawn-

ing. The possibilities of *power* are ranged on a new scale, and Gissing's narrative is patterned according to the efforts of characters either positively to grasp some of this power or at least to align themselves with its field of force. The bitter recognition to which Reardon gives voice is that the increasing power centred in London has resulted in exactly the reverse of a shining cultural capital. He has been attracted by an image of the literary life that he comes to recognise as enshrined in the past. His lament to Biffen echoes Gissing's cry: 'where are the good cultured people?'

> We form our ideas of London from old literature; we think of London as if it were still one centre of intellectual life: we think and talk like Chatterton. But the truth is that intellectual men in our day do their best to keep away from London—when once they know the place. There are libraries everywhere; papers and magazines reach the north of Scotland as soon as they reach Brompton.

But this is meagre consolation for the dispersed, exiled band of lonely cultural 'loyalists', the 'few awake and watching'. Their cultural capital still stands, but it has been taken over by the insurgent forces, the new men. Reardon is deliberately characterised as a mediocre, but genuine talent, to illustrate the *expectations* of such a man to find a role within a controlling cultural élite, such as was recognised to be in control of the major cultural institutions of previous generations, but which has now suffered an irreversible diaspora. At the heart of the novel is this take-over by a new generation of proprietors, businessmen, editors, publishers and writers. The emotional centre of the novel is correspondingly in the bitterness of the minority artist, not merely that he is now (as he has always been) a minority artist, but that this minority is no longer functioning at the centre but at the periphery of the general culture.

The perspective of the narrative is similar to that of **The Nether World**, in that our direct vision is confined to the sphere of the excluded and exploited, while the upper world of the controllers is only glimpsed in the distance. But now this upper world at least holds distinct names, biographies and activities. In **The Nether World**, power was fixed and permanent, but now it is in motion; the owners and controllers are at least identifiable, if not reachable. The key figures, mentioned but never seen, are Clement Fadge and Mrs Boston Wright, the new editors, Jedwood, the new publisher (seen, in fact, once very briefly) and Markland, the popular novelist. These figures are skilfully insinuated into the aspirations and envies of the characters we *do* see, struggling to survive on the sharp edge between success and failure. There are also a number of minor 'presences' that build up the panorama behind the constricted forescene. There is Ralph Warbury, for instance, the 'all-round man of letters', one of the new breed of bright young men from Oxford and Cambridge. In this respect, Warbury bears the same loose resemblance to Andrew Lang, say, as Jedwood to Heinemann, and Markland to Hall Caine: each economically represents a new phenomenon.

Jasper, as always, understands the process of the writer's

socialisation, under the aegis of a Lang's elegance and a Besant's busy-ness. The 'new literary man' is a hard-working professional who hires out his labour at different levels, contributing to different grades of magazine and journal, reviews, essays, literary gossip, perhaps even a leader column for a daily paper. Jasper's model of his working day is the exact antithesis of Reardon's, the well-oiled clockwork regularity and the morose, frantic stuttering. Besant and Arnold Bennett both reproduce with the same relish this image of the respectable and industrious worker, polishing off a series of daily assignments with the professional dexterity of the doctor or lawyer.

The genial athleticism of the freelance is made possible by the blurring of the lines of cultural demarcation that ensued on the breakdown of an earlier truce between quality and popular periodicals. During the middle years of the century, there was little competition between the quality journals of ideas, criticism and reviews, the popular (in this sense, 'middle-class') magazines with their staple diet of sentimental fiction, and the cheap penny magazines. The various markets were well defined and could be served with little conflict. But the 1880s mark a transition from truce to active hostility.

> The new mass magazines, like the urban newspapers, were tailored for all classes and all levels of intellect—at least they levelled all into one homogeneous 'market'—while the magazines once dominant took a secondary place, in the periphery of culture, where they inevitably fell into decadence.

One of the results of this shift in the balance of power is that a new distinction is made, by men like Jasper, between 'Literature' as the transcendental creation of otherwordly men of 'genius', and the work of the professional literary man, prepared to write intelligently on any subject put before him, from cookery to Greek mythology. Andrew Lang took pride in exactly this sort of 'beautiful thin facility', as James derisively called it. Jasper is of course all too ready to concede the perfect ephemerality of this kind of writing. Like all the manuals of advice to young aspirants that appear around this time, he reiterates the absolute distinction between the genius and literary man, the aesthetic and commercial value of a book. But this was precisely the distinction that Gissing had himself made, from the *other* side of the fence, in a letter to Hardy in 1886, when he referred to his resolution 'to pursue literature as distinct from the profession of letters'. It is one thing, however, for a Milvain to concede this division, while paying lip-service to the notion of Great Literature that exists in a transcendent sphere outside the exigencies of getting published and finding readers, let alone enough to eat. It is another for a Gissing to make the desperate rationalisation that 'in literature my interests begin and end'. Beneath both attitudes is the sense that it is the Milvains who have won control of some of the key mediating positions of cultural power, without access to which the idealistic artist, let alone the genius, cannot survive.

The central indictment of the contemporary literary world made by Gissing, is that it has achieved a total industrialisation of writing, and reduction of the world to the status of a thing. Remote from our view are the owners, employ-ers and managers, whose ranks Jasper is determined to join. Close before our eyes are the factory hands, differentiated only by their capacity and willingness to regulate their intellectual energies to the production of so many words per minute, so many articles per day. No wonder that for Marian Yule in the British Museum reading-room, the prospect of an actual 'Literary Machine' is a dream of release. For the machine is the only workable image; the 'old hack horse', the image associated with Alfred Yule, is hopelessly outmoded.

The reading-room itself stands physically at the centre of the novel, as the literal store-house of literary culture. The main characters are differentiated by their attitudes towards and use of it. Alfred Yule is the one most closely associated with it, so totally has his life become determined by the sheer mechanics of scholarship. Gissing makes a quiet but effective distinction between his 'dead' pedantry and his daughter's 'live' use of literary culture, when they are on holiday together at the beginning of the book. Though Marian is so city-bred that she cannot recognise an ash on her country walk, she can use her literary knowledge (two lines from Tennyson) to enrich the physical object before her. Her father is also made to quote two lines of poetry, but for him the country landscape is only the excuse for a sardonic, introverted joke at the expense of the unfortunate poet Cottle. Not only has he lost all capacity to recognise the minimal value of the Shadwells and Settles, he has lost all instinctive response to the world outside him, natural and human. With his 'peculiar croaking' laugh and 'seamed visage', he inhabits an angular, desiccated world of his own, in which a complimentary footnote from a friend is worth more than his daughter's love.

As for the three other main characters, Marian loathes the reading-room; in her is concentrated all the instinctive revolt against the mechanisation of the intellect. Jasper raids the reading-room for smatterings of knowledge to flavour his facile concoctions. But Reardon, like Yule, is at home there; indeed he would gladly curl up into a snug corner, were it not for the all-embracing constraints of earning money. Though he is close to Yule in his proclivity to make literature a substitute for life, Tibullus and Diogenes Laertius are still 'live' literature for him, even if they are as remote from the present as Shadwell and Cyriac Skinner. The classical past to which Reardon and Biffen pay homage offers the image of a genuine ideal, as well as the indulgence of simple escape. Homer, like the Athenian sunset glorified by Reardon, belongs to an ideal world of free creativity ('*that* was not written at so many pages a day') and natural beauty, that stands in polar contrast to the time-bound city of dreadful fog and murk. But the dream, as usual in Gissing, is so distant from the reality that it cannot inter-act or transform; it can only offer temporary consolation. Biffen and Reardon bend passionately over their Greek metres—'as if they lived in a world where the only hunger known could be satisfied by grand or sweet cadences'. Literal hunger always returns. The ideal past is only a dream world, from which the privileged fool is jerked back into reality. As he lies dying, Reardon wakes from his vision of the Greek dawn: 'The glory vanished. He lay once more a sick man in a hired chamber, longing for the dull English dawn'. It is quintessential Gissing, down to the crushing detail of the 'hired chamber'; the narrator's generosity in giving Reardon a 'chamber' rather than a mundane 'room' is painfully undercut by the fact of its being 'hired'.

Both the strengths and the limitations of the vision of the literary world put forward by Gissing can be located in the rigour with which the alternatives are posed; on the one hand Art, on the other Business; success, failure; inclusion, exclusion. It is worth picking up some of the aspects of the objective historical situation already touched upon, in order to define the limits of Gissing's vision of total cultural disaster. For the innovations in publishing that took place in the 1890s, for example, were in fact very far from simply directed towards the exploiting of a new mass market. Gissing was himself soon to benefit from the changing literary scene in several ways. He would discover that a new publisher such as A. H. Bullen could take a much broader view of the 'value' of a writer like Gissing to his firm, than Gissing would have dreamed possible. We can place Gissing's own version of the new publisher, Jedwood, beside one of the actual new publishers, Heinemann. Both are shrewd enough to harness the earning potential of one of the new popular novelists, Jedwood by a literal and Heinemann by a figurative marriage— Heinemann's first published book was Hall Caine's *The Bondman* (1890), which made them both thousands. But Gissing is misguided as well as ungenerous in attributing to his fictional publisher only the pragmatic flair for 'ventures which should appeal to the democratic generation just maturing'. (pp. 139-44)

The major limitation of Gissing's view of the literary world in **New Grub Street** can be stated thus: whatever one's judgements about the personal moral qualities of a figure such as Heinemann, the 'new men' of which he is representative can never be simple evidence of cultural decline in themselves. For the conditions which they are instrumental in shaping can contain possibilities and release energies not necessarily related to the virtues and vices of the individuals apparently 'in control'. The oblique perspective of the novel is, therefore, an evasion of the complexity of historical change, since the narrow angle is based on a crude generalisation about the depravity of the 'new men'. This insistence on proving a case is, from the point of view of historical accuracy, the novel's greatest flaw. Yet it is precisely the single-mindedness with which Gissing carries through this vision of an absolute dichotomy between Art and Trade, 'culture' and 'progress', that is responsible for its creative urgency. There is a strong evolutionary thesis underlying the narrative, according to which physical victory and moral degeneration are interconnected. It is nevertheless part of the novel's strength that it resists the correlative equation of physical defeat with moral nobility.

The action revolves around the problem of who will get the money and the mate. For every winner, there is a complementary loser: Jasper and Reardon, Amy and Marian, Whelpdale and Biffen, Fadge and Alfred Yule. It is characteristic of the neatness of this pattern that Fadge's moment of triumph, the appearance of his illustrated portrait,

should coincide with Alfred Yule's ignominious departure from London. It is a similar neatness that balances the opening scene of the Milvains' family breakfast in provincial straits and longings, with the closing scene of Jasper and Amy's dinner, in metropolitan comfort and fulfilment. Through the narrative drives an undeviating current of power, with which words such as 'progress' and 'the future' are associated, and all the important characters are seen decisively to succeed or to fail in adaptation to this force. This is the point made by the scene in which Jasper and Marian watch the express train thunder beneath the bridge towards London. It is less a question of the train's 'symbolic' function as representing 'both his driving ambition and the disconcerting sexual attraction Marian possesses for him' (as one critic has said), than of the literal effect it has on the two characters. Whereas Jasper is thrilled by the 'dread force and speed' of this 'symbol' of technological progress, Marian is depressed. There are only two ways of reacting to progress, either enthusiasm or revulsion, determination or apathy.

Even a transitory figure such as Mr Baker, Biffen's ambitious student, is carefully aligned according to his capacity to 'succeed'. He will pass the exam for which he is studying, and rise from the status of docker or bargeman to work in the Customs. But he is also the occasion for one of the instructive loopholes in the strait-jacket of the general thesis of cultural degeneration. Along with Jasper's sisters and Amy Reardon, Mr Baker prompts Gissing to a moment of unexpected tolerance for the possibility of *individual* improvement, maturity or expansion, within the overall picture. P. J. Keating lumps him together with the other working-class figures in the novel (Mrs Goby and the furniture-dealer), in order to convict Gissing of a class generalisation of which he is, unexpectedly perhaps, *not* guilty in this novel, at least at this point. 'They are totally insensitive and thus inferior to the people with whom they come in contact'. Gissing in fact goes out of his way to emphasise the innate and moving tact that prompts Mr Baker to pay Biffen for his instruction out of Reardon's hearing. He does indeed belong to the breed of the 'survivors', with his 'robust figure' and 'clenched fist', but his 'intelligent' look, his 'modesty' and 'delicacy' in effect elevate him morally beyond any of the other 'survivors' in the book, except perhaps Dora Milvain. The irony of the wry interchange he has with Reardon over the difficulties of 'compersition' is directed at least equally at the helplessness of the man who can pronounce the word 'properly', as at the uncouthness of the man who cannot.

But such moments as this, or the admission of 'a noticeable maturing of intellect' in Amy after she leaves Reardon, only momentarily disturb the main pattern of the action. The disruptive complexity suggested by Amy's intellectual expansion is swiftly neutralised by reference to the *ersatz* intellectuality of contemporary periodicals. The prevailing thesis dictates that personal qualities such as 'sensitivity' or even 'maturity' are mere nuances beside the biological capacity for 'success' or 'failure'. One belongs either with the 'stronger' or the 'weaker'. In an early scene, Reardon returns home from a dismal trudge round the park, to find Jasper and Amy sitting together. Coming in from the dark, he enters with 'dazzled eyes'; it is as though he were the intruder instead of Jasper, the stranger who blunders in with his burden of gloom to disturb the charmed circle of light and vitality.

It is natural that, given this peremptory schism between the lost and the saved, the key scenes of the novel should be ones of *confrontation* between individuals. These scenes reflect the single most important movement in all Gissing's work towards states of extreme opposition, both within the narrative in thematic terms of class, cultural and personal crisis, and at the level of narrative structure itself. This novel is as concerned with the disintegration of individual human unions as with the disintegration of general cultural unity—the relation between the two is a blunt assumption. There are three central relationships between a man and a woman: between a husband and wife, Reardon and Amy; between a father and daughter, Alfred Yule and Marian; and between potential lovers, Jasper and Marian. Each of these culminates in a scene of crisis.

All the important male characters are afflicted with sexual desire: not even Jasper and Biffen are immune. Yet, as in all other spheres, Jasper is the one who can most successfully adapt to this dangerous force. In exact contrast to Jasper's pragmatism is Reardon's sentimental idealism. The wry, perfunctory tone of the narrator, as he describes Reardon's attraction to Amy, suggests the fatality and irresistibility of sexual desire.

> As for the poor author himself, well, he merely fell in love with Miss Yule at first sight, and there was an end of the matter.

It is of more than passing interest to note that this phrasing is echoed in a Diary entry of Gissing's for 11 August 1890. While staying with his family, he met a girl named Connie Ash a couple of times. His Diary could hardly be more laconic: 'I am in love with her, & there's an end of it'. The relationship came to nothing, as Gissing seems to have expected. Reardon is again drawing on an attitude with which Gissing was closely familiar, when he expresses an extreme Schopenhauerian devotion to the purity of aesthetic contemplation, as an antidote to the embroilments of the will-to-live. The sight of beauty such as his Athenian sunset is 'infinitely preferable to sexual emotion'.

> I have lived in an ideal world that was not deceitful, a world which seems to me, when I recall it, beyond the human sphere, bathed in diviner light.

Yet whatever the degree of Gissing's identification with such an attitude, it is, like all the motions towards escape, checked and placed within the context of *this* human sphere, here and now. Reardon's ideal love, like his ideal literature, can exist only in imagination or memory; the two ideals fuse together when he reads to Amy from Homer the passage of Odysseus's awed admiration of Nausicaa.

Reardon's sentimental idealisation of women has disastrous consequences, for he rapidly regresses towards a male despotism that aligns him closely with Alfred Yule and the appalling Widdowson of ***The Odd Women***. The refusal of both Marian and Amy to conform to their de-

fined roles as ministering angel or acolyte undoubtedly wins our sympathy, though we understand simultaneously the validity of Reardon's complaint at Amy's frigidity. The two central scenes of confrontation between Amy and Reardon reflect the total breakdown of mutual definition, in which the expectations embodied in the Other are decisively discredited. Reardon is not going to be the successful author Amy imagined; Amy is not going to be the devoted helpmeet, soldiering bravely on through thick and thin. When Reardon tells her that he has arranged to return to a job as a hospital clerk, this is the last straw for Amy: 'I am certainly not the wife of a clerk who is paid so much a week.' In the second scene, at Amy's house, we register how well Gissing understands the almost arbitrary physical obstacles preventing two people conversing directly and freely. Amy is instinctively repelled by Reardon's shabby appearance, Reardon by Amy's studied elegance. This is no casual misunderstanding; it grows out of one of Gissing's deepest beliefs, that experience is ruled tyrannically by masks and images of the presented Self, against which the hidden emotions struggle vainly for expression.

This fierce repression of inner emotion is certainly the key to Alfred Yule's household, the emotional locus that in some ways stands at the centre of the novel. Gissing takes pains to draw the parallels between Yule and Reardon in their increasingly desperate possessiveness of their women. Both project their frustration on to the image of a rival—Jasper. Yule aims the same wild accusation of Jasper's evil influence on Marian as Reardon had with regard to Amy. But in his daughter Marian are concentrated most of the positive virtues denied to Reardon, in some ways her natural counterpart in failure and deprivation. For all the evident proximity of Reardon to many aspects of Gissing's own personality and experience, it is unnecessary to see him, as Jacob Korg does, as the 'tragic central character' in the novel. Marian certainly has more right to the first adjective, and, as will be argued, almost as much right to the second.

Marian's refusal to submit to her father's intolerable dictatorship is genuinely moving, where Amy's comparable rebellion only commands acquiescence in its logic, for we feel the extent to which Marian's bid for self-fulfilment makes unexpected demands on her instinctive compassion and gentleness towards others. It is rare indeed for a character in Gissing to transcend his or her innate passivity in this way. The two climactic scenes of confrontation with her father parallel those between Amy and Reardon, and culminate in those typical moments of total opposition, the polarisation of Self and Other: 'Their eyes met, and the look of each seemed to fascinate the other.' These scenes seem inevitably to gravitate towards such exposures of the naked ego, of brute desire and denial, when Reardon seems silently to cry, 'I want sympathy', Amy, 'I want clean sheets', Marian, 'I want love', and Alfred Yule, 'I want to be an editor again'. One of the most moving moments in the novel occurs when Marian hears that she has lost the modest legacy that, as she knows quite well, has persuaded Jasper into offering marriage. When she summons her father to her bedside, the roles are for once reversed between them, she haughtily summoning and curtly dismissing, in the same way in which *he* has been used to treating her. The unexpected but perfectly plausible outburst of bitterness only confirms her humanity and reveals the depth of her desire, at the same time as it retrospectively illuminates the process by which deprivation has soured her father—for it is exactly her father's tone that she uses:

> 'This of course happens to me,' Marian said, with intense bitterness. 'None of the other legatees will suffer, I suppose?'

But it is not only on behalf of herself that Marian challenges her father. Cursed by marriage with a social inferior, Alfred Yule has tried desperately to 'save' Marian from infection by her mother's defects of speech and manner. The resultant tragedy of dissociation between mother and child is conveyed with a delicacy for which Gissing is not often given credit. The mother wears a permanently puzzled look on her face, for she desperately *wants* to understand her daughter, and share her feelings. The situation is closely similar to one in a tale by Hardy, written almost contemporaneously with this novel. In 'The Son's Veto', the clergyman father turns his son into an educated prig rather than allow him to be sullied by his working-class mother, once a servant at the vicarage. Hardy's tale, deliberately a parable in intent, differs from Gissing's treatment of the situation in focus as well as in the extent of the generalisation. For Gissing, it is the 'educated' child who is the centre of attention; for Hardy, it is the mother, uprooted from her native ties and oppressed by a 'culture' from which she is excluded. Mrs Alfred Yule too has been torn away from her native surroundings and ties in the "Olloway Road", and Gissing is well able to suggest the minutiae of class tensions between herself and her envious relatives, who always suspect her of the condescension she tries so hard to avoid. But the differences from Hardy are as instructive as the similarities. For Gissing sees no intrinsic value in Mrs Yule's 'natural ties' as Hardy does in Sophy Twycott's. There is nothing equivalent in Gissing to the suggestion of sexual attractiveness in Sophy's nut-brown hair, and the emotional attachment between her and her old lover Sam Hobson. Mrs Yule has only the redeeming qualities of kindness and gentleness. But, most important of all, the focus of the relationship is not on her at all; it is on her daughter Marian, who is as much the victim of the oppressive education her father has forced on her, as the mother.

It is rare indeed for Gissing to question his deeply-rooted sense of educated 'culture' as an essential good. On his one visit to Max Gate in 1895, it was exactly the inferiority of Hardy's 'culture' to Meredith's that he used to distinguish between the two. (He had recently visited Meredith at Box Hill also.) Yet in this aspect of this novel, at least, he does seem to come nearer than anywhere else to Hardy's questioning of the intrinsic value of an educated 'culture' that produces only at best the pathetic consolations of Greek metrical effects (and, though we know that Gissing revelled in such pedantry himself, in the context of the novel they are meant to be pathetic), and at worst the nightmare sterility of the Yule family. The questioning does indeed stop short of the extreme generalisation, because it is always rigorously conducted under the terms of *this* set of

conditions, with *those* men in control. But Marian's vision of hell in the reading-room, and her sense of 'all literature as a morbid excrescence on life' serve the same function as an extreme generalisation against which the specific circumstances are measured, as the metaphor of the 'nether world' in the earlier novel.

It seems more than likely that Gissing was drawing directly on his own family relationships in depicting some of the tensions in Alfred Yule's household. . . . [The] long summer before the writing of the novel had been spent with his mother and two sisters in their home near Wakefield. This extended period of frustration, of false starts and repeated abandonments, suggests a crisis in his creative life, that could only be solved by a direct confrontation with the problems of the writer's life, as shaped by his personal vision of the sharp oppositions between success and failure, the ideal and the practical. But though he sketched one self-image into Reardon, the self-image of depressive failure centred on the nightmare summer months of 1890, it was into Marian Yule that he projected his deepest desires for emotional fulfilment, and his deepest fears about the value of the education and 'culture' that had taken him so far away from the insular world of his Yorkshire home. Into one sentence in the novel, he puts directly the feelings that he often recorded as the dominant impression whenever he returned home. Of Marian and her mother, we are told:

> The English fault of domestic reticence could scarcely go further than it did in their case; its exaggeration is, of course, one of the characteristics of those unhappy families severed by differences of education between the old and young.

Reardon represents one vital aspect of Gissing's response to the struggle, the Ryecroftian regression towards the safe nooks of scholarly quibbles and the self-indulgent serenity of Athenian sunsets. But Marian's response is true to the best in Gissing, the deep and passionate cry: 'what use are books and learning? I want love'. In Reardon, and even more scathingly in Alfred Yule, Gissing depicts phases of himself: in Alfred, the portrait of the man who knows he is unloved and unlovable, and in Reardon, the man who *fears* he is so. But Marian represents another aspect of desire, the aspect that is not yet inured to loneliness, but still expects, hopes, wants love.

If the novel is as concerned with the tyranny of desire as the pollution of literary culture, it is even more pervasively concerned with the tyranny of money. There is a deep anomaly, however, in the role that money plays in the narrative, an anomaly that links up with the cracks in the version of cultural crisis. According to the encompassing moral vision, it is necessary to endorse a traditional judgement on the degrading effects of the pursuit of money, to which Jasper and his fellow 'new men' are committed. As Robert Selig has pointed out, it is the direct equation between the word and the coin that is this 'new generation's' ultimate blasphemy. But at the same time, there is a quite different thesis offered about the role of money, that applies more narrowly to the *individual's* moral and emotional well-being. For if the pursuit of money degrades, it is even more certain that the lack of money will degrade

First page of a letter from Gissing to Gabrielle Fleury, who had asked permission to translate New Grub Street *into French.*

even further. If it were only Jasper who claimed the interdependence of economic security and fine feelings, we would be rightly suspicious; but the narrative insists at almost every turn that everyday human decency, generosity, tolerance, and love, are only possible, or at least much more likely to be sustained, on the basis of a minimal material security. For Amy's mother, for example, 'life was a battle. She must either crush or be crushed. With sufficient means, she would have defrauded no one, and would have behaved generously to many . . .' The effect that their legacies have on Amy and Marian is, at least initially, to soften and expand the former's attitude to Reardon, and to increase the latter's self-confidence immeasurably. The narrative continually supports Jasper's contention that as a prerequisite for tolerable human relationships as well as individual fulfilment, money is indispensable.

The difficulty is that the generalisation is seen only from the perspective of 'lack', creating, as in the case of the other sharp dichotomies, a dangerously radical opposition between absolute states of poverty and sufficiency. All the characters would agree with Amy that poverty is 'a misery that colours every thought', and with Reardon, that 'this world might be a sufficing paradise to him if only he could clutch a poor little share of current coin'. But in Jasper's case (and to a lesser extent, Amy's), we *do* see a character who succeeds in clutching his little share of current coin, and contrary to the provocative theory put forward that money can ennoble, we see the disappointingly traditional sight of its degradation. This is the reason for the increasing dissatisfaction with which we view Jasper's portrayal, and it points to the underlying discrepancy, suggested in the comments on Mr Baker, between the governing thesis of general cultural and moral decay, and the possibility, indeed positive likelihood, of individual benefit and progress.

In the final scene, we see Jasper and Amy firmly ensconced within the camp of the 'victors'. We recognise that certain virtues are possible within this charmed circle that were impossible outside, but the remarks they make about the now permanently exiled Marian ('only a clever schoolgirl' with 'ink-stains on her fingers') indicate the extent to which these virtues are rigorously referred to membership of the group. The remarks about Marian strike us as peculiarly vicious; but Jasper and Amy must confirm their absolute distance from her. It is not possible, however, for us fully to share in the progress of an individual across the sharp frontier between success and failure. This final scene, so neat, so glib, is not the one demanded by the novel's internal logic. Gissing's deep, humane identification with those who are left outside, requires that the final scene should belong to Marian, and her lonely, loveless vigil in the provincial library.

This, then, is the paradox about money, that the *pursuit* of it must degrade, but the *possession* of it is necessary for the sustenance of all moral and personal good. Although in this novel the paradox is uncontrolled and disruptive, it becomes focused as the central theme of Gissing's next novel, *Born in Exile.* And there it is significant that Gissing concentrates narrowly on the single individual figure trying to cross the boundary between want and security, at the expense of any more general attempt at a coherent social or cultural vision.

If we return to the achievement of *New Grub Street* as a whole, we can reach the following conclusions. The novel represents a partial vision of cultural crisis, conditioned by a personal structuring vision of incompatible dualities. It leaves out of account both the complexity of historical change in the actual conditions of writing, publishing, distributing and reading, and the personal complexity in a Jasper Milvain that might allow him to produce a novel as good as, for example, *The Old Wives' Tale.* Yet despite the qualifications, the core of Gissing's vision seems indisputable, both in fact and in feeling. A radical change *did* take place in the status of 'quality' art and the minority artist, that can fairly be characterised as an unprecedented exclusion from the central positions of cultural power. In our own century, we have seen, on one hand, the further exploration of this exile, and on the other, an increased flexibility and possible interaction between the opposing terms 'minority' and 'mass'. All these developments may seem to place Gissing's sceptical, dogmatic vision of cultural disaster in a distant perspective. But the *questions* he asks, about quality and value, remain close. (pp. 146-56)

Adrian Poole, in his Gissing in Context, *Rowman and Littlefield, 1975, 231 p.*

Jerome H. Buckley   (essay date 1975)

[*Buckley is a Canadian-born American educator and critic who has written and edited works on Victorian literature and poetry. He is also advisor to* Victorian Studies, Victorian Poetry, Clio, *and* Review. *In the following excerpt, Buckley illustrates the autobiographical elements of* New Grub Street.]

One of the many luckless authors who drift into George Gissing's *New Grub Street* is a wispy alcoholic named Sykes, who is writing his autobiography, "Through the Wilds of Literary London," for a provincial newspaper. Few readers, Sykes complains, will credit the grim veracity of his narrative: "Most people will take it for fiction. I wish I had the inventive power to write fiction anything like it." Gissing himself could have said the same for much of *New Grub Street,* where he depends far less on inventiveness than on his personal acquaintance with the London literary jungle.

On its appearance in 1891 the novel was both attacked and defended as a grimly "realistic" exploration of the lower depths of an urban society. Yet the "realism" is strictly limited by the author's well-defined interest in his narrow theme: the struggle for survival of the late Victorian man of letters. Gissing does indeed present sharp impressions of mean streets and dreary lodgings, but only as they contain the lives of his defeated protagonists. He shows no interest in the tribulations of the unaesthetic London poor, their resilience, courage, and laughter; he has no concern with social reform or political protest. He is repelled by indigence and its paralyzing hold on the illiterate unaspiring masses, and firmly convinced, like his Henry Ryecroft, that the average man born to penury cannot suffer so intensely as the impoverished artist, for the "intellectual needs" of most Englishmen are merely "those of a stable-boy or a scullery wench." His sympathy in *New Grub Street* lies with the sensitive, gentle Harold Biffen, a novelist celebrating the "ignobly decent," rather than with the drunken wretch whom Biffen abandons in order to rescue a manuscript from a burning hovel. H. G. Wells found Gissing himself lacking in "social nerve" and bumbling in all practical affairs, with "some sort of blindness towards his fellow-men, so that he never entirely grasped the spirit of everyday life." Gissing's "realism," if it is to be called such at all, does not reach far beyond his private and acutely self-conscious experience.

Within the limits of its vision, however, *New Grub Street* achieves a considerable range. Though not precisely a roman à clef, it offers us a veritable Dunciad of the early 1880s, and we may be sure that the aggressive Jasper Milvain, the gossipy Mr. Quarmby, the redoubtable, querulous Clement Fadge, and a score of others had their living counterparts in the new journalism. Whelpdale's *Chit-Chat* with its blatant appeal to the vulgarity of "the quarter-educated" clearly parodies *Tit-Bits,* the penny paper on which George (later Sir George) Newnes built his fortune. *The Study* and *The Wayside* evidently corresponded to familiar monthlies of the time, and *The West End* and *All Sorts,* representing popular weeklies, actually furnished the titles for new periodicals in the later nineties. Milvain talks knowingly of the demands of the new "market," and Whelpdale projects a quite modern literary agency with a variety of syndicated services. Alfred Yule, on the other hand, insists doggedly on the standards of an old-fashioned pedantic scholarship, and Marian Yule, his daughter and amanuensis, learns to regard herself as a literary machine and to deplore "the hateful profession that so poisons men's minds." From beginning to end we hear much of the jealousies of authors and the scheming rivalries of publishers, of sharp editorial practices, commissioned articles, hostile reviews, rejected manuscripts, ephemeral successes, advertising puffs, libels, and always the drudgery of endless plodding hackwork. And over nearly all of the characters, at some stage of their careers, if not continuously, broods the huge dome of the British Museum, beneath which hosts of readers sit "at radiating lines of desks" like "hapless flies caught in a huge web, its nucleus the great circle of the Catalogue."

Though the detail with which this literary world is evoked is altogether vivid and convincing, the author's attitude toward it is a good deal less than completely objective. Gissing makes no pretense at maintaining the severe disinterest of the thorough-going "realist." Many of his opinions and reactions slip naturally enough into the copious shoptalk of his characters, their circumstantial accounts of their projects, aesthetic principles, and journalistic misadventures. But his presence is felt also behind the narrative, and his personal judgment, either as direct commentary or as grim irony, not infrequently obtrudes upon the action. He is not above haranguing the reader with irritable sarcasm:

> The chances are that you have neither understanding nor sympathy for men such as Edwin Reardon and Harold Biffen. They merely provoke you. They seem to you inert, flabby, weakly envious, foolishly obstinate, impiously mutinous, and many other things. You are made angrily contemptuous by their failure to get on; why don't they bestir themselves, push and bustle, welcome kicks so long as halfpence follow, make a place in the world's eye—in short, take a leaf from the book of Mr. Jasper Milvain? . . .

> It was very weak of Harold Biffen to come so near perishing of hunger as he did in the days when he was completing his novel . . . He did not starve for the pleasure of the thing, I assure you.

Gissing seems to be indicting the reader as much as Amy Reardon when he describes her belated expression of sympathy for Biffen as "so often the regretful remark of one's friends, when one has been permitted to perish." We may guess the depth of his pessimism—outside the fiction—from his complaint, as cheerless as a remark by Hardy's little Father Time, that any pleasure he might have found in observing the antics of a baby was destroyed by "the thought of the anxiety it [was] costing in the present, and of the miseries that inevitably [lay] before it." And we may see a like morbidity in the novel itself in the author's identification of a literary hack and his threadbare wife ("They had had three children; all were happily buried") or even in the naming of an indigent surgeon ("I was christened Victor—possibly because I was doomed to defeat in life"). We are left in little doubt about Gissing's outlook, his loyalties, or the direction of his antipathies.

Written with such prepossessions, *New Grub Street* hovers between embittered satire and a waveringly defensive sentiment. At first glance the satiric element may seem the more conspicuous. The novel was possibly conceived as Jasper Milvain's story, for it begins and ends with Jasper—his is the first voice we hear and his the last word. As the title of the opening chapter suggests, Jasper is "a man of his day": he is emphatically on the side of the "new," and his alignment determines his success, just as Reardon's commitment to the past underlies his abject failure. Jasper's presence, his characteristic gesture, provides a frame: near the beginning he reclines on a sofa, his hands behind his head, as his sister plays the piano; at the end he lies back "in dreamy ease," while his wife, Amy, widow of the defeated Reardon, plays and sings for him. He is preeminently the practical man, selfish, ambitious, adroit, shrewd in his estimate of competition, charming when amiability seems politic, caddish when betrayal appears profitable. He has no delusions of genius or even of great talent as a writer; his objectives are simple and cynical: "Never in my life," he tells Reardon at the outset, "shall I do anything of solid literary value; I shall always despise the people I write for. But my path will be that of success. I have always said it, and now I'm sure of it." Later he warns Marian Yule with the same bluntness, "I shall do many a base thing in life, just to get money and reputation . . . I can't afford to live as I should like to." Marian of course is unwilling to credit his admission, until her inheritance proves too meager to be useful to him and she finds herself accordingly sacrificed to his advancement. Though he is convinced that he can be pleasant if only he has money, his corruption actually increases with his affluence. The very day that the jilted Marian and her father, now blind and broken, leave London, Jasper publishes his calculated eulogy of Yule's old enemy Fadge, to whose post as editor of *The Current* he is shortly to succeed. In the end, when his time-serving strategies have been richly rewarded, he assures Amy, who is likewise practical, that he cannot regret his decision to abandon Marian: "My dearest, you are a perfect woman, and poor Marian was only a clever school-girl. Do you know, I never could help imagining that she had ink-stains on her fingers . . . It was touching to me at the time, for I knew how fearfully hard she worked." We could scarcely ask a more caustic portrait of the cad as man of letters.

As the novel proceeds, however, the satiric intention yields to a stronger autobiographical impulse. Jasper, relegated before long to the background, where he pursues his vision of success, comes forward only at intervals as a foil to less opportunistic and more vulnerable characters. Some of these Gissing attempts to view with a measure of detachment and obliquity, for he diffuses and to some extent disguises his subjective concern. To Whelpdale, who is an essentially comic figure, he assigns his adventures in America, in retrospect more ludicrous than painful: his contributions to the Chicago *Tribune,* his brief career as photographer's assistant, and his resort to a diet of peanuts when penniless in Troy, New York. Alfred Yule, a sharply drawn study of a cantankerous pedant, reflects his respect for scholarship and his trying experience of marriage to a woman beneath him socially and intellectually—though good, long-suffering Mrs. Yule is a steadier more devoted wife than the unfortunate Mrs. Gissing. With Harold Biffen he has a far less constrained sympathy. Often subsisting simply on bread and dripping, Biffen never escapes the dire poverty that Gissing himself knew at least for short periods. As Gissing once did, Biffen plods miles of London streets in the early morning to earn a pittance by tutoring so that he may spend the rest of the day working at his unprofitable novel. If the finished *Mr. Bailey, Grocer* is apparently not much like Gissing's fictions, it suffers similar censure from reviewers who see no excuse for his "grovelling realism" or his failure "to understand that a work of art must before everything else afford amusement." Biffen speaks for Gissing when he describes the dangers of refusing to compromise one's conviction in a world where sensibility can survive only by masking itself in "genial coarseness." And by his last desperate gesture, his death by his own hand, Biffen brings to quiet fulfillment Gissing's recurrent suicidal moods.

When Edwin Reardon, who is the real protagonist of *New Grub Street,* complains that he should have married "some simple, kind-hearted work-girl" instead of the genteel, ambitious, middle-class Amy, Biffen rebukes his fantasy:

> "What a shameless idealist you are! . . . Let me sketch the true issue of such a marriage. To begin with, the girl would have married you in firm persuasion that you were a 'gentleman' in temporary difficulties, and that before long you would have plenty of money to dispose of. Disappointed in this hope, she would have grown sharp-tempered, querulous, selfish. All your en-

> deavours to make her understand you would only have resulted in widening the impassable gulf. She would have misconstrued your every sentence, found food for suspicion in every harmless joke, tormented you with the vulgarest forms of jealousy."

Gissing here writes from sad experience, for Biffen, imagining what Reardon has escaped, pictures just such a union as Gissing endured—and indeed, at the time of writing, was about to repeat. But apart from his marriage to Amy, Reardon's career and character run remarkably close in most details to Gissing's. When we first meet him, Reardon has already reached thirty, the age at which Gissing began the novel. Like Gissing, he has had a sound classical education in a provincial town, has come to London to write, taken miserable lodgings in a back street off Tottenham Court Road, worked for a while as secretary in a hospital, and written several novels, one of which has been successful enough, in terms of sales, to permit him a memorable trip to the Mediterranean. Like Gissing, he eagerly buys old books when he has a spare shilling and reluctantly sells them off when hard pressed for funds. And like Gissing, he is oversensitive to reviews, impatient with people, and badly affected by inclement weather. His conduct surely commands a measure of Gissing's respect. Yet his portrait is no mere exercise in self-justification; it rests upon a deep and far from complacent self-knowledge.

Biffen describes Reardon the novelist as "a psychological realist in the sphere of culture" rather than a devotee of graphic fact and vulgar circumstance; and Gissing himself, in presenting Reardon's character, is very much the psychologist, intensely interested in the analysis yet often clinically detached from it. Despite his manifest virtues, his insight, intelligence, and candor, Reardon is an insecure, unhappy man, subject to sudden revulsions of feeling, a creature of self-pity and irritable pride as well as meekness and compassion. His wrangling with Amy reveals him at his worst, both defiant and abject, now scorning the wife's practicality, now cringing before her common sense. He craves affection and is willing to grovel for it, but when his tears accomplish nothing, then "the feeling of unmanliness in his own position torture[s] him into a mood of perversity," and he becomes cruel in his angry retorts. Ultimately he nourishes his despair; in defeat he regards his seedy clothes "with pleasurable contempt" as "tokens of his degradation," and in the evenings once or twice a week, the masochist of his emotions, he haunts the street where Amy is comfortably housed, so that he may go home hungry to his garret "with a fortified sense of the injustice to which he [is] submitted." His deterioration, paranoid or schizophrenic, is chronicled with an almost Balzacian power and dispassion: "An extraordinary arrogance now and then possessed him; he stood amid his poor surroundings with the sensations of an outraged exile, and laughed aloud in furious contempt of all who censured or pitied him." When we consider the extent of Gissing's identification with this lonely man, we cannot but be shaken by the terror of the self-appraisal.

Reardon's alienation, carrying him at times close to derangement, arises simply from his maladjustment to the

new world of literature and his inability to admit the reality of any alternative existence. Gissing himself, though often disappointed at the reception of his books, was never so great a failure, and his extrapolated fears rather than his direct experience inspired his account of Reardon's collapse. Nonetheless, he shared his hero's commitment to the literary life and especially his literary enthusiasms. Like Reardon, he delighted in the Greek classics and responded warmly to the Greek setting as a reminder of the vanished ancient glory. From Athens in 1889 he wrote lyrical letters of the ruins glowing in the evening light:

> The sunsets are of unspeakable splendour. When you stand with your back to the west and look towards the Acropolis, it glows a rich amber; temples, bulwarks and rock are all of precisely the same hue, as if the whole were but one construction . . . Impossible for you to imagine what I mean. Impossible for any painter to render such scenes . . .
>
> One of the sunsets was rendered extraordinary by the fact that, at the same time, there was a perfect rainbow circling over the whole of Athens, from the foot of one mountain to that of another; the colours of the hills were unimaginable.

A year later, writing *New Grub Street,* he granted Reardon the same aesthetic satisfaction, in almost identical terms. Enraptured by the memory, Reardon tells Biffen of "that marvellous sunset at Athens":

> "I turned eastward, and there to my astonishment was a magnificent rainbow, a perfect semi-circle, stretching from the foot of Parnes to that of Hymettus, framing Athens and its hills, which grew brighter and brighter—the brightness for which there is no name among colours . . . The Acropolis simply glowed and blazed. As the sun descended all these colours grew richer and warmer; for a moment the landscape was nearly crimson."

Biffen thinks it self-torture to remember such pleasures, but Reardon insists that he is sustained by his lost dream: "Poverty can't rob me of those memories. I have lived in an ideal world that was not deceitful, a world which seems to me, when I recall it, beyond the human sphere, bathed in diviner light." Antiquity thus tempts him to escape the human sphere altogether and so to transcend the concerns of a psychological realism and all the demands of his own fiction, which by comparison with the great classics seems "so wretchedly, shallowly modern." And the past awoke a similar vain nostalgia in Gissing himself; *By the Ionian Sea,* the most serene of his books, concludes with the sigh of the classicist manqué: "I wished it were mine to wander endlessly amid the silence of the ancient world, to-day and all its sounds forgotten."

In both his commonplace book and the autobiographical *Henry Ryecroft,* Gissing defines art as "a satisfying and abiding expression of the zest of life." Yet, as Frank Swinnerton observed, there is very little true zest in Gissing's own art and little or no exuberance or striking vitality in his characters. Reardon, convincing in his quiet despair, becomes intensely animated only on the subject of Greece, but it is hard to imagine Reardon's novels, sensitive though they may be, as really zestful on any subject. Like Gissing, Reardon is apparently a careful craftsman with limited range. Gissing is indeed describing much of his own earlier work when he tells us that Reardon's stories, lacking "local colour" and exciting action, are "almost purely psychological" in interest, devoted as they are to the intellectual dilemmas of people of intellect. And even as he is chronicling Reardon's difficulties in padding out the second volume of a three-decker, he himself is facing the problem of inventing appropriate incidents to complete the three-volume structure in which Reardon has his being.

Though it self-consciously contains its own criticism, *New Grub Street* attempts a larger, more general literary statement. Like many later works of fiction and poetry, it concerns itself with the artist, the medium, and the aesthetic act; it is essentially a novel about novelists and the writing of novels. Throughout it is informed by a writer's understanding of the cruel demands of composition, the challenge of the blank page to be filled, the frequent recalcitrance of words, the refusal of the torpid paragraph to come to life and move with grace and logic. When spared the grosser distresses of hunger and poverty, Reardon still knows the anxieties and frustrations of his craft: "Sometimes the three hours' labour of a morning resulted in half a dozen lines, corrected into illegibility. His brain would not work; he could not recall the simplest synonyms; intolerable faults of composition drove him mad. He would write a sentence beginning thus: 'She took a book with a look of——'; or thus: 'A revision of this decision would have made him an object of derision.' Or, if the period were otherwise inoffensive, it ran in a rhythmic gallop which was a torment to the ear." Gissing himself experienced similar woes, but also, we gather from his notebook, moments of a satisfaction usually denied to Reardon: "The pains of lit. composition. How easy any other task in comparison. Forcing of mind into a certain current, the temptation of indolence with a book. Yet the reward, when effort once made." His emphasis, however, falls less on the art of the novel than on the temperament of the novelist as a man apart, the sensibility that seeks creative expression and so sentences itself forever to the discipline of an isolating and harassing creativity.

Harold Biffen, we are told, "belonged to no class." Reardon, too, is an unclassed literary hero, aloof from the grades of society, fallen from a bourgeois economic status and dissociated in any case from philistine tastes and prejudices, living among the poor yet not of them, respecting the rare independent imaginative thinker, impatient with all vulgarity of thought or gesture. Both Biffen and Reardon could declare with Henry Ryecroft (and so with Gissing): "The truth is that I have never learnt to regard myself as a 'member of society.' For me, there have always been two entities—myself and the world—and the normal relation between these two has been hostile." Nonetheless, both draw the materials and settings of their art from the hostile society rather than from an imagination able to transcend or transmute the commonplace. Especially in studying Reardon, Gissing appraises his own attitude and practice with some dispassion and not wholly favorable judgment. *New Grub Street* at its best is a stocktaking rather than a naive apologia. (pp. 223-33)

> *Jerome H. Buckley, "A World of Literature: Gissing's 'New Grub Street'," in The Worlds of Victorian Fiction, edited by Jerome H. Buckley, Cambridge, Mass.: Harvard University Press, 1975, pp. 223-34.*

Gissing relates an anedote concerning *New Grub Street:*

Day in town—Brit[ish] Mus[eum] and London Library. In evening to Blackheath to dine with Whale. Guests: Sidney Lee (ed. "National Dict[ionary] of Biog[raph]y"), Clodd, Shorter, a man named West, and Wheatley, the philologist. Lee told me of an oldish literary hack, who one day came to him in great discouragement, and said he should abandon literature. It turned out that he had been reading ***New Grub Street.***

George Gissing, in his London and the Life of Literature in Late Victorian England: The Diary of George Gissing, *Harvester Press, 1978.*

John Peck   (essay date 1978)

[*Peck is an American poet, educator, and critic. In the following excerpt, from an essay originally published in the July 1978 issue of* The Gissing Newsletter, *Peck, utilizing a formalist approach, assesses the strengths and weaknesses of* New Grub Street.]

Gissing is a remarkably popular novelist with academics who want to write about something other than novels. Turn to any book on social history or cultural history in the Victorian period and Gissing is more than likely to be omitted. Of course this has more than a little to do with the nature of his novels; a point P. J. Keating makes clear in his useful book [*George Gissing: New Grub Street*, 1968]:

> although some critics, most notably Q. D. Leavis and Irving Howe, have had no hesitation in proclaiming it a work of art, its continuing interest for the twentieth-century reader lies in Gissing's astute and probing analysis of the "business" of literature. First and foremost it is a sociological document; a sociological document of genius written in the form of a novel.

This might be overstating the case, but it does describe accurately the nature of much of the critical interest in Gissing. However, recent developments in novel criticism, both in England and elsewhere, have shown a swing away from an approach through content and context, and an increasing emphasis on form. The question this prompts is whether Gissing will receive attention from those who wish to concentrate on the structural and linguistic qualities of fiction, and who show nothing but impatience with the sociology of the novel. Quite simply, if formalism becomes central in the university teaching of fiction, will Gissing be pushed even further towards the fringes, remaining a subject of academic interest only to an ever dwindling minority?

Initially the prospects seem gloomy. In a formalist approach Gissing is of more immediate interest for his weaknesses rather than for his strengths. The shortcomings are easy to list. First of all he is a realist, which in the eyes of some proponents of structuralism is, of course, equivalent to saying that he is not worth bothering with at all. But the real problem with Gissing's realism is that it is often combined with a hectic plot structure. Even in ***Born in Exile,*** where the mechanics of the plot are less obvious than in many of his novels, there are things which arouse suspicion. In particular, Peak's imposture stands out as a piece of ingenuity, a plot device to make the novel happen, which we would not normally expect in a work in this mode. What one admires in a realistic novelist are the insights into character and situation on a vertical scale, whereas the horizontal progression of the story must be something we are all but unaware of, or subtle enough to match the local density. In Gissing the horizontal progression is frequently obvious and awkward. In reading ***New Grub Street*** for example, one's awareness of local insights and felicities is frequently marred by an awareness of the relentless progress of the plot. One's readiness to attest to the credibility of the material is undermined by an awareness of overwhelming artifice. Not that artifice is necessarily a bad thing. But it works, as in a Dickens novel or a Hardy novel, where it is deliberate, whereas Gissing all too often seems to be plundering the storehouse of recurrent situations simply in order to keep the thing going. (pp. 144-45)

But there are problems with this novel besides the artificiality of its plot. One is the mechanical efficiency of Gissing's prose, evident as early as the first sentence: "As the Milvains sat down to breakfast the clock of Wattleborough parish church struck eight; it was two miles away . . . " One can see what the sentence is achieving—the notion of a settled, ordered, community is immediately established through the reference to the church, and the choice of even, rather than odd, numbers. A sort of pastoral calm is conveyed in the name Wattleborough, and we already know a lot about the Milvains, because of the civilised regularity implicit in their taking breakfast at a set hour. But the objection to the sentence is that this complex impression is achieved by a cataloguing of facts which, continued over a long period, can become wearying. There is a lack of metaphoric richness to the prose, and when symbolism is used it seems obtrusive and clumsy. The first page, for example, contains the symbol of a hanged man, but it does not seem to jell with Gissing's preferred method of detailing information. The subsequent picture of Milvain waiting for the train to pass, with the all too apparent parallel of energy between the two, also seems forced, as if Gissing is only really at ease with the most prosaic style. And this prosaic style can seem dull and uninventive.

His language is not the final problem. The opening setting, and the first three chapters, are a piece of obvious pastoralism, which again seems to indicate a certain clumsiness in Gissing's handling of the work. It is not real countryside, but countryside derivative from literature, serving the function of idyllic retreat which countryside so often serves in art. And the dependence upon literary sources is even more obvious when we come on to the minor characters. Whelpdale, for example, is Dickens' perennial hopeless suitor lifted wholesale into another man's work. It is all promising material for the formalist, but material which can be used to denigrate Gissing. Not only do his plots lean upon earlier fictions, but his characters are also derivative.

Cataloguing a novel's shortcomings is a dreary, and not very admirable, critical activity, and it is now probably time to call a halt, but enough has been said to suggest that there are very real problems involved in assessing *New Grub Street* as a work of art. To summarise the problems, they seem to centre on a mechanically relentless plot, a flat prose style, a symbolic poverty, and derivative characterisation. The formalist might concede that the portrait of Reardon is remarkable, but this is only one element in a novel which, as a whole, can seem very shaky. This is the point at which it is tempting to suggest that the novel might have these faults, but that in emphasising them one is likely to overlook interesting things in the content of the work. The extension of this is to point to the limitation of formalist criticism which seems to blind itself to the intrinsic interest of novels for a sterile pursuit of abstractions; but the purpose of this article is to consider the novel from a formal angle, and it seems only appropriate to try and defend it in similar terms.

To make a start, there is one aspect of *New Grub Street* which offers a tempting promise to formalist critics, attracted as they are by novels in the Tristram Shandy tradition, that is, novels about novel-writing, and this is the possibility that the novel itself, in its form, is the perfect illustration of the problems about novel-writing raised in the content of the novel. That is to say, we understand Reardon through the experience of reading a work in which all the strains of writing a three-volume novel are in evidence. It is certainly tempting to emphasise the reflexive qualities of *New Grub Street,* and there seems no limit to the ingenious levels of self-reference a determined critic could discover in the work. But such a reading would seem ingenious rather than perceptive, for one very simple reason, *New Grub Street* is not a bad novel about writing bad novels because it is not a bad novel. However, the view that the formal strains in evidence in the work do add something to our appreciation of the content of the novel should not be dismissed completely. The only objection is to taking the argument too far, to transforming Gissing into a very different novelist from the one he obviously is. In order to defend the novel formally some more straightforward explanation of its formal strength needs to be sought.

In fact, the formal strength of the novel seems to be the frequency with which Gissing heads in a direction which is the mirror opposite of his formal weaknesses. It is most evident when one considers the relentless pace of the plot. Gissing, in his plot, seems reconciled to the simplest form of linear coherence, but at significant stages in the novel this tendency is brilliantly subverted. A novel which is full of action contains some of the best presented moments of inactivity in the whole of fiction. This can be seen in our first view of Reardon. After three brisk chapters of exposi-

tion, in which Reardon has been referred to on several occasions, we are suddenly confronted with the man himself:

> One evening he sat at his desk with a slip of manuscript paper before him. It was the hour of sunset. His outlook was upon the backs of certain large houses skirting Regent's Park, and lights had begun to show here and there in the windows: in one room a man was discoverable dressing for dinner, he had not thought it worth while to lower the blind; in another some people were playing billiards. The higher windows reflected a rich glow from the western sky.
>
> For two or three hours Reardon had been seated in much the same attitude. Occasionally he dipped his pen into the ink, and seemed about to write: but each time the effort was abortive. At the head of the paper was inscribed "Chapter III", but that was all. And now the sky was dusking over; darkness would soon fall.

The obvious, and perhaps rather strained, contrast here is between light and dark: the contrast not really contributing much to the novel because of the lack of reticence so frequently in evidence in Gissing's more poetic writing. But it is a remarkable scene nonetheless, and is so because of its lack of movement, lack of progress, which contrasts so dramatically with the rapid pace maintained for the first three chapters. Up until this point words have rattled forth confidently, but here we are confronted with the novelist with nothing to say. The formal originality is that Gissing has dared to present the sterility of so much of the process of writing by bringing the novel to a complete halt, so that the only encounter is between a man and a blank piece of paper.

Frequently our insights into Reardon are achieved by this sort of formal device, but there is an added richness here due to the contrast with the world of activity. In the man dressing for dinner and the people playing billiards we have a beautifully simple illustration of the world moving along in front of the artist, but the artist unable to enter this world of movement, either in his life or in his work. A scene like this shows up the inadequacy of Irving Howe's comment [in his *A World More Attractive,* 1963] that *New Grub Street* remains in structure a Victorian novel, but the subject and informing vision are post-Victorian . . . " Howe's comment is obviously suspect, because he seems to envisage the possibility of a quite amazing divorce of form and content, in which an old structure can contain a whole new set of perceptions. The obvious riposte is that if the informing vision is post-Victorian then the structure must be as well; and it is such things as these scenes of total inactivity which contribute to the formal and thematic originality of the novel.

Across the novel there is a readiness to experiment with structure in order to present the picture of Reardon, and these experiments always acquire increased force by contrasting so dramatically with the standard story-telling place of the novel. There is, for example, the formlessness of Reardon's days, the description of which necessitates Gissing providing a fairly shapeless passage of prose, in contrast to the shaped structure of the work as a whole. His rows with his wife are similar in structure. They are circular rows, in which, if it were left to Reardon, nothing would be resolved. The point is that we come to know Reardon by contrasting this formlessness not only with the mechanical rigidity of Milvain's day but with the efficient inventiveness of the plot as a whole. Of course, the excessive linear coherence, the over-reliance on neat formulations of plot, can never be fully defended, but the other side of the coin needs to be considered as well. Excessive ingenuity of structure is frequently matched by a brilliantly innovative lack of obvious structure for passages featuring Reardon.

The consequence of these experiments with structure is a picture of Reardon of undeniable brilliance. But it is not only the structural originality that makes the portrait so impressive. There is also Gissing's irony, which affects the presentation at every turn. We are never allowed to lose sight of Reardon's egotism, his selfishness, his readiness to blame others for his failure. It is there in his attitude to his wife and child, and also in his relations with Biffen. An example is the scene of his first encounter with Biffen after the fire which has destroyed the man's home, and nearly destroyed his manuscript. Biffen goes to Reardon's rooms at eleven o'clock at night and finds Reardon sitting by the fire. Biffen speaks first:

> "Another cold?"
>
> "It looks like it. I wish you would take the trouble to go and buy me some vermin-killer. That would suit my case."

In spite of Biffen's near tragedy the conversation thus begins with a discussion of Reardon's problems, who seems too self-absorbed to wonder why his friend might have appeared so late in the evening. In addition, Reardon's conversation is marked by his usual maundering self-dramatisation. And this insistent self-reference is seen whenever he appears in the novel. Yet Gissing never labours the point. He never editorialises in his presentation of Reardon, but trusts to the action to reveal the man. Again we see the credit and debit quality of Gissing's form. His touch with his main character is as certain as it is uncertain with his presentation of minor characters, who are never presented with the same reticence. The conclusion on character presentation is the same as on the mixture of realism and obvious plotting in the novel. Although the novel is over frenetic in its plot there are moments, in the treatment of Reardon, where Gissing reveals a whole new sort of formal sophistication. Similarly with character, here is much in the novel which is derivative, but in the presentation of Reardon Gissing not only shows unusual restraint and artistry but manages to create a character who is radically new.

But where this ability to produce something running counter to his apparent imitations is possibly most in evidence is in the alleged prosaic flatness of his style, and the related lack of any effective symbolic dimension to the work. It is the flat style which creates the impression that it is "First and foremost a sociological document . . ." The implication is that a more flexible style could have led to a more complex novel. Of course, the portrait of Reardon does depend upon a more complicated style, a style which incorporates irony, and it would be absurd to de-

scribe the interest here as merely sociological. But it is possible to feel that the context in which he is presented is principally of documentary interest, because of the fact that the style in which it is presented is the fairly mundane descriptive style of the social historian. But it is possible to argue that there is a mode of aesthetic ordering in the novel which runs counter to the apparent descriptive method. That it has not been widely appreciated is, I think, due to the nature of the traditional content-based criticism the novel has received, which, finding what it wants to find, ignores other qualities in the text. Here is an area where a formalist approach can actually make Gissing seem a better novelist than even an admirer such as Keating would acknowledge.

The alternative mode of ordering in the book is symbolic, but not the rather forced symbolic moments, rather a more thoroughly integrated symbolic structure. It can be seen, for example, in the use of rooms in the novel. Milvain is presented as passing through a series of rooms. In fact, we hardly ever seem to see him in the same set of rooms twice, and we certainly never see him in his own lodgings. They are referred to, but never described, as this might suggest a sense of confinement inappropriate to his personality. Biffen we also see in a series of rooms, but he is oblivious of his surroundings. Whenever he arrives he immediately makes contact with the person without pausing to reflect on his surroundings. In the Yule household we get a sense of separate rooms, of a territory which is Mrs. Yule's, and of a territory which is Yule's, so that when Marian is summoned to her father's rooms there is a sense on his part of extending a privilege. But the character who is most sensitive to rooms is Reardon. We are alerted to this in his response to the British Museum reading-room, which he has come to love although at first it gave him a headache. If it had this effect it is only natural that more dismal rooms will oppress and upset him even more. And the novel makes full use of Reardon in drab and draughty rooms, stripped of furniture, and oppressively closing in on him:

> A street gas-lamp prevented the room from becoming absolutely dark. When he had closed the envelope he lay down on his bed again, and watched the flickering yellowness upon the ceiling.

This makes an impact in itself, but the effect is reinforced by the chapter almost immediately concluding, to be followed by a chapter beginning, "The rooms which Milvain had taken for himself and his sisters were modest, but more expensive than their old quarters." Gissing does not need to underline the fact that as Reardon becomes progressively more confined Milvain finds space to expand. There is, though, a curious ambivalence in Reardon's attitude to the rooms he occupies. He sees them as representing his isolation and loneliness, but they also attract him because they offer the seclusion he craves. So rooms in the novel present a threat but also represent privacy.

The dome of the reading-room also seems to carry the same dual significance. It provides a sheltering roof for the devoted scholar, but it is also an umbrella to a whole network of human problems. It is perhaps only for Reardon that the reading-room represents nothing but a retreat, and a significant feature of the novel is that we never see him at work there. It is those for whom the dome does not have the power of sanctuary who are presented undergoing their daily toil beneath its shadow. It is under the dome that Marian sees Milvain, and it is under the dome that the infighting and politics of the literary world are conducted. It also acts as a central symbol, though, through the sense the novel gives of the reading-room being the hub of a web of literary activity. The novel conveys a clear impression of a grid imposed on London with literary activity in remote parts.

Indeed, a frightening sense of London emerges in the novel. From Reardon's rooms we might glimpse fine views in a pastoral distance, but London itself is hot and polluted, or else cold and foggy. But it is always a London where people wander aimlessly in the streets, or find themselves trapped in lonely rooms. Throughout the novel we gain a sense of people lost in a gigantic maze. Streets and rooms proliferate to the point where we are overwhelmed, and the sense of place is generally confusing and threatening. Frequently what dominates in the novel is not a sense of character, but a sense of alien and changing environments. And there is no escape from this bewildering jungle as the pastoral calm has been left behind in the first three chapters.

Throughout the novel, then, we are wandering through mean streets into bleak and unwelcoming houses. And this sense of a huge unmanageable city is also conveyed by the inclusion of many characters who are referred to but never seen. The object of this is not inclusiveness, but to increase the sense of an anonymous city. The idea of a traditional community, where everybody knows everybody, and where breakfast is at eight o'clock, and where the church is exactly two miles away, is accordingly destroyed. Consequently, Gissing's flat prose style has to be seen not as the norm, but strategic. It is a way of carefully and confidently delineating experience so that he can play off against it a far more intangible sense of the world his characters occupy. As a whole the novel does not present a documentary account in the appropriate style, but moves from this to a sense of human existence which can only be suggested by symbols such as the dome, and rooms, and streets, and London. The accusation of prosaic flatness thus crumbles, for the novel moves beyond realism towards symbolism. But it is a level of richness in the text which can be overlooked if one is too insistent on seeing the novel as a documentary account of literary London.

In fact, by emphasising this formal dimension the conventional view of the novel takes some knocks. It is not going too far to say that, apart from Reardon, the other main characters are not Milvain, Biffen, and the rest, but houses and streets. It begins to seem something other than an "astute and probing analysis of the 'business' of literature . . . " What it begins to seem is a work primarily concerned with the question of the relationship between man and his whole environment, a work about man and the modern city.

Seeing it in these terms, though, inevitably raises the question of the status of all the minor characters. Just what

function are they serving in the novel, beyond being a collection of isolated men in the waste land of London. There is a sense in which nearly all the details of their lives could be sacrificed, and the symbolic force of the novel would remain unimpaired. Indeed, it could be argued that the clumsy derivativeness of their presentation is due to the fact that they are superfluous to the problem Gissing is really exploring. But why then did he not abandon them to produce a more austere, more single-minded, novel? I think it was due to his lack of awareness of just what an original novel he was producing. The novel is moving beyond conventional realism, but Gissing does not seem to be aware of just how powerful his symbolic effects are. So he clings conservatively to conventional characters, even though they are almost irrelevant to the work he was producing. The direction in which the novel is heading is towards the lean integrity of Knut Hamsun's *Hunger,* but Gissing's lack of awareness of his own originality, or possibly his awareness of what novel readers expected, means that some of the force of the novel is dissipated by flaccid character development. But the blundering presentation of minor characters can be overlooked. The novel is a success; but a success, and this is where a formalist approach would come in conflict with a content-based approach, not because of its realistic picture of literary London, but because it turns away from the moral realism of mid-Victorian fiction, to explore a more frightening, more impersonal world, which can only be properly conveyed by a reliance on symbols. (pp. 146-54)

> *John Peck, " 'New Grub Street': An Approach Through Form," in* George Gissing: Critical Essays, *edited by Jean-Pierre Michaux, Vision and Barnes & Noble, 1981, pp. 144-54.*

J. P. Michaux (essay date 1981)

[*In the following excerpt, Michaux examines the symbolic significance of the names Gissing chose for the characters in* New Grub Street.]

By the time Gissing wrote **New Grub Street** it had been a steady practice among writers to use (for their characters) patronymic appellations which carried with them a clear meaning, thus opening the way for the reader's or listener's interpretation. The custom dates back to the Middle Ages with the emergence of the mystery-plays the meaning of which had to be made clear to each and every spectator. It was a widespread practice as far as Elizabethan plays were concerned—such names as Luxurioso, Spurioso or Vincentio were indicative of what functions the *dramatis personae* would carry out. One can link to this practice the theory of humours and the role played by foils which were good means to illustrate the author's thesis.

Apropos of **New Grub Street** it may be worthwhile to try and see whether Gissing like his master Dickens, still made use of those convenient "labels", so to speak, though it was often less obvious than with his predecessors and even sometimes seemed rather *recherché.*

Reardon: The first part of the name of the flawed novelist is composed of the word "rear", suggesting that he is

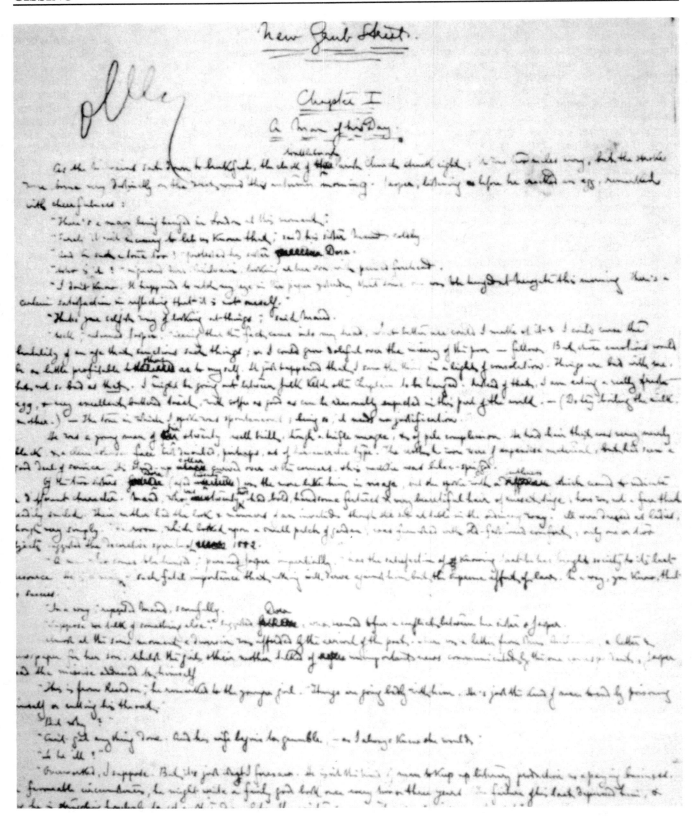

First page of the manuscript for New Grub Street.

somewhat past it or that he is behind the times. He seems to belong to the rearguard of the literary world of *New Grub Street.* Reardon is a foil to Milvain who is a promising careerist belonging to the vanguard, not of an intellectual élite but rather of those who profess that literature is becoming a trade. Thus the military terms are well in keeping with the struggle for survival in the literary jungle of *New Grub Street.* Reardon is also in the rear in the sense that he dreams of the good old days of Dr. Johnson, a time when one could live by one's pen. He fails because he cannot advance or come to the fore; in other words he is unable to adapt to changing ethics. It is no wonder then that Amy will leave him and eventually marry Jasper of the facile pen.

The second part of his name, "don" is a profession which Reardon could well have exercised under better circumstances. Everyone agrees that he is a scholar more fit to write essays about Diogenes Laertius or to talk about Greek metres than for the writing of novels (especially three-deckers), which is a drudge to him. As for his Christian name Edwin, the second syllable stands in ironical contrast with his final failure. Reardon then has been hood-winked by his ideal of classical scholarship throughout the novel. This ideal has made him blind to the harsh reality of commercial success and Jasper Milvain says of him that he "is absurd enough to be conscientious".

Milvain: The first part of his name sounds phonetically the same as mill, a word implying that he is associated with the industrial world which Gissing does not hold in great esteem. Hence the type of work Milvain produces is of a mechanical quality, something made to order or rather according to the well-established law of supply and demand. Milvain himself gives a definition of what his works consist of. Being a success seems to him something which is as automatic as a piece of machinery can be. All he has to do is to follow some recipes: writing according to fashion and public taste ("We people of brains are justified in supplying the mob with the food it likes"), flattering the mass of half-educated readers, or again striking a friendship with influential people. Mr. Bergonzi aptly said [in his essay "The Novelist As Hero," *Twentieth Century,* November 1958] that Milvain today "would be clearly destined for a job in advertising or public relations". This seems to emphasize the fact that Milvain undoubtedly has a turn for business, an enterprising spirit. He examines literature coolly and sees in it all types of marketable commodities. Now a mill can also be a pugilistic encounter, and there is no doubt that here again is underlined the Darwinian theory of adaptability of the survival of the fittest: Milvain loses no opportunity and he sacrifices Marian's love to reach his goal. Though he is not depicted as the total villain, yet we may feel sure that he will make his way even if that means trampling others *en route* ("I shall do many a base thing in life, just to get money and reputation; I tell you this that you mayn't be surprised if anything of that kind comes to yours ears"). This aspect of the character is alluded to by Mrs. Leavis who said [in her essay "Gissing and the English Novel," *Scrutiny,* June 1938]: "When any nineteenth-century novelist names a character Jasper I think we may safely conclude that that character is intended to be the villain."

"Vain", the second syllable of Milvain, seems to imply that his work will be unavailing, that it is doomed to perish very soon. True he is the first one to acknowledge this. Contrary to Reardon, who would like to achieve great fame through laborious hack-work, Milvain wants to achieve a reputation here-and-now, which is in tune with his ability to write quickly and easily on any subject ("It is my business to know something about every subject—or to know where to get the knowledge"). Conversely Reardon needs time to polish his style and do his best. Vain is also Jasper's career as it only tends towards worldly ends. Now Jasper resembles the French *j'aspire* (= I aspire) and there is no doubt about Milvain's aspirations, so the similarity Jasper/*J'aspire* may not be so far-fetched as it first seems, all the more so as Gissing could speak French. Whether conscious, unconscious or just accidental the fact remains and the association of terms is tempting if not wholly credible.

Amy: Amy does not prove to be the ideal *Ami*(e) or companion Reardon wished her to be (not the Mimi or Musette of Murger's *Scènes de la vie de Bohème* anyway). In all circumstances her love does not bear the test of hardship. She first becomes cold towards her husband, who complains about it. Gradually their relationship deteriorates as Reardon's inability to write his *quantum* of pages and to produce anything becomes obvious. A climax is reached when Reardon discloses his intention to resume his job as a clerk. Amy then is definitely not the *Amesoeur* (twin-soul) that her husband dreamt about. The dichotomy Amy/*Ami* is ironical in that she eventually becomes Reardon's enemy and even Biffen's as she is the instrument of their deaths, thus playing the role of a kind of vamp for both of them.

Marian's name is almost transparent. She is a kind of Mary, the Virgin mother, if one may venture the comparison. She has numerous qualities: she is knowledgeable and intelligent. Marian can do a lot of work for her father who trusts her to do many things for him. But as Mary she also suffers: first, her hope of a substantial inheritance is blighted; secondly, her love for Jasper is thwarted and the latter rejects her, preferring to marry Amy Reardon, who benefits from a bigger portion of the Yule inheritance. Thus, after suffering from poverty, an overbearing father and the distaste of hackwork, she ends as a librarian in the country (in the end, unable to escape the world of books altogether). In spite of her good intentions she eventually leads a life poles apart from that of Milvain and Amy, and her doom serves as a good example of the importance of money.

Biffen is the hack-writer who is defeated by fate or receives a smart blow, a biff. It is due not so much to the commercial failure of his realistic novel *Mr. Bailey, Grocer,* as to his realization that he cannot escape the sexual urge. His encounter with Amy is the last straw on the camel's back because he cannot help idealizing her. Amy proves the bane of his life and drives him to commit suicide, quoting Shakespeare's famous phrase from *The Tempest* "We are such stuff as dreams are made on." His suicide is all the more unexpected as he is one who is only happy as long as he can get on with his book. He seems indestructible, indifferent to the slings and arrows of his miserable existence. Content to feed himself on bread and dripping, he is yet always ready to cheer up his friend Reardon.

Whelpdale is also a Grub Street dweller and an inveterate skirt-chaser. He is described as a man who cannot resist a woman's charm. Always madly in love with women, he seems to behave like a young dog, or whelp, unable to refrain from showing his happiness at the sight of his master. Like a whelp he is liable to indulge in many frolics and capers but not all of them are fruitless. He expands his theory of the "quarter-educated" and his idea of a journal called *Chit-chat,* much to Milvain's mirth and disbelief. Yet his venture is successful, and "that ass Whelpdale" finally becomes Milvain's brother-in-law by marrying his sister Dora.

Also he sets up a school to teach people how to write when he himself has failed as an artist, which leads Jasper to comment: "Now that's one of the finest jokes I ever heard. A man who can't get anyone to publish his own books makes a living by telling other people how to write." Yet the adage comes true which says "He laughs well who laughs last", because Whelpdale eventually becomes an important literary figure with his paper. "I believe it is a stroke of genius. *Chat* doesn't attract anyone, but *Chit-chat* would sell like hot-cakes, as they say in America. I know I am right, laugh as you will", says Whelpdale to Milvain.

Yule's Christian name Alfred cannot but remind us of the famous king Alfred the Great. There is nothing great about Alfred Yule and here again we feel the irony in the choice of the name. Alfred Yule has never succeeded in achieving any fame whatsoever and his work consists mainly in writing critical articles anonymously. Besides he has married a lower-class woman whom he has come to dislike because of her ignorance and Cockney-tainted speech. He clings to his last hope to attain literary fame (wreaking revenge on his adversaries at the same time) thanks to his daughter's inheritance, but this last opportunity is denied him and he becomes blind in the end. His surname Yule—an archaic word—suggests pedantry. Alfred Yule is pedantic and only relishes in book-learning and literary rivalry with men like Clement Fadge. Yule is a fount of erudite knowledge but a fount whose water has dried up with the years. A eulogistic footnote on his merits is one of the few joys of his life as P. J. Keating remarked in his [1968] study of **New Grub Street.** Let us notice that the man with whom Yule quarrels bears a rather peaceful Christian name: Clement. As for the word *Fadge* or fudge (fadge being rather obsolete), it recalls a notion of something made up in a dishonest way and this alludes undoubtedly to the literary quarrels and practices of the time.

Mrs. Goby, one of the minor characters, incarnates what Alfred Yule hates: illiteracy of the lower classes. Gissing transcribed their coarse speech phonetically to lay emphasis on their inferiority and ignorance ("I am Mrs. Goby, of the 'Olloway Road, wife of Mr. C. O. Goby, 'aberdasher"). Now in vulgar language a gob is a mouth and also a spittle, so here the character's name bears with it unpleasant connotations linked with the mouth. (Mrs.

Goby cannot express herself properly and Alfred Yule quarrels with her for all that she represents.) The resemblance between Goby and gob is surely not mere coincidence, suggestive as it is.

To my mind the close examination of names and the meanings they carry with them bring evidence that Gissing was perfectly aware of the device which consists in carefully choosing names which evoke certain qualities or defects. We may feel sure that he made use of this device even if he did so more sparingly than Dickens, whom he admired. [P. F. Kropholler], having already perceived this trend to select "meaningful" names, has studied the subject on a large scale in Gissing's works as a whole [in his article titled "On the Names of Gissing's Characters," *The Gissing Newsletter*]. Names have always exerted a fascination on both writers and readers, to such an extent that some of them have come to be used as common denominations. Can we always explain why we have remembered this or that name from a novel or a play? Why do they still resound in our ears? There seems to lie the task of the etymologist who must have recourse to the psycho-analyst—maybe—to account for their deeply-felt power, all the more so as interpretation varies from one reader to another.

Nevertheless we may say that this method contributes to some type of consistency in the drawing of characters as that alluded to by C. J. Francis in his article on heredity and environment: "Not for him [Gissing] are striking changes in character, radical conversions to good or evil such as may be found in romantic novels of the more facile kind. A slow development and alteration of attitudes can be seen in some characters, but it indicates no basic change." We may safely infer that the careful selection or creation of names is directly linked with the delineation of characters, their psychological relationships with other characters, their role, the way in which they react when confronted with specific problems, and to put it briefly with their doom in a novel: be it either success or failure.

Was not Gissing a lover of Greek and Latin authors, is it not justified to think that he kept in mind the notion of *fatum*—the very keystone of Greek tragedy—when writing his novels?

A tendency of Gissing's was morbidity: let us recall the indigent surgeon in **New Grub Street:** "I was christened Victor—possibly because I was doomed to defeat in life." The quotation speaks for itself and we are left little doubt as to Gissing's state of mind. Yet in spite of that, characters are not flat or deprived of any interest, they are not neatly depicted from the start or recognisable at first sight as the incarnations of symbols; for Gissing was perfectly aware of the complexity of human nature. Of Woodstock in **The Unclassed** he says: "Human nature is compact of strangely conflicting elements, and I have met men extremely brutal in one way yet were capable of a good deal of genial feeling in other directions".

Complexity of character does not forcibly entail that they are apt to change radically towards the end of the novel or that a *coup de théâtre* is to be expected every now and then.

So it seems that the notion of fate forces itself upon the reader as he reaches the end of the novels and that men like Reardon have their own essence and cannot witness a complete change. The naming of characters seems to indicate and to further strengthen this impression, and in some way to materialize the abstract notions, the ideas which come to mind in the evocation of Gissing's characters. (pp. 204-210)

J. P. Michaux, "Names in 'New Grub Street'," in George Gissing: Critical Essays, *edited by Jean Pierre Michaux, London: Vision and Barnes & Noble 1981, pp. 204-11.*

Eugene M. Baer   (essay date 1985)

[*In the following essay, Baer inquires if the intrusions of Gissing's personal beliefs manifested in his characters' actions and thoughts are harmful or innocuous to the artistry of* New Grub Street.]

George Gissing's **New Grub Street** poses for the reader the problem of dealing with the numerous authorial intrusions that result from the novelist's social concerns and from his expounding of personal values and beliefs. As Jacob Korg says "[T]he reader is aware of the author at his shoulder, pointing to one detail after another as illustrations of an implicit lesson. Gissing's views [are] . . . in the passages of comment . . . in the tone . . . and [in] his . . . vocabulary."

Critics' reactions to such intrusions vary from Henry James' ideal of the invisible, inaudible author to George P. Elliot's view that intrusions are harmless as long as they do not violate character. Holding a view similar to that of James, Walter Allen says that the artist ought to be like God in creation—omniscient, omnipresent, but invisible. Allen sees both Joyce's *Portrait* and Thackeray's *Vanity Fair,* for example, as flawed because of author intrusions that make characters act, say, or think contrary to reader expectations based upon character qualities.

On the other hand critics such as Percy Lubbock, Norman Friedman, and George Elliott view intrusions much differently. Lubbock maintains that since the general panorama the author displays is a representation of his own experience, the author must be present to assemble and arrange that experience into a tale. Friedman argues that at times the personality of the author has a definite functional role in his work and that "he need not retire behind his work so long as his point of view is adequately and coherently maintained."

George P. Elliott, whose view is similar to Friedman's, indicates that numerous novels considered to be "great representatives of the form are impure and imperfect". He suggests that intrusions consist of several kinds: harmless interruptions to "expound [authors'] theories . . . directly to the reader" so that the reader better understands; harmless, open, "separable from the novel proper", the author tells that reader "This is what you ought to think"; descriptions of nature or of man-made things to present character; shifts of point of view from within the story to authorial omniscience; comments on the behavior of char-

acters. All of these are open and are easily separable from the text, so Elliott says they are harmless. However, if the author imposes his values on a character at the moment of action, of speaking, of thinking, or of choice, he damages the authenticity of the character and, therefore, the artistry of his work.

These other intrusions—open, separable, and relatively obvious—may be amusing, tedious, irritating to the reader, but they do no essential harm. It is only this last type, this imposition of authorial values at crucial moments of speech, action, thought, or choice that is objectionable.

Because of the nature of the Victorian novel, Elliott's criteria seem especially appropriate for **New Grub Street** and are applied in this essay. (pp. 14-15)

One type of usually harmless intrusion in **New Grub Street** is the plot interruption, those instances in which Gissing inserts extraneous portions of exposition, description, narration, or dialogue. These materials are sometimes interesting because of the background they provide, such as the Yule family history and the description of Yule's literary friends, but such material has little to do with the human conflicts of the main plot. Another similar interruption is the Whelpdale American episode. While this episode may offer comic relief and is certainly of interest if one is giving **New Grub Street** a biographical reading, the affair is irrelevant but essentially harmless.

Evidence that these and similar passages are extraneous and may have been inserted to meet the demands of the "three-decker" is supplied by Gissing himself. When Gissing revised **New Grub Street** for Gabrielle Fleury's French translation, he deleted enough material to shorten the novel by the equivalent of 110 pages (of the Penguin edition). His deletions include the three portions cited above. While it is probably true, as Michael Collie states, that Gissing improved the novel by purging it of such material, the reader can easily separate these parts from the plot. He can read them or ignore them; they impose no values on character or reader.

Gissing's comments about his characters are also fairly common and generally harmless. In most cases the comments are easily identifiable, though they may not always be compatible with the readers' view. Such harmless comments abound throughout the novel. Typical are these: "As for the poor author himself, well, he merely fell in love with Miss Yule at first sight, and there was an end of the matter". "Mrs. Yule, of course, understood, in outline, these affairs of the literary world; she thought of them only from the pecuniary point of view, but made no essential distinction between her and the mass of literary people". "His [Reardon's] position was illogical—one result of the moral weakness which was allied with his aesthetic sensibility".

One may not agree with certain of these comments about characters, but they are open and do no violence to the characters. The reader may accept, reject, or ignore.

A passage of commentary on character that may seem objectionable is the following:

Marian often went thus far in her speculation.

Her candour was allied with clear insight into the possibilities of falsehood; she was not readily the victim of illusion; thinking much, and speaking little, she had not come to her twenty-third year without perceiving what a distance lay between a girl's dream of life as it might be and life as it is. Had she invariably disclosed her thoughts, she would have earned the repute of a very sceptical and slightly cynical person.

But with what rapturous tumult of the heart she could abandon herself to a belief in human virtues when their suggestion seemed to promise her a future of happiness!

Collie calls this passage subversive because "Marian does not . . . have a 'clear insight into the possibilities of falsehood'—she is thoroughly misled by Milvain . . . " Collie claims that Gissing intends Marian to be naive, that skepticism, cynicism, and awareness of the "possibility of falsehood" are incompatible with her being. However, the novel does not seem to support this view. Numerous references are made to Marian's awareness of the quality and basis of Jasper's feelings for her: "He scarcely loved her yet . . . ". "His voice was not convincing . . . He did not love her as she desired to be loved". Jasper is quite candid with Marian regarding fame and personal and social aspirations and the necessity of money to achieve these. Only at the very end, when he is trying to break the engagement, does he show some signs of deviousness. Marian's knowledge and understanding of the relationship always includes a significant portion of skepticism. Hungry for passionate love, Marian appears to delude herself. She grasps what Jasper offers, perhaps temporarily shutting out her doubts, doubts which re-emerge even before her (presumably) sexual encounter has ended. The battle between Marian's doubts and her hunger for love continues until Jasper breaks the engagement. By this time Marian may seem to have abandoned herself to belief in Jasper's truthfulness and in his love for her; however, the doubts have periodically intruded into her consciousness throughout the relationship. When the final breakup occurs, Marian admits, "I have felt it for weeks—oh, for months . . . You don't love me Jasper . . . ".

So Marian temporarily deludes herself, momentarily abandoning her doubts. The passage is not subversive. When Gissing says "abandon" he obviously refers to Marian's willingness to be deluded and her cooperation in such delusion. But, as the material immediately following the passage in question illustrates, Marian is so hungry for love that she deludes herself at times, but relinquishes her skepticism only partially and only for a brief interval.

Another comment Gissing makes about his characters may not be as harmless. Gissing says of Alfred Yule's friends, "These men were capable of better things . . . ; in each case their failure . . . was largely explained by the unpresentable wife. They should have waited; they might have married a social equal at something between fifty and sixty". This passage is almost certainly ironic and openly reveals something of the author's bitterness. It seems harmless enough on the surface. However, the concept of wives in this passage might also be viewed as an imposition of values. The passage is the basis for the breakup of the

two central relationships and may be the author's justification for Biffen's suicide.

Passages scattered throughout chapter thirty-five state that the initial cause of Biffen's suicide is his recognition that he will never have Amy or a woman like her. Whether one can accept this and the fact that Biffen, the dedicated artist, changes so rapidly (in approximately five weeks) and so drastically from one who has endured horrible privation to live for art to one without the desire to live at all is another matter. Biffen has exhibited no previous suicidal tendencies. He has been content with the income he earns from tutoring. He is dedicated to writing pure realism. He does not seek wealth or literary fame. He has literally risked his life for art by rescuing his manuscript from the flames. Then, "a beautiful woman had smiled upon him . . . There was an end of . . . peace, . . . labor, . . . endurance of penury". Consequently, he loses all hope, begins to desire death, and calmly realizes the desire by poisoning himself.

If Edwin Reardon had committed suicide, the reader would probably accept the act as consistent with his character as Gissing develops it. However, Gissing seems to have shifted Reardon's traits to Biffen. One suspects that Gissing wishes to dramatize the plight of the poverty-stricken author who is unfit for the competitive literary world and who, worst of all, falls in love with an educated woman. But Biffen's character does not support this final act of despair. One also may suspect that Gissing wishes to attack those women unwilling to share, dutifully and willingly, the poverty of their husbands, but that makes Amy a monster, and Gissing certainly does not portray her as such. While he may portray Amy as faithless and materialistic, Gissing does not portray her as someone desiring to do harm.

Gissing also intrudes to express his views on various world concerns such as the aforementioned marriages between unequals; people trying to better themselves economically by passing examinations; the "worthlessness of current reviewing" of literature; self-pity; the importance of appearance; personalities "wholly unfitted for the rough and tumble of the world's labour market"; the "quarter-educated" and "literature to their taste".

Again, these intrusions are easily identifiable. The reader is free to accept, reject, or ignore. The passages intrude, but do not harm the plot—with at least one exception. That possible exception is found in the views Gissing expresses regarding marriage. Gissing says:

Many a man with brains but no money has been compelled to the same step. Educated girls have a pronounced distaste for London garrets; not one in fifty thousands would share poverty with the brightest genius ever born. Seeing that marriage is so often indispensable to that very success which would enable a man of parts to mate equally, there is nothing for it but to look below one's own level, and be grateful to the untaught woman who has pity on one's loneliness.

However, as cited earlier, Gissing blames the failure of many capable men on unpresentable wives. So, Gissing believes that marriages between social unequals (Alfred Yule and his wife) and economic unequals (Edwin and Amy Reardon) are almost certain to be disastrous. Either the unpresentable, inferior wife will doom the career of her husband, or the intelligent but poor husband will not be able to satisfy the social and economic aspirations of a wife who is his intellectual equal. These are Gissing's stated views, but the reader is not left free to accept, reject, or ignore them because, of course, these views are an essential part of the very texture of the novel. The actualizing of these beliefs is the basis for the two major desertions—Jasper's of Marian and Amy's of Edwin—that are the heart of the novel.

The issue here is whether the desertions are compatible with the characters Gissing has presented. In the case of Jasper, his rejection of Marian seems compatible. He is a man of some honor, but he also wants literary and social success. He has clearly stated that he must marry wealth to achieve that goal, that the goal takes precedence over love. That is why he finds his initial attraction to Marian dangerous—she is poor. That is why he schemes and plots to find reasons and means to end the engagement, including his proposal to Miss Rupert while still unofficially engaged to Marian. He may be dishonorable, faithless, a cad, but he is not inconsistent.

Gissing suggests, as noted above, that when a poor man such as Edwin chooses to marry an educated girl such as Amy, the marriage is doomed because "not one in fifty thousands would share poverty with the brightest genius ever born". Amy does seem to leave Edwin because of his poverty and her aspirations. Her leaving him seems reasonable enough in that light. However, the impediment is removed when Amy receives her legacy. Yet she and Edwin remain separated. Gissing attributes this circumstance to the ravages of poverty, Edwin's appearance and the failure it implies, and stubbornness, among other things. He also implies that the marriage may have been doomed from the start, for other reasons: Edwin seems to have fallen in love with and married "ideal womanhood," not Amy. Also, Amy seems to have married "literary fame," not Edwin. Both are disappointed when the other fails to live up to that which is impossible for each. Then, poverty delivers the *coup de grâce* to the union. On that basis, marriage on false premises and ensuing poverty, Amy and Edwin's inability to reunite seems compatible with their characters. If that is what Gissing had in mind, his imposition of values and his beliefs regarding marriage are not harmful, but are open and harmless intrusions.

Finally, there is that ambiguous episode with which the novel closes, those two scenes depicting the social and private lives of Amy and Jasper. Certainly Gissing intrudes here with his views of the literary world of Jasper and Amy and their ilk and with his views of winners and losers in that world. But the episode can be read either literally or ironically.

If one reads the passages literally, as do Gillian Tindall and Irving Howe, Gissing seems to say that artists lose while those who pander to popular taste and publishers' demands win. In personal relationships the faithful are deserted, die, are banished, but the faithless win happiness. Such a reading suggests either that Gissing sees this con-

clusion as an inevitable product of social Darwinism (heavy handedly presented) or that Gissing cannot resist the urge to vent his bitterness over injustice.

If one reads these passages as ironic, Gissing may be intruding in another way. Then, the words of Jasper and Amy about Fadge may reveal Jasper's insecurity and the kind of duplicity one must practice to survive in that literary world. Read ironically, the words of Amy and Jasper about Marian may reveal a fragility in their relationship, a haunting guilt, and a struggle to be happy in the midst of these. Then, Amy's music and song may represent a sort of deluding drug for the memory and the emotions. If such be the condition in which Gissing leaves Amy and Jasper, one wonders whether the author has intruded to avenge Edwin Reardon, Harold Biffen, and Marian Yule. While occasional, shame, and guilt appear compatible with the characters of Amy and Jasper, haunting fear, shame and guilt do not and may represent a harmful imposition on character.

On the one hand, Gissing's intrusions certainly cannot be overlooked. They tend to be annoyances and they make the novel a flawed work. Yet, with few exceptions they are rather harmless. They are easily detected; they are easily accepted or rejected. They are probably best viewed as Gissing's seeming compulsion to instruct his readers. Finally, they likely make **New Grub Street** more typical rather than atypical of late Victorian fiction. While the novel will probably never share the position of *War and Peace, Huckleberry Finn, Tom Jones,* et al, as "great representatives of the form", it does share with them the authorial intrusions that make it and them "impure and imperfect", yet artistically successful and significant. (pp. 16-23)

Eugene M. Baer, "Authorial Intrusion in Gissing's 'New Grub Street'," in The Gissing Newsletter, *Vol. 21, No. 1, January, 1985, pp. 14-25.*

Pierre Coustillas   (essay date 1986)

[*A French educator and critic, Coustillas is one of the most important authorities on Gissing. He has written and edited numerous works devoted to Gissing and has translated several of the author's novels into French. Coustillas' articles, books, and lectures have helped to revive critical interest in Gissing. Coustillas is also the editor of the* Gissing Newsletter. *In the following excerpt, he addresses Gissing's use of realism and idealism in* New Grub Street.]

Realism is not easy to define; it is a deceptive term. Everyone can distinguish between a romance like Anthony Hope's *The Prisoner of Zenda* (1894), a fantastic story set in an imaginary country, Ruritania, and a novel like **New Grub Street,** with its strong link with reality, its life-like characters and predicaments. Still reality is not quite absent from the former story, and the latter, for all its realism, does not altogether exclude purely subjective elements. Realism is an ever-recurrent notion in studies of nineteenth-century fiction; it is sure to crop up sooner or later in any discussion of aesthetics, especially in the case of the novel which, of all literary media, with the natural exception of biography and autobiography, is the most mimetic. The founders of the novel in the eighteenth century—Defoe, Richardson, Fielding—considered realism, authenticity, the touchstone of their credo. But realism, because the relation of art to reality is an eternal question, has so often been coupled with a qualifying word that is has come to lose its original meaning. In his booklet in the Critical Idiom series, Damian Grant quotes 26 phrases such as "objective realism", "ideal realism", "subjective realism", "militant realism" and "ironic realism". The literary realism instanced by Gissing is closely associated with the effort of the novel, in the nineteenth century and especially in France, to establish itself as a major literary genre. It has been rightly observed that the realism of Balzac and the Goncourt brothers for example—Gissing was well acquainted with these writers' works and did not approve of them indiscriminately—amounted to an assertion that, far from being escapist and unreal, the novel was a particularly apt medium for revealing the truth of contemporary life in society. The realistic and/or naturalistic novelist—Balzac, Flaubert, Zola—saw himself as both an artist and a sociologist, as a scientific historian recording and classifying social types, denouncing social abuses, studying "situations". Hence the graphic descriptions of material surroundings, the cataloguing of men and women according to type, temperament and social environment. Accuracy, physical, topographical and historical, was thought to be of paramount importance, and this proved a pitfall even for the leaders of the movement—witness Balzac's interminable descriptions of Flemish houses in *Les Petits Bourgeois* or Zola's minute delineation of the Jardin du Paradou in *La Faute de l'Abbé Mouret.* Sometimes the frontier between art and history or sociology was so unwittingly crossed that the result was more a document that a work of fiction.

The distinction between realism and naturalism is notoriously unclear. The latter word was little used in England in Gissing's day, partly because there was no naturalist school as in France (but Gissing himself can be said to be a naturalist in some parts of novels such as *Workers in the Dawn* and *The Nether World;* and some of his satellites like Arthur Morrison, Richard Whiteing and the early Somerset Maugham were naturalists after a fashion), partly because the word was disliked and feared by the conventional portion of the reading public. It is safe enough—admittedly vague enough as well—to see naturalism as a bolder form of realism, supported by a mass of theoretical writings, in the front rank of which Zola's *Roman Expérimental* stands forth. Naturalism had scientific pretensions which its predecessor, realism, had widely eschewed. But there is no hard and fast division between the two literary approaches. Gissing was a border-line case. In 1880, when he published *Workers in the Dawn,* he had not yet read any Zola. Yet like him, he already borrowed much from post-Darwinian biology and asserted the wholly *determined* character of man and society. His characters in *New Grub Street,* as indeed in all his preceding novels, are controlled by the coercive forces of heredity and environment. But his incursions into naturalism were not attended by any reasoned and systematic determination to expose the "unclean" aspects of human nature. (A contem-

porary reviewer noted with some relief a propos of *The Nether World:* "Mr Gissing is one of the few persons who can handle pitch without being defiled by it. While he runs Zola close as a realist, his thoughts and language are as pure as those of Miss Yonge herself." The publishers reprinted this time and time again as an advertisement.) Unlike Zola Gissing did not pose as a theorist, probably because he was English and because he fought shy of the dangers of naturalism as exemplified in the work of George Moore, whose early novels (*A Modern Lover, A Mummer's Wife* and *A Drama in Muslin*) are more Zolaesque than any fiction published in England in the last twenty years of the Victorian age.

Realism was then in the air and it was to a large extent accepted as a term of more or less questionable reference even by those critics who objected to it. Undeniably, realism was one of the components of Victorian taste. The middle-class literary critic of the period confronted with a tale of everyday life would frequently resort to the sanction of verisimilitude in order to express his judgment. Such words and phrases as "true to life", "graphic", "a good likeness", often recurred in reviews of the time. Yet too direct an imitation of nature was not permissible. Realism often ran foul of Mrs. Grundy's dictates; so the appearance or semblance of actuality was more valued than actuality itself. The word "realism" was repeatedly discussed in journals—Gissing himself contributed to a symposium on the subject four years after the publication of *New Grub Street*—probably because, even in an age of stability, it was felt to be a changing value. Indeed there had been a noteworthy evolution in the moral climate in England between the moment when Gissing entered his career as a novelist, in 1880, and the middle of the next decade. George Eliot's realism is an adequate term of reference for that year. Her works had been immensely successful and her mild approach to the realities of life was accepted not only by the cultural élite, but by the reading public at large. Her realism, in conformity with that of the Victorian period, put up with the notion that the novel is a slice of life (she made it neither tasteless nor too spicy; she would not hear of *sel gaulois,* which, like Saintsbury, she would have equated with English dirt), that it reflects in a factual way the more ordinary aspects of human experience, but it did not reject the contradictory notion that the reader's aesthetic pleasure is provided only by an artificial selection out of life's material; it did not rule out subjectivity in the act of writing, or the belief that art penetrates to a new, transcendental order of reality. In 1857 she wrote to John Blackwood: "My artistic bent is directed not at all to the presentation of eminently irreproachable characters, but to the presentation of mixed human beings in such a way as to call forth tolerant judgment, pity and sympathy." In 1880 English novelists could venture as far as that—in other words they could produce very tepid stuff. Because Gissing, in *Workers in the Dawn* and *The Unclassed,* chose to probe much deeper than that and had his hero Osmond Waymark say that Dickens's stories were for boys and girls, he was often insulted or ignored by the press.

During the most part of his career—until about 1895—there was an intermittent controversy over realism and naturalism in England. The focal point was the translations of Zola, Flaubert, Maupassant and the Goncourts. The Victorian spirit and boldly realistic fiction were at daggers drawn. The works of the French novelist, even the tamer Daudet, ignored the highly Victorian notion that we have a higher self and a lower self which the sieve of rigid morality separated into two sharply differentiated entities. (Ladies, true, genteel, well-educated ladies, were almost supposed to be sexless.) To those who stuck to the Victorian tradition, naturalistic literature of the bolder continental type was iconoclastic and contaminating. It would "Break the State, the Church, the Throne, and roll their ruins down the slope." It would "sap the foundations of manhood and womanhood, not only destroying innocence but corroding the moral nature." The so-called absence of spiritual ideals in Zola's novel was decried in the press. He and his disciples were treated in a way which nowadays makes entertaining reading: "The underlings of the naturalist school are like dogs battening upon carrion offal. They imitate the master when he is offensive, and go beyond him in reeking foulness." A very few years before Gissing wrote *New Grub Street* those Victorians who abhorred naturalism became militant. They set up the National Vigilance Association with the intention of protecting young people from the dangers of "pernicious literature" and conducted a campaign against the English translations of French naturalistic novels. The campaign resulted in two trials and two convictions for Vizetelly, publisher of Zola, Bourget and Maupassant, who served a prison sentence of three months. His conviction in 1889 was applauded by the press and certainly by a large proportion of public opinion. The following short extracts from newspapers give an idea of the rabid hatred of boldly realistic literature in England at the time: "Zola simply wallows in immorality . . . he gives full rein to filthy, libidinous propensities . . . his books are characterized by dangerous lubricity . . . realism according to latterday French lights means nothing short of sheer beastliness." But as usual in such cases the court verdict had an effect opposite to that reckoned on by the leaders of the National Vigilance Association. If anything the sales of naturalistic literature increased. There was a strong demand, about 1890, for new artistic criteria. The liberal-minded intelligentsia had no respect for the repressive moralism symbolized by Mrs. Grundy and the average three-volume novel read through the circulating libraries. Gissing and George Moore, as is well known, were staunch opponents of it, and *New Grub Street* is, among many other things, a plea for artistic freedom and an attack upon the feeble and sentimental narrative literature typified by the standard commercial novel. About the time Gissing composed his novel of literary life, realism found new supporters in the press. Two extracts will show that the tide was bound to turn. "In England," wrote D. F. Hannigan in the *Eclectic Review* for May 1890, "the artist is either afraid to tell the whole truth, or else he is intellectually incapable of revealing the complicated mechanism of the human heart." "The sample English commodity which circulates in three volumes," commented another critic in the October 1891 number of the *Quarterly Review*, "is a conventional product, an institution like Saturday excursions to Brighton and Margate for half-a-crown, a refuge for distressed

needle-women . . . Our indigenous novel, taken in the bulk, contains little art and no science. And its art is well worn—a feeble echo of Rousseau with insular decorum stifling its too Gallic accents and reducing him to respectable inanity."

So, while realism of the quieter kind was generally taken as a matter of course, its naturalistic excrescence frightened the bulk of the nation; but the evolution of the cultural climate which had prevailed for decades was abruptly hastened on in the early nineties. Gissing marvelled at the turn-about of some influential people when Zola, whose publisher had shortly before been abused and imprisoned and was now ruined, was received by the Lord Mayor of London and all the papers spoke of him in highly respectful terms. This was in September 1893. *New Grub Street* was then in its fifth edition. (pp. 64-8)

New Grub Street offers a complex image of realism. Realism is certainly to be found in the characters' psychology, in the subtle and unvarnished analysis of human motives, but it also appears in the setting for instance, and in the general atmosphere. It includes both material and treatment and, as in Zola's Rougon-Macquart series, is in perfect consonance with an element which transcends whatever seems pedestrian in realism, an element which in Gissing's case may safely be called his humanism. This was felt early enough in his career. The publications of his remarkable travel narrative, *By the Ionian Sea* (1901), was an eye-opener to many purblind critics who, parrot-like, had been complaining repeatedly about the greyness of his world, a world without illusions. But even before that, there were plenty of signs that he was not altogether misunderstood, witness this statement by Arnold Bennett, himself a realist of no mean calibre, about his fellow-novelist in 1899: "To take the common gray things which people know and despise and without tampering to disclose their epic significance, their grandeur—that is realism, as distinguished from idealism or romanticism."

Behind Gissing's realism in *New Grub Street* one feels a number of shaping factors which serve as a framework to human life. In Mrs. Gaskell or George Eliot there were still two worlds, strongly contrasted, the old rural world, slow-moving, unpolluted, pastoral in essence, handicapped though it was by the depressing limitations of human nature, and the world of factories, with its dehumanization, its cult of profit, its mechanization. In Gissing's novels—*New Grub Street* is an average example—the effects of the Industrial Revolution are omnipresent. The scientific discoveries of the nineteenth century forced man to a complete re-assessment of his view of himself as a physical and moral being, also as part of an environment. Man realized more than ever before that he was rooted in time and space, conditioned by the law of supply and demand, by his living conditions, by the spread of industrialization and urbanization. This might be said, beyond literature, to be the subject which is uppermost in the minds of the leading characters in the story. The talents of men like Alfred Yule, Reardon and Biffen are ill-adapted to the new age, with its disquieting characteristics—the acceleration of the tempo of life, the mechanization of book and magazine production, the subservience of literature to the taste of its readers that ever more money may be made in a world where everything has to be paid for in coin of the realm. These men feel that they have to live in cities, almost of necessity in London, where cultural activity has concentrated; they have been sucked into the center of the national whirlpool. Reardon deplores this; Biffen is resigned to it; Milvain—a time-server who swims with the tide—rejoices in it and so does the more ebullient, frothy-minded Whelpdale. Alfred Yule is too absorbed in the petty problems of professional life, too immersed in knowledge for the sake of knowledge, to pause and comment on this aspect of modern life, but he is obviously a victim of it and the reader is made aware of this through his deplorable lack of adaptability. More than any other character, Marian is conscious of the mechanization of the world she lives in. Literature itself, notably of the kind she is herself compelled to turn out, assumes a mechanical character. She senses the absurdity of her own situation when doing fruitless work in the reading-room of the British Museum. Why can't literature be produced entirely by machines? She sighs out in despair: "On, to go forth and labour with one's hands, to do any poorest, commonest work of which the world had truly need!" Her final occupation as a country librarian is a mixed blessing. As Peter Keating notes, she is finally condemned to the very world she had longed to opt out of. Like all the other characters who fail, she feels out of her depth in a swiftly changing world, in which the weakest, the least adaptable creatures, by a process of so-called natural selection with which the Victorians had been familiar for decades, must sooner or later acknowledge themselves defeated. Like Reardon and Biffen she resents the matter-of-factness of modern life, the rendering of which, patient and systematic, is such a weighty element of Gissing's realism. The old ideals were crumbling; spiritual values, admittedly double-edged, were losing their hold upon the mind; the scramble for money and power was now the main incentive to action in many men. One feels that two of Zola's titles, *L'Argent* et *la Curée*, might almost have been used by Gissing for this story of literary life.

Realism uses as means and tools those very elements which it condemns in its assessment of modern life. If realism was not and could not be a science, it nonetheless used a quasi-scientific method. The realists and naturalists of the latter part of the nineteenth century believed that the truthfulness at which they aimed could be gained only from a painstaking observation of reality and a careful notation of fact. Accuracy is the key-word. The characters are accurately described when first introduced—the reader's fancy can only function within a limited space. We know what people look like, how they dress, the tone of their voices; their thoughts, their miseries, their melancholy moods are recorded with a consistency and a constancy which, to the sentimental reader, are of course irritating, but Gissing, like George Moore and Zola, was writing for serious readers, not for optimistic triflers. Each important character's past is recalled in a way which, as often as not, enables one to have some idea of his future development. We are not left free to imagine people in their daily occupations: with their friends and with their own consciences. The only doors that remain closed are those of bedrooms. (Even George Moore closed them, but

he has a way of closing them which suggested that something happened behind, and this horrified many pious, right-thinking people who had an extraordinary capacity for forgetting that they themselves sought and found privacy behind closed doors.) No attempt is made to conceal mental disorder, which mid-Victorians like Dickens described in a roundabout and/or metaphorical way; no borderline is allowed to exist between "normal" and "abnormal" psychology. The characters' fears and desires are explored through both their actions and set pieces of psychological analysis which foreshadow the interior monologue or stream of consciousness technique. The vision of the world described is imposed by the author upon the reader; gravity assumes a variety of forms besides the purely physical one, and we are all the more convinced that these forms, whether social or mental, exist as we watch the characters in their daily struggles. "I want to deal with the essentially unheroic," says Biffen, "with the day-to-day life of the vast majority of people who are at the mercy of paltry circumstances". Gissing did the same: his characters in *New Grub Street,* men as well as women, are average humanity ranging from the semi-educated to the overeducated, and their struggles are essentially unheroic. They are analyzed with intellectual honesty, with accuracy, in an unromanticized manner.

Some contemporary reviewers objected to this form of realism, using two types of arguments. The first is summed up bluntly in the last sentence of an unsigned notice of the story in *Murray's Magazine:* "Deeply interesting as the book is, we feel that it is not Art." In the eyes of that writer, art had to be decorative, an absurd notion by present-day standards. The second argument, which was put forward with the cocksureness of shallow optimism, was that Gissing had held up to nature a distorting mirror. The same anonymous critic ended his sentence with the words: "and we trust that it is not Life." The pioneering character of Gissing's realism in *New Grub Street* appears from the abundance of such comments: "Are there no cakes nor ale, nor any midnight chimes in Grub Street the new?" asked a reviewer ironically. "Are there no men poor, but young and light of heart, in the literary parish? We cannot believe that all the parishioners are gloomy failures, conscientious *ratés*." But surely the writer of that review had not read *New Grub Street* very closely—Whelpdale, not to mention Sykes, comes to mind as a counter-objection. Andrew Lang, a real-life Jasper Milvain whose books sold by tens of thousands—declared he knew no writers like those in *New Grub Street.* He took refuge in the view that the story was unreal through excess of realism in the sense he primly disapproved of. Yet Gissing's unflinching debunking of the romantic notion of literary life, as a close examination of the book testifies, was thought refreshing in its earnestness, and useful as a corrective to many idealised pictures of the literary world.

Besides, for the reader thoroughly acquainted with Gissing's set of literary and philosophical values, the realism of the book is a deceptive appearance. His idealism bursts forth between the seams of his realistic picture. At the age of thirty-three he had not yet succeeded in crushing the seeds of hope that lay deep in his sorely tried ego.

The [anonymous] critic who defined Gissing as "a realist controlled by an ideal" compared him with Zola, Flaubert, George Moore and William Dean Howells, all of them realists in their different ways, and he observed that "with them it is the fact, and the fact only, which seems to count. But it is the fact transfigured by the imagination that one seeks in a work of art; and the finest realism is not found in the record, but in the interpretation of the record." Behind the sordid cares of life recorded in *New Grub Street,* we read Gissing's love of beauty, his defence of lasting human values, his liberal attitude to life. There is always an implicit opposition between the painful realities he describes and the much more acceptable nature of what might have been. It ensues that some of the shafts levelled at, say, Zola for his apparent delight in exposing the unclean or at George Moore for his showy determination to *épater le bourgeois,* if thrown at him, leave him unscathed. One feels that he deplores the sombre situations he creates from the raw material of experience. Perhaps, if *New Grub Street* does not speak for itself, one should turn to other books of his. *The Crown of Life,* that moving love story and most humane plea for peace written on the eve of the Boer War when Gabrielle Fleury was translating *New Grub Street,* is a song of love—his idealism, which he had systematically repressed since his second marriage, gave itself free play in it, because at long last he found a justification for it. Or again his volume of essays, *The Private Papers of Henry Ryecroft,* is an astonishing revelation of his capacity for enjoying life as well as of his modest demands. But let hasty commentators take warning from the title-page: *Hoc erat in votis,* says the pseudo-editor.

Gissing's ideal can be read between the lines in his narration of events that make up the web and woof of ordinary life. He was impatient of material difficulties and all-too-easily depressed by the petty disappointments we experience in our relationships with our fellow-creatures; he hankered for a more dignified existence. For him the phrase "struggle for life" had of course a Darwinian undertone as it has for us, but, because he was endowed with extreme sensitivity (which turned out to be a burden), it meant something much simpler: he found life a struggle, at least whenever—that is, nearly always—he could not turn away from work and enjoy himself. Men's mutual intercourse he thought to be ruled by indifference verging on hostility and, to the sweet-tempered, shy creature he was, this signified a permanent disappointment. His heart goes out to Marian, who is shamefully treated by the callous Jasper Milvain. His sympathy extends to all decent individuals, like her mother, a blameless woman, or the ruined doctor whose wife and child perished in a railway accident. More than most men he felt the pathos of life. An entry in his *Commonplace Book* might serve as an epigraph to the whole of his work: "A frequent source of misery to me is the reflecting on all the frightful physical sufferings through which men have gone. The martyr at the stake, the torture-chamber, the arena etc. etc. These things haunt me in the night." History, whose brightest moments were an intellectual joy to him as it is to Reardon and Biffen, he viewed mainly as "a record of woes". In his novels, far from having to work up pathos, he has to control his natural tendency to judge situations in emotional terms.

George Gissing.

His impatience with stupidity and ignorance, with the tyranny of conventions, his outcries against injustice bear testimony to his valuing the opposite good qualities. He may seem to sneer at the "quarter-educated"; if he does, the reason is that, to his mind, education should be a means of levelling up the cultural patrimony of the country, not of levelling it down, as a simple glance at the evolution of the press between the 1850s and the 1880s testified it did. The spread of education, he thought, was an excellent thing *per se,* but it was being used as a springboard for money-makers and careerists, and Gissing, with his natural tendency to protest against abuses, with the selfconfidence born of his intellectual training, with his keen eye for the seamy side of things, spoke a language which to the modern reader may sound ambiguous. But is the correct view here that of some twentieth-century critics who idealise the masses from their cosy book-room? Or is it rather that expressed by Nathaniel Wedd, whose wife had discussed intellectual matters with Gissing when they were together at the Nayland Sanatorium in 1901? "The two things that Gissing saw most clearly and emphasized with the greatest wealth of illustration," Wedd wrote, "are the vital importance of culture and the degrading effects of poverty on all above a certain low level of spiritual development." The comparison made by Reardon between slavery in ancient times and poverty in nineteenth-century England is fraught with unmaterialized aspirations. Gissing did not choose to depict poverty in his working-class novels, and again in his middle-class stories like *New Grub Street,* because he found it picturesque (there is something of this attitude in his imitators, Arthur Morrison and Richard Whiteing), but because he thought it his duty, given his articulateness, to denounce a state of things which clamoured for redress. Like Matthew Arnold, he wanted to Hellenise the barbarians.

Another significant aspect of his humanism is his love of the classics, which in the days of his direst poverty—Reardon and Biffen are placed in more or less autobiographical positions—he regarded as a safeguard against despair born of the brutalising conditions in which he was living. He reverted to the subject in a section of *The Pri-*

vate *Papers of Henry Ryecroft* in which his devotion to literature in general and to the classics in particular made him wax lyrical. Doubtless when he saw the past through literature, especially through the literature of ancient Greece and Italy, he idealized it, as though the ancient writers' minds had purified it, had cleansed it of its grosser and more cruel aspects. And his love of classical literature and history, which brought him the intellectual comfort of belonging to an *élite,* was part of his love of beauty—the beauty of landscapes (one recalls Reardon's memories of Athens, which, as Gissing's diary confirms, are again pure autobiography), the beauty of people (of course women to whose charm he responded so pathetically) and the beauty of finished artistic work. In *New Grub Street,* the true lovers of beauty, Reardon and Biffen, are perhaps all the more to be pitied as in late nineteenth-century Grub Street their learning, their devotion to the classics, for which contemporary England had little if any use, proves a handicap. The contemplative man, the artist with an incorruptible conscience, thought Gissing, is perpetually at a disadvantage, but especially so in the modern world. Society may destroy him, usually by ignoring him, but it cannot rob him of his aesthetic happiness.

For indeed let us not be deluded by Gissing's realism. It is a tangible phenomenon, but his realism is noticeably different from that of his predecessors and successors. With most of them it is an end in itself or an instrument; with Gissing, it was a means of protest, of self-defence, of revenge against an indifferent or hostile world. Behind his realism we feel, in the noblest sense of the term, a man with a shining intelligence and sensibility. He was never fascinated by trivia; he was not what the Americans of his time called a muck-raker. He was a humanist and an aesthete; inevitably—in whatever he did—he belonged to a minority. He has a message for the world, largely thanks to his classical culture, which he assimilated with both the intelligence of the brain and the generosity of the heart. Samuel Vogt Gapp clearly understood this when he concluded his study of Gissing the classicist with these words:

> He demonstrated the possibilities of his own theory; he showed that intellectual interests are possible even in a life unusually beset by the problems of modern life; he was a living example of the truth that such interests can become the saving features of a man's personality. We might be so bold as to say that he found, in such vital and real intellectual interests as his classic studies afforded, an antidote to neurotic introspection, to the subjectively egocentric tendencies and the morbid self-questionings which were, even in his day, becoming evident in the field of literature.

Herein Gissing stands confessed. (pp. 71-7)

> *Pierre Coustillas, "Some Personal Observations on Realism and Idealism in 'New Grub Street',"* in Cahiers Victoriens & Edouardiens, *No. 24, October, 1986, pp. 63-78.*

<hr>

Gissing on meeting H. G. Wells:

—Great difficulty in getting a red rose, for the Omar dinner, held at Frascati's, Oxford Street. There my guest, John Davidson, met me at 7 o'clock. Sixty-two diners all together. New acquaintances made: W. E. Norris, [J. W.] Mackail (author of *History of Latin Literature*), H. G. Wells and Conan Doyle. Guests of the club were Frederic Harrison and Sidney Colvin. Pleased to meet Hamo Thornycroft again. Wells amused me by rushing up, after dinner, introducing himself hurriedly, (only a minute, as he must go,) and telling me that, when he first read *New Grub Street,* he himself was living in Mornington Road, poor and ill, and with a wife named Amy! Queer coincidence. As he told his story, Mackail, who had been talking with me, stood by and smiled. I rather liked Wells's wild face and naive manner. As usual, not at all the man I had expected.

George Gissing, in his London and the Life of Literature in Late Victorian England: The Diary of George Gissing, *Harvester Press, 1978.*

<hr>

David Grylls   (essay date 1986)

[Grylls is an English educator and critic. In the following excerpt, he provides an analysis of the relationships between the major characters of New Grub Street.*]*

Like all Gissing's finest novels, **New Grub Street** examines how a social problem bites into individual lives. Actually, the problem is really two problems. The first and deepest is poverty, which Gissing classified as a primary corroder not only of happiness and peace of mind, but of decency and self-respect. The conviction that poverty degrades is voiced by virtually every character—a flaw in the novel, Gissing felt, arising from his own bitterness. Given this corrosive power, however, the immediate problem for the characters is how to stay solvent as practitioners of literature—or, more ambitiously, how to float themselves to wealth. The perennial stresses of poverty are applied to the contemporary crisis of letters. The atmosphere of the novel is unrelievedly literary. All the major characters are attempting to survive on the proceeds of print: they are novelists, journalists, editors, agents, or family dependants of these. (The single exception is Harold Biffen: his problem is how to live not by, but while, producing words.) The particular contemporary challenge they face is the commercialization of literature. With the aristocratic patron replaced by the democratic reading public, literature has become just another commodity, exposed to the forces of the modern market—the imperatives of mass production and consumption, the demand for utility or entertainment, the reliance on recently developed techniques of promotion and publicity. But if poverty corrodes, commercialism pollutes. A writer may leap over the pitfalls of penury, but only, perhaps, to slip into the sewers of mercantile compromise.

The dilemma dealt with is Gissing's own—the conflict between moral integrity and material success. This dilemma is nailed into the narrative on a cross-frame of character juxtapositions. The most obvious contrast is that between

Edwin Reardon and Jasper Milvain. Both these men agree that the current standards of the literary world are corrupt; but whereas Reardon rejects them and fails, Milvain exploits them and succeeds. Reardon is a man of the old school (we must specify later what this means) who will not, or cannot, 'make a trade of an art'. Sensitive, conscientious, painfully slow, he strives for work of intrinsic merit rather than ephemeral popular appeal. Jasper is a new man and a tradesman: what he aims at is money and money's benefits—physical comfort, social esteem, travel, luxurious living. Literature for him is a means to this end. Under no illusion about the merit of what he writes, he realizes that success as a writer is not wholly dependent on merit. In the late-Victorian literary market there are other, more serviceable requisites. You must have sufficient capital to finance a flourishing social life: marriage is perhaps the most convenient method of getting your hands on this. You also need influential friends, so that useful reviews can be offered and received, posts can be earmarked, prospects sounded. Recruiting such friends requires diplomatic skills, but also gambler's nerves: patronage from one quarter might well provoke punishment from another. The personal qualities in demand are speed, versatility, cynical detachment and a nose for popular fashion. In short, you must flatter and advertise, cultivate patrons, make connections, and generally pay less attention to your writing than to its successful promotion.

Clearly the difference between Reardon and Milvain is not only moral but temperamental. Reardon is reticent and independent, Milvain sleekly convivial. Reardon is passionate and pessimistic, Milvain cold and cheerful. This character contrast is obvious, but the juxtaposition of types goes further. At the centre of the novel are two parallel relationships—between the married pair, Amy and Reardon, and the lovers, Marian and Jasper. Like *The Emancipated* before it and *The Odd Women* after, *New Grub Street* is based on the affairs of two couples. (pp. 82-3)

In *New Grub Street* the crucial pattern in the action is the way that Jasper's relationship with Marian reduplicates Amy's with Reardon. At first, it is true, what we seem to have is a contrast rather than a comparison. Amy and Reardon are breaking apart; Jasper and Marian, it seems, are uniting. But Gissing makes use of his three-volume format both to build up and to undermine this contrast. The first volume concludes with Reardon's despair, and Amy's pursed dissatisfaction, at his failure to prosper through fiction. The second volume, in which the marriage severs, ends with Jasper and Marian's engagement. Both endings, however, are fraught with foreboding. The second, just as much as the first, is overshadowed by financial worry; and the rapturous betrothal is soon betrayed by Jasper's impatience and selfish concern: 'He rose, though she was still seated . . . When they had parted, Marian looked back. But Jasper was walking quickly away, his head bent, in profound meditation.' The final curtain goes down, of course, on Jasper and Amy united at last, financially secure and emotionally relaxed, harmonious in repulsive bliss.

This ending is apt, and almost preordained, for Jasper and

Amy have much in common. Early in the book Jasper declares that he could never prove attractive to Amy because they are 'too much alike'. His premise is correct though his inference is false. Numerous hints establish the fact that Amy is fascinated by Jasper—by his 'energy and promise of success'. (Jasper, conversely, understanding her well, is rather more sceptical about Amy.) Both are socially ambitious, unromantic, somewhat selfish; at various times they both display a marked disloyalty to Reardon and derive satisfaction from his weakness. They both acknowledge—and more important accept—the moral omnipotence of money, and share the commercial view of literature. They also concur in their conviction that merit must be socially recognized to be of any use. Amy is 'well aware that no degree of distinction in her husband would be of much value to her unless she had the pleasure of witnessing its effect upon others'. When Jasper claims to care only about 'intellectual distinction', his sister Dora sharply objects, 'Combined with financial success'. Jasper's reply is unhesitating: 'Why, that is what distinction means.' Significantly, at the end of the novel, Dora condemns both Jasper and Amy in almost identical terms.

Given these character resemblances, it is scarcely surprising that Jasper and Amy are also alike in their treatment of others. Attracted, perhaps, to their anti-types, they embrace then discard very similar partners. Both Reardon and Marian are introverts whose loneliness has made them sensitive. Warm-hearted but diffident, both hunger for love—hunger being the metaphor used in each case. To Reardon, toiling in poverty, Amy appears like a dazzling light; to Marian, in her bleak life of literary drudgery, Jasper is a 'vision of joy'. Both have moments of murky foreboding, provoked by their partner's responses to money; but in both a craving for sympathy overmasters their suspicion. Marian and Reardon never meet, but Marian closely follows Reardon's path in a downward curve to disaster. Ultimately, the two main relationships are not contrasted but compared. In each a conscientious but nervous *littérateur* seeks escape from isolation through love. Enamoured of ambitious extroverts, both find themselves losing their partners' affection because of a failure to supply them with cash. Just as Amy accepts Reardon's proposal thinking he will one day be wealthy and famous, so Jasper proposes to Marian after news of her inheritance. Reardon's diminishing receipts have their counterpart in Marian's truncated legacy. And as Amy sharply advises her husband to turn out sensational short stories, so Jasper bluntly suggests to his lover that she live by romantic fiction.

The parallels not only run neatly along the narrative, they also plunge down into the characters' emotions. Compare, for instance, the 'fruitless meeting' of the married couple in Chapter 25 with the final meeting, in Chapter 26, of Jasper and Marian in Regent's Park (the latter location chosen by Jasper in order to be 'on neutral ground'—the title of Reardon's book). In the first scene Amy is repelled by Reardon's shabbiness and then begins 'to feel ashamed of her shame'. In the second Jasper notes 'with more disgust than usual, the signs in Marian's attire of encroaching poverty', and yet 'for such feelings he reproached himself, and the reproach made him angry'. The thoughts and feelings of Reardon and Marian, their pride stung by unre-quited love, are also directly analogous. Marian refuses to accept an obviously unwilling offer of marriage: 'Do you wish me to be your wife, or are you sacrificing yourself ? . . . your voice says you promise it out of pity.' This recalls not just Reardon's emotional predicament, but also his actual words to Amy: 'Then you mean that you would sacrifice yourself out of—what? Out of pity for me, let us say.' Other moments, too, are precisely recalled by this final encounter in the park. Much earlier Amy has said to Reardon, of her staunchness under stress of remorseless poverty, 'I can't trust myself if that should come to pass'. In the park Jasper grimly warns Marian that he 'can't trust' himself to remain faithful throughout a pro-tracted engagement. There is even an ironic symmetry in what happens to Marian and Reardon just after they have been abandoned. Marian wrenches herself away to return to work at the British Museum. Reardon resumes his for-mer job as a humble clerk in a hospital. Both return to the very obscurity that preceded their dazzling dreams.

All this might sound rather mechanically schematic, but in fact so gradually are the parallels drawn, and so fully are the individual characters defined, that the dominant pattern of juxtaposition is not obvious until close to the end. The novel is not built simply on the contrast between two men ('Milvain versus Reardon', as one critic has it), but the counterpoint between two relationships, one of which is running ahead of the other, but both of which are eventually played out to a similar plaintive strain. Howev-er, Gissing's initial decision to embody his thematic con-trast between integrity and worldliness not in two men but in two couples has important effects on the subtlety of the novel's characterization. It means that he cannot make his major characters Morality figures of vice and virtue—else why should the 'virtuous' partner in each couple be at-tracted at all to the other? If Amy, say, were merely a mer-cenary succubus, half the book's pathos would be thrown away: Reardon would become just an obtuse dupe, his lasting affection nor more than a neurosis. As it is, Amy is a character with whom at times we sympathize; Jasper, in the earlier part of the book, we might positively admire. Amy's failings are evident enough. She is cold, self-absorbed and sometimes mean—she never once refers to Marian, for instance, without some suggestion of belittle-ment. Although, like her predecessor Rosamond Vincy (and her close contemporary Hedda Gabler), magnetized by the theoretical prospect of being wedded to an eminent man, she cannot help, when poverty comes, putting her-self first: 'What is to become of me—of us?' (Contrast Marian to Jasper: 'And why shouldn't I go on writing for myself—for us?' Amy's correction is a tactical cover-up; Marian's a generous afterthought.) Amy, released from her husband's restrictions, mutates into a perfect high-society animal—purring, glossy, beautifully groomed, but always with a latent hint of savagery as soon as she senses a threat. However, her hardness to Reardon is qualified by impulses of guilt and compassion. And, for quite a time, she is dutiful even by Victorian standards—tiptoeing around the tiny flat, scrupulously attentive to her baby, servicing her husband with silence and meals. What most explains her conduct is her social background. Like her mother, she is instinctively committed to the dictates of

respectability. Refined, intelligent, educated, she is tar-nished and ultimately corroded by the customary re-sponses of her class. Eventually Reardon realizes this, feel-ing that 'It was entirely natural that she shrank at the test of squalid suffering'. Given the book's emphasis on the de-basing power of penury, Amy's flight to security and com-fort is at least comprehensible. Her behaviour is not so much morally outrageous as socially commonplace.

Jasper, too, is no prodigy of evil—but Jasper's personality is a tricky subject that might best be looked into later. Switching for a moment to Reardon and Marian, we find that in their moral portraiture, too, the pigmentation is flecked. Marian is intense, fastidious and decent, but she has enough purely human urges to make her entirely cred-ible. Though timid, she is no paragon of trusting inno-cence. 'Her candour was allied with clear insight', Gissing writes, 'into the possibilities of falsehood; she was not readily the victim of illusion.' This makes her temporary belief in Jasper the more poignant and the less straightfor-ward: it points up the stubbornness of her emotional de-sires, as well as the tantalizing ambiguity of Jasper's over-tures. Her dutifulness as a daughter, too, is carefully dis-tinguished from conventional submission. Though patient to a fault with her fractious father, she resists his sly and presumptuous parleys when he thinks she has become an heiress. Money fortifies her self-respect. And yet, at the same time, her attachment to Jasper makes her 'compro-mise with her strict sense of honour'. She would even find it acceptable, we are told, if he pleaded with her 'to neglect her parents for the sake of being his wife. Love excuses ev-erything, and his selfishness would have been easily lost sight of in the assurance that he still desired her'. Marian responds intensely to Jasper's embraces because what he seems to offer is romantic liberation: 'All the pedantry of her daily toil slipped away like a cumbrous garment'.

Similarly wounded, Edwin Reardon reacts with more self-pity than Marian and less resilience. As Gissing told Bertz, 'Reardon . . . has the *beau rôle*'; yet few leading men could be less charismatic. Reardon is characterized quite deliberately as 'a weak and sensitive man' or, in an-other authorial formulation, a man of 'aesthetic sensibili-ty' allied to 'moral weakness'. This weakness is not lack of principle but rather a shortage of executive power. An exhausted, self-torturing perfectionist, he requires long stretches of time and serenity, as well as large doses of con-nubial affection, to achieve his well-crafted but modest productions. Thrown into the arena of the modern mar-ket, he has no chance against the literary lions who enter-tain the mass audience. Yet Reardon refuses to go down to defeat with the stoic taciturnity of a martyr. Instead he cries out in anxiety and embitterment, vacillates with his wife between bluster and pleading, daydreams, despairs and then frantically resumes his doomed efforts to post-pone his demise. The author firmly resists the temptation to idealize his disintegrating hero. Amy's snappish impa-tience with her husband is rendered quite as understand-able as his moral resentment of her.

Nevertheless, we never lose sight of the fact that Reardon is genuinely a victim of an unjust commercial system. In a penetrating passage at the start of Volume 3, Gissing explains how Reardon survives, after the traumatic parting from Amy, 'by force of commiserating his own lot'. According to conventional moral thinking, there are two distinct categories of victim—those who are genuinely deserving of pity and those who indulge in self-pity. Gissing, however, appreciates that these two categories are often one. Reardon dramatizes his own catastrophe—haunting the streets where his wife is staying, wallowing in elegiac poetry, seeking out the poorest eating-houses, even staring at his image in shop mirrors 'with pleasurable contempt'. Only a facile moral perception would condemn these gestures as *mere* self-pity. Reardon really is in a doleful predicament—impoverished by his scruples, deserted by his wife, virtually bereft of sympathetic friends. It is idle to expect, Gissing seems to say, that those in a pitiable situation should never draw attention to it themselves. On the contrary, that is their best means of survival. A similar emotional pattern emerges in the case of the cantankerous Yule. A monster of domestic asperity, Yule never wins our empathy like Reardon, yet he too, in his plodding and painstaking way, is a casualty of the commercial incursion. Yule, who has very few pleasures in life, is a positive epicure in self-commiseration. Eventually his darkest fears materialize and he learns that he is certainly going blind. Even here, though, the author refuses to remit his sharp scrutiny of Yule's crippled spirit. Announcing his fate to Marian, Yule ghoulishly insists on extracting from her the maximum terror and pity; his speech concludes, Gissing grimly records, 'his voice tremulous with self-compassion'. Again, in view of Yule's history and future, a contemptuously smiling response to this passage would scarcely be appropriate. Yule is disgraceful, but he has indeed suffered; not long after this conversation, he goes blind and dies. The man is undoubtedly pathetic—in every sense of the word.

Despite its almost diagrammatic structure, and the closeness of its thesis to Gissing's own emotions, the characterization in *New Grub Street* is both subtle and unsentimental. Even Dora, an unfailingly kindly girl, is shown to be but human in her self-regard. After Harold Biffen's suicide, Dora awaits further information from Whelpdale, thinking 'more of that gentleman's visit than of the event that was to occasion it'. As in all Gissing's fiction, love is egotistic. As usual, too, there is much shrewd perception of the minor psychological quirks of jealousy and despair. When Biffen tells Reardon that, earlier in the day, he passed Amy, with Milvain, in Tottenham Court Road, Reardon demands incredulously, 'In Tottenham Court Road?' 'That was not the detail of the story', says Gissing, 'which chiefly held Reardon's attention, yet he did not purposely make a misleading remark. His mind involuntarily played this trick.' Soon afterwards, Reardon is abandoned by Amy, and again his mind for a moment slips a notch. Returning to the suddenly empty flat, he lights a fire against the cold: 'Whilst it burnt up he sat reading a torn portion of a newspaper, and became quite interested in the report of a commercial meeting in the City, a thing he would never have glanced at under ordinary circumstances.' This trivial incident is more effective than any extravagant outburst. Reardon's emotions recoil in weariness from the fact that his life is now in ashes. His untypi-

cal absorption is doubly ironic in that it is precisely the commercial world that has led to his sitting there alone.

We need to say more about the commercial world, for a third major source of the novel's vigour, in addition to its structure and its psychological subtlety, is the way it taps energies already released in Gissing's treatment of this subject. The struggling writers are hedged around by an ominous throng of familiar obsessions. Haggling tradesmen buy books and furniture; gambling card-players drive Reardon to distraction. Whelpdale, his novel refused, has to contemplate life as a commission-agent. Reardon actually takes a job as a clerk: 'His face burned, his tongue was parched'. In a commercial society, imaginative literature is of marginal importance to the mass of the people. When Biffen laments to a dealer in oil that all his books have been burnt in a fire, the other responds sympathetically: 'Your account-books! Dear, dear!—and what might your business be?' To pull through, literature must adapt to the market. Repeatedly, the dodges of advertising are recommended by Jasper Milvain, who can see the point of a catchy title (Reardon, conversely, never thinks of a title until the book has been completed). Jasper can also appreciate the potency of well-placed and well-timed reviews. Curtly rejected in his well-meant offer to turn out a laudatory notice for Reardon, he writes it anyway after Reardon's death—and uses it to seduce his widow.

Periodicals often figure prominently in Gissing, and nearly always with unsavoury connections. In **Demos** Mutimer's henchman, Keene, is a journalist who serves him by circulating libel. In both **Born in Exile** and **Our Friend the Charlatan** the hero is descredited by the ruinous discovery of a compromising article in a magazine. **New Grub Street** is the richest repository of this deeply imprinted preoccupation. Its pages are packed with periodical titles—fictional for the most part, though two of them, *The West End* and *All Sorts,* were adopted by real magazines. There is *The Study,* rather formal and old-fashioned, deserted by its editor, the malicious Fadge, for the more contemporary pages of *The Current* (eventually edited by Jasper Milvain, now completely in the swim). There is the *Wayside,* which Reardon falls beside when they turn down his article on Pliny, but from which he gets posthumous recompense when commemorated by Jasper. There is the *Will o' the Wisp,* to which Jasper contributes a slanderous Saturday causerie, and the *Balance,* in which, inappropriately, Alfred Yule makes 'a savage assault upon Fadge'. The list of others is almost endless— the *English Girl* and the *Young Lady's Favourite,* the *Evening Budget* and the *Shropshire Weekly Herald,* and *Chat,* which Whelpdale reduces to *Chit-Chat.* This 'multiplication of ephemerides' (Yule's phrase) is a symptom of changes in the literary market. For Gissing, periodicals were substitutes for books. The wealthy philistine John Yule, who has made his money in paper manufacture, reads little else but newspapers. The ill-educated wife of Alfred Yule sits turning the pages of a coloured magazine. Characters are differentiated by their views on periodical literature. Alfred Yule gains credit with his contention that 'journalism is the destruction of prose style'; he loses it by coveting Marian's money for the purpose of starting up a literary monthly, to be used as an outlet for his grudges. Amy, too, condemns herself by her growing attention to the ephemeral press. Capable of forming purely literary judgements, she switches her attention to financial matters—the implications of gossip columns, 'the practical conduct of journals and magazines'. After leaving her husband she turns even more to 'specialism popularised': pieces on philosophy and social science, potted versions of Darwin or Spencer. Amy reads writing about writing, becomes proficient in substitute achievement. The demands of periodicals encourage this, not only for readers but also for writers. **New Grub Street** is full of journalistic incest, the kind of barren, self-predatory activity that Marian despairs of in the British Museum. Jasper, who studies audiences in order to make his goods fit the consumer, converts this research to more immediate account by producing an article on 'Typical readers'—malicious, satirical, highly successful; a masterpiece of ingrown enterprise. Whelpdale, having failed as a novelist, sets up shop as a literary adviser, instructing failed novelists how to publish and write. Another example is the journalist Sykes: a drunkard whose literary career has dried up, he rescues himself by recounting his scrapes ('Through the Wilds of Literary London') in the pages of a regional paper. Literature about literature, failure metamorphosed into success. Oddly, the supreme example of this is the novel **New Grub Street** itself.

The symptoms of commercialization are consistent with those that appear elsewhere; so too is the historical diagnosis. Throughout the novel the squalors of the present are contrasted with the relative decencies of the past. In the literary sphere the past is represented first by the world of Samuel Johnson, whose own Grub Street, though savagely competitive, was not quite so sordidly commercialized. The *new* Grub Street, Gissing felt, lacked the redeeming features of the old. The title of his book is a sardonic signpost pointing towards a historical chasm rather than an unbroken pathway. Gissing explained to his friend Bertz that when Johnson had defined 'Grub Street' in his dictionary, he had added a Greek quotation meaning 'Hail, O Ithaca! Amidst joys and bitter pains, I gladly come to thy earth'. Gissing commented, 'Is not this delicious? Poor old Sam, rejoicing to have got so far in his Dictionary, and greeting the name "Grub Street" as that of his native land'. Johnson's quotation reveals him as feeling, in the literal sense, nostalgic for Grub Street. So was Gissing: but for Johnson's, not his own. His title, he told Bertz, was not 'altogether' meant contemptuously. One reason is that some of the characters—pre-eminently Reardon, but also Yule—still hanker after Johnson's milieu. All that Jasper has picked up from Johnson is his praise of dogged application.

The past is represented secondly by the non-commercial grandeur of the classics. Ithaca, as Reardon's death scene shows, is no longer a metaphor for Grub Street but a yearningly dreamed alternative to it. Reardon discovers that the classics aren't commercial, but this, for him, is part of their attraction. 'Yes, yes', he reflects, reading the *Odyssey; that* was not written at so many pages a day.' He and Biffen seek temporary refuge from poverty by discussing Greek metres or Euripides' fragments. He plans to go back to Greece once more, to escape from hardship, frus-

tration and struggle. But as he lies dying he dreams of a ship sailing south to the Ionian islands and is grieved to learn that Ithaca 'had been passed in the hours of darkness'. He awakes to the rented shores of Brighton: 'The glory vanished. He lay once more a sick man in a hired chamber, longing for the dull English dawn.

The objections to commercialism in **New Grub Street** are also consonant with those in the rest of Gissing's work. He hated commercialism, we recall, partly because it fomented strife and partly because it pandered to the masses. He also regarded it as antipathetic to the healthy purity of nature. This last is admittedly less important in the novel, though Jasper's progress from the leafy lanes of Finden to the metropolitan corridors of power is no doubt symbolically significant: taking the train from the country at the end of Chapter 3, he 'smiled at the last glimpse of the familiar fields, and began to think of something he had decided to write for *The West End'.* Reardon's attack on London anticipates *The Whirlpool,* and his and Biffen's responsiveness to nature contrasts with Amy's preference for the city. The commercially minded are also urban. More important, they are conquerors in a world of strife. It is no accident that Amy reads Darwin and Spencer. In the elemental struggles of the literary jungle, the survivors only prosper if the failures die out. Some of the characters are linked like pendants, one rising to the rhythm of the other's fall. On the day Yule leaves London, blind and broken, a celebration appears of Clement Fadge—at an earlier period his protégé, later his malevolent rival. Both Whelpdale and Biffen begin by writing commercially fruitless realistic fiction, but while Biffen perseveres into penury, Whelpdale shoots off into lucrative fraud. Though both at first are sexually lonely, Whelpdale succeeds in winning Dora: his bouncy announcement of the joyful tidings tips Biffen into suicide. Ironically, the news of Biffen's death is used as a pretext by Amy and Jasper for a meeting that consolidates their mutual attraction. Whelpdale's success prompts Biffen's suicide; Biffen's suicide clinches Jasper's success. The most sustained personal combat is that between Jasper and Reardon; and since Jasper's reward is Reardon's wife, what begins as a contrast of literary outlooks takes on the appearance of a fight for a mate. The superimposition of sexual struggle on a narrative concerned with commercial strife can be seen in the quasierotic reproaches that Amy directs at her wilting spouse. 'Don't you feel it's rather unmanly?' she remarks, of his failure to satisfy her material desires; and Reardon agrees that it is. He fears that his 'mental impotence' has cost him not only his livelihood but also Amy's love. As he worries about this in the watches of the night, 'The soft breathing of Amy at his side, the contact of her warm limbs, often filled him with intolerable dread'. Financial collapse causes sexual estrangement; the night before they separate, the couple sleep in different beds. The physical aspects of competitive struggle also embrace the question of health. In the drizzly and fog-choked world of **New Grub Street** it is indeed survival of the fittest. While the statuesque Amy is 'gloriously strong', the crumbling Marian has a 'morbid' complexion and suffers from nervous headaches. Reardon is a mournful anthology of ailments—coughs, colds, sore throats, lumbagoes. The contrasts aren't merely sentimental, for Gissing attributes ill health to hardship, both physical (leaky boots, insufficient food) and mental (anxiety, depression, disappointment). The effect, however, is to suggest that survival, physically as well as morally, is a privilege of the coarser-fibred.

Gissing's third objection to commercialism was that it flattered the masses. The anonymous mass audience weighs heavily in the novel, held in contempt by all the main characters, though some, like Jasper, also wish to exploit it. The most measured and successful attempt to do so is that of Whelpdale with his paper *Chit-Chat,* addressed to the 'quarter-educated' and containing no article longer than two inches. Perhaps the best way of assessing the significance of differing attitudes towards the public is by considering them as a factor in the final reason for the novel's power—its skilful reconciliation of its social and personal themes. In books like **Demos** Gissing had argued that personal conduct could not be detached from public policy. He was clumsy, however, in soldering the links. In **New Grub Street** he effects a smoother continuity between the public and the private—or rather between the public (one's literary career), the social (one's appearance at fashionable occasions) and the personal (one's marital and private life). In the novel's moral architecture, the office is connected with the drawing-room, which in turn communicates with the bedroom. The passages between these three areas are no secret. In a commercial society, a lucrative career depends on a flourishing social life; a flourishing social life in turn depends on a prosperous marriage. Behind these crude economic realities are far-reaching moral and emotional implications. Essentially, the novel suggests, the trading attitude to literature is bound to carry over into personal relations. Those who neglect literary value for the sake of money and social esteem will not only be mercenary in private life, they will also display two other faults: first, capitulation to public opinion; secondly, insincerity and dishonesty.

Public opinion: in Gissing's view there was a deep connection between supplying the wants of the vulgar masses and appeasing the whims of a respectable élite. Though the public in question might not be the same, the underlying mentality was. It involved a surrender of individual judgement, an abject deference to prevailing demands. Those who adopted as their literary starting point 'What do the masses want to read?' would take as their be-all and end-all in conduct 'What will people think?' Amy Reardon is a case in point. Her mother is of the 'multitudinous kind' who 'lived only in the opinion of other people. What others would say was her ceaseless preoccupation. She had never conceived of life as something proper to the individual'. Amy is intellectually superior to this standpoint but lacks courage to act on her convictions. Arguing with Reardon, she is constantly apprehensive that their poverty will be publicly talked about, and advises him to forestall such detraction by profitably writing for the masses. Jasper, who likewise believes that intellectuals are justified in catering to the mob, is similarly nervous about public opinion, despite his façade of bold frankness. He guards his tongue in his sisters' company, trims his conversation to flatter his hearers, and carefully avoids putting down in writing any statements that might be used against him. He cultivates a 'diplomatic character' and has 'a scent for

the prudent course'; ultimately, he convinces himself 'that he cannot afford to despise anything that the world sanctions'. Jasper's final public gesture is to frown down his pretty but prattling new wife when she touches on a perilous story. Characteristically, in both print and talk, he assesses his audience.

Another moral corollary of handing over one's judgement to the public is being too easily influenced. Amy is affected by recent impressions just as much as by market trends. Her husband extends her mind in one way, Jasper's magnetism pulls it another. At home she is even 'subtly influenced' by her mother's insistence that her husband is mad. Jasper, conversely, is deeply disturbed when Amy seems to slight his choice of fiancée. By contrast, characters like Reardon and Marian show remarkable fidelity and consistency, in both literary judgement and personal affection. At the opposite extreme from Amy's mother is Biffen, who cares nothing about reviews or readers and finds drawing-room talk an ordeal. It is not that Biffen is a strident rebel: he is scrupulously well-mannered and tries hard to observe propriety of dress. Intellectually, however, he is fiercely independent. This is what Amy pretends to be, but in truth she is not only socially but mentally acquiescent.

Gissing, then, sees an ignominious affinity between serving up literary fare for the masses and waiting on the words of distinguished diners-out. At times, indeed, these two tyrannous publics seem to be almost the same. Biffen speaks of best-selling novelists who 'are in touch with the reading multitude; they have the sentiments of the respectable'. Jasper and Dora see 'a copy of *Chit-Chat* in the hands of an obese and well-dressed man'. As elsewhere in Gissing, plutocratic vacuity keeps company with impoverished ignorance. The commercial mentality, supplying these publics, is cowardly, servile and quite probably insincere. Jasper and Amy are perfectly aware of the limitations of public opinion; but in practice they defer to what in theory they despise. This insincerity is a final link between the novel's social analysis and its treatment of personal relations. Jasper and Amy, in the Ovidian phrase, see and approve the higher course while following the lower. This is true in both literature and life. Amy's discerning intelligence decamps from literary appraisal to commercial assessment. Perceiving that *The Optimist* was unworthy of Edwin, she still exhorts him to write for the market; similarly, though uneasy in conscience, she still makes off to her mother's. Jasper, too, has considerable potential which is ultimately ruined by insincerity—but in his case this is doubly interesting since his pose is one of brutal candour.

The opening scene of **New Grub Street** sketches the essential lineaments of Jasper (as also of his two sisters). As the clock strikes eight, he cheerfully remarks that a man is being hanged at that moment in London (this opening was significant to Gissing: it was earlier recorded in his scrapbook). His sisters immediately object: Maud does not want to hear about such things; Dora is disturbed by her brother's tone. Characteristically, Jasper justifies his flippancy: what better 'use' could he make of this fact; indignation or misery would not be 'profitable' emotions. He adds that his tone 'needs no justification' because it was 'spontaneous'. We have here Jasper's character in epitome: a brusque acceptance of the fall of others, a competitive attitude to human affairs (another's calamity is a 'consolation' to him). At this stage, though, the potential nastiness of his views is apparently excused by his self-awareness. Admitting that his feelings are not exalted, he enters the defence of frank self-interest. For almost the first two-thirds of the book, his cynicism is mitigated, for the majority of readers, by his cheerful acknowledgement of what he is doing. Gradually, however, our responses change. There is no single turning-point, though the first mention of Miss Rupert, in Chapter 22, is an ominous moral creak. Eventually, Jasper's self-awareness only makes him more contemptible. Able to recognize decency (in the person of Marian Yule), even to be moved by it, he abandons it for profitable dishonesty. This personal behaviour is the direct equivalent of his attitude towards literature, in which, though intelligently alert to merit, he commits himself to money-spinning trash.

Jasper Milvain's is a masterly portrait of subtle deterioration. Fundamentally insincere, he has to find means of reconciling his spontaneous responses with his calculated acts. In the case of literature he accomplishes this through an oxymoronic vocabulary: he praises 'good, coarse, marketable stuff', 'the genius of vulgarity', 'Honest journey-work . . . rubbish . . . of fine quality', 'a wholesome commonplace'. More generally, he cultivates a tone of apparently self-critical candour. Continually speaking 'frankly' and 'simply', full of locutions like 'to tell the truth' and 'to put it plainly', he heads off attacks on his stratagems by briskly confessing them first. Jasper's technique might be summarized as 'candour equals self-absolution'. It enables him to justify himself while claiming that he offers no justification. More important, it enables him to lie while gaining credit for the truth. For of course, while always making a show of putting his cards on the table, he is careful to keep quite a few up his sleeve. Jasper degenerates in the course of the novel as the logic of his specious position is worked out. At first his frankness has a genuine connection with his boyish enthusiasm and vigour. Later he exploits it more consciously, luring Marian with 'the unusual openness of his talk', speaking not candidly but 'in a tone of candour'. Jasper's end is implicit in his beginning. His treatment of Marian is ominously latent in his literary manifesto.

New Grub Street takes for granted that literary values are applicable to life. When books are converted to commodities, people are reduced to investments. Gissing facilitates the association by describing literature in moral terms. Reardon shrinks 'from conscious insincerity of workmanship'. Yule might have been more successful had he 'been content to manufacture a novel or a play with due disregard for literary honour' (like his rival Fadge, perhaps, who specializes in 'malicious flippancy'). Biffen tries to write without the suggestion 'of any point of view save that of honest reporting'. He labours over *Mr Bailey, Grocer* 'patiently, affectionately, scrupulously'. Biffen, of course, is a self-styled realist and Reardon, too, though repelled by Biffen's subject, is 'a psychological realist in the sphere of culture'. In 1895 Gissing published an article on 'The place of realism in fiction'. After making a number

of telling distinctions, he concluded by defining realism as 'nothing more than artistic sincerity in the portrayal of contemporary life'. In so far as sincerity is a moral attribute, realism, then, is a literary movement with moral connotations. The relevance to *New Grub Street* is inescapable. Reardon and Biffen are realists not only as novelists but as honest individuals who insist on acknowledging unpleasant facts. The world of Amy and her mother is one of evasion and euphemism. Several of Amy's arguments with Reardon turn on the question of 'realism'—about the admission of their economic plight and the most sensible adjustment to it. Both Amy and Jasper are proud of being 'practical', but their 'practicality' involves untruth. Biffen, hopelessly impractical in their view, is more honestly in touch with the real. Ironically, at the end of the book he allows himself to idealize Amy. The realist dies after fantasy-indulgence: 'He became the slave of his inflamed imagination.'

New Grub Street, an imaginative melting-pot for a number of Gissing's most passionate concerns, is not only an informative sociological document but a skilfully structured psychological study whose social analysis is precisely embodied in its treatment of personal relations. Of course, it has some weaknesses. Written in just under ten weeks—though conceived and planned over a longer period—it occasionally has shoddy patches in the prose and moments of narrative abruptness. Sometimes, too, the tone is disrupted by embarrassingly personal notes: many of these Gissing eliminated when revising the book for a French translation. Overwhelmingly, however, *New Grub Street* survives as a cogent indictment and a moving novel. A tribute to Gissing's will power—'no book of mine', he later confessed, 'was regarded so hopelessly in the production'—it is deeply pessimistic in argument and structure. Its logic is that of a vicious circle: poverty demoralizes; the best escape from poverty is commercialism; but commercialism also demoralizes. Indeed it describes literal circles of frustration: Reardon's false starts and misleading resumptions—'endless circling, perpetual beginning'; his fagged-out pacing in the darkness 'round the outer circle of Regent's Park'; and, at the hub of the novel's action, the great circle of the British Museum Reading-Room, with its figure wandering around the upper gallery like 'a black, lost soul'. In the last analysis, the power of *New Grub Street* is that of a pessimistic parable, an almost infernal conception of injustice. Schopenhauer once said that someone should write a 'tragic history of literature', showing how the truly enlightened authors passed their lives in poverty and misery 'while fame, honour, and wealth went to the unworthy'. In *New Grub Street* Gissing wrote it. (pp. 84-98)

David Grylls, in his The Paradox of Gissing, *Allen & Unwin, 1986, 226 p.*

FURTHER READING

Bibliography

Collie, Michael. *George Gissing: A Bibliographical Study.*

Winchester, England: St. Paul's Bibliographies, 1985, 167 p.
    Comprehensive information regarding the composition, sale, and publication of Gissing's works, including the locations of extant manuscripts.

Biography

Collie, Michael. *George Gissing: A Biography.* Folkestone, England: William Dawson and Sons, 1977, 189 p.
    Biography focusing on the relationship between Gissing's life and his work.

Criticism

Austin, Louis F. "The New Grub Street." *The Illustrated London News* 98, No. 2715 (2 May 1891): 571.
    Contends that Gissing's novel, although well-written, misrepresents the literary world.

Bergonzi, Bernard. "New Grub Street." In his *The Turn of a Century: Essays on Victorian and Modern English Literature,* pp. 45-63. 1973. Reprint. New York: Barnes and Noble, 1974.
    Presents an overview of the major themes and characters of *New Grub Street.*

Bowlby, Rachel. "Making It: Gissing's *New Grub Street.*" In her *Just Looking: Consumer Culture in Dreiser, Gissing and Zola,* pp. 98-117. New York: Methuen, 1985.
    Studies the opinions Gissing and his characters have toward the commercialization of literature.

Collie, Michael. "*The Emancipated* and *New Grub Street.*" In his *The Alien Art: A Critical Study of George Gissing's Novels,* pp. 103-26. Kent: Dawson, 1979.
    Discusses the significance of Gissing's textual alterations to *New Grub Street* in preparation for its French translation by Gabrielle Fleury in 1898.

Colmer, John. "Continuity and Change." In his *Coleridge to Catch-22: Images of Society,* pp. 122-38. New York: St. Martin's Press, 1978.
    Highlights the principal themes and characters of *New Grub Street.*

Cross, Nigel. "Gissing's New Grub Street, 1880-1900," in his *The Common Writer: Life in Nineteenth-Century Grub Street,* pp. 204-40. Cambridge: Cambridge University Press, 1985.
    Describes the London literary marketplace of Gissing's day and categorizes its literary figures according to the various literary types portrayed in *New Grub Street.*

Halperin, John. "The Wrong World, 1889-1891." In his *Gissing: A Life in Books,* pp. 129-73. Oxford: Oxford University Press, 1982.
    Critical biography. The chapter cited above focuses on *New Grub Street.*

Howe, Irving. "George Gissing: Poet of Fatigue." In *Collected Articles on George Gissing,* edited by Pierre Coustillas, pp. 119-25. London: Frank Cass, 1968.
    Assesses Gissing's skill as a novelist and studies the contrasting characters of *New Grub Street.*

Karl, Frederick R. "Five Victorian Novelists." In his *A Reader's Guide to the Nineteenth-Century British Novel,* pp. 323-48. New York: The Noonday Press, 1965.
    Concludes that the overall essence of *New Grub Street* is its overpowering hopeless despair.

Keech, James M. "Gissing's *New Grub Street* and the 'Triple-Headed Monster'." *The Serif* VII, No. 1 (March 1970): 20-4.
    Considers *New Grub Street* a critique of the Victorian three-volume system of publishing novels.

Kropholler, P. F. "*New Grub Street* in Germany." *The Gissing Newsletter* XXIII, No. 2 (April 1987): 39-44.
    Summarizes the opinions of German reviewers on the German translation of *New Grub Street* published in 1986.

Michaux, Jean-Pierre, ed. *George Gissing: Critical Essays.* London: Vision Press, 1981, 214 p.
    This book is divided into two sections: the first consists of general essays about the author; the second section includes thirteen essays about *New Grub Street* by such critics as Angus Wilson, John Goode, George Orwell, and Q. D. Leavis.

Moore, Lewis D. "The Triumph of Mediocrity: George Gissing's *New Grub Street.*" *The Gissing Newsletter* XXIII, No. 1 (January 1987): 1-15.
    Examines the influence of social Darwinism on Gissing's novel.

Murry, J. Middleton. "George Gissing." In his *Katherine Mansfield and Other Literary Studies,* pp. 1-68. London: Constable, 1959.
    Analyzes the autobiographical nature of the characters Edwin Reardon and Alfred Yule.

Pritchett, V. S. "A Chip the Size of a Block." *New Statesman* LV, No. 1422 (14 June 1958): 781-82.
    Discusses the presence of Gissing's reclusive personality in *New Grub Street.*

Selig, Robert L. "Two Major Achievements: *New Grub Street* and *Born in Exile.*" In his *George Gissing,* pp. 53-62. Boston: Twayne Publishers, 1983.
    Summarizes the plot and major issues of *New Grub Street.*

Sloan, John. "The Measure of Success: From *The Emancipated* to *New Grub Street.*" In his *George Gissing: The Cultural Challenge,* pp. 82-102. London: Macmillan Press, 1989.

Explores the aesthetic appeal of Gissing's exposure of the decline of British literary and educational standards.

Additional coverage of Gissing's life and career is contained in the following sources published by Gale Research: *Contemporary Authors,* Vol. 105; *Dictionary of Literary Biography,* Vol. 18; and *Twentieth-Century Literary Criticism,* Vols. 3, 24

Henry James

1843-1916

American novelist, short story and novella writer, essayist, critic, biographer, autobiographer, and dramatist.

The following entry presents recent criticism of James's works. For further discussion of James's entire career, see *TCLC*, Volumes 2 and 11; for discussion of his novella *The Turn of the Screw*, see *TCLC*, Volume 24; for discussion of his novel *The Portrait of a Lady*, see *TCLC*, Volume 40.

INTRODUCTION

James is considered one of the greatest novelists in the English language. He enlarged the scope of the novel by introducing narrative devices unknown before his time. His highly self-conscious narrators prepared the way for the interior monologues of such later writers as James Joyce and Virginia Woolf. Most important, James vigorously advocated a greater realism in American literature, particularly with his criticism and essays on the art of fiction. Besides matters of technical innovation, he brought a number of original themes to American literature. Perhaps the most obvious is the myth of the American abroad—the encounter of the New World with the Old. James incorporated this myth into the "international novel" genre, of which he was both originator and master. But he also dealt with other social and psychological concerns, such as the artist's role in society, the need for both the aesthetic and the moral life, and the benefits of a developed consciousness receptive to the thoughts and feelings of others. According to Van Wyck Brooks, James was most of all a "historian" of his age—an author who interpreted a generation of people on both sides of the Atlantic.

James was born in New York City, the second son of well-to-do, liberal parents. He was a shy, bookish boy who assumed the role of observer beside his active elder brother William, who later became a pioneer of psychological study in America and founder of the philosophical school of Pragmatism. Both Henry and William spent much of their youth traveling between the United States and Europe. They were schooled by tutors and governesses in such diverse environments as Manhattan, Geneva, Paris, and London. Both developed a skill in foreign languages and an understanding of Europe rare among Americans in their time. This constant oscillation between two worlds had a profound effect on James: it became the major theme of his fiction and an attraction throughout his life.

At the age of nineteen James enrolled at Harvard Law School, briefly entertaining thoughts of a professional career. However, this ambition soon changed and he began devoting his study time to reading literature, particularly the works of Honore de Balzac and Nathaniel Hawthorne.

Inspired by the literary atmosphere of Cambridge and Boston, James wrote his first fiction and criticism, his earliest works appearing in the *Continental Monthly,* the *Atlantic Monthly,* and the *North American Review.* He met and formed lifelong friendships with William Dean Howells—then assistant editor at the *Atlantic*—Charles Eliot Norton, and James Russell Lowell. Howells was to become James's editor and literary agent, and together the two could be said to have inaugurated the era of realism in American literature. In 1869 James went abroad for his first adult encounter with Europe. While in London he was taken by the Nortons to meet some of England's greatest writers, including George Eliot, John Ruskin, Dante Gabriel Rossetti, and Alfred Lord Tennyson. The year 1869 also marked the death of James's beloved young cousin Minny Temple, for whom he had formed a deep emotional attachment. This shock, and the intensity of his experiences in Europe, provided much of the material that would later figure in such works as *The Portrait of a Lady* and *The Wings of the Dove.*

James returned to the United States in 1870 determined to discover whether he could live and write in his native country. During this time he wrote his first novel, *Watch and Ward* (unpublished until 1878), and "A Passionate Pilgrim," his first significant American-European tale. However, after a winter of unremitting hackwork in New York, James became convinced that he could write better and live more cheaply abroad. In 1875 he moved permanently to Europe, settling first in Rome, then in Paris, where he was admitted into the renowned circle of Gustave Flaubert, Emile Zola, Guy de Maupassant, Alphonse Daudet, and Ivan Turgenev. He greatly admired the French writers, but felt closest to Turgenev, who confirmed his own view that a novelist need not worry about "story," but should focus exclusively on character. Eventually James settled in London, where he found the people and conditions best suited to his imagination. He wasted no time in producing the early novels which would establish his reputation—*Roderick Hudson, The American,* and *The Europeans.* Though James earned recognition with his first European novels, he did not gain popular success until the publication of *Daisy Miller* and *The Portrait of a Lady.* The latter mark the end of what critics consider the first period in his career. Throughout the following decades he progressed toward more complex effects in his novels and stories. Because of his experiments he eventually lost the popularity that he had achieved with *Daisy Miller* and *The Portrait of a Lady.* Many critics suggest that growing neglect by the public induced him to try his hand as a playwright. However, after several attempts at drama—most notably his dramatization of *The American,* and his new productions, *Guy Domville* and *The High Bid,* all of which failed at the box office—James gave up the theater.

The years 1898 to 1904 were the most productive of James's literary career. During this period he brought out several volumes of stories as well as the consummate novels of his late maturity—*The Wings of the Dove, The Ambassadors,* and *The Golden Bowl.* After 1904 James's health and creativity began to decline. Though he still produced a sizeable amount of work, consisting mainly of his autobiographies, essays, and criticism, he finished only one novel, *The Outcry.* With the outbreak of the First World War, James devoted much of his remaining energy to serving the Allied cause, and when the United States did not immediately back the Allies he assumed British citizenship in protest against his native land. On his deathbed the following year he received the British Order of Merit.

Most critics divide James's career into three periods. In the first, from 1876 to the mid-1880s, he established himself as the originator of the international novel and a masterful portrayer of American character. In such early works as *Roderick Hudson, The American,* and *The Europeans,* James explored the effects of European civilization and corruption on Americans. Both the tragedy and the humor in this situation consist in the protagonists' insistence on partaking of the European experience without sacrificing their New World innocence. Numerous critics have interpreted the stories of James's protagonists as a quest for identity, or, more specifically, as a passion to enter into the history of civilization. In *Roderick Hudson* James first explored his concern with the artist's role in society, a theme which pervades much of his middle and late fiction. Here the European experience is merged with the story of a young American sculptor who struggles between his art and his passions. James ended this first phase of his career by producing what many critics consider the most balanced of all his novels, *The Portrait of a Lady,* which concerns expatriate American society in England and Italy. This novel is considered a profound study of a young woman from upstate New York who brings to Europe her provincialism and moral pretensions, but who also demonstrates a sense of sovereignty and a "free spirit" capable of living greatly at odds with the Victorian world. *The Portrait of a Lady* is a convincing demonstration of James's shrewd insight into character and his understanding of the role power plays in personal relations.

The second period, from the mid-1880s to 1897, is often considered a transitional phase in James's career. Many of the novels and stories written during this time are marked by what critics have described as an advance in form and narrative technique. He also abandoned his "international" theme and began focusing on the clash between art and life, aesthetics and social morality—particularly in such short stories and novellas as "The Lesson of the Master," "The Real Thing," "The Beast in the Jungle," and *The Aspern Papers.* The 1880s also saw the publication of two novels dealing specifically with contemporary social issues: *The Bostonians,* which depicts the struggle between a conservative Southerner living in New England and a man-hating suffragette, and *The Princess Casamassima,* in which James portrayed the downward path of a young man who toys with and is eventually destroyed by revolution. Considered the most significant work of this period

is *The Tragic Muse,* because it signified James's growing interest in the world of drama. Stung over the neglect of his once-large reading public, he turned to the theater during the 1890s in hope of regaining his popularity. His dramatization of *The American* was a modest success, but his attempts at comedy, and his one historical play—*Guy Domville*—proved that James lacked the qualities to become a successful dramatist. However, from his experience he brought back to his novels a new commitment to economy in writing and an extraordinary aptitude for framing fictional situations in a scenic and dramatic manner.

The third and final period of James's career, from 1897 to his death, saw the full development of techniques he had begun using during the 1880s. With the publication of such works as *The Spoils of Poynton, What Maisie Knew, The Turn of the Screw,* and *The Awkward Age,* he refined the methods of "scenic" progression, the point-of-view narration—which he narrowed to a single angle of vision—and the art of "indirect suggestion." The subjects of this period are the expanding consciousness of the individual, the moral education of children, and the clash between subjective and external realities. James even experimented with psychic phenomena—such as projected fantasies and repressed hysteria—and the reliability of language itself in *The Turn of the Screw.* However, the most important works of this final period are the three novels written at the beginning of the century: *The Wings of the Dove, The Ambassadors,* and *The Golden Bowl.* The first of these is the story of a dying American heiress, and, more specifically, of those characters who seek to inherit her fortune. Though the subject borders on the melodramatic, James managed to create a moving study of a well-intentioned individual who becomes the victim of her own graces. Most critics view the character of Milly Theale as the apogee of James's American innocent, a figure so weak and pure that she suggests the Christlike heroines in Fyodor Dostoevsky's stories. *The Ambassadors* again shows James's talent for investing a limited plot with grandeur and elegance. The novel is essentially a high comedy of American and European manners, as a middle-aged, self-satisfied American named Lambert Strether undertakes a mission to Paris to bring back the son of a wealthy provincial family. The irony of the story turns on Strether's accomplishing his mission against his will, for the young man agrees to return home even though Strether, now captivated by Parisian life, urges him to stay. *The Golden Bowl* is James's final novel of significance and is regarded as the most symbolic and richest in poetic imagery of all his works. Among the most complex of James's novels, *The Golden Bowl* incorporates a number of his characteristic themes: the marriage of American and European cultures, the conflict of innocence and experience, the "knowledge" of sin, and—specifically through the character of Maggie Verver—moral redemption.

Critical interest in James's work has risen steadily since the centennial of his birth in 1943. Throughout much of his career he was regarded as a "writer's writer," particularly during his middle and mature years. The average reader was, and often still is, apt to find him verbose, complex, at times awkward, and overly concerned with matters of social propriety. Many early critics accused him of indulging his talents for his own pleasure. The most common attacks held that his stories lacked the necessary action to sustain interest and, more seriously, that they had no relation to events in the real world. The two novels in which James awkwardly tried to deal with social issues—*The Bostonians* and *The Princess Casamassima*—were proof to these critics that he lacked the imagination to produce anything but romantic portraits. This attitude resulted in the author's near obscurity following the First World War, a period when the social and psychological dilemmas of leisured upper-class characters seemed particularly inconsequential. However, through the work of such critics as F. O. Matthiessen, F. W. Dupee, and Leon Edel, a revival of interest in James's work took place in the 1940s and 1950s. Those who approached his work unburdened with stereotypes and prejudices found a skilled technician and a master at presenting the subtleties of human character. By the 1960s most critics realized the depth of James's fiction. No longer were his plots considered mere contests between innocent Americans and a corrupt Europe; discerning readers deciphered his symbols and found a broad philosophical and psychological interest. Many critics began interpreting James's novels and stories according to previously established myths, such as the Fall of Man, the figure of Christ, the Nietzschean notion of the "created self," and the famous battleground of the conscious ego and subconscious alter ego. Today most scholars believe James's position is firmly established as one of the most imposing figures in twentieth-century literature.

PRINCIPAL WORKS

A Passionate Pilgrim, and Other Tales (short stories) 1875
Roderick Hudson (novel) 1876
The American (novel) 1877
The Europeans (novel) 1878
French Poets and Novelists (criticism) 1878
Watch and Ward (novel) 1878
Daisy Miller (novel) 1879
Hawthorne (criticism) 1879
The Madonna of the Future, and Other Tales (short stories) 1879
Confidence (novel) 1880
The Portrait of a Lady (novel) 1881
Washington Square (novel) 1881
*Daisy Miller [first publication] (drama) 1883
The Siege of London. Madame de Mauves (novellas) 1883
A Little Tour in France (travel essays) 1885
The Bostonians (novel) 1886
The Princess Casamassima (novel) 1886
The Aspern Papers. Louisa Pallant. The Modern Warning (novellas) 1888
Partial Portraits (criticism) 1888
A London Life (short stories) 1889
The Tragic Muse (novel) 1890
The American (drama) 1891

The Real Thing, and Other Tales (short stories) 1893
Guy Domville (drama) 1895
Theatricals. Two Comedies: Tenants, Disengaged [first publication] (dramas) 1895
Theatricals, second series: The Album, The Reprobate [first publication] (dramas) 1895
The Other House (novel) 1897
The Spoils of Poynton (novel) 1897
What Maisie Knew (novel) 1897
The Two Magics: The Turn of the Screw, Covering End (novellas) 1898
The Awkward Age (novel) 1899
The Sacred Fount (novel) 1901
The Wings of the Dove (novel) 1902
The Ambassadors (novel) 1903
The Golden Bowl (novel) 1904
English Hours (travel essays) 1905
The American Scene (travel essays) 1907
The Novels and Tales of Henry James. 24 vols. (novels, novellas, and short stories) 1907-09
The High Bid (drama) 1908
Views and Reviews (criticism) 1908
Italian Hours (travel essays) 1909
The Outcry (novel) 1911
A Small Boy and Others (autobiography) 1913
Notes of a Son and Brother (autobiography) 1914
Notes on Novelists, with Some Other Notes (criticism) 1914
The Ivory Tower (unfinished novel) 1917
The Middle Years (unfinished autobiography) 1917
The Sense of the Past (unfinished novel) 1917
Within the Rim, and Other Essays (essays) 1918
The Letters of Henry James. 2 vols. (letters) 1920
Notes and Reviews (criticism) 1921
The Art of the Novel (criticism) 1934
The Notebooks of Henry James (notebooks) 1947
The Complete Plays of Henry James (dramas) 1949

*This drama is an adaptation of the novel *Daisy Miller.*

CRITICISM

William James (letter date 1905)

[*One of the most influential figures in modern Western philosophy, James was the founder of the philosophical movement of Pragmatism. In such works as* The Principles of Psychology (1890) *and* The Varieties of Religious Experience (1902), *James attempted to comprehend and to describe human life as it is actually experienced, rather than formulating models of abstract reality far removed from the passion and pain of life. In the following excerpt, he criticizes his brother's allusive style in* The Golden Bowl *(for Henry James's response, see the excerpt below).*]

It put me, as most of your recenter long stories have put me, in a very puzzled state of mind. I don't enjoy the kind of 'problem,' especially when, as in this case, it is treated as problematic (*viz.,* the adulterous relations between Charlotte and the Prince), and the method of narration by interminable elaboration of suggestive reference (I don't know what to call it, but you know what I mean) goes agin the grain of all my own impulses in writing; and yet in spite of it all, there is a brilliancy and cleanness of effect, and in this book especially a high-toned social atmosphere that are unique and extraordinary. Your methods and my ideals seem the reverse, the one of the other—and yet I have to admit your extreme success in this book. But why won't you, just to please Brother, sit down and write a new book, with no twilight or mustiness in the plot, with great vigor and decisiveness in the action, no fencing in the dialogue, no psychological commentaries, and absolute straightness in the style? Publish it in my name, I will acknowledge it, and give you half the proceeds. Seriously, I wish you *would,* for you *can;* and I should think it would tempt you, to embark on a 'fourth manner.' You of course know these feelings of mine without my writing them down, but I'm 'nothing if not' outspoken. Meanwhile you can despise me and fall back on such opposite emotions as Howells's, who seems to admire you without restriction, as well as on the records of the sale of the book.

William James, in a letter to Henry James in October, 1905, in Henry James: The Critical Heritage, *edited by Roger Gard, 1968. Reprint by Routledge & Kegan Paul, 1986, p. 392.*

Henry James   (letter date 1905)

[*In the following excerpt, James responds to his brother's criticism of* The Golden Bowl *(see the excerpt above).*]

I mean (in response to what you write me of your having read the **Golden B.**) to try to produce some uncanny form of thing, in fiction, that will gratify you, as Brother—but let me say, dear William, that I shall greatly be humiliated if you *do* like it, and thereby lump it, in your affection, with things, of the current age, that I have heard you express admiration for and that I would sooner descend to a dishonoured grave than have written. Still I *will* write you your book, on that two-and-two-make-four system on which all the awful truck that surrounds us is produced, and *then* descend to my dishonoured grave—taking up the art of the slate pencil instead of, longer, the art of the brush (vide my lecture on Balzac.) But it is, seriously, too late at night, and I am too tired, for me to express myself on this question—beyond saying that I'm always sorry when I hear of your reading anything of mine, and always hope you won't—you seem to me so constitutionally unable to 'enjoy' it, and so condemned to look at it from a point of view remotely alien to mine in writing it, and to the conditions out of which, *as* mine, it has inevitably sprung—so that all the intentions that have been its main reason for being (with *me*) appear never to have reached you at all—and you appear even to assume that the life, the elements forming its subject-matter, deviate from felicity in not having an impossible analogy with the life of Cambridge. I see nowhere about me done or dreamed of the things that alone for me constitute the *interest* of the doing of the novel—and yet it is in a sacrifice of them on

their very own ground that the thing you suggest to me evidently consists. It shows how far apart and to what different ends we have had to work out (very naturally and properly!) our respective intellectual lives. (pp. 393-94)

Henry James, in a letter to William James in November, 1905, in Henry James: The Critical Heritage, *edited by Roger Gard, 1968. Reprint by Routledge & Kegan Paul, 1986, pp. 393-94.*

V. S. Pritchett   (essay date 1980)

[*Pritchett is a highly esteemed English novelist, short story writer, and critic. Considered one of the modern masters of the short story, he is also one of the world's most respected literary critics. A twentieth-century successor to such early nineteenth-century essayist-critics as William Hazlitt and Charles Lamb, Pritchett employs much the same critical method: his own experience, judgement, and sense of literary art are emphasized, rather than a codified critical doctrine derived from a school of psychological or philosophical speculation. In the following excerpt, Pritchett comments on James's* The American Scene.]

Henry James's **The American Scene** is still one of the very few excellent books of travel by an American about his own country. He is as exact and prophetic in his own restricted way as the extraordinary and very different Tocqueville was in his. The book is unique in a genre where—strangely enough, among a foot-loose people—American literature is very poor; for penetrating observation and evocation of the land and the cities we have to turn to novels and, above all, poetry. The remarkable thing about the book is that although it was written in 1905, and in spite of the huge changes that have occurred in America since that time, it presents (as Leon Edel says in a troubled introduction) an essential America that is still recognizable.

This ought not to surprise us: great artists are always farseeing. They easily avoid the big stumbling blocks of fact. They rely on their own simplicity and vision. It is factfetishism that has given us those scores and scores of American books on America, the works of sociologists, anthropologists, topical 'problem' hunters, workingparties and statisticians, which in the end leave us empty. Henry James succeeds because he rejects information. He was himself the only information he required.

> It should be unfailingly proved against me that my opportunity found me incapable of imparting information, incapable alike of receiving and imparting it; for then, and then only, would it be clearly attested that I *had* cared and understood.

He was looking for a personal relationship to the scene he had left twenty years before. In so many other books on the country the sense of a relation is lacking; indeed, they leave one with an impression of a lonely continent, uncontemplated, unloved, unfelt by a people who have got so much out of it, as they move on, that they see little in it and give or leave nothing of themselves to the scene. How else to explain that sensation of things, places, even people abandoned which is so painful in the American landscape! How often one has felt what James sensed about certain American scenes, especially in New England:

> And that was doubtless, for the story seeker, absolutely the story: the constituted blankness was the whole business, and one's opportunity was all, thereby, for a study of exquisite emptiness.

Or:

> Charming places, charming objects, languish all round, under designations that seem to leave on them the smudge of a great vulgar thumb—which is precisely a part of the pleading land appears to hint to you when it murmurs, in autumn, its intelligent refrain. If it feels itself better than so many phases of its fate, so there are spots where you see it turn up at you, under some familiar tasteless inflections of this order, the plaintive eye of a creature wounded with a poisoned arrow.

Henry James knew what the poison was. It would eventually wreck the American cities—a process our planners, always out of date, are eager to imitate in England today.

James was a traveller, that is to say, a story-seeker to the marrow. His novels themselves are conscious journeys into the interior. He had started by writing travel sketches of things in France, Italy and Germany and England when he was young; the 'vignettes' of a sentimental traveller, meant to tease the American fancy for the Atlantic trip. *The American Scene* is a totally different matter. Perhaps at the age of sixty the returning expatriate originally promised himself one more sentimental pilgrimage. But in twenty years American life had passed through a crucial change. It could either sink him or raise him by the challenge. He was roused. Half the pleasure of the book comes from the sight of a travelling mind reinvigorated. He met the challenge with a richer and revived analytical gift. He rejected the journalistic temptation. In the twenty years since 1883 a huge immigrant invasion had changed the character of the cities; big business, the great industrial monopolies, had taken total power and had imposed the business ethos; the pursuit of money had become the engulfing and only justifying role. New York had been a rough, low-built sea port with pigs rooting in the streets of lower Manhattan when he left, Central Park was a farmland. He returned to find all Manhattan crammed, and the skyscrapers rising—'simply the most piercing notes in that concert of the expensively provisional into which your supreme sense of New York resolves'.

James ignored the colossal news item. He saw that his subject was not shock and that he was not there to advertise or boost the obvious. His subject was how the consciousness of a half-repentant expatriate would be affected, and what inner meanings and sensibilities he could offer in return. Guilt there would be, but distaste: nostalgia for what was gone, but a feeling for the drama; he would have to be both personal and yet the analyst. He became the seeker. He would have to lay himself open to the full bewilderment of his situation. In his introduction to an earlier edition of this book, W. H. Auden described it as a prose poem; an excellent description. Generously evocative and

labyrinthine in its tact, it also shows a man struggling with love and menace. The skyscrapers are a 'vocabulary of thrift' but there are 'uglier words' for that. With mild but deadly truth they evoke (he says)

> the consciousness of the finite, the menaced, the essentially *invented* state [that] twinkles ever, to my perception, in the thousand glassy eyes of those giants of the market.

Again and again, he remarks on the 'pathos' of a civilization so exuberantly on the move, but bewildered in having to accept itself as temporary. Of the new rich he writes:

> What had it been their idea to *do*, the good people . . . do that is, in affirming their wealth with such innocent emphasis and yet not at the same time affirming anything else.

They live in houses that have

> the candid look of costing as much as they knew how. Unmistakably they all proclaimed it—they would have cost still more had the way but been shown to them; and, meanwhile, they added, as with one voice, they would take a fresh start as soon as ever it should be. 'We are only instalments, symbols, stop-gaps', they practically admitted, and with no shade of embarrassment: 'expensive we are, we have nothing to do with continuity, responsibility, transmission, and don't in the least care what becomes of us after we have served our present purpose'.

And the governing motive:

> To make so much money that you won't, that you don't 'mind' anything.

Not, as it has turned out, the awful sight of American cities. If you do 'mind' you can easily become an un-American activity.

For James, America was 'dancing on the thin crust of a volcano'. In personal relationships

> the most that was as yet accomplished . . . was the air of unmitigated publicity, publicity as a condition, as a doom from which there could be no appeal.

There was the inability to communicate, which was not felt as a loss among the new immigrants, but rather as a gain; they had become American. James, the native, puts his finger on what often dismays the chatty European traveller in his casual contacts: the American chill.

To isolate James's hostile impressions as I have done or to quote his final denunciation of the reigning spirit of the time—a denunciation which did not appear in the first American edition—is to give a misleading impression of a book warm in feeling and rich in texture. Every page contains a picture or a phrase that will bring New York, Boston, the scrub forest of New Hampshire, to the eyes, but backed by his long loving knowledge of the places. He records such deeply American things as allowing the forest to come down to the edges of the innumerable lakes. The story seeker, as he calls himself, continually questions the landscape in relation to himself, and it is the self-questioning which is at the heart of his ability to create the scene in the superb chapter on New Hampshire. Why does it seem to be Arcadian? Why was he always brought back to the thought that the woods and rocks insist on referring themselves to the idyllic? Was it because they bore no burden of history? The thought charms him, but another thought makes him sceptical: perhaps he rhapsodized now, because in Europe he had been deprived

> to excess—that is for too long—of naturalism in quantity. Here it was in such quantity as one hadn't for years to deal with; and that might by itself be a luxury corrupting the judgment.

The irony is subtle; but hasn't James hit exactly upon what drifts through one's mind as one drives the scores of miles through the scrub, the brown rock and grey rock of New England, or stands by some clear cold pond in the woods—the lyrical and, at the same time, crushing quantity of Nature, stupefying the mind? How much the love of quantity, together with its inexorable, umbrageous detail, has meant to an American mind.

James spent about a year as a returned native. Business and immigration were the important themes, alien to him and to his natural nostalgias; no searching was needed as far as business was concerned. That hit one in the face. The immigrants were more difficult, but he took a lot of trouble to see what was happening on New York's lower East Side.

There, as a writer, he was as excited as he was disturbed by what would happen to the language, and to character. How long would the melting take? Then he went South, and any romantic hopes he had were pinched by wretched weather and the general shabbiness. He is still good, but he is better on native ground. He discovered that Washington was the place where, for once, men ruled the conversation. Outside of known, friendly haunts, he had been starved of two things in America: conversation—all that was offered was talk—and privacy. He hated the open interior of the American club and house. But if, inevitably, he harks back to the times when a home was not a house, when locality existed and the tycoons were unknown, if he denounces the new age and sees it will lead to worse, he is soundly American in admiring the drama of the situation and in his feeling for the extravagant.

The search for the story, the inturned Jamesian story, is at once pertinacious and very touching. He creates an America because he creates himself in relation to it. The book is a true work of travel because it is a collaboration and with a living country that scatters a myriad unanswered questions about 'as some monstrous unnatural mother might leave a family of unfathered infants on door steps or in waiting rooms'. (pp. 131-37)

> *V. S. Pritchett, "Henry James 'Birth of a Hermaphrodite'," in his* The Tale Bearers: Literary Essays, *Random House, 1980, pp. 120-37.*

Darshan Singh Maini   (essay date 1982)

[*In the following excerpt, Maini examines James's literary criticism.*]

In the course of his long industry, James had the occasion to comment on some of the major critics of his time, and the long essays on such critics as Matthew Arnold and the French Taine, Saint-Beuve, M. Schérer, in particular, enable him to dwell on the dynamics of criticism and to offer views that in certain ways forestall the modern theories of the New Critics, linguistic and stylistic critics, on the one hand, and of the Geneva critics and the phenomenologists, on the other. All these ramifications . . . help establish his *modernity* in the field of criticism in the same way his novels and tales do in the realm of fiction.

In an important essay called **"The Science of Criticism"** (1891), James regards "the critical sense" as something "absolutely rare" and the critic as the artist's "brother" in vision and exercise, a person made absolute through the energies and economies of his own craft. As he puts it, "in literature criticism is the critic, just as art is the artist." In his essay on Maupassant (1888), James again implies that just as a tale is "a direct impression of life"—a view more fully and insightfully aired in **"The Art of Fiction"** (1884)—a really creative work of criticism is a direct impression of a poem or a play or a novel as it invades the responding imagination. In each case, the intervening temperament or sensibility or psyche brings the sum of impressions to a focus. And he quotes Maupassant's statement to the effect that "every theory is a generalized expression of temperament asking itself questions." And finally, in the article on M. Schérer as a critic, written as early as 1865, James insists upon the same virtues in a critic that he does in a novelist. It is "the moral sense" leading to the "spiritual force" that "animates, coordinates and harmonizes" the mass of opinions and impressions, whether the vessel is one or the other. That is why his criticism and his fiction eventually form a continuing grid of moral energies.

The emerging Jamesian theory of the novel, as it begins to acquire critical weight and to assume the dimensions of a philosophy of fiction . . . , may briefly be summed up thus: The novel, in his view, was the freest form of fabulation and therefore showed an unlimited appetite for all forms and aspects of reality. It could literally appropriate the most complex and intimate as well as the remotest shades of human experience. As he put it in **"The Future of the Novel"** (1899), "it will take in absolutely anything. . . . But for its subject, magnificently it has the whole human consciousness." And though James insists on the directness of the impressions and thus on the authenticity of experience, he is not unaware of the question of typicality. Indeed, what he desires most is a synthesis of the uniquely individual and the known universal in human experience. For he believed that the imagination can appropriate things and that, beyond a point, it turns appropriately into an imagination of proxy. The life of the mind is an experience in itself, and feeding, like the birds of the air, on invisible manna, it goes back homing to the life of the senses—"the aesthetic life" of Kierkegaard.

Again, James's idea of the organic nature of the novel is best seen in his repeated references to the "germs" and "seeds" of his own stories in the prefaces, though he employs such metaphors in relation to the principle of development in the works of those novelists in particular that come closest to his moral-organicistic view of things. It is in this sense that we may regard the Jamesian concept of the novel as an expanding metaphor. Similarly, almost from the beginning of his critical exercise, James stipulates an organic link between form and substance, technique and theme, vision and style. In all his aesthetic gropings and strivings, "the search for form" is almost a mystic pursuit, and the achieved novel a consummation. No wonder the relationship between the theme and the form is viewed, particularly in the prefaces, in terms of "marriage" and "sacrament," etc.

Above all, James is fascinated by the novel as a form of fabulation best suited to bring out the moral energies of man. In that running argument that broadly distinguishes the English novel from the French in scores of reviews and articles, he keeps elaborating the point that the very structure of the novel envisages an engagement of the moral imagination. And he quotes, with approval, the view of one of the Goncourts that "the novel is ethics in action." It is the element of moral lyricism in George Eliot, for instance, that makes her, above everything else, almost Shakespearian in James's view.

There is, to be sure, no hard-and-fast theory of the novel in Henry James. His frequent use of a mixed critical lexicon based on analogies and correspondences from painting, architecture, geometry, tapestry, music, etc., would testify to his unending quest. The virtues he admired most in the novel may be listed as movement, density, vividness, intensity, resilience, economy, objectivity, coherence, moral energy, rhetoric, and poetry. James was not a very original thinker, but the majesty of his critical imagination was so striking as to give his thought a luminous quality.

Though what James looks for in a writer is finally much more than the energies of language, there is no doubt that the question of style has for him an importance that simply overtops everything else. This is because, for him, style is not only the signature of the writer's psyche, carrying the aroma of the personality in action, but is also at once a mode of comprehending reality and an aspect of reality. It has a cognitive function; and it is in this sense that style *becomes* insight, that it informs a writer's *Weltanschauung* in the end. All these ideas that are now commonplaces of stylistic criticism are naturally not aired with any kind of doctrinal belief or urgency in James's own comments on the style of the writers he takes up for consideration, though the underlying assumptions lead one inevitably in that direction. In the essay on Gabriele D'Annunzio, for instance, he observes that "there is no complete creation without style any more than there is complete music without sound," and he goes on to talk even of the "style of substance as well as of form." My purpose here, however, is to confine the question to the poetic aspects of style insofar as poetry relates to the essence of things and to the uniqueness of language. I trust that a sampling of James's comments should suffice to settle the issue.

On Carlyle's style: "its avalanche movement, . . . as if a mass of earth and rock and vegetation had detached itself and come bouncing and bumping forward. . . . the quality of race and soil." Clearly it is the turbulent Protestant and Scottish personality, with its moral monism and the imagination of indignation, that James wishes to highlight in relation to the rhetoric and style of Carlyle.

On Shakespeare: In *The Tempest,* says James, the Bard of Avon after a stormy passage in life achieves "the lucid stillness of his style," and, he adds, Shakespeare "points for us as no one else the relations of style to meaning, and of manner to motive."

On Stevenson: James refers, among other things, to Stevenson's romance of words—"a kind of gallantry as if language were a pretty woman." The jauntiness "of Stevenson's style is seen as his engagement with the romance of boyhood"—the sense of youth and the idea of play. On its uniqueness thus: "His special stock of association, most personal style and most unteachable trick fly away again to him like so many strayed birds to nest, each with the flutter in its beak of some scrap of document or legend, some fragment of picture or story, to be retouched, revarnished and reframed."

On Alphonse Daudet: The French writer's light impressionistic style is something that is a feast for the eye and a music for the ear. Daudet, he says, "discovers everywhere the shimmer and the murmur of the poetic. . . . His style is impregnated with the southern sunshine and his talent has the sweetness of a fruit that has grown in the warm, open air." And yet James is also conscious of the nervous energies of this style: "The author's style has taken on bone and muscle, and become conscious of treasures of nervous agility."

On Théophile Gautier: Gautier, observes James, loved words for their "aroma" and for their "colour"—"a bit of Keats gallicized." Again, "Half the charm of his writing is in the mere curl and flutter of his phrase." However, James is careful enough to add that his enjoyment of Gautier's style did not prevent him from seeing him as "a very philistine of philistines" where the higher moral consciousness is concerned. The "gaiety" of Gautier's style, then, is purely and simply a question of his Gallic temperament.

On George Sand: "Her language had to the end an odour of the hawthorne and the wild honeysuckle." Even as James laments the "want of moral taste" in her, he admires her art, for it is "open to all experience, all emotions, all convictions." Comparing her style with that of Balzac, he adds, "Madame Sand's novels have plenty of style but they have no form. Balzac's have not a shred of style, but they have a great deal of form."

On Pierre Loti: Loti's vivid and striking descriptions of the sea hold James's imagination in awe, and yet he notes with regret that "the French imagination has none but a sensual conscience."

Though all manner of beauties and felicities are found lurking in James's critical pieces, and though some of his remarks on the popular women novelists of his day and on a variety of other writers constitute their own kind and order of criticism, it is only in the case of his favorite novelists (his criticism of contemporary poetry being both meagre and insignificant, on the whole) that his imagination rises to meet the critical challenge in full faith and force. The EML book on Hawthorne, the essay on him, and the essays on George Eliot, Trollope, Stevenson, H. G. Wells, Daudet, Gautier, Loti, Balzac, Flaubert, Maupassant, George Sand, and Turgenev, in particular, carry his most valuable and pondered criticism that in certain ways would always remain something rare and refined, a collector's criticism, if you like. Here is how he sums up Hawthorne's genius in the concluding paragraphs of his book on Hawthorne: "He combined in a singular degree the spontaneity of the imagination with a haunting care for moral problems. Man's conscience was his theme," and later he describes him as "an aesthetic solitary" whose "beautiful, light imagination is the wing that on the autumn evening just brushes the dusty shadow." And who but James could have so penetratingly seen that George Eliot "succeeds better in drawing attitudes of feeling than in drawing movements of feeling?" Even at the age of twenty-two, when he set out to review books, James observed that Trollope was a master of "small effects" but that "nothing" in him "is infused." As for Balzac, James recognizes the French passion for precision, completeness, and symmetry in his work and "that huge, all-compressing, all-desiring, all-devouring love of reality." But to reach this conclusion, he uses one of his favorite forms of criticism—comparative criticism. "When we approach Thackeray and George Eliot, George Sand and Turgenieff it is into the conscience and the mind that we enter, and we think of the writers primarily as great consciences and great minds. When we approach Balzac we seem to enter into a great temperament—a prodigious nature. He strikes us half the time as an extraordinary physical phenomenon." . . . In a late essay, **"The Lesson of Balzac"** (1905), James shows how absorbed he was in the great globe of French life through tireless observation, on the one hand, through intuition and economy of art, on the other. Though the spiritual life of Balzac's characters remains largely costumed, his mastery of the interlocking determinants and of the chemistry of social relationships and societal pressures makes him an unrivalled chronicler of the Gallic temperament and character. Again, in a handsome and high tribute to that "beautiful genius," Turgenev, James admires the marriage of realism and poetry in the work of the great Russian writer. He thus calls him "the novelist's novelist"—a master spirit in worshipful labor, supremely attuned to the moral rhythms of life.

The manner and style of James's criticism, as I have hinted earlier, changes almost imperceptibly from phase to phase in the manner of his fiction. There is a continual shading off of colors and tints. While the earlier apprentice pieces have, at their best, a certain economy of line and shape as in a pencil-sketch, a crystalline purity and a water-color impressionism characterize the criticism of the middle period. As we begin to view the heavy oils of the final phase, we realize that the earlier traits of economy and purity and lambency are not entirely lost; only they are now subsumed in the *chromatics* of his criticism. In short, James's criticism has been moving from the beauty and poetry of a Whistler to the intensity and visionary depth of a Rembrandt. While the earlier criticism is without cobwebs and codicils, on the whole, the later essays and critiques have a density of thought, imagery, and style

that constitute a kind of critical hieroglyphics. An effort of the imagination is needed to decipher the code and to relate the ideas to their rhetorical resonance. In fact, the element of "muddlement" in this criticism has the same aesthetic sanction as it has in the novels of the final phase.

To be sure, James's criticism also shows the same kind of weaknesses and limitations that his fiction does. A curious element of meretriciousness is perilously close to its riches and splendors, and an air of unreality seems to reduce certain pieces to a rhetorical exercise. There is in some of the earliest reviews even a patronizing, presumptuous tone that is as exasperating in its own way as is the gratuitously involved nature of some of his later and larger essays. Also, there is a danger, here and there, of a volume under reviewing disappearing altogether from the scene, leaving the reader with the critic's own whimsies and fancies. Also, it is quite possible, particularly in some of the prefaces and in some later essays, that the reverberations we hear have a hollowness or that in this piece or that what we find at the end of a long ordeal of critical engagement is not a jewel, but a vapour. But these are the hazards of James's criticism, and they are to be accepted as part of the Jamesian effect. For when his critical imagination is in full cry, it goes ahunting with a whip in hand, starting a whole school of hares and then running them to ground with an ease that leaves the reader gasping in awe and admiration. Even in the midst of all such detours and meanderings, so characteristic of the later style, there is a certain kind of intellectual tenacity and single-mindedness that is hard to come by in fiction criticism.

As in the animated and ambassadorial prose of the final phase, there is in his later criticism a tendency toward a very elaborate and complex type of imagery. Apart from a touch of intellectual colloquialism, there is a shift from mechanical to organicistic imagery. For instance, the earlier reviews and articles abound in the imagery of food, house, coin, carriage, etc., while the later essays are rich in the imagery of seed, blossom, fruit, and tree, of germ, birth, and growth. There are even metaphysical turns and twists and leaps quite in keeping with "the indirect vision" of the final years. (pp. 194-98)

It is only when his fiction and his criticism are read in tandem that we may truly realize the nature of the miracle called Henry James.

To sum up, it may be affirmed that James's *genius* has gone into his fiction and his *talent* into his reviews, critical essays, and prefaces, etc. In short, all that is greatest and strongest and most enduring is to be found in his creative writings; all that is collateral, redemptive, and illustrative finds itself mirrored in his criticism. Each has its own unique charm and its own unique place in James's *oeuvre*. Together they make for an *order of writing* that has few parallels and fewer peers in the English language. For anyone who has savored this criticism and lingered in those leafy and tangled arbors would come away with almost the same kind of awe, admiration, and bewilderment as he would after a sojourn in James's subtle and wrought novels and tales of intelligence. In fact, the *aesthetic* pleasure of James's criticism is not a small component of its appeal and effectiveness. The felicity of his "branched thoughts," to use a Keatsian phrase, is fetching. (pp. 198-99)

> Darshan Singh Maini, "Henry James: The Writer as Critic," in The Henry James Review, Vol. 8, No. 3, Spring, 1982, pp. 189-99.

Leon Edel on James's private persona:

Henry James was acutely conscious of having lived into the new age of journalism and its excessive curiosity about the living great. His private life was private indeed. He could push secrecy to a fine art. He confided in no one. His open, ritualistic life was a mask, and in a late essay on George Sand he repeated in more elaborate form what he had said as a young man and also embodied in one of his late ghostly tales, "The Real Right Thing." This tale has a biographer-hero who in the end finds the ghost of his subject planted in the doorway of the study, warning him to abandon his project. In the essay on George Sand, James deplored—and not without some relish—the manner in which the prolific lady's love affairs were unscrambled in public and the way in which her letters of passion, and those of Chopin and Musset, were given to the world. At the same time a mischievous and slightly boastful note creeps in. He would be careful not to reveal himself. No one would turn *his* pockets inside out.

> Leon Edel, in his Writing Lives: Principia Biographica, W. W. Norton and Company, 1984.

Martha Craven Nussbaum (essay date 1983)

[*Nussbaum is an American philosopher and educator who has written extensively on the treatment of ethical themes in classical and modern literature. In the following excerpt, she discusses James's moral philosophy in* The Golden Bowl *as presented in the character of Maggie Verver.*]

She wants, this woman, to have a flawless life. She says to her good friend Fanny Assingham, "I want a happiness without a hole in it big enough for you to poke in your finger. . . . The golden bowl as it *was* to have been. . . . The bowl with all happiness in it. The bowl without the crack"—signaling in this way to us, who know the properties of this remarkable flawed object, that she wishes her life to be (unlike the bowl) a pure and perfect crystal, completely without crack or seam, both precious and safely hard.

Two features of Maggie Verver's moral life, in the first half of this novel, strike us as salient. One is this assiduous aspiration to perfection, especially moral perfection. The other is the exclusive intensity of her love for her father, the oddness of her marriage to the Prince, which, far from effecting the usual reordering of the commitments and obligations of childhood, has permitted her to gratify, to an extraordinary degree, her "wish to remain, intensely, the same passionate little daughter she had always been." This wish to be without flaw and this desire to remain her father's daughter—we suspect that they must be somehow

connected. And yet the nature of the connection is not altogether obvious, especially since it is far from obvious that this refusal to move from father to husband is a perfect way of living for an adult woman. But I believe that a connection, and a deep one, will emerge if we scrutinize more closely the particular nature of Maggie's moral aspiration. This will be a route into the novel, by which we can begin to appreciate the ways in which James is working here with questions about moral ambition, moralism, and the nature of our worldly relation to value. (pp. 25-6)

Maggie, then, wants to be as good as possible; and when she says this, it is evidently moral goodness that is uppermost in her thoughts. If we ask more closely about what, for her, constitutes moral perfection, we find that the central idea is one of never doing a wrong, never breaking a rule, never hurting. "Maggie had never in her life," her father reflects, "been wrong for more than three minutes." The "note of the felt need of not working harm" the "superstition of not 'hurting' "—these are the concerns pressed urgently by her "quite heroic little sense of justice" in every situation of choice. It does not surprise us that her husband should compare her, in thought, to a Roman *matrona,* bearing "the transmitted image of rather neutral and negative propriety that made up, in his long line, the average of wifehood and motherhood." What sharply sets her apart from this sternly upright figure is, above all, the intensity, the note of real fear, with which she insists on the claims of guiltlessness. In a revealing moment, she compares the requirements of morality (and especially its prohibition of certain bad acts) to the "watertight" insides of an ocean liner: "Water-tight—the biggest compartment of all? Why it's the best cabin and the main deck and the engine-room and the steward's pantry! It's the ship itself—it's the whole line. It's the captain's table and all one's luggage—one's reading for the trip." Morality and its rules of not hurting constitute for her a safe world in which to live and voyage, protected against nameless dangers. If ever a breach were made in the walls of that vessel, if even one seam should give way—but she does not dare to imagine that. She avoids it. She sits in the liner (perhaps the same vessel that Fanny refers to later as "Mr. Verver's boat") and reads only what the captain, or father, has provided for the trip.

So, surrounded by her innocence, she goes about straining to keep herself right, to make her life a flawless crystal bowl holding, as far as pleasures go, "nothing, one was obliged to recognize, but innocent pleasures, pleasures without penalties." The novel is dense with images for this splendid aspiration: images of crystal, of roundness, of childhood—and above all, references to the happy innocence which was, as the Prince says, "the state of our primitive parents before the fall." As innocent as these of any knowledge of evil, either for doing or for seeing, they live, she and her father Adam, sheltered by the immaculate white walls and the placid gardens of "monotonous Eaton Square," a place which is the appropriate embodiment of Maggie's Edenic longing: "They knew, it might have appeared in these lights, absolutely nothing on earth worth speaking of—whether beautifully or cynically; and they would perhaps sometimes be a little less trying if they would only once for all peacefully admit that knowledge wasn't one of their needs and that they were in fact constitutionally inaccessible to it. They were good children, bless their hearts, and the children of good children." In this passage, as in Maggie's speech about the steamer, we have a sense that bulwarks of ignorance are being erected against some threat that presses in from the world; that knowledge of some truth is not simply absent, but is being actively refused for the sake of beatitude. (For Adam's *daughter* was not born in Eden; and the "children of good children" must have, in virtue of being this, some connection with original sin.)

Maggie has reached a time in her life at which we might expect her to notice a difficulty attaching to her ideal. She has, specifically, married. She has undertaken to become a woman and to move from her father's home into a husband's. This time might be expected to be a time of conflicting obligations. For the daughter of so exacting a father, a daughter who, moreover, has served for most of her childhood and adolescence as her father's sole traveling companion, friend, and partner, it might be expected to be a time of a painful breaking away from past attachments and commitments. To become a separate woman in her own right and the Prince's wife, this woman, it is clear, will have to give pain. Even if, as Fanny says, natural attachments "may be intense and yet not prevent other intensities," the nature of this particular blood relation, as deep as any marriage, surely makes claims that would block other, complicating loves. But Maggie's conscience so shrinks from the guilt of rendered pain that she cannot bear at all to embark on this job of separation. Her resourceful imagination therefore discovers that in every conflict of loves or of values, one can, by the right sort of effort, reach an allegedly guiltless consistency and harmony—even "that ideal consistency on which her moral comfort almost at any time depended." What is this strategy? "To remain consistent," we are told, "she had always been capable of cutting down more or less her prior term." This image from syllogistic logic means, I suppose, that a promising way to resolve a conflict of obligations is always to rewrite the major premise of the practical syllogism so that the prior term no longer covers the entire extension of the middle term. Instead of "all B are A," we will now have, at most, "some B are A." By this device Maggie can cause a potentially troublesome value term no longer to apply in the given situation. She preserves her comfort by preserving her consistency; she preserves her consistency by "simplifying" her world and even her character, as the Prince observes. In the case at hand, she solves the apparent conflict of marital love with filial duty by "cutting back" the claims of marriage, marrying in such a way that she can still remain her father's, "undivided."

So in a funny way, what began as the noble idea of failing in no duty and cherishing every value ends, consistently pushed through, in an enterprise that cuts back, cuts down, alters values to fit the claims of consistency. Any claim that seems capable of conflicting with her primary duty to her father—a duty which to this good daughter looks identical with morality itself—can be allowed to have validity only insofar as it accords with his requirements, consents, as she and her father say, to be "round"

rather than angular, harmonious rather than discordant. She and her father are, she imagines, in a boat together, sailing away from "luxuriant complications."

Maggie's attachment to moral simplicity brings with it some disturbing consequences. The first is, plainly, an avoidance or suppression of her own adult sexuality. If she allows herself to mature and to experience marriage fully, then she opens herself immediately to complication and to the possibility of a break. She and her father will no longer be "undivided." Therefore Maggie, as she ostensibly matures, has cultivated, increasingly, an androgynous and even an ascetic persona. "Extraordinarily *clear* . . . in her prettiness," she is even described as "prim." Her father recalls that "when once she had been told before him, familiarly, that she resembled a nun, she had replied that she was delighted to hear it and would certainly try to." Later she is compared to "some holy image in a procession;" her character is said by Fanny to be like "that little silver cross you once showed me, blest by the Holy Father, that you always wear, out of sight, next your skin." This deliberate suppression of her womanliness is evidently promoted by her father, who associates womanliness with weakness, the absence of judgment, and the inability to give genuine companionship, and who, on the other hand, thinks of his daughter as his first companion in his spiritual adventures. He is an intellectual and artistic pioneer, a Cortez discovering a new world. When he asks himself whether his wife might have accompanied him in this adventure, he comes quickly to a conclusion that rules out the womanly (or at least women of his own class) altogether: "No companion of Cortez had presumably been a real lady: Mr. Verver allowed that historic fact to determine his inference."

To become a "real lady" is, then, to abandon her father, to wound him by ceasing to be his companion in all things. It is, I think, this moral claim, and not merely some vague girlish fear, that leads Maggie, even in marriage with a man to whom she is deeply attracted, so to repress her womanly responses that Fanny can confidently and, we feel, correctly assert that she has never really "had" the Prince. This link is confirmed by James's subtle use of water imagery in connection with both sexual passion and moral conflict or complication—frequently the two of these together. We have already noticed Maggie's "watertight" steamer, secured against a harm or a violation, and Mr. Verver's boat, which sails safely away from complication. What we can now point out is that the first image is closely joined by Maggie herself to an admission that she does not respond to her husband's "particular self"; in the second case, the complications from which Maggie imagines father and daughter sailing away are "husbands and wives" who had "made the air too tropical." Maggie even asks herself at this point, "Why . . . couldn't they always live, so far as they lived together, in a boat? She felt in her face, with the question, the breath of a possibility that soothed her; they needed only *know* each other, henceforth, in the unmarried relation." Sexuality is seen and feared as a ground of conflict, a threat against the moral safety of not harming. Maggie's fear of water expresses the link between these two refusals—just as, in the passage in which the Prince and Charlotte renew their relationship, imagery of flooding (linked with a picture of breaking through or out of a perfect circle) indicates at once both their mutual sexual response and their acceptance of moral guilt: "Then of a sudden, through this tightened circle, as at the issue of a narrow strait into the sea beyond, everything broke up, broke down, gave way, melted and mingled. Their lips sought their lips, their pressure their response and their response their pressure; with a violence that had sighed itself the next moment to the longest and deepest of stillnesses, they passionately sealed their pledge." This willingness to burst out of the tight circle of harmony, to risk the ocean, is what we know Maggie has so far lacked. In the case of her father's parallel avoidance both of moral guilt and of a full sexual life, we are told in no uncertain terms that the consequence has been physical impotence with his new wife. With Maggie this is less clear and perhaps less important; whatever takes place physically, we are clear that there is a failure, on the level of imagination and emotion, to respond as a separate adult woman to her husband's own separate sexual presence. She is still intact in her innocence; nothing is damaged. "She had been able to marry without breaking, as she liked to put it, with her past."

Another consequence of Maggie's innocence is, plainly, an inability in any area of her life to see values, including persons, emerge as distinct ends in their own right. In every case they are rounded, accommodated, not recognized insofar as their claims collide with other claims. But this is plainly a way of viewing persons—those recalcitrant, inveterately "angular" objects—that leads to a certain neglect. First, there is the neglect of what Maggie calls her husband's "unknown quantity, [his] particular self." She even tells him, "You're not perhaps absolutely unique." And in the famous image of the pagoda at the beginning of Part II she betrays for the first time a curiosity about her situation, of which the Prince is so prominent a part. She desires for the first time to peer inside this odd, tower-like object which for so long has oddly occupied a place at the center of her garden, and into which "no door appeared to give access from the convenient garden-level." It is no wonder that at this point she begins to see, too, that her moral imagination is rather like an unsorted storeroom, full of "confused objects," "a mess of vain things, congruous, incongruous," tossed in, in a heap, and shut behind a locked door. "So it was that she had been getting things out of the way."

And it is not only personal qualitative uniqueness that goes into Maggie's storeroom; it is also, we need to add, personal *separateness,* the value of each person and each end as a distinct item generating its own claims. In the romance of Tristan, whose praise of love's crystalline simplicity James very likely had in view, the lovers' cultivation of simplicity makes them blind to the way in which each commitment and each value is separate from and liable to conflict with each other; in the same way, Maggie sees only roundness where in real life there is angularity, and therefore misses the distinct claims of each particular value. This is, strikingly, true even of her love for her father, as we see from a brief, proleptic scene early in the novel. Returning from church, Maggie finds her father besieged by Mrs. Rance, an irritating woman who wants to marry him. For the first time Maggie perceives that her own marriage *has* begun to entail for Adam the pain of abandonment and of harrassment from would-be companions. And strangely, this idea suddenly gives her, also for the first time, a sense of her father as a separate person: "He was on her mind, he was even in a manner on her hands—as a distinct thing, that is, from being, where he had always been, merely deep in her heart and in her life; too deep down, as it were, to be disengaged, contrasted or opposed; in short objectively presented." Moral objectivity about the value of a person (or, presumably, any other source of moral claims) requires, evidently, the ability to see that item as distinct from other items; this in turn requires the ability to see it not as a deep part of an innocent harmony but as a value that can be contrasted or opposed to others, whose demands can potentially conflict with other demands. In making her father's law normative for a world of harmlessness, Maggie has, ironically, failed to see *him.* It is not until much later that she really takes this in; her next move here is to resolve the conflict and restore the "harmony" by giving him Charlotte as a wife. But because of this scene, *we* are aware of her maneuvers as self-deceptive and false. Knowledge of a good, that is to say a value, in the world requires, we see, knowledge of evil, that is to say of the possibility of conflict, disorder, the contingent necessity of breaking or harming. Without eating this fruit she is just a child, ignorant of the value of the good as well.

We are now in a position to appreciate one of the oddest and most striking features of James's portrait of this idealistic pair of Americans: the inveterate tendency of both father and daughter to assimilate people, in their imagination and deliberation, to fine *objets d'art.* This matter is given considerable emphasis in James's design. One of the most striking incursions of the authorial voice into a narrative told, for the most part, through the consciousness of one or another of its characters begins, "Nothing, perhaps, might affect us as queerer, had we time to look into it, than this application of the same measure of value to such different pieces of property as old Persian carpets, say, and new human acquisitions." And such a strange way of valuing is present too in our very first glimpse of Maggie, where she speaks of her husband as "a rarity, a beauty, an object of price. . . . You're what they call a *morceau de musée.*" We are, of course, invited to take the time ourselves to look into this odd matter.

We soon realize that this propensity for the aestheticization of persons does not precisely indicate that the Ververs neglect the moral, or reduce the moral to the aesthetic. Indeed, it is agreed all round that they are distinguished for their keen *moral* sense, even for their strict moralism. It is rather that the peculiar nature of their moral aim, with its extreme emphasis on flawless living and, because of this, on consistency and harmony, is best supported by a view of persons that tends to assimilate their properties to certain salient properties of works of art. Works of art are precious objects, objects of high value. And yet it is a remarkable feature of our attention to works of art that it appears to spread itself round smoothly and harmoniously. I can, visiting a museum, survey many fine objects with appropriate awe and tenderness. I can devote myself now to one, now to another, without the sense that the objects make conflicting claims against my love and care. If one day I spend my entire museum visit gazing at Turners, I have not incurred a guilt against the Blakes in the next room; nor have I failed in a duty toward Bartok by my loving attention to Hindemith. To live with works of art is to live in a world enormously rich in value, without a deep risk of infidelity, disloyalty, or any conflict which might lead to these. It is the Ververs' brilliantly resourceful idea that the moral life, too, can be flawless and innocent of violation, while remaining full of value, if only persons can be made to resemble aesthetic objects, things to be displayed in a gallery for innocent attention. Closely linked with Mr. Verver's aestheticization of Charlotte is a wish "for some idea, lurking in the vast freshness of the night, at the breath of which disparities would submit to fusion." This idea—that he should marry Charlotte so as to restore the general harmony—comes to him during the very moment at which he sees the precious Damascene tiles "successively, and oh so tenderly, unmuffled and revealed," until they "lay there at last in their full harmony and their venerable splendor." It is surely the splendid order and harmony of these aesthetic objects (each tile lies uncompetitively side by side with its neighbors; the demands of tender attention to all can be faithfully met) which Mr. Verver covets for his human life; and coveting it, he turns Charlotte, by marriage, into the finest piece of all. For Maggie as well, the wonderful idea is that a husband who resembles a "fine piece" can be packed and unpacked, stored and brought out for show—or, if he should become too "big," be sent to American City to be "buried;" in none of these circumstances will its presence place a strain on the deliberation of the collector or spoil the harmony of the museum, or life, which testifies to his rare powers of perception.

In short, then, we have begun with a noble and venerable moral ideal—not just the fancy of a childish girl, but a picture of personal conduct and personal rightness that has very deep roots in the moral tradition of our entire culture. (It is not fortuitous that this combination of moralism and excessive simplicity is attributed to the American characters in this novel—nor that these Americans should be as resourceful in technical deliberation as they are naive in emotional response.) We are shown that this ideal, followed out to its strictest conclusion, generates an extraordinary blindness to value and ends by subordinating the particular claim of each commitment and love to the claims of harmony. And that *is*, we see, the fancy of a childish girl. It does not work on its own terms, since it does wrong to persons and commits acts of blindness and cruelty. (It is not inappropriate that Maggie and her father, as well as the other pair, are, in effect, charged with disloyalty and adultery—for each has been unfaithful to the commitments involved in making a marriage just because of this childlike unwillingness to break away or to experience guilt.) And it is morally objectionable in that it commits the holder to a systematic neglect of certain features of persons—namely, both their separateness and their qualitative uniqueness—on which their specific personal value might be thought to rest. The richness of the novel's moral vision lies in the way in which it both shows us the splendor of a rigorous moralism (for this simple vision attracts not only the Americans but to some extent

every major character in the novel) and at the same time erodes our confidence in this ideal by displaying the guilt involved in such innocence. There is, as Maggie later says, an "awful mixture in things."

The world of *The Golden Bowl* is a fallen world—a world, that is, in which innocence cannot be and is not safely preserved, a world where values and loves are so pervasively in tension one with another that there is no safe human expectation of a perfect fidelity to all throughout a life. (This novel works out this idea in the sphere of human personal love, but *The Princess Casamassima* shows us that James is ready to extend it more broadly to include nonpersonal commitments and values.) In this world our first choice as adults is the choice to pursue our personal goals at the expense of a separation from and a break with the parent. And we cannot ever count on the fact that our love of a husband will not require the spiritual death of a best friend and mentor, that fidelity to a wife will not require cruelty to a former lover. There are better and worse choices, naturally, within this tangled world; but it is childlike to refuse to see that it *is* in this way tangled, for this is a feature of our situation as creatures with values operating in the world of nature. As James wrote in the preface to *What Maisie Knew:* "No themes are so human as those that reflect for us, out of the confusion of life, the close connexion of bliss and bale, of the things that help with the things that hurt, so dangling before us for ever that bright hard metal, of so strange an alloy, one face of which is somebody's right and ease and the other somebody's pain and wrong."

I am claiming, then, that this novel works out a secular analogue of the idea of original sin by showing a human being's relation to value in the world to be, fundamentally and of contingent necessity, one of imperfect fidelity and therefore of guilt; by showing us ourselves as precious, valuing beings who, under the strains imposed by the intertwining of our routes to value in the world, become cracked and flawed. Guilt toward value is here, if not literally a priori, still a feature of our humanness which attaches to us as a structural feature of our situation in nature and in the family, prior to the specific choices and failures that we enter upon in a particular life. The Prince says about crystal, "Its beauty is its *being* crystal. But its hardness is certainly its safety." On this analogy, human beings, like the golden bowl, are beautiful but not safe: they have ideals, but they split. Charlotte's question about the bowl was, "If it's so precious, how comes it to be cheap?" The answer to this question is the story of four human lives.

This novel, I have indicated, is about the development of a woman. To be a woman, to give herself to her husband, Maggie will need to come to see herself as something cracked, imperfect, unsafe, a vessel with a hole through which water may pass, a steamer compartment no longer tightly sealed. Later, as her perception is shifting, she will in fact see herself as a house not perfectly closed against the elements: "She saw round about her, through the chinks of the shutters, the hard glare of nature." And in the world of nature, what Maggie sees is the suffering of Charlotte, caused by her act. Her guilt has entered her vision.

The second half of the novel is the story of Maggie's initiation into knowledge of her fallen world. Beginning to *live* is, for her, beginning to see that meaningful commitment to a love in the world can require the sacrifice of one's own moral purity. To regain her husband she must damage Charlotte. We are fully aware, as is she, that her cruelty and dishonesty to Charlotte are in no way purified or effaced by the fact of Charlotte's own offense. Her love, unlike the ideal of the Tristanic lover, must live on cunning and treachery; it requires the breaking of moral rules and a departure from the comfortable garden.

It would be an important and fascinating task to trace the details of this development: the way, for example, in which exposure to conflict and a womanly exposure to sexuality are linked, here as before, in the imagery of water, as Maggie the passenger becomes a swimmer; the way she comes to see that the value of persons and of objects is partially constituted by the risk they bring of pain and opposition— that "any deep-seated passion has its pangs as well as its joys, and that we are made by its aches and anxieties most richly conscious of it"; the way in which the departure from Eden brings with it the possibility of certain moral emotions which were unknown in that garden—among them shame, jealousy, tenderness, and respect; the way in which, from having seen only clear, splendid objects, Maggie learns, inhabiting a human world, to be a "mistress of shades," a reader of nuance and complexity. (There are no books in Eden.)

But although we do not have space to go into all of this, what we now must notice is that these new dimensions of perception and response begin to amount, strangely, for us and for Maggie, as things go on, not so much to a way of living with imperfection as to a new way of getting at perfection. Maggie, still as exigent and idealistic as ever, discovers a way of remaining a splendidly pure and safe object *within* this fallen world, "as hard . . . as a little pointed diamond." . . . We might describe the new ideal this way: See clearly and with high intelligence. Respond with the vibrant sympathy of a vividly active imagination. If there are conflicts, face them squarely and with keen perception. Choose as well as you can for overt action, but at every moment remember the more comprehensive duties of the imagination and emotions. If love of your husband requires hurting and lying to Charlotte, then do these cruel things, making the better choice. But never cease, all the while, to be richly conscious of Charlotte's pain and to bear, in imagination and feeling, the full burden of your guilt as the cause of that pain. If life is a tragedy, see that; respond to that fact with pity for others and fear for yourself. Never for a moment close your eyes or dull your feelings. The ideal is summarized by James in his preface to *The Princess Casamassima* as one of "being finely aware and richly responsible"; it is nowhere more fittingly and fully embodied than in the long passage of deliberation in which Maggie, picturing vividly Charlotte's silent suffering, decides to urge her husband to speak to Charlotte once more before her departure. Here we feel that Maggie's keen sensitivity to the values of love and

friendship, which she herself is violating, redeems and transfigures the cruelty of her act. If she acts badly of necessity, at least she takes upon herself the conscious guilt for that badness and, by her sense of guilt, shows herself as a person to whom badness is odious. It is not surprising that Maggie repeatedly imagines herself as a sacrificial figure who bears the pain and guilt of the situation through the fine responsibility of her consciousness. This idea of bearing guilt for love's sake is evidently the source of the comparisons of Maggie to the scapegoat of ancient Greek religion, who saves the community by bearing its pollution, and also to Christ, who took upon himself the sins of the world. The difference in her case is that she assumes this world's burden of sin not by going into exile or dying but by sinning, and by seeing that she is sinning, and by bearing, for love, her own imperfection.

But as the end approaches, we are troubled by our sense that this is, after all, a new way of being innocent. We are troubled by Maggie's comparison of herself to a diamond, more angular than the original crystal, but even more safely hard. We note that she is still fond of the language of moral absolutes: " 'consummate' was [a] term she privately applied." She has not so much altered her moral categories as rearranged the items to which she attaches these favored terms; not so much accepted evil in herself as seen a new way to be (internally) safely innocent. We have been put on our guard against projects of safety and projects of perfection, so we wonder whether Maggie's new ideal has itself a crack in it.

And now, as we reflect in this way, it should strike us that in fact, according to the last scene of the novel, Maggie has not yet, as she approaches the final parting with Charlotte and her father and the final confrontation with Amerigo, eaten the fruit of the tree of knowledge of good and evil. It is still hanging before her, just before the end, "the golden fruit that had shone from afar." So the new moral ideal cannot really have been the fruit of that eating, and Maggie, until the very end, is still in some significant sense an innocent, though more responsive and more womanly than before.

What is, then, Maggie's innocent failure of recognition, and what can we discover in the final scene that will explain to us why here, and only here, James presents her as falling from purity? We notice, in her last encounter with Adam and Charlotte, some significant signals. Aesthetic images for persons reappear and multiply. There is talk of the "human furniture required, aesthetically, by such a scene;" there is talk of the emptiness of a house with "half of its best things removed." There is, above all, a marked aestheticization of Charlotte as "incomparable," "too splendid." We are forced to ask why, at this point of triumph for Maggie's new ideal rightness, she should re-import the techniques of the old innocence—why, after so deeply responding to Charlotte's solitude and pain, and after urging Amerigo to do the same, she should suddenly retreat behind these old refusals. An answer begins to emerge along with the question; we begin to sense the discovery for which James is preparing us.

Amerigo has refused Charlotte not only his love, but also his response and his vision. He refuses to see her pain; he allows it to remain at a distance, receiving her as "Royalty" rather than as a woman who has arranged her life around her passion for him. What we now begin to see is that Maggie was wrong to think that it could, should be otherwise. The demands of his love for Maggie will not, in fact, allow the moral luxury of clear sight and generous response. To love one woman adequately he cannot always be tormented by a consciousness of the other. He must, then, of necessity banish the other, wronging her not only, like Maggie, in act, but also in the depths of his imagination and his vision. The demands of the new ideal of seeing are not always compatible with an adequate fulfillment of each of our commitments, for some loves are exclusive and demand a blindness in other quarters. Instead of being "finely aware and richly responsible" we may, in fact, have to become, as lovers, grossly insensitive and careless with respect to other, incompatible claims. The mere fact of being deeply engaged forces a blindness. The moment at which Maggie finally tastes the "golden fruit" is such a moment: on both sides, obtuseness feeds the triumph of love.

> 'Isn't she too splendid?' she simply said, offering it to explain and to finish.
>
> 'Oh, splendid!' With which he came over to her.
>
> 'That's our help, you see,' she added—to point further her moral.
>
> It kept him before her therefore, taking in—or trying to—what she so wonderfully gave. He tried, too clearly, to please her—to meet her in her own way; but with the result only that, close to her, her face kept before him, his hands holding her shoulders, his whole act enclosing her, he presently echoed: ' "See"? I see nothing but *you*.' And the truth of it had, with this force, after a moment, so strangely lighted his eyes that, as for pity and dread of them, she buried her own in his breast.

The Prince, then, sees nothing but Maggie. And Maggie, seeing this singleness of vision, reacts to her sight of Amerigo as to a tragedy—with "pity and dread." For she sees, in truth, that he *does* see only her, that she and he together have brought about, within his imagination, an extinction of vision and a failure of response; and that this has happened of tragic necessity because of the requirements of his commitment to her. Long ago, Maggie did not see that choice among competing values could ever be tragic. Then she saw that it could be tragic, but thought that a heroine of tragedy could still avoid tragedy inwardly by being richly responsible to everything in intellect and feeling. Now she sees in her husband the genuine, unredeemed article, a "hero" violating love for the sake of love, purified by no inner sympathy, no note of higher consciousness.

But at this moment, with the "golden fruit" of knowledge hanging there before her, she discovers, too, that she cannot gaze on this tragedy like the perfectly responsive and responsible spectator, seeing and feeling for everyone, and still have the knowledge of love for which she has sacrificed. Aristotle argued that tragedy brings illumination concerning values: through the "pity and dread" inspired by tragic events, we learn about what matters to us, and

we are clarified. Maggie, in the last sentence of the novel, recognizes that the keen vision and acknowledgment of the good tragic spectator are themselves values which can, in the world of nature, collide with other values. To see all, to be present to all, requires of the spectator a narrowness of love; to surrender to love requires an infidelity of the soul's eyes. To look will be to judge him; to judge him is to fall short of the fullness of his passion. " 'Thank goodness, then,' said Charlotte, 'that if there *be* a crack we know it!' " Here Maggie sees beyond her, seeing that the gifts of love require a gentleness that goes beyond, and covers, knowledge.

So she makes for him the last and greatest sacrifice of all. She gives him her purity of vision, her diamond hardness—as he had given up, for her, his vision of Charlotte's humanity. Once he had, long before, asked Fanny Assingham to give him her eyes, meaning to lend him the higher keenness of her American moral sense. Now his American wife gives him her eyes in fact, burying her own vision, therefore her perfect rightness, in his body.

And does one, as Charlotte asked, make a present of an object which contains, to one's knowledge, a flaw? To that Maggie herself has had, in the deeper moments of her connoisseurship, an answer: "The infirmity of art was the candour of affection, the grossness of pedigree the refinement of sympathy; the ugliest objects, in fact, as a general thing, were the bravest, the tenderest mementos, and, as such, figured in glass cases apart, worthy doubtless of the home, but not worthy of the temple—dedicated to the grimacing, not to the clear-faced, gods."

What are we to say about this? Is there, then, a moral ideal in this novel, or isn't there? Do the insights of the prefaces and of Part II stand or fall? I want to say that they stand, that there is an ideal here. It is not altogether undermined; it is still precious. It is only shown to be, like everything human, imperfect. (And perhaps, as the passage just mentioned suggests, this flaw in it is partly constitutive of its specifically human value and beauty.) The end of the novel does not tell us that it is pointless to become "finely aware and richly responsible"; it only warns us against turning this norm into a new form of watertight purity by showing us that a deep love may sometimes require an infidelity against even this adult spiritual standard. (pp. 26-39)

Martha Craven Nussbaum, "Flawed Crystals: James's 'The Golden Bowl' and Literature as Moral Philosophy," in New Literary History, *Vol. XV, No. 1, Autumn, 1983, pp. 25-50.*

Gore Vidal   (essay date 1984)

[*An American novelist, short story writer, dramatist, and essayist, Vidal is particularly noted for his historical novels and iconoclastic essays. In the following excerpt, he analyzes character and symbolism in* The Golden Bowl.]

In the spring of 1880 Mrs. Henry Adams confided to her diary: "It is high time Harry James was ordered home by his family. He is too good a fellow to be spoiled by injudicious old ladies in London—and in the long run they would like him all the better for knowing and living in his own country. He had better go to Cheyenne and run a hog ranch. The savage notices of his Hawthorne in American papers, all of which he brings me to read, are silly and overshoot the mark in their bitterness, but for all that he had better not hang around Europe much longer if he wants to make a lasting literary reputation." That same year the egregious Bret Harte observed, sadly, that Henry James "looks, acts, thinks like an Englishman and writes like an Englishman."

But the thirty-seven-year-old James was undeterred by public or private charges of un-Americanism; he had every intention of living the rest of a long and productive life in England. Since he was, in the phrase of his older brother William, like all the Jameses a native only of the James family, the Wyoming pig farmer that might have been preferred rooting, as it were (Oh, as it were!—one of his favorite phrases: a challenge to the reader to say, As it were *not?*), for those truffles that are to be found not beneath ancient oak trees in an old country but in his own marvelous and original consciousness. James did nothing like an Englishman—or an American. He was a great fact in himself, a new world, a terra incognita that he would devote all his days to mapping for the rest of us. In 1880 James's American critics saw only the fussy bachelor expatriate, growing fat from too much dining out; none detected the sea-change that was being undergone by what had been, until then, an essentially realistic American novelist whose subject had been Americans in Europe, of whom the most notorious was one Daisy Miller, eponymous heroine of his first celebrated novel (1878).

But by 1880, James was no longer able—or willing?—to render American characters with the same sureness of touch. For him, the novel must now be something other than the faithful detailing of familiar types engaged in mating rituals against carefully noted backgrounds. Let the Goncourts and the Zolas do that sort of thing. James would go further, much as Flaubert had tried to do; he would take the usual matter of realism and heighten it; and he would try to create something that no writer in English had ever thought it possible to do with a form as inherently loose and malleable as the novel: he would aim at perfection. While James's critics were complaining that he was no longer American and could never be English, James was writing *The Portrait of a Lady,* as nearly perfect a work as a novel can be. From 1881, James was the master of the novel in English in a way that no one had ever been before; or has ever been since. Even that Puritan divine, F. R. Leavis, thought *The Portrait* "one of the great novels of the English language."

Over the next twenty years, as James's novels got longer and longer, they became, simultaneously and oddly, more concentrated. There are fewer and fewer characters (usually Americans in a European setting but Americans at some psychic distance from the great republic) while the backgrounds are barely sketched in. What indeed *are* the spoils of the house Poynton? James never tells us what the "old things" are that mother and son fight for to the death. Balzac would have given us a catalog; and most novelists would have indicated something other than an impression

of a vague interior perfection. As James more and more mastered his curious art, he relied more and more on the thing *not* said for his essential dramas; in the process, the books become somewhat closer to theater than to the novel-tradition that had gone before him. Famously, James made a law of the single viewpoint; and then constantly broke it. In theory, the auctorial "I" of the traditional novel was to be banished so that the story might unfold much like a play except that the interpretation of scenes (in other words, who is thinking what) would be confined to a single observer if not for an entire book, at least for the scene at hand. Although James had sworn to uphold forever his own Draconian law, on the first page of *The Ambassadors,* where we meet Strether, the principal consciousness of the story and the point of view from which events are to be seen and judged, there is a startling interference by the author, Mr. James himself, who states, firmly: "The principle I have just mentioned. . . ." Fortunately, no more principles are mentioned by the atavistic "I."

There is the familiar joke about the three styles of Henry James: James the First, James the Second, and the Old Pretender. Yet there are indeed three reigns in the master's imagined kingdom. James I is the traditional nineteenth-century novelist, busy with the usual comings and goings of the ordinary fiction writer; James II is the disciplined precise realist whose apotheosis is *The Portrait of a Lady.* From 1890 to 1895 there is a break in the royal line: James turns to the theater; and most beautifully fails. Next comes the restoration. James returns in triumph to the novel—still James II (for purposes of simile, Charles II as well); and then, at the end, the third James, the Old Pretender, the magician who, unlike Prospero, breaks not his staff but a golden bowl.

After 1895, there is a new heightening of effect in James's narratives; he has learned from the theater to eliminate the nonessential but, paradoxically, the style becomes more complex. The Old Pretender's elaborateness is due, I should think, to the fact that he had now taken to dictating his novels to a series of typewriter operators. Since James's conversational style was endlessly complex, humorous, unexpected—euphemistic where most people are direct and suddenly precise where avoidance or ellipsis is usual—the last three novels that he produced (*The Ambassadors,* 1903; *The Wings of the Dove,* 1902; and *The Golden Bowl,* 1904) can be said to belong as much to the oral tradition of narrative as to the written.

James was fifty-seven when he started *The Ambassadors* and sixty-one when he completed *The Golden Bowl.* In those five years he experienced a late flowering without precedent among novelists. But then he was more than usually content in his private life. He had moved out of London; and he had established himself at the mayoral Lamb House in Rye. If there is an eternal law of literature, a *pleasant* change of house for a writer will produce an efflorescence. Also, at sixty, James fell in love with a young man named Jocelyn Persse. A charming Anglo-Irish man-about-town, Persse was not at all literary; and somewhat bewildered that James should be in his thrall. But, for James, this attractive young extrovert must have been a great improvement over his predecessor in James's affection, Hendrik Andersen, the handsome sculptor of megalomaniac forms. Andersen had been trouble. Persse was good company: "I rejoice greatly in your breezy, heathery, grousy—and housey, I suppose—adventures and envy you, as always, your exquisite possession of the Art of Life which beats any Art of mine hollow." This "love affair" (with the Master, quotes are always necessary because we lack what Edith Wharton would call the significant data) had a most rejuvenating effect on James; and the first rapturous days with Persse coincided with the period in which he was writing *The Golden Bowl.*

A decade earlier (November 28, 1892) Henry James sketched in his notebook the first design for *The Golden Bowl:* " . . . a father and daughter—an only daughter. The daughter—American of course—is engaged to a young Englishman, and the father, a widower and still youngish, has sought in marriage at exactly the same time an American girl of very much the same age as his daughter. Say he has done it to console himself in his abandonment—to make up for the loss of the daughter, to whom he has been devoted. I see a little tale, *n'est-ce pas?*—in the idea that they all shall have married, as arranged, with this characteristic consequence—that the daughter fails to hold the affections of the young English husband, whose approximate mother-in-law the pretty young second wife of the father will now have become." James then touches upon the commercial aspect of the two marriages: "young Englishman" and "American girl" have each been bought. They had also known each other before but could not marry because each lacked money. Now "they spend as much of their time together as the others do, and for the very reason that the others spend it. The whole situation works in a kind of inevitable rotary way—in what would be called a vicious circle. The *subject* is really the pathetic simplicity and good faith of the father and daughter in their abandonment . . . he peculiarly paternal, she passionately filial." On Saint Valentine's Day, 1895, James again adverts to the story, which now demands to be written, though he fears "the adulterine element" might be too much for his friend William Dean Howells's *Harper's* magazine. "But may it not be simply a question of *handling* that?"

Seven years later, James was shown a present given the Lamb family by King George I: it is a golden bowl. The pieces have now begun to come together. James has just completed, in succession, *The Ambassadors* and *The Wings of the Dove.* Comfortably settled in the garden room at Lamb House (later to be inhabited by E. F. Benson's dread Miss Mapp and then the indomitable Lucia; later still, to be blown up in World War II), James wrote, in slightly more than a year, what he himself described to his American publisher as "distinctly the most done of my productions—the most composed and constructed and completed. . . . I hold the thing the solidest, as yet, of all my fictions." The "as yet" is splendid from a sixty-one-year-old writer. Actually, *The Golden Bowl* was to be the last novel that he lived to complete; and it has about it a kind of spaciousness—and even joy—that the other novels do not possess. In fact, *pace* F. R. Leavis, I do not think

James has in any way lost his sense of life or let slip "his moral taste" (what a phrase!). . . . (pp. 8-9)

When I first read *The Golden Bowl,* I found Amerigo, the Prince, most sympathetic. I still do. I also found—and find—Charlotte the most sympathetic of the other characters; as a result, I don't think that her creator does her justice or, perhaps, he does her too much conventional justice, a black cloth on his head as he sentences her to a living death. But then James *appears* to accept entirely the code of the class into which he has placed both himself in life and the characters in his book. This means that the woman must always be made to suffer for sexual transgression while the man suffers not at all or, in the case of the Prince, very little—although the renewed and intensified closeness to Maggie may well be a rarefied punishment that James only hints at when, for the last time, he shuts the door to the golden cage on Husband and Wife Victrix. For once, in James, the heiress has indisputably won; and the other woman, the enchantress, is routed.

I barely noticed Adam Verver the first time I read the book. I saw him as an aged (at forty-seven!) proto-J. Paul Getty, out "to rifle the Golden Isles" in order to memorialize himself with a museum back home—typical tycoon behavior, I thought; and thought no more. But now that he could be my younger brother (and Maggie an exemplary niece), I regard him with new interest—not to mention suspicion. What is he up to? He is plainly sly; and greedy; and although the simultaneous possession and ingestion of confectionery is a recurrent James theme, my God, how this father and daughter manage to both keep and devour the whole great world itself! They buy the handsome Prince, a great name, *palazzi,* the works. They buy the brilliant Charlotte. But they do not know that the two beauties so triumphantly acquired are actually a magnificent pair, destined to be broken up by Maggie when she discovers the truth, and, much as Fanny Assingham smashes the golden bowl into three parts—and pedestal, Maggie breaks the adulterine situation into three parts: Amerigo, Charlotte, and Adam (she is, plainly, pedestal). Then, adulterine world destroyed, Maggie sends Adam and Charlotte home to American City at the heart of the great republic.

Best of all, from Maggie's viewpoint, Charlotte does not know for certain even then that Maggie knows all—a real twist to the knife for in a James drama *not* to know is to be the sacrificial lamb. Once Mr. and Mrs. Adam Verver have gone forever, the Prince belongs absolutely to Maggie. One may or may not like Maggie (I don't like what she does or, indeed, what she is) but the resources that she brings to bear, first *to know* and then *to act,* are formidable. Yet there is a mystery in my second experience of the novel which was not present thirty years ago. What, finally, does Adam Verver know? and what, finally, does he do? Certainly father and daughter are so perfectly attuned that neither has to *tell* the other anything at all about the unexpected pair that they have acquired for their museum. But does Maggie lead him? Or does he manage her? Can it be that it is Adam who pulls all the strings? as befits the rich man who has produced a daughter and then bought her—and himself—a life that even he is obliged to admit is somewhat selfish in its perfection.

As one rereads James's lines in his notebook, the essentially rather banal short story that he had in mind has changed into a wonderfully luminous drama in which nothing is quite what it seems while James's pious allusion to the subject as "really the pathetic simplicity and good faith of the father and daughter in their abandonment" is plain nonsense. James is now giving us monsters on a divine scale.

I think the clue to the book is the somewhat, at first glance, over-obvious symbol of the golden bowl. Whatever the king's christening gift was made of, James's golden bowl proves to be made not of gold but of gilded crystal, not at all the same thing; yet the bowl is massy and looks to be gold. The bowl is first seen in a Bloomsbury shop by Charlotte, who wants to buy a wedding present for her friend Maggie. Charlotte cannot afford anything expensive but then, as she remarks to her lover, Maggie's groom-to-be, " 'She's so modest,' she developed—'she doesn't miss things. I mean if you love her—or, rather, I should say, if she loves you. She lets it go.' " The Prince is puzzled by this use of "let," one of James's two most potent verbs (the other is "know"): "She lets what—?" Charlotte expatiates on Maggie's loving character. She wants nothing but to be kind to those she believes in: "It's of herself that she asks efforts."

At first the bowl enchants Charlotte. But the shop owner overdoes it when he says that he has been saving it for a special customer. Charlotte knows then that there must be a flaw; and says as much. The dealer rises to the challenge: "But if it's something you can't find out, isn't it as good as if it were nothing?" Charlotte wonders how—or if—one can give a present that one knows to be flawed. The dealer suggests that the flaw be noted to the recipient, as a sign of good faith. In any case, the bowl is a piece of solid crystal and crystal, unlike glass, does not break; but it can shatter "on lines and by laws of its own." Charlotte decides that she cannot afford the bowl; she joins Amerigo, who has been waiting for her in the street. He had seen the flaw at once. "*Per Dio,* I'm superstitious! A crack is a crack—and an omen's an omen."

For the moment, that is the end of the bowl itself. But James has now made the golden bowl emblematic, to use a Dickens word, of the relations between the lovers and their legal mates. To all appearances, the world of the two couples is a flawless rare crystal, all of a piece, beautifully gilded with American money. Of the four, the Prince is the first to detect the flaw; and though he wanted no part of the actual bowl, he himself slips easily into that adulterine situation which is the flaw in their lives. Charlotte refused to buy the bowl because she could not, simply, pay the price; yet she accepts the adultery—and pays the ultimate price.

In due course, Maggie acquires the bowl as a present for her father. Although she does not detect the flaw, the dealer believes himself mysteriously honor-bound to come to her house and tell her that the flaw is there. During his confession, he notices photographs of the Prince and

Charlotte; tells Maggie that they were in his shop together. Thus, she learns that they knew each other before her marriage and, as she tells Fanny, "They went about together—they're known to have done it. And I don't mean only before—I mean after."

As James's other triumph of knowledge gained through innocence was called **What Maisie Knew,** so this story might easily have been called *When Maggie Knew.* As the bowl is the symbol of the flawed marriages, so the line: "knowledge, knowledge was a fascination as well as a fear," stands as a sort of motto to this variation on one of our race's earliest stories, Adam and Eve and the forbidden fruit of knowledge which, once plucked, let the first human couple know both the joys of sex and the pain of its shadow, death. But if James was echoing in his last novel one of the first of all our stories, something is missing: the serpent-tempter. Is it Adam Verver? Or is he too passive to be so deliberate an agent? Actually, the shop owner is the agent of knowledge; but he is peripheral to the legend. Fanny Assingham has something slightly serpentine about her. Certainly, she is always in the know, but she is without malice. In fact, she prefers people *not* to know; and so she makes the splendid gesture of smashing the bowl and, presumably, the knowledge that the bowl has brought Maggie. But it is too late for that. Maggie moves into action. She sets out to rid herself of Charlotte because "I want a happiness without a hole in it. . . . The golden bowl—as it *was* to have been."

In the first of a series of splendid confrontations, Maggie tells the Prince that she knows. He, in turn, asks if Adam knows. "Find out for yourself!" she answers. Maggie is now having, as James colloquially puts it, "the time of her life—she knew it by the perpetual throb of this sense of possession, which was almost too violent either to recognize or to hide." Again, "possession." When the suspicious Charlotte confronts her in the garden (of Eden?) at Fawns, Maggie lies superbly; and keeps her enemy in ignorance, a worse state—for her—than even the United States. Finally, Maggie's great scene with her father is significant for what is not said. No word is spoken by either against Charlotte; nor is there any hint that all is not well with Amerigo and Maggie. But James's images of Maggie and Adam together in the garden—again the garden at Fawns (from the Latin *fons:* spring or source?)—are those of a husband and wife at the end or the beginning of some momentous change in their estate. The images are deliberately and precisely marital: "They were husband and wife—oh, so immensely!—as regards other persons." The reference here is to house party guests but the implication is that "other persons" include her husband and his wife. They speak of their social position and its ambiguities; of the changes that their marriages have made. She is a princess. He is the husband of a great lady of fashion. They speak of the beauty and selfishness of their old life.

Maggie remarks to her husband that "I'm selfish, so to speak, *for* him." Maggie's aria on the nature of jealousy (dependent in direct ratio on the degree of love expended) is somewhat mystifying because she may "seem often not to know quite *where* I am." But Adam appears to know exactly where he is: "I guess I've never been jealous."

Maggie affirms that that is because he is "beyond everything. Nothing can pull *you* down." To which Adam responds, "Well then, we make a pair. We're all right." Maggie reflects on the notion of sacrifice in love. The ambiguities are thick in the prose: Does she mean, at one point, the Prince or Charlotte or Adam himself? But when she says, "I sacrifice you," all the lines of the drama cross and, as they do, so great is the tension that James switches the point of view in mid-scene from daughter to father as James must, for an instant, glimpse Adam's response to this declaration: "He had said to himself, 'She'll break down and name Amerigo; she'll say it's to him she's sacrificing me; and it's by what that will give me—with so many other things too—that my suspicion will be clinched.'" Actually, this is supposed to be Maggie's view of what her father senses, but James has simply abandoned her in mid-consciousness for the source of her power, the father-consort. How Adam now acts will determine her future. He does not let her down. In fact, he is "practically *offering* himself, pressing himself upon her, as a sacrifice. . . ." The deed is done. He will take Charlotte back to American City. He will leave the field to Maggie.

Adam has been sacrificed. But has he? This is the question that reverberates. Maggie finds herself adoring him for his stillness and his power; and for the fact "that he was always, marvellously, young—which couldn't but crown, at this juncture, his whole appeal to her imagination." She gives him the ultimate accolade: "I believe in you more than anyone." They are again as one, this superbly monstrous couple. "His hands came out, and while her own took them he drew her to his breast and held her. He held her hard and kept her long, and she let herself go; but it was an embrace that august and almost stern, produced, for its intimacy, no revulsion and broke into no inconsequence of tears."

Where Maggie leaves off and Adam begins is not answered. Certainly, incest—a true Jamesian "horror"—hovers about the two of them, though in a work as delicately balanced as this the sweaty deed itself seems irrelevant and unlikely. It is enough that two splendid monsters have triumphed yet again over everyone else and, best of all, over mere human nature. But then Maggie contains, literally, the old Adam. He is progenitor; and the first cause; *fons.*

It is Adam who places Charlotte in her cage—a favorite Jamesian image; now James adds the image of a noose and silken cord by which Adam leads her wherever he chooses—in this case to the great republic of which Fanny observes to Maggie: "I see the long miles of ocean and the dreadful great country, State after State—which have never seemed to me so big or so terrible. I see *them* at last, day by day and step by step, at the far end—and I see them never come back." It is as if a beautiful, wealthy, American young woman of today were doomed to spend her life entirely in London. But the victorious Maggie believes that Charlotte will probably find life back home "interesting" while she and her father are the real losers because they are now forever parted. But Fanny is on to her. Fanny gets Maggie to confess that what was done not only suits her ("I let him go") but was indeed no more than the

successful execution of Adam's master plan: "Mrs. Assingham hesitated, but at last her bravery flared. 'Why not call it then frankly his complete success?'" Maggie agrees that that is all that is left for her to do.

At the end, Adam has brought together Maggie and Amerigo. James now throws all the switches in the last paragraph:

> [Amerigo] tried, too clearly, to please her—to meet her in her own way; but with the result only that, close to her, her face kept before him, his hands holding her shoulders, his whole act enclosing her, he presently echoed: "'See'? I see nothing but *you.*" And the truth of it had, with this force, after a moment, so strangely lighted his eyes that, as for pity and dread of them, she buried her own in his breast.

The golden cage has shut on them both. She is both gaoler and prisoner. She is both august and stern. In the book's last line the change of the word "dread" to "awe" would have made the story a tragedy. But James has aimed at something else—another and higher state for the novel (for life, too, that poor imitation of art with its inevitable human flaw): he has made gods of his characters; and turned them all to gold.

Years earlier, when James first saw the gilded Galerie d'Apollon in the palace of the Louvre, he had "an immense hallucination," a sense of cosmic consciousness; and over the years he often said that he could, all in all, take quite a lot of gold. At the end of Henry James's life, in a final delirium, he thought that he was the Emperor Napoleon; and as the Emperor, he gave detailed instructions for the redoing of the Tuileries and the Louvre: and died, head aswarm with golden and imperial visions. Fortunately, he had lived long enough to make for us *The Golden Bowl,* a work whose spirit is not imperial so much as it is ambitiously divine. (pp. 9-12)

*Gore Vidal, "Return to 'The Golden Bowl',"
in* The New York Review of Books, *Vol. XXX,
Nos. 21 & 22, January 19, 1984, pp. 8-12.*

John Bayley   (essay date 1986)

[*Bayley is an English literary critic and educator known primarily for his studies of Alexander Pushkin, Leo Tolstoy, Thomas Hardy, and George Eliot. In the following essay, he discusses character, narrative structure, and the use of techniques adopted from drama in* The Wings of the Dove.]

The Ambassadors, The Wings of the Dove, The Golden Bowl, the great works of fiction which are the crown of Henry James's achievement as a novelist, were written in less than five years, between the last year of the old century and the first four years of the new. They are a symbolic achievement in a variety of ways, symbolic of the novel itself, of its majestic achievement in the nineteenth century and its promise of new worlds to conquer in the era to come, and symbolic of James's own endurance and fertility, of his powers of understanding as a writer and a man. No wonder his biographer, Leon Edel, makes the point that these three novels represent James's final feat of self-realization as an artist, the fullest realization—in James's own words—of how 'art *makes* life, makes interest, makes importance', and that after their completion James for all practical purposes bade farewell to the novel, as Shakespeare has been imagined to bid farewell to the stage in *The Tempest.*

Of course he wrote more. He wrote more stories, some of his best, and two unfinished novels, *The Sense of the Past* and *The Ivory Tower.* But in their nature they recall an earlier phase, a time when he was exploring, in the manner of Balzac, the natural history of a society. The three great novels that preceded them are explorations of a different kind. They use all James's vast store of knowledge about society and its ways, all his accumulated wisdom and experience, but they also turn the mastery of art into a process of questioning. James said of the subjects of these novels that they 'dogged him and followed him'. He was investigating the incalculable, things intimated by the deepest processes of living which, for that reason, can never be fully known. In fact he was writing a sort of poetry. And as the critic Northrop Frye put it, 'The poet cannot talk about what he already knows.' James's famous late style is essentially a mode of enquiry.

Lord Mark, in *The Wings of the Dove,* is 'one of those characteristic cases of people in England who concealed their play of mind so much more than they showed it'. James's own late style can give the same impression, because the way it reveals can look like a wonderful imitation, almost a physical analogy, of the probings, queries and hesitations implicit in social intercourse, and of what he referred to as 'the fathomless equivocation' of English life. James was a lonely man, with a loneliness that deepened as he grew older. His later mode of artistic enquiry is a way of overcoming loneliness, of extending an almost tactile intimacy to the potential reader through the mode of words.

The reader, of course, may find it difficult to respond. Indeed when the books came out there was hardly any response at all, and James was chagrined to find with how few spirits his new eloquence struck a chord. No doubt it increased his sense of isolation. But time is changing that; more and more readers today are listening to James's inimitable talk, to the way it indicates truths unreachable in any other way, truths of changeless power and meaning. And they give us the feeling of taking part in a conversation rather than listening to a monologue, not of attending to a display of wit but of being involved in an intimately humorous exchange. The three novels are deeply and as it were naturally funny. *The Wings of the Dove* has situations and dialogues in which humour has a Shakespearean part, as much a part as tragedy, cruelty and pathos.

A sense of intimacy came naturally to James, was indeed an aspect of his loneliness, and is at one with the kind of dialogue projected in the characters—Kate Croy's with her father, with Merton Densher, with Milly Theale. Consciousness (which James usually referred to in the French, *conscience*) seems shared between author, characters and reader, and the participation of the last has its own special rewards and fascinations, which can arise out of bafflement itself. Intimacy is never a matter of being told what

to think. It is like the secret converse of lovers, whose understanding is not dependent on a single authority. In *The Golden Bowl* Charlotte Stant uses that index when she says that her relation with Prince Amerigo was 'everything a relationship could be, filled to the brim with the wine of consciousness'. She makes the point with a rather stagey emphasis, no doubt deliberately procured by the author, but the tone and the method suggested by her speech had become of vital importance to him. He wished above all to avoid the stance of the all-knowing novelist. In a letter to Violet Hunt he spoke of his desire for 'the dramatic and scenic way, without elementary explanations and the horrid novelist's "Now you must know that—" '.

James was writing about *The Ambassadors,* his own favourite among the novels. Its hero was for him an ideal centre of consciousness, tuned exactly to curiosity, discovery, and illusion. But in the two subsequent novels consciousness is much more diffused, and many readers would think more successfully diffused, among several characters, with all of whom we feel a special and personal intimacy. In *The Wings of the Dove* they are the triangle of Kate Croy, Merton Densher, and Milly Theale—the 'Dove' herself. Their relation is of course an intensely dramatic one, and it is in this novel that James most triumphantly fulfils what he called in his *Notebooks* the 'Scenario', the marriage of novelistic with theatrical technique. 'The divine principle is a key that, working in the same *general* way, fits the complicated chambers of *both* the narrative and the dramatic lock.'

Certainly *The Wings of the Dove* offers the most sensational possible combination of a stage drama, indeed a melodrama, with a lengthy and elaborate novel, unfolded with the greatest delicacy and sophistication. At every stage of his career as an artist James had perceived the uses and the potential of melodrama. It was to some extent an American tradition, inherited from Nathaniel Hawthorne and Edgar Allan Poe, but much heightened, in James's middle period, by his ambition to write plays that would succeed on the stage. His dramatic career had been a fiasco, its climax the traumatic first night of *Guy Domville,* when his appearance as author had been greeted from the gallery with hoots of derision. Hardly surprising in a way, for although the dialogue was beautifully written the play was cumbrous in its construction and denouement, and touchingly ill adapted to the public taste.

James had learnt his lesson—in two senses. He would renounce the stage, but he would use his failure there to develop a new style of fiction in which the stage should have a ghostly presence, the characters treading its boards in London parks and drawingrooms, an *auberge* by a river in France, a crumbling Venetian palace, in the thick rich softness of a great country house. The novel should have its big 'moments', just as the theatre had them, but instead of being timed to the revelations of speech and voice they would be timed, with an equal precision, to silent discoveries, gambits and reversals unseen and guessed at only by the power of their effects.

In *The Wings of the Dove,* the middle novel of the three, this process is seen at its most spectacular, the key most triumphantly turned in '*both* the dramatic and the narrative lock'. It is indeed, and for these reasons [as Dorothea Krook wrote in her *The Ordeal of Consciousness in Henry James*], 'the work that many will account James's masterpiece'. So gripping is it, in its own inimitable way, so enthralling the stages by which we are led to the denouement, that the critic has no business to spoil the reader's pleasure by revealing any of them prematurely. But let me note here the deliberation with which James has reversed, in the narrative interest, the most naturally and graphically striking dramatic moments. We do not see the betrayal of the conspiracy, or the scene in which it is revealed. We do not see the effects of the revelation on the heroine, the 'Dove'. We are not present at the scene where she talks to her beloved Densher afterwards, nor can we read the final letter she sends him. Her death takes place offstage.

But the consequences of this invisibility are all the more shattering, more dramatically compelling and far-reaching in their effects. Milly's forgiveness, if that is what it is, destroys from beyond the grave the relationship of Kate Croy and Merton Densher, the lovers whose intimacy has been 'filled to the brim with the wine of consciousness'. What can consciousness do in the face of this soft and silent action, the ambiguous spreading over them of the Dove's wings? They have money now—at least Densher has—they can marry: but the whole basis of their mutuality has undergone a transformation as complete and irreversible as any brought about in classical drama, at the Comédie-Française, or on the stage of *Oedipus Rex*.

Only at the very end of the novel is the play, as it were, allowed its big moment. The lovers confront each other; against all expectation their scheme has come off. But something—perfectly tangible—lies between them, as if it were Othello's handkerchief, or the gun which, as Chekhov observed, if it is visible on the stage must go off before the end of the play. It is a long envelope, containing a letter from Milly's solicitors to Densher. We do not know what is in it, and neither does Kate Croy, but if it is surrendered to Kate, Densher will be wholly in her power, no longer given refuge in his own new-found relationship beneath the Dove's wings. Kate perceives this, and perceives what will happen as a result. Like many great things in the theatre, this moment is dramatic to the point of being histrionic—outside the theatre would we really believe that a letter lying between a pair of lovers could be so fraught?—but the novel has had its say now, and has worked its complex and incalculable magic upon us. It is for the play to complete the tableau, and to complete it by leaving everything settled in terms of the drama, and yet unsettled in terms of the novel, and of life:

> . . . with an intensity now beyond any that had ever made his breath come slow, he waited for her act. 'There's but one thing that can save you from my choice.'
>
> 'From your choice of my surrender to you?'
>
> 'Yes'—and she gave a nod at the long envelope on the table—'your surrender of that.'
>
> 'What is it then?'

'Your word of honour that you're not in love with her memory.'

'Oh—her memory!'

'Ah'—she made a high gesture—'don't speak of it as if you couldn't be. *I* could in your place; and you're one for whom it will do. Her memory's your love. You *want* no other.'

He heard her out in stillness, watching her face but not moving. Then he only said: 'I'll marry you, mind you, in an hour.'

'As we were?'

'As we were.'

But she turned to the door and her headshake was now the end. 'We shall never be again as we were!'

It is the strongest, most unsettling conclusion to any of James's novels; and it fits the expert fusion of novel and melodrama that it can be taken on several levels and in different ways. It is at once a *coup de théâtre,* and what James in his Preface to *The Golden Bowl* was to call 'the appeal to incalculability'. In one sense we don't believe a word of it, as we don't need to believe in the stage effects—those of Corneille, Rostand, or of James's contemporary Maeterlinck—which bring a hush to the audience, and perhaps a tear to the eye. In such a context the theatre fully achieves its own kind of artifice, and removes any distinction between what is emotionally true and what is emotionally satisfying. Densher and Kate are not quite real at this moment, by the highest standards of fictional reality. And yet, in James's hands, the appeal to the stage actually manages to heighten that 'appeal to incalculability'.

How does this come about? A kind of melodrama was instinctive and congenial to James's temperament, although to his friends he often tried to play this down, as he did with what he called his 'pot-boiler', *The Turn of the Screw.* That ghost story has an atmosphere of mystery and incalculability which is not so far away from *The Wings of the Dove,* whose melodramatic subject he also deprecated, in a letter to a friend: 'The subject is a *poor* one, I unaffectedly profess—the result of a base wish to do an amiable, a generally pleasing love-story.' James might seem to have a quaint idea of what the public might consider a pleasing love-story, yet it was also a shrewd one. In writing fiction he still longed for the commercial success which had eluded him on the stage. The 'poor little rich girl' who is made love to for her money, who is mortally ill, and who is wholly generous and forgiving in her death to those who have betrayed her—such a story could be a popular tearjerker in any age.

But James of course had his own sense of what the really fine working out of the subject demanded. The novel must for him be an affair of *consciousness*—here that of Kate Croy and Merton Densher. And in that climactic last scene consciousness is no longer united in their conspiracy of love and desire for each other—it has gone separate ways. Densher has entered a dream of Milly—her sweetness, her pathos, her tender love for him which discovery and disillusion did not change, the whole atmosphere of

Milly, in fact what now seems to him *her* consciousness. The sentimentality of the thing is a positive asset to James's fine sharp sense of how potent such a legacy is to the man, how it brings tears to his eyes, and makes the prospect of Kate's society and marriage seem coarse and banal. Kate is bleakly aware of this, and of how the Densher she conspired with in love and in sex is no longer there. Brilliantly James hits the note of his absence—'I'll marry you, mind you, in an hour.' It is all the more depressing for Kate because it is an undertaking he would certainly honour. But his spirit is still in the mystery of Venice and Milly.

James conveys here, as in **The Golden Bowl,** an incomparable sense of how love requires a mutuality of consciousness, a mutuality which many different things can bring about, and can equally destroy. Mutuality, for Kate and Densher, is in their problem, their problem of love and money. In the letter to his friend Mrs Humphry Ward from which I quoted James goes on to say that

> such as it is, the subject is *treated,* and it wouldn't have been treated if the pair hadn't *met* on the subject of Milly's money. The thing is essentially a drama, like everything I do, and the drama, with the logic, the progression, the objectivised presentation of a drama, is all *in* their so meeting. The main field of it is, as the book is composed in Densher's consciousness; that composition involves, for us, largely, the closing of Kate's, and there is no torment worth speaking of for Densher; there's no consciousness—none, I mean, that's at all dramatic—if their agreement hasn't been *expressed* and this expression hasn't been—above all—the *thing* he has subscribed to.

Mrs Humphry Ward, a tough, genial and intelligent lady, author of the serious best-selling novel *Robert Elsmere,* might have grasped what James was getting at, but would probably also have felt that his interest in treatment was excessively abstract. None the less James had seen what really mattered to the **Wings of the Dove** theme, both as the starkest drama and the most sophisticated novel: that the consciousness of the conspirators—Kate and Densher—is first wholly unified and intimate in their pact, and then separated. Densher's sense of Kate, his love for her, is wholly bound up in their agreement. If he develops any kind of independent consciousness, and if Kate's is closed off by the author, they are bound to be no longer intimate, and that process reaches its climax in Kate's statement at the book's ending: 'We shall never be again as we were!'

The drama whose power is most behind James, even though perhaps unconsciously, is not one of those competently and briskly emotive pieces he had seen and studied in Paris, however much they may have contributed to his feeling for the 'Scenario'. It is the psychological drama at the heart of Shakespeare's *Macbeth.* Shakespeare makes the deep intimacy, the tremendous connubial understanding, of the Macbeths, present to the audience solely and simply by his exhibition of the fact that together they are planning a murder. Macbeth himself might have said, in admiration of his wife, what Mrs Lowder says—'Men haven't, in many relations, the courage of women'—and

have received as reply the straight statement, 'They haven't the courage of women.' Kate has neither pleasure in, nor illusion about, what she is up to, and no trace of hypocrisy; she only remarks that she is strong enough to do what she doesn't like doing.

The dramatic heart of *Macbeth* is the estrangement of mutuality, the eclipse of Lady Macbeth as a 'consciousness' as her husband acquires a dreadful solitude and independence deriving from the growing realization of what they have done. Their closeness cannot survive the success of the scheme which it made possible. James, one might say, goes one further than Shakespeare in exploiting the potential of this. His Macbeth, Merton Densher, is not only separated in the execution of their scheme from his partner's consciousness, but rapt into a wholly different centre of consciousness, that of Milly herself. It is this which Kate perceives so clearly at the quiet climax of their drama, when she takes the stage again with brief authority to pronounce the epitaph on her relationship with Densher. Milly is dead, but her consciousness survives in Densher's awareness of its wings over him, in the knowledge of what she has done for him.

The dramatic irony is that Kate, not a bit jealous, can try at first to see this as her own achievement, and to persuade Densher that she has brought it about. Her view of love is a view of success. Echoing Lady Macbeth she can seek to assure him, 'But we've not failed.' Milly has had her love ('She wanted nothing more. She has had *all* she wanted') and it is now for Kate and Densher to have theirs, on the proceeds. Milly's fabulous wealth metamorphoses itself into love and generosity, from beyond the grave. It is one of the many ironies of this extraordinary book that the Dove's wings are also the wings of money, which can do everything except secure and guarantee the continuance of a love-relation. A much cruder though related irony occurs in **The Portrait of A Lady,** the big novel which made James's name in earlier days, before he evolved the 'divine principle of the Scenario', and was still using the old omniscient mode, 'the horrid novelist's "Now you must know that . . ." ' The irony here is that the rather too perfectly nice and generous and enquiring *conscience,* the invalid Ralph Touchett, arranges that a fortune should be left to his young cousin, Isobel Archer, in order that she should live finely and fully, as he sees her capable of doing. But the gift destroys her, for it brings deception and deprivation and a soon-loveless marriage that 'grinds her in the very mill of the conventional'. All this the young James magisterially displays. But the drama of **The Wings of the Dove** is much more subtle and imponderable. Milly's gift and Milly's love reveals the relation of Densher and Kate, and reveals how close it was. And Milly's own motives remain incalculable. Was her generosity a species of revenge, or was it, as Kate can claim with a comforting dismissiveness, a sign that she wanted not truth but love? Let Densher deceive her so long as he was tender to her, for she loved him 'with passion'. 'She would have taken from you what you could give her,' says Kate, 'and been glad of it even if she had known it false.'

Even in their dramatic solution these things remain richly obscure. Nothing is displayed. And the drama also turns, in its subtle way, the screw of suspense, for in using drama as the mainspring of his novel James is also filling it as densely as he can with 'felt life', with the daily reality of things, and, as Densher 'restlessly reflects' at the time of climax, 'The taste of life was itself the taste of suspense'. Certainly in the climax of the act before the final scene Kate is confident that they have won, that they get their love, and the money, and the Dove too; for the Dove has had what she wanted, and it is the function of life, which Kate embodies, to dismiss death as something suitable for other people. Kate has the same lack of a true sense of others that Lady Macbeth shows when she says about the king, her victim: 'The sleeping and the dead are but as pictures.' Kate insists that Milly's fate has been wholly appropriate, because, after all, she loved Densher. What more could she want?

In the same way, Lady Macbeth assumes it proper that Duncan should die in order to make way for her and her husband. Only afterwards does the reality of the dead get home to her and make her realize, as Kate does, that she has become, in the words of Deflores to Beatrice in *The Changeling,* 'the deed's creature', that she can never again be as she was. For Lady Macbeth the realization means breakdown, and that would not happen to Kate. Indeed for all we know Kate may shrug off entirely, or almost entirely, her sense of what has happened. She is a character in a novel as well as in a play, and by implication the persons in a novel—and especially in James's novels—can be speculated about in our imaginations as if they were real, and continuing, at the novel's end, into the general reality of a life. From the obscure tensions of their last dialogue we infer that Densher, in order to free himself from Kate, offers her Milly's money, and we may also infer that this wounds Kate deeply, more deeply than anything else. Densher's act even resembles Macbeth's indifference, after his crime, to the wife with whom he was once so completely united.

In terms of *The Wings of the Dove* as drama, Densher and Kate are indeed not separate individuals but a 'relationship' pure and simple. James drops the right hint when he tells us that 'they were so much more together than they were anything else', and as he remarks in the letter I quoted, the pair become one in their scheme. It is one of the fascinations of the combined drama and novel, so triumphantly worked out in *The Wings of the Dove,* that their separation from each other places them back again in the novel's world. They—and especially Kate—become individuals, with all the potential of the single, the individuals that they once were when we learnt their history at the beginning of the novel. Something rather similar takes place at the end of *The Golden Bowl,* when the relationship in art of the four participants is dissolved, and they are sent out from the closeness of the drama into the all too open spaces of life.

As an individual character again Kate might do many things. She might take Densher's money—Milly's sumptuous legacy—and make a 'good' marriage elsewhere. Or the dramatic and seemingly so final close might, we feel, be only a lovers' tiff which would resolve itself in the more humdrum intimacies of marriage, even if a marriage from which the first glow of their mutuality had departed. So densely and yet discreetly suggestive is James's art, even when he is putting the finishing touches to his climactic scene, that all such outcomes appear possible. Densher and Kate were caught up in the world of high drama by their relation to Milly. Left by themselves again they seem on the verge of dwindling into the commonplace. Milly herself, however symbolic her role as Dove, as victim and redeemer, never loses her artless American enthusiasm and simplicity, her 'eagerness' that is 'shamelessly human'. She is in one sense a comic figure, as the figures in one of James's wittily perspicuous social investigations can hardly help being, as well as a figure—in her dramatic role—of tragic pathos and mystery.

Even as a Dove Milly's role is ambiguous. Everyone else, caressing and making much of her, calls her that. And Kate, in her interrogatively affectionate chats with the sweet *ingénue* who admires her as not only wonderfully handsome but as mistress of 'the art of seeing things as they were', goes so far in 'her own shades of familiarity' as to use the endearment 'duck'. The touching discrepancy, among the pet names, would not have been lost on James's effortless mastery of the fictionally humorous. Under such pet names Milly is petted and patronized and manipulated, in terms of the complex power mechanisms which the novel reveals, but when she withdraws into the mystery of the drama she is revealed as the Dove descending, the shadow of enfolding wings.

Like many of James's novels *The Wings of the Dove* has more than once been successfully produced as a stage play. Its dramatic impact, its qualities of timing and discovery, are very great indeed, gripping an audience more effectively in the theatre than any of the other adaptations of his stories. But though Milly is a gift to a good actress, and one whose performance could steal the show, she cannot on the stage be other than a unitary manifestation, a victim whose sweetness and stoicism, dignity and forgiveness, is successfully revealed *en clair* in interviews with Kate, with Lord Mark, and finally with Densher. The part on the stage cannot correspond to James's wonderful multiple image in the novel of the charming and vivacious girl, withdrawn by her fate into a mystery which—as is proper to mysteries—is never fully penetrated by those who have sought to make use of her, but which profoundly affects their relationships and their lives. In putting his key into the narrative and the dramatic locks, James turns the former to reveal an expert enquiry into the socially and morally equivocal, and the latter to unfold a mystery, a passion and revelation only vouchsafed through the medium of those on whom it has impressed itself. Drama closes the curtain which fiction is always trying to peep behind.

It is typical of James to involve his whole process, at this stage of his writing, in protean metaphors whose elaboration touches on the verge of comedy. Mrs Lowder of Lancaster Gate, Kate's rich and match-making aunt, loves to contemplate the spectacle of Milly's approaching death, in all 'the perfection of its pathos'. It makes her positively fond of Densher, whom she despises as a suitor for Kate, that he can tell her, however reluctantly, about the dying girl's situation. 'She sat there before the scene, as he couldn't help giving it out to her, very much as a stout citizen's wife may have sat, during a play that made people cry, in the pit or the family-circle. What most deeply stirred her was the way the poor girl must have wanted to live.' The metaphor of the playhouse underlines the brutality which James so inexorably brings out, more subtly and more compellingly even than Tolstoy does in his great story *The Death of Ivan Ilyich.*

Mrs Lowder is not a fiend; she is even in her own way kindhearted, convinced that she 'lives for others', which of course means arranging other people's lives to her own satisfaction. But to her Milly's dying is as good as a play, and nothing shows human and social nature more sharply than James's formal device of having the characters in the novel watch in their own ways the spectacle of death afforded by the play. As the two forms are separate, for all their cunning combination in **The Wings of the Dove,** so Milly's fate is inviolably separate from these who are living with her, by her, on her, and in the contemplation of her case. James himself had always been fascinated by the death of the young and the beautiful, of those who had so much to live for and wanted so much to live. His own cousin, Minnie Temple, had died young of tuberculosis, and though James had been in no sense in love with her he had been charmed by the pathos of her vitality. His own sister, Alice, had died of cancer a few years before he wrote **The Wings of the Dove,** and he had watched for days at her bedside and studied with the closest attention the symptoms of her dying when it came. In a letter to his brother William he had given an extremely minute and moving account of these. They are all the more overwhelmingly present in the novel because of the way in which James's art has elected to suppress all mention of such things. The Dove dies in the odour of mystery, not of medicines. As Kate puts it with her own special kind of hard sympathy, Milly will never smell of drugs.

That hardness of phrase, and what lies behind it, is one of the themes most meticulously explored in what we might call the novelish side of the novel, the side that reveals what the characters are like, or how they have come to be as they are. No novel of James's gets off to a more powerful start. It shows at its most graphic what might be described as his Dickensian side, for the first pages turn the atmosphere of late Dickens into the subtlest and strongest of Jamesian essences. In 1865 James reviewed *Our Mutual Friend* in the *Nation,* and though he criticized the novel severely it is clear that much in it fascinated him. Dickens had always been in his blood. Not even Balzac, whom he so much admired and to whose influence he paid tribute in his essay 'The Lesson of Balzac', had so deep and pervasive an effect on James's art as did his early reading of Dickens. And Dickens, in his later novels, had become absorbed in the problem of how, as individuals, we become as we are, and with the technique of exploring it.

Kate Croy, at the opening of the novel, her face 'positively pale with irritation', is a sister of Bella Wilfer in *Our Mutual Friend,* the girl exasperated by the poverty and constriction of her family circumstances and determined at any cost to fulfil herself by getting money. In his Boffin couple Dickens provided a benevolent version of the function assigned by James to Mrs Lowder. In his portrait of Kate Croy's father James reverses Dickens's benevolent picture of the impractical and indigently lovable Mr Wilfer. The long scene between Kate and her father which opens the book is one of the most masterly in it, and its atmosphere—its effluvia one might say—creeps and spreads right through the unfolding of the story. James's subject is a brutal one, as he is well aware, and here he portrays it in its most subtly brutal aspect. Dickens knew all about hardness and gave it the two sides of a coin—his bad people display its ruffian side and his good characters the sentimental. James reveals, more exploratively, how hardness can be a virtue which goes with the effort to maintain some standards of feeling and behaviour. Kate, who has been driven almost unconsciously into the useful art of 'seeing things as they were', is for that reason a creature of an altogether higher species than her father, whom she in other ways so tellingly resembles. Her hardness consists in seeing clearly what her father and sister, in their genteelly self-assured repulsiveness, take for granted. It is up to her to sell herself in some way so that they may absently, and as of right, come in for the proceeds.

In the course of the wonderful opening scene between Kate and her father it becomes clear that she is making an effort—her last—to assert the proper meaning of the bond between them. She is ready to come to him if he wants her, to look after and keep house for him, as an unmarried daughter traditionally should. Kate makes clear to him how vulnerable she is.

> 'It's simply a question of your not turning me away—taking yourself out of my life. It's simply a question of your saying: "Yes, then, since you will, we'll stand together. We won't worry in advance about how or where; we'll have a faith and find a way." That's all—*that* would be the good you'd do me. I should *have* you, and it would be for my benefit. Do you see?'

Her invocation of the natural bond is touching in its simplicity, containing as it does the quiet centre of a relation which would be so fondly emphasized in the style of Dickens or George Eliot. Kate's lack of the sort of fondness they would find appropriate emphasizes the connection, and also the subtlety with which James is exploring a true instance of what in them would be a cliché. Kate needs her father, even to her own disadvantage, in order that they should 'have faith and find a way'; and the unspoken appeal behind the voiced one is that he should have some sympathy for her in her desire for Densher, and at least lend moral comfort to the perplexities she is in.

But Kate's father, with his 'kind, safe eyes', shows his own kind of stoicism, even gallantry, in rejecting her appeal. 'Her "Father!" was too much, and he met it sharply.' He tells her to pull herself together. For Mr Croy their alliance will be a wholly undercover one, an understanding not between father and daughter but like that of thugs and secret agents. Kate's rich aunt has offered her house room and an entry into the world of possible rich marriages, on condition that she has no communication with her deplorable father. Clearly then it is her duty to accept, and the implication is brought out with James's characteristic humour.

'Of course you understand that it may be for long.' Her companion had hereupon one of his finest inspirations. 'Why not frankly for ever?'

Although we never meet Kate's father again he is present in spirit throughout the book, and the relation he demands of his daughter in giving her up endures too. He is confident that in the end they understand each other, with no filial or paternal rubbish about wanting to be together, to 'have faith and find a way'. Throughout the book James quietly reveals the terrible affinity between the relation the father has chosen and the relation, 'which made anything but confidence a false note for them', growing up between Kate and Densher. In both cases the natural bond—of fathers and daughters, lovers—has been turned into the bond between conspirators in a society which recognizes nothing but power and success.

In his review of *Our Mutual Friend* James had particularly criticized Dickens's handling of his predatory couple, the Lammles, who exemplify in the most emphatic style Dickens's increasingly nightmarish sense of how the members of Society prey upon each other, bartering themselves and their friends for money and position, for social and financial advantage. Duped by each other, for each has been manipulated into thinking the other a good match, the Lammles try to recoup their fortunes by socially kidnapping the daughter of their rich 'friends' the Veneerings. But, as James points out, the operation is so stylized that we cannot believe in it—and consequently in the Lammles themselves—for a moment. They are stock villains in the Dickens theatre, just as the Veneerings themselves are caricatures of his feelings about the behaviour of the new and vulgar rich. James's portrayal of the purposes and preoccupations of Lancaster Gate, the equivalent of the Veneerings' grand house in Chelsea, are far more subtle, though perhaps in the end not much more sympathetic. His use of melodrama never oversimplifies the real complexity of social situations, just as he bestows, like Balzac, an intensity of affectionate observation on such unedifying denizens of his milieu as Lord Mark and Lionel Croy.

If James's vision of Kate Croy and Densher, and the game they come to play, is probably influenced by Dickens's portrait of the Lammles, James pursues with far greater interest than Dickens the idea of conspiratorial intimacy, and where it must ultimately end. Kate and Densher do not take for granted the social ploys which they find themselves practising: indeed they begin as rebels together against the domination of Lancaster Gate. But Lancaster Gate can only be fought with its own weapons, with its own kinds of cunning and treachery. The pair are thus in the classically interesting position, for tragic effect, of knowing the good while practising the bad, of trying to achieve their love and their genuinely high sense of each other by behaving like those around them who take the corruptions of self-interest utterly for granted.

James is charmed by and attentive to those who take themselves thus for granted, but not a bit seduced by them, nor by their peculiarly English self-confidence, a confidence that, for Lionel Croy, 'Life had met him so, half-way, and had turned round so to walk with him, placing a hand in his arm and fondly leaving him to choose the pace.' In the 'shabby sunshine' at his mean digs Croy none the less suggests 'but one thing: "In what perfection England produces them!" ' He has those 'kind, safe eyes, and a voice which, for all its clean fulness, told the quiet tale of its having never had once to raise itself'. In *The Wings of the Dove* and *The Golden Bowl* James is an incomparable observer of that English superiority which marked the Society manners of his time. We see it in Maud Lowder's 'hard fine eyes' and the way they turn from one person to another, in Lord Mark's regarding Milly at the dinner party as an American object to be taken 'imperturbably, irreclaimably, for granted' (that adjective 'irreclaimably' exhibits every particle of Jamesian finesse), even in the odious assumption of Kate's sister Marian, impoverished and *declassée* as she is, that she still retains all the simple imperatives of her class.

That kind of conviction is extremely important to the novel; it is in fact the mainspring of the conduct which James heightens into melodrama and fashions into a plot. It is noticeable how often he comments on the look of eyes, the social index of watchfulness, of verdicts invisibly handed out and invincibility retained. Lord Mark's— 'though it was an appearance they could suddenly lose— were as candid and clear as those of a pleasant boy'. Both Croy and Lord Mark, in their appearance of 'rightness', represent a tactic of James which finds its most elaborate expression in the summing-up of Lady Castledean in his next novel, *The Golden Bowl:*

> Her ladyship's assumption was that she kept, at every moment of her life, every advantage—it made her beautifully soft, very nearly generous; so that she didn't distinguish the little protuberant eyes of much smaller social insects, often endowed with such a range, from the other decorative spots on their bodies and wings.

In his three great late novels, above all in *The Wings of the Dove* and *The Golden Bowl,* James gives to complex metaphor an incalculable life of its own, sinister or touching, now magnificent and now homely, always implicitly humorous, tellingly domestic even when it reaches melodrama, as when Milly is compared to some youthful victim of a revolutionary tribunal, clutching stairs or banister as she is dragged away to execution; or when Charlotte Stant, in *The Golden Bowl,* is described as walking with an invisible silken cord round her neck, its end held by her husband in his pocketed hand. The function of such metaphor is to naturalize the melodrama in the plot, mixing it to the point of complete absorption with James's study of a dense social scene, where motive and behaviour must always be 'subject to varieties of interpretation'. And such a mixture helps to add, as he once put it, 'the sharp taste of uncertainty to a quickened sense of life'. In the same way the observed naturalness of his characters, their eyes, their tone, their almost amiability, mixes into their actions, making them plausible at their most melodramatic. As in Ivy Compton-Burnett's novels, the most evil deeds and deplorable situations are presented in an elegant setting of wit and dialogue, so in *The Wings of the Dove* and *The Golden Bowl* a simple symmetric plot, based on the chessboard of a ruthless power struggle, becomes more peculiar, more moving, even more ramified, from James's immersion of it in metaphor, and from his unerring sense of social appearance.

In his earlier fiction James had often openly contrasted American manners and assumptions with European ones, American innocence and strength with European worldliness and experience. Now the war has gone underground, so to speak, and in these two novels takes a form at once more brutal and more subtle, more humorous and more dramatic. Milly—and it is the most touching thing about her—is the solitary American champion, demonstrating among other things James's own obscure loyalty to the tradition and the country in which he had been born and bred. She is hedged about by English intrigue and deceit, and—much more dangerously—by that, in one sense perfectly genuine, loving and cherishing which makes people coo over her as 'the Dove'. No wonder she 'studies the dovelike', and how 'a dove would act', for like Maggie in *The Golden Bowl* she learns to equal the natives in the subtlety of their own moves, although her subtlety is of a different order, and the metaphor in which it is conveyed often homely. She is touchingly described as drawing up to her chin, like a down comforter, the theory that Merton Densher is indeed in love with the vivid Kate, but that Kate cannot help it, 'could only be sorry and kind'. For Milly the comfort in that Scenario is that Densher may in time turn to her, if she opens her wings to him. But the effect of the image, as of so many others, is to remove from Milly any too obviously dramatic and sentimental presentation—the lonely loving heart betrayed etc.—just as James is so exquisitely careful not to exploit the promisingly pathetic theme of the young girl who is to die.

The homeliness, the lack of insistence, mean that Milly's love for Densher is ordinarily and touchingly commonplace, a hunger for affection, a reaching out for someone with whom to feel at home. Densher, after all, unlike Lord Mark and the Lancaster Gate set, is a figure whose origins and personality bridge the gap between English and American manners, and perhaps his love might do the same? We remember that in *The Portrait of a Lady*—James's first major novel—the heroine rejects both the English and the American prototype hero to choose an international figure. Isobel Archer's decision to marry Gilbert Osmond has disastrous consequences; but James at that time had not in any case the gifts or the experience to convey the impression that she was really in love with him: indeed he makes a virtue out of this inability by suggesting that Isobel married Osmond because it seemed to her the 'right' thing to do. At the time when he was writing *The Wings of the Dove* James had come to know personally what love-longing was all about—young men had come into his lonely and elderly bachelor existence for whom he felt a very great need and affection—and in the sense he gives of Milly's consciousness he marvellously conveys all the softness of love, and the way in which its yearnings are twinned with loneliness and isolation.

Like many successful fictional creations Milly was taken by different readers in different ways. For James's friend William Dean Howells she had a 'lovely impalpability'. More vulgar female readers, on the other hand, had no difficulty in identifying with her at a more sensuous level. A very rich and pushy young American who had been a tycoon's mistress insisted on a meeting. 'Oh Mr James,' gushed Miss Grigsby, 'everyone says I look like Milly Theale. Do *you* think I look like Milly Theale?' We can guess at James's recoil from this approach, and at the care he subsequently took to keep Miss Grigsby out of his life; but she had indicated a certain kind of success in his portrait of Milly, and one which was the logical outcome of his desire to produce a love story to which many readers might respond. In letters to his cronies James was careful to belittle his story on precisely these grounds, but it is significant that both *The Wings of the Dove* and *The Golden Bowl* contain a strong element of popular appeal, an appeal based on James's newfound ability to convey with graphic sensuousness, as well as subtlety, what passionate love and sex were really like. There is an element of *East Lynne,* as it were, in both novels, and the way in which their superb density contains the strongest, most sensuous, emotional elements goes far to explain their ever growing popularity and appeal.

Miss Grigsby no doubt intuited something else. She identified with Milly's hair (hers too was red and beautiful), with her pearls and her palazzo, with everything fated and beautiful about her that is like the Bronzino portrait. But no doubt she also relished an underlying element of sexual speculation which is not far from being purient. As his *Notebooks* show, James himself was conscious of this from his first conception of the subject. Somehow he must keep off the idea that sex was the best treatment, that a girl who was fading out of life might be restored, or at least consoled, by the amorous attentions of a young lover. And of course by so scrupulously keeping off this point James's artistry cannot avoid bringing it in. An erotic element can be most powerfully presented in the novel by certain kinds of exclusion. In keeping sex away from Milly, James in fact surrounds her with its mysterious and disturbing intensities. Kate and Densher, the healthy lovers, are positively ill with its importunacy, which they slake together when she comes alone to his Venice lodging.

The atmosphere of Venice, so powerfully suggested in James's descriptive writing, itself enhances the sexual motif, as it does in Thomas Mann's novella *Death in Venice,* and more recently in Anthony Powell's *Temporary Kings,* the last but one novel in his sequence *A Dance to the Music of Time.* For James as tourist, as well as artist, Venice was a repository of ancient sex, which he had brought to life in his own story, *The Aspern Papers.* Years before, Constance Fenimore Woolson, a middle-aged American lady who had been devoted to him—more devoted than he realized at the time—had fallen to her death one December from the window of her lonely Venetian home. Haunted as it was, the city was a natural setting for the haunting dénouement of his novel-drama. And in the withdrawal of Milly from sight, in that setting, we may feel that she is gathered up into James's own consciousness. She dies in her palazzo, which James identified in a letter as having been inspired by his view of the Palazzo Barbaro, near the Iron Bridge. The name is sufficiently redolent of the old energies and ruthlessness which lurk in the town, conjured up by James to give a new sort of life to his novel.

Venice indeed fills the gap left by James's withdrawal from view of the main action. In his Preface to the novel in the New York edition he draws attention to the technical shortcomings of the work as he sees them. It has a 'makeshift middle' and a 'displaced centre'. The second half 'bristles with "dodges" . . . which would form a signal object-lesson for a literary critic bent on improving his occasion to the profit of the budding artist'. The perspective misleads deliberately, because the artist has had to 'produce the illusion of mass without the illusion of extent'. James's Prefaces may be treasure-houses of technical lore as he conceived it, but from the point of view of the reader they have been overvalued. The novelist, after all, is too close to the bricks and mortar to judge of the building as his reader sees it: the reader indeed may be depressed, even disillusioned, by the writer's view of things. In his Prefaces James comes closer to portentousness, to that 'self-reverence' of which H. G. Wells accused him, than he ever does elsewhere.

Of course *The Wings of the Dove,* like all great novels, has its shortcomings, which the reader can be the best judge of. As in *The Ambassadors* there is perhaps too much emphasis on the *idea* of 'living', and of love as the big part of living: Milly's hunger for both is touching, but is also too much determined, in its directions, by the way the plot has to go. And yet like all great novels this one seems to the reader *true,* deep, a mass of complex and authentic creation, querying, wondering, and revealing. There is a sad tendency today to see the novel as a form purely in terms of its 'literariness', as James himself is apt to do in his Prefaces. It is natural there that he should cover up his own deepest contribution, which is, just as with Tolstoy or Kafka, in his most mature works essentially himself, his own vision of things. He desired, as an artist, to be absent from his creation, as he claimed that Shakespeare was absent—except as an artist—from *The Tempest;* and yet deep down he also knew that the man was present 'on every page'.

And, it may be, in every character. James himself was present, in a deep and subterranean sense, in Isobel Archer of *The Portrait of A Lady,* just as he is present in Kate Croy of *The Wings of the Dove.* Of all such deeply considered heroines he could have said *'C'est moi',* as Flaubert did of Madame Bovary. But there is a special reason why *The Wings of the Dove* holds a symbol of the Jamesian consciousness, a symbol as moving as it is inclusive. He had put himself, very straightforwardly, into *The Ambassadors* as its leading *conscience,* Lambert Strether, and the considered simplicity of the connection is a weakness of that novel. In *The Wings* conscience takes on a form at once more inevitable and more completely and unconsciously dramatized. I have said that when the Dove dies she is gathered up into James's own consciousness. This occurs because James has always been the Dove, has put his own predicament into hers, and his own self-questioning.

Milly's fabulous wealth is James's talent. It does her no good; and James himself had often ruefully considered at this time that his gifts had been betrayed by the public, which had ignored or misunderstood him; that all they

had brought him was isolation, solitude, a state cut off from living and the normal joys of human being. This is the hidden source of the power which the image of Milly presents in the book to the reader. Cut off by his powers from the human race, James will none the less continue to sustain it with his art when he is dead. And yet the artist's faith that his wings will stretch over and comfort the race to come does not mitigate the bitterness of his own private death, his unlived life. 'Fearfulness and trembling are come upon me, and an horrible dread hath overwhelmed me. And I said, Oh that I had wings like a dove! for then would I flee away and be at rest.' So wrote the psalmist in the Fifty-Fifth Psalm, recording the deceit and guile of the world and the despair they bring. But in the Sixty-Eighth Psalm he wrote also, 'Yet shall ye be as the wings of a dove, that is covered with silver wings and her feathers like gold.'

There is nothing especially hermeneutic in such a reading of the novel's powers; certainly nothing portentous. Humour and incongruity are as basic to these great works of James's maturity as are the deep process of questioning and self-questioning in them, the comprehension of class and family not in naturalistic and sociological terms but as contradictory and infinitely complex manifestations of life, driven by personal furies, cloaking determined purposes. Both the serpent and the dove are in James himself; the innocence and openness of the novel are as wonderful as its wisdom and its guile. Milly's fate and her forgiveness, hidden from us as they are, are deeply moving, but they remain humanly subject to what James called 'varieties of interpretation'. More touching still is the image of Milly as the Dove who only wants to be somebody's duck, who wants to be loved as herself. Humour and its incongruities, love and its simplicities, are the breath of life in these novels. As is the power of money. The Dove's feathers are covered with gold, as is the fabulous bowl in the next novel, and these things are not just symbolic. Standing in a very rich lady's gilded drawing-room James once remarked *sotto voce* to a friend: 'I can stand a great deal of gold.'

Gold was power, whose operations at all levels and in all types of psychology James profoundly understood. His knowledge helped him to unlock both the narrative and the dramatic doors, and in this novel to enter both at the same time. It had given him new powers, even when he seemed at his most powerless. His failure on the London stage, the collapse of his hopes as a popular and successful writer, had been compensated by the great novels which came to him in those long monastic hours at Lamb House, Rye, pacing to and fro every morning, confiding to his faithful typist at her machine. (pp. 7-29)

John Bayley, in an introduction to The Wings of the Dove *by Henry James, edited by John Bayley, Penguin Books, 1986, pp. 7-29.*

Michael Kellogg   (essay date 1987)

[*In the following essay, Kellogg discusses the objectives and limitations of James's late style.*]

Teddy Roosevelt dismissed Henry James as "an effete and

miserable snob." HJ returned the compliment by classifying his distinguished contemporary as a "dangerous jingo." The superficial insight and profound injustice of both views should surprise no one. The two men were bound to misunderstand one another, just as Sarah Pocock and Lambert Strether in *The Ambassadors* had no common ground on which to meet. Indeed, the difficulties engendered by such meetings between American forces of nature and European—whether home-grown or naturalized—refinements form a recurring theme in James's works.

Although James could accurately depict the American *type,* it is clear, despite some early sympathetic if wooden portraits—Christopher Newman in *The American* and Casper Goodwood in *The Portrait of a Lady,* for example—that he was in the end wholly of the opposite camp. And the sneaking sympathy we feel with TR's assessment of James is directly linked to a frustration with James's hyper-refinement of both matter and manner. We long at times for a Roosevelt to burst onto the scene of one of James's later novels, particularly *The Golden Bowl,* and disperse the swirls of obscurity by calling a spade, at last, a spade.

Nothing, of course, would be resolved by calling Charlotte a slut, the Prince a cad, Maggie a simpering fool, and Adam Verver an amiable nonentity; nothing, that is, but our craving for exact labels. And it is precisely this craving that James, in his later works, steadfastly refuses to satisfy. For such labels, once applied, free us from further thought about their subjects. They sum them up and dismiss them, as TR, in character, and HJ, in a rare lapse, summed up and dismissed one another.

An aversion to simplistic assessment is the hallmark of the later James. It is, therefore, surprising to find even such perceptive readers as Leon Edel and Gore Vidal subscribing to the conventional wisdom that James's later style was dictated, literally, by his acquisition of a typewriter and amanuensis. On this view, he simply started to write as he talked and James was, by all accounts, a most elliptical talker. But the studied indirection of James's later style and the harmony of that style with James's mission as an artist—as he came finally to understand it—belie such an unselfconscious, that is inartistic, account. Vidal, in particular, has carelessly dismissed as incidental (if not unfortunate) what is in fact James's supreme achievement.

Common speech is a well-worn path from which our thoughts and feelings too seldom stray. Our words for things, by their very familiarity and the ease with which we apply them, become substitutes in a sense for perceiving the things themselves. Or, at least, they make it easy not to perceive too closely or to distinguish too finely. Yet close perception and fine distinction are the essence of James's art. So if language is a grid that we impose upon experience in what his brother William called "the mind's act of self-defense against universal drift and decay," then HJ is determined to break the resultant gridlock and work his way or even drift, if he must, to a newer, fresher vantage point.

The theme of James's later novels is the tragedy of the

commonplace; not the pompous sputtering tragedy of visible disaster, but the hidden and largely silent tragedy of the human spirit in its most homely conditions. It is a theme that cannot be handled directly because of the familiarity of the objects of study. They are too encrusted with our ordinary ways of speaking and, hence, thinking about them. Familiarity may not breed contempt, but it does dull perception. George Eliot made the point most beautifully in *Middlemarch.*

> That element of tragedy which lies in the very fact of frequency has not yet wrought itself into the coarse emotion of mankind; and perhaps our frames could hardly bear much of it. If we had a keen vision and feeling of all ordinary human life, it would be like hearing the grass grow and the squirrel's heart beat, and we should die of that roar which lies on the other side of silence. As it is, the quickest of us walk about well wadded with stupidity.

James's art, then—in search as it is of "that element of tragedy which lies in the very fact of frequency"—is supremely one of indirection. He works not so much with words as around them, seeking the felt quality of everyday experience which is masked by coarse abstractions. What may appear as an old-maidish fastidiousness in his refusal to speak plain is in fact a courageous groping toward that "keen vision and feeling of all ordinary human life" of which Eliot speaks.

James explores the human sensibility layer by layer, as if he were peeling off the concentric coats of an onion—each thinner and more delicate than the last—unbeguiled by the prospect of some simple, easily grasped core. The effect of his later style, with its endless qualifications and intimations, is to aid in that exploration by slowing us down, by preventing our slapping familiar labels on things and then rushing on. It brings us round to things by novel routes and presents them from striking angles. It forces us to listen, to see, and to take account.

In the process, we may lose our bearings and be unable to decide, for example, whether Lambert Strether is reaching towards insight or fumbling in obscurity. But struggling with that uncertainty is fundamental not only to Strether's character, but also to our own task as readers. The clarity for which James strives appears obscure, we might say, because it refuses to be satisfied with what ordinarily passes for clarity and is in fact the most resistant because unnoticed form of obscurity.

Needless to say, however, James's later style is not unproblematic. As he himself said in an essay on *Middlemarch,* "the greatest minds have the defects of their qualities." James's prose is rather like the golden bowl itself, richly gilded but covering a grave flaw.

The inherent limitation of James's method, and of the prose which is allied with that method, lies in the truth of Eliot's statement: even the quickest of us do go about "well wadded with stupidity." We lead, of necessity, rather superficial lives. We do not, cannot organize those lives around discriminations too subtle to be communicated directly. Even if our experience has depth in some areas—and that is no insignificant achievement—we must be content in the others, where the requisite intensity cannot be sustained, to pass smoothly on, buoyed by common speech and common judgments. As a result, quarrying of the sort that James does into the commonplace facts of a human life, will repay the effort only in limited areas. Only certain aspects of the lives of certain types of characters are intricate enough to substain a Jamesian analysis.

Much of the world of action, which thrives on superficialities, is therefore excluded by James's technique. Paste-on labels for things set the stage for action. They provide the confident backdrop necessary for vigorous activity, and without them we cannot "get on." It is the refusal or inability to traffic in such labels that leads to the near paralysis of the Jamesian hero. Thus, Lambert Strether cannot, will not see—until it is directly thrust upon him—the "hard realities," as Woollett might say, of Chad's relations with Madame de Vionnet. Strether sees, rather, the extent to which Chad has been polished and enriched by that relationship. And he sees Madame de Vionnet in all her charm and desperation. Strether is entranced by the deeper, but more elusive, reality of the "virtuous attachment" promised him by Little Bilham.

Sarah Pocock, by contrast, is able to swoop down and collect her too willing prize with a vigor worthy of TR precisely because she sees nothing but the sordid liaison. Strether feels the tragedy of Madame de Vionnet. Sarah Pocock knows nothing but the melodrama of "saving" Chad, a drama in which Strether has miserably failed to play his part.

In *The Golden Bowl* only two actions are directly and vividly portrayed: the kiss of Charlotte and the Prince in Part I and the shattering of the golden bowl by Fanny Assingham in Part II. These two actions, in their ringing clarity, reverberate throughout the novel. They are endlessly dissected and analyzed. All their causes and consequences are exposed. The result is fascinating; but human life, we must insist, consists largely of doing, not of thinking about doing. What James said of Maggie—"Her grasp of appearances was out of proportion to her view of causes"— can be turned on its head and applied to him. James's view of causes is out of proportion to his grasp of appearances. Or, as Marian Hooper Adams more pithily put it: "Henry James chewed more than he bit off."

Since most of us have not time for endless rumination on the springs of conduct, James is also restricted in his cast. He must create for his principal characters persons who are plausibly articulate about the subtle shadings of the spirit, and who have sufficient leisure to be preoccupied with such things. Sarah Pocock doesn't merit much attention because her consciousness isn't rich enough. She is too easily played out, existing as she does on the surface of things and at home as she is in the world of action.

James's style culminates in *The Golden Bowl,* his most perfect and most limited work. The lack of a Sarah Pocock to intervene as *deus ex machina* at least permits him to play out his hand fully, with a fully Jamesian cast. The beauty and poignancy of the analysis are unsurpassed in literature. But one cannot escape a distinct distaste for the idleness, the vacuity of each of the four major characters as

Their endless subtleties and amoral refinements ultimately leave us cold.

When we act we do so admittedly on the illusion of simplicity. But we do act, because we haven't the luxury of constantly playing Hamlet. Yet we need not be as insensitive as Sarah Pocock. There is a balance to be struck and our life as moral beings is a search for that balance. One feels that James, in his horror of coarse simplicity, badly missed the middle ground. The resultant paradox is that one of the greatest students of human nature, to reverse a remark he made about Dickens, understood man but not men.

No writer ever listened harder for the squirrel's heartbeat than Henry James. That is his greatness and his limitation. (pp. 432-36)

> Michael Kellogg, "The Squirrel's Heartbeat:
> Some Thoughts on the Later Style of Henry
> James," in The Hudson Review, *Vol. XL, No.
> 3, Autumn, 1987, pp. 432-36.*

Paul Lukacs   (essay date 1988)

[*In the following essay, Lukacs assesses the use of ambiguity in* Daisy Miller *within the context of James's later novels.*]

Daisy Miller, although widely taught and widely read, is usually dismissed by scholars and critics as a minor work. This cannot be because of its size, as the same commentators inevitably prize the equally concise *Turn of the* ***Screw.*** Nor can it be because of its theme. First published in 1878, this small novel stands as what Leon Edel [in his *Henry James: The Conquest of London*] calls "the prototype" of the international theme that Henry James explored in longer, more critically admired novels such as *The Portrait of a Lady* (1881), ***The Ambassadors*** (1903), and *The Golden Bowl* (1904). Yet, while the theme suggests affinities with James' more celebrated fiction, its presentation suggests an important difference; and clearly this difference is what accounts for the critical dismissal of the novel. When compared to those other novels, both the form and content of ***Daisy Miller*** seem straightforward and accessible. Unlike James' later experiments with narrative point of view, here it is always clear what the observing consciousness is thinking. So too, here the style is clear and direct, and there is little doubt about what happens or even about why it happens. In short, ***Daisy Miller*** is unlike James' more celebrated novels because it seems unambiguous, and precisely because it seems unambiguous, critics tend to view it as little more than light entertainment, in Edel's words, "the equivalent of a pencil sketch on an artist's pad."

Ambiguity, or at least ambiguity of a certain type, is widely considered the hallmark of James' mature style, with some critics going so far as to argue that his use of it amounts to a veritable revolution in the history of the novel. Yet "ambiguity" is itself something of an ambiguous term, and these critics disagree on exactly what type of ambiguity James should be credited with employing. Some consider it primarily stylistic, while others see it as an aspect of narration. Still others view it as a function of plot, since "what happens" in a James novel, especially a novel of his major phase, happens within a character's consciousness moreso than within the social world. Dorothea Krook [in her *The Ordeal of Consciousness in Henry James*] offers a synthesis of these views when, referring specifically to **The Golden Bowl,** she writes:

> [James presents] his story at every point through the consciousness of a single interpreter, so that everything that happens is seen from that interpreter's point of view and no other. . . . [He arranges] the dialogues and interior monologues [so] that they with perfect self-consistency yield two distinct and, in the context, contradictory meanings, one confirming the validity of the interpreter's point of view, the other putting it in doubt.

Scholars clearly do not consider **Daisy Miller** to be ambiguous in this sense. For one, James' style was much more direct in 1878 than in 1904. For another, since the action of the novel is essentially social, "what happens" has little to do with an interpreter's point of view. And finally, while the story is filtered through a character's consciousness, that character's interpretation is never obscure. Put simply, Frederick Winterbourne's opinion of Miss Daisy Miller changes over the course of her story, but what occasions the change always seems perfectly clear.

Yet the *meaning* of such change is not at all clear. At the end of the novel Daisy's Italian companion, Giovanelli, tells Winterbourne that "she was the most beautiful young lady I ever saw . . . [and] the most innocent." This occasions Winterbourne's final change of heart, so confusing him that he is left staring speechlessly at her newly dug grave, a "raw protuberance among the April daisies." What happens here is perfectly clear; even why it happens is clear enough. But what remains unclear all throughout the novel is the *meaning* of such happenings. For if **Daisy Miller** is not ambiguous in the ways that **The Golden Bowl** or **The Ambassadors** are, it nonetheless is far from straight-forward. Indeed, judging from popular rather than critical reaction, it may well be the least straight-forward of all of James' novels. Beginning with its first publication, **Daisy Miller** always has yielded two completely different readings, one which sees Daisy's "innocence" as a virtue, and another which sees it as willful ignorance. This ambiguity is not a matter of technique. Instead, it is a matter of theme. Daisy may well be "the most innocent," but neither Winterbourne nor the reader can ever be certain of what that means.

Nor apparently could James himself be certain. As part of the controversy that the novel produced upon its publication, the English writer Mrs. Lynn Linton wrote to James asking him to explain himself. A heated argument had broken out at one of her usually urbane dinner parties, and the battle-lines were clear. "Did you mean us to understand," Mrs. Linton inquired, "that Daisy went on her mad way with Giovanelli just in defiance of public opinion, urged thereto by the opposition made and the talk she excited?" Or was she "too heedless, and too little conscious of appearance to understand what people made such a fuss about?" James' response could not have been

very helpful. While he affirmed that Daisy was "above all things innocent" and even called her story a "little tragedy of a light, thin, natural, unsuspecting creature," he at the same time noted that she "was very fond . . . of gentlemen's society" and bluntly labeled her "a flirt." When he revised the story for the collected New York edition of his work thirty years later, he tried to avoid the issue entirely: "My supposedly typical little figure," he wrote in his Preface, "was of course pure poetry, and had never been anything else."

But the issue did not go away and Daisy had never been just "pure poetry." Although James dropped the original subtitle as part of his revision, the novel remains "A Study," that is, an investigation of a type or problem. Daisy's type is announced plainly when she is first presented: "Here comes my sister," young Randolph Miller cries out, "she's an American girl." The problem is announced a few pages later. Miss Daisy Miller looks "extremely innocent," thinks Winterbourne:

> Never, indeed, since he had grown old enough to appreciate things, had he encountered a young American girl of so pronounced a type as this. Certainly she was very charming; but how deucedly sociable! Was she simply a pretty girl from New York state. . . . Or was she also a designing, an audacious, an unscrupulous young person? Winterbourne had lost his instinct in this matter, and his reason could not help him.

The problem is how to interpret the type, and by extension, the story that carries her name. As Mrs. Linton's dinner guests well understood, either Daisy is an innocent victim of an unfeeling society or she is a head-strong flirt. Thus her story depicts either an American girl who is destroyed through her contact with the oppressive atmosphere of the "old world" or an American girl who dies as a consequence of being too stubborn and naive to listen to sensible advice. Again, the issue is not whether Daisy is innocent. Instead, the issue is what her being innocent means.

According to one reading, Daisy's innocence means that she is a child of nature as opposed to history. The novel provides plenty of evidence to support this interpretation. When Winterbourne first meets Daisy, he is struck by her "perfectly direct and unshrinking" glance; and when he escorts her to the Castle of Chillon, he notes that she "avoid[s] neither his eyes nor those of anyone else," thus confirming his earlier impression that being with her is not at all like "social intercourse in the dark old city at the other end of the lake." Later, when Mrs. Walker advises her that "it is not the custom" to walk through the Roman streets without a proper chaperone, Daisy bravely declares: "I never heard anything so stiff! If this is improper . . . then I am all improper, and you must give me up." This interpretation sees Daisy's innocence as a virtue that separates her from the unnecessarily "stiff" conventions of an excessively traditional society. If it means that she is inexperienced, it also means that she has nothing to hide. Thus she plays no roles and carries no affectations; and she is innocent also in the sense of being guiltless, innocent, that is, of the charges of vulgarity and indelicacy that repeatedly are brought against her. Indeed, according to this view, those charges actually indict Mrs. Walker and all the other self-appointed arbiters of social *mores* who so cruelly shun Daisy. For since this American flower wants nothing more than the freedom to be herself, their selfishness is the only real impropriety.

This first interpretation has proved especially popular with readers who see **Daisy Miller** as part of a larger pattern in American literature. In their view, the novel is indeed unambiguous, celebrating new world innocence as it condemns old world prejudice. Thus more than one commentator has taken Daisy to be, like Billy Budd, Huck Finn, or Natty Bumppo, a mythic or archetypal figure. . . . Yet a second interpretation has proved equally popular ever since the novel first appeared; and according to it, Daisy is anything but mythic. This second reading takes her innocence to be an inexperience that manifests itself as willful ignorance, and it finds her guilty of the very charges that the expatriate colony brings against her. It agrees with Mrs. Walker's conclusion, that Daisy does "everything that is not done here" because she is "*naturally* indelicate."

What is remarkable about these two readings, and what in turn makes the peculiar ambiguity of **Daisy Miller** so clear, is that they both rely on the same textual evidence. A reader who arrives at the second interpretation will agree that Daisy is a child of nature; he will disagree, however, on what being a child of nature means. According to this reading, she is conceited and self-centered, someone who always "prattle[s] about her own affairs" and insists that no one can "interfere with anything I do." Again, the text provides plenty of evidence. Throughout the novel Daisy simply does not know how to behave properly, and she responds defiantly if anyone bothers to tell her so. For example, when Mrs. Walker cautions her about walking without a proper chaperone, she declares, "I don't think I want to know what you mean. . . . I don't think I should like it." And when Winterbourne warns her to stop flirting openly with Giovanelli, she insists, "in her little tormenting manner," that she prefers "weak tea" to any of his "advice." She is full of herself, always conscious that people are watching her but never willing to entertain the possibility that someone else might know what is good for her. "All I want," she tells Winterbourne when he proposes escorting her to Chillon, "[is] a little fuss!" And near the end of the novel she behaves more and more like a spoiled child, going so far as to exclaim, "I don't care . . . whether I have Roman fever or not!" In short, according to this interpretation, Daisy acts both improperly and irresponsibly so that her death results from her own ignorance, stupidity, and vanity. Continually revealing a lack of standards and principles, she is guilty of willfully ignoring the recommendations of those whose standards are clear.

Early in the novel Winterbourne's aunt, Mrs. Costello, judges Daisy to be "very common," the "sort of [American] that one does one's duty by . . . not accepting." That Daisy *is* common is clear. From beginning to end she is identified as a type, and any attempt to discover some core of character that goes beyond or transcends the type inevitably fails. It fails because in 1878 James steadfastly re-

fused to give her any sort of private or personal identity. Consequently the two interpretations of her also become interpretations of a certain kind of American girl, which is the problem that Winterbourne fails to solve from beginning to end. Initially, when he thinks her "only a pretty American flirt" he is "grateful for having found the formula" that applies to her. Later, however, he defends her because he does not believe that someone so "pretty and undefended and natural" should be "assigned to a vulgar place among the categories of disorder." The problem is clear enough:

> He said to himself that she was too light and childish, too uncultivated and unreasoning, too provincial, to have reflected upon her ostracism or even to have perceived it. Then at other moments he believed that she carried about in her elegant and irresponsible little organism a defiant, passionate, perfectly observant consciousness of the impression she produced. He asked himself whether Daisy's defiance came from the consciousness of innocence or from her being, essentially, a young person of the reckless class.

Every reader of the novel faces this problem, for the same textual evidence yields two radically different readings, one of which praises Daisy for her innocence, another which indicts her for it. The ambiguity comes, however, in there being no interpretive middle ground between these two. This American girl is either naive and unassuming or defiant and calculating, and there simply is no way to resolve the discrepancy.

This problem of Daisy's ambiguous character and the ambiguous theme cannot be resolved because James never presents her mind at work. In this vein, Winterbourne asks exactly the right question: does Daisy have "the consciousness of innocence?" Yet even that question can be interpreted in two ways: Does she have the consciousness, meaning the state of mind, of innocence? Or does she have the consciousness, meaning the awareness, of being innocent? Since answering yes to one of these entails answering no to the other, both Winterbourne and the reader end the novel still unsure. Even James was unable finally to make up his mind. When he judged Daisy to be "pure poetry" he quite clearly sided with her. That judgment came thirty years after he created her, however, when his understanding of both ambiguity and the international theme had changed. In his Preface to the 1909 New York edition, James defended that judgment by asserting that "pure poetry . . . is what helpful imagination, in however slight a dose, ever directly makes for." He supplied some such help in his revisions by emphasizing Daisy's charm and her critics' prejudices. Yet this dose of helpful imagination was indeed slight, for without radically rewriting the whole novel, he could not give Daisy the depth of personal character that would allow her to transcend her type. Thus when he looked back at her at the end of his career, he concluded that because she remained so obviously a type, her story was not really a good one. It suffered, he wrote, from "a certain flatness in my poor little heroine's literal denomination," which is to say that when compared with the fiction he had been writing more recently, it lacked the kind of ambiguity he prized.

The problem with *Daisy Miller,* according to James in 1909 as well as a host of later critics, is its very subject. As a "prototype" of the international theme, however, its subject makes perfect sense. For no matter which interpretation of it one chooses, this novel tells the story of an innocent American girl's experience in Europe. James was to tell similar stories for the rest of his life. Yet beginning with *The Portrait of a Lady,* published three short years after *Daisy,* he began to move away from a presentation of national or social type to a presentation of more personal character. "The germ" of that novel, he writes in its Preface, was "the character and aspect of a particular engaging young woman;" and the problem he faced when writing it was how to endow this "slight personality . . . with the high attributes of a Subject," that is, how to construct a plot that would not reduce the character to a type. Thus the significant movement in Isabel Archer's story does not really involve "what happens" in society, the change in her social status from a single American girl to a married expatriate. Instead, the significant movement involves her consciousness of what happens (or has happened). She begins the novel as a young girl who is essentially unaware of the nature of the world, and she concludes it as a mature woman who sees fully who and where she is. James allows more and more access to Isabel's mind until her consciousness becomes *the* point of view that interprets what happens in the novel. As he put it in the Preface, "the centre of the subject" is not her relation to other characters or other "things that are not herself;" instead, the center of interest is "her relation to herself."

James' interest in representing a character's "relation to herself" led him, twenty years later in the novels of his major phase, to refract virtually all of a protagonist's experiences through his or her individual consciousness. In turn, this emphasis on the individual process of seeing and interpreting led to his celebrated ambiguity, as virtually everything that happens in one of these novels is interpreted through an individual point of view. As James himself writes in his Preface to *The Ambassadors,* "the business of my tale and the march of my action, not to say the precious moral of everything, is just my demonstration of this process of vision." Demonstrating that process compelled him, however, to increasingly portray his protagonists in personal as opposed to social terms. Thus, while Isabel Archer, Lambert Strether, and Maggie Verver are all, like Daisy Miller, Americans abroad, their social and national identities become less and less important in their respective novels until by the end of *The Golden Bowl* Maggie's place in a fictitious "American City" is rendered irrelevant by her place in the ivory tower of a wholly imaginative garden. She never once sees herself as a social type and, consequently, the opposed readings that produce ambiguities have very little to do with her being an American in Europe. As Leon Edel suggests, the theme of this, James' last completed novel, is "personal" and "philosophical" but finally not social.

James presents the action of *The Golden Bowl* through different points of view, culminating with Maggie's, so that everything that happens in the novel can be read or re-read through her individual consciousness. In *Daisy Miller* he steadfastly refuses to present even a hint of his protagonist's point of view, thus leaving her forever typical and representative but not at all individual. This emphasis on personal awareness makes *The Golden Bowl* a bigger book and Maggie a deeper character than Daisy. It does not, however, make either her or her story any more ambiguous. James was led to prize ambiguity by his conviction that "the *whole* of anything is never told." But he was led to that conviction by his realization that the kind of social dilemma he represented in *Daisy Miller* could not be resolved. The thematic ambiguity of his little story of the innocent American girl's experience in Europe has little to do with his technique as a novelist. Indeed, unlike his later, more famous ambiguity, it may never have been completely in his control. Isabel Archer, Lambert Strether, and Maggie Verver all reenact in various ways Daisy's story, but in doing so they become less and less "typical" as their stories become more and more personal. Consequently, in their novels James' international theme becomes increasingly unambiguous and at times even incidental. Yet in *Daisy Miller,* which tells only the story of a social type, the international theme is forever unresolved and forever in the fore. In turn, that unambiguous ambiguity makes this small novel a truly major work, not a pencil sketch but a wonderfully suggestive and complex study. (pp. 209-15)

Paul Lukacs, "Unambiguous Ambiguity: The International Theme of 'Daisy Miller'," in Studies in American Fiction, Vol. 15, No. 2, Autumn, 1988, pp. 209-16.

Lois Hughson   (essay date 1988)

[*In the following excerpt, Hughson examines the historical and biographical perspectives James employs in* The Portrait of a Lady, The Bostonians, The Princess Casamassima, *and* The Tragic Muse.]

While Henry Adams confirmed himself in the belief that historical narrative would never show how things really happened if it continued to be written as a variant of biography, Henry James's fictional narratives also moved away from the model of biography toward the model of history. Written in a span of five years, *The Bostonians* (1886), *The Princess Casamassima* (1886), and *The Tragic Muse* (1890) all constitute . . . a critique of the idea that the world exists for the education of man. They embody a rejection of the Emersonian view that individual consciousness is adequate to the meaning of experience. Rather, they attempt to find coherence and continuity by invoking a realm of action that, as historical, can tolerate the elements of antagonism, contradiction, and real change without diminishing in significance. Dominated by the sense of irony that comes from the confrontation of individual claims to power and actual events and from the variance of intent and outcome, these novels show that what is at stake in the move away from biography toward history is the fate of the individual will. They end in the containment of the explosive forces of history and in the establishment or reestablishment of an equilibrium that was threatened by the action of the narrative.

The Bostonians, The Princess Casamassima, and *The*

Tragic Muse have for some time now been thought of by James scholars as the novels most influenced by the ideas and practice of the French naturalists. Most recently Sergio Perosa described them as "experimental" in Zola's meaning of the word: "marked that is by an awareness of social and environmental problems and by a reliance on the principle of full documentary exposition." Although I am not persuaded that we can best get at these novels through such a term as *documentary,* James clearly had an idea of the novel quite different from the one he embodied in *The Portrait of a Lady* (1881). As he said in the preface to *The Tragic Muse,* the novel is much like a Tintoretto painting in which more than one thing is going on while the subject remains one. Although he did not comment on it, the space in the Tintoretto is public. The difference between *The Portrait of a Lady* and these novels is, indeed, the difference between a portrait and a fresco, between a biography and a history: in the one, the aim is to understand a person, the important actions conceived of as those which are characteristic of the person and explain her essence; in the other, the aim is to understand the relations among a series of events in which character is not wholly private but serves to connect and explain the events. In a history, whether painted or printed, character cannot be understood without reference to a sequence established among the events on the canvas.

We may come to understand better, through James's use of a biographical model in *The Portrait of a Lady,* the attractiveness to him of the more inclusive historical model. *Portrait* is a novel entirely consonant with the view that experience is the education of consciousness. It starts with ignorance and ends in knowledge. Its heroine is all potential at the outset, all finished form at the conclusion. It begins with unmarried innocence and ends in married experience. The birth, growth, maturity, and self-discovery of the heroine through the paradigmatic subject of a choice of husband controls the depiction of a world whose events are never explained in any terms but personal. Individual psychology is sufficient. What Isabel comes to know about herself is her attachment to a certain moral view of life that transcends particular historical moments. She returns not to Osmond but to the idea of marriage. Little attempt is made to give the manners so acutely observed any historical explanation. Even when a novel is so attentive to social detail that it can serve a later age as an historical document, it may not present experience historically because the author does not desire to explain central events or relationships in terms of the relation of past to present or to focus on moments of threatening or actual change.

Yet if we compare the conclusion of *Portrait* with that of any of Jane Austen's novels, in which the heroine enters a social world that complements and continues the self-discoveries that their experience has provided, we see indeed that Isabel Archer's situation is radically different from Emma's or Elizabeth Bennett's. Isabel's education brings her to a knowledge of the discontinuity between herself and the world and a preference for the world of beautiful but completed forms over the contingent world of ongoing choice and contradictory emotions. Like Henry Adams, who chooses the great abstraction of force that can be measured instead of the confusion of events,

Isabel chooses unity and coherence over multiplicity, which she feels as chaos. Like Adams's education and unlike Emma's, Isabel's education is compromised, though not entirely failed. It comes too late; she has already made the marriage that marks her maturity.

In this disjunction between experience and the consciousness it educates and in James's denial of the chance for that knowledge to make a difference in Isabel's happiness, we see an ambivalence toward the relation of consciousness and experience. Her decision to remain with Osmond is in a fundamental way a confirmation of the self that chose him initially. Although in one sense Isabel seems now, by her loyalty to her empty marriage, to have surrendered her girlish ideal that there must be no disparity between what she is and what she seems, her loyalty is also an affirmation of that ideal. She is not tempted by Warburton or Goodwood, because they challenge an idea of herself to which she is already firmly committed. Although she appears finally to be acting as Henrietta told her one day she must—to please no one, not even herself—she is in the most important sense choosing and pleasing herself.

When James moves toward a model of history, the power of the central consciousness is markedly reduced. The explanation of his characters' fates is conceived more broadly than they are able to comprehend. Unlike Isabel, who is raised to her greatest prominence by her final choice, Verena and Hyacinth are in different degrees obliterated. When Basil throws his cloak over Verena and takes her from the Music Hall, part of her self is submerged; her identity is hidden, not proclaimed. Hyacinth not only kills himself, but, in our last view of him, his body is covered by the Princess. Both Hyacinth and Verena, it is true, come to understand many of the determinants of their positions. Neither, however, comes to the full understanding that Isabel achieves, an understanding that allows the reader to feel her triumphant in spite of her losses and denials. The design of the narratives of the two later novels provides, through the more extensive historical significance of the events, a sense of explanation and therefore a sense of external constraint and necessity that is not one of the effects of *The Portrait of a Lady.*

In exploring "the sentiment of sex," as he called it, in late nineteenth-century America, James sought for genuine historical explanations. We can understand *The Bostonians,* and the lives of its characters only through the events of their shared American past. For instance, Miss Birdseye's efforts in the great reform movements before the Civil War are central in forming an estimation of all their lives: "The great work of her life," James calls it without irony, was "her mission repeated year after year, among the Southern blacks. She had gone among them with every precaution to teach them to read and write; she had carried them Bibles and told them of the friends they had in the North who prayed for their deliverance." She brings from the past a belief in justice and social progress that the events of the present do not justify. The awakening of moral sentiment for the eradication of social abuse that she thinks she sees in the ferment of Boston's Gilded Age is in fact a multiple degradation of the ideal of reform. Reform has become a subject for advertisement, newspaper report, and entertainment for the masses, as it will be if Verena speaks at the Music Hall, and for the mindless rich, as it has been when she spoke at Mrs. Burrage's soiree. In its passing from Miss Birdseye to Olive and Mrs. Farrandar, reform has been cut loose from genuine moral consciousness and transferred to the narrow sphere of personal injury and ambition. In Olive, a sharp but limited understanding of social reality combines with a powerful will and intense but poorly understood emotional needs. The energies this combination releases lead her to a martyrdom not entirely unsought and a removal from the arena of social action in which the ideas she carries can have an historical future.

So committed is James to historical explanations that even Basil's love for Verena is presented as best understood from a historical perspective. The defeated Southerner, the embodiment of the chivalric masculinity whose social basis has been destroyed by the war, Basil comes north. Like many young Southern men of his generation, he adopts the commercial ways of the society that has proved itself stronger. Basil's sexual response to Verena is intermingled with his feelings of resentment about the North, which seems on the verge of defeating him again. The result is that his will is made unexpectedly powerful. His need to see himself as the heroic protector of womanhood comes from his fight against psychic disintegration and his drive to reassert his Southern identity as much as from his love for Verena. Out of his need, he sees a truth about Verena. he sees that she is not committed to feminism, that she is a conduit for other people's ideas, and that even in private she falls into stock phrases and mere forms of argument. To the extent that Basil assumes that a fundamental part of human nature can be distinguished from the social forms that express it—that personality is not subsumed wholly by social role—to this extent his views are James's. We ought not to assume that he speaks for James, however, when he asserts that he knows best which social form expresses Verena's essence. In fact, as a social theorist, he is frequently a figure of fun, with his ideas from Tocqueville and Carlyle and his groundless intellectual self-satisfaction. Yet as David C. Stineback points out, his ideas are not wholly deprecated by James. He is also an outsider through whom the commercial, democratic North can be measured. The ambiguities that some readers find in James's attitude toward the woman's movement and toward Basil spring from James's willingness to permit in the characters a multiplicity of conflicting, yet coherent views of experience.

Verena, as she is presented in the novel, is also a product of historical events. She is the daughter of a charlatan in whom the spiritual needs and questions of pre-Civil War New England are transformed into spirit rapping and faith healing. Her father has no essential self apart from his meretricious roles. That is why his wife is never able to catch the slightest private admission from him that there is anything dishonest in his séances, for example, and why his greatest bliss is to find his name in the newspapers. Verena's mother comes from an old abolitionist family now allied, through her impetuousness, with a man who will sell his own daughter. Verena has been taught, then, to believe in social ideals, but her teachers have been hy-

pocrisy and shoddy commercialism. On the basis of the historical model, the novel should move through these conflicts toward victory for the person whose historical dimension provides a connection and fulfillment for a girl with such a history.

To give that victory to Basil's Southern conservatism and sense of sacred private values rather than the Northern reform that Olive stands for makes a handsome formal reversal of the Civil War. The Southern defeat is reversed, yet Miss Birdseye's hope that a real Southerner will be brought around to the cause is, in a witty maneuver, given new hope. Verena's desire for a life's work like Miss Birdseye's mission in the South is given ironic fulfillment in her marriage. She too will have a mission in the South, and it too will be tumultuous. Of those tears she sheds when she leaves the Music Hall with Basil, James tells us, "in the union, so far from brilliant, into which she was about to enter, these were not the last she was destined to shed." With that word *union,* James reminds us that society and individual lives are shaped by the conflicts of the past. Here the ending specifically invites us to see continued conflict, not resolution.

However, there is a narrative force operating against the sense of continuing conflict at the conclusion of *The Bostonians.* When we look at the action from Verena's point of view, we observe the biographical model in operation. Verena is yet unformed when we meet her. Stineback suggests that Olive and Basil are attracted by her "childlike weakness." She is a consciousness waiting to be awakened to herself and to the world. She even agrees to forswear marriage for the movement because she is ignorant of her own sexuality. The drama lies in the emergence and education of her consciousness. For this reason, when Burrage and his friend mock her and Mathias Pardon offers to make a good thing of her financially, Olive's appropriation of her seems defensible because it contributes to a broadening and deepening of Verena's experience. Similarly, in New York, when Olive at her worst is tempted to marry Verena to Henry Burrage, she provides the increasingly amorous Basil an opportunity to seem to be offering Verena a larger, truer life. By the third part of the novel, Verena has been educated to the point where she must make the kind of choice that biographies from their earliest versions as saints' lives and exempla present their subjects; she must choose between good and evil and reveal her own moral essence. The most profound lesson of her education is the lesson of her sexual nature. Her choice of Basil is the choice of a privacy deeper than any he conceives of, for she is not choosing marriage as the social form that most justly embodies sexuality. She is choosing sexuality itself, for the sake of which she must surrender her loyalty to other social forms she admires and endure forms that are sure to bring her pain.

This biographical model of narrative interacts with the historical model to produce a great complexity and richness as well as a degree of uncertainty of interpretation, but it also competes with the historical model in the sense that Verena's choice is made without reference to the historical model. If we understand Verena's decisions as personal and biographical, then the historical conflicts involving past and present, public and private, North and South, and the possibility of changes in relations between men and women seem almost irrelevant. Verena's great summary choice does not seem to illuminate the historical themes.

Still, in spite of the competition between the biographical and historical models, *The Bostonians* seems to be a novel that shows James's confidence that history as an explanation of events in the public realm and biography as the account of the education of consciousness are compatible and that it is possible to make sense out of experience, not merely to be reduced, as was Henry Adams, to measuring it. The fact that we experience the models as competing rather than wholly complementary reflects the strain James sees in the relation of private and social experience, the biographical and the historical determinants of our actions, and the high cost by which consciousness maintains its integrity and masters experience.

In *The Princess Casamassima,* there is almost no difference between the biographical and historical determinants. Like *The Bostonians, The Princess* works toward a public explosion that never takes place. In both novels, a moment of violent social change, the culmination of historical actions represented in the narrative, is averted by a personal violence that contains it. Within Hyacinth's personal experience are repeated enough of the class tensions within society to make us feel that the full range of society is represented, even if on reflection we miss industrial workers. Indeed, James was probably historically correct in omitting a representative of that class from his depiction of the anarchist groups. In *The Bostonians,* Verena's experience can be interpreted in different ways, depending on whether the model of biography or the model of history dominates; in Hyacinth's experience, however, there is very little disparity between the two models. In fact, Charles Anderson, who argues that the social conflicts are to be understood only as an externalization of Hyacinth's internal dilemma and that James's theme was, again, not the coming revolution but the familiar one of awareness, creates a dichotomy that James's narrative avoids.

Hyacinth's awareness, indeed, is embedded in the course of history, to use Auerbach's phrase, and his tragedy is the tragedy of history. The growth of his awareness as the hero of a novel on the biographical model takes him to the point where he cannot carry out his pledge as an anarchist. Once he becomes aware that the glories of civilization and its abominations are inextricable, he cannot act to bring it down. The story of his own family, in which his ill-treated working-class mother murders his aristocratic father, becomes a prophecy he cannot fulfill once he recognizes himself as his father's son. The relationship with the Princess thus represents one possible reparation for the historical injustice that is inseparable from Hyacinth's private life. With her, the injustice, his illegitimacy, is turned to possible advantage in two senses. First, it is the source of his "gentleness," that is, the nobility that makes possible his visit to Medley and his openness to the beauties of social form and art. Second, a relationship with the Princess marks the transcendence of class hostility and initi-

ates the possibility of new kinds of social organization that will make reparation for past wrongs. The danger that Mme. Grandoni warns of is the lack of any basis for such relationship beyond the Princess's whim. The Princess neither seeks to compensate Hyacinth for the suffering her class has inflicted on him, which is Lady Aurora's motivation, nor can she transcend class and establish new relations on the foundation of common humanity. She is drawn to Hyacinth precisely because he is an anomaly within his class, not for any qualities seen independent of class. Her only worry is that having known Lady Aurora, he may not be as fresh a specimen, as innocent of the beauties of civilization, as she had supposed.

Moreover, the relationship with the Princess is marked by fantasy from its beginning, when she is indeed a princess from a romance, the same romance in which Hyacinth imagines he will be recognized by his father's family. After his return from Europe, the fantasy persists in the scenes where he feels a companionable intimacy with her at her fireside in a relationship that mimics the domestic side of marriage. In Pinnie's death scene, James reminds us of this romance, which is such an important part of Hyacinth's relationship with Pinnie, by having her voice the fantasy that during his absence Hyacinth has been with his aristocratic family, who will now recognize him to compensate for the depravations of his life with her.

The meeting of the anarchists, which precipitates Hyacinth's declaration that he will pledge himself to "immediate action," begins with Poupin's sense of the way social injustice is embodied in Hyacinth—in his origin, in his "mother's disaster. . . . He was *ab ovo* a revolutionist." But James provides more than this rather mechanical explanation of Hyacinth's revolutionary impulses. He vividly depicts the miseries of London that Hyacinth absorbs on his long walks, "and as in that lower world one walked with one's ear nearer the ground the deep perpetual groan of London misery seemed to swell and swell and form the whole undertone of life." When Hyacinth learns that Hoffendahl is in England for some purpose yet unknown, he becomes exalted by the vision, "immensely magnified, [of] the monstrosity of the great ulcers and sores of London—the sick, eternal misery crying out of the darkness in vain, confronted with granaries and treasure-houses and places of delight where shameless satiety kept guard." Aware that Paul Muniment is keeping Hoffendahl's secret plans from him, a secret Hyacinth sees as an opportunity for his own devotion, Hyacinth's tension mounts; out-of-doors he attempts to relieve his nerves, but he is caught between the sense of suffering humanity and the abject helplessness and blundering counsels of the people in the room he has left. Alone in the street, he has the vision of action that becomes inseparable for him from Paul Muniment: "If he had a definite wish while he stood there it was that that exalted deluded company should pour itself forth with Muniment at its head and surge through the sleeping world and gather the myriad miserable out of their slums and burrows, should roll into the selfish squares and lift a tremendous hungry voice and awaken the gorged indifferent to a terror that would bring them down." His relationship with Paul contains the alternative resolution to his disinheritance. In the brotherhood of the anarchists,

Hyacinth might find both the emotional fulfillment he craves and the new social relations to replace the class structure that he hopes to destroy.

Hyacinth, James reveals, is as mistaken about what Paul can give him as about what the Princess can. J. M. Luecke argues that Hyacinth's tragedy originates in this fallible consciousness that makes him so misjudge the two people he has most counted on. Such a view is certainly true to the education of consciousness that the novel contains, but it takes an unnecessarily narrow view of the significance of Paul's and the Princess's failing Hyacinth. Hyacinth is not merely experiencing a sense of abandonment by the people he loves in those hours before his suicide. His anguish at the novel's conclusion, although fed by his relationships with Paul and the Princess, stems primarily from his indecision over the rightness of the anarchist views that have brought them together. The fundamental change in his life comes from his visit to Europe, where "the sense of the wonderful, precious things" society has produced came to dominate in his mind "the idea of how society should be destroyed." After his pledge to Hoffendahl, James tells us, "a change had come over the spirit of his dream. He had not grown more concentrated, he had grown more relaxed." Why should it be, as Lionel Trilling maintains, that Hyacinth's decision to give his life to the revolutionary cause frees him "to understand human glory"? What is the connection, never articulated by Hyacinth nor understood by him but contained and explained by the narrative, between the pledge to kill and die and the discovery of the riches of civilization?

Initially, Hyacinth's entry into the world of beauty involves a guilty separation from his foster mother, Pinnie, and a disloyalty to his class as defined by his suffering mother. Pinnie's fantasy of his aristocratic family feeds both his own fantasy and the guilt that accompanies it, which seems to make her death and the denial of his mother the price for his new life. But the pledge of his life to the cause of the suffering poor atones for his guilt and makes possible his acceptance of money from Pinnie and Mr. Vetch. James writes of his "sense that since he was destined to perish in his flower he was right to make a dash at the beautiful, horrible world." Furthermore, the antagonism inscribed in his parentage is between the suffering poor and the exploiting rich. Before he goes to Europe he does not make the identification of beauty and power that will exacerbate his guilt and make it impossible to surrender his pledge. In the Keatsian world of Medley, sensual delight has nothing to do with power.

In Paris Hyacinth identifies with his revolutionary French grandfather and experiences his most exalted vision of history as mixed destruction and creation, as blood and glory:

> he had recognized so quickly its tremendous historic character. He had seen in a rapid vision the guillotine in the middle, on the site of the inscrutable obelisk, and the tumbrils, with waiting victims, were stationed around the circle now made majestic by the monuments of the cities of France. The great legend of the French Revolution, a sunrise out of a sea of blood, was more real to him here than anywhere else; and,

strangely, what was most present was not its turpitude and horror, but its magnificent energy, the spirit of destruction. That shadow was effaced by the modern fairness of fountain and statue, the stately perspective and composition; and as he lingered before crossing the Seine a sudden sense overtook him, making his heart falter to anguish—a sense of everything that might hold one to the world, of the sweetness of not dying, the fascination of great cities, the charm of travel and discovery, the generosity of admiration.

Hyacinth appears to be preparing to take on the mixed guilt and power of a revolutionary, but in the last lines, he withdraws to a life of passive appreciation.

Yet the emotional intensity of the life that Hyacinth imagines as possible for himself becomes clear in the letter he writes to the Princess explaining his new feelings about the cause. Far from forgetting mankind's suffering, he has a more intense sense of the achievements they have been capable of in spite of it:

> They seem to me inestimably precious and beautiful and I've become conscious more than ever before of how little I understand what in the great rectification you and Poupin propose to do with them. . . . The monuments and treasure of art, the great palaces and properties, the conquests of learning and taste, the general fabric of civilisation as we know it, based if you will upon all the despotisms, the cruelties, the exclusions, the monopolies and the rapacities of the past, but thanks to which, all the same, the world is less of a 'bloody sell' and life more of a lark—our friend Hoffendahl seems to me to hold them too cheap and to wish to substitute for them something in which I can't somehow believe as I do in things with which the yearnings and the tears of generations have been mixed.

The cause now appears, not in the image of the French Revolution, which has been a great destroyer and creator, but as a "redistribution" based on "invidious jealousy." He fears this desire to take and to have in himself and ascribes to Hoffendahl the desire to "cut up the ceilings of the Veronese into strips, so that everyone might have a little strip." Experiencing a "deep mistrust of . . . the intolerance of positions and fortunes that are higher and brighter than one's own," he fears, indeed, that such an intolerance has been his motive in the past. To take any part in the action of history, then, is to be guilty. Hyacinth imagines that to be only an admiring spectator of the results of its energy and horror is to be free of both the suffering and the guilt of action. He conceives of his revolutionary act as performed without the desire for possession that would leave the stain of envy on his soul. He cannot abrogate his pledge for he is caught even more surely by a second form of guilt, the guilt that comes from his recognition of the inextricability of beauty from the horror of power. Even scourging envy from his own heart will not free him of that guilt.

To this point in the novel, the claims of the revolutionary attitude have been strongly advanced, principally through Hyacinth's experience of the cruel London streets, based on James's observations of London, and through the pathos of Pinnie's life, with its suffering despite its unquestioning acceptance of social inequity. In a letter of 1886 to Charles Eliot Norton, James remarked that "the condition of [the English upper class] . . . seems to me to be in many ways very much the same rotten and *collapsible* one as that of the French aristocracy before the revolution—minus cleverness and conversation; or perhaps it's more like the heavy, congested and depraved Roman world upon which the barbarians came down. In England the Huns and Vandals will have to come up—from the black depths of the (in the people) enormous misery. . . . At all events, much of English life is grossly materialistic and wants blood-letting."

The Princess, herself, makes much the same comment to Hyacinth at Medley, but her historical judgment is compromised by her manipulations of her husband, the comedy of her sacrifices, her love affair with Paul, and her failure to see that she is being used. Of course, James make clear that every position is compromised by the limits of the people who espouse it. As in **The Bostonians**, here, too, the model of history does not permit a privileged perspective. Because characters are in the midst of history as experience, no one of them can encompass fully the significance of the action as it progresses. And, indeed, James, himself, was ambivalent about social injustice and revolution. Two years before he wrote that England was ready for a blood-letting, he published **A Little Tour in France** (1884) in which he recorded his response to a bombing in Lyons:

> Of course, there had been arrests and incarcerations, and the "intransigeant" and the "Rappel" were filled with the echoes of the explosion. The tone of these organs is rarely edifying, and it had never been less so than on this occasion. I wondered, as I looked through them, whether I was losing all my radicalism; and then I wondered whether, after all, I had any more to lose. . . . I failed to settle the question, any more than I made up my mind as to the possible future of the militant democracy, or the ultimate form of a civilisation which should have blown up everything else.

Like the irresolute James, Hyacinth, on his return from France, makes a half-hearted attempt to repudiate his pledge. In the scene with Paul Muniment at the park, Hyacinth shows that his desire to strike a revolutionary blow is inseparable from his desire to be loved by Paul. He cannot imagine how, if Paul cares for him, he can contemplate Hyacinth's death, and Paul's reasonableness chills him. He says he will not repudiate his pledge, but he seems to want Paul to tell him not to carry it out. Clearly, Hyacinth regards Paul as having arranged his pledge, and the reader is left with the sense that Paul will not let Hyacinth off the hook, exploiting Hyacinth's affection and admiration for himself but giving no emotional response in return. The "healthy singleness of vision" that James credits him with permits him to remember the "immeasurable misery of the people" and to respond to this cause alone. Although there are no contradictions in Paul as there are in the Princess and he never claims to be something more than he is or to disguise his aims, we feel his inhumanity compared

to the pathos and generosity of the Princess. Furthermore, Hyacinth's sense of Paul as a man of action and power makes Hyacinth's yearning to identify with Paul, to be his brother in social action and in love, another source of guilt as well as a reason to stand by his pledge.

Like Hyacinth, who both takes possession of the aristocratic point of view and seeks to repudiate any point of view based on class resentment, the Princess also seeks to free herself from class. She is trapped, however, by her money. In the comedy of her life, we see her trying to make middle-class bad taste take the place of poverty. But in its tragedy, we see her become aware that only the money and the husband she detests give her a chance to be a part of the movement, that her life is at its core a contradiction. Like the contradictions of history, her personal contradictions are the source of her glory and her destructiveness. She is capable of conceiving and projecting a beautiful idea of social revolution, and by this she constitutes yet another tie that binds Hyacinth to the pledge he gave Hoffendahl, even as she becomes ever more anxious to free him from it.

Hyacinth seeks before his suicide to escape the irreconcilable contradictions that are a part of his relations with Paul and the Princess. His desired return to Millicent would be a return to his origins, to unquestioning membership in the class that marked his childhood. Yet James has represented Hyacinth as alienated from this class by the contradictions of parentage and the peculiar upbringing resulting from it. His air of superiority and refinement make him attractive to Millicent, just as it is what involves him with the Princess, and indeed, it is what makes him Hoffendahl's choice for assassin. Furthermore, Millicent lives in the world of appetite and sensuality where history does not exist. He cannot return there.

He has not lived there since the visit to his dying mother in prison with which the book opens. Pinnie feels rightly the decisiveness of that visit, that in taking him there she has done something needing forgiveness, for she gave him then the burden of his own history. Hyacinth tells her quite mistakenly that that "dismal far-off time . . . had ceased long ago to have any consequences for either of them." His last view of his situation before he chooses suicide is that he cannot bear to commit an act that would not only be a personal repetition of his mother's crime but would also be a blow struck at her by bringing her "forgotten, redeemed pollution" again before the world. In Hyacinth's despair lies the final view of history as a crime reenacted in succeeding generations. To such an idea dwindles the magnificent notion of a world-historical action.

At the moment of crisis the two warring visions of the fulfillment of his pledge are embodied by the Princess and his mother. In the last meeting with the Princess, she argues so eloquently and looks so beautiful that "the image of a heroism not less great flashed up again before him in all the splendour it had lost—the idea of a tremendous risk and an unregarded sacrifice." But at the moment before action, he sees again the revolutionary act as a murder committed out of envy. His mother's act blots out the sublime vision of the French Revolution, "a sunrise out of a sea of blood." When Hyacinth expresses to the Princess his horror at the thought that anything should happen to her, he is speaking not only of his love but of his need for the splendor with which she invests history and human action, against which he feels always the tawdry drag of his own experience. She, in contrast, asks why she should be outside common human destiny. She cannot find her way into history from the world of romance and comedy in which Hyacinth along with the other men in her life and her own ambivalence imprison her.

The disagreement in the critical literature over whether Hyacinth's suicide is an act of heroism or weakness comes from confusing the immediate emotions that compel the act and the significance of the act for the view of history the novel embodies. What Hyacinth as a character feels is loneliness, rejection, alienation, guilt, and the desire to expiate what he experiences as his own envy and selfishness. All of this is mixed with shame at not being able to redeem the pledge he made on behalf of the suffering millions whose claim to justice he still recognizes. But the significance of his action is far beyond what he himself understands it to be.

Ironically his suicide is the reenactment of his mother's action, a striking out at the oppressor class made futile by its private character, a denial of the revolutionary act. In a context where history is seen as the bloody transfer of power and the forms of civilization are inseparable from the class that exercises power, Hyacinth's act also denies a vital part of history. Preoccupied with the forms of the past it forgets or has no faith in the capacity of power to create new forms as it is wielded by new hands. Yet the pledge of the revolutionary act had released in Hyacinth both the response to beauty and the belief in his own capacity to create it. Hyacinth's self-destruction aspires not only to expiate the guilt of hunger and the guilt of power but to bring an end to the cycle of blood and sunrise he imagined history to be. His suicide strikes at once at the lust for power and at creativity, for if we identify power and splendor how can we deny our desire for the one without surrendering the other? The identification also dismisses claims to justice, yet the suicide constitutes a refusal to take part in civilization's injustice or in the destruction of its beauty. His alienation from Paul, the Princess, and Millicent speaks to the alienation that is both his birthright and his destiny. It is not merely the revolutionary act he cannot perform; he can undertake no action because he has no foothold from which to act. Yet every life must be lived from a particular point of view. History is made by the collision of warring and self-justifying perspectives, and we all live in history or not at all.

As a novel written on the model of history, *The Tragic Muse* is less occupied with explanations of the present in terms of the past or with consequences of the past than with the attempt to embody the social history of the late nineteenth-century artist in fiction. The idea of social change as a road to more just relationships and the satisfaction of desire among those excluded from the ruling class is given a different turn than in *The Bostonians* and *The Princess Casamassima.* Through Nick and Miriam, James continues to explore the relationship of personal experience and the shared experience of history, but this time the tragic and sardonic elements of the earlier novels give way to a comedy that forbids suffering. James turns his back on the power of historical action to create and destroy. On his way to the entirely private worlds of the later career that open in the end to myth but never again to the power of the historical dimension, he shuts down the possibilities of significant political action and transfers all the energies of men and women competing for power to the world of art.

In the preface, James compares his novel to a play in which there is no "usurping consciousness." In *The Tragic Muse,* there is no central intelligence against which all the events ultimately are measured, nor is there a figure like Verena or Hyacinth who advances on the biographical model to maturity. Miriam's training in her craft is a way of showing what it means to be an actress, not an initiation into selfhood. From the first, the characters exhibit a self-knowledge or a lack of it that is not altered by events. Their ability to muster the courage and perseverance to choose what is right for them and the clash between fully realized ways of being in the world are the main lines of interest in the narrative.

At the heart of the novel is a fundamentally historical action. Nick's choice of art over politics is an act of rebellion, a revolution against a way of life established by his father and maintained by his mother and Julia Darrow. In Lady Agnes's fate are embodied the social consequences—loss of power, privilege, ease, and status—that the choice signifies. James says of the Dormers at the outset, in the scene at the Salon, that they are "finished creatures . . . ranged there motionless on their green bench." The exhibition carries a threat to them in bringing to Nick the feeling of "youth in the air, and a multitudinous newness, for ever reviving, and the diffusion of a hundred talents, ingenuities, experiments."

Nick's revulsion from politics is not based on the realization that he hasn't the talent for it. On the contrary, he seems to have the abilities to make a great career: he has "the trick" of speaking well; he knows how to appeal "to stupidity, to ignorance, to prejudice, to the love of hollow idiotic words, of shutting the eyes tight and making a noise." Nor is the choice of art merely a choice of one great life over another, for Nick sees politics as emptied of the meaning it had in his father's lifetime. He has come to believe that the parties have no programs, only the wish to be in power; Mrs. Dallow cares little for social improvement, wishing merely to preside over a political salon.

In the episode at Mr. Carteret's house, Mr. Carteret's prodigious memory of old cabinets and elections makes the past weigh heavy in politics and cuts politics off from life, as if parliamentary affairs were not ultimately the affairs of the nation. When Nick expects to see 1830 on his wristwatch, the reader feels further that politics was always so, a matter of form and precedence never filled with the excitement and splendor of human aspiration and rivalry. This is the English political sleep that the revolutionaries of *The Princess Casamassima* wish to disturb. Yet amidst the ruins of the Abbey on the grounds of Mr. Carteret's estate, Nick has a vision of England through the centuries, a combination of history and landscape that seems to make serving his country a relation of love reciprocated.

Whatever ambivalence the reader feels is dissipated in the unpleasant air of financial and emotional blackmail by which Mr. Carteret and Lady Agnes seek to maintain Nick in the life of politics. Nick can more easily free himself to perform his revolutionary act than Hyacinth can because what he rejects has little value in his own eyes. What he chooses is not only an affirmation of what he knows to be his authentic self but is a rejection of the hypocrisy and sordid manipulation that politics means to him.

James is not especially successful, as he admits in the preface to the New York edition, in making us feel what the life of art means to Nick. Oscar Cargill claims that James had no "fund of positive ideas" to give Nick the "quality of creative genius." He wishes James had attended the exhibition of the Fauves and laments his conservative taste in painting. However, James knows a great deal about the stage, and through Miriam he is able to make clear the significance of the life of art to Nick and to herself. Through her relationship with the diplomat, Peter Sherringham, we realize the sense of power and freedom that Miriam's life in the theater gives her and the satisfactions art offers to rapacious drives. When Peter first asks her to give up her career to be "a great diplomatist's wife," she asks what he will do about "the demon, the devil, the devourer and destroyer" in her nature. She rejects the notion of keeping it under but approves when he says he "will gorge it with earthly grandeurs." Nevertheless, only when she feels the full extent of her power as an actress does she believe he has felt it sufficiently to make a mere actress his wife. Her anger that he should believe her to be "the perfection of perfection" and yet imagine she should give it up to be "a muff in public" for him is held in check by what she feels she owes him and by the sense of her own splendor, independent of him, transcending anything society can offer in position, money, or privilege.

The egotism and the desire to dominate and manipulate show most crudely at the outset of Miriam's career, and as she discovers her voice and flowers as an actress, they are the source of the prodigious energy of the process that culminates in the splendor of her presence on stage. James celebrates the power that makes her irresistible to Peter and to the audiences that she enthralls. The power, however, has as its dominion the realm of art. James repeatedly shows that Miriam uses gestures and postures from her roles in social encounters, so that we feel how insignificant the "real" Miriam is. The face, voice, step, spirit, turn of head, and wonderful look that Peter imagines will make her supreme in his world as they do on the stage will turn to mere manner in a diplomat's wife, while on the stage they constitute truth. The real Miriam is the woman who marries Dashwood because she needs such a man to manage horses, rehearsals, tickets, and publicity. Only on the stage is she the exalted being Peter loves. The freedom and power of art is not transferable to the realm of action.

The reader cannot suppose that Nick will attain that freedom and power. It is one thing for the classless Miriam, outside convention by racial heritage, to take up a life sub-

versive to society. Nick declares his independence of his father's world, disinherits himself, and by forcing his mother to surrender Broadwood, destroys for his family the way of life it represents. But Nick's fate is a comedy. The world, in the person of Mrs. Dallow, will not let him go, and his love of her speaks of his imperfect freedom from it. She makes good the damage he has caused, restores his family to Broadwood, and marries his sister to Peter. The reader feels the danger of Gabriel Nash's prophecy. Julia and her way of life may prove too tolerant of Nick's art, and he will be integrated into the life of weekends in the country.

Miriam and Nick both rise above the unpleasant life that social and personal history seem to dictate for them. Verena, however, appears doomed to a continuation of the Civil War and fails to achieve freedom along with her sexual identity. In *The Bostonians,* James represented heterosexuality as a powerful conservative force, but it does not remove Verena from political life. Such a removal is Basil's fantasy, but the reader sees that such a fantasy itself is part of the political world. Every act in the earlier novel is political and part of history. Hyacinth, however, is destroyed by the contradictions of history and politics, for which James could imagine no resolution and no transcendence and whose explosive force he feared. The "demon, devourer, and destroyer" in Miriam that are inseparable from her artistic drive are a part of every action insofar as action is conceived of as the expression of the desire to possess, to dominate, to transform, even to enjoy.

Although Gabriel Nash is a version of the English aesthete, Quentin Anderson, in seeing him as a version of James's father, points to an important link between the way James was brought up to see action in the world and his devotion to art. James, senior, advocated being as superior to doing, just as Nash does, because it is in doing that the demon is unleashed. In the world of *The Princess Casamassima,* there is no way to have something without taking it away from someone else. In the world of haves and have-nots, the have-nots can become haves only by destruction and expropriation. In *The Bostonians,* Olive Chancellor's character is developed with a sharp eye to its self-delusion, its narrowness, its intellectual and emotional ungenerosity in the first half of the narrative, and Olive reaches her moral nadir in the pages where she seems ready to conspire with Mrs. Burrage to marry off Verena in a way that will secure Olive's emotional dominance. At this moment in the narrative, Basil appears as a liberator, and to love him appears to be the choice both of self and of a larger life. Yet as Basil becomes more powerful and persistent, he becomes more problematic a figure, while Olive is given the moving scene on Cape Cod where she is overwhelmed by shame and loss, and Verena feels the cost of her alliance with Basil. Ultimately Basil is represented as capturing and carrying Verena off in a demonstration of domination more ungenerous than anything we have seen in Olive. In Paul Muniment, as in Basil, we see the singleness of vision that James associates with successful action, while both Verena and Hyacinth are torn by their awareness of contending perspectives. Both Paul and Basil share the rapaciousness that Miriam is aware of in herself but that is harmlessly expressed in the symbolic domination and possession of her art, while Nick does not.

All three of these narratives are carried forward by the interaction of different centers of consciousness with antagonistic ways of seeing events and organizing experience. They are pervaded by the ironies arising from these multiple perspectives, and therefore they withhold from the reader a firm moral center. In both *The Bostonians* and *The Princess Casamassima,* the past is morally equivocal, creative and destructive. The present is the continuation, not the resolution of that conflict. In *The Tragic Muse,* James envisions the artist as being able to free himself from history and live without the burden of ambiguous morality: freedom and power without guilt. But in the life of action, those who exercise power tend to be morally obtuse. In James's view of history, both as past and as contemporary social experience, power and justice cannot be united. All the revolutionary forces that James evokes in these novels are held in check by the very moral equivocality that brings them into existence. (pp. 83-102)

> Lois Hughson, "History as a Model for the Novel: Henry James," in her From Biography to History: The Historical Imagination and American Fiction, 1880-1940, *University Press of Virginia, 1988, pp. 83-102.*

James on the distinction between history and fiction:

Historians and story-tellers work each in a very different fashion. With the latter it is the subject, the cause, the impulse, the basis of fact that is given; over it spreads the unobstructed sky, with nothing to hinder the flight of fancy. With the former, it is the effect, the ultimate steps of the movement that are given; those steps by which individuals or parties rise above the heads of the multitude, come into evidence, and make themselves matters of history. At the outset, therefore, the historian has to point to these final manifestations of conduct, and say sternly to his fancy: So far thou shalt go, and no further. A vast fabric of impenetrable fact is stretched over his head. He works in the dark, with a contracted forehead and downcast eyes, on his hands and knees, as men work in coal-mines. But there is no sufficient reason that we can see why the novelist should not subject himself, as regards the treatment of his subject, to certain of the obligations of the historian; why he should not imprison his imagination, for the time, in a circle of incidents from which there is no arbitrary issue, and apply his ingenuity to the study of a problem to which there is but a single solution.

Henry James, in his Literary Reviews and Essays, *Vista House Publishers, 1957.*

Wendy Lesser (essay date 1989)

[*In the following essay, Lesser explores the role of gender in James's fiction.*]

Ambiguity is a moral value in James because it enables one to see both sides of a question; that is, ambiguity is itself

the technique that lifts both the writer and his readers out of their personal selves. James's insistent tortuousness forces you, as it forces him, to leave behind the simpler black-and-white discriminations that we find it so much easier to exercise on a daily basis. Yet the words "insistent" and "force" belie James's actual technique, which is one of seductively witty conversation. It is a pleasure to yield ourselves to those charming, flattering sentences: their very length and digressiveness mark, for us, the author's respect for *our* conversational subtlety, *our* impressionability to nuance and detail. James does not stoop to conquer; he draws us in as equals.

The Jamesian style places a premium on certain attributes that are linked to an appreciation of ambiguity: sympathy, receptivity, wit. And the fictional plots themselves confirm and affirm these judgments. The characters who are best at exercising sympathy, who are most receptive to the tonal ambiguities of the world, and whose wit softens the severity of those perceptions, are the ones we like best: I'm thinking particularly of Ralph Touchett in *The Portrait of a Lady,* or Fanny Assingham, whose enlightening presence in *The Golden Bowl* makes its obscurities somewhat more penetrable. Yet it is impossible to read James's novels as morality tales about the triumph (or even the tragic failure, which is triumph reversed) of virtuous qualities like sympathy, receptivity, and wit. For even those qualities are not unmixed blessings. If you truly believe in ambiguity as a moral force, then *no* quality can be an unmixed blessing. The triumphant Jamesian character can never simply arrive at the perception of a virtue and then carry it to its extreme conclusion; he (or, more often, she) must constantly be teetering in the balance between the extremes, seeking to placate the authorial fates by darting first in one direction and then in its opposite. That there are so few "triumphant" Jamesian characters testifies to the difficulty of the enterprise. More often, James's figures flounder in their efforts to pursue singlemindedly a supposed Jamesian virtue. Thus Fleda Vetch in *The Spoils of Poynton,* John Marcher in "The Beast in the Jungle," and Merton Densher in *The Wings of the Dove* all get hoist by the petard of their own passive receptivity: they are so busy embodying Jamesian appreciations of ambiguity that they fail to live their own lives. James never lets us forget that the opposite of sympathy is discrimination; the opposite of receptivity is will; and the opposite of wit is moral seriousness. These too are virtues, and ones he deeply appreciates, for James is always willing to have it both ways, even if neither his readers nor his characters can fully go along with him. (And yet that "always" marks a moral flaw too, for anything undiluted by its opposite is dangerous. James's premium on ambiguity is so infinitely regressive that even he cannot escape its toils: he teaches us to hold his own unremitting ambiguity against him.)

I promised, in the title, to talk about James and gender, and I do intend to get around to that subject in a moment. But the preliminaries I've devoted myself to in the preceding paragraphs are not, I hope, mere throat-clearings. They define the terms on which one must take James's "statements"—not only about women, but about everything else. They point, that is, to the trickiness involved in the effort to figure out what James is saying about women: one can't pin him down to an absolutely unambiguous position, nor can one simply throw up one's hands and say, "He's just being ambiguous." That would be the John Marcher solution, the tactic of a creature so fearful of making a mistake that he can never exercise a single option. James advises us that we *must* choose something, even if the choice is bound to be partially wrong. And I think that in regard to his portraits of women this pressure to formulate some attempt at a conclusion is even greater than usual—not just because you or I might think "the woman question" is important, but because James himself did. He may not have viewed it as narrowly as Olive Chancellor and her fellow sufferers and suffragettes do in *The Bostonians,* but James was nonetheless extremely interested in the rules, instincts, privileges, and characteristics that defined—and perhaps still define—the feminine. For James, the behavior of women in civilized society (with "civilization" carrying all of its Freudian drawbacks as well as virtues) was crucially tied to the poles of moral understanding he repeatedly explored: sympathy versus discrimination, passive receptivity versus energetic exercise of will, wit versus seriousness. (To these I would also like to add, at this point, knowledge versus innocence and renunciation versus possession. The latter is not quite the same thing as passivity versus will, for the effort to renounce must often be an extremely powerful one.) How these polarities get worked out in James's vision of women will be the subject of the rest of this essay. It's important to keep in mind, however, T. S. Eliot's notion that James's mind was "so fine that no idea could violate it." Often misappropriated as an insult, this remark is instead a wise admonition about keeping our own crude "ideas" separate from James's infinitely painstaking workings-out.

When Elizabeth Hardwick was once asked, during a panel discussion about American literature, to name "our greatest female novelist," she promptly responded "Henry James." The remark's wit lies in part in its accuracy. James's sympathy for his female characters would be unusual in any country and in any era; but coming as they do from the same culture that gave us Melville's sailors, Twain's picaresque heroes, and Howells' businessmen, James's women are nothing short of thrilling. They leap whole from his brain as Athena did from Zeus's—and, like Athena, they dominate the intellectual atmosphere of their respective cities. (In fact, James's urbanism seems intimately linked to his feeling about women. It is only in cities that women can achieve the full flowering of their social and intellectual powers—which is why so many Jamesian heroines, like their author, end up fleeing provincial America for urban Europe.) There is something capacious and awe-inspiring and incomparable about the masculine fiction of nineteenth-century America; I'm not in any way trying to downplay the virtues of *Moby-Dick* or *Huckleberry Finn.* But there is also something discomforting about the process of actually reading these great books. They are prickly and a bit cold, like a cave; whereas James's novels are like a beautiful house whose hostess has prepared everything to suit her own exquisite taste and our comfort. (The discomfort comes only after the visit, when we wonder what our charmingly gossipy hostess is saying about *us* to her subsequent guests. In other words, James's novels are pleasurable to read but difficult to re-

solve; there's always something that nags and festers, preventing us from feeling safely finished with the book.) James made the American novel habitable.

Like Elizabeth Hardwick, I had always assumed that the pleasure I felt in reading James's novels stemmed in part from their congenial feminine sensibility. (Harold Brodkey has called James's "an invented female voice.") So it was with some surprise that I first discovered the feminist anger at James. This reaction tends to be set off, primarily and perhaps predictably, by *The Bostonians.* I taught it one year to undergraduates at UC Santa Cruz and was met with cries of outrage on the part of my more vociferously feminist students, who felt that James was travestying Olive Chancellor. And then I found the same kind of complaints in *The War of the Words,* the first volume of Sandra Gilbert's and Susan Gubar's projected three-part feminist study, *No Man's Land.* What Gilbert and Gubar essentially do is to take Basil Ransom—"the impoverished southerner who speaks for masculine values in *The Bostonians*"—as a stand-in for Henry James. They argue "that Basil's aesthetic is an essentially Jamesian one, a belief that a man of letters must set himself against 'an age of hollow phrases and false delicacy' . . . and that Basil's rescue of Verena from the diseased clutches of Olive and her band of fanatical acolytes reflects James's desire to tell women that 'Woman has failed you utterly—try Man.' " They also make a glancing reference to "James's suspicion that Olive's lesbianism is a symptom of social disorder."

This take on Henry James is so different from my own that my first tendency is merely to gasp with disbelief: can we really be speaking about the same novel? However, misrepresentations and inaccuracies like Gilbert's and Gubar's (which I will address in some detail later) arise from the same sources as the outrage of my undergraduates—and outrage, when honestly felt, generally points to something worth looking at. In other words, while I feel that the feminists are wrong in their specific interpretations of *The Bostonians,* I'm persuaded that their feeling of violation springs from real disturbances created by James's novel. For somewhat different reasons, the book caused outrage when it was first published in 1886; and, perhaps because he never got over that adverse reaction, James failed to include the novel in his definitive New York edition. *The Bostonians* is not the comfortable, well-appointed house that most James novels are: it has lovely architectural features and a charming color scheme, but it also has unexpected trap doors and hidden pincushions in the overstuffed chairs. Any discussion that deals seriously with James's feeling about his female characters must surely take account of *The Bostonians,* and I intend to make it the centerpiece of my discussion. But I propose to approach it in reverse, by beginning at the end of James's career and working backward in time to the composition of *The Bostonians.* Only in comparison to later works that reworked similar patterns—specifically, in comparison to *The Golden Bowl* and *The Wings of the Dove* and, to a lesser extent, *The Spoils of Poynton* and *The Portrait of a Lady*—does the true complexity of *The Bostonians* emerge. I will start, then, with *The Golden Bowl,* which is in many ways the most perfect and triumphant example of James's intentional ambiguousness.

The central geometric pattern in fiction (and perhaps, if we agree with Freud, in life) is the triangle. But in James's fiction the figure is more likely to be a lopsided quadrangle: the usual three (with two "suitors" battling over one "object") and a fourth character situated somewhere between participant and observer. This fourth character is not divorced from the action; on the contrary, the outcome of the battle will affect him (or her) significantly, and he often has a great deal of influence on that outcome. But for some reason—having to do with family relationships, or prior history, or inappropriate age and gender, or mere lack of animal appeal—he is not an object of sexual desire for any of the other three, nor is he allowed to possess fully the one of the three that he desires. And therefore he (or, as I say, she) is outside the triangle of competition.

In *The Golden Bowl,* this peripheral figure is Adam Verver. The real fight is between Maggie and Charlotte over the Prince; Adam is merely married to Charlotte, for convenience (for Maggie's convenience, as both he and Maggie acknowledge). The true object of Adam's desire is Maggie, his own daughter. For obvious reasons, he cannot keep her forever. (By desire I do not necessarily mean overt sexual desire; in this case, it rather refers to a more domestic feeling, a wish to be with the other person intimately and continuously, as in fact Maggie and Adam *have* been together up until her marriage to the Prince.) There is no way, given the structure of things, that Adam is going to end up with all his wishes gratified; the best he can do is to sacrifice himself on behalf of the person he loves. This he does by removing both himself and Charlotte from the scene, thus leaving the Prince completely to Maggie. Whether this final "act" is due to his or Maggie's decision is never made quite clear: their understanding is so complete that whatever one intimates, the other feels.

Like the other objects of triangular desire in James's work (for example, Merton Densher, Owen Gereth, and Verena Tarrant), Prince Amerigo is something of a black hole; or perhaps it would be more accurate to say he's a deep, dark well into which one peers intently without ever being sure how much water (if any) is at the bottom of it. The Prince is, almost by definition, subtle and intelligent. If he weren't so on his own, centuries of family history—all those bound volumes of archives Maggie is so fond of consulting—would combine to make him so. He possesses enormous taste and discrimination. It is he who instantly spots the flaw, the crack, in the eponymous golden bowl, and leaves the Bloomsbury shop so as not to have to listen to the dissimulating sales pitch; while Charlotte, who *wants* the bowl, and therefore wants it to be desirable, stays on. But, like the other "dark wells" of Jamesian fiction, the Prince is on some level stupid, or at least obtuse. At best, he is only passively intelligent. Throughout most of the novel, he depends on Charlotte's superior intelligence, her willingness to lay things out for him. "What in fact most often happened was that her rightness went, as who should say, even further than his own," James tells us, speaking for the Prince's own perceptions; "they were conscious of the same necessity at the same moment, only it was she, as a general thing, who most clearly saw her way to it." Yet as the novel hurtles to its close and Maggie clearly stands

to win, the Prince abruptly changes sides, betraying both himself and Charlotte, as they were at their best. " 'She's stupid,' he abruptly opined," giving his wife his final take on Charlotte. But in delivering this opinion—based, as he says, on his sense that Charlotte doesn't know Maggie "knows"—the Prince reveals his own stupidity. Taste alone fails him, and self-protection triumphs over acute perception. He takes Charlotte's proud, pained performance for the real thing, though even Maggie sees through it: " 'She knows, she knows!' Maggie proclaimed."

Knowledge is a central question for Maggie, and her own changing relationship to it determines our shifting sympathy for her. In the first half of the novel, when she's innocent and ignorant, it's hard to be either for or against her: she's simply not much of a factor, whereas the Prince and Charlotte are both wonderful. In the second half, as she increasingly becomes the most knowledgable character in the drama, our feelings for her undergo a strange transformation. We both respect her more (because she's intelligent) and pity her more (because she perceives she's been betrayed); but, as she begins to use this knowledge to alter her situation, we also begin to draw back from—what to call it?—her exercise of power, her manipulation, her (almost) tyranny. Why should it be worse for her to manipulate Charlotte, after discovering the adulterous affair, than for Charlotte to manipulate *her* during the affair? Because Charlotte knows she's being manipulated, and Maggie knows she knows; and in this novel, knowledge is everything, the source of all pain and all power. No—knowledge and money together are everything, as Maggie and Adam triumphantly demonstrate. Neither alone is sufficient to carry one very far.

Charlotte, of course, understands this from the beginning. She understands that her tragedy is to be poor, that poverty prevents her from having what she most wants in life—namely, the Prince, whom she meets and falls in love with before Maggie ever sees him. If Charlotte is materialistic, she is no more so than the novel as a whole, or than any Jamesian novel; James was never one to underestimate the importance of money. Yet Charlotte never allows gross materialism to dampen her passions: she knows that life is to be lived, not to be speculatively evaluated for its possible worth. She has more courage than any of the other three comfort-seekers. "Don't you think too much of 'cracks,' and aren't you too afraid of them?" she says to the Prince, in a conversation that alludes to more than the gilt-crystal bowl itself. And then she accurately remarks about herself: "I risk the cracks." She has enormous pride (it's her pride that forces her, in the end, to pretend that *she* has urged Adam to make the move back to drearily provincial "American City"), but she's even willing to abandon that pride when it's in contest with love. Just before the Prince's marriage, having wangled an hour alone with him, she makes a declaration of her love: "I don't care what you make of it, and I don't ask anything whatsoever of you—anything but this. I want to have said it—that's all; I want not to have failed to say it." That willingness to reveal herself is perhaps another and even deeper kind of pride.

Charlotte is the culmination of one tradition of Jamesian

heroine. She bears a physical and situational resemblance to Isabel Archer: they are both poor, both "independent," and both attractive in an extremely American, "free" way. But in some ways she's much more comparable to Kate Croy of *The Wings of the Dove.* Both Kate and Charlotte are capable of feeling and engendering deep love for and in a man—a man, whether it be Merton or Amerigo, who cannot necessarily rise to the high levels of courage they themselves exemplify. Both refuse to marry in poverty (Kate has excellent reasons, with the example of her sister's sordid domesticity always before her), and both choose less direct and less socially acceptable ways of possessing their beloved. Finally, both attain their ends by manipulating an innocent young woman (Milly/Maggie) whose discovery of the deceit destroys the Kate/Charlotte plot; and both nonetheless, and surprisingly, remain sympathetic characters.

Yet they too differ in important ways. Kate is a far more active manipulator, a far more culpable perpetrator of morally dubious "plotting," while Charlotte merely falls (though knowledgably, it's true) into her complicated situation. And Milly's victory over Kate is ambiguous—Milly is, after all, dead—whereas Maggie's victory over the banished Charlotte is complete. Charlotte, as victim, thus has something in common with an entirely different order of Jamesian heroine: the Fleda Vetch type, the "renouncer." And Charlotte too renounces, not only at the novel's beginning, in her last meeting with the as-yet-unmarried Prince ("What she gave touched him, as she faced him, for it was the full tune of her renouncing. She really renounced—renounced everything, and without even insisting now on what it had all been for her"), but also at the end, when she agrees to be packed off to America. In the famous metaphorical passage with which James describes her submission to Adam Verver's will, it is our sense of Charlotte's initial proud freedom that makes her final entrapment all the more painful: "Charlotte hung behind, with emphasised attention; she stopped when her husband stopped, but at the distance of a case or two, or of whatever other succession of objects; and the likeness of their connection would not have been wrongly figured if he had been thought of as holding in one of his pocketed hands the end of a long silken halter looped round her beautiful neck. He didn't twitch it, yet it was there; he didn't drag her, but she came."

The connection between marriage and possession is one that James stresses in *The Golden Bowl.* Critics have often commented (I have myself, elsewhere) that Adam and Maggie buy their spouses outright. This both is and is not true. Certainly neither marriage would have taken place if great sums of money were not involved. If money were not an object, Amerigo and Charlotte could have married each other prior to the beginning of the book, and we would have had no book. James is not just saying that money is always, to some extent, an object (though he is, I think, saying that); he is also remarking on the kinds of non-financial "possession" entailed in marriage, and even in love outside of marriage—a topic he explored repeatedly in the novels preceding *The Golden Bowl.*

Near the beginning of *The Wings of the Dove* is a beautiful image of what it means to fall in love at first sight, as Kate and Merton do at the party where they first meet: "They had found themselves looking at each other straight, and for a longer time on end than was usual even at parties in galleries; but that, after all, would have been a small affair if there hadn't been something else with it. It wasn't, in a word, simply that their eyes had met; other conscious organs, faculties, feelers had met as well, and when Kate afterwards imaged to herself the sharp, deep fact she saw it, in the oddest way, as a particular performance. She had observed a ladder against a garden wall, and had trusted herself so to climb it as to be able to see over into the probable garden on the other side. On reaching the top she had found herself face to face with a gentleman engaged in a like calculation at the same moment, and the two inquirers had remained confronted on their ladders." It seems impossible that this image of perfect mutuality, perfect equality, could ever be shattered; and yet that feeling of liberated recognition does give way eventually to the coercive tone with which Merton insists Kate must "come to him"—must allow him to possess her, sexually—if he is to continue submitting to her will in the plan regarding Milly.

The entire trajectory of Kate's and Merton's love affair, from magical pairing to entrapment and loss, is mimicked in one sentence of *The Golden Bowl,* where Maggie contemplates what has become of the love affair between her husband and Charlotte Verver: "Behind the glass lurked the *whole* history of the relation she had so fairly flattened her nose against it to penetrate—the glass Mrs. Verver might, at this stage, have been frantically tapping, from within, by way of supreme, irrepressible entreaty." The transparent but solid material that once enclosed the two lovers in their own impenetrable world now serves only to imprison Charlotte. She alone, and not the equally culpable Prince, suffers the consequences of the affair's discovery.

This is not just because society is harder on women—though James isn't above making that point as well. Look at the way, for instance, he deplores, in *The Spoils of Poynton,* "the cruel English custom of the expropriation of the lonely mother. Mr. Gereth had apparently been a very amiable man, but Mr. Gereth had left things in a way that made the girl marvel. The house and its contents had been treated as a single splendid object; everything was to go straight to his son, and his widow was to have a maintenance and a cottage in another country. No account whatever had been taken of her relation to her treasures." Society and its laws *were* unfair to women, but that, from James's viewpoint, wasn't the worst of it. Women suffered more because, in his view, they were capable of suffering more: their sympathy, their intelligence, their knowledge made them suffer, whereas men were generally, like the Prince, protected by a layer of self-serving obtuseness. In all of James's work, there is no marriage in which the man understands more than the woman. (The possible exception is in *The Portrait of a Lady,* where the husband at first seems more intelligent and knowledgeable than his wife. But what Osmond possesses in the realm of taste and knowledge, he lacks in terms of the capacity to transmute that knowledge into feeling; his intentional coldness finally makes him stupid, while Isabel's suffering makes her wise, or at least wiser.) And especially in *The Golden Bowl,* the pattern is one of men taking the lead from women: Charlotte always formulates their mutual idea before the Prince can put it into words; Adam marries at Maggie's hinted suggestion; Fanny Assingham has to explain every nuance of the plot to her endearingly dense husband Bob; and Maggie takes the responsibility for saving everybody at the end, while the Prince, relying on her to fix things up, merely and passively waits. James suggests near the beginning of the novel that this had always been Amerigo's self-confessed way of dealing with women (and, by extension, every man's way of dealing with every woman): "This was *his,* the man's, any man's position and strength—that he had necessarily the advantage, that he had only to wait, with a decent patience, to be placed, in spite of himself, it might really be said, in the right. Just so the punctuality of the performance on the part of the other creature was her weakness and her deep misfortune—not less, no doubt, than her beauty."

James's novels are, in part, about mutuality in love; but there is a limit to how mutual love can be if one member of the pair is invariably morally, emotionally, and intellectually superior. Men in James are always being a little dense: " 'I say, you know, Kate—you *did* stay!' had been Merton Densher's punctual remark on their adventure after they had, as it were, got out of it; an observation which she not less promptly, on her side, let him see she forgave in him only because he was a man." It might even be their stupidity that makes them lovable. That seems, for instance, to be Owen Gereth's chief appeal to the intelligent Fleda Vetch: "He had neither wit nor tact, nor inspiration . . . He had clean forgotten that she was the girl his mother would have fobbed off on him; he was conscious only that she was there in a manner for service—conscious of the dumb instinct that from the first had made him regard her not as complicating his intercourse with that personage, but as simplifying it. Fleda found it beautiful that this theory should have survived the incident of the other day." This built-in disparity between the sexes gives even James's most tragic novels an affinity with screwball-comedy movies (where the women are also braver and more intelligent than the men, and where individual jokes as well as entire plots get constructed on this discrepancy). There is a way in which James always seems to be hinting that men and women ought to aspire to a marriage of equals, even if one sex (the feminine) is a little more equal than the other.

The degree to which James favors his females may backfire with some readers. "The endings," Harold Brodkey has said of the novels, "tend to be overdetermined and cruel in their attribution of *real* impotence to the men: the male characters are granted their success, if they are allowed any, by women—often caryatid-like, androgynous women, or an angelic one here and there—and by their own efforts never, except their efforts of understanding the monsters, the sphinxes and angels, that James posits." This is, of course, an exaggeration. But it's based on enough truth to give one pause. How, if he always makes women superior to men, can James be credited with true fairness in the realm of gender? Fairness is not, of course,

the only criterion of aesthetic achievement; but in the novel, where the author by definition starts with a stacked deck, it's an extremely important one. We've got to feel that the author is giving all his characters their due—giving each one a fair shake, as it were—if we are to sympathize at all with their fates. Their tragedies, to move us, must seem dealt by an impartial (or close to impartial) universe rather than by a crooked dealer. I said above that James "always" hints that women are superior, that "every man" asks to be saved by "every woman." But what James actually does is to couch that expression of "the man's, any man's, position" in the words of Amerigo's perceptions: even this casual generalization inevitably derives from, and is qualified by, a very individual point of view. For James, the specifics of character always matter more than generalities and categories—even, or especially, when the category is as enormous as gender.

That, in a way, is the central point of *The Bostonians.* As a work of moral instruction, it sets out to question the degree to which any generalizations can safely be made about men and women. And as a work of literature, it does so by overturning the sexual patterns that James was to work so hard constructing elsewhere in his fiction. If Olive Chancellor is wrong, it is not because she believes women to be superior (as James apparently did) or is attracted to her own sex (as James apparently was). It is because she allows those private beliefs and feelings to influence her vision of what a completely moral universe would look like: she wants the world to be as she is. Yet Olive is no more wrong than Basil Ransom, who is equally monomaniacal in his vision of the world. The fact that they are a woman and a man is—for once, in James—irrelevant. They are a perfect match in terms of strength of will, intensity of desire, intelligence, discrimination, and force of personality. It is as if Kate had reached the top of her ladder to confront, not the face of her beloved, but that of her absolute enemy.

In the lopsided quadrangle that underlies *The Bostonians'* structure, Adam Verver's participant-observer role is played by Miss Chancellor's sister, Adeline Luna. Like Adam, Mrs. Luna is desired by none of the other three and herself desires someone she can't have (Basil Ransom). The reason she can't have him, however, is merely that he doesn't find her attractive—an insult so immense that it fuels her lunatic behavior, which in turn pushes along the plot. It is Mrs. Luna who, out of self-destructive willfulness, keeps Basil from listening to most of Verena's New York speech. (This gives rise to one of the best scenes in the novel, where Basil's urge to abandon Mrs. Luna is brought into direct conflict with his Southern chivalry we relish his squirming dilemma and at the same time emphathize with his palpable desire to get rid of her.) This trick of hers, by keeping him from Verena, actually makes him more aware of how much he loves the girl. Mrs. Luna then trots off to Olive to tell her about Verena's hidden relationship with Basil, perversely insuring that Olive will cling tighter and Verena will inevitably have to break away. Mrs. Luna accomplishes nothing that will either help herself or injure Ransom (her two conscious motives); she succeeds only in ultimately harming Olive.

Verena Tarrant is possibly the darkest of James's deep wells of desire, in that it is almost impossible to understand why two intelligent people are so wildly attracted to her. Even James doesn't have much to say in her favor, aside from the fact that she's pretty. "Her ideas of enjoyment were very simple," he comments early on; "she enjoyed putting on her new hat, with its redundancy of feather, and twenty cents appeared to her a very large sum." This is innocent ignorance carried to a ludicrous extreme: Maggie is Charlotte's twin, by comparison. Even Ransom, who loves Verena, perceives her silly side, though he merely finds it charming: "There was indeed a sweet comicality in seeing this pretty girl sit there and, in answer to a casual, civil inquiry, drop into oratory as a natural thing. Had she forgotten where she was, and did she take him for a full house?" Yet Basil doesn't appreciate having anyone else notice her silliness: "The only thing our young man didn't like about Doctor Prance was the impression she gave him (out of the crevices of her reticence he hardly knew how it leaked), that she thought Verena rather slim." By this late point in the novel, we have come to know that Dr. Prance is the closest thing James gives us to the authorial viewpoint, the voice of sense and reason.

In most of the other Jamesian triangles, two women are in competition for a man: Charlotte and Maggie battle it out for Amerigo, Milly and Kate for Merton Densher, Fleda Vetch and Mona Brigstock for Owen Gereth, and so on. The prominent exception to this pattern, other than **The Bostonians,** is **The Portrait of a Lady,** where Gilbert Osmond, on the one hand, and Caspar Goodwood, on the other, compete for Isabel. (Lord Warburton represents a mere diversion from Goodwood, like a small path off that particular road—the road not taken.) But even the exception proves the rule, for that plot still involves two adventurous, strong-minded women (Madame Merle and Isabel) revolving around and determining the fate of one essentially passive man. **The Bostonians** turns this pattern upside down and inside out. Not only is the object of contention a woman (which shifts the charge of being passive and insubstantial from the male gender to the female), but the competitors—for the first and only time in all James's work—are of opposite sexes. Everywhere else, the structure relies on pitting one woman's feelings against another's, and the essential story lies in their differing capacities for willed action, deep passion, renunciation, and suffering. But here the novel pits a woman against a man, and *their* respective capacities for feeling and action are accordingly brought under consideration. The mold is broken, and all the usual bets about gender are off.

One of the most troublesome questions in the novel is the extent to which James identifies with, sympathizes with, or even likes Basil Ransom. (In that sense, he's very clearly the Maggie of this book.) For reasons not entirely clear to me, Gilbert and Gubar assume that the identification is nearly total. Is this because James and Ransom are both men? That hardly does justice to James's sympathetic portraits of women throughout his books. Is it because Ransom is occasionally given the linguistic wherewithal to poke fun at the women's movement? But so is Mrs. Luna (some of her comments are really hilarious), and hers can

hardly be considered the moral or emotional viewpoint of the novel. Gilbert and Gubar feel that "Basil's aesthetic is an essentially Jamesian one"—but James clearly finds something amusing in the response of the editor who told Ransom "that his doctrines were about three hundred years behind the age; doubtless some magazine of the sixteenth century would have been very happy to print them." It is almost impossible to take Basil seriously as a writer. If the possession of "doctrines" alone were not enough to warrant his exclusion from the Jamesian "aesthetic," we would still have his naïve careerism (he is ready, for instance, to marry on the financial and reputational strength of one accepted but not yet published article). Perhaps some of this spurious "writer" issue is what accounts for Gubar and Gilbert's even more incomprehensible statement to the effect that "Basil's male bonding with the fallen Union dead memorialized in the Harvard library reflects James's own fellowship with lost New England forefathers." For one thing, Harvard's Memorial Hall, where Basil has his epiphany, is not a library, so there are no books present to remind James of either his or Basil's literary connections. (People who don't know James well always tend to overestimate his identification with the act of writing. In fact, authorship most often appears in his fiction as a highly suspicious activity.) But, more importantly, Basil's sympathy for his brave Civil War opponents would seem to acknowledge the importance of reaching across barriers to sympathize with one's enemies, rather than just reaching backward to one's own antecedents. Basil's sympathetic journey from South to North could be taken as a mirror for James's from North to South (James did, after all, lose family in the war, and yet he found himself able to create a brave Southern veteran). If James identifies with Basil at all in this novel, it is precisely through the act of reaching out of himself toward an opposite. For a writer like James, it is much harder to get inside a man like Basil Ransom than it is to imagine oneself a Jamesian heroine.

Though feminist readers have felt impelled to rescue Olive Chancellor from James's diseased clutches, it is Basil Ransom who is in many ways the easy mark of this novel. Olive stands on her own: she has a force, a character, even a degree of appealing inconsistency, that suggest she has earned her author's ultimate respect. Basil, on the other hand, at times comes so close to being a caricature that James feels impelled to step in and protect him from us. Thus the moments at which James most obviously distances himself from Ransom are the very moments when, subtly and ironically, he also criticizes *us* for our distance. For instance, he says of Basil: "When I have added that he hated to see women eager and argumentative, and thought that their softness and docility were the inspiration (the highest) of man, I shall have sketched a state of mind which will doubtless strike many readers as painfully crude." The presentation of Basil seems to call into question the whole enterprise of authorship, as if James wants to shirk the responsibility for having created such a creature (resting it instead, perhaps, on our societal shoulders) and simultaneously to take credit for inventing and sympathizing with such an alien character. In what is perhaps the prime example of this ambivalence, he remarks: "The historian who has gathered these documents together does not deem it necessary to give a larger specimen of Verena's eloquence, especially as Basil Ransom, through whose ears we are listening to it, arrived, at this point, at a definite conclusion. He had taken her measure as a public speaker. . . . From any serious point of view it was neither worth answering nor worth considering, and Basil Ransom made his reflections on the crazy character of the age in which such a performance as that was treated as an intellectual effort, a contribution to a question." We are both totally inside Basil and entirely removed from him here, just as James is both an objective "historian" and a judgmental member of the listening "we." The ironies are such that any feminist readers who feel Basil's stance is "neither worth answering nor worth considering" are forced, if they are honest, to recognize the parallel between their own prejudices and his.

One of Basil's chief flaws is that he consistently underestimates Olive Chancellor; and if we view her as a caricature of the typical suffragette, we are ourselves guilty of Ransom-like obtuseness. A bundle of nerves wrapped around a core of iron, Olive is one of the most human and admirable of James's creations. She has chosen to lead a life in which everything material gets sacrificed to abstractions, yet she's plagued by an underlying level of excellent taste. She's sincere but never stupid—as opposed to her sister Adeline, who is both dense and dishonest. In fact, James shows Olive to best advantage whenever he compares her to Mrs. Luna. In a relatively late scene, where Adeline is tattling on Verena and Basil, James gives us the following:

> Olive kept these reflections to herself, but she went so far as to say to her sister that she didn't see where the "pique" came in. How could it hurt Adeline that he should turn his attention to Verena? What was Verena to her?

> "Why, Olive Chancellor, how can you ask?" Mrs. Luna boldly responded. "Isn't Verena everything to you, and aren't you everything to me, and wouldn't an attempt—a successful one—to take Verena away from you knock you up fearfully, and shouldn't I suffer, as you know I suffer, by sympathy?"

> I have said that it was Miss Chancellor's plan of life not to lie, but such a plan was compatible with a kind of consideration for the truth which led her to shrink from producing it on poor occasions. So she didn't say, "Dear, me, Adeline, what humbug! you know you hate Verena and would be very glad if she were drowned!"

The wit in that last paragraph is both Olive's and James's; in this moment of narration, the intimate "I" and the seemingly distant "Miss Chancellor" are inextricably intertwined. Elsewhere James comes right out and praises Olive in terms that truly reflect a "Jamesian aesthetic": "In reality, Olive was distinguished and discriminating, and Adeline was the dupe of confusions in which the worse was apt to be mistaken for the better." (This also says something, by implication, about Ransom, who is hated by the discriminating Olive and loved by the confused Adeline.) Part of what makes Olive discriminating, to James's mind, is her ability to let specific sense data triumph over her own abstract theories; it is this ability that

gives her a charming inconsistency. Her passion for the cause of women does not prevent her, for instance, from noticing the foibles of her sex: "Olive was sure that Verena's prophetic impulse had not been stirred by the chatter of women (Miss Chancellor knew that sound as well as anyone); it had proceeded rather out of their silence." It is Olive's admirable capacity for both discrimination *and* sympathy that enables her to draw this conclusion.

If innocence versus knowledge is the polarity that informs **The Golden Bowl,** with will versus passive acceptance structuring **The Wings of the Dove** and possession versus renunciation infusing **The Spoils of Poynton,** then sympathy and discrimination define the spectrum along which **The Bostonians** runs. It is a novel whose ostensible "subject" is discrimination (against women by male society) and sympathy (on the part of women for their less fortunate sisters). It is also a novel that functions largely by influencing our tendencies toward sympathy and discrimination, as James skips and hops between the characters, first dropping a kind word and then a snide remark, or simultaneously attacking and defending with irony. Sympathy and discrimination are both high Jamesian values, and they are also the values that most dispose us toward reading his novels: without sympathy we wouldn't care about his characters; fates, and without discrimination we would never appreciate the fine nuances of his sentences. In **The Bostonians,** these polar oppositions are intermittently juxtaposed, enabling us to realize that sympathy without discrimination is relatively worthless, while discriminating taste without a shred of tenderness is hardly worth calling taste. Nowhere is this point made so clearly as in the portrait of Miss Birdseye.

When James first published **The Bostonians** serially in 1885 and 1886, the Boston responses to the book focused on the character of Miss Birdseye, whom people took to be mockingly modeled on one Miss Peabody. To a letter from his brother William on the subject, Henry answered with pained surprise: "I have the vanity to claim that Miss Birdseye is a creation. You may think I protest too much: but I am alarmed by the sentence in your letter—'It is really a pretty bad business,' and haunted by the idea that this may apply to some rumour you have heard of Miss Peabody's feeling *atteinte.* . . . Miss Birdseye is a subordinate figure in **The Bostonians** . . . But though subordinate, she is, I think, the best figure in the book, she is treated with respect throughout, and every virtue of heroism and disinterestedness is attributed to her." In other words, she's *not* Miss Peabody, but even if she were, Miss Peabody should be flattered rather than insulted. This explanation didn't wash too well with the Boston crowd, and it may have been in part the bad aftertaste from this reaction that kept James from re-publishing the book twenty years later in the definitive edition of his novels.

When you turn from James's self-defense to the novel itself, Miss Birdseye's presentation is likely to come as something of a shock: "She was a little old lady, with an enormous head . . . She had a sad, soft, pale face, which (and it was the effect of her whole head) looked as if it had been soaked, blurred, and made vague by exposure to some slow dissolvent. The long practice of philanthropy had not given accent to her features; it had rubbed out their transitions, their meanings . . . She belonged to the Short-Skirts League, as a matter of course; for she belonged to any and every league that had been founded for almost any purpose whatsoever. This did not prevent her being a confused, entangled, inconsequent, discursive old woman, whose charity began at home and ended nowhere, whose credulity kept pace with it, and who knew less about her fellow-creatures, if possible, after fifty years of humanitary zeal, than on the day she had gone into the field to testify against the iniquity of most arrangements." Treated with respect throughout? Every virtue of heroism? Surely, we think, James is being disingenuous. But then we realize that this portrait of Miss Birdseye, though presented as if objective, is actually framed by Basil Ransom's perceptions. And we begin to understand that though the harsh description is in part James's own critique of unmitigated sympathy, it is also a critique—by implication—of the purely discriminating viewpoint that can't see the value of a Miss Birdseye. We get the same "objective" information presented in a totally different tone in the last paragraph of the chapter, when we are looking at Miss Birdseye through another set of eyes: "Olive Chancellor looked at her with love, remembered that she had never, in her long, unrewarded, weary life, had a thought or an impulse for herself. She had been consumed by the passion of sympathy; it had crumpled her into as many creases as an old glazed, distended glove. She had been laughed at, but she never knew it; she was treated as a bore, but she never cared. She had nothing in the world but the clothes on her back, and when she should go down into the grave she would leave nothing behind her but her grotesque, undistinguished, pathetic little name. And yet people said that women were vain, that they were personal, that they were interested! While Miss Birdseye stood there, asking Mrs. Farrinder if she wouldn't say something, Olive Chancellor tenderly fastened a small battered brooch which confined her collar and which had half detached itself." James ends the chapter there, with Olive's tender gesture, as if to say: yes, Miss Birdseye's unremitting sympathy is laughable; and yes, discrimination makes things hard-edged, distinct, meaningful, while too much sympathy produces soft vagueness, meaninglessness, the "crumpled" quality of an old glove; and yes, it requires discrimination (on Olive's part as well as Basil's) to perceive the limits of sympathy. But sympathy, in the form of a tender gesture, is nonetheless the final point. It's Olive's sympathy in the face of her ability to discriminate, rather than Miss Birdseye's easier, undiluted variety, that James encourages us to admire. Yet if we take this encouragement too far—if we choose to respect Olive and merely to laugh at Miss Birdseye—we show ourselves less capable of discriminating sympathy than Olive herself is.

Part of the way James plays on our own sympathies, in the competitive triangles he sets up in his novels, is to distribute power in unexpected ways. In *The Golden Bowl,* Maggie is innocent and somewhat dull, while Charlotte is witty, knowing, and beautiful; on the other hand, Maggie is enormously rich and Charlotte is poor. So at the end, when the marriage triumphs, our sense of virtue rewarded is somewhat mitigated by the fact that money won out. Similarly in the case of *The Wings of the Dove:* Milly, the rich, weak girl, wins by dying; Kate, who survives, fails to profit from her exercise in manipulation. You may admire Milly or Kate more, but whichever you choose, you can't make the sum come out entirely in your favor. Milly, too, is a manipulator (through her passive acceptance of others' tribute) and Kate, too, is subject to the corruption of money. Milly's death is neither a complete tragedy nor a complete transcendent victory, and Kate's final loss is neither entirely her own fault nor entirely imposed on her. In extremely unequal ways, they are a fair match in the competition for Merton Densher.

In *The Bostonians,* Olive is the competitor who has money (Basil is notoriously and self-proclaimedly poor), yet Olive eventually loses the prize. Is this supposed to make us feel that untarnished virtue, unaided by filthy lucre, has for once triumphed? I doubt it. In the other comparable case, where Isabel Archer chooses the poor man (Gilbert Osmond) over the rich one (Caspar Goodwood), we live to see her regret that choice—not for financial reasons, but because she initially mistook poverty for virtue. *The Bostonians* doesn't let us peek past the final curtain of the marriage, doesn't let us confirm the rightness or wrongness of Verena's choice. But James does say of Verena's tears (in a final sentence that doubles back on itself with numerous ironies): "It is to be feared that with the union, so far from brilliant, into which she was about to enter, these were not the last she was destined to shed." The voice sounds pompously snobbish, like that of Mrs. Farrinder or Mrs. Burrage; but James has by now had nearly five hundred pages to train us in the distinction between personal appeal and veracity. Even if the voice is dislikable, it might still be telling the truth. The author, in any case, is not going to guarantee that Verena's choice (which, as sentimental novel readers, we might consciously or unconsciously have wished for) is going to prove the right one. More than any other James novel except possibly *The Wings of the Dove*—more, certainly, than the unsatisfyingly non-committal *Portrait of a Lady—The Bostonians* leaves us with a truly ambiguous ending.

Much critical hay has been made of the fact that Olive "buys" Verena (she actually hands over large checks to Mr. Tarrant) whereas Basil wins her through pure sex appeal alone. But, as I suggested in talking about *The Golden Bowl,* James seems to feel that love in any form is virtually inseparable from possession. What Olive is after, and what the money merely helps smooth the way toward, is a mutual and freely-entered-into compact of possession between herself and Verena. Verena has possessed Olive's affections practically since their first meeting; Olive only wants something similar in return. She is quite direct about explaining her notion of possession (or possessiveness) when she answers Verena's query as to why she won't visit the Tarrant's house: "Olive expressed her reasons very frankly, admitting that she was jealous, that she didn't wish to think of the girl's belonging to any one but herself." Basil Ransom feels the same way, which is why he won't let Verena belong to him and to her public at the same time (not to mention, of course, Olive). But Basil assumes such sentiments are his rightful prerogative as husband and lover, whereas Olive offers them in a somewhat self-deprecating manner as mere personal description. The crucial difference between the two is that Basil wants to win Verena through pure force of personality—wants, effectively, to overpower her will—while Olive wants Verena freely to choose her. Olive has, constitutionally, as strong a will as Basil's, and as detailed a knowledge of her own desires, but she doesn't want that will and those desires to be the only determining force. Early on in the novel, Verena offers to "renounce," to promise never to marry; but Olive refuses to accept the renunciation at that point because she wants the decision to be knowledgeable and mature, not the result of a weaker will submitting to a stronger one. A great part of Olive's tragedy, it seems to me, is that she overestimates Verena, presuming her to be equal to herself. (This is also, I think, Kate's tragedy with regard to Merton and Charlotte's with regard to Amerigo; and it is to all of their credit that they make this mistake.) It doesn't really matter whether Basil overestimates Verena, because for his purposes—a household angel to worship, and an admiring slave to be worshipped by—an inferior will do just as well.

I am doing an injustice to Basil here. In a Basil-like manner (as he does, for instance, with Olive), I am exaggerating someone's flaws and underestimating his subtlety solely because his principles are at odds with mine. In fact, Basil Ransom is in many ways an engaging character, and if I were being as fair and as sex-blind as I take James to be, I would admire his ruthless exercise of will as I do, say, Kate Croy's. Like numerous readers over the years, I have unwittingly slipped into viewing *The Bostonians* as a battle between Olive Chancellor and Basil Ransom in which we must choose one or the other—and, in doing so, choose either women or men.

It's easy to see, with a novel like *The Golden Bowl,* that whom you side with and how you feel about the outcome depends on where you stand at a particular moment in time. As Gore Vidal appealingly suggests: "I barely noticed Adam Verver the first time I read the book. I saw him as an aged (at forty-seven!) proto—J. Paul Getty, out 'to rifle the Golden Isles' in order to memorialize himself with a museum back home—typical tycoon behavior, I thought; and thought no more. But now that he could be my younger brother (and Maggie an exemplary niece), I regard him with new interest—not to mention suspicion." Vidal views Amerigo and Charlotte as the tragic victims of the plot; for him, Maggie and her father are "monsters on a divine scale." John Bayley, in an equally astute but much more balanced reading of the novel, says in *The Characters of Love:* "Certainly the victors in such a contest are not likely to appear in an agreeable light, and especially when the economic scales are weighted so heavily in their favour. I think, though, that James, the least sentimental of writers, would not feel himself bound to side with penniless passion and wrongdoing in defeat." Vidal and Bayley end up on different sides of "the Maggie question," but their discussions both acknowledge that one might, under other circumstances, come to the opposite conclusion. *The Golden Bowl,* in other words, has provoked criticism as intelligent as it is.

The Bostonians, on the other hand, tends to sort readers vigorously into two opposing camps, with little or no acknowledgment that things could be seen another way. I do not think this is due to the inferiority of the earlier novel. Rather, I think it's because we—*unlike* James—do not have the capacity to take Olive's and Basil's roles equally seriously. It is we, and not James, who find a woman's love for a woman incommensurable with a man's. For James, Basil and Olive are intensely individual, tragically matched suitors competing for the hand of a specific (if not terribly worthwhile) love object. For us, they inevitably become symbols of two opposing sets of principles and two conflicting ways of life. But it is always a mistake, in James, to let the general prevail over the specific (in this case, to let gender matter more than individual identity). In *The Bostonians,* we find ourselves siding with Dr. Prance whenever she opens her mouth, and toward the end we understand why: "Olive had perfectly divined by this time that Doctor Prance had no sympathy with their movement, no general ideas; that she was simply shut up to petty questions of physiological science and of her own professional activity." It's the "petty" questions that, as a novelist, James finds professionally interesting: the questions about how specific people will act under given circumstances and how we will respond to those actions, regardless of the "general" social laws or moral regulations.

I don't want, however, to suggest that James finds all outcomes morally neutral. (Dr. Prance is, after all, interested in curing her patients, not merely in exploring their respective physiologies.) Part of the reason for the heatedness of the critical discussions, whether about *The Bostonians* or about the other novels, is that the difference in the conflicting outlooks matters. It would be possible, of course, to write Jamesian criticism that suggested "tolerance" as the ultimate good, and that advocated equal sympathy for Maggie and Charlotte, for Kate and Milly, for Olive and Basil. Such criticism, in fact, might well have been written by Henry James's brother William, who cheerfully defined his pragmatic philosophy as simply a matter of making appropriate distinctions.

In the second chapter of *Pragmatism,* William James tells a story about being on a camping trip during which a philosophical disagreement took place. In discussing a hypothetical squirrel circling a hypothetical tree so as to remain out of view of a hypothetical observer, one side insisted that the circling observer *did* "go round" the squirrel and the other that he did not. William was called upon to solve the dispute: " 'Which party is right,' I said, 'depends on what you *practically* mean by "going round" the squirrel. If you mean passing from the north of him to the east, then to the south, then to the west, and then to the north of him again, obviously the man does go round him, for he occupies these successive positions. But if on the contrary you mean being first in front of him, then on the right of him, then behind him, then on his left, and finally in front again, it is quite as obvious that the man fails to go round him, for by the compensating movements the squirrel makes, he keeps his belly turned towards the man all the time, and his back turned away. Make the distinction, and there is no occasion for any farther dispute. You are both right and both wrong according as you conceive the verb "to go round" in one practical fashion or another.' "

To the reader of this passage, it becomes instantly clear that William and Henry James grew up in the same family but drew totally different attitudes toward life from that experience. Both are believers in multiple viewpoints; both insist that the "right" answer differs as you shift from one position to another. But whereas William's ambiguity is completely resolvable—"Make the distinction, and there is no occasion for any farther dispute"—Henry's is not. In order to put William's procedure into effect, you simply need to be sure of all the pertinent variables. But Henry would say, as he has Fanny Assingham say in *The Golden Bowl:* " 'One can never be ideally sure of anything. There are always possibilities.' " In William's vision of the world, one can use knowledge to make choices fearlessly and without regret; in Henry's, knowledge is always imperfect, and some loss is inevitable.

To announce sunnily that Maggie and Charlotte, or Olive and Basil, can be "both right and both wrong" would be to do a terrible violence to Henry James's complicated vision. It would be to become vague, crumpled organs of undiluted sympathy, like Miss Birdseye—or, as I suggested near the beginning of this essay, to become cowardly, passive John Marchers, afraid of committing ourselves to any choice. James's novels demand active choice, demand discriminations of sympathy, even as they suggest the dangers and insufficiencies of taking these positions. However carefully we make our choices, we can't, as readers of a James novel, have everything our way. That's what makes them like life. (pp. 176-99)

> Wendy Lesser, "Henry James and the Battle of the Sexes," in Southwest Review, Vol. 74, No. 2, Spring, 1989, pp. 176-99.

Dorothea Krook   (essay date 1990)

[*Krook is a Latvian-born Israeli educator, critic, translator, and poet who has written extensively on James. In the following essay, she examines the two types of ambiguity present in* The Ambassadors.]

There is scarcely a page in Henry James's *The Ambassadors* (1903) that is not ambiguous in the common loose sense of the word, in which 'ambiguous' means simply obscure, puzzling, mystifying, baffling, and the like. This passage or this sentence could mean this, or that, or something else, we say to ourselves as we gaze at it, often blankly, trying to make out *what* it could reasonably mean. Here is a typical example. It is the last passage in a long colloquy between Strether and Maria Gostrey late in the story, ending the chapter (Book XI, Chapter 2) which is immediately followed by Strether's fateful day in the French countryside (Book XI, Chapter 3). Maria says:

> 'Mr. Newsome and Madame de Vionnet may, as we were saying, leave town. How long do you think you can bear it without them?'
>
> Strether's reply to this was first another question. 'Do you mean in order to get away from me?'

> Her answer had an abruptness. 'Don't find me rude if I say I should think they'd want to!'

> He looked at her hard again—seemed even for an instant to have an intensity of thought under which his colour changed. But he smiled 'You mean after what they've done to me?'

> 'After what *she* has'.

> At this, however, with a laugh, he was all right again. 'Ah but she hasn't done it yet!'

It is James's elliptical, allusive late style that makes the difficulties, of course. The key questions to be answered are: Why should Chad and Madame de Vionnet want to get away from Strether? What is the thought in Strether's mind that makes him change colour? Why, having evidently pushed aside this thought whatever it was, does he smile when he says 'You mean after what they have done to me?' And what *have* they done to him?—what does *he* think they have done to him? And what does Maria mean when she corrects him, saying, No, after what *she* (Madame de Vionnet) has done to him? What *has* 'she' done to him? And why is Strether relieved ('at this . . . he was all right') to think that it's what she has done to him, whatever it is, that makes them want to get away from him? Finally, what does Strether mean when he says 'with a laugh' that she hasn't done it yet—whatever it is she is supposed to have done?

The list of questions is longer than the passage that raises them; but this is not surprising—it takes less space to produce an obscurity than to explain why it is obscure. I give my gloss for what it is worth. Maria is telling Strether that Chad and Madame de Vionnet want to get away from him because they are beginning to find his constant surveillance nerve-racking. The thought that passes through Strether's mind, making him change colour, is that they are finding his surveillance nerve-racking because their 'virtuous attachment' is not virtuous, and they are getting tired of having to conceal this from him. Having pushed this disagreeable thought aside, he takes refuge in an alternative explanation of Maria's cryptic remark: they want to get away from him because it oppresses them to think how they are 'exploiting' him in the interests of maintaining their relationship, and in particular what he has *lost* as a consequence of their 'exploitation' (Mrs Newsome, and all the benefits for him of marrying her). This is what they have 'done' to him; but it is Marie de Vionnet in particular, Maria reminds him, who had 'done' it, because her need of Chad is greater than his of her (a point already sufficiently established). In that case, Strether's last remark ('Ah but she hasn't done it yet!'), the most cryptic of all, may mean that she hasn't yet caused him to lose all, because he is still within the six-week's period of grace allowed him by Sarah Pocock, and may yet decide to join them (with Chad, of course) at Liverpool for the voyage back to America—in which case 'all losses are restored' and it is paradise regained for Strether.

An alternative reading is to give Maria's words a simpler, less portentous meaning. When she says 'Don't find me rude if I say I should think they'd want to [get away from you]', what she means, and what Strether understands her to mean, is that he is simply becoming a bore to them with his perpetual hanging around them, and they just want to be on their own for a bit. This is the thought that makes Strether change colour: he finds it most disagreeable to suppose that the brilliant pair, and especially of course Marie de Vionnet, are beginning to be bored by him. So he pushes the thought aside, and suggests instead (as on the first reading) that they want to get away from him because of their bad conscience about what they have been the cause of his losing, this being what they have 'done' to him, and she, Madame de Vionnet, in particular. The meaning of Strether's last statement, 'Ah but she hasn't done it yet!', would then be the same as on the previous reading.

These are both possible readings of the passage. But one cannot be *sure* that either is correct—that there may not be another, quite different reading that 'covers' the elusive data at least as well or perhaps better; and it is significant that neither of the readings I have proposed appears to be decisively confirmed by anything—any act or speech—elsewhere in the book. Perhaps this passage, among others, ought to be treated as a Jamesian 'crux', analogous to a crux in Shakespeare, which will require time and the cumulative labours of many James scholars to discover its best reading.

I cite another passage which, as is stands, is equally obscure, baffling, and 'ambiguous'. It is the dialogue in Book IX, Chapter 1 between Strether and Madame de Vionnet in the scene in which she tells him about the marriage that has been 'arranged' for Jeanne. It too comes at the end of the scene, and starts when Madame de Vionnet pronounces the words 'And—willingly, at least—he [Chad] would never hurt *me*'. At this, there flashes upon Strether 'a light, a lead' that, together with the expression of her face, tells him 'her whole story' as never before. The light grows, becoming ever more luminous as the passage proceeds to its close, its revelation apparently reinforced by 'the refined disguised suppressed passion of her face'. What *is* this light, this lead?—you ask yourself. What *is* the momentous revelation Strether has had by it? There is no clue, no hint, in the passage itself, and you gaze at it baffled, wondering whether the answer might be this, or that, or something else, without much confidence in any of your hypotheses.

But in this instance salvation is just round the corner. In the very next chapter, Strether briefly gives Maria Gostrey the gloss we need. Chad had helped to arrange Jeanne's marriage as a proof to Madame de Vionnet of his unwavering 'attachment' to her following her cold treatment by Sarah Pocock: 'The act is his answer to Mrs Newsome's demonstration', he tells Maria; 'she [Madame de Vionnet] asked for a sign, and he thought of that one'. What Strether had seen in Marie de Vionnet's face was presumably the intense happiness and relief it was to her to have had this 'sign' from Chad, and this had been for him the 'light', the 'lead', for understanding the depth of her feeling for Chad and the 'suppressed passion' behind and beneath it.

This is how Strether interprets Madame de Vionnet's presumed happiness and relief, along with the 'the refined disguised suppressed passion of her face'. But the reader, who knows—as Strether doesn't yet—'the deep deep truth' about her relationship with Chad, may legitimately see more in and behind Chad's demonstration. He may, more cynically, see the marrying off of Jeanne as a means also of getting out of the way an unmarried daughter whose presence in the house would be an impediment to the mutual pair's complete freedom to pursue their relationship. And he may even see Jeanne's departure as, in her mother's eyes, the removal of a possible rival, even though Chad had plainly shown that it was the mother not the daughter he wanted. Nevertheless, if in her last scene with Strether Marie de Vionnet can call herself 'old and abject and hideous', even if only in the self-despising mood of that moment, she might well be happy and relieved—in the depths of her subconscious, of course—to have a beautiful young daughter safely removed by marriage from the possible role of temptress to a lover who happened to be closer in age to the daughter than to the mother.

The ambiguity I have so far talked about is mainly a function of James's late style, which deliberately resorts to the cryptic, the elusive, the mystifying for its own special ends. There is however another kind of ambiguity to be considered, where 'ambiguous' has a more precise meaning than just obscure, puzzling, baffling, and so forth. It is to be found in only a limited number of James's works, the paradigms being *The Turn of the Screw* (1898) and *The Sacred Fount* (1901). The remaining works are *The Lesson of the Master* (1892), *The Figure in the Carpet* (1896), and *The Golden Bowl* (1904). But there are patches or 'pockets' of this kind of ambiguity in (for example) *The Aspern Papers* (1888), *The Spoils of Poynton* (1897) and *The Wings of the Dove* (1902); and, as we shall see, in *The Ambassadors.*

In the paradigm works, everything can be read in two and *only* two ways. The text—meaning, every key episode, dialogue, and even utterance—admits of two alternative and contradictory readings, each self-complete and wholly consistent with all the data. In *The Turn of the Screw,* one of the two possible readings is that of the first-person narrator, the governness. On this reading, the children are being hideously corrupted by the apparitions of the two depraved servants, Peter Quint and Miss Jessel, and the governess is the Jamesian saviour figure trying to redeem them from the evil to which they have succumbed. The alternative and contradictory reading is that the governess is psychically disturbed (from 'sex-repression', or whatever) and has imagined it all; in which case the apparitions are hallucinations of her deranged brain, the children are totally innocent of the depravity she attributes to them, and the governess herself is hideously guilty—of pursuing and harassing the children with her pathological suspicions, leading the girl to a nervous breakdown and the boy to his death. These and only these are the two possible readings of the story; and there is nothing to tilt the balance decisively in favour of one or the other, thus leaving the ambiguity total and unresolved.

In *The Sacred Fount* the ambiguity is of the same kind, though the outcome is not tragic as it is in *The Turn of the Screw.* Either the first-person narrator's observations and explanations are valid, in which case the strange changes he sees in the principals are real and his 'vampire' hypothesis to explain the changes is confirmed. Or the narrator is wholly and pathologically deluded, in which case the supposed changes are imaginary, and the narrator is an unsavoury *voyeur* who deserves his final exposure by the energetic Mrs Brissenden.

The Ambassadors as a whole is by no means ambiguous in this special sense. But it has one great 'pocket' of this kind of ambiguity; and it turns on Chad's transformation. The matter of Chad's transformation is obviously of key importance in Strether's 'process of vision' and his trans-valuation of values vis-a-vis Woollett. It is the foundation of his case for betraying his original mission, for pleading with Mrs Newsome to let Chad stay back with the wonderful woman who has wrought the transformation, for pleading with Chad never to abandon the wonderful woman, and for himself suffering the loss of Mrs Newsome and the security, the affection, the esteem he would have had by marrying her. If Chad was *not* transformed, or even less radically transformed than Strether supposed, all Strether had built on it collapsed—'cracked' and 'crumbled', in his own words.

So it is disconcerting to find the question suddenly arising in Strether's mind: Is Chad's transformation real; or is it a figment of his imagination (which we know to be highly developed)? Is he seeing something that is objectively there to be seen, or is he just 'seeing things'? The momentous and potentially shattering question springs up for him on the day of the Pocock's arrival (Book VIII, Chapter 2), on his drive from the station with Jim Pocock; and his intense reflections on it proceed by three stages.

First, having observed that neither Sarah Pocock nor Jim has remarked on the change in Chad that he himself had found so overwhelming from his first encounter with Chad in the theatre box, he firmly dismisses their 'sightlessness' as a function of their philistine lack of imagination or their bad faith or both:

> It all suddenly bounced back to their being either stupid or wilful. It was more probably on the whole the former; so that would be the drawback of [Sarah's] bridling brightness . . . Their observation would fail; it would be beyond them; they simply wouldn't understand. Of what use would it be then that they had come?—if they weren't to be intelligent up to *that* point.

Immediately, however, in the same breath, the great doubt about his own 'observation' leaps up in his mind, and grows and grows like a spreading fire from the moment he asks himself whether he himself might not be 'utterly deluded and extravagant':

> Was he, on this question of Chad's improvement, fantastic and away from the truth? Did he live in a false world, a world that had grown simply to suit him, and was his present slight irritation—in the face now of Jim's silence in particular—but the alarm of the vain thing menaced by the touch of the real? Was this contribution of the real possibly the mission of the Pococks—had they come to make the work of observation, as he had practised observation, crack and crumble, and to reduce Chad to the plain terms

in which honest minds could deal with him? Had they come in short to be sane, where Strether was destined to feel that he himself had only been silly?

Strether's copiousness in drawing out the implications of his moment of self-doubt stands in sharp contrast to the spareness of the governess in *The Turn of the Screw* when, shortly before Miles dies, the terrifying thought crosses her mind that the child may after all be innocent: 'If he *was* innocent, what then on earth was *I*?' she cries to herself. And the narrator in *The Sacred Fount,* when he sees his wonderful 'palace of thought' crack and crumble (Strether's terms exactly fit his case) in his showdown with Mrs Brissenden, is likewise more succinct: 'What if she *should* be right?' he murmurs inwardly. But the point is the same; it is the moment of radical self-doubt and self-misgiving, which is a crucial element in the pattern of the Jamesian ambiguity of the kind I am describing.

The third stage of Strether's process of coping with the frightening thought that he may have been deluded about Chad's transformation is also integral to the pattern. It is the justification, or re-justification, of his own perception by mentally reviewing the witnesses who have confirmed its validity:

> He glanced at such a contingency ['that he himself had only been silly'], but it failed to hold him long when once he had reflected that he would have been silly, in this case, with Maria Gostrey and little Bilham, with Madame de Vionnet and little Jeanne, with Lambert Strether, in fine, and above all with Chad Newsome himself. Wouldn't it be found to have made more for reality to be silly with these persons than sane with Sarah and Jim?

So Strether concludes that he is, must be, 'all right' after all if his vision is supported by such a cloud of distinguished witnesses. But the reader experienced in the subtleties of the Jamesian method of ensuring that the ambiguity shall remain totally unresolved will recognise that Strether's supposed witnesses are either not witnesses at all, or are not 'reliable' because not disinterested witnesses. Maria Gostrey is the first to be struck off Strether's list. Maria never knew Chad before his supposed transformation—so how could she know whether he had or hadn't been transformed? The answer is, she doesn't know; she has only taken Strether's word for it that there *has* been a transformation, and that it is as marvellous as he says. Madame de Vionnet and Chad, being the most interested 'parties' in the case, are *ipso facto* ruled out as objective witnesses. Little Bilham, as a close friend of Chad and wholly committed to his 'cause', is likewise ruled out; and it is surely significant that when he appears to be explicitly confirming the change in Chad, he immediately throws in the qualification: 'But I'm not sure that I didn't like him about as well in his other state'. And later again:

> 'He wasn't so bad before [the transformation] as I seem to have made out that you think—'(says Little Bilham).

> 'Oh I don't think anything now!' Strether impatiently broke in . . . 'I mean that originally, for

her [Madame de Vionnet] to have cared for him—'

'There must have been stuff in him? Oh yes, there was stuff indeed, and much more of it than ever showed, I dare say, at home'.

These may be intended as hints to the reader that the change in Chad is not as great or remarkable as Strether sees it to be, and that little Bilham's honesty obliges him delicately to correct Strether's 'exaggerated' view. Or it may even mean that there is no change at all, and Bilham's seeming confirmation of it is just another 'technical lie' in support of Chad, of a piece with his lie about the 'virtuous attachment'.

As to 'little Jeanne': there is no mention anywhere of her having perceived a change in Chad; and Strether can be drawing on her as a witness only because he assumes that, being Madame de Vionnet's daughter, she must necessarily 'see' what *maman* sees; or, alternatively, because he assumes that, if she is secretly in love with Chad, she could only be in love with him if he *had* been transformed. Finally, there is Mamie Pocock: whom Strether does not include in his list of witnesses because at this point he has not yet had his private meeting with her. The case of Mamie is particularly interesting. Strether tells Madame de Vionnet even before he has had his talk with Mamie that 'she sees him [Chad] as different'. Then, at their meeting in Sarah's hotel salon, he feels he has received all the confirmation he wants of Mamie's 'seeing' what Sarah and Jim have failed to see; and afterwards, in his talk with little Bilham, inspires his young friend to develop his great theory, about Mamie's being unable to be in love with Chad because she came out to 'save' him, but seeing him already 'saved' had nothing to do in that direction. However, when we re-read Strether's long talk with Mamie in search of evidence for his conviction that she 'sees', we discover that Mamie has actually said nothing—not a word—about it. Strether has merely inferred from her behaviour that she must have seen the change in Chad; and is so certain about his inference that he treats it as a fact. But it is *not* a fact; and the disposition of a mind like Strether's to mistake inferences and assumptions for facts *and* convince others of the factuality of the non-facts is exactly one of the psychological phenomena that Henry James cunningly exploits as a device for creating and sustaining his ambiguity.

What we discover, then, is that there is no reliable independent confirmation of Strether's perception of the change in Chad, which is the starting point of his drama of consciousness, and, consequently, that a huge question-mark hangs over the validity of Strether's vision. This does not mean of course that Strether's perception has been proved to be false. On the contrary, his vision of a Chad transformed remains intact as one of the two possible *true* interpretations of the data. The transformation may be exactly as Strether sees it—as radical and portentous; Waymarsh and the Pococks who don't see it may be exactly as 'sightless' as Strether says they are; the cloud of witnesses he invokes (Chad, Madame de Vionnet, little Bilham) may all be speaking the objective truth in confirming his vision; and about those who don't speak (Jeanne and Mamie) his inference that they see the change in Chad may be totally correct. In short, just as in *The Turn of the Screw* the governess' account of what happened at Bly may be completely valid, so may Strether's of what happened to Chad.

This precisely is the design of the Jamesian ambiguity: to leave the reader faced with two and only two interpretations of the data, which are mutually exclusive (meaning, that if one is true, the other is necessarily false—Chad cannot both be and not be transformed); yet each of which is wholly consistent with all the available evidence—in this instance, the evidence of the witnesses, which may be read both ways, as confirming one interpretation (Strether's) and disconfirming the other (the Pocock's), or confirming the Pocock's and disconfirming Strether's. Nor is there a single piece of evidence that decisively tilts the balance in favour of one interpretation or the other; that there shall be none is another basic rule of the Jamesian ambiguity. Consequently, there are no grounds *on the basis of the evidence*—in other words, no 'rational' grounds—for choosing one interpretation as more valid than the other.

If you do choose—as Strether does, as the governess in *The Turn of the Screw* does—you can choose only on the basis of something other than the evidence. You can choose, in a word, only by an act of faith—'blind' faith—in the validity and integrity of your own vision. And this is the deep truth about human experience and human knowledge that the Jamesian ambiguity is designed to dramatise. When in life a crucial act of choice has to be made between two and only two possible lines of action, figured in the two and only two possible interpretations of the Jamesian fiction, and the facts or data constituting the evidence are intractably ambiguous in supporting with equal force and decisiveness *both* of the two and only two alternatives, the crucial choice can only be made by an act of faith—which in effect by-passes, ignores, and transcends the evidence, leaving you with your lone unsupported vision of things as the sole basis of your choice. (pp. 148-55)

Dorothea Krook, " 'The Ambassadors': Two Types of Ambiguity," in Neophilologus, *Vol. LXXIV, No. 1, January, 1990, pp. 148-55.*

Larry A. Gray (essay date 1990)

[*In the following excerpt, Gray examines the recurrent imagery of sibyls, seekers, and sacred founts in James's fiction.*]

James's novel *The Sacred Fount,* published in 1901 but not included in the New York Edition, has been a puzzle for readers ever since it appeared. Often apologetically, critics have disagreed about what really happens in the story and what it all means. But aside from questions of the literary merits of the book in isolation, it has clearly proven to be important in any study of James's career. Few would dispute its characteristic Jamesian quality, and often it has been viewed as a pure exercise in method, as if the author had managed to write a work of this length without the benefit of "substance." Because James himself deprecated it the few times he referred to it in letters, most discussions of the work try to avoid any extraordinary claims. What I would suggest is that this tale, which grew to novel length as James wrote it, represents an adept combination of both types of "sacred fount" situation that James used, usually only one or the other, in shorter works throughout his career.

In the novel, the narrator is a habitual seeker of knowledge. His preoccupations hardly appear to transcend the level of gossip, however, as he seems intent on learning who is intimate with whom at a weekend visit to an English country estate. What raises his inquiry to a higher or different level is his testing of a predatory theory of human relationships. His cynical hypothesis proposes that, in an intimate couple, one person feeds off the other in vampire fashion and thereby increases either in youthful appearance or in mental vigor, while the other is correspondingly depleted. In observing the Brissendens, the narrator states the theory to his companion as follows:

> "One of the pair . . . has to pay for the other. What ensues is a miracle, and miracles are expensive. . . . Mrs. Briss had to get her new blood, her extra allowance of time and bloom, somewhere; and from whom could she so conveniently extract them as from Guy himself? She *has,* by an extraordinary feat of legerdemain, extracted them; and he, on his side, to supply her, has had to tap the sacred fount. But the sacred fount is like the greedy man's description of the turkey as an 'awkward' dinner dish. It may be sometimes too much for a single share, but it's not enough to go round."

The narrator here allies himself with the "greedy man's" outside view of the situation, which naturally ignores mutuality and emphasizes the limitations of quantity. Yet what if intimate relations do involve sacrifice, but there *is* enough to go round? And what if, therefore, the sacrifice is not as one-sided as a greedy observer might assume, but is essentially reciprocal? This is not to say that intimacy is or will appear to be perfect, but that to view it greedily from the outside is to miss the "tone" of whatever is actually there.

In the last scene of the story Mrs. Briss seems to defeat the narrator and his cynical hypothesis by no longer understanding the similar theory they have played with earlier in the day, in reference to Gilbert Long and *his* unidentified source of mental vitality. Various critical interpretations of this conclusion have been offered, ranging from Mrs. Briss's protecting her own secret affair with Long to her "proving" that the narrator is actually mentally unbalanced. Although Jamesian ambiguity makes a definite answer beside the point and all but impossible, my own view is that Grace is simply protecting her marriage from a nosy intruder as best she can. But whether or not she is protecting Long as well as her husband, the unmarried narrator must accept her assertive refusal to talk further and is left only with the prospect of returning to London alone with his theory forever unresolved. He has not been proven wrong so much as irrelevant. His ultimate failure to analyze the sibyllic Grace and her relation to the sacred fount of her husband leaves him lost as a seeker of the human truth behind the other's marriage.

But this configuration of a man puzzling over a couple's intimacy is just one of the two sacred fount situations that James uses in this novel and in the tales. The other way makes use of the seeker's own potential role as a sacred fount—his opportunity for becoming involved in a successful intimate relation with another person.

In this other configuration, the seeker usually fails to realize his role in time, and the sibyl is left far more "depleted" than any intimate partner we ever see. In the course of *The Sacred Fount,* the narrator investigates May Server as the potential source, now showing signs of depletion, for Gilbert Long's wit. Midway through the book there occurs a climax in which the narrator, quietly and ignorantly, fails to understand May, just as Marcher fatally fails his sibyl of the same name, in the tale published two years later. The narrator, perplexed all day by the mystery of Mrs. Server's nervousness in his presence and by her enigmatic smile, finally engages her in a dialogue alone in the garden. Trying to test her as a candidate for his theory, he makes riddling references to the other guests and in the process sincerely hints that he himself feels a special attachment to her, apart from them. The subject of love thus comes up, and the narrator puts forth his peculiar idea that Guy Brissenden loves her, to which she answers, logically enough, "How can that be when he's so strikingly in love with his wife!" The narrator, preoccupied with his theory, plays on "strikingly" as being a reference to the invigorating effect of a vampire relation on Mrs. Briss's appearance. Yet this is an inference May could not possibly follow; her denial of Guy's love for herself seems, to the reader, rather to open the way for the seeker's own declaration of love and his accepting the role of mutual intimate. So when the narrator next puts forth the idea of "being in love by the day," as contrasted to a longer period of time, such as with the Brissendens' marriage, May's response demonstrates a waiting for clarification in reference to intimacy with herself that never comes:

> "But isn't there such a state also as being in love by the day?" . . . and, while I vaguely sought for some small provisional middle way between going and not going on, the oddest thing, as a fruit of my own delay, occurred. This was neither more nor less than the revival of her terrible little fixed smile. It came back as if with an audible click—as a gas-burner makes a pop when you light it. It told me visibly that from the moment she must talk she could talk only with its aid. The effect of its aid I indeed immediately perceived. "How do I know?" she asked in answer to my question. "I've never *been* in love."

Her impassive remark is her only defense against his delay, his attempt at a "middle way" that equally avoids both a declaration of real intimacy and the suggestion of a "by the day" assignation. In fact he was considering neither option, but all the same he has forced her to deflect the point in such a way that the moment of possibility passes.

After this half-noticed climax, the narrator's chance for intimacy with May takes on the dimension of a missed opportunity with serious implications for her, though he never quite articulates what has taken place between them. Soon after, he senses her passing, as if into death, as the party listens to music. May becomes an enigmatic symbol to him of the quiet beastliness that he sees in the relations formed in "our civilised state":

> What, for my part, while I listened, I most made out was the beauty and the terror of conditions so highly organised that under their rule her small lonely fight with disintegration could go on without the betrayal of a gasp or a shriek, and with no worse tell-tale contortion of lip or brow than the vibration, on its golden stem, of that constantly renewed flower of amenity which my observation had so often and so mercilessly detached only to find again in its place. This flower nodded perceptibly enough in our deeply stirred air, but there was a peace, none the less, in feeling the spirit of the wearer to be temporarily at rest. There was for the time no gentleman on whom she need pounce, no lapse against which she need guard, no presumption she need create, nor any suspicion she need destroy. In this pause in her career it came over me that I should have liked to leave her; it would have prepared for me the pleasant after-consciousness that I had seen her pass, as I might say, in music out of sight.

Perhaps it is not altogether too late for the narrator to love, but clearly any potential for a closer relation to May and a truer understanding of her has vanished. His pity for her sibyllic smile, the signal he might have interpreted as a promise of true intimacy, should he reciprocate it, allows him to keep her nostalgically distant; his theoretical pursuits throughout the rest of the book prevent any change in this view.

The Sacred Fount thus offers both patterns James used in depicting this configuration of characters in the tales. Mostly in middle period works like **"The Liar"** (1888) and *The Turn of the Screw* (1898), on the one hand, the sacred fount dimension is embodied in the sibyllic figure's marital intimacy; the seeker actively attempts to solve the mystery, often exceeding the boundaries of ethics in the process. . . . [The] seeker implicitly envies the omniscience suggested by the sibyl's intimacy with a third person. In works like **"The Pupil"** and *The Turn of the Screw,* James equates this settled omniscience of invulnerably married couples with the precocious, nonanalytical knowledge of children. And when children are under the seeker's scrutiny, they are especially vulnerable to the destructive quality of his or her well-meant desire for privileged knowledge.

In early and late works like *Daisy Miller: A Study* (1878) and **"The Beast in the Jungle"** (1903), on the other hand, the sacred fount role represents something potential in the seeker, a failed opportunity or route not taken: his inability to be such a mutual partner with the sibyl constitutes an essential failure. He chooses the detached analytical approach to truth, rather than the intuitive and immediate, and as a result his quest always reaches an idle pass. In the extreme but representative case of Marcher and May, the seeker's complex ignorance both of the sibyl's depth of devotion to himself and of his participation in her "knowledge" results in nothing less than her death. Whether or not sibyl or seeker would have been depleted by a closer relation becomes irrelevant, in these works, because abso-

lute damage to both results even without the potential problems of intimacy. And even when a late tale like **"The Bench of Desolation"** (1909-10) depicts a long-delayed reconciliation of sibyl and seeker, the portrait of human loss often seems at least as vivid as its resolution.

James used each sacred fount situation in deft tales written during his apprentice years of the sixties and early seventies. In these works the seeker is a relatively weak figure who believes he is controlling his fate until the final twist of plot humbles him. The sibyl, by contrast, is a strong-willed creature whose virtual omniscience stretches credibility as, almost with authorial power, she puts the seeker in his place. In **"A Landscape-Painter"** (1866) the seeker-narrator, a rich artist, has escaped a mercenary fiancée in the city only to meet a sea captain's daughter in rustic New England. Keeping his wealth a secret, he finally decides he will marry the innocent woman and then calmly observe her well-earned happiness as she learns her good fortune; after the wedding, however, she surprises him with the news that she knows his secret, having read his diary while nursing him in illness, the unselfish act that had finally convinced him to choose her. When she reveals her deception of the complacent narrator, she justifies herself with chilling logic: "I said I would be your wife. So I will, faithfully. . . . It was diamond cut diamond. You cheated me and I mystified you. . . . A false woman? No, it was the act of any woman—placed as I was placed." The young James thus makes his sibyl invulnerable, and her mystification of the seeker a conscious act of deception. And though the narrator accepts rather than fails the opportunity of marriage, his essential ignorance of the sibyllic woman seems almost more culpable than her lie. As she taunts him at the end, "I am incapable of more than one deception.—Mercy! didn't you see it? didn't you know it? see that I saw it? Know that I knew it?"

"Osborne's Revenge" (1868) provides an early example of the seeker prying into another's intimacy. The duped central consciousness is a young lawyer who seeks to avenge his friend's suicide by somehow foiling the career of the cold woman who jilted the friend just before his death. Osborne tries to attract her love so that he may jilt her in return, but ultimately he learns that she has been engaged for some time to a Mr. Holland: the friend's death was the result of a self-created obsession, and Osborne's attempted revenge thus amounts to a pale, almost unnoticed repetition of this obsession. Again we must wait for a final twist of plot, but when all is revealed we see that a seeker has been meddling with another's marriage. Had Osborne succeeded in his plan, he would have consciously created the failed opportunity situation: he would have gained the woman's love and then destroyed her by rejecting it. These clever stories anticipate James's many uses of the two sacred fount situations, but they are immature in that the characters seem mainly to serve a too arbitrary plot. The more mature works will provide more equal competitors for the conflict, resulting in deeper character interactions and moral resonance.

In *Daisy Miller* and **"The Diary of a Man of Fifty"** (1879), the Jamesian seeker fails to perceive his responsibility for the heroine, and she dies. By the late seventies

James had thus arrived at his story of the "poor sensitive gentleman" and his "too late" recognition. After Daisy's death, Winterbourne often thinks of the girl and her "mystifying manners," and he realizes "on his conscience that he had done her an injustice." Having earlier concluded from her questionable actions, culminating in her midnight visit to the Colosseum with Giovanelli, that "She was a young lady whom a gentleman need no longer be at pains to respect," he yet finally admits to his aunt that he was wrong: "She sent me a message before her death which I didn't understand at the time. But I have understood it since. She would have appreciated one's esteem." Winterbourne is more perceptive about Daisy than the other Americans and more sincerely sympathetic about her mistakes, for the most part, so his esteem is significant. Failing to understand the essential moral fact of his own involvement in her innocence, he chooses to judge her objectively: the result is her death.

The heroine of **"The Diary of a Man of Fifty"** has died long before the present action, but her daughter conveys the message of the narrator's failure, in his youth, to esteem the Countess as she had deserved. As in ***Daisy Miller,*** the seeker's passive moral complacency leads to the heroine's fate, apparently preventable by him alone. The analogy that the man of fifty insists will prove him correct in his past condemnation of the Countess actually suggests just the opposite conclusion. Young Stanmer is courting the daughter, who is a young widow, as her mother was, and who lives in the same villa. The narrator predicts that Stanmer will discover some dark secret about the present countess and abandon her, but instead the young man marries her and is happy. He writes to the narrator after the marriage: "You talked me into a great muddle; but a month after that it was all very clear. Things that involve a risk are like the Christian faith; they must be seen from the inside." Stanmer thus offers the great reproach to all seekers in James who, tragically or ignorantly, try to understand their relation to an "other" only from the outside. The man of fifty will never know how happy his own marriage might have been; the real fruit of his experience is even more negative, however—he must live with the guilt for his past repudiation of the Countess. Similar to that of John Marcher, his bitter fate is to have deliberately condemned himself to an outside view and to have learned nothing for certain except his own failure.

From the mid-eighties until the end of the century, James's tales usually depict a more active seeker who, determined to gain an inside view, victimizes an innocent sibyllic figure or intimate couple. Instead of Winterbourne failing Daisy, we see Oliver Lyon self-righteously tormenting the Capadoses in **"The Liar"** (1888) or the governess questioning Miles to death, for his own good, in ***The Turn of the Screw*** (1898). Characteristically, James expresses his seeker's mistakes in these tales indirectly through an unconsciously revelatory point of view. And in works like **"The Impressions of a Cousin"** (1883), **"The Aspern Papers"** (1888), and **"The Way It Came"** (1896), similarly, the narrator's degree of responsibility is communicated to the reader far beyond the teller's penitent admissions. Most of James's unreliable or unsympathetic first-person narrators appear in the tales of the middle period.

A representative third-person seeker of the middle period is Oliver Lyon, central consciousness of **"The Liar."** James depicts this respectable, discerning portrait painter as a man who unconsciously uses his artistic intelligence in a progressively malignant way as he pries into the private marital secrets of Colonel and Mrs. Capadose. Having failed in courting the wife during their youthful days, Lyon becomes obsessed with demonstrating his own present superiority over her affable "liar platonic" of a husband. At first, apparently sympathetic, he is satisfied merely to imagine her suffering over the embarrassments that the Colonel's exaggerated stories cause in society; later, however, he feels compelled to paint the husband's portrait with such "truth" that he will seem monstrous to his wife and the rest of society. After the portrait is destroyed by the baffled Colonel, who understands only that it upsets his wife, Lyon must rest content with a cynical assessment of the marriage that excludes him: "She was still in love with the Colonel—he had trained her too well." As Lyon leaves them on this note, abandoning his blind cruelty for a future of blind ignorance about such marital unselfishness, the reader is left to draw the true conclusion about his moral inversion.

When other seekers of the middle period actually destroy innocence, their mistake seems all the worse because they victimize the one who most deserves and expects their trust. The woman who narrates **"The Way It Came"** ruins her own marriage plans by jealously refusing to believe her fiancé's word that he has been visited by the woman friend he had never previously seen on the night that the friend died. The narrator's jealousy becomes so acute that, their marriage abandoned, she hails it as "a direct contribution to my theory" that he soon dies, still unmarried and still devoted, she madly assumes, to the dead woman. The governess's similar mistakes and inflictions in ***The Turn of the Screw*** have been frequently discussed. Flora is driven away in illness, and Miles is frightened to death by suffocating inquiry and extremes of agitation, all owing to the governess's exaggerated desire to perform her task and get at the truth behind the presumed deceitful innocence of the children.

Probably the most tragic case of cruelty to a blameless child in the tales of the middle period is the failed opportunity of **"The Pupil"** (1891), in which Pemberton destroys his charge, Morgan Moreen, at the moment of their apparent liberation from his vulgar parents. The boy, a preadolescent like Miles, is similarly of precocious intelligence, with great insight into the character of those around him. The tutor laments his inability to help the pupil throughout the tale, in which the Moreens are painted as shamelessly vulgar and stubborn when it comes to any plan that will really suit their unappreciated jewel of a son. When the parents finally agree, for selfish reasons, that the boy can be placed in the tutor's protection "for as long as Mr. Pemberton may be so good," we witness an instantaneous life or death drama based on the tutor's reaction to this news. Seeing the boy's excitement and open affection for himself, the tutor is frightened and feels he "should say something enthusiastic" to meet the pupil's feeling; though he hesitates for a mere instant to show the reciprocity the boy expects, in that moment he disappoints

Morgan to death. Their situation differs in its tragedy from those involving Daisy and May Bartram because their teacher-student intimacy is intense and deep but necessarily doomed, either by Morgan's adulthood or his death. What occurs at the end, in a sense, is the pupil's literally fatal recognition of this doom. As readers, however, we share the tutor's view and mainly feel his helpless sense of personal and universally human guilt. Pemberton is the most passive and sympathetic seeker of the middle period, but his one lapse places him with the others in their destruction of innocence.

The late tales are typically third-person works with a "poor sensitive gentleman" as the seeker. James returns to the emphasis of the early period on failed opportunity, and the late seekers share and exceed Winterbourne's capacity for a final awareness. And though the late stories usually involve real human loss, the guilt is not so easy to assign as in the cruel acts of the middle period works. The mystery of ideal intimacy is no longer embodied in a blameless "other" or in another's actual marriage. Often the sibyl, like May Bartram, shares the seeker's peculiar ignorance for most of the journey, though in the end she blazes the way for his enlightenment. Yet if the later sibyl characteristically perceives the truth sooner, this does not mean that she contains it: she merely seems to embody it, at first, to the newly awakening seeker. These are dramas of revelation, of a developing consciousness, and frequently the development is collaborative in the late works. The exaggerated value that the middle seekers envy in another's marriage or innocence has thus become a real, possible value; and its attainment is often at least symbolically achieved in the reconciliation that often draws the late tales to a close.

Peter Brench, central consciousness of **"The Tree of Knowledge"** (1900), is representative of these more sensitive late seekers. Having spent his bachelor life befriending Mr. and Mrs. Mallow because, like Lyon, he secretly loves the wife, this seeker is unselfish enough to desire that she be spared the truth of her husband's mediocrity. Brench claims, early on, that he has "the misfortune to be omniscient," but the tale goes on to show that his sparing Mrs. Mallow the embarrassment is a superfluous act: she has known and accepted the truth of mediocrity all along. It is Brench who must learn the real truth, that their marriage is self-sufficient in a way that he has never discerned from the outside. The revelation diminishes Brench's imagined importance, but his position as friend is secure. As with the other late seekers, true knowledge, even when it excludes him, makes up in some degree for the previous misapplication of his life.

Brench is always much closer to the truth than Lyon of the middle period; even before his final revelation, he accepts the fact that the Mallows are essentially solid in their marriage: "They were, at all events, deliciously formed, Peter often said to himself, for their fate; the Master had a vanity, his wife had a loyalty, of which success, depriving these things of innocence, would have diminished the merit and the grace." He is intuitively right, though condescending; Peter still must learn the essential fact that their ignorance of Mallow's artistic mediocrity is not what

makes the marriage work so well. Mrs. Mallow tells Brench, in their one scene alone together, that in Paris her son Lance will learn what the Master already "knows": "Quiet joy." The knowledge of mediocrity that Peter fears so much on their account seems thus to matter little to the sibyl: when she thinks of what her husband knows, it is the true bliss of a successful marriage and not the more abstract matter of artistic proportion in statuary. When Peter learns that she has quietly "known" about the mediocrity all along, he finally understands that she has viewed life with a far better sense of proportion than he has himself.

For Peter Brench and John Marcher, the women with whom they might be intimate are impossible to marry; the seeker's knowledge of what he has missed must suffice. But in **"Broken Wings"** (1900), **"The Jolly Corner"** (1908), **"Crapy Cornelia"** (1909), **"Mora Montravers"** (1909), and **"The Bench of Desolation"** (1909-10), the seeker is able to confront the mistakes of his past doubts and misguided inquiries, and then to accept the role of husband or intimate friend with a woman whose moral understanding is close enough to the real thing. In **"Broken Wings"** Stuart Straith and Mrs. Harvey have equally "blundered, as sensitive souls of the 'artistic temperament' blunder, into a conception not only of the other's attitude, but of the other's material situation at the moment, . . . their estrangement had grown like an evil plant in the shade." Their caring for each other has had to wait ten years to be revived, but in the end the light does pierce the shade in time for them to reconcile their artistic temperaments and work together intimately.

Even more notable for its resolution of difficulties is the late reconciliation of Herbert Dodd and Kate Cookham in **"The Bench of Desolation."** In spite of the damage Dodd has sustained throughout life, in the end he can accept both Kate herself and the fivefold repayment of past losses; it is a second chance at the true path he abandoned years before. The autumnal, fairy-tale resolution of this work characterizes it as a late tale. Dodd's innocence is recoverable, despite the pain that he and his lost family have suffered. Guilt and blame become mostly irrelevant in the dusky light of final understanding.

Throughout his long career, James himself only rarely attempted a close depiction of a marriage from the inside. Among the novels, we have the latter part of *The Portrait of a Lady* (1881) and *The Golden Bowl* (1904), but the wife in both of these cases must become a seeker herself because the husband's intimacy is possibly or certainly with someone else, tainting the marriage that defines her life. And of the tales, only **"The Abasement of the Northmores"** (1900), **"The Birthplace"** (1903), and **"Mora Montravers"** (1909) feature a married central consciousness; unlike the couples in the novels, however, all three of these are of the settled, intimate sort. **"Mora Montravers,"** the last tale James wrote, is a fitting conclusion to his lifelong concern with the seeker's imaginative consideration of his own and others' intimacy. In it, Sidney Traffle must confront the problematic issue of young Mora, his wife's niece, whose unconventional behavior is mildly scandalizing the quiet, middle-aged Wimbledon couple. Jane Traffle assumes that Mora, having moved into her art teacher's studio, must therefore be his mistress, but the more Sidney investigates the situation the more he sees himself and Jane as spotless but unadventurous while Mora is decisive, pure, and daringly unselfish. She is a sibyllic descendant of Daisy Miller, and the ultimate effect of her behavior is to spark into life Jane's basic generosity and moral resilience. Traffle's simple wife becomes a kind of sibyl in the end, and the "importunate fiend of fancy" that characterizes him as a seeker is redirected from Mora to Jane in the final sentences of the story: "Lord, the fun some people did have! Even Jane, with her conscientious new care—even Jane, unmistakably, was in for such a lot." Traffle's revelation about his wife, and about himself through his wife, is not absolute; even in an achieved sacred fount marriage, there are further human mysteries for the seeker to ponder. (pp. 192-200)

> *Larry A. Gray, "Sibyls, Seekers, and Sacred Founts in the Tales of Henry James," in* The Henry James Review, *Vol. 11, No. 3, Fall, 1990, pp. 189-201.*

Alison Lurie (essay date 1991)

[*Lurie is an American novelist and critic who typically explores the world of the American middle class. In the following essay, she analyzes character in* The Bostonians *and argues that the novel can be read as both a fairy tale and a political allegory.*]

Though **The Bostonians** is set in New England, it was written by someone who had already chosen to live abroad for nearly six years, and after the death of his parents in 1882 would not set foot in his native country again for twenty more.

Returning to America in the early Eighties, James felt estranged and depressed. He was repelled rather than attracted by post—Civil War prosperity and commercial expansion, and thought Boston both ugly and noisy. He was also struck by the domination of society by women; he spoke of a "deluge of petticoats." There was some basis for this impression; the heavy casualties of the Civil War and the departure of many men for the Western territories had produced a population imbalance in the East; and women, for the first time, were moving into the professions.

In his **Notebooks,** James planned **The Bostonians** as "a very *American* tale, a tale very characteristic of our social conditions." He asked himself "what was the most salient and peculiar point in our social life." The answer was "the situation of women, the decline of the sentiment of sex, the agitation on their behalf."

In the new movement for women's rights to vote and for equality in education, James saw the subject for a novel set in the city which for decades had been a center for reform. On the simplest level, **The Bostonians** is a romance: the story of Olive Chancellor and Verena Tarrant, two intensely committed young women's rights activists, and

Olive's cousin, the antifeminist Southerner Basil Ransom, who comes between them.

As might have been expected of a book with such a controversial subject, **The Bostonians** had a mixed reception when it was published in 1886. Henry James considered it his best work to date, and his friend William Dean Howells called it "one of the greatest books you have written." Yet the reviews were all unfavorable, and the novel was nearly forgotten for over fifty years.

In the conservative 1940s and Fifties **The Bostonians** was rediscovered by critics who saw James's portrait of Olive Chancellor and her fellow reformers as admirably satirical and disparaging. Some, like Lionel Trilling, were full of praise for the handsome, ambitious, deeply conservative hero, and quite content that the book should end with his near abduction of the beautiful young feminist Verena. More recently, feminist critics such as Judith Fetterly have concentrated on the defects of Verena's suitor, and seen her attraction to him either as a regrettable erotic enthrallment, or as a martyr's wish to experience firsthand the "sufferings of women" of which she has spoken so movingly.

At the beginning of **The Bostonians** the city itself seems to suffer not only from commercial ugliness but from "the decline of the sentiment of sex" which James wrote of in his **Notebooks.** It is barren and solitary; the landscape visible from Olive Chancellor's window is described as "empty," "lonely," "anomalous," "cold," and "brackish," adjectives that seem to apply equally to Olive's spinster existence.

Indoors things are not much better. Olive's parlor, though evidently that of a cultured person, is compared to a corridor, and her friend Miss Birdseye's to "an enormous street-car"; the suggestion is that these are not cozy homes, but places one passes through on the way to somewhere else. Later on, when Verena comes to live with Olive Chancellor, the view from her house has become even more unpleasant:

> The western windows of Olive's drawing room, looking over the water, took in the red sunsets of winter; the long, low bridge that crawled, on its staggering posts, across the Charles; the casual patches of ice and snow; the desolate suburban horizons, peeled and made bald by the rigour of the season; the general hard, cold void of the prospect. . . . There was something inexorable in the poverty of the scene, shameful in the meanness of its details, which gave a collective impression of boards and tin and frozen earth, sheds and rotting pipes, railway lines striding flat across a thoroughfare of puddles. . . .

Verena thinks the view "lovely," but the implication is that her life with Olive, who would like Verena to promise never to marry, will also be desolate, hard, cold, void, and perhaps even shameful.

New York, where Basil Ransom lives and tries to practice law, is less bleak but hardly more attractive. Outside Ransom's shabby boarding house is a smelly grocery and a "relaxed and disjointed roadway, enlivened at the curbstone with an occasional ash-barrel or with gas-lamps drooping from the perpendicular," and there is a mechanical demon even more sinister than the crawling and staggering bridge over the Charles River:

> the fantastic skeleton of the Elevated Railway, overhanging the transverse longitudinal street, which it darkened and smothered with the immeasurable spinal column and myriad clutching paws of an antediluvian monster.

But in *The Bostonians* it is not only cities that are ugly and depressing. Even in full summer the New England countryside appears stunted and barren, at least in Basil Ransom's eyes:

> The shadows grew long in the stony pastures and the slanting light gilded the straggling, shabby woods . . . there was nothing in the country . . . that seemed susceptible of maturity: nothing but the apples in the little tough, dense orchards, which gave a suggestion of fruition here and there.

In the Cape Cod village where Olive and Verena go for a vacation with two other unmarried feminists, the ancient reformer Miss Birdseye and the sexless Dr. Prance, the houses are "low, rusty, crooked, distended, . . . with dry, cracked faces and the dim eyes of small-paned, stiffly-sliding windows." The cottage Olive has rented is separated from the bay by a "small, lonely garden" and the littered remains of a shipyard.

A skewed vision of the landscape in which he sets his story is not James's only method of stacking the deck against the reformers. All of them are in some way flawed. Mrs. Farrinder, "the great apostle of the emancipation of women," is a large, cold, smooth, self-important person with an insignificant husband. Mrs. Tarrant, Verena's mother, is an overweight, beaten down, socially ambitious frump who has joined her disreputable husband in fradulent séances and a dubious free-love community; her only claim to respectability is that she is the daughter of a famous male abolitionist. Dr. Prance is "spare, dry, hard, without a curve, an inflection, or a grace" though lively and intelligent. She is perhaps too intelligent for the point James wanted to make, for at the end of the book, quite illogically, we learn that she is no longer in favor of women's rights.

Miss Birdseye, the former abolitionist who has been "in love . . . only with causes" all her life, is described by James at the start of the novel as a dim, comic character: "a confused, entangled, inconsequent, discursive old woman." As the story progresses, however, James warms toward her, seeing her as the last representative of New England transcendentalism. "She was heroic, she was sublime, the whole moral history of Boston was reflected in her displaced spectacles." Yet his admiration is valedictory and incomplete. Miss Birdseye's eyesight is weak metaphorically as well as actually, he implies: she cannot see clearly, or discriminate between the noble causes of her youth and the foolish ones of the present day, and her decline in the final chapters signals the end of "the heroic age of New England life."

James's most subtle, tragic, and devastating portrait of the contemporary feminist is Olive Chancellor, with "her light-green eyes, her pointed features, and nervous manner," who is "unmarried by every implication of her being," and deeply hostile to men. Olive is a serious young woman of independent means, an intellectual who reads Goethe and listens raptly to Beethoven. Her greatest wish is to devote all her energy to the feminist cause; but in fact she has great difficulty in liking most of the people who support it. Though it offends her sensibilities, Olive—like many reformers today—must deal with celebrity-crazed journalists, greedy lecture agents, and society patrons for whom Verena's remarkable talent as an inspirational "speaker" is merely an occasion for an expensive party.

Olive, who has something of the nervous temperament of James's invalid sister, Alice, is also afflicted with a New England conscience. She is given to constant self-doubt and questioning of her own motives; almost the first thing we learn about her is that she is "subject to fits of tragic shyness, during which she was unable to meet even her own eyes in the mirror."

If all this were not enough, James has chosen as his central character and public spokeswoman for feminism a heroine who is essentially and ironically totally unliberated. Verena Tarrant is a reformer only by accident of birth. On her first public appearance, under the mesmeric influence of her father—a shady character who would today probably be making his living as a New Age healer—she repeats the advanced opinions about women's rights that she has heard at home. One reason her gift for public speaking is valuable to the movement is that she not only presents herself as, but actually is, "feminine" in the most conservative sense of the word. "I am only a girl, a simple American girl," she tells her audience, "and of course I haven't seen much, and there is a great deal of life that I don't know anything about."

In spite of this disclaimer, Verena is a charismatic figure; at once inspired and ignorant, a late and ambiguous descendant of famous New England preachers from Jonathan Edwards to Ralph Waldo Emerson. This, James seems to imply, is what the great tradition had come to.

Though Verena is innocent herself, she is the cause of very questionable behavior in others. As James tells us, she "had always done everything that people asked." "What was a part of her essence was the extraordinary generosity with which she would expose herself, give herself away, turn herself inside out, for the satisfaction of a person who made demands on her." She is also somewhat masochistic: James informs us that "it was in her nature to be easily submissive, to like being overborne." It is this self-denying wish to please, perhaps even more than her youth, beauty, and extraordinary talent as an orator, that makes her so attractive to both men and women.

James's fiction, of course, is full of innocent American girls who come to a bad end. Often it is their best qualities that bring about their destruction, by attracting exactly the wrong sort of men: Isabel Archer's wealth and wish to do something great in life, or Daisy Miller's eagerness for experience and naive disregard of convention. Verena's beauty, generosity, and histrionic gifts have the same effect.

The central conflict in *The Bostonians* is over who will have possession of Verena. Because she is both naive and passive, her own wishes have little to do with the outcome. Early in the novel she is literally sold by her father to Olive Chancellor for "a very considerable amount"—a transaction which Verena accepts without difficulty: "She had no worldly pride, no traditions of independence, no ideas of what was done and what was not done."

Olive's appropriation of Verena, from the start, is compared to a kidnapping:

> Olive had taken her up, in the literal sense of the phrase, like a bird of the air, had spread an extraordinary pair of wings, and carried her through the dizzying void of space. Verena liked it, for the most part; . . . she felt that she was seized, and she gave herself up.

Mr. Tarrant's, Olive's, and Basil Ransom's influence over Verena are all spoken of as a "charm" or a "spell." The mythical or magical overtones are no accident; *The Bostonians* can easily be read as a fairy tale. The closest parallel is to the story of Rapunzel, with Verena as the heroine given up by her parents to a witch in exchange for green stuff (not money in the original story, but a leafy vegetable known as *rapunzel* in German and *rampion* in English). Her name itself suggests green things—veridian, verdure—and her masses of brilliant hair, like Rapunzel's, are an important feature of her appearance. Verena is also rescued by a prince from a distant country (in *The Bostonians*, the deep South), with the metaphoric name of Ransom.

But Basil Ransom is no fairy-tale hero. His feeling for Verena is not so much love as a wish to dominate and overpower, perhaps even to destroy. ("So long as he made her do what he wanted he didn't care much how he did it.") Ransom's political views, including his attitude toward women, are deeply reactionary—"about three hundred years behind the age," according to an editor who has rejected one of his articles. Where Olive reads Goethe and dreams of the future, he reads Carlyle and reveres the past.

Ransom is convinced that women are "essentially inferior to men, and infinitely tiresome when they declined to accept the lot which men had made for them." They were, he believes, created to make the other sex happy:

> that was the way he liked them—not to think too much, not to feel any responsibility for the government of the world. . . . If they would only be private and passive! . . .

"For public, civic uses," he tells Verena, women are "perfectly weak and second-rate." There are hints that as a Southerner Ransom thinks of the world in terms of superior and inferior, even of master and slave.

Basil Ransom is also very ambitious, with an "immense desire for success." Unfortunately, he himself is a failure. His family has lost its property and slaves in the war, and he is unable to publish his reactionary articles or make a living as a lawyer in New York: "He had had none but small jobs, and he had made a mess of more than one of them." So discouraged is he by his prospects that at one point he thinks seriously of marrying Olive Chancellor's rich, frivolous sister, Mrs. Luna, who is eager to acquire an aristocratic and decorative husband; in effect, to buy him as Olive has bought Verena. He excuses the transaction by asking himself if it is not in fact his duty to marry Mrs. Luna, so that he will have the leisure to express his political views and the money to publish them.

Verena, on the other hand, is a tremendous success in her career. She is already aware of this at the beginning of the book; the first words we hear her speak are: "*I* had a magnificent audience last spring in St. Louis." It has been suggested that one of the reasons Ransom wants, as he puts it, "to take possession of Verena Tarrant" is envious spite; he wants to own her in order to, as he says, "shut her up."

Basil Ransom's courtship of Verena has also been seen as an act of political revenge against Olive Chancellor and all she stands for, including the New England abolitionists whom many Southerners thought responsible for the Civil War. From this point of view his campaign is a kind of terrorism. Judith Will has noted that Ransom's first exclamation on learning of Olive's political opinions is "Oh, murder!"—a phrase he repeats twice more: once when he hears Verena practicing the speech she intends to give in Boston, and finally just before he goes to the Music Hall to prevent this performance. Later, as he waits there, he feels as if he had "made up his mind, for reasons of his own, to discharge a pistol at the king or president." And when he succeeds in tearing Verena away from her friends, her family, and the huge audience waiting to hear her speak, it almost seems as if a murder of some sort has taken place.

The Bostonians can also be read as a political allegory, a more subtle and sour version of the many postwar novels in which the main theme was the need for reconciliation between North and South. Often, in these tales, the radical, democratic views and long winters of the North were contrasted with the aristocratic society, lush climate, and sensual warmth of the South, and their political reunion was echoed in a romantic bonding of two former opponents.

In this reading, Ransom's kinship to Olive is metaphorically appropriate: like North and South they are closely related but become bitter enemies. His abduction of Verena and the destruction of her career is the South's revenge for the ravages of the Northern armies, as well as a symbolic marriage. Appropriately, the central scene of the book takes place when Verena and Basil Ransom visit Harvard's Memorial Hall. Ransom is moved by the inscriptions commemorating Harvard students who died in the war: "They touched him with respect, . . . he forgot, now, the whole question of sides and parties. . . ." Verena is also moved; moreover, she almost immediately betrays Olive Chancellor ("I tell her everything") by promising to conceal this meeting.

But whereas most post-Civil War romances ended happily, the final scene of *The Bostonians* is ominous. Ransom's mere appearance at the Music Hall is enough to make

Verena unable to give her speech. Backstage her parents, Olive, her lecture agent, and the attendant journalists are nearly in hysterics; outside the audience begins to roar and stamp. James's description suggests that they are a mob waiting for its victim; even that the Music Hall is a kind of Roman Colosseum, where Verena is to be thrown to the lions. Instead, it is Olive who goes out to meet the angry crowd as if "offering herself to be trampled to death and torn to pieces" while Ransom drags Verena away in tears. In the famous last sentence of the book, James remarks: "It is to be feared that with the union, so far from brilliant, into which she was about to enter, these were not the last she was destined to shed."

Men and women cannot easily be reconciled as equals, nor can North and South. James's conclusion is pessimistic, but it is one that history over the next hundred years was in large part to justify. (pp. 23-4)

> *Alison Lurie, "A Fine Romance," in* The New York Review of Books, *Vol. XXXVIII, No. 8, April 25, 1991, pp. 23-4.*

V. S. Pritchett on the young James:

Our usual picture of James comes from the later, old Pretender period when he seems to be genuflecting, somewhere in space, before the image of Art, mysteriously sustained by an invisible private income. The young James with the glossy beard is quite a different person: dashing, shrewd about ways and means, burning with energy. There is vast confidence in his malice and his ironic laughter. He is absolutely professional. He delights to earn his living; he is tough with editors; he is prompt and clever with his pot-boilers; he has an eye to serials and commissions. He was longheaded enough to know, within six months, when he would be able to switch to greatness. He arrived in London for the publication of a work of serious criticism and of his early novels, which were unknown here. A few rapid moves and he knew everyone. At first agog, but soon he was in the clubs—a 'member' in the full, soporific sense. A word from Henry Adams—the supreme Yankee snob and expert at the game—and he was staying in the best houses. The lazy, genial Thackeray had been ruined by dining out; for James it was part of the plan. In his second winter, he had dined out 140 times and in the best society—'behold me after dinner conversing affably with Mr Gladstone.'

V. S. Pritchett, in his The Tale Bearers: Literary Essays, *Random House, 1980.*

Clare R. Goldfarb   (essay date 1991)

[*In the following excerpt, Goldfarb contends that much of James's fiction is a critique of the Victorian ideal of domestic bliss.*]

"Home sweet home" is not a major theme of Henry James's work; there are no examples of positive family relationships in his early, middle, or late periods. No conjugal bliss, no nurturing home life; instead a parade of widows and orphans marches through the novels. Wife and husband battering, child and parent abuse, alcoholism, depression, and suicide—all appear in the Jamesian account of the home. Implicitly and explicitly, James condemns the cult of domesticity so dear to the hearts of his contemporaries. (p. 43)

Malignant, abusive relationships appear again and again in [James's] fiction as early as *Roderick Hudson,* as important as *The American,* and as slight as *The European.* The tale that brought him his first fame, *Daisy Miller,* concludes with its heroine's death caused, in large part, by the lack of loving, but firm, guidance. *Watch and Ward,* his first finished novel, depicts Nora Lambert, a twelve-year-old girl impulsively adopted by a wealthy bachelor. Nora's father is an alcoholic and a suicide, and her mother has died "outwearied and broken-hearted."

A family matrix of maternal martyrdom and paternal abandonment appears only once in *Watch and Ward,* but it appears several times in *Roderick Hudson,* the work James preferred to call his first attempt at a novel. James is careful to tell us not only who is who but also who was who in his international collection of truncated families where widows and orphans are the rule. The hero Roderick is a second son living with his widowed mother, whose husband, Roderick's father, drank himself to death. The orphaned narrator is Rowland Mallet, whose father, a "chip off the primal Puritan block" made homelife miserable for his wife.

When the two young men, Roderick and Rowland, go to Italy, they meet a mother and daughter with a lurid family history of their own. The widowed Mrs. Light, James tells us, is the daughter of an American painter and an abusive woman. Before finally abandoning her family in order to run off with an English lord, this woman beat her husband and neglected her child. The battered husband returned to America to die in an asylum. Not one good marriage exists or seems to have ever existed in the kinship histories of *Roderick Hudson.* What does exist are examples of spouse abuse.

In addition to abusive wives there are abused wives on both sides of the Atlantic. Roderick's mother is longsuffering, but James treats Madame Grandoni with a lighter hand; she appears again in *The Princess Casamassima.* Madame is the victim of a Neopolitan husband who beat her with his fiddle-bow and then left her for a *"prima donna assoluta."* As light as James's touch may be in describing Madame Grandoni, the theme of spouse battering is an ominous one which foreshadows the union between Christina Light and her Prince, for *Roderick Hudson* concludes with a desolate marriage that promises no future contentment for either party.

Christina Light has a mother who first neglects her, then smothers her with attention and finally blackmails her into a miserable marriage; remember that Christina also lays claim to a spouse-battering grandmother. As such, she is a stereotypic case study for modern sociologists. Victims of family abuse and neglect often themselves become perpetrators of violence. It would come as no surprise to investigators of family violence to discover that Christina Light becomes a cruel, capricious wife to Prince Cassamassima. Her history of abuse seems to make her an heiress of maltreatment, a human being victimized by her upbringing.

Motherhood comes in for a great deal of criticism in the early works. In **Roderick Hudson,** Christina Light must accede to her mother's domination. In **The American,** the heroine, Claire de Cintre, must retreat to a Carmelite convent to escape the machinations of her scheming mother.

But James did not allow husbands and fathers to provide alternatives to such schemers as Madame de Bellegarde or Mrs. Light. Males provide neither a safe haven for their offspring nor a comfortable existence for their wives. In **Roderick Hudson,** *paters familiae* are distant, bad memories: in **The American,** Claire's father has died before the novel begins, perhaps a victim of his wife's scheming, perhaps an adulterer, but most certainly an ineffective father, incapable of providing any kind of protection for his daughter. When Christopher Newman promises Claire that marriage to him will be a safe haven and that she will be safe with him, as safe as in her father's arms, a reader can understand why she refuses his proposal. A father's arms have provided no security for Claire, and home is no safe haven. Better the cloister of a strictly female universe than the bonds of family.

When it is the turn of a father to be widowed and to dominate a family, James depicts Dr. Sloper of **"Washington Square."** Richard Poirier calls him the Cruel Father of a "melodramatic fairy tale." Dr. Sloper rules a household shared with his widowed sister and daughter, never letting them forget that they are no compensation for the deaths of his beautiful wife and promising young son. Both his sister and his daughter are on the receiving end of Dr. Sloper's generally low opinion of females and "female characteristics." Neither woman is a match for his wit and irony, weapons he uses freely in his dealings with them. Rarely does he speak to his daughter openly, and never with warmth or affection. Towards Lavinia, his tone is even sharper and more impatient.

As cruel as Dr. Sloper may seem in his verbal assaults, he is even more threatening in the power he possesses as the male head of the household. If his daughter and sister do not do as he wishes, he can disinherit them. Homelessness and poverty are very real possibilities for both Lavinia and Catherine in the world they inhabit, the Washington Square home governed by a domineering father whose idea of child-rearing is shaped by the idea of obedience.

Child neglect replaces child rearing in much of Henry James's fiction. Morgan Moreen of **"The Pupil"** dies at the end, a victim of his weak heart, but also a victim of parental neglect and the inability to find a satisfactory and nurturing family life. Neglect and banishment also follow Miles and Flora in **"The Turn of the Screw."** The myriad interpretations of that famous tale have one trait in common, family neglect and abuse. An abundance of surrogate parents seem ready to assume the care of these children, but none of them is capable of giving the children the home they need.

Critics have discussed the vulnerability of James's little boys, and his little girls do seem tougher; Flora lives at the end of **"The Turn of the Screw"** albeit numbed by hysteria and terror. One exception to the rule of female survivorship is little Effie Bream in **"The Other House."** She is drowned by a jealous candidate for the role of her stepmother.

But the proverbial wicked stepmother has no corner on cruelty. Biological parents can behave just as badly towards their children, and a biological mother, Ida Farrange of **What Maisie Knew,** is more than unkind to her child. Through Maisie's perceptive young eyes, Ida is a nightmare figure with "huge painted eyes." She rarely speaks to her daughter, and Maisie receives her share of physical abuse from a mother whose "manual motions" she has been trained from an early age to watch. Mrs. Farrange is quite capable of dashing her child almost to the bottom of the stairs, when her talk displeases her.

Maisie's biological parents have used her as an object of their hatred of each other, and when they finally reject her, they do so with words that would scar any child. Maisie's mother loathes her, says her father, and Ida insists, quite vociferously, that Maisie's father wishes she were dead. Unfortunately her step-parents, though not as blatantly abusive, are also failures at parenting.

Mrs. Beale, like Ida Farrange, has never accepted the consequences of her relationship to a dependent, and faced at the end of the novel with Maisie's decision to reject both her and Sir Claude, she is furious. "In an incoherence of passion," Mrs. Beale snatches and jumps at Maisie. The child she once tenderly embraced and who once loved her more than she did her own papa, now is an "abominable little horror," "a hideous little hypocrite" with "a dreadful little mind." Such physical and verbal abuse merely repeats what Maisie has come to expect from "home, sweet home."

Jamesian children often suffer because they are unwanted. Parents and relatives such as the Moreens in **"The Pupil,"** the Uncle in **The Turn of the Screw,** and the Farranges of **What Maisie Knew,** do not want children, and they disown, banish, or dispossess them with a fair amount of ease. Children are an interference to such parents. Effie Bream's presence interferes with the marriage plans of her widowed father; Miles and Flora interfere with the bachelor life of their uncle. These children pay a heavy price finally for their interference.

Even children born to artists may suffer in the Jamesian world; some may die. In **"The Lesson of the Master,"** Henry St. George proclaims that children are a curse. Lamenting his own failure to accomplish "the great thing," St. George blames his family for the loss, declaring that he has sacrificed his talent to placing his children and dressing his wife. "One's children interfere with perfection. One's wife interferes. Marriage interferes." At least St. George's children survive to attend public school; other offspring born to artists are not as fortunate. After reading the latest work by her husband, **"The Author of Beltraffio,"** Beatrice Ambient lets their child die rather than grow up to read such a book.

Children suffer and die in families; wives and husbands suffer physical and verbal abuse. But parents too may be the victims of neglect and dispossession. Jamesian children may be as guilty of parental abuse as Jamesian parents are of child abuse. When parents become elderly or when mothers are widowed, they become vulnerable and, all too often, victims of abusive behavior meted out by their children. Mothers with insensitive, eldest sons may endure a restricted life away from the homes which they have helped to create.

Dispossessing offspring turn their widowed mothers out to dower houses. Such places may be picturesque, but the heroine of **"A London Life"** doesn't like the custom "of the expropriation of the widow in the evening of her days, when honour and abundance should attend her more than ever." James's concern over this legal iniquity dating back to medieval times was strong enough that he referred to dower houses in at least two other works, *The Tragic Muse* and *The Spoils of Poynton.*

In *The Tragic Muse,* Percival Dormer—who never appears personally—roams about the world "taking shots which excited the enthusiasm of society, when society heard of them, at the few legitimate creatures of the chase the British rifle had up to that time spared." But he is not too busy to turn his mother out of the country home she adores so that he may rent it to an American. Likewise, Owen Gareth banishes his mother in *The Spoils of Poynton,* and Mrs. Gareth recognizes that such usage is not common in other countries, for example, France. If James were flouting the Victorian cult of domesticity in his fiction, he could have done so no more effectively than by drawing figures of dispossessed mothers, growing old away from their children and their homes.

Ranging from neglect of the elderly to mere indifference to outright cruelty and violence, the examples of familial abuse in James's fictional families are abundant. James depicted tragedies happening behind elegantly closed doors, tragedies involving broken families, orphans, child and parent abuse, as well as battering parents and spouses. If, for sociologists and anthropologists, the individual family provides a microcosm of the larger world, then James's vision of family life is indeed sombre. As the Victorian Age came to a close, the Victorian icon of a family as a "walled garden," a haven of stability, a model of deference and discipline, crumbled and fell. As scholars have looked behind the walls of those gardens, they have discovered that violence was too often a component of family life. Students of family life need look only to the novels of Henry James for further corroboration of such a conclusion. (pp. 44-50)

> *Clare R. Goldfarb, "Home Sweet Home: Henry James's Critique of the Cult of Domesticity," in* The Midwest Quarterly, *Vol. XXXIII, No. 1, Autumn, 1991, pp. 43-51.*

Stuart Hampshire   (essay date 1991)

[Hampshire is an English philosopher and critic. In the following excerpt, he argues that James's literary achievement was primarily one of form and structure.]

Henry [James] famously shifted the narrative of the "old-fashioned English novel," which included even *Middle-march,* into a narrative of consciousnesses, using the inherited devices of drama to keep the separate consciousnesses vividly before the reader. He took over from Jane Austen, particularly from *Persuasion,* the novelistic soliloquy in which a character's conscious thoughts appear in direct, and now largely Jamesian, speech. Notoriously he also used, and perhaps overused, the confidant of classical drama as a device to multiply the shifts of consciousness within the story.

The confidant Fanny Assingham, for instance, probed secrets in *The Golden Bowl.* Henry James was fascinated by secrecy in all its forms, by the maneuvers of concealment and by the thrill of sudden revelations, when the long-guarded truth is dragged from the shadows and made explicit. For him sexuality was indissolubly connected with secrecy and concealment, with the unsaid and the unspeakable thing that exists behind the flow of civilized behavior, with locked doors and with hints and allusions kept studiously vague. Max Beerbohm's marvelous cartoon shows James earnestly kneeling to examine two pairs of shoes left to be cleaned in a hotel corridor, a scene of Edwardian adultery probed. The prurient curiosity implied is not incidental but deep-seated; it was the engine of James's imagination. The Maisie of *What Maisie Knew* is present in one form or another in almost all his best stories and in most of the novels.

He has often been rebuked, by Wells and by other critics, for omitting any frank representation of physical passion, such as can be found in Maupassant or Lawrence. I agree with Millicent Bell [in her *Meaning in Henry James*] that this is a misunderstanding of James, and it is a misunderstanding, also, of the normal ways that the human imagination works. For many men and women the most intense feeling, whether it is sexual or religious feeling, requires as a condition of its intensity mystery, concealment, privacy, and a sense of the unspeakable. When James returned on a visit to America from Europe, he was disgusted by the dominance of newspapers and by the rage for publicity in American life, a disgust expressed in his stories. The only life worth living, and that has authentic vitality, is one that preserves and enjoys the felt tension between the civilized, social self and the hidden recesses of the inner and unclothed self. Otherwise there is a universal flatness and no place for art and for dramatic fiction, as in the unlivable-in America he thought he saw in his last visits, the land of celebrity which must soon turn literature into journalism.

Henry James had one master and only one: not Dickens, as might be expected, but Balzac. Balzac had conveyed delight in depicting greed and lust and the unregarded victims caught in the naturalized inferno, Paris. James was a supremely worldly man, driven by a vast curiosity about the three mechanisms of London's social life, money, rank, and sexual passion, and in the great novels of his maturity, *The Wings of the Dove* and *The Golden Bowl,* he found a fitting form. On re-reading some of the other works, one is very easily bored by the sentimental educations of Roderick Hudson, Rowland Mallet, Christopher Newman in *The American,* and, most of all, by Lambert Strether in *The Ambassadors,* who seems particularly leaden in his awakening. James always wrote more memorably about women than about men, and Gilbert Osmond, a convincing and subtle villain, is arguably the only interesting male to be set alongside Isabel Archer or Madame Merle or Milly Theale or Maggie Verver or Charlotte Stant. The perception that sets light to the great novels is a perception of the cost of high civilization and of the unavoidable corruption of the new money in London, the new Babylon, and of the discarding of the poor, teeming in their slums. [In his *The Jameses: A Family Narrative*, R. W. B. Lewis] quotes, from *The Princess Casamassima*, a description of the London scene:

> It's the old regime again, the rottenness and extravagance, bristling with every iniquity and every abuse, over which the French Revolution passed like a whirlwind; or perhaps even more a reproduction of the Roman world in its decadence, gouty, apoplectic, depraved, gorged and clogged with wealth and spoils, selfishness and skepticism, and waiting for the onset of the barbarians.

"Gouty" is again a pure Jamesian epithet in the context. Millicent Bell quotes a letter that James wrote to Charles Eliot Norton, just after *The Princess Casamassima* had appeared, in which in similar style he compared the English ruling class to the French aristocracy before the Revolution: he predicted that "in England the Huns and Vandals will have to come *up*—from the black depths of the (in the people) enormous misery." He expected the doom of social upheaval, some "blood-letting" as he called it, but the bloodletting he actually encountered was the wholly unexpected horror of the First World War.

James, supremely self-conscious, knew that his own aesthetic attitudes were the enjoyment of an inherited privilege. He knew that, unlike his brother, he was always a superior tourist everywhere in the world, brought up to record at leisure, and to exploit for literary gain, the picturesque features of the lives being lived around him, without ever being fully involved in them, as William was for many years at Harvard. [In his *Henry James and Revision*] Philip Horne quotes a revealing passage from *Italian Hours:*

> To travel is, as it were, to go to the play, to attend a spectacle; and there is something heartless in stepping forth into foreign streets to feast on "character" when character consists simply of the slightly different costume in which labour and want present themselves.

The great novels, *The Wings of the Dove* and *The Golden Bowl,* coming more than twenty years after *The Portrait of a Lady,* combine a vision both of the elevating and debasing effects of accumulated wealth, of the gross power of money that turns into refinement as well as into cruelty. Millicent Bell writes: "It is easy to see that *The Wings of the Dove* is all about money." So it is, no less than *Eugénie Grandet:* so also was *The Golden Bowl.*

Living in the age of Frick, Morgan, the first Rockefellers and Harrimans, the Ververs in *The Golden Bowl,* "wonderful" little Maggie and the elusive, sinister Adam Verver together outwit their European dependents, Charlotte Stant and the adulterous Prince. They buy them up and take them over, as if they were subsidiaries, underfunded assets from an older and negligent culture. Sensitive principally to social surfaces, Charlotte and the Prince pathetically underestimate the cunning, ruthlessness, and controlled energy that were needed to make a great fortune in the fierce struggles of capitalist concentration in America.

The Ververs' simplicity is all surface, not substance, and Charlotte, parading sophistication, turns out to be an innocent who has strayed into a jungle, and for her impulsiveness she suffers the terrible penalty of accompanying her commercial, cautious, and calculating husband to an unmentionable city somewhere in the middle of America. The famous end of this wonderful story, Charlotte obediently showing visitors her husband's treasures, led, as it were, by a silken cord, is black and harsh, and almost tragic, in its Jamesian style. Money wins. The darkness of the plot helps to explain James's statement that he could never sincerely propose marriage because that would imply that he thought better of human life than he actually did. (pp. 4, 6)

Philip Horne's record of the revisions that Henry made for the New York Edition of the novels, together with the prefaces, suggests one qualification in the measure of [James's] greatness: Henry's conception of the art of fiction was predominantly a matter of structure, and of form and sustained dramatic tension in the storytelling, and of the elimination of the inessential.

Perhaps—and a tentative "perhaps" is certainly needed—from another point of view the most enduring achievement of fiction is in the art of illusion, in the invention of characters who have the particularity that distinguishes the actual from the merely possible, in a trick played upon nature: as with Leopold and Molly Bloom, Françoise and Charlus and Madame Verdurin, Prince Andrew, Mrs. Proudie, Miss Havisham and Sam Weller, Mr. Woodhouse and Emma Woodhouse, Evelyn Waugh's Apthorpe, Isherwood's Mr. Norris and Sally Bowles—the list could obviously be prolonged indefinitely. All these have an irresistible presence as distinct persons, living still by their inessential particularities.

This power of illusion James did not possess. He was too intensely involved in communicating the joys of representation, as the New York Edition's revisions show, and as he records them in several of his short stories—in **"The Figure in the Carpet"** and **"The Lesson of the Master,"** for example. He did not try to break out of the circle of his own sensibility. Rather he exulted in the exuberance of his own phrase-making, and the wit, which welled up in his diction and writing reflected his delight in his own conversation. (p. 6)

Stuart Hampshire, "What the Jameses Knew," in The New York Review of Books, *Vol. XXXVIII, No. 16, October 10, 1991, pp. 3-4, 6.*

FURTHER READING

Bibliography

Budd, John. *Henry James: A Bibliography of Criticism, 1975-1981.* London: Greenwood Press, 1983, 190 p.

Lists recent criticism and other secondary works.

Ricks, Beatrice. *Henry James: A Bibliography of Secondary Works.* The Scarecrow Author Bibliographies, No. 24. Metuchen, N.J.: Scarecrow Press, 1975, 461 p.

Comprehensive bibliography of James criticism.

Biography

Edel, Leon. *Henry James.* 5 vols. Philadelphia: J. B. Lippincott Co., 1953-73.

Definitive biography for which Edel was awarded the Pulitzer Prize.

Criticism

Bell, Ian F. A. "Language, Setting, and Self in *The Bostonians.*" *Modern Language Quarterly* 49, No. 3 (September 1988): 211-38.

Discussion of vocabulary, imagery, and characterization in *The Bostonians.*

Born, Brad S. "Henry James's *Roderick Hudson:* A Convergence of Family Stories." *The Henry James Review* 12, No. 3 (Fall 1991): 199-211.

Analysis of James's early novel, *Roderick Hudson,* in the light of his relationships with his father and brother.

Carton, Evan. "The Anxiety of Effluence: Criticism, Currency, and 'The Aspern Papers.'" *The Henry James Review* 10, No. 2 (Spring 1989): 116-20.

Discussion of themes and imagery in "The Aspern Papers."

Joseph, Mary. "Suicide in Henry James's Fiction: A Socio-logical Analysis." *CLA Journal* XXXIV, No. 2 (December 1990): 188-211.

Applies Emile Durkheim's late nineteenth-century definition of suicide to sixteen of James's novels and tales.

Krook, Dorothea. "'The Aspern Papers': A Counter-Introduction." In *Essays on English and American Literature and A Sheaf of Poems,* edited by J. Bakker, J. A. Verleur, J. v.d. Vriesenaerde, pp. 223-34. Amsterdam: Rodopi, 1987.

Discusses the structure and meaning of "The Aspern Papers."

Moon, Heath. "Saving James from Modernism: How To Read *The Sacred Fount.*" *Modern Language Quarterly* 49, No. 2 (June 1988): 120-41.

Analyzes the motifs and ambiguity of *The Sacred Fount.*

Veeder, William. "Henry James and the Uses of the Feminine." In *Out of Bounds: Male Writers and Gender[ed] Criticism,* edited by Laura Claridge and Elizabeth Langland, pp. 219-51. Amherst: University of Massachusetts Press, 1990.

Exploration of James's portrayal of gender, focusing on *The Portrait of a Lady* and the late novels.

Weiman, Robert. "Realism, Ideology, and the Novel in America (1886-1896): Changing Perspectives in the Work of Mark Twain, W. D. Howells, and Henry James." *Boundary 2* 17, No. 1 (Spring 1990): 189-210.

Explores sociopolitical themes in *The Bostonians, The Princess Casamassima,* and *The Tragic Muse.*

Wiesenfarth, Joseph. "*The Portrait of a Lady:* Gothic Manners in Europe." In *Reading and Writing Women's Lives: A Study of the Novel of Manners,* edited by Bege K. Bowers and Barbara Brothers, pp. 119-39. Ann Arbor, Mich.: UMI Research Press.

Discussion of James's concept "horror of respectability" as presented in *The Portrait of a Lady.*

Additional coverage of James's life and career is contained in the following sources published by Gale Research: *Contemporary Authors,* **Vol. 104;** *Dictionary of Literary Biography,* **Vols. 12, 71, 74;** *Concise Dictionary of American Literary Biography, 1865-1917; Major 20th-Century Writers; Short Story Criticism,* **Vol. 8; and** *Twentieth-Century Literary Criticism,* **Vols. 2, 11, 24, 40.**

Franz Kafka

Das Schloss (*The Castle*)

Austro-Czech novelist, short story writer, and diarist.

The following entry presents criticism of Kafka's novel *Das Schloss,* first published in 1926 and translated into English in 1930 as *The Castle.* For general discussion of Kafka's career, see *TCLC,* Volumes 2 and 6. See *TCLC,* Volume 13, for a discussion of Kafka's novella *Die Verwandlung* (*The Metamorphosis*) and *TCLC,* Volume 29, for a discussion of his novel *Der Prozess* (*The Trial*).

INTRODUCTION

Although left unfinished at the time of Kafka's death, *The Castle* is often considered the best-developed of his novels. The narrative describes the struggles of a protagonist, known only as K., to be acknowledged as Land Surveyor by the officials of a mysterious castle and the distrustful peasants living in the Castle village. Related from the perspective of a character who may be mentally unstable, *The Castle* is a multivalent work that has given rise to a wide variety of critical interpretations, including philosophical, religious, and psychological readings.

Published posthumously, *The Castle* is Kafka's last major work. It is generally believed he began writing the novel during one of several trips he took to recover from the painful effects of tuberculosis, which he was diagnosed as having in 1917. Some commentators date the writing of *The Castle* as early as Kafka's 1918 sojourn to the village of Zürau, some as late as the time he spent convalescing in the village of Planá during the summer of 1922. Max Brod, Kafka's friend and literary executor, has noted the existence of a fragment from Kafka's diaries, "Temptation in the Village," which was composed in 1914 as a preliminary study for the opening scenes of *The Castle.* The bulk of the novel was finished by July 1922; it was among the material Kafka gave to Brod and ordered destroyed after his death. Contrary to his wishes, however, Brod assembled the unrevised manuscript and published it as *Das Schloss* in 1926. The novel was translated into English in 1930 by Willa and Edwin Muir; a 1954 translation by Eithne Wilkins and Ernst Kaiser includes appendices containing fragments of unfinished chapters and different versions of the opening paragraphs.

The plot of *The Castle* centers on K., a man who insists he has been called to act as Land Surveyor to Count Westwest, the ruler of an enigmatic, dilapidated castle situated above a snowbound village. Once K. is inside the village, however, Castle officials as well as villagers refuse to recognize his claim. The remainder of *The Castle* traces K.'s passage from arrogant self-assurance to doubt, exhaustion, and death. The novel also focuses on one village

household, the Barnabas family, that has fallen out of favor with the Castle because one of their daughters refused the rapacious advances of a Castle official. Mirroring K.'s situation, the family's plight at the hands of an alternately exploitative and indifferent bureaucracy, as well as the related stories of Frieda, a barmaid, and Pepi, a servant, lend readers objective insight into circumstances that K. himself fails to perceive.

In many critical readings of *The Castle,* connections have been drawn between Kafka's life and the characters and events in the novel. The Castle, for example, has been characterized as a satiric portrait of the Austro-Hungarian Empire's bureaucracy, with which Kafka was well acquainted through his position with a government insurance company. The cold reception K. receives from the villagers has been similarly likened to the virulent anti-Semitism Kafka experienced during his lifetime. Like Kafka, K. seeks marriage and a place in society, yet pursues a career that would place him outside society's conventional boundaries; he suffers from exhaustion and sickness and endures social alienation as a result of this ambivalence. Some critics maintain that the character of Frieda represents Kafka's Czech translator, Milena Jesenská Pollak. Married to an abusive husband, Milena became involved in a love affair with Kafka but found herself unable to leave her husband and wed Kafka; she eventually ended the relationship. In *The Castle,* Frieda is initially involved with Klamm, a brusque and demanding Castle official. She has a brief affair with K. but abandons the liaison to return to the powerful Klamm and the security of her position as a barmaid. While such biographical comparisons have been determined to provide some insight into *The Castle,* many critics have maintained that they do not in themselves constitute a total view of the work.

One of the most prominent readings of *The Castle* was first advanced by Max Brod, who proposed that the novel functions as a religious allegory much like John Bunyan's *Pilgrim's Progress* (1678). Numerous commentators have suggested that the Castle and its servants represent a divine agency that is inscrutable in its indifference to K., who has been characterized as a potential messiah or twentieth-century seeker who faces unknown pitfalls and setbacks in seeking the path to God. Erich Heller and others argue that this theory ignores the neurotic and inhuman behavior of the Castle officials, which seems to support the idea that the Castle represents a bastion of evil, a "heavily fortified garrison of a company of Gnostic demons" who effectively resist the advances of K.'s soul. A third group of critics have asserted that the inefficient bureaucracy of the Castle, which seems to reward rebellion and punish conformism, may represent an ambiguous and indeterminate symbol of good or evil that frustrates all attempts at rational comprehension.

The truth of K.'s claim to the position of Land Surveyor is another issue disputed by commentators. Many critics argue that K. may be lying about being summoned by Count Westwest, since he has no letter of appointment and no surveying apparatus. As others have noted, however, K. also receives official letters from and is assigned two assistants by the Castle, seeming to confirm his appointment. This type of contradiction recurs throughout the novel, creating a dramatic sense of indeterminacy and ambiguity. In his *A Hesitation Before Birth,* Peter Mailloux asserts that *The Castle* succeeds because its ambiguities and outright contradictions produce in the reader the same feelings of confusion and alienation which K. suffers in his endeavors to reach the Castle.

Kafka's ability to express ambiguous ideas in a meticulously clear prose style has prompted epistemological and structuralist interpretations in which K.'s task, like that of the reader, is viewed as an attempt to break the code of the Castle's symbolic structure. As many recent critics have noted, each rational interpretation of *The Castle* is countered by an equally valid opposite interpretation and thereby serves to frustrate any notion of unequivocal meaning in the text.

CRITICISM

Christopher Lazare   (essay date 1941)

[*In the following review of* The Castle, *Lazare highlights the novel's ambiguity and compares its main characters and themes to those of* The Metamorphosis *and* The Trial.]

The reissuance of **The Castle** is a good sign and we should like to think of it as the result of popular demand. Kafka has too often been regarded as a sport of literature, strange and esoteric in his preoccupations, and limited in his appeal. And yet his work possesses a quality which should immediately establish him as a "master" in the public mind, the quality of meaning all things to all readers. Thus, in the *Miscellany,* Dr. Slochower convincingly proves him a "pre-fascist exile" while Edwin Muir no less persuasively identifies him with religious mysticism, and if one examines the bulk of critical writing inspired by his output, one finds him variously announced as Expressionist, Freudian, Marxist, Surrealist, a cross between Kierkegaard and Lewis Carroll, Plato and Bunyan, Goethe and Lautréamont. These contradictory evaluations are neither due to Kafka's vagueness nor to any profound misapprehension on the part of his critics. On the contrary, they are a mark of his creative resilience; Kafka's devices, which have much in common with poetry, draw upon the individual *conscience* and subjectivity of the reader and since they present a new system of metaphors for human experience (in the sense that the "Castle" or Gregory Samsa, the vermin-man of **Metamorphosis,** are metaphors) it is not surprising that they should give rise to disparate interpretations. The arbitrary and the ambiguous are familiar elements in Kafka's reality and it is a tribute to his talent that they still persist as a dissociate kind of literary after-effect in the appraisals of his work. We hesitate to add a version of our own to the list; it would be simpler to merely describe Kafka's explicit and structural characteristics.

In **The Trial,** Joseph K., a bank manager, is falsely arrested; the charge is never revealed to him and *although he is under arrest he maintains his position at the bank.* He is finally executed without having been judged. The hero of **Metamorphosis** turns into an insect; he continues to lead a "conventional" life and dies an insect *although he has retained human consciousness throughout.* The protagonist of **The Castle** (who is also designated by the initial, K.) is summoned by the "Castle" to act as a land surveyor; once he arrives in the Village, however, the "Castle" refuses to recognize him and he is discredited by the Village. *Although K's presence is never acknowledged by the "Castle,"* he persists in his efforts to gain admission and dies of exhaustion without having accomplished his purpose. It is at this point that the "Castle" sends word that K. may remain and work in the Village even though he has no right there. (The conclusion is the one outlined by Kafka to Max Brod.)

All of Kafka's heroes (those letters in the human alphabet!) seem to exist on the borderline of two worlds: the one, physical, inferior, senseless, the empiric world with its degraded patterns based on function and use; the other spiritual, inscrutable, authoritative, overshadowing the first. The hero is exposed to a simultaneous awareness of both, which excludes him from an absolute participation in either. He lives in a "pun" reality; he has only an umbilical connection with experience and not one of his acts or movements proceeds from his own volition or is complete without its *correspondence.* He longs to escape, not into the fantastic or miraculous, but into the universe itself—into some positive state common to all man.

In *Metamorphosis,* the family (as a domestic community) represents this state and the hero, Gregory Samsa (who has been given a name but deprived of his externally human characteristics) lives in its midst as the most alien and despicable form of household life, a vermin. Yet he retains his consciousness as a man and is aware of what is happening to him as an insect. The situation in *The Trial* is analogous. K. is a criminal working in the most sanctimonious of institutions, a bank; his awareness of his own innocence is like Samsa's possession of his human faculties. In the end both of them must die in an identity which is not completely their own. The other K. achieves his closest contact with the "Castle" when he is permitted to become the schoolhouse janitor in the Village where he has never been wanted.

The disorientation outlined is not based on any *confusion en Dieu.* Thomas Mann emphasizes this point in his introductory "Homage" to *The Castle:* " . . . he (Kafka) did not yearn after a blue flower blossoming somewhere in a mystical sphere; he *yearned after the 'blisses of the commonplace.'* " That phrase without depriving Kafka of his originality, relates him to the main tendencies of twentieth century literature, the product of insecurity, shifting values, peace, war and depression, the disenfranchisement of the individual and the humanization of the machine. It is reflected in Gide's quest for the *"rapprochement infini,"* in Joyce's attempt to invent a new mode of communication, in Proust's inverted clairvoyance and Stein's destruction of the character-identity in narrative. They are all attempts to reorientate man in a world that has deprived him of belief—whether it is Magic, Religion or Science. Freud rationalized the Original Sin; Kafka restored it to poetry. (pp. 69-71)

Christopher Lazare, "The Human Alphabet,"
in Decision, *Vol. 1, No. 4, April, 1941, pp. 69-71.*

Walter J. Ong   (essay date 1947)

[*Ong is an American educator, theologian, and linguist best known for the theoretical study* Orality and Literacy *(1982). In the following excerpt, Ong demonstrates how the philosophy underlying Kafka's* Castle *directly conflicts with current Western philosophy.*]

To those who feel acutely the always urgent need of giving common habits of thought and feeling a good going over, the way in which Kafka contests much that goes into the false surface which persistently forms on life is a further guarantee of the worth of his perceptions. Here is one whose irony, moving soberly and relentlessly within the framework of the bourgeois milieu itself, will confute in a determined and circumstantial fashion the bogus consistency of a merchandizing civilization which will allow only such critiques of reality as can begin and end with a cheery grin. Kafka's effect in areas such as this is unmistakable. But much good writing reaches this far.

One can perceive that the general force of Kafka's irony carries it much further still. However, the implications of his irony in all the quarters to which it extends are not always so clear. When it engages with forces which are still more complex and resistant to analysis, although there can be no doubt that something is happening, one is often enough at a loss to say just what this something is. Thus the question continues to suggest itself as to what Kafka implies concerning the religious tradition of the West. How does his irony apply to the Christian or to the Jewish-Christian ethos? There are certainly at least some who feel that the numbing swirl of frustration in which Kafka's heroes move is somehow at odds with this ethos in a very radical sense.

Kafka is, after all, primarily concerned with the region of religious activity, and it is in this region that his interminable series of frustrations arise. In *The Castle* the hero, K., seeks in vain to get to the seat of authority controlling the village to which he has come—indeed, seeks in vain even to contact the Castle, for all his interviews with Castle officials turn out to be suspect of unreality in every way, each recurrent attempt to come to grips with the officials only plunging K. into a further frustration which reinforces the foregoing ones.

Now the Castle certainly in some way suggests God. Kafka's friend, Max Brod, who, by a fortunate disregard of Kafka's instructions to destroy his manuscripts, also became Kafka's literary executor, assures us that the Castle should be equated directly with divine guidance. Yet the Castle not only is the focus of all of K.'s frustrations but even in itself appears dim and ambiguous enough. The more he looks at it, the more it seems to K. to be not a castle at all but a group of insignificant houses, not unlike those of his own home village, grouped in an unimpressive huddle.

Moreover, a curious turn is given to Kafka's thought here. For, strangely enough, if he does make out divine guidance to be an illusion, Kafka seems to side with it anyhow. He does not really give K. any leg to stand on, any claim on the Castle at all. K.'s very presence in the Castle village is unaccountable and a source of constant embarrassment to himself. His questionable position here makes it seem only right that he wear himself out fighting for an illusion. You are given the impression that the illusion has a sort of right to mislead him.

Here is a speciously new and an intriguing sophistication in the recipe for eating your cake and having it: divine guidance is indeed an illusion, but it's a good thing precisely because of this fact. You have the cake precisely because you eat it. That is to say.

Such an interpretation of Kafka would be less convincing did it not seem to tie in so readily with a set of reactions extremely widespread, if often veiled, today, when the theme of imagination and imaginative illusion is capable of suffusing man almost inevitably with a glow of satisfaction. Down at the level of the commonalty, the attractiveness of the illusion motif is attested by such things as the sure-fire popularity of stories and movie shorts in which the psychiatrist is the central figure. Here preoccupation with the motif ties in rather bluntly with feelings of satisfaction and a general euphoria: uniformly, the psychiatrist shorts all turn out happily, and the grisly fact that psychiatry, like everything else, has in many cases dismally failed is kept well out of sight.

But far above the commonalty and through the higher ground of advertising campaigns, the apotheosis of illusion still carries on. It trips lightly through Disney's pretty fantasy worlds with their insistent insinuation that life is really like this. It makes itself more expressly felt in O'Neill's pleonastic rehearsal of the pipe-dream theorem in *The Iceman Cometh* (one critic has remarked that the term "pipe dream" occurs about two hundred times in the play). But it goes on far beyond these areas, where its claims are somewhat ill-defined, to occupy dizzy intellectual fastnesses in the field of comparative religion, from which points of vantage it manages periodically to swoop out in quiet attempts to swallow up Christianity in its own ambiguous gentlemanly way.

Clearly, there is continuity in the picture. At the bottom you have the movie-goer who comes to feel really sharp when he is made aware that however ill-founded a phobia or hysteria may be, it *is* real in terms of the way it works on a man's life. At the top you have the devotee of comparative religion occupied in validating religions principally in terms not of what they are founded upon—which would seem to be the vital question—but in terms of what they do to you if you have them. "Imagination," Sir James Frazer eventfully observes, "acts upon man as really as does gravitation, and may kill him as certainly as a dose of prussic acid." The drive to concern oneself with religion on these terms readily runs down through the other levels to connect with the drive which gives popular psychiatry its appeal.

It is with the sort of remark just quoted that Frazer's thought, and the type of thinking it represents, slips beneath the wealth of detail it has accumulated and scrapes bottom. It is not strange that in doing so it immediately gives off a ring like that of an apothegm out of S. S. Van Dine. The two writers are face to face with the same state of mind. At almost any intellectual altitude people now want to operate in this commodity of illusion. And they are all hoping for the same heady dividends: the somewhat esoteric sense of being in the know and the *élan* which this sense brings with it. You get paid a little more at the higher levels, but everywhere you get paid in this sort of currency.

In its appeal on this basis, the apotheosis of illusion is quite epidemic, and its epidemic proportions make it a tempting enough context in which to consider Kafka. It is a sizable and rich enough context to be plausible for even so competent and important an artist.

And this context is worth the time here given it because

it is certain that in a discussion of Kafka's impact on his milieu such a context will never be irrelevant. So it must always be kept in mind. And yet it would most certainly not at all provide *the* frame in which to interpret Kafka. For Kafka has significance deeper and more radical than any which mere association with such thinking could give.

Whatever else it does, Kafka's ironic futility implies a head-on attack on the dominant religious psychology of Western man. This is a basic, if not the basic, reason why it bites so forcibly and deeply into our consciousness.

Kafka's world is governed by the sense that man's actions are carried on in a setting to which they are irrelevant. The Kafka hero is set at large in an environment which does not engage at all with the achievement which enters into human actions but only with the radical insufficiency which is inseparable from them. *The Castle* can be taken as typical here. K., according to Kafka's plan explained by Max Brod in his concluding note to *The Castle,* was to have played out the entire remainder of his life in vain negotiations to achieve contact with the Castle, and then at the end of his life was to have been informed that he would be allowed to live and work in the Castle village "for certain auxiliary considerations." The irrelevance of K.'s activity is absolute and final.

Kafka carries through his design with a disconcerting simplicity and lack of compromise, and the dominant note in the life of the Kafka hero thus becomes one of *plight.* This plight arises from the fact that the hero's universe, in the last analysis and the only analysis that counts, is dominated by something *different* from himself—different not in a half-hearted way but quite intransigently.

At this point Kafka's thought cuts straight athwart the current which has chiefly determined the direction characteristic of the modern Western milieu. The force of this current has been to inhibit, more and more, recognition of the fact of a plight at the center of man's life. Kafka contests this fiction which has long tended to dominate the West and which in the wake of the tin can and the *Reader's Digest* is now trailing over into the East—the fiction of the life with no deep-seated plight, no chronic distress, at its center, the fiction of man in a universe with plenty of problems indeed but with none which overwhelms him with embarrassment and the sense of a deep and incurable weakness inseparable from his very being.

Kafka will not assume the view, more often stoutly implied than expressed, that in contact with reality the paramount design is in what you catch. He enforces the notion that it is in what you miss, and that not only on those special occasions when you set out deliberately to catch a design, but always and in everything: the paramount design is what you are always engaged in missing.

In this view one cannot say or imply, as the Western fictionists would, that your grasp of reality need only be extended to more and more things, amplified by increasing the number and sharpness of your concepts, pushed out at the edges. Rather, your grasp on reality stands always in need of being complemented by a radically new grasp. Furthermore, since *the* design of reality lies outside your experience, and since your own life is to be lived *by you* within the framework of such reality, in so far as you are acting on your initiative you are in a plight, and there's no getting around it ever. This is the position of Kafka's Barnabas who, when he gets to the Castle, "doesn't venture to speak to anybody for fear of offending in ignorance against some unknown rule and so losing his job." Barnabas, unlike, for instance, George Bernard Shaw, senses in his own being a quality which compels him to approach everything else with supreme deference.

Most of the larger movements which have characterized modern Western thought and feeling give evidence of a more or less conscious effort to repress the notion that at the center of man's life there is this plight, that man is faced with a world which does not adequately present, much less explain, itself on the side he reaches it from, but opens out on to another side to which man cannot reach save through the inadequate medium of the world itself. Certainly the growth of thought which occupies the strategic position in the Western world—that growth which, for example, gathered to a head in the *Aufklärung,* which stood pretty much for order, had a converse, even this converse, typical Western movement that it was, worked toward the same end. The forces of disorder which came to term in the French Revolution give evidence, strangely enough, of the same urge to make up everything in convincing little packages.

For when you look for concrete effects of the French Revolution, what do you find? Not only certain accouterments of freedom but other things, things like the metric system for weights and measurements—the tremendous psychological effect of the symbolism attaching to this achievement must not be forgotten, nor its spread with the revolution all over the world—and superdepartmentalized governments. Everywhere the finger of the revolution has been laid, right down to Stalin's Russia, you see signs of the same passion for getting things into self-contained systems once for all—and that on a cosmic scale.

Behind Stalin's universalism, as behind Lenin's, there is a deep psychological urge much more fundamental than Marxism, which was only a shellac for the urge to universalism, though a shellac manufactured from the same elements as the universalist urge itself.

James Burnham has made the point that Stalinism is not a departure from Marxism but simply pure theoretical Marxism reduced to practice. It might help also to observe that there is a basic commodity much more widespread than Marxism or Stalinism which enters into and determines the characteristic direction of both. It is the great fiction of the West: the self-possessed man in the self-possessed world, the fiction which seeks to erase all sense of plight, of confusing weakness, from man's consciousness, and which above all will never admit such a sense as a principle of operation.

This same fiction has asserted its influence over all modern Western philosophy and, indeed, is one of the chief referents in terms of which most modern philosophy in the West is constituted the organized whole which, despite the rival claims of various "systems," it has, by general admission, always been.

A tendency to develop an idealistic philosophy is chronic with man. It is one of the threats constantly present because of the structure and peculiar imperfections of the human intellect. And yet the extreme popularity, the sense of exhilaration and achievement attending such philosophy in the modern West is symptomatic of the development of the great fiction.

What could be more satisfying to a mind bent on denying that there is a real plight—of any genuinely critical sort—at the center of man's life than a philosophy which sets out to construct man himself and everything else out of the absolute unity of the Idea? Here is a self-possessed world if there ever was one. In such a world the tranquility of man is totally uncompromised by any threat of anything genuinely different. Indeed, this world is so self-possessed that in *The Phenomenology of Mind* Hegel himself owns the supreme difficulty there is in getting such a world to *do* anything once you have it knocked together.

It might be objected here that since the East has known and still knows monisms and pantheisms which are every bit as airtight as the idealistic product which modern Western man has found so comforting, this feature of modern Western thought is not distinctive of it at all. But there is a difference between the East and the modern West here, and a sizable one. However its theorizing may go, the East still preserves superstitions on a large operative scale. And, however false they are in other ways, the superstitions tend to keep alive an appreciation of the aspect of reality which the modern Western has found it increasingly difficult to be aware of.

The superstitious man lives in the presence of an acute sense that there is something in the world which is different, something which keeps escaping him. He habitually deals with things in terms of forces which do not yield to understanding. By virtue of his superstitions he engages in operations within precisely the area where his thought is deficient. He cannot yet afford to ignore this area, as can the man with a greater store of understanding to occupy his attention. The superstitious man, by his very superstitions, keeps reminding himself of his plight.

It is because it senses these implications of superstitiousness and not particularly because superstitions are *unfounded* beliefs that the Western mind now finds the notion of superstition so bitterly distasteful. Unfounded beliefs can still be as high-handed as ever so long as they do not imply the plight for humanity that superstitions imply.

Not opposition to unfounded belief as such, but the subconscious urge to do away with this sense of plight is the key to the characteristic religious operations of the modern Western mind. This subconscious urge gave force and direction to the greatest religious crisis which modern Western thought has ever known—the crisis which was generated when in the fifteenth and sixteenth centuries this thought attained the maturity to which it had been growing during the Middle Ages—and the same subconscious urge has been operative in distinctively Western religion ever since.

The Christianity invented in and distinctive of the modern West, as against the Christianity which the modern West shares with the ancient West and the modern East, is a Christianity without a sacramental system and the Mass. Both these items tend strongly to convey the sense of something other, something different and inviolable in reality, and thereby to keep alive in man the sense of his plight. To the growing inhibitions of the Western mind such things appeared hair-raising enough, and it is little wonder that where the inhibitions fully asserted themselves the sacramental system and the Mass went into the discard.

The sacramental system underlined the presence of something other, something different in the workaday world by indicating certain precise points (without excluding others) at which sensible phenomena opened out into the quite different world beyond. The sacraments were visible signs of invisible grace. It is clear that they were objectionable because of their intimate implication with this sense of something different and beyond man's own reach. For the two sacraments of baptism and the Eucharist which the modern Western inhibitions consented to keep were retained only after they had been thoroughly purged of such an implication by being made merely commemorative rites with only an external or surface value.

It is noteworthy how local this crisis was: despite its opposition to Rome, the East never experienced the crisis at all, and the implications of sacramentalism remain the impassable gulf between the dissident Eastern churches and the Western phenomenon of Protestantism to this day.

In the light of recent findings it can be seen how the same state of mind made the Mass a critical issue in Western Europe at the same time as the sacraments. The psychological import of the Mass made quite inevitable some sort of conflict between it and the growing Western inhibitions.

Psychological effects and implications of ritual exist long before they are isolated and identified by scientific study. Indeed, as in the case of many psychological facts, isolation and identification is here often extremely difficult and at times practically impossible. It is therefore not strange that during the fifteenth and sixteenth-century conflict concerning the Mass, and long thereafter—until the past few decades—neither those who protested against the Mass nor those who fought for it nor anyone else could state the exact psychological issues involved.

Recent findings, however, make them clearer, for it is now known, through the work of Maurice de la Taille and others, that the psychological import of the Mass as a sacrificial act—and this is the ground on which it was assailed—is, among other things, the giving of oneself to God by means of a gift which symbolizes oneself. Without going into the detailed questions concerning the manner of identification of oneself with the gift peculiar to the Mass, one can in this aspect of the Mass setting readily recognize implications of the sort which distress the new Western mind. For here you have the material world—in terms of the gift—again put to use in a way which dramatizes the fact that it opens out to something that is beyond, different, inviolable within being. The fiction of a self-contained man in a self-contained world will not admit of this sort of maneuver. Seeing himself in a world of this sort, man

is inevitably reminded of his weak and inadequate grasp of reality.

It is informative to note that as scholars have ransacked every possible source for material throwing light on the psychological implications of the Mass setting, they have found little relevant material where the modern Western mind has had its own way: Catholics themselves in the Western milieu find the psychological implications of the Mass comparatively difficult to catch. The encyclopedic findings of modern psychology at work on the Western consciousness have not been particularly helpful at all. The greatest light has come from anthropological studies of cultures outside the modern Western milieu.

One of the most notable religious phenomena in the modern West has been the marked tendency automatically to identify Catholicism with superstition. This, again, is a local phenomenon, for other milieux have been at odds with Catholicism for quite different, and even totally opposite, reasons. Yet, although Catholicism and superstition in terms of reason are worlds apart, Catholicism quite unlike superstition maintaining that it can meet all of reason's claims both in the large and in detail, and presenting a tremendous volume of scholarly and popular literature to substantiate its assertion, still the tendency in the West to link Catholicism and superstition is quite understandable. For the fact is that they both oppose the West's favorite fiction, the fiction of the self-possessed man in the self-possessed world, the fiction of man in a world some of which is far away but no part of which is inviolable to his gaze. (pp. 439-50)

In effectively contesting this fiction, Kafka does something extremely difficult to do. Catholics, who readily enough smell out the fiction, have seldom succeeded in contesting it in terms which do not at the same time suppose it, and those, like Newman, who have succeeded are accordingly likely to find their thought emasculated by simplistic interpretations—proposed even by Catholics who fail to take stringent measures against the fiction as it touches their own minds.

The Western Catholic will not even readily conceive of himself as having an entrée to the world of superstition which the rest of the West does not have. He is likely to regard such entrée as an altogether uncomplimentary qualification, forgetting that even so gross a thing as superstition must doubtless be based on some sort of facts and that when certain objectionable features have been routed out of one's life, they not infrequently have carried some more desirable things with them.

The Western Catholic's interests have been turned in the other direction. For centuries now, Catholic activity in the West has been concerned in great part with maintaining itself in and effecting a *rapprochement* with the milieu in which recognition of man's plight has been more and more inhibited. Leaving aside the radical deficiency of human action, Western Catholic apologetic has applied itself to making explicit and elaborating what one might call the cold-blooded or hard-headed type of rational approach to Christianity, the approach which emphasizes almost nothing but man's reasoning in its positive, conclusive aspect.

This approach does not keep in the forefront of attention this sort of thing: You are, being what you are, in a difficult and embarrassing position. What are you to do about it? Rather, devoting full energy to validation of the Church's claims in terms of the historical intransigency of the New Testament and trenchant exegesis of records, the emphasis of the Western approach is more like this: Follow your reason. It's the thing that gets you places. Needless to say, the claims of reason can be equally honored in either approach, although they occur at different times in the two different psychological patterns. And each approach has its own dangers. The latter is likely to write off everything other than reason as though other things always led man in the opposite direction than that of reason itself (this approach, for example, occasions the distinct dislike for ceremonial of any sort which plagues the West). The former is likely to forget that reason is the only sure *test* by which all natural reality is to be evaluated when the time for evaluation occurs.

By concentrating in the West on the one approach which appeals to the Western mind, even the Catholic Church, which in common with Kafka does not find itself committed to the great Western fiction, is nevertheless so occupied with the Western mind that one must look to the Church outside the modern Western milieu to come to the question of the relation of Kafka's un-Western textures to the Christian ethos. Here where the Church is not concerned with the modern Western inhibitions one finds a world more sympathetic to Kafka which the Church accepts pretty much on its own terms.

In an earlier state of Western culture, as she still does in much of the East, the Catholic Church dealt regularly with a mind dominated by a reverence born of a sense of contact with something different, something inviolable, in reality. Without worrying this mind with too detailed explanation, she dealt with it as far as possible by quietly detaching this reverence from the bogus objects to which it had attached itself and transferring it to her cult of the One God. The history imbedded in much Catholic ritual is ample evidence of her procedure here.

This is the kind of mentality also dealt with by the Hebrew prophets with whom Christian teaching connects. "Holy, holy, holy," the cherubim in Isaias say of the Lord God of Israel—*Kadosh, kadosh, kadosh,* the root meaning of which is *separated, separated, separated.* The notion of *separated,* of something different, beyond, not to be intruded upon, inviolable, something with which man cannot presume directly to engage, is the accepted notion by which Yahweh is identified for His Hebrew people. All Hebrew worship centered about the Holy of Holies, the *separated* place—first in the portable tabernacle, later in the Temple at Jerusalem—which dramatically applied to Yahweh this basic concept of separation and inviolability by providing Him with a chamber so separate, so different from anywhere else in the world, that it was closed off permanently in absolute darkness and was never entered by anyone save by the high priest once a year.

The Old Testament nowhere needs bother to vindicate the notion of *kadosh.* This notion is the common property of the whole milieu in which the Hebrews lived. The prophet's business was not to instill this notion in the people but to teach them that this notion belongs to Yahweh above all and not to the world of foolish superstition with which they were surrounded. (pp. 452-55)

[The] concept of *kadosh* is more than suggested in Kafka, the Slavo-Germanic Jew, whose sensibilities were doubtless not closed to Eastern influences. Kafka cuts far back of the Western fiction to the area where the Jewish, Catholic, and many other worlds meet, though it be to go their separate ways. His position here is made quite explicit in his short story **"Ein Hungerkünstler,"** which appeared the year of his death and in which a thinly veiled allegory brings out a deep regard for a milieu like that in which the early fathers of the desert flourished, a milieu "superstitious" enough to endorse unreservedly lives given to nothing but fasting and prayer.

These are lives practically unknown in the modern West save among Catholics. Even in the Catholic Church they are more common in regions of Eastern culture than they are in the West today, where asceticism, in keeping with its milieu, has emphasized the element of visible accomplishment—educational, charitable, or other. The earlier form of monasticism based on the keen sense of the futility and inconclusiveness which attends even such things viewed as "accomplishments" has, for the time being, waned in the West, where practically speaking only a few older orders such as the Trappists maintain it in its pure form.

But it is still *the* monasticism of the Oriental rites. And in Kafka's **"Hungerkünstler,"** who fasts with such passionate abandon, although one notes a tendency to exhibitionism somewhat out of line with the monastic ideal, one also sees plainly the urges at work on the Eastern cenobite.

One also sees these urges depicted in clean-cut opposition to the modern Western milieu. Kafka's star comes into ascendancy when the psychological setting which has so long framed Western thought stands badly shaken—although whether irreparably so remains to be seen. The neat structure of the Newtonian physics on which so much depended gave way some time ago. Lately even idealism has been more and more threatened as attention has been drawn off to the line of thought which runs through Kierkegaard, Heidegger, and Jaspers to turn up in M. Sartre's *Existenz* philosophy where the universe occasions not self-confidence, self-possession, but nausea—which, it is plain enough, is a kind of manifestation not unconnected with the sense of plight, the sense of there being an indomitable otherness in the universe. (Kafka, who read Kierkegaard devotedly, is of course definitely connected with this course of thought.)

Then the atomic bomb has not failed to add its own impressive threat to the great Western fiction. It has become almost impossible to allow one's life to be suffused with the vague impression that the local control over various phenomena achieved by the human race is going to power a cosmic managerial revolution. Spectacular enough to penetrate the subconscious, where the fiction has had its real supports, the atom bomb has rather relieved man of the exhilarating feeling of having a machine by the throttle and substituted the more dismaying sensation of having a bear by the tail. (pp. 456-57)

Kafka's work, like all great art, can be made almost as prolific of truth and error as the real world can be. Beneath its impressive, simple immediacy, it is sufficiently complex to attract all sorts of philosophical "systems" scouting for material they can utilize, legitimately or otherwise. It is not to be denied, either, that—like, I suppose, all art—Kafka's work can be, on the whole, made more productive of error than reality itself can. Being selective, art does not provide all the counteractions that reality does for the psychological forces it sets in motion.

The momentums which Kafka's sensibility develops can, indeed, run wild. They can be accelerated in all sorts of directions and to varying speeds. But as Kafka's sensibilities go in themselves, whatever else they do, they restore to the West movement in a dimension to which the West has long been trying, though never with complete success, to relinquish its claim.

Brod says that Kafka's message is a *non liquet* written over all of life. Whatever this *non liquet* may be in Kafka, it is not quite the same as the verdicts to be rendered concerning life itself, and for Brod to put the matter just this way perhaps already accelerates some of the forces even in

Kafka at the expense of others. Yet in something like this lies Kafka's significance for his milieu. For the great fiction with which the West has hypnotized itself has obscured the realization that the sensible world with which man directly engages has in itself no answer to give, that what it is always and inevitably engaged in is not the process of satisfying man but of egging him on, and that there just isn't going to be any verdict returned in terms of the world man rubs his nose against. No one anywhere is moving an inch toward returning one. Because there's none returnable. (In so far as it connects in one way or another with this fact, the interest in illusion is a legitimate interest of the modern West in its own case history.)

In its devotion to its weird fiction, seldom has the modern West been able to grasp in full dimension the implications of the reality it feels before itself—the implications caught in Augustine's dictum that "Our heart is restless till it rests in Thee." This does not mean, as one commonly finds it made to mean, merely that man must expect recurrent spells of restlessness, that incidents, each quite pat in itself, become a little cloying from time to time—a sort of turn-about-is-fair-play arrangement, and you'll get over it if you only wait. Such an understanding of man's plight is not worth its own weight in words.

To assimilate Kafka, the West will have to do a lot better than that. It will have to capture again the sense it once had of man's deep plight on this earth, not as a transient and dilettante mood, but as an inevitable component of every action. (For K. the Castle is after all like his own home village, and the implication is that whatever goes for it goes for everything.) Until its vision and sensibilities are freely operating here, the West will never be aware what the reality that confronts it really is. (pp. 459-60)

Walter J. Ong, "Kafka's Castle in the West," in THOUGHT, *Vol. XXII, No. 86, September, 1947, pp. 439-60.*

Ronald Gray (essay date 1956)

[*Gray is an English educator and critic specializing in German literature. In the following excerpt, Gray interprets the events of K.'s stay in the Castle village not on the basis of the protagonist's subjective experience, but from a detached exterior perspective.*]

It is time now to stop seeing [**The Castle**] through K.'s eyes and to look for those inter-relationships and significances which he, being part of the story, is unable to perceive. K. is never in a position to reflect, for example, on the sequence of events in the final chapters, where he is first abandoned by his assistants, their work being apparently done, then summoned to Erlanger and, having withstood temptation, feels in harmony with the officials. A document has been torn up, a victory seemingly celebrated, and K. is content to imagine Klamm in the most loving relationship with Frieda. It is not K.'s business to inquire into the meaning of all this. Yet it is not unreasonable for an outsider to assume a pattern unifying these apparently unconnected events. With good will towards the castle, the pattern is clear—K. has been persuaded of his insignificance, his humility has been subjected to an exact-

Pen sketches by Kafka.

ing test, and his endurance is rewarded. It may at least be so, and while it would be presumptuous for K. to claim it, it is less presumptuous in a reader. Adopting, then, a more well-disposed point of view towards the castle and to K.'s environment in general, what picture emerges?

To take a point at random, there is Klamm's second letter to K., which he regarded at the time with such suspicion:

> To the Land-surveyor at the Bridge Inn. The land-surveying you have carried out so far meets with my approval. The work of your assistants is also praiseworthy, you manage to keep them hard at it. Do not slacken in your zeal. Continue your work to a good conclusion. Any interruption would make me embittered. For the rest, be of good cheer, the question of wages will be decided shortly. I am keeping you in mind.

In the light of the reward K. does receive at the end, this makes much better sense. Casuistry is needed to interpret K.'s spying out the land as surveying, and this must be accounted a fault, from the present point of view. Apart from that, the letter is straightforward. As with the first letter from Klamm, it is in the main K.'s unquiet conscience ('an unquiet, not a bad one') that hinders him from trusting Klamm's word. He rejects the assurance because the castle merely insists that he knows enough already. The fact that in the first letter the words 'as you know' are added to the statement destroys its value in his eyes. Given a quiet conscience he need have troubled no further.

Almost from the outset, K. is encouraged to see events and people in a friendlier guise. It is not a simple matter, however, to ascribe good motives, and may need passionate determination as well as trust. Frieda indicates this to K. when she says 'If only you knew, with what passion I search for a grain of goodness for myself in everything you do and say, even if it hurts me.' His fashion of interpretation is a matter of his disposition, as hers is; things are to him as he is disposed to see them. He can at least recognize this, though he cannot himself change his disposition. That, at least, is how both villagers and castle present the situation to him from the first day of his stay.

The choice between sympathy and hostility, trust and suspicion, is first presented to K. by the carrier Gerstäcker, who offers to drive him back to the Bridge Inn after his brief visit to the laundry in Lasemann's house. K. is puzzled by this act of kindness, which he imagines to be in conflict with the strict ordinances of the castle, and calls out after a while to ask whether Gerstäcker has permission to drive him around on his own responsibility. Receiving no answer he throws a snowball full in the man's ear. This brings Gerstäcker to a halt, but although he makes no reply, the sight of his wretched face compels K. to put his question in a different tone of voice. 'What he had said before out of spite he now had to repeat out of sympathy.' This time he asks whether Gerstäcker will not be punished for giving him a lift. Gerstäcker's answer ends the first chapter on a note of choice: ' "What do you want?" ['Was willst du?'] asked Gerstäcker uncomprehendingly, but awaited no further explanation, called to his horses, and they drove on.'

From K.'s point of view, Gerstäcker simply does not un-

derstand what K.'s question means. The phrase 'Was willst du?' implies, like the French 'Que veux-tu?', some weary resignation. At the same time it can be read as asking 'What do you want? Do you choose that I shall be punished or not? Will you put the question in spite or in sympathy?' The fact is that Gerstäcker has already suffered for his action, not as the result of any intervention by the castle but at K.'s own hands. The question asked in spite carries its own punishment. A good deal of the real or imagined hostility towards K. arises similarly from the assertiveness or presumptuousness of the villagers; when he suffers, as he does at the hands of Gisa, the castle has no hand in it. Indeed the castle bell has just rung out in its ambiguous fashion (as it seems to K.), 'with rhythmic gaiety' and 'painfully too': it can be heard in both ways, and there is a second bell for those who will make no choice at all, a 'weak and monotonous chime' that seems to K. at this stage to suit the weary journey through the village. There is nothing pure, certain or unchangeable about it as yet.

Shortly afterwards Gerstäcker's question is repeated to K. by an official at the castle. When K. has explained (though falsely) his situation and desires over the telephone, the answer comes 'Was willst du?' There is no possibility of weary resignation in the words this time, it is a direct question. But K. scarcely hears it; convinced that nothing can come of this conversation he makes an insincere inquiry and hangs up. A little later, he sees the fact of choice quite consciously. Looking at Klamm's letter, 'he saw in it . . . an open choice presented to him; it was left to him to make what he wanted of the orders in the letter.' But the recognition of the fact cannot alter the choice he does make. He is disposed towards suspicion and acts accordingly.

For a great part of the novel K. realizes the good intentions of others almost against his will. The schoolmaster strikes him at once as 'a really domineering little man', and K. fancies he is flattered by his position of authority and the attentiveness of his pupils. Yet the schoolmaster's first words are 'more mild' (or 'more meek'— 'sanftmütiger') 'than K. had expected.' A little later, when Gerstäcker offers to take K. home, K. feels that 'the whole scene did not give an impression of particular friendliness,' although he has been treated in a 'not unfriendly' fashion for the last hour or so. Similarly, in his conversation with the hostess at the Bridge Inn, the woman's laughter sounds 'mocking, but much more gentle than K. had expected.' K.'s expectation is disappointed in this way on other occasions. He is unwilling to be persuaded that he has 'a host of good friends at the castle', and treats the suggestion with mockery. Not until after the horrifying experience of freedom and isolation in the Herrenhof courtyard is it said of K. himself that he had 'grown more mild.'

All this is a matter of K.'s mood. In saying that the villagers and the castle are hostile, dictatorial, well-disposed or acting in K.'s best interests, one is saying that they appear so to him. Yet the mere fact that he has an inkling of their good will, even when on the whole he expects only hostility from them, is an indication that in his transformed mood at the end he might be prepared to reflect on his past experiences differently. And since we are now taking a bird's-eye view denied to K. it may become possible to observe significances of which K. is oblivious.

An episode where, if K.'s limited viewpoint is adopted, there is a sense of frustration and meaninglessness, whereas from the general viewpoint there is possible meaning, is that in Lasemann's house. This follows immediately on K.'s first and only attempt to reach the castle on foot; utterly exhausted, he leaves the 'straitening street' ('die festhaltende Strasse') for a narrow alleyway. Seeing a house, he enters and finds himself in a room filled with smoke and steam, surrounded by people who seem not particularly pleased to see him. He is told to sit down, water is splashed in his face, and since nobody takes any further notice of him he falls asleep. Nevertheless, on waking, he offers thanks for hospitality, only to be more or less dragged to the door and sent out into the snow again. From K.'s point of view the whole affair looks rude, inconsequential and inhospitable. There is, however, another aspect of which even he seems partially aware. He cannot be wholly aware of it since he cannot know the pattern of events later in the book. K. arrives at the house, as he arrives for the Bürgel interview, at a moment when he has at least temporarily given up hope of entering the castle. The sight of the house he interprets as a sign that he is 'not abandoned'. And there *are* suggestions, at least to begin with, that the inhabitants are well disposed towards him: a 'friendly' peasant welcomes him in, and a woman's hand reaches out to save him from stumbling. Thus far there is normality. Inside, the scene has more of a dream-like quality. In the rolling smoke and steam K. stands 'as though in clouds'. Not, it should be noted, in 'clouds of steam', not the usual metaphor, but as though he were actually standing in clouds, as if he were taken out of his earthbound existence. A voice then calls to K. asking who he is, and the narrator's comment on his reply again has overtones of meaning. ' "I am the Count's land-surveyor", said K., and sought thus to justify himself before the still invisible ones' ('und suchte sich so vor den noch immer Unsichtbaren zu verantworten'). Why should these villagers be described as 'invisible ones', instead of by the more normal phrase, 'these invisible people?' A vague sense of mystery is conjured up by these words. The mystery increases when K.'s attention is suddenly caught by the sight of a woman suckling a child in the corner. This is the woman whose appearance has already been described, and which suggests indistinctly the figure of the Virgin in some Nativity scene. K. himself finds her surprising, though he is unable to say wherein the surprising element consists. For the reader, there comes a feeling that the scene is of some importance for K., though he too is unable to say why. The girl seems to preside over the scene—K.'s attention is repeatedly drawn to her, and before he leaves he actually jumps round so as to face her. As soon as he does so, however, he is dragged away by a man at each elbow, much as he is dragged away later from the officials' corridor by the landlord and his wife. Has all this any recognizable significance?

Scarcely—it remains for the most part a mystery. But as K. leaves there is a small incident, for which no explanation is given, but which seems more readily placeable.

'All this had lasted only a minute, and at once K. had one of the men to right and left of him and was being dragged by them, as though there were no other means of making themselves understood, silently but with all their strength towards the door. The old man was delighted over something in all this, and clapped his hands. The washerwoman too started laughing, and the children suddenly shouted like mad.'

Is this applause for K., or are they delighted to see the last of him? K. in his present mood would be more likely to assume the latter, though once again he is too weary to speculate about it. Yet the same question of dual interpretation arose after the Bürgel interview, when the bells seemed to proclaim a joyous victory, while the landlord heard them expressing exasperated anger. It may well be applause here; the peasants have been by no means unfriendly towards K., and there is a sense in which he seems to have benefited by his stay in the house. He is refreshed, he moves 'more freely' than before, and when he arrives outside the scene seems 'a little brighter'. He has also become 'rather more sharp of hearing', as though he were better able to interpret what he hears than formerly. It is conceivable that K. has been present at some strange ceremony of whose meaning he has been only dimly aware through the impressive figure of the girl, and that the clapping of the old man, the laughter of the woman, the shouting of the children was a rejoicing at its happy conclusion. The fact that K. is not allowed to remain does not contradict this—he is, as one of the villagers observes, an exceptional case, whereas they are content to remain where they are. The mystery that still envelops the scene is of the kind that must accompany any supposed contact with spiritual forces.

Kafka's style always compels the reader to adopt first the standpoint of the character whose story is related, since only the reflections of this character are actually recorded. The rest is related without causal or logical connection. Friedrich Beissner has observed this effect in Kafka's story *Die Verwandlung,* in which Gregor Samsa is transformed into a repulsive insect. Since only Samsa's account is given, the reader is gradually forced into accepting it. Beissner recalls however that in an early edition Samsa was portrayed in a text-illustration as a man, suggesting that to all outward appearance he remained one. Similarly, K.'s subjective experience here is not solely valid. From the villagers' point of view, this episode in Lasemann's house may have represented K.'s first acceptance by the castle, to be confirmed almost at once by the arrival of the two assistants.

The actions of the castle are often perceived thus dimly in the background, being related to the events in the narrative much as the text-illustration is related to the story of *Die Verwandlung.* They are not openly asserted because of the limitation of the narrator to K.'s position. The task of a reader at his second reading is to inquire what other interpretation may be placed on the events other than that presented to him through the eyes of K. Thereupon the contours of the castle are perceived surrounding the story like the air round an open hand. The difficulty lies in forcing one's gaze away from the hand and concentrating it on the enveloping insubstantiality. This is of course the difficulty with all religious or metaphysical thought, but to imagine the hand without the air about it is even more difficult. (pp. 83-92)

Ronald Gray, in his Kafka's Castle, *Cambridge at the University Press, 1956, 147 p.*

James R. Baker   (essay date 1957)

[*Baker is an American educator and critic. In the following excerpt, Baker argues that K.'s monomania makes him capable of seeking, but not finding, a resolution to his plight.*]

In the more than two decades of critical commentary on Kafka's *The Castle* a great many interpretations have been offered. In view of this diversity we might say of K's adventures, as someone in the novel remarks of Klamm's enigmatical messages, "The reflections they give rise to are endless." But much of this critical work had been in agreement on one point: K's experiences have some sort of allegorical significance. When it comes to estimation of the character and dimension of the allegory, however, there has been no happy consensus. The source of K's frustrations has been located on almost every level of his experience, political, social, sexual, and so on. If there has been a failing in these efforts it is that, too often, the insights available through the specialized approach (Freudian, Marxian) are incomplete. Their very consistency becomes a danger, tempting us to abstract from a highly complex and sometimes ambiguous image of experience only those elements which "fit" the special reading.

It is not the purpose of this essay to disparage the various interpretations of *The Castle* which have appeared in the past. On the contrary, it is through the medium of the work that has been done that we have come to understand that K.'s problem is one that manifests itself on every level of his experience. This is something that we can see clearly from our present perspective. It is now obvious that K's difficulty brings into play his *total being*. Criticism which fails to take this fact into account cannot hope to reveal the proportion of the allegory or the complex and finally irresolvable structural problem which Kafka encountered.

K. is summoned to the village by the count of the castle to operate as a land-surveyor. His exact duties, however, are unclear, and in an effort to determine the nature of his work K. tries to contact the castle authorities. All of his attempts end in frustrating failure. Thwarted in direct contact, K. appeals to the officials of the village. Immediately he becomes involved in a maze of confusion, incompetence, and petty jealousy. Eventually it becomes apparent that he is a land-surveyor only in name and that he spends all of his time surveying his own situation. "Never had K. seen vocation and life so interlaced as here, so interlaced that one might think they had exchanged places."

It is through recognition of this identity of life and vocation that we can realize the enormity of K's problem and see that it must, inevitably, confront him in every phase of his experience. In the latter stages of his effort to clarify his mission he finds that he is denied the comfort of asking

limited questions and that he has miscalculated the dimension of his inquiry. The comprehensive question—What is my life-purpose?—comes to be the only relevant inquiry. And in the mature pessimism which K. attains near the end of the narrative, even this question sometimes appears vain, for judging empirically, in terms of the record of his experiences in the village, it seems foolish to expect an end to seeking, foolish to assume that vocation and life can ever be disentangled. This vision of his situation is K.'s great achievement. His ability to withstand such a vision—to persist in spite of it—marks him as a hero as noble in his spiritual odyssey as is Christian in his *Progress*.

From the vantage of K.'s mature perspective we can assess the significance of certain of his adventures in the village. Shortly after entering the community K. discovers that he is not to be favored with unique privileges. He therefore assumes that if he is ever to obtain clarification of the original assignment he must solicit the aid of his fellow-villagers. K. needs no encouragement. His perseverance is inexhaustible. But he is not strong enough, in these initial steps in his progress, to do without the hope that advice will show him the proper line of procedure. But as he grows more familiar with the villagers and their officials he becomes skeptical of outside sources of help. The opportunities for reliable guidance and congenial relations seem to be almost nil; but K. learns to accept this. He reasons: "All that sort of thing could be put up with, it belonged to the ordinary continual petty annoyances of life, it was nothing compared to what K. was striving for, and he had not come here simply to lead an honored and comfortable life."

K.'s persistence dictates the nature of his relations with everyone he contacts. Even before he realizes fully that vocation and life have merged, this persistence often operates sub-consciously. His rejection of the two assistants sent to him by Klamm is motivated by his failure to perceive that they function to keep him occupied with the prime question, and thus deter him from irrelevant activity, such as his attempt to work out satisfactory relations with Frieda. But by the time K. drives them off, their mission is completed, for they have so frustrated his time with Frieda that he rejects her willingly. And having done so, K. finds that he is able to take up his attempt to make contact with renewed energy and enthusiasm. Eventually the succession of dead-end relationships with villagers convinces K. that the community offers scant comfort and little in the way of sound advice. Trustworthy guidance, he concludes, can come only from outside the human community.

At the same time, the few communications he receives from Klamm (one of the castle dignitaries) exasperate him because they seem to evidence confusion and even ignorance of his plight.

> The surveying work you have carried out thus far has been appreciated by me. The work of the assistants too deserves praise. You know how to keep them at their jobs. Do not slacken in your efforts. Carry your work on to a fortunate conclusion. Any interruption would displease me. For the rest be easy in your mind; the question

of salary will presently be decided. I shall not forget you.

Yet, unless he is to lose faith in the integrity of the castle, K. must conclude that it is his logic, not Klamm's, that is inadequate. His own powers of reasoning must be unable to bridge the gulf between himself and the mysterious attentions of the castle authorities. But though K. experiences this failure of rational strength again and again, he never loses faith in the belief that the castle forces have the power to define his position. Heroically, he sacrifices his own ego in order to preserve his faith in the Supreme Authority.

K.'s refusal to accept the advice or values of the villagers, his refusal, in short, to accept the human situation, has its sources, paradoxically, in his great skepticism and in his great faith. Experience has shown him that the mind is capable of (or doomed to) continual dialectic, that it cannot achieve finality in its own terms. Thus he stands convinced that finality must come from a supra-rational source, an authority outside the community of men.

The great majority of the villagers find K.'s persistence irritating and absurd. His monomania, they feel, blinds them to all of the virtues and pleasures of village life. He appears inhumane and, at times, insane—unwilling to accept what they regard as the normal, the common, condition. His uniqueness provokes resentment, criticism, and on certain occasions, outraged opposition. K. then, is not representative, that is, he is certainly not Man, as He habitually operates. He is the inquiring spirit, abstracted and epitomized; he represents the "dark" side of the sensibility, which normally prefers sleep and oblivion to the tortures of active seeking for reliable authority.

It is hardly surprising that Kafka found himself unable to complete the allegory. Within the extremely narrow frame of values in which his hero operates there can be no resting place. The satisfactions available in the human community are for K. so transient and minimal that they must be wholly discounted. He comes to look upon them as distractions or "petty annoyances" which inhibit the efficient direction of all energy toward the resolution of his question.

When the narrative breaks off there is little of promise in K.'s situation. But Max Brod's summary of Kafka's verbal outline of the proposed conclusion suggests a reason for the reluctance of the writer to finish his tale:

> The ostensible Land Surveyor was to find a partial satisfaction at least. He was not to relax in his struggle, but was to die worn out by it. Round his death-bed the villagers were to assemble, and from the castle itself the word was to come that though K.'s legal claim to live in the village was not valid, yet, taking certain auxiliary circumstances into account, he was to be permitted to live and work there.

Apparently Kafka could envision for his hero only a continuation of frustrating adventures similar in nature to those detailed in the manuscript we have. Such an extension would have been superfluous, because in the final analysis *The Castle* would have remained what it is in its present form—an allegory of seeking, not of triumph or fulfillment.

The biographers have made it amply clear that this inconclusiveness was consistent with Kafka's own psychology. But we have only to examine K.'s reactions to see that his fate must be dictated by the question which possesses him. His refusal to accept any of the traditional "answers" held out to him by the villagers insures his continued isolation, his frustration on every possible level of experience, and his final defeat. To allow K. eventually to "run down," "to die worn out by it," is indeed the only means of bringing his quest to a close: on the one hand K. refuses the compromises which the villagers, for the sake of expediency, have made; at the same time he dedicates himself to the pursuit of an authority which, because it is suprahuman, must always appear to him to be incomprehensible and elusive.

Had Kafka completed his structure in the way he sketched for Brod, it is doubtful that we could have regarded K. as heroic. An uncompromising rejection of the communal values (inadequate as they may be) would have dehumanized K. entirely. He would have become over-obvious abstraction, so far removed from ordinary values as to destroy our sympathy and feeling of kinship. The aim of my conjecture has been to suggest two things. The first was to trace the logical consequence of K.'s monomania, and the second to point out the structural problem which grows out of Kafka's self-defeating wisdom. (pp. 74-7)

James R. Baker, " 'The Castle': A Problem in Structure," in Twentieth Century Literature, *Vol. 3, No. 2, July, 1957, pp. 74-7.*

Heinz Politzer   (essay date 1962)

[*Politzer was an Austrian-born American educator and the author of several studies of Kafka's works. In the following excerpt, Politzer uses established critical commentary to examine the major motifs in* The Castle.]

K. has contemplated the Castle from the main street of the village. But this road "did not lead to the Castle Hill; it only made toward it and then, as if deliberately, turned aside; and though it did not lead away from the Castle, it led no nearer to it either." The village is built along this street which, for very good reasons, "seemed to have no end": as far as can be ascertained the road describes a circle. Along this street are located the various stops on K.'s way: near the bridge is the Bridge Inn where he spends his first night; then comes the school where he finds employment as a porter; and finally the Herrenhof Inn where he meets Frieda in the taproom and is able to espy Klamm. The Herrenhof is also the scene of his meeting with secretary Bürgel, and it is here that the novel breaks off during his conversation with the landlady. Since the Herrenhof is also on the village street, K. at the novel's end has come not a single step nearer to his goal, the Castle.

He moves along a perimeter in the center of which the Castle Hill and the Castle itself are situated. It is his intention to leave the periphery and advance toward the center, but all kinds of real and imagined obstacles bar his way.

He learns only a little about the region which separates him from the center, the realm of the "intermediate figures," the officials and the messengers; and whatever information he gathers is second hand, obtained by hearsay. Olga, for example, reports about the barriers which her brother, the messenger Barnabas, has encountered in the offices of the Castle:

> He is admitted into certain rooms, but they are only part of the whole, for there are barriers behind which there are more rooms. . . . You must not imagine that these barriers form a definite border line. . . . There are even barriers through which he is able to pass, and they look exactly like the ones he has never yet passed, and therefore one must not jump to conclusions and suppose that behind these latter barriers the offices are essentially different from the others.

The image presented by the offices—barriers which can be passed before others which protect a last inner chamber which remains inaccessible—is derived from the age-old pattern of the labyrinth. A possible ground plan for the interior of Kafka's Castle could be found on the late Renaissance wooden ceiling of the ducal palace in Mantua. There a deceivingly simple system of bars and passageways is organized around a center which dominates the whole design. Another less classical model is the glass-covered round box in which a little ball has to be steered to the middle through winding runways interrupted by walls and intertwined with other corridors. This box, a favorite toy, must have come to Kafka's notice at a very early time in his life. The maze has proved attractive to the human imagination at various stages of its development, primarily the early ones and those when man was in search of a lost primitivity.

Although K. is never admitted to the interior of the offices, he succeeds at least in advancing into the Herrenhof, where the senior officials occasionally put up for a night. In the end he even penetrates the region of these sleeping quarters, seemingly an extension into the village of the Castle's secret:

> In the hall they were met by an attendant who led them . . . into the entry and through the low, somewhat downward sloping passage. . . . Everything was on a small scale, but well and daintily appointed. The space was utilized to best advantage. The passage was just high enough for one to walk without bending one's head. Along both sides the doors almost touched one another. The wall did not quite reach the ceiling, probably for reasons of ventilation, for here in the low cellar-like passage the tiny rooms could hardly have windows.

This corridor, subterranean, carefully constructed according to a well-considered design, interrupted by a multiplicity of closed doors, is still only the fringe of a labyrinth.

That Kafka's tortuous ways of thinking predisposed him to adopt the labyrinth as a central image has long been recognized. One has only to think of the intricate script the execution machine produces in **"In the Penal Colony,"** of the meandering interpretations of the Law in which both Titorelli and the Prison Chaplain indulge in *The Trial,* or

of the "tormenting complications of the labyrinth" which, in one of Kafka's last stories [**"The Burrow"**], make up an unnamed animal's Burrow. The image of the maze must have suggested itself to Kafka with undiminished urgency during all the phases of his life. He would have had to invent it if it had not come down to him from tradition in untraceable ways.

But Hermann Pongs both oversimplifies and complicates matters unduly [in his *Franz Kafka: Dichter des Labyrinths*] when he calls Kafka the "poet of the labyrinth." Pongs defines the labyrinth as "an effective image of a world out of joint" and uses it in opposition to what he terms a "symbolism of light." Comparing, not quite fairly, Kafka's world with the "universal mystery" of Goethe's *Faust,* in which the "struggle between god and devil, light and darkness" has been more fully presented, Pongs arrives at the judgment that Kafka's labyrinthine world is nothing but "some sort of shrunken form." Throughout his disquisition Pongs sees in the labyrinth a dark and vague counterimage to the glories spread through the ages by solar myths.

Archeology, however, has shown that from its very inception the labyrinth was informed with the duality inherent in a universal image. [In the essay "The Labyrinth" in S. H. Hooke's *The Labyrinth*], C. N. Deedes, who has followed the shape and function of the labyrinth from its origins in Egyptian art to the European Middle Ages, concludes: "Above all, the Labyrinth was the centre of activities concerned with those greatest of mysteries, Life and Death. There men tried by every means known to them to overcome death and to renew life." Even Gustav René Hocke, who seems to have inspired Pongs's Kafka interpretation, is ready to admit that for the earlier civilizations "the labyrinth was a metaphor unifying the calculable and the incalculable elements of the universe. The roundabout way leads to the center. Only the roundabout way leads to perfection." This original duality of the labyrinth reappears in **The Castle,** stated, to be sure, as the basic paradox upon which the novel is built.

Hocke followed up the tradition of the labyrinth from the Middle Ages to the present day. His work, a *catalogue raisonné* of the suprarealistic achievements in European civilization since the late Renaissance, points to Kafka's native city, Prague, as a "focal point" of long standing for all types of "mannerism," that is, of exercises which lead the human mind beyond the classical canons of literature and art. Under Rudolf II of Habsburg (1552-1612) Prague became a center of cabalistic thought as well as of astrological and alchemistic practices. The labyrinth, being a Hermetic figure of prime importance, seems to have survived by some secret intellectual osmosis from those golden and gold-making days until it reappears in Kafka. Hocke at least points emphatically to the following aphorism in Kafka's notebooks (October 1917):

> Seen with the terrestrially sullied eye, we are in the situation of travelers in a train that has met with an accident in a tunnel, and this at a place where the light of the beginning can no longer be seen, and the light of the end is so very small a glimmer that the gaze must continually search for it and is always losing it again; and further-

more, both the beginning and the end are not even certainties. Round about us, however, in the confusion of our senses, or in the supersensitiveness of our senses, we have nothing but monstrosities and a kaleidoscopic play of things that is either delightful or exhausting.

According to Hocke [in his *Manierismus in der Literatur*], of all the mysteries of the "mannerists" at least the "secret malady" of being spellbound by the darker sides of divinity has survived in Kafka. This malady, then, degenerates in Pongs's view to "some sort of paralysis," a diagnosis which is even at first sight contradicted by K.'s feverish activities with regard to *his* labyrinth, the Castle.

There exists in any case an atmospheric connection between the Castle of Rudolf II on the Hradžany Hill and the Castle of Kafka, who lived near Rudolf's palace during the winter of 1916-1917 in the small Zlatá ulička (the "Golden Lane"), supposedly the street of the Emperor's alchemists. [In his *Franz Kafka*] Brod assures us that "Franz did not choose this quarter at all from any mystic or romantic inclination, except perhaps subconsciously." No critic will be such a mystic as to postulate with conviction a direct relationship between the two castles; yet, considering the strange and devious ways in which the imagination of a writer often works, one cannot resist the temptation to reinforce Brod's all-too-timid observation, "except perhaps subconsciously."

With these qualifications in mind we may notice that the images of the Castle and the Labyrinth merge in the *Amphitheater of Eternal Wisdom* (1609) of the Rosicrucian and alchemist Heinrich Khunrath. This Amphitheater

represents the secret doctrine in the form of the dragon of Hermes, who lives in an impregnable fortress. It has twenty-one entrances which seem to invite the seeker to enter the sanctum, yet twenty of these ways lead him to closed compartments. The bewildered student of the occult may wander from one to the other without ever reaching the drawbridge of which Hermes is the watchman.

With Hermes the watchman even the figure of a doorkeeper is added to what appears in outline and design as a labyrinthine castle.

The Czech polymath and Moravian brother Jan Amos Komensky (Comenius—1592-1670) leads us still closer to Kafka's Castle. His treatise, *The Labyrinth of the World and the Paradise of the Heart* (1623), contains, as its title indicates, a warning against black magic rather than an introduction into its secret practices. Its hero, a pilgrim, in the end resigns from the world, perhaps not quite convincingly, and commends his soul to his creator. Yet at the outset of his wanderings he meets an associate named Searchall or Impudence, who introduces him both to the world of the labyrinth and the world as a labyrinth. They are soon joined by a strangely hermaphroditic being called Falsehood. These two companions are emissaries from the same labyrinth through which they are going to lead the pilgrim. They correspond in function and to a certain degree even in character to the two assistants K. obtains from his Castle. Komensky's three wanderers climb a

tower from which they view the maze of the world, which appears to them as a city: "I counted six principal streets all running from east to west side by side," says the pilgrim, "and in the centre of them there was a large, round square or market-place; behind it there stood to the west, on a rocky, abrupt hillock, a high and splendid Castle, at which almost all the inhabitants of the town gazed." This Castle of ultimate wisdom has a sister palace, dedicated to Fortune. Door images abound. Yet the most striking anticipation of Kafka is in the dim view Komensky's pilgrim seems to take of Land-Surveyors. He passes in review the conditions of man, his trades and avocations, and meets, between the philosophers and the musicians, "those who measured and weighed" the place.

Others, again, measured the hall itself; and almost everyone measured it differently. Then they quarrelled and measured afresh. Some measured a shadow, as to its length, width, and breadth; others also weighed it in a balance. They said generally that there was nothing in this world nor out of it which they were unable to measure rightly. But having watched this their craft for some time, I observed that there was more boasting than use.

The combination of Castle, Labyrinth, and Land-Surveyorship, as well as the conception of "measuring" as an incommensurable boasting (*Anmassung*), would suggest that Kafka was influenced, perhaps directly, by Komensky. The suggestion is supported by Kafka's interest in Czech literature, which makes it more than probable that he was familiar with the labyrinth of his predecessor. But even if we could establish beyond doubt that Komensky's allegory served as a source of Kafka's symbolic parable, we would have contributed little to our understanding of the later writer. After all, Komensky fully explains the meaning of his castles by giving them names. Kafka, on the other hand, confronts us with an unanswerable question in the very moment when he gives us, instead of the name of his Castle, that of its master the Count Westwest.

Brod's theological interpretation of the Castle in the postscript to the German editions has been most eloquently contradicted by Erich Heller [in *The Disinherited Mind*]:

The Castle of Kafka's novel is, as it were, the heavily fortified garrison of a company of Gnostic demons, successfully holding an advanced position against the manoeuvers of an impatient soul. I do not know of any conceivable idea of divinity which could justify those interpreters who see in the Castle the residence of "divine law and divine grace."

Ascribing a Gnostic heritage to the Castle officials, Heller has undoubtedly fathomed deeply the regions where Kafka gathered the material for his demonology. Yet he avoids touching upon the secret of the Castle's innermost chamber.

[In his *Wilder den misverstandenen Realismus*] Georg Lukács enters there, somewhat brazenly, when he explains: "Kafka's god, the Senior Judges in *The Trial*, the real administration of *The Castle*, represent the transcendence of Kafka's allegories: nothingness." Presupposing the existence of a "real" master of the Castle and as a materialist disbelieving unreality, Lukács is quite consistent in eliminating this master once and for all from the pages of the book. "If a god is present here," he continues, "he is a god of religious atheism: *atheos absconditus.*" This characterization of the Castle's master as a hidden un-god is wittier than it is profound. It simply projects the "emptiness," with which the exterior of the Castle impressed K. at first sight, into the innermost center and replaces Kafka's warning qualification that this emptiness is only "apparent" with a certainty, the certainty of absolute negation. Negating the godhead absolutely, Lukács comes close to Brod, who posits it—closer in any case than it may be pleasant for either critic to realize: both are translating what appears to them as an allegory into conceptual language. If Lukács's interpretation proves anything to be true, then it is our suspicion that atheism is a theology turned upside down.

In order to gain at least a measure of the paradoxicality of this Castle we have, as usual, to consult Kafka's language. Again his choice of names is revealing—revealing, that is, of his intention to mystify his reader. The lord of the Castle is identified very early in the first chapter as "the Count Westwest." [In his *Franz Kafka*] Emrich has observed that "this name could refer to the absolute end, the region of death beyond the sunset, but also to the transcendence, the conquest, of death." Looking more closely, we can see Kafka at work playing a most intricate word game with the reduplication of the syllable "West." Assuming that "West," like the Hotel Occidental in *Der Verschollene,* is indicative of decline, then its repetition underscores the signs of decomposition that welcomed K. on his arrival: the crumbling of the Castle walls, the crows around the tower, the long stretches of darkness, the snow of winter. Yet the negative emphasis provided by repetition is counteracted by the law of logic according to which a double negation results in a reinforced affirmation. The West of the West may indicate the decline of the decline, that is, an ascent. Then Kafka would have alluded here to eternal life, would have attempted to say in his opaque way what a more believing soul, the Dean of St. Paul's, John Donne, expressed in the line: "And Death shall be no more; Death, thou shalt die."

The secret of the inner chamber consists in the complete ambivalence it represents between life and death, descent and resurrection, heaven and hell. It is both; at least it seems to waver constantly between the poles of man's physical and spiritual existence. Kafka succeeded here in concentrating into two syllables all the uncertainties and indecisions, the doubtful expectations and hopeful fears, that the hero of *The Trial* poured out in the veritable flood of his last questions.

Kafka took great care to sustain this ambiguity throughout the imagery of the novel. There are bells in the Castle, as if it were a church. First "a bell began to ring merrily up there, a bell that for at least a second made his heart tremble . . . as if it threatened him with the fulfillment of his vague desire." The menace of having one's desire fulfilled is still the expression of K.'s personal ambivalence, a psychological remark indicating the state of a mind that feels threatened at the prospect of finding his wishes terminated by fulfillment. Yet K.'s subjective ambivalence is soon followed by the objective observation that the place of the merry bell was "taken by a feeble, monotonous little tinkle," the very opposite of the first. To blur the image still further, Kafka adds that this tinkle "might have come from the Castle, but might have been somewhere in the village."

He uses this technique more subtly when it comes to K.'s entry into the Herrenhof. He describes the scene as follows: "The front steps had a balustrade, and a fine lantern was fixed over the doorway. When they entered, a piece of cloth fluttered over their heads; it was a flag with the Count's colors." K., eager to establish his future master's identity, could be expected to study the emblem of this flag or at least make a guess at the character of the Westwest family by observing the color scheme of the piece of cloth fluttering over his head. Exactly the opposite comes to pass. K. concentrates on the details of the door and the doorway, although "all the houses in the village resembled one another more or less." The flag, however, is described as having colors without actually displaying any, and whatever heraldry Count Westwest may boast of in his coat of arms remains undisclosed.

Still more intricate is an exchange K. has with the village teacher. Asked whether he knows the Count, the teacher first replies in the negative, and when K. insists, adds in French, "Remember that there are innocent children present." Superficially this uncalled-for admonition may heighten [what Emrich terms] the "sinister, perhaps macabre and disreputable, or even infernal and obscene aspect" of the Castle, since it implies that the Count is so depraved that his name must not be mentioned before infants. Yet it may also mean that K. tries to pronounce in vain the name of a superior being, violating something like the Third Commandment and committing a sin that innocent children should not be allowed to witness. Either interpretation may serve as a reason for K.'s taking this rebuke as a "justification" to invite himself into the teacher's house: he may suspect that the teacher is the accomplice of an infernal procurer or that he is a piously reticent apostle of his most mysterious Lordship.

Kafka did not, could not, decide on the identity of the Castle's "afflicted inhabitant" whom K. had imagined. As usual, he left this question open. Thus the Count seems to be *both* sublime *and* satanic, someone *and* no one, and what K. actually perceives are mirrorings of his own doubts.

In *The Castle* Kafka introduces us to a greater number of characters than in any other story, and for the first and only time the female element prevails among them. These figures, female as well as male, are engaged in almost uninterrupted conversations about one another, and since their characters are highly unusual, they approach one another at the strangest angles and from the most unexpected directions. The distortions of reality generally characteristic of Kafka's style present themselves here as a matter of course. Moreover, these figures cannot avoid talking about the Castle; the Castle forms the continual background of their conversations; it colors their relations with one another and informs them with its own enigmatic presence, whether they are villagers or officials. It seems to speak through them all, but what it communicates is the insoluble puzzle of its existence. If the ground plan of this village is a labyrinth, then Kafka has complicated the wanderings of his hero still further by using K.'s dialogues with his antagonists as an elaborate constellation of mirrors reflecting the Castle, each other, and K., all simultaneously. One of the most perfect labyrinths is the mirror cabinet, and Kafka seems to use similar techniques to delay K.'s progress on a way where "deceptions are more frequent than changes." [In a footnote, the author provides the German original: "Täuschungen sind häufiger als Wendungen." He adds: "The German *Wendungen* ("turns") points still more distinctly to the labyrinthine nature of K.'s way"].

While still at the beginning of his way, K. receives a letter from the Castle, which begins, "My dear Sir, as you know, you have been engaged for the Count's service." The three words, "as you know," are the reflection mirroring K.'s wishes and intentions rather than the statement of an actuality; he has not been told by anyone before that he has been accepted. Noticing the letter writer's mental reservations, K. suspects a hidden trap: the letter, he observes, does not "gloss over the fact that if it should come to a struggle, K. had had the audacity to make the first advances; it was very subtly indicated and only to be sensed by an uneasy conscience—an uneasy conscience, not a bad one; it lay in the three words 'as you know.'" These three words disturb his conscience because they throw the responsibility for all future developments back upon him. As a whole, the letter does not really welcome him; it does not authorize his position; it only reflects his arrival.

The signature on the document is illegible, but Barnabas, the messenger, names powerful Klamm as the sender. [Heller writes that] Klamm's name certainly suggests "straits, pincers, chains, clamps, but also a person's oppressive silence." Klamm also shares his initial with K., so that, theoretically speaking, the name of his so-called employer could be abbreviated to indicate the name of the Land-Surveyor. This does not mean to suggest that Klamm exists only in K.'s imagination nor that he merely embodies K.'s subjective ideas about the Castle officials. A real person appears to K. soon afterward, a man who is if anything the Land-Surveyor's extreme opposite: the epitome of bourgeois sedateness, a towering image of trivial virility. [The critic adds in a footnote, "It can be argued that, in Klamm, Kafka drew a likeness of his father; this would be another reason for K.'s and Klamm's names beginning with the same letter"].

The identity of their initials does indicate, however, that a basic and fundamentally inexplicable connection exists between them. That K. has no hope whatever to clarify this connection (which, of course, represents his relation to the Castle as a whole), he can see from Klamm's letter: printed beside the illegible signature it shows as the sender's official rank the designation "Chief of the Department X." This "Department Number Roman Ten" is also the unknown department, since X stands for an undefined quantity in German as it does in English. K. is at liberty to replace this X with any figure he chooses, yet this X,

the secret at the Castle's center, will never fit without a remainder in any of his calculations. The struggle upon which he enters is a struggle against an unknown, an unknowable opponent. It is also a struggle of letters, K. versus X, a cabalistic battle, and our man from the country is ill-advised when he solicits human help to gain it.

K.'s first move in this unpromising fight is the conquest of Frieda, the barmaid at the Herrenhof:

> An unobtrusive small girl with fair hair, sad eyes, . . . but with a surprising look, a look of special superiority. As soon as her eye met K.'s, it seemed to him that her look decided something concerning himself, something which he had not known to exist, but which her look assured him did exist.

K. hardly notices Frieda's frame, nor does her appearance warrant any special attention. Her attraction for him lies in her eyes—Kafka resorts again to the rather primitive expedient of mentioning her eyes and looks six times in two sentences—or rather in the "something," existing and not existing, which is mirrored in them. He is struck by the "decision," which he has projected into her looks and which her eyes reflect back to him, a decision, we may safely assume, made with regard to K.'s claims on the Castle. When she reveals herself as Klamm's mistress, he decides to win her as an ally in his fight, because of the "special superiority" he has noticed in her glances. "In your eyes," he says, "I read far more the conquests still to come than the conquests past." These future conquests are to end his own struggles, and since Frieda's eyes seem to bear good tidings as to their outcome, he tries to seduce Frieda from her allegiance to Klamm to the serving of his own purposes. He succeeds, to a certain degree: their embrace, consummated "among the small puddles of beer and other refuse scattered on the floor" of the taproom is a perfect parody of a Wagnerian *Liebestod*. What dies in this embrace, however, is primarily Frieda's relation to Klamm. After this night the Chief of Department X does not call her any more; the "special superiority" fades from her eyes, and with it any reflection of the Castle. When Frieda professed to be Klamm's mistress, her glance swept "triumphantly" over K.; now that K. has deflected her eyes and concentrated them upon himself, he has extinguished the triumphant view of the Castle in them and replaced it with his own image. For Frieda will not tire of reflecting his weakness in endless curtain lectures, a process during which he paradoxically develops an ever-growing affection for her. When Frieda is ready to leave him, K. actually seems to love her. Mirrors make bad allies.

K.'s first informant after his night with Frieda is not his new mistress but her "Little Mother," Gardena, the landlady of the Bridge Inn. He learns that Gardena herself had entertained tender relations with Klamm; thus her conversation is inevitably tinged with nostalgia for past glories and present aversions to K., the intruder upon her cherished memories. He has to hear, by way of an introduction, that the landlady's "poor head cannot understand how a girl who had the honor of being known as Klamm's mistress—a wild exaggeration in my opinion—should have allowed you even to lay a finger on her." Rather than informing K., the landlady offends him. The only intelligence he obtains consists in the doubts that Gardena casts on the relation that exists between Frieda and Klamm, a thoroughly negative sort of information since it suggests that K.'s strategy, which is based on this very relationship, is nothing but tomfoolery. A little while later Gardena declares, "You put me in mind of my husband, you are just as childish and obstinate as he is." Instead of the desired picture of Klamm, K. is shown here his own self-portrait, with which the likeness of the landlord is blended, to K.'s disadvantage. His own image is tarnished as well as blurred in the eyes of the landlady.

The further K. progresses in his wanderings, the less positive is the information that he is able to gather about Klamm. Gardena, for example, speaks about her long-lost lover in tones reminiscent of the teacher's warning. "Don't use Klamm's name," the landlady says. "Call him 'him' or something, but do not mention his name." With the utmost piety she speaks of a being with whom, after all, she has enjoyed herself in a most human way: "The fact that he had ceased to summon me was a sign that he had forgotten me. When he stops summoning people, he forgets them completely." She seems to explain her own resignation to her fate, but she also mirrors here the collapse of K.'s hopes which were to use Frieda as a decoy in *his* relations with Klamm.

Whatever intelligence K. succeeds in gathering is not only scarce but contradictory. Olga, Barnabas' sister, calls Klamm rude: "He can apparently sit for hours and then suddenly say something so brutal that it makes one shiver." Gardena, on the other hand, infers "that he is terribly sensitive." But she touches on his secret, the letter X, when she concedes, "How it is in reality, we do not know." Erlanger, his secretary, maintains that "Klamm's job is, of course, the biggest"; yet K. never learns in what this job actually consists. He only finds out some duties which Klamm shirks: he does not read any protocols nor does he wait for messages from the village; he is downright irritated when a messenger approaches him. Thus we are not surprised in the end when we hear that Barnabas, who has been assigned to Klamm as a messenger and receives his instructions by word of mouth, doubts that the official referred to as Klamm in the Castle is really Klamm. What could be called Klamm's protean nature is also the effect produced by the mirrors of the labyrinth, which distort and refract everybody and everything that presents itself to them.

There is, however, one thing in which all the accounts about Klamm agree with one another: "He always wears the same clothes, a black morning coat with long tails." Only what is arbitrarily changeable remains rigidly unchanged—his solemn and sinister attire, which truly befits a secretary of Count Westwest. Klamm's toilet harmonizes with the monotony surrounding the Castle; its funereal character agrees with the general mood of decline, the dark cloth being, so to speak, an expression of the darkness, the unknowable, which it covers. Yet it would be a mistake to draw any conclusions from Klamm's coat about his real nature. "Woe to him," says an old adage from the cabala, "who takes the mantle for the law." This mistake, however, K. made when, looking through the

peephole in the taproom, he mistook Klamm's orderly appearance and bourgeois propriety for human qualities against which he could pitch his energies. Klamm's "mantle" hides a secret which is just as impenetrable as the Law of *The Trial.*

The law according to which *The Castle* is administered touches K. once more in the form of a letter. This time the document is unsigned, as if the sender had wanted to disappear completely. Paradoxically the letter commends K. for labors he has not even begun. It reads in part: "The surveying work that you have carried out thus far has been appreciated by me." But K. has done no surveying yet. Quite the contrary, he has just accepted the job of porter at the village school. To make things worse he has also sullied Klamm's sleigh—another of his "mantles." "The work of the assistants too deserves praise," the official document continues. Yet the assistants have not done anything either; they have engaged in all kinds of mischief; they have followed K. against his strict orders and are molesting him at the very moment when he peruses the letter, so that he has to drive them away with his elbow. "Carry your work to a fortunate conclusion," the letter ends, "I shall keep an eye on you." The last phrase indicates that the author of this missive is identical with the writer of the first letter, K.'s "decree of appointment." There the sender had promised "not to lose sight of you" (*Sie nicht aus den Augen zu verlieren*); here he takes the phrase up again to give his promise a still more positive turn. This turn, however, leads K. to the realization that he has neglected his duties, disavowed his own claims to be a Land-Surveyor, and gone astray. The praise is perverted to scorn.

Again, the images of eye and sight are used to function as mirrors with the purpose of confusing K.'s sense of direction. Klamm "keeps an eye" on K. and, by doing so, impresses upon him how far he has strayed from the path of providence. But the phrase has also a less metaphorical meaning, for Klamm has dispatched Arthur and Jeremias, the assistants, not so much to help the Land-Surveyor as to watch him. "Messengers of Klamm," Frieda describes them. "Their eyes—those ingenuous and yet flashing eyes—remind me somehow of Klamm's eyes; yes, this is it: it is Klamm's glance that sometimes pierces me from their eyes." At the same time these spies and "eyes" of Klamm mimic K., shadow him, intrude into the privacy of his bed, and covet Frieda; one of them, Jeremias, will actually steal K.'s mistress as K. has stolen Klamm's. [According to Ronald Gray in his *Kafka's Castle,* the spies] "enact one long parody of K.'s persistence"; on the other hand, they will fade out of sight and vanish as soon as he has dismissed them, thus depriving them of the object of both their vigilance and mimicry. If they are Klamm's eyes, they are also K.'s mirrors.

Yet Kafka has refined still further the play of mirrors in this labyrinth. As there is on the stage a play within the play, there is an occasional mirror-within-mirror effect in this novel. The most intricate and most confusing among these maneuvers of deception occurs in the thirteenth chapter when Frieda repeats to K. the landlady's utterances about him. At this time a genuine sympathy for Frieda and pity for her lot have begun to get the better of his proprietary instincts. It is in the cadence of a consolation and a compliment that he tells her, "Before I knew you I was going about in a blind circle." Quite some time elapses, and one of the most telling scenes of the book, K.'s meeting with Hans Brunswick, intervenes before Frieda returns to his words:

> How startled I was . . . when you said some time today that before you knew me you had gone about in a blind circle. These are perhaps the same words that the landlady used; she too says that it is only since you have known me that you have become aware of your goal. That is because you believe you have secured in me a sweetheart of Klamm's, and so possess a hostage that can only be ransomed at a great price.

This serves as the introduction to a long tirade in which Frieda enumerates the gloomy views the landlady holds with regard to K. Her recital ends with the following words:

> But the landlady said finally, when you see then that you have deceived yourself in everything, in your assumptions and in your hopes, in your ideas of Klamm and in his relations to me, then hell is going to begin for me . . . , since you have no feeling for me but the feeling of ownership.

The interplay of various reflections is almost inextricably involved. Who speaks? Frieda or Gardena? Frieda never indicates the occasion at which Gardena said these words, nor does she fully identify with them and take the responsibility for them. She reproduces, however, with utter satisfaction something that originates in a word that K., and not the landlady, has spoken. He said it in good faith and with the best of intentions. And yet his own statement was strangely twoedged. Anyone who is as hostile to him as the landlady can easily turn it against him. He himself had conceded that he needed Frieda very much. Nor can it be denied that he first approached her from utilitarian motives. Gardena certainly displayed considerable ingenuity in reading these motives and spelling them out, but she falls victim to her own animosity when she deduces the course of Frieda's future from K.'s past. His very words which started the conversation prove that K. has developed other sentiments for Frieda than a mere "feeling of ownership."

Frieda then, only seemingly passive, blends K.'s self-reflection and the landlady's reflection of it, twists and turns them, and throws the image back at him. In this process K.'s words have lost all warmth of human kindness and show him to be nothing but a caricature of his former self. Mercilessly exposing the ulterior motives that have inspired K. and just as coldly anticipating the conclusion that his future actions will spring from similar calculations, Frieda exposes K. as a monster. But ulterior motives are at best partial truths, and their discovery usually produces the effect to be expected from splinters, a fragmentation and distortion of reality. In this cruel mirror-within-mirror play Frieda sends K. back to the "blind circles" of the labyrinth along which he had wandered before meeting her. Thereby she demonstrates that their meeting has indeed been in vain. Long before she deserts him in actual fact, she abandons him here. And yet she acts with a cer-

tain painful logic: having been taken for a mirror, she shows K. nothing but himself. (pp. 229-43)

> *Heinz Politzer, in his* Franz Kafka: Parable and Paradox, *Cornell University Press, 1962, 376 p.*

Martin Greenberg   (essay date 1968)

[In the following excerpt, Greenberg analyzes the role of Land Surveyor in The Castle.*]*

[In *The Castle*] K. arrives in Count Westwest's domain "late in the evening" and goes to sleep beside the stove of the public room in the Bridge Inn. He is waked up by the son of an under-castellan and asked to show his permit, for "this village belongs to the castle, and whoever lives here or passes the night here does so, in a manner of speaking, in the castle itself. Nobody may do that without the Count's permission." K., apparently still dazed by sleep and not knowing where he is, repeats what he has just been told in the form of questions, "as if he wished to assure himself that what he had heard was not a dream"—like Gregor Samsa in *The Metamorphosis*, K. wakes up into a dream of truth which commences with the assurance that it is no dream.

If he must have a permit, the now fully roused K. says, why, then, he'll just have to go and get one.

> "And from whom, pray?" asked the young man.
>
> "From the Count," said K., "that's the only thing to be done."
>
> "A permit from the Count in the middle of the night!" cried the young man, stepping back a pace.
>
> "Is that impossible?" inquired K. coolly. "Then why did you waken me?"
>
> At this the young man flew into a passion. "The manners of a tramp! [*Landstreichermanieren*]" he cried. "I insist on respect for the Count's authority! I woke you up to inform you that you must quit the Count's territory at once."

K.'s disrespect consists, not in his presuming to impose himself upon the Count in the middle of the night, but in his presuming to impose himself upon the Count at all; not in his insouciant tramp's manners, but in his daring to tramp into the Count's territory in the first place—the insignificant question of decorum masks an ultimate question so that the surface of the work presents a ludicrously pedantic appearance. The concealed ultimate question is: Can K. as a concrete individual impose himself upon, directly confront the impersonal automatism of the world? Can K. compel the all-determining system of necessity which rules the world to take account of him as a self-determined person? Can K. compel the Count, who is a lord of files and cases—that is, units in a system of control—officially to admit him into his territory as an uncontrolled individuality? K. wishes to live in the world, which is a world of necessity, and yet be free ("I want to be free always")—in that consists his disrespect for the Count's authority. Because he wishes to be a wandering unfixed element *in* a world of fixities and iron determinations, the castellan's son calls him a tramp (*Landstreicher*).

"Enough of this comedy," K. retorts and announces himself as the land-surveyor (*Landvermesser*) whom the Count has sent for. The comedy K. has had enough of is his own pretense of not knowing where he is or what he is up to—his own pretense of not knowing. What he is sick and tired of is Joseph K.'s role: acting the sleeping innocent who refuses to take responsibility for who he is. K. says straight out that he is a land-surveyor and that there is "no sense in acting the sleeper" (*den Schlafenden zu spielen*). In the universal dream landscape of **The Castle** land means life, the spiritual terrain of human life. One who comes to survey land in such a universal world is a life-surveyor, a thinker who tries to grasp the whole of life in the survey of his consciousness. Land-surveyor K. is a knowledge-seeker, a philosopher, or rather a philosopher-poet since he does not address himself, to an abstract universal knowledge but to the concrete universal of "castle stories." He is the artist-protagonist of modern literature whose lineage goes back to the philosopher-poet whom Coleridge found under the prince's disguise of Hamlet. One way to state the novel's theme is: Can the poet-as-knower (i.e. the modern poet) live in the world? Can Dostoyevsky's Underground Man, "the man of acute consciousness" who will not submit to the "whole legal system of nature," nevertheless live above ground? To be, and at the same time to survey and understand one's being reflectively—is that possible?

The young man Schwarzer circumspectly telephones the castle to verify K.'s claim that he is the Count's land-surveyor, reporting how he found K., "a man in his thirties, a really ragged fellow, sleeping calmly on a bag of straw with a tiny rucksack for pillow and a knotty stick within reach." This describes a tramp. And after the castle calls back in reply, Schwarzer hangs up angrily, crying: "Just what I said! Not a trace of a land-surveyor [*Landvermesser*]. A common, lying tramp [*Landstreicher*], and probably worse." Schwarzer, peasants, landlord, and landlady seem about to fall on K. together, and he scurries underneath his blanket, when the phone rings again and he hears Schwarzer say: "A mistake, is it? . . . How am I to explain it all to the land-surveyor?"

For Schwarzer (and for K. too) it is a case of K.'s being either a *Landstreicher* or a *Landvermesser* and he has little doubt which K. is when he telephones the castle. The castle's first thought is to agree with him—after it calls back the first time K. is about to be thrown out of the village as a tramp. But upon second thought the castle acquiesces in his claim and K. is allowed to stay. However, the initial hesitation of the castle casts a shadow over its recognition of K. The ambiguity is deepened by K.'s own attitude toward his being named land-surveyor: it is "unpropitious" for him on the one hand, he reflects, though on the other hand it is "propitious"; and he observes to himself that the castle "was accepting battle with a smile." Recognition does not give K. "rest" (*Ruhe*) and shelter in the bosom of the community, it starts a battle for existence (" . . . my existence is at stake, [it] is threatened by a scandalous official bureaucracy . . . "), a frantic "pursuit" (*Jagd*) in

which he careers wildly about the village for six days and never reaches a sabbath conclusion. In a deleted passage, an official protocol sums up K.'s early history in the village as follows: "The land-surveyor K. first of all had to endeavor to establish himself in the village. This was not easy, for no one needed his work. . . . So he roamed about in a seemingly aimless way, doing nothing but disturb the peace of the place." His later history is no different: ". . . [H]e's always prowling around the Herrenhof, like the foxes around the henhouse, only in reality the secretaries are the foxes and he is the hen." K. has tramped a long distance through life, after renouncing wife and child, to find a regular job as the castle's land-surveyor and he hopes for acceptance into the community of men, but instead he encounters the most exasperating uncertainty about his appointment and each night there is even a problem about where he is to sleep—the foxes have holes and the birds of the air have nests, but land-surveyor K. has nowhere to lay his head.

What K. does not understand—what he *will* not understand—is that to be a *Landvermesser* is necessarily to be a *Landstreicher*: the two are one. To be a thinker about life is to be cast out of life, a tramp and vagabond. The very word *Vermesser*, which rubs against the words *vermessen* and *Vermessenheit* with all their suggestions of temerity, presumption, overstepping limits, whispers the fate reserved for its bearer: that as a surveyor of life he must forever be a trespasser on it. K. says about himself early in the book: "I don't fit in with the peasants, nor, I imagine, with the castle." He cannot join the peasantry in the village and immerse himself in concrete, unselfconscious, unilluminated being, because what he seeks is just precisely being illuminated by consciousness and consciousness is the castle's business (" 'Nothing here is done without taking thought,' said the Village Head"). On the other hand, he cannot join the "gentlemen" of the castle and give himself entirely to abstract knowledge without forfeiting his earthly weight, his concrete existence. He cannot be a villager without forfeiting knowledge (the universal); he cannot be an official without forfeiting concreteness. He is and must remain a land-surveyor: somebody who strives to unite concreteness and universality, that is, the poet. For "concrete universal" defines art. K. is an artist whose "high, unfulfillable demands" are only fulfillable in art, not in life. **The Castle** is the fruit of K.'s land-surveying, an imagined concrete universal about striving for an impossible real concrete universality. In this sense Kafka's religious goal is to aestheticize life, to make the concrete universal real. Underneath their unfinished exteriors his works are complete aesthetically; it is only as religious efforts *in life* that they are incomplete. But that was what Kafka cared about most of all—the religious goal of aestheticizing life—and could not stop content at the aesthetic goal of writing works of literature. Hence his testamentary requests to Max Brod to burn whatever of his writings he had.

K. seeks being and consciousness, the innocence of Paradise and the freedom of self which the Tree of Knowledge confers; he wants to have Adam's apple and eat it too. He wants to unite the village and the castle. Now it is true that the village and the castle are already united: as the teacher tells him, "There is no difference between the peasantry and the castle." Peasants and officials are united in abjectness under the yoke of the laws of life. The peasants, "with their open mouths, coarse lips, and literally tortured faces—their heads looked as if they had been beaten flat on top, and their features as if the pain of the beating had twisted them to the present shape—" are beaten flat by the flailing tail of the Leviathan world. And the castle gentlemen are tired with the infinite fatigue of overworked officials dozing at their desks with never a moment's relief from the eternal burden of upholding the world-as-it-is. "He's asleep," Frieda says about Klamm after K. has viewed him through the peep hole of the Herrenhof barroom:

> "Asleep?" cried K. "But when I peeped in he was awake and sitting at the desk." "He always sits like that," said Frieda; "he was sleeping when you saw him. . . . That's how he sleeps, the gentlemen do sleep a great deal. . . ."

The castle and the village are united in their subjection to a world of necessity, a world in which being is enslaved by ignorance to automatism, and knowledge is that automatism become conscious of itself and haughtily elevated above the life it controls. They are united in disjunction—the very image of man's self. But K. wishes to conjoin castle and village so that the two merge into one: to free being through knowledge and to vivify knowledge through being. He wishes to recover innocence through *increased* consciousness—as Kleist put it, he wants to "eat of the Tree of Knowledge a second time in order to fall back into the state of innocence." K.'s "high, unfulfillable demand" is for a second Fall of the fallen world forward out of history back into Paradise.

Much of the surface confusion of the novel is due to the fact that K. strives simultaneously after two contradictory goals—to settle in the village (life) and to penetrate into the castle (thinking-about-life)—without his recognizing the contradiction. He is the man in the joke who rushes out of the house in opposite directions. His failure to recognize the contradiction is ignorance of the world, of reality, which is why the landlady of the Bridge Inn, that expert on reality, calls him "the most ignorant person in the village." But what is confusion, madness, impossibility in the perspective of the world and its reality, is courageous effort in the perspective of the spirit. K.'s worldly confusion (ignorance) is at the same time spiritual effort (awareness). What is senselessness on the surface of the novel, on the level of reality, as the manifest content of K.'s dream, is spiritual purpose in its depths, at the level of symbol, as the latent dream content. In the world, K. is foolish, childish, crazy (*meshuggah*) [The author adds in a footnote that "Meshuggah" was "Kafka Sr.'s Yiddish epithet for his son"]; in the spiritual realm he is a dangerous fox—reality and spirit, in the modern world of mere matter of fact, stand at daggers drawn. The marvelous truth of the art of *The Castle,* of the dream-narrative form at the height of its development, lies in its faithfulness to the protagonist's confusion of life as well as to his spiritual effort. It is not a case of the life-confusion not mattering, spirituality being all. The confusion matters as much as, is as true as, the spiritual meaning: the Kafka nightmare is as true as

its interpretation and is not something simply to be worked through. K. the ignorant stranger to life, the ineffectual blunderer about the world who, though "he's been living here among us in the village long enough," is still "capable of getting lost in the three streets there are in the village," is not the price Kafka willingly pays down for K. the poet, the spiritually conscious K. K.'s life-failure is not justified as spiritual distinction; it *is* failure. He does not, thumbing his nose at the world, turn life-failure into spiritual success. "The spirit only becomes free," Kafka aphorized, "when it ceases to be a stay"—a support and consolation. Because spirit without world, knowledge without power, is not spirit or knowledge. And so K. is not a hero and *The Castle* is not an epic if an epic needs a hero; he is a confused man struggling with himself and with the world.

Early in the novel K. recognizes the world's dilemma: in the inconsistencies of Klamm's first letter to him, about his appointment to the Count's service, he perceives a "frankly offered choice" as to "whether he preferred to become a village worker with a distinctive but merely apparent connection with the castle, or an ostensible village worker whose entire job was in reality decided for him by the messages which Barnabas brought" from the castle—the choice is between really settling in the village and having an apparent connection with the castle, or ostensibly settling in the village and really working for the castle. K. does "not hesitate in his choice" when faced with this clear alternative; with fine decisiveness he chooses—both courses! the village and the castle: "Only as a worker in the village, removed as far as possible from the sphere of the castle, could he hope to reach anything in the castle itself, these village folk who were now so suspicious of him would begin to talk to him once he was, if not exactly their friend, their fellow citizen, and if he were to become indistinguishable from Gerstäcker or Lasemann—and that must happen as soon as possible, everything depended on that—then all kinds of roads would surely be opened to him at one stroke, which would remain not only forever barred to him but quite invisible if it were solely a question of the favor of the gentlemen up above." K.'s life-confusion, his inability to choose between the two realms so that he incoherently rushes off in opposite directions, is at the same time a coherent spiritual effort to unite the two realms. The perplexity and confusion of the reader is K.'s own perplexity and confusion at trying to live impossibly, to reconcile the irreconcilable. What mystifies in *The Castle* is the truth—the truth of a world in which reality and spirit stand opposed—and not an obscurantist art. (pp. 162-70)

Martin Greenberg, in his The Terror of Art: Kafka and Modern Literature, *Basic Books, Inc., Publishers, 1968, 241 p.*

W. G. Sebald (essay date 1972)

[*In the following excerpt, Sebald explores Kafka's use of death symbolism in* The Castle.]

The smooth surface of Kafka's work has remained an enigma in spite of what his interpreters have managed to dredge from its depths. It has preserved its integrity against the advances of criticism. What it conveys is the infinitely sombre gaze of the five year old boy who, dressed in a sailor suit and with a shiny black walking stick and a straw hat in his hand, was dragged into the gloomy exoticism of a photographer's studio in Prague. Critics have singularly failed to come to terms with this gaze, they have overlooked the yearning, fearful images of death which pervade Kafka's work and which impart that melancholy whose onset was as early as it was persistent. Sickness unto death, unless purged by suicide, has always been suspect in the eyes of society. It is therefore ignored, and instead one strives to wrest some positive meaning from Kafka's work—if necessary, in the spirit of the existentialist *volte face* whereby freedom emerges from the very absurdity of an endeavour. Such interpretations have been attempted in defiance of the obvious fact that Kafka felt constrained to hide any happiness he may have experienced like a physical deformity. It would mean a form of absolution for society if one could place a positive interpretation on K.'s desire for death, since it was society that instilled this grim, deep-seated desire in him in the first place and death—at least according to common supposition—is only a cipher for salvation.

Towards the end of the story K. converses with the landlady of the Herrenhof. ' "Didn't you once learn tailoring?" the landlady asked. "No, never," K. said. "What actually is it you are?" "Land Surveyor." "What *is* that?" K. explained, the explanation made her yawn. "You're not telling the truth. Why won't you tell the truth?" "You don't tell the truth either." ' He is not a surveyor then, he does not have anything with him to substantiate his claim, he is merely a wanderer, a figure who first appears with a 'minute rucksack' and a 'knotty stick'. Psycho-analysis designates the image of a journey or a hike as a symbol of death, and Adorno [in "Schubert" in *Moments Musicaux*] describes the scenario of Schubert's two great song cycles as follows: 'They link up with poems in which again and again the images of death present themselves to the man who wanders among them as diminutively as Schubert in the Dreimäderlhaus. A stream, a mill and a dark desolate wintry landscape stretching away in the twilight of mock suns, timeless, as in a dream—these are the hallmarks of the setting of Schubert's songs, with dried flowers for their mournful ornament.' Brown Bohemian earth, where at the end of the Middle Ages another German poet had once talked with death, also surrounds the Castle, as the pictures edited by Klaus Wagenbach show, and Kafka deliberately avoided introducing the brighter green of organic nature into his landscape as a source of comfort. The ground is covered in frost and snow, a still-life, a *nature morte* which precludes any hope of regeneration; this is reinforced by Pepi's statement that winter is long in these parts, so prolonged that in her recollection spring and summer appear to last barely more than two days, 'and even on those days, even during the most beautiful day, even then sometimes snow falls.' K. complains often enough that it is difficult to make any progress across this landscape. Aggravated by the monotony, the wanderer who tries to cross it always retraces his own tracks. 'The eccentric structure of this landscape, where each point is equidistant from the centre, is revealed to the wanderer who traverses it without making any headway: every development is its own perfect antithesis, the first step is as close to death as the last, and the dissociated points of the landscape are visited in a circle, without it ever being left behind. For Schubert's themes wander just like the miller or the lover abandoned in winter by his mistress. They have no history but are merely viewed from different angles. The only change is a change of light.' There can seldom have been a more apposite description of the way in which the avowedly unmusical Kafka circles about the geometric location of his yearning than in these lines of Adorno's on the structure of Schubert's work. The debate about K.'s 'development' suddenly seems egregious, for at the point where in the first section of the book he crosses the wooden bridge over the stream and invades the territory of the Castle, he is like 'those wretched souls who travel hither and thither but have no history' [as Walter Benjamin writes in his "Über einige Motive bei Baudelaire" in *Illuminationen*]. The busyness in the *paysage mort,* all the to-ing and fro-ing of coaches and litigants, and every attempt to attain some goal in the domain of death bear the marks of immense futility. So too folk lore tells us that in that undiscover'd country one takes three steps forward and three steps back. In the Berliner Ensemble production of *Mother Courage* the heroine marched against a revolving stage through the devastated lands of the Empire with no hope of ever changing her situation. K. too, the first time he tries to press on into the Castle, experiences a paralysis of the will to proceed imposed by some external force. 'At last he tore himself away from the obsession of the street and escaped into a small side-lane, where the snow was still deeper and the exertion of lifting one's feet clear was fatiguing; he broke into a sweat, suddenly came to a stop, and could not go on. Kierkegaard describes the humorous equivalent of a progression directed against its own teleology in a passage devoted to the old Friedrichstädter Theatre in Berlin and a comedian called Beckmann.

> He can not only go, he can come and go at the same time. That's something quite different, to come and go simultaneously, and through this genial accomplishment he can improvise the whole physical setting and can not only represent a wandering journeyman but also come-and-go like one. We see it all, looking up from the dust of the highway towards a welcoming village and hearing its quiet sounds, glimpsing the very path which skirts the village pond where one turns off by the smithy—and there we see Beckmann approaching with his small haversack, his stick in his hand, carefree and cheerful. He can come-and-go followed by urchins whom one cannot in fact see.

> [Quoted by Adorno in "Zweimal Chaplin" in *Ohne Leitbild.* The author comments in a footnote that "The quotation comes from an early piece entitled *Repetition* which Kierkegaard wrote under a pseudonym."]

Adorno cites this passage in an essay on Chaplin. But Chaplin of whom we are reminded by the adventures of Karl Rossmann and by many photographs of Kafka himself—Chaplin who became hopelessly entangled in his own hastiness—was the hero of a modern entertainment which Kafka described to Janouch [in *Conversations with Kafka*] as 'the magic lantern of a neglected youth,' and all his life the neglect of youth appeared to him like a premature death.

We learn only very little about the Castle itself, the imaginary centre of the landscape of death. However, the figures that emerge from it in the course of the story allow us to draw certain conclusions about its nature. There is first of all Schwarzer who wakens the weary K. from his unauthorized sleep. The name draws attention to the colour that seems to be dominant in the Castle; its inhabitants, like the assistants, wear close-fitting black clothes as a sort of uniform. Yet the assistants themselves in spite of their sometimes importunate liveliness, do not appear properly alive. When Artur returns to the Castle in order to lodge a complaint about his master, the latter realizes for the first time what he finds so repugnant about Jeremias, the assistant who remains behind—it is 'this flesh which sometimes gave one the impression of not being properly alive.' And shortly afterwards the appearance of Jeremias confirms his uncanny suspicion:

> As he stood there, his hair rumpled, his thin beard lank as if dripping with wet, his eyes painfully beseeching and wide with reproach, his sallow cheeks flushed, but yet flaccid, his naked legs trembling so violently with cold that the long fringes of the wrap quivered as well, he was like a patient who had escaped from hospital, and whose appearance could only suggest one thought, that of getting him back in bed again.

The tousled hair, the soaking beard, the eyes held open only with difficulty, the loose flesh—it is as if Jeremias were already in a state of decomposition, a corpse escaped from the grave. After all, 'bed' and 'sleep' often stand for the abode and condition of the dead, in this and other literature. When Frieda lets K. peep through the spy-hole into Klamm's room, the latter is sitting completely immobile at his table. The only sign of life is a cigar smoking in his motionless hand and the glint of the pince-nez which hides his eyes—the most vital part of a man. Immediately afterwards K. wonders if Klamm is disturbed by the rowdiness of the servants. ' "No," said Frieda, "he's asleep." "Asleep?" cried K. "But when I peeped in he was awake and sitting at the desk." "He always sits like that," said Frieda, "he was sleeping when you saw him. Would I have let you look in if he hadn't been asleep? That's how he sleeps, the gentlemen do sleep a great deal. . . . " ' Sleep is the brother of death and is assiduously cultivated by the inhabitants of the Castle. When they leave their bureaux to attend a hearing, they prefer to do it at night and even then they like to settle themselves in bed like Bürgel, that image of a regressive existence to which K. so fervently longs to return. Bürgel spends a large part of his time in bed, he deals with his correspondence in bed and interrogates plaintiffs from his bed. Unlike other officials Bürgel is plagued by insomnia. K. too is a restless spirit. This may be why Bürgel is willing and able to indicate a way out for K. Yet K., overcome by irresistible weariness, forfeits the chance of revelation, like the character in a Yiddish story who sleeps through the Day of Judgement. Sortini too,

whom K. encounters only through Olga's story, is a harbinger of death. He is not one of those officials bloated with age, like Klamm, or one of those with child-like faces, like Bürgel: his features are rather different. Olga describes him as a small, weak, thoughtful person, and goes on, 'and one thing about him struck all the people who noticed him at all, the way his forehead was furrowed; all the furrows—and there were plenty of them although he's certainly not more than forty—were spread fanwise over his forehead, running towards the root of his nose. I've never seen anything like it.' A physiognomy such as Olga describes here reminds one readily of a mummy distorted by a shrinking process. However, it is not only this which makes the haggard Sortini an envoy of death, but also the scene where with legs stiffened by his sedentary occupation he leaps across the shaft of the fire engine to approach Amalia who is decked out like a bride. Politzer recognizes the fire service party where Sortini meets Amalia as a *sacre du printemps* but he omits to point out the affinity between the archetype of this ritual and that of death, even though the death symbolism surrounding the sacrificial feast of the maidservants can be shown to be a literary *topos*. Adrian Leverkühn, for instance, is oppressed at the wedding of his sister by the fact that 'the white shroud of virginity, the stain slippers of the dead' are used. Amalia is prepared for the firemen's festival in precisely the same manner. The 'dress was specially fine', Olga recalls, 'a white blouse foaming high in front with one row of lace after the other, our mother had taken every bit of her lace for it.'' Olga then describes the necklace of Bohemian garnets and reports her father as saying, 'To-day, mark my words, Amalia will find a husband.' But Amalia rejects Sortini's advances, is alarmed by the ghastly character of the spring rites and the absence of any conciliatory aspect which she may have hoped for in her more obscure presentiments. There are no tokens of any luxuriant scenery promising carefree procreation; of the requisites of the vernal season we glimpse only the bare date, 3 July; and the centrepiece of the feast is a mechanical monster in the shape of the fire engine. For this reason Amalia refuses the next day to obey Sortini's summons which reaches her, according to Olga, in the form of a pornographic document drafted in copper-plate handwriting. For this reason too she brings down execration upon her family. Henceforth her father trudges each day up to the Castle entrance or to that of the cemetery, in order to draw the inhabitants' attention to himself and the sad lot of his family as they drive past in their carriages.

> In his best suit, which soon becomes his only suit, off he goes every morning from the house with our best wishes. He takes with him a small Fire Brigade badge, which he has really no business to keep, to stick in his coat once he's out of the village. . . . Not far from the Castle entrance there's a market garden, belonging to a man called Bertuch who sells vegetables to the Castle, and there on the narrow stone ledge at the foot of the garden fence father took up his post.

The best suit, soon to be the only one he will have left, the blessing of his family, the small medal, the market garden, the name of the gardener and the narrow stone ledge, all this recalls—if one translates the surreal fantasy images back into rational concepts—funerals and grave yards. The fact that shortly afterwards his wife follows the father on his excursions again adds to this picture of the death of the old couple. When Olga reports 'We often went out to them, to take them food, or merely to visit them, or to try to persuade them to come back home' here too the empirical equivalent is a visit to the cemetery and the graveside, the leaving of food for the wandering souls, still perpetuated in the sprinkling of holy water. Indeed the attempt to persuade the departed to return home is an archaic residue which had a great impact on Döblin when during a journey to Poland [recounted in his *Reise in Polen*] he visited the Jewish cemetery in Warsaw on the eve of the Day of Atonement. At home, however, the parents have left behind their stiff and helpless bodies which Amalia dresses and undresses, puts to bed and feeds, very much like Nag and Nell in *Endgame*.

When K. tries to reach the Castle, as he twice does at the beginning of his stay in the village, images of home well up involuntarily in his mind's eye. On the occasion of his first attempt, which ends with the regeneration scene in Lasemann's house, he is struck by the similarity between the Castle and the small town where he grew up, and he wonders whether it would not have been better to return home again instead of pressing on towards the Castle. The second time he believes himself to be approaching the Castle arm in arm with Barnabas, again a memory of home is conjured up.

> They went on, but K. did not know whither, he could discern nothing, not even whether they had already passed the church or not. The effort which it cost him merely to keep going made him lose control of his thoughts. Instead of remaining fixed on their goal they strayed. Memories of his home kept recurring and filled his mind. There, too, a church stood in the marketplace, partly surrounded by an old graveyard which was again surrounded by a high wall. Very few boys had managed to climb that wall, and for some time K., too, had failed. It was not curiosity which had urged them on. The graveyard had been no mystery to them. They had often entered it through a small wicket-gate, it was only the smooth high wall that they had wanted to conquer. But one morning—the empty, quiet marketplace had been flooded with sunshine, when had K. ever seen it like that either before or since?—he had succeeded in climbing it with astonishing ease; at a place where he had already slipped down many a time he had clambered with a small flag between his teeth right to the top at the first attempt. Stones were still rattling down under his feet, but he was at the top. He stuck the flag in, it flew in the wind, he looked down and round about him, over his shoulder, too, at the crosses mouldering in the ground, nobody was greater than he at that place and that moment.

Just as death has always been considered the second home of mankind, so images of his first home flit through K.'s imagination on his way to the Castle. Moreover Adorno reminds us that Schubert too, 'in the cycle revolving

around the words "All my dreams are ended", uses the name of "inn" only for the graveyard.' The precise significance of such a notion can be seen from K.'s clear memory of climbing the wall. What a crude psychology is so quick to interpret as an unambiguous orgastic symbol, in view of the ramming home of the flag and its taut fabric—a symbol that conveys the conquering of death by the power of life—is in fact anything but unambiguous even in K.'s mind. On the contrary, the brief moment of triumph when to the boy looking over his shoulder the crosses seem to sink into the ground is treated as the expression of a short-lived surrender to personal happiness. The cemetery exists just as before and then the teacher, a representative of realism, arrives and with a mere glance brings down the whole house of cards. A more appropriate tool to help us understand this episode and the context in which it appears would be Freud's theory, developed in his later years, of the identity of the life and the death wish. Freud regarded both as conservative, inasmuch as both were concerned to escape from a state of spiritual and physical individuation and to enter that condition of painlessness which is beyond the birth trauma. Kafka considers this combination to be at once comforting and hopeless in those passages where K. and Frieda try to lose themselves in one another. We should not, of course, overlook the significant but remote moment when, shortly after his arrival, K. experienced in Frieda's arms the joy of a timeless alienation from himself; yet this mirror of salvation is shattered by the description not long afterwards of their futile endeavour to recreate this *unitas unitatis*.

> There they lay, but not in the forgetfulness of the previous night. She was seeking and he was seeking, they raged and contorted their faces and bored their heads into each other's bosoms in the urgency of seeking something, and their embraces and their tossing limbs did not avail to make them forget, but only reminded them of what they sought; like dogs desperately tearing up the ground they tore at each other's bodies, and often, helplessly baffled, in a final effort to attain happiness they nuzzled and tongued each other's face. Sheer weariness stilled them at last and brought them gratitude to each other. Then the maids came in. "Look how they are lying there," said one, and sympathetically cast a coverlet over them.

As so often with Kafka, a single isolated gesture at the end of a description seems to sum up its whole meaning. A sheet is spread over the twisted bodies who have died in love. It is well known that all the women characters in Kafka's novels remain tied to a stage of evolution that preceded the emergence of human life. There is, for example, the bloated Brunelda in ***America,*** or Fräulein Bürstner, or Leni who has a bind of web between the middle and the fourth finger of her right hand as a token of her origins in some prehistoric swamp; and Frieda too, described as an etiolated creature who shuns the light, belongs to this group, as does Pepi who has risen from the chthonic depths of the Brückenhof, and Gardena, vegetating in her bed like a carnivorous plant. Walter Benjamin [in "Franz Kafka" in *Angelus Novus*] saw early on that these creatures belonged to a stage 'which Bachofen calls the hetaeric.' Its manifestation is that of self-forgetful life, and thus also of death. Just as the rotational correspondences of 'hetaera esmeralda' haunt the compositions of Adrian Leverkühn after his exposure to the sting of death in the prostitute's embrace, so too Kafka's novels are permeated by the sombreness of a world where the dark forces of matriarchal figures unsex their male partners. These matriarchal figures, however, stand at the gates of Hell, for as Berthold von Regensburg tells us [in Vol. IV of his *Handwörterbuch des Deutschen Aberglaubens*] Hell lies at the heart of earth's steamy swamps. Such is the terrible ambivalence which cripples the power of life in Kafka's work. The death wish of love has its pendant in the message which K. believes he hears in the tolling of a bell, when Gerstäcker drives him back to the Brückenhof on his sleigh after the first fruitless expedition. 'The Castle above them, which K. had hoped to reach that very day, was already beginning to grow dark, and retreated again into the distance. But as if to give him a parting sign till their next encounter a bell began to ring merrily up there, a bell which for at least a second made his heart palpitate for its tone was menacing, too, as if it threatened him with the fulfilment of his vague desire.' As the promise is transformed into a threat of death, the tolling soon dies away, to be replaced by a less ambiguous sound, 'by a feeble monotonous little tinkle which . . . certainly harmonized better with the slow-going journey, with the wretched-looking yet inexorable driver.'

In the context of this argument, it would seem appropriate to explore the messianic traits which Kafka, more modest but also more serious than any of his contemporaries, bestows on his alter ego K. The limits of his messianic vision correspond to the great scepticism with which Kafka regarded the possibility of transcending the human predicament. Admittedly, since K. refuses to disclose to the village secretary Momus details of his identity and thus evades the regular admittance procedure into the realm of the dead, it could be argued he intends to invade the Castle as a living person and annual death's anathema on life. But all the other messianic hopes are imputed to him by others rather than being his on pretensions, and are therefore an example of those projections held to be the basis of human religion. K. initially represents a hope of this kind for Barnabas' family, a hope which even Olga fears towards the end of her tale is perhaps only an 'illusion,' for this family has always awaited the day when 'someone in the long procession of visitors would arrive and put a stop to it all and make everything swing the other way again.' But to bring the process to a halt, to dissipate the mythic power that reproduces itself in an eternal recurrence by forcing it to reverse its direction—this does not lie in K.'s power any more than in that of the young observer in Kafka's story *In the Gallery*. Like him, K. is dazzled and disoriented by the surface events, is himself drawn into the spectacle and thereby becomes guilty of complicity. 'Then,' Olga says, 'we should have lost you, and I confess that you now mean almost more to me than Barnabas's service in the Castle.' For Pepi too, the maid who lives in a damp cellar, K. represents the epiphany of a better life. 'At that time', we read, 'she had loved K. as she had never loved anyone before; month after month she had been down there in her tiny dark room, prepared to spend years there,

Kafka, circa 1922, in front of the apartment building where his family lived.

or, if the worst came to the worst, to spend her whole life here, ignored by everyone, and now suddenly K. had appeared, a hero, a rescuer of maidens in distress, and had opened up the way upstairs for her.' The outcome of these hopes is familiar. After a short respite behind the bar Pepi has to return to the world from which she came, and it looks as if K. goes with her, after losing Frieda and his job as a caretaker. The saviour cannot come up to the great expectations held of him and sinks to the level of those who on his arrival looked up to him in hope. In this connection the episode with Hans Brunswick takes on a curious ambivalence. K. mentions to him that at home he used to be called ' "The Bitter Herb" on account of his healing powers.' The 'bitter herb' can stand for gentle hippocratic healing or be a symbol of death. The doctor is a secularized messiah who expels sickness from the suffering body but he is also the accomplice of death. This ambiguity, present at an early stage in Kafka's work, can be seen in the child's attitude to the stranger. The optimistic energy of the child—for [as Kafka writes in his **"Hochzeitsvorbereitungen auf dem Lande"**] 'nobody is more eager to change things than a child'—tries to overcome K.'s ambivalence, and out of the contradiction there arises in him the belief that though for the moment K. was wretched and looked down on, yet in an almost unimaginable and distant future he would excel everybody. And it was just this absurdly distant future and the glorious developments which were to lead up to it that attracted Hans; that was why he was willing to accept K. even in his present state. The peculiar childish-grown-up acuteness of this wish consisted in the fact that Hans looked on K. as on a younger brother whose future would reach further than his own, the future of a very little boy.

Hans' desires, themselves conditional, do not inspire K. to any messianic gesture; rather they arouse 'new hopes in him, improbable, he admitted, completely groundless even, but all the same not to be put out of his mind.' Thus all hope remains circular and in the end it is no more than a 'misunderstanding', as Bruno Schulz, Kafka's Polish translator, put it [in *Die Zimtläden*]. Yet the messianic ideal is imputed to K. once again. Towards the end of the novel he finds himself by mistake in Bürgel's room on his way to an interrogation and there falls into a heavy sleep while the secretary imparts to him vital information that will lead him out of his dilemma. As though under some kind of compulsion Bürgel explains to the sleeping K. the threat which at that very moment he poses to the totality of the system. 'It is a situation', Bürgel elaborates, 'in which it very soon becomes impossible to refuse to do a favour. To put it precisely, one is desperate; to put it still more precisely, one is very happy. Desperate, for the defenceless position in which one sits here waiting for the applicant to utter his plea and knowing that once it is uttered one must grant it, even if, at least in so far as one has oneself a general view of the situation, it positively tears the official organization to shreds: this is, the worst thing that can happen to one in the fulfilment of one's duties.' This is the promise of apocalyptic destruction, but the potential messiah has fallen asleep from weariness—in other words, has succumbed to the brother of death—and he does not hear the summons directed at him. At precisely the point when he draws closest to his own salvation and to the salvation he could offer to the rest of the world, he is also furthest away from it, because of the eccentric structure of Kafka's world. At precisely the moment when his spirit is called, K. is asleep. Bürgel's words which from the outset K. hears only as a distant murmur, fail to rouse him to a new life but rather lull him into a sleep from which there will not readily be an awakening. ' "Clatter, mill, clatter on and on," he thought, "you clatter just for me." ' In falling prey to the temptation of sleep and thus offending against Pascal's metaphysical commandment 'Thou shalt sleep no more', K. averts the danger which an individual such as he represents for the Castle. Though this may be inevitable, it also conveys the crazy irony of all human endeavour to escape from the limitations of one's own existence. 'One's physical energies last only to a certain limit;' explains a Mephistophelian Bürgel, 'Who can help the fact that precisely this limit is significant in other ways too? No, nobody can help it. That is how the world itself corrects the deviations in its course and maintains the balance. This is indeed an excellent, time and again unimaginably excellent arrangement, even if in other respects dismal and cheerless.' However, the latent messian-

ic mission to invade the realm of the dead as a living saviour can be interpreted in another way, if one equates the realm of the dead with the place where one's forefathers are assembled. This search for a buried ancestral tradition is represented by one of those insignificant gestures which seem to offer a key to the Kafka enigma.

> . . . the support of the arm above was no longer sufficient; involuntarily K. provided himself with new support by planting his right hand firmly against the quilt, whereby he accidentally took hold of Bürgel's foot, which happened to be sticking up under the quilt.

This surrealist detail is a memory of orthodox Judaism, in which one sought to ensure a lasting contact with the departed by touching the feet of the corpse. Kafka has this gesture in mind at another point when he writes [in his diary]:

> In Hebrew my name is Amschel, like my mother's maternal grandfather, whom my mother, who was six years old when he died, can remember as a very pious and learned man with a long, white beard. She remembers how she had to take hold of the toes of the corpse and ask forgiveness for any offence she may have committed against her grandfather.

Klaus Wagenbach has moreover demonstrated the topographical similarity between Kafka's Castle and that of the village Wossek, from where his father's family originated. K.'s attempt to penetrate the rambling wings of this castle may then be interpreted as an effort to re-enter the spiritual traditions of his forefathers. Kafka often regretted how remote they seemed to him, alienated as he was by the process of assimilation. 'I am as far as I know the most typical Western Jew among them', he writes in a letter to Milena, 'this means, expressed with exaggeration, that not one calm second is granted me, nothing is granted me, everything has to be earned, not only the present and the future, but the past too—something after all which perhaps every human being has inherited, this too must be earned, it is perhaps the hardest work.' Small wonder if at the conclusion of the novel (which cannot be too distant from the point where the extant fragment tapers off) K. would, according to Max Brod, have died of exhaustion; small wonder indeed if he has to pay with his life to achieve proximity with his ancestors.

There are other images of death in the landscape surrounding Kafka's Castle. Folk lore [Benjamin writes in his *Handwörterbuch des deutschen Aberglaubens*] teaches us that the inn is an ancient symbol of the underworld. It is the place where the dead assemble before descending into Hell, and in legend the devil's tavern is the last stage on the journey of the dead. Like the Brückenhof it stands on the border of the other world. Even the architecture of the Herrenhof has something of a subterranean atmosphere, above all when the servant leads K. across the yard and

> then into the entry and through the low, somewhat downward-sloping passage. . . . The servant put out his lantern, for here it was brilliant with electric light. Everything was on a small scale, but elegantly finished. The space was utilized to the best advantage. The passage was just

high enough for one to walk without bending one's head. Along both sides the doors almost touched each other. The walls did not quite reach to the ceiling, probably for reasons of ventilation, for here in the low cellar-like passage the tiny rooms could hardly have windows.

And then the noise is described, a chaos of sound, of dictating and conversing voices, the clink of glasses and the blows of a hammer—a cacophony which may well have appeared as the most appropriate image of Hell to a Kafka notoriously sensitive to noise. The fact that coaches are used for travelling about similarly fits into the landscape of death, as does the telephone, that mystagogic instrument to which Proust and Benjamin paid such eloquent tribute. It is from the telephone that K. hears the same eleusinian humming which many of us remember from childhood walks beside the telegraph wires and which made a peculiarly melancholy impression. But the clearest evidence that the administrative apparatus of the Castle is occupied with the endless cataloguing of the dead comes from the claim that despite of all confusion and contradictions nobody can slip through the official net. What strikes us as the most disconsolate aspect of this sphere of death is the fact that even here, just as in life, the powerful and the helpless are separated, that (again in accordance with folk lore) the village people dwell together in one room beneath the earth, while the gentlemen occupy a castle as in their previous existence. Finally a particularly valid argument for K.'s proximity to death when he enters the village is proffered by Ronald Gray's book on the *Castle*. In his interpretation of the last scene of the novel fragment, Gray does not, admittedly, arrange the death symbols which he discusses into the kind of pattern described above; in his view K. encounters death here almost by accident: it appears as a reflection of a narrative convention rather than a long since anticipated event. The landlady of the Herrenhof talks in this passage about her strange old-fashioned and over-crowded wardrobe, about dresses reminiscent of the *pompes funèbres* to whose dusty vulgarity K. has taken exception. 'If the dresses', Gray writes [in his *Kafka's Castle*] 'are the disguises which the hostess is accustomed to wear when she announces to men the moment of their death, a good deal falls into place.' The landlady as Mistress World, as a barmaid in an inn belonging to the Devil, occurs in a poem by Walter von der Vogelweide, and Rilke in [the fifth of his *Duino Elegies*] dedicated to travelling acrobats pays homage to the very same allegorical persona as Kafka when he recalls the place 'where the modiste Madame Lamort / winds and binds the restless ways of the world, / those endless ribbons, to ever-new / creations of bow, frill, flower, cockade and fruit, / all falsely coloured, to deck / the cheap winter-hats of Fate.' It is, then, safe to assume that Gray is correct in his interpretation of this last scene and after all that has been said, it is manifest that the Kafka fragment could scarcely have found a more precise ending; here the fragmentary character of the novel transcends itself. This ending is appositely summarized in Gray's commentary as follows:

> The Charon-like figure of Gerstäcker already has K. by the sleeve, to carry him away on his flat, seatless sledge. On the preceding page the

hostess seemed to be giving him instructions about K.'s destination. And now the hostess concludes with the possibly ambiguous remark: "Tomorrow I shall be getting a new dress; perhaps I shall send for you".

That K. has attained the end of his natural course can only be regarded as a source of comfort and salvation as one compares it with the alternative that might have befallen him: to remain an eternal 'stranger and pilgrim' on earth, as in the legend of Ahasver, the Wandering Jew. And to avoid this fate, K. seeks out the land of death of his own accord, for as he says in rejecting Frieda's dream of emigrating to Spain or the South of France, 'What could have enticed me to this desolate country except the wish to stay here?' The yearning for peace which in K.'s world only death itself can provide, and the fear of being unable to die (like the hero of Kafka's *Gracchus the Huntsman*), the fear of a perpetual habitation in the no-man's land between man and thing—that yearning, that fear must be reckoned the ultimate motive for K.'s journey to the village whose name we never learn. Yet this village is at once the place where Jean-Paul causes the souls who have reached it to sigh, 'At last we are in the courtyard of eternity and but one more death and we shall see God'. (pp. 22-34)

W. G. Sebald, "The Undiscover'd Country: The Death Motif in Kafka's 'Castle'," in Journal of European Studies, Vol. 2, No. 1, March, 1972, pp. 22-34.

Richard Sheppard (essay date 1973)

[*In the following excerpt, Sheppard examines the ambiguously threatening and benevolent nature of the Castle, its officials, and their relationship to K.*]

The question of the status of the Castle authorities in Kafka's novel is fraught with difficulties. It is not necessary to go very far into the immense amount of secondary literature to discover that these difficulties have caused commentators on *Das Schloß* to take a bewildering variety of attitudes to the mysterious Castle and its elusive occupants. So, before an attempt is made here to come to any conclusions about this intricate problem, it is useful to be clear about the questions which are asked about the Castle authorities and to consider the various answers which have been given to them. On the whole, two questions tend to be asked: Is the Castle an allegory of God? and: Are the Castle authorities benevolent or malevolent? (p. 190)

On the basis of what the reader is told, the Castle appears to be all-too-human and yet endowed with divine powers of observation and intervention; to be both benevolent and malevolent. Because the Castle is so complex and ambiguous a phenomenon, it is not surprising that some commentators seem to compound confusion when they try to define its status. Thus, Marthe Robert, apparently unaware that she is contradicting herself, claims [in her book *L'Ancien et le Nouveau*] that the Castle is actively malevolent and yet implies that it is in some respects benevolent seeing that it does not chase K. out of the village even though he has no official right to stay there. She claims that the Castle exercises a secret power over the villagers' lives and yet concludes in the last few pages of her book that it is a *Neutrum:*

> Le Château est neutre, il entérine les initiatives individuelles, prend note de ce qui se passe et se fait, mais n'intervient pas dans le cours des événements . . .

> The Castle is neutral, it ratifies individual initiatives, takes note of what happens and what is done, but it does not intervene in the course of events . . .

(pp. 203-04)

The reader of **Das Schloß** knows the Castle under three aspects. He knows it as K. experiences it; he knows it as K. interprets that experience; and he knows it as K. hears about it from other people. Or, to put it another way, the reader knows the Castle as K. encounters it directly; he knows it as K. projects his own preconceptions upon it; and he knows it, via K., as the object of local folklore. Again, Marthe Robert's work implies that she understands these distinctions, but because her very stimulating analysis of **Das Schloß** pays relatively little attention to narrative structure, she turns distinctions between categories of information into unresolved contradictions. Thus, she can look at the officials as gods, yet speak of the Castle administration as though it were nothing but a man-made organisation and affirm that the Castle is simply a product of K.'s fantasy.

K.'s interpretation of his experience of the Castle differs from the reality of his experience of the Castle in two ways. On the one hand, . . . K. evolves an image of the Castle as a malevolent, super-efficient and monolithically purposeful bureaucracy which is not legitimised by his actual experience of the Castle authorities. And on the other hand, K. is blind to the mythic dimension of the Castle authorities to which frequent reference has been made. Thus, despite the image of the Castle which exists in K.'s mind, no one tries to eject him from the village or deprive him of anything that is not properly his, and nobody engages in any struggle with K. which he has not initiated himself. Indeed, it is possible to go further and to say that for all K.'s grandiose mental picture of the Castle, that institution, as a bureaucratic machine, is singularly ineffectual. Administratively, it rarely intervenes in K.'s life, and when it does so, its interventions are usually pointless. Thus, from the point of view of administrative efficiency, Klamm's first letter is vague to the point of uselessness and his second letter meaningless. The choice of Barnabas as messenger is, administratively, a mockery and the assistants do anything but assist in their official capacity. From the point of view of officialdom, it seems immaterial whether K. co-operates with Momus or not. The Village Superintendent's office is one huge muddle. Erlanger's directive that Frieda should return to the *Herrenhof* taproom comes at a point when she has already done so. And just before K.'s interview with Bürgel, Frieda is said to be amazed that K. keeps talking instead of taking her by the arm—an indication perhaps that even at this late stage in the narrative, K. could have carried off Frieda again without any interference from the officials.

Furthermore, although the officials present themselves to K.'s experience as mythic beings who invite him to undergo elemental experiences of death and rebirth, K. is consistently blind to that aspect of his experience and neglects it when he has to interpret his experience. As has been argued, there is a pattern in K.'s experience of which K. himself is ignorant. Throughout the novel, the authorities seem to be trying to tell K. how it is possible to live fully and creatively within the Castle world, to be using official channels or everyday experience in order to communicate a message whose import is more than official and more than immediate. Thus, although Klamm's letters are administratively absurd, both of them tell K. something about himself as a person. Although the assistants and Barnabas are useless from an official point of view, both have something vital to say to K. Although Erlanger's directive is futile, what K. hears about Erlanger communicates something to him about the real meaning of his descent into the *Herrenhof.* Although K. learns little or nothing that is reliable about the workings of the Castle administration during his interview with the Village Superintendent, there are elements in his experience during that interview which impart much more fundamental information to K. about the status of the Castle bureaucracy.

Throughout **Das Schloß,** the officials present themselves to K. under two complementary aspects to both of which K. is blind. They are simultaneously the ineffectual administrators of a man-made bureaucratic system and *agents not allegories* of a power working actively for K.'s good. K.'s prejudices, however, prevent his interpretation of the Castle authorities from doing justice to their twofold nature and it is only when K. has died to his prejudices, rid himself of his obsessive image of the Castle that he becomes capable of developing an attitude towards the Castle which is appropriate to its ambiguous nature. Only after K. has penetrated to the 'goodness' which lies behind his image of a massive father-figure, does K. learn to be indifferent towards the officials as the executives of an administration and respectful towards them as 'the impenetrable executives of Providence'.

Many of the villagers whom K. meets seem similarly incapable of appreciating that the Castle operates at two levels. Indeed, some, notably Frieda and Gardena, are caught in the vicious trap of paying the kind of respect to the officials as men which is properly due to them only in their capacity as agents. Because Gardena is mesmerised by her memory of Klamm the man, she fails to see how Klamm, in his capacity as an agent of Providence, is working to free her from himself. Because Frieda has excessive respect for the institutions and taboos of the Castle world, she fails to see that the Castle may desire to liberate her, through a relationship with K., from those selfsame institutions and taboos. Because the village girls are flattered by the attentions of the officials as men, Amalia is censured for not sleeping with Sortini the man, and the real significance of Amalia's act, her implied rejection of the mythic experience of death and rebirth, seems to get overlooked. (Incidentally, this same confusion underlies Max Brod's interpretation of the Amalia episode. Because Sortini the man and Sortini the demi-god are merged in

Brod's mind, the refusal of Sortini's bed becomes *in itself* the refusal of divine grace. In contrast, it might have been more helpful to regard Amalia's refusal of Sortini's bed simply as one indication among many that Amalia is refusing to be human.) Because Mizzi regards the Castle administration as a necessary but man-made fiction and seems to serve it out of that spirit, she can only tell K. of the emptiness of that fiction. What she cannot do is tell K. of a creative power from beyond which works through that fiction. Finally, because the teacher's respect is directed to the officials as men and to their institutions as human institutions, he, like the *Herrenhof* landlady, is aggressive and authoritarian in his guardianship of those institutions. If Count Westwest, the all-too-human divinity, is dead, then the children must not know of it, for in the view of the teacher, besides the institutions whose central figure he is, there is nothing. Thus, if the world of the Castle and village looks bleak because of K.'s failure to comprehend adequately what he sees, then that world is made doubly bleak by the persistent failure of others of its inhabitants to understand that a power of good may flow through it secretly and work through them obliquely.

Surprisingly enough, in view of his damning judgement on the Castle [in his "The World of Franz Kafka" in *The Disinherited Mind*], Erich Heller seems to have recognised something of that secret power which flows through the Castle and its executives. Having suggested that Kafka's fictional world is the symbol of a real world which 'has been all but completely sealed off against any transcendental intrusion', and having demolished any suggestion that the Castle authorities can be equated with God, he goes on to say:

> . . . although the cursed rule of the castle is the furthest point of the world to which his wakeful mind can reach, there dawns, at its extreme boundaries, a light, half suspectingly perceived, half stubbornly ignored, that comes from things outside the scope of Klamm's authority.

The choice of the word 'light' is particularly apposite, for the light of which Heller speaks here is the light which appears from behind the Law in Kafka's parable *Vor dem Gesetz (Before the Law)* and the light which K. perceives in the blue of the sky behind the Castle buildings when first he sees them:

> Nun sah er oben das Schloß deutlich umrissen in der klaren Luft und noch verdeutlicht durch den alle Formen nachbildenden, in dünner Schicht überall liegenden Schnee.

> Der Turm hier oben . . . war ein einförmiger Rundbau, zum Teil gnädig von Efeu verdeckt, mit kleinen Fenstern, die jetzt in der Sonne aufstrahlten . . . , und einem söllerartigen Abschluß, dessen Mauerzinnen . . . sich in den blauen Himmel zackten.

> Now he could see the Castle above him clearly outlined in the clear air, its form made even more distinct by the thin layer of snow which lay everywhere, forming a crust over everything.

> The tower up above him here . . . was uniformly round, and, mercifully, concealed in part by

> ivy, pierced by small windows which were glittering now in the sun . . . , and topped by a kind of garret, the crenellation . . . of which stood out jaggedly against the blue sky.

But, having noticed that, it is possible to go further than Erich Heller is prepared to, and to say not simply that that light and that blueness are visible *behind* the Castle, at the farthest corner of the Castle world, but also that they are to be found *within* the world of the village. For instance, when K. reaches his point of greatest dereliction at the end of the eighth chapter, the narrator says explicitly that even after all the electric lights had been extinguished in the *Herrenhof* courtyard, a faint gleam of light still remained visible from the wooden gallery above, providing a certain point of stability for K.'s wandering gaze. Although K. then overlooks this one remaining gleam of light, its very existence seems to suggest that even after K. has done his utmost to antagonise the Castle authorities to the limit of their endurance and has cut off all official connections with them, they still refuse to break off all unofficial contact with him. Throughout *Das Schloß,* K., when he is out in the open and away from the harsh artificial glare which illuminates the inside of many of the village buildings, encounters similar 'guiding lights'. The assistants above all are associated with lanterns, and although their lanterns are described as 'schwankend' ('bobbing', 'swaying', 'unsteady'), the very nature of these lanterns seems to symbolise the fluctuating, sporadic and secret ways in which positive influences are at work on K.'s personality and within the world of the village. Similarly, it is perhaps not too much to suggest that the blue which K. sees in the eyes of Olga and the man who sits at table with his children at the end of the sixth chapter is also the blue which he had seen behind the jagged turrets of the Castle. [The critic adds in a footnote, "Surprisingly enough, we never hear the colour of Frieda's eyes."] Admittedly, it takes K., 'the man from the country', a long time to sense the presence of the 'beyond' amid the 'self-sufficient finitude' of the Castle world. Consequently, it takes the reader an even longer time to develop the same sense. Nevertheless, it is possibly that sense which caused . . . Marthe Robert to concede at one or two points that the Castle may not be entirely evil.

It is often assumed that the fact that K.'s perspective monopolises the foreground of *Das Schloß* is a cause for despair, an indication that nothing can be said about the world of the village and Castle with any certainty. If, however, the reader is prepared to devote close study to the text, then that very limitation may become an advantage. K. sees more than he is aware of seeing, and if the reader can accustom himself to looking for those elements in K.'s experience which K. himself overlooks or leaves out of account, then there appears, behind and through the mind of K., a world of mythic beings and archetypal events which work together for the benefit of those people who are open to their power. Perversely paradoxical though the claim may seem, Klamm, the assistants, Sortini and the rest are, in their strange ways, the agents of a power that is benevolent at the same time as they are, respectively, the bureaucrat who helps mesmerise the villagers, the tormentors of K. and the lecherous pursuer of the village women. Outrageous though the claim may seem, a power which invites people to become what they are meant to be is working upon K. through the labyrinthine medium of the ossified Castle bureaucracy, upon Frieda through her relationship with the stronger K. and upon Amalia through the apparently destructive medium of Sortini's lust. Absurd though the claim may seem, the neurotic, childish and frequently inhuman officials are the executives of a power of enlightenment, even if that light is, as often as not, obscured by the neuroses, infantilism and apparent inhumanity through which it has to travel before it can reach its fore-ordained destination.

The foregoing analysis should, if nothing else, have helped to modify the idea that it is a question in *Das Schloß* of a simple opposition between a 'good' heroic K. and a 'bad' Castle authority, or between a malevolently assertive K. and a godlike and benevolent Castle authority. In reality, the relationship between K. and the Castle authorities is much more complicated, and it is with a brief consideration of this relationship that this chapter will conclude.

If the preceding argument holds good, then K. should not be regarded as an existential hero on the Sartrean model, or rather, if he is regarded as such, this should be taken as an indication of the mistakenness of his way of life rather than its commendability. In ["Kafka und Sartres Existenzphilosophie," *Arcadia* 5 (1970)], a recent article in which he relates Kafka to Sartre's existential philosophy, Walter Sokel describes Sartre's picture of the 'human condition' and Kafka's image of man thrown into a world of tortured uncertainty, and concludes that there is a:

> . . . Gleichstimmigkeit der beiden Autoren und ihrer Seh- und Dar-stellungsweise der menschlichen Realität.

> . . . close similarity between the two authors and between the way in which they see and depict reality.

According to Sokel, K. is the archetypal existential hero, who, compelled to make sense of a world in which there is nothing given, no essence and no *a priori* meaning to existence, does so by creating an identity for himself:

> K., von dessen Vergangenheit und Motivierung wir nichts Bestimmtes kennen und daher auch nichts ihn Bestimmendes, ist identisch mit seinem Vorhaben. Abgesehen davon ist K. nichts.

> Er muß sich selbst eine Funktion, eine Stellung als Stelle, er muß sich selbst Natur und Wesen geben. Auch bei ihm geht Existenz der Essenz voran.

> We know nothing determinate about K.'s past and motivation: we therefore know nothing about the circumstances which have determined him. K. is identical with his intention and nothing apart from that.

> He has to give himself a function, a position as a place in life; he has to provide himself with a nature and an essence. For K. too, existence precedes essence.

By now, the weakness of this position should be obvious.

Sokel talks here as though K.'s perspective were identical with Kafka's: as though Kafka were endorsing K.'s way of seeing and doing things. In contrast, this book has tried to show that K.'s vision is initially much narrower than that of the narrator who stands behind him, and that, as the novel progresses, K. comes to realise that the world around him which he had assumed was a featureless nothingness has a secret life of its own, is full of hidden signs which could reveal to him, among other things, who he really is. Where Sartre and K. posit 'le néant', Kafka posits 'le tout'. Then again, it is not true to say that K. is identical with his intention. As has been shown, K. is more than an amalgam of conscious mind and intentional will, and as the novel progresses, so K. begins to discover something of that *a priori* essence whose existence Walter Sokel seems to doubt. Indeed, *Das Schloß* could be said to represent the complete rebuttal of Sartrean existentialism. Using as his central character a man whose assumptions, it is true, are remarkably like those of the Sartre who wrote *L'Etre et le Néant,* Kafka proceeds to demonstrate the inadequacy of those assumptions.

Nor is K. a Prometheus who has consciously come to free an oppressed community from a collection of omnipotent but flippant gods. K. arrives in the village with a propensity for struggle. He therefore projects his own aggressiveness onto the Castle and villagers without any justification for doing so. The result of this is that he derives a neurotic and precarious 'negative identity' from his fantastic struggle with a Castle which is, to a great extent, the product of his own imagination. Despite K.'s cryptic remarks about his final aims and his general air of messianic purposiveness, the fact is that K., far from wanting to break the hold of the Castle over himself and the villagers, actually needs to believe in the monolithic oppressiveness of the Castle so that his false identity as a victimised landsurveyor and his obsessive struggles may be legitimised and perpetuated. Out of this spirit, K. says to himself towards the end of the second chapter that he preferred those villagers who sent him away or were afraid of him to the Barnabas family who offered him hospitality. Whereas the antagonism of the former helped him to concentrate his powers, the friendliness of the latter diverted him and contributed to the dissipation of those powers. Appearances to the contrary, it actually makes life simpler for K. if he demonises the Castle, for by so doing, he can avoid seeing the complexity of the experiences which he undergoes in the village. This vicious circle, in all its childish simplicity, is only broken because the Castle authorities, being more than [what Klaus-Peter Philippi calls in his *Reflexion und Wirklichkeit: Untersuchungen zu Kafkas Roman, Das Schloß*] the 'subjective projection' of an 'absolute' aim of K.'s own', act as the agents of a power from beyond themselves which cuts into K.'s wilfulness and opens up what appears to be a hopeless situation.

Nevertheless, the Promethean, messianic image which K. presents to the world is convincing enough to worry some of the villagers and encourage others. The landladies and the teacher, those guardians of the myth of the Castle's absolute and unassailable authority, are seriously agitated by the implications of K.'s behaviour, for they know that if he is what he appears to be and persists in his struggles, then he will destroy Castle society. What they fail to realise, however, is that K. needs the Castle, that he has arrived in the village without any real purpose and that he himself is unaware of the threat which his behaviour poses to the system. K.'s unawareness shows itself fairly early on in the novel when he sees that he has disturbed Gardena in some way and begins, metaphorically speaking, to 'open the door' to some ultimate knowledge about the frailty of the apparently impregnable Castle authorities:

> '. . . was fürchten Sie also? [sagte K.] Sie fürchten doch nicht etwa—dem Unwissenden scheint alles möglich,' hier öffnete K. schon die Tür—, 'Sie fürchten doch nicht etwa für Klamm?'

> ' . . . so what are you afraid of ? [said K.] You're surely not afraid—everything seems possible to an ignorant man', at this point K. was already opening the door—, 'You're surely not afraid *for* Klamm?'

But Gardena does not admit that this is so, and because ultimate knowledge is not K.'s aim, he does not pursue the point and carries on much as he had done before. Similarly, in Chapter Nine, Gardena mentions that everyone is afraid 'um Klamm', 'for Klamm', and does their best to protect him. Then again, right at the end of the book, the *Herrenhof* landlady betrays her fear of K. and tries to elicit from him, by asking him about her clothes, just how far he is conscious of the implications of his earlier conduct. K., she says, is either a fool or a child or a very wicked, dangerous person. And although he may be nothing but the former, the possibility remains that he may be the latter, that he may be dedicated to discovering that the Castle is in one sense nothing and to liberating the village from its frail authority by means of that knowledge. But the *Herrenhof* landlady need not have worried, for one of the great ironies of *Das Schloß* is that K., despite his appearance of messianic assertiveness, is no messiah and all but completely innocent of the depth of fear that he has the power to cause in the minds of the guardians of the myth.

Conversely, during his stay in the village, K. meets several people who seem to need a messiah figure to liberate them from the constrictions of village society. Although Frieda has been sent by Klamm to 'still K.'s hunger' (during their first night on the *Herrenhof* floor, she sings a little song to K. just as the collective voice of the Castle sings a song down the telephone and the blue-eyed father sings to his children), she discovers that she needs K. to exorcise her childishness just as much as K. needs her love, and immediately before their final parting, K. remarks to Frieda on his ability to free her from illusions. The Barnabas family, too, regard K. as a kind of saviour. From the outset, this family, alone of the villagers, welcome K., and Olga tells him that he has come to mean almost more to her than all of Barnabas' work in the Castle. To quote Wilhelm Emrich [in his *Franz Kafka*]:

> K. hat die Aufgabe, Olga und Amalia ins Leben zurückzuführen, ohne ihre höhere kritische Bewußtseinsstufe zu opfern.

> K. has the task of bringing Olga and Amalia back into life without sacrificing their higher critical faculties.

During the interview with Gardena, K. cuts through the self-deceptions and illusions with which she has palliated her inner pain for years in a way that none of the villagers could, and young Hans Brunswick implies that he regards K. as a man who will do great things. When K. first looks at the peasants in the second chapter, he feels that they want something which he does not understand, and although it may be a delusion, it is just possible that they half-expect K. to act as a kind of saviour in Castle society. Furthermore, more than one hint is given that the officials themselves would like K. to tear down the dead structures of the Castle in the same way that the messengers in Kafka's *Betrachtung* would like someone to put an end to their meaningless official lives. Bürgel describes the possibility of the destruction of the Castle apparatus with something of the lascivious eagerness of a voluptuary contemplating an orgasm, and concludes:

> . . . wie wird es aber nachher sein, wenn es vorüber ist, die Partei, gesättigt und unbekümmert, uns verläßt und wir dastehen, allein, wehrlos im Angesicht unseres Amtsmißbrauches—das ist gar nicht auszudenken! Und trotzdem sind wir glücklich. Wie selbstmörderisch das Glück sein kann!

> . . . but how will it be afterwards, when it is all over, when, sated and free of care, the applicant leaves us and we stand there, alone, defenceless in the face of our misuse of official power—that does not bear thinking about! And yet we are happy. How suicidal happiness can be!

When K. finds himself in the corridor outside after this interview, one of the officials begins to crow like a cock, a sound which perhaps means that the officials are both celebrating K.'s awakening *and* pointing to the possibility that they have been betrayed. The man who can cause them so much discomfort has, in the end, failed to destroy them. But, despite the hints that are given him, K. is as impervious to the fact that the village needs a kind of messianic figure as he is to the fears of the landladies that he may be one. Because he is obsessed by his egocentric struggle with an opponent who is largely imaginary, K. is unaware of the wider possibilities inherent in that struggle. Another of the great ironies of *Das Schloß* is that the village seems to need a man of K.'s intelligence who could pierce the mystification which surrounds the Castle authorities, but K. has neither the vision to see the necessity of that task, nor the sense of responsibility to those who would suffer as a result of such surgery, nor the compassion towards those who need a healing herb that is not 'bitter' [The critic adds in a footnote, "The reference is to K.'s long conversation with Hans Brunswick, during which it transpires that K. has considerable abilities as a doctor and was known as 'the bitter herb' before he came to the village."]. Thus, the bowed heads and averted eyes which K. uncomprehendingly encounters as he moves through the world of the Castle perhaps signify respect for him as a potential messiah, fear of him as a potential destroyer of the system and shame for him as one who is ignorant both of his potential ability and of his potential destructiveness.

The relationship between K. and the world of the Castle seems therefore to have two levels. At one level, because the Castle is the indirect agent of a benevolent power, its representatives seek to turn K. from his aimless, solipsistic striving and to reconcile him with himself and the village. But, because the Castle is, at a second level, a decrepit human institution, its officials secretly desire K. to become aware of the revolutionary implications of his conduct and to destroy their bureaucratic system which is, by any standards, rotten. These two levels interpenetrate throughout the novel. On the one hand, the Castle does not exist and K. is an adult in a world of children because his conduct suggests, deceptively as it turns out, that he realises this metaphysical truth. On the other hand, the Castle does exist and K. is a child in a world of adults because he wilfully refuses to see the transcendent quality of benevolence which operates obliquely, through the Castle authorities and the institutions of the village.

Marthe Robert writes of **Das Schloß:**

> Entre toutes les possibilités que lui offre le Château, Kafka ne sait pas plus que K. ce qu'il décide de choisir: il reste en suspens, aussi clairvoyant qu'irrésolu, condamné à tout comprendre sans jamais prendre un parti. De là vient la beauté si captivante de son œuvre, mais aussi le sens réactionnaire, si ce n'est politiquement dangéreux de son message.

> Kafka has no more idea than K. which of the possibilities offered him by the Castle he will decide to choose. He remains in suspense, as clearsighted as he is irresolute, condemned to understand everything without every committing himself to anything. From that arises not only the captivating beauty of his work but also the reactionary and even politically dangerous tendency of its message.

Although it is not all difficult to see why Mme Robert should have passed this judgement on the novel, it may be somewhat misplaced. K., it is true, chooses nothing, but there is a very real sense in which events and experiences choose K. in order to bring about a change in his personality, and an equally real sense in which the agents of this change are the elusive beings who inhabit the Castle. If then **Das Schloß** is, politically speaking, a conservative and even a reactionary novel, it needs to be understood that its conservatism is of a very peculiar order. During his career as a writer, Kafka developed a very subtle sense that, despite all evidence to the contrary, the world as it stood had a life of its own, that there was, in the end, a rightness about the way in which the world was moving, and that the greatest mistakes a man could make were to ignore or to impede that movement. Hence the question mark which finally hangs over **Das Schloß.** There is a sense in which the world of the Castle is in need of a social revolution, and yet, Kafka seems to suggest, perhaps that action would have the effect of irreparably destroying the channels through which a kind of grace still flows. The village community is in need of a messianic figure—but it needs someone who, unlike K., understands the secret workings of that community, knows that a revolutionary movement might disrupt or interfere with those workings and is prepared to accept the responsibility which such knowledge brings. In an indirect way, **Das Schloß** is about

the problem of revolution and the strange conclusion that Kafka seems to reach is that revolution can only take place on the basis of a willingness to accept what already exists. K., for most of the novel, does not possess this quality of acceptance and learns it only when he is near his death. Thus, for the want of a revolutionary who understands the depths of the problem of revolution, the Castle, ramshackle yet transparent, all-too-human and yet the executive of a kind of Providence, is permitted to stand. (pp. 205-18)

> *Richard Sheppard, in his* On Kafka's Castle: A Study, *Barnes & Noble Books, 1973, 234 p.*

Erich Heller   (essay date 1975)

[*Heller was a Czechoslovakian-born English educator, critic, and editor who wrote extensively on German literature. In the following excerpt, Heller contests the critical interpretations of* The Castle *as a religious allegory.*]

It has been said that **The Castle** is a religious allegory, a kind of modern *Pilgrim's Progress;* that the unattainable building is the abode of divine law and divine grace. This would seem to be a misapprehension reflecting a profound religious confusion, a loss of all sureness of religious discrimination. Where there is a spiritual famine, *anything* that is of the spirit may taste like bread from Heaven, and minds imbued with psychology and "comparative religion" may find the difference negligible between Prometheus, clamped to the rock, and the martyrdom of a Christian saint; between an ancient curse and the grace that makes a new man.

The Castle is as much a religious allegory as a photographic likeness of the devil in person could be said to be an allegory of Evil. Every allegory has an opening into the rarefied air of abstractions and is furnished with signposts pointing to an ideal concept beyond. But **The Castle** is a terminus of soul and mind, a *non plus ultra* of existence. In an allegory the author plays a kind of guessing game with his reader, if he does not actually provide the answers himself; but there is no key to **The Castle.** It is true that its reality does not precisely correspond to what is commonly understood in the "positive" world as real, namely, neutral sense perceptions of objects and, neatly separated from them, feelings (hence our most authentic and realistic intellectual pursuits—natural sciences and psychology; and our besetting sins—the ruthlessness of acquisitive techniques and sentimentality). In Kafka's novels there is no such division between the external sphere and the domain of inwardness, and therefore no such reality. There is only the tragic mythology of the absolutely incongruous relationship between the two worlds.

Kafka's creations are at the opposite pole to the writings of that type of romantic poet, the true poetical representative of the utilitarian age, who distills from a spiritually more and more sterile external reality those elements which are still of some use to the passions, or else withdraws from its barren fields into the greenhouse vegetation of inwardness. The author of **The Castle** does not select for evocative purposes, nor does he project his inner experience into carefully chosen timeless settings. Kafka does not, after the manner of Joyce, give away, in the melodious flow of intermittent articulation, the secret bedroom conversations which self conducts with self. There are no private symbols in his work, such as would be found in symbolist writing, no crystallized fragments of inner sensations charged with mysterious significance; nor is there, after the fashion of the expressionists, any rehearsing of new gestures of the soul, meant to be more in harmony with the new rhythm of modern society. Instead of all this, the reader is faced with the shocking spectacle of a miraculously sensitive soul incapable of being either reasonable or cynical or resigned or rebellious about the prospect of eternal damnation. The world which this soul perceives is unmistakably "real," a castle that is a castle and "symbolizes" merely what all castles symbolize: power and authority; a bureaucracy drowning in a deluge of forms and files; an obscure hierarchy of officialdom making it impossible ever to find the man authorized to deal with a particular case; officials who work overtime and yet get nowhere; numberless interviews which never are to the point; inns where the peasants meet, and barmaids who serve the officials. In fact, it is an excruciatingly familiar world, but reproduced by a creative intelligence endowed with the knowledge that it is a world damned forever. Shakespeare once made one of his characters say: "They say miracles are past; and we have our philosophical persons, to make modern and familiar, things supernatural and causeless. Hence it is that we make trifles of terrors; ensconcing ourselves in seeming knowledge, when we should submit ourselves to an unknown fear." In Kafka we have the abdication of the philosophical persons. (pp. 102-04)

The Castle is not an allegorical, but a symbolic novel. A discussion of the difference could easily deteriorate into pedantry, the more so as, in common and literary usage, the terms are applied rather arbitrarily. It will, however, help our understanding of Kafka's work if we distinguish, in using these two terms, two different modes of experience and expression. I shall therefore define my own use of these words.

The symbol is what it represents; the allegory represents what, in itself, it is *not*. The terms of reference of an allegory are abstractions; a symbol refers to something specific and concrete. The statue of a blindfolded woman, holding a pair of scales, is an *allegory* of Justice; bread and wine are, for the Christian communicant, *symbols* of the Body and Blood of Christ. [The author adds in a footnote: "I should like to beg the indulgence of the reader for disregarding the established theological terminology. The following discussion will, I hope, to some extent justify my apparent arbitrariness, which I do not wish to maintain outside the scope of this particular argument."] Thus an allegory must always be rationally translatable; whether a symbol is translatable or not depends on the fundamental agreement of society on the question of what kind of experience, out of the endless range of possible human experience, it regards as significant. The possibility of allegorizing will only vanish with the last man capable of *thinking in abstractions* and of forming *images* of them; yet the validity of symbols depends not on rational operations but on complex experiences in which thought and feeling merge in the act of spiritual comprehension. The sacra-

mental symbols, for instance, would become incommunicable among a race of men who no longer regard the life, death, and resurrection of Christ as spiritually relevant *facts*. An allegory, being the imaginary representation of something abstract, is, as it were, doubly unreal: whereas the symbol, in being what it represents, possesses a double reality. (pp. 107-08)

There are, however, allegorical elements to be found in *The Castle:* for instance, the names of many of the characters. The hero himself, who is introduced with the bare initial K. (undoubtedly once again an autobiographical hint—the novel was originally drafted in the first person— and at the same time, through its very incompleteness, suggesting an unrealized, almost anonymous personality), is a Land Surveyor. Kafka's choice of this profession for his hero clearly has a meaning. The German for it is *Landvermesser,* and its verbal associations are manifold. The first is, of course, the Land Surveyor's professional activity, consisting precisely in what K. desperately desires and never achieves: to produce a workable order within clearly defined boundaries and limits of earthly life, and to find an acceptable compromise between conflicting claims of possession. But *Vermesser* also alludes to *Vermessenheit,* hubris; to the adjective *vermessen,* audacious; to the verb *sich vermessen,* to commit an act of spiritual pride, *and* also to apply the wrong measure, make a mistake in measurement. The most powerful official of the Castle (for K. the highest representative of authority) is called Klamm, a sound producing a sense of anxiety amounting almost to claustrophobia, suggesting pincers, chains, clamps, but also a person's oppressive silence. The messenger of the Castle (as it turns out later, self-appointed and officially never recognized) has the name of Barnabas, the same as that man of Cyprus who, though not one of the Twelve, came to rank as an apostle; "Son of Consolation," or "Son of Exhortation," is the Biblical meaning of his name, and it is said that his exhortation was of the inspiring kind, and so built up faith. And the Barnabas of the novel is indeed a son of consolation, if only in the desperately ironical sense that his family, whom the curse of the Castle has cast into the lowest depths of misery and wretchedness, in vain expects deliverance through his voluntary service for the authority. To K., however, his messages, in all their obscurity and pointlessness, seem the only real link with the Castle, an elusive glimmer of hope, a will-o'-the-wisp of faith. Barnabas's counterpart is Momus, the village secretary of Klamm and namesake of that depressing creature, the son of Night, whom the Greek gods authorized to find fault with all things. In the novel it is he whose very existence seems the denial of any hope which Barnabas may have roused in K. Frieda (peace) is the girl through whose love K. seeks to reach the goal of his striving; Bürgel (diminutive of *Bürge,* guarantor) is the name of the little official who offers the solution without K.'s even noticing the chance; and the secretary, through whom K. does expect to achieve something and achieves nothing, is called Erlanger (citizen of the town of Erlangen, but also suggestive of *erlangen,* to attain, achieve).

This discussion of names provides an almost complete synopsis of the slender plot of *The Castle.* Someone, a man whose name begins with K., and of whom we know no more, neither whence he comes nor what his past life has been, arrives in a village which is ruled by a Castle. He believes that he has been appointed Land Surveyor by the authorities. The few indirect contacts that K. succeeds in establishing with the Castle—a letter he receives, a telephone conversation he overhears, yet another letter, and above all the fact that he is joined by two assistants whom the rulers have assigned to him—*seem* to confirm his appointment. Yet he himself is never quite convinced, and he never relaxes in his efforts to ascertain it. He feels he must penetrate to the very center of authority and wring from it a kind of ultra-final confirmation of his claim. Until then he yields, in paralyzed despair, broken by only momentary outbursts of rebellious pride, to the inarticulate yet absolutely self-assured refusal of the village to acknowledge him as their Land Surveyor: "You've been taken on as Land Surveyor, as you say, but, unfortunately, we have no need of a Land Surveyor. There wouldn't be the least use for one here. The frontiers of our little estates are marked out and all officially recorded. So what should we do with a Land Surveyor?" says the village representative to him.

K.'s belief appears, from the very outset, to be based on both truth and illusion. It is Kafka's all but unbelievable achievement to force, indeed to frighten, the reader into unquestioning acceptance of this paradox, presented with ruthless realism and irresistible logic. Truth and illusion are mingled in such a way in K.'s belief that he is deprived of all order of reality. Truth is permanently on the point of taking off its mask and revealing itself as illusion, illusion in constant danger of being verified as truth. It is the predicament of a man who, endowed with an insatiable appetite for the absolute certainty that transcends all half-truths, relativities, and compromises of everyday life, finds himself in a world robbed of all spiritual possessions. Thus he cannot accept the world—the village—without first attaining to that certainty, and he cannot be certain without first accepting the world. Yet every contact with the world makes a mockery of his search, and the continuance of his search turns the world into a mere encumbrance. After studying the first letter from the Castle, K. contemplates his dilemma, "whether he preferred to become a village worker with a distinctive but merely apparent connection with the Castle, or an ostensible village worker whose real occupation was determined through the medium of Barnabas." From the angle of the village, all K.'s contacts with the Castle are figments of his imagination: "You haven't once up till now come into real contact with our authorities. All those contacts have been illusory, but owing to your ignorance of the circumstances you take them to be real." The Castle, on the other hand, seems to take no notice whatever of the reality of K.'s miserable village existence. In the midst of his suffering the indignity of being employed as a kind of footman to the schoolmaster, and never having come anywhere near working as a Land Surveyor, he receives the following letter from Klamm: "The surveying work which you have carried out thus far has been appreciated by me. . . . Do not slacken in your efforts! Carry your work to a fortunate conclusion. Any interruption would displease me. . . . I shall not forget you." From all this it would appear that it is, in fact, the village that disobeys the will of the Castle, while de-

feating K. with the powerful suggestion that he misunderstands the intentions of authority. And yet the authority seems to give its blessing to the defiance of the village and to punish K. for his determination to act in accordance with the letter of its orders. In his fanatical obedience it is really he who rebels against the Castle, whereas the village, in its matter-of-fact refusal, lives the life of the Law.

Kafka represents the absolute reversal of German idealism. If it is Hegel's final belief that in the Absolute truth and existence are one, for Kafka it is precisely through the Absolute that they are forever divided. Truth and existence are mutually exclusive. From his early days it was the keenest wish of Kafka the artist to convey this in works of art; to write in such a way that life, in all its deceptively convincing reality, would be seen as a dream and a nothing before the Absolute: " . . . somewhat as if one were to hammer together a table with painful and methodical technical efficiency, and simultaneously do nothing at all, and not in such a way that people could say: 'Hammering a table together is nothing to him,' but rather 'Hammering a table together is really hammering a table together to him, but at the same time it is nothing,' whereby certainly the hammering would have become still bolder, still surer, still more real and, if you will, still more senseless." This is how Kafka, in the series of aphorisms "He," describes the vision of artistic accomplishment which hovered before his mind's eye when, as a young man, he sat one day on the slopes of the Laurenziberg in Prague. Has he, in his later works, achieved this artistic justification of nonentity? Not quite: what was meant to become the lifting of a curse through art, became the artistically perfect realization of it, and what he dreamed of making into something as light as a dream, fell from his hands with the heaviness of a nightmare. Instead of a vindication of nothingness, he achieved the portrayal of the most cunningly vindictive unreality.

It is hard to understand how *The Castle* could possibly be called a religious allegory with a pilgrim of the type of Bunyan's as its hero. Pilgrimage? On the contrary, the most oppressive quality of Kafka's work is the unshakable stability of its central situation. It takes place in a world that knows of no motion, no change, no metamorphosis—unless it be the transformation of a human being into an insect. Its caterpillars never turn into butterflies, and when the leaves of a tree tremble it is not due to the wind: it is the stirring of a serpent coiled round its branches. Pilgrim or not, there is no progress to be watched in *The Castle*, unless we agree to call progress what Kafka describes in "A Little Fable" as the "progress" of the mouse: " 'Alas,' said the mouse, 'the world is growing smaller every day. At the beginning it was so big that I was afraid, I kept running and running, and I was glad when at last I saw walls far away to the right and left, but these long walls have narrowed so quickly that I am in the last chamber already, and there in the corner stands the trap that I must run into.' 'You only need to change your direction,' said the cat, and ate it up." It has been said that Kafka has this in common with Bunyan, "that the goal and the road indubitably exist, and that the necessity to find them is urgent." Only the second point is correct. Indeed, so urgent is it for Kafka to discover the road and reach the goal that life seems impossible without this achievement. But do road and goal exist? "There is a goal, but no way; what we call the way is only wavering," is what Kafka says about it in "Reflections on Sin, Suffering, Hope, and the True Way." And is there really a goal for him? This is the answer that Kafka gives to himself in "He": "He feels imprisoned on this earth, he feels constricted; the melancholy, the impotence, the sickness, the feverish fancies of the captive afflict him; no comfort can comfort him, since it is merely comfort, gentle head-splitting comfort glozing the brutal fact of imprisonment. But if he is asked what he actually wants he cannot reply, for—that is one of his strongest proofs—he has no conception of freedom."

Kafka's hero is the man who *believes* in absolute freedom but cannot have any conception of it because he *exists* in a world of slavery. Therefore it is not grace and salvation that he seeks, but either his right or a bargain with the powers. "I don't want any act of favor from the Castle, but my rights," says K. in his interview with the village representative. But convinced of the futility of this expectation, his real hope is based on Frieda, his fiancée and Klamm's former mistress, whom K. is obviously prepared to hand back to him "for a price."

In K.'s relationship to Frieda the European story of romantic love has found its epilogue. It is the solid residue left behind by the evaporated perfume of romance, revealing its darkest secret. In romantic love, as it has dominated a vast section of European literature ever since the later Middle Ages, individualism, emerging from the ruins of a common spiritual order, has found its most powerful means of transcendence. The spiritually more and more autonomous (therefore more and more lonely) individual worships Eros and his twin deity within the romantic imagination, Death, as the only gods capable of breaking down the barriers of his individualist isolation. Therefore love becomes tragedy: overcharged with unmanageable spiritual demands it needs must surge ahead of any human relationship. In its purest manifestations, romantic love is a glorious disaster of the soul, carrying frustration in its wake. For what the romantic lover seeks is not really the beloved. Intermixed with his erotic craving, inarticulate, diffuse, and yet dominating it, is the desire for spiritual salvation. Even a "happy ending" spells profound disillusionment for the romantic expectation. Perhaps it is Strindberg, deeply admired by Kafka, who wrote the last chapter of its history. It is certainly Kafka who wrote its postscript.

For K. loves Frieda—if he loves her at all—entirely for Klamm's sake. This is not only implied in the whole story of K. and Frieda, but explicitly stated by Kafka in several passages that he later deleted, probably because their directness seemed to him incompatible with the muted meaning of the book. As an indictment of K., it is contained in the protocol about his life in the village which Momus has drawn up, and in which K. is accused of having made up to Frieda out of a "calculation of the lowest sort": because he believed that in her he would win a mistress of Klamm's and so possess "a pledge for which he can demand the highest price." On the margin of the protocol there was also "a childishly scrawled drawing, a man

with a girl in his arms. The girl's face was buried in the man's chest, but the man, who was much the taller, was looking over the girl's shoulders at a sheet of paper he had in his hands and on which he was joyfully inscribing some figures." But perhaps still more conclusive than Momus's clearly hostile interpretation is another deleted passage giving K.'s own reflections on his love for Frieda:

> And then immediately, before there was any time to think, Frieda had come, and with her the belief, which it was impossible to give up entirely even today, that through her mediation an almost physical relationship to Klamm, a relationship so close that it amounted almost to a whispering form of communication, had come about, of which for the present only K. knew, which however needed only a little intervention, a word, a glance, in order to reveal itself primarily to Klamm, but then too to everyone, as something admittedly incredible which was nevertheless, through the compulsion of life, the compulsion of the loving embrace, a matter of course. . . . What . . . was he without Frieda? A nonentity, staggering along after . . . will-o'-the-wisps. . . .

The desperate desire for spiritual certainty is all that is left of romantic love. K. *wills* his love for Frieda because he *wills* his salvation. He is a kind of Pelagius believing that he "can if he ought," yet living in a relentlessly predestined world. This situation produces a theology very much after the model of Gnostic and Manichaean beliefs. The incarnation is implicitly denied in an unmitigated loathing of "determined" matter, and the powers which rule are perpetually suspected of an alliance with the devil because they have consented to the creation of such a loathsome world. Heaven is at least at seven removes from the earth, and only begins where no more neighborly relations are possible. There are no real points of contact between divinity and the earth, which is not even touched by divine emanation. Reality is the sovereign domain of strangely unangelic angels, made up of Evil and hostility. The tedious task of the soul is, with much wisdom of initiation and often with cunning diplomacy, gradually to bypass the armies of angels and the strong points of Evil, and finally to slip into the remote kingdom of light.

The Castle of Kafka's novel is, as it were, the heavily fortified garrison of a company of Gnostic demons, successfully holding an advanced position against the maneuvers of an impatient soul. There is no conceivable idea of divinity which could justify those interpreters who see in the Castle the residence of "divine law and divine grace." Its officers are totally indifferent to good if they are not positively wicked. Neither in their decrees nor in their activities is there any trace of love, mercy, charity, or majesty. In their icy detachment they inspire certainly no awe, but fear and revulsion. Their servants are a plague to the village, "a wild, unmanageable lot, ruled by their insatiable impulses . . . their scandalous behavior knows no limits," an anticipation of the blackguards who were to become the footmen of European dictators rather than the office boys of a divine ministry. Compared to the petty and apparently calculated torture of this tyranny, the gods of

Shakespeare's indignation who "kill us for their sport" are at least majestic in their wantonness.

From the very beginning there is an air of indecency, indeed of obscenity, about the inscrutable rule of the Castle. A newcomer in the village, K. meets the teacher in the company of children. K. asks him whether he knows the Count and is surprised at the negative answer: " 'What, you don't know the Count?' 'Why should I?' replies the teacher in a low tone, and adds aloud in French: 'Please remember that there are innocent children present.' " And, indeed, what an abhorrent rule it is! The souls of women seem to be allowed to enter the next realm if they surrender their bodies, as a sort of pass, to the officials. They are then married off to some nincompoop in the village, with their drab existence rewarded only by occasional flashes of voluptuously blissful memories of their sacrificial sins. Damnation is their lot if they refuse, as happens in the case of Amalia, Barnabas's sister, who brought degradation upon herself and her family by declining the invitation of the official Sortini.

No, the Castle does not represent, as some early interpreters believed, divine guidance or even Heaven itself. It is for K. something that is to be conquered, something that bars his way into a purer realm. K.'s antagonism to the Castle becomes clear from the very first pages of the book. This is how he responds to the first telephone conversation about his appointment which, in his presence, is conducted between the village and the authorities:

> K. pricked up his ears. So the Castle had recognized him as the Land Surveyor. That was unpropitious for him, on the one hand, for it meant that the Castle was well informed about him, had estimated all the probable chances and was taking up the challenge with a smile. On the other hand, however, it was quite propitious, for if his interpretation were right, they had underestimated his strength, and he would have more freedom of action than he had dared to hope.
>
> (pp. 115-25)

Erich Heller, in his Franz Kafka, *The Viking Press, 1975, 140 p.*

Frederick R. Karl   (essay date 1977)

[*Karl is an American critic who has written extensively on English literature and literary figures of the eighteenth, nineteenth, and twentieth centuries. He is particularly known for his studies of the life and works of Joseph Conrad. In the following excerpt, Karl studies the interplay of time and space in Kafka's novels* The Trial *and* The Castle.]

Enclosure tells us that in stasis, inertness, paralysis, hesitation, hovering between life and death there is an entire life and that that life is by no means negative. Withdrawal does not mean loss of personal self, nor does refusal deny any alternate existence. Resistance to life without any apparent resolution of conflicts can prove meaningful to the individual. Such an "alternate" culture of unresolved elements has its own directions, its own space-time considerations, its own myths and interrelationships. Narcissism, self-reflected images, mirror-reflections, refractions of reality, retreat into holes and rooms—all of these suggest enclosure; and they appear to establish their own line of development, even their own matter and spirit. Enclosure, we should stress, is as separated from "nil," the "void," and "nothingness" as it is from the active life.

Enclosure provides its own countering culture. Its space and time considerations have affinities with those in myth, archetypes, the experience of the shaman, nightmare and memory—although enclosure remains distinct from all of them. It thrives on countermovement, alternate experiences, withdrawal, burrowing. Unlike Existentialism, which appears superficially similar, it involves no leap into belief, no sudden break in the thread of existence. It is not death-oriented, although burrowing does suggest death. It can be heroical, while mocking heroism. *What is certain:* enclosure as it develops fully resists action, progress, activity.

In Proust and Kafka, enclosure reaches its highest creative point, and in Kafka, in particular, it has profound reverberations in cultural terms; for such enclosure represents those time and space considerations which have dominated our thought since the eighteenth century.

One of the more remarkable passages in **The Trial** occurs when Joseph K. visits the painter Titorelli. Like the later scene in the Cathedral, this long interlude with Titorelli, and the passages leading up to it, is archetypal Kafka. Altogether, they combine nearly every aspect of his work: time and space elements removed from our usual temporal-spatial expectations; the sense of enstiflement and suffocation; a surrealism of scene and personage; the suggestion of Hades, hell, Lucifer, and Heaven; the sense of individual will trying to impose itself on a situation that defies change, development, or improvement; the presence of an artist figure—a landscape painter who lives in a stuffy attic; the caged quality of the protagonist, a functionary who functions in vain.

Kafka needed in this scene the physical equivalent of those choices Titorelli will later present to Joseph, an objective correlation of K.'s decisions. The initial description of Titorelli's locale leads in by way of images of hell: "disgusting yellow liquid," fleeing rats, a shrieking infant, untended, a deafening din from the tinsmith's workshop, apprentices beating on a sheet of tin which casts "a pallid light," stifling air, the presence of the scurrying children, led by a "slightly hunchbacked" thirteen-year-old. Salvation, Joseph K. had led himself to believe, lies here. It is typical Kafka despair: deeply urban, full of corruption of civilization and human values, not unlike an animal's noisome lair, replete with his detestation of human progress and modernity. Neither light nor space nor expansive time enters here. Yet Joseph K. is seeking a painter.

Even before K. enters Titorelli's suffocating quarters, we have noted Kafka's denial of time and space. Once into the scene, however, he does not simply negate, but does so against a backdrop of the painter's "wild heathscapes," the outside world that exists somewhere as a lost paradise. K. can only obtain the wild heathscape through payment; he cannot experience it. The room itself—from which Joseph had intended to "soar" beyond the confines of his case—only further confines his case. A mockery of a room for a painter, its one window allows almost no light, no beyond.

The spatial conception of the painter's attic is a standard one in Kafka. That is, space *up* is always negated by space enclosed. The former may be a room at the top of something—building, warehouse, tower—but it is, also, space denied. There is no vista, no horizon, no sense of things opening out. We shall see this point demonstrated most obviously in *The Castle,* which dominates the village and is situated somewhere in heaven, and yet its very spatiality in the distance is negated by the stuffy rooms which, apparently, lead toward it, or so K. thinks. Kafka never gives us a true feeling of space but presents only enough of it for purposes of denial. Thus, *The Castle* finds its counterpart in **"The Burrow," "The Investigations of a Dog,"** even in **"The Great Wall of China."**

In a curious play of spatial-temporal concepts, Joseph K. in the painter's studio is swallowed up not by immensity and endless horizons, but by a "wretched little hole." Titorelli's attic is representative of all space in *The Trial.* Few critics have commented upon Joseph K.'s bank as a locale, and yet it, too, consists of a maze of rooms, a burrow, even though the end function of the bank is to convey limitless wealth to a seemingly unending procession of clients. Once again, we have a large, apparently ceaseless organization or function embodied in tiny stages, small rooms, cramped quarters. Joseph K. in his bank is little different, given the physical change, from Gregor Samsa in his room. Double doors, openings, entrances, exits, labyrinths, paths, roads and their like dominate. The endlessness of space and sweeps of time become enclosed spatiality and severely restricted temporality.

In these and other ways, Titorelli's attic is the perfect setting for the choices the painter will offer Joseph K. We note that K.'s deepest insights into his case come from the painter and in that stuffy attic. For the first time, he is presented with alternatives, and what had before been incomprehensible chaos becomes, now, comprehensible chaos. Also, when K. does learn of the three alternatives, he is so uncomfortable, so near suffocation, he barely listens. Titorelli has to keep repeating. The alternatives are themselves enclosure patterns, since the choices offered are not really choices. The three possibilities are "definite acquittal, ostensible acquittal, and indefinite postponement." The first is out of the question, so that choice fixes on the other two. The second, ostensible acquittal, calls for great but temporary concentration, whereas the last, indefinite postponement, is less taxing, but requires steady application. All involve escape; all are traps. Even with knowledge, K. is in a limbo. For our immediate purposes, the three have spatial-temporal dimensions indistinguishable from their conditions.

The placement of these choices in the attic indicates a correlation between the space and time dimension of the locale and the space and time considerations implicit in decision making. Part of the suffocation we feel in Kafka's work is not merely physical; it extends to the intimate relationship between locale and content. His is a philosophy

of life stretched out between points that go everywhere and nowhere. Titorelli, after explaining these choices, then opens up startling new vistas of the case for Joseph K. A new arrest is possible at any time after acquittal. Foreshortening and distancing are implicit in Titorelli's impressions: "Even while they are pronouncing the first acquittal [he tells Joseph] the Judges foresee the possibility of the new arrest."

As befitting a painter, Titorelli speaks of "distant" prospects and "foreshortened" ones, "vistas" and "immediate" objects. He speaks of not letting the "case out of your sight"; he tells Joseph to keep the case going "only in the small circle to which it has been artificially restricted." He mentions that the "Judges foresee" new possibilities and vast considerations, which they can deny. Being caught in such uncertain dimensions reinforces the terrible loneliness and isolation every Kafka protagonist experiences despite his considerable activity. With space and time so different from his expectations, he walks the paths of a world which lacks color, texture, and affect. The landscape of a Kafka novel is absolutely flat, even though there are steps, buildings, and attics. Only sea level counts.

A scene paralleling Titorelli's attic occurs in the Cathedral. In the first, the spatiality of the case is denied by the stuffiness of the quarters; in the second, the constrictions of the case are dwarfed by the spatiality of the quarters. In the attic, Joseph K. seemed too large for the pettiness of the choices; in the Cathedral, he is too small for the spaciousness of the opportunity. Kafka is opening up and closing down, closing down and opening up, like a gigantic accordion expanding and contracting to fit the particular music. The sequences introductory to the Cathedral scene indicate Joseph's hesitance to leave his work even for a short time, for fear he will not be permitted to return. Such indecision, common in Kafka's fiction, is part of Joseph's allegiance to the cramped quarters of the bank, his fear of the unknown, and his rejection of a spatial dimension, in the form of the Cathedral, that might "open up" his case. As is typical of a Kafka protagonist, he grips tenaciously and obsessively the very thing that will diminish him, a trait quite characteristic of both neurotic and healthy behavior. As much as Joseph wishes to find the court, he is pleased the court cannot find him.

The Cathedral experience is filled with uncertainties. The Italian whom he is to meet speaks a dialect Joseph cannot understand—part of the synesthesia which accompanies Kafka's derangement of spatial-temporal dimensions. This verbal isolation is a foreshadowing of the physical isolation Joseph will experience when he enters the Cathedral Square and the Cathedral itself. It is Kafka's way of augmenting the spatiality of the Cathedral, which already diminishes Joseph, and presenting a dimension of endless, ahistorical, primitive time sequences—the Cathedral as having existed since time began and as continuing long after Joseph's demise. Kafka writes that " . . . the size of the Cathedral struck him as bordering on the limit of what human beings could bear." Yet it encloses Joseph, for the priest who calls him, as if from Mount Sinai, identifies himself as a prison chaplain; and we are suddenly involved in the evocation of space and time denied, the familiar prison image that runs throughout Kafka's work. Revelation may mean Armageddon.

The Cathedral takes on the Paradise-Hades aspect of enclosure: what may offer salvation is, equally, the source of eternal damnation. The machine that tenders eternal bliss also imposes excruciating physical suffering. The priest, who is God's representative, is a chaplain of prisons. Joseph is caught by his case at every turn, and the spatiality of the Cathedral, as well as its endless temporal dimension, is negated by what fills it. It is a limitless shell or maze stuffed full of void. Once we have experienced this Paradise-Hades aspect of the scene, through space-time, we are thrown into the famous section on the law, the parable called "Before the Law." It, too, is an instance of Paradise-Hades, of enclosure potentialities.

Although there are as many interpretations of this section as there are Kafka scholars and critics, and we find no reason to deny the validity of many of them, nevertheless, the fact remains that the "moment," a temporal dimension, and the "beyond," a spatial dimension, are crucial. The parable of the law is full of Kafkan temporal-spatial illusions and delusions. The law itself becomes both very close and very distant, and one's understanding seems immediate and then infinitely difficult. The law, as well as nearly every other ambiguous phenomenon in Kafka, is like that accordion mentioned earlier, opening and then closing out of phase with the observer. Kafka's protagonists always mistime and "mis-view" their situations. The parable of the law indicates how timing and placing determine a life-and-death role.

At this point we cross with enclosure, whose paradoxes involve an intensity of vision based on seeming paralysis, inwardness, even death. For enclosure writers, death is the epitome of infinite space and limitless time, to the extent death entangles itself with every aspect of life. In enclosure, it is only through death or something akin to it that the protagonist can reach more vital ground, *if* he or she ever does. With death as absolute, the individual is miniaturized, diminished, dwarfed, made to seem part of the fateful or circumstantial destiny that was so much a part of the late nineteenth-century psyche. Kafka's figures striving for art, and like Prometheus being neglected or left to rot, are striving to overcome a fate that discards individuals. Working in time and space, Kafka's protagonists face a losing struggle against endless sweeps of space and time.

In one of his letters to Milena, the young Czech writer whom he met in early 1920, Kafka writes that his "life lasts one night." In fact, many of these letters, which unfortunately are undatable, overlap with the writing of *The Castle.* Evidently, as Kafka's physical condition worsened and his remaining years appeared fewer, his stress on time and space became more insistent. While the theme of artist and art remains strong throughout his career, the parallel theme of space given and then denied and of time opened up and then closed down appears more emphatic in the later years of composition.

Not unusually, the Milena letters are full of spatial and temporal considerations. Kafka repeatedly sees himself as

Milena Jesenská Pollak.

a small thing, as diminished against the vast framework of other people and events. In comparing his life to Milena's with her husband, he speaks of himself as "the mouse in the 'great household' who is allowed at best once a year to run freely across the carpet." He tells her of the death wish we have as children and of his desire, when in the classroom, of fleeing from the strong and fearful schoolteacher into an open, freer world. Finally, in an image that runs parallel to Joseph K. in the Cathedral, he speaks of himself as burrowing and tunneling his way to her "out of the dark hole" and then discovering that, instead of encountering her, he encounters "the impenetrable stone." The result is that he has to "wander back along the tunnel (which has been dug so quickly) and fill it up." "In the end," he says, "one will make new paths again—old mole that one is!"

Such spatial-temporal imagery defines *The Trial.* Kafka repeatedly measures Joseph K. against others, so that he is dwarfed by their gigantic stature. In the bank, the manufacturer and the Assistant Manager appeared "as though two giants of enormous size." In the Cathedral scene, the priest comes down from a distant pulpit and speaks in a voice that commands the entire building. Even Block, who seems to grovel, turns on K. and berates and menaces him for the pitiful nature of his case. Kafka is always working with perspectives. And he continues in this manner, in works that are incomplete, until the Laocöon-like protagonist is caught in ambiguity and ambivalence, whose serpentine coils are those of space and time.

If *The Trial* limns an internal labyrinth, *The Castle* describes one that is open to the sky, but not for that less labyrinthine. Infinite spatiality, Kafka demonstrates, can be as claustrophobic as enclosed, stuffy space. Distancing and denial of it is implied in K.'s role as a land surveyor—one who deals in space, horizons, measurement. He is, we recognize, the other side of Joseph K., not only in name but in function. Whereas the latter works in the cramped quarters of a bank and must confront sweeping time-space, the land surveyor works in the outside but must confront inner mazes. They double each other, as it were, so that they can demonstrate the "tower" and "pit" aspects of the Kafkan vision. A bank clerk deals in time—payments, interest, bills falling due, mortgages, quarterly, semi-annual, annual sums—and a land surveyor deals in space—measured, calculated, enclosed, boundaries, and perimeters. The "time" of Joseph K. is tied to measurement, while the "space" of K. is also a matter of limits—so that the two together describe the outlines of Kafka's temporal-spatial world, with its measurable frontiers, as against that time-space which lies beyond and which belongs to the artist and the quester. The problem is always in reaching that beyond, escaping from a measured hell into an infinite paradise.

Yet Kafka's world exists with mirrors: the infinite reflects cramped space, and eternity comes back as a measured span of time. Distortion is the key, so that reflection, refraction, optical illusions—as in Proust—are always changing the nature of the content, creating that treadmill effect of furious activity leading nowhere. *The Castle* is a model demonstration of this process: of a mirror held up to nature not to reflect *it,* but Kafka. The counterpart to the extended spatial dimension of the castle is the "limited" spatiality implicit in K.'s employer, Klamm, the symbol of authority in the novel. Klamm's name in German has associations of tightness, closeness, compactness, narrowness, even numbness. It is a name connected to burrows, holes, subterranean caves, and especially labyrinths. Whatever the castle holds out in spatial potential, the word (and person) represented by *klamm* takes away.

The Castle, unfinished and unrevised, might go on and on, although Brod in his Note to the novel says Kafka had indicated a concluding chapter. Ideologically, however, there can be no conclusion, except with the death of the author, since the novel is a process of life held in tension between castle (with its space-time associations) and Klamm (with his). In between, K. tries to make do with a limbo existence of arbitrary episodes. The novel need not have been completed because the episodes, like bamboo sections, can replace each other at nearly any point or be extended to any length. There is no possible conclusion, because Klamm represents a subterranean labyrinth and the towering castle suggests the promise of a beyond. As long as the two work at counterpurposes, the novel continues. For even if K. were to discover some gap which indicated a different approach to the castle, spatial dimensions would shift to close up the hole and make it impossible for him to penetrate the interstices.

In actuality, K. uses the outside space surrounding the castle approaches as a means of getting from one small space to another. He lives in rooms, in measured, cramped quarters, even though his mission is to survey large distances and enclose *them.* Early in the novel, K. calls out to Barnabas, the castle messenger, and the name rings out into the night, only to echo from a great distance. Yet distances have no relationship to human capability, for Barnabas has just left K.'s side and yet is already so far off that K.'s voice seems to carry for miles. The effect upon us and upon K. is disruptive of normal spatial expectations, so that even in this scene, which occurs outdoors, we are carried back into hollows and concave spaces, into Kafka's world of space exaggerated and distorted.

About midway through *The Castle,* K. tries to grapple with the idea of freedom and/or imprisonment, although the formulation is full of his typical paradoxes. Almost completely ignored:

> . . . it seemed to K. as if at last those people had broken off all relations with him, and as if now in reality he were freer than he had ever been, and at liberty to wait here in this place usually forbidden to him as long as he desired, and had won a freedom such as hardly anybody else had ever succeeded in winning, and as if nobody could dare to touch him or drive him away, or even speak to him; but—this conviction was at least equally strong—as if at the same time there was nothing more senseless, nothing more hopeless, than this freedom, this waiting, this inviolability.

This mixture of liberation and imprisonment within the space-time considerations of enclosure paradox is, apparently, the subject of *The Castle.* We note the religious, political, and social overtones, but we must resist seeing Kafka's work as anything but the tensions and conflicts themselves. Allegory is a dangerous game with any modern author, but even more perilous with Kafka. The paradoxes exist for themselves, as they did in Kierkegaard, whose *Fear and Trembling,* Politzer points out, often runs parallel to episodes in *The Castle.* For Kafka's characters—whom Brod called "Nihilistic ideas arising in God's mind"—to succeed in their quest would contradict the very ideology underlying them. Kafka refers to this paradox when, in his letter of June 26, 1913, to Felice Bauer, he speaks of writing as akin to death itself: "Writing . . . is a sleep deeper than that of death, and just as one would not and cannot tear the dead from their graves, so I must not and cannot be torn from my desk at night." This is far more than romantic posturing. It is entrance into that incredibly resonant limbo, peculiar to mythical ventures and enclosure fiction, where tension between opposites is everything, where no resolutions can exist, and where writer and protagonist are caught in seeming paralysis and stasis.

Since Kafka leaves behind the usual categories of novel expectations, his work requires a critical vocabulary that is *sui generis:* a different landscape demands a different approach. One of the major space-time considerations in *The Castle,* for example, is its movement toward the infinitude (or abyss) of the castle by way of trivia and trivial means. K. explains to Frieda his interest in the boy Hans, telling her that "one must take advantage of everything that offers any hope whatever." K. must hang on to connections, he must never lose threads of arguments, he must be sure Barnabas has actually spoken to Klamm, he must ascertain the precise nature of each lead and each path. For every aspect of this little world—a maze or labyrinth—is proportionate to the big world, that of castle, Klamm, and Prince.

Every detail of that individual life must somehow find the scale of the outer world. K. hopes that if he finds the order of his own experience he will divine the pattern and order, even the fundamental idea, of what lies beyond. He can forsake no detail, for that, like the homunculus or the microcosm, may contain the whole. In this little world, all people and all information are connected, although their particular pattern of relationship is not apparent. One must remain vigilant, however, for the missing clue can surface, and then one will learn precisely how to react to discover a resolution. The anxiety and anguish implicit in every Kafka fiction comes not only from the nature of the maze itself, but from the frantic desire every protagonist has not to lose any fragment of that maze.

This need to fit oneself into unknown spatial and temporal elements shrouded in fog, mist, and snow is attached to Kafka's persistent theme of the protagonist-artist trying to ply his art. Although K. is a craftsman, not a creative artist, his role is presented as that of the artist who must journey into the unknown in order to understand the nature of his craft. Politzer quotes from a letter Kafka wrote to Max Brod, on July 5, 1922, in which the former expresses his role as writer as a journey through hell. "This descent to the dark powers, this release of spirits which are bound by nature, these dubious embraces and whatever else may occur down there unknown to someone up here who is writing stories in broad daylight. . . . What right have I, who was not at home, to be startled when the home suddenly collapses; for I do know what has gone on before the collapse; have I not exiled myself, leaving the house at the mercy of all evil forces?" The imagery is of the Orphic descent into a different space-time pattern from that obtained aboveground, a descent into the labyrinth or maze that characterizes most of Kafka's fiction.

This maze may be underground *or* aboveground. In *The Castle,* the labyrinth is of village paths and roads, which may or may not lead to the castle. The maze, wherever it may lead, however, contains its own spatial and temporal dimensions, and the man traveling through it must come to terms with the nature of art and the artist. Kafka prepares us well for this role-playing, of the artist cutting himself off—almost in Joycean terms—and then descending by stages into something whose precise terms he cannot comprehend, where temporal and spatial concepts will never form a satisfactory whole. The maze will "amaze" him, in its purest sense of creating wonder, awe, astonishment. We are close to the workings of mythical man in that border area where enclosure categories, fictional ideas, and shamanistic derangement come together.

Kafka's land-surveyor, that K. who once refers to himself as Joseph K., is the typical deracinated artist figure of 1910-1925 literature. Cut off, alienated, forsaking his past, he journeys to the village to take up a post the precise nature of which he does not foresee. He is a dedicated man, a bachelor who, having once mentioned a family in his old country, never refers to it again. The very indistinctiveness of his goal becomes significant if we judge him as an artist; for he has come to measure, think, contemplate, and then try to put together. In his role as artist, his encounter with labyrinths is not unexpected, since to penetrate into the intricacies of the maze is to embrace mysteries invisible to common sense. That labyrinth or maze, in fact, is the testing ground for the artist, for the Orphic figure must encounter a different space-time when he descends.

While the sexual component of penetration and labyrinth is inescapable and psychologically revealing, the more fruitful area of inquiry is in those myths akin to the making of art. None of this denies that Kafka's mazes, and his protagonists' inability to find their way, run parallel to his own sexual disorientation: his alternating desires to "penetrate" the female world and his terrible fear and anxiety about the threatening coils at the female center. None of this denies further that the circuitous routes Kafka plots both above and below ground are tubes, canals, vaginal walls, to which entrances are closed off, denied. And, finally, none of this denies that such places contain Eleusian mysteries, terrible rites of initiation, locales of death, and indeed seem protected by the *vagina dentata.* To recognize all this, however, is to observe that the sexual component, which is not at all a contradictory note, is subsumed in the artistic process.

Despite all of K.'s movement and activity, he never leaves the periphery of the village, he never finds the path or road that leads to the castle or the castle compound, and he never finds clues to the labyrinthine process in which he finds himself. Even the time sequencing of *The Castle* throws K., and the reader, off balance. The expectation is of temporal infinity: the castle as a mythical place seems caught in endless time. It has always existed and will continue so shrouded in fog and mist long after K.'s quest—whatever *that* is—has ended. That is one line of temporal expectation. Set alongside or against that is the actual time span of the novel, in all seven days, the Biblical and magical seven. Thus far, then, we have a temporal dualism in which the parts cannot possibly harmonize. Further: the amount of page space given to K.'s quest splits the seven days into approximately one-seventh of the book's length for the first three-and-a-half days and the other six-sevenths of length for the final three-and-a-half days. That means that K. and the reader, speeded along with the expectation of about fifteen to twenty pages for each day of the week, suddenly come up against a holding action that expends the entire rest of the novel on half a week, at the rate of one hundred or more pages a day. Accordingly, temporal factors become increasingly complicated: castle infinitude remains, while foreground is played out in varying shifts from concentrated to extended time, with neither crossing our expectations.

This calculation fails to take into account the village with its own temporal expectations and its relationship to castle eternality. When K. enters into village life, there is virtually no way in which he can carry over clock, calendar, or empirical time from his earlier life. Like the artist when he inserts himself into the temporal dimensions of his work, K. must try to balance time sequences which exist within his experience and those which he must comprehend to exist in village and castle. In a way, Kafka takes us within that crazy-quilt world of creativity, into the very inexplicables he must grapple with in order to present K.'s own journey. With village time an unclear factor, castle time mysterious and ahistorical K. himself living in empirical time, K. must discover a formula which consistently eludes him. This formula is more than a way for reaching Klamm or any other of the castle officials; it is no less than how to grasp distorted forms of experience, unexpected states of mind, and different levels of time.

If time is a labyrinth, space is also a maze of possibilities and potentialities. Spatially, Kafka uses the various emissaries and minor officials—Erlanger, Bürgel, Barnabas, the two Assistants—as ways of increasing distance between K. and the castle. In realistic fiction, the presence of an intermediary indicates one has approached the seat of power; one can negotiate with the minor official, who acts as a stand-in for the principal officer. Kafka scrambles this spatial concept by making the intermediary separate K. even further from the seat of power. The minor official indicates not how close he has come, but how distant decisive action may be, how shrouded in fog that principal officer really is. Yet such distancing ironically works at crosspurposes with K.'s expectations, which are that the sight of any intermediary is a sign of his having made contact with the castle. Accordingly, space, like time, is opening up and closing down, becoming the labyrinthine way which is Kafka's metaphysical principle.

We can then see the inset story of Amalia and Sortini, which so dominates *The Castle,* as a mirror image of K. and his dealings with officialdom. By a great act of will, Amalia has transcended the sordid intentions of Sortini, although, as a consequence, her family must almost perish. Amalia is a rare character in Kafka's fiction, in that she has learned to act independently of a decision which would, normally, have consigned her to destruction. Although she teeters on the edge of disaster, as does her family, she has, through an act of will, moved beyond the maze with all its traps and snares. She has nested in the village amidst the forces of annihilation, defied the labyrinthine manner of the castle, and defined her own style. In Amalia, Kafka represented an alternate position to K.'s obsessive need to approach the castle and to assume his post as land-surveyor, if that indeed is even his true fate. Amalia has moved outside the spatial-temporal terms of the artist and his creative-self-destructive mode of proceeding. What she has learned about her own style has brought her to empirical time and measured space, those dimensions which will always elude someone like K., who must seek clues within the labyrinth.

In these mirror images, of Amalia and K., we have the antipodes of Kafka's fiction: she is the Tower of Babel, whereas K. is the pit of Babel. Yet the artist can exist only as K. does, caught in the inexplicables of space-time. Nor-

mal life, with pain, anguish, suffering, is represented by Amalia: she has broken from the maze, not to find happiness, which is impossible anyway, but to experience independence of the self-destructive impulses which accompany the artist's existence. Rejecting those impulses, she has evaded the enclosure space-time dimensions which grip K. At one point in Olga's story, K. asks, ". . . since nothing happened and you had no definite punishment hanging over you, what was there to be afraid of ? What people you are!" The question indicates that (1) K. will never really understand that Amalia has broken out of the cycle which claims him; or (2) K. cannot accept her experience since his function is to struggle against space-time patterns which *must* baffle him.

The mirror image perhaps exists in order to show him a life, also shrouded in fog, mist, and snow, that can never be his. He will never become independent of the law and courts, as Gregor is wedded to his family and room, as Kafka's army of insects, moles, and other small forms is attached to burrows and holes, caught in a maze which *is* their experience. That Amalia could break out, with all its attendant anguish and personal reverberations, indicates that Kafka saw alternatives in the distance; narrated by a secondary character, perhaps distorted in the telling, nevertheless such experiences suggest a way out of the artistic-self-destructive dilemma. Whereas Amalia would never create anything except the shaky terms of her own life, K. and his legion of doubles in the human, animal and insect world are forever caught by spatial-temporal implications that indicate another kind of world which disallows final choice, independence, or normalizing experience. (pp. 424-36)

Frederick R. Karl, "Space, Time, and Enclosure in 'The Trial' and 'The Castle'," in Journal of Modern Literature, *Vol. 6, No. 3, September, 1977, pp. 424-36.*

Charles Bernheimer   (essay date 1977)

[*Bernheimer is an American educator and critic. In the following poststructuralist treatment, he analyzes the failure of many critics to interpret ambiguous textual and symbolic relationships in* The Castle.]

The typical Kafka text derives much of its powerful effect from the intensity with which it simultaneously invites and frustrates interpretation. The necessity to interpret engages the reader of Kafka at a particularly intimate level because it is exactly the failure of the Kafka protagonist to interpret his situation successfully that leads to his destruction within the text. The existential implication of a failed hermeneutic is death, be it that of Georg Bendemann, Gregor Samsa, Joseph K. or the Land-Surveyor K. Defending themselves against this dire consequence of misreading, critics often reproach Kafka's protagonists for their blindness to the existential or psychological meaning of their fictional situations. In making this reproach, the critic is implicitly asserting his belief in the continuity between the images presented in Kafka's text and the outside world. Text and existence, mimetic image and semantic content, stand in symbolic relation to each other and the critic's job is to elucidate these relationships to which the protagonist himself is blind. Thus the critic's viewpoint is moral and prescriptive, guiding his reader to those life-enhancing values the deluded Kafka protagonist has ignored. Gregor Samsa, it is argued, should realize that the meaning of his metamorphosis is right there in the metaphor he has become. Gregor fails to profit from this potential revelation because of his unwillingness to read his new body symbolically. Similarly, this prescriptive criticism attacks Joseph K. for not realizing that the meaning of his trial resides in his own guilt feelings. The metaphor of being-on-trial, if read correctly, is an invitation to self-analysis, and to self-choice, an invitation which K. refuses at each opportunity thereby condemning himself to continued guilt and to early death. But the critic saves himself from a similar condemnation by accepting the invitation, elucidating the terms of the metaphor, giving it an existential relevance that K., in his guilty blindness and oedipal delusion, is unable to see. Different critics may read the metaphor in different ways, but what they have in common is a conviction that its significance is elucidated by, rather than contained within, its own metaphoric structure.

Now this, of course, is exactly K.'s attitude in **The Castle.** As Land-Surveyor, K.'s vocation is to delimit differences, to map out boundaries, in order to establish the symbolic principle relating possession to authority, ownership to its origin, material presence to an absent but recuperable presence. His ambition is to be a successful reader of the Castle's symbolic structure, and he feels that his very existence depends on this success. For him, as for many critics of Kafka's texts, symbolic interpretation ensures not just the meaningfulness of life but even its continuation. The Castle within the novel plays the same role for K. as does the text of the novel for the meaning-hungry interpreter. Thus K.'s defeat is emblematic of the failure of symbolic interpretation to bridge the gap between life and literature, existence and text, meaning and sign.

The bridge K. crosses in the very opening paragraph of the novel takes him into a purely textual world out of which no exit can be articulated. The "illusory emptiness" his searching gaze seeks to penetrate from this bridge suggests, through its ambiguous reference to either a momentarily absent presence or the permanent void of an illusion, the kind of shifting play of signification which will henceforth determine K.'s existence in a state of suspension. This play deconstructs one of Western culture's central images of hierarchic and differential order: the powerful castle dominating a subservient village at its feet. K., surveyor of differences, assumes that the function of this order is to define the sacred and the profane, a principle of inclusion and exclusion, standards for legality and transgression, the existential terms of significant freedom and random absurdity. But from the outset the crucial difference between Castle and village is subverted, and with it the very possibility of a symbolic structure such as K. seeks to establish.

This subversion is subtly initiated when, in the first speech of the novel, Schwarzer informs K. that "this village is the property ('Besitz') of the Castle and whoever lives here or

passes the night here does so, in a manner of speaking ('gewissermassen'), in the Castle." But it is the description of K.'s initial view of the Castle that most explicitly collapses the distinction between it and the village. That difference is upheld as long as K. views the Castle from a sufficient distance to allow him to consider it entirely in terms of a literary and historical tradition that has infused the word "castle" with associations of power, authority and inviolability. A closer view, however, disappoints K. for the Castle then appears to be nothing more than "a wretched-looking little town thrown together out of village houses." The disturbing resemblance of the reputed center of signifying order to the peripheral dependency in which K. finds himself causes him to remember nostalgically the clear symbolic organization of his home town. There the church tower, though "an earthly building—what else can we men build?—[had] a loftier goal than the surrounding cluster of low-built houses and a clearer meaning than the muddled ('trübe') work-a-day life." Meaning is clear in this structure because earthly images, recognized as distinctly different from and other than metaphysical ideals, function analogically to symbolize a transcendental meaning. This is the function of the symbol in most Romantic theory. Coleridge, for instance, [in *The Statesman's Manual*] writes that "the symbol is characterized by the translucence of the special in the individual, or of the general in the special, or of the universal in the general; above all of the eternal through and in the temporal." But even Saussure's linguistic approach insists on the link within the symbol between the representative and the semantic functions of language: "One characteristic of the symbol," Saussure states [in his *Course in General Linguistics*], "is that it is never wholly arbitrary; it is not empty, for there is a rudiment of a natural bond between the signifier and the signified."

The Castle demonstrates no such bond but seems rather to be an arbitrary structure without a constitutive center. Its tower belongs to a private house and is of uncertain significance. It is pierced with windows that glitter in an "insane" manner and is topped by battlements of "unsure, irregular, broken" design. Confused by his perceptive faculties, K. finally resorts to a metaphor to describe the appearance of the Castle. But the image he chooses, of a deranged ("trübselig") tenant breaking through the roof and lifting himself up to show himself to the world, is clearly a reflection of his own deranged state of mind. (Later he notes that "the gaze of the observer could not remain concentrated [on the Castle] but slid away.") Observation of the Castle has generated metaphor which in turn has created a doubling effect the existential meaning of which is madness. The Castle acts as a mirror, apparently other but constantly dissolving this otherness into the reflexive play of repetition. Its function is the essence of metaphoricity: the maintenance of differences that are simultaneously condensed into sameness.

In a diary entry of January 16th, 1922, the time when Kafka was just beginning to write **The Castle,** he analyses a recent psychic breakdown ("Zusammenbruch") in terms of the madness to which the wild tempo of introspective pursuit may well lead him. Then he considers the nature of the limit to which he might be brought were he able to hold his own in this pursuit. "Pursuit," he writes, "is indeed only a metaphor ("Bild"); I can also say 'assault on the last earthly frontier,' an assault, moreover, launched from below, from mankind, and since this also is only a metaphor, I can replace it by the metaphor of an assault from above, aimed at me from above." Thus at the limit of human sanity is the substitutive activity of metaphor itself, an activity which suspends the differences between active and passive, above and below, inside and outside, in a theoretically endless play of interchangeability. "Literature," Kafka adds, "is an assault against the limit."

K.'s assault on the Castle is not literary in the sense Kafka proposes here. Rather, his is a vain assault undertaken from within literature against its very structure. K.'s central concern is to distinguish and define village and Castle so that he can establish a coherent and stable symbolic bond between them. The function of such a bond will be to anchor the permutations of the structure by giving it a center, the Castle, that is somehow within its perimeters yet outside its freeplay. This attempt to determine a center is evident in K.'s response to the choice he feels is being put to him "whether he preferred to become a village worker with a distinctive but merely apparent connection ("Verbindung") with the Castle, or an apparent village worker whose real occupation was determined through the messages conveyed by Barnabas." His decision, which he considers an unhesitating determination, is phrased as follows: "Only as a worker in the village, removed as far as possible from the gentlemen of the Castle, could he hope to achieve anything in the Castle itself." This may at first seem like no decision at all and, in fact, K. has not chosen either of the alternatives he defined at first. What he's done is to abolish the word "apparent" from his earlier formulations, thereby establishing both existential possibilities as equally "real" and simultaneously available. By firmly delimiting the distance between village and Castle, he hopes to maintain their difference as distinct presences and thus be in a position to survey their interrelated significance. The Castle as presence will make available the Castle as unique origin, as governing center that regulates the structure of meaning and forms it into a coherent totality.

The demand for a transcendent presence, both physical and verbal, is the cornerstone of K.'s strategy to decode the Castle's duplicitous structure. "First I want to see [Klamm] at close quarters," he tells the landlady, "then I want to hear his voice." Much of K.'s energy is engaged in an effort to fight off the absorption of what he calls his "actual person, me myself" into "what is transacted in the offices and can be construed again officially this way or that." By resisting the mediation of written texts, K. hopes to avoid becoming subject to the kind of annihilating interpretive work by which the Mayor reduces Klamm's letter to nothing more than "a signature on a blank sheet of paper," an illegible signature at that. Thus he asks Barnabas to memorize his request that he, K., be allowed to speak in person before Klamm because a written letter "would only go the same endless way as the other papers." Similarly, he refuses to respond to Momus' protocol, despite the landlady's claim that it provides the only road to Klamm, because he does not want his answers to be "in-

corporated into the hostile text." He sees no possible connection between the protocol "over which just now Momus was breaking a salt-covered pretzel, which he was enjoying with his beer, in the process covering all the papers with salt and caraway seeds" and his own image of Klamm as an eagle, remote, silent, self-determining. The text is a material object, debased in K.'s eyes through its contiguity with other physical things. The kind of communication he yearns for is unmediated, direct, through eyes and ears, the vocalization of Klamm's silence, the lifting up of his "downward-pressing gaze" (139; 151). K. is, in the terms introduced by Jacques Derrida, resolutely logocentric and phonocentric, an undeviating believer in the metaphysics of presence.

One of the results of this belief is that K. can respond to immediate presence only in so far as it refers to a transcendent signified. This is particularly evident in his relationship to Frieda. When she declares to K. that it is he and not Klamm that she misses, K., we are told, "paid attention to only one thing" and asked "Is Klamm then still in communication ('Verbindung') with you?." "Verbinden," to bind, unite, join, connect, link, that is K.'s obsession, for "Verbindung" serves the purpose of "vergleichen" to compare, reconcile, equalize, which in turn makes "vermessen" possible, to measure, survey. It is hard not to agree with the landlady's interpretation of K.'s motives when she declares (as Frieda reports her sentiments) that K. has "no feeling for [Frieda] but the feeling of ownership ('Besitz')" and that this property is of little value to K. except as a means to reach Klamm and bargain directly with him. K., it would seem, regards Frieda as one term in symbolic connection, a term which he thinks can be used to force the other, absent one, to present himself. This is vividly illustrated, in a passage Kafka deleted perhaps due to its very explicitness, by the drawing scrawled on the margin of the protocol concerning K.'s relationship to Frieda. It shows "a man with a girl in his arms. The girl's face was buried in the man's chest, but the man, who was much the taller, was looking over the girl's shoulder at a sheet of paper he had in his hands, on which he was joyfully inscribing some figures. Physical presence, for K., is a semantic lack that requires the supplement of symbolic inscription. This inscription corresponds to a use of language that Kafka explicitly condemns: "For all things outside the phenomenal world," Kafka writes in a crucial aphorism, "language can be employed only in the manner of an allusion ('andeutungsweise') but never even approximately in the manner of a comparison ('vergleichsweise') since in accordance with the phenomenal world it is concerned only with property ('Besitz') and its relations." The symbolic mode of comparison constitutes an attempt to appropriate the metaphysical realm in terms of the physical, sensual world. It "makes the same" (the literal meaning of "vergleichen") the transcendent and the immanent by including both in a centered structure of property relations susceptible to being surveyed.

But K. is a Landsurveyor in a quicksand of shifting signs. The Castle refuses to confront him on his own terms, refuses to be conjured into presence. Instead it insists on the purely allusive nature of its textuality. "Andeutung" is its mode, that is, hinting, intimating, alluding, pointing to a meaning that is always elsewhere ("deuten" means to interpret, explain, signify, while "an" as prefix refers to a temporal future or spatial remove). At one point K. complains that, although he is fighting "for something vitally near ('etwas lebendigst Nahes'), for himself," the Castle repeatedly denies him the possibility of battle, thereby displacing him (the German word here is "verlegen" which also has the temporal meaning of "to delay or postpone") into an "unofficial, totally unintelligible, opaque, alien life." By constantly shifting away from a confrontation, infinitely postponing it, the Castle is causing K.'s life to take on some of the opaque ("trübe"—a word which reminds us of the "trübselig" inhabitant K. imagines in the Castle tower) and unintelligible, ("unübersichtlich," literally "unoverseeable") qualities of its own allusive metaphoricity. On this occasion, K. clearly foresees the existential consequence of this progressive absorption into a de-centering, deconstructing movement: psychic breakdown ("Zusammenbruch") followed by death. Yet he perseveres in the attempt to control this movement by determining that it has a generative center.

Olga's description of the Castle anteroom, based on Barnabas' account of his experience there, is the nearest K. gets to a perception of what is at the Castle's core. But her description subverts any notion of center or originating presence and reveals the radically textual nature of the Castle's structure. Officials in the anteroom stand reading huge books which lie open on a long desk stretching from wall to wall. The officials move from one book to another at will and occasionally dictate at a whisper to scribes ("Schreiber," literally, "writers") sitting on low benches. The scribes jump up to catch the officials' words, sit down quickly to make note of them, then jump up once more. It is not known whether what is dictated originates in the book the whispering official is reading or is his private invention. All these writings, obviously full of gaps and errors, accumulate in piles under the scribes' tables and are occasionally disseminated when a particular scribe happens to remember that he has a letter addressed to someone. The messages consequently have no necessary temporal correlation to the situation at hand nor, as we know from the letter K. receives praising him for surveying work he has never done, is their content necessarily relevant. Thus the textuality of the Castle is defined as displacement, fragmentation, postponement, duplicity. The plurality of books on the table is indicative of the fissure that has always-already occurred in some hypothesized original, unified Text, the indelible inscription of a paternal Logos. These books are already interpretations of interpretations, signifiers of previous signifiers, references within a library. They are the parricidal traces of a deconstructed Logos. Both the movement of officials between books and the discontinuous form of their dictation to the scribes illustrate that writing, including, of course, Kafka's own, is generated in a continuous displacement from origin, a displacement which inscribes writing into a temporal movement of deferral and the text into a semantic structure of deceit.

The scene of the distribution of files provides another comic illustration of the process of textual dissemination. Files of papers are handed out to the gentlemen in their rooms by servants who wheel a heavily laden cart up and down a long corridor. The servants match file numbers with door numbers in order to ensure correct delivery but they often make mistakes and must then engage in devious negotiations to persuade the reluctant officials to return the inappropriate files. Once all files have been distributed, one little piece of paper remains. Given that he has often been told that his case is the smallest of the small, K. imagines that this might very well be his own file. One of the servants, however, tears it up, a seemingly irregular act that K. excuses on the grounds of the accumulated irritation experienced by the hard-working servant. But this remaindered text may be seen as exactly that excess which, according to Derrida's analysis [in "Structure, Sign and Play in the Discourse of the Human Sciences" in *The Languages of Criticism and the Sciences of Man,* Macksey and Donato, eds.], is produced as a supplement in every signifying act. The servant attempts to achieve a rigorous adjustment of message to referent but finds such totalization impossible. The "Unregelmässigkeit" (irregularity, unruliness, nonconformity) of his tearing the paper into pieces is a necessary function of the Castle's textual productivity. K.'s reluctant identification with this paper has a significance he does not understand: he is himself irretrievably "irregular," in excess, supplementary. There is no integration possible for him within the "hostile text" which tears his being into scripted fragments.

In effect, K.'s quest inscribes him more and more deeply into the very textual freeplay he seeks to ground and delimit. He becomes a kind of hermeneutic machine, having to interpret every aspect of what he sees, hears and reads. Although he does not file reports and protocols, K.'s meditations and conversations have the same interpretive function as the Castle's official writings. In searching for the "Vergleich," he achieves only the "Andeutung." While trying to establish his difference from the Castle, he functions increasingly like it. If displacement, fragmentation, postponement and duplicity define the Castle's textuality, they are also the terms of K.'s existence.

K.'s possible duplicity is first suggested by his ambiguous response to the Castle's recognition of his title in the telephone communication to Schwarzer. "That was unpropitious for him, on the one hand," K. reflects, "for it meant that in the Castle they were well informed about him, had estimated all the probable chances, and were taking up the challenge with a smile. On the other hand, however, it was quite propitious for, if his interpretation was right, it proved that they had underestimated his strength and that he would have more freedom than he had initially dared to hope for." Why, the reader asks himself, should K. consider his professional activity a "challenge" to the Castle? How does the Castle's recognition of his official role give him more freedom than he had initially expected to have? K.'s meditation puts the reader in a hermeneutic quandary not unlike that experienced by Olga and Barnabas in their attempt to determine the importance of the letters Barnabas delivered to K. The reader is tempted to conclude about K.'s motives as Olga concludes about the letters that "to estimate their just value is impossible, they themselves change value perpetually, the reflections they give rise to are endless, and chance alone determines where one stops reflecting, so even one's opinion is a matter of chance." K.'s inwardness is just as opaque and problematic for the reader as the communications emanating from within the Castle are for K. In both cases the nature of the problematic involves a confusion as to whether the source of authority is internal or external.

Basing themselves on K.'s reaction to the Castle's confirmation of his post and on other supposed "evidence" scattered throughout the text, critics have argued that K. is in fact an impostor who simply invents a calling for himself and then fights to get this subjective fiction recognized by the Castle authorities. But it would be more accurate to say that what K. is fighting for is a world in which the critical categories of subject and object, fiction and reality, truth and fraud are clearly distinct and hence effectively usable, for instance to label him an impostor. This is K.'s challenge to the Castle in his determination to survey its land as it is the challenge offered by the reader of Kafka's novel in his determination to interpret it symbolically. K. imagines that the Castle takes up his challenge with a smile, as well it might, since the very formulation of K.'s response indicates that he is already caught in that duplicitous play of perspectives he allegedly wants to fight off and since the Castle's telephonic acknowledgment of his employment, like all such communications, is, as the Mayor explains, "merely a practical joke."

The only "real and reliable thing" transmitted by the local telephones, the Mayor declares, is "the humming and singing" which had seemed to K. "as if out of the hum of countless children's voices—but this was not really a hum, rather the song of distant, of very distant voices—as if out of this hum there rose up, in a close to impossible manner, one single high but strong voice that struck the ear as if it were demanding to penetrate beyond mere hearing." This pure sound is the undifferentiated murmur of language engaged in its own temporal process. Any attempt to evoke this integral flow of voices can only proceed through a potentially infinite series of "as if" phrases, metaphoric allusions to the forever elusive. "There is no fixed telephonic connection ('Verbindung') with the Castle," says the Mayor, "no central exchange that transmits our calls further." To reach the Castle is to be displaced from any possible center into a stream of language that allows no individual articulation to interrupt its autonomous movement. (pp. 367-75)

Castle discourse is most frequently represented as an ambiguous play with the subject-object, inner-outer distinction. Thus when Klamm, or rather the Chief of department X, writes to K.: "As you know, you have been engaged for the Count's service," this duplicitous statement perpetuates the uncertainty as to whether the authority for K.'s appointment rests with him or with the Castle. The fluctuating character of Klamm's appearance initiates a similarly deceptive game in the field of perception. Olga tells K. that Klamm "is supposed to look completely different when he comes into the village and when he leaves it, different before and after having drunk beer, different awake and asleep, different alone and in dialogue and, what is easily understood from this, almost entirely different up in the Castle." Yet there is a constant in the reports of Klamm's appearance: it is agreed that he always wears a black morning coat and long tails. In typical Castle fashion, sameness is mixed with difference, the sameness in this case being of a peculiarly sinister nature (one remembers the crows K. observes circling around the Castle tower). Olga explains Klamm's metamorphoses by asserting that "they depend on the momentary mood of the observer, on the degree of his excitement, on the countless gradations of hope and despair he finds himself in when he sees Klamm, which can usually happen only for a moment." This explanation, which places the source of difference within the perceiving subject, clearly simplifies the situation. For Olga herself suggests later on that officials may imitate Klamm's "sleepy, dreamy style," making the original hard to distinguish from his doubles, and much earlier the landlady maintained that neither K. nor she herself was "capable of seeing Klamm as he really is." Thus it becomes impossible to determine when Klamm himself is changing, when he is being imitated, and when the observer's imagination is projecting a change upon him. He seems to exist fundamentally as a name, as that name [described in Lacan's "D'une Question Préliminaire à Tout Traitement possible de la Psychase" in his *Écrits*] which designates paternal authority by tracing it in the very transformations of metamorphic structure; the Lacanian "nom-du-père" Klamm's power is a function of his capacity for displacement and substitution. The images in terms of which he is "seen" are supplements operating to in-face what is essentially effaced, absent, empty, without center or origin. Like the Castle itself, from which the gaze can only "slide away," Klamm subverts the epistemological value of perception and inscribes the observer into a reflexive play of mirrors and doubles. (pp. 375-76)

The rapacious brutality of the officials' letters summoning women reflects the violence of the break caused by desire in the Castle's substitutive and displacing structure. Olga remarks of this break that: "Of course, we're all supposed to belong to the Castle and there's supposed to be no distance ('Abstand,' a word which may also mean 'difference') between us, and nothing to be bridged over, and that may be true enough usually but we have unfortunately had the occasion to see that, just when something depends on it, it doesn't hold." The Castle's play with the reflexive permutations of identity and difference remains an abstract supposition for the village community. What the villagers actually perceive violates this play by expressing the violence of desire arching towards a particular object. But the officials never allow themselves to be more than briefly and inconsequentially distracted from the mode of the play. Their affairs are always short-lived, no attachments are made and, after a woman is dismissed, she is completely forgotten "not only as far as the past is concerned," Gardenia informs K., "but literally for the entire future as well." Thus sexuality institutes no significant "Verbindung" between Castle and village; it is no more than a slight tear, or momentary fold, in the Castle's textual fabric. (p. 377)

The majority of the village women evaluate a sexual connection with an official much as K. does. It appears to represent for them the perfect union between the physical and the spiritual-made-flesh, the embodiment of symbolic order. What they fail to realize is that, as Kafka puts it in an aphorism, "there is nothing besides a spiritual world; what we call the world of the senses is the evil in the spiritual world; what we call evil is only a necessary moment in our endless evolution." The physical, phenomenal, sensual world cannot form a bridge linking it to the spiritual sphere because it is always-already included in that sphere, as its evil, its temporality, and one might add, its verbal articulation. The women who valorize their sexual bond with the Castle are overlooking its genesis in a rupture of the officials' textual freeplay, a freeplay into which, as members of the reflexive village-Castle structure, they are unavoidably inscribed from the beginning. Desire is subsumed by the force of its absence.

Amalia alone rejects the debased use of language characteristic of the officials' demands for sexual satisfaction. She tears up Sortini's summons and throws the fragments into the messenger's face. K. remarks of this act that "the more you say about it, the less clearly can it be decided whether it was great or small, clever or foolish, heroic or cowardly," but K. seems in many ways singularly unqualified to judge Amalia. For Amalia has done what K. and the villagers hold back from doing: she has repudiated the need for "Verbindung" with the Castle. She refuses to accept that any viable bond could exist between the brutal exaction of sexual service and an authentic political or spiritual authority. Her tearing up of Sortini's letter differs significantly from the act of tearing K. witnesses in the Herrenhof corridor. There it is the verbal supplement, the excess signification, that is destroyed, to K.'s regret since he imagines himself written into that textual left-over. Here it is Amalia's body that is being requisitioned as if it were a text subject to being ripped apart. The language of the letter is crassly referential and appropriative. Nothing is "left over," except perhaps the ambiguity of the address "to the girl with the garnet necklace"—not much of an ambiguity given that Amalia had been wearing the necklace when Sortini saw her. So by ripping the letter to pieces, Amalia is refusing the rapacious connection forged by desire between language and physical presence.

The consequence of this refusal is self-enforced silence on Amalia's part, ostracism by the community, and frantic activity by Amalia's family to achieve a new "Verbindung" with the Castle. Amalia's silence is the result of her radical divorce from the energy of desire. She is not interested in the "Castle stories" that are K.'s sole concern and spends her time caring for her debilitated parents. Her position is much like that K. achieves when, left alone in the courtyard of the Herrenhof, he feels "as if all connection ('Verbindung') with him had now been broken off" leaving him "freer than ever," no one being allowed "to touch him or drive him away, or even speak to him; but—this conviction was at least equally strong—as if at the same time there was nothing more senseless, nothing more hopeless than this freedom, this waiting, this inviolability." For K., significance is entirely a function of "Verbindung" and necessarily involves a certain violation of radical individual freedom. Amalia, on the other hand, is capable of living within that freedom, as Olga recognizes when she says of her sister "Amalia not only bore the suffering but had the understanding to see through it; we saw

only the effects, she saw into the causes ("Grund"); we hoped for some small remedy ("Mittel," also "means" or "medium"), she knew that all was decided; we had to whisper, she had only to be silent; she stood eye to eye with the truth and lived and endured her life then as now." However, the truth Amalia has confronted is, in fact, not the truth of the Castle's textual plurivocity but rather a violation of it. The Castle can never be encountered "face to face." It always slips away, shifts to the side. What Amalia retreats from is the Castle's debased manifestation in the world, as evil, as a compulsion towards possession ("Besitz"). And since all language deals with possession, she must retreat outside of words into a silent absorption in the present moment. "She's never alarmed, never afraid, never impatient," Olga says. Amalia has almost managed to exit from the text.

The other members of her family, however, do not share her "heroic" strength with the consequence, in Olga's view, that they "betrayed Amalia, tore [themselves] loose from her command of silence," being unable "to go on living without hope of any kind." Their betrayal consists in their adoption of the villagers' surmise that Amalia's act was an affront to the symbolic law linking village and Castle. Assuming that their only "hopeful *Verbindung*" with the Castle had been the supposedly insulted Sortini, they set out to reestablish their connection through written petitions, personal encounters, Olga's prostitution, Barnabas' service as messenger. But now the Castle retreats into its mirror-function. It denies that there has been any insult to it or that any guilt exists to be forgiven Amalia's family. It gives "no outward sign" of being in any way affected by the desperate activities of the various family members. However, Olga maintains that these members were aware that, in order to "make everything all right," they had need only "show through our behavior that we had overcome the incident, no matter in what way, and reassure public opinion that it was never likely to be mentioned again, whatever its nature may have been." In other words, authority rested with the family itself but it was incapable of authorizing its conduct. Instead, it became absorbed in discussing the story of the letter "back and forth, in all its known details and unknown potentialities," thereby, says Olga, "plunging deeper and deeper into what we wanted to escape from." Amalia's act of tearing up a text has in turn become a text subject to infinite interpretation by her anxious family. By reinscribing Amalia into the hermeneutic mediations ("Mitteln") of the village-Castle structure, her family betrays her courageous authorization of her being in silence. And this betrayal is doubled by our own. For as readers interpreting the meaning of Amalia's conduct, we also violate her muteness, force her actions to speak words they were intended to hush. Almost despite ourselves we follow the lead of the Barnabas family in becoming more and more deeply immersed in that very hermeneutic quicksand from which Amalia has deliberately extricated herself.

The paradox that the act most deliberately resistant to hermeneutic molestation, closest to being outside the text, generates the most elaborate enterprise of textual recuperation receives its most extensive illustration in the scene of K.'s interview with Bürgel. Bürgel is, significantly, a

"Verbindungssekretär." His title alone points to his special competence in furthering K.'s ambition. Moreover, his name means "little guarantor" or "little castle." K. stumbles upon Bürgel late at night when, dead tired already, he is looking for Erlanger's room. Bürgel then proceeds to explain to K., at enormous length, that exactly their current situation is of such a nature that the applicant "can dominate everything and to that end need do nothing more than somehow put forward his plea, for which fulfillment is already waiting." This, of course, is a fairy-tale promise: the assurance that language will have an immediate effect upon reality, that a spoken wish will come true. It is a promise of "Verbindung" as "Vergleich" in its most radical form: language will have the power to appropriate both the transcendent and the phenomenal worlds. Being purely constitutive, it will require no interpretation. Such has been the goal of K.'s desire all along and, in fact, some of the reasons Bürgel gives for his peculiar susceptibility at this time coincide with points in K.'s strategy to attain his goal: the private, more humanly sensitive point of view adopted by the officials at night, the effective power of the applicants' "mute presence," of his physical "proximity."

But Bürgel's offer is destroyed in the very process of its being made. The primary purpose of his chatter is not the fulfillment of K.'s desire but rather of his own, which is to fall back to sleep in the course of conversation. Moreover, he is aware that K. is exhausted and that "one's physical energies suffice only to a certain limit," to precisely that limit which is "full of meaning in other ways." This, he says, cannot be helped, for "in this manner the world corrects itself in its course and maintains the balance." The "world" in question is that of the text, embodied here in the temporal flow of Bürgel's "quiet, self-satisfied voice" droning on in what seems to be an effort to approximate the mesmerizing hum of voices on the castle telephone line. What is to be "corrected" is the possibility offered within this verbal flow to somehow get outside it. Bürgel speaks of this possibility as a "tearing apart" of the official organization, as a breaking open of its "Lückenlosigkeit," its being-without-gaps. But he also explains that "such opportunities are in accord with the general situation in so far as they are never made use of," that they "actually exist only by way of rumor," and that "there is no room for such a case in this world." This hypothetical case has many of the same qualities as the text the servants in the Herrenhof corridor tear into shreds. Both are in excess, supplementary, irregular. Yet both have been produced by the very structure they add themselves to and are in turn erased by this structure. Bürgel's loquacity rips his offer to pieces just as effectively as the servants' action destroys the remaindered document. Nothing, finally, is changed. K., at the end of Bürgel's speech, is fast asleep "closed off ('abgeschlossen') from all that was happening."

The Castle (the German word for "castle," "Schloss," can also mean "lock" or "closure") can survive as a structure only so long as K. is excluded from it. The fate of the ripped text and of the Bürgel offer are homologous to K.'s own fate. For he also is a supplement produced by the constitutive lack in the Castle's textual play. The Castle's seamless "Lückenlosigkeit," its perfectly self-sufficient finite closure, is generated paradoxically by a gap, a tear, in the place of its center. This gap always-already exists and can never be filled, if the signifying movement of the text is to remain open to a freeplay of repetitions, permutations and substitutions. Thus K. is supplementary from the beginning, from the moment he crosses the bridge, but he is also from that moment, and at every subsequent one, blindly engaged in the process of completing a finite ensemble to which his activity is essential. His failure to penetrate the apparently completed structure of the Castle is the never-completed process that structures *The Castle.* K. goes around seeking an official position from which he is constantly displaced and deferred. He is unable to recognize that this movement actually performs his textual function and constitutes that "world" from which he is concurrently excluded.

Relating this to the mirror analogy, we note that insofar as the Castle functions as a mirror it is in itself devoid of images, of representational content. Yet it can be perceived only as a reflect or framing the observer's world. The absence within the mirror enables the observer to see the world as representation while the enabling absence itself must always remain occulted. Thus the observer's perspective creates a mimesis that constitutes his world, and perhaps himself, within the framework of what may be called a text. The observer cannot enter this text except as an image reflected in the mirror. Yet he is always supplementary to that void that constitutes the mirror's essence, its own empty self-reflection.

Hence the importance of the limitation of the narrative perspective to K.'s point of view. In his search for the Castle, K. must be unaware that he is already within *The Castle.* His position can only be one of blindness and ignorance for, as Kafka states in an aphorism, "Truth is indivisible, therefore cannot know itself; anyone who desires to know it must be a lie." K.'s perspective is moral in this way: as a supplement, he always feels himself to be somehow illegitimate, excessive. But the minimal presence of a narrator standing apart from K. implicitly asserts the "true" perspective of structural necessity. As Joseph K. remarks in *The Trial,* such an assertion, that "one must accept everything as necessary, . . . turns lying into a universal principle." This turn is evident in *The Castle* when the narrator tells us that K. was "abgeschlossen" to Bürgel's offer. Here the narrator speaks independently of K.'s consciousness for what is arguably the only time in the novel. He does so at the very moment when the possibility has been articulated that K.'s supplementary function could be resolved into the structure it supplements. Through his self-conscious pun on the word "schloss," the narrator comes to the fore to stress the necessity of K.'s inclusion in the exclusionary activity of the Castle which generates *The Castle.* The lie of the supplement is necessary to the truth of the text, a truth the supplement always defers outside articulation.

This brings us back to the problematic role of the critic—interpreter of Kafka's duplicitous text. *The Castle* mirrors the critic no matter how hard he tries to efface the individual direction of his gaze. The fundamental opacity of the text solicits supplements which can only lie as they add themselves to the history of hermeneutic endeavor initiated by K. himself. The symbol-hunting critics reveal their nostalgia, similar to K.'s, for a lost world bound together by a language of felt analogies. The structural approach I have employed here has perhaps the advantage of attempting to analyze the genesis within Kafka's novel of its own necessarily "excessive" character. Yet my analysis would not be true to the nature of its own life if I did not confess to believing that I have achieved some significant *Verbindung* with the text, if only by acknowledging the inevitable failure of my effort. (pp. 379-83)

> *Charles Bernheimer, "Symbolic Bond and Textual Play: Structure of 'The Castle',"* in The Kafka Debate: New Perspectives for Our Time, *edited by Angel Flores, Gordian Press, 1977, pp. 367-84.*

Alan Klein   (essay date 1984)

[*In the following excerpt, Klein interprets the Castle as a symbol of Hell and K. as a would-be Messiah in the tradition of Hasidic folk tales.*]

Franz Kafka's novel **The Castle** has become one of the most enigmatic masterpieces of our time. From its earliest appearance, **The Castle** has been received as a parable about an individual's search for salvation. In an "Homage" written in 1940, Thomas Mann saw K., the protagonist, as an alienated member of the faith, who wishes "to get into the community and attain to the state of grace." This somehow does not ring true upon a reading of the text. We find K. not to be Everyman struggling for salvation, but rather extraordinary in his vision and persistence.

However, Kafka wrote and spoke of a "secret cabbala" behind **The Castle,** a frame of reference which would provide the key to his thinking. One discussion of the novel has to some extent provided that key. [In "The Law of Igrominy: Authority, Messianism and Exile in *The Castle,*" an essay collected in *On Kafka,* edited by Franz Kuna] W. B. Sebald has pointed out, in passing, the similarity between the Hebrew word for Land-Surveyor, K.'s title in the novel, *meshgeach,* or in the diminutive *mesheoach,* and the Hebrew word for Messiah, *meshiach.* [In his *Franz Kafka: A Biography*] Max Brod, Kafka's executor and earliest biographer and editor, has noted Kafka's extensive knowledge of Hebrew. Confident therefore that Kafka had sufficient knowledge of Hebrew to be conscious of any double-meaning in the Hebrew equivalent of titles he had assigned his characters, we should examine any further double-meanings in order to reassess the text that Kafka has presented for our unraveling.

We find that the modern Hebrew word for "castle" is *Tzreach.* However, in Biblical Hebrew *Tzreach* refers to "cave" or "cellar." In addition, the ruler of the Castle is named Count Westwest. The Hebrew for "west" is *ma'arov.* Its closely related noun is *ma'aroh,* meaning again "cave" or "cavern."

The nature of K.'s central struggle with the Castle now be-

comes clear. The Castle is not a symbol of Heaven, of what is above, of grace, but rather of hell. It is an outpost of what is below. It is the fortress of evil that has subdued the villagers and even blocked any knowledge of the path to redemption. Count Westwest, given our new understanding of the Hebrew double-meaning of his name, becomes the leader of the cave, the leader of the fortress of evil blocking our connection with God. Count Westwest might even be Satan, the representatives of the Castle his legions of demons.

Thus, the novel is no longer about a Job-like figure trying to retain his faith in the face of an incomprehensible God. The Messiah has no need to attain salvation; he grants it. Instead, if we are to see K. as the Messiah in the tradition of the Hasidic folk tales upon which Kafka was obviously drawing, but filtered through his unique sense of the ironic and the comical, a whole, new, fresher, and wittier understanding of the novel comes alive for us.

The moment and the atmosphere of K.'s introduction of himself, for example, take on a whole new meaning. The passage could be read, "Let me tell you that I am the Messiah whom the Count is expecting. 'Messiah?' he heard the hesitating question behind his back and then there was a general silence." There is something amiss in the townspeople's reaction to the introduction of K., if we are to assume he is the Messiah. They do not regard this event as a miracle, as their redemption—"Oh, I know all about you, you're the Messiah, and then adding: 'But now I must go back to my work,' she returned to her place behind the bar. . . . " The townspeople do not realize that they are in need of any sort of redemption; the Castle and its ethic have come totally to dominate their lives.

It is part of the paradoxical irony of the book that K. cannot enter into the struggle with the Castle unless the Castle fights back. The second paradox weaving its way through the novel is the utter blindness of the villagers to their state. The Castle has come to control the minds and acts of the villagers so completely that they have lost even their desire for redemption. It is the mark of the power of the Castle that in the course of K.'s struggle he is subsumed by the very forces against which he is working. He begins to lose even his power of self-determination.

Perhaps **The Castle** is a statement of the condition of mankind in a war-torn, secular world, where not only have all individuals become oblivious to the need for redemption, but even the Messiah, were he to come to earth, would also be forced to succumb to the forces of evil which block our faith in God. (pp. 43-5)

> *Alan Klein, in a review of "The Castle," in* The Explicator, *Vol. 42, No. 3, Spring, 1984, pp. 43-5.*

Ron Smetana   (essay date 1986)

[*In the following excerpt, Smetana attributes the Castle's lack of centralized authority to its diffusion of power amongst the villagers.*]

Is the Castle a monolithic, impersonal, dictatorial bureaucracy? Just the opposite. Castle power is diffused through the entire village population. It is not that K. is unable to make headway against the Castle's power because of its solidity, but because it is not there at all (in one place, on the hill).

Some readings of *The Castle* [such as that of Günther Anders in his book *Franz Kafka*] have found "a totally institutionalized, indeed, a totalitarian, world of authority" that preserves [what Frederick A. Olafson, in his "Kafka and the Primacy of the Ethical," terms] "the integrity of the Castle's system." Villagers are repressed and powerless [observes W. G. Sebald in "The Law of Ignomiy: Authority, Messianism and Exile in *The Castle*"] as is K. in "his head-on clash" with the "self-contained and self-perpetuating" Castle power [Franz Kura in his *Franz Kafka: Literature as Corrective Punishment*].

But what is on the Castle hill? There is a fouled-up switchboard. There are toppling stacks of papers. There are lost documents. There are officials who will not cooperate with one another. There are pranksters. What is not on the hill is clear, uniform, central authority. The mayor to K.: "The first Control officials . . . recognize that there is an error. But who can guarantee that the second Control officials will decide in the same way, and the third and all the others?" In his attempt to assault Castle power, K. is not beating his head against a brick wall, he is pressing on an all-too-yielding revolving door.

K. should have known better. He is told forthrightly that "there is no difference between the peasantry and the Castle," and the Castle's physical appearance is consistent with this notice. The Castle is "only a wretched-looking town, a huddle of village houses." The Castle is no different from the village; in fact it is in the village—individuals and their daily lives—where most power lies.

The outstanding example of this is K. himself. His life in the village is spawned from Schwarzer's childish challenge and his own braggadocio about having a right to be in the village. The simple fact that he remains in the village proves he does not need an official permit to stay. K., however, does not realize his "success" or that it comes through his own decision and power and the supportive actions of those villagers who provide him with food and shelter. As for the villagers, they defy the only two explicit orders that come from the Castle. The mayor disobeys a "categorical" order to hire a surveyor, and Amalia rejects Sortini's demand.

K. goes in search of an official validating power to which he can press his claim to be a land surveyor. There is no resistance whatever to this claim, much less systematic, totalitarian resistance. The petty quarrel with Schwarzer is "won," but K.'s quest for bureaucratic confirmation is a failure because of the *lack* of central authority.

The Castle presents a world without absolutes. K. is free to leave, to stay, to call himself a surveyor. But he is too free; he is at a loss because of the absence of given structure in his new life. "Divested of illusions and lights, man feels an alien, a stranger. . . . This divorce between man and his life, the actor and his setting, is properly the feeling of absurdity" [writes Albert Camus in *The Myth of Sisyphus and Other Essays*]. This is the nightmare of *The Cas-* *tle*—not claustrophobia from authoritarian bureaucracy, but the agoraphobia and falling sensation of unhappy existentialism—K.'s endless free-fall plunge through yielding, gravityless society and existence. (pp. 47-8)

> *Ron Smetana, in a review of "The Castle," in* The Explicator, *Vol. 45, No. 1, Fall, 1986, pp. 47-8.*

Peter Mailloux (essay date 1989)

[*In the following excerpt, Mailloux relates* The Castle *to events in Kafka's life and discusses the novel's major themes.*]

Although it is Kafka's most complex novel, a work so tightly woven that it is almost impossible to isolate single strands of it, every incident, every setting being inextricably connected to all the others, *The Castle* does begin, like most of Kafka's stories, with a simple situation. A stranger arrives in a village and asks for a place to sleep. Compared to Gregor Samsa's transformation into a bug or Joseph K.'s sudden and inexplicable arrest, this is not a premise of particular power or promise. It does not require a leap of faith on the reader's part. It does not even forcibly dislocate him from his usual context. It is probably, in fact, the simplest, most straightforward initial situation that Kafka ever described. (pp. 518-19)

The castle is, of course, the central symbol of the novel, and it is presented much more fully than its obvious counterpart, the court in *The Trial*. But it nonetheless seems just as vague, mysterious, and ultimately ambiguous as the court is, and not just to K. Consider, for instance, its relation to the village. According to the villagers, the castle, like the court in *The Trial*, is an omnipotent organization with a vast, largely invisible hierarchy that controls their lives entirely. Everything in the village belongs to the castle, and nothing is done there without the villagers' first considering the castle's possible response to the action. The officials, particularly the chief official Klamm, but also the least significant among them, are treated with a respect verging on veneration. Nothing they do, however arbitrary, is questioned; everything is simply accepted as correct and necessary. So dominant is the castle, in fact, that K.'s notion that there should be rules governing it and some freedom under it is regarded by the villagers as proof of his lack of understanding. The castle is not to be questioned; it is not to be understood; it is just to be obeyed.

The castle, in other words, is regarded by the villagers much as a particularly autocratic parent might be regarded by his particularly docile child. (Kafka's themes never change.) At the same time, however, there seems to be little basis for its authority. The fear and veneration may be constant, but they are also theoretical, since the castle rarely seems to direct or demand. It is what it is because the villagers make it so; on its own, it is just there. Even this is hardly certain, in fact, since none of the villagers go to the castle, and most have only the most ephemeral contact with the few officials who occasionally leave their closed world (so closed that its atmosphere—and here too there is a parallel to *The Trial*—is rumored to make villagers faint) to venture into the village. (p. 520)

There is, then, nothing definite about the castle, except perhaps its inaccessibility to K. This is emphasized throughout, it is stated as well as shown, but even here there is the ambiguity of exactly what prevents K. from reaching his goal. He himself claims that the obstacles are all external. Sometimes he blames the hostility of the villagers. Sometimes he blames the inefficiency or ill will or even the fear of the castle officials, who force him to go through quasi-official intermediaries like the Mayor (a direct descendant of the lawyer Huld [in *The Trial*]) and mire him in innumerable documents that, like the court records, propagate themselves perpetually but never seem to settle anything, in part because they are uninterpretable except by the initiated, in part because it is never clear who in the castle reads them. Sometimes he blames the incompetence of his two assistants provided him by the castle. Sometimes he just blames unlucky circumstances.

These claims are countered, though, by other suggestions that K. is himself his own worst enemy. He is told continually, for instance, that he misunderstands everything about the castle, that everything he does is exactly the wrong thing to do, that his very desire to reach the castle is premised on a misunderstanding. K. insists that he wants no favors, that he has been summoned by the castle (although this too is actually ambiguous: at one point K. also seems to admit that it is all a pretense) and therefore is only demanding his rights. For the villagers, however, this makes no sense, since as an outsider K. has no rights. Anything that is done for him is by definition a favor.

To misunderstand is the essence of being a stranger, of course, but K.'s misunderstanding, according to the villagers at least, is greater than that: it is the misunderstanding of a child in an adult world. "If you wouldn't always talk about things like a child, as if they were for eating," he is admonished once, and after that the epithet arises again and again. He is as ignorant as a child, as blundering as a child, as naïve as a child, as dependent as a child. Perhaps most important, he is as impatient as a child. He wants to establish contact with the castle immediately, in one bold stroke, on his terms, and so he takes a series of drastic steps, each of which only seems to further jeopardize his chances. The boldest of these steps is his attempt to waylay Klamm when Klamm is getting ready one night to leave the village. K. hides in Klamm's waiting carriage, but the only thing that he achieves by this is preventing Klamm from showing himself. The carriage, the entire courtyard in which the carriage waits, once forbidden to K., are now ceded to him, giving him the sense that he has won a freedom "such as hardly anyone else had ever succeeded in winning." At the same time, though, what he has won is completely desolate and meaningless, a freedom than which there is "nothing more senseless, nothing more hopeless."

The audacity of this kind of attempt—an audacity already implicit in K.'s ostensible function of land surveyor (in German, *Landvermesser,* a word easily related to *vermessen,* meaning "audacious")—combined with his stubborn refusal to believe anything he is told and his childish conviction that his perception of the castle he has barely seen is the only correct one, make it plausible that K.

should fail in his efforts. But despite these qualities he is presented with one apparently real opportunity to achieve his goal, an opportunity that it is certainly his own fault for missing. One night he is summoned for an interview with a minor official and wanders by mistake into the room where another official named Bürgel is sleeping. Bürgel's name (*Bürge* means "guarantor" in German) suggests that he might be able to bail K. out of his trouble, and the fact that his immediate superior is named Friedrich (suggesting *Frieden,* "peace") reemphasizes the suggestion. Bürgel himself admits as much, in fact: he tells K. that the one sure way to circumvent the castle's bureaucracy is to surprise an official in his sleep. This rarely happens, he says, but if it does, if the applicant, not even knowing what he has done, manages to slip, like a tiny grain through an almost perfect sieve, through the network that makes the officials so inaccessible, then the official inevitably yields to the intruder and takes up his case. This is just the opportunity K. has been seeking since coming to the village, the answer to his prayers, the miracle in which he has almost ceased to believe; but even as Bürgel is telling him of it, is guaranteeing him that if he makes the slightest response now his problems will be solved, and he will be accepted by the castle, K. is already falling asleep, betrayed by his body at the crucial moment, just as Kafka had been so often betrayed by his. He sleeps, in fact, through the rest of Bürgel's monologue and so forfeits his last chance, perhaps his only chance, to make contact with the castle.

Still other explanations for K.'s failure are stated or implied throughout *The Castle.* Perhaps it is because his case is such an unimportant one (as he is told by the Mayor, "one might almost say the least important among the unimportant"). Perhaps—as the Mayor also tells him—it is because K. is too sensitive, too quick to interpret lack of welcome as rejection. Perhaps he asks too much. The very number of explanations is itself a possible explanation. If K. had one certain obstacle to overcome, he could concentrate on that. As it is, however, he never knows exactly what to do, and so, after each failed attempt, he can only try again and fail again and try again and fail again, apparently ad infinitum. In fact, the futility of his efforts very quickly becomes the only constant, so pervading and dominating the novel that it finally obscures everything else, including the question that might be expected to be paramount: why K. wants to get to the castle in the first place.

In *The Trial* this is an easier question to answer since the court, while vague, does at least have one concrete association. It is the Law, something an arrested man, a man obsessed with proving himself innocent, would naturally want to reach. (As the man from the country says, explaining his own quest, "Everyone strives to attain the Law.") But a concrete association, as we have already seen, is precisely what the castle does not have. The more it is examined, the less clear it becomes, for the reader as well as for K. With so little specified and so much implied, the castle is in fact a perfect candidate for allegorizing, which is the way many readers, beginning with Max Brod, have approached it, turning *The Castle* into a latter-day *Divine Comedy* or *Pilgrim's Progress.* The details change from reader to reader, but summarized most baldly the interpretations go something like this. K. represents modern man, particularly Jewish modern man (as Brod says [in his *Franz Kafka: A Biography*], "Kafka in *The Castle,* straight from his Jewish soul, in a simple story, has said more about the situation of Jewry as a whole today than can be read in a hundred learned treatises", in pursuit of religious truth, as represented by the castle. This truth is inexplicable, unpredictable, inaccessible, unappeasable (in other words, divine), and so K., with the best will in the world, can never attain it. His attempt is doomed to frustration, and yet he must continue to make it, just because it is a pursuit of religious truth. His final reward, we are left to assume, will come later, after the book, after the life, in another world entirely.

There are several obvious advantages to this kind of interpretation. For one thing, it does plausibly answer the question of why K. wants to get to the castle. It also serves to make the book seem less bleak, and Kafka less despairing, since frustration in the service of transcendent truth is somehow less frightening, somehow more acceptable, than frustration in pursuit of earthly goals. (In the former case, there is at least the implied happy ending: satisfaction will come later, in that vague other world.) The problem, however, is that Kafka was never as interested in religious truth as Brod, who did have a genuinely religious perspective on life, liked to think. The distance between the real world and a transcendent world, between physical man and spiritual values, great as it was, was not for Kafka the crucial gulf. Rather, it was the distance between man and men, between the individual, as exemplified by himself particularly, and the world in which he was forced to live that preoccupied him. The word "God" almost never appears either in Kafka's stories or his personal writing. The salvation he sought was almost always human.

In itself, this orientation is enough to raise questions about a religious remodeling of *The Castle,* but there is also the fact that the castle is not, as Kafka describes it, a particularly persuasive representative of grace or transcendent truth or spiritual values. If anything, in fact, it is more demonic than divine. It is lorded over by a count whose name, K. is told, should not be mentioned around innocent children. It is run by officials whose primary contact with the village seems to take the form of seducing and then abandoning the village's young women. Power and authority the castle certainly has, but these never seem to be used for worthwhile ends and may ultimately be countermanded by the pandemonium that also seems to reign there. (When K. first calls the castle on the phone, for instance, all he can hear is a buzz "like the hum of countless children's voices.") There is even a continual undercurrent associating the world of the castle with death. Situated in a wasteland of snow and ice, where winter lasts most of the year and summer seems to shrink to several days (and even during these days it often snows,) where the day seems to pass in several hours, while the nights last interminably, the castle is a place primarily characterized by stillness. Even the count's name, Westwest, suggests a region beyond decline, a west further west than that where the sun sets.

A more plausible interpretation of the castle, and of K.'s reasons for wanting to get there, one that takes into account its negative associations as well as its separation from the village and its inaccessibility, might therefore be that it represents the world of writing, something that always concerned Kafka and that particularly preoccupied him during the writing of *The Castle.* His definitions of writing—as a "descent to the dark powers," a kind of death in life—parallel exactly his descriptions of the castle. K.'s inexplicable but irresistible attraction to it corresponds exactly to Kafka's impulse to write. His failure to get there reproduces Kafka's own conviction that he had not yet succeeded in writing the kind of work he wanted. Most striking of all, the irony that Kafka developed throughout the winter of 1922, that he intimated whenever he talked about his writing—that writing, while the most important thing to him, was also the reason he had not yet managed to be part of life—is clearly present in K.'s relation to the castle. For him, the castle may be the place he most wants to get to, to the point that his very existence seems to be at stake if he cannot establish contact with it. It may be defined simply as the one place he cannot reach. But for Kafka it is also what prevents K. from achieving anything else. It is, in other words, not only K.'s ultimate goal; it is also his ultimate obstacle.

To understand this, it is necessary to return to the question of why K. wants to get to the castle, a question to which there is in fact a simple, if often overlooked, answer. Without permission from the castle he cannot stay in the village, and this is what he claims, at least initially, that he really wants to achieve. The fact that K. soon forgets this and transforms the castle from a means to an end obscures this for the reader, who sees the novel primarily through K.'s eyes. But there is nonetheless little doubt that the village, for Kafka, is much more than just a launching pad for K.'s efforts to reach the castle. It is, in fact, the novel's version of the real life of which Kafka was always claiming he wanted to be a part.

Appropriately (since it is a version of real life), Kafka describes the village in much more detail than he does the castle, and he also describes it with a surprising lack of idealization. Peacefulness, camaraderie, productivity, the pleasure of being close to the soil: always before, when Kafka had described places like Zürau, these had been the qualities he had emphasized, until it seemed as if any village, by the very fact of its being a village, somehow partook of the essence of Eden. Kafka's envy, and not his eye, always seemed to underlie these descriptions. Because he wanted to share this life, because he believed it must be the Promised Land, he ignored the wretchedness he might otherwise have seen.

In *The Castle,* however, perhaps because his time at [his sister Otta's house in] Planá had corrected some of Kafka's myopic perspective, there is none of this sentimentalizing. Now, the people in the village are gruff, inhospitable, and inarticulate, and their lives are poor and shabby. They live in one-room cottages, grandparents, parents, and children all crowded together, forced to work, bathe, eat, and sleep in this single room, a corner of it devoted to each activity. They are dominated, more-

The resort village of Spindelmühle, where Kafka began writing The Castle *in 1922.*

over, by fear and suspicion, and there is not a single scene in the novel in which one of them seems even moderately happy. As K. says of the village, "it is a fine setting for a fit of despair." Nonetheless, it is here that K. decides he wants to live ("What could have enticed me to this desolate country except the wish to stay here?" he says at one point), if only the villagers will let him.

That, though, as far as K. is concerned anyway, is just what they won't do. Everyone in the village seems to know him, or to have heard of him, and most, if forced to talk with him, are polite, perhaps because his still ambiguous relation to the castle makes them afraid to reject him explicitly. There are also hints that his supposed freedom to do what he wants, the freedom that results from his having no defined function or identity, is somewhat admired by some of the villagers, even if it also causes them to treat him condescendingly. But generally, especially initially, the villagers' response to K. is to avoid him as much as possible. No one will give him a place to sleep. He is not allowed in one of the two village inns. He is snubbed and bullied by the teachers. He is told by the landlady of the inn where he is allowed, reluctantly, to sleep for several nights that if she had had her way he would have been kicked out the moment he arrived. Even his footprints have to be carefully removed from the snow after the one occasion when K. does manage to pass beyond the boundaries set up for him. As the landlady tells him, summarizing the villagers' attitude, "You are not from the castle, you are not from the village, you aren't anything. Or rather, unfortunately, you are something, a stranger, a man who isn't wanted and who is in everybody's way, a man who's always causing trouble. . . . " If K. would just leave, or if he could be made to disappear as easily as can his footprints, then nearly all would be happier.

Or so K. assumes, although there is (as always in *The Castle*) room for doubt. It may be that the same qualities that seem to prevent him from getting to the castle also cause him to exaggerate the village's rejection. (As the Mayor tells him: "The very uncertainty about your summons guarantees you the most courteous treatment, only you're too sensitive, by all appearances. Nobody keeps you here, but that surely doesn't amount to throwing you out.") Perhaps he only needs to be patient, to allow the villagers time to accept him. Instead, however, K.'s response, based on his assumption that if the castle accepts him, the villagers will have to also, is to redouble his efforts to get to the castle. Everyone he meets in the village he immediately evaluates solely according to his or her presumed capacity to help him achieve this goal. He does this with his two assistants (who have actually, we later learn, been sent to make him more frivolous, less anxious about the castle). He does it with Barnabas, with the landlady, with the Mayor, with the little boy Hans who is one of few villagers to admire him. He even does it with Frieda, whose genuine love for him he should be able to recognize. All of them become for K. just means to an end, pawns to manipulate in the game he assumes he is playing with the castle.

The irony of this manipulation, of course, is that it makes no sense in terms of K.'s original goal. Because means and end have been reversed, the ultimate result is that K. continues to pursue his false goal even after his real goal has apparently been achieved. Once he wins Frieda, after all, K. actually is well on his way to becoming part of the village. By the very fact of his relationship with her he is no longer so completely isolated, and the involvement also serves to change the attitude of the other villagers. They become more willing to accept K., so that all he has to do, as he is told again and again, is forget about the castle and accept his present condition. Nobody explicitly says it, but the implication is clear: K. must choose between the two worlds. It is only his preoccupation with the castle that prevents him from becoming part of the village.

Lest there be any doubt of this—for K. or the reader—Kafka provides for both an explicit parallel to K.'s situation in the story of Amalia and Sortini, which he tells, significantly, immediately following the scene in which Frieda, because of his manipulation of her, finally breaks with K. The connection between K. and Barnabas's family has in fact been set up from the beginning of the novel. Like him, they are outcasts. Like him, they are obsessed with reaching the castle. And like him, they have so far been unsuccessful in their attempts, until finally, in desperation, they have even turned to him for assistance. At the same time, he is regarding them, the only people in the village whom he had originally had no desire to meet, whom he has continually been warned by all in the village to avoid, as his last chance for help.

The story of the family's decline, as K. is told it by Olga, is a long and complicated one; the fact that Kafka devotes almost one-fifth of *The Castle* to it is itself proof of its importance. But it can be summarized briefly. Once one of the village's most respected families, they have lost their position because of one unfortunate incident, the propositioning of Amalia, the younger daughter, by an official of the castle named Sortini. (There is, by the way, a significant redundance here: K.'s troubles began with an official named Sortini.) In itself, Olga tells K., this was not shameful. It was in fact an honor, an opportunity of which any other young woman in the village would have immediately taken advantage. Amalia, however, has rejected the proposition, and it is this rejection that has turned the village against the family. From that day on, their every effort (excepting Amalia's, who has remained aloof from the situation, devoting herself solely to taking care of her parents, the ones most affected by the tragedy) has been directed toward contacting the castle and receiving forgiveness from it.

Olga's description of these efforts is the longest part of her story, and it contains all of the ironies that K. has already discovered through his own efforts. First their father had tried to contact the castle, expending all of his energy in the attempts until he was transformed from a relatively young and still vigorous man into an invalid. Then Olga and Barnabas continued the struggle, Barnabas by presenting himself at the castle as an unofficial messenger, Olga by "entertaining" the servants of the officials at the Herrenhof. Despite these efforts, though, they have obtained no satisfaction, not even the satisfaction of having their guilt acknowledged. According to the castle, they cannot be forgiven because they have not been guilty of anything; if they want to be forgiven, they must therefore first prove themselves guilty.

This is bad enough, but the real irony, the one from which K. should be able to learn a lesson, is that while the family cannot prove themselves guilty to the castle, they do, by the very fact of their continued attempts to contact the castle, prove themselves guilty to the town. In fact, the decline of the family is specifically linked, not to their first difficulty, but to their later attempts to rectify it. As Olga herself acknowledges, "If we had quietly come forward again and let bygones be bygones and shown by our behavior that the incident was closed, no matter in what way, and reassured public opinion that it was never likely to be mentioned again, whatever its nature had been, everything would have been made all right in that way too, we should have found friends on all sides as before, and even if we hadn't completely forgotten what had happened, people would have understood and helped us forget it completely." All they had to do, in other words, was forget about the castle and continue living their lives as they had previously. Instead, however, they have only plunged deeper and deeper into what they had originally wanted to escape from.

The ironic futility exemplified in this story applies to K. too, of course, and it is the final, and most poignant, irony of *The Castle,* an irony made even more poignant by the fact that K. even misses this last opportunity to recognize and rectify his mistake. He remains trapped between the two worlds of the village and the castle, just as Kafka felt trapped between the worlds of writing and real life. And what is worse, he remains trapped there apparently unnecessarily. Like Kafka, he has apparently had his chances to escape—most explicitly with Frieda, but also with Bürgel and even with Amalia, who has provided him with one last alternative by her example of stoic indifference to her position—but he has missed them all. And so he ends as he began, a man hesitating before birth, apparently doomed to continue his futile efforts indefinitely.

Interpreted thus, *The Castle* really is a despairing book, Kafka's definitive analysis of his own isolation, loneliness, and futility. But there are two important qualifications that remain to be made. The first is the unwritten conclusion of the book, which Max Brod claims was once told him by Kafka. According to Brod, K. was to continue his struggle until he was finally worn out by it. Then, as he lay on his deathbed, surrounded by the villagers, word was to come from the castle that although his legal claim to live in the village was not valid, he was nonetheless to be permitted to live and work there. K. would then die, having at last achieved at least this "partial satisfaction."

Whether or not this would have been the ending is uncertain, of course, and it is even less certain that it really, as Brod says, represents a positive ending. Ultimately, however, the question may not matter anyway, since *The Castle* is more than simply an analysis of K.'s—or Kafka's—particular dilemma. The dilemma is in fact expanded to a universal one, one that the reader shares in the very experience of reading the book, and it is this expansion that finally qualifies Kafka's apparent despair. It is also what makes *The Castle* Kafka's most complete artistic success.

Appropriately, another irony, that the reader of *The Castle* is as trapped and helpless as K., that he in fact becomes, in the course of reading the book, another version of K., lies behind this expansion. In most good novels, there is, of course, some identification between reader and hero, some sympathetic sharing of the hero's plight. The desire for such identification, for expanding, if only vicariously, one's world of experience, is a primary reason for reading novels in the first place. But Kafka forces a much more active role, and therefore a much deeper identification, on the reader. And he also refuses to allow the reader any legitimate escape from the identification. At the end of the book, we too are still trapped, just as K. is, foiled in all of our attempts so far to understand *The Castle,* but not yet convinced that an understanding of it is beyond our grasp. We may, that is, be ready to read the book again, in the hope that this time we can make sense of it.

Attempt followed by conditional failure followed by further attempt; a book that always seems within reach but that never actually gets understood: metaphorically, these circumstances alone make the reader a version of K. But the parallels can be made more explicit still. Consider, for instance, the implications of K.'s ostensible function as land surveyor. It makes K. someone who tries to create a workable order within clearly defined boundaries; in other words, a reader of sorts. Beyond that, everything that K. sees, everything that happens to him, he immediately interprets, trying to fit it into a larger picture. Another way of defining his dilemma in the novel would, in fact, be to say that he is a bad reader. He misinterprets everything.

Examples of this can be found throughout *The Castle.* When K. is shown a picture of a messenger and asked to analyze it, his guesses, as the landlady tells him, are "quite wrong." When he receives a letter from Klamm, he misconstrues it entirely, at least according to the Mayor. When he first sees Barnabas, he is deceived by his jacket (K. tends to be a literal reader, a reader of surfaces) and wholly misunderstands Barnabas's importance. When he hears Olga's story about Amalia, he immediately jumps to the wrong conclusion about it. The villagers' response, when faced with the same opportunity for interpreting, is almost inevitably not to make the attempt, and K.'s continual failures make that understandable. The more K. interprets, the further from the truth he seems to get.

And so, unfortunately, does the reader, who not only has a reason comparable to K.'s for wanting to interpret—the desire to understand *The Castle*—but also has even more opportunities for it. He has too, at least initially, sound reasons for assuming that his efforts will be rewarded. The very names of the characters, for instance, seem both to demand and to reward interpretation. The eponymous K. easily leads back to Kafka; the fact that the primary representative of authority, the book's inevitable father figure, also has a name beginning with K seems to make the autobiographical link still more explicit. The self-appointed messenger is appropriately named Barnabas, "son of consolation," after the Biblical figure who, although not actually one of the twelve apostles, came to rank among them. Klamm's village secretary, who sees people only at night and is one of those who most contradict K.'s hope of reaching the castle, is called Momus, "the son of night," after the figure appointed by the Greek gods to find fault with all things. The significance of the names of Frieda and Bürgel has already been mentioned. And then, finally, there is Erlanger, the official from whom K. does expect to get some help. His name suggests *erlangen,* German for "to attain or achieve."

The fact that there is so much interpretation in the book, so many examples to follow, is a further inducement to readers to persevere in our attempts, but there is no doubt that as the book continues, these attempts become just as futile as K.'s. The problem is that there are too few facts, too many conflicting explanations, too much uncertainty. The guiding narrative voice that is always missing in Kafka's stories is even more egregiously absent now, and it is replaced by a cacophony of conflicting opinions. Everything that happens is explained and reexplained with the result, as K. protests once, that the more that is said, the less clear all becomes. Readers end up not knowing what to believe, if anything. We end up, that is, in the same position as K., who knew as much about the castle after his first view of it as he ever learns afterward. Then it seems both there and not there, palpable yet invisible, a place embodying authority, yet not to be reached. The "truth" of *The Castle* is similarly unattainable.

Kafka's success, then, consists in a perfect uniting of form and content in *The Castle.* In a book about isolation, he isolates the reader. In a book about futility, he frustrates the reader. He does not do so in any facile way, moreover, nor just for the aesthetic effect. The only way truly to write *The Castle* was as Kafka wrote it, since certainty of any sort would have been absolutely out of place in the novel. And there was, finally, one last implicit advantage to the method, an advantage of which Kafka himself may not have been fully aware. His method does suggest the one "happy ending" that is not inconsistent with K.'s dilemma. There is no way out of the dilemma, that is clear. But the dilemma, by the end, is just as clearly shown to be not only K.'s (or Kafka's) fault. For a long time, part of Kafka's despair had been based on his conviction that his problems were his alone, that they resulted from his own inability to get along in the world. Now, however, he would seem to have recognized that this was not necessarily the case. In *The Trial,* while pretending to show Joseph K.'s innocence, Kafka had actually proven him guilty. But in *The Castle,* while apparently accusing K., he ultimately excused him, just by demonstrating the universality of his dilemma. In *The Castle,* in other words, Kafka finally managed to achieve what he had always wanted. He placed himself back in the mainstream of life, and without denying his essential loneliness. Instead, he forced the reader to share it. (pp. 521-30)

Peter Mailloux, in his A Hesitation before Birth: The Life of Franz Kafka, *University of Delaware Press, 1989, 622 p.*

FURTHER READING

Bibliography

Flores, Angel. *A Kafka Bibliography: 1908-1976.* New York: Gordian Press, 1976, 193 p.
     Checklist of works by and about Kafka.

Biography

Brod, Max. *Franz Kafka: A Biography*. Rev. ed. Translated by G. Humphreys Roberts and Richard Winston. New York: Schocken, 1960, 275 p.

Study of Kafka's life by his friend and literary executor. Includes reminiscences by two of Kafka's companions and samples of Kafka's handwriting and pen sketches.

Hayman, Ronald. *Kafka: A Biography*. New York: Oxford University Press, 1982, 349 p.

Critical biography. Includes a comprehensive chronology of Kafka's life and works.

Janouch, Gustav. *Conversations with Kafka*. Rev. ed. Translated by Goronwy Rees. New York: New Directions, 1971, 219 p.

Recounts Kafka's discussions with Janouch on such topics as life and literature.

Wagenbach, Klaus. *Franz Kafka: Pictures of a Life*. Translated by Arthur S. Wensinger. New York: Pantheon, 1984, 223 p.

Reproduces photographs of Kafka, his family, and places and objects associated with his life. Also includes a chronology of Kafka's life and brief commentary on the illustrations.

Criticism

Arneson, Richard. "Power and Authority in *The Castle*." *Mosaic* XII, No. 4 (Summer 1979): 99-113.

Reflects on the pseudo-religious nature of the political powers in *The Castle* and views K. as a "romantic individualist" in revolt against this Castle cult.

Fickert, Kurt J. "Kafka's Assistants from the Castle." *The International Fiction Review* 3, No. 1 (January 1976): 3-6.

Discusses Kafka's use of the double in *The Castle*.

Knapp, Bettina L. "Kafka: *The Castle*—The Archetypal Land-Surveyor." In her *Archetype, Architecture, and the Writer*, pp. 67-83. Bloomington: Indiana University Press, 1986.

Discusses K. and the Castle as archetypes of self-seeking and spiritual knowledge.

Kudszus, W. G. "Meeting Kafka." In *Franz Kafka (1883-1983): His Craft and Thought*, edited by Roman Struc and J. C. Yardley, pp. 141-51. Waterloo, Canada: Wilfrid Laurier University Press, 1986.

Uses a single passage from *The Castle* to explore the reader's "entry" into and subsequent understanding of the novel.

Lawson, Richard H. "*The Castle*." In his *Franz Kafka*, pp. 103-24. New York: Ungar, 1987.

Examines the novel's major themes.

Mueller, William R. "The Lonely Journey." In *Celebration of Life: Studies in Modern Fiction*, pp. 232-50. New York: Sheed and Ward, 1972.

Maintains that Kafka's treatment of ambiguity in *The Castle* reflects his "bewilderment" at his life experiences.

Neider, Charles. "The Secret Meaning of *The Castle*." In his *The Frozen Sea: A Study of Franz Kafka*, pp. 122-52. New York: Oxford University Press, 1948.

Offers a Freudian interpretation of *The Castle* and concludes that Kafka was influenced by psychoanalytic theory.

Neumeyer, Peter F., ed. *Twentieth Century Interpretations of The Castle: A Collection of Critical Essays*. Englewood Cliffs, N. J.: Prentice-Hall, 1969, 124 p.

Reprints articles by Edwin Muir, Herbert Tauber, Walter Sokel, Max Brod, and other Kafka authorities.

Olafson, Frederick A. "Kafka and the Primacy of the Ethical." *The Hudson Review* XIII, No. 1 (Spring 1960): 60-73.

Uses examples from *The Castle* to argue against the common perception that Kafka's ethical system is descended from Kierkegaardian philosophy.

Robbins, Jill. "Kafka's Parables." In *Midrash and Literature*, edited by Geoffrey H. Hartman and Sanford Budick, pp. 265-84. New Haven, Conn.: Yale University Press, 1986.

Uses the methods of *midrash*, biblical commentaries by Jewish sages of the first through third centuries, to interpret self-contradictory discourses in *The Castle*.

Ronell, Avital. "Doing Kafka in *The Castle*: A Poetics of Desire." In *Kafka and the Contemporary Critical Performance: Centenary Readings*, edited by Alan Udoff, pp. 214-35. Bloomington: Indiana University Press, 1987.

Studies the appeal of Kafka's *Castle* for literary theorists.

Scott, Nathan A., Jr. "Franz Kafka: The Sense of Cosmic Exile." In his *Rehearsals of Discomposure: Alienation and Reconciliation in Modern Literature*, pp. 11-65. New York: Columbia University Press, 1952.

Argues that Kafka's protagonists struggle to attain unity with God.

Steinberg, Erwin R. "K. of *The Castle*: Ostensible Land-Surveyor." *College English* 27, No. 3 (December 1965): 185-89.

Argues that K. lies about his appointment to the position of Land-Surveyor.

Tauber, Herbert. "*The Castle*." In his *Franz Kafka: An Interpretation of His Works*, translated by G. Humphries Roberts and Roger Senhouse, pp. 131-85. New Haven, Conn.: Yale University Press, 1948.

Examines the major events and themes of the novel.

Thorlby, Anthony. "The Novels." In his *Kafka: A Study*, pp. 68-83. Totowa, N. J.: Rowman and Littlefield, 1972.

Introduces major critical concerns in a section about *The Castle*.

Vincent, Deirdre. " 'I'm the King of the Castle . . . ': Franz Kafka and the Well-Tempered Reader." *Modern Language Studies* XVII, No. 4 (Fall 1987): 60-75.

Argues the inevitability of diverse critical responses to Kafka's works, especially *The Castle*.

Webster, Peter Dow. "A Critical Examination of Franz Kafka's *The Castle.*" *The American Imago* 8, No. 1 (March 1951): 36-60.

> Freudian interpretation of *The Castle* which argues that the novel illustrates the conflict between K.'s ego and his "total psychic past centered in an infantile trauma."

Additional coverage of Kafka's life and career is contained in the following sources published by Gale Research: *Contemporary Authors,* **Vols. 105, 126;** *Dictionary of Literary Biography,* **Vol. 81;** *Short Story Criticism,* **Vol. 5; and** *Twentieth Century Literary Criticism,* **Vols. 2, 6, 13, 29.**

Frigyes Karinthy

1887-1938

Hungarian humorist, short story writer, novelist, playwright, poet, critic, and translator.

INTRODUCTION

Karinthy is noted for his numerous satirical and parodic essays and short stories. Critics praise his best works for their insight into the grotesqueries and inanities of individuals living out what Karinthy perceived to be the tragedy of modern life. After the beginning of the First World War, Karinthy produced fewer satirical works and began writing pieces that directly protested social and political injustice. His last book, *Utazás a koponyám körül* (*A Journey Round My Skull*), a memoir describing his affliction with a brain tumor from diagnosis through surgery, is considered a unique autobiographical accomplishment.

Karinthy was born in Budapest in 1887. He published his first novel, *Nászutazás a föld középpontja felé* in 1902, and began publishing regularly in 1906. He entered the University of Budapest to study mathematics and natural science, then attended medical school for a time. Because the rigorous discipline of his course of study prevented him from pursuing his wide range of intellectual interests, Karinthy left the university and became a journalist. He soon gained acclaim as a brilliant member of Budapest's café society and as a writer of skillful parodies of well-known European authors; his first collection of these works, *Így írtok ti,* appeared in 1912. After the outbreak of World War I, he openly criticized the devastating effects of the war; he also translated Jonathan Swift's *Gulliver's Travels* into Hungarian during this period. His two sequels to Gulliver's journal, *Utazás faremidóba* and *Capillária* were published in 1917 and 1921, respectively. Karinthy frequently wrote for cabarets, theaters, and a number of influential Hungarian periodicals until he began experiencing the psychic disturbances which accompany a brain tumor; early in 1938, he submitted to an operation to remove the tumor. Although the surgery was successful, Karinthy died of a brain hemorrhage in August, 1938.

Karinthy's best works use humor as a vehicle for sociopolitical and philosophical commentary. While much of his writing is entertaining, Joseph Remenyí observes that even Karinthy's " 'trifles' have a metaphysical shadow. . . . [The reader] is aware of a *thinking* writer." Such works as *Capillária* and *A Journey Round My Skull* exemplify Karinthy's ability to make serious subject matter amusing. *Capillária* recounts relationships and conflicts between men and women in the form of a traveller's journal, allowing Karinthy to comment on the disparate conceptions that men and women hold of each other. *A Journey Round My Skull* is Karinthy's account of his

brain disease, beginning with his first suspicions of the disorder and culminating in his precise description of the operation, which was performed using only a local anesthetic. The memoir presents a detailed picture of his physical and mental state through the course of his brain disease, during which Karinthy scrutinized the slow disconnection of the link between intellect and body and attempted to understand the nature of that link. In *A Journey Round My Skull,* Karinthy applied to his own experience the intense powers of observation that are displayed in his social commentary. While some critics maintain that Hungary's social and political upheaval prevented Karinthy from consistently producing the quality of work of which he was capable, he is nevertheless credited with producing works notable for their wit and insight.

PRINCIPAL WORKS

Nászutazás a föld középpontja felé (novel) 1902
Így írtok ti: paródiák. 2 vols. (parodies) 1912

Holnap reggel (drama) [first publication] 1916
Tanár úr kérem! (short stories) 1916
  [*Please Sir!*, 1968]
*Utazás faremidóba (novel) 1917
*Capillária: regény (novel) 1921
The Drama: A Farce-Satire in One Act (drama) 1922
Ki kérdezett? (essays) 1926
Nem mondhatom el senkinek: versek (poetry) 1930
Még mindig így írtok ti (parodies) 1934
Utazás a koponyám körül (memoir) 1938
  [*A Journey Round My Skull*, 1938]
Grave and Gay: Selections from His Work (collected works) 1973
Three Plays: The Singing Lesson: The Long War; The Magic Chair (drama) 1982; published in the journal *Performing Arts*

* These works were translated and published as *Voyage to Faremido. Capillaria* in 1965.

CRITICISM

G. W. Stonier (review date 1939)

[*In the following excerpt, Stonier offers a favorable review of* A Journey Round My Skull.]

Pirandello once wrote a brilliant little play called *The Man with the Flower in his Mouth.* . . . The title predisposes to gaiety, and the curtain goes up on two men chatting outside a café. As often happens in conversation between strangers, one wishes to talk while the other settles down to listen; the bottle must fill the glass. In this case the talker sets out to charm and to impress his singularity on his companion; he has been shopping, and describes in fascinating detail, as though he were cataloguing a Spring morning, the way in which the shop assistant has spoken to him and flourished his hands, how the parcel has been wrapped up, the change snatched from the overhead railway, and so on. This delight in small acts daintily performed has become the passion of his life, and as he goes on talking, with nervous insistence, we begin to guess his secret. He is ill, of course; it all comes out—the doctor has given him three months, the flower in his mouth is a cancer. And the scene ends when he gathers up his parcels and goes to rejoin his wife, who has been watching from the corner of the street.

Frigyes Karinthy reminds one of Pirandello in a number of ways. Indeed, if Pirandello had found himself in the situation of the character of his play, this is just the sort of book, absorbed and ironically detached, we should expect him to have written. He could not have written it better. *A Journey Round My Skull* is the autobiography of nine months of illness (tumour on the brain) which everyone expected to end fatally. The first hint that anything was wrong occurred one evening when the author, a well-known Hungarian writer, was sitting in a café studying a crossword. It was his habit to do this crossword every evening, and he was always baffled by one or two clues referring to "well-known proverbs" he had never heard of.

At that very moment the trains started. Punctually to the minute, at ten past seven, I heard the first one.

I looked up in surprise to see what was happening. There was a distinct rumbling noise, followed by a slow increasing reverberation, as when the wheels of an engine begin their unhurried movement, then work up a louder and louder roar as the train glides past us, only to fade into silence, like the song of the Volga boatmen straining at their craft. I decided that it might have been a lorry and returned to the mysterious proverb.

Only a minute had gone by when the next train started.

After that, the trains returned every evening; they became a habit and at times even amused him. The next symptom was more alarming: a fainting fit which he took at first for a stroke. He went to a doctor who diagnosed nicotine poisoning. Though his own feeling was of something far more serious, and he suspected a tumour on the brain long before any of the specialists would pronounce, he found himself instinctively acting and thinking as though such an illness were *impossible*. . . . Once the nature of his malady was recognised, he accepted it completely, discussing it, walking round it, bouncing it eagerly here and there on the springboard of theory. His knowledge of medicine (he had been trained to be a doctor) as well as his professional curiosity as a writer made him the perfect reporter of such an experience. The various phases and components of his illness—rapid physical deterioration, enhanced dreaming, freedom from responsibility—are conveyed with extraordinary acuteness. There is, too, a lightness, a transparency in his descriptions (such as one gets sometimes in the writings of opium-addicts) which may be due to the advances of the disease but more probably to his own bounding egotism. It would be impossible to have a better imaginative record of a disease, from the first discovery of the tumour to its removal during an operation of four hours, three of which Karinthy experienced without losing consciousness; but at the same time we are aware on every page of the author himself, interested, ironically assertive, as capable of knowing how he appears to others as of recording his own musings. Obviously he is the type of writer who is also an actor; he believes in the Pirandellian theatrical philosophy of human life. In one charmingly extravagant passage he refers to "the apple-tree merely playing the part of an apple-tree, while the stars have their role in the great *ensemble* of heaven."

We may read *A Journey Round My Skull* in order to discover what it is like to suffer from a tumour on the brain—and on that point M. Karinthy satisfies our curiosity. Those indeed who are horrified at the thought—he was threatened by blindness, paralysis and idiocy, if not death—will no doubt be horrified by parts of the book. It is, however, a triumph of writing, of stoical insight, and like Baudelaire's *Une Charogne*, leaves us finally curious about its author. Who is Frigyes Karinthy? He has an unnerving talent. . . . He is popular as a wit and humorous journalist, and spends most of his time in cafés. His serious work is placed high by critics. He has written plays, novels and stories and introduced nonsense writing to Hungary, "in order to break up conventionalities of language." He seems, so far as one can discover, to enjoy in Budapest the sort of reputation which Altenberg has long enjoyed in Vienna. Such talents do not always export well. But to judge from *A Journey Round My Skull*, Frigyes Karinthy may well be a writer as interesting and original, say, as Italo Svevo. There are not many humorists witty enough to remark "Humour is no joke to me" (a phrase I notice in his book). Let us hope that Mr. Vernon Duckworth Barker, a personal friend of Karinthy, who has translated admirably the present volume, will be encouraged to give us some of his other work. Meanwhile, *A Journey Round My Skull* is, what the publishers claim for it, a very remarkable book. (pp. 180, 182)

G. W. Stonier, "A Strange Record," in The New Statesman & Nation, Vol. XVII, No. 415, February 4, 1939, pp. 180, 182.

Sir Flinders Petrie   (review date 1939)

[*In the following excerpt, Petrie gives a mixed review of* A Journey Round My Skull.]

[*A Journey Round My Skull*] is a queer book. The author, a Hungarian man of letters, was discovered to be suffering from a tumour on the brain, was operated on and made a complete recovery. Crudely speaking, he has written up all that he thought, felt and suffered during the months between his first symptons of disease and his restoration to health. Those who are not particularly robust in mind or stomach where sickness and surgical operations are concerned will find the book uncomfortable. Others will be interested but may wish the author were less fond of philosophical embroideries of fact. . . .

What makes the book odd reading in the first place is his habit of poeticizing his sensations or of drawing profound thoughts from them. Then there is his unappeased curiosity in physiological and clinical detail. It may be that this was some sort of morbid condition of his disease; but at the same time the author's intellectual interests appear to have been such as to take him, in the ordinary course of events, to a film of an operation on the brain or on a visit to a slaughter-house or to meditate upon the metaphysical significance of cremation. It was after several visits to doctors, specialists, sanatoria and a neurological clinic in Vienna, where he observed some rare cases of dementia, that he was given treatment to assist in diagnosis. The consequences of his disease, failing a successful operation, were pointed out to him, though he had already made himself acquainted with them; and, after a bad period of illness and hallucinations, he was taken to a celebrated clinic in Stockholm and the surgeon got to work.

The author gives us his sensations, or the memories of his sensations, during the lengthy operation. He is, no doubt naturally enough, too interested in what happened to deny the reader any of the details. [*A Journey Round My Skull*] is not without imaginative quality and is well writ-

ten in its way, but it can hardly avoid giving the impression of a literary exercise. And it may be doubted whether every experience is suitable material for a literary exercise.

Sir Flinders Petrie, "A Literary Exercise on Disease," in The Times Literary Supplement, No. 1933, February 18, 1939, p. 101.

Joseph Reményi   (essay date 1946)

[*Reményi was a Hungarian-born American writer who was widely regarded as the literary spokesperson for the Hungarian-American community during the first half of the twentieth century. His novels, short stories, and poetry often depict Hungarian-American life, and his numerous translations and critical essays have been instrumental in introducing modern Hungarian literature to American readers. In the following excerpt, Reményi discusses Karinthy's major works.*]

Between the first and second World Wars the spiritual bankruptcy of Europe, the freakish ensemble of European powers, the conflict of the extreme right and the extreme left wing in politics, made concentration on realizable ideals almost impossible. It is not surprising then, that much of the writing of this period should be grotesque. The *Teatro del Grottesco* in Rome produced Luigi Chiarelli's *The Mask and the Face* in 1916. The name of the theatre and the title of the play were an indication of their purpose; they justified extravaganzas and approved of a fantastic defiance of reality. Ramon Gomez de la Serna, the Spanish writer, created maxim-like verbal pictures, called *greguerias,* motivated by a bizarre view of life. Carl Sternheim's, the German writer's, sardonic expressionism represented a devastating attitude, no doubt out of place on the pages of a Sunday supplement. Frigyes Karinthy, the Hungarian writer, possessed a unique idiom. Some of his work impresses one as if his mind was performing summersaults in the presence of the reader—a perfectly turned idea balanced by wit. Karinthy was a skeptic in that Greek sense which associated doubt with examination and not with negation. Dogmas did not interest him, rather the reason why people submit to dogmas. His brain never seemed idle. He could be startling, exquisite and gay. Yet the sum total of his work is fragmentary. His fragmentariness is a reflection upon himself as well as upon his times and environment.

Karinthy, as a humorist, was somewhat of a literary wizard. Nevertheless he should not be classified solely as a humanist. His metaphysical curiosity prevented his ignoring the obscure and incomprehensible features of life. He maintained that living was a polyphonic experience, that variety sang through the universe, that the key of life's composition indicated infinite possibilities. His joviality was speculative; but he was sufficiently the artist who felt the pathetic unmeaningness of many things and happenings, and was hurt by them, but, in a creative sense, was also intrigued with their place in human destiny. His jesting articulateness, his vivacious communicativeness jeopardized his reputation as a "serious" writer; his "slang", the argot of "literary" cafés, detracted from his reputation as a genuine literary artist—a reputation, however, to which he was entitled. In a world of political and social masqueraders it was easy to mistake his nimbly expressed, but not light work for sheer virtuosity. He had the solitariness of a clown, with no sneering contempt for his fellowman whom he amused, but possessing a mastery of facts, understanding and adroitness of expression that made him superior to his surroundings. There was cosmic conviviality in Karinthy, the source of which was his sense of universality. Most of his work gives the impression that unless man learns his relationship to the universe, his provincialism of thinking or heedlessness will eventually destroy him. The tragedy of man is that in his anxiety to sustain himself and seeking happiness on a rather low scale, he becomes separated from the greatness of human fate. Each day is a part of eternity, but everyday people are far too often not even conscious of mortal obligations. Ennui is the trite condition of man's tragic lot. These are stereotyped views, but Karinthy's searching intelligence and imagination made them interesting.

Karinthy did not lead a well regulated life. His vibrant personality toyed with the sophisticated moods of Budapest, with the city's colorfulness and poverty, with its breeziness and indolence. He was as much as institution of the literary life of the Hungarian capital, as was Aristophanes in Athens. . . . His entire life was characterized by a consciousness that apprehended and expressed the peculiar status of a highly individualized sensitivity in a clever and hectic environment. Much of this environmental cleverness—in its political, social and literary aspects—was superficial. None-the-less this easy going and seemingly irresponsible writer was, in some respects, the *custos morum* of a society that was rather lax in its norm. Karinthy, of course, did not moralize, but practiced the responsibility of creative imagination in a fashion which made of him an unauthorized, but authoritative judge in an era of paralogisms. He knew how to apply Horace's view; that is, to tell the truth with a laugh.

The *entrefilet* and *croquis,* brief reflective articles of Budapest dailies, were forms of expression in which his fancy and his intellect excelled. He also wrote a great deal for cabarets. His sense of parody was extraordinary. All these writings revealed a flexible intelligence, an agile mind, an authentic though not specific knowledge. In his youth Karinthy attended lectures at the University of Budapest, but he was more or less an auto-didact with an insatiable hunger for learning. One could imagine him in the company of Dr. Johnson, discussing intricate problems. He liked to read in an "irregular manner" like the great English conversationalist. He might also have been a friend of Diderot and one of his collaborators in editing the Encyclopedia. However, he was essentially, a twentieth century spirit, recognizing in the unreasonableness of this age the dislodged position of reason, the perishableness of values. When he died in 1938 at the age of fifty many of his countrymen mourned the death of a distinguished writer, and even those who consistently underrated him had to admit that in those dismal times his writings afforded pleasure and satisfaction.

In a preface to a collection of plays and dialogues, entitled *Szinhaz* (*Theatre*), Karinthy declares categorically that the form of the world is *motion,* its essence is *calm.* In this same preface he states that he was always seeking the *Absolute,* that his art was an endeavor for the awareness of the totality of life in all its moments. This endeavor implies a *tragicomic* disposition; it reveals the writer's relationship to the deceptiveness of life, conditioned by limited free will. Goethe's advice: *sterbe und werde* (die and become) dignifies human struggle; on its journey the spirit of man can reunite with the purpose of destiny. One discerns such views in the works of Karinthy; one also feels his mockery of such heroism. As he did not look upon literature as an opiate for loneliness, he could not accept the nauseating egoism of those litterateurs who pretended to solve the perplexing problems of existence with temporary slogans. His aim was to discover the sense of living. On the other hand the dreamlike haze of the undefinable, the esoteric vagueness of the unknown seemed an ambush, a betrayal of reason. Consequently, thinking as a metaphysical procedure was a tragicomic effort, and it was this tragicomic effort, this partly pathetic, partly baffling contact with rationalizable illusions that determined the tone and psychology of Karinthy's work.

All his writings, even the inconsequential ones, are directed toward a hypothetical goal. They are actuated by an irrepressible urge for comprehension. One hears the questing, crying, shouting voice of solitariness, rejecting the idea that life is ridiculous. "I was a soul, I fought" we read in one of his poems. Sometimes his voice is ineffectual, at times it seems futile. It can be harsh in the equality of the fight, it can be graceless, especially when he uses words that are formless when in contact with the idea they wish to express. Too often he succumbs to a belletristic manner, to slips of taste, to mental indiscretions that amused those of similar taste, but were really wordplays or just "smart." He could not escape the influence of a crumbling civilization; indeed, his yearnings, his jocose star-gazing afflictions, his scientific flirtation with heavenly bodies rather than with earthly luminaries, his insistence upon the substantiality of life, were expressions of a tragicomic nature in need of more than the vehicle of lively literary journalism.

His only book of poems (somewhat inferior to his prose) has the characteristic title: **Nem Mondhatom El Senkinek.** (*I Cannot Tell It To Anyone.*) In the foreword he says that, as he could not tell his secret to anyone, he had to tell it to everyone. But his interest in eternal values did not lessen his critical interest in actualities. He had common sense, but it was like common sense in a circus, like a caricature in a church. Two of his popular books, **Így Írtok Ti** (**This Is How You Write**) and **Még Mindig Így Írtok Ti** (**You Still Write Thus**) are travesties of known writers; they show Karinthy's ability to identify himself with the voice and spirit of contemporaries who in many ways were alien to his spirit. In some instances the pastiche is more genuine than the original. His imagination could be nurtured by other imaginations without losing its identity. Karinthy's abhorrence of arrogant timeliness did not prevent his recognizing the convenient ideas of the moment. As a journalist he learned not to be unduly vexed or bewildered by ephemeral activities.

The elasticity and buffoonery of his humor, the satirical

originality of his observations, were, as a rule, expressed in an idiom in tune with the idea he wished to express or criticize; and though some of his yarns sound like twice-told tales, the reader is well repaid by the attractive wit of the writer. His humor stresses the importance of spiritual rescue, an honest regard for the sacredness of life. In one of his stories we meet a musician who became a trapeze "artist". He was unable to appear before the public as a concert violinist, his one aim in life. Finally he achieved his dream, surmounting incredible difficulties; he played the violin up in the air, on the trapeze bar, and the public was compelled to listen. In this story—as in many of his other stories and sketches—one senses the writer's sympathy for the dreams and eccentricities of his fellowmen. His lyricism is coherently objectified in a manner which aptly measures his art against those writers of short stories who could be simple and suggestive about the most complicated patterns of human problems.

Even his "trifles" have a metaphysical perspective, a tragicomic shadow. In *Gorbe Tukor (Crooked Mirror)* and in other works of similar ironic intention and intonation, in his sketches and stories, e.g. in *Tanar Ur Kerem (Professor, Please)*, *Talalkozas egy Fiatalemberrel (Meeting with a Young Man)*, *Ballada a Nema Ferfiakrol (A Ballad of Silent Men)*, *Krisztus vagy Barabas (Christ or Barrabas)*, *Gyilkosok (Killers)*, one is aware of a *thinking* writer, endowed with a turn of mind that even in its disillusioned moods did not dissociate itself from the rage and hopes of mankind. His collection of essays, *Ki Kérdezett? (Who Asked?)* shows the contradiction of words in their obvious and hidden meaning. Karinthy's sense of the grotesque sometimes bordered on metaphysical irritability; generally, however, it was a truly boundless interest in incongruous human actions and reveries.

As in the case of other humorists, Karinthy, too, knew bitterness and despair. Mark Twain's accustomed humor is certainly missing in *The Mysterious Stranger;* in Karinthy's works humor sometimes was scoffing, jeering, condemning. He was hurt by the grimness of male-female relationships and the resulting heartaches; by the overrefined lies of such existence; by man's capacity to make a fool of himself and by woman's capacity to abuse the male. With less misogynic restlessness than August Strindberg and adhering to his grotesque inclinations, Karinthy wrote a story entitled *Capilláría,* which he called a sequel to Swift's *Gulliver's Travels.* It seems that while he was translating Swift's story into his native tongue, he conceived the idea of continuing Gulliver's diary. First he wrote a book, entitled *Utazás Faremidóba (A Journey to Faremido)*, imitating the tone and manner of Gulliver's travels in strange lands. But *Capilláría,* the country of women, is really his expression of scorn blended with despair. The writing of his *Faremido* story was prompted by the desire to liberate the soul from the frailties of the body; several of his stories deal with madness; others with sad incompatibility of man's pacifistic notions and the unscrupulous and wretched struggle for survival. But *Capilláría* is the voice of the male whose sense of humor prevents his becoming an out and out misogynist, but could not prevent his pondering on questions related to man and woman in a manner that was not flattering to that remark-

able objective of a male's desire. *Capilláría* as a work of art is persiflage; it shows man's degradation in a world where women prefer power to love. One recalls Tolstoy's remark that when a man woos he says things to a woman he later forgets, but the woman does not forget them, though she has ceased to love the man. One also recalls Ibsen's Nora, the emancipated nineteenth century woman; Karinthy implies that in the twentieth century it is man who should be emancipated from the domineering and demoralizing influence of women.

Some critics accused Karinthy of having a distorted view about male-female problems. Others recognized his astuteness, the dark depth of his despair, the intensity of his satire. It was Karinthy, the psychologist and Karinthy, the poet, who in novel-form expressed the male's disappointment in his dreams of the opposite sex; he also expressed the frenzied loneliness of the male who would like to remain a troubadour, but whom woman expects to be a provider and a guinea pig on which to try out her emotional and materialistic inconsistencies. Karinthy would like women to remain women, and not to be golddiggers or feminists to the detriment of their femininity.

Holnap Reggel (Tomorrow Morning) is Karinthy's most representative dramatic achievement. It is a three-act play and had a consecutive run of one hundred and fifty performances in a Budapest theatre, though some critics called it a closet drama, and some asserted that Karinthy remained a novice of the stage. The writer called his play a tragicomedy. In the ingenious preface of the printed version he says that as a rule the beginning of a tragicomedy is gay and the ending sad, whereas in his play the beginning is sad and the ending gay. The plot concerns an engineer who is also an aviation expert and an inventor. His name is Sandor Ember. "Ember" means *man* in Hungarian; it also means *human.* The symbolism of the protagonist of the play is obvious. He is in love with a singer; she, however, prefers an aristocrat, Count Beniczky, a man without complexities, but strong and virile. After various psychologically well motivated preliminaries we meet Sandor Ember one morning on the city outskirts; he is expected to do experimental flying in the presence of two army officers, his friends, Maria Lehotay, the singer and her lover, the count. The day before, Count Beniczky and Sandor Ember had an "American duel". The count drew the red ball, the engineer the black one, hence he had to die. His intention was to commit suicide during the experimental flying. Instead of committing suicide, he returns safely, and feels superior to the people who heretofore considered him weak and vacillating. His last words are, turning to the singer: "How happy I am, Maria . . . I do not love you anymore!"

One gathers the impression that the chief character of the play is one whose lack of selfconfidence and courage was caused by unrequited love. Flying his plane away from the pettiness and habitual selfishness of humans he suddenly developed a sense of proportion and recognized the ghost of his fears. He had taken the measure of human evaluations and pride and became spiritually and emotionally independent.

Utazás a Koponyám Körül (A Journey Round My Skull)

is Karinthy's only book that has appeared in English. It was translated by Vernon Duckworth Barker, an English writer who lived a few years in Budapest. It was first published in England, then in America. Thomas Sugrue, the American novelist, calls it "a strange, a wistful, and a lovely book, though its subject matter is neither wistful nor lovely, only strange." Karinthy's curiosity never forsook him; his ailment, a brain tumor, his state of mind because of it, the operation in Stockholm by Herbert Olivecrona, the famous surgeon, were experiences to which he reacted with all the alertness of his intelligence and imagination. This is a book of consciousness in the shadow of possible death; an amazing document of human awareness. One of the most significant statements is the following: "It is important that I should relate what happened in a sober, clear style, undisturbed by my present frame of mind. If only for this reason I could not do otherwise than put on record the fact that throughout my illness I was the victim of a sense of guilt which has only now reached the threshold of consciousness. I had the feeling that I was guilty of some forgotten sin that had never been condoned because the memory of it remained outside my conscious mind. This perhaps explains why, from the first to last, I am incapable of complaining or rebelling against my fate."

The sober tone, especially in reporting the operation, is unusually effective considering that the writer was facing death (he passed away a year after the operation), yet on this outbound journey he did not silence his creative intelligence. His sense of guilt in the paralyzing unreasonableness of modern life is an admission of a need of values, of a sense of duty expressed in many of his writings. This explains his overtaxed sensibility, his grotesque pattern of profaneness and spirituality, his tragicomic relationship to the concept of heroic living.

As before stated, Karinthy was a fragmentary writer, a relativist in search of the absolute, an integration-seeking individual tempted and repelled by disintegrating western culture. The vacuum and hokum of the modern world, the humbug, hooliganism and satanism of man in this kind of a world, affected his sense of humor and his sense of values which were interconnected terms. The basic element of his outlook was tragicomic, indeed; within the scope of his Hungarian experiences he recognized the pathos and bathos of the human adventure in its universal aspect. The quality of his humor (*mirth, farce, mischievousness, nonsense, acridity, irony, satire*) was determined by the quality of his expectations regarding realizable ideals. He had a critical point of view, and laughed for reasons that Bergson identified with the mechanical violation of one's natural rhythm. But he was also saddened by the fact-accepting Martial's axiomatic wisdom—that the good man is always a beginner, that goodness is but an attempt at being human.

His work is of varying merit. Much of it is random-creativeness. He combined deliberateness with instinctive freedom, and in substance his sense of the grotesque is but a grinning awareness of an age in which there was a terrible cleavage between the ideal and the real. His comic sense, his drollness, his broad smile and his burning sense of truth were not always woven harmoniously into the fabric of art, therefore parts of his work do not exhibit an unswerving attachment to aesthetic integrity. To a certain extent the social, political and economic structure of his times explains the defects, but they were also congenital defects. None-the-less, whatever shortcomings he had, his observing intelligence, keen imagination, creative power were undeniable. Wit was Karinthy's stock-in-trade, banality his phobia, smugness his aversion, truth his dream.

As a thinker and *causeur* Karinthy had much in common with the eighteenth century *philosophes*. This affinity, however, was rather in the enlightened manner of expression than in its ideological perspective, and it had a twentieth century intonation. Nandor Varkonyi, the Hungarian literary critic, aptly said that in Karinthy's world one experiences things as they are and at the same time as they should be. Karinthy was interested not only in the biological reality of things, but also in their logical existence in reference to ideas and ideals. He abhorred mannerisms, yet used mannerisms of expression to fight them. He had a critical mind, a sense of dissonance, a fear of imperfection, a vision of perfection that was excluded from the realm of facts. What makes him especially significant in relationship to the modern Hungarian literary scene was his concern with the clarification of intellectual terminology applied to the commonplace inconsistencies of everyday life and to the conceit of its humdrum character. Hungarian literature is rather meager in philosophical traditions, and Karinthy's imaginative contribution to the intellectual qualities of Hungarian letters is undeniable. It must be stressed that in an age of science he used his scientifically inclined imagination as a speculative vehicle for aims, that in themselves were not scientific, yet his manner of writing suggested the relationship of belles lettres to scientific purposes and expressions. Like Matthew Arnold in the nineteenth century Karinthy was aware of the dilemma of modern life as a consequence of an iconoclastic interpretation of nature and human nature and of scientific inventions. This comparison does not imply a similarity between the literary aptitude and significance of the two writers; it merely indicates the similarity of alternatives—science and faith, science and poetry, science and morality—that thinking writers, with entirely different backgrounds, face in modern times because of a confused and confusing sense of spiritual orientation. Of course, in substance, Karinthy was remote from the ideological and actual world of Matthew Arnold.

As a popular writer, he was primarily acclaimed for his humorous spirit, his wit, caustic intelligence and for his unprejudiced attitude. His laughter was logical, although it reached many illogical souls. He enjoyed mental anagrams. As a humorous writer he differed from his predecessors inasmuch as his humor was urbane and sometimes complicated; it was antithetical to the rural jokes and conventional reflections of other humorists, and to the smartaleck chattering of pseudo-modernists. He was a master of that irony which Edgar Johnson, the American critic, identifies with "double talk" in a meaningful sense, and not as mere gibberish. Karinthy permitted himself a latitude in expression and taste that made his humor sometimes rather loud than vital at the price of authentic creativeness; on the other hand, because of his genuine ability, he never joined the braggarts of fun whose humor and satire was fostered by the cheap expectations of every-day standards. (pp. 69-79)

Joseph Reményi, "Frigyes Karinthy, Hungarian Humorist: 1888-1938," in Poet Lore, *Vol. LII, No. 1, Spring, 1946, pp. 69-79.*

Paul Tabori   (essay date 1966)

[*Tabori was a Hungarian-born English journalist, novelist, editor, and translator. In the following excerpt from the introduction to his translation of* Voyage to Faremido. Capillaria, *Tabori provides an overview of Karinthy's career and briefly discusses his literary influences.*]

Karinthy began as a humorist; he rose to fame as a fun-maker and parodist. The two volumes of parodies he published under the title [*Így írtok ti*] made him respected and feared almost overnight. He also published innumerable short sketches and provided the Budapest cabarets (modelled on the famous Munich *Elf Scharfrichter* and the later Viennese *Kellerbühnen,* and originally inspired by Montmartre) with some of their best pieces.

As a parodist he was without peer. I love Stephen Leacock's *Literary Lapses* and respect Robert Neumann's vitriolically accurate work in this field. I know a good many other writers who have dabbled in this particular literary form—yet I have no hesitation in saying that none of them could touch Karinthy. He had a wonderful ability of grasping the essential quality, the basic nature of any writer, Hungarian or foreign. His parodies could be wild and mad exercises of the imagination running amuck (Perelman is perhaps the closest in this respect); but in most cases they were of high literary quality in themselves. Whether it was Ibsen or Conan Doyle, Dickens or Zola, the Hungarian Endre Ady or Ferenc Molnár whom he picked for his victim, the persiflage and satire were pinpointed brilliantly, showing up the faults or exaggerations of the most eminent authors. He was like a master taxidermist; his stuffed animals were so life-like that they almost moved. Because his hits were so palpable, he made quite a few enemies; but even those who suffered the most cruel punishment at the point of his pen yielded in the end to the power of his heroic laughter. It became quite an honour, at least in Hungary, to be parodied by Karinthy.

But his mind was too sturdy and independent to be content with basing his work on the creations of others. His own original humour was abundant and irresistible; he must have written a couple of thousand 'funny pieces,' not counting his stage sketches. He usually started from an everyday premise, carrying it to its witty absurd extreme. A commonplace problem, a humdrum situation blossomed magically into a boisterous farrago of nonsense in his hands. Nothing is more difficult and futile than to analyze humour, and long studies have been devoted to the difference in the sense of the ridiculous between various nations and ages. But Karinthy's pieces, I believe, have a universal appeal. Whether he writes about a school-boy explaining his bad school report (and telling his father that he cannot call on the headmaster as the front-door of the school has

been removed for an indefinite period) or the effete young poet complaining bitterly that his own mother didn't know him (only to discover in the end that the woman was not his mother at all); whether he traces the gradual development of murderous rage in a man longing to make a pet of a rabbit but being foiled by the animal's stupidity; or whether he relates his own adventures in trying to educate his children—he has the rare talent of provoking belly-laugh and happy chuckle alike. That is, his wit is both robust and subtle; and it has a slight bitter taste that is thought-provoking.

A good example of Karinthy's biting humour is his one-act play, **The Magic Chair,** of which he has written two or three versions, one considerably longer than the others. It is the story of the inventor, Dr. Genius, who has been kept kicking his heels in a Minister's anteroom for years. In the meantime he has invented perpetual motion, split the atom and found the formula for external youth—but the Minister is far more interested in a match-box that plays the National Anthem whenever a match is struck and in a picture frame that lights up when the sun sets. Years of frustration have embittered Dr. Genius. The moment of his revenge has now arrived. For he has invented a chair which is a kind of automatic lie-detector that will make everybody who sits in it speak nothing but the absolute truth. The one-act play shows him smuggling his invention into the Minister's room—and the chair doing its work only too well. The chair shows up the politician for the ridiculous windbag he is; the private secretary as a corrupt lickspittle; the wife as a hysterical and cheap tart; the best friend, a "sensitive poet," as a vulgar and vain publicity hunter; the doctor a humbug who lives off the ignorance of his patients. The revenge of the inventor is complete; and though the fun becomes fast and furious, it is also in a way quite terrifying. This short play contains a modicum of Swift's fearful and majestic misanthropy. The laughter it awakens is mixed with the humble realization how little integrity the human race possesses. It was Karinthy's delight in many of his works to pierce inflated balloons and to show up the pretensions, frailties and contemptible vices of his fellow-men. As a good humorist he did not spare himself either. Bureaucrats, warmongers, pompous office-seekers, money-bags were all fair game to him. One of his most amusing pieces describes an interview with "the Bank." He applies for a small loan but "the Bank" spins him such a moving hard luck story that in the end it is *he* who hands over his last banknote. With all his flights of fancy, with all his absurdity, there is a deep layer of social criticism even in his lightest and most frivolous writing.

Karinthy was also a poet of considerable depth and originality. He wrote comparatively little verse; his whole life's output amounts only to a couple of volumes entitled **Message in the Bottle** and [**Nem mondhatom el senkinek**]. But he was a master of rhyme and rhythm, and he stood quite alone in Hungarian poetry, without ancestors, companions or followers. In the introductory poem of his first volume he sums up his *ars poetica;* the following free translation may give an idea, however faint, of his poetic gifts.

(The poet is asked why he no longer writes
poems.)
(A few lines illegible, then . . .)

. . . my fingers
are frozen. This bottle in my left. The right
holds the joystick. It has grown very stiff.
Thick ice on the wings. I don't
know whether the engine can take it. Queer
snoring noises it makes, in here. It's terribly
   cold.
I don't know how high I am
(or how deep? or how far?).
Nearness and distance, all empty. And all
my instruments are frozen. The scales
of Lessing and the compressometer of the Academy;
the Marinetti altimeter, too. I think
I must be high enough because the penguins
no longer lift their heads as my propeller
drones above them, cutting across
the Northern Lights. They no longer hear me.
   Here are
no signs to see. Down there some rocky land.
   New land?
Unknown? Ever explored before? By whom?
   Perhaps
by Scott? Strindberg? Byron, Leopardi?
I don't know. And I confess
I don't care. I'm cold, the taste
of this thin air is bitter, horribly bitter . . .

                                    (pp. xi-xiv)

Here I am, at the Thirteenth Latitude of Desolation,
the Hundredth Longitude of Shame,
the Utmost Altitude of teeth-gnashing Defiance,
somewhere far out, at the point of the Ultimate,
and I still wonder whether it is possible to go any
   farther . . .

"And I still wonder whether it is possible to go any
farther . . ." That was, in a sense, the basic idea of all
Karinthy's poetry. Whether he re-told the Parable of Talents or sang of the Invisible Prison that enfolded all men,
he was on a quest, and his unquenchable curiosity accompanied him to the very end of his life. (p. xv)

It was his deep curiosity that left him discontented with
past and present and turned him into a writer of utopias,
a very early but breathtakingly prophetic practitioner of
science fiction. Many people familiar with his *œuvre* agree
that some of his most important ideas were embedded in
the two short novels contained in this present volume, the
sequels to Swift's *Gulliver's Travels*. *Faremido* and *Cápillaria*, I feel, combine Karinthy's qualities and interests as
poet, humorist, philosopher, scientist and visionary. The
first was written in 1917, the second, in 1921—and these
dates are important. When he published *Faremido*,
Čapek's *R.U.R.* with the first appearance of the robots
had not yet been seen on any stage or printed in any book.
Automation was something no one even dreamt of; cyber-
netics was far in the future and in the mind of Dr. Norbert
Wiener. If ever a man was ahead of his time, the author
of *Faremido* could be said to have marched in the distant
vanguard. The point needs no labouring. The reader, if he
keeps the date of the book's original appearance in mind,

will find proof of this startling prophetic power on every
page. Karinthy's utopias owe nothing to any predecessor;
to Swift himself he owes only his framework, and even the
character of Gulliver becomes transmuted through his
magic.

Faremido was in a certain sense a prologue to the longer
and more complex *Cápillaria.* Basically both have the
same theme: the utter inadequacy of Man, the futility of
all our endeavours, the ridiculous pretence that we are
sentient beings capable of progress. In *Faremido* Karinthy
contrasted Man and Machine; in *Cápillaria* he juxtaposed
Man and Woman. The latter is a tale that would have delighted Schopenhauer or that Prince of Misogynists, Otto
Weininger. (pp. xvi-xvii)

Basically Karinthy was much more than a humorist, parodist, writer of utopias, poet or philosopher. As a Hungarian critic and biographer points out in a brief study, Karinthy was really an encyclopaedist in the truest sense of this
almost forgotten word. All his life he fought against the
barriers to social progress, against prejudice and superstition, against power-myths and false legends. "He was a
fighter . . . and a forlorn hope. He was a champion of the
Rule of Reason and of the Government by Intellect."

More than twenty-five years after his death his work is just
as alive in his native country as it has been for many years.
Hardly a day passes without a Karinthy sketch being produced in some literary cabaret or on the radio; hardly an
hour goes by without someone quoting one of his famous
bons mots. But his greatest, most original achievements
are still lacking general acknowledgment. Many collections of his stories and sketches are being published. Even
his early diaries and notes, his correspondence and his
translations are printed—but his popularity, as it was in
his lifetime, remains one-sided. Fundamentally he hated
to be considered the eternal clown, a 'real card,' a
'scream.' Those of us who knew him well, to whom he
talked of his real purpose and hope, knew well enough that
he was annoyed whenever he was classified as a lightweight funny man. Most publishers, magazines, dailies,
for which he worked, demanded 'something amusing'
from him; no wonder that he was for so long misunderstood by his compatriots. Yet Mihály Babits, the great
Hungarian poet, translator and critic, wrote in 1926 in answer to the enquiry of a foreign publisher:

If someone asked me who was the Hungarian
writer with the most to say to Europe, beyond
the frontiers of Hungary and independently of
our tragic problems, I would name Frigyes
Karinthy without the slightest hesitation. His
work carries the most universal message about
our deepest common human problems. We have
great writers beside him whom Europe does not
know or knows insufficiently, and whom it
would be well worth for the whole world to
know; for they have created pictures of the life
and emotions of a much-suffered and amazingly
complex nation. In the colours of these pictures
you will discover the basic elements of all that
is eternally human. But in Karinthy's work
these elements are not presented in Hungarian
colours, through Hungarian problems. In his
writing the people are not wearing Magyar gar-

ments—no, I'm tempted to say, they wear no clothes at all. They are completely and unashamedly naked . . .

To be sure, Karinthy has always tried to present the very essence of people and events. Where he has succeeded in his quest, he has sought the simplest manner to express the basic ideas so that all men could understand him.

He made no secret that he wanted to be considered one of Diderot's successors; if he had had his way, he claimed, he would have devoted all his time and ingenuity to create a new encyclopaedia. By this he meant nothing as simple and ordinary as a series of illustrated and morocco-bound volumes to grace a glass-fronted book-case. Even in his bondage of having to write too much and too fast, he retained a deep nostalgia for his original conception. Although he was unable to work systematically on the new definition of ideas, he did at least produce many scattered, occasional pieces under the various headings of his imaginary *New Encyclopaedia*. He used quite often the subheading "an article in the New Encyclopaedia" for his essays; even his humorous pieces, sketches, short stories, novels were all part of a great comprehensive plan. His only full-length play, [*Holnap reggel*] was also conceived as a link in this encyclopaedic chain—it served to give an entirely new interpretation to the problems of fear and courage.

Nor can one exclude from his basic design the parodies of [*Így írtok ti*]. In a preface he wrote to the third or fourth edition of this collection, Karinthy emphasized that he was not trying to produce simple parodies, travesties or mere banter but literary caricatures, to show up sharply and faithfully the basic qualities of his victims. If he had been aiming at easy laughs, he would have chosen bad or second-rate writers and their most vulnerable works—Pinero instead of Wilde, Ohnet instead of Proust. But he parodied the best writers and their finest work; in his caricatures he reduced them to their essence, to nudity—and created further headings for his *New Encyclopaedia*.

In his introductory letter to **Cápillaria,** Karinthy explained forcefully why he considered the French encyclopaedists, Diderot and the other liberal humanists, his models and forerunners. They "called themselves encyclopaedists deliberately and consciously," he wrote, "they already knew that analysis was the basis of the great work of enlightenment. The terribly confused complex of ideas, whose mistaken association is shown by their practical result, the frightful state of the world, must be unravelled, taken apart, broken up if there is no other way; we must find the pure, simple elements of ideas so that we can reassemble them in a natural, healthy way."

Some of his critics have compared him to Swift (and Swift was perhaps the strongest influence upon the encyclopaed-

ists), yet the two sequels to *Gulliver's Travels* show how different Karinthy was from his great predecessor. While Dean Swift disliked (and even hated) humanity, condemning all men because of their sins, Karinthy loved human beings and loved life. In his eyes man was not essentially bad; he needed help just as social reforms had to be achieved in order to cure the *malaise* of the world.

In some ways, Swift considered individual and collective faults almost original sins. In the same mistakes and crimes Karinthy saw errors of education and the failings of social institutions. In the preface to **Cápillaria** he explained that the anomalies in the relations of the sexes were due not to inborn viciousness but to a faulty social system—a system that accepted the idiotic premise that a woman's love should require other rewards and returns than the love of a man. He urged a revolution, to put an end to sexual misery; but he knew that in order to achieve this, its economic causes must be also removed. "After the revolution of our everyday bread," he wrote, "we must start the revolution of everyday happiness, of everyday love . . . "

He was a pacifist with a searing hatred of war; but he hated inequality and injustice just as deeply. " . . . there is a greater crime than murder, there is something worse than death—it is slavery," he wrote. "And war means slavery. If man lived for ever and not for just the biblical threescore-and-ten, then indeed the supreme treasure of which he could be robbed would be his life and killing the supreme sin. But as we all have to die sooner or later, he who robs me of the meaning of my life commits a graver sin than a murderer. And the meaning of life is freedom. War is the destroyer of human liberties. The antithesis of war is not peace but the revolution of ideas . . . " (pp. xviii-xxi)

Paul Tabori, in an introduction to Voyage to Faremido. Capillaria *by Frigyes Karinthy, translated by Paul Tabori, Living Books, Inc., 1966, pp. vii-xxi.*

FURTHER READING

Szalay, Károly. "Frigyes Karinthy (1887-1938)." In *Grave and Gay: Selections from His Work,* by Frigyes Karinthy, edited by István Kerékgyártó, pp. 239-46. Budapest: Corvina Press, 1973.

Biographical and critical overview.

Edwin Markham

1852-1940

(Full name Charles Edward Anson Markham) American poet.

INTRODUCTION

Once internationally famous as the author of "The Man with the Hoe," Markham was a popular American literary figure of the first half of the twentieth century whose works espoused progressive social and spiritual beliefs. In contrast to the experimentalism and pessimism that generally characterized poetry of this era, Markham's quatrains, sonnets, and heroic verse celebrate peace, love, and socialist utopian reform.

Markham was born in Oregon City, in the Oregon Territory. His parents separated several years after his birth, and in 1856 the young Markham moved with his mother to a farm at Suisun, in central California. Although in later years Markham romanticized his childhood and adolescence, he found his youthful pursuit of knowledge frustrated by his mother's refusal to buy books or to finance his education. Only after Markham ran away from home for two months in 1867 did she agree to allow him to enter Vacaville College. Markham earned his teacher's certificate from Vacaville in 1870, and later attended the San Jose Normal school. After teaching in California for several years and taking courses at Christian College in Santa Rosa, Markham became superintendent of schools at Placerville.

In 1876 Markham abandoned the Methodist faith of his childhood and became a follower of the spiritualist and utopian socialist Thomas Lake Harris. Harris's doctrine, which espoused social harmony and universal charity, became a major force in Markham's life. Markham had begun writing poetry as early as 1872, but he did not sell his first poem until 1880. For the next nineteen years, he contributed poems to *Harper's, Century,* and *Scribner's,* and cultivated friendships with such eminent American literary figures as Edmund Clarence Stedman, Hamlin Garland, and Ambrose Bierce.

During the last week of December 1898, Markham completed a poem that changed his career overnight. Entitled "The Man with the Hoe," the poem was based on the painting of the same name completed by the French artist Jean-François Millet in 1862. Millet's painting depicts a stooping peasant with a brutish expression on his face who in Markham's poem becomes the embodiment of the suffering of oppressed labor throughout world history. Markham read the poem to an editor of William Randolph Hearst's San Francisco *Examiner* at a New Years' Eve party, and that newspaper published the work two weeks later. "The Man with the Hoe" attracted wide public no-

tice and was reprinted in newspapers across the United States. Its appeal for better treatment of the working class became the subject of national debate and launched Markham's career as a poet, transforming him into a national celebrity. Markham enjoyed this immense public prestige until his death in 1940.

Markham's poetry is characterized by its highly rhetorical nature and expresses his advocacy of social reform as well as his desire for the unity of humankind through spiritual faith. "The Man with the Hoe," as well as his subsequent poetry, was hotly debated by critics. William Jennings Bryan wrote: "There is a majestic sweep to the argument; some of the lines pierce like arrows," while Ambrose Bierce railed: "As a literary conception it has not the vitality of a dead fish. It will not carry a poem of whatever excellence otherwise through two generations." Although Markham's first collection of poetry, *The Man with the Hoe, and Other Poems,* was subject to the same controversy, critics generally viewed Markham as a poet of much promise. With each successive collection, however, he encountered disfavor with critics. When *Gates of Paradise, and Other Poems* was published in 1920, Herbert S. Gorman wrote: "Markham became a poet when he wrote 'The

Man with the Hoe' and when he penned the last line he ceased to be a poet." Nevertheless, Markham always remained popular with readers, and his distinguished appearance—tall, ruggedly featured, and bearded—impressed many people as the ideal of a great American poet. In 1922 Markham, on invitation from former president William Howard Taft, read his poem "Lincoln, the Man of the People" at the dedication of the Lincoln Memorial; in 1932, on the occasion of Markham's eightieth birthday, he was regaled at New York's Carnegie Hall, a celebration to which thirty-five nations sent representatives. Despite the decline in his reputation after his death, Markham remains an important figure in American poetry of the early twentieth century.

PRINCIPAL WORKS

The Man with the Hoe, and Other Poems (poetry) 1899
Lincoln, and Other Poems (poetry) 1901
Children in Bondage (nonfiction) 1914
California, the Wonderful (nonfiction) 1915
The Shoes of Happiness, and Other Poems (poetry) 1915
Gates of Paradise, and Other Poems (poetry) 1920
New Poems: Eighty Songs at Eighty (poetry) 1932

CRITICISM

Edward B. Payne   (essay date 1899)

[*In the following excerpt, Payne outlines the initial critical controversy surrounding the publication of "The Man with the Hoe."*]

As a literary production Edwin Markham's poem, **"The Man with the Hoe,"** needs no argument—its exceptional merit in that particular being almost universally conceded. . . . [The] poem has been, and is yet, the center of a remarkable controversy bearing on the social problems of modern times. Walt Whitman prophesied of a future for these states when "Their presidents shall not be their common referee so much as their poets shall," and the widespread and earnest attention accorded to this poem may be taken as an illustrative instance of the power of the poet to stir and direct the thoughts of men. Here is a case in which men are deeply moved and sharply aroused, not by an act of legislation, not by a scientific demonstration, not by a logical argument, but by a few lines of verse sung out from the frontier West by one hitherto but little known, but now at once recognized as a leader of the people, girded with moral purpose and inspired by urgings of social justice.

The newspaper clippings referring to the poem indicate a remarkable itinerary for **"The Man with the Hoe"** since its first publication in the San Francisco *Examiner*, January 15, 1899. Daily and weekly papers republished it, generally with extended comments, first throughout California and the Pacific States; then in the Mississippi valley; on into New York and New England; over the line into Canada; and even across the sea stretch to the Hawaiian Islands. It appears to have everywhere stimulated thought upon social problems, and to have called out vigorous and diversified expressions of opinion all along the line of its course.

Mr. Bailey Millard, literary editor of the *Examiner*, was the first to record an opinion. He greeted Mr. Markham as "a new voice, deep-toned, sonorous, singing grandly," and pronounced the poem "a piece of virile verse, one of the very few true poems, written by Californians"; adding that "it is tense, sympathetic, interest compelling, and, above all, heroically human." Forthwith, that distinguished critic, whose pen is sharper than a locust thorn, Ambrose Bierce, took issue with Millard's judgment. He prophesied for Mr. Markham, as he has done before, an "eventual primacy among contemporary American poets," and recognized the "noble simplicity and elevation of his work" in general; but urged several objections to this particular poem, chiefly because of "the sentiment of the piece, the thought that the work carries." To the sense of Mr. Bierce this is but an echo of "the peasant philosophies of the workshop and the field; the thought is that of the sandlot—even to the workman threat of rising against the wicked well-to-do and taking it out of their hides." Regarding the origin of **"The Man with the Hoe,"** Mr. Bierce had this to say:

> He is not a product of the masters, lords, and rulers in all lands; they are not, and no class of men are, responsible for him, his limitations and his woes—which are not of those that kings or laws can cause or cure. The masters, lords, and rulers are as helpless in the fell clutch of circumstance as he—which Mr. Markham would be speedily made to understand if appointed dictator. The notion that the sorrows of the humble are due to the selfishness of the great is natural, and can be made poetical, but it is silly. As a literary conception it has not the vitality of a sick fish. It will not carry a poem of whatever excellence otherwise through two generations. That a man of Mr. Markham's splendid endowments should be chained to the body of this literary death is no less than a public calamity. If he could forget now, what the whole world will have forgotten a little later, that such a person as William Morris existed, it would greatly advantage him and prove the excellence of his memory.

At once, following this beginning of controversy, the critics began to arise, right and left, making what Mr. Loomis characterized in "The Land of Sunshine" as "an audible noise." The newspapers received hundreds of manuscripts, and for a time accorded as much space to **"The Man with the Hoe"** as to prize fights and "police stories." The clergy made the poem their text; platform orators dilated upon it; college professors lectured upon it; debating societies discussed it; schools took it up for study in their literary courses; and it was the subject of conversation in social circles and on the streets. It was extolled, ridiculed, jested at, cartooned, assailed, anathematized, defended; and there is not yet an end.

A curious episode in the controversy was the entire misapprehension of the spirit and purport of the poem, by some of the working people; that is, if some writers were not concealing their true sentiments under a masque. One, for instance, regarded the poem as a direct assault on the American farmer, and assured Mr. Markham that "agriculture is a peaceful, ennobling, and independent calling."

Some came to the defense of the poem, and made good points for its doctrine, by a facetious assumption of character and idea. One who announced that he was himself **"The Man with the Hoe"** declared it to be "not his fault that he had no steam plow." The steam plows were all in the hands of the men who held two hundred thousand or more acres of land; and yet, he added, "nature has given to every man two hundred thousand acres of land. Some of it is in the moon, some of it on other planets, but the circumstance that we cannot get at it is not the fault of the rulers, landlords, and masters. Why should I blame the millionaire when he merely follows his instinct and aids nature in her great evolutionary work—the production of millionaires instead of men? Let him stand on my neck."

The poem has not been spared at the hands of those grotesque critics whose humor is chopped out with a meat axe. A writer on the staff of the San Francisco Evening Post pronounced it "driveling nonsense, written in a futile effort to find out who made the 'thing that grieves not and never hopes,'" and recommended to Mr. Markham, as fit material for his poetic attempts, "the statistics of the Chamber of Commerce, and the facts concerning the export and import trade of the city." "Surely," he says, "our laureate of the clod and hoe may not disdain to ask his withered muse for inspiration to write a poem paraphrasing the shipping news and idealizing the fiscal statements of the collector of the port." The editor of the San Francisco Wave found the Markham idea a subject for contempt:

> It strikes us as the veriest twaddle. The burden of Mr. Markham's lay is, that the man with the hoe has been brutalized by his superiors. His brow is low, his face without intelligence, his whole make up, mental and physical, a libel on man as Mr. Markham thinks he should be. Mr. Markham's ideal man with a hoe should be a person with a four-story forehead and the front of a leading actor in a genteel comedy company. Being a genuine poet, Mr. Markham entirely overlooks the important fact that if some portion of the human race was not horny fisted and beetle browed, few of the fields would be plowed or reaped, and railroad building, hod carrying, sewer digging, and other kindred callings would become lost arts. When humanity is invested with very high foreheads and razor edged intellects sharpened by a college course, it opens doctors' or stockbrokers' offices, or practises law. It carefully avoids hoes, spades, and pick axes. It is plain, therefore, that if the world were run on Mr. Markham's plan he would never have written his famous poem, for there being no man

willing to use a hoe, the inspiration of his great effusion would have been lost. All of which tends to show that writing poetry is one thing, and thinking common sense is quite another.

The philosophy of the poem has been more seriously and intelligently dealt with by the president of Stanford University, David Starr Jordan, who has used it as the theme of a lecture delivered in many places throughout the Coast. He acknowledges the existence of **"The Man with the Hoe,"** something like him being found in all lands, but chiefly in France where we should be content to let him remain. But as to responsibility for him, the lords and masters may claim a partial alibi. His slant brow and brute jaw only mark the primitive character. Labor in itself is not the cause of his condition; but he suffers from the fact that he labors for others instead of for himself. He is chained to the wheel of toil, and that degrades. He is crushed under the burdens of excessive taxes, and militarism, and the aggressions of aristocracy and intolerance. In Europe his status is due conspicuously to the degenerating processes of the Latin races. His hope is not in the whirlwinds of rebellion. Regeneration must come from peace, from tolerance, from justice, and from a chance to labor, not for the nation, but for himself. Men straighten up for self, and for self alone.

In one of his lectures, President Jordan affirmed that the real and radical reason for the slanted brow of "the man with the hoe," and his brute jaw, is that his "father and mother had them,"—an explanation which had already been advanced by an earlier critic in a fable:

> Said the chicken to the eggshell from which it had just emerged, "Why didn't you give me a nice, long tail and four legs like the horse over there?" "Blame my mother for that," replied the egg, "she laid out the plan of your existence."

In an article written from the standpoint of a theosophist, Dr. Jerome A. Anderson has attempted to correct Mr. Markham's philosophy, by asserting that the poem "is built upon entirely wrong conceptions of human life"; that it is "an example of the curiously perverted views prevailing in this era of ignorance"; that it is "founded on the theological assumption that man is not the fashioner of his own destiny"; that it smacks of "grace" and "vicarious atonement" which engender "the exceedingly vicious habit of blaming misdeeds upon somebody other than the true author"; that the hoe man is "a product of the law of cause and effect"; that he has already existed through many incarnations, and his condition is due to "individual causes set in action by the individual in previous lives." This, of course, relieves the "masters, lords, and rulers," from responsibility. The hoe man is not their handiwork, but a thing of his own fashioning.

Mr. Markham has been censured for that he denounces the "immemorial infamies" and "perfidious wrongs" from which the hoe man has suffered, without suggesting the remedy—the same mistake, albeit, as some one has pointed out, that Thomas Hood made in writing "The Song of the Shirt." Mr. Markham does indeed leave it to others to answer his question, "How will you ever straighten up this shape?" The answers volunteered in the discussion have

Man with the Hoe, the subject of Markham's famous poem, painted between 1860 and 1862 by the French artist Jean-François Millet.

been diversified from the recommendation to "let things drift" to a demand for the radical reconstruction of society. On the one hand it is held that there is nothing to do, because the "slave of the wheel of toil" is providentially and wisely destined to his task, a foreordination of God, calling for general gratitude; as one writer, an alleged "poetess," puts it, the "man with the hoe" is:

> The man the Lord made and gave;
> For which we should most thankful be—
> That we have tillers of the soil—
> Tillers giving us our prosperity.

On the other hand it is proposed to organize "a universal trust embracing all the means of production and distribution, and including in the combine labor as well as capital, while as the beneficiaries of such trust are included all the people—a trust of the people, for the people, and by the people. The followers of Henry George have not missed their opportunity. Joseph Leggett, one of their foremost leaders on the Coast says: "Single taxers have no difficulty in answering the question, Who made the man with the hoe? To them it is rank blasphemy to say that God made him. It is absolutely impossible to conceive of the existence of such a creature under conditions that secured to all men the right of access to the land which God made and gave up to the children of men. No man with the hoe could be found among the Indians who occupied this continent before the white man came. Low in the scale of being as were the aborigines of Australia, there was no man with the hoe among them. That dread shape came in with the landlord. In the Golden Age of English labor, of which Prof. Thorold Rogers tells us, there was no man with the hoe in England. He appeared on the scene contemporaneously with the English landlord, and he will remain there until the landlord is eliminated. The man with the hoe came into existence in this country contemporaneously with the giving out of our supply of government land, and he will stay with us until the adoption of the single tax secures to every child of man within our borders the right to the use of the earth." Another "single taxer" says: "The man wants his own land to hoe, and that will end most of the woe; that will put light in his eye and uplift him and his jaw, and give him a stiff upper lip. He is in no particular need of theology, religion, free silver, or rag money."

The value of this discussion lies in that it illustrates the loose but intricate tangle of modern thought as touching the conditions, the possibilities, the obligations of civilization; and how tradition, self-interest, prejudice, and passion, as well as sincerity, good-will, and the love of truth and justice are all potent factors in determining the variant opinions and irreconcilable purposes of men. We are far from any such consensus of opinion as might enable us to effect wise and speedy readjustments looking to improved conditions for the masses of men. It will probably be a long time yet, before we shall be able to unite all the energies of society in a general committal to any adequate movement for progress and reform. The voices of men are discordant, their motives at variance, their aims contradictory. The worst of it is, that the majority seem still to be skeptical of any great possibilities for human society. To any voice crying aloud in behalf of the primary rectitudes as between man and man, the multitude is still disposed to respond, "Crucify him!" This seems to prove that the hoe man is not the only man of whom it may be said that the light has been extinguished within his brain. We have all been brutalized under this régime of interior and ever intensifying competition. We cling to and defend the traditional business and social procedures, despite their radical iniquities. Only the few appear to see that these iniquities are anything more than incidental—mere infelicities of a system which, on the whole, is regarded as good enough, if indeed it be not exalted to the plane of divine beneficence. This general lack of moral insight into the essential meanness and degradation of our system is the dark fact of our times, the hopelessness of humanity. It makes room within us for a sometimes flippant and sometimes sullen skepticism as to the plain simplicities of social truth and righteousness. We need, more often than we hear it, the clear voice of the bard and the prophet challenging our indifference and unbelief. There should be many Markhams. (pp. 17-24)

> Edward B. Payne, "The 'Hoe Man' on Trial,"
> in The Arena, Boston, Vol. XXII, No. I, July,
> 1899, pp. 17-24.

W. N. Guthrie   (essay date 1899)

[*In the following review, Guthrie enthusiastically praises* The Man with the Hoe, and Other Poems.]

Every true citizen of the great American republic, who is also born or naturalized in the greater republic of letters, one not of equal rights but, apart from difference of divine endowment, of equal chances, longs to hear of the advent of some first-rate American singer—whose song shall be not echoes from over the sea, but the utterance of our life as it strives to fulfill itself in individual loveliness. It is hard to be critical. We are so desirous. Any firefly seems a star, any meteor a sun. Witness Mr. Stedman, easily our most meritorious American critic. What a contrast between him of the "Victorian Poets" and him again of the "Poets and Poetry of America?" In the former a Matthew Arnold is esteemed a minor, in the latter a Longfellow a major poet! To Mr. Stedman, by the way, is dedicated the little book of verse of which it is our lot to speak and surely if he was "first to hail," as also "to caution," its author he did well both by him and us. At all events neither poet nor critic has cause for shame.

Our first word shall be one of gratitude—not passionate, for our deepest self has been scarcely stirred, but gratitude nevertheless. A choice diction, great sonorousness within the line unit of his blank verse, skillful and effective use of the noble sonnet form, perfect mastery of the old heroic stanza of Dryden's "Annus Mirabilis" and Gray's "Elegy," as in **"The Wail of the Wandering Dead"** and the far nobler **"Song to the Divine Mother,"** and lastly a felicitous handling of the free dithyrambic rhythm and rhyme, as in **"The Desire of Nations"** and **"A Lyric of the Dawn."** All these things, greatly to the credit of Mr. Edwin Markham, it is a pleasure to note for the edification of some prospective reader, since any one who has already perused the contents of *The Man with the Hoe, and Other Poems* needs not even to be reminded of these technical virtues of our poet.

It is ungracious, on the other hand, to fault his blank verse for being purely cumulative in its power, metrical line upon line, no flow of period, consequently none of the larger eloquence which is found in some of his rhymed work? And this not only in the title poem, but in **"A Look into the Gulf," "In Death Valley," "At the Meeting of Seven Valleys,"** and in **"From the Hand of a Child."** Does not fairness require the statement that a number of short pieces, unfortunately included in the volume, are mere poetic experiments of doubtful value even as such, the feminine rhymes occasionally leading what thought or feeling there is into predicaments which bring it to the brink of nonsense or dissipate it into ghosthood; such an echo as

> Wail, wail, wail,
> For the fleering world goes round,

partaking more of parody than of imitation; the free rhythm of such a piece as **"The Man under the Stone,"** whatever its merits otherwise, having little that reminds us of the splendid success of Heine in his "Nordsee" or of Arnold in such a piece as "The Future."

We may deplore such poetic self-consciousness, learned of Wordsworth, as (**"To the Cricket"**),

> *Lead* thou the starlit night with merry notes,
> And I will *lead* the clamoring day with rhyme;

or (**"To Louise Michel"**),

> And here now at the parting of the ways,
> I lay a still hand lightly on your head.

Fancy the picture, and smile not! We may regret that he is disposed to indulge that self-pitying mood, vulgarly called the "blues," which no man is hypocrite enough to deny having experienced, but which no benevolent person desires by literary expression to transmit; for are there not too many poems on death and the dead which suggest that afterlife may be as bad as, if not worse than, the "blues," from internal causes or got by the contagion of unmanning sympathy, cause this present life to seem?

We may chuckle at the survival of the supposition that "only man is vile" the dear little ants knowing no competition, no caste system, no warfare (**"Little Brothers of the Ground"**); and, in sympathy with this the traditional treatment of nature, little effect being noticeable of botany or mythology, etc. Here surely Lanier set an example worth following!

What shall be said now in honest, sincere praise? **"The Man with the Hoe,"** though an undeveloped creature, is mistaken for a degenerate, and all the other socialistic pleas are sincerely eloquent, dignified, impressive. Such sonnets as **"The Elf Child," "The Goblin Laugh," "A Leaf from the Devil's Jest Book," "A Meeting," "The Last Furrow," "The Warp of Dreams,"** are each in its way excellent, the last two being peculiarly strong. These alone would not let our poet's name easily pass away with the somewhat hysterical vogue of **"The Man with the Hoe,"** although it is grace of fancy rather than virile strength of imagination which impresses us in them. His **"Lyric of the Dawn,"** though it recalls at times poems by greater poets, and becomes once almost dangerously didactical, is a charming piece of verse.

"The Desire of Nations" has in it things of great beauty from which we should like to quote freely, particularly that beautiful identification of the Christ with Balder, Apollo, Osiris, and the Ideal Socialist.

And lastly his **"Song to the Divine Mother"** is sustained and eloquent as well as technically remarkable, in which Gray's "Elegy" stanza has a prophetic swiftness, a passionate fullness of sweep, though the pessimism of certain stanzas is only the artistic elaboration of the "blues."

In conclusion let us say that the volume well deserves to obtain the attention which the title poem by the chance of newspaper notoriety may bespeak for it, and some of us heretics, who are quite sure that "The Recessional" is not Kipling's greatest, would like to whisper in the dear public's ear—if it will not betray us to the inquisitors of the press—that neither also is **"The Man with the Hoe"** Mr. Edwin Markham's masterpiece. (pp. 499-502)

> *W. N. Guthrie, "Markham's Poems," in* The Sewanee Review, *Vol. VII, No. 4, October, 1899, pp. 499-502.*

William Morton Payne   (review date 1899)

[*The longtime literary editor for several Chicago publications, Payne reviewed books for twenty-three years at the* Dial, *one of America's most influential journals of literature and opinion in the early twentieth century. In the following excerpt, Payne contends that Markham's artistic strength lies in his nature poems.*]

It is not our intention to make any contribution of our own to the discussion of that over-discussed poem, **"The Man with the Hoe."** We have known Mr. Markham as a poet for many years, and have held the sturdy vigor of his verse in high esteem. It is merely an inexplicable caprice of the public that has singled out this particular poem for extravagant laudation or censure, as the case may be, and has achieved for its writer a reputation that his previous years of work had not won for him. We wish only to say that in his assumption that society has made "the man with the hoe" what he is, there is a begging of the whole question. We are rather inclined to think that men make themselves instead of being moulded by pressure from without, and

that men with hoes and other useful implements play a proper part in the social economy. And we are also minded to quote a few apposite sentences from one of Stevenson's essays. "When our little poets have to be sent to the ploughman to learn wisdom, we must be careful how we tamper with our ploughman. When a man in not the best of circumstances preserves composure of mind, and relishes ale and tobacco, and his wife and children, in the intervals of dull and unremunerative labor,—when a man in this predicament can afford a lesson by the way to what are called his intellectual superiors, there is plainly something to be lost, as well as something to be gained, by teaching him to think differently. It is better to leave him as he is than to teach him whining." The popular success of Mr. Markham's single poem has, however, had the excellent effect of bringing out a volume of verse which might otherwise never have seen the light, and which was certainly worth printing. It is not alone in the titular poem that the author has elected to wear the prophet's mantle, for the same plea for the oppressed and the same vision of a coming human brotherhood is the strain of most of his songs. The ideal is of the noblest, if here somewhat vaguely conceived, and we cannot have too many poets for whom the message comes in such words as these:

> Go, be a dauntless voice, a bugle-cry
> In darkening battle when the winds are high—
> A clear sane cry wherein the God is heard
> To speak to men the one redeeming word.

In his **"Song to the Divine Mother,"** which is perhaps the finest of his poems, the passionate socialism of the author achieves an expression that would not have been unworthy of Morris. But for all the deep human feeling with which these songs of the "Fraternal State" are charged, we are bound to say that Mr. Markham appeals to us more strongly when he forgets man and turns to the consolations of nature, or when, giving free rein to the imagination, he has such a vision as this of **"The Wharf of Dreams."**

> Strange wares are handled on the wharves of sleep:
>   Shadows of shadows pass, and many a light
>   Flashes a signal fire accross the night;
> Barges depart whose voiceless steersmen keep
> Their way without a star upon the deep;
>   And from lost ships, homing with ghostly crews,
>   Come cries of incommunicable news,
> While cargoes pile the piers, a moon-white heap—
>
> Budgets of dream-dust, merchandise of song,
> Wreckage of hope and packs of ancient wrong,
>   Nepenthes gathered from a secret strand,
> Fardels of heartache, burdens of old sins,
> Luggage sent down from dim ancestral inns,
>   And bales of fantasy from No-Man's Land.

> *William Morton Payne, in a review of* The Man with the Hoe, and Other Poems, *in* The Dial, *Chicago, Vol. XXVII, No. 319, October 1, 1899, p. 242.*

Ellen Burns Sherman   (essay date 1899)

[*In the following essay, Sherman argues that in the light of Charles Darwin's theory of evolution, sympathy for the working classes, as displayed in "The Man with the Hoe," defies reason.*]

Perhaps no poet really expects an answer to the stately interrogations which he levels against the universe or mankind at large; above all, when such interrogations are couched in rhetoric so seductive and masterly as in **"The Man with the Hoe."** And yet, and yet—between the almost breathless appreciation which the reader is compelled to give each stanza of this remarkable poem and one's afterthoughts there must often have been an unconscious protest. Possibly the bygone habits of school-days, when questions had to be answered, have asserted themselves, and the reader has felt a few nebulous answers gathering amid this chaos of poetical queries. Such answers would be especially likely to obtrude with gentle heresies if the reader had chanced to study Mr. Markham's poem immediately after the reading of a chapter from some work on evolution, like Drummond's "Ascent of Man." In the light of the processes of evolution, the throes of sympathy, and all the bitter Job-old misgivings excited by the man with a hoe, become subdued and transformed into a calm and complacent tranquillity, that need feel no worse pangs at the sight of the man who is "dead to rapture or despair" than in contemplating his more remote furry ancestor, or a nearer one whose "vestigial structures" were still more marked than his.

While it is undoubtedly well, now and then, to give the world a "mental and moral nudge" to accelerate the movements that uplift mankind, it is also well to temper one's sympathy with the remembrance that it has not been "man's inhumanity to man," alone, that has produced the semi-brutish condition of the hoe-handling class, but also certain conditions imposed by Nature upon those who first wrestled with her, unaided by the discoveries and inventions of later days. As long as Nature forced men to delve and drudge for their bare sustenance, it was most mercifully ordained that there should be a clod-like correspondence between their sensibilities and their tasks. For the same reason, the ox, with an ox's work to do, is a happier and more useful animal than he would be with anything more than an ox-light in his brain. Nobody "blew out the light" within the brain of the man with a hoe. The time has not come for it to be lighted, but the materials were in existence for kindling it in some succeeding generation. One might as logically mourn for the absence of the marvelous coloring of the butterfly in its grub state, as to sigh o'erlong over the too slanted brow of the toiling peasant, who is only a man "in the making"—a making that requires many patient centuries. And when these centuries are all completed, there will probably be a vaster difference between the highest type of the man that is to be and the one that now is, than exists between our wisest sage and **"The Man with the Hoe."**

If a sigh comes up at the thought of the gulfs between the seraphim and **"The Man with the Hoe,"** how measure one's suspiration when he contemplates the still greater chasms that lie between the seraphim and the barbarous African tribes whose language is a series of mere clicks, or the Eskimo who burrows in the snow, eats his meat raw, never ablutes, and leaves his female offspring out in the cold to perish?

One finds, too, the same widely varying range of gift and intelligence among the lower animals. The nightingale, if given to those comparisons which Dogberry says are "odorous," might well lament over the gulfs between it and the goose, the pouter pigeon, or the duck, and the trained racehorse would surely feel a pang of sympathy for the dull-witted mule or dromedary.

"The descent of man from the animal kingdom," says Drummond, "is sometimes spoken of as a degradation. It is an unspeakable exaltation." On his way to higher stages man was obliged to pass through the condition of the man with a hoe, but one should not pause too long in considering any one stage of evolution. A poet such as Mr. Markham should also sing a song of exultation over the illumination that inevitably awaits the remote descendants of **"The Man with the Hoe."** (pp. 1033-34)

Ellen Burns Sherman, " 'The Man with the Hoe' Again," in The Critic, *New York, Vol. XXXV, No. 869, November, 1899, pp. 1033-34.*

The first publication of "The Man with the Hoe":

On December 31, 1898, Markham and his wife went to a New Year's Eve party at Carroll Carrington's. In Markham's pocket was a just-finished draft of a long poem inspired by Jean Franҫois Millet's painting *The Man with the Hoe,* which had been on exhibit in San Francisco. When Markham read it at Carrington's request, Bailey Millard, one of Hearst's editors, asked to print it in the *Examiner.* Hearst had made Millard editor of the Sunday edition, a department separate from the dailies. Aware that he had been put in charge to boost circulation, Millard, having learned from Hearst the value of sensationalism, needed some color. . . . Markham's poem seemed perfect for Millard's needs. Underneath a reproduction of the Millet painting, Millard set the poem in heavy type and blocked it in with a floral border. Below that he added an "appreciation" of Markham's "virile verse." Set exactly in the middle of the front page of the culture section of the Sunday, January 15, 1899, issue, it was an aggressive display.

Joseph W. Slade, in Prospects, *Vol. 1 1975.*

Leonard D. Abbott   (essay date 1902)

[*In the following excerpt, Abbott acclaims Markham as the poetic voice of labor and socialism.*]

"Markham is played out," said a friend to me the other day. "He has only written one great poem, and that has been much over-rated." The view-point indicated by these remarks has found not infrequent expression, especially in the newspapers. It is based chiefly, I think, on the carping criticism of literary hacks, who write to tickle the palate of a conservative and orthodox public. Most of the "critics" were amazed, not to say chagrined, when Markham's magnificent poem of revolt, **"The Man with the Hoe,"** won him world-wide fame. What right had this man, with his revolutionary thought, his championship of the proletaire, his terrific indictment of the "masters, lords and rulers in all lands," within the sleek and sacred precinct of letters? He has left all the beaten tracks; he has refused to confine his verse to love motives, or to trees and flowers. In his poetry is the voice of the oppressed and the outcast, and he hurls their fierce resentment in the very teeth of the "Gray Privilege" of to-day. No wonder the old-time litterateurs quaked at the vision of this portent and tried to belittle it, for in Markham they beheld a new force, and the germ of a new epoch, in literature.

Such is the feeling inspired by a reading of Markham's last book of poems, a book that is dedicated from its first page to its last to the Free Spirit of Democracy. One of the poems in this volume, **"The Sower,"** is pronounced by no less a critic than Max Nordau to be "more than on a level" with **"The Man with the Hoe;"** and **"Lincoln"** may fairly challenge comparison with Markham's masterpiece. To this latter poem Jack London pays the following tribute:

> Not forgetting Walt Whitman's 'O Captain, My Captain,' wet with tears and halting with half-sobs, it is not too much to state that in Mr. Markham's **'Lincoln'** the last word has been said. The poem itself is a 'stuff to wear for centuries.' In the centuries to come it is inevitable that

Markham, "the dean of American poets."

it shall be coupled with the name of Lincoln. If its author had made no other bid for fame, this one bid would suffice. It is an inspired biography, an imperishable portraiture of a man, and so long as the memory of Lincoln endures will it endure.

Hardly less great is **"The Sower,"** a poem written after seeing Millet's picture of that name and instinct with the Socialist spirit. Of this sower, who typifies the working class of the world, Markham writes:

> He is the stone rejected, yet the stone
> Whereon is built metropolis and throne.
> Out of his toil come all their pompous shows,
> Their purple luxury and plush repose!
> The grime of this bruised hand keeps tender white
> The hands that never labor, day nor night.
> His feet that know only the field's rough floors
> Send lordly steps down echoing corridors . . .
> This is the World-Will climbing to its goal,
> The climb of the unconquerable Soul—
> Democracy whose sure insurgent stride
> Jars kingdoms to their ultimate stone of pride.

And ever this thought recurs, that "the strong young Titan of Democracy" shall one day become conscious of his strength and power, and take his own. The great Leader shall arise at last—

> Lover of men, thinker and doer and seer,
> The hero who will fill the labor throne
> And build the Comrade Kingdom, stone by stone;
> That kingdom that is greater than the Dream
> Breaking through ancient vision, gleam by gleam—
> Something that Song alone can faintly feel
> And only Song's wild rapture can reveal.

America's is to be the proud destiny of winning the new era in human progress. Hers is the mission to "take the toiler from his brutal fate—the toiler hanging on the Labor Cross." Already Germany "hears the great Labor Angel down the night, crying, 'Behold my judgments are at hand!' " And France and Belgium "feel the young pulses of the days to be, and hear far voices call them to aspire." America shall lead them all:

> But harken, my America, my own,
> Great Mother, with the hill-flower in your hair!
> Divine is that light you bear alone,
> That dream that keeps your face forever fair . . .
> The armed heavens lean down to hear your fame,
> America: rise to your high-torn part!
> The thunders of the sea are in your name,
> The splendours and the terrors in your heart.

Edwin Markham's democracy is as inclusive as Nature itself. All his verse is permeated by "the tang and odor of the primal things." "The winging whisper of a homing bird," "the gladness of the wind that shakes the corn," "the pity of the snow that hides all scars,"—such are some of his wonderful phrases. He makes us fall in love with Nature anew, and draws us nearer to the great common life of the world. He has written no more lovely poem than that on **"The Wall Street Pit,"** in which he contrasts the "surge and whirl" of its mad faces with the sane life "on stiller ways." He writes:

> Thrice happier they who, far from these wild
>   hours,
> Grow softly as the apples on a bough.
> Wiser the ploughman with his scudding blade,
> Turning a straight fresh furrow down a field—
> Wiser the herdsman whistling to his heart,
> In the long shadows at the break of day—
> Wiser the fisherman with quiet hand,
> Slanting his sail against the evening wind.
>
> The swallow sweeps back from the south again,
> The green of May is edging all the boughs,
> The shy arbutus glimmers in the wood,
> And yet this hell of faces in the town—
> This storm of tongues, this whirlpool roaring on,
> Surrounded by the quiets of the hills;
> The great calm stars forever overhead,
> And, under all, the silence of the dead!

Edwin Markham is the first real poet of Labor. It is true that Shelley has given us some stirring revolutionary ballads, and many beautiful lines alive with the social passion. Morris, too, has bequeathed to the world a little sheaf of exquisite Socialist poems. Some of the minor poets have written "labor" poems that will live. But Edwin Markham, more than any other poet in the English language, can claim the honor of being the Bard of Labor,—the true product of the last great movement that is destined to shake the world to its base. (pp. 74-5)

> *Leonard D. Abbott, "Edwin Markham: Laureate of Labor," in* The Comrade, *Vol. 1, No. 4, January, 1902, pp. 74-5.*

Evolution of "The Man with the Hoe":

[Markham's] notebook for 1896 already contained a first draft of "The Man with the Hoe," though with material incorporated which went back to 1885. One of his efforts in this area is curious, in that he attempted to make a sonnet of his feelings. There must be few American poems which had drawn so much thought, over so long a time before they consummated themselves in verse. What there was of the sonnet came to Markham in this wise:

> This is the Abyss, the goal to which we creep
> This is the Gulf that hangs below the race.
> The terror of that dull indifferent face,
> Stolidly beyond the reach of words that weep
> Beyond despair & hope—a human heap,
> An Emptiness wherein there is no place
> For the white feet of beatitude & grace
> More terrible than Dante in the Deep

He continued to struggle with this vision and with related thoughts while his more decorous verses increased in number, as *Scribner's* and *Century* and the *Atlantic Monthly* responded to his contributions.

> *Louis Filler, in his* The Unknown Edwin Markham, *The Antioch Press, 1966.*

David G. Downey   (essay date 1906)

[*In the following excerpt, Downey demonstrates that the message of Markham's poetry is its call for social unity.*]

To Edwin Markham poetry is not a byplay, not the recreation of an idle hour. It is not offered as an easy substitute for thought, something that one may read merely for the pleasure of the rhyme, or to satisfy a soft and sensuous sentimentality. Poetry to him is a vocation, a high and heavenly calling, the fit vehicle for the expression of the truth that will not be silent. As Paul cried, "Woe is me if I preach not the gospel," so this man hears the command that pushes him along his appointed way. To fail is to be recreant to the deepest convictions of his soul. His it is to speak whether men will hear, or whether they will forbear. That he realizes the urge of his mission, and that to him it is a duty that may not be shirked without meriting the coward's fate, is evident in his description of **"The Poet":**

> His home is in the heights: to him
> Men wage a battle weird and dim,
> Life is a mission stern as fate,
> And Song a dread apostolate.
> The toils of prophecy are his,
> To hail the coming centuries—
> To ease the steps and lift the load
> Of souls that falter on the road.
>
> He presses on before the race,
> And sings out of a silent place.
> Like faint notes of a forest bird
> On heights afar that voice is heard;
> And the dim path he breaks to-day
> Will some time be a trodden way.
>
>   . . . . .
>
> O men of earth, that wandering voice
> Still goes the upward way: rejoice!

Poetry to him is not only a high and serious vocation; it takes on somewhat of the nature of revelation. He is not more poet than prophet. Something of the inspiration and authority of the prophets of truth and righteousness he would claim, I fancy, for himself. The life-giving quality of moments of vision, the swift and sure deduction from some inspirational glimpse into the heart of things—all this he realizes and holds. One cannot read **"The Whirlwind Road"** without being reminded of Paul's experience in the third heaven, where he heard things that could not be uttered in human speech. So our poet, in moments of inspiration, and on the Mounts of Vision, sees and feels truths and ideals that at best can only be shadowed forth and suggested in human song and speech:

> The Muses wrapped in mysteries of light
> Came in a rush of music on the night;
> And I was lifted wildly on quick wings,
> And borne away into the deep of things.
> The dead doors of my being broke apart;
> A wind of rapture blew across the heart;
>
> The inward song of worlds rang still and clear;
> I felt the Mystery the Muses fear;
> Yet they went swiftening on the ways untrod,
> And hurled me breathless at the feet of God.
>
> I felt faint touches of the Final Truth—

Moments of trembling love, moments of youth.
A vision swept away the human wall;
Slowly I saw the meaning of it all—
Meaning of life and time and death and birth,
But cannot tell it to the men of Earth.

And how beautifully does he illustrate and illume the
same thought in these simple and musical lines!—

She comes like the hush and beauty of the night,
  And sees too deep for laughter;
Her touch is a vibration and a light
  From worlds before and after.

And then again, how vigorously and vitally does he conceive the poet's mission! Here is no mystical muse singing
of the joy of quiet and rest, of the virtue of meditation and
inaction in monastery and cell, but instead the clear voice
and the bugle call of a twentieth century knight of labor
and toil; one whose business and mission it is to inspire
men to ideals and deeds of noble and heroic sacrifice and
service: his mission, that of the bard or skald of ancient
times who sang the glory and strength of the fathers for
the inspiration and strengthening of the sons; of the bugler
of to-day who on the field of fight by his clarion note
nerves the soldiery for the onset and charge of victory:

O Poet, thou art holden with a vow:
The light of higher worlds is on thy brow,
And Freedom's star is soaring in thy breast.
Go, be a dauntless voice, a bugle-cry
In darkening battle when the winds are high—
A clear sane cry wherein the God is heard
To speak to men the one redeeming word.

. . . . .

Let trifling pipe be mute,
  Fling by the languid lute:
Take down the trumpet and confront the Hour,
And speak to toil-worn nations from a tower—
Take down the horn wherein the thunders sleep,
Blow battles into men—call down the fire—
The daring, the long purpose, the desire;
Descend with faith into the Human Deep,
And ringing to the troops of right a cheer,
Make known the Truth of Man in holy fear;
Send forth thy spirit in a storm of song,
A tempest flinging fire upon the wrong.

And as for the outcome of his song, that too must be practical and find its fulfillment as it is embodied in individual
life and in the social order. It will not content this singer
that his readers shall be touched to sentimentality, so that
they will speak sweet and honeyed praises for his message,
and then go their ways all unheeding its deeper import and
purpose. He is not willing that either he or his message
shall simply be conceived "as a very lovely song of one
that hath a pleasant voice, and can play well on an instrument: for they hear thy words, but they do them not." He
knows full well that the value of his song is in proportion
to its incarnation in thought and life. Just as God's richest
and finest thought comes to fruition in the Word made
flesh, so our poet realizes that it is the Song forceful and
fruitful in speech and deed that has power and efficacy. All
this is clearly and strongly set forth in his **"Song Made
Flesh":**

I have no glory in these songs of mine:
  If one of them can make a brother strong,
It came down from the peaks of the divine—
  I heard it in the Heaven of Lyric Song.

The one who builds the poem into fact,
  He is the rightful owner of it all:
The pale words are with God's own power
  packed
    When brave souls answer to their bugle-call.

And so I ask no man to praise my song,
  But I would have him build it in his soul;
For that great praise would make me glad and
  strong,
    And build the poem to a perfect whole.

When we come to a consideration of the message of Markham, when we ask, "what is his special and central contribution to the thought of to-day?" the answer is not difficult. He is the poet of humanity—of man in relations. Always in his thought is the consciousness of the social bond
that binds, or ought to bind, men into associations and organizations for common weal. His muse is tuned to the
key of social brotherhood. It is one theme, with many and
delightful and suggestive combinations and variations.
Just as the musician combines and unites the simple notes
of the octave into the complexities and harmonies of ora-
torio and symphony, so the poet weaves out of this simple
theme the harmony and symphony of life. And this must
not be taken as depreciation, for even the greatest and
most influential singers and thinkers have their one central
theme. And it is only as we understand that, that we have
the key and clue to the meaning of their singing and speaking. Stopford Brooke says of Browning: "When *Paracelsus*
was published in 1835 Browning had fully thought out,
and in that poem fully expressed, his theory of God's relation to man, and of man's relation to the universe around
him, to his fellow men, and to the world beyond. . . .
Roughly sketched in *Pauline*, fully rounded in *Paracelsus*,
it held and satisfied his mind till the day of his death." And
he adds that Browning escapes monotony "by the immense variety of the subjects he chooses, and of the scenery in which he places them"—in other words, singleness
of theme with variety of treatment. The myriad-minded
men are few. Indeed, the day of cyclopedic information is
gone. The world is too vast, the subjects too many, for the
individual to grasp and hold. So we live in the age of specialization. In physics, mechanics, literature, and art men
set themselves to the doing of one thing. And it must not
be forgotten that the man who would do one thing well
must of necessity know many things with precision and
clearness. The most many-sided man of his day was Paul,
but he never lost sight of his objective. "This one thing I
do" was ever present in his thought and efficient in his effort. He toiled and traveled, he suffered and endured, he
wrote and spoke, but always with one clear outstanding
purpose—the exaltation and depiction of Christ as Redeemer and Lord. So Markham sings in various keys,
treats divers subjects, but always keeps his main theme—
the Social Man—in view.

Nature for him adumbrates, suggests, and illustrates this
truth. Religion is interpreted as a social bond. Divine Fa-
therhood is the ground and seal of human brotherhood.

The will of God is the will of the social welfare of the holy brotherhood. Government—municipal, state, and national—is for the uplift and betterment, for the closer joining in fellowship and service, of the units that now too frequently struggle, and fight, and fail, being alone. How clear this is may be seen in **"Brotherhood,"** a poem that undoubtedly goes to the heart of his message:

> The crest and crowning of all good,
> Life's final star, is Brotherhood;
> For it will bring again to Earth
> Her long-lost Poesy and Mirth;
> Will send new light on every face,
> A kingly power upon the race.
> And till it come, we men are slaves,
> And travel downward to the dust of graves.
>
> Come, clear the way, then, clear the way:
> Blind creeds and kings have had their day.
> Break the dead branches from the path:
> Our hope is in the aftermath—
> Our hope is in heroic men,
> Star-led to build the world again.
> To this Event the ages ran:
> Make way for Brotherhood—make way for Man.

In Markham the sense of humanity, of the worth and dignity of the individual—first heralded in the gospels, then dropping out of sight, coming into view again in the French Revolution and in the passionate outbursts of Shelley and his compeers, finding fit phrasing in Burns's melodious verse, voicing its hope in Tennyson's "Golden Year" and "Locksley Hall"—comes into full view and has ample range and play. Without doubt he is endeavoring to hasten the day foreseen by Burns when he sang:

> Then let us pray that come it may,
>   As come it will for a' that,
> That sense and worth, o'er a' the earth
>   May bear the gree, and a' that,
> For a' that, and a' that,
>   It's coming yet, for a' that,
> That man to man, the warld o'er,
>   Shall brothers be for a' that.

Anxious he is to have something to do with the quick in-bringing of the time foretold by Tennyson:

> When wealth no more shall rest in mounded heaps,
> But smit with freer light shall slowly melt
> In many streams to fatten lower lands,
> And light shall spread, and man be liker man
> Thro' all the season of the golden year.

In his portrayal of the social bond, in his call to a brotherly kindness and helpfulness that shall be real, organic, and universal, he becomes of necessity the poet of the spiritual and ideal, as against the material and the merely utilitarian conception of life. When men conceive material possessions as the highest good, when every man is striving for position and power, when acquisition is uppermost in every thought and most evident in endeavor—then men are in the fires of fiercest and bitterest competition; then selfish greed and passion have the mastery, and men are asking in the spirit and speech of Cain, "Am I my brother's keeper?" Markham holds that the way out is the spiri-

tual interpretation of the world, and its organization in the spirit of the Sermon on the Mount. He is no singer of a brotherhood that rests in the materialistic conception of life. **"The Muse of Brotherhood"** declares this truth:

> I am in the Expectancy that runs:
>   My feet are in the Future, whirled afar
> On wings of light. If I have any sons,
>   Let them arise and follow to my star.
>
> And at the first break of my Social Song
>   A hush will fall upon the foolish strife,
> As though a joyous god, serene and strong,
>   Shined suddenly before the steps of life.
>
> Cold hearts that falter are my only bar:
>   Heroes that seek my ever-fading goal
> Must take their reckoning from the central star,
>   And follow the equator: I am Soul.

In the thought of our author, brotherhood is the outspring of spirituality—the deep truth latent at the heart of the gospel—so that he does not hesitate to make his **"Muse of Brotherhood"** say:

> I am Religion by her deeper name.

The same truth is taught in **"The Mighty Hundred Years."** In these man has come to self-knowledge and self-revelation as never before. With all that has been gained he is ready for new conquests and adventures. But the higher fields of knowledge, the finer adventures of the future, lie in the realm of the immaterial and spiritual:

> It is the hour of man: new Purposes,
>   Broad-shouldered, press against the world's slow gate;
> And voices from the vast eternities
>   Still preach the soul's austere apostolate.
> Always there will be vision for the heart,
>   The press of endless passion: every goal
> A traveler's tavern, whence he must depart
>   On new divine adventures of the soul.

So too in **"The World-Purpose."** Men are saying that the pursuit of the ideal and the spiritual is in vain. It is all a vague and foolish dream. Let us eat and drink, for to-morrow we die. It is the cry of the materialist and pessimist of every age. It is heard especially to-day in this age of stupendous material power, of forces well-nigh inconceivable, and of wealth hitherto unimaginable. Against all this the poet lifts his passionate protest. The Spiritual Power is not sleeping or dead. It still keeps watch and ward. As Lowell saw the triumph of truth through the presence of the Eternal God "keeping watch above his own," so Markham sees, and speaks his faith in ringing words of hope and cheer:

> All that we glory in was once a dream;
> The World-Will marches onward, gleam by gleam.
> New voices speak, dead paths begin to stir:
> Man is emerging from the sepulcher!
> Let no man dare, let no man ever dare
> To mark on Time's great way, "No Thoroughfare!"

And perhaps best embodiment of all in this respect is his call **"To Young America"**—this nation so signally fa-

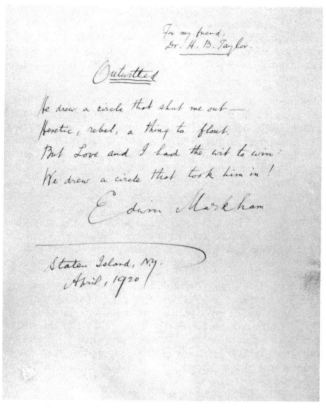

Fair copy of "Outwitted," *which was collected in* The Shoes of Happiness, and Other Poems.

vored, so highly prospered, endowed with a wealth of crude material and native resource that cannot be computed or estimated, just emerging as a world-force, as a factor in the mighty movements of modern life! Realizing perhaps for the first time the greatness of her opportunity, the richness of her privilege; tempted as mayhap no nation has ever been to worship the god of Mammon, to believe that man lives by bread and bread only, how true and timely the vision and the message of this singer of to-day!—

> In spite of the stare of the wise and the world's
>   derision,
> Dare travel the star-blazed road, dare follow the
>   Vision.
>
> It breaks as a hush on the soul in the wonder of
>   youth;
> And the lyrical dream of the boy is the kingly
>   truth.
>
> The world is a vapor, and only the Vision is
>   real—
> Yea, nothing can hold against Hell but the
>   Winged Ideal.

(pp. 84-95)

David G. Downey, "Markham's Message: An Interpretation," in his Modern Poets and Christian Teaching: Richard Watson Gilder, Edwin Markham, Edward Rowland Sill, *Eaton & Mains, 1906, pp. 84-95.*

Harriet Monroe   (review date 1915)

[*As the founder and editor of* Poetry, *Monroe was a key figure in the American "poetry renaissance" that took place in the early twentieth century.* Poetry *was the first periodical devoted primarily to the works of new poets and to poetry criticism, and from 1912 until her death Monroe maintained an editorial policy of printing "the best English verse which is being written today, regardless of where, by whom, or under what theory of art it is written." In the following review, Monroe expresses approbation for* The Shoes of Happiness, and Other Poems, *but remarks that Markham's poetry has lost its "poetic magic."*]

In certain of his poems Mr. Markham's democracy bridges the gulf between rhymed eloquence and poetry. In **"The Man with the Hoe,"** especially, the passion for social righteousness fuses into a white heat and is molded by the poet into a pure form of austere beauty. Here, as with Isaiah and Ezekiel, social righteousness becomes spiritual beauty, and thus a lofty poetic motive.

But when the muse, jealous of other passions, deserts her over-burdened votary, the verse, however noble in motive, loses poetic magic. This is the trouble with **"The Chant of the Vultures," "Love's Hero-World," "The Jews," "Freedom,"** and other poems suggested by the great war or other problems of modern politics. It is the trouble also with Lowell's "Commemoration Ode," which may stand as our most conspicuous American example of a noble poem *manqué*—social passion not quite fused into a form of perfect art, and achieving therefore merely rhymed eloquence instead of poetry.

Two or three of Mr. Markham's best quatrains in this manner may serve to emphasize the point. The first is from **"Freedom":**

> Man is the conscript of an endless quest,
> A long divine adventure without rest.
> Each hard-earned freedom withers to a bond:
> Freedom forever is beyond—beyond.

The second is from **"The Fear for Thee, My Country":**

> I fear the vermin that shall undermine
> Senate and citadel and school and shrine—
> The Worm of Greed, the fatted Worm of Ease,
> And all the crawling progeny of these.

And here is the most eloquent quatrain from **"Virgilia,"** which is in the same class with the others, though its motive is personal rather than social passion:

> One thing shines clear in the heart's sweet rea-
>   son,
>   One lightning over the chasm runs—
> That to turn from love is the world's one treason
>   That darkens all the suns.

The present volume contains many poems of this kind—a kind not without honor, even though the honor be not the muse's own award. The *Six Stories* are excellently told; they move with a light, swinging gait, from a heart full of sympathy and humor. **"The Shoes of Happiness"** is perhaps the best of these—at least it is the gayest; but in **"How Oswald Dined with God"** and **"How the Great**

Guest Came" the motive of social righteousness is expressed in tales poignant and beautiful. Mr. Markham knows when to stop in telling a story; all his tales end with a good climax.

But the book has more magical moments—poems or parts of poems, which prove once more that Mr. Markham is a poet. **"At Friends with Life"** contains this fine stanza:

> There on the Hills of summer let me life
> On the cool grass in friendship with the sky.
> Let me lie there in love with earth and sun,
> And wonder up at the light-foot winds that run,
> Stirring the delicate edges of the trees
> And shaking down a music of the seas.

The brief poem, **"San Francisco Falling,"** is one of the best in the book, its eighth line being especially beautiful:

> A groan of earth in labor pain,
> Her ancient agony and strain;
> A tremor of the granite floors—
> A heave of seas, a wrench of shores,
> A crash of walls, a moan of lips,
> A terror on the towers and ships;
> Blind streets where men and ghosts go by;
> Whirled smoke mushrooming on the sky;
> Roofs, turrets, domes, with one acclaim
> Turned softly to a bloom of flame;
> A thousand dreams of joy, of power,
> Gone in the splendor of an hour.

And in **"Wind and Lyre,"** perhaps the finest of his lyrics, Mr. Markham gives us an impassioned and beautiful prayer-song:

> Thou art the wind and I the lyre:
>   Strike, O Wind, on the sleeping strings—
>   Strike till the dead heart stirs and sings!
> I am the altar and thou the fire:
>   Burn, O Fire, to a snowy flame—
>   Burn me clean of the mortal blame!
> I am the night and thou the dream:
>   Touch me softly and thrill me deep,
>   When all is white on the hills of sleep.
> Thou art the moon and I the stream:
>   Shine to the trembling heart of me,
>   Light my soul to the mother-sea.

(pp. 308-11)

Harriet Monroe, in a review of "The Shores of Happiness and Other Poems," in Poetry, *Vol. VI, No. 6, September, 1915, pp. 308-11.*

George Hamlin Fitch   (essay date 1916)

[*In the following excerpt, Fitch favorably appraises Markham while discussing the major themes and concerns of his poetry.*]

Edwin Markham I have taken as the foremost of the new writers of our period because of his moral force and his keen sympathy with the struggles of those who work with their hands. Coming up, as he did, from the ranks of manual labor, securing an education by hard work and painful self-denial, he has a feeling for the working classes which no one can share who has not earned his bread in the sweat of his brow. Had he written nothing more than **"The Man**

With the Hoe"** he would have been worthy of a place among the great laureates of labor; but in both prose and verse he has done fine work in helping to secure better conditions in mills and factories, and especially in protecting young children from the selfishness of parents and employers.

Markham's natural method of expression is a free blank verse, which he handles with great ease and power. As he says himself, his thought unconsciously crystalizes in this form of verse, although he is skilful in handling various poetical metres. Before he wrote the poem which suddenly flashed his fame around the world, he had written some fine sonnets and other poems, all of which were tinged with his deep earnestness. Early in his career he was profoundly stirred by a photographic reproduction of Millet's "The Man With the Hoe", and some of the thoughts which it inspired he cast in poetic form. More than a decade later he saw the original painting in the art gallery of a San Francisco millionaire. As Markham himself says:

"Millet's 'The Man With the Hoe' is to me the most solemnly impressive of all modern paintings. As I look upon the august ruin that it pictures I sometimes dare to think that its strength surpasses the power of Michael Angelo. . . . For an hour I stood before the painting, absorbing the majesty of its despair, the tremendous import of its admonition. I stood there, the power and the terror of the thing growing upon my heart, the pity and sorrow of it eating into my soul. It came to me with a dim echo in it of my own life—came with its pitiless pathos and mournful grandeur."

Markham was so deeply moved by this study of Millet's picture that he took up his original draft, expanded it, and produced the poem as it stands today. At a meeting of a literary club in San Francisco he read this poem, which so greatly impressed Bailey Millard, then Sunday editor of the San Francisco *Examiner* that he secured the manuscript for publication in his paper. The day it appeared correspondents of several Eastern newspapers telegraphed it to their journals and it was cabled to London. Markham's name as a world poet was thus flashed over the land and under the sea, and in a single day he found himself famous! (pp. 137-40)

Markham is not a poet of occasions, although some of his best work, like his **"Lincoln"**, was written for anniversary celebrations. He does not write until the spirit moves him. Hence the gap of more than a decade between his second and third books of verse. He does not always reach the height toward which he aims, but it can be said for his work that it maintains a higher level than the work of any other living American poet. Some may prefer Whitcomb Riley, but to me Markham seems to sound a finer note of a broader humanity than the Hoosier poet, sweet and wholesome and genuine as is all Riley's work. In other words, Markham is what the late Alfred Russell Wallace so aptly called him, "the greatest poet of the Social Passion that has yet appeared in the world."

Markham seems to feel the woes of the heavy-laden as no other poet of our time has felt them. The burden of poverty, the hopelessness of the poor creatures who are always clinging to the slippery edge of the abyss of want and crime, the injustice of fate that keeps some of the finest natures forever in bondage of debt—these are the themes which bring forth the lightning of his wrath, the thunder of his scorn. His heart is so moved by the spectacle of the world's unfortunates that he compels the reader's pity and tears. He loses all count of time and space when the spirit moves him. Hence his shortest lyric seems to have the freshness of the first morning, and there is none of the smell of the lamp on any of his work, no matter how careful may be the finish of the verse.

Without apparent effort Markham also seems to select the right word in every line and his rhymes are never awkward nor far-fetched. In fact, when he wears his singing robes and is under the spell of his powerful imagination, language seems to become plastic under his hands. He uses words as the potter uses the clay on his wheel, with a few deft movements making the shapeless lump take on varied forms of beauty. This power is seen more signally in **"Virgilia"** than in anything Markham has written. That poem breathes inspiration in every line, and it has a sweep of imagination, a wealth of imagery and a rare kind of prophetic power that bears one along to the noble end.

In **"Virgilia"** the poet gives a fine conception of the meeting of his first self with his soul-mate, the woman who was formed to feed his imagination and to give him courage to struggle against fate, and then of his fruitless quest for her throughout the ages. Here are a few lines from the conclusion of this poem, with the splendid sweep of the verse:

> I will go out where the sea-birds travel,
> And mix my soul with the wind and the sea;
> Let the green waves weave and the gray rains ravel,
> And the tides go over me.
>
> The sea is the mother of songs and sorrows,
> And out of her wonder our wild loves come;
> And so it will be through the long tomorrows,
> Till all our lips are dumb.
>
> She knows all sighs and she knows all sinning,
> And they whisper out in her breaking wave;
> She has known it all since the far beginning,
> Since the grief of that first grave.
>
> She shakes the heart with her stars and thunder
> And her soft, low word when the winds are late;
> For the sea is Woman, the sea is Wonder—
> Her other name is Fate!

Many of our poets, when they have caught the ear of the public, have hearkened to the voice of the publisher and have put forth poor work. But Markham has written only when the spirit moved him. Hence he has only three books of verse to his credit: *The Man With the Hoe, and Other Poems, Lincoln, and Other Poems* and *The Shoes of Happiness, and Other Poems.* Hence, also, there is no mediocre verse in these volumes.

It is not often that a poet has an opportunity to celebrate the State which gave him his inspiration as Markham has celebrated California. Though not born in the Far West, Markham spent all his early impressionable years in the country across the bay from San Francisco. There he learned what it was to earn his bread in the sweat of his brow, and there as a farmer's boy, he stored up those pictures of the heavens and the earth which give distinction to his verse. In *California, the Wonderful,* Markham has produced a unique book. It gives a mass of information about the resources, the history, the scenic beauty and the marvelous development of the Golden State, but all the prosaic details are touched with poetry. The man who witnessed these wonders was a poet, and he was unable to write this history in any other form than poetical prose. This book was prepared to let the world know what the Panama-Pacific Exposition at San Francisco was designed to commemorate. When the great Exposition was fairly under way, Markham was invited to visit it and to write his impressions. He took the occasion to visit all parts of the State, and the reception that he received was so hearty and so enthusiastic that it quite overcame the modest poet. It showed him that the bard, unlike the prophet, might be honored in his own home.

The poet's other book of prose is *Children in Bondage,* a startling description of the many American industries in which young children are stunted and ruined, morally and physically, to satisfy the greed of parents and employers.

Markham's hair is white but his eyes are keen and his voice is vibrant with strength and feeling. So we may expect more poems from his pen that will help the world to live the spiritual life. (pp. 141-45)

> *George Hamlin Fitch, "Markham: Poet of the American People," in his* Great Spiritual Writers of America, *Paul Elder and Company, 1916, pp. 136-45.*

Mark Sullivan (essay date 1927)

[*In the following excerpt, Sullivan analyzes the reception of "The Man with the Hoe" in relation to social conditions of the time.*]

During Christmas week of the year 1898, a California school-teacher, Edwin Markham, living on the heights back of Oakland, in a cottage that looked down upon the bay and city of San Francisco and the Golden Gate, utilized his vacation to complete a poem. For years he had been haunted by the memory of a painting he had seen reproduced in *Scribner's Magazine* in 1886, "The Man With the Hoe," by the French peasant-artist Millet. Then he had the great joy of seeing the original painting in San Francisco. He described the experience subsequently:

> I sat for an hour before the painting and all the time the terror and power of the picture was growing upon me. I saw that this creation of the painter was no mere peasant, no chance man of the fields, but he was rather a type, a symbol of the toiler, brutalized through long ages of industrial oppression. I saw in this peasant the slow but awful degradation of man through endless, hopeless, and joyless labor.

The poem was first published in the San Francisco *Examiner,* January 15, 1899. (p. 236)

The poem flew eastward across the continent, like a contagion. As fast as the mails carried it, newspapers printed it as a fresh focus of infection, first California and the Pacific Coast, then the Mississippi Valley, on into New York and New England, over the line into Canada. Within a week, phrases and couplets from it were on every lip. Newspaper editions containing it were exhausted and publishers reprinted it, together with editorials about it, and the hundreds of manuscripts of comment received from the public. The newspapers, a historian of the day remarked, as a unique phenomenon, "gave as much space to **'The Man With the Hoe'** as to prize-fights and police stories. The clergy made the poem their text, platform orators dilated upon it, college professors lectured upon it, debating societies discussed it, schools took it up for study. . . . The president of Leland Stanford University, Doctor David Starr Jordan, used it seriously and intelligently as the theme of a lecture delivered in many places"; "and," said *The Arena Magazine* six months after the poem's publication, "there is not yet an end."

Not only did the poem become general as the average man's symbol for the political and economic mood of the time. Within the narrower world of literature, critics hurried to place an estimate on the newly arrived poet. Up to this time they had not noticed him, although for years he had been sending verse to Eastern magazines and had won some slight recognition as a poet with a bent for esthetic themes.

Among critics who looked to the effect of **"The Man With the Hoe"** on the social ferment of the day, it "was hailed by many as 'the battle cry of the next thousand years.' " The New York *Herald* asked: "Has a great poet arisen in the teeming West? Is . . . a revolution impending in America—a bloodless revolution this time, fought not with bullets but with ballots? If so, Edwin Markham will prove to be at once its despised prophet and its accepted high priest." Another newspaper said: "This poem comes as the cry of the zeitgeist." Equal elevation of tone appeared in all the comment that looked primarily at the relation of the poem to the common mood of the day. Applause of the poem and its author included such expressions as: "One of the greatest thinkers of the world." ". . . touches the high-water mark of American achievement in verse." "The foremost name in poetical literature since Tennyson and Browning." The San Jose (Calif.) *Mercury,* moved, perhaps, by local California pride, assured all doubters that " **'Man With the Hoe'** is the strongest, most meaningful, and most striking poem, with the single exception, perhaps, of Kipling's Recessional, that has been written in any country in the last quarter of a century." Many quite temperate persons compared "**The Man With the Hoe**" with Thomas Hood's similar appeal to a similar zeitgeist, "The Song of the Shirt":

> With fingers weary and worn,
> With eyelids heavy and red,
> A woman sat, in unwomanly rags,
> Plying her needle and thread. . . .
>
> "O men with sisters dear!
> O men with mothers and wives!
> It is not linen you're wearing out,
> But human creatures' lives!

> Stitch-stitch-stitch!
> In poverty, hunger, and dirt—
> Sewing at once, with a double thread,
> A shroud as well as a shirt!"

To Americans of a later generation, it may seem fantastic that the average man of 1900 should have taken Markham's poem as meaning him; that he should have seen in "**The Man With the Hoe**" a mirroring of himself; that he should have read "slave of the wheel of labor," and thought of himself; that he should have regarded "masters, lords, and rulers in all lands," as something that might oppress him, here in America; that he should have looked upon himself as "plundered, profaned, and disinherited," and as the victim of "perfidious wrongs, immedicable woes." Yet that is precisely what did happen, and that is why the poem had such an enormous vogue.

Sociologists, editors, political leaders, all who were close to the heart of the crowd or concerned with it, seized upon "**The Man With the Hoe**" as an expression of the prevailing mood of the American people. William Randolph Hearst, with true journalistic instinct, realizing that William J. Bryan was the outstanding spokesman of the sort of protest the poem expressed and appealed to, asked Bryan to write about it for the New York *Journal.* Bryan made the poem the text for a characteristic summing up of the complaints of the times. Ominously, he quoted Victor Hugo's description of the mob as "the human race in misery." On his own account Bryan said:

> It is not strange that "**The Man With the Hoe**" created a profound sensation. It is a sermon addressed to the heart. It voices humanity's protest against inhuman greed. There is a majestic sweep to the argument; some of the lines pierce like arrows. How feeble in comparison have been the answers to it.
>
> The extremes of society are being driven further and further apart. Wealth is being concentrated in the hands of a few. At one end of the scale luxury and idleness breed effeminacy; at the other end, want and destitution breed desperation. . . .

Markham himself had not anticipated the kind of acclaim that came to his poem, and certainly not the volume of it. He had looked upon Millet's powerful painting, he had been moved to an ecstasy, and had written a poem. Apparently it took time for him to find just the significance that the country saw in the poem instantly, its direct relation to concrete conditions in America. Asked by a magazine editor to tell how he came to write it, he said:

> I was born a man with a hoe. I am a child of the furrow. All my youth was passed on a farm and cattle ranch, among the hard, severe conditions that go with that life. Of course, I do not mean to say that there are not happy phases of farm life. I enjoyed as a boy the horseback rides on the long ranges of hills. The smell of the furrow was pleasant to me. I knew and loved animals, the horses and cattle. But with all this I felt, too, the privations and scraping poverty that are the frequent accompaniment of the farm boy's life.

Merely to see **"Man With the Hoe"** as the poetic assertion of an analogy between a French peasant and an American farmer was sentimentalism and fallacy. Nevertheless, supporters of the established order saw, or affected to see, only this limited application, and wrote ready answers. To reply by the device of giving a true picture of the American farmer, in contrast with the French peasant, was obvious and frequent. One critic said:

> Markham's **"Man With the Hoe"** is an insult to every farmer and every farmer's son in America. It draws a picture that has no foundation in fact. It is utterly vicious in that it degrades honorable labor and promotes contempt for work, and dissatisfaction, unrest, and despair where there should be hope, happiness, and courage. It and all similar woeful wailings are worse than worthless trash.

A more honest criticism was written by E. P. Powell, author of "Our Heredity from God," who said:

> Mr. Markham shows us the workman of civilization, not going up from the animal, but going down from what God made him. . . . Such an interpretation of man and labor, especially of agricultural labor, at this time, puts the poem in alignment with that pessimism and explosive arraignment of social order in which sentimentalism strikes hands with brute force.

Powell, reversing Markham's point of view, rewrote the poem as he thought it should be:

> Lifted by toil of centuries, he leans
> Upon his hoe and gazes on the heavens,
> The glorious light of ages on his face . . .
> What gulfs between him and the anthropoid.

But the true symbolism of **"The Man With the Hoe,"** as applying to the average man—artisan, clerk, small businessman; and the effect the poem was having on the social feeling of the time, was not missed by those who had most reason to apprehend it. They sought ways to offset it. An anonymous donor—it was revealed to be Collis P. Huntington, a railroad multimillionaire, after he died in 1900—offered a prize of $700 through the New York *Sun* for the best poetical answer to **"The Man With the Hoe."** In making the offer, Huntington affirmed, anonymously, that Markham's poem did injury to a great class of agricultural toilers who would resent the statement that they were "brothers to the ox." He said that this poem would add to the tendency, already too strong, of young Americans to look on field labor as distasteful.

The fallacy of this kind of reply, the insincerity of some who made it, angered those who felt Markham had made an unanswerable indictment. Bryan retorted:

> The literary sycophants who strew rhetorical flowers in the pathway of the successful . . . complacently throw the responsibility for failure in life upon God, or Nature, or upon the man himself.

It was Bryan, too, who tied Markham's poem directly to existing American conditions, translated Markham's generalizations into an indictment with specific counts. Some of Bryan's accusations were aimed at conditions already

passed or passing; others pointed straight at the heart of conditions that were causing wide-spread discontent. When Bryan asked:

> Is it the fault of God or Nature . . . that our tax laws are so made . . . that the poor man pays more than his share and the rich man less?

he was referring to the Supreme Court's invalidation, in 1895, of the attempt to have an income-tax law, and attempt that had to wait for success until 1913.

But when Bryan asked:

> Is it the fault of God or of Nature that children are driven into factories?

he was referring not only to child labor (then coming to be generally looked upon as deplorable), but, in a broader sense, to the increase of factory life in America, the economic condition that was increasingly taking American families from the farm to the factory—a transition which, in connection with what had previously been the ideal of life in America, was a principal cause of social fretfulness.

And when Bryan asked:

> Is God or Nature responsible for the . . . trust? Is God or Nature responsible for private monopolies?

he was putting his hand on the name for the particular institution which, in that year, and for fifteen years afterward, was the country's outstanding political issue, regarded as its outstanding social menace. (pp. 239-49)

The year of the publication of Markham's poem, 1899, and the following year, saw the publication of twenty-eight books about "Trusts," and more than 150 magazine articles, in addition to several of the nineteen volumes of the official report of the United States Industrial Commission which had spent many months hearing testimony about monopolies. (p. 253)

> *Mark Sullivan, "A Picture, A Poem, and the Times," in his* Our Times: The United States 1900-1925, America Finding Herself, Vol. II, *Charles Scribner's Sons, 1927, pp. 236-53.*

Sister Mary James Power   (essay date 1938)

[*In the following excerpt, Power examines the Swedenborgian philosophy present in Markham's poems.*]

Edwin Markham is the Prophet of a Kingdom Coming. The kingdom that he foretells is to be established when all men will be "inbrothered." Then will they live for and not on one another; they will love one another not only as much as themselves, but more than themselves. The Kingdom of Christ will have come upon earth to make the world one vast Brotherhood of Man, a Fraternal State, governed by Love radiating from the Divine Christ Who is its centre.

Markham's attitude toward religion is, therefore, one of belief in an industrial and social federation that man should organize here upon earth, a confraternity that enjoins no faith in rigid dogma, but, on the contrary, functions through the spirit of Christianity only. In a quatrain, the poet sings his credo:

> Here is the Truth in a little creed,
> Enough for all the roads we go:
> In Love, is all the law we need,
> In Christ, is all the God we know.

That is the essence of Swedenborgianism. To the followers of Swedenborg, the seer of the eighteenth century, there is one God, in whom there is a Divine Trinity: He is the Lord Jesus Christ. They are saved by believing in Him, by avoiding evil because it is of and from the Devil, by doing good actions because they are of and from God, and by doing them as a man from himself, yet, believing at the same time, that they are done from the Lord with him and by him. These seminal principles one finds in the work of Edwin Markham. In verification, we quote his acknowledgement of Swedenborg's philosophy:

> I wish to express my gratitude for the vast light that his teaching has shed upon my mind and upon all my volumes of verse.

As an adherent of Swedenborg, Markham believes, also, that the highest expression of God is in man. That faith is the foundation of Markham's Utopia, his Brotherhood of Man. Early in life the vision of that Utopia came to him. Through the economic and social injustice that he saw befogging the world, it burned its image on his heart. Millet's painting of the toiler, misshapen by the greed of the few, awakened him to the outrage committed against the divine in man, and he responded with **"The Man with the Hoe,"** a loud rebuke to overpowering Capitalism:

> O Masters, lords and rulers in all lands,
> Is this the handiwork you give to God,
> This monstrous thing distorted and soul-
>   quenched?
> How will you ever straighten up this shape;
> Touch it again with immortality.

As Markham visions the Kingdom Coming, he sees always in proximity and in outstanding contrast the conditions of labor working toward a Nemesis. So far removed from the spirit of the Gospel of the Labor Christ, in Whom he sees the Ideal of Fraternity, are men who discover work not a blessing but a curse,

> For the toilers have the least,
> While the idlers lord the feast.
> Yes, our workers they are bound,
> Pallid captives to the ground;
> Jeered by traitors, fooled by knaves,
> Till they stumble into graves.

Everywhere in society is there the plunder of the many by the few. The haggard faces of the poor look out upon the world of plenty. The toiler hangs upon the "Cross of Labor." Humiliated men receive no merited rest, and traitors misspend His Bread. Yet in the prospect of the Fraternal State, Markham sees a New Heaven and a New Earth, when the Brotherhood of Man, the working form for Christ on earth, will right all wrongs. Service to others, Love in Action, will be its act of homage to its White Comrade,

> Sweeter are comrade kindnesses to Him

> Than the high harpings of the Seraphim.

But now, in time, even among the lower forms of life, he finds his ideal of Brotherhood. The ants, he observes, "bound by gentle Brotherhood," working with gay and busy toil, evenly distribute the yield; men, he observes, "shriveled up with hates," sharing unequal burdens, plunder the profits. Similarly, the birds prefigure the equality that will dominate the Kingdom. In contrast to the disspiritedness that he senses among builders who are constructing a spacious hall nearby, he hears the rapturous song of the throstles as they build their nests. Trees, furthermore, stand on an equal footing on the floor of God's kingdom, sharing their leafy comfort with all God's children, representing the plan of the Great Designer for democracy among men,

> . . . since the first star they have stood
> A testament of Brotherhood.

Despite the apparent triumph of the Capitalist that Markham notes contrary to the principles of the Federation of Man, Labor has a dedicated patroness. Revering the Swedenborgian tenet of the Brotherhood, that "God is man absolute," she wears for her crown the passion-flower, and she stands beside the nail-torn God. Hearing the lamentations of nations oppressed, she breaks the infamous chain with which Greed has bound the earth. She is the Light in Darkness, the Muse of Labor. To dispel the evil of the centuries that men may dream of "The Kingdom of Fraternity foretold," is her sacred mission. And she performs it in the spirit of high joy, for she says that she is song. Wherefore, she warms the heart of man, when, in the midst of almost broken hopes, he hears her sing:

> I am Religion and the Church I build
>   Stands on the sacred flesh with passion
>   packed;
> In me the ancient gospels are fulfilled—
>   In me the symbol rises into Fact.

Still he hopes for more tangible protection against the foe of his Ideal that will dominate the twentieth century. Along the road of the century there will watch a new Sphinx, Labor, that will ask the dreaded question and demand an answer or the destruction of the Brotherhood. Thus, he awaits a leader, one who will "Fill the labor throne and build the Comrade Kingdom, stone by stone."

Early in life Markham declared faith in divine intervention to direct the ways of universal brotherhood. The Desired One, long since sung in prophecy by Isaiah, the One Who was to come to Israel, Whose name "shall be called Wonderful, Counsellor, The Mighty God, the everlasting Father, the Prince of Peace," is, he knows, the Desire of Nations. Prophet-like, he visions the Star of Hope that will reappear this time to shine upon a hero-world standing beneath the unfurled standard of Fraternity. But the promise in the sky will not herald the advent of the Glory of the Lord, veiled in a Child or in the pomp of a Hero-King preached by "tedious argument and milkless creed,"

> But in the passion of the heart-warm deed
> Will come the Man Supreme.
> Yea, for He comes to lift the Public Care—
> To build on Earth the Vision hung in air.

This is the one fulfillment of His Law—
The one Fact in the mockeries that seem
This is the Vision that the Prophets saw—
The Comrade Kingdom builded in their dream.

That the coming of the Kingdom, despite the seeming fading of the Vision among men whose hearts are held by the meshes of gain, is inevitable, Markham impresses through its Divine origin. He says that "the vast inbrothering of man—the glory of the universe" began with time. Uninterruptedly the purpose has moved down through the centuries, unwavering in its determination to establish justice. The idea has been the music of the spheres; it was the song of the shepherds on that first Christmas night when reverberating the heavenly messengers they might have sung the Kingdom that had come in Mary's Child. For He came in the spirit of Brotherhood, an elder Brother, "a Common Man at home with cart and crooked yoke." And throughout His earthly mission, he preached the gospel of the New Republic. His Sermon on the Mount is the essence of the Kingdom.

That fundamental principle embodied in the Master's teaching: All things unto all men, Markham uses in specific examples for the progress of his State. Ivan, the watchman of Moscow, sharing his coat with the beggar, Elizabeth, who forgot herself in brother-love, and Hilary who "flung the psalter by and hurried to a brother's cry," are all the gospelers of the prophet who has formulated this, another creed for the members of his Utopia:

There is a destiny that makes us brothers:
　None goes his way alone:
All that we send into the lives of others
　Comes back into our own.

And in the same key, the stories of Oswald's beneficence to the hungry of his realm, the gold that accused the king of wrong done to his people, the guest that came to Conrad, and the Juggler of Touraine who gave in worship to Mary his all, "fingers and body and feet," are parables sufficient to interpret the Kingdom that Markham prophesies. Functioning through men united in a Leader Whose "Esse" is infinite love, it is by virtue of this all-embracing charity that the Kingdom must be perpetual. Contrariwise, history records cities built and deeds done for a single glory merely. And where Tyre and Babylon, Greece and Rome, Thebes, Troy, and Carthage were, was felt once to be eternity, but time has taught the truth that

No house can stand, no kingdom can endure
Built on the crumbling rock of Self-Desire:
Nothing is Living Stone, nothing is sure,
　That is not whitened in the social Fire.

Fired with the hope of those heroes who have felt with the poet that the Vision cannot fail, Markham would conscribe all to the Dream. Like Lincoln, Mazzini, Lamennais, St. Francis, and even Cromwell, who have been of "The company of souls supreme," Americans have a special vocation in the Brotherhood. Other nations, he feels, are not privileged to have been held, as it were, in the hollow of God's Hand to carry out the Divine Will. From **"The Errand Imperious"** comes the voice to America:

'Tis yours to bear the World-State in your
　dream,
To strike down Mammon and his brazen breed,
To build the Brother-Future, beam on beam;
Yours, mighty one, to shape the Mighty Deed.

As a tribute to her policy of arbitrating with rival states in South America and of commemorating the occasion with an heroic statue of Christ surmounting the highest peak of the Andes, Markham dedicates a prayer in verse to the Divine Pacificator, imploring for the world on the eve of the great war this protection:

O Christ of Olivet, you hushed the wars
Under the far Andean stars:
Lift now your strong nail-wounded hands
Over all peoples, over all lands:
Stretch out those comrade hands to be
A shelter over land and sea!

The war itself, entirely opposed to his Ideal of Brotherhood, the Federation of the Peoples, the Parliament of Man, moved him to frequent utterance for peace through the mediation of Love and Justice. These fragmentary lines are significant:

Peace, peace, O men, for you are brothers all—

. . . . .

Do you not know you came
Out of one Love and wear one sacred name?
Comrades, read out His words again:
They are the only hope for men!
Love and not hate must come to birth;
Christ and not Cain must rule the earth.

And in the Red Cross League he saw the kindness and the mercy that symbolize that league of infinite kindness which will be "In ages when the agonies are done, When all will love and all will lift as one."

Time has not weakened the prophet in Markham. To him the Kingdom built on democracy and comrade-love shines as the morning star of eternity. Quoting Laplace, he holds that despite all the findings in science, one thing alone remains: Love that constitutes the pillars of his State. It is the self-subsisting force of the universe. Through it Christ became divine, "having no self to serve, no will That does not seek the welfare of All." This is truly Swedenborgian philosophy. And the prophet would extend it even to the realms of romance and call it the "Romance of the Infinite"; He would take his "winged mate" beyond the natural and cry out to his soul in the spirit of Gethsemane's great Love, "The Heart's Cry,"

Can you be true to Love in spite of all,
　Be true as granite in the mountain wall?

while the answer to the question self-imposed is the prayer that he

. . . shall stand full-armed in life's last hours—
In the great night of death white and tall.

This, too, is Swedenborgian in that all must be done for the sake of Love alone. Nor does the thought of Heaven as a reward influence the motive of the deed.

At eighty, the poet injected other specifically Swedenbor-

gian philosophy. Adoring the Lord Christ not according
to orthodox belief but as the embodiment of the Trinity,
he emphasized the "nail-torn Christus" as the Omnipotent One, departing from the dogma of God as the Provi-
dent Father. And the quatrain which is the epitome of his
gospel of the Parliament of Man plays likewise into the tenets of the philosophy by such a title as **"The New Trinity"** by its suggestive refutation:

> Three things must a man possess if his soul
>   would live,
>   And know life's perfect good—
> Three things would the all-supplying Father
>   give—
>   Bread, Beauty and Brotherhood.

His interpretation of Heaven is from Swedenborg as well:
It is a real world reached only by those who have passed
through the preparatory schools of the angels. There also
souls experience the long drama of Love, for heaven rests
on the two great loves—the marriage love and the fraternal love. Fugitive lines like these carry the thought:

> A little while men eat this earthly bread,
> Then pass on to the nations of the dead.

> To the austere sifting of the vanisht crowds,
> Till on some souls the eternal sleep is shed.
> No, not immortal but immortale.

> For she will be immortally my own—
> Mine in the marriage of eternity.

At eighty, also, the prophet is inspired by another toiler.
A reflection on Rodin's statue, "The Thinker," reimmor-
talizing labor, harks back to Markham's first thoughts in
verse to celebrate the Brotherhood and elicits the daring
line, "How patient he has been with God!" It leads on to
a consideration of the same theme, reversing the subject
to the oppressor when Markham as the prophet, scanning
the streets and finding only consequences of self-love
among all: the clergy and the laity, ask

> Who would welcome the Workman in,
> This Workman from Nazareth?

Fittingly many poems of his last book, [*New Poems:*]
Eighty Songs at Eighty, are a prospect and a retrospect
over all he has sung, for in essence he sings that the Kingdom is coming and that

> The crest and crowning of all good,
> Life's final star, is Brotherhood.

Though the poet feels the glow of the Brotherhood of
Man, unfortunately he does not enjoy the warmth of intimacy with a Personal God in Whom all things are one.
(pp. 85-93)

> *Sister Mary James Power, "Edwin Markham:*
> *The Prophet of a Kingdom Coming," in her*
> Poets at Prayer, *Sheed & Ward, 1938, pp. 83-
> 93.*

Louis Filler   (essay date 1963)

[*Filler is a Russian-born historian, biographer, and critic. In following essay, he discusses the attitudes among
American readers, critics, and academics that account
for the eclipse of Markham's reputation.*]

Edwin Markham has not been well remembered. Among
those who have had some sense of his presence, he has
been conceived of as old-fashioned and passé: an amiable
and naive old man. Droves of school children were introduced to a charming and unexpectedly lively ancient;
droves of club-women and joiners of professional and fraternal groups knew him as an after-dinner speaker who
could be depended upon to say the expected, the unchal-
lenging.

More significant is that fact that he has not seemed to warrant substantial consideration by the evident pillars of our
living literature, and particularly by our critics of our poetry. The Gregory and Zaturenska *History of American
Poetry, 1900-1940* thought Markham a "sad" figure because he had been "serious"—serious, that is, but incapable, thanks to his "incorrigible optimism," and his having
been "trapped in a fatal circle of literary reminiscence."
Other words which occurred to these critics (who have
also written verse) included "confused," "boyish," "simple," and "rhetoric." The latter word also seemed the
proper word to Louis Untermeyer, who thought Markham was less good a poet than even Joaquin Miller, having
the latter's rhetoric without the resonance of his more exuberant moments. Miller's latest biographer, one M. M.
Marberry, who thought his subject a *Splendid Poseur,*
writes Markham down as being "as wretched a poetaster
as ever lived." The dignified Spiller, *et al., Literary History
of the United States,* in as typical a passage as can be found
in its two volumes of impressionistic chapters, has a low-
pulsed passage upon Markham best described as high-
level ignorance; suffice it here that it is pompously deroga-
tory. Louis Wann's *The Rise of Realism* is another typical
academic production: it dutifully reproduces three of
Markham's standard poems; but its brief notice of Markham's life, filled with inadequacy, is not calculated to stir
any response in the reader whatsoever.

And yet Markham's is not only a famous name: it is one
of the most famous names in poetry. Innumerable people
have as distinct a sense of the reality of his **"The Man With
the Hoe"** as of any other poem. The William Rose Benét-
edited *Fifty Poets: An American Auto-Anthology* published
"The Man With the Hoe" first, as by the Dean of American Poets, and "because we regard it as a permanency in
American literature." Three of Markham's poems rate in
Merle Johnson's *You Know These Lines!,* a professional
bibliography of the most quoted verses in all American poetry. Even Louis Untermeyer, who has all his life reflected
the *à la mode,* in his *Concise Treasury of Great Poems,*
both English and American, from Chaucer to Dylan
Thomas, reproduces **"The Man With the Hoe"** and **"Lincoln, the Man of the People."** He reproduces nothing by
Miller.

It is generally understood, I believe, that Markham was
a product of "the age of reform," which hoped to reorga-
nize society in the interests of its depressed classes, its least
articulate voices. In general, too, it has been assumed that
this human sympathy with the downtrodden distinguished the writings of Markham and other "reformers."

Markham at age sixteen.

It has also been assumed that these "reformers" oversimplified the social problem, substituted sentiment for art in their work, and were rightly, therefore, relegated to things no longer relevant, no longer repaying study. (There has been some recent effort to indicate that they were desperately confused, and even dangerous. This line of thought serves variously expedient purposes.)

These are all assumptions I find so fantastic on their very face that I study them all the time, as time permits, in order better to understand how they can be held with any degree of intellectual comfort. I take it that art reflects human complexities and experiences, that it concentrates the conscious and the unconscious in terms which reveal an age and the role of the individual in that age; and that high art stirs in us a sense of our own qualities, as compared with those of our predecessors. To think of the "reformers" as simple-minded men is so strange when one recalls that they include such very different figures as Josiah Flynt, Lincoln Steffens, Finley Peter Dunne, and Edwin Markham—who, in many senses, were not primarily reformers at all—that it raises the question of just why these gargoyles have persisted as accurate representations of the originals.

I take it that there is relatively little interest in the "truth" of things—that our emphasis, as a society, has been upon what works, what induces success, what is practical. To be sure, this is nothing new in American life. Hard-headed Americans made life fairly difficult for Whitman, Melville, Emily Dickinson, and many another who had something to say about the innermost feelings of his countrymen and women. Americans "appreciated" and will continue to "appreciate" Poe, as they later did Thoreau and in some measure Twain, for the wrong reasons. But Americans who turned away from them, or ignored their intentions, were very often engaged in worthy enterprises of their own. Would anyone claim that abolitionists were lesser folk than artists?—that Wendell Phillips and Emerson and Theodore Parker and John Quincy Adams and Lincoln are lesser names than those of Melville and Poe? That Henry George and Justice Holmes are lesser names than that of their contemporary, Twain? They all competed in public, along with many others who also had versions of "truth" to peddle, and confronted their readers with a spectrum of opinion which permitted the public more or less to go where it wanted to go.

I assume that if the public had wished an accurate and representative account of its past fifty or so years, and of Markham's life and development in them, such an account would have been provided. For example, Lincoln Steffens' helpful autobiography had a certain vogue in the 1930's and is still read; but through such a screen of misconception as to be practically meaningless. It was used to close gates, not to open them. I do not care to labor this point. My interest is in what the public has wanted, rather than in what it has not wanted. Why has it preferred inadequate and even absurd views of Edwin Markham and his work?

To begin with, the basic characteristic of the reform period in which Markham was a dominating figure was its grassroots quality. The muckrakers were *popular:* they were familiar faces and names to most Americans anywhere. It seems important to emphasize this point, because there is something in many of us which finds this fact difficult to swallow. I recall writing an article on the youth movement, so called, which *The Reporter* had solicited (it was later published in the *Southwest Review*), in which I referred to the "powerful and popular" muckraking movement. One of *The Reporter* editors pencilled in the margin: "But it wasn't!" He had no information, of course; but why was it important for him to think so?

Collier's—the self-same *Collier's* which recently went out of existence—was a popular magazine of reform, run by the scholarly Norman Hapgood. So was the *American,* also recently defunct, and once run by a large body of judicious editors. So were *McClure's, Success, Cosmopolitan, Everybody's*—a name of significance—and many others. They were much more important than the *Atlantic, Harper's, Scribner's,* and similar "class" publications; they had better and more challenging writers. The significant novelists, essayists, and personalities wrote for them. Markham was one of the central pillars of this citadel of reform and, as such, had a national audience and international fame.

As a poet, his position was somewhat more complicated. Poetry had never been much of a democratic weapon since Lowell had levelled his dialect verses at slavery and Whittier had published his agitational and folk poems. Poetry had, in the post-Civil War period, become a symbol and sign of conventional gentility, rather than a medium for expressing universal thoughts and feelings. Whitman, for all his democratic apostrophes, in no way affected the masses, who preferred "The boy stood on the burning deck," and " 'Give us a song!' the soldiers cried." Whitman's reputation was shielded and sustained by a cult during these cold decades of the pre-reform period. It is generally imagined, now, that it took a special revolution to break a vicious cycle of artificial versifying. Peter Viereck echoes much of this opinion when he thinks that the older poetry was hamstrung by "thee's" and "thou's." What is most inadequately realized is the length and breadth of the revolution in poetry in the 1890's and 1900's. Much more than the relative popularization of Whitman's massive effort was involved. The efforts of numerous individuals who followed after him were poured into the problem of American expression. Even James Whitcomb Riley, for all his sentimentality and commonplaceness, was exploring common speech for uses in verse. Edwin Arlington Robinson was vastly more traditional in his techniques than is realized, but he probed natural utterance as well as a most un-American pessimism. William Vaughn Moody attempted to speak on topics and attitudes of the 1900's. I need not develop this theme, here. I intend only to underscore that much more than Markham's reputation is involved in attitudes and impressions of him and his work. The reputations of several score of his most distinguished contemporaries are also dusty with casual clichés.

I go further. I claim that poetry has by now practically ceased to be effective in our society, and that the presence or absence of "thee's" and "thou's" has close to nothing to do with the case. Let us, for the moment, assume Markham's inadequacy: he is "as wretched a poetaster as ever lived," except, of course, for **"The Man With the Hoe"** and . . . What poetry do *you* read? For which poet do *you*, today, have a real—I said, a real—regard? From whose verse do *you* anticipate catharsis? From Edna St. Vincent Millay? From Vachel Lindsay? Or Carl Sandburg? Or Robinson, or e. e. cummings? And how many of you are there? We are worlds away from Lewis Mumford, who recalls that he used to carry *Leaves of Grass* around, and, on the sands of Ogunquit, Maine, "that I bayed those verses to the ocean." Would *you* do this, and do you know anyone who would?

The cold fact is that we are, today, back in the 1890's, poetrywise, before reform broke down the spiked gates of American culture. One of the more amusing games one can play is to conjecture who, in due course, will emerge as our present-day equivalents of Thomas Bailey Aldrich, Edmund C. Stedman, Richard Watson Gilder, and other strong and conventional arms of nineties poetry . . . . How did we manage this return to the nineties? Weren't we going in a direction *away* from them?

Poets did not succeed in learning the secret of popularity during the popular reform period of pre-World War I years, with the single exception of Edwin Markham. He published his verses, read them in his rich voice before large and varied audiences, and had them read for him. Other poets were confined to "magazine verse" and poorly read volumes. Of epochal—and abortive—significance, therefore, was Vachel Lindsay's campaign, in the latter part of the 1900's: his attempt to live upon the countryside by exchanging poems for food and shelter, while seeking converts to his "gospel of beauty." It is worth pausing to ask which poet today would have the courage and conviction—the sheer gall—to approach his fellow Americans with verses or (in Lindsay's phrase) *Rhymes to Be Traded for Bread.*

The 1910's were a period of enormous poetic excitement. One can add up in it practically all the names he can actually think of, setting aside voices which were too young to have been present in any form and which may have status today but not stature. Untermeyer, in his autobiographical *From Another World,* notes that he and his fellows of the 1910's were under the impression that they were shaking down all values in poetry; upon reconsideration, he is astonished to see how little they were changing. And yet, this was the age of John Reed as well as of the Ezra Pound of villanelles and ballades, of Edgar Lee Masters as well as of T. S. Eliot, of Robinson and H. D., of Amy Lowell's "experiments" and Robert Frost's fulfilling poems. It even included Hart Crane as a very young man, like many of his age about to be thrown into the powerful currents of the 1920's.

My purpose here is not to accuse anybody of anything, but merely to point up our present poetic circumstances. The youth movement of the 1910's should have been a charming and lovely thing, even with the ugly smear of World War I across its face. In some ways it was. The reform generation had been stiff and not wholly flexible: it had preconceptions and attitudes which needed to be supplemented by a bold and experimental youth. The tragedy was that the reformers, Markham included, were not supplemented but superseded. Their youthful successors were unwilling to build upon their elders' achievements and to study their very human American experience. No doubt the youngsters—some of them not particularly young—could not help themselves. They reflected the atomization of American society, its march to the cities, its turn toward "specialization" and impersonality. The younger generation thought it was protesting against conformity and anonymity. It lacked insight to see that its free verse and free love and free thought were anything but free, that their experiments constituted no more than a kind of random stitching on the reverse side of mass production—which they were impotent to influence. And that their "freedom" served no truly liberating function. It merely reflected society's traumas.

Do you understand me? Do you know what I am talking about? I am saying that poetry in the 1910's, as lovely as some of it was, became disassociated from other American experience. That, increasingly, we were being skewered together not by deep-rooted traditions, race and family memories, historical obligations, but by half-formulated creeds and accidents of time and place. The first World

War only completed this tragic process of disassociation. I believe it is the task of the present generation—if it wishes to live—to reformulate our lives and give them some minimal consequence.

Markham had been one of the great men of the 1900's: the author of a dozen poems besides **"The Man With the Hoe"** which had rugged strength and poetic inevitability. Read his first two books of poems, if you don't credit this statement. He had been America's conscience, voicing its concern for humanistic and humane causes, in "Edwin Markham's Eyrie," which he conducted in *Success Magazine,* and in other publications. He had struck off one of the great prose series of the age: "The Hoe-Man in the Making." This became the battle-cry of the anti-child labor crusade. He had been, to the great novelists and statesmen around the world, America's greatest living poet. But as Progressivism slipped away, under the pressure of forces which we are still unwilling to face and understand, Markham's fame, and, indeed, the quality of his verse, declined.

Markham, by the middle of the 1910's, had clearly ceased to be the pivotal figure in American culture and society he had recently been. But you will have to be receptive, open-minded, imaginative to accept the fact that he still was very much of a pivotal figure—even then, even in the 1910's. But not, of course, in the eyes of the new and "vital" poets, the bohemians and socialists and others who revolved about the anything but popular "little" magazines.

I put "vital" into quotation marks not to suggest doubt about the value of the new poets (by the way, there were many more than one might think), but because their vitality has been impugned by younger poets on the make. John Ciardi, for example, reviewing Edna St. Vincent Millay's career in the *Saturday Review,* wrote in an impressionistic vein of the purest irony. Vachel Lindsay has scarcely been mentioned in poetry "circles" since his death; he might just as well be Markham, with two set pieces for anthologies, for all the attention he has received! And so with all the figures of the "renaissance" of the 1910's.

The world of poetry, in the 1920's, continued to grow: it became richer and fuller with aspirants, more powerful, more complex, and it continued to cast a net which took in Edwin Markham as well as Elinor Wylie and the more abstruse intellectuals of Vanderbilt University. It would have taken more dedicated and penetrating minds than were available anywhere in America to appreciate how fragile were the relations of our living poetry with the grassroots, how easily they could die or be killed. Suffice it here that Markham was still very much around in the 1920's, but that his status had by then become dependent on his living presence: that his past had already been committed to limbo with the age of which it was part. There is no present point to discussing his work in the 1920's: it includes a great poem, I say—**"Ballad of the Gallows Bird,"** published in *The American Mercury,* August, 1926—and a great anthology of poetry. But American poetry, like much else in American culture, had cast loose from its moorings and was completely at the mercy of circumstances. There would be no way, thereafter, of learning from our experience. There would be, indeed, no way of judging the state of our poetry, or the status of our poets, by any comparative measure. Small wonder, then, that the year 1929 fell on both like a cyclone on a hothouse.

With all the studies of poetry—and there is scarcely a press too small to offer its farthing of toll to the mendicants of "explication"—we have still no study of poetry in the 1930's. We could use one; and we would no doubt be astonished to discover that Markham is still with us. In what capacity? The newest set of new voices, in that grim time, did not bother to ask. The American past (now including the twenties) was deemed deader than ever. The youngest young were as eager to dance on its grave as the twenties, as their sister tens, had been to dance upon the grave of pre-World War I reform. The vicious idea of the "usable past"—which meant, in practice, that there was little in the past which needed to be so much as given a glance—was freshly interpreted to mean that nothing which did not bear on the economic crisis could be important: that it could only be decadent, "individualistic," bourgeois. I do not think it necessary to work over the dead dog of neo-communism and "proletarian literature," except to say that it had an influence totally out of proportion to its real meaning to Americans. Americans in their hearts of hearts cared little about "social significance." Only a trickle of them had any consistent and material concern for our culture, and even fewer for our poetry. But these few ran much of the culture enterprise of the thirties, and ran it with small regard for what might be real or fantasy. Consider the confused, simple, rhetoric of the *New Masses!*—its naiveté!—its incorrigible optimism! It was everything that Markham has been called except boyish. It was too old in essence to be that: it was old—old—old in the way of all opportunists and fair-weather heroes.

And here, hastily, I drop the 1930's. And Markham, too, finally passes out of sight—he died in 1940—and into a silence which is only less profound than that which surrounds the poetic spokesmen of social significance. For we have all heard of **"The Man With the Hoe"** and have some sense of its survival values. But what thoughts have we had, what do we *read,* of the "proletarian" verse of Alfred Hayes, Clement Greenberg, Edwin Rolfe, Willard Maas, Joy Davidson, Genevieve Taggard, Isidor Schneider, Rolfe Humphreys, H. H. Lewis—even Kenneth Fearing? Here, too, I drop consideration of reform and leftism and liberalism, except, finally, to explain why *The Reporter* editor felt compelled to say of the "powerful and popular" muckraking movement, "But it wasn't!" For *The Reporter* wishes to reform, and it can only imagine reformers in its own image—as lonely birds and wise-guys. It cannot believe that once—once upon a time—reform could appeal to a substantial section of the American public and be guided—for better and worse, to be sure—by its spontaneous instincts and interests and corrections. . . .

Poetry, in the 1930's, had been only a secondary art, and more disassociated from the active reading public than ever. The Popular Front had bawled doggerel hymns about the working class; it had almost no sense of individual differences and needs. Then, in the 1940's, poetry, except for what was offered at poetry socials and in schoolroom anthologies, fell into the hands of the cloistered: the modern equivalent of the mediaeval monks, except that not a few of them had just recently been marching with red flags in the mighty and unconquerable vanguard of the unshakable and triumphant working class. With the raising of T. S. Eliot to stardom, with the logical acceptance of Ezra Pound and his ragbag of ideas, including fascism, poetry no longer needed to appeal to anyone. It was "thoroughly small and dry,/Smaller and dryer than the will"; the work of a few explicators of a few verses—sometimes merely their own—to a few acolytes. I recall a student (this was some seven years ago, when Eliot was still in full apotheosis among the elect) describing to me his impressions of Eliot's *Ash Wednesday,* and indicating vaguely that he would like to know some Latin, though he had no intention of doing anything about it. I asked him just what his interest was in the poem; so far as I knew, he was an atheist, at most, and had no concern whatever for the "soul." With remarkable appositeness, he answered: "Oh, I know it's snobbish. *But anybody can join in.*"

An éliteness for the masses. A time for private worlds, sanatorium silence, all carefully supervised by a glossary of criticism, telling the patient what to think, how to think, the right poets, and the O. K. concepts. A time for poetry having nothing to do with people, communities, issues, ideas, or feelings. Here, indeed, is a cosmos in which Markham can have no place. But, note, I have not asserted that he does. I have simply undertaken to explain how a man can have been plainly in the public eye for some forty years, and, in the end, be totally unknown, as I expect to demonstrate in due course. But not Markham alone. Vachel Lindsay can have no place in such a world, nor Edwin Arlington Robinson, nor anyone, in a real and personal sense. Reputations come and go. Special issues of periodicals are put out on one person or another, for specialists. The young men fight for fellowships and Fulbrights. Everyone can use a vacation. . . .

I suppose this must be qualified. There are folk-singers. There are campus poets. And there are genuine talents like Peter Viereck and Robert Lowell and even Muriel Rukeyser, a survivor of the thirties. America has never lacked talents. Our problem has been with their ability to grow, to feed the American psyche, to find pathways to one another. Folk songs aren't lyrics, even though we sometimes call them that. Forties poets sneering at twenties poets are being neither gracious nor helpful. There is nothing wrong with being a campus poet, or looking through ivy-covered glasses at the world, so long as one is feeding from the world and nourishing it in turn. There have been egomaniacs who were patent geniuses. But there are limits to the amount of atomization a civilization can sustain. Myopia becomes a habit. There are, in fact, thousands of persons, today, who give lip-service to Edwin Markham, as there are thousands who do the same for Robinson Jeffers and T. S. Eliot and others in different circles and geographic sections. But everyone feels the difference between such lip-service and the social effort and hope embodied in the public acclaim which was accorded Carl Sandburg and Robert Frost. And everyone knows

that two such swallows add up to no more than a hope of better things.

It happens that Markham's life contains some presently unknown quantities; but they are not secrets in the sense that Shakespeare's life is a secret. Markham's is actually available to anyone, as is Lindsay's. Elements of them have been revealed from time to time. Other elements could have been deduced or reconstructed, and still others readily solicited. It makes no difference. The point was and is that the secrets were not demanded, were not sought. They were rejected, first, by an optimistic time—the Progressive era—which, in effect, thought that bygones ought to be bygones, and that (this was before World War I) peace on earth was about to bloom as a perennial. And those secrets were rejected, next, by our own pessimistic decades which have failed to see any value in the experiences of their elders and sought guides to understanding in dogmas, preconceptions, and personal equations. We function so regularly in terms of clichés and generalizations that for some minds a full-dimensioned treatment of our times—and of a Markham within them—may well seem like a personal attack, impugning their understanding.

Poetry continues, at this hour of American time, to be a specialty, a ritual conducted by Fellows of the Library of Congress, the Bollingen Award type of person, and teachers in small seminars. It needs to begin to consider ways back to people—not "the Peepul," whoever they are, but to whole persons and personalities. But first of all those concerned for poetry need to realize how simply inadequate have been the hasty impressions of its status which, in terms of our poets, have been conducive to corrupt and juiceless thought. Can poetry recapture its sense of multiplicity, of rhythm as well as thought, of occasion as well as "meaning"?

Can it recapture its courage—even so much as the courage of an old-timer like E. C. Stedman, who was drearily genteel but secure in his sense of right and wrong, enough so to consider the case of Walt Whitman at length, in broad daylight? We have developed sly tricks, in recent decades, which he would have spurned. It now seems natural to assume that one does not deal with arguments of which one does not approve. One does not give space to personalities whose ideas conflict with one's own. Let them publish their own magazines and books.

And they do. Each idea has its own magazine, its own followers, its own vocabulary. And so ideas proliferate, but human relations are stunted and immature.

Is it too hopeful to think that, so far as our poetry is concerned, we may be coming to the end of a dry road—that demand increases for substance and variety? My own chips are on the youngest young. If I may again advert to my article, mentioned before: "Our Youth: Aspiring or Tiring?" in the Summer, 1951, *Southwest Review.* In it, I referred to "the silent generation," by which I meant *the older generation,* "with nothing to say, and disappointed that its juniors have nothing to suggest." *Time Magazine,* in its better known article, "The Younger Generation," published November 5, 1951, called *the younger genera-*

tion "the silent generation." One can see why: *Time* is bought in greater quantities by papa than by junior; no use offending the breadwinner and magazine-buyer. But Thornton Wilder in his amiable article on the same subject in *Harper's,* or the *Atlantic,* or some such, was quite right to wonder what the phrase meant, as applied to the young. I suggest it meant nothing. And that we can all gain from candor and an open exchange of understandings about Markham, and poetry in general, and what have you. (pp. 447-59)

> *Louis Filler, "Edwin Markham, Poetry, and What Have You," in* The Antioch Review, *Vol. XXIII, No. 4, Winter, 1963-64, pp. 447-59.*

FURTHER READING

Biography

Stidger, William L. *Edwin Markham.* New York: The Abingdon Press, 1933, 287 p.
    Adulatory biography.

Criticism

"The Religion in Markham's Poetry." *Current Literature* XLII, No. 3 (March 1907): 317-18.
    Examines the religious elements in Markham's poetry.

Filler, Louis. *The Unknown Edwin Markham: His Mystery and Its Significance.* Yellow Springs, Ohio: The Antioch Press, 1966, 205 p.
    Analysis of why Markham's reputation as a poet declined so dramatically after his death.

Fleissner, Robert F. "Markin' the Frost Line: On Robert Frost and Edwin Markham." *South Carolina Review* 16, No. 2 (Spring 1984): 120-24.
    Suggests that Frost's poem "The Objection to Being Stepped On" satirizes Markham's "The Man with the Hoe" and compares lines of several of Frost's poems to those of Markham.

Flower, B. O. "Edwin Markham: A Prophet-Poet of the Fraternal State." *The Arena* XXVII, No. 4 (April 1902): 391-411.
    Characterizes Markham as a "great poet" who "ranks with the noble few of the ages whose almost every line suggests a colossal picture or an awe-inspiring truth, and who above all are the servants of God and the light-bearers of their age and time—sincere, unselfish, conscience-guided souls singing in a world of self-absorption and expediency."

Goldstein, Jesse Sidney. "Escape of a Poet." *The Pacific Humanities Review* XIII, No. 3 (September 1944): 303-12.
    Romanticized account of the alleged adventures of Markham during the two months he ran away from home as a teenager.

———."Two Literary Radicals: Garland and Markham in Chicago, 1893." *American Literature* 17, No. 2 (May 1945): 152-60.
    Examines the literary relationship between Markham and Hamlin Garland and the influence of Garland's work on Markham's poetry.

Graham, D. B. "Yone Noguchi's View of Edwin Markham." *The Markham Review* 6 (Winter 1977): 39-40.
    Describes the unfavorable impression Markham made on a Japanese writer visiting New York in 1906.

Gregory, Horace, and Zaturenska, Marya. "Edwin Markham." In their *A History of American Poetry, 1900-1940,* pp. 51-4. New York: Harcourt, Brace and Co., 1942.
    Overview of Markham's life and work.

Phelps, William Lyon. "Edwin Markham." In *Commemorative Tributes of the American Academy of Arts and Letters, 1905-1941,* pp. 405-07. Reprint. Freeport, N.Y.: Books for Libraries Press, 1968.
    Obituary tribute.

Slade, Joseph W. " 'Putting You in the Papers': Ambrose Bierce's Letters to Edwin Markham." *Prospects* 1 (1975): 335-68.
    Publishes correspondence between Ambrose Bierce and Markham, tracing the course of their literary friendship.

Wisehart, M. K. "Edwin Markham's Three Glimpses of God." *The American Magazine* 106 (September 1928): 26-7, 69-70, 72, 74.
    Biographical sketch and interview with Markham.

Additional coverage of Markham's life and career is contained in the following source published by Gale Research: *Dictionary of Literary Biography,* Vol. 54.

Rafael Sabatini

1875-1950

Italian-born English novelist, playwright, short story writer, and historian.

INTRODUCTION

A prolific author in several genres, Sabatini is considered a masterful practitioner of historical fiction. Eschewing modernist literary movements, Sabatini fashioned an idiosyncratic fictional mode partially modeled on adventure novels of the seventeenth and eighteenth centuries, and at the same time he transcended the category of popular period romances through his erudition, droll dialogue, authentic use of historical detail, and his command of archaic idioms. He viewed the work of the historical novelist as similar to that of the historian: both require in-depth research, treat historical personalities and events with accuracy, and go beyond a mere recording of facts to analyze the subtexts of history.

Sabatini was born in the medieval walled town of Jesi, Italy, to an Italian father and an English mother. At least one critic has suggested that Sabatini's childhood among the romantic ruins of churches and palaces from earlier centuries could have predisposed him toward a fascination with the past. Due to the dual nationalities and the encouragement of his parents, Sabatini received a cosmopolitan education. He learned English from his mother and later wrote his fiction in that language. After studying at the Ecole Cantonale in Zoug, Switzerland, and the Lycée of Oporto, Portugal, where he showed an interest in history, he traveled throughout Europe and then settled in England, intending to pursue a career in business. However, Sabatini decided upon a writing career after finding employment on a Liverpool newspaper. During the war years of 1917-18 he worked in the Intelligence Department of the British War Office. Sabatini continued writing into his early seventies. He died in 1950 in Adelboden, Switzerland.

All of Sabatini's novels are set in the historical past, ranging from medieval and Renaissance Italy to France of the Revolution. *The Carolinian* is his sole fictional work set in the Americas. Sabatini's first novel, *The Lovers of Yvonne,* went largely unnoticed. With *The Tavern Knight,* Sabatini began producing a series of extremely popular adventure novels, including *Bardelys the Magnificent, St. Martin's Summer, The Sea-Hawk,* and *The Banner of the Bull: Three Episodes in the Career of Cesare Borgia.* The publication in 1921 of *Scaramouche: A Romance of the French Revolution,* however, established Sabatini's reputation as a popular novelist throughout the English-speaking world. Described by Edwin McAlpin as a novel of "sin and its consequences," *Scaramouche* is, nevertheless, also a tale of high adventure and swordsmanship. The

novel takes its title from a sequence in which the hero, André-Louis Moreau, after numerous encounters with his arch-enemy, the Marquis d'Azyr, joins a strolling band of actors and assumes the stage name of Scaramouche. In this work Sabatini extracts a bitter moral from the rivalry between Moreau—a young and idealistic monarchist-turned-Republican—and the cruel, licentious marquis. At the novel's conclusion the marquis is made to regret his youthful transgressions when he learns that Moreau, the man he has plotted to defeat, is his own son, fathered out of wedlock many years before.

The success of *Scaramouche* was surpassed by that of *Captain Blood: His Odyssey,* and its sequels, *Captain Blood Returns* and *The Fortunes of Captain Blood.* Probably the best known of Sabatini's works, this trilogy is set in one of his favorite milieux—the high seas during the seventeenth century. Sabatini's vivid character, Captain Blood, was partially based on a historical personage, a gentleman English surgeon named Henry Pitman who was sold into slavery at Barbados, but who later escaped. Sabatini evidently based subsequent developments in the first novel on written collections of buccaneer tales and adventures. In the latter portion of *Captain Blood,* in which the unjustly treated Englishman commits himself to the life of a pirate on the Spanish Main, his actions are, nevertheless, ruled by a code of honor and virtue that is typical of Sabatini's heroes.

Political intrigue was a favorite theme of Sabatini, and he found generous material from which to fashion his plots in the political machinations of the Popes, the Inquisitors, and the secular rulers who populate European history. His lifelong fascination with the Borgias prompted Sabatini to treat this calculating Italian dynasty in three different literary genres. A controversial volume of history, *The Life of Cesare Borgia of Grance,* in which Sabatini argued that the celebrated sins of the Borgias have been perpetuated over time in popular belief but lack support in documentary evidence, was followed by his novel, *The Banner of the Bull.* From this novel, Sabatini adapted a play, *The Tyrant: An Episode in the Life of Cesare Borgia,* successfully produced in Birmingham and London in 1925. *The Minion* (published in the United States as *The King's Minion*) belongs to the same category, that of the novel of political deceit. Set at the court of James I, *The Minion* concerns the historical events surrounding the murder of Sir Thomas Overbury, confidant to King James and a commoner, who was knighted in 1608. Overbury's influence with the monarch made him the object of jealousy on the part of the notorious divorcée, Frances Howard, Countess of Essex. Sabatini's plot follows from his study of the historical sources, from which he concluded that two separate conspiracies to murder Overbury had become confused in the historical accounts. Finally, in Sabatini's history *Torquemada and the Spanish Inquisition* he draws a powerful character study of the Grand Inquisitor.

Critics have frequently compared Sabatini's art to that of Alexandre Dumas, *père,* the nineteenth-century French writer and acknowledged master of the romantic adventure novel. Some critics have faulted the author for allegedly relying on overworked narrative strategies of such romantic writers as Stanley Weyman and Robert Louis Stevenson. Nevertheless, Sabatini's witty and self-conscious bows to the artistry of an earlier literary period are considered by most commentators to transcend a simple reworking of traditional themes. Critics are nearly unanimous in commending Sabatini's inventive and stirring plots, impressive command of the English language, his thorough and convincing historical settings, and the compelling characterizations of both his novels and plays. Critics have praised such novels as *The Sea-Hawk, Scaramouche, Captain Blood, The Carolinian,* and *Bellarion the Fortunate* for their swiftly moving, adventurous plots that involve numerous sharply defined characters. Sabatini is also admired for such subtle, fully developed historical portraits as those of Cesare Borgia and Tomás de Torquemada, which integrate the imaginative with the historically authentic.

Although written in the twentieth century, Sabatini's novels and plays consciously bask in the emotions, settings, and mores of the popular romantic fiction that flourished in the eighteenth and nineteenth centuries. Such recognized requirements of Romanticism as exotic settings and the elemental emotions of love, hatred, revenge, conquest,

and power illuminate Sabatini's adventure tales. Most indicative of the Romantic outlook is Sabatini's cultivation of historicism. The desire to reanimate the past—not simply to recreate it but actually to enter into the past by leaving the present behind—was one of the definitive elements of the Romantic attitude. In his fiction, Sabatini sought to recapture this past by sheer force of energy and bring it to life.

PRINCIPAL WORKS

The Lovers of Yvonne (novel) 1902
The Tavern Knight (novel) 1904
Bardelys the Magnificent (novel) 1906
St. Martin's Summer (novel) 1909
Bardelys the Magnificent [with Henry Hamilton] (drama) 1910
The Life of Cesare Borgia of Grance (history) 1911
The Lion's Skin (novel) 1911
Torquemada and the Spanish Inquisition (history) 1913
The Banner of the Bull: Three Episodes in the Career of Cesare Borgia (novel) 1915
The Sea-Hawk (novel) 1915
The Historical Nights' Entertainment. 3 vols. (short stories) 1917-38
Scaramouche: A Romance of the French Revolution (novel) 1921
Captain Blood: His Odyssey (novel) 1922
Scaramouche (drama) 1923
In the Snare [with Leon M. Lion] (drama) 1924
The Carolinian (novel) 1925
The Carolinian (drama) 1925
The Tyrant: An Episode in the Life of Cesare Borgia (drama) 1925
Bellarion the Fortunate (novel) 1926
The Minion (novel) 1930; also published as *The King's Minion,* 1930
Captain Blood Returns (novel) 1931
Scaramouche the Kingmaker (novel) 1931
The Black Swan (novel) 1932
Heroic Lives (history) 1934
Venetian Masque (novel) 1934
The Fortunes of Captain Blood (novel) 1936
The Sword of Islam (novel) 1939

CRITICISM

Lewis Melville (essay date 1924)

[*In the following excerpt, Melville surveys several of Sabatini's novels, praising his story-telling powers, his gift for characterization, plot invention, and daring adventure sequences.*]

Rafael Sabatini is our outstanding "costume" novelist. He is also an historian of repute, a dramatist . . . , and author of a play for the screen that has scored one of the greatest successes of recent years. It is needless to add that he is now a "best seller." (p. 307)

A perusal of his books makes it clear that he has always been a student of history, European as well as British. He has in fact an encyclopædic knowledge of this branch of learning and (like his own heroes) he, with never a care, treads century after century underfoot. Incidentally, he is a terror to the modern biographer, because in comparatively few pages he can tell the story of the person he decides to honour, whereas it takes another and a lesser man a volume or two to do the same thing.

When Mr. Sabatini is not writing novels . . . , or historical works (he is the historian of Cæsar Borgia and of *Torquemada and the Spanish Inquisition*), he occupies his leisure in throwing off thumb-nail sketches of interesting incidents of the past. Many of these last he has gathered together in the two series of *The Historical Nights' Entertainment.* Some idea of the wide range of knowledge of this author may be gathered from the contents of this work. Take a few of the titles gathered at random: **"Casanova's Escape from the Piombi," "Count Philip Königsmark and the Princess Sophia Dorothea," "The Murder of Amy Robsart," "The Story of the St. Bartholomew," "The Betrayal of Sir Walter Ralegh."** Who else could do this so easily and at the same time so thoroughly?

In these days we are rather apt to forget that the first duty of the storyteller is to tell a story. Judging from modern fiction as a whole, this first step is the most difficult.

At least it is less and less frequently attempted. The book that is described as psychological may be a very admirable treatise, it may make most interesting reading, but it can only be dubbed a novel by courtesy. And after all, when all is said and done, the novelist should write novels.

Mr. Sabatini believes surely that in a story something should happen—even in life something happens every now and then, though many present-day novelists have tacitly agreed to ignore the fact that there is in life anything more than character and dialogue. Since as a matter of fact there are thrills in life (one can imagine Mr. Sabatini saying), why should there not be thrills in pen-pictures of life?

The only trouble for what I will call the adventurer-novelist is that, be his inventive faculties however great, everything has been done before in real life. (pp. 307-08)

Mr. Sabatini, however, takes his chances like a man, and he has been well rewarded for his courage. He has gathered unto him a host of readers and has delighted [all] of them. He is read with avidity in every English-speaking country, and I suppose his books have been translated into most languages. A man of simple, gracious manner, humble as to his achievements, albeit naturally not without some appreciation of his work, he has the defects of his qualities—from the point of the interviewer. I had the pleasure lately of a conversation with him that lasted more than an hour. My object was to lead him on to talk of his art; yet I came away without the subject being touched

upon. I am sure however that he likes (as which of us does not?) discerning praise: I can only hope that he will think such praise as I humbly mete out is discerning.

What I particularly like about Mr. Sabatini's heroes is that they are so splendidly human. Sometimes they do silly things—just for all the world as men do in life. Did not Lord Randolph Churchill at the critical moment in his career "forget" Goschen? Often the heroes are unduly trusting; but if they were not, how could the author use his splendid ingenuity in extricating them from tangles into which their blind faith has led them?

Also, many of the heroes have a flaw in them. I mention this as a merit. Marcel de Bardelys, when in wine, wagers that he will win for his wife a girl unknown to him and in whom he has no interest whatsoever. Even the fact that the period is that of Louis XIII is not an excuse, for however the morality of such a thing was then regarded, Bardelys is too much the *grand seigneur* to justify it to himself. He makes amends and, after much tribulation and many really serious inconveniences such as his life being in danger, he loses his wager and wins his delightful bride. Captain Blood is at least as real a character as that namesake of his who in the reign of Charles II contrived to steal the Crown Jewels from the Tower. He had already had an adventurous career before Mr. Sabatini takes his story in hand. He then acquires a grievance in that, though innocent, he is at the Bloody Assizes sentenced to death for treason by Jeffreys himself—the sentence being commuted to a living death as a slave in Barbados. Of course, Blood escapes. Perforce he becomes a pirate—a man of iron will, coolness, resource and courage—an admirable, gentlemanly pirate. He makes his mistakes, he none the less overthrows his enemies and ends as Governor of Jamaica. So may all gentlemanly pirates flourish! Perhaps the most amazing thing in *Captain Blood* is the fact that Mr. Sabatini shows the same intimate knowledge of eighteenth century ships and seamanship as he does of Mary Queen of Scots or Marat, or fencing at the old Italian Commedia dell' Arte.

One more example. This from *The Snare,* an admirable story of the Peninsular War. General O'Moy, Adjutant-General of the Forces in Portugal, for once in his life behaves badly. He believes his wife to be unfaithful to him with his friend, and disgraces himself utterly in his blind rage. He too, when his suspicions are proved unfounded, repents in sackcloth and ashes, and is forgiven by all concerned, including the reading public and (in this case) the theatre-going public, for Mr. Sabatini (with him, as the lawyers say, Mr. Leon M. Lion) has dramatised this novel.

Mr. Sabatini has the pleasant habit of introducing real characters into his historical romances. Thus in *Bardelys the Magnificent* you have Louis XIII in his habit as he lived; in *The Snare* there is Wellington to the life at the time of the construction of the Torres Vedras lines; in *Captain Blood* you have a pen-portrait of Jeffreys, not the Jeffreys as whitewashed by Harry Irving, but the traditional ruffian as depicted by Macaulay. The only difference is in person—Mr. Sabatini presents him as he appears in a little known portrait:

Blood beheld a tall, slight man on the young side of forty, with an oval face that was delicately beautiful. There were dark stains of suffering or sleeplessness under the low-lidded eyes, heightening their brilliance and their gentle melancholy. The face was very pale, save for the vivid colour of the full lips and the hectic flush on the rather high but inconspicuous cheek-bones. It was something in those lips that marred the perfection of that countenance; a fault, elusive but undeniable, lurked there to belie the fine sensitiveness of those nostrils, the tenderness of those dark liquid eyes, and the noble calm of that pale brow.

In *Scaramouche,* a story that opens in France in 1788, Mr. Sabatini presents Robespierre, Marat, Desmoulins and Danton. His hero is lawyer, actor and dramatist, a master of fence, and in the end a successful lover. The canvas is immense, the atmosphere admirable—one can see the thunder-clouds of revolution gathering until the storm overtakes the monarchy and (for the time being) upheaves France.

Mr. Sabatini has in his novels the sanity of the historian; to his histories he imparts the gifts of which he is possessed that make his works of fiction so fascinating. He has the power of being dramatic without being melodramatic. He is more realistic than Scott and more romantic than Thackeray. It is no exaggeration to say that in his historical romances he has the sure touch of Dumas—and I do not know how to pay him a higher compliment; but to this I may certainly add that in every book Mr. Sabatini has written his own personality is stamped in it. If you pick up a volume by Mr. Sabatini and put it down before you have finished it, believe me the fault is not his. (p. 308)

Lewis Melville, "Rafael Sabatini," in The Bookman, *London, Vol. LXVI, No. 396, September, 1924, pp. 307-08.*

Edward Shanks   (essay date 1925)

[*Shanks was an English poet, novelist, critic and editor of the* London Mercury *from 1919 to 1922. In the excerpt below, Shanks commends* The Tyrant: An Episode in the Life of Cesare Borgia *as a well-written play but asserts that Sabatini has presented an implausibly sympathetic portrayal of his protagonist.*]

Like Mr. Rafael Sabatini, I hate to think that any really bad man ever really existed; and so long as I have breath in my body I shall be prepared to go on proving that there were none. I therefore welcome Mr. Sabatini's efforts in this admirable cause. His play, **The Tyrant** . . . is a memorable and most noble attempt towards what we both have at heart.

Mr. Sabatini, I notice, has weakened a little. Dismayed (one can but suppose) by the outcries of those for whom the wickedness of the Borgias is a sacred tradition, he has volunteered an explanation. Nothing, it seems (and I can confirm the assertion, though the importance of the fact at first escaped me) is said on behalf of Cæsar Borgia, except by himself. Nevertheless, as Cæsar presents the case with immense skill and no one important contradicts

him . . . the audience does go away with the feeling that he has been terribly maligned. Cæsar was an enlightened statesman. Lucrezia was a martyr to her philanthropic propensities, but otherwise rather dull. It is true that Alexander VI. had three illegitimate children; but as a matter of fact he was a strong opponent of the doctrine of the celibacy of the clergy, and he begot and acknowledged his family purely as a matter of conscience. Some of these arguments are mine; but I am proud to claim them. I will never be behind Mr. Sabatini in the rehabilitation of historical characters. I am afraid that in the English courts, no action for libel by a descendant of the Borgias—if there are any, though I did once meet a gentleman of that name—would lie. All the more reason therefore for Mr. Sabatini and me to do our best in our effort to explain the real inwardness of the Borgia policy.

But at the same time I am of the opinion that Mr. Sabatini goes too far. I am prepared to believe that Cæsar was really a brilliant statesman, that his career was dictated by a liking for order and organisation, and that the persons he overthrew had all his vices without his genius or his public spirit. Mr. Sabatini could forget more than I ever knew about the Italian Renaissance and still give me points and a beating; and I welcome his testimony in favour of a view which I have always held. But at the same time he must not ask us to accept the notorious Cæsar as a blameless person motivated by eminent Christian virtues, nor must he put forward excuses which strike at the very root of dramatic ethics.

Mr. Matheson Lang once played, and with very great effect, as "The Bad Man," but he must not, or so it seems, ever be put forward as a bad man. And hence an attempt to star Cæsar Borgia as a sympathetic and benevolent character, which, on whatever reading of history, he never can be.

Solignola is a little hill-town of Umbria or thereabouts; and the lord of Solignola is, with others, concerned to terminate the victorious career of Cæsar Borgia. One plot fails. Another is devised in which Panthasilea (so spelt, I know not why), daughter of the lord of Solignola, is to figure as a conscious and willing decoy. Cæsar detects the plot. He takes all that Panthasilea has to give, and evades the conspiracy. Solignola is taken. At a banquet, a poisoned cup of wine is offered to Cæsar. But Panthasilea drinks it and dies instead of him.

As a brisk and moving sword-and-cloak play this is really excellent. Mr. Sabatini, if my recollection is accurate, has never before written for the stage unaided. If this is his first single venture, then he is very warmly to be congratulated. His piece moves with admirable vigour and briskness from the first line to the last, and makes an opportunity for a quite remarkable display of stage-setting in decoration and costume.

And Mr. Sabatini's defence is ingenious. Cæsar is the only person who contradicts the libels directed against him, and he does so to a girl whose passion for him is the central theme of the play. But he makes his assertions very easily and no one will deny that, lovesick as the girl may be, she accepts them with astonishing ease. Now Cæsar Borgia is, in the first place, one of the most interesting characters in modern history. His methods and his whole cast of thought anticipated those of a score of modern statesmen. It is possible that he just failed to secure a commanding position in Italy and to create a great power among the earliest great powers. It is certain that in Italy of that period no man in public life could afford to neglect the lie, the phial, and the dagger, any more than to-day a public man can afford to neglect the wireless or the press agency. All this is true; but Mr. Sabatini has not really tackled it. Cæsar Borgia, truthfully expounded, might be made a very sympathetic figure to persons to whom had been equally truthfully expounded the conditions of the age in which he lived and worked. Mr. Sabatini tries to make him sympathetic by an illegitimate procedure, which clashes with the ideas of those who have any real information upon the period. Cæsar's aims may have been enlightened; but he did use treachery, and he did use poison and the dagger, in pursuit of them. They may make for dramatic intensity, but are not necessarily high ethics.

It is further to be remarked that the Borgias have become almost a myth, and that modern myths are few enough. Don Juan and the Wandering Jew have passed safely into this category; and there are a few historical figures who are candidates for it. Mary Stuart is one, and the dramatists and the novelists rightly do what they will with her. Cæsar Borgia is another; and, on the whole, I think it is probably desirable that the concept which the popular idea of him represents should, if necessary, triumph over historical truth. At any rate, in this conflict there is no room for a compromise between legend and historical truth: let us have no second-rate article which is partly one and partly the other. Let us have definitely one thing or the other.

I repeat that Mr. Sabatini's play is an admirable piece of work, not to be criticised adversely except upon these somewhat high grounds. Mr. Sabatini is that somewhat unexpected figure, an historical novelist who has a real curiosity about, and knowledge of, history, and is often preferable, on questions of real truth, to accepted historians. There is no doubt, for example, that he has given us a picture of Jeffrey infinitely preferable to that given by Macaulay. My complaint against this play is that, shirking a problem of immense psychological interest, he adopts half measures with the Borgia.

Edward Shanks, "The Blameless Borgias," in The Outlook, *Vol. LV, No. 1417, March 28, 1925, p. 217.*

Graham Sutton (essay date 1927)

[*In the excerpt below, Sutton praises the play* Scaramouche *for its "fresh and ingenious" handling of a political plot.*]

[Sabatini's play **Scaramouche**] deals only incidentally with the old tribe. They loom largely; but they are there not so much for their own picturesque sake (though in this respect the author makes good use of them) as to provide an asylum for the hero, a young Monarchist who is induced to espouse the Republican cause for the sake of a private vengeance. The political outline of this play—one

may say its ethical outline—is extremely fresh and ingenious. I am no politician; but if I were, I should be tempted to expend the rest of my article on tracing the nice vacillations of public opinion, which have resulted in the balance of this play being poised as we see it. Time was, within fairly recent memory, when the Sans-culotte was the inevitable villain of French Revolution tales. The balance shifting, Aristocrats came in for their share of stage abuse. To-day opinions are so divided that it is no longer safe to put all one's dramatic eggs in one political basket. So here we have young André-Louis Moreau, a fervent aristocrat, driven against his logical convictions to attack the Marquis d'Azyr on a point of individual tyranny. Moreau proves such a force that he ends as one of the bright particular stars of the new Republican government; after which he sees the error of his ways, and declaring that republicanism will be only the substitution of a new tyranny for the old, resigns his portfolio and goes into voluntary exile. The whole theme is admirably handled, though it is much less stressed than my account of it may imply. I emphasise it here because in our theatre a costume-play with any genuine thought in it is so rare as to be a portent. Most costume-playwrights are content to assert themselves with a few "gadzooks" or "marrys" or "citoyens," as the period demands, and with a rehash of stock judgments: just as most star managers are apt to insist on plays with no live parts but their own. That is not Mr. Rafael Sabatini's way—nor Sir John Martin Harvey's only way, either. The play is both intelligent and well written. . . . (pp. 247-48)

Graham Sutton, "Artists All," in The Bookman, *London, Vol. LXXII, No. 430, July, 1927, pp. 247-48.*

The tale [of *Scaramouche*] is simply alive with incident. . . . It will appeal to those readers who sometimes lament that they cannot longer find books of the type the elder Dumas poured forth so brilliantly.

—*R. D. Townsend, in a review of* Scaramouche *in* Outlook, *1921.*

St. John Adcock (essay date 1928)

[*A prolific English author, Adcock served as editor of the London* Bookman *from 1923 until his death in 1930. In the excerpt below, he explains how and why Sabatini's fiction transcends the limitations of the popular romantic adventure novel.*]

Sabatini has acquired a richer vocabulary and writes an easier, more virile and vigorous English than do many distinguished authors who were born in England and expensively trained in its Public Schools and Universities. Coming to England, he made his home at Liverpool, and worked for a while on a Liverpool newspaper. He wrote short stories and, like most beginners, had manuscripts rejected and accepted by the magazines; and during this time, and before and after this, he must have devoted himself largely to that wide study of Italian, Spanish and French history which was to bear such good fruit in the romances, plays, biographies and historical works that were ultimately to yield him his due meed in money as well as in fame—ultimately, for the due meed was in no haste to bestow itself upon him, and he had a lingering interval of hopes deferred and difficulties to be overcome such as have soured and embittered many authors, but he seems to have taken the worst as he has taken the best of things with a philosophical impartiality, so that success has left him what he was in the days of his probation, one of the kindliest, most gracious and most modest of men. I daresay it was his native modesty that helped to prolong the period of his waiting. I have the best of reasons to know that he never had any skill in pushing himself, and that he had not even a rudimentary knowledge of that art of self-advertisement which others use to such prompt and profitable effect. His only method seems to have been to do his books, and do them well, and to leave them to do all the rest, and in the end they have done it in the most satisfactory and triumphant manner.

Born in 1875, he is now a year or two over fifty, and his first novel, *The Tavern Knight,* appeared when he was close on thirty, in 1904. In these twenty-four years he has written over twenty books and some three or four plays; and you realise what this must have meant in unremitting industry if you remember that the books included, apart from imaginative fiction, such exacting and scholarly histories as *The Life of Cæsar Borgia,* and *Torquemada and the Spanish Inquisition,* though he cannot have given much less time to reading and research for the groundwork of his historical romances and for the brilliant series of historical studies and stories in his two volumes of *The Historical Nights' Entertainment.*

His second novel, *Bardelys the Magnificent,* is a gallant, picturesque romance of the France of Louis XIII, written with a gusto and imaginative power that should have carried him straightway into a resounding popularity; if it fell short of doing that, it at least established him alike with the public and with the critics as a novelist who knew how to tell an excellent story and to tell it, moreover, with more of literary art than commonly goes to the making of popular novels. I have seen this and other of his stories compared with the tales of Dumas, and certainly Dumas would have gloried in the dashing, riotously romantic Bardelys, who, flown with wine, wagers that he will win and marry a girl who is a stranger to him, and is too fine a gentleman not to repent of this swaggering boast but, having gone through desperate adventures which cunningly hold the reader in continual expectation and suspense, ends by gaining the lady after he has lost his wager. There is a Dumas-like breeziness and gusto in the telling of all this, but there is more finish of style, and a subtler psychology in the presentation of character than were ingredients in the magic of the great French master.

Following Bardelys at yearly intervals came *The Trampling of the Lilies, Love at Arms, The Shame of Motley, St. Martin's Summer, Anthony Wilding, The Lion's Skin,*

then, in 1912 (with the *Life of Cæsar Borgia* in the same year) *The Justice of the Duke;* in 1913 (with the history of *Torquemada* in that same year) came *The Strolling Saint,* and in the next four years *The Gates of Doom, The Sea Hawk, The Banner of the Bull,* and *The Snare.* These last three added very appreciably, I think, to Sabatini's steadily increasing vogue. In 1918 and 1919 came the two volumes of *The Historical Nights' Entertainment;* then, after an interval of two years, we had *Scaramouche,* with *Captain Blood* and *Fortune's Fool* on its heels in 1922 and 1923, and the "Sabatini boom" had begun.

It seemed to begin suddenly with *Scaramouche,* but might very well have started with any of the three preceding novels if they had not been published during the war—with *The Sea Hawk,* a glamorous, robust story of Barbary corsairs and a great sea-rover, Sir Oliver Tressilian, whose wild adventures are related with touches of grim humour and in the finest spirit of romance; with *The Banner of the Bull,* written round the dazzling, strange career of Cæsar Borgia and alive with the intrigues and clashing ambitions and rich in the scenic magnificence of mediæval Italy; with *The Snare,* a vividly dramatic romance of Portugal during the Peninsular War, which he adapted for the stage, a little later, in collaboration with Leon M. Lion, who produced it successfully at the Savoy Theatre.

Meanwhile Sabatini had already produced, with less success, three other plays, including a version, dramatised in collaboration with Henry Hamilton, of *Bardelys the Magnificent;* and had occupied himself for a while as partner in a London publishing firm. But he had done with publishing when *Scaramouche* appeared, to take the reading world by storm and set an enthusiastic public asking for his earlier books and stir the publishers to run after him, who had hitherto been running after them.

He had fared until then no better in America than in his own country, and I have heard that no sooner was his name one to conjure with than certain American houses made various efforts to secure novels of his they had formerly declined to accept.

Scaramouche was filmed, and triumphed sensationally on both sides of the Atlantic; and, in a word, after twenty years in the wilderness Sabatini had emerged into a long-promised land that is flowing with milk and honey every pint and pound of which he had paid for in honest, hard work long before the goods were delivered to him.

Most writers of romance avoid the risk of overstraining their imaginations by inventing a formula at the outset, and thereafter make all their books according to that pattern. One of the charms of Sabatini's work results from his never having adopted that easy-going plan. Each new romance of his has been always a new one and never the old one artfully retold with variations. It has not only the freshness of a new plot but usually of different surroundings. Bardelys flourished in seventeenth century France; *The Justice of the Duke* is another Borgian story; *The Sea Hawk* is all of the sea and piracy; *The Snare* takes you into the Napoleonic wars, and *Scaramouche* into the horrors and heroisms of the French Revolution. *Captain Blood* grows out of the Monmouth rising and the tyrannies of

Bloody Jeffreys. Sabatini has a delicate skill in the creation of heroines, but the love element is only one of various threads of interest in his stories. He handles the facts of history imaginatively, and turns them to effective account when they serve his purposes; when he introduces real notabilities into his narrative he draws them with fullness of knowledge and yet with such deftness that though they are clothed in all the actuality that once belonged to them that are so nicely toned to his general scheme that they do not overshadow or take anything from the lifelikeness of his fictitious persons. His Louis XIII in *Bardelys the Magnificent* is a masterpiece of realistic portraiture; as that is of Jeffreys in *Captain Blood;* there are graphic sketches in *The Snare* of Wellington and of the famous secret service agent, Colonel Colquhoun Grant; and notable pen-pictures of Robespierre, Danton and Marat on the crowded canvas of *Scaramouche.*

I remember reading an interview in which Sabatini laid it down that, whatever his *genre,* the aim of every novelist should be the achievement of realism; that however imaginative a story may be it should be so written that a reader may feel able to accept it as true. He protested against the "over-educated sterility" of the school of novelists who, making realism an end in itself, instead of a means to an end, laboriously overload their pages with minute and sometimes unsavoury details, as if the business of the artist were not to learn how to achieve an effect of reality by selecting his material and suggesting more than he in fact revealed, but to rest content in a slavish imitation of the mechanical work of the average photographer. If grimness and drabness and squalor are not excluded from Sabatini's romances, they are never introduced for their own sakes, but only when they happen to be an indispensable part of his story. He is a romancist in grain, and an artist in romance, and, like the true artist, mixes his colours, as Sir Joshua said they ought to be mixed, "with brains".

The passion for romance is too deeply rooted in our nature ever to be eradicated, but it is not always potent; it has its winters. There are fashions in fiction, as in everything else, but yesterday's modest will be in favour again to-morrow. Romance was in the ascendant once more, some years ago, when Stanley Weyman, Rider Haggard, Anthony Hope, J. M. Barrie were young; we have wandered since through arid regions of psycho-analytical experiment where no romance brightened, and Sabatini's mistake was in getting born out of his due time. But it is a hopeful augury nowadays that so many have come and are coming to him, and to such as him, drawn to his and their books for change and refreshment, as travellers are attracted to a welcome oasis in a desert. (pp. 281-88)

> *St. John Adcock, "Rafael Sabatini," in his* The Glory That Was Grub Street: Impressions of Contemporary Authors, *The Musson Book Company Limited, 1928, pp. 279-88.*

Edwin A. McAlpin   (essay date 1928)

[*In the following excerpt, McAlpin summarizes the swiftly moving plot of* Scaramouche *with its unexpected twists and turns of fate.*]

Scaramouche, by Sabatini, is a tragedy with sin as its motive. The book opens with André Louis Moreau and his friend, Philippe de Vilmorin, in conflict with the Marquis de la Tour d'Azyr over the killing of a peasant who had been caught poaching on the Marquis's land. André did not know who his mother was, but believed himself to be the natural son of his godfather, M. de Kercadiou. André's friend, Philippe, was a candidate for Holy Orders and a pronounced revolutionist. The Marquis was a gentleman of the old régime. He was a sensualist, but a man of his word. His culture was a veneer for a hard and brutal materialism. He was an accomplished swordsman and a bachelor whose intrigues with other men's wives were notorious. The Marquis had at last decided to get married and was paying court to the beautiful Aline de Kercadiou, the niece of André's godfather.

Philippe and André met the Marquis at the château of M. de Kercadiou.

The Marquis, angered by the revolutionary sentiments of Philippe, cleverly forced a duel upon the inexperienced seminarian and killed him. André was so infuriated by the murder of his friend that he denounced the Marquis to his face, and when that gentleman admitted he had killed Philippe because of his eloquence, André decided to become the voice of Philippe.

André threw himself into the revolutionary movement and discovered he also had a gift for the eloquence that the Marquis feared. André visited Rennes and Nantes in an effort to obtain justice. The Courts were deaf to his appeals, but he stirred up the mob. The government officials sought to kill him because of his activities, and, therefore, he had to flee.

By accident he stumbled upon a troupe of traveling players. This troupe needed a man, and André joined them as Scaramouche. In their company he knew he had an excellent chance of escaping his enemies. His experiences as an actor make a delightful interlude in the tragedy that is being developed by the plot of the story. He fell in love with the leader's daughter, Climène, and they became engaged. Under the influence of André, the troupe improved their performances and had a successful season at Nantes. The pretty and vivacious Climène attracted many admirers. Along with others the old roué, the Marquis de la Tour d'Azyr, succumbed to her charms. The poor little actress had her head turned by his elegant manners, immense wealth, and social position. She yielded to his advances and was swept off her feet. When she returned from a night with the Marquis at his château, André, in his bitter anger, stirred up the revolutionary sentiments of the audience and turned them against the Marquis. The play broke up in a riot.

André fled to Paris and succeeded in getting a position in a school of fencing. On the death of the fencing master André took over the school and became a finished swordsman. His Republican friends discovered him in his new occupation. They told André the nobles had developed a system of forcing duels upon the revolutionists and then killing these inexperienced swordsmen in cold blood. They suggested that he be elected as a delegate to the convention and retaliate by beating the nobles at their own game. At first he refused; he accepted only when he learned that his old enemy, the Marquis de la Tour d'Azyr, was one of the leading duelists. He became a delegate to the convention to punish the Marquis for the dastardly murder of Philippe de Vilmorin. . . . André's purpose was to kill the old rascal, but the Marquis partially parried one of André's lunges, and instead of being killed the Marquis only had his arm torn open.

At the end of the story the reader discovers the Marquis is André's father. The roué and libertine finally sees how this life, which had sprung from his youthful sin, had been used by fate to rob him of all the things he most desired. André had been instrumental in blocking the Marquis's efforts to marry the beautiful Aline de Kercadious, whom the Marquis loved and eagerly desired. It was André's action in stirring up the riot at Nantes that had deprived the Marquis of the pretty Climène, a mistress he was deeply interested in. It was André who destroyed the Marquis's reputation as a swordsman. It was André, as a representative Republican, who took away the Marquis's estates, wealth, and eminent social position.

Scaramouche is a tragedy of sin. The sins of a man's youth have an uncanny way of remaining dormant and finally rising up to destroy all those things that make life beautiful and happy. (pp. 39-43)

> Edwin A. McAlpin, "Sin and Its Consequences," in his Old and New Books as Life Teachers, *Doubleday, Doran & Company, Inc.,* 1928, pp. 36-49.

Richard J. Voorhees   (essay date 1979)

[*In the essay below, Voorhees discusses why Sabatini deserves to be read by a new generation of readers and places the author's best novels above the typical period fiction of his time, emphasizing his nimble dialogue and vivid, literary prose. He reproduces some of Sabatini's own words concerning the uses of history in the construction of his novels and examines the role of women in Sabatini's fiction.*]

"He was born with a gift of laughter and a sense that the world was mad. And that was all his patrimony." In the twenties and thirties some thousands of readers probably would have recognized with pleasure the opening of *Scaramouche* (1921). By 1975 only readers well stricken in years would have been likely to have a clue to the sentences or to the man who wrote them. The case may be altered yet again, for Ballantine Books, starting in March of 1976, has reissued eight titles by Sabatini, including *Scaramouche.*

For a number of reasons Rafael Sabatini (1875-1950) deserves to be widely read again. First of all, he writes far better English than most creators of historical romance and high adventure, though he is not altogether immune from the kind of stylistic infection that is endemic to the genre. Part II of *The Sea Hawk* (1915) begins with the following piece of overheated prose: "Sakr-el-Bahr, the hawk of the sea, the scourge of the Mediterranean, and the terror of Christian Spain, lay prone on the heights of Cape

Spartel." More characteristic of Sabatini is a manner caught from the dramatic literature of the seventeenth and eighteenth centuries, with a diction composed in part of rare or archaic words, French phrases, Latinate forms. He prefers "what time" to "meanwhile" and "he nothing heeded" to "he paid no attention to." He is so fond of saying that someone "stood at gaze" that characters often seem to be standing at gaze all over the landscape. He must have stopped more than a few people in their tracks with the "rich muliebrity" of a vicomtesse, a "ramage" of trees, and "armigerous" Whigs.

These, however, are harmless affectations, no more debilitating to Sabatini's brisk prose than lace and perukes to his sinewy heroes. The prose, indeed, is not only much better than that of most popular novelists; like Wodehouse's, it is better than that of many a more significant novelist. Sabatini is lucid and flexible, never monotonous or awkward, always in control of his sentences, no matter how long some of them may be. The passage quoted from *The Sea Hawk,* though it is flamboyant, is at least parallel in structure. At their best, Sabatini's sentences are as graceful as his swordsmen.

From the seventeenth and eighteenth centuries Sabatini derives a kind of metaphor which, if a trifle self-conscious, is entertaining, and sometimes witty. When André-Louis Moreau ("Scaramouche"), a young lawyer compelled to abandon his practice, seeks work as an assistant to a fencing master, Sabatini remarks, "The position, you see, had its humiliations. But if André-Louis would hope to dine, he must begin by eating his pride as an hors d'oeuvre." Informed that his duties will include sweeping out the fencing room, André-Louis says, "And so the robe yields not only to the sword, but also to the broom."

Sabatini's dialogue is obviously not the equal of Congreve's but it does not look bad beside that of the ordinary comedy of the Restoration, for it is as full of thrust and riposte as the swordplay that Sabatini describes with such liveliness and authority. Because André-Louis, now a fencing master, has fought duels with aristocrats, the Marquis de La Tour d'Azyr demands, "Are the men who have opposed you men who live by the sword like yourself?" "On the contrary, M. Le Marquis," André-Louis replies, "I have found them men who die by the sword with astonishing ease." As the following exchange between a young girl and her highly respectable aunt indicates, there is something of George Bernard Shaw in Sabatini's use of shock and paradox:

> "It is not my chastity that is in question, but that of M. de La Tour d'Azyr."
>
> "Wherever did you learn that dreadful, that so improper word?"
>
> "In Church."

Sabatini also likes to exercise himself in aphorisms. Since he is an entertainer, he tosses off his quota of light ones, but when the occasion requires it, he can crack a maxim as dark as those of La Rochefoucauld. Of a woman who has been no better than she should have been, he writes, "With her, expiation had begun as it does when it is possible to sin no more."

Though Sabatini has a very thorough knowledge of the periods about which he writes, it sometimes looks as if he has studied history in Hollywood. Too frequently the heroes are like matinee idols, the heroines like romantic actresses, the villains like character actors reveling in the hokum which, in the movies, often passes for wickedness. The costumes, properties, and sets appear to have been drawn from the vast cornucopia of the old M.G.M. studios. The wardrobes are a fop's delight, and the inventory of gold and precious stones amounts, as Doctor Johnson would say, to wealth beyond the dreams of avarice. Remote places and people call up the Cecil B. De Mille in Sabatini: the Algerian sections of *The Sea Hawk* abound in a kind of Hollywood exoticism: palace intrigue, shrewd eunuchs, ingenious and barbaric cruelties, torchlight flickering on the scimitars of black-robed janizaries.

Sabatini's best writing, however, is infinitely superior to the usual period fiction of his time. Sabatini is concerned with character as well as costume, so that the invented heroes are not brass monuments of bravery and good looks, the invented heroines not waxen dolls. The historical characters are not mannequins on which to drape the robes of justices, the vestments of bishops, the uniforms of generals. Nor are they simplified figures from historical legend. The Judge Jeffreys of *Captain Blood* is an example of the latter. Not only in legend but also in Macaulay and those historians who, into the twentieth century, wrote under the influence of Macaulay, Jeffreys is a blood-thirsty monster and nothing else. Researching and writing in the early twenties, Sabatini concludes that the monster is a fiction, and responsible historians publishing in the late sixties agree with him. "It is significant," says P. J. Helm, "that the trials in which Jeffreys is said to have behaved unfairly are usually those of which no official account has survived." Sabatini does not try to convince the reader that Jeffreys was such a tenderhearted fellow that he could not swat a fly in his courtroom, but he indicates that he was not quite the supreme example of what George Orwell called "that gouty old bully, the English hanging judge." Still in his thirties, as he was indeed at the time of the "Bloody Assizes" (he died at forty-one), Sabatini's Jeffreys has a delicately handsome face and a melancholy air. He observes proper rules of procedure and tries to restrain the bursts of fury that prisoners and witnesses provoke him to. A powerful irony presides over the court: as Jeffreys sentences men to death, he endures terrible pain from the kidney disease that will kill him in a few years. In Jeffreys the reader sees a man, not a poison-breathing dragon.

The ordinary life of various times and places moves through Sabatini's pages; dockworkers and itinerant actors, attorneys and tradesmen go about their affairs. The reader discovers odd generalizations (all the leading French Revolutionaries were exceptionally pockmarked), technical details, significant distinctions. Even one who nods occasionally over Sabatini (if there is such a reader) will eventually learn that in the seventeenth and eighteenth centuries men removed their shoes to fight duels with swords, and that a pirate and a buccaneer are not one and the same.

His essay **"Historical Fiction"** in *What Is a Book?* (1935), edited by Dale Warren, shows that Sabatini takes history and the historical novel with equal seriousness; he has equal contempt for the careless historian and the novelist of the sex-and-"Gadzooks!" school. The writer of historical fiction, he considers, is obliged to research the entire life of the period that he chooses so thoroughly that he is quite at home in it. If he knows his business, his book will not be cluttered with his knowledge, but "informed and enlightened by it." A period novel may concern itself "entirely with historical characters and historical happenings." Or it may "present an invented story developed by means of imaginary characters but set against a real background to which story and characters must bear some real and true relationship." Or it may blend "events that are real with events that are reasonably and logically imagined, and characters that lived with characters that the author has invented."

Among his own novels, Sabatini notes, *The King's Minion* (1930) illustrates the first procedure. He did not invent a story, and he "scarcely invented even a minor character." He imagined a solution to the mystery of the murder of Sir Thomas Overbury, but only after "close study and close reasoning." *Scaramouche* illustrates the second procedure. The hero is an invented character, but he moves against a true historical background, and he is "the natural offspring of the circumstances and habits of mind into which he is born." *Captain Blood* illustrates the third procedure. Blood is not a historical character, but much of his life is borrowed from "the lives of men who actually lived," and the early part of his story is largely the story of Henry Pitman, a surgeon and traveler of the seventeenth century.

> The writer of historical fiction . . . is obliged to research the entire life of the period that he chooses so thoroughly that he is quite at home in it. If he knows his business, his book will not be cluttered with his knowledge, but [in Sabatini's words] "informed and enlightened by it."
>
> —*Richard J. Voorhees*

Sabatini's categories do not stop him from inventing a number of documents which confer an appearance of reality on imaginary happenings and characters. The introductory note to *The Sea Hawk* informs the reader that the authority for the novel is Lord Henry Goade (a character in the novel), who, though a great seaman, was inclined to intrigue. He was therefore removed from his command by Elizabeth and appointed Queen's Lieutenant of Cornwall. In his leisure he wrote a history in eighteen folio volumes, the last thirteen of which deal with the events of his own day. The opening of chapter 13 of *Captain Blood* announces that the greater part of the narrative is derived from Jeremy Pitt (a character in the novel), who kept the log of the *Arabella* "as no other log that I have ever seen was kept." Some of the sheets are mutilated; others are missing, and Sabatini pretends to suspect that Esquemeling (a real buccaneer, traveler, and writer) stole them so that he could attribute Blood's exploits to "his own hero, Captain Morgan." He omits the fact that a part of the novel has a solid basis in the life of Henry Pitman.

The "documentation" of **Scaramouche** is scattered through the text. Sabatini quotes from his hero's letters and from a volume called his *Confessions.* Old copies of newspapers and playbills in the Carnavalet Museum confirm critical dates. The very absence of documents creates an air of authenticity: "Diligent search among the many scenarios of the improvisers which have survived to this day has failed to bring to light the scenario of *Les Fourberies de Scaramouche.* . . ." In instances like these Sabatini plays a game not unlike that which George Macdonald Fraser plays when he pretends to be no novelist but rather the editor of "The Flashman Papers." The game involves a slight hazard or two. Though no deception is intended, an ingenuous reader may be deceived: at least one reviewer took the first Flashman novel for a genuine memoir. And whereas the Flashman novels work perfectly as regards point of view (Flashman simply relates what he has experienced), Sabatini's do not. No Henry James, Sabatini does not bother his head over such matters.

Whatever their exact relation to history, Sabatini's best novels are first-rate adventure and melodrama. Among the devices of melodrama which Sabatini employs with great skill are disguise and impersonation. Because his skin is dark and he speaks perfect Spanish, Captain Blood can pass as "Don Pedro Sangre, an unfortunate gentleman of Leon," and damn the English, those "heretics" who hold Barbados. Blood wears the uniform of a Spanish admiral, and André-Louis Moreau actually wears theatrical makeup and mask. A fugitive, he attaches himself to a company of strolling actors and hides behind a false nose as they pass through a village. Sabatini's novels are also rich in what John Buchan called, in a memorable phrase, "escapes and hurried journeys." These are vivid and concrete, not only because Sabatini is blessed with the gift of the storyteller, but also because he has acquired a detailed knowledge of military and (especially) naval strategy and tactics. His accounts of the virtuosity of Captain Blood, Charles de Bernis, or Sir Oliver Tressilian have the bright color of romance and the conviction of the expert witness.

Sabatini's world is in some ways remarkably pure. The air rings with the clash of swords and is acrid with the smell of gunpowder, yet gratuitous violence, sensationalism, and even rough talk are as exceptional in Sabatini as they are typical in more recent writers of adventure novels. At the time he wrote, he was obliged to represent Danton's obscenities with dashes, but one supposes that he would do the same thing if he were writing today. He does not pretend that piracy and war are not accompanied by rape, but he refrains from using the word, and he does not (as later writers do) make a Roman holiday of the fact. Rape takes place offstage. Onstage, the villain does no more than rip the heroine's bodice.

Accustomed to high casualty rates in Sabatini, the reader will probably be shocked nonetheless by an episode in **The Black Swan** (1932). The villain is Tom Leach, a pirate on whose head Henry Morgan has put a price of five hundred pounds. At the close of the novel Charles de Bernis tosses Leach's head at the feet of Morgan. A man not easily shaken, Morgan protests, as he may well do, "You're damned literal, Charles." But Sabatini is more likely to note pathos and irony in death than to exploit ghastliness. When a young divinity student unskilled in the sword is provoked into challenging a skillful aristocrat to a duel, they meet on a bowling green behind a tavern, the scene of more innocent competitions. And when two women arrive too late to stop André-Louis Moreau from going to a duel in the Bois, they hear in the midst of their frantic thoughts an ordinary street cry: "A raccommoder les vieux soufflets!"

Sabatini's heroes offer the reader of historical romances much that he expects, but they also spring a few surprises on him. They are more often than not foppish, for Sabatini is convinced that adventurers love clothes. Taffeta, satin, and silk glamorize their figures, and billows of Mechlin lace embellish their wrists. When he is under full sartorial sail, Captain Blood affects not only a cane but a cane well decorated with ribbons; on his head is a meticulously curled wig and on that a broad hat surmounted by a plume. If he did not carry a rapier as well as a cane, if his eyes did not have a "steely" look, he might seem to be no more than a foolish and cowardly fop straight off the Restoration stage, a Sir Fopling Flutter of the seas. In fact, he and Sabatini's other well-dressed heroes are not only brave fellows but also, in the words of the dramatis personae of Restoration comedy, "men of wit and sense," except where women are concerned.

The bravery of the hero is exceeded by his purity. Though he may follow the trade of pirate or buccaneer, he is, by all the available evidence, as chaste as any Victorian curate. (Captain Blood and Charles de Bernis have, as it were, no mistresses but their ships.) The result is an orgy of woman-worship which takes one back to the Middle Ages. The very memory of Arabella Bishop is a "bittersweet purifying influence" upon Captain Blood, and Sir Oliver Tressilian (defending his checkered career) puts it more strongly: "No lover since the world began was ever so cleansed, so purified, so sanctified by love as I was." De Bernis thinks that because he has plundered and killed, he is probably beyond redemption. As he tells the story of his adventurous life to Priscilla Harradine—the scene is a clear echo of *Othello*—she drops a tear on his hand. "I thank you," he says, "for that tear dropped on the grave of a lost soul," but he feels later that some of his wickedness has been washed away. Devotion to a woman is the only religion of the hero. Blood, though born and bred a Catholic, is "a papist when it suits him" (when, for example, he is impersonating a Spaniard). Sir Oliver, indignant at Christian hypocrisy, renounces Christianity and, because it is obviously the politic thing to do, embraces Mohammedanism.

Again and again Sabatini's heroes are good and innocent men turned, through no fault of their own, to fugitives and outlaws. From these circumstances Sabatini creates high dramatic interest and ironic repercussions, but never a hero comparable to those of Stevenson or Kipling. Blood, however, has special points of interest, as Sherlock Holmes would say, and André-Louis Moreau has dimensions which bring him close to the heroes of major novelists. When the reader first meets him, Blood is practicing medicine at Bridgewater, but he has behind him several years of adventure by land and by sea. Shortly after taking his degree at Trinity College, Dublin, he served with the Dutch under the great de Ruyter in the war against France, was imprisoned for two years in Spain, and fought with the French in their war on the Spanish Netherlands. For treating the wounds of one of Monmouth's officers, he is sentenced to death, but his sentence is commuted to transportation as a slave to Barbados. There he steals a ship and embarks on his piratical career. He is a kind of marine Raffles, an outlaw but in his way a patriot. He abominates James II, but he admires William III as Raffles admires Queen Victoria.

Educated not only in medicine but also in the classics, Blood is especially devoted to Horace and Suetonius, and he could scarcely function without Latin writers: preparing for a hazardous enterprise, directing a sea fight, rejected by a woman, he recalls an appropriate passage. That Blood is both pirate and surgeon, a man who destroys life and preserves it, sheds blood and stops it, makes him more fascinating than the hero of the ordinary adventure story and produces such drama as the encounter between Blood and Judge Jeffreys. During his trial for treason Blood has observed Jeffreys with a doctor's eye, and at the close of the trial he shakes the Judge by saying, "The death to which you may doom me is a light pleasantry by contrast with the death to which your lordship has been doomed. . . ."

André-Louis Moreau has twice as many careers as Blood has. He trains himself to be an all-round man of the theater and takes the part of Scaramouche, but he is also lawyer, revolutionary orator, and fencing master. The last three professions have, of course, a touch of the theater in them, and Sabatini's implications about the resemblances between the theater and all of life have in turn a touch of Pirandello. There is further interest in the fact that while doing his heroic deeds André-Louis protests that he is not a man of action but a man of thought, and that he thinks heroics are probably useless. He does so with some reason, for with him even fencing becomes an intellectual pursuit, so that a passage of arms is like a game of chess. Though politically engaged, he insists that he has no interest in political change, and again with good reason. It is only the death of a friend that provokes him to revolutionary activity. Disgusted by the excesses of the Revolution, he retires from it, and at the end of the novel he makes a more or less plausible claim to have been a classical republican all along. Cynically he identifies himself with the character he plays in his troupe, but in this respect he is wrong: he stirs up trouble, all right, but he is otherwise the reverse of Scaramouche.

The women in Sabatini, like the women in most adventure stories (even those of Stevenson, Buchan, and Chesterton) are less satisfactory characters than the men. At least one of them is remarkably epicene: "Miss Arabella Bishop—this . . . slip of a girl with her rather boyish voice and her almost boyish ease of movement." But Arabella's cheeks blush as readily as those of the other heroines, and her eyelids flutter as much.

Stranger and more important is the cruelty with which these odd goddesses treat their worshippers. Is it a deliberate imitation of the literature of courtly love? Is it a reflection of a bitter episode in Sabatini's life (of which very little is known), an obsession? If Sabatini's novels were no longer than the ordinary adventure novel, there could be no reconciliation between the hero and one kind of heroine, for a hundred thousand words go by before she wakes up to his virtues. "I do not number thieves and pirates among my acquaintances," Arabella says glacially to Blood, and there follows a shocking spectacle: Blood besotted with rum, unshaved, his wig uncurled, and his clothes a complete mess. Rosamund Godolphin is even worse, for there is absolutely no pleasing her. When Sir Oliver Tressilian (who sleeps across the threshold of her cabin like a dog to guard her) tells her that he has betrayed his corsairs and risked his own life to save hers, she replies that he should have consulted her first.

Most of Sabatini's villains are stock characters. Don Diego Espinosa is treacherous and cruel because he is a Spaniard. Colonel Bishop, who whips Jeremy Pitt with a bamboo cane till it splits, is a sadist out of the silent movies. Tom Leach, who slavers when he sees Priscilla Harradine swimming naked, belongs to that category of the old melodrama called "beast" or "fiend." An exception is the Marquis de La Tour d'Azyr (who is really a kind of spoiled hero), intolerably arrogant, ruthless in the defense of the privileges of his class but convinced of the rightness of its cause, a brave man and in his way an honorable one.

Why should a revival of Sabatini not be a success? Characterization, to be sure, is not the strong point of his novels. The ships are more real than some of the men who sail them; the gowns are more attractive than some of the women who wear them. But if his characters are worlds away from Dickens's, they are not so far from Arthur Conan Doyle's. His prose is more literary than that of most popular writers, but his polite language is no more artificial than (say) Raymond Chandler's tough one, and his metaphors are actually less extravagant than Chandler's. A happy combination of the researcher and the imaginative writer, he is as trustworthy as he is entertaining. He catches most admirably the spirit of a man, a town, a time. His description of a French port in *Scaramouche,* for example, compares favorably with Virginia Woolf's description of an English one in *Orlando.* Even his weaker novels have fine narrative momentum, masterful suspense, and gunplay and swordplay expertly recounted. Now that he has returned from the limbo of novelists, his swordsmen and his seamen ought to display for great numbers of new readers their purity and their gallantry, their discipline and their enterprise, their wardrobes and their wit. (pp. 195-204)

Richard J. Voorhees, "The Return of Sabatini," in South Atlantic Quarterly, *Vol. 78, No. 2, Spring, 1979, pp. 195-204.*

FURTHER READING

Douglas, Norman. "Theology." In his *Experiments,* pp. 69-79. New York: Robert M. McBride & Co., 1925.
    Remarks on the absence of anti-Catholic sentiment in Sabatini's novel of the Inquisition, *Torquemada.*

Frank R. Stockton

1834-1902

(Full name Francis Richard Stockton; also wrote under the pseudonyms Paul Fort and John Lewes) American short story writer, novelist, poet, satirist, writer of fairy tales, and author of fiction for children.

INTRODUCTION

Stockton was one of America's most popular and prolific writers during the final two decades of the nineteenth century, and his works were widely read throughout the English-speaking world. He is remembered today chiefly as the author of children's fantasy tales and the short story "The Lady, or the Tiger?" Stockton's varied output included science fiction and local color stories, as well as novels and poetry.

Born in Philadelphia in 1834, Stockton was one of nine children. His father never approved of his desire to write fiction and apprenticed him to a wood-engraver following high school. However, Stockton's mother and his brother John encouraged his literary efforts, and he published his first story, "A Slight Mistake," in 1855, while working as an engraver. In 1864 Stockton became a journalist for the Philadelphia *Press and Post* and continued working as a magazine and newspaper writer and editor for the next two decades. Stockton first gained wide attention with a series of children's fantasy tales published in various magazines during the 1860s and later collected together as *Ting-a-ling.* In 1873 Mary Mapes Dodge invited Stockton to work as her assistant on the newly founded *St. Nicholas Magazine,* a publication for children. Stockton not only performed editorial work, but wrote articles, poetry, and stories under his own name and the pen names Paul Fort and John Lewes. In addition, he produced his first major work for adults, a group of tales published serially and later collected as *Rudder Grange.* Stockton maintained a grueling schedule between *St. Nicholas* and his other writing until 1878, when failing eyesight, attributed to eye strain suffered as a wood-engraver, as well as generally poor health, forced him to take a part-time position with *Scribner's Magazine.* Eventually his eyesight became so impaired that he retired from publishing entirely. Warned by doctors to read and write as little as possible, Stockton composed his fiction mentally and dictated the finished works to his wife or relatives. In this way the majority of his most famous works were written: *The Late Mrs. Null, The Casting Away of Mrs. Lecks and Mrs. Aleshine, The Bee-Man of Orn, and Other Fanciful Tales, The Squirrel Inn, The Adventures of Captain Horn, Mrs. Cliff's Yacht,* and *The Great Stone of Sardis.* Stockton died in 1902 while visiting Washington, D.C.

Critics note that the most characteristic trait of Stockton's fiction is the subtle humor which he conveyed through

whimsical situations and eccentric characters. His children's fantasies, which he termed "fanciful tales" rather than fairy tales in order to avoid the sentimental connotations of the traditional designation, contain such mythical creatures as dryads and dwarves who behave much like ordinary people, reacting with the mixture of pragmatism and believable emotion that Stockton referred to as "common sense." The juxtaposition of unusual situations and characters with credible responses creates much of Stockton's humor, both in the children's tales and elsewhere. Stockton was also acclaimed for such fantasies written for adults as *The Great Stone of Sardis,* which often involve fictitious scientific discoveries, and for witty local color stories which are usually set in Virginia. While Stockton was praised by his contemporaries for his sympathetic portrayals of African-American and white Southerners in *The Late Mrs. Null* and other works, some modern readers have found his use of dialect condescending and his characters stereotypical. Throughout Stockton's tales, authority is generally undercut, and the wisdom of the common people, especially women, is championed. For example, in "The Griffin and the Minor Canon," the Minor Canon, the lowest official of a medieval cathedral, faces the terrifying Griffin—who has come to the city to see his sculpted likeness on the cathedral—when his superiors all prove themselves cowards and flee. Impressed by the Canon's devotion and courage, the Griffin threatens to destroy the city if its people ever mistreat the Canon, who eventually is made Bishop as a result. Intellectuals who would direct the lives of the unlettered are parodied in "The Bee-Man of Orn," where a meddling Sorcerer asserts that a poor, ignorant, ugly beekeeper has been transformed from another state into his present one. The Bee-Man, previously content with his life, decides to find out what he once was, and eventually, after much tribulation, remembers that he was once a baby. The Sorcerer transforms him into a baby, only to discover, forty years later, that the baby has grown up to be the same dirty, illiterate man as before. In many of his stories, Stockton presented strong female characters, notably in *The Late Mrs. Null* and *Mrs. Cliff's Yacht*. In *The Casting Away of Mrs. Lecks and Mrs. Aleshine,* two middle-aged housewives find themselves adrift at sea after a shipwreck and save themselves and a male companion by relying on their own ingenuity and determination.

Stockton's most famous work, "The Lady, or the Tiger?," was originally composed to provoke discussion at a party. It is the story of a young commoner in a "semi-barbaric" land whose love for his princess is discovered by the king. The youth is condemned to the king's arena, where he must choose which of two doors to open. Behind one of the doors is a young woman in love with him whom he may marry; behind the other is a ravenous tiger. The princess discovers which door conceals which fate, and points the young man to the door on the right. The story ends with the latter walking to the door as the narrator explains that the princess has long been torn between pity for the youth and jealousy at his belonging to the other woman. "The Lady, or the Tiger?" brought Stockton fame and provoked years of debate, but almost ruined Stockton's career. For more than a year after the publication of the story, publishers refused Stockton's submissions, demanding an equal performance to "The Lady, or the Tiger?" Stockton parodied his plight in "His Wife's Deceased Sister," a tale in which a writer slowly rebuilds his career after failing to satisfy expectations raised by one brilliant success. The writer eventually composes another story which is even better, and orders his wife not to release it until after his death. Acceding to reader demand for a sequel to "The Lady, or the Tiger?," Stockton wrote "The Discourager of Hesitancy," which preserves the ambiguity of the first tale by posing another unsolvable puzzle for *readers* to answer before they are told the outcome of the original tale. Though readers received the sequel with some amusement, critics paid it little attention.

Stockton was primarily a storyteller who entertained his audience with fanciful tales, rather than a creator of serious plots or complex characters, so his popularity began to wane even before his death, as changing public taste demanded more emphasis on intricate action and less on whimsical narration. The decline in Stockton's popularity has also been attributed to the seemingly condescending tone of some of his stories about African-American and white Southerners, and the datedness of his scientific fantasies. However, such critics as Suzanne Rahn find a number of his novels and short stories, especially his children's tales, to contain a wisdom belying their apparent simplicity and deem them worthy of wider appreciation than they have received in recent decades.

PRINCIPAL WORKS

"A Slight Mistake" (short story)   1855; published in *American Courier, A Family Newspaper*
Ting-a-ling (fairy tales) 1870
Roundabout Rambles in Lands of Facts and Fancy (essays and short stories) 1872
What Might Have Been Expected (novel) 1874
Rudder Grange (short stories) 1879
The Floating Prince, and Other Fairy Tales (fairy tales) 1881
Ting-a-ling Tales (fairy tales) 1882
The Lady, or the Tiger? and Other Stories (short stories) 1884
The Transferred Ghost (short stories) 1884
The Casting Away of Mrs. Lecks and Mrs. Aleshine (novel) 1886
The Christmas Wreck, and Other Stories (short stories) 1886
The Late Mrs. Null (novel) 1886
*The Bee-Man of Orn, and Other Fanciful Tales (fairy tales) 1887
*The Queen's Museum (fairy tales) 1887
The Dusantes: A Sequel to The Casting Away of Mrs. Lecks and Mrs. Aleshine (novel) 1888
The Great War Syndicate (novel) 1889
Ardis Claverden (novel) 1890
The Squirrel Inn (short stories) 1891
The Adventures of Captain Horn (novel) 1895
Mrs. Cliff's Yacht (novel) 1896
The Great Stone of Sardis (novel) 1898
John Gayther's Garden (short stories) 1899
The Vizier of the Two-Horned Alexander (short stories) 1899
The Novels and Stories of Frank R. Stockton. 23 vols. (novels, short stories, fairy tales, and satires) 1899-1904

*These two collections are almost identical and were issued simultaneously.

CRITICISM

William Dean Howells   (essay date 1887)

[*Howells was the chief progenitor of American realism and an influential critic during the late nineteenth and early twentieth centuries. He stands as one of the major literary figures of his era; having moved American literature towards realism and away from the sentimental romanticism of its early years, he earned the popular sobriquet "the Dean of American Letters." Despite his prefer-*

ence for realism, Howells respected Stockton's work. Here, Howells compares the techniques of Stockton with those of realist novelists.]

Mr. Stockton's readers have a right to look a little askance at the title and general air of the two volumes [**Stockton's Stories,** First and Second Series], recently published, bearing his name. Is it intimated that this story-teller, having developed into a novelist, finds it a convenient time to bring together in a complete form all his short stories, and thus to take leave of the company? (p. 130)

Mr. Stockton, more, perhaps, than any recent writer, has helped to define the peculiar virtues of the short story. He has shown how possible it is to use surprise as an effective element, and to make the turn of a story rather than the crisis of a plot account for everything. In a well-constructed novel characters move forward to determination, and, whatever intricacy of movement there may be, it is the conclusion which justifies the elaboration. We are constantly criticising, either openly or unconsciously, a theory of novel-writing which makes any section of human life to constitute a proper field for a finished work; however many sequels may be linked on, we instinctively demand that a novel shall contain within itself a definite conclusion of the matter presented to view. But we do not exact this in a short story; we concede that space for development of character is wanting; we accept characters made to hand, and ask only, that the occasion of the story shall be adequate. Take, for example, one of Mr. Stockton's cleverest stories, **"The Remarkable Wreck of the Thomas Hyke."** The actual release of the imprisoned passengers is not the point toward which the story moves, and the righting of that singular vessel is only one of a number of happy turns, all starting from the one original conception of a vessel with water-tight compartments, sinking bows foremost, and held in perpendicular suspense. On the other hand, the story . . . **"The Christmas Wreck"** disappoints one, for the reason that the occasion of the story is inadequate, and has neither the wit of an amusing situation nor the surprise of an unexpected one. It may be said in general that Mr. Stockton does not often rely upon a sudden reversal at the end of a story, to capture the reader, although he has done this very happily in **"Our Story,"** but gives him a whimsy or caprice to enjoy, while he works out the details in a succession of amusing turns. Thus the story of Mr. Tolman, which comes nearer than his other stories to being an undeveloped novel, rests upon the delightful fiction of a man, tired of commonplace success, creating for himself an entirely new situation in life, and watching therein a bright little love-comedy.

Indeed, this figure of Mr. Tolman might almost be taken as an idol of the author himself. Like that respectable man of business, Mr. Stockton turns his back on the world in which he finds himself going a dull round, and takes a journey to another country, where he finds the same world, indeed, but stands personally in no sort of relation to it. He is relieved of all responsibility, and sets about enjoying the lives of the men and women whom he observes. There is thus in his stories a delicious mockery of current realistic fiction. He has an immense advantage over his brother realists. They are obliged to conform themselves to the reality which other people think they see, and they are constantly in danger of making some fatal blunder; making the sun, we will say, strike a looking-glass hung upon a wall in a house so topographically indicated as to be easily identified by the neighbors, who concur in testifying that the sun by no possibility could touch the glass, day or night. Mr. Stockton, we repeat, has an immense advantage over other realists. His people are just as much alive as theirs, and they are all just as commonplace; they talk just as slouchy English, and they are equally free from any romantic nonsense; but they are living in a world of Mr. Stockton's invention, which is provided with a few slight improvements, and they avail themselves of these with an unconcern which must fill with anguish those realistic novelists who permit their characters to break all the ten commandments in turn, but use their most strenuous endeavors to keep them from breaking the one imperious commandment, Thou shalt not transgress the law of average experience. Mr. Stockton's characters, on their part, never trouble themselves about the ten commandments,—morality is a sort of matter of course with them,—but they break the realist's great commandment in the most innocent and unconscious manner. There is not the first sign of conscious departure from rectitude in the character who, by his ingenious invention, demonstrates the law of negative gravity, and the husband and wife who bury deep in the water the key which turns the lock upon the fatal manuscript, in the story of **"His Wife's Deceased Sister,"** are as natural and healthy in action as their friend Barbel with his superpointed pins.

To return for a moment to that quality in a short story which Mr. Stockton has so admirably illustrated, of immediate wit independent of definite conclusion, a capital example exists of combined success and failure in his recent fantasy . . . *The Casting Away of Mrs. Lecks and Mrs. Aleshine.* The first part of that story is inimitable, and if it had been left unfinished it would, if we may be pardoned the bull, have been complete. We suspect that the people who have worn away their nights guessing the riddle of **"The Lady or the Tiger?"** would have wasted their days in trying to account for the barred entrance to the enchanted island in the Pacific. As it turns out, Mr. Stockton himself had no intention of accounting for the island. He invented it,—he would have invented a continent if his story had required it,—and he leaves it and the Dusantes equally unexplained; but he seems to have felt a certain compulsion to develop his characters, and to carry forward the energetic lives of those two illustrious women who are henceforth immortal. To be sure, we can forgive the platitude of the two succeeding parts of the story for the sake of a longer companionship of Mrs. Lecks and Mrs. Aleshine, and the incident of the ginger jar was worth embalming, yet in our stern capacity of literary judges we are compelled to repeat the well-known decision: Not guilty, but don't do so again.

We may observe here that Mr. Stockton falls easily into the autobiographic form, and that his peculiar gift gains by this device. In actual life we listen to a man who can tell a wonderful story of his own experience, and our incredulity vanishes before the spectacle of his honest, transparent face and the sound of his tranquil, unaffected voice. Thus Mr. Stockton, in his ingenious assumptions, brings

to bear upon the reader the weight of a peculiarly innocent, ingenuous nature, for the figures that relate the several stories carry conviction by the very frankness of their
narratives. They come forward with so guileless a bearing
that the reader would be ashamed of himself if he began
by doubting, and the entire absence of extravagance in the
manner of the story continues to keep his doubts out of
the way.

This low key in which Mr. Stockton pitches his stories,
this eminently reasonable and simple tone which he
adopts, is the secret of much of his success. One discovers
this especially by reading **"A Piece of Red Calico,"** and
then fancying how Mark Twain would have treated the
same subject. Both writers take on an air of sincerity, but
one retains it throughout, and never seems to be assuming
it; the other allows his drollery to sharp, and before he is
done his voice is at a very high pitch indeed.

As we had occasion to point out when considering *The
Late Mrs. Null.* Mr. Stockton finds a congenial field in the
delineation of negro character. We are sometimes tempted
to think that his finest success lies in such inimitable
sketches as **"The Cloverfields Carriage"** and **"An Unhistoric Page."** When he enters the world of negro life, he
finds already existing just that independent logic of fact
and irresponsibility which he enjoys creating. He has only
to help himself to what he sees, and it would be a hard
question to answer whether he made up **"An Unhistoric
Page"** or overheard it.

We began with the expression of a fear lest these two volumes were an informal announcement that their author
had abandoned short stories for novels. A re-reading of
the books and an inquiry into the secret of Mr. Stockton's
well-won and honorable success reassure us. Whatever
ventures he may make in the field of novel-writing, and
however liberal may be his interpretation of the function
of the novel, we cannot believe that he can escape the demands of his genius. The short story, either by itself or as
an episode in a novel, so completely expresses his peculiar
power, it makes such satisfactory use of his intellectual caprice, and it avoids so easily the perils which beset one
who builds a novel upon a whim that, for his own pleasure,
we are sure that Mr. Stockton will go on entertaining the
public in a style where he is his only rival. (pp. 130-32)

> *William Dean Howells, in an originally un-
> signed essay titled "Stockton's Stories," in The
> Atlantic Monthly, Vol. LIX, No. CCCLI, Jan-
> uary, 1887, pp. 130-32.*

Edith M. Thomas with Frank R. Stockton
(conversation date 1893)

> [*The following excerpt is from a conversation between
> Thomas, an American poet, and Stockton. Stockton
> talks about the sources of his story ideas.*]

[Frank R. Stockton]: I owe a great many [suggestions for
stories] to day-dreams. I used to entertain myself in this
way constantly when a schoolboy. In walking home from
school I would take up the thread of a plot and carry it
on from day to day until the thing became a serial story.

The habit was continued for years, simply because I enjoyed it—especially when walking. If anybody had known
or asked me about it I should have confessed that I
thought it a dreadful waste of time.

[*Edith M. Thomas*]: But it proved, I dare say, a sort of
peripatetic training-school of fiction.

Perhaps it might be called so. At any rate, years after, I
used to go back to these stories for motives, especially in
tales written for children. But there was another way in
which, in later years, I have made use of day-dreams. I
often woke very early in the morning—too early to think
of rising, even if I had been thriftily inclined—and after
some experimenting I found that the best way to put myself to sleep again was to construct some regular story.

Some regular story carried through to the end. I would
begin a story one morning, continue it the next, and the
next, until it ran into the serial. Some of these stories lasted
for a long time; one ran through a whole year, I know. I
got it all the way from America to Africa.

*Perhaps you anticipated reality. For a friend of mine who
reads every book of travels in Africa which she can lay
hands on, firmly believes that the Dark Continent will be
opened up as a pleasure and health resort for the whole
world! But what became of the story?*

Well, a long time after, a portion of it came to light again
in *The Great War Syndicate.* The idea of **"Negative Gravity"** was taken from another day-dream, the hero of which
invented all sorts of applications of negative gravity, and
from these I made a selection for the printed story.

*Delightful—for we may hear from this hero again. I hope
he is inexhaustible. How fortunate to have a treasure-house
of characters and exploits. You have only to open the door
and whatever you want comes out! You don't have to go to
any "Anatomy of Melancholy" or Lemprière, or Old Play,
where somebody else is going, too, and will anticipate you—
the hard luck of some of the rhyming fraternity!*

Of course, some suggestions are wholly involuntary. You
do not know how or whence they come. I think of a good
illustration of this involuntary action of the mind in con-
juring up suggestion for a story. Some time ago, as I was
lying in a hammock under the trees, I happened to look
up through the branches and saw a great patch of blue sky
absolutely clear. I said to myself: "Suppose I saw a little
black spot appear in that blue sky." I kept on thinking.
Gradually the idea came of a man who *did* see such a little
spot in the clear sky. And now I am working up this notion in a story I call **"As One Woman to Another."**

*You literally had given you less than the conditions given
for describing a circle, for you had but a simple point to
start with. One might conclude, all that is necessary is to
fix upon some central idea, no matter how slight, and then
the rest will come, drawn by a kind of mysterious attraction
toward the centre.*

Ah, but it will not do for the professional writer to depend
upon any such luck or chance, for if you wait for suggestions to come from the ether or anywhere else, you *may*
wait in vain. You must begin something. If the mind has

been well stored with incident and anecdote, these will furnish useful material, but not the plot. It is often necessary to get one's self into a proper condition for the reception of impressions, and then to expose the mind, thus prepared, to the influence of the ideal atmosphere. If the proper fancy floats along it is instantly absorbed by the sensitive surface of the mind, where it speedily grows into an available thought, and from that anything can come. (pp. 469-70)

[The] subject of suggestions, and how they come, is an interesting one. It reminds me of what the astronomers tell us of certain methods they employ. For instance, they expose, by means of telescopic action, a sensitive photographic plate to the action of light from portions of the heavens where nothing is seen. After a long exposure they look at the plate, and something may be seen that was never seen before—star, nebulæ, or perhaps a comet—something which the telescope will not reveal to the eye. As an instance of my use of this exposure plan I will mention this: some years ago I read a great deal about shipwrecks—a subject which always interests me—some accounts in the daily papers and some sea stories, such as those of Clark Russell, who is my favorite marine author, and the question came into my mind: "Is it possible that there should be any kind of shipwreck which has not been already discovered?" For days and days I exposed my mind to the influence of ideas about shipwrecks. At last a novel notion floated in upon me, and I wrote **"The Remarkable Wreck of the *Thomas Hyke*."** I have since had another idea of an out-of-the-way shipwreck, which I think is another example of a wreck that has never occurred; but this is a variation and amplification of a wreck about which I read.

Has it ever happened that any of your fancies turned out to be actual fact? Truth is said to be stranger than fiction.

In some instances just that thing has happened. In one story I had a character whose occupation was that of an analyzer of lava, specimens being sent to him from all parts of the world. In this connection a foreigner inquired of him if there were any volcanoes near Boston, to which city he was on his way. This preposterous idea was, of course, quickly dismissed in the story. But I received a letter from a scientific man in New England who thought I would like to know that, not far from Boston, but in a spot now covered by the ocean, there existed in prehistoric times an active volcano. As to the practical application of some of my fanciful inventions, I may say that two young ladies on Cape Cod imitated the example of Mrs. Lecks and Mrs. Aleshine, and having put on life preservers, and each taking an oar, found no difficulty in sweeping themselves through the water, after the fashion of the two good women in the story. I will also say that the Negative Gravity machine is nothing but a condensed balloon. As soon as a man can make a balloon which can bear his weight and can also be put in a money belt, he can do all the things that the man in the story did. I may also say that naval men have written to me stating that it is not impossible that some of the contrivances mentioned in **"The Great War Syndicate"** may some day be used in marine warfare. I myself have no doubt of this, for there is no reason why

a turtle-backed little ironclad, almost submerged, should not steam under the stern of a great man-of-war like the *Camperdown,* and having disabled her propeller blades, tow her *nolens volens* into an American port, where she could be detained until peace should be declared. (pp. 472-73)

But we were speaking of the necessity of having a definite purpose at the outset of a piece of work.

It amounts to a necessity, almost. For instance, if I am about to write a fairy tale, I must get my mind in an entirely different condition from what it would be were I planning a story of country life of the present day. With me the proper condition often requires hard work. The fairy tale will come when the other kind is wanted. But the ideas of one class must be kept back and those of the other encouraged until at last the proper condition exists and the story begins. But I suppose you poets do not set out in this way. (p. 473)

I have been thinking why it is that very often the work of an author of fiction is not as true as the work of an artist, and I have concluded that the artist has one great advantage over the author of fiction, and over the poet, even. The artist has his models for his characters—models which he selects to come as near as possible to what his creations are going to be. The unfortunate author has no such models. He must rely entirely upon the characters he has casually seen, upon reading, upon imagination. How I envy my friend Frost! Last summer, when he wished to sketch a winter scene in Canada, he had a model sitting with two overcoats on, and the day was hot. Now, I couldn't have any such models. I should have to describe my cold man just by thinking of him.

Or learn to shiver, yourself, like the boy in Grimm's Tales—*and describe that!*

But it is a serious matter. The best artists have live models to work from. But your writer of fiction—how, for instance, can he see a love scene enacted? He must describe it as best he can, and, although he may remember some of his own, he will never describe those. (pp. 474-75)

Frank R. Stockton and Edith M. Thomas, in an interview in McClure's Magazine, *Vol. I, No. 6, November, 1893, pp. 466-77.*

Henry C. Vedder (essay date 1894)

[*In the excerpt below, Vedder assesses Stockton's work in several genres, arguing that, despite Stockton's neglect of many of the normal dicta of literature, most of his work has literary value and unique humor.*]

As no reader will have failed to infer, Mr. Stockton is first of all a clever writer of short stories. Collections of his magazine stories have been made at various times since 1884: *The Lady or the Tiger?, The Christmas Wreck, The Bee-Man of Orn, Amos Kilbright, The Clocks of Rondaine,* and *The Watchmaker's Wife,*—each volume containing, besides the title story, several other tales. These volumes show Mr. Stockton's peculiar powers at their best, and they give him an unquestioned place in the front rank of American story writers. It is true that these tales of his violate certain conventions of literary art. They seldom have a plot; they frequently have no dialogue, consisting wholly or mainly of narrative or monologue; there is not much description, and no apparent attempt at effect. One would say that stories constructed on such a plan could hardly fail to be tedious, however brief, since they lack so many of the things that other story tellers rely upon for effects. Mr. Stockton's method is vindicated by its success, not by its *a priori* reasonableness. There is such a thing, no doubt, as "good form" in every performance that demands skill; but, after all, the main point is to do the thing. David's smooth stones from the brook seemed a very ineffective weapon with which to encounter a giant, and every military authority of the age would have pronounced his attempt hopeless; but Goliath found, to his cost, that the shepherd's sling was mightier than the warrior's sword and spear. The Western oarsmen who rowed by the light of nature, and nevertheless beat crews trained trained to row scientifically, explained that theirs was called the "git thar" stroke. Mr. Stockton's method of story-telling may be similarly defined; it succeeds with him, but in another's hands it would very likely be a failure.

It must not be inferred that these stories lack literary merit. The contrary is the fact, as a critical study of them discloses. Take one of the purely narrative stories, for example, like **"A Tale of Negative Gravity."** It is told with so much of positive gravity, in so matter-of-fact a style, that one almost swallows it whole,—almost, but not quite. Now let one analyze that story, try to imitate its simple style, and however practised he may be in the art of expression he will finish his experiment with a new respect for the author's purely literary gifts. From one point of view Mr. Stockton may almost be said to have no style. There is nothing, one means, in the mere turn of his sentences, in his method of expression, that can be seized upon as characteristic, and laid away in memory as a sort of trade mark by which the author's other work may be tested, judged, and identified. It is very plain, simple, flowing English, this style of Stockton's, the sort of writing that appears to the inexperienced the easiest thing in the world to do—until they have tried. The art that conceals art, until it can pass for nature itself,—that, we are continually told, is the highest type, and the secret of that Mr. Stockton has somehow caught.

These tales stamp their author as one of the most original of American writers. Though his style lacks mannerism or distinctive flavor, it is not so with the substance of his work. That has plenty of flavor, flavor of a kind so peculiar that his work could never by any accident be mistaken for that of any other writer. It might be not the easiest of tasks to tell whether an anonymous essay or story should be fathered upon Mr. Howells or Mr. Aldrich; but it requires no such nicety of literary taste to recognize a story of Mr. Stockton's. One who has sufficient accuracy of taste to distinguish between a slice of roast beef and a raw potato, so to speak, will know the savor of his work wherever it is met. Other writers may be as original, in the strict sense of that term, but few, if any, are so individual, so unmistakably themselves and nobody else.

Most writers of short stories sooner or later are tempted to try their wings in the longer flight of a novel. It seems to be just about an even chance whether they succeed or fail, so different are the conditions of the two classes of fiction. One dislikes to use the word failure in connection with any of Mr. Stockton's work, yet **The Late Mrs. Null** and **The Hundredth Man** fall very far short of the relative excellence of his tales. The plots are very ingenious, the mystery surrounding Mrs. Null until the very last being quite worthy of Wilkie Collins; the dialogue is bright and amusing; considerable power of characterization is shown in these novels, a thing almost wholly absent from the tales. Yet withal there is a lack of power, and while the books are clever *tours de force* they are not work of lasting worth.

Why this should be is something of a puzzle, since writers of far less originality and force than Mr. Stockton have produced better novels. The ingenious reader may easily propose to himself several explanations, of which the following may be the most satisfactory, since it seems to fit all the facts known to the public. Mr. Stockton's peculiar power is best described by the word "droll." He excels in that juxtaposition of incongruities that is the essence of humor. Only, in his case, the incongruity is commonly not of ideas but of acts and situations; the incongruity of ideas is not put into words, as is the wont of most humorists, but suggested to the reader, suggested often with great delicacy and subtlety. The production of this effect on the mind of the reader is one that cannot be prolonged beyond a certain point without wearying him. A joke that a friend takes fifteen minutes to tell us is not likely to have a very sharp point when the end finally comes, and a writer who spins out his drollery to three hundred pages will find it becoming a weariness to the flesh. The very thing that constitutes Mr. Stockton's power in a story that can be read in a half-hour constitutes his weakness in a novel.

There is one other excellence in his novels for which Mr. Stockton has not yet been given credit. He has succeeded, at least in [**The Late Mrs. Null**], in giving his story plenty of "local color." He was at one time a resident of Virginia, and the negro dialect and character have seldom been represented with a more sympathetic accuracy than by him. He may not have penetrated so deeply into the very heart of the negro as Mr. Page in his "Marse Chan" and other companion stories, but he has made himself not a bad second to the acknowledged first in this field.

As might, perhaps, be expected, Mr. Stockton has succeeded better in novelettes. Here he is almost as much at home as in the brief tale. **The Casting Away of Mrs. Lecks and Mrs. Aleshine** and its sequel, **The Dusantes,** reach pretty nearly, if not quite, the highwater mark of our author. The first named of these stories is one of the best illustrations possible of his peculiar gift. The motive of the tale is the simplest possible: it is to show how two good New England women, bred in a narrow round of duties, and wonted to a certain moral and social standard of action until it had become second nature, would continue to act after their kind in whatever unaccustomed and startling circumstances they might be placed. The humor of the story consists almost wholly in the incongruity between the incidents of a shipwreck, involving a stay on a desert island, and the ingrained notions and habits of these women. This theme is treated with so much ingenuity, and with a touch so deft as to make of the story one of the most humorous things in literature. A little knowledge of New England village life is necessary to its fullest appreciation, but the reader is to be pitied whose imagination is not tickled by many of the scenes and incidents of this adventure.

One notes, in reading this story, what he cannot have failed to observe elsewhere, that the author has caught the trick of lifelike narration. The tale, in its sober, matter-of-fact style and its verisimilitude, might have been the work of Defoe or Hale. Neither of these writers is destitute of humor, especially Dr. Hale, but neither of them could have supplied the element in Stockton's stories that is their chief charm. The three are alike only in their faculty of telling a story so as to give it, while one is reading at least, all the semblance of the truth itself.

The young folks know a good story-teller by instinct, and Mr. Stockton has from the first been a prime favorite with them. As we have seen, his first book [*Ting-a-ling*] was composed of stories for children, and he has gone on writing for his youthful readers until his "juveniles" make quite a row, seven or more volumes. The best of these stories show a gift very similar to that which wins the favor of older readers, though it is rather a fantastic imagination than pure humor that inspires the best of them. Children, as a rule, have a quite rudimentary sense of humor, yet they are not incapable of appreciating droll things. They perceive most easily, however, that sort of humor which builders embody in gargoyles and other similar ornamentations,—grotesque distortions of types with which they are familiar in every-day life. Some of Mr. Stockton's fairy tales show a fertility of imagination that surpasses anything he has done in his other writings, and their whimsical absurdities are so gravely set forth that many a staid father while reading them to his children has been half inclined to accept them as veritable histories. It is noteworthy that in these stories the narrow line separating the fanciful from the burlesque is never crossed. Nobody could suspect from the writer's manner that he does not himself firmly believe in the reality of his marvellous creations. A false note here would be fatal, and none would be quicker to detect it than the readers of *St. Nicholas,* where most of these tales have first appeared.

One of these books is of a more conventional sort, *A Jolly Fellowship.* It is a very good story, only—and this is the worst one could say of it—a dozen other men might have written it as well as Mr. Stockton. It so completely lacks his distinctive qualities that, despite its general brightness, it must be ranked among his few failures; or, if that seem too harsh a word, his partial successes.

Mr. Stockton gives no signs of having exhausted his vein. He has made for himself a place unique and unapproachable in the regard of those who love good literature. Original to the verge of eccentricity, he provokes no comparisons with any writer. Nobody has ever thought of calling him "The American somebody or other,"—a title bestowed on his fellow craftsmen, doubtless with an intent to compliment, though it is really the direct insult that can be offered to a man of letters, since it accuses him of being the weak echo of some European celebrity. No, the author of *Rudder Grange* is not "The American Lamb" nor the American anybody else, he is just Frank R. Stockton. (pp. 292-300)

Henry C. Vedder, "Francis Richard Stockton," in his American Writers of To-Day, Silver, Burdett and Company, 1894, pp. 288-300.

Arthur Quiller-Couch   (essay date 1895)

[*Quiller-Couch was an English man of letters especially noted as the author of* The Golden Spur *(1899), the editor of* The Oxford Book of English Verse *(1900), and as a contributor to various periodicals under the pseudonym "Q." In this excerpt from an essay originally published in* The Speaker *in 1895, he describes Stockton's fall in popularity and recommends his fiction to contemporary readers.*]

[*Rudder Grange,* "The Lady or the Tiger?" and "A Borrowed Month"] are almost classics. That is to say, they have the classical qualities, and only need time to ripen them into classics: for nothing but age divides a story of the quality of "The Lady or the Tiger?" (for instance) from a story of the quality of "Rip Van Winkle." They are full of wit; but the wit never chokes the style, which is simple and pellucid. Their fanciful postulates being granted, they are absolutely rational. And they are in a high degree original. Originality, good temper, good sense, moderation, wit—these are classical qualities; and he is a rare benefactor who employs them all for the amusement of the world.

At first sight it may seem absurd to compare Mr. Stockton with Defoe. You can scarcely imagine two men with more dissimilar notions of the value of gracefulness and humour, or with more divergent aims in writing. Mr. Stockton is nothing if not fanciful, and Defoe is hardly fanciful at all. Nevertheless in reading one I am constantly reminded of the other. You must remember Mr. Stockton's habit is to confine his eccentricities of fancy to the postulates of a tale. He starts with some wildly unusual—but, as a rule, not impossible—conjuncture of circumstances. This being granted, however, he deduces his story logically and precisely, appealing never to our passions and almost constantly to our common sense. His people are as full of common sense as Defoe's. They may have more pluck than the average man or woman, and they usually have more adaptability; but they apply to extraordinary circumstances the good unsentimental reasoning of ordinary life, and usually with the happiest results. The shipwreck of Mrs. Lecks and Mrs. Aleshine was extraordinary enough, but their subsequent conduct was rational almost to precision: and in story-telling rationality does for fancy what economy of emotional utterances does for emotion. We may apply to Mr. Stockton's tales a remark which Mr. Saintsbury let fall some years ago upon dream-literature. He was speaking particularly of Flaubert's *Tentation de Saint Antoine:*

The capacities of dreams and hallucinations for literary treatment are undoubted. But most writers, including even De Quincey, who have tried this style, have erred, inasmuch as they have endeavoured to throw a portion of the mystery with which the waking mind invests dreams over the dream itself. Anyone's experience is sufficient to show that this is wrong. The events of dreams as they happen are quite plain and matter-of-fact, and it is only in the intervals, and, so to speak, the scene-shifting of dreaming, that any suspicion of strangeness occurs to the dreamer.

A dream, however wild, is quite plain and matter-of-fact to the dreamer; therefore, for verisimilitude, the narrative of a dream should be quite plain and matter-of-fact. In the same way the narrator of an extremely fanciful tale should—since verisimilitude is the first aim of story-telling—attempt to exclude all suspicion of the unnatural from his reader's mind. And this is only done by persuading him that no suspicion of the unnatural occurred to the actors in the story. And this again is best managed by making his characters persons of sound every-day common sense. "If *these* are not upset by what befalls them, why"—is the unconscious inference—"why in the world should *I* be upset?"

So, in spite of the enormous difference between the two writers, there has been no one since Defoe who so carefully as Mr. Stockton regulates the actions of his characters by strict common sense. Nor do I at the moment remember any writer who comes closer to Defoe in mathematical care for detail. In the case of the *True-born Englishman* this carefulness was sometimes overdone—as when he makes Colonel Jack remember with exactness the lists of articles he stole as a boy, and their value. In the *Adventures of Captain Horn* the machinery which conceals and guards the Peruvian treasure is so elaborately described that one is tempted to believe Mr. Stockton must have constructed a working model of it with his own hands before he sat down to write the book. In a way, this accuracy of detail is part of the common-sense character of the narrative, and undoubtedly helps the verisimilitude enormously.

But to my mind Mr. Stockton's characters are even more original than the machinery of his stories. And in their originality they reflect not only Mr. Stockton himself, but the race from which they and their author spring. In fact, they seem to me about the most genuinely American things in American fiction. After all, when one comes to think of it, Mrs. Lecks and Captain Horn merely illustrate that ready adaptation of Anglo-Saxon pluck and business-like common sense to savage and unusual circumstances which has been the real secret of the colonisation of the North American Continent. Captain Horn's discovery and winning of the treasure may differ accidentally, but do not differ in essence, from a thousand true tales of commercial triumph in the great Central Plain or on the Pacific Slope. And in the heroine of the book we recognise those very qualities and aptitudes for which we have all learnt to admire and esteem the American girl. They are hero and heroine, and so of course we are presented with the better side of the national character; but then it has been the better side which has done the business. The bitterest

critic of things American will not deny that Mr. Stockton's characters are typical Americans, and could not belong to any other nation in the world. Nor can he deny that they combine sobriety with pluck and businesslike behaviour with good feeling; that they are as full of honour as of resource, and as sportsmanlike as sagacious. (pp. 212-15)

Nationality apart, if anyone wants a good stirring story, *Captain Horn* is the story for his money. It has loose ends, and the concluding chapter ties up an end that might well have been left loose; but if a better story of adventure has been written of late I wish somebody would tell me its name. (p. 215)

Arthur Quiller-Couch, "Mr. Stockton," in his Adventures in Criticism, *G. P. Putnam's Sons, 1925, pp. 211-15.*

William Dean Howells   (essay date 1901)

[*In the following excerpt, Howells considers Stockton's view of life and its relation to his fiction.*]

When one is reading some of Mr. Stockton's ingenious and serious stories, *The Great Stone of Sardis,* for example, or **"The Water-Devil,"** or *The Great War Syndicate,* one is tempted to speculate what would have happened had the author of these tales been caught early and shut up in the shop, say, of an electrical engineer, and had his mind turned in the direction of mechanical inventions. His seriousness is never more effective than when he is carefully explaining some of those contrivances, upon the successful working of which his story depends. Perhaps a reader trained in electrical science would detect the suppressed factor, but the ordinary reader is more likely to grow a little impatient, and wonder why Mr. Stockton is explaining so patiently his invention or his mechanism; he is quite ready to accept the results of so plainly an accomplished mechanic, and wishes he would hurry on with his story. In truth, Mr. Stockton is really an exceedingly clever juggler, who rolls up his sleeves, places his apparatus under a calcium light, puts on an innocent face, deprecates the slightest appearance of deception, and then performs his extraordinary feats. There is a nimbleness of movement, an imperturbable air, and the thing is done.

The supreme quality which Mr. Stockton possesses as a novelist is his inventiveness. He is an Edison amongst the patient students and gropers after the dramatic truths of human life. As one surveys the eighteen volumes which gather the greater part, but by no means the whole of his product in fiction, one is amazed at the fertility of invention brought to light, and the careless ease with which each piece of work is thrown off. One might think his *Adventures of Captain Horn* had exhausted the capacity of the story-teller dealing with hid treasures, but *Mrs. Cliff's Yacht* follows in its wake, and one gets, not the leavings of the former story, but a fresh turn of absorbing interest. Mr. Stockton has hinted at the author's predicament who has struck twelve once, and vainly hopes to be heard when he strikes eleven, in his witty story of **"His Wife's Deceased Sister;"** but he himself followed the inimitable tale of *The Casting Away of Mrs. Lecks and Mrs.*

Aleshine with *The Dusantes,* and seems to delight in explaining one mystery by another.

Inventiveness is so dominant a note that human character itself is presented as a cleverly put together toy. The persons in these stories are usually matter of fact in their manner, but the springs which work the characters are often marvels of ingenuity. Thus, when Mr. Stockton first proposed to himself to write novels in distinction from stories, he sought in each of the leading cases a central character, set, so to speak, like an alarm clock, to go off, when the striking time came, with a great whir. His Mrs. Null is carefully constructed thus to go through all the motions of a human being, yet to have a concealed mechanism which is the ultimate explanation of her conduct. So, too, Mr. Horace Stratford, in *The Hundredth Man,* has a whim upon which the whole structure of the book is nicely balanced, like a rocking stone; and in *The Girl at Cobhurst,* Miss Panney is like the linchpin to a very ramshackle sort of vehicle,—pull it out, and the whole wagon falls to pieces.

Perhaps this is the explanation why so many of Mr. Stockton's stories are autobiographic in form. When the narrator is himself the hero, he is bound to a certain modesty of behavior, and the low key in which his narrative is pitched allows of more extravagant incident, because the sincerity of the narrator cannot easily be called in question. The soberness, almost melancholy, with which the brother-in-law of J. George Watts tells of **"The Remarkable Wreck of the *Thomas Hyke*"** is like a seal set to the verity of the tale. Defoe seeks to give authenticity to one of his fictions by calling one or two witnesses into court who are just as fictitious as his hero. Mr. Stockton uses a better art when he makes his narrator's manner corroborate his invention. But it is easier to conceal an invention than both the inventor and the invention, and so, when he has some highly improbable tale to tell, Mr. Stockton is apt to resort to this device. The story-teller was himself a part of the story, and how can you disbelieve the story when the teller is so careful in his narrative, so manifestly unwilling to pass beyond the bounds of the actual fact? If you have not to account for the inventor, if he is the sober reality on which everything leans, then you have removed the greatest obstacle to confidence. Mr. Stockton realizes to the full the advantage which accrues from a trustworthy narrator, and he makes his narrator trustworthy by abdicating his own place as invisible story-teller, and giving it to one who was himself an actor in the story.

That human life is treated as a piece of mechanism, a stray bit of a Chinese puzzle, appears not merely from the deliberateness with which each part is fitted into its place, but from the entire absence of the emotional element, except as it is supplied now and then by the inventor to lubricate his machinery a little. Mr. Stockton is rarely more droll than when he lets his lovers disport themselves as lovers. It sometimes seems as if he looked up lover's words in the dictionary. At times, he hastens over the critical passages with a shamefaced alacrity; at others, he makes his lovers go through the motions with praiseworthy carefulness, almost as if he were rehearsing them for some real scene. Love-making is for the most part merely one of the inci-

dents in a merry career, and one of the great charms of Mr. Stockton's stories is that entertainment is furnished without any undue excitation of the nerves. Even the murders that are committed occasionally in his books are like those one encounters in the *Arabian Nights,*—necessary parts of the plot, but bringing no discomfort to any one. There is often a tremendous clatter and banging in temptestuous scenes, but likely as not the mind carries away as the permanent effect some highly amusing byplay; as when, in the story of *Mrs. Cliff's Yacht,* we hear above the roar of battle the torrent of virtuous oaths delivered with stunning effect by Miss Willy Croup.

The one exception to the mechanical theory of inspiration of character in these stories is found in Mr. Stockton's use of the negro. Once in a while, to be sure, his negro is a sort of jack-in-the-box, as good little Peggy in *The Late Mrs. Null,* who takes a very deliberate part in pulling the strings; but for the most part Mr. Stockton seems to assume that nature has been so munificent in endowing the negro with incalculable motives and springs of conduct, that he need only stand by, admiring, and faithfully record these whimsical inventions. The very fidelity with which he attends to this business results in far greater successes than any he wins by his own motion. In this same story of *The Late Mrs. Null* he has a character—Aunt Patsy—so vivid, so truthful, and so appealing to the imagination that one familiar with the great company of Mr. Stockton's characters can find no other so triumphant in its art.

It is, perhaps, an inevitable consequence of a view of human life which concerns itself but little with the great moments of emotion, that there are frequent failures in proportion. The elaborate fiction, for example, of Mr. Stull as the real proprietor of Vatoldis, but concealed behind the screen of social dignity, leads Mr. Stockton into a great deal of humorous but rather wearisome detail; and in *The Girl at Cobhurst,* the highly specialized cook seems to be boosted into an important part in the evolution of the story. Yet the delicacy, the refinement of mind, which give almost an old-fashioned air,—Mr. Stockton's "madam," in his conversations, is a courtly bow,—are conspicuous by the entire absence of the burlesque. If Mr. Stockton hurries over the emotional, there is not the slightest taint of cynicism, nor any approach to the vulgarity of making fun of the secrets of the heart. Grotesquerie there is in abundance, and dry drolling; but both artistic restraint and a fine reserve of nature render the work always humane and sweet.

Where, indeed, in our literature shall we find such a body of honest humor, with its exaggeration deep in the nature of things, and not in the distortion of the surface? The salt which seasons it, and may be relied on to keep it wholesome, is the unfailing good humor and charity of the author. The world, as he sees it, is a world peopled with tricksy sprites and amusing goblins. When he was telling tales for children, these gnomes and fairies and brownies were very much in evidence. He does not bring them into evidence in his stories for maturer readers, except occasionally, as in **"The Griffin and the Minor Canon"**; but they have simply retired into the recesses of the human spirit. They do their work still in initiating all manner of caprices and whimsical outbreaks; but they are concealed, and this story-teller, who knows of their superabundant activity, goes about with a grave face the better to keep their secret. (pp. 136-38)

> *William Dean Howells, in an originally unsigned review of "The Novels and Stories of Frank R. Stockton," in* The Atlantic Monthly, *Vol. LXXXVII, No. DXIX, January, 1901, pp. 136-38.*

Harper's Weekly   (essay date 1902)

[*In the excerpt below, the anonymous reviewer treats Stockton's use of the combination of the whimsical with the commonplace to create his humor.*]

Those who like the subtle differentiation of flavors, will have their peculiar pleasure in recognizing the variance of the Middle State types abounding in Stockton's books from the New England types of a more prevalent tradition. Here are Jersey people, Pennsylvania people; Americans of a softer accent and a laxer fibre, not so nervous, not so strung-up in their lives or characters as the children of the Puritans whom we know in the pages of Miss Wilkins and Miss Hewett. Their story tends less to tragedy, and to pathos and more to the good-endings dear to the average. We find them true in the midst of the most delicious impossibilities of shipwreck, landslide, burglary, negative gravity, and what-not and they are always Americans of the sort that abound on the lines of emigration westward from the Atlantic to the Pacific, between the New England populations on the north and the Virginia populations on the south. In his books they are less distinguished by dialect than the persons of Northern or Southern fiction, and they are for the most part transposed from their native environment into circumstances of the author's invention. There is singular comfort in that: they make you feel at home in whatever region of the air or depth of the sea you happen to meet them.

If Stockton's humor were to be analyzed it would not be humor. What one can say of it with absolute security is, not that it is like no other humor, but that it is finally his in such degree that the effort of recalling like humor is yours when you have ceased to read, and that it does not itself currently suggest the humor of any other American. Of course it is of a dry seriousness which forms the best medium of preposterous suggestion, and it is in a manner ironical. All humor is ironical, but in Stockton's irony there is no touch of cruelty. . . .

[The] most poignant delightfulness of his art lay in his power of investing his comic fairyland with the familiar scenery and the wonted personality of our every-day ambient. What chiefly makes you laugh is the touch by which a character in the mid-air of impossibility does just what that character would do in New Jersey or Pennsylvania, and feels and thinks as such a character would with its feet on its own ground.

> *"Francis Richard Stockton," in* Harper's Weekly, *Vol. XLVI, No. 2367, May 3, 1902, p. 555.*

Griffin on the nature of Stockton's "fanciful tales":

The stories in *The Floating Prince* are by no means . . . moral capsules. . . . The fairy tales of Oscar Wilde are remembered for their color and their simplicity; but the stories of Stockton are memorable for more important reasons. They are, in so far as they were written for children, mature; they are, in so far as they were written for mature minds, of deceptive simplicity. Their flavor is elusive, their charm dependent upon the attitude of the reader. It was Stockton's desire that they should be "discovered" by adults, and be accepted for what they are—shrewd commentaries on human nature and human blindness.

> *Martin I. J. Griffin, in his* Frank. R. Stockton: A Critical Biography. *University of Pennsylvania Press, 1939.*

Edwin W. Bowen   (essay date 1920)

[*An American literary critic and classicist, Bowen here characterizes Stockton's writing by examining several of his major works.*]

[Stockton] first gave evidence of wider promise when he contributed to *Scribner's Magazine* a set of sketches running as a serial, and subsequently (in 1879) issued in the volume entitled *Rudder Grange.* These sketches contained a fresh and entertaining portrayal of a picturesque phase of American life and centred about the novel idea of a young married couple keeping house on a canal-boat and taking a boarder to boot. The book was written in a quaint, droll vein, and displayed much skill. Its bounding humor imparts to it indefinable charm. The characters of the wife Euphemia and the maid Pomona are very cleverly detailed. The original of Pomona was an orphan girl acquired by the Stocktons from an orphan asylum in New York for their own home, and she was therefore to a large extent sketched from life. The book is extremely amusing, and does not pall on one's taste but may be read and re-read with keen interest and pleasure.

The conception of *Rudder Grange* was a happy idea, and the book served to make the author's reputation as a humorist. In it Stockton shows a delightful quality of humor,—not boisterous, irreverent or exaggerated, like Mark Twain's earlier humor, but sly, unobtrusive and refined. It is not forced but spontaneous and sparkling, bubbling up as if from an inexhaustible fountain. For *Rudder Grange* is as entertaining and amusing as when the sketches first appeared as a serial in the forerunner of the present *Century Magazine.* It still holds its own in the trying test of time.

After this success Stockton undertook to win fame by the short story. The result was a distinct triumph in **"The Lady or the Tiger?"** This story is said to have been written chiefly as the author's contribution to an evening's entertainment of a company of congenial friends, when Stockton was living at his Rutherford home in New Jersey. The posing of a problem so neatly balanced is a clever device that attests Stockton's gift of humor as well as his genius.

The story has awakened a great deal of curiosity and provoked no little discussion. It has often been made the subject of debate, but still remains unsolved. For no decision has been accepted as final, the general result has been at best a Scotch verdict, or a hung jury. (pp. 453-54)

The variety of Stockton's stories makes classification difficult. Some of them, like *John Gayther's Garden,* seem to cluster round a common subject and form a more or less humorous group. But most of the volumes are simply casual collections which their author issued from time to time in book form after the publication of his *Lady or the Tiger?* collection in 1884. Some of the stories may be roughly described as sea tales, as for instance, **"The Remarkable Wreck of the *Thomas Hyke*"**. This is one of Stockton's most clever stories. It is ingeniously invented and worked out in detail with unusual skill. The original conception is that of a ship with watertight compartments sinking bow foremost and held in perpendicular suspense. The tale contains a number of happy turns and the entire plan is skilfully executed. Yet the final effect is something of a disappointment to the reader because the occasion appears inadequate, offering neither an amusing situation nor a surprise. **"The Christmas Wreck"** is another story of this group. A second class of Stockton's stories may be called stories of surprise and plot-reversal. A notable example is furnished in **"Our Story."** It proved a successful device in Stockton's hands, as it did later and oftener in the hands of O. Henry. Stockton more commonly begins with a caprice or a whimsy for the reader's amusement and then elaborates a succession of ingenious and entertaining turns leading up to the desired conclusion.

One of Stockton's typical stories is entitled **"A Tale of Negative Gravity."** This may serve to illustrate a third class. It is a narrative story—a monologue—setting forth in a straightforward manner how an elderly gentleman and his wife take a long, rough walk of fifteen miles, burdened with a knapsack and a lunch-basket, and accomplish this arduous athletic feat in a few hours, without effort or fatigue. The explanation is found in an ingenious contrivance of the gentleman's invention—a little machine carried in his knapsack which counteracts the force of gravity by adjusting the gauge to the carrier's weight. How this ingenious device is constructed, we are not informed, it being assumed as a *fait accompli* at the outset of the story. Years afterwards the author confessed that this tale was taken from a day-dream, the hero of which devised all sorts of applications of the principle of negative gravity. Despite the assumption of this impossible device as a matter of course, the story is told in such a sober, matter-of-fact manner as almost to allay suspicion and compel belief. But with all the author's mastery of his art, the illustration is not entirely complete, so that the reader eventually awakes to the realization that he has simply been under Stockton's magic spell.

There is a marked peculiarity of Stockton that differentiates him from most story-writers. His realism—for he is a realist—transcends the average human experience. Most realists in their stories scrupulously observe the rule of normal experience. That is, they do not introduce into their tales anything that transcends the average experience of every-day life. They may allow their characters to break the ten commandments, but the law of average experience is regarded by them as the one imperious commandment which must not be transgressed. Not so with Stockton. His characters are, without exception, moral men and women who are strict observers of the decalogue, who nevertheless have no compunctions about breaking the great commandment of realism, and who appear just as innocent in the act as if they never once dreamed of the operation of this law in the realm of fiction. Thus, the leading character in the story above mentioned, by his ingenious invention, demonstrates the law of negative gravity and moves and acts in supreme unconsciousness of any infraction on his part of a universal law of nature. Likewise the husband and wife in **"His Wife's Deceased Sister"** appear perfectly natural in their conduct when they bury deep in the water the key to the strong-box containing the fatal manuscript.

The explanation of Stockton's disregard and apparent contempt for this law of realism is that he places his characters in a world of his own invention, in which certain improvements and advantages above the average of common experience are assumed as a matter of course. He transports his characters out of the humdrum round of our daily experience into a far country. They are still in this same world, to be sure, but they do not appear to stand in any personal relation to it. This is an attendant circumstance of the glamor of Stockton's art. Thus there is in his stories, as a critic has expressed it, a delicious mockery of current realistic fiction which gives him an immense advantage over his brother realists.

It must be conceded, then, that Stockton's stories contravene certain conventions of literary art. Moreover, while they show great ingenuity of invention, they seldom show much plot. Indeed, plot is a weak spot in Stockton's equipment. In this respect he is the very antithesis of Poe with his ingenious and intricate plots, and of his disciple, Sir Arthur Conan Doyle. Again, Stockton's tales are frequently mere narrative or monologue. Not a few of them are without dialogue—a method which most story-tellers rely upon as a convenient method of portraying their characters. It has also been pointed out as a defect in some of Stockton's stories that he does not make sufficient use of description to localize the scene of his story.

It must be admitted, nevertheless, that Stockton produces his effects successfully, even though by other than the conventional literary methods. His methods are self-justified, although they would probably prove a signal failure if generally adopted. He is critically familiar with his art and has so mastered it that he is able to impart a delightful plausibility to queerly motivated plots. (pp. 454-57)

Stockton, like many another short story writer, attempted the bolder flight of the novel. But he did this gradually,—step by step, as it were, not by a leap or a bound. For his *Casting Away of Mrs. Lecks and Mrs. Aleshine,* which appeared in the same year (1886) as some of the volumes of his short stories, forms an easy transition from the short story to the domain of the novel. This fantasy in a novelette and the first part of it (which is far more clever than the latter part) might readily pass for a first-class short story. The truth is that the first part of this novelette represents the high-water mark of Stockton's achievement in fiction. It is quite up to the standard of his best short stories. Like the short story, this brief novel afforded him ample field for the display of his rare literary gifts. *The Casting Away of Mrs. Lecks and Mrs. Aleshine* has a very simple plot. It seeks to show how two commonplace New England women who have moved only in the narrow, circumscribed sphere of their home life will remain true to type when suddenly thrust into unusual and startling surroundings. The ship on which they had sailed from San Francisco for the Orient suddenly goes down in the middle of the Pacific, and these two good women find themselves, with a male survivor, in a small leaky boat which the three are compelled later to abandon for the merciless sea. Throwing themselves into the water, and relying upon life-preservers, they succeed in keeping afloat until they reach a desert island, where they find food and shelter in an unoccupied house. Here, as if marooned, they live in some degree of comfort until they are joined by another small company of shipwrecked persons, including a returning missionary and his daughter. Mrs. Lecks and Mrs. Aleshine set to work to make a match between their rescuer and the missionary's daughter. When the match is made, a ship opportunely appears and brings the entire shipwrecked company back to America. (pp. 457-58)

The narrative abounds in amusing turns, and the humor depends largely upon the incongruity between the incidents of the shipwreck and the innate habits of the two New England women. The theme is handled with much ingenuity and deftness of touch, and the tale of the adventure is told with all the interest and freshness of an eye-witness. The style is simple and matter-of-fact, with no effort at rhetorical embellishment, very much after the manner of Defoe, with which, indeed, it invites comparison. All in all, *The Casting Away of Mrs. Lecks and Mrs. Aleshine* forms a really thrilling narrative, and has every semblance of an actual experience; for Stockton has shown himself here a master of the art of lifelike narration. The latter part of the story is unworthy of the first part, which is inimitable. If the author had left the story incomplete, it would have been a finer piece of art. It was a mistake to explain the barred entrance to the enchanted island of the Dusantes. Stockton ought to have left this an enigma, as in **"The Lady or the Tiger?"**

The sequel of *The Casting Away of Mrs. Lecks and Mrs. Aleshine* is *The Dusantes.* The Dusantes are the supposed owners of the unoccupied house on the enchanted island. This tale is not much inferior to the novelette just described. Another tale, deserving of mention is *The Great War Syndicate,* one of Stockton best. It is somewhat after the manner of H. G. Wells's fiction. The assumptions in such fiction seem too visionary, even though the tales are admirably told. These novelettes form the transition to Stockton's longer tales—his novels. It will prove interesting to consider certain representatives of this form of his fiction.

Stockton's first long tale or novel was *The Late Mrs. Null,* published in 1886. It is a good novel, with a rather ingenious plot, and provides plenty of mysterious and amusing situations. The mystery surrounding the personality of

Mrs. Null is ingeniously conceived, and the details of the entire story are well worked out. Mrs. Null first appears as a private secretary in an information bureau in New York City when a patron applies there for information about a male cousin of hers. Mr. Null, her putative husband, contributes to the mystery of the tale until he is discovered toward the end to be a mere myth. Mrs. Null finally reveals her identity as the attractive young woman, Annie Peyton, when in Virginia Lawrence Craft, the hero of the novel, falls in love with her as a kind of reaction after his rejection by Roberta March. The most picturesque character in the book is Mrs. Null's disagreeable old aunt, the widow Keswick, who is portrayed with much droll humor. Her ruthless persecution of her quondam suitor Robert Brandon, the wealthy old bachelor and uncle of the charming Roberta March, is extremely amusing, especially her revenge as described in the wedding scene. Here, by the way, Stockton reverts to his occasional device of end-surprise by representing the widow as flatly refusing at the marriage altar to accept for her husband the bachelor Brandon whom she had forced into that embarrassing situation merely in order to wreak her revenge upon him.

Unlike some of Stockton's stories, *The Late Mrs. Null* has much local color. The author was quite familiar with the country he described, the scene being for the most part Virginia, of which state he was once a resident and from which came his mother and his wife. He introduces the negro into this novel and represents the negro dialect with sympathetic accuracy. Indeed, Stockton appears to have found a congenial field in delineating the negro character. The characters in *The Late Mrs. Null* stand out distinctly, being drawn with especial boldness of outline, and the novel is rather a clever effort, though below the level of its author's best short stories. It certainly deserved more commendation than some critics were disposed to give it when they characterized it, along with *The Hundredth Man,* as a mere *tour de force.*

After producing several other novels, including *The Adventures of Captain Horn* and its sequel *Mrs. Cliff's Yacht* (published in 1895 and 1897, respectively), Stockton wrote *Ardis Claverden,* which ranks as one of his most pretentious novels. For the setting of this novel he selected that region of Virginia about Monticello. The novel portrays well-bred Virginia and English society. The bewitching heroine is finely drawn, and is a happier creation than the hero. But her conduct in the Georgia incident, when she goes on the escapade to find her lover Roger Dunworth, is decidedly unconventional and very improbable. The motive for this escapade as described seems entirely inadequate. It is said that of all the female characters of his fiction Stockton expressed his preference for the racy and piquant Ardis Claverden. The name made a strong appeal to him, because Ardis is said to be a name hereditary in the family of the novelist's mother. The portrait as here drawn has much to attract and charm, but the novel as a whole is a rather uneven production and hardly above mediocre.

In 1898 Stockton published a very interesting long story containing some romance, but hardly worthy to be classed as a novel,—*The Great Stone of Sardis.* This story is somewhat after the manner of his **Great War Syndicate,** and was probably suggested by Jules Verne's *Journey to the Centre of the Earth* and *Twenty Thousand Leagues Under the Sea.* It purports to be the record of a marvelous scientific expedition to discover the North Pole by the aid of a submarine boat kept in touch with its point of departure by a kind of telephonic connection. After the return, another startling adventure is undertaken, and is narrated in the latter part of the tale. This is the project of sinking a bottomless shaft by means of a tremendous shell in order thus to discover the centre of the earth, which is found to be an immense diamond. The conception was bizarre and grotesque enough, but the author developed it into a fascinating tale, incidentally injecting into it a good deal of drollery and fun. The tale shows that aspect of Stockton's genius that is inclined to the whimsical and chimerical, as well as the mechanical turn of his invention. (pp. 458-61)

One of Stockton's last novels,—perhaps the very last he wrote before his death in Washington in 1902—was **Kate Bonnet.** Although the last of his long stories, this is believed by some critics to be first in point of merit. It is a story of sea-life, the romance of a pirate's daughter. The action of the story centres about Jamaica in the West Indies, and the story itself contains some thrilling incidents of pirate life on the high seas. The heroine is a clever creation, but hardly seems to be the daughter of a pirate. She is well sketched, as is also her rough old father and, indeed, all the other leading figures. The author exhibits no ordinary skill in delineating and contrasting Kate Bonnet's two rival suitors. This novel possesses strong narrative interest and shows its author's return to the source of inspiration that induced his previous sea tale—*The Casting Away of Mrs. Lecks and Mrs. Aleshine.* The setting and characters are entirely different, however, from those that figure in that captivating novelette. In these two rather long sea tales Stockton is almost up to the quality of his very best work.

It is critically agreed that Stockton's novels are inferior to his short stories. He was far more successful with this form of literature than with the novel. The secret of his success with the short story lies in his droll humor, which is more effective in acts and situations of brief duration than in long-spun-out tales. He was above all things a humorist, and it is of the very essence of humor to juxtapose incongruities. Now Stockton's type of humor consisted in the incongruity of acts and situations rather than ideas, hence his humor is better adapted to the short story than to the novel. Yet his achievement as a novelist was creditable, and his valuable contribution to juvenile fiction deserves recognition. He had the gratification of seeing some of his stories and tales translated into various European tongues,—a sign of wide appreciation.

An examination of Stockton's accomplishment as a man of letters shows conclusively that as a writer of books for children, as a writer of short stories, as a novelist and, above all, as a humorist, he has placed American literature under a lasting obligation to his genius and art. He has attained to no little distinction in each of these several departments, but preëminently, as concerns form, in the

short story, where he challenges comparison with the leading American creators of this type of literature. (pp. 461-62)

Edwin W. Bowen, "The Fiction of Frank R. Stockton," in The Sewanee Review, *Vol. XXVIII, No. 3, Summer, 1920, pp. 452-62.*

Martin I. J. Griffin   (essay date 1939)

[*In the following excerpt, taken from his biography of Stockton, Griffin argues that, although Stockton is a secondary figure when compared with such contemporaries as Henry James, Mark Twain, or William Dean Howells, he is still an important writer and an accomplished stylist.*]

Any just estimate of the contribution of Frank R. Stockton to American literature must inevitably place him in the second rank of those who were carrying the standard of American literary achievement during the last quarter of the nineteenth century. Led by the artistry and the philosophy of William Dean Howells (1837-1920), who exercised a double influence through his realistic novels and his urbane critical papers in *The Atlantic Monthly* and later in *Harper's Magazine,* the period during which Stockton was quietly dictating his best stories was one of intensive literary activity. Mark Twain (1835-1910) was a dominant figure whose *Tom Sawyer* had been published in 1876 while Stockton was still writing the **Rudder Grange** papers for *Scribner's Monthly,* and Twain's *Personal Recollections of Joan of Arc* (1895) coincided with one of Stockton's periods of greatest productivity. Henry James's (1843-1916) realistic studies of international contrasts, like *The Portrait of a Lady* (1881) and *The Tragic Muse* (1890), together with his great story of the supernatural, "The Turn of the Screw" (1898), were setting a standard of artistic achievement which has not since been equaled, except by Edith Wharton. Bret Harte (1836-1902), most artistic representative of the story of moral contrast, was exerting a marked influence on younger writers through the years that Stockton was quietly adding to his own reputation. These were the giants of those days, and the front-rank quality of their work is unquestionable. (p. 144)

Stockton's work reveals clearly how little he was influenced by the literary trends of his times. He was an individualist, indifferent to literary movements, indifferent to geography when the local-colorists were hymning of their own parishes, a practioner of his craft with the matter-of-factness of the accomplished artificer. He was never a "literary" writer, and although many of his stories—*The Casting Away of Mrs. Lecks and Mrs. Aleshine, Rudder Grange,* "The Griffin and the Minor Canon," "The Lady, or the Tiger?",* to mention but a few—are permanent additions to American literature, Stockton never persuaded himself that he was creating immortal fiction. He was a professional story-teller, interested in the life about him with the interest of the journalist, the editor, the author, who knows the requirements and the impermanence of the popular magazine. Unlike many of his contemporaries, William Dean Howells, James Lane Allen, Thomas Bailey

Aldrich, for example, Stockton was not, in any scholarly sense, deeply read in the stream of English literature, although he did at times express his pleasure in Defoe and Dickens. In part this was due to defective sight, in greater part to the simple fact that he was not interested. On the few occasions when he discussed things literary, he wrote not as the critic, but as one activated by a personal and subjective purpose which concerned itself not at all with what other men had written. His scant half-dozen essays serve to illuminate his own work, express his working definitions of the essential difference between realism or romanticism, or his own methods of working up his stories.

Although he was born in Philadelphia, and lived there until his marriage, Stockton's tastes were for rural life and for the country scene. Seldom did he lay the entire scene of a story in the city, although this represented no revolt against urban life, nor did it reflect any adherence to the provincial movement. It was, rather, that he felt he could do more with his characters in the country. His urban characters are never as convincing as his country people, just as his fairies and his ghosts are more real, and more sympathetic, than his young men in love. A curious, but in an artist by no means unusual, quality existed in Stockton. Reality, for him, was meaningless unless it was webbed with fancy, but there was nothing of the impractical about his attitude toward his work. He asked for, and received, good prices from editors for his stories, and he utilized his time and his material with scrupulous thoroughness and economy. He sought no publicity, and rather shunned public references to his private life, except in such published interviews as any successful writer must submit to. Yet he has clearly set down in his stories more details of his life and travels than most men include in their formal biographies. Boyhood pranks, school experiences, love, marriage, house-hunting, the servant problem, travel, and the casual observations of day-by-day are all utilized effectively. He realized clearly the fact that anything in life, however incidental, is interesting if it is interestingly presented. Through the apparently simple process of vitalizing the commonplace by an ingenious overlay of the uncommon, Stockton produced story after successful story, when lesser writers would long since have been written out.

Stockton looked upon life with a passive but receptive interest. A clear thinker, but never a deep one, he was neither a philosopher seeking first causes, nor a cynic happily pointing out life's limitations. The human relationships he depicted in his stories are often superficial, but his attitude is always warmly sympathetic. He is writing at his best when he portrays homely, rural people who meet extraordinary circumstances, as do Mrs. Lecks and Mrs. Aleshine, or the Minor Canon, or Euphemia's husband (nameless hero!), with unamazed practicality. He is writing at his best when he is serenely contemplating the eminent *rightness* of disordered natural laws, like **"Negative Gravity"** or the doleful plight of **"The Transferred Ghost."**

The interest in Stockton's stories arises chiefly from character and situation, hardly ever from plot. While his short stories usually come to a neatly rounded point, his novels,

from the standpoint of structure, consist chiefly of a series of connected episodes. But again generalization is dangerous, for in a type of fiction in which one would expect Stockton to be least successful, he produced, in **Kate Bonnet,** at least one well-articulated plot.

The style of Stockton's writing, because of its studied simplicity, is frequently overlooked by commentators on his work. Stockton is a stylist in a very real sense, even though his style belongs to an older and perhaps mellower tradition than that which has grown progressively less intelligible during the three decades since his death. His method is to strip his writing of all ornament, deliberately to remove any "literary" quality. The result is that he achieves his effects quickly, but with no appearance of haste—with, rather, a definite sense of leisure. His tones are chatty, informal, and he has that precision of phrase which adroitly conceals its own art. It seems, indeed, to be a style in keeping with the quill pens with which he wrote, suited to the easy pace of his stories, urbane and restrained. His diction follows definite patterns, but he has fewer irritating mannerisms than most authors who have written as voluminously. If he has not given us memorable phrases, it is because his diction is an instrument, and not an effect. It is the medium through which he produced his memorable pictures, the deft method whereby he created memorable people. (pp. 145-48)

Martin I. J. Griffin, in his Frank R. Stockton: A Critical Biography, *University of Pennsylvania Press, 1939, 178 p.*

Henry L. Golemba   (essay date 1981)

[*Below, Golemba discusses the effect the expectations of Stockton's readers had on his writing.*]

Stockton's audience read him essentially for one reason: to be refreshed by wit so that they could return to their business with renewed vigor. They expected his art to be like the magic kiss in **"Old Pipes and the Dryad"** which makes the recipient ten years younger. They went to his books as later audiences went to the silent screen comedies, not for art nor for philosophy but for humor and escape. They formed "Pass-it-on Societies" to spread **"The Buller-Podington Contract,"** not because the story was a plea for people even of antipathetic interests to cooperate but because they thought the plot was funny. They loved **"The Lady, or the Tiger?"** not for its cosmology, nor for its depiction of the joy and terror of sex, nor for its concern whether passion and selfishness or reason and morality were the greater forces in human behavior, but because the story gave them an excuse to debate among themselves, perhaps peppering their remarks with sexist or anti-sexist jokes. They read about Pomona because she was eccentric, not because she raised questions of feminism, class bias, or American culture. If this audience were told that Gertrude Stein, an admirer of Stockton's, had borrowed the inversion of point of view he used in **"Our Story"** (1883) to write her famous *Autobiography of Alice B. Toklas* (1933), they would shrug their shoulders politely; they would not be impressed.

This audience also liked its literature to be straightforward. When Stockton in **"The Knife That Killed Po Hancy"** (1889) set out deliberately to render the split-personality concept of Robert Louis Stevenson's Jekyll and Hyde (1886) in a more complex fashion, his audience considered the complexity a distraction instead of an asset; they much preferred Stockton's earlier, less complex efforts such as **"The Transferred Ghost"** (1882) and **"The Spectral Mortgage"** (1883). They favored Charles Dickens's "A Christmas Carol" (1843) over Stockton's **"The Baker of Barnbury"** (1884), in part because Scrooge's belief that Christmas is a humbug is proved wrong, whereas the baker's suspicion is more sinister. He believes Christmas celebrants are hypocrites and their celebration a fraud.

Similarly, when this audience praised Stockton's women, they were far more generous to his conventional characterizations of older widows, as in *The Casting Away of Mrs. Lecks and Mrs. Aleshine* (1886), than to his vigorous, aggressive, sexually charged young heroines, as in *Ardis Claverden* (1890)—a response that was in inverse proportion to Stockton's own evaluation of these two books. That they recognized the significant contribution to the development of the short story achieved in **"The Lady, or the Tiger?"** (1882) is to their credit, but they were unable to perceive Stockton's far more subtle and sophisticated use of this technique in *John Gayther's Garden* (1902) and *The Vizier of the Two-Horned Alexander* (1899). When Stockton introduced genuine tragedy into the comic texture of *The Girl at Cobhurst* (1898), he confused his audience. Even today when people study his evil women—and he has created some truly fine ones—they highlight characters like Maria Port in *The Captain's Toll-Gate* (1903) who is rendered innocuous by the other women in the novel, and they ignore more menacing females like Mrs. Keswick in *The Late Mrs. Null* (1886) who is capable of destroying people and driving some to suicide.

This audience preferred the obvious to the complex, the simple to the sinister, because they and their families, to paraphrase Victoria, wished to be amused. Consequently, anything beyond the frankly humorous had to be buried in the substrata of the story for the appreciation of that minority within his popular audience whom Stockton called "a chosen few." Ardis Claverden's sexual drives were described in terms of thrilling horseback rides or seemingly innocent paintings. Sexuality is discussed in an apparent digression about the relative merits of cucumbers and gherkins. Marriage on the rebound to an unsuitable mate is characterized by the wedding gift of a corkscrew. The age-old double entendre of "dying" to mean sexual intercourse is so deftly interwoven into **"The Water-Devil: A Marine Tale"** as to be unnoticed on first glance, even though flirtation is an obvious element of the story.

Stockton's stint at the children's magazine *St. Nicholas* was a useful apprenticeship for this type of work because children's literature provides many levels of interpretation, from the most innocent to the dangerously profound, and the reader, depending on his maturity, can probe as deeply as he dares. Writing adult literature at a time still influenced by official and social censorship, Stockton en-coded his stories with suggestive themes and let the reader decide whether to decipher them.

As it was with sex, so it was with other taboos. The void—or the meaninglessness of existence—and the absurd—or the vision of a universe of total ambiguity—intrigued Stockton as it did Melville, Hawthorne, and Poe, but where the last three faced the void and absurdity full face, sometimes even revelling in them, Stockton gave them only passing glances. He would nod an acknowledgement of their presence and then get on with his plot. In *Ardis Claverden* he gives two portraits of the void, one in black, the other in white; one in a cave, the other lost in a snowy wood. Having presented these pictures of nothingness, he quickly extricates his characters and hurries them into the complexities of an everyday world that seems significant by comparison because it is all they have. Stockton assures them and his readers, quite as quickly, that that world is more than enough.

I call this technique indirection; the most serious statements are made covertly, by suggestion, clue, hint, innuendo. It is the essence of the Western Tall Tale, but Stockton knew it better in the guarded speech of oppressed American blacks such as Uncle Isham in *The Late Mrs. Null.*

One might imagine that the limits imposed by his middle-class, middle-brow audience would have greatly frustrated Stockton. Sometimes he did see these limits as an unavoidable prerequisite of his craft, but generally he identified closely with the values of middle-class Americans. Where Walt Whitman might sing the praises of the divine common and Frank Norris might view mankind as so many stupid sheep, Stockton genuinely liked his bourgeois readers. He saw their values as a necessary bulwark against greed and selfishness, privilege and riot, monopoly and chaos.

He saw middle-class women especially as the one sane sector in a world bent on destruction and war. Much has been made of this era of "bloomers," symbol of increased mobility, but Stockton also liked the top part of the Gibson girl's outfit: the tie, the blouse with broad shoulders or enlarged arms symbolic of a willingness to carry the weight of the world or to do the world's work, and her hat—no floral, awkward, immobilizing hat, but a plain, direct statement that she was ready to do the right thinking society required. This thinking involved an opposition to war, imperialism, monopoly, wealth, sexism, selfishness, ignorance, and oppression, and promoted those genteel virtues necessary to make a garden flourish, to put a house in order, to allow a family to grow.

Stockton's auctorial posture was as though he were regarding this pageant from the Kitchell astronomical observatory in the tower of his beloved home called "The Holt." Theodore Roosevelt had played there when a child, and the two sides of Roosevelt—the conservationist, "Teddy Bear" side, and the aggressive "Big Stick" side—aptly pinpoint Stockton's allegiance: firmly opposed to imperialism, positively in favor of conserving the most humane elements of American civilization. His narrative persona may seem detached as if in a tower, but his concern was immediate as if he spent countless hours behind a telescope making close scrutiny of society's complex activity. The noted critic Edmund Gosse reported that Robert Louis Stevenson had "adored these tales of Mr. Stockton's, a taste which must be shared by all good men," little knowing that in the twentieth century the concept of the "good man" would be ridiculed as incredibly naive or woefully inadequate.

Stockton felt that of all segments of society his middle-class readership was the most admirable, even though they had many faults. His identification with this class provided many of his strengths and some of his most glaring weaknesses. By allying himself with this social stratum, he developed a distaste for the powerfully rich, believing with Lord Acton that power corrupts. His bourgeois sympathies made him neglectful of the lower classes at the other end of the social scale. In his essay **"Funny Darkies,"** for example, he dehumanizes both rich and poor. He satirizes "million-heirs" who have inherited wealth but can not enjoy life and contrasts them with poor but happy blacks. A medium between the two extremes would theoretically be the middle class.

Such wholehearted identification with the bourgeoisie made him dislike immigrants of all ethnic persuasions, including the British, as well as blacks, labor unions, and the working class in general. Occasionally, as with Pomona in a series of novels and with the heroine of **"Derelict: A Tale of the Wayward Sea"** (1891), he would sympathize with individuals in the lower class as he did with the upper classes in *The Great War Syndicate* (1889); but generally his values lay with the new phenomenon of the vast middle class which bought his books.

Although Stockton liked middle-class values, he would sometimes criticize them, but his delicate satire was easy to miss. In two cases, for example, he uses a nest of birds to cap the contract between his hero and heroine to begin a family. In *The Girl at Cobhurst* the scene is intentionally overwritten as a parody of the Sentimental Romance; in *The Great Stone of Sardis* (1898) a similar bird scene is meant as an honest tribute to the couple's love and their individual growth.

The same quiet satire can be seen at work in the one political issue Stockton felt strongly about—imperialism and its handmaiden, war. He attempted to nudge his readers gently from the path of imperialism. People who smiled at a humorous story were not in the mood, he hoped, to wage international war, a prospect that loomed inevitable to his generation. An enthusiast about the conservationist dimension of Teddy Roosevelt and America, he loathed the "Big Stick," "Rough Rider," and "Great White Fleet," which he saw as the Hyde half of America's national character. Stockton stood for what he called "the Spirit of Civilization," little suspecting that this virtue, like Stevenson's "good man," would so soon be seen as a farce, as when D. H. Lawrence in the early 1920s proclaimed, "Civilized society is insane."

If by "civilized society" Lawrence meant etiquette, narrow conventionality, and suppression of individualism, Stockton would agree, since he himself criticized those qualities as threats to self-growth, in **"My Translataphone"** and **"Derelict,"** for example. But Stockton would draw the line where self-growth risked becoming self-indulgence. To him, sound civilization was based on its elemental nucleus—the individual who has come to a sufficient understanding of himself or herself that he or she can enter into a mutually rewarding relationship with another human being. In **"Derelict"** he presents two couples—one has achieved this monad of civilization; another has merely become married.

In stories like **"The Christmas Shadrach"** (1891) and **"The Magic Egg"** (1894) Stockton demonstrates exactly how difficult this twin goal of self-understanding and growth through human relationships can be. In novels like *Ardis Claverden* and *The Girl at Cobhurst* he shows that the goal is especially difficult, since the human imagination can so easily fool itself that it has accomplished what it has not. The goal is also imperative since society seemed about to fall apart, as the frequent shipwrecks in Stockton's stories suggest. This concern for an imperiled civilization led Stockton to follow the success of *The Adventures of Captain Horn,* the best-selling American novel for 1895, with a sequel, *Mrs. Cliff's Yacht* (1896), in an effort to channel the spirit of adventure in the direction of domesticity. He hoped he could help make the common problem of living well seem as exciting as any great enterprise from Polar exploration (*The Great Stone of Sardis*) to piracy (*Kate Bonnet,* 1902). His characters, as in *Kate Bonnet,* are motivated by complex, powerful forces which sometimes resemble Poe's Imp of the Perverse. Their universe seems often corrupt, chaotic, or absurd. Small wonder Stockton saw civilization as no easy or cozy quest.

In 1936, Walter L. Pforzheimer declared about Stockton, "The people who know the author know the epoch [1880-1900], and the two are interchangeable; the author is the age incarnate; rarely has a man so reflected his period." This assessment is probably hyperbolic, and the opinion expressed in *Harper's Weekly* in 1902 is more balanced: Stockton "was as distinct an embodiment of the American spirit in one sort as Mark Twain was in another." The safest statement is that Stockton does reveal much principally about the middle-class, middle-brow, generally female audience of his day. While Richard Harding Davis's women were striving to become regal, as in *The Princess Aline* (1895), and while Frances Hodgson Burnett's mother would sacrifice anything to see her American child become an aristocrat in *Little Lord Fauntleroy* (1886), Stockton's women were becoming self-reliant individuals, his children realistic American children. Of his thirty novels, only one—*The House of Martha*—seems boring to modern readers, and that is because it is a creature of its time. Widely popular in 1891, *Martha* is a reverse of *Pygmalion* or *My Fair Lady;* a woman who lives like a reclusive nun doffs her cap to reveal hair as rich as Hester Prynne's and becomes a doctor and a lover. Unlike Hawthorne, Chopin, and James, Stockton celebrates the transformation without ambivalence.

Reading Stockton can reveal much about the era, its values, customs, economy, fashions, problems, housing, transportation. His children's novel, *What Might Have*

Been Expected (1874), a forerunner of *Huckleberry Finn* (1884), tells how much flour costs, how Christmas was celebrated, how sumac was collected and processed for tanning, and other practical information. To me, however, the most fascinating quality of Stockton's art is how conscious he was of his readership, an attention that foreshadows recent trends in recreative fiction and apperceptive criticism wherein what the reader does with the book before him is of great importance.

In the assembly of auditors in *John Gayther's Garden,* as one example, we learn how diverse his audiences were even when they shared the same socioeconomic class. They range from the liberated Next Neighbor, to the conventional Master of the House, to the astute but conservative Mistress of the House and her Daughter, who shows much promise and much confusion as a representative of the next generation of reader. In *The Vizier of the Two-Horned Alexander* the wife takes no part in the action, yet she is the focus of the novel as a test of whether her idealism or her local prejudices will win out, a trial that mirrors Stockton's conception of his readers' possible responses.

To his further credit, it is clear these achievements were deliberate, not happenstance. In a series of writings, ranging from stories like **"The Pilgrim's Packets"** (1873) to sketches like **"Plain Fishing"** (1888) to articles like **"Mark Twain and His Recent Works"** (1893) to his introductions to story collections like *Afield and Afloat* (1900) and *A Story-Teller's Pack* (1897), he makes clear what he believes are the special qualities of his art. He acknowledges that his uniqueness prevents him from being classed easily in any of the literary movements of his era—not strictly a Naturalist, Realist, Western humorist, local colorist, satirist, nor regionalist—although his work touches upon each of these categories. He will not risk losing his audience by indulging in the literary experimentation of a James or a Crane, and yet he will not stoop to the hack writing of a Davis, an Alger, or a Burnett. He realizes that because his writings are generally humorous their deeper philosophy will be ignored. He knows his artistry seeks to gather "fair flowers that verge on the deep ravine" and that many will not see the philosophical abyss because of the floral display. In a nightmare he had toward the end of his career, he dreamed that the house of fiction he had built up had burned down, but I doubt he suspected how complete the conflagration would be. He went from being as widely known as Mark Twain and as highly respected as Henry James in his day to all but total obscurity in modern times.

For one who accomplished so much and knew what he was doing, such neglect is unjust. The British marvel that Stockton is better known and esteemed in England than he is in his native land. . . . Unless the effort is made to preserve Stockton for American literary culture, he may continue to suffer what Frederick Lewis Pattee feared in 1923: "He has receded far into the shadow, the gloom of which bids fair to become total." (pp. 147-53)

Some writers are lost due to the whim of history; others for understandable reasons. Stockton belongs to this latter class of victim. Eight major factors can be cited as cause for his obscurity. First, he was enormously popular, and for many decades popular writers have been disdained. While this problem has been rectified somewhat since scholars have discovered they can learn much about American culture by studying its popular literature, the focus remains on lesser writers than Stockton like Crawford, Davis, and Alger. Ironically, had Stockton been a hack writer, he might be better known today. But he insisted on quality within the limits of his middle-brow audience. This audience may have lacked the sensitivity, education, and energy to appreciate Henry James fully, but it resented literature that was trashy, facile, or formulaic.

Second, Stockton was basically a humorist, and for years because of some puritanical twist it was thought that if some one is funny he can not be serious; if the reader laughs, he can not be learning—a rupture of the Lucretian dictum that good literature should entertain and instruct. Even Mark Twain's philosophy was long neglected because he seemed a comedian, and it required the effort of Stockton as well as others like Howells to argue that humorists too have serious statements to make.

Paradoxically, Stockton's efforts on Twain's behalf may have helped plunge him into Twain's shadow. Twain's humor is of the broad, Western variety, whereas Stockton's is subtler, gentler, more Eastern. One knows when Twain has made a joke, but can not always be sure with Stockton. . . . It took Howells more than a decade to figure out Stockton's humor completely; the majority of the world has not yet caught on. In an epoch noted for humorous literature Stockton with Harris and Twain is one of the most notable humorists.

That epoch is a third reason for Stockton's obscurity, because for most of this century it was seen, as Henry Seidel Canby remarks, as "a small town joke" or as a germinal phase before Naturalism. But America in the last quarter of the nineteenth century was fraught with significant issues, such as industrialization, the rise of labor unions and the city, the influx of immigrants, social mobility, the "Negro question" and the "servant question," the threat of war, and America's growing stature as a world power.

In fact, two cultural issues are so major as to be classed by themselves as causes of Stockton's obscurity—the neglect of feminist history and the poetics of domesticity. For the first half of this century there was no wide interest in the history of feminism; Kate Chopin, Stockton's contemporary, for example, was not seriously studied until 1956. I know of no American writer who investigates the question of women's liberation in so many permutations who has been as summarily neglected as Stockton. (pp. 155-56)

Domesticity as a literary subject has suffered as much neglect as feminist history, in part because we have not had adequate tools to analyze this esthetic, although William C. Spengemann's 1977 book has made a valuable contribution. Indeed, the poetics of domesticity might strike some as Stockton's most fascinating quality. Again, he is poles apart from Twain, whose Huck Finn makes "siviliz-in' " sound like some dread disease. In contrast, Stockton may be the last capable American author to be a stalwart defender of civilization not as an abstraction but as a concrete manifestation in the form of love, marriage, and the family—a belief that literature appears to have abandoned, though it has its champions in the other arts, as witnessed by the sculptor Henry Moore.

Stockton's uniqueness is the sixth cause for his neglect. Though he confronts social determinism and evolution, he is not a Naturalist. Though he captures places in points of time, he is no local colorist and no regionalist. Though he gives accurate portraits of people and places from New England, New York, and the Old South, he is too inventive to be a staunch Realist alone. As he specified in **"The Pilgrim's Packets,"** he fits none of the categories of the period's literature. Dreiser's *Sister Carrie* (1900) does triple duty; in reading it, one knows the novel, has a taste of Dreiser's entire canon, and gains a sense of what Naturalism is. By reading Stockton's *The Girl at Cobhurst,* one knows only that novel, and can not be sure that his next chronological production will be similar. In fact, *Cobhurst* is followed in a span of three years by the science-fiction novel *The Great Stone of Sardis,* then the history of piracy *The Buccaneers and Pirates of Our Coast,* then the fantasy novel on immortality *The Vizier of the Two-Horned Alexander,* and the satire on Transcendentalism in *The Associate Hermits,* then the facile children's adventure story *The Young Master of Hyson Hall,* followed by one of his best story anthologies *Afield and Afloat,* which is equalled in quality by the picaresque romance *A Bicycle of Cathay,* and so forth.

The seventh major shortcoming is that Stockton wrote no single novel that stands head and shoulders above the rest. Melville's *Moby Dick,* Hawthorne's *The Scarlet Letter,* Dreiser's *Sister Carrie* are essential to their canon and are the foundation for much of their reputation. Henry James's *The American, The Portrait of a Lady,* and *The Ambassadors* are convenient novelistic shorthand which represent his three major phases. With Stockton, no one novel is preëminent. To understand his canon, one must read his canon. To comprehend adequately his views on feminism, at least half a dozen volumes must be perused.

To augment the problem, somewhat encouraged by his being paid by length and by his audience's leisurely reading habits, his style is often prolix. When a witty conceit strikes him, he will take a few paragraphs to explore it. Some of his crucial scenes, as when John Asher in *The Captain's Toll-Gate* confronts the evil Maria Port, could be reduced from four paragraphs to four lines by a writer like Hemingway. Indeed, Stockton's willingness to give a leisurely cast to his novels is his one true fault as an artist. They lack the terseness, concision, and economy modern reading tastes demand.

For that reason, a beginning Stockton reader should start with his short stories, which are tighter than his novels. Some suggestions are **"The Magic Egg,"** which stands comparison with Sherwood Anderson's "The Egg"; **"The Knife That Killed Po Hancy,"** which can be compared to Poe and Stevenson; **"Mr. Tolman"** as Stockton's peculiar form of Realism; **"The Christmas Shadrach"** as a study of psychology and feminism; **"Ghosts in My Tower"** as a study of racism; **"The Philosophy of Relative Existences"** as a fine philosophical fantasy, **"Our Story"** as an experi-

ment in point of view; **"Derelict: A Tale of the Wayward Sea"** which plays with the modes of Realism, Romance, and Absurdism; and **"The Wreck of the *Thomas Hyke*"** which demonstrates Stockton's quirky perspective on reality.

The eighth and final point highlights Stockton's technique of "indirection," by which much of his serious matter is hidden behind the humorous gloss which sold his books. Irvin Ehrenpreis has recently offered a useful terminology by which this trait may be understood, though he modestly applies it exclusively to poetry. [In his essay "At the Poles of Poetry," *The New York Review of Books,* August 17, 1978, Ehrenpreis] distinguishes between "the poetry of limits" and "the poetry of extremes," in which the former "depends on form, on gradations of tone, on language that is deliberate, obviously selected," whereas the latter "depends on deep, often shocking images, on sudden leaps of mood, unpredictable reversals of tone, on language that sounds uncalculated." The poetry of limits "suggests clarification emerging from uncertainty; the poetry of extremes suggests mysterious emotions in conflict."

When one recalls Stockton's essential belief that the universe is likely a vertiginous chaos of absurdity, one can appreciate Ehrenpreis's belief that, "In the poetry of limits the common relation between form and meaning is ironical. The form is tangible and suggests design bringing order to chaos. The meaning suggests chaos pressing against form." While the "poetry of limits" seems a valuable construct for appreciating Stockton's work, Stockton complicates the matter by being a humorist to boot. The challenge about humorists as with their satirist cousins is knowing when they are being flippant and when they have discovered the still, oracular balance. One way to view Stockton is as a Henry Adams in motley, however much such a metaphor helps.

Stockton would be best served by being thrust into the throes of objective criticism. He sorely needs a test conducted by a number of informed minds to determine just how important a writer he is. No doubt he would emerge as one of the finest humorists, Twain and Harris included, of the last twenty-five years of nineteenth-century American literature. Among his contemporaries, Stockton is not as fine an artist as Henry James nor so idiosyncratically a genius as Stephen Crane, but that is no reason he should be totally discarded. Of the hundreds of writers who flourished in America in the last decades of the nineteenth century listed in Howells's *Literature and Life* and in Thomas Beer's *The Mauve Decade,* very few deserve immortality. Stockton is one who does. Were his entire canon matched against Twain's, Stockton would emerge a close rival, although no one of his books can match the greatness of *Huckleberry Finn.*

Certainly in terms of scope Stockton is impressive. Consider the gamut he ranges in *A Chosen Few* (1895): the local color sketch **"Asaph"** and the speculative philosophy of **"Relative Existences,"** the science-fiction story **"A Tale of Negative Gravity"** and the fairy tale **"Old Pipes and the Dryad,"** the ghost story **"The Transferred Ghost"**, and the realistic, Thurberesque **"A Piece of Red Calico,"** even the significant triumph of **"The Lady, or the Tiger?"**

whose popularity and problems Stockton commented on in **"His Wife's Deceased Sister."** If one desired a literary garden filled with everything from discreet purple violets to tall, bold sunflowers, few candidates could emulate Stockton's achievement. My hope is that [my study] will plunge him into "The King's Arena" of close literary criticism, whether to be devoured by tigers or to be embraced in admiration, but in any case to be rescued from the oblivion and from the naive enthusiasm he does not at all deserve. (pp. 156-59)

Henry L. Golemba, in his Frank R. Stockton, *Twayne Publishers, 1981, 182 p.*

Suzanne Rahn   (essay date 1988)

[*In the excerpt below, Rahn presents an overview of Stockton's themes and techniques, comparing his works to those of L. Frank Baum and portraying Stockton as a forgotten pioneer of children's fiction.*]

[Stockton] is not only the first but the greatest American master of the original fairy tale for children. Yet today he seems to be known, if at all, only by **"The Lady, or the Tiger?"** (a story for adults), **"The Griffin and the Minor Canon,"** and **"The Bee-Man of Orn"**—and by the latter two only because Maurice Sendak turned them into picture books. Sendak himself confessed that Stockton "had always been, quite honestly, 'The Lady or the Tiger?' man. I had never read anything else. Reading 'The Griffin and the Minor Canon' was very much like opening a treasure chest."

There are . . . good literary-historical reasons for remembering Frank Stockton's role in the development of American fantasy for children, but the treasure chest of his stories deserves reopening for its own sake. His blending of traditional folktale motifs and characters with his own common-sense logic, quirky humor, sardonic satire, and pervasive personal philosophy is mellow and distinctive. Stories like **"The Griffin," "The Bee-Man," "The Floating Prince," "The Magician's Daughter,"** and **"Prince Hassak's March"** are fun for children and worth investigating for adults. (p. 224)

Stockton's fairy tales began appearing at a time when little fantasy of any kind, and less of any quality, had been written in America for children, other than Hawthorne's retellings of Greek myths in *A Wonder-Book* and *Tanglewood Tales.* (p. 225)

Like Andersen and Ruskin before him, Stockton himself seems to have taken off into fantasy straight from the traditional tales of Europe and the Near East that he had known as a child:

> I was very young when I determined to write some fairy tales because my mind was full of them. I set to work, and in course of time, produced several which were printed. These were constructed according to my own ideas. I caused the fanciful creatures who inhabited the world of fairy-land to act, as far as possible for them to do so, as if they were inhabitants of the real world. I did not dispense with monsters and enchanters, or talking beasts and birds, but I

obliged these creatures to infuse into their extraordinary actions a certain leaven of common sense.

These first stories, about a small fairy named Ting-a-ling, were published in 1870 (as *Ting-a-ling,* later *Ting-a-Ling Tales*) as Stockton's first book. Compared to his later fairy tales, they are crudely done, an unamalgamated mixture of an Arabian Nights setting with the diminutive fairies of Western literary tradition and a boyishly violent humor. But the combination of "fanciful creatures" and "common sense" was to be a fruitful one, and became the trademark of his fairy tales. Two volumes of these tales appeared in the following decade, *The Floating Prince and Other Fairy Tales* (1881) and *The Bee-Man of Orn and Other Fanciful Tales* (1887).

L. Frank Baum has been hailed by many as the originator of distinctly American fantasy for children, but the road to Oz runs through Frank Stockton country. Stockton employs a more traditional setting and cast of characters, small kingdoms and villages like those in Grimms' tales with a chiefly prince-and-peasant population, plus a wide range of "fanciful creatures" from Greek and Near Eastern mythology and European folklore—fairies, dryads, sphinxes, afrits, wizards, giants, dwarfs, hobgoblins, genii, gnomes, griffins, and hippogriffs, all mingling nonchalantly with each other. His protagonists, whether princes or peasant girls—he is quite even-handed in his choice of sexes—are natives, and seldom surprised by encountering a sphinx or a fairy on the road. Baum enlists a much higher proportion of invented creatures (though Stockton also invents a few) in a continuing saga, so that one gets to know them and their land, and he plays off their oddity against astonished newcomers from our world. But his basic narrative strategy (such as we see in *The Wizard of Oz, The Road to Oz, The Lost Princess of Oz,* etc.) is very like Stockton's and may have been learned from him: the naive protagonist journeying through a strange land, meeting a succession of eccentric yet generally sensible and friendly creatures, who may join themselves to the traveling party. And Baum, like Stockton, makes a point of how such an assorted group can co-exist harmoniously. The talking beasts and seemingly helpless old woman whom the folktale protagonist may encounter are the forebears of these characters, but although the creatures of Stockton and Baum may play the part of animal-helpers in assisting the protagonist in a quest, they have more "rights" as characters; they have quests and motivations of their own. For both authors, fairyland is more than a little American, being multi-ethnic and, despite the kings and queens, democratic; there is little of the bickering over status and power that goes on constantly in Carroll's worlds.

Both Stockton and Baum, again, take great pleasure in imaginary inventions and labor-saving devices, such as were in real life the pride of pre–World War I America. Baum's prototype robot, the clockwork Tik-tok, would feel at home in the mechanical city of Stockton's **"How the Aristocrats Sailed Away,"** which must also be wound up periodically (on its revolving stairway) to stay awake. Such Stockton stories for adults as **"A Tale of Negative Gravity"** (1884), **"My Translataphone"** (1900), and *The*

Great War Syndicate (1889) and a story for children called **"The Tricycle of the Future"** (1885) are not even fantasy but early technological science fiction. Howells, who found Stockton enjoyable but perplexing, complained that this "Edison" of authors presented "human character itself" as "a cleverly put together toy"—that "the emotional element" was entirely absent from his stories, "except as it is supplied now and then by the inventor to lubricate his machinery a little."

For a novelist of character and emotion (like Howells himself) these traits would be serious limitations, and Stockton's "straight" novels, though they have their defenders, are not his most memorable work. For a writer of nonsense fantasy, however, it is logic, humor, and invention that are essential—character and emotion that must be subordinated to the smooth operation of the whole. In this field, Stockton, like Baum and Carroll, is superb.

Most Stockton fairy tales are based on familiar folktale patterns. The simplest are about children who meet some supernatural figure in the woods near their homes, and in which their good will and good sense earn them some reward. Such stories remind us of folktales like "Toads and Diamonds," save that Stockton's homes are happy, though humble, to begin with, and the reward correspondingly more modest. Selma is hired by gnomes as a tutor for their prince and takes home a generous salary in gold in **"The Emergency Mistress."** Colin and his little sister win Christmas decorations and a doll from two dwarfs in **"The Sprig of Holly."** The ideas expressed in these stories are also relatively simple; you can call them "morals" and not be far off. Colin refuses to trade a year, or even a day, or even a minute of service for the holly sprig, and his father praises him afterwards for his " 'steady refusal to make a rash bargain, even for a very short time'."

A larger and more interesting group of stories includes **"The Floating Prince," "The Magician's Daughter," "The Queen's Museum," "The Banished King," "The Philopena,"** and **"Prince Hassak's March."** Here, the protagonists are older and of royal blood, their affairs involve whole kingdoms, and their quests take them far from home. Not one but several varieties of supernatural beings may be encountered. These stories often end with a royal marriage, in classic folktale fashion, and may remind us of such tales of quests and journeyings as "The Water of Life," "The Golden Bird," or "The Seven Ravens."

The third group of Stockton's fairy tales are the hardest to classify and seem farthest from folktale origins. They too may involve a journey and encounters with strange beings, but their protagonists are lowly and their problems universal rather than royal—old age in **"Old Pipes and the Dryad,"** destiny in **"The Bee-Man of Orn,"** human evil in **"The Griffin and the Minor Canon."** Their outcomes are not strongly positive; the Bee-Man ends where he began, and the other two stories conclude with the deaths of the dryad and griffin who have aided the protagonists, so that the conventional happy ending is neutralized.

Like Andersen, Ruskin, Thackeray (in *The Rose and the Ring*), even Baum, Stockton built on traditional foundations of setting, characters, and plot. But in all his fairy tales these traditional elements are outweighed by his consciously modern and critical approach to them. "I obliged these creatures to infuse into their extraordinary actions a certain leaven of common sense." The incongruity of common sense from a giant or a hippogriff becomes both a source of humor and a way of parodying the irrationality of the folktale. But an affectionate parody—Stockton, unlike Mark Twain, felt none of the urge to destroy the European past that took form in *The Prince and the Pauper* and *A Connecticut Yankee in King Arthur's Court.* His **Personally Conducted,** a European travelogue series published in *St. Nicholas* in 1887-88, encourages young readers to overcome their nationalistic prejudices and learn new "merits and virtues" from "the people we meet" in England, Germany, Italy, Switzerland, and France.

And Stockton's targets for satire only begin with the folktale; that same fondness for common sense led him to poke fun at political follies, the unrealistic expectations of reformers, and human vanity itself, especially in his second, and largest group of fairy tales. In **"The Floating Prince,"** for example, Prince Nassime has been cast out of his kingdom by a usurper and decides to found a new realm of his own. " 'The first person I meet,' " he declares, " 'shall be my chief councilor of state, the second shall be head of the army, the third shall be admiral of the navy, the next shall be chief treasurer, and then I will collect subjects of various classes'." The first person he meets is a five-inch-tall fairy named Lorilla—who, in fact, makes an excellent chief councilor. A giant becomes his general, a shepherd on stilts his admiral, a clam-digger his treasurer, a class of schoolboys his aristocrats, and so on. This random yet logical method produces a happy and prosperous community, leading us to the conclusion that whatever, clearly inferior, method is used to form a government in the real world must have even less logic behind it. **"The Clocks of Rondaine,"** one of Stockton's few short stories for children that hovers just on this side of fantasy, was written in 1887 and satirizes the current passion for reform. (pp. 226-29)

["Prince Hassak's March"] is typical Stockton in its inventiveness, its picaresque structure and miscellaneous characters, its final irony. It is also typical in its attitude toward a Prince who thinks he can march straight to his goal; its true hero is not the would-be heroic Hassak, whose foolish pride is deflated, but the Jolly-cum-pop, who looks foolish but acts wisely in accepting cheerfully whatever life brings to him. When he is the only prisoner too fat to escape through the narrow window of the jail, even this does not trouble him:

> "It is the most ridiculous thing in the world," he said. "I suppose I must stay here and cry until I get thin." And the idea so tickled him, that he laughed himself to sleep.

Later, when he has finally tired of the jail, he decides on a simple stratagem and frees himself single-handed.

This view of life, which in **"Prince Hassak's March"** is expressed by a journey, is symbolized through architecture in one of Stockton's novels for adults, *The Squirrel Inn* (1891). The inn of the title is a building of eccentric design, which exerts a peculiar and unsettling influence on the lives of its assorted inhabitants. At one point Susan, the innkeeper's wife, remarks with some exasperation, " 'Things didn't turn out as I expected them to, and I suppose they never will; but it always was my opinion, and yet, that nothing can go straight in a crooked house.' " To which her husband replies:

> "It strikes me, Susan, that our lives are very seldom built with a hall through the middle and the rooms alike on both sides. I don't think we'd like it if they were. They would be stupid and humdrum. The right sort of a life should have its ups and downs, its ins and outs, its different levels, its outside stairs and its inside stairs, its balconies, windows, and roofs of different periods and different styles. This is education. These things are the advantages that our lives get from the lives of others.
>
> "Now, for myself, I like the place I live in to resemble my life and that of the people about me. And I am sure that nothing could be better suited to all that than the Squirrel Inn."

Like Susan, Hassak wanted things to "go straight." But to have succeeded in marching straight to Yan would have taught him nothing. The Prince learns from "the people he meets" and the unforeseen things that happen to him—in fact, from the very failure of his quest.

The quest that fails to "go straight" is a common motif in Stockton's stories for children. Arla does not succeed in reforming the clocks of Rondaine. The protagonist of **"The Banished King"** does not learn, as he sets out to do, how to rule more wisely; he becomes a perpetual wanderer, leaving the kingdom in the competent hands of his queen. The three foolish young men are not allowed to reach the island where live three good, pretty, and intelligent sisters in **"The Sisters Three and the Kilmaree,"** until the Fairy Godmother has educated them by harsh experience, to "take the nonsense out of them"; their quest fails until they deserve to succeed. Loris and the Ninkum never do reach the fabled **"Castle of Bim,"** where everything is " 'positively charming, and everybody is just as happy and gay as can be' "; " 'I don't believe any of us will find that place,' " concludes a more sensible character. And the Bee-Man's quest for a more impressive "original form" ends finally in his becoming a humble bee-man again.

Even Stockton's less fantastic stories often follow the same pattern. The boy who invents the ingenious horse-powered **"Tricycle of the Future"** sees his invention destroyed. Several of Stockton's best stories for adults—for example, his fine comic novel *The Casting Away of Mrs. Lecks and Mrs. Aleshine* (1886)—deal with shipwrecks, the classic symbol for the random destruction of human hopes and plans.

The motif is especially striking, however, in his stories for children, for it is almost the rule both in folktales and in children's literature that a quest should succeed. Stockton advises children to expect failure and frustration. Nassime, in **"The Floating Prince,"** is an exception that proves the point; he is able to found his kingdom because he does not attempt to march straight forward toward his

goal, but "floats," learning readily from "the people he meets" and taking what opportunities come his way. "This," said Frank Stockton, "is education."

There is something stoical, in a pleasant way, about this philosophy, and indeed, like many humorists, Stockton used humor as a defense against his own melancholy. His wife Marian remembered that "He hated mourning and gloom. They seemed to paralyze him mentally until his bright spirit had again asserted itself and he recovered his balance." And he spoke with an inside understanding of the darkness of his great contemporary Mark Twain:

> It is well known that the actor of comedy often casts longing glances toward the tragic mask, and when he has an opportunity to put it on, he often wears it so well that one cannot say that he has no right to it. The same pen-point that will make a man laugh out in church, if gently pricked by it, will not only slay a bride at the altar, but will go entirely through her and kill her father who is giving her away.

Occasionally, in Stockton too, one feels an increased pressure of the pen-point. In **"The Lady, or the Tiger?"** readers must identify with a princess choosing between her lover's marriage to another and his death. Stockton subtly weights the story—then, by ending with the famous question, forces his readers to choose the tiger themselves. And the underlying melancholy in some of his best children's stories gives way to an even bleaker view of human nature in **"The Griffin and the Minor Canon."**

The story was inspired by Stockton's visit to Chester cathedral, with its strange carvings in wood and stone, and he completed it in Chester itself. It tells of a church with a great stone griffin carved above its porch, and how a real Griffin (who had never known what he looked like) comes flying one day from the wilderness to see this portrait of himself. The townspeople are terrified, and the only one with courage to approach the monster is a minor canon of the church, "a young man of a kind disposition," who is used to performing the duties no one else cares for—conducting weekday services for a congregation of three old women, visiting the sick and poor, counseling people in trouble, and teaching a school of bad children. The Minor Canon leads the Griffin to the church, where he is much struck by the fine statue. But even after several days, the Griffin shows no sign of leaving. He conceives a liking for the Minor Canon and begins to follow him as the young man goes about his duties.

As the autumn equinox approaches, when the Griffin is known to take his semi-annual meal, the townspeople become more and more apprehensive. They order the Minor Canon to banish himself to the wilderness, assuming that the Griffin will go to look for him. But instead the Griffin begins to take on some of the duties that his friend had performed. . . . (pp. 230-33)

When at last the desperate townspeople bring up the subject of the Griffin's equinoctial dinner, they learn that the monster despises them all too much to have any wish to eat them:

> "They appear to be all cowards, and, therefore,

mean and selfish. . . . In fact, there was only one creature in the whole place for whom I could have had any appetite, and that was the Minor Canon, who has gone away. He was brave and good and honest, and I think I should have relished him."

"Ah!" said one of the old men very politely, "in that case I wish we had not sent him to the dreadful wilds!"

And now, learning of this for the first time, the Griffin is furious. He announces that he will go to find the Minor Canon and bring him back. . . . Wrenching the statue from the church, the Griffin carries it to his cave in the wilderness, then finds the Minor Canon slowly dying of starvation and nurses him back to health, and finally returns him one night to the town. Here the young man at last receives the treatment he deserves, "and before he died, he became a bishop." (pp. 233-34)

Stockton may well have meant the story as a parody of such hero-versus-monster legends as St. George and the Dragon. In his variation, the monster is of far nobler character than his potential victims; the hero triumphs not by an act of slaughter but by kindness, humility, and self-sacrifice; and the *monster* rescues *him*. Such twists would have pleased a man with a personal distaste for violent solutions—one who opposed the Spanish-American War; who published an unsuccessful but heartfelt pamphlet in 1860 called *A Northern Voice,* suggesting that the South be allowed to secede; and who wrote such strongly pacifist fiction as (for adults) *The Great War Syndicate* (1889) and (for children) **"Derido; or, The Giant's Quilt"** (in *The Floating Prince*).

But the implications of the story only begin with parody. In most Stockton fairy tales the more serious failings are assigned to foolish individuals, like Hassak in **"Prince Hassak's March"**—though it is true that the most sensible characters are often non-human. In **"The Griffin,"** the townspeople seem to represent the generality of humanity, a cowardly, selfish, and foolish humanity who are willing enough to take advantage of their one hero, without ever recognizing him for what he is. Stockton underlines this indictment with sly jabs of his pen. These folk are afraid that the Griffin will devour their children, but ready "to mention that there was an orphan asylum in the next town." When the Griffin takes over the Minor Canon's visit to the poor, the poor virtually disappear:

> All those who had depended upon charity for their daily bread were now at work in some way or other, many of them offering to do odd jobs for their neighbors just for the sake of their meals—a thing which before had been seldom heard of in the town. The Griffin could find no one who needed his assistance.

Even the Griffin notices the irrelevance of the church to these people's lives—that nobody goes there. And while Stockton allows that in time the people learned "to honor and reverence their former Minor Canon without the fear of being punished if they did not do so," he ends the story by commenting, with devastating understatement, on the Griffin's death, "It was a good thing for some of the people of the town that they did not know this."

The Minor Canon himself is plainly Christ-like in his personal qualities, in his self-imposed duties, and in his rejection by the very folk he saves. His banishment is reminiscent of the traditional identification of Christ with the scapegoat, laden with the sins of the people and driven out into the wilderness. Stockton's echoing of Biblical phrases—"their daily bread," "bow yourselves before him," "put him in the highest place among you"—and, of course, the centrality of the church also guide the reader toward a religious interpretation of the story. Stockton seems to suggest that Christian virtues are no more appreciated today than they ever were, that if Christ reappeared he would once more be crucified, and that—since the Minor Canon's rank is so low in the church hierarchy,—the religious establishment has itself lost sight of its true priorities.

But what, then, of the Griffin? If the Minor Canon represents Christ, one might expect him to vanquish a Devil-monster. This does not happen; indeed, the Griffin saves the life and ensures his advancement. And it is the Griffin, not the Minor Canon, who acts as the protagonist of the story, and gives it its special quality. Again, as in **"The Lady, or the Tiger?"** Stockton persuades us to confront the monsters within ourselves. But the Griffin is a being of such rich ambiguity as to make that tiger look like the simple big cat that it is. (pp. 234-35)

Here, on the church, among a myriad other sculptures of "saints, martyrs, grotesque heads of men, beasts, and birds" representing all creation, the griffin seems the untamed force of nature itself, subject only to God. And indeed, as the Griffin's companion, the Minor Canon discovers that the whole world of nature lies open to him:

> "It is like reading an old book" said the young clergyman to himself; "but how many books I would have had to read before I would have found out what the Griffin has told me about the earth, the air, the water, about minerals, and metals, and growing things, and all the wonders of the world!"

At the same time, the Griffin is neither omnipotent nor omniscient. In the beginning, he does not even know what he looks like; his motive for leaving the wilderness is simple curiosity. (p. 236)

An intriguing ambiguity characterizes the Griffin's moral character as well. He seems noble in his attraction to and appreciation of the Minor Canon, in his scorn of the townspeople, and in his lofty refusal to take vengeance on them. Maurice Sendak seems to have admired him. "Our friend the griffin," he wrote [in *The Griffin and the Minor Canon,* 1963], "is strong, proud, imperious, vain, intelligent, good—and, best of all, lion-hearted." But he is not simply good (like the Minor Canon). He *is* vain, as we can see from his delight in the fine statue of himself, and one cannot overlook his intentions toward the Minor Canon:

> "Do you know," said the monster . . . "that I have had, and still have, a great liking for you?"

"I am very glad to hear it," said the Minor Canon, with his usual politeness.

"I am not at all sure that you would be," said the Griffin, "if you thoroughly understood the state of the case. . . ."

Surely the Griffin's assumption that he has the right to devour the Minor Canon is the height of egotism—and yet it does not strike us, somehow, as wholly outrageous or impossible. Ingestion is, after all, an act of union, and there is a strange interdependence between the young man and the monster. For all his virtue, the Minor Canon is ineffective without the Griffin's help; it is the Griffin who succeeds in curing the sick, teaching the bad children, and banishing poverty from the town. But it is also the Minor Canon who inspires the Griffin to carry on his work, and without him, in the end, the Griffin can find no reason to live. Each needs the other to make himself complete—as the spiritual and the animal make up the fully human being. Was Stockton suggesting, long before the Jungians, that we need the primitive strength and natural, instinctive wisdom of the animal within ourselves?

Or was he aware of the traditional symbolism associated with the griffin, that made its likeness appropriate for a cathedral? In Christian iconography, the griffin, half eagle and half lion, symbolized the union of two natures in Christ—the divine (bird) and the human (animal). (So a griffin appears in Dante's *Purgatorio*, Canto 29, drawing the triumphal chariot of Beatrice.) But it was not necessary for Stockton to know this in order to see his own Griffin as something monstrous, yet somehow divine. Between them, the Griffin and the Minor Canon may represent two aspects of a complex God—the terrifying Jehovah of the Old Testament and the self-sacrificing Jesus of the New. It fits perfectly that the townspeople do not honor the Minor Canon for his own sake, but only when the Griffin's vengeance threatens them. They need a God of Fear—and it is as well, Stockton suggests, that they do not realize when that God is dead.

It is odd that **"The Griffin and the Minor Canon"** has always been a favorite with children, for the story is Stockton's darkest fairy tale. In it, human nature is portrayed as cowardly, selfish, and despicable, incapable of appreciating either the simple goodness of the Minor Canon or the rich mysteries of meaning summed up by that complex monster, the Griffin. And it suggests that something of value is diminishing, withdrawing forever into the wilderness. It ends not with the Minor Canon's elevation to a bishopric—which we could accept as a happy ending—but with the Griffin's lonely death and the disappearance of the great statue from the church. Its last word is "gone."

Stockton himself, who took pleasure in writing fairy tales

and counted the best of them among his finest work, wondered if they could really be for children, and clearly they are not for children alone. But children deserve the chance to enter Stockton's world, to enjoy his humor, puzzle over his logic, share his sensible, sardonic view of human society and government and his vision of life at the Squirrel Inn. (pp. 236-38)

Suzanne Rahn, "Life at The Squirrel Inn: Rediscovering Frank Stockton," in The Lion and the Unicorn, *Vol. 12, No. 2, December, 1988, pp. 224-39.*

FURTHER READING

Bowen, Edwin W. "Frank R. Stockton." *Sewanee Review* XI, No. 4 (October 1903): 474-78.
    Analysis of story and plot in Stockton's short stories.

Buel, C. C. "The Author of 'The Lady, or the Tiger?'" *Century Magazine* XXXII, No. 4 (July 1886): 405-13.
    Discussion of Stockton's use of humor and fantasy to explore human nature.

Chislett, William, Jr. "The Stories and Novels of Frank Stockton." *Moderns and Near Moderns: Essays on Henry James, Stockton, Shaw, and Others,* pp. 67-97. 1928. Reprint. Freeport, N.Y.: Books for Libraries Press, 1967.
    Summary and appreciation of Stockton's better-known works, intended to revive readers' interest in them.

Cloud, Virginia Woodward. "In Lighter Vein: 'The Lady, or the Tiger?'—A New Solution." *Century Magazine* LI, No. 4 (February 1896): 638-39.
    Fictional dialogue demonstrating contemporary debates over the outcome of Stockton's tale.

Howells W. D. Review of *A Story-Teller's Pack. Harper's Weekly* XLI, No. 2110 (29 May 1897): 538.
    Considers the technique and effect of Stockton's subtle humor.

Mabie, Hamilton W. "Frank R. Stockton." *The Book Buyer* XXIV, No. 5 (June 1902): 354-57.
    Memorial tribute praising Stockton's humor.

Pforzheimer, Walter L. "The Lady, the Tiger, and the Author." *The Colophon* n.s. I, No. 2 (Autumn 1935): 261-70.
    Detailed discussion of the genesis and reception of "The Lady, or the Tiger?"

Additional coverage of Stockton's life and career is contained in the following sources published by Gale Research: *Contemporary Authors,* Vol. 108; *Dictionary of Literary Biography,* Vols. 42, 74; and *Something about the Author,* Vols. 32, 44.

August Strindberg

Fröken Julie (Miss Julie)

(Full name Johan August Strindberg; also wrote under pseudonym of Harved Ulf) Swedish playwright, novelist, short story writer, poet, essayist, and journalist.

The following entry presents criticism of Strindberg's play *Fröken Julie* (*Miss Julie*), which was first performed in 1889. For a discussion of Strindberg's complete career, see *TCLC*, Volumes 1, 8, and 21.

INTRODUCTION

Miss Julie is considered the masterpiece of Strindberg's naturalistic period and a major text in the evolution of modern drama. Subtitled "A Naturalistic Tragedy," the play focuses on the destructive relationship between the aristocratic Miss Julie and her ambitious servant, Jean. Highlighting themes of class and sexual conflict, Strindberg's use of such experimental theatrical techniques as pantomime and monologue has anticipated many of the trends in twentieth-century drama.

Closely observing the traditional dramatic unities of time and place, *Miss Julie* opens in the kitchen of a Swedish manor house on Midsummer Night and closes there the following morning. Strindberg employed the one-act form with a view to keeping the audience's attention continuously directed toward events on the stage. The first scene begins with interplay between Kristin, the cook, and Jean, the valet, and reveals information principally about Miss Julie. She is perceived as mentally unstable, the product of her recently broken engagement and the conflicting strains of an ancestry that is both aristocratic and humble. As the action unfolds, Strindberg implies that what follows is to a large degree a biologically determined struggle between the oppositional pairs of male and female, strong and weak, nobly and humbly born. Jean, who has been singled out as Miss Julie's dancing partner during the Midsummer Night festivities, engages in a subtle battle of wills with his mistress that ultimately leads to their mutual seduction. Both characters define themselves in terms of their aspirations. Jean wishes to ascend the ladder of social success, whereas Miss Julie imagines a life free of the restrictions of her social class. After Jean declares his longstanding attraction to Miss Julie, the couple escapes to Jean's room in order to avoid a group of peasants who enter the kitchen to continue their merrymaking. The seduction takes place off stage, and when Jean and Miss Julie return to the kitchen the flirtatious banter of the play's first half is replaced by frenzied fantasizing and argument. They discuss fleeing Sweden and running a hotel on Lake Como, with Jean eventually buying a Romanian noble title. This romantic dream quickly dissolves as barriers between the pair assert themselves, and the balance of power dramatically shifts as Jean begins to display open

contempt for Miss Julie. Feeling herself to be simultaneously under Jean's powerful influence and morally compromised, Miss Julie leaves the kitchen to commit suicide, while Jean is reduced to cringing servility when summoned by her father, the count.

Strindberg wrote *Miss Julie* in 1888, during the first phase of his artistic maturity (1884-1892), before the spiritual crisis dissected in his autobiographical novel, *Inferno,* and previous to adopting the expressionistic style of his late plays. Some critics have viewed *Miss Julie* as a symbolic presentation of Strindberg's disastrous marriage to Siri von Essen. Without denying the validity of a biographical approach to Strindberg's art (V. S. Pritchett has referred to him as "the perpetual autobiographer who has at least three albatrosses—his three wives—hanging from his neck"), many scholars have preferred to locate the dramatic power of *Miss Julie* in a broader context. Drama in the 1880s had been revolutionized by the adaptation of Emile Zola's novel *Thérèse Raquin* (1867) and its attack on what Strindberg called "the patent-leather themes" of romantic drama. Naturalism proper, as advocated by Zola, centered on the lucid exposition of action, the use of factual stories, realistic depiction of ordinary characters, and conversational dialogue. Strindberg furnished *Miss Julie* with a preface expounding his naturalistic philosophy of the theater which has exerted a profound influence in its own right. In view of Zola's criticism of Strindberg's *The Father* (1887), commentators have read the preface to *Miss Julie* as a placatory gesture aimed at the new drama's founding father. Scholars are unanimous, however, in pointing to the distinctive character of Strindberg's naturalism, which makes *Miss Julie* an amalgam of tragic, romantic, and naturalistic perspectives. In particular, Strindberg's personal conception of Naturalism placed greater emphasis on life as a conflict of wills and a battleground for the struggle between flesh and spirit, rather than the struggle against heredity and environment that is characteristic of Naturalism. Moreover, Strindberg shaped and selected the elements of his story, which was based on fact, in a conspicuously artistic manner that Naturalism sought to avoid.

Criticism of *Miss Julie* has often used the claims of Strindberg's preface as its starting-point. In particular, critics have noted the dichotomy between the conception of simplified characters representing social and psychological types set out in the preface and the actual complexity of Miss Julie and Jean. Whereas early reactions to Strindberg's drama were characterized by distaste for what was perceived as outright misogyny, some later critics have maintained that Strindberg demonstrated an affinity for both of *Miss Julie*'s main characters, and consider the play as a whole to be the embodiment of its author's psychological contradictions and ambiguities. While clarifying Strindberg's originality regarding the presentation of sexual psychology, scholars have also placed *Miss Julie* in its intellectual milieu and have argued that Strindberg made significant use of ideas and motifs derived from the nineteenth-century movements of Romanticism, Symbolism, and Decadence. The play has had a lasting impact on the techniques and concerns of twentieth-century drama as well as pioneering what Strindberg's biographer, Michael Meyer, has called "the depiction of men and women driven by love, hatred, jealousy or a mixture of all three to that nightmare border country where hysteria abuts on madness."

CRITICISM

Martin Lamm   (essay date 1948)

[*Lamm was a professor of literary history at the University of Stockholm and a member of the Swedish Academy. At the Academy's request he wrote* August Strindberg, *one of the foundations of Strindberg research and criticism. In the following excerpt from this study originally published in Swedish in 1948, Lamm examines the characterization and structure of* Miss Julie.]

Strindberg offered *Miss Julie* to the publisher K. O. Bonnier in a letter on August 10, 1888, describing the play as "the first Naturalistic Tragedy in Swedish Drama." He continued: " '*Ceci datera!*'—this play will be recorded in the annals." It was an accurate prophecy. *Miss Julie* is a masterpiece of naturalistic drama. Whereas other attempts made in the 1870's and 1880's to bring naturalism into the theatre are today often of interest only to literary historians, *Miss Julie* is still performed regularly. It is bolder and more original in design than its contemporaries, and it is executed with greater artistic integrity.

The preface to *Miss Julie* shows that Strindberg observed the demands for technical reforms advocated by Zola and the Théâtre Libre. He wanted to remove the footlights, replace kitchen utensils painted on the scenery with real ones, allow actors to speak their lines in profile or with their backs to the audience, introduce dumb show, and so forth. All this was in conformity with naturalism's striving to transform the stage into a room whose fourth wall has been replaced by the proscenium opening.

Strindberg also took pains to emphasize that he had depicted a "case," that he had chosen, as he states in the preface, a "theme from a true story I heard a number of years ago, which made a strong impression on me." (A letter written . . . in October, 1888, indicates that the model was a certain titled young lady who seduced a stableman.) Strindberg's sensational story, partly drawn from life, supposedly proved (again in accordance with Zola) a natural law: the stronger survive in the struggle for existence.

Miss Julie is the last representative of a noble house whose blood line has run thin. She is doomed to be destroyed; whereas the valet Jean is a "species originator" with a fresh appetite for life and without any cumbersome feelings about honor. Strindberg, using the terminology of "Cultivated Fruit," says in the preface that "the thrall has this advantage over the nobleman: he lacks a fatal preoccupation with honor. And in all of us Aryans there is something of the nobleman or of Don Quixote." The word "Aryans" suggests that Strindberg had discovered Nietzsche, but these ideas had been in his mind earlier, and they were intensified by his association with Heidenstam [Verner von Heidenstam was then a young writer and friend of Strindberg; he was awarded the Nobel Prize in literature in 1916]. Heidenstam represented himself as belonging to "the vanishing inheritance nobility"—too refined, too unbarbaric to be able to stay on its feet in the struggle for existence; whereas he regarded Strindberg as a representative of "the new intellectual nobility, which will have its own House of Lords." Strindberg obviously recalled this remark when he wrote in the preface that Miss Julie is "a relic of the old warrior nobility now giving way to the new intellectual nobility or aristocracy of great minds." Strindberg tries to persuade himself that he will welcome this inevitable development:

> When we grow as strong as the earliest French revolutionaries, we shall feel unconditionally happy and relieved to see the national parks cleared of rotting, overage trees which have stood too long in the way of others equally entitled to a period of growth—as relieved as when we see an incurable invalid die!

The spectator is not similarly relieved, because Strindberg, in spite of his approval of her fate, portrayed Miss Julie's downfall as tragedy. She is an aristocrat with high-strung emotions who has lost her way among the lower classes who do not understand her; they trample her ideals, are amused by her humiliation, and hound her to death. It is possible that when Strindberg first approached the subject he identified more with the socially ambitious "species originator," Jean, but during the writing he was drawn to Miss Julie, with whose hypersensitive nervousness he felt an affinity. Strindberg felt that the superman was a vanishing race and that the earth would be dominated by "the lowly." Another example of his interpretation of the superman cult is in the novel *In the Outer Skerries.* Like Miss Julie, the well-educated fishing commissioner Borg is defeated in his struggle with representatives of the lower classes—the crude fishermen and their families.

Strindberg was not content to discuss the "problem of social climbing and falling" in the preface and then have it confirmed in the play's outcome. In his eagerness to underscore the importance of the problem he has the two protagonists, Miss Julie and Jean, make specific reference to it in the dialogue. They talk extensively to each other about their origins, obsessions, and inherited tendencies. Miss Julie had had a recurrent dream in which she climbs to the top of a column and longs to fall down; Jean often dreams that he is lying under a tall tree and longs to climb to the top. In a long, impassioned speech Miss Julie forecasts the extinction of her line and the ritual smashing of her family's coat of arms against her coffin; Jean tells of his ambitious plans to rise above his lower-class status.

Strindberg undoubtedly realized how improbable it was for such reflections to be made in the same fateful hour when Miss Julie becomes a victim of Jean's opportunism and is driven to suicide. In a passage omitted from the preface he justifies the reflections by maintaining that it was permissible in modern drama for characters to discuss Darwinism, and he points out that the gravedigger in *Hamlet* spoke "Giordano Bruno's philosophy."

Apart from Miss Julie's and Jean's discussion of the problem of degeneration and their tendency to analyze each other's feelings, the play is a strict application of Zola-esque principles. Zola had acknowledged the legitimacy of the classical unities because they were in keeping with his demand for an illusion of reality, but in his own plays he was only able to observe the unity of place, since he was fettered by the cumbersome plots he was dramatizing. Strindberg criticized him in the essay **"On Modern Drama and Modern Theatre" ("Om modern drama och modern teater")** especially his overemphasis on the importance of realistic décor and his failure to recognize the necessity for unity of time. In *Thérèse Raquin,* for example, Zola made "the mistake of having a year elapse between the first and second acts." For Strindberg, classical French drama was the model to follow: "With Molière, French drama had entered a phase in which all scenic effect was abandoned, and the nuances of emotional life became the most important element. Observe how the delicious vivisection of Tartuffe takes place in one room furnished with two taborets." In *Miss Julie,* the action occurs in one setting so that the characters can "develop in their milieu." And although it is evident in the early drafts that Strindberg originally planned an act division, "as an experiment," he dispensed with having the curtain fall during the play and made the action continuous.

The one-act form necessitates drastic simplification in terms of number of characters and plot. *Miss Julie* contains three speaking roles and only a few rudiments of an Ibsen-like intrigue. For example, the opening scene is a symbolic foreshadowing of the future action: Kristin, the cook, is preparing food for Miss Julie's bitch Diana who has displeased her mistress by sneaking out with the gate-keeper's pug-dog. When Kristin later learns of Miss Julie's indiscretion, she recalls that Miss Julie's pride was such that she wanted Diana shot. Ibsen's method of illuminating future action through parallel scenes is used in the later episode with the greenfinch: Miss Julie insists on taking her pet bird with her on her flight abroad to prevent its falling into the hands of strangers. When Jean kills it, she becomes hysterical: "Kill me too! Kill me! You, who can butcher an innocent creature without blinking an eye!"

In his next play Strindberg would simplify even further. He felt that *Miss Julie* was a "compromise with romanticism and stage decoration" but that *Creditors* was "thoroughly modern" and a better play: "three characters, a table and two chairs—and no sunrise!" Obviously, it now displeased him that in the final scene in *Miss Julie* he had—as Ibsen hand done in *Ghosts*—allowed the sunrise to establish a jarring contrast to the mood of desperation within the room.

Strindberg's rules for dramatic characterization set forth in the preface are actually only an application of Théodule Ribot's concept of the ego as a complex of multiple, often mutually hostile, impulses. In his autobiography, Strindberg had already criticized the tendency on the parts of novelists and dramatists to conceive of character as "a very simple, mechanical contrivance. . . . A 'character' and an automaton seem almost identical. Dickens's famous characters are organ-grinders' puppets, and 'characters' in the theatre are required to be automatons." The same criticism appears in the preface to *Miss Julie,* where Strindberg is opposed to "simple stage characters" whose psychological identity can be expressed in a single word and whose uniqueness is evidenced through a physical defect, a habitual gesture, or a constantly repeated expression. Instead, he claims to have made his fingers "characterless" in order to show "how rich soul-complex is." Therefore, he has depicted them:

> vacillating, disintegrated, a mixture of old and new . . . My souls (characters) are conglomerations of past and present phases of civilization, bits from books and newspapers, fragments of humanity, torn pieces of once-fine clothing that has become rags, patched together as the human soul itself.

Strindberg's intention was to go beyond simple explanations for actions and to present the multiplicity of conscious and unconscious motivations upon which actions are based. In his preface he lists the circumstances that led inevitably to Miss Julie's seduction: "the mother's basic instincts, the father's wrong methods in rearing the girl, her own nature, and her fiancé's influence on a weak, degenerate mind; also, and more immediate—the festive mood of Midsummer Eve." When Georg Brandes found the heroine's suicide psychologically unbelievable, Strindberg enumerated a large number of motivations contributing to her decision in his letter of reply: "Notice that Miss [Julie] left to herself would have lacked the power, but now she is driven and tormented by the multiple motives."

Even as Strindberg worked to simplify the play's structure, he tried to complicate its internal mechanism, although to a certain degree these attempts remained drawing-board fantasies. The preface was written after the play, and Edvard Brandes was probably correct in his suspicion that *Miss Julie* was not the result of the application of conscious theory. Strindberg best realized his intentions in the portrayal of the heroine. Miss Julie wavers under the influence of many different impressions and is torn between the most contradictory feelings: tenderness and contempt, ecstasy and irony, vanity and the wish to degrade herself, erotic desire and chaste modesty. She is capricious, unrestrained, tactless, sometimes cruel and heartless. We are, nevertheless, touched by sympathy for her. She matures as a person under her misfortune, whereas Jean becomes more despicable in his mood of triumph. Her inherited pride, which earlier found expression in a rigid and insecure haughtiness, takes on a tragic dimension when she goes to her doom with the razor in her hand.

The personalities of the other two characters in the play are more simplified and do not present the psychological enigma Miss Julie does. Jean is an exuberant figure drawn with grotesque humor: innately vulgar and yet possessing fastidious habits and manners. "Polished, but coarse underneath," is the way Strindberg describes him in the preface. Particularly in the beginning of the play, when Jean poses as a fussy connoisseur of food, wine and feminine beauty, his cockiness is irresistible. Unfortunately, Jean displays a sophistication that is not consistent with his character at the beginning of the play. Without intentionally caricaturing him, Strindberg provides Jean with witty repartee that one does not expect to hear from a valet with lower-class origins.

Kristin—with her sullenness, her uncharitable religiosity, and her inveterate respect for class distinctions—is a typical representative of one aspect of the Swedish national temperament. Her class consciousness is so great that she is unable to be jealous of Miss Julie. "No, not of her," she says to Jean. "If it had been Clara or Sofi, I would have scratched your eyes out! Yes, that's the way it is. Why—I don't know. - - - Oh, it's disgusting!"

As in his subsequent naturalistic dramas, Strindberg begins *Miss Julie* at a brisk pace by avoiding obvious exposition. The opening line by Jean—"Miss Julie is crazy again tonight, completely crazy!"—thrusts the spectator immediately into a situation that is quickly made clear through the servants quarreling. The description of the mistress of the house is corroborated by her first entrance: She is at once artistocratically condescending, coquettish, and provocative; and we are reminded of Jean's story about her mother who wore blouses with dirty cuffs, but insisted that all her buttons have the Count's coronets on them. Not until after the seduction are we motivated to shift our sympathy from Jean to Miss Julie. Strindberg depicts effectively the shifts in Julie's emotions from numbed shock to the terrifying discovery that this man to whom she has given herself is more despicable than she could have dreamed possible.

The final scene is perhaps the best in the play, containing that blend of naturalism and fantasy that is so typical of the later Strindberg. The final effect, however, was produced only after repeated revisions. An early draft shows that Strindberg originally thought of having Miss Julie grab the razor away from Jean after all possibilities of escape were blocked and the Count's bell had sounded to summon his valet. She slashes her wrists in full view of the audience, crying triumphantly: "You see, lackey, you weren't capable of dying." Fortunately, Strindberg's interest in the phenomenon of suggestion provided the impulses for a different resolution. In the published version Miss Julie wants to commit suicide, but cannot do it of her own free will. She must be compelled to it by an external command. She asks Jean if he has ever seen a hypnotist in a theatre: "He says to his subject: 'Take the broom,' and it's taken. He says: 'Sweep,' and the person sweeps." When Jean protests that the subject has to be asleep, Miss Julie answers ecstatically: "I'm asleep already . . . the whole room is like a cloud of smoke . . . and you look like a stove . . . shaped like a man in black with a tall hat . . . and your eyes glow like coals when the flames die down . . . and your face is a white patch like ashes." The

sunshine streams into the desolate room, and Miss Julie rubs her hands as if warming them before a fire: "It's so nice and warm . . . and so bright . . . and so peaceful!" Jean puts the razor in her hand and whispers in her ear that she must take it with her to the barn. But once again her courage deserts her, and Jean feels himself growing powerless as he thinks of the Count's bell and the police. Not until the bell rings sharply twice again can he straighten himself up: "It's horrible. But there's no other way out . . . Go!" Miss Julie now has the determination necessary to go to her death.

In the preface Strindberg maintains that he had not made his people into catechists who sit and ask stupid questions in order to elicit clever replies:

> I have avoided the symmetrical, mathematical and contrived construction of the dialogue in French drama, and have let people's minds operate as irregularly as they do in real life where, in conversation, no subject is completely exhausted, and one mind finds a cog in another mind with which to engage. Consequently, the dialogue, too, wanders, gathering in the opening scenes material which is later picked up, reworked and repeated, developed and embellished, like the theme in a musical composition.

Strindberg is not, however, as free from contrivance as he believed; the rambling purposelessness of *Miss Julie* is more apparent than real. The play contains some old-fashioned theatrical repartee, and Strindberg did not attempt to write dialogue that sounded like the ordinary everyday speech that Zola recommended and later naturalistic dramatists like Granville Barker and Chekhov pushed to extremes. But in comparison with Strindberg's earlier dialogue, the language in *Miss Julie* is denser and richer in texture, probing beneath surface reality into the unconscious: the characters become intoxicated by their own words, and while they speak about one thing, their minds are elsewhere.

The scenes after the seduction offer clear examples of how Strindberg attempted to put into practice his principles of naturalistic dialogue. Jean, who alternates between a feeling of triumph and a fear of the consequences of his action, talks rhapsodically of the future, of traveling with Julie to Switzerland and founding a hotel with the daughter of a count as cashier. Julie, her feelings torn between shame and erotic longing for the man who conquered her, is only half listening and she responds anxiously: "That's all very well! But Jean. . . . Say that you love me!" When talking has finally restored Jean's composure, he says to her: "Sit down there! I'll sit here and we'll talk as if nothing has happened." She bursts out desperately: "Oh, my God! Have you no feelings?" To which Jean replies: "Me! No one has more feelings than I do, but I know how to control myself." Strindberg constantly reminds us of the disparity between what people say they want and what they really want. Jean talks about his ambitious plans for the future while his thoughts are constantly occupied with how to get rid of Julie and retain his position on the estate. Julie pleads for assurances of affection in order to preserve at least the illusion that she committed her indiscretion for love. Deep down she feels a burning shame at having given herself on a whim to a man for whom she has no feelings. Not surprisingly, their mutual pledges of love and devotion turn into exchanges of bitter invective in a matter of minutes.

When Kristin prevents them from fleeing at the decisive instant, Julie hits upon the kind of bizarre idea common in moments of desperation: all three of them will go to Switzerland. She now tries to sell to Kristin the same travel plans, the same proposal for starting a hotel on the shores of Lake Como with which Jean had regaled her earlier. Her speech becomes more and more agitated as her courage sinks. Then, when Kristin asks her if she really believes what she is saying, she collapses: "I don't know. I don't believe anything any more."

Contained in these passages are all the innovations in revelation of character that Strindberg wanted to express through dialogue: the irregular operation of the mind, the contrast between thought and speech, the reiteration of the same theme with new psychological implications. Perhaps the author's intentions are too obvious, but they are brilliantly executed.

During the writing of **Miss Julie,** Strindberg was eager to create a prototype for naturalistic drama, a counterpart to what the Goncourt brothers produced for the novel. In the preface he declares that he chose their "documentary novels" for models since they "appealed to me more than any other contemporary literature." "Modern people" are not satisfied to see something happen; they want to know how it happens. "We want to see the wires, watch the machinery, examine the box with the false bottom, pick up the magic ring to find the join, look at the cards to see how they are marked." It is the presence of this "machinery" that makes **Miss Julie** less spontaneously moving than **The Father.** (pp. 212-20)

> *Martin Lamm, in his* August Strindberg, *edited and translated by Harry G. Carlson, Benjamin Blom, Inc., 1971, 561 p.*

Raymond Williams　　(essay date 1952)

[*Williams is an English educator and critic whose writing is informed by his socialist ideology and his belief that a reader's perception of literature is directly related to cultural attitudes which are subject to change over the course of time. He is best known for* Modern Tragedy *(1958), which asserts that modern tragedy derives from the inadequacies of social systems rather than weaknesses of character, as in classical tragedy, and for* Drama: From Ibsen to Eliot, *a study of the development of modern drama. In the following excerpt from the latter study,* Williams *elucidates* Miss Julie's *theatrical innovations in the light of objectives set forth in the preface.*]

Strindberg was, perhaps, in revolt against the same things as was Zola, against the "patent-leather themes" of the romantic drama. But his own ideas for reform were different, and the experiments into which his ideas led him represent a unique and quite separate dramatic form. His position is more justly represented by the opening paragraph of his *Preface* to **Lady Julie** (1888).

Dramatic art, like almost all other art, has long seemed to me a kind of *Biblia Pauperum*—a bible in pictures for those who cannot read the written or printed work. And in the same way the dramatist has seemed to me a lay preacher, hawking about the ideas of his time in popular form—popular enough for the middle classes, who form the bulk of theatrical audiences, to grasp the nature of the subject, without troubling their brains too much. The theatre, for this reason, has always been a board school, for the young, for the half-educated, and for women, who still retain the inferior faculty of deceiving themselves and allowing themselves to be deceived: that is to say, of being susceptible to illusion and to the suggestions of the author. Consequently, in these days when the rudimentary and incompletely developed thought-process which operates through the imagination appears to be developing into reflection, investigation, and analysis, it has seemed to me that the theatre, like religion, may be on the verge of being abandoned as a form which is dying out, and for the enjoyment of which we lack the necessary conditions. This supposition is confirmed by the extensive theatrical decline which now prevails through the whole of Europe, and especially by the fact that in those civilised countries which have produced the greatest thinkers of the age—that is to say, England and Germany—the dramatic art, like most other fine arts, is dead. In some other countries, however, it has been thought possible to create a new drama by filling the old forms with the contents of the newer age; but, for one thing the new thoughts have not yet had time to become sufficiently popular for the public to be able to grasp the questions raised; moreover, party strife has so inflamed people's minds that pure, disinterested enjoyment is out of the question. One experiences a deep sense of contradiction when an applauding or hissing majority exercises its tyranny so openly as it can in the theatre. Lastly, we have not got the new form for the new contents, and the new wine has burst the old bottles.

The Father (1887) and especially **Lady Julie** (1888) are attempts at such a new form. By this time, of course, Ibsen's prose plays were widely known. Although Strindberg was in many ways openly contemptuous of Ibsen—he called him "that famous Norwegian blue-stocking"—Ibsen's established practice was a very definite part of Strindberg's new dramatic consciousness. (pp. 100-01)

[In **Lady Julie** Strindberg] attempted to fashion new conventions. The "new wine had burst the old bottles"; or, more precisely, the old bottles had soured the new wine.

> In the present drama I have not tried to do anything new—for that is impossible—but merely to modernise the form in accordance with what I imagined would be required of this art from the younger generation. . . . In regard to the character-drawing, I have made my figures rather characterless, for the following reasons:

> The word "character" has, in the course of the ages, assumed various meanings. Originally, I suppose, it signified the dominant characteristic

of the soul-complex, and was confused with "temperament." Afterwards it became the middle-class expression for the automaton. An individual who had once for all become fixed in his natural disposition, or had adapted himself to some definite rôle in life—who, in fact, had ceased to grow—was called a "character". . . . This middle-class conception of the immobility of the soul was transferred to the stage, where the middle-class has always ruled. A "character" on the stage came to signify a gentleman who was fixed and finished: one who invariably came on the stage drunk, jesting, or mournful. For characterisation nothing was required but some bodily defect—a club-foot, a wooden leg, a red nose; or the character in question was made to repeat some such phrase as "That's capital," "Barkis is willin' ", or the like. . . .

This analysis of characterisation remains a central text for the study, not only of the later romantic drama, but also of the naturalist drama. Strindberg, however, sees the function of the naturalist author differently:

I do not believe in simple characters on the stage. And the summary judgments on men given by authors: this man is stupid, this one brutal, this one jealous, etc., should be challenged by naturalists, who know the richness of the soul-complex, and recognise that "vice" has a reverse side very much like virtue. . . .

(The "richness of the soul-complex" is certainly the serious author's concern, but he may frequently be able to express it through just such summary judgments as Strindberg rejects, since his concern is the general structure of experience rather than portraiture.)

. . . My souls (characters) are conglomerations from past and present stages of civilisation; they are excerpts from books and newspapers, scraps of humanity, pieces torn from festive garments which have become rags—just as the soul itself is a piece of patchwork. Besides this, I have provided a little evolutionary history in making the weaker repeat phrases stolen from the stronger, and in making my souls borrow "ideas"—suggestions as they are called—from one another.

In so far as this method of characterisation is concerned, Strindberg's theory was at this time in advance of his practice. Julie and Jean are not "characters", it is true; one could define them in Strindberg's terminology as "souls", as "elemental." Julie is the aristocratic girl, fixed in the conscience of inherited debt, consumed by romantic ideals of honour, and in practice a predatory "half-woman." Jean, the valet, by contrast, is "on the up-grade"; "sexually, he is the aristocrat"; he is adaptable, has initiative, and hence will survive. When they meet, when they clash sexually, it is Julie who goes to pieces. Their love-act has no meaning:

Love, I think, is like the hyacinth, which must strike root in the dark *before* it can produce a vigorous flower. In my play, it shoots up, blossoms, and runs to seed, all at the same time, and that is why the plant dies quickly.

The clash of Julie and Jean is, then, a convention to express a fact which Strindberg has perceived in relationship. And although the relationship is specific, it is hardly personal. The "drama is enacted by symbolic creatures formed out of human consciousness." But Strindberg's definition of his method of characterisation ("my souls . . ." (above)) hardly seems relevant to his practice in this play, although it is certainly relevant to his later, expressionist, pieces. It is true that Jean, as the stronger, imposes his ideas on Julie, the weaker, but this is rather the specific situation than an instance of the general method of the play's development.

Finally, as to the dialogue: I have rather broken with tradition in not making my characters catechists who sit asking foolish questions in order to elicit a smart reply. I have avoided the mathematically symmetrical construction of French dialogue and let people's brains work irregularly, as they do in actual life, where no topic of conversation is drained to the dregs, but one brain receives haphazard from the other a cog to engage with. Consequently my dialogue too wanders about, providing itself in the earlier scenes with material which is afterwards worked up, admitted, repeated, developed and built up, like the theme in a musical composition.

Strindberg was right, of course, as Ibsen was right, in rejecting the vapid artifice of French romantic dialogue. But what he proposes to substitute is not a controlled, literary medium, but, at first sight, simply haphazard conversation. In his last phrase, it is true, the idea of a verbal theme—what came later to be called "contrapuntal dialogue"—is stated, and Strindberg's use of this method is important in such pieces as ***Dreamplay*** and ***Ghost Sonata.*** But it would be extravagant to see in the dialogue of ***Lady Julie*** an example of this method. In such passages as the following, phrases that have been used earlier are repeated, but only as a means of argument—the one casting the other's words back in a reversal of a previous situation:

JULIE. So that's the sort of man you are. . . .

JEAN. I had to invent something: it's always the pretty speeches that capture women.

JULIE. Scoundrel!

JEAN. Filth!

JULIE. And now you've seen the hawk's back.

JEAN. Not exactly its back.

JULIE. And I was to be the first branch. . . .

JEAN. But the branch was rotten.

JULIE. I was to be the signboard at the hotel. . . .

JEAN. And I the hotel.

JULIE. Sit inside your office, lure your customers, falsify their accounts.

JEAN. *I* was to do that.

JULIE. To think that a human soul could be so steeped in filth.

JEAN. Wash it then.

JULIE. You lackey, you menial, stand up when I'm speaking.

JEAN. You mistress of a menial, you lackey's wench, hold your jaw and get out. Are you the one to come and lecture me on my coarseness? No one in my class has ever behaved so coarsely as you have tonight. Do you think any servant girl attacks a man as you did? I have only seen that sort of thing among beasts and fallen women.

In this passage, at least, we are back to something very like the "catechism."

The prose of **Lady Julie** is effective, not so much by pattern, as by force. It has a vigour wholly consonant with the dramatic speed of the action: (although this vigour is hardly conveyed by the orthodox English translations; the idea that the prose could be better translated in "American" than English is probably just). From the first words:

JEAN. Lady Julie's mad again tonight, absolutely mad.

to the closing scene where Jean sends Julie out to suicide:

JULIE. I am asleep already—the whole room seems like smoke. And you look like an iron stove, a stove like a man in black clothes with a tall hat. And your eyes are like coals when the fire is going out, and your face is a white patch like the ashes . . . it's so warm and lovely . . . and so light—and so peaceful.

JEAN. (*putting the razor in her hands*) There is the broom. Now go, while it's light—out to the barn—and . . . It's horrible. But there's no other possible end to it. Go!

the language has the explicit, calculated violence of the whole dramatic method; but it is always the rush of passionate statement rather than the patterned verbal theme which Strindberg, in the *Preface*, seems to have in mind.

The whole virtue of **Lady Julie** is its speed. In this, Strindberg's new formal devices play their part:

In order to provide resting-points for the public and the performers without allowing the public to escape from the illusion, I have introduced three art-forms, all of which come under the heading of dramatic art, namely, the monologue, the mime, and the ballet: all of which, too, in their original forms, belonged to ancient tragedy, the monody now becoming the monologue, and the chorus the ballet.

Most impressive is the "ballet" where the peasants sing a Midsummer Eve drinking song while Jean and Julie are alone in the bedroom. Kristin's mime is less successful; it has the air of simple defiance of normal theatrical practice, and serves little dramatic purpose. Strindberg, it seems, felt the need of formal devices of this kind, but felt it theoretically rather than practically. It is interesting to note that he considers the possibility of the actor working independently, being encouraged to improvise in these interludes. But in **Lady Julie,** where so much energy is concen-

trated for a clear single effect, it seems vital that a singular control should be retained. Only a dramatist writing for a specific company would be wise to allow this improvisation, of which Strindberg's description "creative art" could be misleading.

Strindberg suggests other experiments in performance:

As regards the scenery I have borrowed from impressionist painting its symmetry and its abruptness. . . .

(backcloth and furniture are set diagonally);

Another perhaps not unnecessary novelty would be the abolition of footlights . . . Would not the use of sufficiently powerful sidelights . . . afford the actor this new resource—the strengthening of his powers of mimicry by means of the face's chief asset—the play of the eyes?

He would like to

turn the stage into a room with the fourth wall missing

but thinks this might be premature.

Strindberg's *Preface*—and the partial exemplification of its theories in **Lady Julie**—are very interesting evidence of the disturbance produced in the mind of an original and serious dramatist by the state of the stage of his day—where dramatic conventions had virtually disappeared under the weight of theatrical conventions, and where conventionalism, as a result, conveyed only the idea of false artifice. If parts of the *Preface* now fall a little coldly on our ears, it is because we have seen "experimental drama" come to mean no more than theatrical experiment, and are as far as ever from significant *dramatic* conventions. But the *Preface* retains a genuine interest, in spite of its having become, consciously or unconsciously, a major document of the "experimental theatre." Perhaps at this point it will suffice to quote Strindberg's own judgment (in *An Open Letter to the Intimate Theatre*—1909):

As the Intimate Theatre counts its inception from the successful performance of **Lady Julie** in 1906, it was quite natural that the young director should feel the influence of the Preface, which recommended a search for actuality. But that was twenty years ago, and although I do not feel the need of attacking myself in this connection, I cannot but regard all that pottering with stage properties as useless.

This comment should be everywhere reprinted with the *Preface.* (pp. 104-09)

> *Raymond Williams, "August Strindberg," in his* Drama: From Ibsen to Eliot, Chatto & Windus, 1952, pp. 98-125.

Harold Clurman   (essay date 1956)

[*Highly regarded as a stage director and drama critic, Clurman was an important contributor to the development of the modern American theater. In 1931, with Lee Strasberg and Cheryl Crawford, he founded the Innovative Group Theatre, which served as a forum for the works of budding playwrights, including Clifford Odets, William Saroyan, and Elia Kazan, and as an experimental workshop for actors. In the following excerpt, Clurman views* Miss Julie *as an embodiment of Strindberg's inner conflicts.*]

Strindberg's **Miss Julie** is not an easy play to understand, to stage or to write about. . . . [It] is a landmark in European drama and a work of undeniable power and superb craftsmanship . . . . (p. 127)

The difficulty and fascination of the play reside in a complexity of which the author was thoroughly aware, a complexity arising from the contradictory drives and preoccupations within the dramatist himself—a man of genius in whom there raged, without ultimate resolution—all the psychological, social, intellectual battles of the late nineteenth century. Strindberg was an ardent romantic poisoned by the prick of rationalism, a traditionalist whose rebellious mind could not abide the answers tradition gave, a misogynist who mistrusted men, a revolutionist with autocratic impulses, a man of many marriages who was possibly homosexual. His plays are thus dense with explosive material and not readily assimilable. The realist Strindberg wrote the first and most enduring expressionistic plays; this sick man had the energy and creative force to produce more than fifty plays, sixteen novels, seven autobiographies and nine other works—and he is still a stranger to us.

In **Miss Julie** the web of complexity is drawn from two separate strands: the deep need of the young countess—whose mother, a rabid feminist, taught her daughter contempt of men—to satisfy her sexual cravings which she experiences as a form of abasement, and the conflict of classes in a still strongly stratified society. In the play, the aristocracy is corrupt and the cowed working class is stricken with a venomous sense of inferiority. The girl wants to be loved but also wants to be dominated. She begs to be mastered, but she finds reason in her man's vulgarity and base origin to revile him. She no longer has the support of any religious faith, but she desperately needs something to believe in, to cling to. She must destroy herself, but her valet lover, with his craven fear and envy of his master, will undoubtedly escape, and by virtue of materialistic shrewdness will find prosperity.

The play is no mere woman-hating melodrama. Strindberg embodies himself more in Miss Julie than in her lover. There is no question here of "sympathy." The play is a dramatization of the author's inner life in which his turbulent subjective emotions are objectified by his ferociously realistic mind in acutely observed figures from the society of his day. The play—written in 1888—is psychoanalysis and sociology—lucid nightmare and impassioned treatise. It is a horrendous masterpiece. (pp. 127-28)

Harold Clurman, in a review of "Miss Julie", in his Lies Like Truth: Theatre Reviews and Essays, *The Macmillan Company, 1958, pp. 127-29.*

F. L. Lucas   (essay date 1962)

[*Lucas was an English man of letters who is best known as the editor of John Webster's works. Noted for what one critic termed the "eighteenth-century" qualities of the "bluff common sense and man-of-the-world manners" in his criticism, Lucas was antagonistic to modernist trends in poetry and criticism. In the following essay, Lucas praises* Miss Julie's *structure, while judging the play as a whole to be melodramatic and mediocre when compared with the work of Ibsen.*]

[**Miss Julie**] seems to me better than **The Father.** For hero and heroine, it has a lout and a trollop, instead of a half-wit and a hag. Not much more attractive; but, at least, rather more interesting; and considerably more credible.

A Count's daughter seduces a valet; then, after eating the forbidden fruit, this terrified daughter of Eve cuts her own throat with a razor obligingly provided by the valet—a proletarian tough who remains at least less decadent than the degenerate aristocrat.

Strindberg said he had heard of a similar case where a Swedish girl, nobly born, seduced a groom; though *she* ended, not like Miss Julie as a suicide, but, less romantically, as a barmaid.

The play's plot is not pretty; but, for Strindberg, it reflected some of his own pleasure at having carried off, son of a waitress though he was, the aristocratic Siri von Essen, Baroness Wrangel. And if, in some moods, he came to believe that he had been not so much her seducer as himself the seduced, that only heightened the likeness.

Some, indeed, may feel that, monstrous though Strindberg was in impaling past friends and lovers on his poisoned pen, the photograph of Siri at the date of her marriage to him does suggest, with all its charm, a certain decadence not inappropriate to the part of Julie; which she herself later performed in Copenhagen. Fairness must add, however, that there seems no evidence for believing Strindberg's frenzied charges against her. Here the witness of their daughter, Karin Smirnoff, appears vastly more reliable than his.

But though this harsh picture in **Miss Julie** of the highborn girl and the squire of low degree may have owed something—if far less than **The Father**—to Strindberg's own relations with Siri, the play appears to have been based more immediately on one of the strangest episodes in his strange life, which Strindberg was actually living through at the time of writing.

In 1887 the exiled writer, with his three children, and the unhappy wife he could neither live with nor without, removed his hunted and haunted existence to Denmark. The winter of 1887-8 he spent, tormented by poverty and neurosis, at Klampenborg and Taarbaek, a few miles north of Copenhagen. In the spring of 1888, to economize, he took rooms in the eccentric home of a lady of family, the last of her race, at Skovlyst near Holte, a few miles north-west of the capital.

This lady, Fröken Frankenau, was a grotesque, yet tragic figure. Daughter and only surviving child of a so-called Count and Countess Frankenau, she had been left by her parents' death a lonely and impoverished spinster. Now forty, the unhappy woman was grown half-crazed. Denied human affection, she had turned to pet animals. Her house became a smelly ruin, a chaos of rubbish and lumber, a kind of mad menagerie. Staring neighbours would watch the poor eccentric rambling about her ramshackle home and carrying in her arms now a pet duckling, now a lamb, now a senile cock, eighteen years old, half-blind and half-bald, which she used to wash with sand and scrubbing-brush, and to call 'my old angel-boy'.

Now Fröken Frankenau's father, eleven years after her birth, had begotten a natural son on some girl whom, like Ibsen's Old Werle, he quickly married off to a poor husband. When Fröken Frankenau was thirty-six, she persuaded this half-brother of twenty-five to share her loneliness at Skovlyst, and run her ruined estate. But, to save their dead father's good name, the pair concealed their real relationship. Loyal; but not very prudent. For naturally the neighbourhood assumed them to be lovers. And so did their new tenant, Strindberg. Hence in July 1888, imagining himself to be living under the roof of a Count's daughter who had given herself to her bailiff, he wrote *Miss Julie,* with its theme of a Count's daughter who gives herself to a servant.

That Strindberg had wholly misunderstood the real situation matters little now. He had found a plot for his play. But, for him, the sequel proved more serious.

To tell the whole fantastic and fascinating story would here take too long. Briefly, what happened was this. At first Strindberg made friends with the bailiff, Ludvig Hansen; then, as often with Strindberg, this friendship changed to vehement enmity. Partly because there was in the house a half-sister of the bailiff's, in her teens, named Martha Magdalena, to whom Strindberg in a rash moment once allowed himself to make love. The result was, according to Strindberg's version, that the bailiff first tried to blackmail him for hush-money; then made life intolerable for the whole Strindberg family—he burst into their rooms, he filled the house with uproar, he fired pistols outside in the small hours of the night. So Strindberg was forced to leave Skovlyst. But he revenged himself by telling an acquaintance in the Danish police that he suspected Hansen of being at the bottom of certain mysterious burglaries in the neighbourhood. A posse of policemen took the road for Skovlyst. Hansen was arrested and tried. But, to his horror, Strindberg now found himself summoned to give evidence in court. Panic-stricken, he fled to Berlin; and was only with difficulty brought back by a friend to Copenhagen. Then Martha Magdalena, furious on her half-brother's account, testified in court that Strindberg had seduced her. Naturally the Copenhagen press rang with delighted scandal and *Schadenfreude* over this amorous escapade of the famous misogynist. Finally, for lack of evidence, Hansen was acquitted. And Strindberg, returning to Sweden, took the shabby revenge of writing and publishing a long short-story, *Tschandala* (1889), in which a thinly disguised Hansen was caricatured as the villain. Though Strindberg transferred the time and place of his tale to seventeenth-century Sweden, the world was not de-ceived by this thin disguise; and for the rest of his long life poor Hansen never lived it down.

The real end of this tragi-comedy was perhaps more truly tragic than anything imagined in *Miss Julie.* Poor Fröken Frankenau was finally compelled by poverty to sell the home of her fathers. But her half-brother, Hansen, instead of behaving like the scoundrel depicted by Strindberg, devotedly supported her till she died; then gave her an epitaph as 'the last of a noble race'. Hansen himself survived into a fretful and forgetful old age, much astonished to find himself sought out and eagerly interrogated by Strindberg-scholars.

As so often, real life has here produced a piece of fiction and drama odder and more amazing than most works of imagination. But, fond though Strindberg was of basing his own fictions on facts, that practice remains artistically dangerous. For in history or biography we can be fascinated by fantastic improbabilities. Knowing them true, we are more gripped, the more improbable they are. But with most fiction and drama the case is exactly opposite. We take these to be fictitious; yet we wish, for the nonce, to believe them true; therefore, as a rule, they must *seem* convincingly probable. Improbability, instead of a gain, now tends to become a serious loss. For it provokes us to cry: 'Pshaw! How far-fetched!' In fine, truth is so often stranger than fiction just because good fiction can so seldom afford to be as strange as truth.

Now the plot of *Miss Julie* remains perfectly possible. None the less I find it hard wholly to suspend disbelief. This play seems, indeed, more impressive than *The Father,* which I find a tragic farce; yet there are details in *Miss Julie* where the illusion wears thin.

The time is Midsummer Eve, when the Swedish countryside could wake again the spirit of pagan revelry, and ghosts come back to walk the earth. The scene is a Count's kitchen, where stand symbolically visible its lowly pans and kettles; while in the background, no less symbolically, a glass door reveals the Count's patrician garden with its towering poplars and blooming syringas, fountain, and its statue of the God of Love.

Kristin, an odious kitchen-wench of thirty-five, is busy cooking. To her enters Jean, the valet, a man of thirty, carrying his master's riding-boots. Tonight the Count is away from home. But, even in absence, his menacing shadow will fall, from first to last, darkly across the play.

Miss Julie, says Jean, is crazy *again* tonight. She has been waltzing like a madwoman, first with the gamekeeper, then with Jean himself. Drily Kristin replies that Miss Julie has grown only crazier since, fourteen days ago, her engagement was broken.

For Miss Julie, it appears, had tried making her betrothed jump over her whip, like a circus-dog, and then slashing at him. The third time she did this, the young man, one is glad to hear, snatched her whip, snapped it in two, and walked off.

Evidently this young lady is an arrogant sadist; and, it will soon appear, a masochist as well.

While the valet appreciatively sips his master's claret, the cookmaid brews some emetic mess for Miss Julie's bitch, Diana. Diana, despite her austere name, has recently disgraced herself by flirting with mongrels—more symbolism of her mistress's coming fall; but perhaps a little too obvious. It seems clumsy beside Ibsen.

Enter Julie, to ask if her dog's mess is ready. Kristin mutely indicates to her the presence of the valet. And the valet grows impudent.

> JEAN. (*gallantly*).   Have the ladies secrets between them?
> JULIE. (*flipping her handkerchief in his face*).   That's inquisitive!

As Jean had remarked shortly before, whenever the upper classes try unbending towards common people, they tend only to grow common themselves.

Miss Julie invites Jean to dance. But he hesitates; because, first, he has promised the dance to his betrothed, Kristin; secondly, people might talk. But Julie brushes his objections aside. They go out, and there is heard from the garden the fiddling of a Scottish reel, while Kristin busies herself with the kitchen dishes.

Jean returns alone, and puts an ingratiating arm round Kristin; but is pursued back into the kitchen by Miss Julie, who little relishes the sight of this caress. However, she proceeds to praise Jean's dancing; and to praise his appearance when he has changed his coat—'Très gentil, Monsieur Jean!' To her surprise, he caps her French (for once upon a time he served in a Lucerne hotel)—'Vous voulez plaisanter, Madame!' And now Kristin falls asleep in her chair—perhaps a trifle too conveniently.

> JULIE. She'll make a pleasant wife, she will! Perhaps she snores, too.
> JEAN. No, she does *not*. But she talks in her sleep.
> JULIE. How do *you* know she talks in her sleep?
> JEAN. I've heard her.
>
> (*Pause.*)

Then Julie makes him sit down; makes him drink beer (he had much preferred his master's stolen wine); makes him toast her, and kiss her shoe. At this point Jean begins to grow alarmed; but also to grow tempted.

Kristin shuffles drowsily out. And Jean warns his lady against demeaning herself. In vain. If he thinks her queer, she says, for that matter everything in life is queer.

> I have a dream that comes back to me now and again. I remember it *now*. I am sitting perched up on a column, and I can't see how to get down. I feel dizzy when I look down; but down I *must* get; yet I haven't the courage to throw myself down. I can't keep my hold, and I long to be able to fall!; but I can't. Yet I can find no rest till I *have* got down—down to the ground! And when I *have* got down to the ground, I want to get under the earth. . . . Have you ever been through anything like that?

This dream-symbolism is again obvious—still more obvious, in certain of its details, since Freud.

At once Jean caps Julie's dream with a dream of his own—a little too neatly its opposite. *His* dream is of wanting to climb a tree with its top in sunlight, and a nest of golden eggs. Yet he can never contrive to reach the bottom branch—could he but do *that*, the rest would be easy.

All this becomes curiously like the seduction-dreams told by Vittoria to Brachiano, or exchanged by Francesco and Zanche the Moor, in Webster's *White Devil;* just as Miss Julie's wooing of her servant may recall the Duchess of Malfi's wooing of her steward. But such likenesses only accentuate the contrast. Whatever Webster's crudities and horrors, his remains a more sinister and imaginative power.

Julie invites her valet out into the park. But, as they go to the door, with a coquetry like the Widow Wadman's in Sterne, Jean pretends to have a speck in his eye. Julie removes it, or pretends to; then taunts him as a prudish Joseph; then boxes his ears when he embraces her. He asks to be allowed, since it is now past midnight, to go away and clean his master's boots. She tells him to put the boots away.

Then Jean relates how, as a poor boy housed in a hovel with seven brothers and sisters, plus a pig, he used to be employed to weed the Count's grounds. There one day he saw the girlish Julie in her pink dress and white slippers; and hid himself under a weedheap. After that, in his mad passion for her, he tried to drown himself in the mill-pool; and slipped in to see her at church; and again tried to kill himself by sleeping on elder-blossom.

> JULIE. You're a charming story-teller, you know! Have you been to school?
> JEAN. A little. But I've read lots of novels, and been to the theatre. Besides, I've listened to fine folk talking, and it's from them I've learnt most.

Julie now tells him to get the boat and row her out on the lake, to watch the sunrise. In reply, he advises her to go to bed. But now approaches a chorus of singing peasants. Afraid of being found together, the two take refuge in Jean's room; and, entering the kitchen, the farm-hands dance and sing a song with mocking innuendoes aimed at Julie and Jean.

When at last these revellers have departed, the guilty pair reappear—like Adam and Eve after tasting the forbidden fruit.

Now with social misalliances the danger is that, though the masses may be morally as good as their so-called betters, yet aesthetically they often make their so-called betters wince. That is one of the risks inevitably incurred by young ladies who, whether to please themselves, or to annoy their parents or husbands, elope with the baker or the gamekeeper. In the long run the risks of such romance are high. And marriage can come to seem a very long run. To the question why married men live longer, a cynic replied: 'They don't; it only seems so.' But it can certainly seem so.

No doubt Jean, though brute, lout, and cad, is less decadent than Fröken Julie. In the Darwinian struggle for survival, it will be he that survives. None the less he now shows himself, more clearly than ever, to be crude, vulgar, ugly-mannered—a churl. And Julie is quickly made to feel it. She craves desperately for his love—the only romantic justification for her fall. But the sated Jean becomes callously practical.

They must run for it. For the scandal will be frightful. She agrees. He suggests Switzerland, or the Italian Lakes—they can start a hotel.

> JEAN.   That's a life, take my word for it. All the
> time new faces, new languages. Not a
> minute left for brooding or nerves. No
> search for a job—the work comes of it-
> self. Night and day, bells ringing, trains
> whistling, buses coming and going. And
> all the while the gold pieces keep rolling
> into the office. *That's* a life.
> JULIE.   Yes, that's living. And what about *me*?
> JEAN.   Mistress of the house—the ornament of
> the whole business! With *your* looks—
> and *your* manners—oh, a sure thing.
> Kolossal! You just sit like a queen in the
> hotel-office, and set your slaves moving
> with a touch on the electric bell. The
> guests'll pass in review before your
> throne. You can't think how people
> dither when they get their bills handed
> them. I'll salt the charges, and you'll
> sugar them with your sweetest smile.
> Ah—let's be off!

Practical man that he is, Jean even whips out an international time-table—Malmö, 6.30 p.m.—Hamburg, 8.40 a.m.—Frankfort—the St Gothard—Como. (But could a Swedish lackey really conjure continental time-tables so pat from his pocket—as if he were a Cook's agent on the platform at Bâle?)

Still higher soars Jean's imagination—money—a decoration bought in Rumania?—why, he might end as a Count himself!

But Julie wants, not dreams of squalid eminence hereafter, but love, love, love—and *now*!

> JEAN.   I'll say it a thousand times—later on!
> Only not here! Above all, no senti-
> ment!—or it's all up with us.

Then he lights a cigar.

> JEAN.   Sit down, now! *I*'ll sit here, and let's talk
> as if nothing had happened.
> JULIE.   My God! Have you *no* feelings?
> JEAN.   Oh yes, there's not a fellow so full of
> feeling as me. But *I* can keep a hold on
> myself.
> JULIE.   A moment ago you could kiss my shoe!
> And now!
> JEAN.   (*harshly*). Yes, that was *then*. *Now* we've
> other things to think of.
> JULIE.   Don't speak harshly to me!
> JEAN.   No—but sensibly. One folly's been
> done. Don't do any more. The Count
> may be here any moment. . . .

But money? Jean replies that money is *her* affair. But she has none. Yet she dare not wait to face her father. She

weeps. Jean comforts her with some of his wine. Suddenly realizing that it is pilfered, she cries in revulsion—'Thief!' *Now* yawns clear before her the abyss of her own degradation. 'A servant,' she sneers, 'is always a servant!' But Jean's retort is only too easy—'And a whore's a whore!'

Their recriminations grow hideous; then Jean softens again and tries to kiss her. But she shrinks as from a rat.

At this point, however, the action takes, for me, a strangely unrealistic turn. Though at any moment the Count may arrive, and therefore every instant is precious, Julie plunges into a long story of her past, on the pathetic plea that, perhaps, if they learn to know each other better . . . ? This digression should surely have come sooner, if at all.

There follows the usual Strindberg story of woman's wickedness. Her mother, Julie explains, was a feminist! She denounced marriage—yet married the Count, her social superior. She did not want a child; but, when Julie was born, brought her up as a hoyden—the victim of stupid dreams about sex-equality. (Echoes of *The Father* grow clear.) Then this demon-Countess ruined her husband, the Count, by setting fire to the house, after carefully intercepting the fire-insurance premium he had just duly paid. Thus she got him into the clutches of her lover, a rich brick-manufacturer; who then rebuilt the house.

Consequently Julie herself has grown up to loathe *all* men. Now she would like to shoot Jean. However, let them get away—enjoy a few days of delirium—then die.

But Jean has not the least desire to die. Already he is bored to death with *her*. Brutally he flings on the table a silver coin to pay her services. After all, he sneers, what does her nobility amount to? All sprung from a miller long ago, whose wife became a king's mistress!

By now Julie is paralysed and broken. Jean takes command. Let her go—dress—and get hold of some money. She goes; and Kristin enters, dressed for church. Almost at once she guesses all. She will not stay in such a house of iniquity. She will leave. Then she and Jean can marry.

The brief Swedish midsummer-night is over. (A bleak contrast to Shakespeare's!) Through the window glints the sun of dawn, like the fatal sun that rises at the end of Ibsen's *Ghosts*. Miss Julie returns, in travelling-dress, with her beloved pet bird in a cage. She has stolen her father's money. But Jean *must* come with her. She cannot face that long midsummer-day's journey among strange crowds, alone. Jean consents. But he will have no baggage; and no pets. With a meat-chopper he decapitates the wretched bird. Julie shrieks with horror; then blazes out into a blood-lust of hatred. 'Kill *me* too! Kill *me*! You that can kill an innocent creature, without one qualm! Oh, I hate and loathe you! There's blood between us. I curse the hour I saw you. I curse the hour I quickened in my mother's body.'

> JEAN.   What's the good of cursing? Go!
> JULIE.   No, I *won't* go yet. . . . You think I
> can't look on blood! You think I'm so
> weak—ah, I should like to look at *your*
> blood, at *your* brain on a chopping-

> block—I'd like to see your whole sex
> swim in a sea of blood like that . . . I
> think I could drink from your skull—
> yes, I'd like to bathe both feet inside
> your ribs, and eat your heart baked
> whole.

Strange that critics have lavished luxuriant praises on a play that sinks to melodrama so crude. Further, this slaughtered bird seems quite wantonly dragged in, simply to give occasion for this frenzied rant. What need to butcher the wretched thing, when it would have been so simple to leave it behind?

One can, of course, argue that this lout craves some victim on which to vent his blood-thirsty exasperation. One can plead that the bird is a symbol both of Julie herself, and of sex. One may compare that passage in Strindberg's novel **Black Banners** (1904) where a young reveller coming home at dawn and greeted by the song of *his* pet-bird, whips out a revolver and shoots it; realizing only long afterwards that it symbolized his own evil conscience, which he craved to kill. Possibly enough, Julie's siskin is descended from that other dramatic fowl, Ibsen's wild duck. But, if so, the comparison seems to kill the siskin more completely even than Jean's chopper.

The English reader may also recall Heathcliff in *Wuthering Heights,* hanging his dear Isabella's little dog—'and when she pleaded for it, the first words I uttered were a wish that I had the hanging of every being belonging to her except one: possibly she took that exception for herself'. But, though *Wuthering Heights* is in parts a wonderful book, this seems to me one of those places where, like some passages in Elizabethan tragedy, it sinks to the depths of a penny dreadful.

Kristin re-enters, prayer-book in hand, on her way to church. Desperately Julie appeals to her—let her come abroad with them, and run the hotel-kitchen.

Here again it is hard not to be chilled into scepticism. Why should Julie wish for the company of this odious wench, who is also her rival? And what earthly sense in trying to tempt Kristin with prospects of seeing Munich—its Raphaels and Rubenses? Much this greasy baggage would care for Raphael or Rubens! As well lure a pig with eau-de-cologne.

Kristin's reply, of course, is cold contempt. With great relish she patters off pious phrases about the rich having less hope of entering heaven than the camel of passing the needle's eye; then she goes out to warn the stable-boy not to let the fugitives have horses.

In her final despair, Julie's eye falls on the razor with which Jean has just shaved. Suddenly the Count's bell rings. (One recalls the far more poetic knocking at the gate in *Macbeth.*) Automatically Jean relapses into the complete flunkey, and answers obsequiously through the speaking-tube. Julie begs him to hypnotize her into doing her ghastly deed. He hands her the razor; whispers in her ear; and she goes out to the hayloft, blade in hand. Curtain.

It may still be doubted whether this decadent neurotic would really have resolved on suicide. What, in fact, was to prevent Miss Julie from simply absconding like the noble young lady in Strindberg's source-story, who ended as a barmaid? One may suspect poor Julie of being one of those numerous characters in fiction and drama who kill themselves mainly for the author's convenience. Very obliging. But readers or audiences do not feel, as a rule, much gratitude.

None the less, whether one likes or loathes **Miss Julie,** the historic fact remains that it became a landmark in naturalistic drama; as Strindberg from the first was confident it would. *'Ceci datera,'* he told his publisher; 'it will mark an epoch.' It did.

'It has already,' wrote Lamm (perhaps Strindberg's best critic) in 1924, 'long outlived the naturalist plays of Zola, Henri Becque, and Hauptmann; and it surely will outlive those of Galsworthy and Chekhov.' One wonders. Particularly so far as Chekhov is concerned.

Miss Julie was first performed in Copenhagen in 1889, with Strindberg's wife Siri as the heroine. Unfortunately Strindberg became so jealous of the young actor playing Jean, that he threatened Siri with his revolver. 'Shoot!' said she. 'No,' he retorted, 'you are not worth powder.' And, rather feebly, walked away.

In 1893, at Antoine's Théâtre Libre in Paris, the piece created 'une énorme sensation'. And no play of Strindberg's has remained so widely known. It has been acted as far afield as Russia and South Africa; and even in Esperanto.

It seems to me at least a better play than **The Father.** Why?

First, plot. This is constructed with a neatness and lightness, a simplicity and unity, even more marked than in Strindberg's previous work. It is a technical feat that Ibsen himself might have admired. For the whole tragedy is compressed into a single act, a single night, a single room.

Even the opening sentence plunges effectively into the central theme. 'This evening,' says Jean, 'Miss Julie is mad *again,* completely mad.' And, apart from Miss Julie's rather ill-timed reminiscences about her past, when one would have expected her to be bolting for the station, this masterly compression is maintained to the end.

Further, this skill is quite conscious and calculated. Strindberg's native impatience and impetuosity liked to cut out inessentials, and hurry to the point. Hence few dramatists have been so fond of plays in a single act. 'In France,' he wrote to Brandes, 'I always ate five mutton-cutlets, much to the amazement of the natives. Each cutlet consisted of half a pound of bone, and two inches of fat—which I left. In the middle was a ball of back-muscle, "la noix". That I ate. "Give me 'la noix', 'the nut'," say I to the dramatist.' Considering how rare is the virtue of brevity, one may well agree. Again, the plot, though brutal, seems at least more convincing than that of **The Father.** Miss Julie is, no doubt, what Carlyle might have called (as, with less reason, he did call Browning's *The Ring and the Book*) 'an Old Bailey story'. Still Old Bailey stories frequently occur; and can possess human interest.

But it is still more in characterization that *Miss Julie* seems superior to *The Father.* Strindberg is here a careful 'naturalist'; like Zola, who had wanted to make drama more scientifically physiological and psychological, with full respect for natural laws, especially those concerned with heredity and environment.

Thus, thought Zola, instead of being squeezed into some artificial plot, dramas should more clearly mirror life. And this theory Zola had practised in dramatizing his own *Thérèse Raquin* (1873)—a picture of the retribution pursuing a husband-murdering wife and her lover. In a way this was a reversion from the Romantic drama, with its whirl of violent action, to that classic concentration on psychology found in Racine or Molière; though Racine and Molière, no doubt, would still have thought Zola and Strindberg crude barbarians.

Further, as Strindberg explained in this play's important preface, he tried to make his characters still more natural and lifelike by giving them the incoherence of real life. He wanted to supersede the over-simplified personalities and one-track types of dramatic convention. He aimed at creating, not puppets, not Jonsonian 'humours', but souls vibrating, like his own, with half a dozen contradictory impulses at once. Lady Macbeth or Coriolanus may be driven onward by a single 'ruling passion'; but Jean and Miss Julie veer like weathercocks in a whirlwind.

Similarly with causation. Glib theorists may try explaining a number of effects by a single cause; but Strindberg here prefers, like Nature, to base a single effect on a number of causes.

Thus Julie's ruin follows from (1) her mother's passionate instincts; (2) her own foolish upbringing; (3) the dangerous intoxication of Midsummer Eve.

Again, Strindberg took deliberate pains to get away from those artificially neat repartees of the conventional stage which too much resemble the rallies of a tennis-court, or the thrust and counter-thrust of a fencing-match. Instead, his characters talk with the disconnected incoherence of real life. They speak at cross-purposes, not listening to each other (Chekhov does this better); or they say things they think they think, but do not really think at all. Thus when Julie depicts to the sneering Kristin how they will live abroad, Kristin brutally retorts—'Do you really believe all that yourself?' And at once poor Julie collapses— 'I don't know. I don't believe anything any more.'

Yet one may doubt whether all this effort to heighten realism really makes much practical difference. Many stage-conventions are the height of unreality: yet they work. What more unreal than the choruses of Greek tragedy, or its stiff patches of line-for-line, Cat-and-Puss duologue? What more artificial than the Alexandrines of Racine? Yet *Antigone* or *Athalie* seems likely long to outlive *Miss Julie.* The neat repartees of Sheridan or Wilde may be too bright to be true; yet they delight us still.

A more important superiority of *Miss Julie* over *The Father* comes, I think, from its being less autobiographical, less of a misogynist tract, less of a biased self-vindication. Strindberg here becomes at least more detached, more objective, more impartial. He can view the degenerate Julie more calmly than he could the fiendish Laura, who was so close to his hated wife. He can see the brutish Jean more steadily than he could the maudlin Captain, who was too much Strindberg's own self-pitying self. And so in this later play the balance is at least held far more fairly in the duel between the sexes.

Indeed this balance seems to have been improved by a shift in Strindberg's own attitude during the actual course of composition. Originally he had viewed Miss Julie's fate quite coldly and scientifically, with the eyes of a Darwin or a Nietzsche, as a battle for existence between decadent aristocrat and robust proletarian, in which the fitter survived. And for the doomed victim he felt no pity.

His own words are definite enough. 'That my tragedy is depressing to many, is their own fault. If we become strong like the first men of the French Revolution, it must give us a completely good and happy impression to watch this clearing of the forests, whose rotten superannuated trees have stood too long in the way of others with an equal right to grow for their allotted period—just as good an impression as when one sees an incurable invalid expire.'

This sounds very jaunty and jolly. Yet not all of us are so anxious to resemble 'the first men of the French Revolution'. What decent being wants to be like Robespierre or Marat? Is it very civilized to enjoy the anguish of this wretched girl, like *tricoteuses* knitting round the guillotine? And then what a curious notion that the deathbeds of the incurable are so exhilarating! Indeed one wonders why, if the death of poor Julie was so pleasant to contemplate, Strindberg ever called his play 'a tragedy'. He seems to have forgotten the importance, particularly in tragedy, of a thing called pity.

But though, when he took pen in hand, it was often as if a devil entered into Strindberg; though he could sometimes find in ink a sort of brutal intoxication; none the less he was not always cruel; and here his own sympathies seem in the end to have shifted a good deal from Jean to Julie.

He had sided at first with Jean, the healthy boor, against Julie, the decadent aristocrat. For he was himself the son of a poor maidservant; and Siri, a patrician. But Strindberg's personality was double. He was the son, not only of a maid-servant, but also of a better-class father; and so he could sympathize not only with proletarian against aristocrat, but also, at other times, with aristocrat against proletarian. Hence his temporary cult for Nietzsche. So now Julie might be a woman; but she was also a lady. And Strindberg came, I think, to feel that a lady, however fallen, remained in some ways more sympathetic than a callous cad. Indeed, he thought at one moment of giving Julie a more spirited suicide. Snatching the razor from Jean, she cut her own throat on the stage, with the cry of scorn— 'See, you lackey, *you* don't know how to die.'

So an unusual touch of pity found its way into the play after all. And this seems to me to help a good deal towards making it better than *The Father.* With the Captain it is hard to feel any patience; with Julie, one would be hard to feel no compassion.

But, when all is said, what value should one attach to imaginative literature of this type? Plato or Tolstoy would doubtless have condemned *Miss Julie* out of hand, as sordid and immoral. Strindberg himself in later years made Harriet Bosse promise never to act Julie (as Siri once had done). One can plead, of course, that this is one side of real life; and those who wish to see life steadily and whole may wish to see this side also. A week in Wapping would, no doubt, be unlikely to leave one as buoyant, healthy, and sane, as a week in the high Alps. Still a week in Wapping might be curious and instructive. In the words of Crabbe, once himself a surgeon:

> Come, search within, nor sight nor smell regard,
> The true physician walks the foulest ward.

Such literature might be called medicinal.

It could be further argued, that so far as influence-value is concerned, *Miss Julie* is at least superior to *The Father*. *The Father* is an exposure of domineering women; *Miss Julie* is an exposure of decadent women. Now the danger of domineering women, though it can exist, became with Strindberg a grotesque obsession; but the danger of decadence remains all too real.

The crucial objection to Miss Julie seems to me not so much its subject as its treatment. In this one senses a certain hardness and brutality. In all fiction and drama the most important of all the characters remains, I believe, the author. He may be unseen; but, constantly, for those who have real feelings, he is felt. Between the lines of every epic, story, or play there looks out the author's face. It may be a shadowy face, as with Homer or Shakespeare; it may be a face more clearly revealed, as with Ibsen or Hardy; but, with all these, the face is impressively fine. Many readers, no doubt, are blind. They never glimpse those faces between the lines. But if they cannot, they will never, in my belief, make much of criticism. They had better go back to Anglo-Saxon grammar or Gothic roots.

Now the face seen here, and often elsewhere, between the lines of Strindberg seems to me forbidding—too much a demoniac among the tombs. 'A lazar-house it seemed.' He tends to make men at large appear worse than they are. That I feel to be, in any writer, a defect. To treat men as worse than they are has a tendency to make them really worse. And that is a poor service to humanity.

Therefore, whatever his genius, it seems to me a betrayal to rank Strindberg, even for a moment, on a level with Ibsen or Chekhov. Had this subject been treated by Chekhov, or Flaubert, or Hardy, I believe that the effect might have been far finer and far more moving. For they were more human.

Therefore the pleasure-value of *Miss Julie* seems to me mediocre; its influence-value, for most people, still more dubious. Critics have extolled it. But critics have often shown, I think, a like lack of measure in flattering the fellow-dramatists of Shakespeare. Many of these could write superb scenes; a few could occasionally compose impressive plays. But often their drama reminds me, in one re-

spect, of opera. For in opera the music may be superb; but, too often, the libretto is miserable. Similarly in Elizabethan plays the music of the verse can be magnificent; but the rest—plots, characters, ideas—is too frequently as poor and artificial as the average opera-libretto.

This point has been admirably put by Jusserand: 'When one has read some dozens of these pieces—muddy, macabre caricatures, combining overpraised literary gifts with crudities unparalleled, then—when all has been weighed, recollected, and judged, when one has duly recalled the indulgent appreciations of Charles Lamb and the passionate advocacies of Swinburne—one feels seized by an irresistible longing to climb up to Saint-Étienne du Mont and bear a branch of laurel to the chapel where sleeps Racine.'

Bjørnson summed up *Miss Julie* much more briefly, in one syllable—'svinsk'—'swinish'. That is perhaps oversimple. But I would far rather be Bjørnson than Strindberg.

Indeed there are moments when one may feel Miss Julie to be tragically symbolic of this twentieth century of ours which, like her, was born with high traditions from the past, and has so often, like her, surrendered itself politically and artistically to the vulgar, the cruel, and the mean. (pp. 363-81)

> *F. L. Lucas, " 'Fröken Julie' (1888)," in his* The Drama of Ibsen and Strindberg, *The Macmillan Company, 1962, pp. 363-81.*

Robert Brustein   (essay date 1962)

[*An American drama critic and the artistic director of the American Repertory Theatre Company, Brustein is well known and highly respected for his devotion to excellence in all aspects of theater production and his belief in theater's "higher purpose." As the dean of Yale University's School of Drama from 1966 to 1979, Brustein introduced many innovative dramatic techniques, often considered controversial, which gave Yale a reputation as one of the leading drama schools in the nation. Brustein's criticism, including* The Theatre of Revolt, The Culture Watch *(1975), and* Critical Moments: Reflections on Theatre and Society, 1973-1979 *(1980), is highly regarded for the way it places drama within a social context and for its prose style. In the following excerpt, Brustein argues that the characters Jean and Miss Julie incarnate Strindberg's ambivalent moral attitudes.*]

[*Miss Julie*] embodies, in abundance, those qualities which Strindberg associates exclusively with the male: discipline, control, self-sufficiency, cruelty, independence, and strength.

In the fine preface he has appended to the work— obviously composed in a mood of brashness, confidence, and high spirits—Strindberg documents his achievement, giving these male virtues their aesthetic and philosophical equivalents. For here he expounds his theory of Naturalism. Beginning by ridiculing the debased ideas found in the commercial theatre, Strindberg goes on to repudiate, as well, all drama with an ethical motive, where the spectator is induced to take sides or pass judgments. . . . *Miss Julie,* at least, is offered as a work without tendency, moralizing, or subjective prejudices: a simple scientific demonstration of the survival of the fittest. Strindberg concedes that the fall of his heroine may arouse pity, but he attributes this response to the spectator's "weakness," and looks forward to a time when, through the progress of science, audiences will be strong enough to view such things with indifference, having dispensed with those "inferior and unreliable instruments of thought called feelings." Echoes like these of Darwin and Nietzsche, Strindberg's scientific and philosophical authorities during his "male" period, resound throughout the preface, and so do echoes of Zola, Strindberg's masculine dramatic theoretician. For *Miss Julie* is undoubtedly the closest thing to a Naturalist drama that Strindberg is ever to write. The hero and heroine—as "characterless" as real people—have been provided with an elaborate social-psychological history, and are controlled by their heredity and environment; the action is loose, natural, and compact without being plotty; the dialogue has the aimlessness of real speech; and the acting style, makeup, costumes, settings, and lights have all been designed for a minimum of artificiality.

Yet, despite all these unusual concessions to the "real," *Miss Julie* is not, strictly speaking, a Naturalistic work—partly because of the ballet, mime, and musical interlude Strindberg introduces into the work in the middle, but mostly because the author is constitutionally incapable of Naturalist impartiality. [The critic adds in a footnote: "It is doubtful if such a thing as Naturalist impartiality can ever be absolute, since the need for some principle of selection ultimately invalidates the fiction of artistic detachment. Yet, even a casual comparison of *Miss Julie* with, say, any work of Chekhov's, will show how far short Strindberg falls of objectivity. Actually, Strindberg's anger against emancipated women, his attraction to aristocratic Supermen, and his revulsion to dirt are attitudes which suggest he does not really share the Naturalist temper—a temper usually democratic, egalitarian, 'advanced' on such social questions as female rights, and rather obsessed with the more sordid aspects of life."] . . . [If the play has an appearance of detachment, this is because an entirely new element has been introduced which balances Strindberg's sympathies. For if, formerly, Strindberg was mainly concerned with the sexual war between men and women, he is now examining a social conflict as well, between a servant and an aristocrat. And while he is still identifying with the male as a Hercules in combat with Omphale, he is also identifying with the female as a Don Quixote in conflict with an unscrupulous thrall. In short, Strindberg has not suspended his partialities, he has merely *divided* them. Both Jean and Julie are projections of the splits in the author's nature—the male versus the female, and the aristocrat versus the servant—and, in each case, he is defending himself against the side that he fears more.

Strindberg's split sympathies can be detected even in the preface, though in disguised form. Despite his pretense at scientific impartiality, for example, his misogyny is still perfectly clear, for he characterizes Julie as a "man-hating woman," a type that "forces itself on others, selling itself

for power, medals, recognition, diplomas, as formerly, it sold itself for money." Similarly, though he affects a Darwinian indifference to the supersession of the "old warrior nobility" by the "new nobility of nerve and brain," he admits that the aristocrat's code of honor was "a very beautiful thing," and that the new man rises in the world only through base and ignoble tactics. Strindberg's admiration for the sexual aristocracy of Jean, in fact, is qualified by his sense of the servant's inherent vulgarity: "He is polished on the outside, but coarse underneath. He wears his frock coat with elegance but gives no assurance that he keeps his body clean." Jean's lack of cleanliness is not something designed to endear him to Strindberg, who throughout his life had an intense revulsion to dirt; but it signifies that if Jean is the sexual aristocrat, he is the social slave, just as Julie is the sexual slave but the social aristocrat. In each case, Strindberg's sympathies, despite his protestations of neutrality, are enlisted firmly on the side of the aristocracy.

The dramatic design of *Miss Julie* is like two intersecting lines going in opposite directions: Jean reaches up and Julie falls down, both meeting on equal grounds only at the moment of seduction, in the arms of the great democratizer, sex. Both are motivated by strong internal (in Julie's case, almost unconscious) forces which propel them towards their fate—underscored by social-sexual images of rising and falling, cleanliness and dirt, life and death. These images inform the entire play but are unified in two contrasting poetic metaphors: the recurring dreams of Jean and Julie. In Julie's dream, she is looking down from the height of a great pillar, anxious to fall to the dirt beneath, yet aware that the fall would mean her death; in Jean's, he is lying on the ground beneath a great tree, anxious to pull himself up from the dirt to a golden nest above.

The crossover is the crux of the action: Jean seduces Julie during the Midsummer Eve festivities, and then induces her to cut her throat in fear that their impossible liaison will be discovered. Julie's descent, therefore, is a movement from spirit to flesh, motivated by her attraction to dirt and death. She unconsciously desires to degrade herself, to be soiled and trampled on, and when she falls, she ruins her entire house. Born, like Strindberg, of an aristocratic father and a common woman (her mother is associated with dirt through her fondness for the kitchen, the stables, and the cowsheds), Julie finds in her parentage the source of her problems. Her father's weakness has taught her to despise men, and the influence of her mother, an emancipated woman, has encouraged her to dominate and victimize them. Jean has seen her with her weakling fiancé, forcing him to jump over her riding crop like a trained dog; and in the torrent of abuse which pours from her after she has been seduced, her hatred of men is further underlined. On the other hand, neither her class arrogance nor her sex hatred is total. Her fiancé has filled her with egalitarian ideas, so that she tempers her aristocratic impudence with democratic condescension ("Tonight we're all just happy people at a party," she says to Jean. "There's no question of rank"). And her natural sexuality, heightened by suggestions of masochism, weakens her masculine resolve ("But when that weakness comes, oh . . . the shame!"). Like Diana, her wayward bitch, she is a thoroughbred who consorts with the local mongrels, since her unconscious impulses lead her, against her will, to roll herself in dirt.

By contrast, Jean's ascent is associated with cleanliness and life, and is a movement from the flesh to the spirit. He wishes to be proprietor of a Swiss hotel; and his highest ambition is to be a Rumanian count. Like Julie, he is trying to escape the conditioning of his childhood—a childhood in which filth, muck, and excrement played a large part. As we learn from his story of the Turkish outhouse, his strongest childhood memory is of himself on the ground yearning towards cleanliness. Having escaped from the Turkish pavilion through its sewer, he looked up at Julie in "a pink dress and a pair of white stockings" from the vantage point of weeds, thistles, and "wet dirt that stank to high heaven." At that time, he went home to wash himself all over with soap and warm water. Now he is still washing himself, in a metaphorical sense, by trying to rise above his lowly position and aping the fastidious manners of the aristocracy. For just as Julie is attracted to his class, so is he impelled towards her. He has become a lower-class snob through his association with his betters, wavering between an aristocratic affectation of French manners and tastes, and a slavish servility amidst the Count's boots.

The contrast between the two characters is further emphasized by their conflicting views of the sexual act and the concept of "honor." Despite her mother's influence, Julie believes rather strongly in Romantic love and Platonic ideals, while Jean, despite his rather pronounced prudishness, regards love merely as an honorific term for a purely animal act—as Iago would put it, as "a lust of the blood and a permission of the will." Jean, indeed, is the Elizabethan Naturalist come to life in the modern world, though, unlike the Elizabethan dramatists, Strindberg does not make the Naturalist a villain. Jean is superstitious, and pays lip service to God (a sign, Strindberg tells us, of his "slave mentality"), but, in effect, he is a complete materialist, for whom Platonic ideals have no real meaning whatsoever. Though he admires Julie's honor, he knows it is only a breath; truth, like honesty, is wholly at the service of his ambition, for he will lie, cheat, and steal to advance himself; and as for conscience, he might say, had he Richard III's eloquence, "It is a word that cowards use." It is because of his pragmatic materialism that Jean so values reputation, whereas Julie, the idealist, seems to scorn it. For like the Elizabethan Machiavel, Jean knows that it is external appearances rather than personal integrity that determines one's success in the world. Strindberg undoubtedly views this unscrupulous valet as a link in the evolution of the Superman. And though he secretly disapproves of all his values, he is willing to countenance Jean, in spite of his baseness, because of his effective masculine power.

Jean, therefore, differs from the Captain [in Strindberg's earlier play *The Father*] in his toughness, self-sufficiency, and total lack of scruples; but Strindberg has apparently decided that Iago's ruthlessness, rather than Othello's romantic gullibility, is the necessary element in achieving victory over the female. Yet, if Jean is no Othello, then Julie is no Desdemona either; and just as Julie learns that Jean is not a shoe-kissing cavalier, so Jean is disillusioned in his expectations of Julie. Jean's disenchantment is signified by his growing realization that the aristocracy is also tainted. For, in getting a close look at Julie, he sees that she, too, has "dirt on your face," and that the inaccessible golden nest is not what he had hoped:

> I can't deny that, in one way, it was good to find out that what I saw glittering above was only fool's gold . . . and that there could be dirt under the manicured nails, that the handkerchief was soiled even though it smelled of perfume. But, in another way, it hurt me to find that everything I was striving for wasn't very high above me after all, wasn't even real. It hurts me to see you sink far lower than your own cook. Hurts, like seeing the last flowers cut to pieces by the autumn rains and turned to muck.

Julie, in short, has achieved her unconscious desire. She has turned to muck, and been cut to pieces by the rain. And now there is nothing left for her but to die.

In this act of expiation, Jean serves as Julie's judge and executioner; but it is in her death that she proves her social superiority to Jean, even though she has been sexually defeated by him. In the most obvious sense, of course, her suicide signifies his victory; just as he chopped off the head of Julie's pet songbird, so he must chop off hers, lest she decapitate him (the sermon in church that morning, significantly, concerned the beheading of John the Baptist). But if Jean triumphs as a male, he is defeated as a servant, for her honorable suicide, a gesture he is incapable of, makes his survival look base. Strindberg dramatizes Jean's ignobility by his servile cringing at the sound of the Count's bell. Slobbering with uncontrollable fear, he hypnotizes Julie into going into the barn with his razor. But despite this display of will, it is Julie, not Jean, who is finally redeemed. Hitherto convinced of her own damnation because of the biblical injunction that the last shall be first and the first last, Julie discovers that she has unwittingly attained a place in paradise through her fall. For she learns that "I'm among the last. I *am* the last"—not only because she is last on the ladder of human degradation, but because she is also the last of her doomed and blighted house. As she walks resolutely to her death, and Jean shivers abjectly near the Count's boots, the doubleness of the play is clarified in the conclusion. She has remained an aristocrat and died; Jean has remained a servant and lived; and Strindberg—dramatizing for the first time his own ambiguities about nobility and baseness, spirit and matter, masculine and feminine, purity and dirt—has remained with them both to the very end. (pp. 113-19)

Robert Brustein, "August Strindberg," in his The Theatre of Revolt: An Approach to the Modern Drama, *Little, Brown and Company, 1964, pp. 85-134.*

An excerpt from The Confession of a Fool:

About this time much interest was aroused in what has been called the "woman question." The famous Norwegian male blue-stocking had written a play on the subject, and all feeble minds were obsessed by a perfect mania of finding oppressed women everywhere. I fought against those foolish notions, and consequently was dubbed "misogynist," an epithet which has clung to me all my life.

August Strindberg, in his The Confession of a Fool, *The Viking Press, 1925.*

A. Cleveland Harrison   (essay date 1970)

[In the following essay, Harrison discusses Strindberg's transcendence of strict naturalism in Miss Julie.*]*

When Emile Zola wrote *Thérèse Raquin* (1873), he used its preface to introduce a credo of naturalism that he tried unsuccessfully to illustrate in his play. Although the French novelist-turned dramatist set out to avoid old formulas and conventions in *Thérèse Raquin,* he merely succeeded in producing another melodrama, but this time one which stressed the sordid and unsavory drabness of the French lower middle class instead of the customary peccadilloes of the well-to-do bourgeoisie. Zola himself never wrote a dramatic masterpiece of any kind, nor did he create a prototype of the naturalism he sought. In time, he recognized that others must create a drama meeting the essentials of the form that he described again in 1881 in "Le Naturalisme au theatre": "I am waiting for someone to put a man of flesh and bones on the stage, taken from reality, scientifically analyzed, and described without one lie. I am waiting for someone to rid us of fictitious characters, of these symbols of virtue and vice which have no worth as human data. I am waiting for environment to determine the characters and the characters to act according to the logic of facts combined with logic of their own disposition."

August Strindberg was perhaps the most generative playwright to satisfy many of Zola's naturalistic requirements. He achieved what Zola only sensed, the compatibility of realistic devices with classical form to produce a more lifelike drama. By combining the two, he created *Miss Julie.* This ordered product of an artist transcended the haphazard slice-of-life interpretation of many Zola followers while establishing several of the mode's distinguishing characteristics.

In his polemic, Zola made specific demands for the naturalistic form. First, in contrast to the novel, plays should be characterized by conciseness and clearness through the briefer analysis of action and words. The implication of this remark is that on stage a single well-chosen word, spoken with a particular inflection and accompanied by a gesture with certain tension and direction, can together render a deeper, more vivid, concrete analysis than extended description and exposition in a novel. Secondly, Zola asked for a real and logical story to show the "double influence of characters over facts, of facts over characters."

In substance, he pleaded for playwrights to stop making neat plots with artificial situations and abstract characters and to concentrate instead on adopting characters with real traits who act as people do every day. Third, Zola required that characters, behaving as ordinary people, should be placed in a setting that duplicates a real environment and relates its multiple influences to the characters' actions. Zola's fourth demand was for dramatists to write dialogue that embodies the "natural" word choice, emotions, and tones of conversational speech appropriate to each character.

Particularly interesting, considering the form later evolved by Strindberg for *Miss Julie,* Zola discerned no contradiction between his demand for scientific method in playwriting and his partial endorsement of the classical formula represented by the three "unities." But he was not consistent in his viewpoint. Looking at popular playwrights of the period, like Augier, Dumas *fils,* and Sardou, Zola acquiesced to their rather diffuse, romantic handling of place, implying that it is false but justifiable if "one ray of truth" about life is thus disengaged. He was even more clearly in sympathy with romantic treatments of time in his overt statement that "one must cheat a little." A naturalistic, one-to-one relationship between the passage of time in a plot and the elapsed time in performance to him was obviously not necessary. Zola assumed, for instance, that a condensation of fifteen days into three hours on stage remained within the bounds of naturalism. Yet his other naturalistic requirements suggest more than the mere rattle of conventional plotting that such a compromise implies. He called for an "action of ideas"—not the artificial excitement of a sequence of nervous leaps from time to time and place to place, but a slow flow of sentiments, sensations, motives, and unfolding discoveries for both the play's characters and audience.

These aspects of Zola's dramaturgy, as Strindberg practiced them, demonstrate that Zola's intuition, about the value of combining scientific method with classical form, was more on target than his acceptance of romantic uses of time and place. Although Strindberg later called *Thérèse Raquin* "the first milestone of naturalistic drama," he was not blind to Zola's inconsistency in allowing a year to elapse between the first and second acts. More forceful than his recognition was Strindberg's request that in a production the first act be removed altogether to assure a "more unified impression." As if to prove the validity of his criticism, when he wrote his own version of Zola's brand of naturalism he concentrated a single event into one hour and a half of continuous action, in order to avoid disturbing the audience's "capacity for illusion."

Strindberg wrote *Miss Julie* in 1888. It was one of the fourteen plays he conceived during his so-called naturalistic period between 1886 and 1893. But the play's chronology is not so relevant, perhaps, as its philosophical lineage and relationships. Its immediate predecessor in 1887 was *The Father,* which only in part fit the naturalistic themes and techniques of Zola, who criticized the play for being too calculated in design. This apparent calculation led

Alrik Gustafson [in his "The Scandinavian Countries," in *A History of Modern Drama,* ed. by Barrett H. Clark and George Freedley] to conclude that, despite Strindberg's focus on then-current psychological theories, he meant *The Father* to be a nineteenth-century version of a Greek tragedy. In the realization of his aim, he found it difficult to confine himself to Zola's well-defined but restrictive naturalistic objectives. Yet, quite likely Strindberg wanted to please Zola, the influential authority of the new theatre in Europe, while avoiding what he considered the mode's limitations as art. In any event, Strindberg began *Miss Julie* in December, 1888, drawing from *The Father* the incipient motif that became the central pattern of all his so-called naturalistic plays: "The head-on, savage collision of two wills, usually those of a man and a woman, each seeking absolute mastery over the other, neither willing to yield, and with the weaker though finer being finally crushed by the stronger, less scrupulous will" [Gustafson]. Such a collision of wills forms the nexus of the action in *Miss Julie.*

Strindberg obviously based his work on readings of the physical and social scientists of the day. In Bernheim and the Nancy School of psychologists, he found a preoccupation with suggestion and hypnosis, dramatized in Julie's suicide. From Buckle, he took the notion that as an individual's circumstances and social position change, the truth to him also changes. He demonstrated some aspects of this idea in the rise of the middle-class Jean above the sinking aristocrat, Julie. From biology, he drew the idea of man as a bio-chemical entity, and revealed through Julie and Jean how physiology can be a determinant of human behavior. Finally, from Darwin he extracted the motif of natural selection and the survival of the fittest that appears in the play. Miss Julie, a decadent aristocratic girl, dies by her dated code of honor while her servant-seducer survives by natural selection.

But Strindberg's intellectual borrowings were synthesized in the characters, for Strindberg's principal concern, as advocated by Zola before him, is with human problems in a frame of reality. Miss Julie's search is a very human one; she wants someone truly to love her and through this love to find an image of herself that she can understand. Jean's ambition, also, is an eternally relevant one: how best to rise in the world to a position as nearly coincident with one's ideal as possible. Christine's aim, too, is never outdated: the servant who wants to do what she knows how to do, thus unconsciously filling her time while assuaging her conscience with decorous maxims. The psychology of these characters is both representative and individual.

To meet Zola's double demand that heredity and environment mutually reinforce each other, Strindberg slowly unfolds simultaneously the past and present lives of Julie and Jean, often motivating the disclosures through devices that are firmly grounded in the play's environment. The mid-summer celebration is fraught with conditions which could easily precipitate violent thoughts or acts. The absence of Julie's father on such an occasion holds dangerous potential. The whole complex of Julie's break-up with her fiance, her menstrual cycle, and her ever-present

search for a feminine identity through sexual love eventually cannot be denied under such circumstances.

Strindberg avoids the invented story which Zola inveighed against. The Swedish playwright, in the preface to his play, claims that he took the theme from real life after hearing it a few years before when it made a deep impression on him. E. M. Sprinchorn, a recent translator of Strindberg, insisted that the play "concentrates into ninety minutes the nine years of Strindberg's life with Siri Von Essen up to the time of the marital crisis." Whether or not the play is a revelation of his marriage, certain interesting parallels do exist between Strindberg's own childhood and that of Julie: he too felt unwanted and in the way, desired to be caressed, praised, and loved, lost his mother while still a child, lived in a cold and loveless atmosphere, and constantly sought a mother substitute. These parallels are not incidental in either Strindberg's life or revelations of Julie's character.

The atmospheric tonality of *Miss Julie* is built of sensual details, both verbal and physical. The conversation throughout the first half turns upon such things as the sadistic scene in the barn between Julie and her fiance; Jean's changing clothes while Julie is present; the question of whether or not Christine snores in her sleep; Julie's figure, her breasts, her horseback riding; the intimacies of engaged couples; and Julie's dog getting herself in a "fix" with the gatekeeper's mongrel. Equally important to the voluptuous texture are the many objects in the environment that assail the senses: flowers, beer, wine, a canary bird, a cutaway coat, boots, and scented handkerchiefs. There are acts between Julie and Jean that reinforce the overall "physicalness" of the action: Julie flips Jean with her handkerchief, and feels his biceps; Jean kneels in front of Julie and kisses her foot; later he grabs her about the waist and kisses her on the mouth, whereupon Julie slaps him. All these titillations precede the seduction as a kind of preliminary to complete sexual intimacy. Enough of Zola's requirements for naturalism have been applied to Miss Julie to demonstrate sufficiently how Strindberg fulfills the French novelist's naturalistic objectives, not only in general but in specific terms as well.

Strindberg, however, reaches beyond ordinary naturalism. The question remains as to whether *Miss Julie* is in total effect more nearly a superb example of the best in realism or whether it is sufficiently bizarre and sordid, bestial and mechanistic to represent naturalism fully. A lack of moderation in these directions doomed most naturalistic efforts to theatrical failure. Strindberg, on the other hand, shows admirable restraint in his play and cannot rightfully be accused of some of the excesses which characterize the works of others before and after *Miss Julie.* For example, his exploration of Julie's character is tame beside the murder of the unwanted husband by Therese and her lover in Zola's *Thérèse Raquin* (1873), or the preying upon a dead man's family and fortune in Becque's *The Vultures* (1882), or the illicit love, drunkenness, and murder in Tolstoy's *The Power of Darkness* (1886). Strindberg explores misery in *Miss Julie,* but not crime and perversion in the usual sense, except perhaps at the very end when Jean perpetuates his hypnotic suggestion of self-destruction. The play

Meryl Streep as Julie in a 1969 Vassar College production of Miss Julie.

would be as valid, and Julie's suicide just as likely, with this bit of mesmerism removed.

Not once does Strindberg succumb to *tranche de vie,* or the "slice-of-life" approach, with its negation of dramatic effects, lacking in excitement, suspense, and form. Yet neither does he appear to impose arbitrarily a form; instead, he discerns a form of action, as Francis Fergusson suggests of the realists in *The Idea of a Theatre.* In fact, the more obvious naturalistic surfaces of ***Miss Julie*** may obscure the art of its composition. The extreme heightening of experience that the play represents sets it apart from typical naturalism. Strindberg stressed that art is the effect not the photographic reproduction of life. He eschewed techniques aimed at achieving detailed realistic accuracy. Instead, he sought a symbolic form appropriate to the play's sexual significance—two parts: love play and aftermath. But because he was interested in ideas, his two-part form may be viewed as embodying cause and effect also. For the play is an argument that develops and elaborates the ideas he wants to advance. Symbolically and rhetorically, the fulcrum and dividing point for the two parts is the sexual act offstage. ***Miss Julie*** seems even faintly Ibsen-Shavian in that the entire second half of the play is a discussion of what occurred in the first part and how it will affect Julie's life. It may also be viewed as a kind of

reversal of the Pygmalion-Galatea legend; for in the human act of kissing Galatea (Julie), Pygmalion (Jean) destroys her. Julie has heretofore been a doll manipulated by heritage and teaching, and now she falls apart under the centrifugal tug of her real passions and the vacillation of her mind.

These patterns confirm Strindberg's obvious concern with ideas as an instructive artist; despite his analogical intent, he is not content to let the audience draw its own conclusions altogether. He takes pains to stimulate the audience's thinking about his ideas by fully revealing them discursively as well as metaphorically on stage. The characters not only act, they think, and they discuss their thoughts. Their discussion may lead some to question the probability of Julie's awareness of the sources of her disruptive urges, but the fact that Julie can see her behavior and its relation to how her mother lived and how her father educated her is not contradictory as it may seem on the surface. Human beings very often recognize what is within them and may in moments of insight trace their apparent sources; nevertheless, this insight is not a force of will of the sort that ordinarily would be necessary to interrupt behavior which, in Julie's case, is compulsive in its intensity. Through such delving "out loud," Jean and

Julie's dialogue becomes an action, an investigation, a verbal tug-of-war.

The compactness of the play is classic: one place, one uninterrupted period of ninety minutes, one lover's triangle, one organic action. In *The Weavers* (1892), another naturalistic prototype, Hauptmann uses the exact opposite development, a diffuse form. *The Weavers* has five separate and distinct locales; it takes place over several days' time; it presents a cross-section of people (the mob as protagonist); and it synthesizes fragments of arguments from every economic class represented. In its own way, *The Weavers* is as artfully designed as **Miss Julie.** *The Weavers,* however, shows us an expanding analysis of a condition in which outer event is emphasized while **Miss Julie,** by contrast, is a contracting analysis in which inner event has greater significance. *The Weavers* reflects more the theatrical conventions from which it is emerging, while **Miss Julie** is an echo of classic and neo-classic form as well as a prediction of things to come.

Miss Julie's striking resemblance to the classic Greek tragedy with its single fated action, moving unmistakably to the implied violence of Miss Julie's suicide, realizes even the purported Greek fastidiousness about showing violent acts. Julie is fighting to free herself from what must be a growing sense of the ever-narrowing tunnel of her life. The play opens *in medias res* just before Julie starts her terrifying run, immediately before she has the throat-locking realization that there may not be a shining exit hole at the end of the darkness. The action of the play is Julie's running—her hysterical, wall-pounding, flight into the *cul-de-sac* of her heredity and the maze-threading search of her environment where she finds no exit, no means, no terms, no nourishment beyond herself to extend her life. Julie wants someone truly to love her. Her suffering in the course of the play—the gradual emotional build-up to the point of seducing, being seduced, through all her asking for an answer when she finds she has been used—this seeking, finding, pleading, slipping, grasping, and finally succumbing *is* the form of the life of the play.

In the person of Julie, Strindberg realized Gorki's injunction to the naturalistic playwright about the process that should be observed in the development of characters: "The characters of the drama should act independently of the volition of the dramatist, in accordance with the law of their individual natures and social environment; they must follow the inspiration of their own destiny, and not that of any other destiny arbitrarily imposed upon them by the author. They must be driven by their own inner impulses, create the incidents and episodes . . . and direct the course of the play, being permitted to act in harmony with their own contradictory natures, interests, and passions."

Moreover, Strindberg reached beneath the realistic surface details and beyond the natural volition of characters to produce poetic qualities. The atmosphere of the Swedish Midsummer Eve is a romantic setting with local color, folk touches, dance, and music. The speeches by Julie and Jean about their pasts and hopes for the future are suggestive and metaphoric speeches. The rich suggestion emanating from "things" is not naturalistic but poetic. The count's black boots, the canary, the straight-razor, the beer and the wine—all "mean" something on more than one level. Fergusson speaks on realism's "hidden poetry, masquerading as reporting," which similarly applies to Strindberg's dialogue in **Miss Julie,** still another element which sets the play somewhat above and outside the naturalistic mode.

Miss Julie is both an essence and an anomaly of naturalistic play structure. In it, Strindberg observed the principles of naturalism, but he went beyond them by demonstrating: (1) selectivity in the choice of materials, (2) compactness in the plot structure, (3) suggestiveness in his dialogue and the demonstration of character relationships, (4) poetic symbolism in his use of properties, and (5) rhetorical soundness in the care with which he builds the case of the truth about Julie. (pp. 87-92)

A. Cleveland Harrison, " 'Miss Julie': Essence and Anomaly of Naturalism," in The Central States Speech Journal, *Vol. XXI, No. 2, Summer, 1970, pp. 87-92.*

Birgitta Steene   (essay date 1973)

[*In the following excerpt, Steene contends that* Miss Julie*'s dramatic strength is psychological rather than social.*]

It was part of Strindberg's Naturalistic ambition to construct a full-length play as a concentrated one-acter. In **Miss Julie** interludes like a mute midsummer eve's dance and a pantomime performed by the cook, Kristin, take the place of conventional intermissions. Furthermore, in his desire to maintain the illusion of a real drama taking place before the audience, Strindberg followed the Naturalistic demands for unity of time, place, and action. One also senses the impact of Naturalism in the story itself, which Strindberg was eager to emphasize as being "a case, a motif from life itself as I heard it spoken of a number of years ago, when the episode made a strong impression on me." Finally, the playwright's desire to prove, with his drama, a law of nature—in this case the survival of the fittest—was in accordance with Zola's decrees.

The concentrated plot of Strindberg's drama concerns Miss Julie, a twenty-five-year-old woman of the nobility, who flirts with her father's valet, Jean, during a midsummer eve. After seducing Julie, Jean suggests that they flee to Switzerland in order to avoid a scandal at home but later changes his mind. Vacillating between despair and hope of escape, between disgust for and dependence on Jean, Julie finally chooses suicide, but only after Jean has exerted a hypnotic influence on her.

Jean, the opportunist who was once a laborer's son but has learned to live in the style of a gentleman, is, to quote from Strindberg's famous preface to the play, a "race-builder," a man of the future, representing "the new nerve-and-brain nobility," to whom Julie must succumb. It was Strindberg's belief that the evolution he depicted in **Miss Julie** was not only inevitable but also desirable. If it depressed anyone, said Strindberg in his preface, to see the downfall of a tragic figure, it was the spectator's own fault;

instead of being sentimental about Julie he should realize that the time would come when "we shall be happy and relieved to see the national parks cleared of ancient rotting trees which have stood too long in the way of others equally entitled to a period of growth—as relieved as we are when an incurable invalid dies." A modern audience is not, however, likely to view the conflict between the hypersensitive Julie and the socially pretentious but brutal Jean with any great feelings of comfort. The reason for this is obvious: Strindberg's portrait of Julie in the play is much more sympathetic than his view of her in the preface.

The preface was written after the play, and its tone reveals a conscious attempt on Strindberg's part to disengage himself from his characters. The effort to transcend his private daemon, noticeable in the drama itself, was completed as Strindberg proceeded to view his dramatis personae as objectified products of his controlling artistic intellect. His cool analysis of Miss Julie as a creature of indeterminate sex is a case in point.

> Miss Julie is a modern character, not that the half-woman, the man-hater, has not existed always, but because now that she has been discovered she has stepped to the front and begun to make a noise. *The half-woman is a type* who thrusts herself forward, selling herself nowadays for power, decorations, distinctions, diplomas, as formerly for money. The type implies degeneration; it is not a good type and it does not endure; but it can unfortunately transmit its misery.

One might argue that because Strindberg felt compelled to develop *Miss Julie* within very limited bounds of time and place, its action is allowed to accelerate to a point where it becomes detrimental to the psychological plausibility of the drama. What Strindberg gives us in *Miss Julie* is a kind of dramatized synopsis of a relationship. Yet the concentrated swiftness with which he unravels the story of Jean and Julie has its fitting counterpart in the labile, hysterical mood of the title figure and in the brusqueness of Jean's character. It does not lead to a simplification of the dramatis personae; in that respect Strindberg remained true to his original intention of complicating the inner mechanism of the drama while simplifying its outer form. He departed from the classification in conventional drama of characters according to stereotypes, and in the spirit of French psychologist Ribot he attempted to dramatize a whole complex of human traits. As a result Jean is depicted as both servile and aggressive; Julie as both domineering and submissive.

The strength of the drama is psychological. Its social situation seems hardly relevant today, and if it is acceptable to us at all, it is because Strindberg works it into the subliminal texture of the play. The idea of social rising and falling compels Strindberg to include the exchange of dreams between Jean and Julie in the early half of the drama; Julie sees herself sitting on a high pillar, longing to fall down; Jean has a vision of lying under a high tree, wishing to climb to the top. Fortunately these dreams also function on a psychological level and reinforce the feeling that two incompatible people are driven together and that the catastrophe is almost a *fait accompli*.

Through Jean's seductions of her, Julie becomes a fallen woman, not only in the puritanical sense (which was relevant enough to Strindberg) but in a social-ethical sense as well; she loses her *noblesse oblige,* the trait that is the very foundation of life among the warrior nobility of which Julie is a relic. Julie is, in Strindberg's words, "the last of her race"; what becomes extinct with her is more than her personal family line; it is a way of life based on such concepts as pride, courage, and honor.

As a social upstart, Jean's conquest of Julie is a victory, the fulfillment of a childhood dream; as a small boy he watched Julie in a pink dress and white socks while he himself lay among the weeds and "wet dirt that stank to high heaven." Remembering Strindberg's common association of soil and manure with sexuality, Jean's memory refers not only to a dream of social egalitarianism but to a sexual fantasy as well. Now when Julie has been socially degraded and Jean has possessed her in body, the roles have been reversed; the valet sees his mistress as a flower turning to muck; and in a literal sense Julie, dressed sloppily and with a dirty face, looks as if she had been soiled and trampled on, whereas Jean retains his fastidious elegance, brushing off any speck as easily as he turns away Julie's pleadings.

Yet, the final scene of the play shifts once more the parts of the two lovers. For while Julie walks to her death holding her head high, Jean cringes in fear before the count's bell. The servant is victorious as a male, but he remains a servant. The aristocrat is defeated sexually and socially, but she dies nobly. In an early draft of the play Strindberg made this development even more clear by having Julie die on her own initiative. Pulling the razor out of Jean's hand, she said scornfully: "You see, servant, you could not die." Even in the final version of the play Julie's suicide is to be regarded—as Strindberg suggests in his preface—as "the nobleman's *harakiri,* the Japanese law of inner conscience which compels him to cut his own stomach open at the insult of another."

Strindberg claims in the preface to *Miss Julie* that he has challenged the rhetorical style and stilted dialogue of older drama: "I have avoided the symmetrical, mathematical construction of French dialogue, and let people's minds work irregularly, as they do in real life where, during a conversation, no topic is drained to the dregs, and one mind finds in another a chance cog to engage in. So too the dialogue wanders, gathering in the opening scenes material which is later picked up, worked over, repeated, expounded and developed like the theme in a musical composition."

This statement, which brings to mind Chekhov's art, could actually serve as an accurate description of a dramatic technique found much later in Strindberg's production, in *A Dreamplay* and in his chamber plays. But when applied to *Miss Julie,* it becomes only a half-truth; in this drama Strindberg's dialogue is still quite conventional even though one can see attempts at an allusive speech pattern, especially in the scene following the seduction.

But the counterpoint technique of the later dramas is hardly developed yet in *Miss Julie.* Instead Strindberg relies rather heavily on a symbolic pattern reminiscent of Ibsen's dramas—he uses objects or situations as metaphors designed to foreshadow the dramatic conflict. In the opening scene, Kristin is busy preparing a brew for Diana, Miss Julie's purebred bitch who has been consorting with a bastard dog—an all too obvious parallel to Miss Julie's own fate later on in the play. The ending is anticipated in much the same way—Julie gives Jean her delicate cage bird and, without hesitation, he breaks its neck, thus revealing both his own unfeeling nature and the role he will play in Miss Julie's final fate.

Such a calculating technique is hardly convincing in the work of a dramatist who usually aims at a more instinctive layer of our psyche. In the final analysis the technical design of *Miss Julie* seems too well made and the play rather survives in spite of it; it lives not on its Naturalistic premises or Ibsenite technique but on its emotional tempo, as always a very essential part of Strindberg's dramatic talent.

We know that Strindberg had difficulty with the ending of *Miss Julie* and that he questioned Julie's previous explanatory revelation of her past. These are precisely the passages which are set up according to Strindberg's Naturalistic conception of the human psyche; hence we must assume that the playwright sensed the incompatibility of some aspects of the contemporary literary approach to character and his own personal feeling for dramatic efficacy. (pp. 52-7)

> *Birgitta Steene, in her* The Greatest Fire: A Study of Strindberg, *Southern Illinois University Press, 1973, 178 p.*

John Ward   (essay date 1980)

[*In the following excerpt, Ward rejects Strindberg's analysis of* Miss Julie *in the preface, arguing that the play possesses a hybrid nature combining lyricism and realism.*]

While it is an historically important document as well as a superbly combative theatrical manifesto, the Preface to *Miss Julie* is not a reliable guide to the theme and content of the play. It was written after the play and in some senses is a rationalisation. Certainly it offers an interpretation which is both stimulating and coherent but it is more relevant to a discussion of Strindberg's intentions than to his achievement.

Miss Julie is Strindberg's first tragedy about a woman and his first purely *sexual* tragedy. The other plays of this period dealt with the difficulties of male-female relationships, marriage as a battlefield and the role of children but Julie is the only Strindbergian character so far who is destroyed by her sexuality. Still she is not the corrupt human being, that Lind-af-Hageby variously describes as a 'weak, neurotic, aristocratic Miss', 'the useless, unnatural, pleasure-loving hysterical woman of the leisured classes whom he detested' and 'the pretty, neurotic sexual useless woman, blue-blooded and empty-minded, destined to total extinc-

tion in the process of natural selection.' Nor, *pace* F. L. Lucas, is *Miss Julie* simply 'an exposure of a decadent woman'.

The evidence for this critical abuse of Julie's character, and the implied praise of Jean, is to be found principally in Strindberg's Preface. There he declares that Julie is 'a relic of the old warrior nobility which is now disappearing in favour of the new neurotic or intellectual nobility'. She is an aristocrat whose role and function is being superseded by the evolutionary process. She is a member of a virtually extinct class who is destroyed by the representative of a lower, more dynamic class. This was certainly Strindberg's conception but, as the play developed and he delved deeper into the characters, the moral and psychological issues became more complicated. In the Preface he was concerned to provide a purely naturalistic account of the play that would serve both as a reply to Zola's criticisms of *The Father* as insufficiently naturalistic and as a declaration of the aims of naturalism. But, in practice, his Darwinian prejudices faded before the complexity of the characters and both Julie and Jean emerge as much more than the class stereotypes described in the Preface. Julie is more sympathetic, while Jean is more contemptible.

The analysis contained in the Preface will be rejected because, as we shall see, it makes *Miss Julie* a poorer play than in fact it is. Certainly Julie and Jean are imprisoned by class bonds and their relationship is crippled by social prejudices but it is far too simplistic to conclude: 'Thus the servant, Jean, lives; but Miss Julie cannot live without honour. The slave has this advantage over the knight, that he lacks the latter's preoccupation with honour'. This theme can be found in the play but it provides neither a sufficient, nor an unambiguous, explanation of the drama as a whole. Julie, especially, is too complex to be the symbol of a class or to be a pawn in a Darwinian strategy. Jean, too, emerges most powerfully as an individualised human being rather than as a social type. The dramatic force of the play is to be found precisely at those points where it goes beyond social theory and portrays the passionate interrelationships of the characters stripped of their incredible pretensions.

In fact, in the process of composition, neither Julie nor Jean turned out to be plausibly typical of their class. She is declassé as a result of her sexuality, while he is uneasily class conscious as a result of his vague ambitions. In view of the text, it seems strange that so sensually vital a woman was ever intended to represent the last of an etiolated aristocratic line or that such an insensitive, swaggering lackey as Jean should be regarded as the successful representative of the newly emerging dominant class. To explain this we must remember that Strindberg prudishly regarded Julie's hypersensitivity and morbid sexuality as evidence of her decline, while he saw Jean's hard-headed materialistic ambition as a source of social power. The anomalies between Strindberg's declared intentions in the Preface and his much greater achievement in the play reflect the way in which the psychological conflict centering on Julie took over in his mind from his original concern with class issues.

Unlike his other protagonists of this period, Julie is not

and has not been married; this fact alone would make the play unusual. Unexpectedly, Julie is in many respects a sympathetic and certainly a pitiable woman; though this should not make us suppose she is fundamentally different from the rest of her sex when her interests are threatened. In common with Strindberg's other women, she can be cruel, as when she takes Christine by the nose and makes fun of her; superior ('I, the lady of the house, honour my servants by attending their dance'); domineering, as when she tries to force her fiancé to jump over her riding whip like a dog; and contemptuous ('Quite the little aristocrat, aren't you'). By exploiting the allegiances of her own sex, she tries to enlist Christine against Jean. Given the chance, her pride and conceit would compel her to dominate any man as she tries to dominate Jean. But in his case there are two things which prevent her from being successful; her class and her strong sexuality. The one makes marriage out of the question, the other inspires a fatal attraction. Fatal because for a woman to compete with a man outside marriage is dangerous and, for an aristocratic woman, disastrous. As Strindberg has shown us, married life is a woman's home front; there she has all the advantages. But it is not too difficult to conceive of a situation in which a man has the odds. And this is precisely what Strindberg does in *Miss Julie.*

Julie is a woman of strong sensuality who is repressed by social convention. She is essentially a modern woman in a feudal setting. There is nothing domestic or abashed about her; she possesses none of the modest 'virtues' of her time. Rather she titillates Jean unmercifully during the first part of the play. She is self-assured, self-opinionated, sensual and considers herself the equal of any man and the superior of most. Although she is likeable in many respects and sexually appealing, we must be careful not to overlook her failings or to exaggerate Jean's brutality. But equally, we must realise that the driving force of the drama is Julie's character. The play is not entitled *Jean the Valet.* Julie is the more interesting and complicated character into whom Strindberg has poured much of his own contradictory nature. Jean articulates attitudes of social resentment, ambition and humility which were, at the time, part of his creator's nature but the sexual conflict that constantly dominated Strindberg is primarily to be found in Julie not in Jean.

By making her a single woman who had not been corrupted by marriage, he was able to invest her with the gaiety and enchantment he had always sought in women. Nevertheless, Julie presents a problem. When presented with a sensual woman Strindberg's feelings of insecurity usually reasserted themselves. Yet he does not vilify Julie. He presents her with all her shortcomings but there is no edge to his voice when he portrays her. The explanation would seem to be that Julie is not directly a dramatic portrait of anyone from his own personal life. She is a projection of his personal needs and fears, of course, but in general he distanced his life from the characters of this play more than he did normally.

Julie is an aristocratic Estelle and Jean is a plebeian Bentley Drummle but she is also a nineteenth-century Connie Chatterley and he is her Mellors. In a long Rousseauesque

speech Julie tells Jean how her mother brought her up as a '*boy* of nature' so that I might stand as an example of how a woman can be as good as a man', while 'on the estate, all the men were set to perform the women's tasks and the women the men's'. To this degree she is a victim of her upbringing. Quite naturally, she wishes to join uninhibitedly in the peasants' Midsummer revelries and escape from the restrictions of her social position, so that she might 'burrow my way deep into the earth'. But she has also had passed on to her a deep hatred of men which though normally suppressed is blatantly revealed at times of stress. So she humiliates her fiancé and generalises from the example of Jean, after he has butchered the greenfinch: 'I'd like to see all your sex swimming in a lake of blood'.

Rousseau like Strindberg would blame this on her childhood education. In *Emile,* the French philosopher offers some advice which was very close to Strindberg's heart: 'Love childhood, indulge its sports, its pleasure, its delightful instincts.' In **Miss Julie** to point up the truth of Rousseau's doctrines, Strindberg has Julie's mother wilfully misinterpret them. Instead of bringing her child up in a state of nature appropriate to its sex, she provides Julie with a natural environment and then imposes an unnatural series of human relationships upon her. Rousseau warns that 'a perfect man and a perfect woman should no more be alike in mind than in face' and so 'it follows that their education must be different'. Julie's mother ignores this and instead literally puts into practice a remark that Rousseau intended to be ironical. 'Who is it that compels a girl to waste her time on foolish trifles? . . . What have men to do with the education of girls? What is there to hinder their mothers educating them as they please? . . . Well then, educate them like men.'

Thus, at one level, the tragedy of Julie is a demonstration of the truth of Rousseau's educational ideas and a dramatic realisation of his theory that the more women are like men, the less influence they will have over men, and that everything which cramps and confines nature, for example, in girls the development of grace, is in bad taste. This interpretation is confirmed by Strindberg in the Preface; the half women, the men haters 'are a poor species, for they do not last, but unfortunately they propagate their like by the wretchedness they cause; and desperate men seem unconsciously to choose their mates from among them . . . but fortunately they go under because they cannot adapt themselves to reality or because their repressed instincts break out uncontrollably'. Here Strindberg suggests that the feminist conspiracy of women, which aims at undermining human society, endeavours to gain strength and continuity from a conspiracy of mothers which hands down to daughters a desire to dominate and humiliate men, while creating in sons a need to be the victims of women.

However, Julie's position is not quite as simple as this because, as she admits, when asked if she has ever loved her father:

> Yes, enormously, but I've hated him too. I must
> have done so without realising it. But it was he
> who brought me up to despise my own sex, made
> me half woman and half man. Who is to blame

for what has happened—my father, my mother, myself? Myself? I haven't any self. I haven't a thought I didn't get from my father, not an emotion I didn't get from my mother . . .

From her father she has inherited her urge towards self-abasement and her lack of emotional control. Most of the time she is her mother's child but occasionally she is her father's weakling; from the one she derives her will, from the other her tendency to make a fool of herself over men. Julie, then, is a psychological hermaphrodite, torn between an urge to power and a need for humiliation, between passion and caution, love and hate, grossness and refinement, the masculine and the feminine: 'tenderness and contempt, ecstasy and irony . . . erotic desire and chaste modesty'. Without Julie, Jean would have remained an ambitious, resentful, common man whose life would never have touched the heights of tragedy. By contrast Julie would have been a tragic figure with any man.

From the perspective of sex, Jean is a much more straightforward person; his complexity lies in his class attitudes. He is a daydreamer who is almost completely cowed by his social environment. When he resists Julie's advances and warns her of the danger, at one point ordering her to leave him, 'For your own sake I beg you . . . if they find us together you are lost', his concern is double edged. An innate sense of what is socially, and therefore morally, proper makes him think it inconceivable that the lady of the house should make a fool of herself with a servant. But he also fears for his own skin.

> JEAN. (*frightened*) You must go away at once. I can't come with you—then we'd be finished—you must go alone—far away—anywhere.

These are the words of a desperate man who is placing responsibility on a woman because he is hamstrung by 'this damned lackey that sits in my blood'. Without Julie's encouragement he would never have had the courage to sleep with her (though once aroused he is a very passionate man), let alone the will to make her kill herself. The notion that Jean hypnotises Julie is both unconvincingly portrayed and artistically inappropriate. Nothing in the play leads up to its introduction and when Julie mentions hypnosis, she uses it as an example of the power of command. She tries to will Jean to behave like a man, like an aristocrat. To explain the suicide, it is more natural to discuss her hysteria which is apparent throughout the play. In a sense, Julie decides to kill herself; Jean merely says the words. If anyone is controlled or conditioned, it is Jean by the bell, not Julie who, for reasons that will appear, makes her own decision. Yet Strindberg intended that the stronger will of Jean should be the determining factor in Julie's suicide, so the ambivalence of the final scene would seem to be misplaced. On the other hand, the play acquires both credibility and subtlety if we largely discount hypnotism and explain Julie's decision in terms of her psychology.

Jean's essential feelings towards Julie are rooted in fantasy. Although he suggests later that his story of his childhood encounter with her is false, the intensity with which he relates it indicates, at least, that it represents a pro-

found yearning on his part. Julie is the ideal, the beautiful girl in 'the Garden of Paradise' who is to be worshipped, but once she has 'soiled' herself with 'a peasant's child', his sense of social order and morality are destroyed. When he discovers 'that the eagle's back was as scabbed as our own, that the whiteness of those cheeks was only powder, that those polished fingernails had black edges, that the handkerchief was dirty though it smelt of perfume', all his disappointed puritanism bubbles over—'Servant's whore, lackey's bitch . . . Have you ever seen any girl of my class offer her body like that? I've only seen it among animals and prostitutes'. The beautiful Turkish Pavilion turns out to be a latrine, his ideal woman becomes a slut and his Eden is degraded into a Gomorrah.

On different occasions, Jean manifests casual brutality, animal sensuality and a rather pathetic tendency to daydreaming which is devoted to evading the need to act. He is a most un-Nietzschean character; his power is simply the brutal failure of a born peasant with resentments he is unable to live out. The framework which holds these qualities together and unifies them is class, though even in Jean's case it is not the basic driving force of his behaviour. He is an embodiment of the myth of working-class virility in which such artists as Strindberg and Lawrence seem to have believed. The myth did not haunt Strindberg permanently as it did Lawrence, but in *Miss Julie* he had his peasant display more overt sensuality than any of his more sophisticated characters in the other plays: 'You are like hot wine, strongly spiced.' Jean's memory images are insistently sensual. 'Have you ever noticed how beautiful cats are? Soft to the touch like human skin.' Indeed, it is his coarseness, his brutal sensuality that Julie finds sexually appealing. In contrast to the attitudes expressed in the vast majority of his plays, Strindberg writes in the Preface: 'Jean has the whip-hand of Miss Julie simply because he is a man. Sexually he is an aristocrat by virtue of his masculine strength, his more finely developed senses and his ability to seize the initiative'.

Their mutual social and sexual roles are schematised by the two dreams they narrate. Julie's dream does not simply mean that she wishes to escape from the isolation of her social position, it is also a symbolic expression of the sexual needs that Jean can satisfy: 'I long to fall . . . I know I shall find no peace till I come down to the ground. And if I get down I should want to burrow my way deep into the earth'. For Julie, Jean's attraction is that he is 'a great strong lout', who in her mind is the opposite of her weak fiancé. Although she knows that an affair with Jean will degrade her, her ambivalent personality draws her to him. Time and again, in outbursts that are the product of despair and regret, she demands to be punished: 'Hit me, trample on me, I've deserved nothing better'. 'Kill me too! Kill me!'. 'Hurt me more'. Of course, she wants him to help her, she desperately wishes she had not 'fallen', she is afraid of her father and ashamed of the social disgrace but it would be a simplification of her character to ignore the element of self-indulgence in her degradation, which is expressed so superbly in her dream speech.

In a similar way, Jean's dream expresses his will to power and his desire to ascend the social ladder, while at the same time communicating his masculinity in specifically phallic terms. 'And I climb and climb, but the trunk is so thick and slippery'. Alone he cannot escape from his class; his ostensibly virile self-confidence is not sufficient. This is evident in his encounters with Julie for his masculine bravado and cynical cruelty alternate with a sense of kinship and affection for her. Moreover, every occasion on which she makes him feel powerful is balanced by another occasion when she makes him feel inadequate. He can never be content with being 'just your animal' and is painfully aware that he can never make her love him. So eventually Jean admits defeat. Julie is altogether too complex for him, the class situation too overawing and his ambitions too fragile for him to be socially effective. Beneath the virile role he plays is a servant who conquers the world in his dreams and causes havoc among the ladies from time to time. But when he finds the waters too deep, his puritanism asserts itself and he self-righteously abuses Julie and primly admonishes Christine: 'Kindly express yourself more respectfully when you refer to your mistress'.

Contrary to F. L. Lucas's opinion, the unimaginative Christine is the perfect mate for the valet. She will be impressed by his smattering of French, his 'refined' tastes and his physical vigour. She will remain a solid support who will listen to his stories without leading him into danger. Christine is too stupid to see through him, too much of a peasant to tempt him to realise his ambitions, but enough of a snob to appreciate his pretensions. We can imagine, after years of married life when they are still valet and cook, Jean self-pityingly blaming his failure on Christine's inhibiting lack of drive and imagination. She is the perfect excuse for his inadequacies and the perfect foil for his self-esteem. That he should choose her as his wife is conclusive evidence of his class conservatism. For once, Strindberg is correct when he writes in the Preface: 'She is a female slave, utterly conventional, bound to her stove and stuffed full of religion and morality which serve her both as blinkers and scapegoats'. She is a perfect embodiment of Nietzsche's slave morality, herd mentality. This insight suggests that he was not entirely unperceptive about the qualities of her natural mate.

Even though she exhibits a slave mentality, Christine is a far more decisive and self-willed character than either Julie or Jean. For instance, Julie's decision to commit suicide is stimulated less by Jean's brutality than by Christine's pietism. Underlying the perfectly adequate account provided by Julie's hysteria, the sexual and class impasse and her deep sense of personal shame, Strindberg suggests that her death has a religious context, which is provided by Christine. In the servant's character he embodies much of the narrow-minded, ungenerous pietism embraced by his stepmother and which, after a brief conversion in his youth, he found utterly distasteful. In words which could equally be applied to Christine he has written [in his ***Son of a Servant***] of his stepmother: 'John saw how she had succumbed to the sin of pride. She really believed she was far ahead of others on the road to blessedness and already a child of God'. In Christine, the pietistic self-righteousness of the Nurse in ***The Father*** is made even more extreme and unattractive by the insularity of the

peasant. By portraying Christine so unfavourably when it would have been quite easy to show her as the long suffering victim of class conflict and other people's vices, Strindberg effectively condemns pietism and peasant conservatism.

Christine is more responsible than Jean for Julie's death because she is stronger than he is. Jean, at least, has the excuse that he is paralysed by fear of 'his lordship' because he knows that in terms of the class morality he has done wrong, but there is nothing to prevent Christine from helping Julie. Yet when Julie desperately appeals to her as another woman to help her against Jean, all Christine can do is moralise.

> CHRISTINE. The blessed Saviour suffered and died on the cross for all our sins and if we turn to Him with a loyal and humble heart, He'll take all our sins upon Him.
>
> JULIE. Do you believe that, Christine?
>
> CHRISTINE. With all my heart, as surely as I stand here . . . And where the sin is exceeding great, there His mercy shall overflow.
>
> JULIE. Oh, if only I had your faith! Oh if !
>
> CHRISTINE. Ah, but you can't have that except by God's special grace, and that isn't granted to everyone.
>
> JULIE. Who has it then?
>
> CHRISTINE. That's God's great secret, Miss Julie. And the Lord's no respecter of persons. There shall the last be first.
>
> JULIE. Then He has respect for the last?
>
> CHRISTINE. (*continues*) And it is easier for a camel to pass through the eye of a needle than for a rich man to enter Kingdom of Heaven.

After piously affirming her own comforting theology, confident of course that she has 'God's special grace' and that the Lord does respect *her* person, she concludes with a cold-blooded act of class propriety:

> That's how it is, Miss Julie. Well I'll be going— and as I pass the stable I'll tell the groom not to let any of the horses be taken out before his lordship comes home, just in case. Goodbye (*goes*).

In the scenes quoted above, Christine signs Julie's death warrant by suggesting an image of redemption after death without in any way trying to comfort her as a woman. If she had shown Julie by an act of kindness that someone could sympathise with her, the girl might have had some hope; but provided with such cold comfort, all Julie can do it despair. Julie's final words, 'And the first shall be last', ironically supplement Christine's self-satisfied, 'There shall the last be first', and clearly remind us of the servant's moral responsibility for her death.

In terms of mood and style ***Miss Julie*** is ostensibly a hybrid play which falls into two separate parts. Once Julie and Jean have slept together, the midsummer magic dissipates, the scents and the sounds of revelry fade as if the sun had indeed set, their pretences are torn aside and

Strindberg depicts a furious sex battle to the death. At the same time, the class war is joined with a bitterness we had rarely glimpsed in the earlier half where both Jean and Julie play out their class / sexual roles without revealing the two rather desperate human beings behind them. At first, Jean plays his part as the virile young servant who is handsome, ambitious and daring enough to distinguish himself among his class while remaining securely within it. By contrast, Julie is the Lady who believes she can occasionally join in peasant fun and games without demeaning herself and falling from aristocratic grace. They both enjoy living a little dangerously but remain and wish to remain what they are; a peasant, who despite his fantasies, knows his place, and an aristocrat, who despite her taste for social slumming, remains the Lady of the Manor.

But when they make love the danger becomes real and what was originally a game develops into tragedy. They are thrust out of the class roles which have shielded them; he from the painful discrepancy between his ambitions and his servility, she from her perilous sensuality. They find they have committed themselves not merely sexually but socially. They have rebelled against a sexual code that is part of a wider social code and a very important part. Their intimacy has been witnessed, if only circumstantially, and they can do nothing together but live beyond the social pale or die. The inevitability of their tragic situation is portrayed by defining the social conflict in terms of increasing sexual aggression. Neither of the latter forces would be sufficient to account for Jean's brutality or Julie's hysteria but together they make inevitable such scenes as the butchery of the greenfinch, the suicide decision and Julie's outburst against the male sex. The conclusion of the play is reached by an intensification of those social and psychological factors which had been established earlier. So, although the surface texture of the play changes, its deeper emotional structures remain constant.

Yet there are definite stylistic differences between the two halves, even though their social and emotional drives are continuous. And curiously enough it is the first part of the play, the least intense and volatile, which is stylistically more experimental. While the closing sequences of *Miss Julie* are clearly naturalistic, the first half presents critical problems which are unusual among the pre-Inferno plays. These problems can best be introduced by recalling the dream speeches. In a predominantly naturalistic play we might suppose that such lyrical invocations would be out of place.

There is something incantatory about Julie's repetitions, 'drifts, drifts on and across', 'it sinks, sinks', 'I long to fall, but I don't fall', which is echoed in Jean's dream speech. In fact, these are stylised dream speeches uttered mesmerically for theatrical effect so that Strindberg can carry the audience with him, while he makes a number of points in a highly succinct and ostensibly undramatic manner. The rhythms of the speeches are designed to suspend the disbelief which would be a normal response to such a blatant cancellation of naturalism. If we examine the extract closely, we shall hardly fail to notice how precise it is, much too neatly juxtaposed to be real, much too full of pastoral imagery to be more than a lyrical expression of

Jean and Julie's experiences, and much too tightly constructed to be part of natural dialogue. In about twenty lines of dialogue Strindberg presents Julie's misanthropy, her sensuality, her class discontents, her sexual ambivalence, and precisely contrasts them with Jean's class ambitions, his Eden fantasies, his phallicism, his aggression and his inevitable sense of failure. The contents of these two speeches are models of stylised simplicity but they are no more like actual dreams than they are like actual dialogue.

The first half of the play is impregnated with non-naturalistic effects. Up to the ballet sequence that is contemporaneous with their love-making, the play is written as a subtle mixture of lyricism and realism which might be seen as metaphor of Strindberg's view of courtship. Even the physical setting combines the mundane with the bucolic. Kitchen utensils mingle with 'a statue of Cupid, lilac bushes in bloom and tall Lombardy poplars', the tiled stove meticulously provided 'with a section of an overhead hood to draw away fumes' is also decorated with birch leaves; this kitchen contains as well as a sink and an ice-box 'a big Japanese spice-jar containing flowering lilacs'. These contrasts are justified by its being Midsummer eve but the fact that Strindberg chose this time of year gives the earlier section of the play a magical quality. The mood is heavy with heat, lust and gaiety. No one, except Christine, behaves conventionally, as the mood of the festival heightens their responses.

And yet there are numerous realistic touches which anchor the play. Strindberg asked for a realistic decor in the kitchen without 'painted saucepans'. The 'filthy mess' Christine is cooking to abort Julie's pug, Jean's butchering of the greenfinch and Christine's reference to Julie's 'monthly' to account for her crazy behaviour, must have been quite shocking to nineteenth-century audiences. But even these 'realities' play a dual role. The symbolism of the pure-bred pug's sexual association with a mongrel prefigures Julie's fall, while the greenfinch has several symbolic overtones; as a beautiful caged bird denied its natural freedom it represents Julie but as the present of her former fiancé it represents his and Jean's servitude and hence Julie's aristocratic authority (which Jean eventually destroys).

But Strindberg is not content merely to contrast reality and fantasy, he orchestrates them into movements which lyrically express his characters' yearning for some ideal. The magic of Midsummer Night intensifies Jean's longing for the ideal aristocratic life and Julie's desire for an Arcadia where she can behave simply as a woman, without incurring the social stigma that would normally be attached to such conduct. Their flirtation scenes, by remaining at the level of romantic parody, safely express a sporadic desire to become each other's equals. Julie can drink beer and allow a servant to kiss her shoe and Jean like a young gallant can flirt with her. Both can interpret these scenes to suit their own fantasies; but such an ideal is possible only because it is the creation of a special occasion and something utterly apart from social realities. This indeed is an unusual evening when everyone (even Christine during her mimed soliloquy) is affected by the strange, undefined longing created by song and dance, scent and flowers.

A further example of the way Strindberg uses unreality to heighten real psychological and social conflicts is in Jean's long childhood reminiscence. The story he tells is real enough (whether it is true is irrelevant) but the style in which he narrates it is extremely high-flown. One has to be careful here because this is not simply a description of a childhood experience by an adult, it is an attempt on his part to recreate the experience as *felt* by that child. Strindberg is portraying a grown man's recollections of his childhood attitudes. Most of us tend to fall into an exaggerated, rather stilted, consciously literary style of speaking when we try to express our childhood feelings, as if we believed that a child's mind was full of palaces and kings, absolute beauty and ugliness, pure good and evil. And this is precisely the habit that Strindberg is exploiting through Jean's speech; but for purposes beyond those of verisimilitude.

As before, the contrasts are too neat, the social and sexual references too appropriate to the present situation, the imagery too typical of the speaker's role and the narrative too much under control, to be Jean's natural reminiscence. This speech with its romantic evocations ('the Garden of Paradise and there stood many evil angels with flaming swords to guard it', 'a Turkish pavilion in the shadow of jasmine trees and overgrown with honey-suckle'), the self-conscious drama, the Dickensian pleading for pity and the religious overtones, serve the functions of allegory as well as those of psychological revelation. Certainly, it is a very romantic outburst bereft of the bitterness we should expect of Jean. The emotional discharge, 'Oh, Miss Julie! Oh! A dog may lie on the Countess's sofa, a horse may have its nose patted by a young lady's hand, but a servant . . . !', is too self-consciously literary to be genuine class bitterness; it is much closer to romantic despair.

In view of these lyrical qualities, to what extent do Strindberg's naturalistic techniques determine the impact of the play? Zola had criticised *The Father* for the absence of particular milieu. In *Miss Julie,* Strindberg sought to remedy these 'failings' and, as he admits in the Preface, 'I have therefore not suggested that the motivation was purely physiological nor that it was exclusively psychological'. Apart from the psychological drives, which have been examined in detail, a multiplicity of motives is given. Physiological (Julie's menstruation), hereditary, physical (presence of the razor), mental (hypnotism, the stimulus of the count's bell and the blood of the bird) and environmental (the Midsummer night, the odour of the flowers etc) causes supposedly impel Julie's sexual fall and suicide. Certainly each of these factors plays a part, but they are not separately or jointly what makes *Miss Julie* a unique, profound and credible drama. The psychological naturalism of the play, as it blends social and sexual frames of reference within an economical physical setting, is what raises the play to the level of great writing and great theatre. If each of the causal elements, enumerated by Strindberg in the Preface, were to take full effect, they would distract from the concentration of the piece. *Miss Julie,* indeed, has a background of references that gives it body but

they are not each fully-fledged causes. These are to be sought in the characters of Jean and Julie, which Strindberg has developed with even more complexity than those of the Captain and Laura.

The milieu in *Miss Julie* defines character in broad outline but not in detail. Christine's environment is the kitchen, the domain of a peasant. Jean, the servant with noble pretensions, occupies the kitchen and the master's bedroom. Julie, the slumming aristocrat, commutes between the manor house and the kitchen. These parallels neatly relate character, social class and location to each other but they are not allowed to dominate the play. In *Miss Julie* the born dramatist fortunately triumphed over the theoretician. In fact, Strindberg followed his own injunction to seek out those points in life where the great conflicts appear (*faire grande*) and, as a result, neither Julie nor Jean are loose bundles of responses united by a firm personality. Whatever Strindberg intended, he created eminently rounded, flesh and blood people. This is the principal reason why *Miss Julie* is arguably his finest pre-Inferno play and, for its size and scale, one of the great masterpieces of the Western theatre. This is also why Julie's death is convincingly tragic, contrary to the following incredibly wrong-headed assessment by Dahlström: 'Julie's fall is not a moral one, rather it is a superficial social disturbance . . . Even for Strindberg, Julie's fall is not genuine. He gave her nothing to lose but false pride and nothing to stain, but an already badly stained name. *Miss Julie* cannot succeed as a tragedy because the author failed to give it adequate tragic substances.' Against this, as a conclusion of the foregoing analysis, we can simply state that she is a character for whom an audience can feel sympathy, whose social and sexual dilemma is convincing and whose considerable potentiality as a human being is tragically wasted. (pp. 57-71)

> *John Ward, in his* The Social and Religious Plays of Strindberg, *The Athlone Press, 1980, 337 p.*

Evert Sprinchorn (essay date 1982)

[*Sprinchorn is an American educator and critic who has produced numerous important studies and translations of Scandinavian literature, focusing on the works of Henrik Ibsen and August Strindberg. The following excerpt contains material that originally appeared in "Strindberg and the Greater Naturalism," The Drama Review, Winter, 1968, and in Essays on Strindberg, edited by Carl Reinhold Smedmark, published by the Strindberg Society, Sweden, 1966. In it, Sprinchorn highlights the originality of Miss Julie by placing it in the context of late nineteenth-century theatrical practice in Paris and by comparing it to Greek tragedy and the work of Ibsen and Jean Genet.*]

[Strindberg] always regarded theatre as a kind of poetry, as the most heightened form of artistic expression, in which much more happens in each moment than in the sluggish and dilatory prose of the novel. In an age when verse was rapidly disappearing from the drama, he had to bring a different kind of poetry into the theatre. The main line of Strindberg's development, the line that leaps over all the apparent contradictions in his philosophical and religious development, is the line that traces his constant efforts to enhance the expressiveness of theatre. It is this ceaseless experimentation with theatrical art that has bewildered critics as much as it has stimulated dramatists.

Even such comparatively simple and straightforward plays as *The Father* and *Miss Julie* can easily be misunderstood and deprecated if regarded only as realistic or naturalistic works. In certain crucial respects they are much less realistic than *The Wild Duck* or *The Three Sisters*. Zola, the chief apostle of naturalism, was quick to find fault with *The Father* as a naturalistic play. Even *Miss Julie,* the drama that most fully answers the requirements of Zola's naturalism, is less naturalistic than Strindberg, in his preface, claims it to be. He labeled **The Father** simply "a tragedy," but he gave *Miss Julie* the subtitle "a naturalistic tragedy." This subtitle and the greater attention to physical detail in the play were probably due to Zola's criticism of **The Father.** In contrast to many readers and spectators who have been misled into thinking that that play was written in white heat by an inspired madman, Zola found the design of the play and the characters in it too obviously the product of careful calculation. The persons were too abstract, too manifestly the figures in a mathematical formula contrived to produce the desired result. Furthermore, the action was so radically truncated that the illusion of reality was bound to be shattered.

Having taken the pains to prepare his own French translation, which he mailed off to Zola with a covering letter asserting that the play had been "composed according to the experimental formula," Strindberg was undoubtedly upset by the Frenchman's criticisms. He might well have replied that in a tragedy the characters should appear larger than life and possess a somewhat abstract quality and that too much attention to realistic detail would detract from the grandeur of the design. *The Father,* after all, was meant to be a nineteenth-century version of Greek tragedy, and of Agamemnon in particular. But the rebellious Swede knew that unless he could find an audience outside his own country, stolid, philistine Sweden would silence him or force him to write only for the ladies' magazines. Having alienated the Swedish conservatives with his socialism and the liberals with his anti-feminism, he felt that his whole career as an original writer depended on attracting a following outside Sweden. No wonder then that he took Zola's criticisms to heart when he wrote his next play, *Miss Julie.* And having written it and made one or two fair copies, he perhaps feared that the play still would not seem naturalistic enough. Hence the preface, which has come to be recognized as the most concise and comprehensive statement of naturalistic theatre.

The two people Strindberg most wanted to please with his play were Zola and Antoine, the theoretician and the practitioner of the new movement. *The Father* was written before Antoine opened the doors of his Théâtre-Libre to the non-Boulevard drama, but *Julie* was written over a year later, by which time Antoine had become the most talked-about producer in Paris. The *Julie* preface shows very clearly how alert Strindberg was to what was happening in the French capital. There is scarcely a thought in this manifesto of naturalism that is original with him.

Zola's experimental formula meant a concentration on the inner drama, an avoidance of theatrical tricks, a simplification of sets, and an adherence to the unity of time—in other words, a return to the principles of Racinian neoclassic drama. Echoing Zola, Strindberg averred that the theatre had reached a crisis, that the conventional intrigue drama was dead, and that only psychological drama could hold the interest of modern audiences. From Zola, too, comes the Darwinistic remark about humanity sloughing off its feelings as it evolves into a higher species that will not allow emotions to inhibit its thinking. From the Goncourt brothers come the idea of literature as case history, in which the writer is little more than a doctor's recording secretary or a court stenographer, and the conviction that the theatre is a declining art form fit only for women and children. From the French psychologists Théodule Ribot and Jean-Martin Charcot comes the theory that the ego consists of contradictory impulses, many of which may be buried beneath the level of conscious thought. From Hippolyte Bernheim comes the notion that hypnotic suggestion is a powerful force in life and much more common than generally supposed. From his familiarity with the European stage, as reflected in the Parisian papers and journals, derives Strindberg's call for solid rather than painted scenery (already in use in theatres that could afford it); for asymmetrical sets (frequently used in French melodrama, sometimes in opera, and also in some productions of the Meiningen players); for real props (a fetish of the duke of Saxe-Meiningen); for the abolition of footlights to make facial expressions more true to life (the aim of theatre designers ever since the stage moved indoors in the seventeenth century); and for acting that would permit the performer occasionally to turn his back to the audience (already practiced by Porel as actor in the 1870s and as director in the 1880s at the Odeon theatre—Strindberg had seen him in 1876). Even the pantomimed action that Strindberg wants to substitute for an intermission is probably due to the growing interest in pantomime plays in Paris in the 1880s. In making these points he seems to be addressing himself mainly to the provincial theatres, urging them to catch up with the latest trends. Ten years after Strindberg wrote his preface, Stanislavsky at the Moscow Art Theatre was still trying to get rid of canvas doors that billowed when they should have been slammed.

It is in Strindberg's plea for an intimate theatre that Antoine's influence is most apparent. Antoine's recent and unprecedented success was partly the result of having staged his plays in a small rented hall. Since his untrained actors did not know how to project in the manner of the skilled performers at the Boulevard theatres, they spoke in a natural conversational tone and acted pretty much as people do in real life. Thus, by a fluke, Antoine hit on the right acting method for the naturalistic drama. The acting and the theatre were in almost perfect harmony. For Strindberg the great virtue of the intimate theatre was that it could be supported by a small intellectual coterie so that the dramatist would not be forced to write down to his audience. Secondarily, it offered the opportunity for subtle effects, the play of expression on the faces of the actors, the small gesture, the intimate tone of voice—all of which could not be "read" in the typical large theatre.

The writing of the *Julie* preface, like the opening of Antoine's theatre, occurred at a time when the naturalist movement was actually quite far advanced. Taine, Zola, the Goncourts had scored major victories all along the cultural front, and the theatre, that almost impregnable fortress of tradition and conservatism, had been the last area to be invaded. It was, however, at a critical juncture. The movement had won a major breakthrough in 1887 because of Antoine's young and enterprising spirit, but a group of young novelists, including some former Zolaites, had estranged themselves from the movement because of the sordidness of Zola's *La Terre.* At the same time, the Decadents, some of whom had begun as naturalists, were gathering their forces and in the next decade, under the banner of Symbolism, would outflank the naturalists. Consequently, when Strindberg leaped into the naturalistic saddle, he rode off in all directions.

Underneath this literary opportunism Strindberg had drawn up his own naturalist platform. Up to the mid-1880s his principal concern had been with social questions. These he had resolved, at least temporarily, in *The Author,* the fourth volume of his autobiography, written in 1886. He thereupon turned inward for his material, a course that would lead eventually to *A Dream Play.* This change reflected the interest in abnormal psychology that developed parallel with the rise of naturalism. During August 1886 he steeped himself in the "literature of insanity," and a few months later he wrote *The Father.* He felt, undoubtedly, that he was on the right track because of recent tendencies in the work of Zola and Ibsen.

The bedrock of his philosophy lay in the conviction that life was to be viewed less as a struggle against heredity and environment, as the naturalists insisted, than as the struggle of minds, each seeking to impose its will on other minds. Powerful minds were like charged particles attracting weaker particles, thus building up magnetic fields of influence. He found scientific support for his theory in the writings of Bernheim. Following up the latter's idea that "all who may be hypnotized are susceptible to suggestions," he wrote **"The Battle of Brains"** (1887), an essay in experimental psychology in which the Darwinian idea of the struggle for existence and the Spencerian idea of the survival of the fittest were applied to the life of the mind. Physical battle was obsolete; brawn had been conquered by brain and now it was a question of mind against mind and the power of suggestion. "Suggestion is only the stronger brain's struggle with and victory over the weaker," wrote Strindberg, "and this process is at work unconsciously in everyday life," in political, religious, and artistic controversies, as well as in domestic squabbles. This essay, which anticipates the age of propaganda, of Madison Avenue and public opinion polls, provides the key to Strindberg's view of theatre and helps to define his position in the naturalist movement.

At first he had aligned himself with the naturalists because he saw them as exposers of the sham and "humbug" of modern civilization. If they did not precisely long for a return to nature, as the Rousseauistic Strindberg did, at least

they were opposed to the social establishment. At the same time he characterized realism (*not* naturalism) as the tendency in art to create illusion by the careful rendering of significant details. This was in 1882, before he had written his naturalist tragedies. A few years later, however, having written *Miss Julie* and having acquainted himself with the plays of the Théâtre-Libre, he felt it was necessary to dissociate himself from at least one branch of the naturalist movement and to distinguish between the "greater" and the "lesser" naturalism—which he proceeded to do in his essay **"The Modern Drama and The Modern Theatre,"** written in 1889. Here he says that the greater or higher naturalism is the naturalism

> which seeks out those points where the great battles take place, which loves to see what one doesn't see everyday, which revels in the conflict of natural forces, whether they are called love and hate or the spirit of rebellion and the instinct for association, and which cares not whether a thing is beautiful or ugly as long as it is magnificent.

The lesser naturalism allows no scope for the personality of the artist; it is merely a faithful imitation of nature, a kind of photography so inanely accurate that even "the speck of dust on the lens was included as part of the picture." The lesser artist presents ordinary events and cannot see the forest for the trees, while the greater artist singles out the significant motif, which usually has something to do with life as struggle.

The greater naturalist follows the path blazed by the Zola who wrote *Germinal* and *La Terre,* not the Zola who in allowing *L'Assommoir* to be adapted for the theatre emphasized the environment of the action by having an extraordinarily realistic tavern and laundry erected on the stage. The lesser naturalist follows in the footsteps of Becque, whose *Vultures,* a realistic rendering of middle-class life, lacks temperament. This represents the objective approach loved by those "who lack personality, the soulless ones, as they should be called." To Strindberg the great drama, the drama of Shakespeare, Racine, and Molière, was essentially psychological drama, a conflict of wills, in which the stage apparatus was reduced to a minimum. Shakespeare required scarcely any sets at all, and Molière's "marvelous vivisection" of Tartuffe "takes place on a stage with two taborets." For the battle of brains no naturalistic set is needed. *The Father* and *Miss Julie* can be performed with a table and two chairs and a few props, such as a birdcage, a lamp, and a straitjacket.

Nevertheless, to judge from the preface to *Miss Julie,* Strindberg, in accord with naturalist thinking, wanted the set to be an active force in the drama. Environment and heredity were to be the jaws of the vise that would crush Miss Julie. The preface was written, however, to sell the play rather than to explain it. If we look at the play itself, we see what Strindberg actually had in mind for this set. He describes a manor-house kitchen of which the audience sees only the corner containing the large glass doors leading to the yard. This vaulted entry is a little stage-left of center. The other walls and the ceiling of the kitchen are masked by the teasers and tormentors, which means that in making some of their exits and entrances the actors would not use any doors. They would, in a sense, just fade in and out of the picture. Furthermore, the long deal kitchen table is cut off by the drapes or curtains serving as tormentors, for the audience is supposed to see only one end of it. "As far as the set is concerned" wrote Strindberg,

> I have borrowed from the impressionists the idea of an asymmetric, truncated picture, and believe I have thereby enhanced the illusion, since, by not seeing the whole room and all its furnishings, the spectator will be induced to exercise his imagination to complete the room.

This is a rather remarkable set that Strindberg prescribes, especially for this particular play, in which the heroine is to be trapped in the kitchen and forced to enter the valet's bedroom. One would have surmised that both the action of the play and the naturalist concern with milieu would have led the dramatist to specify a closed-in box set. Yet Strindberg manifestly sought to avoid both this and the old-fashioned wing-and-drop set and endeavored to create instead the kind of effect the impressionist painters were achieving on canvas, presenting a corner of a room rather than the whole space. The incompleteness of the impressionist composition drew the artist and the viewer into closer personal contact, placing the viewer in the scene and compelling him to identify with the artist at a particular moment. From being "the representation of nature through imagination," as Humboldt had defined it at the beginning of the Romantic era, art had become, in Zola's definition, "a corner of creation seen through a temperament."

In this, as in his replacement of the customary intermissions with a pantomime and a ballet and his reduction of the playing time to ninety minutes, Strindberg's ulterior purpose was to ensnare and hold an audience. If life to him was a battle of brains, the theatre was a submission of minds, achieved by the spectator's willing suspension of disbelief and the dramatist's hypnotic skills. If the subject matter was morally unpleasant or logically impossible, a conflict of minds would arise and the author-hypnotist would have to enhance the spell. Conventional naturalism created the illusion of reality by the accumulation of details (though its primary theoretical purpose was to establish the force of environment), whereas Strindberg assumed that the spectators could best be spellbound if they could be lured into the spirit of the game and made to supply what was missing. The dramatist's task was to supply what was significant.

One way of doing this was to give the selected objects a symbolic meaning. This is, of course, a basic artistic method, but Ibsen the realist and Zola the naturalist employed it with more than usual thoroughness, and Strindberg always appreciated the latter more as a symbolist than as a naturalist. Symbols now were not to be linked to the realms of the ideal and the supernatural; they were meant to adumbrate an inner, psychological action, to provide a focus for the mass of realistic detail, and to enlarge the scope of the work. In Zola's *La Bête humaine* the locomotive becomes a recurring symbol of the bestial drives of the engineer, just as in *La Curée* the entwining flowers (their

names taken from seed catalogues) in the hothouse suggest the irresistible force of the sex drive. Ibsen's method is most apparent in *The Wild Duck*, but even in *A Doll's House* the denuded Christmas tree in the last act speaks vividly of the change in the Helmer household. In *Miss Julie* the boots waiting to be polished and the gaping speaking tube convey the haunting presence of Julie's father, the count. The songbird in the cage, the bird that Julie insists is her only friend and that Jean so brutally kills, underscores almost too heavily the situation in which the aristocratic girl finds herself. The set itself, the kitchen—naturalistic in that it takes us away from the parlors and drawing rooms of conventional realistic plays and speeds us on the way down to Wesker's kitchen and LeRoi Jones's toilet—is symbolic of the servants' world into which Julie has lowered herself. In contrast to most naturalistic plays, *Miss Julie* shows us a character out of her milieu. (pp. 23-9)

[The] mantle of naturalism did not sit comfortably on Strindberg's shoulders. When he wrote *Miss Julie,* naturalism had already arrived at a crossroads. Some of its adherents attempted to make the novel and the stage painstakingly accurate copies of life. Arno Holz, for example, set forth in the 1890s his theory of a "consistent naturalism," which he summed up in the formula: Art $=$ Nature $-$ X, X representing such factors as the artistic means employed and the artist's personality. Strindberg would have no truck with this trifling naturalism. "All my literary endeavors," he said toward the end of his life, "have been in reaction against *Kleinkunst* and petty realism." The formula for an artistic realism and a heightened naturalism would read: Art $=$ Nature $+$ X. The kind of acting he wanted in his plays would unite realism with grandeur, but, as in Talma's definition of great acting, it would be a union of grandeur without pomp and nature without triviality. (p. 33)

[In his preface Strindberg] had much more to say about psychology than about theatre and gave the impression that *Miss Julie* is a thoroughly naturalistic presentation of a woman driven to suicide, a casebook study fully documented. He has given so many reasons for Julie's suicide that one feels her death is overdetermined in a way that Hedda Gabler's, for instance, is not. There is Julie's lack of a will to live and her desire to put an end to the family of which she is the last and weakest member. There is her aristocratic shame at having sullied herself through intercourse with a lower species of life. Further, there are the more immediate and precipitating causes: suggestions prompted by the sight of the songbird's blood, the presence of the straightedge razor, the fear of discovery of the theft, and the final command given by Jean, the servant with a thirst for life. Although Strindberg was justifiably proud of this multiplicity of motives, I doubt that the spectator can be aware of all of them when Julie walks off stage to end her life. And if he were, the play, however successful it might be as a nineteenth-century case history, would fail as a tragedy.

Nowadays the Julies of this world do not commit suicide. They cohabit with their butlers, servants, stable grooms, and chauffeurs and manage to live as happily with them as their sisters do with the proper young men they meet at their coming-out parties. The same was true in Strindberg's time, though to a lesser extent. Strindberg said that one of his models for Miss Julie was a certain Emma Rudbeck, the wellborn daughter of a general. She seduced a stable boy, moved to Stockholm, and became a waitress. She did not kill herself. Whatever may be the principal cause of Julie's suicide, it cannot lie simply in class conflict. In the course of the last half-century, the class barriers that loomed so large to Strindberg and his audiences have been partially washed away by the currents of democracy and have left the true foundations of the play all the more clearly exposed. The rise of one class and the fall of another that are augured in *Miss Julie* have come to pass. Moreover, the drama itself has developed along the lines laid down by Strindberg so that his technique is no longer so bewildering. The result is that we are now in a position to see *Miss Julie* less as a social problem play than as a type of modern tragedy.

From the dramaturgical point of view, the first thing that strikes one is the degree to which the story material has been concentrated. Earlier one-act plays almost always concerned themselves with relatively trivial incidents and avoided any deep exploration of character. A joke, a *quidproquo,* a contretemps sufficed for a one-act comedy; a *méprise* or an unfortunate coincidence, for a one-act tragedy. In most cases, one felt the material was being stretched to cover thirty or forty minutes. With *Miss Julie,* one feels just the opposite. Although the play runs for an hour and a half, it is so crammed with story and motivation that the performers and the director must single out the important strands of the action or risk losing their audience.

The density of texture in Ibsen's plays has often been remarked, but Ibsen's kind of concentration differs from Strindberg's in that the Norwegian is intent upon withholding information until the most effective moment while the Swede is eager to tell all he knows at once. Ibsen constructs his plays like mystery stories that come to an end when the last and most vital piece of information is revealed. Strindberg, as he himself said, tends to spill everything immediately in his realistic plays, and only after his Inferno crisis does he learn to hold back and mystify his audiences. Ibsen is more concerned to explore the past while Strindberg, even in a naturalistic work like *Miss Julie* in which those forces of the past, heredity and upbringing, have such a large part to play, seeks to depict the present. Ibsen's plays are constructed on the Scribean model and contain an exposition, a development leading to a climax, and then a denouement or catastrophe. The technical novelty in Ibsen's method was not, as Shaw says it was, the introduction of the discussion scene, but it was, rather, the penetration of the exposition into the rest of the play. The climax in an Ibsen play either consists in or is triggered by some crucial revelation of the past. Hence Ibsen's characters often seem to be patients on Freud's couch or ghosts clutching at cobwebs in some dingy Victorian mansion.

Miss Julie is different. Even though the past haunts Julie's mind and permeates nearly every moment of the play, the emphasis is on the present. Whereas Ibsen's plays are all exposition, *Miss Julie* is all climax and catastrophe. Bearing in mind the three-part structure of a conventional play, we may say that Ibsen stresses the first part, Strindberg the last. Ibsen's method is certainly more typical of the post-Renaissance drama and probably more sensible, for in drama, as in sex, the climax cannot be prolonged indefinitely; and when Strindberg finally came to write *Miss Julie* he had to reduce the playing time from the two or three hours of a standard play to ninety minutes—and of course he had to eliminate the act divisions, for an interrupted climax is no climax at all. I say when he finally came to write *Miss Julie,* for it is apparent that Strindberg could not have achieved this extraordinary degree of concentration, by which the nine years of his love life with Siri are distilled into ninety minutes of pure drama, without first having written his short stories about marriage, the plays *Sir Bengt's Wife* and *Comrades,* and the autobiographical novel *A Madman's Defense.* In a sense these took the place of the extensive notes and drafts that Ibsen made.

It is also clear, as Carl Reinhold Smedmark has pointed out [in his "Introduction to *Fröken Julie,*" *August Strindbergs dramer*], that Strindberg did not embrace the one-act form as soon as he sat down to write about Julie. Indeed, Strindberg originally may have had a three-act play in mind, the first act ending with the dance of the peasants that forces Julie to retreat into Jean's room, the second act ending when Julie exits to pack her things and elope with Jean. But that scene is not nearly strong enough to serve as a second-act curtain, and Strindberg had to keep the action rolling on beyond this point without a break, even though it meant telescoping Midsummer Night so violently that it would have given pause to any realistic dramatist. When Strindberg set out, either consciously or unconsciously, to create one long stretch of rising action, intermissions had to be discarded and replaced with a dance and with pantomimes, landings that would permit the spectator to rest and relax on the way to the climax but not to escape from the influence of the author-hypnotist. Strindberg was experimenting with a form that improved on Zola's *nouvelle formule*—make it true to life, make it grand, and keep it simple—by making the spectator's agony brief and by letting the action rush to its conclusion without interruption. Commenting on the concentrated form of *Miss Julie,* Strindberg said,

> In every play there is one real scene. That's the one I want. Why should I bother with what's leftover and give six or eight actors the trouble of taking care of it.

> In France I always ordered five mutton chops, much to the astonishment of the autochthons. A mutton chop has half a pound of bone and two inches of fat. Within is the ball of lean meat—*la noix.* That I ate. Give me the nut is what I tell playwrights.

In its final shape, *Miss Julie* bears only slight traces of its embryonic three-part form. It more resembles a two-act play formed by lopping off the exposition, with a consequent shift in the position of what used to be known as the peripety or plot reversal. Ordinarily, this would come at the end of the second act in a three-act play, the function of the third act being either to spell out the consequences of this reversal in the case of a tragedy or to restore the fortunes of the protagonist in the case of a comedy. In *Miss Julie,* however, about 40 percent of the play is rising action and 60 percent, catastrophe.

Apart from its position in the structure of the play, the peripety is a true peripety, bringing a change of fortune for both Jean and Julie. Once they seduce each other, their lives are changed irrevocably, and the world in which they move and think is turned upside down. The two-part structure of the play accords perfectly with the social and sexual reversal. (Dickens's *Little Dorrit,* which Strindberg, as a devotee of its author, may well have read, has the same structure, the second half of the story reversing the social relationships of the chief characters in the first half.) The first part of the play pictures Jean as slave and Julie as mistress; the second part shows Julie as slave and Jean as master. In the first part, Julie despises Jean for being vulgar, boorish, and animal-like; in the second part, Jean despises Julie for being dirty, impure, and unable to control herself. The noble lady lowers herself beyond the possibility of redemption while the slave rises above her. The aristocrat in the social sphere becomes the slave of the valet; the valet becomes the aristocrat in the sexual sphere. Much of the richness of this play, as of Strindberg's other writings in the 1880s, derives from his ability to fuse social and psychological motives. In his own marriage, the antagonism between him and his wife was, as he admitted, "the clash between the upper class and the lower class." But the sexual, psychological, and inner conflicts are fundamental to the play; the social conflict is there to enhance the sexual conflict.

To focus more sharply on the basic conflicts, Strindberg makes use of small symbolic actions and parallels, devices that were to become the hallmarks of his dramatic technique in later years. The fact that Julie's pet dog Diana (!) has become pregnant by a mongrel foreshadows the peripety of the play, just as Jean's brutal beheading of Julie's pet songbird Serena (!) anticipates the final scene. The two dreams that Julie and Jean relate in the play complement each other so perfectly that one feels the ordering hand of the playwright more strongly here than elsewhere. In her recurrent dream, Julie finds herself on top of a high pillar from which she wants to climb down but cannot. Jean, in contrast, dreams of climbing up the thick, slippery trunk of a tree to rob a nest of its golden eggs. The transparent sexual imagery scarcely calls for comment, nor does the way in which these two dreams prefigure the action of the drama. Julie dreams of debasing herself—and will do so; Jean dreams of rising to the top—and will do so, at least for a moment. And in realizing their dreams, both will be disillusioned.

Concentrating on Julie we tend to forget that Jean experiences a minor tragedy. Once he mounts above Julie and robs her nest of its golden eggs, he is deprived of an object of worship. His is the slave's mentality, and without anything or anyone to look up to his life loses its meaning. Fortunately, there are always other masters to whom he can attach himself. Julie's father, the Count, is still there to inspire him with respect, as Strindberg says, even after

Jean has possessed the daughter and seen how empty that pretty shell is. It is because there are always masters around and because Jean is a slave first, last, and always that he can retire from the battlefield unharmed, or at least not fatally wounded. Jean's life is defined by those above him, and, consequently, it has an aim and a purpose and a meaning. Without the aristocracy, God would not exist for Jean.

In contrast, Miss Julie's life lacks definition because there is nothing she can lastingly respect and revere. What one part of her being desires, the other part finds repulsive. She wants her fiancé to kowtow to her; she makes him jump over her riding crops as if he were a trained dog; but she has only contempt for him because he obeys her. When he refuses to jump, she hates him for that too. She enjoys seeing Jean kiss her shoe; she wants him to seduce her; she teases him until he does; but once he has blackened his lips on her shoe and ejaculated his seed into her, she hates him and herself for what they have done. Yet half an hour later she wants to repeat the whole business. Life for her is a balancing act in which she teeters between being slave and being master. As long as she plays her role in society, she can maintain her balance, but the moment she abandons that role and fully commits herself, she plunges from the pillar that haunts her dreams. Julie is destroyed because the game she has been playing becomes real.

To appreciate how this comes about, we have to consider another parallel that Strindberg employs, a parallel that is as essential to *Miss Julie* as exposition is in a conventional three-part play. Before the seduction, Jean tells Julie that as a small boy he stole apples from the Count's orchard, which is pictured as a Garden of Eden with its tree of life and, by implication, its tree of knowledge of good and evil. On another occasion he came into the grounds to work in the vegetable gardens. Driven by curiosity, he stole into the outhouse, a beautiful Turkish pavilion hung with honeysuckle. (Opulent bathrooms and air fresheners were not invented by Americans.) While he was in there, he heard people approaching. He was trapped. "There was only one way out for the upper-class people. But for me there was one more. And I had no choice: I had to take it." Covered with muck and excrement, he ran through the strawberry patches and the raspberry and rose bushes until he caught sight of little Miss Julie. In her pink dress and white stockings, she appeared like an angel to him, a symbol of the hopelessness of ever rising above the class into which he was born. This was a crucial experience to Jean, and his whole view of life was shaped by this childhood expulsion from the Garden of Eden. The rest of his story about trying to commit suicide because he realized the impossibility of entering again the Eden out of which he had been cast is romantic exaggeration, reflecting his own daydreams, no doubt, but primarily intended, as he later admits, to impress Miss Julie.

Jean's parable serves as a background against which the rest of the play must be seen. When Julie is in the kitchen with Jean, and the farmhands and servants are heard approaching, Julie is in the same position as the boy Jean was. Now she is out of her milieu, enjoying the unsophisticated pleasures of the lower class. From the kitchen, which is in the servants' quarters and unconnected with the house, there is one proper way out for Jean and his class; but for Miss Julie there is yet another way—Jean's room—and she has no choice but to take it. And when she leaves Jean's room, covered with shame, she faces the black-liveried valet, a symbol of the hopelessness of ever changing her way of life.

This sense of physical entrapment is essential to a proper working of the play on stage. Without it, all the motives for Julie's end that Strindberg adduces seem only intellectual rationalizations. With it, they gather together to create a force of irresistible dramatic power. Before the seduction, Julie is a wild animal, hunted and pursued by her own desires. After the seduction, she is a trapped and caged creature hurling herself against the bars that imprison her. Jean's offer to elope with her is not an invitation to freedom but a temptation to enter a smaller, darker, narrower cage. Her suicide should have the same effect on us as the deliberate death of a wild animal that prefers to die rather than live in captivity.

Julie, however, is not only a wild creature; she is also a sophisticated human being. What distinguishes the human being from the animal is masochism, and what makes Julie the fascinating modern woman she is, is the extent to which she is half-man, half-woman, both hunter and hunted, both on top of the pillar and at the bottom of it, both master and slave. It is her unconscious desire to be trapped, her inner compulsion to defile herself that makes her modern—not, as Strindberg points out, because her type has not always existed but because it is now coming forward and attracting attention. Or, he might have said, because it is now being understood.

Julie kills herself not because she is an aristocrat but because she is Julie. Jean is ultimately no more than a part of her own being, a willing and convenient actor who can be assigned a major role in the drama she is constantly rehearsing and never finishing. But this time the drama is carried out to its logical end. By committing suicide Julie escapes from the net of conflicting desires. As with Hedda Gabler, her last moments are her noblest moments. Ibsen may have written *Hedda Gabler* (printed 1890) as a counterstatement to *Miss Julie* (printed 1888 and first performed 1889) or to Strindberg's short story **"Upon Payment"** ("Mot betalning," published in the collection entitled *Married II,* 1885), in which the sexually ambiguous woman who finds motherhood repulsive first appears. That Ibsen meant Hedda to be a sister under the skin to Helen, the woman in Strindberg's story, is obvious. He took the opening lines of the story and built on them. "Her father was a general, and she was quite young when her mother died. After that the visitors to the house were mostly men. And her father took charge of bringing her up." In writing *Hedda Gabler,* Ibsen was invading Strindberg's territory and challenging him on his own ground. But Hedda's suicide is like Julie's in one important respect: there is a note of triumph sounded in it. If Hedda and Julie had chosen to live on as the vassals of Brack and Jean, we could speak of a defeat; but not now. Hedda's fear of scandal, her contempt for the philistine Judge Brack, her awareness that she has failed to realize her

ideals—either immediately in her own life or vicariously in Lövborg's—constitute the negative aspect of her suicide. But she also kills herself because she wants to bring back into the world some of the glamour and grandness it lost when the middle class took power; she wants to show Brack that there are more things in heaven and earth than are dreamt of in his philistinism ("People don't do such things!"); she wants to prove to herself that Lövborg's ideals and hers can be realized, if only fleetingly, and she wants for once in her life to do something exciting instead of just hearing about it from Lövborg's lips. Much of this complex motivation must inevitably escape the attentive spectator and even the careful reader because Ibsen, working within the formal limits of the *pièce bien faite,* had to rush his ending. Hence Hedda's decision to kill herself appears impulsive, irrational, and capricious, rather than arrived at step by step. Strindberg, on the other hand, by minimizing the exposition and prolonging the catastrophe, painstakingly carves out each of the steps that carry Julie to her end.

More instructive than Ibsen's play is a group of long one-acts written in France since 1940. The superficial similarity of Genet's *Deathwatch* and *The Maids* and Sartre's *No Exit* to **Miss Julie** and **Creditors** is immediately apparent and testifies to the vitality of a form that Strindberg may be said to have reinvented: the ninety-minute one-act spellbinder, long enough to allow the full development of a rich subject, short enough to demand and receive the audience's complete concentration. *No Exit* is a three-character drama in which all three are trapped in situations that represent their lives. But since they are all dead there can be no change or resolution as there can be for Miss Julie. *The Maids,* Genet's most revealing play, strikes me as being modeled both in form and content on Strindberg's **Miss Julie.** Here is the essence of Genet's thought. Everything he wrote before it was in preparation for it; everything he has written since is an elaboration on it.

Genet presents a sado-masochistic ritual in which two maids play the roles of mistress and maid; that is, maid A plays the mistress, and maid B plays maid A. In taking the part of the tyrannical mistress and in reviling B, A is simultaneously achieving the position she herself both hates and envies, heaping abuse on the position she in fact occupies, and providing B with the pleasure of being spat on. After a bit of this the roles can be switched, so that every nuance of sadism and masochism can be enjoyed. Nothing could be more perfect, except to have it go on forever. This it cannot do, for reality in the person of Madame always threatens to arrive on the scene and interrupt their pretense. Hence an alarm clock must be set to warn them of their mistress's expected arrival. Regrettably, the maids trap themselves by unsuccessfully trying to betray Madame's lover to the police. When Madame finds out what they have done, their game will have to end once and for all. They must either destroy their mistress or themselves. They therefore decide to play the game in earnest and act out the ritual to its ultimate conclusion. They will poison their mistress, and they will act out the poisoning. As the real mistress approaches, the weaker of the two maids takes the part of the mistress and proves herself the stronger by commanding the other maid, who is of course playing the weaker maid, to give the mistress-maid the poisoned tea. In this manner, the weaker maid manages to combine in herself both the sadist and the masochist, both the slave and the master. In her last moments she ecstatically achieves the synthesis that in life could only be hers in pretense. She dies both by her own hand and by that of another.

The end of *Miss Julie* is remarkably similar. Julie's problem is twofold. She herself is the mistress and therefore cannot "play" that role, and she has found no one who can play the game with her and keep it at the desired pitch of excitement. But as her father the Count approaches, she does find a partner who will play the game to the end. She orders Jean to order her to kill herself. She, the weaker of the two, who has not strength enough to kill herself, seems stronger at the end when she tells Jean what to do. Jean seems weaker because he is incapable of acting until the Count rings the bell. Like Genet's Madame, the Count is the primum mobile in this universe of slaves and masters rotating around each other, and Strindberg was wiser than Genet in keeping this force offstage. As in Strindberg, class distinctions are used in *The Maids* to earmark the master and the slave, the sadist and the masochist. Other distinctions can serve the same purpose. In *Deathwatch*, for instance, which is set in a prison cell, degrees of criminality separate the envied from the envious, the glorified ones from the self-haters; and in *The Blacks* Genet expresses the distinction in terms of the white and black races. In nineteenth-century Europe, the sado-masochistic relationship could best be suggested by using the social class structure. In twentieth-century America, it is most forcefully brought out by using black skins and white skins to distinguish the players in the game. It would be quite in keeping with the inner spirit of Strindberg's play to adapt it for present-day American audiences by making Jean a black man and Julie a white Southern belle, as has often been suggested. On the other hand, Tennessee Williams's *A Streetcar Named Desire*, which struck many Swedes as a Southern version of *Miss Julie*, differs fundamentally from Strindberg in that the heroine's behavior is motivated by her feelings of guilt. She knows she is responsible for destroying her husband who killed himself when confronted by her revulsion at his homosexuality. Guilt, which plays such a large part in Ibsen's works and accounts for his use of the retrospective technique, is not an important factor in Strindberg's naturalistic works, nor in the ritualistic works of Genet. "The naturalist has wiped out guilt along with God," said Strindberg in his preface to *Miss Julie*—and so has the existentialist. The roots of the sado-masochistic relationship may quite possibly lie in the sex act, so that the male-female conflict that Strindberg emphasizes in his works may be the psychological and physical basis of the social conflict of classes. Nevertheless, as Genet's homosexual plays make clear, male and female should be understood as representing attitudes rather than organs.

Just as *Miss Julie* is an attempt by Strindberg to reduce or distill the action of the conventional well-made play to nothing but climax and catastrophe, so Genet in *The Maids* has in effect extended and prolonged the last moments of *Miss Julie*. The whole of Genet's play spells out what happens on the last pages of Strindberg's play. At that point, Jean and Julie are no longer the comparatively free creatures they were at the beginning. The possibility of keeping Julie as his mistress on the estate does not appeal to Jean when he is reminded of the consequences, the pregnancy and scandal that will come inevitably if their affair continues. On the other hand, the possibility of eloping with Julie is cut off by the cook Christine. Julie is confronted by the alternative prospects of a life with Jean or a life with father. Either way, she is faced with humiliation, degradation, scandal, her own unhappiness, and that of others. The situation is stalemated with both Jean and Julie knowing that the only real end must be Julie's suicide. But neither of them is able to bring about this resolution: Julie because she is weak, Jean because he is afraid. Only something that can give her strength and him courage can make them move. The only thing that can give her strength is something outside her, and the only thing that can give him courage is some greater fear. Not until the Count rings the bell are Jean and Julie able to act.

To bring off the end, which obviously gave Strindberg some difficulty, he had to steal a sunrise from Ibsen and some hypnosis from the French school of psychology. These two devices were necessary to lift the play from the level of realism to the ritualistic level on which Genet's play is enacted. The spirit of the end is violated by realistic acting and realistic sets. To escape realistic acting, Strindberg calls for Julie to be hypnotized, and her last long speech is spoken in an ecstasy. To rid himself of the realistic set for which he had argued so eloquently in his preface but which at this moment would betray the spirit of Julie's speech, Strindberg calls for the long slanting rays of the early morning sun to fall on Jean alone. But I have never seen a production in which this direction is followed. The spectator should be aware of nothing but a black, undefined object in the sun and the voice of the transported Julie. To realize Strindberg's intentions the audience must be as hypnotized as Julie.

Under hypnotic suggestion, largely self-induced, Julie has jumped from one orbit to another, where Jean cannot follow her. If the audience were aware now of the psychological motives for her death, they would be left behind with Jean. The ending will not work unless the world of reality momentarily fades away. The gaping mouth of the speaking tube is ominously present throughout the play and functions dramaturgically in much the same way as the gods do in Greek tragedy. When it speaks, Jean and Julie are forced to act. But Julie can act only by entering her play-world where to act in one sense means to act in another. When she is hypnotized and transported, the stage world of audience and actor coincides with the play-world of Julie. In the rest of the play, the setting and the performers are imitations of the world the audience knows. In this last scene, the audience is at one with Julie, no longer watching but participating, and the real world has ceased to exist for both. When the bell rings again for the last time, this mood is shattered, and Julie is shoved over the edge of the abyss to her death, for by this time the real world stands for death. Although Strindberg at first planned to have Julie die on stage, it is not necessary for us to see her die. We experience the effect of the razor slash when the bell rings. Here Strindberg succeeds better than Ibsen did in *Rosmersholm*. Rosmer and Rebecca talk each other into a double suicide, and they too must be in some exalted state that belies the heavy Victorian set in which they stand. Ibsen follows their last exit with a speech by the housekeeper, in which she describes their deaths, and it results in a fatal collapse of the action to the realistic level.

Miss Julie demonstrates both the effectiveness and the limitations of stage realism. It enables the spectator to identify to a certain extent with the protagonist and with the situation on stage, but it inhibits the expansion of the spirit. When considered in relation to the end of the play, the long uninterrupted stretch of action and its realistic basis serve as a runway for a flight into another realm. The audience should take off with Julie, experiencing with her the growing terror of entrapment, the ecstasy of escape, and then, for one brief instant, the blow that brings oblivion. In that lies the essence of romantic theatre. The spectator begins as a witness to a realistic event and ends as a participator in a ritual.

Genet's technique consists in beginning the ritual in medias res. On anyone not in a frame of mind to accept his peculiar ritual, his play will have the same effect as the Catholic liturgy on a nonbeliever, who may find the ceremony curious, instructive, and beautiful but who will not share in it directly. Genet's world is a world of fantasy with piquant touches of reality. His characters are not real, nor are they meant to be. Genet capitalizes on the fact that theatre is an illusion by presenting his world of illusions as theatre. His evil is not evil in any practical sense since it exists only in the form of fantasy; as soon as his ritual of sadism and masochism becomes real, it comes to a halt.

In contrast to Genet, Strindberg gradually entices the spectator into the ritual. For him, the ritual in the play reflects a ritual in real life. When Genet's maid dies, only a marionette dies; when Julie dies, a woman dies and a world with her.

A proper understanding of the ending of *Miss Julie* goes a long way to answering the objections raised against the play as tragedy. In the view of most critics, neither this play nor *The Father* is tragic because the naturalistic philosophy implicit in them allows for no spiritual meaning in the universe. The Darwinian scheme imposes no moral order on existence, and without that there can be no tragedy, tragedy being irreconcilable with chaos. As part of a spiritual universe, the tragic hero enjoys a measure of free will allowing him, for a moment at least, to become godlike, as Oedipus does when he plucks out his eyes and astonishes even the gods by going beyond the fate they had ordained for him. In the naturalistic view, mortal man lacks free will and is simply the victim of heredity and physical circumstances. Because of the way in which they were raised, Miss Julie is neurotic and the Captain paranoid.

Strindberg met these objections head on, and in writing *Miss Julie* and *The Father* he deliberately set out to emulate ancient tragedy. Whereas Ibsen sought to avert odious comparisons by giving *Ghosts* the modest and ironic subtitle "a domestic drama," Strindberg pointedly called *Miss Julie* "a naturalistic tragedy" and gave it the length and structure of ancient Greek tragedy. (pp. 34-46)

To make tragedies out of *The Father* and *Miss Julie,* Strindberg had to find a modern equivalent for the Greek sense of fate. In *The Father* fate, he said, takes the form of erotic passion, by which he meant the incestuous aspect of the lovemaking of the Captain and his wife. In *Miss Julie* the heroine's faulty upbringing, her weak constitution, and her social position all add up, as Strindberg remarks in his preface, to an equivalent of fate or the universal law of the Greeks. Then, having deprived his protagonists of free will by seeing them as creatures in a Darwinian world, he gave it back to them when he made them the final arbiters of their fates. Miss Julie makes the decision to kill herself and stages her own death. The Captain has all along been acting out his destiny, his wife only playing the part he has assigned her. He is an Othello who creates his own Iago. Though they are the slaves and victims of their passions, Julie and the Captain end up being more free than any Greek hero because they are their own oracles. The god is within them. Hearing its voice, Julie tells Jean what he must do, and the Captain lets the nurse play mother to him and slip the straitjacket over him. As surely as the heroes of Greek tragedy, Julie and the Captain embrace their fates, Julie taking in her hand the razor that represents the masculine element in her and the Captain submitting to the straitjacket that represents the oedipal longings that have determined the course of his life.

These are rationalistic answers to those who feel that *The Father* and *Miss Julie* do not belong in the august company of the great tragedies of the past. But there is more to the argument. Strindberg knew that tragedy was essentially irrational and that the paradox of tragedy was that it produces a sublime effect while dealing with the most horrible acts and disclosing the most awful truths. The tragic catharsis results from seeing what lies beyond reason and reasoning beyond what is seen. The strict naturalist could not view life tragically because he limited himself to things he could explain, never venturing into the heart of darkness. He was satisfied to reason about what happened in the world by studying the facts. The tragedian wanted to explain the facts, which meant going beyond them. That was why Strindberg sought a higher naturalism. He was not content to reproduce reality as accurately as possible. He needed to create a second reality, an exaltation of life.

Writing in 1887 on the intrigues and machinations of men and women in the battle of the sexes, Strindberg said, "All these ideas and schemes that I have ascribed to human beings, and especially to women, I have purely and simply transferred from the unconscious, the obscure realm of the instincts, to the conscious realm."

He said this before he wrote the plays. It was easy enough for the polemicist to discourse in an essay on man's unconscious thought; it was quite another matter to bring the unconscious on stage with such immediacy that the spectator would feel that he has actually entered the world where fantasies are the only real facts and where the inner life becomes the outer life. This was the challenge the dramatist faced, the challenge that he answered in the strongest scenes of *The Father* and *Miss Julie.* He wanted to raise the viewer to the sphere in which Julie exists at the moment when she decides to end her life and to let him fall with the Captain into the pit of madness. (pp. 48-9)

> *Evert Sprinchorn, in his* Strindberg as Dramatist, *Yale University Press, 1982, 332 p.*

Strindberg on Zola's drama:

Thérèse Raquin is a new departure, but since it is adapted from a novel it is still not perfect in form. The author has had the feeling, however, that through greater unity of place his audience would receive a more complete illusion, by which the action would impress its main feature more forcefully on the spectators. At every curtain rise, the spectator had to be haunted by the memories of the preceding act and thus through the impact of the recurring milieu be captivated by the action. But because of the difficulty in having a before and after the crime sequence, Zola commits the error of letting a year elapse between the first and second acts. Presumably he did not dare offend against the prevailing law about a year's widowhood, otherwise a day between the acts would have been enough, and the play would have made a more unified impression. I therefore once suggested to a director of a theatre, whom I wanted to persuade to produce *Thérèse Raquin,* that he remove the first act.

August Strindberg, in his Samlade Skrifter, Vol. XVII, *Albert Bonniers Forlag, 1913.*

Edmund A. Napieralski   (essay date 1983)

[In the following excerpt, Napieralski examines the fairy-tale motifs in Miss Julie.*]*

In a letter to Karl Otto Bonnier on 10 August 1888, Strindberg hailed *Miss Julie* as "the first Naturalistic tragedy in Swedish drama." Since its first production, critics and audiences have understood Strindberg's indebtedness to the French naturalistic tradition as well as his own prefatory explanation of the play's naturalistic elements: its tight and simple form, its definition of elemental, hereditary, and environmental forces that appear to motivate the characters, its verisimilitude, and the testimony it seems to give to the law of nature that says the fittest shall survive. While few would contest the distinctive contribution Strindberg made to theatrical naturalism in this play as well as in others like *The Father* (1887) and *Creditors* (1888), the entire Strindberg canon clearly defines another strain in the art of this complex genius: antinaturalistic, romantic, expressionistic, even mystical. What is commonly thought, however, is that this strain evolved after or at least outside his naturalistic period and came to full bloom in later works like *A Dream Play* (1902) and *The Ghost Sonata* (1907). But even in *Miss Julie,* Strindberg shows through his use of fairy-tale motifs that naturalism could not satisfy him and that its narrow definitions could never contain his vision of tragic human experience.

Strindberg's interest in fairy tales, legends, and folk tales runs throughout his career. In the 1870's, for example, he helped to translate the tales of one of his favorite authors, Hans Christian Andersen; in 1882 he wrote a fairy-tale play, *Lucky Peter's Travels;* in the 1890's he started to collect Swedish folk ballads and melodies; in the early 1900's he composed *Swanwhite* (1901), *The Crown Bride* (1901), and *Abu Casem's Slippers* (1908), all using legends and fairy-tale elements; and in 1903 he published his own collection of original tales, *Sagor,* Strindberg's interest in legends and fairy tales, then, was not something casual, accidental, or temporary, nor was it limited to a specific period in his life. It should come as no real surprise, then, that fairy-tale elements should appear elsewhere in Strindberg's work, even in *Miss Julie.* In a recent article ["Fairy Tales, the Unconscious and Strindberg's *Miss Julie*" (*Literature and Psychology* #28, 1978)], Philip Dodd notes allusions in the play to a magic brew, to dreams, to a Garden of Paradise. He also mentions Jean's depiction of himself as a swineherd, and the possibility of the lovers' flight to Lake Como, "redolent of the lived-happily-ever-after conclusion of many fairy tales." Dodd's purpose, however, is to explore Strindberg's indebtedness to Andersen's "The Snow Queen" and to Eduard von Hartmann's *Philosophy of the Unconscious* (1884), and he claims that the fairy-tale motifs in *Miss Julie* "do not saturate the texture of the play." The fairy-tale elements in *Miss Julie* are present, however, as more than mere allusions or ornaments and, in fact, function as structural components to intensify the power of the play as tragedy.

Allusions to fairy tales and legends as such run throughout the drama. While Julie and Christine are mixing a potion for Julie's sick dog, Diana, Jean asks, "Is this some magic brew you ladies are preparing on midsummer eve, which will reveal the future and show whom fate has in store for you?" After they have shared their dreams with each other, Jean suggests, "We must sleep with nine midsummer flowers under our pillow tonight, Miss Julie, and our dreams will come true!" Before the ballet, Jean describes himself as one of "those princes in the Arabian Nights, who couldn't eat or drink because of love". At the end of the play, with the coming of sunrise, Jean claims that now the Devil must surrender his power. Trying to persuade Christine to accompany them to Switzerland, Julie promises that they will see King Ludwig's palaces, "just like in the fairy tales."

In addition to these allusions, other fairy-tale elements so pervade *Miss Julie* that they invite the audience to examine the possibility that they define the structure of the play as tragedy. First, there is the romantic setting of the play in Midsummer, a time of enchantment as well as a time for the celebration of fertility. A princess and a commoner—whom she can transform into a prince by her love—dance, share drink and their dreams, and make love. They can escape the powers of her wicked mother and father by journeying to a green world, a journey to be made in the company of a greenfinch and a helpful servant. Elements such as these—elements that can be recognized in such classic tales as "Snow White" and "Cinderella"—are reshaped by irony to make the audience sense the extent of Miss Julie's frustration, the depth of her tragedy.

Strindberg's ironic use of the fairy tale begins with the play's setting itself. In keeping with the playwright's intention in his *Preface,* that setting appears to be realistic to avoid the artificialities of canvas stage doors and painted saucepans. Yet that setting includes the time of Midsummer, the biggest secular holiday of the year, which led Strindberg to weave together elements of Swedish custom and elements of the fairy tale. The festival, traditionally celebrated on June 24, was called "St. Hans's Day," "Hans" being an abbreviation of Johannes or John, for St. John the Baptist. Houses were thoroughly cleansed and ornamented with flowers and green boughs. The night was filled with drinking, feasting, singing, and with dancing around bonfires and a Maypole. Christian and pagan beliefs merged to promise that the powers of trolls and other evil spirits could be nullified, illnesses cured, and that maidens could, by following a carefully prescribed ritual, dream of their husbands-to-be. It is to this ritual that Jean refers when he suggests to Miss Julie that they sleep with nine midsummer flowers under their pillows. Jean's offering her beer in the same scene may also refer to the belief that during the dream a maiden would be offered a delicious beverage by the prospective lover. These and other traditional elements of Swedish custom, like birch leaves decorating the stove and juniper twigs strewn on the floor of the kitchen, blend with features like the fountain with the statue of Cupid to create a setting that suggests romance and idyll. As in many fairy tales, the environment holds forth the promise of fertility, the union of male and female, a rich harvest and new life.

Next, while making perfectly good sense on a naturalistic plane, all characters in the play, seen and unseen, also represent fairy-tale figures. Miss Julie has characteristics of the classic princess: an aristocratic upbringing, a code of honor, physical attractiveness, modesty, tenderness, and vulnerability. Whereas Strindberg asserts in the **Preface** his approval of her downfall at the hands of the socially ambitious Jean, many critics have noticed, as audiences have felt, the playwright's ambivalent attitude toward her. Martin Lamm notes [in his *August Strindberg*], for example, that while trying to be true to the naturalistic credo, Strindberg was drawn to Miss Julie, "with whose hypersensitive nervousness he felt an affinity." Børge Madsen also claims [in his *Strindberg's Naturalistic Theatre*] that Strindberg saw Miss Julie as a victim of heredity and environment, a tragic character "in a desperate struggle against nature." By endowing her with fairy-tale qualities, Strindberg could be sympathetic towards her without betraying his naturalistic thesis.

Miss Julie's character as fairy-tale princess is further defined by her relationship to her parents. Miss Julie speaks of her mother, although her natural parent, in terms that suggest the fairy-tale stepmother. She claims, first, that she came into the world "against my mother's wish." Then, like a stepchild, she was forced to wear boys' clothes and to look after the stable horses. As if casting a spell, the mother also taught her to hate men and to be an emancipated woman. The mother's spell extended even to the estate, where she forced men to do women's tasks and women the men's. Finally, after suffering convulsions and hiding herself in attic and garden, the mother set fire to the house, stables, and cowshed, and betrayed her husband with a lover. Like the fairy-tale witch, she is portrayed as violent and destructive. Although not as fully developed, Miss Julie's father has also contributed to her confused condition: "But it was he who brought me up to despise my own sex, made me half woman and half man." In a sense, her parents hold Miss Julie in thrall. Their non-appearance on stage makes both figures of mother and father all the more shadowy and menacing. Confused in her identity, Miss Julie struggles desperately to escape their curse.

In *The Uses of Enchantment,* Bruno Bettelheim explores ways in which fairy tales contribute, on both conscious and subconscious levels, to the child's development of an identity, an integrated self. The struggles of fairy-tale heroes and heroines to escape the clutches of a wicked witch or stepmother, or the tyranny of a brutal father, mirror the child's need to put the influences and the apparently despotic authority of parents into perspective so that the individual self can mature. Bettelheim sees the central motif of "Snow White," for example, as the "pubertal girl's surpassing in every way the evil stepmother who, out of jealousy, denies her an independent existence—symbolically represented by the stepmother's trying to see Snow White destroyed." Strindberg's heroine, however, is denied the consolation of the fairy-tale heroine: " . . . Snow White, betrayed by her stepmother, was saved by males—first the dwarfs and later the prince." Miss Julie's father provides no liberation, and her prince no rescue.

Jean represents an ironic mixture of fairy-tale lovers. On one plane, he may be the handsome prince capable of transporting his princess to a new Eden; on another, he may be the pauper capable of being transformed, metamorphosed by the love of his princess to a new nobility. These apparently contradictory possibilities and Jean's failure to fill either role are appropriate to Strindberg's ironic perspective in the play. Lamm sees both Miss Julie and Jean as characters full of contradictions. Miss Julie, he notes, is "torn between the most contradictory feelings: tenderness and contempt, ecstasy and irony, vanity and the wish to degrade herself, erotic desire and chaste modesty." At the same time, the critic sees Jean as "innately vulgar and yet possessing fastidious . . . manners. 'Polished, but coarse underneath,' is the way Strindberg describes him in the preface." These contradictions testify to Strindberg's own ambivalence toward the two characters: cognitively or rationally he can analyze them as classes in a social revolution or as natural forces in an elemental struggle for survival; affectively, however, he can sympathize with them as romantic fairy-tale figures.

Allusions, setting, and characterizations in **Miss Julie** come together in an action that mirrors the action of a fairy tale. At the beginning, Miss Julie—charming and flushed with the mood of the festival, and flirtatious—teases Jean with her commands. After they come in from a dance, she insists that Jean take off his livery. He complies by putting on black tails and a bowler hat, a costume more appropriate to courting a princess. While their love potion is only beer, Miss Julie commands that he drink her health, then kiss her shoe, pick lilacs for her, and take her for a moonlight row on the lake. After she removes a speck of dirt from his eye, she orders him to kiss her hand. The entire interlude is playful and romantic—the coy princess and her shy suitor.

In this happy mood, and as they become more intimate, it is natural for Miss Julie and Jean to share their dreams. Both their dreams can be interpreted within a naturalistic framework to signify Miss Julie's wish to descend from the heights of her socially superior class and Jean's wish to climb above the confinement of his lower class. Among other critics, Maurice Valency [in his *The Flower and the Castle*] claims that the symbolism of the dreams is simple: "the upper class is suicidal, the lower class aspiring; and this is the consequence of a destiny which, in Strindberg's opinion, is a biological phenomenon."

On the other hand, both dreams can make good sense within a fairy-tale framework. Jean's dream offers the best clue to this possibility:

> I dream that I'm lying under a high tree in a dark wood. I want to climb, up, up to the top, and look round over the bright landscape where the sun is shining—plunder the bird's nest up there where the gold eggs lie.

Jean appears to be the fairy-tale figure, perhaps as in "Jack and the Beanstalk," confronted with a dangerous task or quest: climbing out of darkness into light to gain a magical prize—gold eggs. In spite of its social and sexual implications, Miss Julie's dream can also be understood in a fairy-tale perspective. Her lonely and precarious position on top of a pillar is the result of her being forced there by her noble birth and the perverse influences of her parents. Like the fairy-tale princess imprisoned in a tower, she is in desperate need of escape or rescue.

Jean's subsequent confession of his childhood infatuation with Miss Julie also fits the fairy-tale scheme. As a young boy, he watched from afar the comings and goings of lords and ladies in the house of the Count, whose walls were hung with pictures of kings and emperors, and whose garden—a "Garden of Paradise"—held "a Turkish pavilion in the shadow of jasmine trees and overgrown with honeysuckle." He pined after Miss Julie, dressed in pink dress and white stockings, and like the distraught, hopeless lover, wanted to die for being unable to possess her.

The approach of the peasants signals the gradual distortion of the fairy tale by irony. On the one hand, Jean may be behaving gallantly by giving Miss Julie refuge in his room: "I'll bolt the door. And if anyone tries to break in, I'll shoot." But on the other hand, he exploits her trust and vulnerability by making love to her. Dressed in their best clothes and wearing flowers, the peasants dance—a ballet certainly in harmony with romance and with a festival celebrating fertility—but their dance is accompanied by what Jean calls "a filthy song," about two bad girls who had thrown their greatest treasures away.

On their emergence from his room, Jean promises Miss Julie escape to a green world, to Switzerland, the Italian Lakes, where they will live an eternal summer. He pictures Miss Julie at the hotel they will own as a queen before whose throne guests will file and lay tribute on her table.

But even in his initial description, the dream paradise begins to tarnish and fade, for he will "salt" the bills of their guests. From this point until the end of the play, irony twists the dream into nightmare, the fairy tale into tragedy.

The contrasts between the beautiful and romantic details of the play's first part and the inversion of those details in the second part are sharp and cruel. Instead of pride and joy, Miss Julie feels shame and sorrow. The flattery and playfulness of the first part turn into mutual recrimination, disgust, and bitter name-calling in the second. Jean fails to be metamorphosed, and instead puts his livery back on and gives Miss Julie wine that he has pilfered from her father. The green world of Lake Como becomes, in Jean's words, "as beautiful as a puddle," and a place where lovers quarrel and leave estranged.

Even in the last painful moments of the play, shreds of fairy-tale motifs appear. By accompanying Miss Julie and Jean on their escape, Christine could be the helpful servant. Instead, she condemns both of them and promises to frustrate their flight by ordering the groom not to allow horses to be taken out before the Count's return. Miss Julie's greenfinch, a clear symbol for her caged and powerless condition, may also be the helpful animal of the fairy tale. Rather than providing the comfort and companionship that such animals give fairy-tale princesses, the animal is destroyed by Jean in a brutal act that foreshadows the death of the princess herself.

Jean's abetting of Miss Julie's death wish is his last brutal act of the play which runs counter to the audience's expectation of a prince who helps his princess. Jean is able to cast his own spell here, a spell which combines with those of her parents to lead to Miss Julie's doom. With no will of her own, Miss Julie asks Jean to order her to kill herself. Fabricating another fairy-tale figure, she imagines Jean as a hypnotist: "a man dressed in black, with a tall hat—and your eyes shine like coals, when the fire is dying—and your face is a white smear, like ash. . . ." And Jean does enchant the princess: putting his razor into her hand, he says, "Here's the broom." As Ibsen did in *Ghosts*, Strindberg makes ironic use of the sunrise at this point: there is no hope or new life for Miss Julie, but only despair and death.

The tragic ending of **Miss Julie** is a direct antithesis of the fairy-tale ending. In *The Uses of Enchantment*, Bettelheim explains the importance of happy endings:

> The happiness and fulfillment which are the ultimate consolation of the fairy tale have meaning on two levels. The permanent union of, for example, a prince and a princess symbolizes the integration of the disparate aspects of the personality—psychoanalytically speaking, the id, ego, and superego—and of achieving a harmony of the theretofore discordant tendencies of the male and female principles. . . . Ethically speaking, that union symbolizes, through the punishment and elimination of evil, moral unity on the highest plane—and, at the same time, that separation anxiety is forever transcended when the ideal partner has been found with

whom the most satisfying personal relation is established.

There is no question, of course, that Miss Julie and Jean
fail to achieve either psychological or moral unity. Miss
Julie goes off to kill herself, and Jean responds automatically to the Count's bell: "since his lordship spoke to
me—I can't explain it properly, but—oh, it's this damned
lackey that sits in my blood—I think if his lordship came
down now and ordered me to cut my throat, I'd do it on
the spot." Both persons remain enslaved, unintegrated,
unredeemed.

Strindberg's use of fairy-tale allusions, characters, and action in *Miss Julie* may be understood and accepted within
the context of his entire work. On the one hand, as his
Preface asserts, he wished to create in this play a classic
of naturalism. On the other hand, fairy tales and legends
were so much a part of his creative imagination that they
came to be interwoven with naturalistic elements. The
Preface gives us the cognitive Strindberg; the play, the affective Strindberg as well. Lamm narrates how Strindberg
felt that *Miss Julie* was " 'a compromise with romanticism and stage decoration,' " but that *Creditors* was
" 'thoroughly modern' " and a better play: " 'three characters, a table and two chairs—and no sunrise!' " On an
intellectual or rational level, Strindberg could approve the
earlier play's representing the desirability of the lower
class overcoming the higher, the victory of the strong over
the weak in society as well as in nature. His use of fairy-
tale motifs, however, allowed an emotional Strindberg to
sympathize with Miss Julie, to feel her desolation as he
would the loss of a fairy-tale princess.

Strindberg's use of fairy-tale motifs most certainly affects
the way an audience responds to *Miss Julie.* While the
work may be a textbook example of naturalistic theatre,
it is certainly not that aspect which explains the universal
appeal of the play and its repeated successes in performances for almost a hundred years. Like Strindberg, an
audience may see class conflict and an elemental struggle,
but what it feels—as is true of all great works of art—can
explain the stature of this play as a classic. Fairy tales are
a part of everyone's childhood, regardless of time and culture. The fairy-tale motifs in *Miss Julie* allow the audience not only to understand the conflicts in the play, but
also, by sensing the ironic distortion of those motifs, to feel
profoundly the depth of its tragic vision. (pp. 282-88)

> *Edmund A. Napieralski, " 'Miss Julie': Strind-
> berg's Tragic Fairy Tale," in* Modern Drama,
> *Vol. XXVI, No. 3, September, 1983, pp. 282-
> 89.*

John Eric Bellquist   (essay date 1988)

[*In the article excerpted below, Bellquist analyzes
mythopoeic elements associated with the late nineteenth-
century movement of Symbolism in* Miss Julie.]

The pages that follow on Strindberg's *Fröken Julie*
(1888), with initial reference to his play *Fadren* (1887), are
part of a longer study of Strindberg's development in the
1880s, when he seemed to be moving towards a mythopoe-

ic means of literary expression and a mythic interpretation
of life, a transition made at least a decade earlier than his
celebrated Inferno crisis and his recognized turn to occultism and religious myth. Recent critics tend to see Strindberg's recourse to myth in the 1890s as suggesting a "polyphonic" modernist technique, but it is doubtful that
Strindberg employed mythology primarily in order to impart structures to his literary works. Strindberg turned to
the mythologies of the world's great religions (Christian
in *Easter* [1902], Hindu in *A Dreamplay* [1901; 1906],
Buddhist in *The Ghost Sonata* [1907]) or of esoteric religious sources (Swedenborg, for example) because he recognized in them ways in which he already saw or conceived the world on his own. He was not a mythographic,
but rather a mythopoeic, author; he created myths, he did
not just borrow them.

To apply such a view to Strindberg in the 1880s is as yet
relatively unorthodox, although it has often been indirectly hinted at by others—especially by those who see signs
of expressionism in Strindberg's earlier work. One speaks
more commonly of Strindberg in the 1880s as a naturalist,
not a poet of myth. In the present essay, the ideological
term "naturalism" is used in Strindberg's own sense, particularly as he develops it in the foreword to *Miss Julie.*
Because of this naturalism, in *Miss Julie* certain basic elements of Strindberg's increasing inclination toward
mythopoesis are suppressed, but they remain there as an
undercurrent nevertheless. Any creative director could
easily bring them to the fore should he or she so wish. To
summarize in advance: there are discernible intimations of
Strindberg's mythopoesis in the play's references to sleep
and dreams; in the exchange with the cook Kristin, when
Julie despairingly gives voice to Strindberg's characteristic
existential theme; and in the image of Salomé, which as
a central icon of Symbolism is also related to sleep and
dreams, to the Symbolist poet's landscape of the mind.
These elements may not at once seem to suggest myth, but
as Ernst Cassirer argues, to the mythic consciousness
sleep, dreams, and waking life are synonymously interrelated; and for Strindberg, who came more and more to
view life as a chaotic dream, demonic myth was a means
of giving meaning to the existential threat of life's possible
meaninglessness. Dreams can point two ways: toward in-
tegrative images and symbols and, hence, myths or to surreal, chaotic discontinuity. For Strindberg they suggested
both.

The Father and, in particular, *Miss Julie* have traditionally been defined as naturalistic, in part because they seem
to present psychological studies of pathological confrontations between the sexes. Each play presents a slice taken
from the lives of a small number of characters, but in *Miss
Julie* Strindberg emphasizes the detailed description of heredity and environmental influences, especially upon Julie
herself. The boundaries of *The Father*'s peculiar world
reach beyond either such naturalistic representation or the
dramatic presentation of prefreudian psychological analysis. Much of the power of *The Father* rests, first, on the
play's existential theme as it is portrayed in the Captain's
struggle and, second, in the play's cosmos of myth. The
existential theme is what Carl Reinhold Smedmark refers
to when he calls *The Father* a tragedy of atheistic deter-

minism; Strindberg develops the theme subtly throughout the play, beginning with the opening scene in which a child's paternity is called into doubt. The myth appears not merely in the play's pattern of mythological allusions (to Hercules, for example), but in that house of women who suggest warring religious and occult visions of life, in the song of the Angel of Death, and in the ghosts who haunt the Captain and Laura's attic. These mythic elements do not imply any spiritual consolation but rather constitute a demonically mythopoeic expression of the possibility of life's absolute meaninglessness (which, as suggested above, is typical of Strindberg's mythopoesis). This mythic meaninglessness is what the Captain must tragically face. One could apply to the world of *The Father* the remark that the protagonist makes in *Inferno* (1897), only in reverse: in *The Father* the positivists have become spirits, and the realists have become divinities. But this means that they are negative divinities, divinities of the absence, rather than the presence, of any consolatory metaphysical meaning.

When we turn to *Miss Julie* on the other hand, we encounter what may at first seem a different world. Here Strindberg's avowed naturalism has become an applied doctrine, which he sketches in the play's foreword both in terms of the theory of hereditary and environmental influences upon human character and by means of contemporaneous theories of psychology. According to such psychology, any particular human being's character consists of a constant flux of chaotic drives or energies that originate both within and without the self, both externally and internally, so that human beings are thus really "characterless." Strindberg writes elsewhere that this fluidity of human character ought to be presented or represented in what he calls "constructionless" literature, but in the foreword to *Miss Julie,* too, he uses similar language when he rejects "the constructed dialogue of French drama". Here naturalism, even as it denotes the determinism of heredity and the environment (upon which Strindberg elaborates at great length), also signifies characterless characters presented in constructionless literature. All but *Miss Julie*'s conclusion, which, since it reflects the psychology of suggestion, clearly foreshadows the intersubjective mythopoeic vision of life that Strindberg portrays during his Inferno period, may therefore seem to resemble an intensified, naturalistic version of *Upstairs, Downstairs;* but we must be sure to take the term naturalism in Strindberg's complex sense. *Miss Julie* involves a servant and a daughter of the nobility who engage in a steamy and seamy seduction and its aftermath, set in a kitchen where we can smell the meat frying on the stove; Jean and Julie are presented as characterless characters; and the play's action, compared with that of Ibsen's drama and most drama before him, is constructionless. Yet Strindberg's doctrine of naturalistic representation, presented by means of the psychology of the characterless, accounts for only part of the play's lasting power: hidden, or perhaps not so hidden, within the play's psychological naturalism are the other elements of Strindberg's mythopoesis to which I have already alluded.

To begin with, one should remember that *Miss Julie,* like *The Father,* displays that "ineradicable subjectivity"

which even critics who call these plays naturalistic can recognize. Part of *Miss Julie*'s dramatic rhythm consists of the ebbing and flowing of Julie and Jean's streams of consciousness, verbalized in the dialogue. The constant interweaving of mental contents deriving from the past and the present, rather than the patterned action of plot, gives the play its primary means of development or movement. But as with any modern stream-of-consciousness novel, this means that Strindberg must resort to other devices if he wishes to give the play an aesthetic shape: among them are the imagery of rising and falling and allusions to Biblical myth. Another pattern of reference that has also been noticed, though perhaps not stressed, involves the imagery of sleep, dreams, and waking. As early as 1924, Martin Lamm wrote that Julie's actions resemble those of a sleepwalker; and even before, in 1908, Strindberg told Manda Björling to play Julie's final moments precisely in that way. The imagery of sleep and dreams and the structure of the action that it accompanies indicate that *Miss Julie* can be taken as a covertly prospective study in Strindberg's later dreamplay technique, and that, like a Symbolist poem, it can therefore be seen as subtly suggesting or presenting a mental landscape—which is how one can view *The Father* as well, though in that play Strindberg's mythopoeic subjectivity is much more obvious.

On one level the references to sleep and dreams in *Miss Julie* may simply be explained by the play's naturalism. After all, the action occurs on Midsummer's Eve, and it lasts all night until sunrise. Certainly anyone who stays up that long will be tired and likely to talk about it. Yet the imagery of sleep and dreams also provide not only a mimetic realism and a poetic structure, but also a dreamlike atmosphere within which the characters converse and move. To understand this atmosphere, which is associated with the play's *midsommarnattsstämning* or 'Midsummer's Eve atmosphere', one may turn to Richard Bark, who in his study of Strindberg's dreamplay technique has shown that playwrights who represent dreams or mental realities on the stage tend to follow certain conventions. As Bark says, dramatic characters stand before us in the flesh, so we cannot look into their minds the way we look into characters' minds in novels. Therefore—to cite one set of examples—a dramatic character may enter into a dreaming state and yet remain on the stage; other characters, who represent or suggest the dreams's contents, can then proceed to act, perhaps on another plane, in a space set off from that of the dreamer. We can see this in Shakespeare's *Tempest* (c. 1611) or in the modern American dramatist Ruth Wolff's *The Abdication* (1969), a play about Queen Kristina; we see it in *To Damascus* (1898) and *A Dreamplay,* too.

In *Miss Julie* a similar situation is introduced: early in the play, in the mysterious kitchen where the cook Kristin has prepared an "infernal" dish for Julie's dog and where Kristin and Julie are imagined by Jean to be concocting a *trollsoppa* or a 'magic soup' that might enable them to envision the future, Kristin peculiarly falls asleep. The transition to this state proceeds through a pantomime to a further dialogue, in which Kristin's role gradually recedes, while Julie and Jean's erotic encounter develops. Kristin's sleep introduces the theme of eroticism more explicitly, permitting Jean's provocative allusion to his having slept with her; and once she is asleep, Jean and Julie begin to act in a more overtly romantic manner, with Jean histrionically raising his glass and kissing Julie's foot. This seems to suggest at least as much the enactment of a romantic fantasy as it does a naturalistic fact. We learn at this point that Kristin's sleep has an esoteric or occult significance, apparently reflecting folk belief: sleep, says Jean when Julie attempts to awaken her, must be respected, and sleepers may not be disturbed. After this, in the older editions, Kristin exits as the stage direction says, *sömndrucken* or 'drunk with sleep'. In the new edition, the direction appears after Jean and Julie have spoken of sleeping on Midsummer's Eve's flowers and recounted their recurrent dreams of rising and falling, a directional change that permits Kristin's presence on the stage even longer and reminds us of the dream all the more. In the play sleep, then, is a recurrent symbolic motif as well as a structural device, and although Kristin does leave the stage, repeated references to her remind us that she is in effect constantly present. Beginning with Kristin's dozing off, one may conceive Jean and Julie to be enacting, or acting in, a kind of dream, just as Sebastian and Antonio do in *The Tempest* while Gonzalo and Alonso are asleep.

This is not to say that what we perceive on the stage is in fact Kristin's dream, although one could certainly play it that way as an experiment if one wished; no more are Antonio and Sebastian necessarily enacting the dreams of Alonso and Gonzalo when they are about to kill Alonso. Instead, while a character or characters are asleep and others remain as if awake, we are reminded, just as in *The Tempest* and in *A Dreamplay,* that art and life are like a dream and that human actions as well as thoughts resemble the dream's contents. "Here I stand, talking about dreams with you," says Julie just after she and Jean have recounted their recurrent dreams of rising and falling, to which Jean replies that tonight they may become *sanndrömmade* and thus their dreams may become true. Of course they do: "Have I been walking in a dream this night?", Julie asks after their sexual consummation; and the answer is that she has. Throughout the play she and Jean move as if they are in a dream, and the dream is in turn associated with the many references to intoxication and to magic—to that *förtrollningen* or 'enchantment' from which one "awakes." Here again the imagery at first may seem simply concrete and naturalistic—the characters are drinking beer and wine; *trollet* or 'the troll' is said to have walked abroad during the night—but soon it becomes symbolically suggestive: magic, intoxication, music, and the fragrance of flowers, all contribute to the play's intersubjective, dreamlike atmosphere. That Julie walks offstage to her suicide just after she has been in a hypnotic trance, during which she has said that she is asleep, is but a fitting culmination to a play in which she has been a sleepwalker almost all along. The stage direction tells us she is awake at this point, but she herself says she is going to her rest—a rest suggested not only by Jean's whispers in her ear, but by the play's constructionless dream of her characterless life, in which impulses toward death and self-destruction have repeatedly accompanied her expression of erotic desire.

If one grants that *Miss Julie* in certain respects might be a dreamplay, one must ask why Strindberg resorted to the dream as a means of dramatic representation. As previously suggested, one might argue that he does so for purposes of structural symbolism, just as would a writer of a stream-of-consciousness novel; but as has also been suggested above, there are at least two more answers to this question. One is that Strindberg's theory of the psychology of the characterless presupposed a world so chaotically subjective that the dream was the only way to account for it; the other is that, for mythopoeic thinking, dreams and life are continuous in ways that for empirical thought they are not. In *The Father* and *Miss Julie,* one can see Strindberg's mythopoesis taking shape, even though it is by no means as developed as it would be beginning with his Inferno period. Mythopoesis, for him, was a metaphysical means that could account for the chaos of modern life, a chaos that the characterlessness of Jean and Julie reflects. It is important to remember these facts when one considers Strindberg's psychological theory: *The Father,* he wrote in a letter from mid-October 1887, presented "the modern fate in the form of an erotic passion;" that modern fate, he added less than a month later, in another letter wherein he described himself as a dreaming sleepwalker, had given rise to "the new world-view, indeterminism". Shaped into a mythic dream, this world-view, along with the psychology of characterlessness that reflects it, constitutes the implicit basis of *Miss Julie* as well, though it was a world-view that remained submerged in the text because he was seeking to create a categorically naturalistic work.

As the end of *Miss Julie* approaches, both Jean and Julie are tired. Once again this is on one level merely naturalistic: they have been up all night, engaging in dalliance. But especially in Julie's case, the tiredness is existential: the flux of impulses that together constitute her character—all those determining impulses, both internal and external, that Strindberg lists in the foreword—have worn her out. She is, she says, "so tired, so endlessly tired." At this point the dream is temporarily ceasing, for along with the sunrise, Kristin is about to bring waking reality into the picture; the trolls, we are told, have gone away. Julie, however, still speaks the language of the dream, pouring forth an impressionistic stream of images that echoes Jean's proposals about opening a hotel by Lake Como. To this Kristin replies:

KRISTIN. Hör nu! Tror fröken själv på det där?
FROKEN. (*tillintetgjord*) Om jag tror på det själv?
KRISTIN. Ja!
FROKEN. Jag vet inte; jag tror inte på någonting mer. . . . Ingenting! Ingenting alls!

KRISTIN. Listen! Does madame herself believe in all that?
FROKEN. (*annihilated*) Do I believe in it myself?
KRISTIN. Yes!
FROKEN. I don't know; I don't believe in anything any more. . . . Nothing! Nothing at all!

Only a few moments later, Julie in turn questions Kristin

about her faith, asking her if she really believes that the Lord will take our sins upon Himself if we are faithful and penitent. Then Julie laments, "Alas, if only I had your faith! Alas, if . . . ." Julie's lack of faith does not just derive from the night's activities or from her problematic upbringing. She is a fundamental Strindbergian type, suffering from the indeterminism of modern life:

> FROKEN.　　. . . Vems är skulden till vad som skett! Min fars, min mors, mitt eget! Mitt eget! Jag har ju intet eget? . . . Vems är felet?—Vad rör det oss vems felet är; det är ändå jag som får bära skulden! bära följderna!

> FROKEN.　　. . . Whose is the fault for what happened! My father's, my mother's, my own! My own? I have nothing of my own? . . . Whose is the fault?—What does it concern us whose fault it is; it is still I who must bear the consequences!

The point here is not merely that Julie's character is naturalistically determined by impulses from her father, her mother, or from anything else. It is that such determining influences cut across each other at such cross purposes that the individual has nothing to hang on to. Unlike Kristin, Julie is, as she herself says, "too proud . . . and too wise" to shift the blame onto Christ. She is the characterless, ultimately existential human being, who lives in the void created by indeterminism and who must therefore create her own fate. This she does, first by reentering the dream state in order to prepare herself to commit suicide and then by walking off stage completely "awake." For her, the dream of characterlessness has led to the moment of existential choice: she elects to die, and death, as in *A Dreamplay,* is linked with waking from the dream of life. By committing suicide, she is, however pessimistically, making a tragically noble response to modern life's indeterminism.

By means of the word existential, I want to turn to what may be called the romantic tradition, for existentialism can be thought of as a philosophical extension of romantic thought. Romantic poets, faced with the death of the past and its structures of meaning—faced, that is, with the fundamental existential dilemma—seek to recreate them or replace them through various means, such as myth. *Miss Julie* is in this sense a romantic play by a romantic author concerned with existential problems. It culminates with Julie's suicide, which is an example of what has been called, with respect to other authors, the aesthetic, or the romantic, image. Julie's suicide is foreshadowed by the decapitation of the siskin; the decapitation of the siskin is preceded in turn by Kristin's declaration that she is on her way to a sermon on the beheading of John the Baptist. Julie herself, at the height of her rage, says she would like to see Jean's brain on the chopping block; she is like Salomé here, but the image is developed in still more brutal terms, as if she were a maenad dismembering Orpheus. Even if one were to insist that my interpretation of *Miss Julie* as a dreamplay about a human being's ultimate confrontation with the abyss only implies relations with Symbolism and its obsession with the dream or with the abyss, nevertheless in this concluding image the play enters the world of Symbolism and decadence explicitly.

Albert Finney and Maggie Smith, from a 1966 production of Miss Julie *in London.*

Among the Symbolists or decadents the image of Salomé and John the Baptist was a central icon or motif, for Salomé embodied simultaneously the dance and the femme fatale. She thus suggested the fatal price of the pursuit of ideal beauty, the alienation of the poet who sought to achieve it, the inescapable presence of death in life and life in death. In *Miss Julie,* the romantic image of the death of John the Baptist and of Julie as Salomé becomes a focusing myth or symbol, just as the Angel of Death in *The Father.* Nor should this be surprising: Strindberg was a painter, which may be one reason why the iconography of his mythic dreamplays *The Father* and *Miss Julie* resembles that of paintings by Puvis de Chavannes (1824-98), Gustave Moreau (1826-98), Odilon Redon (1840-1916), Fernand Khnopff (1858-1921), Emile Fabry (1865-1966), Bellery Desfontaines (1867-1910), or Carlos Schwabe (1866-1926). This is not a matter of influence; of these painters, only Moreau and Puvis de Chavannes were early enough to have earned Strindberg's attention before the writing of *Miss Julie:* at the Salon of 1876, for example, 500,000 people are said to have viewed Moreau's Salomé paintings, which the critics of the day repeatedly described as dreams or hallucinations; and Puvis de Chavannes, who first exhibited his *Beheading of St. John the Baptist* in 1870, was well-known even earlier. We have, however, no evidence of Strindberg's knowledge of such painters until later on, in the 1890s; nor did he read Huysmans' *A Re-*

bours (1884), in which not only Moreau's *Salomé,* but also the works of Redon and Bresdin (1825-85) are described, until February 1889. Yet the list above still illustrates affinities. It could be expanded by references to literature, of course, beginning with the appearance of Hérodias in Heine's *Atta Troll, ein Sommernachstraum* (1843) and continuing through Mallarmé's *Hérodiade* (c. 1864) and Flaubert's story "Hérodias" (1877) to Wilde's play *Salomé* (1894), illustrated by Aubrey Beardsley, among the more obvious examples. A great artist such as Strindberg does not need to have actually encountered such works in order to have arrived at a vision that so many writers and painters of his age so readily shared.

Miss Julie closes, then, with Strindberg's version of the aesthetic image, in order to sum up the consequences of the threat of nihilism in a modern world that seems but an indeterminate dream. Julie elects to enact that image because, as a characterless character, she finally comes to understand this indeterminism so clearly. Unable to stand the beheading of the bird, she is incapable of playing Salomé to Jean. Instead she herself becomes as Salomé and John the Baptist fused into one. She has danced for Jean's head; she has found that eroticism wanting. Although she does not demand Jean's destruction, she openly considers it; yet she cannot face the role of reenacting the image again and again in further sexual encounters. So she martyrs herself rather than someone else. Even as she embodies the aesthetic image, she suggests the self-negation of the work of art rather than the alienation of the artist who, while seeking an ideal, yet impossible, beauty, creates it—a fitting consummation for the Strindberg who was suspicious of art and said it should be constructed in constructionless terms. In effect the characterless Julie could say of herself, as Strindberg once said of himself, that . . . "in an often recurring night dream I feel myself flying, without weight, find it completely natural, just as also all concepts of right, unright, true untrue in me are dissolved, and . . . everything that occurs, no matter how unusual it is, seems that it must be." As Strindberg said, too, in the same context, "det är ju rätta konsekvenserna af den nya verldsåskådningen, indeterminism" ("these are of course the proper consequences of the new world view, indeterminism").

To return to my opening remarks: *Miss Julie* is an instructive text for anyone who wishes to trace the development of Strindberg's mythopoesis. Myth was Strindberg's ultimate response to the horrifying threat of the indeterminism of modern life, which made even the waking hours seem to him like a dream in which he moved as a sleepwalker. The image of Salomé, while properly a legend rather than a true myth, appealed to him simply because it summarized, in symbolic form, an essential type of erotic encounter within the indeterminate dream of life: that erotic longing of both sexes which can become a destructive rather than a constructive force. The image of Salomé, as Strindberg reinterprets it, also summarizes the action of the play. Dramatically he was not interested in the beauty of Salomé, but in the contradictory violence within her attraction, a violence that in his version turns inward upon itself. Such eroticism appeared in Strindberg's work not simply because he was a man who had problems with

women, but because it was part of his negative mythology of life. Later on, in the 1890s, he would at times turn to religions and occult sources that resembled the myths he had also conceived on his own; in the end of *Miss Julie* he was drawn to a Biblical legend that fit with the mythic view of the world that had been developing deep within his consciousness. Either case, the myth created or the myth or legend borrowed, expressed the underlying vision of the author, which itself was mythic and which resulted in either covertly or overtly mythopoeic works. (pp. 1-10)

John Eric Bellquist, "Rereading 'Fröken Julie': Undercurrents in Strindberg's Naturalistic Intent," in Scandinavian Studies, *Vol. 60, No. 1, Winter, 1988, pp. 1-11.*

Michael Meyer on Strindberg's narrative technique:

Strindberg achieved an economy beyond Ibsen's; he proudly pointed out that the plots of *Miss Julie* and *Creditors* would each have sufficed for a five-act play, but that he had reduced each of them to a single act of ninety minutes or less. Take a lamb cutlet, he said; it looks large, but three-quarters of it is bone and fat, containing a kernel of meat. I strip off the bone and fat and, like the Greeks, give you the kernel.

Michael Meyer, in his Strindberg: A Biography, *Secker & Warburg, 1985.*

Freddie Rokem   (essay date 1988)

[In the essay below, Rokem illuminates Strindberg's stage techniques in Miss Julie.*]*

Strindberg succeeded in arriving at theatrical effects that resemble the way a photograph "cuts out" a piece of reality: not a symmetrical joining of one wall to the other walls in the house—the basic fourth-wall technique of the realistic theater—but rather an asymmetrical cutting-out. Furthermore, Strindberg used cinematographic techniques resembling zoom, montage, and cut, which are highly significant from the strictly technical point of view and for the meaning of the plays. Historically, photography and movies were making great strides at the time and were art forms to which he himself—as photographer and as movie writer—gave considerable attention and interest. During Strindberg's lifetime, both *The Father* and *Miss Julie* were filmed as silent movies by the director Anna Hofman-Uddgren and her husband, Gustaf Uddgren, writer and friend of Strindberg, but only *The Father* has been preserved.

Strindberg thus developed dramatic theatrical techniques that, like the movie camera, can bring the viewer very close to the depicted action and, at the same time, can quite easily change the point of view or direction of observing an event or succession of events. The disappearance or near disappearance of the static focal point is largely the result of the introduction of these different photographic and cinematographic techniques. When the characters, the action, and the fictional world are continuously presented, either from partial angles or from constantly changing ones, it is often impossible for the spectator to determine where the focal point is or what the central experiences are in the characters' world. This in turn is a reflection of the constant and usually fruitless search of the characters for such focal points in their own lives.

Whereas Hedda Gabler's lack of will to continue living was based on her refusal to bear offspring within the confines of married life, Miss Julie's despair primarily reflects her unwillingness merely to exist. Of course, there are external reasons for her suicide, and Strindberg has taken great care both in the play and in the preface almost to overdetermine her final act of despair. Nevertheless, as several critics have pointed out, there are no clear and obvious causal connections between her suicide and the motives presented. Instead, this final act of despair is triggered by an irrational leap into the complete unknown, as she herself says "ecstatically" (according to Strindberg's stage direction) in the final scene when she commands Jean, the servant, to command her, the mistress, to commit suicide: "I am already asleep—the whole room stands as if in smoke for me . . . and you look like an iron stove . . . that resembles a man dressed in black with a top hat—and your eyes glow like coal when the fire is extinguished—and your face is a white patch like the ashes." These complex images within images resemble links in a chain, and they illustrate the constant movement or flux of the despairing speaker's mind. For Miss Julie there is no fixed point in reality, no focal point, except her will to die, to reach out for a nothingness.

In Strindberg's description of the set in the beginning of *Miss Julie,* he carefully specifies how the diagonal back wall cuts across the stage from left to right, opening up in the vaulted entry toward the garden. This vault however, is only partially visible. The oven and the table are also only partially visible because they are situated exactly on the borderline between the stage and the offstage areas. The side walls and the ceiling of the kitchen are marked by draperies and tormentors. Except for the garden entry, there are no doors or windows. As the play reveals, the kitchen is connected only to the private bedrooms of the servants Jean and Kristin; there is no direct access to the upper floor where the count and his daughter, Julie, live except through the pipe-telephone.

In his preface to the play, Strindberg explained: "I have borrowed from the impressionistic paintings the idea of the asymmetrical, the truncated, and I believe that thereby, the bringing forth of the illusion has been gained; since by not seeing the whole room and all the furnishings, there is room for imagination, i.e., fantasy is put in motion and it completes what is seen." Here Strindberg describes the imaginative force of this basically metonymic set. But rather than following the custom in realistic theater of showing the *whole* room as part of a house that in turn is part of the fictional world of the play, Strindberg very consciously exposes only *part* of the room. He claims it should be completed in the imagination of the audience. As Evert Sprinchorn comments: "The incompleteness of the impressionist composition drew the artist and the viewer into closer personal contact, placing the viewer in the scene and compelling him to identify with the artist at a particular moment."

The audience comes closer not only to the artist through this view of the kitchen from its interior but also, by force of the diagonal arrangements of the set, to the characters inside the kitchen. This is because the fourth wall, on which the realistic theater was originally based, has been moved to an undefined spot somewhere in the auditorium, the spectators are in the same room as the dramatic characters. It is also important to note that, to achieve this effect, Strindberg also removed the side walls from the stage, thus preventing the creation of any kind of symmetrical room that the spectator could comfortably watch from the outside. Furthermore, the audience is not guided regarding the symmetries, directions, or focal points in the set itself, which the traditional theater strongly emphasized. The only area that is separated from the kitchen is the garden, visible through the vaulted entry, with its fountain and, significantly enough, its statue of Eros. Thus, the physical point of view of the audience in relationship to the stage is ambiguous.

What is presented is a "photograph" of the kitchen taken from its interior, drawing the audience's attention to different points inside or outside as the play's action develops. The set of *Miss Julie* can, furthermore, be seen as a photograph because while the spectators get a close view from the inside of the kitchen, they also experience an objective perception of it and the events taking place there through the frame of the proscenium arch. The comparison between Strindberg's scenic technique in *Miss Julie* and the photograph is compelling because of the very strong tension between intimacy and closeness on the one hand and objectivity and distance on the other; this sort of tension has often been observed to be one of the major characteristics not only of the play but also of photography, as the practice of documenting and preserving large numbers of slices of reality. The photograph also "cuts" into a certain space from its inside, never showing walls as parallel (unless it is a very big space photographed from the outside), at the same time it freezes the attention of the viewer upon the specific moment. In photography the focus is on the present (tense), which is "perfected" into a "has been" through the small fraction of a second when the shutter is opened. Barthes even goes so far as to call this moment in photography an epiphany.

This is also what happens in *Miss Julie* when the attention of the audience is continuously taken from one temporary focal point to the next by force of the gradual development of the action. Our eyes and attention move from the food Jean is smelling to the wine he is tasting, to Miss Julie's handkerchief, to Kristin's fond folding and smelling of the handkerchief when Jean and Miss Julie are at the dance and so on. In *Miss Julie* these material objects force the characters to confront one another and to interact. They are not objects primarily belonging to or binding the characters to the distant past toward which they try to reach out in their present sufferings—as are the visual focal points in Ibsen's plays or even the samovars and pieces of old furniture in Chekhov's plays. The objects in *Miss Julie* are first and foremost immersed in the present, forcing the characters to take a stance and their present struggles to be closely observed by the audience.

In *Miss Julie* the past and the future have been transformed into fantasy, so the only reality for the characters is the present. Because Jean and Miss Julie are forced to act solely on the basis of the immediate stimuli causing their interaction, and because the kitchen has been cut off diagonally leaving no visually defined borders on- or off-stage, it is impossible to locate any constant focal points, either outside or inside the fictional world of the play and the subjective consciousness of the characters. This "narrative" technique achieves both a very close and subjective view of the characters and a seemingly objective and exact picture of them. The temporal retrospection has also been diminished because Jean and Miss Julie are not as disturbed by irrational factors belonging to a guilt-ridden past as, for example, the Ibsen heroes are. Strindberg's characters are motivated primarily by their present desires.

This of course does not mean that there are no expository references to the past in *Miss Julie,* on the contrary, there are a large number of references to specific events in the lives of the characters preceding the opening of the scenic action. The play, in fact, begins with a series of such references, all told by Jean to Kristin. Thus, we learn that Miss Julie is "mad again tonight" (inferring that it is not the first time this has happened), as represented by the way she is dancing with Jean. And to give her behavior some perspective (just before her entrance), Jean relates to Kristin how Miss Julie's fiancé broke their engagement because of the degradations he had to suffer, jumping over her whip as well as being beaten by it. These events are, however, never corroborated by other characters in the play. Miss Julie's subsequent behavior does to some extent affirm Jean's story, but we can never be completely sure.

What is specific to Strindberg's plays is not the omission of the past—which absurdist drama emphasizes—but rather a lack of certainty regarding the reliability of what the characters say about that past. And since in many of Strindberg's plays there is no source of verification other than the private memory of the character speaking, the past takes on a quite subjective quality. Miss Julie gives *her* version of *her* past and Jean relates *his,* and the possible unreliability of these memories is confirmed when Jean changes his story of how he as a child watched her in the garden. (pp. 112-15)

The major outcome of past actions, guilt, is objectified in Ibsen's plays. That is the reason why it can be given a specific geographical location in the outside world, which becomes the "focus" (in all respects) for it. In Strindberg's fictional worlds there is definitely an awareness of past actions, that is of guilt, but it exists as a private limbo in the subjective consciousness of the individual characters and thus cannot be projected onto the objective outside world. That is why in Strindberg's plays there is either no visual focus or a constantly moving one.

In *Miss Julie* the two principal characters continuously try to turn their respective opponents into the focal point onto which their own guilt and related feelings of inadequacy and general frustration can be projected. That is one of the major reasons for their sexual union and the distrust and even hatred to which it leads. Just how fickle those focal points are, however, can also be seen as in Miss Julie's last desperate attempt to find some kind of support in Jean for her step into the unknown realm of death. Jean's face has become a white spot, resembling to Miss Julie the ashes of a fire because the light of the sun—which is rising at this point in the play—is illuminating him. Again the present situation becomes the point of departure for her wishes. And when Miss Julie wants to die, her wish is thus focused on Jean's illuminated face. In *Ghosts* Ibsen used the same images (the fire and the sun) at the end of the last two acts as objective focal points. Strindberg has compressed these images into one speech in which they are projected onto Jean by the fantasy of Miss Julie's subjective consciousness. Ibsen gives a "scientific" explanation of Oswald's madness for which the sunset is a circumstantial parallel, whereas Strindberg lets the sunset motivate the outburst of Julie's death wish, as expressed from within. Thus the preparations for the introduction of expressionism, wherein everything is projection, had already been made in Strindberg's pre-Inferno plays. (pp. 115-16)

> Freddie Rokem, "The Camera and the Aesthetics of Repetition: Strindberg's Use of Space and Scenography in 'Miss Julie', 'A Dream Play', and 'The Ghost Sonata'," in Strindberg's Dramaturgy, *edited by Göran Stockenström, University of Minnesota Press, 1988, pp. 107-28.*

M. L. K. Lally   (essay date 1990)

[*In the following essay, Lally analyzes the symbolism of decapitation in* Miss Julie.]

In August Strindberg's *Miss Julie,* a fascinating study of a complex and naturalistic heroine, there is an odd reference to the Sunday lesson, which Kristen is anxious for Jean to hear. The subject is, as Strindberg informs us, the beheading of John the Baptist. Of what possible relevance to our understanding of the drama is this rather pointed reference?

We recall that after the seduction of Jean (John) by Miss Julie, or Julie by Jean, the valet prepares for Sunday services to keep his promise to his fiancée, Kristen. Jean complains that the lesson of the day, the beheading of John the Baptist, will be a long one.

> KRISTEN. It's about the beheading of John the Baptist, I think.
> JEAN. That's sure to be horribly long. Hi, you're choking me! Oh Lord, I'm so sleepy, so sleepy!

All through this interchange, Kristen is helping Jean to dress by putting on his "bib and tucker." The comment, "you're choking me," refers to Kristen's actions, but also to Jean's emotional state as he is being threatened and pressured by both his fiancée and the distraught Julie.

Shortly thereafter, Jean beheads Julie's caged greenfinch.

This act has several meanings. On the literal level, the bird is an encumbrance that must be eliminated if their escape is to succeed. On the symbolic level, however, it is a symbol for Julie herself, imprisoned in her sex and her social class, helpless before the razor that will end her life. But just as the bird threatens the couple's ease of escape, Julie herself poses a threat to Jean, to his current secure position, and to his ambitious plans for himself. As the couple reproach one another, agonizing over what to do, Julie says,

> You think I'm a coward and will run away. No, now I'm going to stay—and let the storm break. My father will come back . . . find his desk broken open . . . his money gone. Then he'll ring that bell—twice for the valet—and then he'll send for the police . . . and I shall tell everything. Everything.

This threat of exposure Jean cannot bear. As Julie makes a half-hearted appeal to Kristen to join Jean and herself in their escape, Jean is seen in the door of his room, "sharpening his razor on a strop." Later, Julie fingers this same razor, asking Jean,

> If you were in my place, what would you do? (*picking up the razor and making a gesture*) This?

Jean responds affirmatively, saying that he, unlike Julie, would not actually take his own life, implying perhaps that she should. Julie then comments that her father couldn't commit suicide either.

> JEAN. No, he didn't want to. He had to be revenged first.
> JULIE. And now my mother is revenged again, through me.

Julie's comment is a curious one that is more fully understood in the light of the reference to John the Baptist made shortly before. Julie's comment recalls Salome's mother's revenge on John the Baptist, first through his imprisonment by Herod and then through his beheading, which Salome obtains for her mother by dancing before the king. In the cases of both Salome and Julie, the mothers of the girls are revenged, first in their own right and then through the agency of their daughters. Julie's second revenge on her father will come when and if the Count is disgraced by his daughter's shameless behavior with the valet. Both Julie and Jean recognize that this behavior may have "consequences," including even the bastardization of the Count's bloodline.

But the double revenge against the Count is never realized, because Jean cannot run the risk of being exposed as a seducer. He hears "the two sharp rings on the bell" to which Julie had alluded earlier when she was threatening him. At once he becomes the subservient lackey. Whereas several hours ago Jean had total control over his actions (beheading Julie's bird without a moment's hesitation), he wavers now in indecision while Julie pleads with him to order her to cut her own throat. Desperate, trapped by his social class, and unmanned by the Count's presence, Jean reflects,

> To be so frightened of a bell! Yes, but it's not just

a bell. There's somebody behind it—a hand moving it—and something else moving the hand—and if you stop your ears—if you stop your ears—yes, then it rings until you answer—and then it's too late. Then the police come and . . . and . . . (*The bell rings twice loudly. Jean flinches, then straightens himself up.*) It's horrible. But there's no other way to end it . . . Go!

The command is clear. Julie, with the razor Jean has put into her hand, walks firmly out to the barn to end her own life, a ritual severance similar to the beheading commemorated in the lesson of the day. (pp. 196-98)

> *M. L. K. Lally, "Strindberg's 'Miss Julie'," in* The Explicator, *Vol. 48, No. 3, Spring, 1990, pp. 196-98.*

Alice Templeton   (essay date 1990)

[*In the following excerpt, Templeton examines the conflict between naturalism and tragedy in* Miss Julie.]

Reading *Miss Julie* against rather than through the preface is made possible by the tension between naturalism and modern tragedy within the play. Naturalism and tragedy appear to be contradictory literary and philosophical stances, since naturalism implies a determined world, while tragedy depends on the possibilities of moral choice and of error. An unfortunate outcome in a determined world is usually considered pathetic, while the same outcome in a world where individual will asserts itself is considered tragic. It would seem, then, that naturalism and tragedy could not coexist without serious qualifications of both concepts.

Strindberg attested to the importance of the dialectic between these apparently contrary effects by subtitling the play "A Naturalistic Tragedy." The subtitle is usually understood to mean that the play employs naturalistic dramatic techniques, that it validates naturalistic beliefs about heredity and environment, and that it shows, through Julie's unfortunate demise, the fallacy of attempting to live outside those biological and social laws. (p. 470)

In the preface Strindberg suggests that this same antagonism between naturalism and tragedy structures the play. He describes Miss Julie as

> a tragic type, offering us the spectacle of a desperate fight against nature; a tragic legacy of romanticism, which is now being dissipated by naturalism. . . .

Julie's "desperate fight against nature" is of course embodied in her struggle with Jean, the spokesman in the play for naturalism. Her romanticism is primarily a profound discontent with the sexual and class conventions of her day and an accompanying desire to abandon those socially-defined differences, at least for the holiday night during which the play takes place. According to Strindberg, Julie's tragedy is that she is caught in the middle of indifferent life-forces that doom her to weakness and death. But also in large part her tragedy is that she is not a naturalist: in the first half of the play she does not or cannot give in to a deterministic worldview, and she will not accept her "natural" destiny as woman and as aristocrat. As a result, she appears to pursue her own destruction.

The preface again emphasizes the antagonism between naturalism and tragedy when it speculates about the audience's responses to *Miss Julie.* According to Strindberg, to respond to Miss Julie's destruction as tragedy is to depend on "those inferior and unreliable mechanical apparatuses called emotions": if Miss Julie wins the audience's sympathy, it is because "we are still too weak to overcome the fear that the same fate might overtake us." Strindberg looks forward to the time when audiences are able to respond with "indifference" to "the brutal, cynical, and heartless spectacle that life offers us" because for him the "alternate rising and falling provides one of life's greatest pleasures . . . " To sympathize with Julie, a requirement for understanding the play as a tragedy in the broadest sense of the term, is then to respond to the play with outmoded romantic emotion: it is to fail, along with Julie, as a naturalist.

Strindberg's comments, considered along with the criticism that praises the play for its tragic and romantic effect, imply that the tragic dimension of *Miss Julie* arises from a breach in naturalistic vision, perhaps even from the failure of naturalism as an effective aesthetic. The difficulty is in locating the rift in naturalism: is it in the character of Julie, in the play taken as a whole, in the audience, or in all of these? The preface contends that the vestigial emotions of the audience, like Julie's vestigial romanticism, are to blame; however, the text itself can be read as an indictment of the naturalistic vision the preface claims the play celebrates. *Miss Julie* can be understood as "a naturalistic tragedy" not because Julie is victimized by naturalistic forces but because she falls victim to a naturalistic worldview.

The "tragic legacy of romanticism", as Strindberg defines it in the preface, is consonant with rebellion against nature, but in the play Julie rebels against the social systems of class and gender. In this sense she possesses "revolutionary" desire, impulsive and ill-defined though it may be. Julie wants to abandon, at least for Midsummer's Eve, the arbitrary, oppressive roles that are expected of her as an aristocratic woman: "Tonight we're all just having a good time. There's no question of rank." She may be alternately contemptible and pathetic, victimizing and victimized, but she is profoundly discontented with conventional gender and class relations, as her treatment of her fiancé and her dream about falling indicate. Because her "revolution" lacks a method, and because she has no satisfying means of expression, her discontent is self-destructive. With no program for change, with no means of expression of her own beyond those rooted in class and gender, and with subtle coaxing from Jean, she pursues transformation through sex. The idea of sexual pairing as deliverance from class oppression is a common one in folktales (Cinderella, for example) and in literary works from Richardson to Lawrence. Strindberg reverses the usual structure, making his female character the discontented aristocrat who wishes to fall rather than the lower class victim who

is helped up the social ladder by a fortunate marriage. This arrangement enables the play to emphasize the undirected, inexpressible quality of Julie's desire even as Strindberg provides multiple, yet finally inadequate explanations of her discontent. Further confounding any constructive expression of her desire is Julie's dependence on the very privileges of sex and class identity that she denounces.

Jean, who in a very different play might sympathize with Julie's predicament, also feels trapped in the class system, but his response opposes hers. Rather than reject the system, he seeks to beat it, to rise within it—"to get up, up to the very top"—and so he is dedicated to its perpetuation. Ironically, Jean is both the discontented servant who possesses an uneasy class consciousness and the play's central spokesman for social and biological determinism. As such he is both an encouragement and an adversary to Julie's revolutionary, if inarticulate, desire. Julie's romanticism offers Jean the opportunity of sexual conquest, and with it a possible means up the social ladder, but it also threatens to expose his complicity in his own class oppression and his cruel role as sexual oppressor. The sexual interlude is the play's symbolic center. Sex is the act by which, paradoxically, both characters believe they can, at least temporarily, legitimate their visions and accomplish their personal and class transformations.

The conflict between the two characters takes the form of a power struggle to control the symbolic significance of the major actions in the play, sex and suicide. Although the characters waver, change roles as master and servant, and speak from complex unconscious motives, the conflict between Julie as revolutionary and Jean as determinist motivates the entire action and language of the play. The uniqueness and fineness of the play reside in the way the desires of both Julie and Jean emerge spontaneously in reaction to each other and take forms that have decidedly destructive consequences. In Birgitta Steene's words, the play "lives . . . on its emotional tempo."

While neither character is deliberately "political," their struggle reveals them to be pawns moved by the political effects of their own language and actions. In addition, the intoxicating odor of flowers, the half-light, the alcohol, and the Midsummer's Eve saturnalia contribute to the impulsiveness of the characters and lend the play the accidental, circumstantial atmosphere characteristic of both tragedy and naturalistic literature, though in each case that aura has contrary philosophical and political significance.

Jean's calculated, harshly realistic views of sex and of class difference constantly undercut yet strangely encourage Julie's desire to abandon her place in the traditional gender and class structure. In the first half of the play, leading up to the offstage sexual interlude, Jean appears to be the voice of reason and restraint, warning the foolish and haughty Miss Julie to protect her reputation. That is, he seems to be the worldly naturalist celebrated in the preface, who knows too well "the brutal, cynical, and heartless spectacle that life offers." But much as honest Iago twists appearances to reveal their seediest side, Jean drops the sexual insinuations that lead Julie to her downfall:

JEAN. Frankly, Miss Julie, I don't want to hurt your feelings, but I wonder if it's wise—I mean for you to dance twice in a row with the same partner. Especially since the people around here love to talk.

MISS JULIE (*bridling*). What do you mean? What kind of talk? What are you trying to say?

When Julie orders Jean to change out of his livery on this holiday, Jean again calls attention to their sexual difference by saying, "I'd have to ask you to leave for a minute. My black coat is hanging right here—." The presence of the sleeping Christine, his fiancée, also enables him to display his sexuality in front of Miss Julie, as he corrects Julie's cruel observation that Christine probably snores: "No, she doesn't. But she talks in her sleep." Jean thus taunts Julie by reminding her of his sexuality, the one sphere in his life in which she, as aristocrat, has no immediate privilege. Far from being the indifferent, rational understanding of life's laws portrayed in the preface, the naturalism that Jean professes is a self-interested passivity that protects him while it fixes a locus for Julie's desire.

In the same way that he projects his sexuality in terms of his concern for Julie's reputation, Jean also reveals his aristocratic tastes and worldliness in the disguise of servility. When Julie compliments him in French, to her surprise he responds in French. Also he rejects her compliments as "flattery," explaining in formal language that "My natural modesty would not allow me to presume that you were paying sincere compliments to someone like me. . . ." His display of aristocratic language leads to other revelations about his travels, his acting ability, and his exposure to upper class culture. In fact, his very servility to Miss Julie is the primary way he foils her attempt to dispense with class difference on Midsummer's Eve. By being all servant, Jean forces Julie to be the mistress she claims not to want to be:

MISS JULIE. Why don't you sit down?

JEAN. I wouldn't take the liberty in your presence.

MISS JULIE. Not even if I ordered you?

JEAN. Of course I'd obey.

Ironically, she must command him to be her equal. Although his servility thwarts her desire to relate on a human rather than a class level, his show of cultivation renders the arbitrariness of class structure even more clear, and so encourages Julie's pursuit.

Along with flaunting his sexuality and aristocratic polish, Jean further inflames and fixes Julie's desire by implying that their sexual alliance is forbidden by the very rules of class structure that Julie longs to defy. Jean's and Julie's views of the lower class are at odds throughout the first section of the play. Their difference in attitude toward the crowd again reveals the difference between his determinism and her revolutionary desire. Julie believes that on this Midsummer's Eve rank can be erased, while Jean constantly insists that by dancing with the people, and by dancing with him more than once, Julie compromises her reputation as mistress of the estate. When Jean warns her

not to "climb down," Julie replies, "I have a higher opinion of these people than you do. Let's see who's right! Come on! (*She gives him a long, steady look*)." Her challenge is as much a political one as it is sexual; sex will be the test of whose vision is "right," his naturalism or her romanticism.

Not only does Jean at once deflect and intensify Julie's sexual desire by his overstated allegiance to the "laws" of the class structure, but he also overstates his naturalistic view of sex. Once again, though the preface would lead us to think otherwise, the play reveals Jean's stance to be far from disinterested. For Jean, sex is a drive, not a matter of choice or will, and for that reason it is not a matter for which he is responsible. As she orders him to kiss her hand, he warns Miss Julie that he is only a man, that he is "young," and that it is "dangerous to play with fire." Sex is simply a need, not an expression of complex desires and certainly not an experience particularly related to love. When Julie asks Jean about his experiences with "love," he replies, "We don't use that word around here." In his description of his adolescent attraction to Julie, love is seen more as a sickness to be cured, an inconvenience to be eliminated, than as an experience with any unique significance. Thus after the sexual interlude when Julie begs him to say he loves her, Jean denies her, depriving her of any possible redemption that could come from even so confused an attempt at emotional human connection.

While Jean is the spokesman for naturalism in the play, the play itself shows his stance to be an "unnecessary determinism." Not only is it a strategy that potentially allows him to advance materially and sexually and at the same time escape personal responsibility for his inaction and for Julie's demise, but the play repeatedly demonstrates the fallacy of social and sexual determinism. (pp. 470-75)

The power struggle between Julie and Jean is not easily resolved because the two characters wish to carry out the seduction on their own very different terms; in fact, it is only at the moment when the crowd is pressing toward the kitchen that Jean's determinism completely overpowers Julie's romanticism. He is able to convince her that just as in his boyhood he had only one way out of the lovely outhouse, so she now has only one way out of the situation that threatens her reputation with the people: according to Jean, "You can't fight them; you can only run away." Christine's room is not an option because Jean has already exposed Julie's insensitivity toward the working class when she tried to awaken Christine at the table. Julie is driven into Jean's room by what appears to be "necessity," and sexual union with Jean is robbed of any symbolic significance as an expression of desire broader than that of immediate sexual need. In this way Jean succeeds in defining their sexual liaison as an act of desperate necessity, and thus he robs Julie of the symbolic, political significance that might have affirmed or empowered her desire. Julie's "coming down" is accomplished not in her own terms but in Jean's, though his motives are carefully disguised by his continual reference to the "natural" and "factual" necessities over which he has no control—namely, his manhood and the malicious mob.

The irony and tragedy of the play reside in the fact that, as Jean warns, the sexual interlude does have political and social consequences, but it does not bring the transformations that either character intends. In the last half of the play the characters continue to struggle for control over the symbolic meaning of their sexual intimacy, and, at the end, they battle over the meaning of Julie's suicide. After their liaison Jean's tone and language greatly change. Though Jean insists on calling her "Miss Julie" as long as they are in the Count's house, Julie clearly no longer commands deference from Jean as mistress of the house. She is now more woman than aristocrat, and he abandons his attitude of servility toward her. But she also cannot command respect from him as his lover. In fact, he refuses to speak of love:

> I'll tell you a thousand times—but later! Not now. And not here. Above all, let's keep our feelings out of this or we'll make a mess of everything. We have to look at this thing calmly and coolly, like sensible people. (*He takes out a cigar, clips the end, and lights it.*) Now you sit there and I'll sit here, and we'll talk as if nothing had happened.

He even acknowledges that his story of wanting to die for her was only part of the story: "When I was lying in the onion beds, looking up at you on the rose terrace, I—I'm telling you the truth now—I had the same dirty thoughts that all boys have." Jean thus reduces love and desire to a "natural" sexual urge.

As Julie becomes more disaffected with Jean's calculated coldness, she tries to reassert her class power but is harshly reminded of her own failing, her now-vulgarized sexuality. Jean also reminds her again of her upper-class insensitivity and selfishness:

> JEAN. Why be miserable? Look at the conquest you've made! Think of poor Christine in there. Don't you think she's got any feelings?
>
> MISS JULIE. I thought so a while ago; I don't now. A servant's a servant—
>
> JEAN. And a whore's a whore!

When Julie tries again to assert her former power as aristocrat—"You lackey! You shoeshine boy! Stand up when I talk to you!"—Jean denies any responsibility for the seduction and hurls half-truths at her:

> You lackey lover! You bootblack's tramp! Shut your mouth and get out of here! Who do you think you are telling me I'm coarse? I've never seen anybody in my class behave as crudely as you did tonight. Have you ever seen any of the girls around here grab at a man like you did? Do you think any of the girls of my class would throw themselves at a man like that? I've never seen the like of it except in animals and prostitutes! . . . do you think a person in my position would have dared to look twice at you if you hadn't asked for it?

Although he vacillates between being brutal and being comforting, throughout the last section of the play Jean treats Julie as an inferior woman, not as the mistress of the house. Furthermore, rather than speaking from his earlier role as a deferential servant who knows his place all too well, he speaks openly as a man concerned with the material consequences the situation might offer him. Jean's change of tone reinforces the reader's sense of the political, coercive foundations of his naturalism, despite claims to the contrary by Jean and by the preface.

As John Ward has pointed out [in his *The Social and Religious Plays of August Strindberg*], the second section of *Miss Julie* is characterized by the growing sexual aggression of the characters toward each other. It may be more accurate to say that sexually aggressive language provides the harshest, most violent expression for the power struggle between Jean and Julie. As Julie attempts to regain some power for herself, she tries various attacks that might provide her with some position other than the one Jean's naturalistic worldview has put her in. Just as Jean expresses his disgust with Julie's sexuality, so Julie viciously rages at Jean after he coldly beheads her bird:

> Oh, how I'd love to see your blood, your brains on that chopping block. I'd love to see the whole of your sex swimming in a sea of blood just like that.

Immediately after this outburst Julie turns to Christine for help and protection from Jean; significantly, Christine is "cold and unmoved," refusing to sympathize with Miss Julie and even reinforcing Jean's naturalistic worldview with her own brand of Christian determinism and classism.

Ward argues that Christine's pietism is more responsible for Julie's death than Jean's coldness is; not only does she prevent their escape by telling the stable boy not to let out any horses, but she also encourages Julie's death with her ideas of predestination and her belief in the paradox "the last shall be first." But blaming Christine for not being a "sister" to Julie seems extreme, especially after the abuse Julie has aimed at Christine earlier in the play. Still, like Jean, Christine overwhelms Julie and her revolutionary desire with a determinism that says, "That's how things are, Miss Julie." Both Christine and Jean condemn Miss Julie for breaking the conventional sexual and class rules, and both in their own ways reduce Julie's desire to one-dimensional need. Christine's Christian vision denies the fullness of Julie's human predicament as completely as Jean's naturalism warps Julie's desire into a scenario of sexual desperation, an ironic reversal of Julie's belittlement of Christine earlier in the play.

The ending of *Miss Julie* is the most troublesome part of the play for readers and audiences of Strindberg's drama. Critics offer various, often conflicting interpretations of the manner and significance of Julie's turn toward suicide. For example, Maurice Valency emphasizes [in his *The Flower and the Castle: An Introduction to Modern Drama*] that the end of the play focuses as much on Jean's destruction as on Julie's, given that in sexual and class terms Strindberg identifies more with Jean than with Julie. Lamm writes that the play "leaves us with the impression that [Julie's] suicide is not the result of clear deliberation but of a moment of fortuitous hysteria." Other critics conclude that Julie's suicide is both believable and deliberate, and because it is inspired by her aristocratic code of honor, her self-destruction in some way assures her triumph over Jean's mean, materialistic existence. The preface supports this conclusion: "Miss Julie would take vengeance on herself . . . because of that inherited or acquired sense of honor" possessed by the upper class. In contrast, naturalists "have banished guilt along with God." For this reason, according to Strindberg's preface, "the servant Jean lives on; but not Miss Julie, who cannot live without honor."

In this instance, too, the play provides for more complex meanings than the preface indicates. Julie's suicide is more than a display of an aristocratic code of honor. At the end of the play, upon learning that the Count has returned, Julie turns to Jean to help her destroy herself:

> . . . Oh, I'm so tired. I can't bring myself to do anything. Can't repent, can't run away, can't stay, can't live . . . can't die. Help me, Jean. Command me, and I'll obey like a dog. Do me this last favor. Save my honor, save [the Count's] name. You know what I ought to do but can't force myself to do. Let me use your willpower. You command me and I'll obey.

Suicide, Julie realizes, is what she "ought to do," but she has no conviction either to do it or not to do it. It is simply the course she should take, given the scheme of things that Jean has so convincingly impressed on them both. Though Jean himself is hesitant and weak, pitifully reduced to a powerless servant at the first sound of the Count's voice through the speaking tube, he finally does give in to Julie's plea: "It's horrible! But there's no other way for it to end.—Go!" With these final words of the play, Julie turns toward the barn, razor in hand.

If Julie's suicide can be seen as motivated by an upper-class code of honor, it is not a code that personally or inwardly moves her but rather one that she feels she "ought" to act on. It is made clear at the end of the play, through the characters' desperation, Jean's fear of the Count, and Julie's hypnotic fantasy, that neither character is particularly controlled, willful, or committed: they are equally exhausted and powerless. The naturalistic worldview that Jean so readily endorses as he seduces and then condemns Julie has reached a fatal conclusion, and the characters are left with no choice but to see the logic through to its "horrible" end. Rather than being triumphant over Jean because of her finer sense of honor—rather than destroying herself in opposition to Jean—Julie destroys herself *within* the logic of the naturalistic worldview that Jean so effectively imposes on them both throughout the play. She is, therefore, a victim, but paradoxically it is only by Julie's destroying herself *within* the logic of a naturalistic worldview that the play, understood as a whole, can symbolically censor that reductive, finally fatal vision. The play's critique of naturalism is thus larger than any one character's representation of it.

Regardless of her degree of consciousness or willfulness in implicating Jean in her death, the manner of Julie's suicide does clearly make Jean and the naturalistic vision he stands for culpable. Perhaps more important than forcing Jean to play an actual role in her death is the fact that in a larger sense the very innocence of Julie's suicide ensures the triumph of her romantic worldview over Jean's naturalistic interpretation. According to Strindberg's prediction in the preface, audiences who, like Christine, might have harshly judged Julie had she lived on or had her suicide been purposely vindictive, will respond sympathetically to her predicament. In this way Julie's death breaks the hold of the naturalistic worldview.

In *The Critical Difference*, Barbara Johnson writes, "What is often most fundamentally disagreed upon is whether a disagreement arises out of the complexities of fact or out of the impulses of power." Johnson identifies the critic's dilemma in dealing with *Miss Julie.* Does the fatal struggle between Jean and Julie dramatize given, naturalistic facts of social and sexual difference? Or does the play present for our analysis an ideological power struggle, a confrontation for which Julie is sadly unprepared, equipped only to be complicitous in her own destruction? In the preface, Strindberg claims that it is the complicated facts of sexual and class difference—of nature—that result in Julie's tragedy. However, the play's action seems to be propelled toward its tragic conclusion by the impulses of power on the part of both characters.

Both characters fall into the trap of naturalism which Jean has set to rationalize his own cruel opportunism, though certainly the cost is much higher for Julie than for him. Both Julie and Jean are reduced to caricatures in the end: he to the whimpering, ineffectual slave, and she to the female suicide ruined by sexual and social scandal. In the sense that the play depicts the waste brought about by a deterministic attitude toward human relations, individual power, and sexual and class politics, *Miss Julie* is "a naturalistic tragedy."

The play leaves us not with a vision of determinism but with an understanding of the determination with which the characters engage in destructive sexual and class politics. Julie's actions are ultimately as misdirected and self-destructive as Jean's maintenance of class and gender systems. The play finally impresses on us the fruitlessness of her rebellion and of any revolution that is unable to construe power in a new way. It dramatizes the sometimes pitiable, sometimes contemptible, vulnerability of one whose changing consciousness cannot create commensurate expression and one whose desires are easily twisted against her own interests.

Read against the preface, as well as against Jean's judgments of Julie, the play conveys not a degenerate falling woman, but a woman who is beginning to move toward social and gender consciousness. Her recklessness attests both to her ignorance of self and world, and to her desperation. Her determination to satisfy her desires, which are more likely satisfied through social and personal change, leave Julie vulnerable to Jean's deterministic reduction of desire to vulgarized sexual need. Although her determination to fall is translated by the preface as determinism, it can also be read as an expression of Julie's utter discontent and her complete lack of alternate means of power or expression, other than through conventional sexual and class politics. That is, read against the preface, the play can be understood not as an indictment of Julie's misguided desires to rebel against nature but as an indictment of the social forces that waste her human worth. Most important, however, the play can be read as an indictment of the naturalistic interpretation of those social forces, a powerful and destructive ideology which, by affirming sexist and classist power relations as natural, would reduce women's revolutionary desire to a conventional scenario of female sexual desperation. (pp. 476-80)

Alice Templeton, " 'Miss Julie' as 'A Naturalistic Tragedy'," in Theatre Journal, *Vol. 42, No. 4, December, 1990, pp. 468-80.*

FURTHER READING

Biography

Meyer, Michael. *Strindberg: A Biography.* London: Secker & Warburg, 1985, 651 p.

Critical biography of Strindberg that emphasizes the revolutionary sexual realism of *Miss Julie.*

Criticism

Carlson, Harry G. *Strindberg and the Poetry of Myth.* Berkeley: University of California Press, 1982, 240 p.

Study of mythic elements in Strindberg's drama that includes a chapter devoted to *Miss Julie.*

Greenway, John L. "Strindberg and Suggestion in *Miss Julie.*" *South Atlantic Review* 51, No. 2 (May 1986): 21-34.

Discussion of Strindberg's general scientific interests with particular reference to his use of mesmerism in *Miss Julie.*

Kagan-Moore, Patrick. "Dramatic Time and the Production Process: Reading for Rhythm in *Miss Julie* and *The Duchess of Malfi.*" In *Text and Presentation: The University of Florida Department of Classics Comparative Drama Conference Papers Volume VIII,* edited by Karelisa Hartigan, pp. 103-16. Lanham, Md.: University Press of America, 1988.

Analysis of time-related imagery in *Miss Julie.*

Lamm, Martin. "*Miss Julie.*" In *Strindberg: A Collection of Critical Essays,* edited by Otto Reinert, pp. 105-16. Englewood Cliffs, New Jersey: Prentice Hall, 1971.

Early essay by Lamm comparing *Miss Julie* with the criteria expressed in Strindberg's preface.

Parker, Brian. "Strindberg's *Miss Julie* and the Legend of Salome." *Modern Drama* XXXII, No. 4 (December 1989): 469-84.

Examination of *Miss Julie* with reference to the Salome legend as presented in works by writers and artists associated with the late nineteenth-century movements of Symbolism and Decadence.

Tornqvist, Egil. "*Miss Julie* and O'Neill." *Modern Drama* 19, No. 4 (December 1976): 351-64.

Traces *Miss Julie*'s influence on O'Neill's Electra trilogy and other plays.

Tornqvist, Egil, and Jacobs, Barry. *Strindberg's "Miss Julie": A Play and Its Transpositions.* Norvik Press, 1988, 302 p.

Discussion of *Miss Julie* focusing on its performance and adaptation history.

Williams, Raymond. "Private Tragedy: Strindberg, O'Neill, Tennessee Williams." In his *Modern Tragedy,* pp. 106-20. London: Chatto and Windus, 1966.

Discusses the social and psychological aspects of *Miss Julie.*

Additional coverage of Strindberg's life and career is contained in the following sources published by Gale Research: *Contemporary Authors,* Vol. 104; and *Twentieth-Century Literary Criticism,* Vols. 1, 8, 21.

Yokomitsu Riichi

1898-1947

Japanese novelist, short story writer, essayist, playwright, and poet.

INTRODUCTION

Yokomitsu's fiction exemplifies the tenets of the Shinkankakuha movement, which existed in Japan from 1924 to 1927. In response to the naturalist school of Japanese literature represented by the Shirakaba writers, who concerned themselves with the realistic presentation of life, Yokomitsu and other members of the Shinkankakuha group held that writing should present readers with an unsubjective record of their characters' sensations. Although Yokomitsu adopted some of the techniques of the "I-novel"—the predominant Japanese prose form of his day, in which authors related actual events of their lives through highly detailed confession yet made use of dialogue, narrative, and other devices of fiction—he sought to avoid the subjectivity of the I-novel by objectively describing situations separate from his own experiences.

Yokomitsu endured an unsettled and often lonely youth; his father was a surveying engineer for new railways, which demanded that the family move frequently from one job site to another. Yokomitsu entered Waseda University in 1916 but gradually lost interest in his studies and decided to pursue a career as a writer. In 1923 he began contributing short stories to literary magazines and in the same year published *Nichirin,* his first novel. The devastating Kantō earthquake, which levelled much of Tokyo in September 1923, instilled in Yokomitsu a sense of being at the mercy of uncontrollable natural forces. According to Mitsuo Nakamuro, Yokomitsu believed that this experience of powerlessness in the face of nature had a great effect on the thought of the upcoming generation of writers. In October, Yokomitsu founded the Shinkankakuha movement with Kawabata Yasunari. By 1927, the movement was considered to have outlived its usefulness as an experimental forum, and many of its writers had defected to Japan's proletarian school of literature. With other non-Marxist writers Yokomitsu formed a new group that continued the modernist ideal of "art for art's sake" and emphasized the subjective process of psychological experience. He journeyed to China in 1928 to research *Shanhai,* the novel which marked the end of his experimentation with Shinkankakuha techniques. Over the next few years, he established himself as Japan's most popular novelist. His last novel, *Ryoshū,* is based on the clash of Eastern and Western cultures he experienced while traveling in Europe during the 1930s. With the advent of World War II, Yokomitsu virtually ceased writing. The few works he published during and after the war advocated the superiority of traditional Japanese culture to Western culture and re-

flected his despair over the Japanese defeat by Allied forces. He died in 1947.

In his short stories and novels, Yokomitsu strove to reform the predominant conception of the modern Japanese novel, which at the time served as either a vehicle for confession or propaganda. He believed that the I-novel, which was intended to express the author's state of mind, was incapable of conveying the effects of tragedy on the human psyche. He also maintained that the proletarian novel, basically an I-novel concerned with social reform, obscured the psychological motivations of characters due to its political intent. Although Yokomitsu's novels achieved enormous popular success in the 1930s, these works as well as his criticism and literary theories are viewed as simplistic by many modern scholars. Critics reserve their praise instead for several of Yokomitsu's short stories. Early stories such as "Maketa otto" (1924; "The Defeated Husband") and later stories such as "Kikai" (1930; "The Machine") reflect his shift from an emphasis on his characters' external sensory perception to one emphasizing their internal psychological states. "The Defeated Husband" centers on the developing jealousy of a husband who suspects his wife of infidelity. Written during Yokomitsu's Shinkankakuha period, "The Defeated Husband" relies heavily on characters' actions, details of setting, and dialogue to reveal his protagonist's psychological trauma. In "The Machine," which examines a character who believes his ideas are being appropriated by his rivals at a small factory, Yokomitsu balances sensory details with confessional narrative to expand on the perceptions presented in the main character's confessions. On the basis of these and other stories, Yokomitsu is regarded by Western critics as an innovative writer whose works anticipated the more conspicuous emergence of modernist literary forms which took place in Japan following World War II.

PRINCIPAL WORKS

"Hae" (short story) 1923; published in journal *Bungei shunjū*
["The Fly," 1965; published in journal *Japan Quarterly*]
Nichirin (novel) 1923; published in journal *Shin'-shōsetsu*
"Atama narabi ni hara" (short story) 1924; published in journal *Bungei jidai*
Onmi (short stories) 1924
Haru wa basha ni notte (short stories) 1927
Shanhai (novel) 1928-31; published in journal *Kaizō*
Shin'en (novel) 1930-32; first half published in newspaper *Ōsaka mainichi shinbun;* second half published in journal *Bungei shunjū*
Kikai (short stories) 1931
Monshō (novel) 1934
*The Roof-Garden, and Other One-Act Plays (drama) 1934
Oboegaki (memoirs) 1935
†Ryoshū (novel) 1937-46
‡Young Forever, and Five Other Novelettes (novellas) 1941
Yoru no kutsu (diary) 1945
§Kanashimi no daika (novel) 1955
Yokomitsu Riichi zenshū. 12 vols. (complete works) 1955-56
|Time, and Others (short stories) 1965
|Love, and Other Stories of Yokomitsu Riichi (short stories) 1974

---

*This collection includes a translation of Yokomitsu's one-act play, *Shimaranu kāten* (*The Curtain Would Not Draw*).

†This work was published in installments in one or more journals.

‡This collection includes a translation of Yokomitsu's novella *Seishun* (*Young Forever*).

§This work was written in 1920.

|These works include translated portions of *Onmi* and *Haru wa basha ni notte.*

CRITICISM

Mitsuo Nakamura   (essay date 1969)

[*In the following excerpt, Mitsuo discusses Yokomitsu's involvement in the Shinkankakuha school of Japanese literature.*]

Yokomitsu Riichi in his **Oboegaki** (**Memoir**) finished around 1935, says, "When we look back from our present perspective it is clear that the Great Kantô Earthquake in 1923 influenced the Japanese people as much as the First World War. It seems that everyone thinks that way." He remarks, however, that almost no one has tried to think of the influence of this Earthquake on literature, which is an unpardonable oversight on the part of the scholars of literature. He adds, "One does not wish to think of great misfortune, perhaps because one finds in it a basis of anything one does."

It might be a little exaggerated to say that the earthquake disaster influenced the Japanese people as a whole as much as World War I influenced the European nations. However it was indeed a major event almost comparable to World War I as far as citizens of Tokyo and Japanese culture concentrated in the area were concerned. It is not a mere accident that the new art movements in Europe after World War I were transplanted to Tokyo after the Great Kantô Earthquake; but what is more interesting is that Yokomitsu recognized that men of letters who had been influenced a great deal by this Earthquake did not try to think of it in connection with literature, and that he attributed to a sense of unbearable misfortune.

When misfortune spreads so much as to become an experience shared by everyone, people no longer wish to speak of it. The problem, then, is to escape from such an unhappy state; and in order to supply energy necessary for doing so, they have to give it some emotionally satisfactory significance.

An earthquake disaster, unlike that of a war, is a natural disaster beyond the volition of human beings. If there is any point reproachable on the side of men, it is only that they were unprepared. The feeling of being thrown off their guard made some people assert "the doctrine of divine punishment," regarding the earthquake disaster as Heaven's vengeance (a theory held by a group of businessmen and men of letters), and it also made others entertain nihilistic ideas resembling those of Western naturalists seen in the words of Kikuchi Kan that "I thoroughly came to know that the idea that Nature is ever favorable to mankind is not true. . . . " All these ideas are considered to be the expression of their desire to give some significance to the natural calamity. Naturally the opinion of the generation whose view of life had already been established was centered in man and was in some sense ethical.

Compared to them, Yokomitsu interpreted the disaster in a slightly different way. In **"Shin Sai"** (**"The Earthquake Disaster"**), the description of his impressions written right after the disaster, he says,

> Immediately after the Earthquake, all men alike
> gave opinions on the merits and demerits of such

an earthquake. Those who experienced this calamity . . . received compensation for the terror they felt in their heart. Because it was a once-in-a-lifetime calamity, they could not help asking compensation for it in something. For the rest of their life whenever they speak of their own terror, they will feel proud of their experience.

It is no longer ethics but psychology that he is interested in.

Yokomitsu has no such intention of looking at the real condition of society or the correct way of living as Kikuchi Kan had by taking advantage of the earthquake disaster. That which he is interested in is the psychological development in the human mind which could not but seek for "compensation" even from this kind of disaster, and the way this is expressed in words. Meeting with this "very rare" historical event, he is vaguely conscious of witnessing the birth of a myth. This proves that he is assuming the attitude of an onlooker, as it were. He is looking at the event in a manner very conscious of his profession as a novelist. He cannot forget his profession. However, from this way of living, a step removed from ordinary people, he has acquired the standpoint that he regards the earthquake disaster itself as one cultural event.

> Whoever has ever lived in the vicinity of Tokyo must have anticipated, it seems to me, such an earthquake as this sooner or later. . . . In spite of this, why have they so excessively exaggerated the scale of this disaster? The reason can definitely be said in a word: 'Because men have been too utilitarian.' People have forgotten to take time for speaking out loudly and warning against it. . . . Meanwhile, the earthquake has been steadily fulfilling its period under the ground.
>
> Once the cycle is fulfilled, people . . . immediately began to anticipate further disasters to come. . . . 'Well, but we shall no longer be living at that time.'—The words which our race will eternally repeat must be this terribly utilitarian expression. . . . Thus the struggle of science with nature which makes disasters worse, will be more and more fierce. What defeats us is not the earthquake. It is the culture produced out of our utilitarianism.

This impression of the twenty-five-year old youth, not only forecasts his lifework, but vaguely anticipates the characteristics of the novelists in the Showa era.

Just as the strong impression given in one's boyhood decides the sensibility of one throughout his life, the earthquake disaster, to this young novelist, is no longer an accidental calamity, but the very basis on which Japanese culture itself is founded; and all that is "founded" on it is nothing but "the anticipation of disaster." From this point of view, "science" is after all what "makes a disaster worse" and "the culture produced out of utilitarianism" is entrusted with a task that eventually destroys human beings.

To this young man, all human efforts looked empty and meaningless. To him who has seen real society and actual

life in that way, the world of literature must have appeared as the only reality; therefore, the revival of fiction in a decorative style seemed to him the way out of the "I" novel of the Taisho era.

The literature of the New Sense School, with Yokomitsu as the central figure in the magazine *Bungei Jidai* (*Literary Age*) which was established in the year following the earthquake disaster, invited much comment among people. Such inclination to make the unstable social condition his own form of existence, however, was not only his own but was shared by many of his contemporaries. (pp. 18-21)

The movement of the New Sense School is apt to be considered as an intangible phenomenon in fashion in the literary world, or as an experimental literary technique which was tried by the young writers and failed. It was indeed a phase that could be considered in that way, but it, in fact, was more than that, and was something which could not be defined so simply. (p. 21)

By replacing the real fact in life or the record of mind and heart which ruled over the world of literary circles at this time with the sense fused into the condition of the object, the writers of this school tried to cut the iron links called the reproduction of the fact.

"The sensuous expression of the New Sense School is, in a word, an intuitive catalysis of subjectivity which deprives nature of its external appearance, and springs into objectivity itself " (**"Kankaku-Katsudô"** or **"Of Sensuous Activity"**). This definition by Yokomitsu clearly shows their intention.

Kataoka Teppei also says, "I dare say that the sense catches an object, and poetry flashes between the primary sense and the second life which then begins."

The words "an intuitive catalysis of subjectivity" and "poetry flashes" show that the expression which they sought was to fix a moment, and so it is not appropriate for a long novel even if it is suitable for poetry or short stories. (p. 23)

The most remarkable feature of Yokomitsu is the desire to create something new by any means to have his individuality recognized. This characteristic is common to all the modern artists, but it is especially strong in his case, and it becomes the very motif of his creative work.

"Hae" is a work in which a tranquil, peaceful mountain village is described. The hero of the story is a fly with "big eyes" which settles on the horse of an omnibus. When the omnibus falls into a ravine, the fly soars into the sky and looks down on the accident as if nothing had happened. Though it is short, the characteristics of the author are conspicuous in the work. The atmosphere produced by the stubborn residents of the mountain village, was well expressed in a kind of flowery style, and the foolish manners of human living are alluded to. But it gives the impression of being too abrupt in the way the omnibus falls into the ravine at the end. Moreover, its allegorical style results in a certain artificiality.

Probably Yokomitsu wished to say that he had created something fresh and new which had never been seen before. He was aiming at creating style and story, and it was his program to escape from "I" novel type realism. For him, sense is the synonym of style, but he himself knew very well that it was impossible to construct a novel with it only. The frame which he chose for supporting "sense" (what Kataoka mentions as life) was the paradoxical elucidation of the opposing elements of human psychology. This characteristic is already seen in **"Nanboku" ("North and South,"** Feb., 1921). When human beings appear, his attention is always paid to the mental activity for outdoing the other party, and the mutual misunderstanding and complications are observed mainly from the viewpoint of victory and defeat. To him the human deeds are, like words, partial and therefore, an incomplete expression of psychology; hence ethics becomes meaningless.

Not only in Yokomitsu but also among other New Sense School writers, this sense of loss of ethics was common, which causes their literature to be called the literature of de-humanization. The Taisho writers considered that it is ideal to have no gap between their life and their works, and that their sense of beauty and ethical view or social outlook should overlap in the same form. With the dissociation of these two, begins the literature of the Showa era. At the bottom of Yokomitsu's resolution to sacrifice himself for style lies a horror of inscrutable reality.

However, it is true that he has found a new place for his work in such a psychological world as this, and it is considered his originality that he believed it the ethics of a writer to live in the very place where ethics is meaningless. His plan was to make another person enter his works, and to make the works themselves a different world from that in which the author lives.

The works, in which the illness and death of his wife are dealt with such as **"Haru wa Basha ni Notte" ("Springtime in a Carriage,"** 1926), **"Ga wa Dokonidemo Iru" ("Everywhere There are Moths,"** Sept. 1926), **"Hanazono no Shisô" ("Thoughts in the Flower Garden,"** Feb. 1927), are "I" novel-like in material, but are different from the traditional "I" novel in character in the point that he does not describe "life," but contents himself intentionally with writing the "sense" of the husband, and creates another world by making use of the excited nerves of the husband as the movement of the style. (pp. 25-7)

> *Mitsuo Nakamura, "New Sense School (Shin Kankaku-ha)," in his* Contemporary Japanese Fiction: 1926-1968, *edited by John Krummel, translated by Ryôko Suetsugu, Kokusai Bunka Shinkokai, 1969, pp. 18-27.*

Dennis Keene (essay date 1974)

[*In the following excerpt from his introduction to Yokomitsu's* Love, and Other Stories, *Keene assesses the importance of Yokomitsu's writings to twentieth-century Japanese literature.*]

Yokomitsu Riichi was born in 1898, and thus belongs to what one might call the third generation of modern Japanese writers, the first generation being those born around 1870 (the "naturalists," such as Shimazaki Toson), the

second those born around 1885 (the "Shirakaba" writers, such as Shiga Naoya). The division of writers into fifteen-year generations is a game that perhaps creates more questions than it answers, and the distinctions it makes obviously lose their validity, or at least their edge, with the passage of time; and yet it is necessary to see any writer within the situation in which he began to write, and since the literary situation in Japan was altering so rapidly during those early years of the twentieth century when Yokomitsu was growing up, some emphasis upon the facts of literary history is required.

Put very simply, what happened during the first decade of the twentieth century was that the colloquial language established itself as the medium for literary prose at the same time as "naturalism" became the main literary movement, and the two are clearly linked. "Naturalism" meant a concern with the "real," with what life was "really" like, and since the life that the writer really knows about is his own, there was a tendency for Japanese "realism" to be concerned with personal confession, a development no doubt encouraged by the fact that there is a long tradition in Japan of the diary as a literary form. This concern with the real as that which is personally experienced was also shared by the next generation of writers, of whom Shiga Naoya is the supreme representative, although the dramatic, confessional aspects of the naturalists are hardly present in his work, since his realism is that much closer to real life in which dramatic events rarely occur. The tone of any work by Shiga Naoya is constantly under control, played down, a control reflected in a style where the colloquial language finally becomes a medium in which a writer can work with ease. This emphasis upon the experience of the "I" is shown in the name of the basic literary genre of the Taisho period (1912-26), which is referred to as the "I-novel." It was against this image of literature, according to his own account, that Yokomitsu wanted to write; he wished to create "fictions" and not record the falsification, "the enormous lies" that go under the name of a diary. This does not mean that he then avoided the autobiographical, since he did not, and perhaps no novelist ever totally does; instead he wished to transform that life into a fictional work of art, unlike Shiga Naoya, who seemed to feel that life as it had been lived was a work of art already.

European modernism of the 1920s also began as a reaction to the idea of the "real" in literature (the opening of Breton's first surrealist manifesto is an attack upon the way Dostoevsky describes the objects in a room), and although the connections between what happened in literary Paris at that period and what happened in literary Tokyo are tenuous (Japanese dadaism, for example, is a marginal affair, and has virtually nothing to do with the parent manifestations in Europe), the starting points of both modernist movements have something in common. Also, if one believes that the avant-garde in the West was, if not created, at least given great impetus by World War I, then a counterpart also occurred in Tokyo with the great earthquake of 1923. Yokomitsu himself certainly believed that the effects of both events upon their respective cultures were similar. Again, if one sees European modernism as a continuation of the symbolist movement in literature, then it is of some interest that Yokomitsu saw his own modernist writings as symbolist also, and not so much as the "literature of sensations" that the manifesto statements of his literary group, the "Shinkankakuha," claimed it to be.

The importance of Yokomitsu's early literature . . . is that it is perhaps the one serious attempt in Japanese to write a modernist literary prose, a prose which has something in common with what was going on in Europe in the 1920s. It is certainly true that one can find things written in Japanese in the 'twenties which seem much closer to European counterparts, such as futurist poems and manifestos, cubist and surrealist poems, prose works more aggressively modernist than Yokomitsu's, but these look now like merely the sad detritus of dead fashions, and even in terms of literary history it is difficult to give them any kind of serious attention. Dada, for example, made a real impact in Paris, whereas in Tokyo it was the plaything of a small and ignored number of individuals; and Jean-Paul Sartre, despite his loathing of surrealism, at least felt himself obliged to admit that it was the one important poetic movement in France in the twentieth century, an admission which no antagonist of Japanese surrealism, if one could be said to exist, would feel impelled to make. Such manifestations in Japan reflected little more than a sensitivity toward European fashion, and that only on the part of a small minority. Yokomitsu's modernism, although obviously sharing some of that superficiality, produced a literature which even if not outstandingly good is at least real. Yokomitsu's prose *is* Japanese modernism of the 1920s, the only literary modernism of that period in Japanese which can be read with an interest that goes beyond mild curiosity. That is his historical importance. (pp. ix-xi)

> *Dennis Keene, in an introduction to "Love,"* and Other Stories of Yokomitsu Riichi, *translated by Dennis Keene, University of Tokyo Press, 1974, pp. ix-xxii.*

Yokomitsu on his continuing development as a writer:

I first began by writing poems, then plays, then symbolist novels, then novels of pure description. I then worked on ways of heightening the sense of reality in my writings, then I went back to symbolism again which was my "Shinkankakuha Period." And now I'm back to realism again, where I want to settle down for a bit.

Implicit in this was a changing way of looking at the world, at things. At first objects were seen in a fantasy world, and then I concerned myself with attempting to see them in the normal, everyday way. I gradually lost interest in that, and attempted to see things in personal terms, using the viewpoint of the self as the basis for description. However, that also became uninteresting, so I concentrated on the way the sensations take in the world. While attempting this I got an obsession with structure, with seeing things as a whole, as a form. Yet recently I've got rather tired of that too.

Yokomitsu Riichi, in his "Mazu nagasa o," translated by Dennis Keene in his Yokomitsu Riichi: Modernist, *Columbia University Press, 1980.*

Noriko Mizuta Lippit (essay date 1980)

[*In the following excerpt, Lippit demonstrates how Yokomitsu used the techniques of the traditional "I-novel" to present modernist themes of alienation and spiritual malaise.*]

The introduction of avant-garde European art and literature to Japan began around the ninth year of Taisho (1920). At that time, the poets and writers who were associated with such journals as *Shinkō Bungaku* (*New Emerging Literature*) and *Aka to Kuro* (*The Red and the Black*) began actively to develop the Dadaist and expressionist movements in Japan, paving the way for the New Perceptionist movement (*shinkankakuha*) led by Yokomitsu Riichi. The Japanese avant-garde movement was closely related to nihilistic decadence and revolutionary anarchism. Dadaist art, combining individual decadence and revolutionary class consciousness, became engaged in rebellion against and destruction of established art and indeed of the entire social system. Such representative Dadaist writers as Tsuboi Shigeji, Kawasaki Chōtaro, Hagiwara Kyōjiro and Tsuji Jun all believed their art to be the forerunner of revolution. The manifesto of *Aka to Kuro* reads:

> What is poetry? What is the poet? Throwing away all the concepts of the past, we declare baldly, "Poetry is a bomb! The poet is a black criminal who throws a bomb at the thick walls and doors of the prison."

The so-called terrorists of the literary circle, regarding the reality which surrounded them as a prison, tried to destroy the social system and the poetic concepts which were fostered by it.

Their creative and revolutionary élan was expressed in their spirit of negation and commitment to destruction:

> Our existence is negation itself! Negation is creation! Creation is nothingness! . . . Negate! Negate! Let us pour all our force into negation! Only then can we exist!

They considered artistic creation to be a form of action, and their negation and destruction were directed at both the establishment in art—"class art"—and the social system—capitalist imperialism—which sustained it.

The avant-garde movement was divided into many small groups because the writers and artists, basically anarchistic, naturally tended to be quite individualistic, yet most of the groups remained close to the Marxian socialist proletarian literary movement. Considering themselves to be terrorists engaged in class struggle within the literary circle, they shared with the proletarian revolutionaries the feeling that the reality of the machine culture created by capitalism was oppressive to art and human life, and both shared the common purpose of destroying the oppressive class system and the art which served as its "running dog."

Both the avant-garde art movement and the proletarian movement received a great blow from the Kanto earthquake of 1923. *Shinkō Bungaku* and *Aka to Kuro,* along with *Tanemaku Hito (Sowers),* which had been established in 1921 as the first journal for proletarian literature, had to cease publication. By 1925, when the new Peace Preservation Law was passed to provide added legal sanction for limiting radical activities, the anarchists had clearly parted from the Marxists, and with the defeat of terrorism, avant-garde art seemed to have lost its revolutionary élan. In the thirteenth year of Taisho (1924), a year after the earthquake, two new journals which were to be the center of early Showa (1926-present) literary activities were established. One was *Bungei Sensen (Art and Literature Battlefront),* a journal which sought to establish a new united front for proletarian literature, and the other, established by Yokomitsu Riichi, Kawabata Yasunari, Nakagawa Yoichi and others, was *Bungei Jidai (The Age of Art and Literature),* a modernist journal which took a leading role in the so-called New Perceptionist movement.

Bungei Jidai started without any consciously formulated ideological or methodological manifesto, except to state that it was committed to the development of a "new art and literature, based on a new life," as Kawabata stated [in his "Atarashii Seikatsu to atarashii bungei" ("New Life and New Art and Literature")] in the first issue. The members of the group which published the journal were very close to the Dadaists and expressionists of *DAMDAM* and *MAVO,* and to other avant-garde writers who had been active before the earthquake. The fact that the New Perceptionists emerged from the Taisho (1912-1926) avant-garde movement is reflected in Kawabata's article "The New Directions of the Newly Emerging Writers," in which he attempted to explain "the theoretical basis of New Perceptionist expression." The elements he considered vital in the New Perceptionist movement are reflected in the four parts into which he divided the essay: (1) the emergence of the new art and literature, (2) the New Perception, (3) expressionistic epistemology, and (4) Dadaistic expression. [In his essay **"Kankaku Katsudo— Kankakukatsudo to Kankaku sakubutso ni taisuru hihan e no gyakusetsu"** ("Perceptional Activities—A Reappraisal of the Criticism of Perceptional Activities and Perceptional Creation"),** published in] the second issue of *Bungei Jidai,* Yokomitsu wrote, "I recognize futurism, cubism, expressionism, Dadaism, symbolism, structuralism, and a part of actualism as belonging to the New Perceptionism."

Although Yokomitsu, Kawabata and others had not yet established their own literature, they were sure that their literature would be the totality of the new avant-garde art in that it would reflect the perception of the new age, absorbing the results of the theoretical and methodological experiments of its forerunners. Yokomitsu's **"Atama narabi ni hara"** ("The Head and the Stomach," 1924), published in the first issue of *Bungei Jidai,* contains the famous line describing a rapidly moving express train, "The small station was ignored like a pebble," and this line alone was taken by writers and critics as a stylistic revolution.

New Perceptionism soon lost its coherence as a movement because it had lacked a firm theoretical structure from the start, but the lack of internal cohesion became particularly apparent when some members left *Bungei Jidai* to join the proletarian literary movement. Yokomitsu, who was seriously concerned with the validity of Marxian dialectics as a means of grasping reality, tried to show that the New Perceptionism was as radical as Marxism in its epistemological method and insisted that its art was not bourgeois or antidialectical. Despite Yokomitsu's effort to bridge the gap between Marxism and New Perceptionism without changing his original theoretical stance, however, the journal could no longer accommodate the writers who were inclined toward proletarian literature, and it ceased publication after the May 1927 issue.

While the proletarian literary movement, led by such writers as Aono Suekichi and Kurahara Korehito, continued to develop actively, leading to the formation in 1928 of the Japanese Proletarian Artists' Federation (NAPF), those of the young modernist writers who were not basically Marxist formed in the same year a new group to publish the journal *Bungei Toshi (The City of Art and Literature).* Joining such writers as Abe Tomoji and Funabashi Seiichi was the young Kajii Motojiro, whose dozen short stories stand as the crystallization of the modernist aesthetics of Japan. Although Nakagawa Yoichi, a New Perceptionist, later joined the group, it differed from the New Perceptionists in the stand it took against proletarian art. The manifesto of the group, written by Abe Tomoji, reads as follows:

> On a plain from which old things disappear
> without leaving any trace, we technicians
> will make the plan for a new city materialize.
> We will build this truly strong, healthy and
> multi-angled, three-dimensional city.

Declaring its anti-Marxist position openly, the group supplied the basis for the formation of the Shinko Geijyutsuha (New Emerging Art School) in 1929. Although the anti-Marxist stance of Yokomitsu and Kawabata became more apparent after the so-called debate on "formalism" carried out between the New Perceptionists and the Marxists (represented by Nakano and Kunahara), they did not join the New Emerging Art School. Instead, they began to publish their own journal, *Bungaku (Literature),* in 1929, through which they continued their basically aesthetic, art-for-art's-sake literary activities.

Bungaku, with *Poetry and Poetics* and *Poetry-Reality,* new journals for avant-garde poetry, took the role of introducing new artistic and literary ideas and movements from Europe; *Poetry and Poetics* was concerned mainly with surrealism, while *Poetry-Reality* published Itō Sei's translation of *Ulysses,* and *Bungaku* published a translation of Proust's *A la Recherche du Temps Perdu.* Kajii's first important work, "The Lemon" (1925), and most of his works which were later collected in *The Lemon* (1931), were published in *Poetry-Reality.*

The translations of Joyce and Proust had a significant influence in Japan's literary circle, especially on Yokomitsu, to whom they suggested a new direction after his initial, experimental stage as a New Perceptionist. Itō Sei had already written several essays in which he advocated highly sophisticated literary expression, and he was establishing himself as a new theorist who considered the novel as basically a literary method. In a series of essays which were collected in *New Psychological Literature,* he criticized the New Perceptionists' impressionistic description of outer forms and phenomena, and suggested they should move to a more direct expression of inner psychology. At the same time, Yokomitsu, moving away from New Perceptionism, was writing an essay entitled **"Poetry and the Novel,"** an essay which was later revised into his famous **"On the Pure Novel."** In it he argued that literature must present an autonomous world of human experience, a world including inner psychological experience and experience in human relations.

Among the avant-garde writers whom *Poetry and Poetics* actively introduced were Rimbaud, Valéry, Proust, Eliot and in particular such surrealist poets as Eluard, Breton and Aragon; the journal focused on their exploration of the subconscious and their use of automatic writing and stream of consciousness. Yokomitsu's **"Kikai"** (**"Machine,"** 1930) was the major outcome of his shift from New Perceptionism to psychological realism. With Kawabata's "Suishō genso" ("Crystal Fantasy," 1931) and Hori Tatsuo's "Sei kazoku" ("The Sacred Family," 1930), it is among the first and most successful products of Japanese modernism, which reached its maturity after going through initial stages of anarchism and struggle against Marxian proletarian literature. While "Machine" was received as a sensational achievement by such critics as Kobayashi Hideo and Itō Sei and was to become one of the most influential works of the decade, Kajii's works, although they were among the most brilliant products of the modernist movement, were received enthusiastically only among his close friends. Even among them, Kajii's works were generally considered to be unique but highly personal writings, writings which reflected, in essence, his disease-sharpened sensibilities [The critic adds in a footnote, "Kajii contracted tuberculosis when he was nineteen years old and died in 1932 at the age of thirty-one"]. While Yokomitsu was always at the forefront of literary activities and was always influential, Kajii, quietly perfecting and nurturing his literary world, lacked social recognition to the end. In Kajii's works, however, we can recognize one extreme form of decadent aestheticism which, purified as visionary imagination and combined with the method of inner realism, resulted in an achievement which fully parallels that of Yokomitsu.

Both **"Machine"** and such works by Kajii as "The Lemon," "Under the Cherry Tree," "Copulation" and "Instrumental Fantasy," tracing the manner in which extremely sharpened, "abnormal" sensibilities build a solid wall to defend against an aggressive, threatening outer world, deal with an estranged inner world of "madness." **"Machine"** is the story of a young man from a remote area of Japan who, working under exploitative conditions at a small, family-operated factory in Tokyo, gradually develops a persecution complex. The factory produces such products as name plates, and the owner of the factory, a middle-aged, "hen-pecked" man, is constantly experi-

menting with ways to improve the chemical treatment of metals.

The protagonist, who swears his loyalty to the owner, becomes involved in a "dangerous" secret experiment which would place the factory in a better position in this highly competitive and unstable small industry. Doing so awakens his suspicions of two fellow workers, Karube and Yashiki, each of whom he believes is involved in stealing his "secrets" and those of the factory, and he comes to believe that they suspect him of stealing their secrets and those of the factory. In this way, a triangular relationship of suspicion is created. Each becomes involved in a highly tense psychological play, trying to outdo the others and to trap them into revealing their evil intentions, first allying with one and spying on the other and then reversing the alliance. Mutual hatred and a desire for revenge bring them to physical confrontations in which each hits the others and is himself beaten.

In the center of the factory, and in fact in the center of the protagonist's mind, is a "dark room" where the experiments are carried out, a room whose key is kept by the master himself. Eventually the protagonist gains access to the room and, becoming concerned that the others may go there as well, keeps trying to catch them at it. When he himself enters the room, he becomes earnestly involved in experimenting with chemicals whose poisonous effects corrode his skin and mind. In fact, working at the factory is itself like yielding to the gradual, corrosive effects of a poison.

> Once in the slot, I found my skin and my clothes wearing out under the corrosive attacks of ferric chloride. . . .

The factory is constantly in a state of financial crisis. The protagonist blames this on the master's "failings," one of which is his habit of losing money—especially the earnings of the factory from which the salaries of the employees are to be paid. The protagonist's involvement in the experiment in the dark room is partly due to his sincere wish to help the master improve the financial situation of the factory and partly due to his desire to obtain the "secret" that would also rescue him from the intolerable work at the factory. Yet the more he frequents the dark room, the more deeply he becomes haunted by suspicion and fear of persecution, and the more deeply he becomes locked in the paranoiac relations with the other two, creating a psychological hell with no exit.

The night when the master loses all of the earnings for which the workers had worked without sleep and under intense psychological pressure, they turn to drinking. The next morning, the protagonist finds that Yashiki, the more clever of the other two, had mistakenly drunk poison (ammonium dichromate) and was dead. The protagonist suspects that Karube, the other worker, might have killed Yashiki to prevent him from stealing the secret, yet for the same reason he suspects that he himself might have been the murderer. The story ends with his loss of himself:

> Perhaps I murdered him. I knew better than anyone where the ammonium dichromate was. Before drunkenness overtook me, I kept think-

ing about Yashiki and what he would be doing somewhere else the next day, when he would be free to leave. And if he had lived, would I not have lost more than Karube? And had not my head, like the master's, been attacked by ferric chloride?

I no longer understand myself. I only feel the sharp menace of an approaching machine aimed at me. Someone must judge me. How can I know what I have done?

Since the story is told by a first-person narrator, the situation is regarded only through the perspective of the protagonist. As the story progresses, the reader begins to suspect that the tense psychological situation that exists among the three may simply be the product of the protagonist's fantasy, and at the end, the reader is left sharing the protagonist's suspicion that he himself may be the murderer. By following the protagonist's understanding of reality—of his situation in the factory—the reader is actually looking into the deranged inner world of the protagonist. Affected by the poisonous chemicals of reality, the protagonist steadily becomes mad as the alienation of his inner world from the outer reality deepens and he loses his grip on himself. The more deeply he looks into his "dark room"—a metaphor for his inner world—for the purpose of finding a way to recover from the alienation, the further his madness progresses. Once this process is initiated by the "law" of reality, there is no way to arrest it or escape from it. The law is that of the "machine," the machine which controls not only the physical reality of those who live in it, but their very minds as well. The protagonist gradually becomes a part of the machine. The protagonist discovers this soon after he starts living in the factory:

The discovery that in the tiniest things a law, a machine, is at work came to me as the beginning of a spiritual awakening.

The protagonist is, of course, a modern man suddenly placed in a modern machine-culture which exploits the body and the mind of both the capitalist and the laborer; as the protagonist notices, the owner of the factory has long been affected by the poisonous chemical fumes of "the dark room." Yet the protagonist may be interpreted more specifically as a modern intellectual who has lost the way to relate himself to the new industrial reality and thus lost himself as well. His sharp observation, cleverness and skill tend to support this understanding. His struggle is that of an intellectual who believes that he has the key to the secret to save himself and others from destruction in a hostile society, yet the very method he employs for the purpose—coiling into the dark room in search of the secret—deepens his alienation from reality and thus hastens his collapse into madness; the "experiment" he carries out there is a "dangerous" one which eventually leads to his self-destruction. Although the work lends itself to symbolic interpretation, however, it also presents realistically the condition of the exploited laborers in capitalist Japan. Yokomitsu is successful thus in integrating the socio-historical reality into his story of the psychological distortion of modern existence.

The atmosphere of the factory—reality—is filled with a

sense of threat, immediately evoking the protagonist's fear and anxiety. His psychological play with the others—one of persecution and victimization—is the result of his sense of threat and his struggle against impending destruction. The more he struggles, however, the more deeply he becomes caught, and in the end, he reaches a state of total despair at the height of madness.

Using the madman's point of view skillfully, the story dramatizes the growing alienation of the protagonist in a threatening modern civilization. The protagonist believes until the very end that he is the only sane person, while the others are madmen or criminals. The sense of superiority with which he views the others brings out both the pathos and the irony of the situation. Oppressed and insulted, he is a victim—and is consequently mad—but the reality which surrounds him and is responsible for his madness is more insane and pernicious than he is. The irony of the sanity-insanity paradox inherent in the madman's point of view reveals the tragic condition of modern man. The oppressed and the insulted turn on and attempt to destroy one another. The protagonist's deadly serious, "mad" involvement in the psychological play among them and his despair at the end is at once tragic and comic. (pp. 104-13)

Yokomitsu and Kajii conceived of the fear caused [in] their protagonists by their helplessness before impending annihilation as a universal ontological problem. **"Machine"** reflects a specifically capitalist exploitative condition which is governed by the law of the machine, and Kajii's "abnormal sensibilities" are specifically referred to as stemming from his disease and from the anxiety and loneliness which resulted from his sense of impending death. Their protagonists' sense of threat, inner confusion and desperate struggle to escape, however, reflect the condition of the modern Japanese of the late Taisho and early Showa periods, a time characterized by the rise of imperialism, ruthless police repression, economic depression, and the failure of anarchism and socialism.

The police repression threatened all avant-garde literary activities, not just those of the proletarian literary movement. It was a period characterized by anxiety. The writers of the period wavered between proletarian literature and decadent modernist literature, experimenting in every possible way in their search for a method and an ideology which would reflect the new human situation.

In addition to the ideological conflict between Marxism and modernism, a conflict which affected most of the writers in one way or another, the questions of form, expression and language raised vital issues for the writers of this period. Neither proletarian writers nor modernist writers could be satisfied any longer with the easy identification of the writer with the work—the I-novelists' conception that regarded literature as self-expression. Akutagawa's escape into a well-constructed world of stories had revealed only the futility of intellectual aestheticism as a response to the new human condition. Possibly as much as for any writer of the period, Yokomitsu's literary activities reflected its conflicts and questions. After extensive experiments with language (which he called the struggle with his native tongue), expression and form during his New

Perceptionist period, he shifted toward "the pure novel" of realism with **"Machine,"** the first major result of his search for a new direction. Yokomitsu's ironic use of the dramatic confession creates a dual perspective—irrational and rational or an involved inner perspective and a detached critical perspective—leading to the integration of the inner psychological novel with the realistic social novel. Although Yokomitsu's theory of the pure novel called for creating works which would present just such an integration of the psychological and the social novel, **"Machine"** achieved this objective far more successfully than the works written consciously according to the dictates of the theory, most of which proved to be much more inclined toward the novel of social manners.

Kajii, who admired Shiga Naoya and tried to combine modernistic perception with realism and plain language, was also in the forefront of the search for a new literary method. The transcendental vision which Kajii's heightened sensibility revealed is conveyed by plain language, and his presentation of his inner landscape attains a simplicity and unaffectedness close to that of Shiga Naoya's I-novels. His works can properly be called verbal paintings. Like **"Machine,"** Kajii's works use the stream-of-consciousness method to delve into the psychic realm of the protagonist. Although **"Machine"** is not an I-novel, but a dramatization of an intellectual's understanding of the human condition, by incorporating the most characteristic techniques of the I-novel—first-person narration, the use of a single point of view presented by the narrator-protagonist, direct description of the inner reality of the protagonist, and the use of plain language and realism—the work draws the reader into the inner world of the alienated hero, subjecting the reader to the same feeling of sympathy for and closeness to that world as that created by the I-novel.

Kajii's short stories, on the other hand, are written in a form basically akin to that of the I-novels in that the author intends to present a certain state of his own consciousness, a state which he attains at a certain moment in his life; yet the highly distilled (although realistic) description of that state itself becomes a metaphor, imparting a poetic character to the works. Kajii's works are the best examples of the modern lyrical novel. If **"Machine"** is a successful example of the use of psychological realism to dramatize the understanding of social life and abstract ideas, Kajii's unique short stories are successful examples of the use of inner realism and stream of consciousness to create a new reality which transcends both immediate inner and outer reality. He achieves this by projecting the subconscious onto the outer reality. Thus, following the protagonist's stream of consciousness or "gaze" reveals not only his inner reality, but the inner nature of phenomenal reality as well. The phantasmagoric visions created by Kajii's "diseased sensibility," by his decadent, Baudelarian sensibility, are the results of his "gazing" at reality. His visionary imagination is attained, therefore, through his conversion into a pure gaze. The excitement the protagonist experiences at the moment of vision stems from a heightened sense of reality, from a renewed sense of life.

In the works of both Yokomitsu and Kajii, the basic meth-od of realism achieves a symbolic representation of the human condition. The modernist perception of the human soul as diseased, as estranged from itself and existing in a threatening environment, is dramatized by inner or psychological realism. In the context of Japanese literature, their achievement meant the transcendence of the I-novel through the use of I-novel techniques. (pp. 117-19)

> *Noriko Mizuta Lippit, "Disease and Madness in Japan's Modernist Literature: Yokomitsu Riichi's 'Machine' and the Short Stories of Kajii Motojiro," in her* Reality and Fiction in Modern Japanese Literature, *M. E. Sharpe, Inc., 1980, pp. 104-19.*

Donald Keene   (essay date 1984)

[*Keene is one of the foremost American translators and critics of Japanese literature. In the following excerpt, he examines Yokomitsu's contribution to modern Japanese literature.*]

Most critics who have written about Modernism in Japanese fiction trace its origins to the group of writers known as the Shin-kankaku-ha (New Sensationalist school), a label first attached to them in 1924. The group was never large, but it included several distinguished writers, and its organ, the magazine *Bungei Jidai* (*Literary Age*), which first appeared in October 1924, exercised a disproportionate influence, especially on the younger writers. The New Sensationalist movement lasted only from 1924 to 1930, by the most generous estimates, and it tended increasingly to be associated with one man, Yokomitsu Riichi, but even among Yokomitsu's works only a few corresponded closely to the professed ideals of his group. The New Sensationalist school, however, had another significance: in the late 1920s, when the proletarian literature movement threatened to sweep before it all but the most firmly entrenched of the established writers, the New Sensationalist group stood for literary rather than ideological principles, and for experimentation in the new techniques that had been created in Europe after World War I.

In the first issue of *Bungei Jidai* Yokomitsu published what appears to have been a hastily written essay explaining the significance of the appellation "New Sensationalism." Like most of his essays, the writing was dense to the point of being impenetrably obscure in places. For example, the following passage elucidates the meaning of "new" in New Sensationalism:

> The difference between sensation and new sensation is this: that the objectivity of the object that bursts into life is not purely objective, but is rather the representation of that emotional cognition which has broken away from subjective objectivity, incorporating as it does both a formal appearance and also the generalized consciousness within it. And it is thus that the new sensationalist method is able to appear in a more dynamic form to the understanding than the sensationalist method by virtue of the fact that it gives a more material representation of an emotional apprehension.

It is doubtful whether even Yokomitsu had a clear grasp

of what he meant by this pronouncement. No doubt he was attempting to lend an air of authority to a vaguely apprehended set of ideas by using the terminology of Western philosophy and aesthetics, then enjoying a vogue among Japanese intellectuals. If such pronouncements were all there was to Yokomitsu, he would certainly not rank as an important literary figure, even within the framework of the late 1920s, when there was relatively little of importance written after the death of Akutagawa in 1927. Yokomitsu was, however, a writer of considerable talent who was devoted to literature as literature at a time when many other writers had become convinced that literature was no more than a means to achieve social or political ends. (pp. 644-45)

Yokomitsu's early stories, written between 1917 and 1923, are intermittently effective, though marred by overingenuity; in general, Yokomitsu's most successful works, both at this early stage of his career and much later on, are those that describe personal experience in the least consciously "artistic" manner. Dennis Keene wrote, "His successes come when the material is close to home, when the literary attempt springs from a concrete personal necessity rather than from a more abstract ideological one." The same is true of other important Japanese writers, but in Yokomitsu's case his frequently expressed dislike for autobiographical fiction and his insistence on the literary theories associated with the New Sensationalist school make it seem paradoxical that his successes should have resulted from the use of materials similar to those that commonly inspired openly confessional writing.

Of the early stories the best is **"Ommi"** (**"Dear,"** 1921), the account of a man's love for his niece, a girl of two or three who rebuffs his every gesture of affection. In the hopes of ingratiating himself, he performs foolish antics, despising himself for these vain efforts to induce her to show more interest in him. The relationship between the man and the little girl is adroitly evoked and is given special poignance by the additional meaning the story had for Yokomitsu: he transferred to this account of a man's love for his niece the closer, more urgent experiences he had with the woman who later became his wife. Even without a knowledge of this extra dimension to the work, the reader can hardly fail to be moved by this unaffected, entirely believable account of love and rejection.

A similar heightening of an event of the past with the more intense feelings of a recent experience characterizes **"Kanashimi no daika"** (**"The Price of Unhappiness"**), a story written around 1920 but not published until after Yokomitsu's death. Although Kawabata Yasunari, who first called attention to the story in 1955, insisted that this account of a wife's infidelity with her husband's friend must not be considered as autobiographical in any sense, it is clearly not pure invention, and it succeeds to the degree that it reflects the author's deep feelings; Yokomitsu's more polished, more artistic later reworkings of the same materials are certainly less moving. Most critics tend to imply that Yokomitsu's career began with his New Sensationalist stories, but Kawabata characterized **"The Price of Unhappiness"** as "the bedrock of the man who was Yokomitsu Riichi."

The first two works by Yokomitsu to appear in commercially published magazines were the short story **"Hae"** (**"The Fly"**) and the novella *Nichirin* (*The Sun*), both of which had been in progress for some years but were not published until May 1923. Although entirely dissimilar in style and content, they were equally unlike Yokomitsu's earlier works, and both were acclaimed on publication.

"The Fly" is the brief, ironic account of a horse carriage that takes passengers from a mountain village to the nearest town. The hunchbacked driver, who has few other pleasures in life, loves to eat, and he has stuffed himself with so many buns that he nods off to sleep while driving the horse. Without his guidance the carriage plunges over a cliff. The only survivor is the fly that has been feeding off the horse. Commentators have pointed out the irony of the story: something so trivial as a coachman's having eaten too many buns is responsible for the deaths of a carriageful of people (and a horse); and it is not one of the passengers, each full of his own importance, but a common fly that survives and calmly contemplates the scene after the disaster. Yokomitsu recalled that he originally intended the story to be a satire, but

> under the burning summer sky the chattering of a collection of human beings suddenly gives way to silence; and in its place, far off, a single fly begins its lively, fresh activity. Once I had conceived of this circumstance, a mysterious sensation that burst the bounds of satire began to radiate from it. I was conceited enough to suppose that if I could express this sensation adequately, a philosophy symbolic of life and fate would emerge from a mere sensation.

Yokomitsu's belief that a sensation, if adequately evoked, could stand for all of human life and destiny was appropriate at this stage of his career, when he was evolving the principles of New Sensationalism; however, a fascination with trivial occurrences ran through his whole career, and led ultimately to a defense [put forth in his 1935 essay **"Junsui Shōsetsu Ron"**] of coincidence as a legitimate and vital element of fiction. The ingenuity of **"The Fly"** seems to have been inspired by Yokomitsu's belief that man is controlled less by his own volition than by trivial external factors. This discovery was too obvious to be more than momentarily interesting; Yokomitsu's mechanistic view of the world would be more fully and better expressed in later works.

Yokomitsu's attempt to distance himself from his stories, in contrast to the "I" novelists, who remained intimately associated with their materials, is even more pronounced in *The Sun*. In this work bloody events that occurred during the reign of the legendary Queen Himiko are treated in detail. Unlike usual historical novels, which give the impression that although the characters lived long ago they were moved by the same emotions as contemporary people. *The Sun* emphasizes the distance separating the readers from the past. [Dennis Keene, in his *Yokomitsu Riichi: Modernist*, notes that] Yokomitsu was undoubtedly influenced to adopt this approach to his materials by Ikuta Chōkō's translation of Flaubert's *Salammbô*, published in 1913. Flaubert conveyed an impression of remoteness and alienness by deliberately not imparting to his characters familiar, easily recognized traits; the result is cold, sometimes repulsive, but also fascinating. Ikuta compounded the effect of distance by making his translation read like a translation; he violated normal principles of Japanese style and translated literally expressions that would seem totally foreign to Japanese readers, though not intended by Flaubert to be bizarre. Yokomitsu, who read Ikuta's translation with absorption, achieved a similar style in *The Sun*. The sentences are short, the diction archaic, and the vocabulary peculiarly constricted. This was not the only influence from *Salammbô;* the description of acts of brutality and sadism in an uncommitted, detached style was clearly derived from Flaubert, and the narrative, like that of *Salammbô*, consists mainly of visual images, with only a minimum of psychological reflection. The lack of attention to what passed through the minds of the characters as they performed their various acts of mayhem underlined the fact that a world was being treated that bore few resemblances to our own.

The Sun is unique not only among Yokomitsu's writings but among all works of modern Japanese literature. The style, period, and themes so impressed the first readers with their novelty that Yokomitsu gained immediate recognition. *The Sun* is still read and included in standard selections of Yokomitsu's works, no doubt because the mixture of ancient history and brutality is so unusual; but it is a bad novel that can hardly be read with a straight face by anyone with the least touch of irreverence in his attitude. The uncouth short sentences are reminiscent less of Flaubert than of Tarzan; at best they suggest a primitive people who had yet to discover subordinate clauses, and the language is not only unhistorical but often plain silly.

The failure of *The Sun* was by no means apparent in its time. Not only was it widely read, but it was made into a successful film in 1925, a pioneering attempt at Modernism in the Japanese film. But the ultimate significance of *The Sun* was that it was clearly an experiment, an attempt to destroy the prevailing modes of Japanese fiction. The group of writers who would soon be known as the New Sensationalists would have as their common bond an impatience with the establishment and a desire to create a new, specifically modern literature. (pp. 645-48)

Yokomitsu's style is the most distinctive feature of New Sensationalism. The story **"Atama narabi ni hara"** (**"Heads and Bellies"**), which appeared in the first issue of *Bungei Jidai*, opened with the lines: "It was noon. The crowded express train raced at full speed. The small wayside station was ignored like a stone." The simile, typical of Yokomitsu at this stage of his career, became the focal point of attack of all those who dislike his new style. **"Heads and Bellies,"** though an inferior story, is often considered as the first cry of the infant literary movement. Other scholars consider **"Maketa Otto"** (**"The Defeated Husband"**), the rewriting of **"The Price of Unhappiness"** published in the October 1924 issue of *Bungei Jidai*, to have been the first New Sensationalist work, if only because it is literarily superior to **"Heads and Bellies."** The style in these early works is marked by short sentences and by "jumps" from one statement to the next without logical connections. The short sentences owe much to Ikuta's

translation of *Salammbô*, but the "jumps" are more likely derived from the Japanese translation of Paul Morand's novel *Ouvert la nuit*, a work much admired at the time. A typical passage from **"The Defeated Husband"** will suggest Yokomitsu's style:

> When he left the house it was already dark outside. He began to walk at once in the direction of the bookshop. A little girl with perfectly normal legs was limping hurriedly along imitating a cripple. After her came a truck racing along jammed tight with policemen. The load of policemen stood silently protruding above the cab like black stamens. A car followed after them. There was a girl inside who was tired. The wooden bridge shook as the vehicles passed over. He came to the main road and turned right. Several trams flew by shaking their human bundles to the rear. The crammed flesh ricocheted inside the square trams. Whirlpools of sickly fragrant lust, bounding and leaping.

It was typical of the New Sensationalist style to use the third person, rather than the first person as in the "I novels" and Naturalist fiction. Personification, another conspicuous feature of New Sensationalist literature, also occurs in this passage, though less startlingly than in some works. Above all, it is the detached observations—sense impressions that are registered but not commented on or explicitly linked to the main body of the narration—that mark this as New Sensationalist writing. Instead of commenting on what passed through his hero's mind as he set out for the bookshop where he hoped to meet another man's wife, Yokomitsu presents a series of ominous images—the pretended cripple, the load of policemen protruding from the top of the truck, the tired girl in the car—leading up to the statement that the trams were shaking their human bundles in a manner suggestive of the "sickly fragrant lust" that the hero is experiencing. Yokomitsu later referred to this period as one during which he fought a fierce battle with the Japanese language and lost, by which he meant that his attempt to change the language between 1918 and 1927 (the dates he gives) by violating normal grammatical principles had ended in failure. Such specifically New Sensationalist stylistic features gradually disappeared from Yokomitsu's writings, but even in his works of New Sensationalism it was not possible, except in stories so brief that they might almost be taken for prose poems, to maintain a consistency of style. At the time he was writing these experimental works Yokomitsu took greatest pride in their surfaces: "The symbol is the surface brilliance that allows the inner life to shine forth. . . . That which attempts the most brilliance in its symbols I have come to call the New Sensationalist School."

It was about this time, in the spring of 1925, that Yokomitsu's wife fell ill. They moved to the seashore at Hayama in Kanagawa Prefecture in the hopes that the wife, Kimiko, would recover in the purer air, but her condition steadily deteriorated. In the spring of 1926 he nursed her, virtually without assistance, devoting himself to satisfying her every whim, but she died in June of that year, only twenty years old. The experience was an overpowering tragedy for Yokomitsu. It was also the kind of experience that again and again had induced writers of the "I novel" to turn to autobiography. Yokomitsu had expressed only contempt for what he considered to be the in-artistic nature of the "I novel," which sets down facts without imparting a structure to them, yet he felt compelled to describe his painful experience in several stories, one of which, **"Haru wa basha ni notte"** (**"Spring Riding in a Carriage,"** 1926), is considered by many critics to be his masterpiece. The story opens when the wife is already seriously ill. The husband is informed by the doctor that there is no hope for his wife's recovery. The wife, suspecting that the doctor has given him bad news, asks the husband to buy morphine so that she can die quickly and painlessly. She tells him then that she knows he loves her, and blames her sickness for her frequent outbursts of jealousy. One day someone sends sweet peas, the first scent of spring. He offers them to his wife, explaining, "They came riding here in a carriage, along the shore of the sea, scattering the first seeds of spring as they came." The wife buries her pale face among the flowers, entranced.

Given in outline, the story fits easily within the category of autobiographical fiction, but there is none of the self-pity characteristic of that genre. Everything is described with clarity:

> Out at sea the afternoon waves broke on the rocks and scattered. A boat leaned and rounded the sharp point of the headland. Down on the beach two children sat like scraps of paper, steaming potatoes in their hands, against a background of deep, surging blue.

> The waves after waves of suffering that came in upon him had never been something to be evaded. The origin of those waves of suffering, each different in each onslaught, existed in his very flesh, had been there from the beginning. He had decided to taste this suffering as the tongue tastes sugar, to scrutinize it with the total light of his senses.

Yokomitsu's concern over his wife's suffering has led some critics to claim that **"Spring Riding in a Carriage"** is not a New Sensationalist work; it certainly seems to demonstrate that the New Sensationalist manner was not suited to portraying anything as immediate as the approaching death of a man's wife.

In **"Hanazono no shisō"** (**"Ideas of a Flower Garden,"** 1927) Yokomitsu was at greater pains to transform the facts of his wife's last days by underlining the formal elements of composition. The story takes place in a hospital that is surrounded by flowers, which bring life and death to the patients. One night the husband, walking in the garden, buries his face among the night flowers:

> As he wept he passed his face from one cold flower to another, drinking in their perfume like an insect. As he smelled the perfume he began to start praying violently.

> "Please, God, save her. Please, God, save her."

> He picked up a handful of primroses and wiped his face with them. The sea was pale and secret before the rise of the moon. A night crow drew an uncanny curve in the air, then flew over the flower beds like a sharp shadow. Like grief itself he walked countless times around the quiet fountain, until his own heart quieted too.

This is skillful writing, more obviously artistic than any comparable passage in **"Spring Riding in a Carriage,"** but it is also less affecting. It is difficult to accept the man's actions literally, and as symbolic gestures they are unsatisfying. Yokomitsu succeeded in creating a polished artistic surface broken only momentarily by the cry to God for help, but instead of intensifying the cry, the descriptions tend to call attention to their own beauty, to their pretentiousness. Most Japanese critics prefer **"Ideas of a Flower Garden"** to **"Spring Riding in a Carriage"** because of the greater degree of accomplishment, but it is hard to escape the feeling that Yokomitsu, in persisting in his quest for modernity and for artistic expression, was doing violence to his natural talents. (pp. 650-54)

Shanghai, Yokomitsu's first full-length novel, was published in segments between November 1928 and January 1931. The main incident is the May 30th Movement of 1925, when Chinese workers at Shanghai, incensed over the killing of several of their fellows by guards at a Japanese spinning mill, staged a general strike, to the astonishment and consternation of the resident foreign population. This was precisely the kind of material that proletarian writers had treated, and Kuroshima Denji's novel *Armed Streets,* published in 1930, described another strike by Chinese workers against foreign capitalists. The proletarian novels about strikes had embodied the message that the workers must some day rise against their oppressors. Yokomitsu's **Shanghai** has no such message nor, for that matter, is it an apology for the Japanese capitalists who were exploiting Chinese workers. It is an attempt to evoke the turbulence of a period of violent clashes, and to capture the essence of the strange city of Shanghai, especially the foreign concessions. Yokomitsu, even before going to China, had been intrigued by the concessions, islands of foreign domination in China where the parks were said to have signs forbidding dogs and Chinese to enter. The concessions seemed to him like a foretaste of the world to come, when people would surrender their pride in their own culture as they engaged in the uninhibited pursuit of money and sex.

Yokomitsu was successful in communicating the atmosphere of the festering city. One can imagine him filling notebooks with his observations as he walked the streets. Yokomitsu wrote **Shanghai** in 1935, when the definitive edition was published, that it had cost him the most effort of any of his works. He went on, "At that time, though it is no longer true, I felt obliged to concentrate my mental powers on observation of the external world, and so Shanghai became in this work a seaport revealed as the state of flux of an external world that included nature." Kawabata considered **Shanghai** the novel in which Yokomitsu moved from observation of the external world to that of the internal world, from the methods of sensation to those of psychology. He expressed the belief that **Shanghai** was the grand summation of the methods of the New Sensationalist school.

The descriptive passages in **Shanghai** rank among Yokomitsu's most successful, if only because the objects portrayed were of intrinsic interest and needed no tantalizing "symbolic" significance; the vignettes of Shanghai are the most memorable parts of the novel. The technique is sensationalist, rather in the manner of Lawrence Durrell's *Alexandria Quartet,* and the effect is similar, emphasizing the alienness of the surroundings.

> A crowd thronged the dusty outdoor stalls. Boiled eggs piled on bamboo trays. Heads of birds losing their shapes in the stalls, monkey trainers between the rotten bean curd and the hot peppers. Lard constantly set a-tremble by the sound of people's feet. A mango that had rolled among the throng of gaping-mouthed old shoes, glittering coals, broken eggs, women with bound feet scuttling round swollen fish bladders.

The differences between Japan and China are emphasized by such passages or by the descriptions of the putrefying Shanghai canals, filled with every kind of refuse that human beings produce; these are implicitly contrasted with the clean Japanese landscapes that linger in the minds even of Japanese who have spent most of their lives in Shanghai. The Japanese characters in the novel sometimes justify the Japanese presence in China in terms of the lack of natural resources, which forces the Japanese to exploit the Chinese; if they did not, the English or Americans would. Some of the Japanese are Pan-Asianists, the forerunners of those who proclaimed the Greater East Asia Co-Prosperity Sphere, but most, even if they smoke opium or wear Chinese dress, are as alien to China as the Europeans and Americans; in Yokomitsu's work Asia definitely is not one.

Shanghai contains exciting scenes and the work is rarely pretentious in the New Sensationalist manner. Its great weakness lies in the characterization. None of the characters exists except on a surface level, and some are implausible from the start. Each is given some effective moments but lacks the weight of a real human being. This was perhaps by design; even so, it suggests that the New Sensationalist methods could not easily be applied to an extended work, or perhaps that Yokomitsu, now on the point of abandoning New Sensationalism as his guiding principle, had become increasingly aware of its limitations.

Shanghai was not successful, though some critics welcomed the apparent shift away from New Sensationalism. One went so far as to label *Shanghai,* along with a recent novel by Miyamoto Yuriko, as an example of "New Naturalism," and others suggested that Yokomitsu, who began his literary career while at Waseda University, the bastion of Naturalism, but refused to follow that style because he despaired of ever surpassing the realism of Shiga Naoya, had at length reverted to his literary origins. Admittedly there is greater reliance on straightforward description in *Shanghai* than in "Ideas of a Flower Garden," and such sections as the account of, say, how one woman became a prostitute would not be out of place in a Naturalist novel, but surely it was not in order to tell her story that Yokomitsu wrote *Shanghai.* An unfriendly critic wrote: "The author was absolutely determined to describe only the atmosphere on the surface of Shanghai. That may be why his novel is the kind of work in which not a single real

human being exists within its atmosphere. . . . *Shanghai* no doubt typifies an age when humanity itself has been lost."

Such comments probably would not have unduly distressed Yokomitsu. He was clearly attempting to create an atmosphere, and not three-dimensional characters. Stereotypes suited his purposes just as well as believable human beings. *Shanghai* was the apotheosis of the New Sensationalist style, which Yokomitsu had labored to create, but it was also its death knell, as he undoubtedly was aware.

In 1930, while *Shanghai* was still appearing in installments, Yokomitsu published the story **"Kikai"** (**"The Machine"**), a work that created such a sensation that Yokomitsu was elevated by his admirers to the rank of "god of literature"; but it has also been argued that this success destroyed him as an artist. The impact that **"The Machine"** made on its first readers, especially those concerned with specifically modern writing, is suggested by this passage [from *Shinkō Geijutsu-ha to Shin Shinri Shugi Bungaku*] written by Itō Sei in 1950, recalling his reactions at the time:

> Yokomitsu Riichi suddenly changed in 1930 with the publication of **"The Machine"** in the September issue of *Kaizō.* This was just at the time when our translation of *Ulysses* was appearing, and **"The Machine"** also clearly revealed its indebtedness to the translations of Proust which had appeared in *Bungaku.* I began to read **"The Machine"** as I walked along the main street in Ushigome, holding in my hand the magazine I had just bought. The story so powerfully impressed me that it all but took my breath away. Yokomitsu had without warning abandoned the New Sensationalist method of narrative that he had employed until *Shanghai,* relating impressions by skips and jumps, and now wrote the flexible, associational style that Tanikawa Tetsuzō called "arabesque." The pages were now crammed with words, sentence following sentence without a break and hardly a change of paragraph. Not to mince words, I felt as if this bull-headed predecessor of ours had succeeded in creating a form that was at least possible with the Japanese language. Hori [Tatsuo] and I were still struggling to accomplish this, but without success, no doubt because we were insufficiently equipped for the task. The literary world was set on its head. The story was acclaimed as a masterpiece, and Kawabata Yasunari and Kobayashi Hideo described it with excitement. But it was baffling that none of the reviews mentioned that **"The Machine"** was influenced by the new French and English literature, which had been systematically presented in *Shi to Shiron* during the previous two years.

Yokomitsu surely had read the translations of Proust and Joyce as they appeared in *Shi to Shiron* (*Poetry and Poetics*) and other avant-garde journals that introduced to the Japanese recent European literature. Some scholars believe that the long sentences and interminable paragraphs of **"The Machine"** were imitative of Proust, but even if Yokomitsu was influenced by the appearance of a page of

Proust, nothing could be remoter in expression or content from Proust than **"The Machine."** If any influence deserves special mention, it is probably that of Paul Valéry. Yokomitsu read Valéry in 1929 with such admiration that, he declared in one letter, he felt like throwing away his pen. What impressed him most in Valéry was the nihilism at the center of individual consciousness, and a rejection of the intellect. Quite possibly Yokomitsu misunderstood Valéry, a difficult writer in French and even more obsure in Japanese translation. Yokomitsu nowhere reveals the kind of intelligence needed to cope with the problems of Valéry's expression, but whether his understanding was correct or not, he *thought* he was being influenced by Valéry in his discovery of the folly of wisdom, and it is possible to interpret his writings of the period in the light of this influence.

"The Machine" is the story of four men who work in a factory where metal plates are made. The owner is a man of childlike innocence, goodnatured to a fault, and absolutely incapable of carrying money without losing it. Karube, the senior employee, is devoted to the owner, and suspects the unnamed narrator of attempting to steal the owner's secret inventions. Karube is an uncouth and even brutal man, but not totally devoid of decency. The fourth man, Yashiki, has been taken on as an extra hand to help with an unusually large order. The narrator is attracted to the congenial Yashiki, though he suspects him of trying to steal secrets. These suspicions are confirmed when Karube observes Yashiki leaving the room where the secret formula is kept. Karube assaults Yashiki and also the narrator when he urges Karube to relent. When the order is filled the next day, the owner loses the money on the way home, and he cannot pay the men. They decide to get drunk together. The next morning Yashiki is found dead. He drank some acid, taking it for water. The narrator wonders if this was Karube's doing. Or perhaps he himself was responsible for leaving the acid in such a place. The story concludes, "I have reached the point where I no longer understand myself. All I feel is that there is the sharp point of some machine coming slowly toward me, getting closer and closer to me. Let somebody take my place and judge me. For if you are to ask me what I have done, how can I be expected to know?"

The machine has been mentioned earlier in the story when, after the fight, the narrator discovers he cannot be sure what the others think of him. "But even if I could not calculate these things, there was somewhere within our midst something that could, some mechanism that we could not see, a machine which was unceasingly making calculations about us and which then directed our actions according to the light of these calculations." The machine seems to stand for fate, which controls the lives of people who imagine that they act of their own free will. The lives of the four men are dominated by their job, which involves using poisonous chemicals to make thousands of nameplates, a process suggestive of the endless torments of hell, and their labor is of course unrewarded. The narrator, unable to tell what caused the death of Yashiki, senses only the presence of the terrible machine.

The meaning of the story has intrigued readers since the first appearance. Kobayashi Hideo's interpretation of the story [*Bungei Hyōron*] was published soon afterward. It is clear that he had a high opinion of **"The Machine,"** but that is about all that is clear. Kobayashi declared that **"The Machine"** was wholly original, without precedent either in Japan or abroad. The particular excellence of **"The Machine,"** in Kobayashi's opinion, was that it was "a book of ethics written in words not found in the vulgar vocabulary." Anyone who could not detect the "odor of ethics" in the work was urged to read something more amusing. The key to the work was the narrator, who is innocence itself. He offers no resistance to Karube, but this very lack of resistance is in fact his resistance. "Karube's violence is no more than movements of the machine. To oppose it would constitute a collision between machine and machine. But the narrator does not endure Karube's violence because he recognizes this principle. He endures it because it is his innocence which has angered Karube."

Kobayashi had little to say about purely literary techniques. He was absorbed instead by the spiritual message, which he characterized as a "song of sincerity" (*seijitsu*). But, he added, this is not sincerity in the worldly meaning, which involves an unclean satisfaction in one's own sincerity. "The sincerity of the narrator is a sincerity that goes to its death without feeling the least self-satisfaction." Kobayashi concluded, "Mr. Yokomitsu is the only author of today on whom I can bestow the adjective 'tragic.' "

Kobayashi's analysis of **"The Machine"** requires exegesis of its own. His insistence on the ethical implication of the work, as opposed to its literary qualities, is difficult to accept, if only because nothing previously written by Yokomitsu, whether his fiction or his essays, suggested philosophical depth; on the contrary, his views are almost always muddled, and he showed little understanding of the works of European criticism for which he professed the greatest admiration. But **"The Machine"** demonstrated Yokomitsu's exceptional literary ability. There is something at once nightmarish and funny about the narration, and its effectiveness is immeasurably heightened by the oppressive atmosphere engendered by the long sentences and paragraphs. The unremitting pressure does not permit the reader to put down the book; the reader who did so could never pick it up again.

Although Kobayashi urged those insensitive to the ethical implications of **"The Machine"** to try something more frivolous, it was Yokomitsu, rather than the readers, who took this advice. **"The Machine"** established Yokomitsu as a central figure in the literary world, though until then he had been considered only of peripheral importance. The success of the story naturally led to many orders from the newspapers and magazines for others. Yokomitsu became a popular author, and in order to satisfy his new readers (but perhaps also because he was weary of his struggle to create a specifically modern literature) he abandoned the complexities of style and themes that had marked his earlier works. His writings were nevertheless superior to those of most novelists of the 1930s, and some of his later works have their defenders. But whatever success Yokomitsu would score from this time onward would be a betrayal of his earlier career as a writer. . . . (pp. 655-61)

The defeat in the war naturally affected Yokomitsu with particular severity, and may have contributed to his death at the end of 1947. One last story, written shortly before his death, **"Bishō" ("Smile")**, was perhaps his finest work in fifteen years. It is set during the last months of the war and tells of a young naval officer, a mathematician, who claims he has invented a death ray that, when perfected, will win the war for Japan. At first the notion seems preposterous to the narrator, but Seihō (the name the officer uses as a haiku poet) has a marvelous smile that inspires confidence. The narrator suspects that Seihō may be insane, but there seems to be no other hope for Japan, and he therefore vacillates between belief and incredulity. Tokyo is bombed, despite Seihō's assurance that not an enemy plane will get through. Soon after the war ends, a brief article in the newspaper states that Japan had possessed a death ray effective to a height of three thousand meters. The inventor is reported to have gone mad with frustration at not having been able to perfect the ray in time to save Japan from defeat. Perhaps Seihō was telling the truth, but the only clear thing now is that he had a wonderful smile. The story is told with economy and Seihō is depicted with a mixture of affection and misgivings, suggesting the complexity of Japanese feelings as the war entered on its final stages.

The success of **"Smile"** is a reminder of the exceptional talent that Yokomitsu possessed. This last story contains nothing smacking of Modernism, whether of the New Sensationalists or any other school formed under European influence during the 1920s and 1930s. For that matter, there is none of the philosophical theorizing that is usually disastrous in Yokomitsu's works. There is not even a "return to Japan." Instead, we have a writer responding to his experience, distancing it, and giving it depth in the manner that good writers have instinctively followed at all times even without the benefit of literary theory.

The New Sensationalist school failed. Yokomitsu Riichi, despite some real successes and great popular acclaim, also failed to create a consistent style. [In *Fūzoku Shōsetsu Ron*] Nakamura Mitsuo once labeled the influences Yokomitsu had received from foreign literature as no more than new clothes worn as a lark. But it would be a mistake to infer from his failures that little had been achieved. Itō

Sei wrote in 1931 that nothing had changed the techniques of Japanese literature as much as the New Sensationalist writings; when people spoke of "new literature" it meant works in that vein. The next generation of Modernists would carry the struggle for Modernism further, though it would not acquire much authority until after 1945. The failure of Yokomitsu was tragic and more deeply affecting than any of his works of fiction. His career and the Japan he lived in are mirrored in the novels, and even if a time should come when they are no longer read as works of pure literature they will remain a memorable segment of the continuing effort of Japanese writers to join the mainstream of modern world literature. (pp. 665-66)

> *Donald Keene, "Modernism and Foreign Influences," in his* Dawn to the West, Japanese Literature of the Modern Era: Fiction, Vol. 1, *Holt, Rinehart and Winston, 1984, pp. 629-719.*

FURTHER READING

Bibliography

International House of Japan Library. "Riichi Yokomitsu." In *Modern Japanese Literature in Translation: A Bibliography*, pp. 276-78. Tokyo: Kodansha International Ltd., 1979.
　　Lists existing translations of Yokomitsu's works in books and journals.

Criticism

Allen, Louis. "Strictly Sensational." *The Times Literary Supplement*, No. 4071 (10 April 1981): 404.
　　Negative review of Dennis Keene's *Yokomitsu Riichi: Modernist*. Defends Yokomitsu's writings against Keene's "consciously destructive" treatment.

Keene, Dennis. *Yokomitsu Riichi: Modernist*. New York: Columbia University Press, 1980, 231 p.
　　General study of the *Shinkankakuha* (New Sensation) movement and of Yokomitsu's works. Includes an overview of Yokomitsu's life and times.

Twentieth-Century
Literary Criticism

Cumulative Indexes
Volumes 1-47

This Index Includes References
to Entries in These Gale Series

Authors in the News (AITN) reprints articles from American periodicals covering authors and members of the communications media. Two volumes.

Bestsellers (BEST) furnishes information about best-selling books and their authors for the years 1989-1990.

Black Literature Criticism (BLC) provides excerpts from criticism of the most significant works of black authors of all nationalities over the past 200 years. Complete in three volumes.

Children's Literature Review (CLR) includes excerpts from reviews, criticism, and commentary on works of authors and illustrators who create books for children.

Classical and Medieval Literature Criticism (CMLC) offers criticism on the works of world authors from classical antiquity through the fourteenth century.

Contemporary Authors encompasses eight related series: *Contemporary Authors (CA)* provides biographical and bibliographical information on more than 99,000 writers of fiction, nonfiction, poetry, journalism, drama, and film. *Contemporary Authors New Revision Series (CANR)* provides updated information on active authors previously covered in *CA. Contemporary Authors Permanent Series (CAP)* consists of updated listings for deceased and inactive authors removed from revised volumes of *CA. Contemporary Authors Autobiography Series (CAAS)* presents commissioned autobiographies by leading contemporary writers. *Contemporary Authors Bibliographical Series (CABS)* contains primary and secondary bibliographies as well as bibliographical essays on major modern authors. *Black Writers (BW)* compiles selected *CA* sketches on more than 400 prominent writers. *Hispanic Writers (HW)* compiles selected *CA* sketches on twentieth-century Hispanic writers. *Major 20th-Century Writers (MTCW)* presents in four volumes selected *CA* sketches on over 1,000 of the most influential writers of this century.

Contemporary Literary Criticism (CLC) presents excerpts of criticism on the works of creative writers who are now living or who have died since 1960.

Dictionary of Literary Biography comprises five related series: *Dictionary of Literary Biography (DLB)* furnishes illustrated overviews of authors' lives and works. *Dictionary of Literary Biography Documentary Series (DLBD)* illuminates the careers of major figures through a selection of literary documents, including letters, interviews, and photographs. *Dictionary of Literary Biography Yearbook (DLBY)* summarizes the past year's literary activity and includes updated and new entries on individual authors. *Concise Dictionary of American Literary Biography (CDALB)* and *Concise Dictionary of British Literary Biography (CDBLB)* collect revised and updated sketches that were originally presented in *Dictionary of Literary Biography.*

Drama Criticism (DC) provides excerpts of criticism on the works of playwrights of all nationalities and periods of literary history.

Literature Criticism from 1400 to 1800 (LC) compiles significant passages from criticism on authors of the fifteenth through the eighteenth centuries.

Nineteenth-Century Literature Criticism (NCLC) reprints significant passages from criticism on authors who died between 1800 and 1899.

Poetry Criticism (PC) presents excerpts of criticism on the works of poets from all eras, movements, and nationalities.

Short Story Criticism (SSC) offers critical excerpts on short fiction by writers of all eras and nationalities.

Something about the Author encompasses four related series: *Something about the Author (SATA)* contains biographical sketches on authors and illustrators of juvenile and young adult literature. *Something about the Author Autobiography Series (SAAS)* presents commissioned autobiographies by prominent authors and illustrators of books for children and young adults. *Authors & Artists for Young Adults (AAYA)* provides students with profiles of their favorite creative artists. *Major Authors and Illustrators for Children and Young Adults (MAICYA)* contains in six volumes both newly written and completely updated *SATA* sketches on nearly 800 authors and illustrators for young people.

Twentieth-Century Literary Criticism (TCLC) contains critical excerpts on authors who died between 1900 and 1960.

World Literature Criticism (WLC) contains excerpts from criticism on the works of over 200 major writers from the Renaissance to the present. Complete in six volumes.

Yesterday's Authors of Books for Children (YABC) contains heavily illustrated entries on children's writers who died before 1961. Complete in two volumes.

Literary Criticism Series
Cumulative Author Index

A. E. . . . . TCLC 3, 10
  See also Russell, George William
  See also DLB 19

A. M.
  See Megged, Aharon

Abasiyanik, Sait Faik 1906-1954
  See Sait Faik
  See also CA 123

Abbey, Edward 1927-1989 . . . . . . CLC 36, 59
  See also CA 45-48; 128; CANR 2

Abbott, Lee K(ittredge) 1947- . . . . . . CLC 48
  See also CA 124

Abe Kobo 1924- . . . . CLC 8, 22, 53
  See also CA 65-68; CANR 24; MTCW

Abell, Kjeld 1901-1961 . . . . CLC 15
  See also CA 111

Abish, Walter 1931- . . . . CLC 22
  See also CA 101; CANR 37

Abrahams, Peter (Henry) 1919- . . . . . CLC 4
  See also BW; CA 57-60; CANR 26;
  DLB 117; MTCW

Abrams, M(eyer) H(oward) 1912- . . . CLC 24
  See also CA 57-60; CANR 13, 33; DLB 67

Abse, Dannie 1923- . . . . CLC 7, 29
  See also CA 53-56; CAAS 1; CANR 4;
  DLB 27

Achebe, (Albert) Chinua(lumogu)
  1930- . . . . CLC 1, 3, 5, 7, 11, 26, 51
  See also BLC 1; BW; CA 1-4R; CANR 6,
  26; CLR 20; DLB 117; MAICYA;
  MTCW; SATA 38, 40; WLC

Acker, Kathy 1948- . . . . CLC 45
  See also CA 117; 122

Ackroyd, Peter 1949- . . . . CLC 34, 52
  See also CA 123; 127

Acorn, Milton 1923- . . . . CLC 15
  See also CA 103; DLB 53

Adamov, Arthur 1908-1970 . . . . . . CLC 4, 25
  See also CA 17-18; 25-28R; CAP 2; MTCW

Adams, Alice (Boyd) 1926- . . . CLC 6, 13, 46
  See also CA 81-84; CANR 26; DLBY 86;
  MTCW

Adams, Douglas (Noel) 1952- . . . CLC 27, 60
  See also AAYA 4; BEST 89:3; CA 106;
  CANR 34; DLBY 83

Adams, Francis 1862-1893 . . . . NCLC 33

Adams, Henry (Brooks)
  1838-1918 . . . . TCLC 4
  See also CA 104; 133; DLB 12, 47

Adams, Richard (George)
  1920- . . . . CLC 4, 5, 18
  See also AITN 1, 2; CA 49-52; CANR 3,
  35; CLR 20; MAICYA; MTCW;
  SATA 7, 69

Adamson, Joy(-Friederike Victoria)
  1910-1980 . . . . CLC 17
  See also CA 69-72; 93-96; CANR 22;
  MTCW; SATA 11, 22

Adcock, Fleur 1934- . . . . CLC 41
  See also CA 25-28R; CANR 11, 34;
  DLB 40

Addams, Charles (Samuel)
  1912-1988 . . . . CLC 30
  See also CA 61-64; 126; CANR 12

Addison, Joseph 1672-1719 . . . . LC 18
  See also CDBLB 1660-1789; DLB 101

Adler, C(arole) S(chwerdtfeger)
  1932- . . . . CLC 35
  See also AAYA 4; CA 89-92; CANR 19;
  MAICYA; SATA 26, 63

Adler, Renata 1938- . . . . CLC 8, 31
  See also CA 49-52; CANR 5, 22; MTCW

Ady, Endre 1877-1919 . . . . TCLC 11
  See also CA 107

Afton, Effie
  See Harper, Frances Ellen Watkins

Agapida, Fray Antonio
  See Irving, Washington

Agee, James (Rufus)
  1909-1955 . . . . TCLC 1, 19
  See also AITN 1; CA 108;
  CDALB 1941-1968; DLB 2, 26

Aghill, Gordon
  See Silverberg, Robert

Agnon, S(hmuel) Y(osef Halevi)
  1888-1970 . . . . CLC 4, 8, 14
  See also CA 17-18; 25-28R; CAP 2; MTCW

Aherne, Owen
  See Cassill, R(onald) V(erlin)

Ai 1947- . . . . CLC 4, 14, 69
  See also CA 85-88; CAAS 13; DLB 120

Aickman, Robert (Fordyce)
  1914-1981 . . . . CLC 57
  See also CA 5-8R; CANR 3

Aiken, Conrad (Potter)
  1889-1973 . . . CLC 1, 3, 5, 10, 52; SSC 9
  See also CA 5-8R; 45-48; CANR 4;
  CDALB 1929-1941; DLB 9, 45, 102;
  MTCW; SATA 3, 30

Aiken, Joan (Delano) 1924- . . . . CLC 35
  See also AAYA 1; CA 9-12R; CANR 4, 23,
  34; CLR 1, 19; MAICYA; MTCW;
  SAAS 1; SATA 2, 30

Ainsworth, William Harrison
  1805-1882 . . . . NCLC 13
  See also DLB 21; SATA 24

Aitmatov, Chingiz (Torekulovich)
  1928- . . . . CLC 71
  See also CA 103; CANR 38; MTCW;
  SATA 56

Akers, Floyd
  See Baum, L(yman) Frank

Akhmadulina, Bella Akhatovna
  1937- . . . . CLC 53
  See also CA 65-68

Akhmatova, Anna
  1888-1966 . . . . CLC 11, 25, 64; PC 2
  See also CA 19-20; 25-28R; CANR 35;
  CAP 1; MTCW

Aksakov, Sergei Timofeyvich
  1791-1859 . . . . NCLC 2

Aksenov, Vassily . . . . CLC 22
  See also Aksyonov, Vassily (Pavlovich)

Aksyonov, Vassily (Pavlovich)
  1932- . . . . CLC 37
  See also Aksenov, Vassily
  See also CA 53-56; CANR 12

Akutagawa Ryunosuke
  1892-1927 . . . . TCLC 16
  See also CA 117

Alain 1868-1951 . . . . TCLC 41

Alain-Fournier . . . . TCLC 6
  See also Fournier, Henri Alban
  See also DLB 65

Alarcon, Pedro Antonio de
  1833-1891 . . . . NCLC 1

Alas (y Urena), Leopoldo (Enrique Garcia)
  1852-1901 . . . . TCLC 29
  See also CA 113; 131; HW

Albee, Edward (Franklin III)
  1928- . . . CLC 1, 2, 3, 5, 9, 11, 13, 25, 53
  See also AITN 1; CA 5-8R; CABS 3;
  CANR 8; CDALB 1941-1968; DLB 7;
  MTCW; WLC

Alberti, Rafael 1902- . . . . CLC 7
  See also CA 85-88; DLB 108

Alcala-Galiano, Juan Valera y
  See Valera y Alcala-Galiano, Juan

Alcott, Amos Bronson 1799-1888 . . NCLC 1
  See also DLB 1

Alcott, Louisa May 1832-1888 . . . . NCLC 6
  See also CDALB 1865-1917; CLR 1;
  DLB 1, 42, 79; MAICYA; WLC;
  YABC 1

Aldanov, M. A.
  See Aldanov, Mark (Alexandrovich)

Aldanov, Mark (Alexandrovich)
  1886(?)-1957 . . . . TCLC 23
  See also CA 118

Aldington, Richard 1892-1962 . . . . . . CLC 49
  See also CA 85-88; DLB 20, 36, 100

Aldiss, Brian W(ilson)
  1925- . . . . CLC 5, 14, 40
  See also CA 5-8R; CAAS 2; CANR 5, 28;
  DLB 14; MTCW; SATA 34

Alegria, Fernando 1918- . . . . CLC 57
  See also CA 9-12R; CANR 5, 32; HW

Aleichem, Sholom . . . . TCLC 1, 35
  See also Rabinovitch, Sholem

Aleixandre, Vicente 1898-1984 . . . **CLC 9, 36**
See also CA 85-88; 114; CANR 26;
DLB 108; HW; MTCW

Alepoudelis, Odysseus
See Elytis, Odysseus

Aleshkovsky, Joseph 1929-
See Aleshkovsky, Yuz
See also CA 121; 128

Aleshkovsky, Yuz . . . . **CLC 44**
See also Aleshkovsky, Joseph

Alexander, Lloyd (Chudley) 1924- . . **CLC 35**
See also AAYA 1; CA 1-4R; CANR 1, 24,
38; CLR 1, 5; DLB 52; MAICYA;
MTCW; SATA 3, 49

Alfau, Felipe 1902- . . . . **CLC 66**
See also CA 137

Alger, Horatio Jr. 1832-1899 . . . . . **NCLC 8**
See also DLB 42; SATA 16

Algren, Nelson 1909-1981 . . . . **CLC 4, 10, 33**
See also CA 13-16R; 103; CANR 20;
CDALB 1941-1968; DLB 9; DLBY 81,
82; MTCW

Ali, Ahmed 1910- . . . . **CLC 69**
See also CA 25-28R; CANR 15, 34

Alighieri, Dante 1265-1321 . . . . **CMLC 3**

Allan, John B.
See Westlake, Donald E(dwin)

Allen, Edward 1948- . . . . **CLC 59**

Allen, Roland
See Ayckbourn, Alan

Allen, Woody 1935- . . . . **CLC 16, 52**
See also CA 33-36R; CANR 27, 38;
DLB 44; MTCW

Allende, Isabel 1942- . . . . **CLC 39, 57**
See also CA 125; 130; HW; MTCW

Alleyn, Ellen
See Rossetti, Christina (Georgina)

Allingham, Margery (Louise)
1904-1966 . . . . **CLC 19**
See also CA 5-8R; 25-28R; CANR 4;
DLB 77; MTCW

Allingham, William 1824-1889 . . . **NCLC 25**
See also DLB 35

Allston, Washington 1779-1843 . . . . **NCLC 2**
See also DLB 1

Almedingen, E. M. . . . . **CLC 12**
See also Almedingen, Martha Edith von
See also SATA 3

Almedingen, Martha Edith von 1898-1971
See Almedingen, E. M.
See also CA 1-4R; CANR 1

Alonso, Damaso 1898-1990 . . . . **CLC 14**
See also CA 110; 131; 130; DLB 108; HW

Alta 1942- . . . . **CLC 19**
See also CA 57-60

Alter, Robert B(ernard) 1935- . . . . . . **CLC 34**
See also CA 49-52; CANR 1

Alther, Lisa 1944- . . . . **CLC 7, 41**
See also CA 65-68; CANR 12, 30; MTCW

Altman, Robert 1925- . . . . **CLC 16**
See also CA 73-76

Alvarez, A(lfred) 1929- . . . . **CLC 5, 13**
See also CA 1-4R; CANR 3, 33; DLB 14,
40

Alvarez, Alejandro Rodriguez 1903-1965
See Casona, Alejandro
See also CA 131; 93-96; HW

Amado, Jorge 1912- . . . . **CLC 13, 40**
See also CA 77-80; CANR 35; DLB 113;
MTCW

Ambler, Eric 1909- . . . . **CLC 4, 6, 9**
See also CA 9-12R; CANR 7, 38; DLB 77;
MTCW

Amichai, Yehuda 1924- . . . . . . **CLC 9, 22, 57**
See also CA 85-88; MTCW

Amiel, Henri Frederic 1821-1881 . . **NCLC 4**

Amis, Kingsley (William)
1922- . . . . . . **CLC 1, 2, 3, 5, 8, 13, 40, 44**
See also AITN 2; CA 9-12R; CANR 8, 28;
CDBLB 1945-1960; DLB 15, 27, 100;
MTCW

Amis, Martin (Louis)
1949- . . . . **CLC 4, 9, 38, 62**
See also BEST 90:3; CA 65-68; CANR 8,
27; DLB 14

Ammons, A(rchie) R(andolph)
1926- . . . . **CLC 2, 3, 5, 8, 9, 25, 57**
See also AITN 1; CA 9-12R; CANR 6, 36;
DLB 5; MTCW

Amo, Tauraatua i
See Adams, Henry (Brooks)

Anand, Mulk Raj 1905- . . . . **CLC 23**
See also CA 65-68; CANR 32; MTCW

Anatol
See Schnitzler, Arthur

Anaya, Rudolfo A(lfonso) 1937- . . . . **CLC 23**
See also CA 45-48; CAAS 4; CANR 1, 32;
DLB 82; HW; MTCW

Andersen, Hans Christian
1805-1875 . . . . **NCLC 7; SSC 6**
See also CLR 6; MAICYA; WLC; YABC 1

Anderson, C. Farley
See Mencken, H(enry) L(ouis); Nathan,
George Jean

Anderson, Jessica (Margaret) Queale
. . . . **CLC 37**
See also CA 9-12R; CANR 4

Anderson, Jon (Victor) 1940- . . . . **CLC 9**
See also CA 25-28R; CANR 20

Anderson, Lindsay (Gordon)
1923- . . . . **CLC 20**
See also CA 125; 128

Anderson, Maxwell 1888-1959 . . . . . **TCLC 2**
See also CA 105; DLB 7

Anderson, Poul (William) 1926- . . . . **CLC 15**
See also AAYA 5; CA 1-4R; CAAS 2;
CANR 2, 15, 34; DLB 8; MTCW;
SATA 39

Anderson, Robert (Woodruff)
1917- . . . . **CLC 23**
See also AITN 1; CA 21-24R; CANR 32;
DLB 7

Anderson, Sherwood
1876-1941 . . . . . . **TCLC 1, 10, 24; SSC 1**
See also CA 104; 121; CDALB 1917-1929;
DLB 4, 9, 86; DLBD 1; MTCW; WLC

Andouard
See Giraudoux, (Hippolyte) Jean

Andrade, Carlos Drummond de . . . . . . **CLC 18**
See also Drummond de Andrade, Carlos

Andrade, Mario de 1893-1945 . . . . . **TCLC 43**

Andrewes, Lancelot 1555-1626 . . . . **LC 5**

Andrews, Cicily Fairfield
See West, Rebecca

Andrews, Elton V.
See Pohl, Frederik

Andreyev, Leonid (Nikolaevich)
1871-1919 . . . . **TCLC 3**
See also CA 104

Andric, Ivo 1892-1975 . . . . **CLC 8**
See also CA 81-84; 57-60; MTCW

Angelique, Pierre
See Bataille, Georges

Angell, Roger 1920- . . . . **CLC 26**
See also CA 57-60; CANR 13

Angelou, Maya 1928- . . . . **CLC 12, 35, 64**
See also AAYA 7; BLC 1; BW; CA 65-68;
CANR 19; DLB 38; MTCW; SATA 49

Annensky, Innokenty Fyodorovich
1856-1909 . . . . **TCLC 14**
See also CA 110

Anon, Charles Robert
See Pessoa, Fernando (Antonio Nogueira)

Anouilh, Jean (Marie Lucien Pierre)
1910-1987 . . . . . . **CLC 1, 3, 8, 13, 40, 50**
See also CA 17-20R; 123; CANR 32;
MTCW

Anthony, Florence
See Ai

Anthony, John
See Ciardi, John (Anthony)

Anthony, Peter
See Shaffer, Anthony (Joshua); Shaffer,
Peter (Levin)

Anthony, Piers 1934- . . . . **CLC 35**
See also CA 21-24R; CANR 28; DLB 8;
MTCW

Antoine, Marc
See Proust,
(Valentin-Louis-George-Eugene-)Marcel

Antoninus, Brother
See Everson, William (Oliver)

Antonioni, Michelangelo 1912- . . . . . **CLC 20**
See also CA 73-76

Antschel, Paul 1920-1970 . . . . **CLC 10, 19**
See also Celan, Paul
See also CA 85-88; CANR 33; MTCW

Anwar, Chairil 1922-1949 . . . . **TCLC 22**
See also CA 121

Apollinaire, Guillaume . . . . **TCLC 3, 8**
See also Kostrowitzki, Wilhelm Apollinaris
de

Appelfeld, Aharon 1932- . . . . **CLC 23, 47**
See also CA 112; 133

Apple, Max (Isaac) 1941- . . . . **CLC 9, 33**
See also CA 81-84; CANR 19

Appleman, Philip (Dean) 1926- . . . . . **CLC 51**
See also CA 13-16R; CANR 6, 29

Appleton, Lawrence
See Lovecraft, H(oward) P(hillips)

Apuleius, (Lucius Madaurensis)
125(?)-175(?) . . . . **CMLC 1**

Aquin, Hubert 1929-1977 . . . . **CLC 15**
See also CA 105; DLB 53

Aragon, Louis 1897-1982 . . . . **CLC 3, 22**
See also CA 69-72; 108; CANR 28;
DLB 72; MTCW

Arany, Janos 1817-1882 . . . . **NCLC 34**

Arbuthnot, John 1667-1735 . . . . **LC 1**
See also DLB 101

Archer, Herbert Winslow
See Mencken, H(enry) L(ouis)

Archer, Jeffrey (Howard) 1940- . . . . **CLC 28**
See also BEST 89:3; CA 77-80; CANR 22

Archer, Jules 1915- . . . . **CLC 12**
See also CA 9-12R; CANR 6; SAAS 5;
SATA 4

Archer, Lee
See Ellison, Harlan

Arden, John 1930- . . . . **CLC 6, 13, 15**
See also CA 13-16R; CAAS 4; CANR 31;
DLB 13; MTCW

Arenas, Reinaldo 1943-1990 . . . . . . **CLC 41**
See also CA 124; 128; 133; HW

Arendt, Hannah 1906-1975 . . . . **CLC 66**
See also CA 17-20R; 61-64; CANR 26;
MTCW

Aretino, Pietro 1492-1556 . . . . **LC 12**

Arguedas, Jose Maria
1911-1969 . . . . **CLC 10, 18**
See also CA 89-92; DLB 113; HW

Argueta, Manlio 1936- . . . . **CLC 31**
See also CA 131; HW

Ariosto, Ludovico 1474-1533 . . . . **LC 6**

Aristides
See Epstein, Joseph

Aristophanes
450B.C.-385B.C. . . . . **CMLC 4; DC 2**

Arlt, Roberto (Godofredo Christophersen)
1900-1942 . . . . **TCLC 29**
See also CA 123; 131; HW

Armah, Ayi Kwei 1939- . . . . **CLC 5, 33**
See also BLC 1; BW; CA 61-64; CANR 21;
DLB 117; MTCW

Armatrading, Joan 1950- . . . . **CLC 17**
See also CA 114

Arnette, Robert
See Silverberg, Robert

Arnim, Achim von (Ludwig Joachim von
Arnim) 1781-1831 . . . . **NCLC 5**
See also DLB 90

Arnold, Matthew
1822-1888 . . . . **NCLC 6, 29; PC 5**
See also CDBLB 1832-1890; DLB 32, 57;
WLC

Arnold, Thomas 1795-1842 . . . . . . **NCLC 18**
See also DLB 55

Arnow, Harriette (Louisa) Simpson
1908-1986 . . . . **CLC 2, 7, 18**
See also CA 9-12R; 118; CANR 14; DLB 6;
MTCW; SATA 42, 47

Arp, Hans
See Arp, Jean

Arp, Jean 1887-1966 . . . . **CLC 5**
See also CA 81-84; 25-28R

Arrabal . . . . **CLC 2, 9, 18**
See also Arrabal, Fernando

Arrabal, Fernando 1932- . . . . **CLC 58**
See also Arrabal
See also CA 9-12R; CANR 15

Arrick, Fran . . . . **CLC 30**

Artaud, Antonin 1896-1948 . . . . . **TCLC 3, 36**
See also CA 104

Arthur, Ruth M(abel) 1905-1979 . . . . **CLC 12**
See also CA 9-12R; 85-88; CANR 4;
SATA 7, 26

Artsybashev, Mikhail (Petrovich)
1878-1927 . . . . **TCLC 31**

Arundel, Honor (Morfydd)
1919-1973 . . . . **CLC 17**
See also CA 21-22; 41-44R; CAP 2;
SATA 4, 24

Asch, Sholem 1880-1957 . . . . **TCLC 3**
See also CA 105

Ash, Shalom
See Asch, Sholem

Ashbery, John (Lawrence)
1927- . . . **CLC 2, 3, 4, 6, 9, 13, 15, 25, 41**
See also CA 5-8R; CANR 9, 37; DLB 5;
DLBY 81; MTCW

Ashdown, Clifford
See Freeman, R(ichard) Austin

Ashe, Gordon
See Creasey, John

Ashton-Warner, Sylvia (Constance)
1908-1984 . . : . . . . **CLC 19**
See also CA 69-72; 112; CANR 29; MTCW

Asimov, Isaac 1920- . . . . **CLC 1, 3, 9, 19, 26**
See also BEST 90:2; CA 1-4R; 137;
CANR 2, 19, 36; CLR 12; DLB 8;
MAICYA; MTCW; SATA 1, 26

Astley, Thea (Beatrice May)
1925- . . . . **CLC 41**
See also CA 65-68; CANR 11

Aston, James
See White, T(erence) H(anbury)

Asturias, Miguel Angel
1899-1974 . . . . **CLC 3, 8, 13**
See also CA 25-28; 49-52; CANR 32;
CAP 2; DLB 113; HW; MTCW

Atares, Carlos Saura
See Saura (Atares), Carlos

Atheling, William
See Pound, Ezra (Weston Loomis)

Atheling, William Jr.
See Blish, James (Benjamin)

Atherton, Gertrude (Franklin Horn)
1857-1948 . . . . **TCLC 2**
See also CA 104; DLB 9, 78

Atherton, Lucius
See Masters, Edgar Lee

Atkins, Jack
See Harris, Mark

Atticus
See Fleming, Ian (Lancaster)

Atwood, Margaret (Eleanor)
1939- . . . . **CLC 2, 3, 4, 8, 13, 15, 25, 44;**
SSC 2
See also BEST 89:2; CA 49-52; CANR 3,
24, 33; DLB 53; MTCW; SATA 50; WLC

Aubigny, Pierre d'
See Mencken, H(enry) L(ouis)

Aubin, Penelope 1685-1731(?) . . . . **LC 9**
See also DLB 39

Auchincloss, Louis (Stanton)
1917- . . . . **CLC 4, 6, 9, 18, 45**
See also CA 1-4R; CANR 6, 29; DLB 2;
DLBY 80; MTCW

Auden, W(ystan) H(ugh)
1907-1973 . . . . . **CLC 1, 2, 3, 4, 6, 9, 11,
14, 43; PC 1**
See also CA 9-12R; 45-48; CANR 5;
CDBLB 1914-1945; DLB 10, 20; MTCW;
WLC

Audiberti, Jacques 1900-1965 . . . . . . **CLC 38**
See also CA 25-28R

Auel, Jean M(arie) 1936- . . . . **CLC 31**
See also AAYA 7; BEST 90:4; CA 103;
CANR 21

Auerbach, Erich 1892-1957 . . . . **TCLC 43**
See also CA 118

Augier, Emile 1820-1889 . . . . **NCLC 31**

August, John
See De Voto, Bernard (Augustine)

Augustine, St. 354-430 . . . . **CMLC 6**

Aurelius
See Bourne, Randolph S(illiman)

Austen, Jane
1775-1817 . . . . **NCLC 1, 13, 19, 33**
See also CDBLB 1789-1832; DLB 116;
WLC

Auster, Paul 1947- . . . . **CLC 47**
See also CA 69-72; CANR 23

Austin, Mary (Hunter)
1868-1934 . . . . **TCLC 25**
See also CA 109; DLB 9, 78

Autran Dourado, Waldomiro
See Dourado, (Waldomiro Freitas) Autran

Averroes 1126-1198 . . . . **CMLC 7**
See also DLB 115

Avison, Margaret 1918- . . . . **CLC 2, 4**
See also CA 17-20R; DLB 53; MTCW

Ayckbourn, Alan 1939- . . . . **CLC 5, 8, 18, 33**
See also CA 21-24R; CANR 31; DLB 13;
MTCW

Aydy, Catherine
See Tennant, Emma (Christina)

Ayme, Marcel (Andre) 1902-1967 . . . **CLC 11**
See also CA 89-92; CLR 25; DLB 72

Ayrton, Michael 1921-1975 . . . . **CLC 7**
See also CA 5-8R; 61-64; CANR 9, 21

Azorin . . . . **CLC 11**
See also Martinez Ruiz, Jose

Azuela, Mariano 1873-1952 . . . . **TCLC 3**
See also CA 104; 131; HW; MTCW

Baastad, Babbis Friis
See Friis-Baastad, Babbis Ellinor

Bab
See Gilbert, W(illiam) S(chwenck)

Babbis, Eleanor
See Friis-Baastad, Babbis Ellinor

Babel, Isaac (Emanuilovich) . . . . **TCLC 13**
See also Babel, Isaak (Emmanuilovich)

Babel, Isaak (Emmanuilovich)
1894-1941(?) . . . . **TCLC 2**
See also Babel, Isaac (Emanuilovich)
See also CA 104

Babits, Mihaly 1883-1941 . . . . **TCLC 14**
See also CA 114

Babur 1483-1530 . . . . **LC 18**

Bacchelli, Riccardo 1891-1985 . . . . . **CLC 19**
See also CA 29-32R; 117

Bach, Richard (David) 1936- . . . . **CLC 14**
See also AITN 1; BEST 89:2; CA 9-12R;
CANR 18; MTCW; SATA 13

Bachman, Richard
See King, Stephen (Edwin)

Bachmann, Ingeborg 1926-1973 . . . . . **CLC 69**
See also CA 93-96; 45-48; DLB 85

Bacon, Francis 1561-1626 . . . . **LC 18**
See also CDBLB Before 1660

Bacovia, George . . . . **TCLC 24**
See also Vasiliu, Gheorghe

Badanes, Jerome 1937- . . . . **CLC 59**

Bagehot, Walter 1826-1877 . . . . . . **NCLC 10**
See also DLB 55

Bagnold, Enid 1889-1981 . . . . **CLC 25**
See also CA 5-8R; 103; CANR 5; DLB 13;
MAICYA; SATA 1, 25

Bagrjana, Elisaveta
See Belcheva, Elisaveta

Bagryana, Elisaveta
See Belcheva, Elisaveta

Bailey, Paul 1937- . . . . **CLC 45**
See also CA 21-24R; CANR 16; DLB 14

Baillie, Joanna 1762-1851 . . . . **NCLC 2**
See also DLB 93

Bainbridge, Beryl (Margaret)
1933- . . . . **CLC 4, 5, 8, 10, 14, 18, 22, 62**
See also CA 21-24R; CANR 24; DLB 14;
MTCW

Baker, Elliott 1922- . . . . **CLC 8**
See also CA 45-48; CANR 2

Baker, Nicholson 1957- . . . . **CLC 61**
See also CA 135

Baker, Ray Stannard 1870-1946 . . . **TCLC 47**
See also CA 118

Baker, Russell (Wayne) 1925- . . . . . . **CLC 31**
See also BEST 89:4; CA 57-60; CANR 11;
MTCW

Bakshi, Ralph 1938(?)- . . . . **CLC 26**
See also CA 112; 138

Bakunin, Mikhail (Alexandrovich)
1814-1876 . . . . **NCLC 25**

Baldwin, James (Arthur)
1924-1987 . . . . . **CLC 1, 2, 3, 4, 5, 8, 13,**
15, 17, 42, 50, 67; DC 1; SSC 10
See also AAYA 4; BLC 1; BW; CA 1-4R;
124; CABS 1; CANR 3, 24;
CDALB 1941-1968; DLB 2, 7, 33;
DLBY 87; MTCW; SATA 9, 54; WLC

Ballard, J(ames) G(raham)
1930- . . . . **CLC 3, 6, 14, 36; SSC 1**
See also AAYA 3; CA 5-8R; CANR 15, 39;
DLB 14; MTCW

Balmont, Konstantin (Dmitriyevich)
1867-1943 . . . . **TCLC 11**
See also CA 109

Balzac, Honore de
1799-1850 . . . . **NCLC 5, 35; SSC 5**
See also DLB 119; WLC

Bambara, Toni Cade 1939- . . . . **CLC 19**
See also AAYA 5; BLC 1; BW; CA 29-32R;
CANR 24; DLB 38; MTCW

Bamdad, A.
See Shamlu, Ahmad

Banat, D. R.
See Bradbury, Ray (Douglas)

Bancroft, Laura
See Baum, L(yman) Frank

Banim, John 1798-1842 . . . . **NCLC 13**
See also DLB 116

Banim, Michael 1796-1874 . . . . . **NCLC 13**

Banks, Iain
See Banks, Iain M(enzies)

Banks, Iain M(enzies) 1954- . . . . **CLC 34**
See also CA 123; 128

Banks, Lynne Reid . . . . **CLC 23**
See also Reid Banks, Lynne
See also AAYA 6

Banks, Russell 1940- . . . . **CLC 37, 72**
See also CA 65-68; CAAS 15; CANR 19

Banville, John 1945- . . . . **CLC 46**
See also CA 117; 128; DLB 14

Banville, Theodore (Faullain) de
1832-1891 . . . . **NCLC 9**

Baraka, Amiri
1934- . . . **CLC 1, 2, 3, 5, 10, 14, 33; PC 4**
See also Jones, LeRoi
See also BLC 1; BW; CA 21-24R; CABS 3;
CANR 27, 38; CDALB 1941-1968;
DLB 5, 7, 16, 38; DLBD 8; MTCW

Barbellion, W. N. P. . . . . **TCLC 24**
See also Cummings, Bruce F(rederick)

Barbera, Jack 1945- . . . . **CLC 44**
See also CA 110

Barbey d'Aurevilly, Jules Amedee
1808-1889 . . . . **NCLC 1**
See also DLB 119

Barbusse, Henri 1873-1935 . . . . **TCLC 5**
See also CA 105; DLB 65

Barclay, Bill
See Moorcock, Michael (John)

Barclay, William Ewert
See Moorcock, Michael (John)

Barea, Arturo 1897-1957 . . . . **TCLC 14**
See also CA 111

Barfoot, Joan 1946- . . . . **CLC 18**
See also CA 105

Baring, Maurice 1874-1945 . . . . **TCLC 8**
See also CA 105; DLB 34

Barker, Clive 1952- . . . . **CLC 52**
See also BEST 90:3; CA 121; 129; MTCW

Barker, George Granville
1913-1991 . . . . **CLC 8, 48**
See also CA 9-12R; 135; CANR 7, 38;
DLB 20; MTCW

Barker, Harley Granville
See Granville-Barker, Harley
See also DLB 10

Barker, Howard 1946- . . . . **CLC 37**
See also CA 102; DLB 13

Barker, Pat 1943- . . . . **CLC 32**
See also CA 117; 122

Barlow, Joel 1754-1812 . . . . **NCLC 23**
See also DLB 37

Barnard, Mary (Ethel) 1909- . . . . **CLC 48**
See also CA 21-22; CAP 2

Barnes, Djuna
1892-1982 . . . **CLC 3, 4, 8, 11, 29; SSC 3**
See also CA 9-12R; 107; CANR 16; DLB 4,
9, 45; MTCW

Barnes, Julian 1946- . . . . **CLC 42**
See also CA 102; CANR 19

Barnes, Peter 1931- . . . . **CLC 5, 56**
See also CA 65-68; CAAS 12; CANR 33,
34; DLB 13; MTCW

Baroja (y Nessi), Pio 1872-1956 . . . . **TCLC 8**
See also CA 104

Baron, David
See Pinter, Harold

Baron Corvo
See Rolfe, Frederick (William Serafino
Austin Lewis Mary)

Barondess, Sue K(aufman)
1926-1977 . . . . **CLC 8**
See also Kaufman, Sue
See also CA 1-4R; 69-72; CANR 1

Baron de Teive
See Pessoa, Fernando (Antonio Nogueira)

Barres, Maurice 1862-1923 . . . . **TCLC 47**

Barreto, Afonso Henrique de Lima
See Lima Barreto, Afonso Henrique de

Barrett, (Roger) Syd 1946- . . . . **CLC 35**
See also Pink Floyd

Barrett, William (Christopher)
1913- . . . . **CLC 27**
See also CA 13-16R; CANR 11

Barrie, J(ames) M(atthew)
1860-1937 . . . . **TCLC 2**
See also CA 104; 136; CDBLB 1890-1914;
CLR 16; DLB 10; MAICYA; YABC 1

Barrington, Michael
See Moorcock, Michael (John)

Barrol, Grady
See Bograd, Larry

Barry, Mike
See Malzberg, Barry N(athaniel)

Barry, Philip 1896-1949 . . . . **TCLC 11**
See also CA 109; DLB 7

Bart, Andre Schwarz
See Schwarz-Bart, Andre

Barth, John (Simmons)
1930- . . . . . . **CLC 1, 2, 3, 5, 7, 9, 10, 14,**
27, 51; SSC 10
See also AITN 1, 2; CA 1-4R; CABS 1;
CANR 5, 23; DLB 2; MTCW

Barthelme, Donald
　　1931-1989 . . . . . **CLC 1, 2, 3, 5, 6, 8, 13,**
　　　　　　　　　　23, 46, 59; SSC 2
　　See also CA 21-24R; 129; CANR 20;
　　DLB 2; DLBY 80, 89; MTCW; SATA 7,
　　62

Barthelme, Frederick　1943- . . . . **CLC 36**
　　See also CA 114; 122; DLBY 85

Barthes, Roland (Gerard)
　　1915-1980 . . . . **CLC 24**
　　See also CA 130; 97-100; MTCW

Barzun, Jacques (Martin)　1907- . . . . **CLC 51**
　　See also CA 61-64; CANR 22

Bashevis, Isaac
　　See Singer, Isaac Bashevis

Bashkirtseff, Marie　1859-1884 . . . **NCLC 27**

Basho
　　See Matsuo Basho

Bass, Kingsley B. Jr.
　　See Bullins, Ed

Bassani, Giorgio　1916- . . . . **CLC 9**
　　See also CA 65-68; CANR 33; MTCW

Bastos, Augusto (Antonio) Roa
　　See Roa Bastos, Augusto (Antonio)

Bataille, Georges　1897-1962 . . . . **CLC 29**
　　See also CA 101; 89-92

Bates, H(erbert) E(rnest)
　　1905-1974 . . . . **CLC 46; SSC 10**
　　See also CA 93-96; 45-48; CANR 34;
　　MTCW

Bauchart
　　See Camus, Albert

Baudelaire, Charles
　　1821-1867 . . . . **NCLC 6, 29; PC 1**
　　See also WLC

Baudrillard, Jean　1929- . . . . **CLC 60**

Baum, L(yman) Frank　1856-1919 . . . **TCLC 7**
　　See also CA 108; 133; CLR 15; DLB 22;
　　MAICYA; MTCW; SATA 18

Baum, Louis F.
　　See Baum, L(yman) Frank

Baumbach, Jonathan　1933- . . . . . . **CLC 6, 23**
　　See also CA 13-16R; CAAS 5; CANR 12;
　　DLBY 80; MTCW

Bausch, Richard (Carl)　1945- . . . . . . **CLC 51**
　　See also CA 101; CAAS 14

Baxter, Charles　1947- . . . . **CLC 45**
　　See also CA 57-60

Baxter, James K(eir)　1926-1972 . . . . **CLC 14**
　　See also CA 77-80

Baxter, John
　　See Hunt, E(verette) Howard Jr.

Bayer, Sylvia
　　See Glassco, John

Beagle, Peter S(oyer)　1939- . . . . **CLC 7**
　　See also CA 9-12R; CANR 4; DLBY 80;
　　SATA 60

Bean, Normal
　　See Burroughs, Edgar Rice

Beard, Charles A(ustin)
　　1874-1948 . . . . **TCLC 15**
　　See also CA 115; DLB 17; SATA 18

Beardsley, Aubrey　1872-1898 . . . . . **NCLC 6**

Beattie, Ann　1947- . . . **CLC 8, 13, 18, 40, 63**
　　See also BEST 90:2; CA 81-84; DLBY 82;
　　MTCW

Beattie, James　1735-1803 . . . . **NCLC 25**
　　See also DLB 109

Beauchamp, Kathleen Mansfield　1888-1923
　　See Mansfield, Katherine
　　See also CA 104; 134

**Beauvoir, Simone (Lucie Ernestine Marie
　　Bertrand) de**
　　1908-1986 . . . **CLC 1, 2, 4, 8, 14, 31, 44,
　　　　　　　　　　　　　　50, 71**
　　See also CA 9-12R; 118; CANR 28;
　　DLB 72; DLBY 86; MTCW; WLC

Becker, Jurek　1937- . . . . **CLC 7, 19**
　　See also CA 85-88; DLB 75

Becker, Walter　1950- . . . . **CLC 26**

Beckett, Samuel (Barclay)
　　1906-1989 . . . . . **CLC 1, 2, 3, 4, 6, 9, 10,
　　　　　　　　　　11, 14, 18, 29, 57, 59**
　　See also CA 5-8R; 130; CANR 33;
　　CDBLB 1945-1960; DLB 13, 15;
　　DLBY 90; MTCW; WLC

Beckford, William　1760-1844 . . . . **NCLC 16**
　　See also DLB 39

Beckman, Gunnel　1910- . . . . **CLC 26**
　　See also CA 33-36R; CANR 15; CLR 25;
　　MAICYA; SAAS 9; SATA 6

Becque, Henri　1837-1899 . . . . **NCLC 3**

Beddoes, Thomas Lovell
　　1803-1849 . . . . **NCLC 3**
　　See also DLB 96

Bedford, Donald F.
　　See Fearing, Kenneth (Flexner)

Beecher, Catharine Esther
　　1800-1878 . . . . **NCLC 30**
　　See also DLB 1

Beecher, John　1904-1980 . . . . **CLC 6**
　　See also AITN 1; CA 5-8R; 105; CANR 8

Beer, Johann　1655-1700 . . . . **LC 5**

Beer, Patricia　1924- . . . . **CLC 58**
　　See also CA 61-64; CANR 13; DLB 40

Beerbohm, Henry Maximilian
　　1872-1956 . . . . **TCLC 1, 24**
　　See also CA 104; DLB 34, 100

Begiebing, Robert J(ohn)　1946- . . . . . **CLC 70**
　　See also CA 122

Behan, Brendan
　　1923-1964 . . . . **CLC 1, 8, 11, 15**
　　See also CA 73-76; CANR 33;
　　CDBLB 1945-1960; DLB 13; MTCW

Behn, Aphra　1640(?)-1689 . . . . **LC 1**
　　See also DLB 39, 80; WLC

Behrman, S(amuel) N(athaniel)
　　1893-1973 . . . . **CLC 40**
　　See also CA 13-16; 45-48; CAP 1; DLB 7,
　　44

Belasco, David　1853-1931 . . . . **TCLC 3**
　　See also CA 104; DLB 7

Belcheva, Elisaveta　1893- . . . . **CLC 10**

Beldone, Phil "Cheech"
　　See Ellison, Harlan

Beleno
　　See Azuela, Mariano

Belinski, Vissarion Grigoryevich
　　1811-1848 . . . . **NCLC 5**

Belitt, Ben　1911- . . . . **CLC 22**
　　See also CA 13-16R; CAAS 4; CANR 7;
　　DLB 5

Bell, James Madison　1826-1902 . . . **TCLC 43**
　　See also BLC 1; BW; CA 122; 124; DLB 50

Bell, Madison (Smartt)　1957- . . . . . . **CLC 41**
　　See also CA 111; CANR 28

Bell, Marvin (Hartley)　1937- . . . . . **CLC 8, 31**
　　See also CA 21-24R; CAAS 14; DLB 5;
　　MTCW

Bell, W. L. D.
　　See Mencken, H(enry) L(ouis)

Bellamy, Atwood C.
　　See Mencken, H(enry) L(ouis)

Bellamy, Edward　1850-1898 . . . . . . **NCLC 4**
　　See also DLB 12

Bellin, Edward J.
　　See Kuttner, Henry

Belloc, (Joseph) Hilaire (Pierre)
　　1870-1953 . . . . **TCLC 7, 18**
　　See also CA 106; DLB 19, 100; YABC 1

Belloc, Joseph Peter Rene Hilaire
　　See Belloc, (Joseph) Hilaire (Pierre)

Belloc, Joseph Pierre Hilaire
　　See Belloc, (Joseph) Hilaire (Pierre)

Belloc, M. A.
　　See Lowndes, Marie Adelaide (Belloc)

Bellow, Saul
　　1915- . . . . . **CLC 1, 2, 3, 6, 8, 10, 13, 15,
　　　　　　　　　　25, 33, 34, 63**
　　See also AITN 2; BEST 89:3; CA 5-8R;
　　CABS 1; CANR 29; CDALB 1941-1968;
　　DLB 2, 28; DLBD 3; DLBY 82; MTCW;
　　WLC

Belser, Reimond Karel Maria de
　　1929- . . . . **CLC 14**

Bely, Andrey . . . . **TCLC 7**
　　See also Bugayev, Boris Nikolayevich

Benary, Margot
　　See Benary-Isbert, Margot

Benary-Isbert, Margot　1889-1979 . . . **CLC 12**
　　See also CA 5-8R; 89-92; CANR 4;
　　CLR 12; MAICYA; SATA 2, 21

Benavente (y Martinez), Jacinto
　　1866-1954 . . . . **TCLC 3**
　　See also CA 106; 131; HW; MTCW

Benchley, Peter (Bradford)
　　1940- . . . . **CLC 4, 8**
　　See also AITN 2; CA 17-20R; CANR 12,
　　35; MTCW; SATA 3

Benchley, Robert (Charles)
　　1889-1945 . . . . **TCLC 1**
　　See also CA 105; DLB 11

Benedikt, Michael　1935- . . . . **CLC 4, 14**
　　See also CA 13-16R; CANR 7; DLB 5

Benet, Juan　1927- . . . . **CLC 28**

Benet, Stephen Vincent
　　1898-1943 . . . . **TCLC 7; SSC 10**
　　See also CA 104; DLB 4, 48, 102; YABC 1

Benet, William Rose　1886-1950 . . . **TCLC 28**
　　See also CA 118; DLB 45

Benford, Gregory (Albert) 1941-.... **CLC 52**
See also CA 69-72; CANR 12, 24;
DLBY 82

Benjamin, Lois
See Gould, Lois

Benjamin, Walter 1892-1940..... **TCLC 39**

Benn, Gottfried 1886-1956........ **TCLC 3**
See also CA 106; DLB 56

Bennett, Alan 1934-.............. **CLC 45**
See also CA 103; CANR 35; MTCW

Bennett, (Enoch) Arnold
1867-1931 .... **TCLC 5, 20**
See also CA 106; CDBLB 1890-1914;
DLB 10, 34, 98

Bennett, Elizabeth
See Mitchell, Margaret (Munnerlyn)

Bennett, George Harold 1930-
See Bennett, Hal
See also BW; CA 97-100

Bennett, Hal .... **CLC 5**
See also Bennett, George Harold
See also DLB 33

Bennett, Jay 1912-.............. **CLC 35**
See also CA 69-72; CANR 11; SAAS 4;
SATA 27, 41

Bennett, Louise (Simone) 1919-..... **CLC 28**
See also BLC 1; DLB 117

Benson, E(dward) F(rederic)
1867-1940 .... **TCLC 27**
See also CA 114

Benson, Jackson J. 1930-......... **CLC 34**
See also CA 25-28R; DLB 111

Benson, Sally 1900-1972 .... **CLC 17**
See also CA 19-20; 37-40R; CAP 1;
SATA 1, 27, 35

Benson, Stella 1892-1933........ **TCLC 17**
See also CA 117; DLB 36

Bentley, E(dmund) C(lerihew)
1875-1956 .... **TCLC 12**
See also CA 108; DLB 70

Bentley, Eric (Russell) 1916-....... **CLC 24**
See also CA 5-8R; CANR 6

Beranger, Pierre Jean de
1780-1857 .... **NCLC 34**

Berger, Colonel
See Malraux, (Georges-)Andre

Berger, John (Peter) 1926- ...... **CLC 2, 19**
See also CA 81-84; DLB 14

Berger, Melvin H. 1927-......... **CLC 12**
See also CA 5-8R; CANR 4; SAAS 2;
SATA 5

Berger, Thomas (Louis)
1924-......... **CLC 3, 5, 8, 11, 18, 38**
See also CA 1-4R; CANR 5, 28; DLB 2;
DLBY 80; MTCW

Bergman, (Ernst) Ingmar
1918-..................... **CLC 16, 72**
See also CA 81-84; CANR 33

Bergson, Henri 1859-1941........ **TCLC 32**

Bergstein, Eleanor 1938-......... **CLC 4**
See also CA 53-56; CANR 5

Berkoff, Steven 1937-............ **CLC 56**
See also CA 104

Bermant, Chaim (Icyk) 1929- ...... **CLC 40**
See also CA 57-60; CANR 6, 31

Bernanos, (Paul Louis) Georges
1888-1948 .... **TCLC 3**
See also CA 104; 130; DLB 72

Bernard, April 1956- .... **CLC 59**
See also CA 131

Bernhard, Thomas
1931-1989 .... **CLC 3, 32, 61**
See also CA 85-88; 127; CANR 32;
DLB 85; MTCW

Berrigan, Daniel 1921-............. **CLC 4**
See also CA 33-36R; CAAS 1; CANR 11;
DLB 5

Berrigan, Edmund Joseph Michael Jr.
1934-1983
See Berrigan, Ted
See also CA 61-64; 110; CANR 14

Berrigan, Ted.................... **CLC 37**
See also Berrigan, Edmund Joseph Michael
Jr.
See also DLB 5

Berry, Charles Edward Anderson 1931-
See Berry, Chuck
See also CA 115

Berry, Chuck.................... **CLC 17**
See also Berry, Charles Edward Anderson

Berry, Jonas
See Ashbery, John (Lawrence)

Berry, Wendell (Erdman)
1934- .... **CLC 4, 6, 8, 27, 46**
See also AITN 1; CA 73-76; DLB 5, 6

Berryman, John
1914-1972 ..... **CLC 1, 2, 3, 4, 6, 8, 10,
13, 25, 62**
See also CA 13-16; 33-36R; CABS 2;
CANR 35; CAP 1; CDALB 1941-1968;
DLB 48; MTCW

Bertolucci, Bernardo 1940- .... **CLC 16**
See also CA 106

Bertrand, Aloysius 1807-1841 .... **NCLC 31**

Bertran de Born c. 1140-1215 ..... **CMLC 5**

Besant, Annie (Wood) 1847-1933 ... **TCLC 9**
See also CA 105

Bessie, Alvah 1904-1985........... **CLC 23**
See also CA 5-8R; 116; CANR 2; DLB 26

Bethlen, T. D.
See Silverberg, Robert

Beti, Mongo.................... **CLC 27**
See also Biyidi, Alexandre
See also BLC 1

Betjeman, John
1906-1984 .... **CLC 2, 6, 10, 34, 43**
See also CA 9-12R; 112; CANR 33;
CDBLB 1945-1960; DLB 20; DLBY 84;
MTCW

Betti, Ugo 1892-1953 .... **TCLC 5**
See also CA 104

Betts, Doris (Waugh) 1932-.... **CLC 3, 6, 28**
See also CA 13-16R; CANR 9; DLBY 82

Bevan, Alistair
See Roberts, Keith (John Kingston)

Beynon, John
See Harris, John (Wyndham Parkes Lucas)
Beynon

Bialik, Chaim Nachman
1873-1934 .... **TCLC 25**

Bickerstaff, Isaac
See Swift, Jonathan

Bidart, Frank 19th cent. (?)-....... **CLC 33**

Bienek, Horst 1930-............ **CLC 7, 11**
See also CA 73-76; DLB 75

Bierce, Ambrose (Gwinett)
1842-1914(?) ..... **TCLC 1, 7, 44; SSC 9**
See also CA 104; CDALB 1865-1917;
DLB 11, 12, 23, 71, 74; WLC

Billings, Josh
See Shaw, Henry Wheeler

Billington, Rachel 1942-........... **CLC 43**
See also AITN 2; CA 33-36R

Binyon, T(imothy) J(ohn) 1936- .... **CLC 34**
See also CA 111; CANR 28

Bioy Casares, Adolfo 1914-.... **CLC 4, 8, 13**
See also CA 29-32R; CANR 19; DLB 113;
HW; MTCW

Bird, C.
See Ellison, Harlan

Bird, Cordwainer
See Ellison, Harlan

Bird, Robert Montgomery
1806-1854 .... **NCLC 1**

Birney, (Alfred) Earle
1904-................ **CLC 1, 4, 6, 11**
See also CA 1-4R; CANR 5, 20; DLB 88;
MTCW

Bishop, Elizabeth
1911-1979 ..... **CLC 1, 4, 9, 13, 15, 32;
PC 3**
See also CA 5-8R; 89-92; CABS 2;
CANR 26; CDALB 1968-1988; DLB 5;
MTCW; SATA 24

Bishop, John 1935-.............. **CLC 10**
See also CA 105

bissett, bill 1939- .... **CLC 18**
See also CA 69-72; CANR 15; DLB 53;
MTCW

Bitov, Andrei (Georgievich) 1937-... **CLC 57**

Biyidi, Alexandre 1932-
See Beti, Mongo
See also BW; CA 114; 124; MTCW

Bjarme, Brynjolf
See Ibsen, Henrik (Johan)

Bjoernson, Bjoernstjerne (Martinius)
1832-1910 .... **TCLC 7**
See also Bjornson, Bjornstjerne; Bjornson,
Bjornstjerne (Martinius)
See also CA 104

Bjornson, Bjornstjerne .... **TCLC 37**
See also Bjoernson, Bjoernstjerne
(Martinius)

Bjornson, Bjornstjerne (Martinius) ... **TCLC 7**
See also Bjoernson, Bjoernstjerne
(Martinius)

Black, Robert
See Holdstock, Robert P.

Blackburn, Paul 1926-1971 ...... **CLC 9, 43**
See also CA 81-84; 33-36R; CANR 34;
DLB 16; DLBY 81

Black Elk 1863-1950 .... **TCLC 33**

Black Hobart
See Sanders, (James) Ed(ward)

Blacklin, Malcolm
See Chambers, Aidan

Blackmore, R(ichard) D(oddridge)
1825-1900 .... TCLC 27
See also CA 120; DLB 18

Blackmur, R(ichard) P(almer)
1904-1965 .... CLC 2, 24
See also CA 11-12; 25-28R; CAP 1; DLB 63

Black Tarantula, The
See Acker, Kathy

Blackwood, Algernon (Henry)
1869-1951 .... TCLC 5
See also CA 105

Blackwood, Caroline 1931- .... CLC 6, 9
See also CA 85-88; CANR 32; DLB 14;
MTCW

Blade, Alexander
See Hamilton, Edmond; Silverberg, Robert

Blair, Eric (Arthur) 1903-1950
See Orwell, George
See also CA 104; 132; MTCW; SATA 29

Blais, Marie-Claire
1939- .... CLC 2, 4, 6, 13, 22
See also CA 21-24R; CAAS 4; CANR 38;
DLB 53; MTCW

Blaise, Clark 1940- .... CLC 29
See also AITN 2; CA 53-56; CAAS 3;
CANR 5; DLB 53

Blake, Nicholas
See Day Lewis, C(ecil)
See also DLB 77

Blake, William 1757-1827 .... NCLC 13
See also CDBLB 1789-1832; DLB 93;
MAICYA; SATA 30; WLC

Blasco Ibanez, Vicente
1867-1928 .... TCLC 12
See also CA 110; 131; HW; MTCW

Blatty, William Peter 1928- .... CLC 2
See also CA 5-8R; CANR 9

Bleeck, Oliver
See Thomas, Ross (Elmore)

Blessing, Lee 1949- .... CLC 54

Blish, James (Benjamin)
1921-1975 .... CLC 14
See also CA 1-4R; 57-60; CANR 3; DLB 8;
MTCW; SATA 66

Bliss, Reginald
See Wells, H(erbert) G(eorge)

Blixen, Karen (Christentze Dinesen)
1885-1962
See Dinesen, Isak
See also CA 25-28; CANR 22; CAP 2;
MTCW; SATA 44

Bloch, Robert (Albert) 1917- .... CLC 33
See also CA 5-8R; CANR 5; DLB 44;
SATA 12

Blok, Alexander (Alexandrovich)
1880-1921 .... TCLC 5
See also CA 104

Blom, Jan
See Breytenbach, Breyten

Bloom, Harold 1930- .... CLC 24
See also CA 13-16R; CANR 39; DLB 67

Bloomfield, Aurelius
See Bourne, Randolph S(illiman)

Blount, Roy (Alton) Jr. 1941- ...... CLC 38
See also CA 53-56; CANR 10, 28; MTCW

Bloy, Leon 1846-1917 .... TCLC 22
See also CA 121

Blume, Judy (Sussman) 1938- ... CLC 12, 30
See also AAYA 3; CA 29-32R; CANR 13,
37; CLR 2, 15; DLB 52; MAICYA;
MTCW; SATA 2, 31

Blunden, Edmund (Charles)
1896-1974 .... CLC 2, 56
See also CA 17-18; 45-48; CAP 2; DLB 20,
100; MTCW

Bly, Robert (Elwood)
1926- .... CLC 1, 2, 5, 10, 15, 38
See also CA 5-8R; DLB 5; MTCW

Bobette
See Simenon, Georges (Jacques Christian)

Boccaccio, Giovanni 1313-1375
See also SSC 10

Bochco, Steven 1943- .... CLC 35
See also CA 124; 138

Bodenheim, Maxwell 1892-1954 ... TCLC 44
See also CA 110; DLB 9, 45

Bodker, Cecil 1927- .... CLC 21
See also CA 73-76; CANR 13; CLR 23;
MAICYA; SATA 14

Boell, Heinrich (Theodor)
1917-1985 ... CLC 2, 3, 6, 9, 11, 15, 27, 39
See also Boll, Heinrich (Theodor)
See also CA 21-24R; 116; CANR 24;
DLB 69; DLBY 85; MTCW

Bogan, Louise 1897-1970 ..... CLC 4, 39, 46
See also CA 73-76; 25-28R; CANR 33;
DLB 45; MTCW

Bogarde, Dirk .... CLC 19
See also Van Den Bogarde, Derek Jules
Gaspard Ulric Niven
See also DLB 14

Bogosian, Eric 1953- .... CLC 45
See also CA 138

Bograd, Larry 1953- .... CLC 35
See also CA 93-96; SATA 33

Boiardo, Matteo Maria 1441-1494 .... LC 6

Boileau-Despreaux, Nicolas
1636-1711 .... LC 3

Boland, Eavan 1944- .... CLC 40, 67
See also DLB 40

Boll, Heinrich (Theodor)
1917-1985 ... CLC 2, 3, 6, 9, 11, 15, 27, 39, 72
See also Boell, Heinrich (Theodor)
See also DLB 69; DLBY 85; WLC

Bolt, Robert (Oxton) 1924- .... CLC 14
See also CA 17-20R; CANR 35; DLB 13;
MTCW

Bomkauf
See Kaufman, Bob (Garnell)

Bonaventura .... NCLC 35
See also DLB 90

Bond, Edward 1934- .... CLC 4, 6, 13, 23
See also CA 25-28R; CANR 38; DLB 13;
MTCW

Bonham, Frank 1914-1989 .... CLC 12
See also AAYA 1; CA 9-12R; CANR 4, 36;
MAICYA; SAAS 3; SATA 1, 49, 62

Bonnefoy, Yves 1923- .... CLC 9, 15, 58
See also CA 85-88; CANR 33; MTCW

Bontemps, Arna(ud Wendell)
1902-1973 .... CLC 1, 18
See also BLC 1; BW; CA 1-4R; 41-44R;
CANR 4, 35; CLR 6; DLB 48, 51;
MAICYA; MTCW; SATA 2, 24, 44

Booth, Martin 1944- .... CLC 13
See also CA 93-96; CAAS 2

Booth, Philip 1925- .... CLC 23
See also CA 5-8R; CANR 5; DLBY 82

Booth, Wayne C(layson) 1921- ..... CLC 24
See also CA 1-4R; CAAS 5; CANR 3;
DLB 67

Borchert, Wolfgang 1921-1947 ..... TCLC 5
See also CA 104; DLB 69

Borges, Jorge Luis
1899-1986 ... CLC 1, 2, 3, 4, 6, 8, 9, 10,
13, 19, 44, 48; SSC 4
See also CA 21-24R; CANR 19, 33;
DLB 113; DLBY 86; HW; MTCW; WLC

Borowski, Tadeusz 1922-1951 ...... TCLC 9
See also CA 106

Borrow, George (Henry)
1803-1881 .... NCLC 9
See also DLB 21, 55

Bosschere, Jean de 1878(?)-1953 ... TCLC 19
See also CA 115

Boswell, James 1740-1795 .... LC 4
See also CDBLB 1660-1789; DLB 104;
WLC

Bottoms, David 1949- .... CLC 53
See also CA 105; CANR 22; DLB 120;
DLBY 83

Boucolon, Maryse 1937-
See Conde, Maryse
See also CA 110; CANR 30

Bourget, Paul (Charles Joseph)
1852-1935 .... TCLC 12
See also CA 107

Bourjaily, Vance (Nye) 1922- .... CLC 8, 62
See also CA 1-4R; CAAS 1; CANR 2;
DLB 2

Bourne, Randolph S(illiman)
1886-1918 .... TCLC 16
See also CA 117; DLB 63

Bova, Ben(jamin William) 1932- .... CLC 45
See also CA 5-8R; CANR 11; CLR 3;
DLBY 81; MAICYA; MTCW; SATA 6,
68

Bowen, Elizabeth (Dorothea Cole)
1899-1973 ..... CLC 1, 3, 6, 11, 15, 22;
SSC 3
See also CA 17-18; 41-44R; CANR 35;
CAP 2; CDBLB 1945-1960; DLB 15;
MTCW

Bowering, George 1935- .... CLC 15, 47
See also CA 21-24R; CAAS 16; CANR 10;
DLB 53

Bowering, Marilyn R(uthe) 1949- ... CLC 32
See also CA 101

Bowers, Edgar 1924- .... CLC 9
See also CA 5-8R; CANR 24; DLB 5

Bowie, David .... CLC 17
See also Jones, David Robert

Bowles, Jane (Sydney)
1917-1973 .... CLC 3, 68
See also CA 19-20; 41-44R; CAP 2

Bowles, Paul (Frederick)
1910- .... CLC 1, 2, 19, 53; SSC 3
See also CA 1-4R; CAAS 1; CANR 1, 19;
DLB 5, 6; MTCW

Box, Edgar
See Vidal, Gore

Boyd, Nancy
See Millay, Edna St. Vincent

Boyd, William 1952- .... CLC 28, 53, 70
See also CA 114; 120

Boyle, Kay 1902- .. CLC 1, 5, 19, 58; SSC 5
See also CA 13-16R; CAAS 1; CANR 29;
DLB 4, 9, 48, 86; MTCW

Boyle, Mark
See Kienzle, William X(avier)

Boyle, Patrick 1905-1982......... CLC 19
See also CA 127

Boyle, T. Coraghessan 1948- .... CLC 36, 55
See also BEST 90:4; CA 120; DLBY 86

Brackenridge, Hugh Henry
1748-1816 .... NCLC 7
See also DLB 11, 37

Bradbury, Edward P.
See Moorcock, Michael (John)

Bradbury, Malcolm (Stanley)
1932- .... CLC 32, 61
See also CA 1-4R; CANR 1, 33; DLB 14;
MTCW

Bradbury, Ray (Douglas)
1920- .... CLC 1, 3, 10, 15, 42
See also AITN 1, 2; CA 1-4R; CANR 2, 30;
CDALB 1968-1988; DLB 2, 8; MTCW;
SATA 11, 64; WLC

Bradford, Gamaliel 1863-1932..... TCLC 36
See also DLB 17

Bradley, David (Henry Jr.) 1950-... CLC 23
See also BLC 1; BW; CA 104; CANR 26;
DLB 33

Bradley, John Ed 1959-........... CLC 55

Bradley, Marion Zimmer 1930-..... CLC 30
See also AAYA 9; CA 57-60; CAAS 10;
CANR 7, 31; DLB 8; MTCW

Bradstreet, Anne 1612(?)-1672 .... LC 4
See also CDALB 1640-1865; DLB 24

Bragg, Melvyn 1939- .... CLC 10
See also BEST 89:3; CA 57-60; CANR 10;
DLB 14

Braine, John (Gerard)
1922-1986 .... CLC 1, 3, 41
See also CA 1-4R; 120; CANR 1, 33;
CDBLB 1945-1960; DLB 15; DLBY 86;
MTCW

Brammer, William 1930(?)-1978 .... CLC 31
See also CA 77-80

Brancati, Vitaliano 1907-1954..... TCLC 12
See also CA 109

Brancato, Robin F(idler) 1936-..... CLC 35
See also AAYA 9; CA 69-72; CANR 11;
SAAS 9; SATA 23

Brand, Millen 1906-1980 .... CLC 7
See also CA 21-24R; 97-100

Branden, Barbara .... CLC 44

Brandes, Georg (Morris Cohen)
1842-1927 .... TCLC 10
See also CA 105

Brandys, Kazimierz 1916- .... CLC 62

Branley, Franklyn M(ansfield)
1915- .... CLC 21
See also CA 33-36R; CANR 14, 39;
CLR 13; MAICYA; SATA 4, 68

Brathwaite, Edward (Kamau)
1930- .... CLC 11
See also BW; CA 25-28R; CANR 11, 26

Brautigan, Richard (Gary)
1935-1984 .... CLC 1, 3, 5, 9, 12, 34, 42
See also CA 53-56; 113; CANR 34; DLB 2,
5; DLBY 80, 84; MTCW; SATA 56

Braverman, Kate 1950- .... CLC 67
See also CA 89-92

Brecht, Bertolt
1898-1956 .... TCLC 1, 6, 13, 35
See also CA 104; 133; DLB 56; MTCW;
WLC

Brecht, Eugen Berthold Friedrich
See Brecht, Bertolt

Bremer, Fredrika 1801-1865 ..... NCLC 11

Brennan, Christopher John
1870-1932 .... TCLC 17
See also CA 117

Brennan, Maeve 1917-............. CLC 5
See also CA 81-84

Brentano, Clemens (Maria)
1778-1842 .... NCLC 1

Brent of Bin Bin
See Franklin, (Stella Maraia Sarah) Miles

Brenton, Howard 1942-........... CLC 31
See also CA 69-72; CANR 33; DLB 13;
MTCW

Breslin, James 1930-
See Breslin, Jimmy
See also CA 73-76; CANR 31; MTCW

Breslin, Jimmy .... CLC 4, 43
See also Breslin, James
See also AITN 1

Bresson, Robert 1907- .... CLC 16
See also CA 110

Breton, Andre 1896-1966... CLC 2, 9, 15, 54
See also CA 19-20; 25-28R; CAP 2;
DLB 65; MTCW

Breytenbach, Breyten 1939(?)- .. CLC 23, 37
See also CA 113; 129

Bridgers, Sue Ellen 1942- .... CLC 26
See also AAYA 8; CA 65-68; CANR 11,
36; CLR 18; DLB 52; MAICYA;
SAAS 1; SATA 22

Bridges, Robert (Seymour)
1844-1930 .... TCLC 1
See also CA 104; CDBLB 1890-1914;
DLB 19, 98

Bridie, James..................... TCLC 3
See also Mavor, Osborne Henry
See also DLB 10

Brin, David 1950-................ CLC 34
See also CA 102; CANR 24; SATA 65

Brink, Andre (Philippus)
1935-................. CLC 18, 36
See also CA 104; CANR 39; MTCW

Brinsmead, H(esba) F(ay) 1922-.... CLC 21
See also CA 21-24R; CANR 10; MAICYA;
SAAS 5; SATA 18

Brittain, Vera (Mary)
1893(?)-1970 .... CLC 23
See also CA 13-16; 25-28R; CAP 1; MTCW

Broch, Hermann 1886-1951....... TCLC 20
See also CA 117; DLB 85

Brock, Rose
See Hansen, Joseph

Brodkey, Harold 1930-........... CLC 56
See also CA 111

Brodsky, Iosif Alexandrovich 1940-
See Brodsky, Joseph
See also AITN 1; CA 41-44R; CANR 37;
MTCW

Brodsky, Joseph .... CLC 4, 6, 13, 36, 50
See also Brodsky, Iosif Alexandrovich

Brodsky, Michael Mark 1948- ..... CLC 19
See also CA 102; CANR 18

Bromell, Henry 1947-............. CLC 5
See also CA 53-56; CANR 9

Bromfield, Louis (Brucker)
1896-1956 .... TCLC 11
See also CA 107; DLB 4, 9, 86

Broner, E(sther) M(asserman)
1930- .... CLC 19
See also CA 17-20R; CANR 8, 25; DLB 28

Bronk, William 1918-............. CLC 10
See also CA 89-92; CANR 23

Bronstein, Lev Davidovich
See Trotsky, Leon

Bronte, Anne 1820-1849.......... NCLC 4
See also DLB 21

Bronte, Charlotte
1816-1855 .... NCLC 3, 8, 33
See also CDBLB 1832-1890; DLB 21; WLC

Bronte, (Jane) Emily
1818-1848 .... NCLC 16, 35
See also CDBLB 1832-1890; DLB 21, 32;
WLC

Brooke, Frances 1724-1789 .... LC 6
See also DLB 39, 99

Brooke, Henry 1703(?)-1783 .... LC 1
See also DLB 39

Brooke, Rupert (Chawner)
1887-1915 .... TCLC 2, 7
See also CA 104; 132; CDBLB 1914-1945;
DLB 19; MTCW; WLC

Brooke-Haven, P.
See Wodehouse, P(elham) G(renville)

Brooke-Rose, Christine 1926-...... CLC 40
See also CA 13-16R; DLB 14

Brookner, Anita 1928-...... CLC 32, 34, 51
See also CA 114; 120; CANR 37; DLBY 87;
MTCW

Brooks, Cleanth 1906- . . . . CLC 24
See also CA 17-20R; CANR 33, 35;
DLB 63; MTCW

Brooks, George
See Baum, L(yman) Frank

Brooks, Gwendolyn
1917- . . . . CLC 1, 2, 4, 5, 15, 49
See also AITN 1; BLC 1; BW; CA 1-4R;
CANR 1, 27; CDALB 1941-1968;
CLR 27; DLB 5, 76; MTCW; SATA 6;
WLC

Brooks, Mel. CLC 12
See also Kaminsky, Melvin
See also DLB 26

Brooks, Peter 1938- . . . . CLC 34
See also CA 45-48; CANR 1

Brooks, Van Wyck 1886-1963. . . . . . CLC 29
See also CA 1-4R; CANR 6; DLB 45, 63,
103

Brophy, Brigid (Antonia)
1929- . . . . CLC 6, 11, 29
See also CA 5-8R; CAAS 4; CANR 25;
DLB 14; MTCW

Brosman, Catharine Savage 1934-. . . . CLC 9
See also CA 61-64; CANR 21

Brother Antoninus
See Everson, William (Oliver)

Broughton, T(homas) Alan 1936- . . . CLC 19
See also CA 45-48; CANR 2, 23

Broumas, Olga 1949- . . . . CLC 10
See also CA 85-88; CANR 20

Brown, Charles Brockden
1771-1810 . . . . NCLC 22
See also CDALB 1640-1865; DLB 37, 59,
73

Brown, Christy 1932-1981. . . . . CLC 63
See also CA 105; 104; DLB 14

Brown, Claude 1937- . . . . CLC 30
See also AAYA 7; BLC 1; BW; CA 73-76

Brown, Dee (Alexander) 1908- . . CLC 18, 47
See also CA 13-16R; CAAS 6; CANR 11;
DLBY 80; MTCW; SATA 5

Brown, George
See Wertmueller, Lina

Brown, George Douglas
1869-1902 . . . . TCLC 28

Brown, George Mackay 1921-. . . . CLC 5, 48
See also CA 21-24R; CAAS 6; CANR 12,
37; DLB 14, 27; MTCW; SATA 35

Brown, Moses
See Barrett, William (Christopher)

Brown, Rita Mae 1944- . . . . CLC 18, 43
See also CA 45-48; CANR 2, 11, 35;
MTCW

Brown, Roderick (Langmere) Haig-
See Haig-Brown, Roderick (Langmere)

Brown, Rosellen 1939-. . . . . CLC 32
See also CA 77-80; CAAS 10; CANR 14

Brown, Sterling Allen
1901-1989 . . . . CLC 1, 23, 59
See also BLC 1; BW; CA 85-88; 127;
CANR 26; DLB 48, 51, 63; MTCW

Brown, Will
See Ainsworth, William Harrison

Brown, William Wells
1813-1884 . . . . NCLC 2; DC 1
See also BLC 1; DLB 3, 50

Browne, (Clyde) Jackson 1948(?)-. . . CLC 21
See also CA 120

Browning, Elizabeth Barrett
1806-1861 . . . . NCLC 1, 16
See also CDBLB 1832-1890; DLB 32; WLC

Browning, Robert
1812-1889 . . . . NCLC 19; PC 2
See also CDBLB 1832-1890; DLB 32;
YABC 1

Browning, Tod 1882-1962 . . . . CLC 16
See also CA 117

Bruccoli, Matthew J(oseph) 1931- . . CLC 34
See also CA 9-12R; CANR 7; DLB 103

Bruce, Lenny. CLC 21
See also Schneider, Leonard Alfred

Bruin, John
See Brutus, Dennis

Brulls, Christian
See Simenon, Georges (Jacques Christian)

Brunner, John (Kilian Houston)
1934- . . . . CLC 8, 10
See also CA 1-4R; CAAS 8; CANR 2, 37;
MTCW

Brutus, Dennis 1924- . . . . CLC 43
See also BLC 1; BW; CA 49-52; CAAS 14;
CANR 2, 27; DLB 117

Bryan, C(ourtlandt) D(ixon) B(arnes)
1936- . . . . CLC 29
See also CA 73-76; CANR 13

Bryan, Michael
See Moore, Brian

Bryant, William Cullen
1794-1878 . . . . NCLC 6
See also CDALB 1640-1865; DLB 3, 43, 59

Bryusov, Valery Yakovlevich
1873-1924 . . . . TCLC 10
See also CA 107

Buchan, John 1875-1940 . . . . TCLC 41
See also CA 108; DLB 34, 70; YABC 2

Buchanan, George 1506-1582 . . . . LC 4

Buchheim, Lothar-Guenther 1918- . . . CLC 6
See also CA 85-88

Buchner, (Karl) Georg
1813-1837 . . . . NCLC 26

Buchwald, Art(hur) 1925-. . . . . CLC 33
See also AITN 1; CA 5-8R; CANR 21;
MTCW; SATA 10

Buck, Pearl S(ydenstricker)
1892-1973 . . . . CLC 7, 11, 18
See also AITN 1; CA 1-4R; 41-44R;
CANR 1, 34; DLB 9, 102; MTCW;
SATA 1, 25

Buckler, Ernest 1908-1984. . . . . CLC 13
See also CA 11-12; 114; CAP 1; DLB 68;
SATA 47

Buckley, Vincent (Thomas)
1925-1988 . . . . CLC 57
See also CA 101

Buckley, William F(rank) Jr.
1925- . . . . CLC 7, 18, 37
See also AITN 1; CA 1-4R; CANR 1, 24;
DLBY 80; MTCW

Buechner, (Carl) Frederick
1926- . . . . CLC 2, 4, 6, 9
See also CA 13-16R; CANR 11, 39;
DLBY 80; MTCW

Buell, John (Edward) 1927-. . . . . CLC 10
See also CA 1-4R; DLB 53

Buero Vallejo, Antonio 1916- . . . CLC 15, 46
See also CA 106; CANR 24; HW; MTCW

Bugayev, Boris Nikolayevich 1880-1934
See Bely, Andrey
See also CA 104

Bukowski, Charles 1920- . . . . CLC 2, 5, 9, 41
See also CA 17-20R; DLB 5; MTCW

Bulgakov, Mikhail (Afanas'evich)
1891-1940 . . . . TCLC 2, 16
See also CA 105

Bullins, Ed 1935- . . . . CLC 1, 5, 7
See also BLC 1; BW; CA 49-52; CAAS 16;
CANR 24; DLB 7, 38; MTCW

Bulwer-Lytton, Edward (George Earle Lytton)
1803-1873 . . . . NCLC 1
See also DLB 21

Bunin, Ivan Alexeyevich
1870-1953 . . . . TCLC 6; SSC 5
See also CA 104

Bunting, Basil 1900-1985. . . . CLC 10, 39, 47
See also CA 53-56; 115; CANR 7; DLB 20

Bunuel, Luis 1900-1983 . . . . CLC 16
See also CA 101; 110; CANR 32; HW

Bunyan, John 1628-1688 . . . . LC 4
See also CDBLB 1660-1789; DLB 39; WLC

Burford, Eleanor
See Hibbert, Eleanor Burford

Burgess, Anthony
. . CLC 1, 2, 4, 5, 8, 10, 13, 15, 22, 40, 62
See also Wilson, John (Anthony) Burgess
See also AITN 1; CDBLB 1960 to Present;
DLB 14

Burke, Edmund 1729(?)-1797. . . . . LC 7
See also DLB 104; WLC

Burke, Kenneth (Duva) 1897- . . . . CLC 2, 24
See also CA 5-8R; CANR 39; DLB 45, 63;
MTCW

Burke, Leda
See Garnett, David

Burke, Ralph
See Silverberg, Robert

Burney, Fanny 1752-1840 . . . . NCLC 12
See also DLB 39

Burns, Robert 1759-1796. . . . . LC 3
See also CDBLB 1789-1832; DLB 109;
WLC

Burns, Tex
See L'Amour, Louis (Dearborn)

Burnshaw, Stanley 1906- . . . . . CLC 3, 13, 44
See also CA 9-12R; DLB 48

Burr, Anne 1937- . . . . CLC 6
See also CA 25-28R

Burroughs, Edgar Rice
1875-1950 . . . . TCLC 2, 32
See also CA 104; 132; DLB 8; MTCW;
SATA 41

Burroughs, William S(eward)
1914- . . . . **CLC 1, 2, 5, 15, 22, 42**
See also AITN 2; CA 9-12R; CANR 20;
DLB 2, 8, 16; DLBY 81; MTCW; WLC

Busch, Frederick 1941- . . . **CLC 7, 10, 18, 47**
See also CA 33-36R; CAAS 1; DLB 6

Bush, Ronald 1946- . . . . **CLC 34**
See also CA 136

Bustos, F(rancisco)
See Borges, Jorge Luis

Bustos Domecq, H(onorio)
See Bioy Casares, Adolfo; Borges, Jorge
Luis

Bustos Domecq, H(onrio)
See Borges, Jorge Luis

Butler, Octavia E(stelle) 1947- . . . . . **CLC 38**
See also BW; CA 73-76; CANR 12, 24, 38;
DLB 33; MTCW

Butler, Samuel 1612-1680 . . . . **LC 16**
See also DLB 101

Butler, Samuel 1835-1902 . . . . . . **TCLC 1, 33**
See also CA 104; CDBLB 1890-1914;
DLB 18, 57; WLC

Butor, Michel (Marie Francois)
1926- . . . . **CLC 1, 3, 8, 11, 15**
See also CA 9-12R; CANR 33; DLB 83;
MTCW

Buzo, Alexander (John) 1944- . . . . . . **CLC 61**
See also CA 97-100; CANR 17, 39

Buzzati, Dino 1906-1972 . . . . **CLC 36**
See also CA 33-36R

Byars, Betsy (Cromer) 1928- . . . . **CLC 35**
See also CA 33-36R; CANR 18, 36; CLR 1,
16; DLB 52; MAICYA; MTCW; SAAS 1;
SATA 4, 46

Byatt, A(ntonia) S(usan Drabble)
1936- . . . . **CLC 19, 65**
See also CA 13-16R; CANR 13, 33;
DLB 14; MTCW

Byrne, David 1952- . . . . **CLC 26**
See also CA 127

Byrne, John Keyes 1926- . . . . **CLC 19**
See also Leonard, Hugh
See also CA 102

Byron, George Gordon (Noel)
1788-1824 . . . . **NCLC 2, 12**
See also CDBLB 1789-1832; DLB 96, 110;
WLC

C.3.3.
See Wilde, Oscar (Fingal O'Flahertie Wills)

Caballero, Fernan 1796-1877 . . . . . **NCLC 10**

Cabell, James Branch 1879-1958 . . . **TCLC 6**
See also CA 105; DLB 9, 78

Cable, George Washington
1844-1925 . . . . **TCLC 4; SSC 4**
See also CA 104; DLB 12, 74

Cabrera Infante, G(uillermo)
1929- . . . . **CLC 5, 25, 45**
See also CA 85-88; CANR 29; DLB 113;
HW; MTCW

Cade, Toni
See Bambara, Toni Cade

Cadmus
See Buchan, John

Caeiro, Alberto
See Pessoa, Fernando (Antonio Nogueira)

Cage, John (Milton Jr.) 1912- . . . . . . **CLC 41**
See also CA 13-16R; CANR 9

Cain, G.
See Cabrera Infante, G(uillermo)

Cain, Guillermo
See Cabrera Infante, G(uillermo)

Cain, James M(allahan)
1892-1977 . . . . **CLC 3, 11, 28**
See also AITN 1; CA 17-20R; 73-76;
CANR 8, 34; MTCW

Caine, Mark
See Raphael, Frederic (Michael)

Caldwell, Erskine (Preston)
1903-1987 . . . . **CLC 1, 8, 14, 50, 60**
See also AITN 1; CA 1-4R; 121; CAAS 1;
CANR 2, 33; DLB 9, 86; MTCW

Caldwell, (Janet Miriam) Taylor (Holland)
1900-1985 . . . . **CLC 2, 28, 39**
See also CA 5-8R; 116; CANR 5

Calhoun, John Caldwell
1782-1850 . . . . **NCLC 15**
See also DLB 3

Calisher, Hortense 1911- . . . . **CLC 2, 4, 8, 38**
See also CA 1-4R; CANR 1, 22; DLB 2;
MTCW

Callaghan, Morley Edward
1903-1990 . . . . **CLC 3, 14, 41, 65**
See also CA 9-12R; 132; CANR 33;
DLB 68; MTCW

Calvino, Italo
1923-1985 . . . . **CLC 5, 8, 11, 22, 33, 39;
SSC 3**
See also CA 85-88; 116; CANR 23; MTCW

Cameron, Carey 1952- . . . . **CLC 59**
See also CA 135

Cameron, Peter 1959- . . . . **CLC 44**
See also CA 125

Campana, Dino 1885-1932 . . . . **TCLC 20**
See also CA 117; DLB 114

Campbell, John W(ood Jr.)
1910-1971 . . . . **CLC 32**
See also CA 21-22; 29-32R; CANR 34;
CAP 2; DLB 8; MTCW

Campbell, Joseph 1904-1987 . . . . **CLC 69**
See also AAYA 3; BEST 89:2; CA 1-4R;
124; CANR 3, 28; MTCW

Campbell, (John) Ramsey 1946- . . . . **CLC 42**
See also CA 57-60; CANR 7

Campbell, (Ignatius) Roy (Dunnachie)
1901-1957 . . . . **TCLC 5**
See also CA 104; DLB 20

Campbell, Thomas 1777-1844 . . . . **NCLC 19**
See also DLB 93

Campbell, Wilfred . . . . **TCLC 9**
See also Campbell, William

Campbell, William 1858(?)-1918
See Campbell, Wilfred
See also CA 106; DLB 92

Campos, Alvaro de
See Pessoa, Fernando (Antonio Nogueira)

Camus, Albert
1913-1960 . . . **CLC 1, 2, 4, 9, 11, 14, 32,
63, 69; DC 2; SSC 9**
See also CA 89-92; DLB 72; MTCW; WLC

Canby, Vincent 1924- . . . . **CLC 13**
See also CA 81-84

Cancale
See Desnos, Robert

Canetti, Elias 1905- . . . . **CLC 3, 14, 25**
See also CA 21-24R; CANR 23; DLB 85;
MTCW

Canin, Ethan 1960- . . . . **CLC 55**
See also CA 131; 135

Cannon, Curt
See Hunter, Evan

Cape, Judith
See Page, P(atricia) K(athleen)

Capek, Karel
1890-1938 . . . . **TCLC 6, 37; DC 1**
See also CA 104; WLC

Capote, Truman
1924-1984 . . . . . **CLC 1, 3, 8, 13, 19, 34,
38, 58; SSC 2**
See also CA 5-8R; 113; CANR 18;
CDALB 1941-1968; DLB 2; DLBY 80,
84; MTCW; WLC

Capra, Frank 1897-1991 . . . . **CLC 16**
See also CA 61-64; 135

Caputo, Philip 1941- . . . . **CLC 32**
See also CA 73-76

Card, Orson Scott 1951- . . . . **CLC 44, 47, 50**
See also CA 102; CANR 27; MTCW

Cardenal (Martinez), Ernesto
1925- . . . . **CLC 31**
See also CA 49-52; CANR 2, 32; HW;
MTCW

Carducci, Giosue 1835-1907 . . . . **TCLC 32**

Carew, Thomas 1595(?)-1640 . . . . **LC 13**

Carey, Ernestine Gilbreth 1908- . . . . **CLC 17**
See also CA 5-8R; SATA 2

Carey, Peter 1943- . . . . **CLC 40, 55**
See also CA 123; 127; MTCW

Carleton, William 1794-1869 . . . . . . **NCLC 3**

Carlisle, Henry (Coffin) 1926- . . . . . . **CLC 33**
See also CA 13-16R; CANR 15

Carlsen, Chris
See Holdstock, Robert P.

Carlson, Ron(ald F.) 1947- . . . . **CLC 54**
See also CA 105; CANR 27

Carlyle, Thomas 1795-1881 . . . . . . **NCLC 22**
See also CDBLB 1789-1832; DLB 55

Carman, (William) Bliss
1861-1929 . . . . **TCLC 7**
See also CA 104; DLB 92

Carpenter, Don(ald Richard)
1931- . . . . **CLC 41**
See also CA 45-48; CANR 1

Carpentier (y Valmont), Alejo
1904-1980 . . . . **CLC 8, 11, 38**
See also CA 65-68; 97-100; CANR 11;
DLB 113; HW

Carr, Emily 1871-1945 . . . . **TCLC 32**
See also DLB 68

Carr, John Dickson 1906-1977 . . . . . . **CLC 3**
See also CA 49-52; 69-72; CANR 3, 33;
MTCW

Carr, Philippa
See Hibbert, Eleanor Burford

Carr, Virginia Spencer 1929- . . . . **CLC 34**
See also CA 61-64; DLB 111

Carrier, Roch 1937- . . . . **CLC 13**
See also CA 130; DLB 53

Carroll, James P. 1943(?)- . . . . **CLC 38**
See also CA 81-84

Carroll, Jim 1951- . . . . **CLC 35**
See also CA 45-48

Carroll, Lewis . . . . **NCLC 2**
See also Dodgson, Charles Lutwidge
See also CDBLB 1832-1890; CLR 2, 18;
DLB 18; WLC

Carroll, Paul Vincent 1900-1968 . . . . **CLC 10**
See also CA 9-12R; 25-28R; DLB 10

Carruth, Hayden 1921- . . . . **CLC 4, 7, 10, 18**
See also CA 9-12R; CANR 4, 38; DLB 5;
MTCW; SATA 47

Carson, Rachel Louise 1907-1964 . . . **CLC 71**
See also CA 77-80; CANR 35; MTCW;
SATA 23

Carter, Angela (Olive)
1940-1991 . . . . **CLC 5, 41**
See also CA 53-56; 136; CANR 12, 36;
DLB 14; MTCW; SATA 66; SATO 70

Carter, Nick
See Smith, Martin Cruz

Carver, Raymond
1938-1988 . . . **CLC 22, 36, 53, 55; SSC 8**
See also CA 33-36R; 126; CANR 17, 34;
DLBY 84, 88; MTCW

Cary, (Arthur) Joyce (Lunel)
1888-1957 . . . . **TCLC 1, 29**
See also CA 104; CDBLB 1914-1945;
DLB 15, 100

Casanova de Seingalt, Giovanni Jacopo
1725-1798 . . . . **LC 13**

Casares, Adolfo Bioy
See Bioy Casares, Adolfo

Casely-Hayford, J(oseph) E(phraim)
1866-1930 . . . . **TCLC 24**
See also BLC 1; CA 123

Casey, John (Dudley) 1939- . . . . **CLC 59**
See also BEST 90:2; CA 69-72; CANR 23

Casey, Michael 1947- . . . . **CLC 2**
See also CA 65-68; DLB 5

Casey, Patrick
See Thurman, Wallace (Henry)

Casey, Warren (Peter) 1935-1988 . . . **CLC 12**
See also CA 101; 127

Casona, Alejandro . . . . **CLC 49**
See also Alvarez, Alejandro Rodriguez

Cassavetes, John 1929-1989 . . . . **CLC 20**
See also CA 85-88; 127

Cassill, R(onald) V(erlin) 1919- . . . **CLC 4, 23**
See also CA 9-12R; CAAS 1; CANR 7;
DLB 6

Cassity, (Allen) Turner 1929- . . . . **CLC 6, 42**
See also CA 17-20R; CAAS 8; CANR 11;
DLB 105

Castaneda, Carlos 1931(?)- . . . . **CLC 12**
See also CA 25-28R; CANR 32; HW;
MTCW

Castedo, Elena 1937- . . . . **CLC 65**
See also CA 132

Castedo-Ellerman, Elena
See Castedo, Elena

Castellanos, Rosario 1925-1974 . . . . . **CLC 66**
See also CA 131; 53-56; DLB 113; HW

Castelvetro, Lodovico 1505-1571 . . . . . **LC 12**

Castiglione, Baldassare 1478-1529 . . . **LC 12**

Castle, Robert
See Hamilton, Edmond

Castro, Guillen de 1569-1631 . . . . **LC 19**

Castro, Rosalia de 1837-1885 . . . . . **NCLC 3**

Cather, Willa
See Cather, Willa Sibert

Cather, Willa Sibert
1873-1947 . . . . . . **TCLC 1, 11, 31; SSC 2**
See also CA 104; 128; CDALB 1865-1917;
DLB 9, 54, 78; DLBD 1; MTCW;
SATA 30; WLC

Catton, (Charles) Bruce
1899-1978 . . . . **CLC 35**
See also AITN 1; CA 5-8R; 81-84;
CANR 7; DLB 17; SATA 2, 24

Cauldwell, Frank
See King, Francis (Henry)

Caunitz, William J. 1933- . . . . **CLC 34**
See also BEST 89:3; CA 125; 130

Causley, Charles (Stanley) 1917- . . . . . **CLC 7**
See also CA 9-12R; CANR 5, 35; DLB 27;
MTCW; SATA 3, 66

Caute, David 1936- . . . . **CLC 29**
See also CA 1-4R; CAAS 4; CANR 1, 33;
DLB 14

Cavafy, C(onstantine) P(eter) . . . . . . **TCLC 2, 7**
See also Kavafis, Konstantinos Petrou

Cavallo, Evelyn
See Spark, Muriel (Sarah)

Cavanna, Betty . . . . **CLC 12**
See also Harrison, Elizabeth Cavanna
See also MAICYA; SAAS 4; SATA 1, 30

Caxton, William 1421(?)-1491(?) . . . . . **LC 17**

Cayrol, Jean 1911- . . . . **CLC 11**
See also CA 89-92; DLB 83

Caedmon fl. 658-680 . . . . **CMLC 7**

Cela, Camilo Jose 1916- . . . . . **CLC 4, 13, 59**
See also BEST 90:2; CA 21-24R; CAAS 10;
CANR 21, 32; DLBY 89; HW; MTCW

Celan, Paul . . . . **CLC 53**
See also Antschel, Paul
See also DLB 69

Celine, Louis-Ferdinand
. . . . **CLC 1, 3, 4, 7, 9, 15, 47**
See also Destouches, Louis-Ferdinand
See also DLB 72

Cellini, Benvenuto 1500-1571 . . . . **LC 7**

Cendrars, Blaise
See Sauser-Hall, Frederic

Cernuda (y Bidon), Luis
1902-1963 . . . . **CLC 54**
See also CA 131; 89-92; HW

Cervantes (Saavedra), Miguel de
1547-1616 . . . . **LC 6**
See also WLC

Cesaire, Aime (Fernand) 1913- . . **CLC 19, 32**
See also BLC 1; BW; CA 65-68; CANR 24;
MTCW

Chabon, Michael 1965(?)- . . . . **CLC 55**

Chabrol, Claude 1930- . . . . **CLC 16**
See also CA 110

Challans, Mary 1905-1983
See Renault, Mary
See also CA 81-84; 111; SATA 23, 36

Chambers, Aidan 1934- . . . . **CLC 35**
See also CA 25-28R; CANR 12, 31;
MAICYA; SAAS 12; SATA 1, 69

Chambers, James 1948-
See Cliff, Jimmy
See also CA 124

Chambers, Jessie
See Lawrence, D(avid) H(erbert Richards)

Chambers, Robert W. 1865-1933 . . . **TCLC 41**

Chandler, Raymond (Thornton)
1888-1959 . . . . **TCLC 1, 7**
See also CA 104; 129; CDALB 1929-1941;
DLBD 6; MTCW

Chang, Jung 1952- . . . . **CLC 71**

Channing, William Ellery
1780-1842 . . . . **NCLC 17**
See also DLB 1, 59

Chaplin, Charles Spencer
1889-1977 . . . . **CLC 16**
See also Chaplin, Charlie
See also CA 81-84; 73-76

Chaplin, Charlie
See Chaplin, Charles Spencer
See also DLB 44

Chapman, Graham 1941-1989 . . . . . . **CLC 21**
See also Monty Python
See also CA 116; 129; CANR 35

Chapman, John Jay 1862-1933 . . . . . **TCLC 7**
See also CA 104

Chapman, Walker
See Silverberg, Robert

Chappell, Fred (Davis) 1936- . . . . **CLC 40**
See also CA 5-8R; CAAS 4; CANR 8, 33;
DLB 6, 105

Char, Rene(-Emile)
1907-1988 . . . . **CLC 9, 11, 14, 55**
See also CA 13-16R; 124; CANR 32;
MTCW

Charby, Jay
See Ellison, Harlan

Chardin, Pierre Teilhard de
See Teilhard de Chardin, (Marie Joseph)
Pierre

Charles I 1600-1649 . . . . **LC 13**

Charyn, Jerome 1937- . . . . **CLC 5, 8, 18**
See also CA 5-8R; CAAS 1; CANR 7;
DLBY 83; MTCW

Chase, Mary (Coyle) 1907-1981 . . . . . . **DC 1**
See also CA 77-80; 105; SATA 17, 29

Chase, Mary Ellen 1887-1973 . . . . **CLC 2**
See also CA 13-16; 41-44R; CAP 1;
SATA 10

Chase, Nicholas
See Hyde, Anthony

Chateaubriand, Francois Rene de
1768-1848 .... NCLC 3
See also DLB 119

Chatterje, Sarat Chandra 1876-1936(?)
See Chatterji, Saratchandra
See also CA 109

Chatterji, Bankim Chandra
1838-1894 .... NCLC 19

Chatterji, Saratchandra .... TCLC 13
See also Chatterje, Sarat Chandra

Chatterton, Thomas 1752-1770 .... LC 3
See also DLB 109

Chatwin, (Charles) Bruce
1940-1989 .... CLC 28, 57, 59
See also AAYA 4; BEST 90:1; CA 85-88;
127

Chaucer, Daniel
See Ford, Ford Madox

Chaucer, Geoffrey 1340(?)-1400 ..... LC 17
See also CDBLB Before 1660

Chaviaras, Strates 1935-
See Haviaras, Stratis
See also CA 105

Chayefsky, Paddy .... CLC 23
See also Chayefsky, Sidney
See also DLB 7, 44; DLBY 81

Chayefsky, Sidney 1923-1981
See Chayefsky, Paddy
See also CA 9-12R; 104; CANR 18

Chedid, Andree 1920- .... CLC 47

Cheever, John
1912-1982 ..... CLC 3, 7, 8, 11, 15, 25,
64; SSC 1
See also CA 5-8R; 106; CABS 1; CANR 5,
27; CDALB 1941-1968; DLB 2, 102;
DLBY 80, 82; MTCW; WLC

Cheever, Susan 1943- .... CLC 18, 48
See also CA 103; CANR 27; DLBY 82

Chekhonte, Antosha
See Chekhov, Anton (Pavlovich)

Chekhov, Anton (Pavlovich)
1860-1904 ...... TCLC 3, 10, 31; SSC 2
See also CA 104; 124; WLC

Chernyshevsky, Nikolay Gavrilovich
1828-1889 .... NCLC 1

Cherry, Carolyn Janice 1942-
See Cherryh, C. J.
See also CA 65-68; CANR 10

Cherryh, C. J. .... CLC 35
See also Cherry, Carolyn Janice
See also DLBY 80

Chesnutt, Charles W(addell)
1858-1932 .... TCLC 5, 39; SSC 7
See also BLC 1; BW; CA 106; 125; DLB 12,
50, 78; MTCW

Chester, Alfred 1929(?)-1971 ...... CLC 49
See also CA 33-36R

Chesterton, G(ilbert) K(eith)
1874-1936 .... TCLC 1, 6; SSC 1
See also CA 104; 132; CDBLB 1914-1945;
DLB 10, 19, 34, 70, 98; MTCW;
SATA 27

Chiang Pin-chin 1904-1986
See Ding Ling
See also CA 118

Ch'ien Chung-shu 1910- .... CLC 22
See also CA 130; MTCW

Child, L. Maria
See Child, Lydia Maria

Child, Lydia Maria 1802-1880 .... NCLC 6
See also DLB 1, 74; SATA 67

Child, Mrs.
See Child, Lydia Maria

Child, Philip 1898-1978 .... CLC 19, 68
See also CA 13-14; CAP 1; SATA 47

Childress, Alice 1920- .... CLC 12, 15
See also AAYA 8; BLC 1; BW; CA 45-48;
CANR 3, 27; CLR 14; DLB 7, 38;
MAICYA; MTCW; SATA 7, 48

Chislett, (Margaret) Anne 1943- .... CLC 34

Chitty, Thomas Willes 1926- .... CLC 11
See also Hinde, Thomas
See also CA 5-8R

Chomette, Rene Lucien 1898-1981 .. CLC 20
See also Clair, Rene
See also CA 103

Chopin, Kate .... TCLC 5, 14; SSC 8
See also Chopin, Katherine
See also CDALB 1865-1917; DLB 12, 78

Chopin, Katherine 1851-1904
See Chopin, Kate
See also CA 104; 122

Christie
See Ichikawa, Kon

Christie, Agatha (Mary Clarissa)
1890-1976 ...... CLC 1, 6, 8, 12, 39, 48
See also AAYA 9; AITN 1, 2; CA 17-20R;
61-64; CANR 10, 37; CDBLB 1914-1945;
DLB 13, 77; MTCW; SATA 36

Christie, (Ann) Philippa
See Pearce, Philippa
See also CA 5-8R; CANR 4

Christine de Pizan 1365(?)-1431(?) .... LC 9

Chubb, Elmer
See Masters, Edgar Lee

Chulkov, Mikhail Dmitrievich
1743-1792 .... LC 2

Churchill, Caryl 1938- .... CLC 31, 55
See also CA 102; CANR 22; DLB 13;
MTCW

Churchill, Charles 1731-1764 .... LC 3
See also DLB 109

Chute, Carolyn 1947- .... CLC 39
See also CA 123

Ciardi, John (Anthony)
1916-1986 .... CLC 10, 40, 44
See also CA 5-8R; 118; CAAS 2; CANR 5,
33; CLR 19; DLB 5; DLBY 86;
MAICYA; MTCW; SATA 1, 46, 65

Cicero, Marcus Tullius
106B.C.-43B.C. .... CMLC 3

Cimino, Michael 1943- .... CLC 16
See also CA 105

Cioran, E(mil) M. 1911- .... CLC 64
See also CA 25-28R

Cisneros, Sandra 1954-............ CLC 69
See also AAYA 9; CA 131; HW

Clair, Rene...................... CLC 20
See also Chomette, Rene Lucien

Clampitt, Amy 1920- .... CLC 32
See also CA 110; CANR 29; DLB 105

Clancy, Thomas L. Jr. 1947-
See Clancy, Tom
See also CA 125; 131; MTCW

Clancy, Tom...................... CLC 45
See also Clancy, Thomas L. Jr.
See also AAYA 9; BEST 89:1, 90:1

Clare, John 1793-1864 .... NCLC 9
See also DLB 55, 96

Clarin
See Alas (y Urena), Leopoldo (Enrique
Garcia)

Clark, (Robert) Brian 1932-........ CLC 29
See also CA 41-44R

Clark, Eleanor 1913- .... CLC 5, 19
See also CA 9-12R; DLB 6

Clark, J. P.
See Clark, John Pepper
See also DLB 117

Clark, John Pepper 1935- .... CLC 38
See also Clark, J. P.
See also BLC 1; BW; CA 65-68; CANR 16

Clark, M. R.
See Clark, Mavis Thorpe

Clark, Mavis Thorpe 1909- .... CLC 12
See also CA 57-60; CANR 8, 37; MAICYA;
SAAS 5; SATA 8

Clark, Walter Van Tilburg
1909-1971 .... CLC 28
See also CA 9-12R; 33-36R; DLB 9;
SATA 8

Clarke, Arthur C(harles)
1917- ...... CLC 1, 4, 13, 18, 35; SSC 3
See also AAYA 4; CA 1-4R; CANR 2, 28;
MAICYA; MTCW; SATA 13, 70

Clarke, Austin C(hesterfield)
1934- .... CLC 8, 53
See also BLC 1; BW; CA 25-28R;
CAAS 16; CANR 14, 32; DLB 53

Clarke, Austin 1896-1974........ CLC 6, 9
See also CA 29-32; 49-52; CAP 2; DLB 10,
20

Clarke, Gillian 1937- .... CLC 61
See also CA 106; DLB 40

Clarke, Marcus (Andrew Hislop)
1846-1881 .... NCLC 19

Clarke, Shirley 1925- .... CLC 16

.... CLC 30
See also Headon, (Nicky) Topper; Jones,
Mick; Simonon, Paul; Strummer, Joe

Claudel, Paul (Louis Charles Marie)
1868-1955 .... TCLC 2, 10
See also CA 104

Clavell, James (duMaresq)
1925- .... CLC 6, 25
See also CA 25-28R; CANR 26; MTCW

Cleaver, (Leroy) Eldridge 1935- .... CLC 30
See also BLC 1; BW; CA 21-24R;
CANR 16

Cleese, John (Marwood) 1939- ..... **CLC 21**
See also Monty Python
See also CA 112; 116; CANR 35; MTCW

Cleishbotham, Jebediah
See Scott, Walter

Cleland, John 1710-1789 .... **LC 2**
See also DLB 39

Clemens, Samuel Langhorne 1835-1910
See Twain, Mark
See also CA 104; 135; CDALB 1865-1917;
DLB 11, 12, 23, 64, 74; MAICYA;
YABC 2

Clerihew, E.
See Bentley, E(dmund) C(lerihew)

Clerk, N. W.
See Lewis, C(live) S(taples)

Cliff, Jimmy..................... **CLC 21**
See also Chambers, James

Clifton, (Thelma) Lucille
1936- .... **CLC 19, 66**
See also BLC 1; BW; CA 49-52; CANR 2,
24; CLR 5; DLB 5, 41; MAICYA;
MTCW; SATA 20, 69

Clinton, Dirk
See Silverberg, Robert

Clough, Arthur Hugh 1819-1861.. **NCLC 27**
See also DLB 32

Clutha, Janet Paterson Frame 1924-
See Frame, Janet
See also CA 1-4R; CANR 2, 36; MTCW

Clyne, Terence
See Blatty, William Peter

Cobalt, Martin
See Mayne, William (James Carter)

Coburn, D(onald) L(ee) 1938- ...... **CLC 10**
See also CA 89-92

Cocteau, Jean (Maurice Eugene Clement)
1889-1963 .... **CLC 1, 8, 15, 16, 43**
See also CA 25-28; CAP 2; DLB 65;
MTCW; WLC

Codrescu, Andrei 1946- .... **CLC 46**
See also CA 33-36R; CANR 13, 34

Coe, Max
See Bourne, Randolph S(illiman)

Coe, Tucker
See Westlake, Donald E(dwin)

Coetzee, J(ohn) M(ichael)
1940- .... **CLC 23, 33, 66**
See also CA 77-80; MTCW

Cohen, Arthur A(llen)
1928-1986 .... **CLC 7, 31**
See also CA 1-4R; 120; CANR 1, 17;
DLB 28

Cohen, Leonard (Norman)
1934- .... **CLC 3, 38**
See also CA 21-24R; CANR 14; DLB 53;
MTCW

Cohen, Matt 1942- .... **CLC 19**
See also CA 61-64; DLB 53

Cohen-Solal, Annie 19th cent. (?)- .. **CLC 50**

Colegate, Isabel 1931- .... **CLC 36**
See also CA 17-20R; CANR 8, 22; DLB 14;
MTCW

Coleman, Emmett
See Reed, Ishmael

Coleridge, Samuel Taylor
1772-1834 .... **NCLC 9**
See also CDBLB 1789-1832; DLB 93, 107;
WLC

Coleridge, Sara 1802-1852...... **NCLC 31**

Coles, Don 1928- .... **CLC 46**
See also CA 115; CANR 38

Colette, (Sidonie-Gabrielle)
1873-1954 ...... **TCLC 1, 5, 16; SSC 10**
See also CA 104; 131; DLB 65; MTCW

Collett, (Jacobine) Camilla (Wergeland)
1813-1895 .... **NCLC 22**

Collier, Christopher 1930- .... **CLC 30**
See also CA 33-36R; CANR 13, 33;
MAICYA; SATA 16, 70

Collier, James L(incoln) 1928- ..... **CLC 30**
See also CA 9-12R; CANR 4, 33;
MAICYA; SATA 8, 70

Collier, Jeremy 1650-1726.......... **LC 6**

Collins, Hunt
See Hunter, Evan

Collins, Linda 1931-............. **CLC 44**
See also CA 125

Collins, (William) Wilkie
1824-1889 .... **NCLC 1, 18**
See also CDBLB 1832-1890; DLB 18, 70

Collins, William 1721-1759 .... **LC 4**
See also DLB 109

Colman, George
See Glassco, John

Colt, Winchester Remington
See Hubbard, L(afayette) Ron(ald)

Colter, Cyrus 1910- .... **CLC 58**
See also BW; CA 65-68; CANR 10; DLB 33

Colton, James
See Hansen, Joseph

Colum, Padraic 1881-1972........ **CLC 28**
See also CA 73-76; 33-36R; CANR 35;
MAICYA; MTCW; SATA 15

Colvin, James
See Moorcock, Michael (John)

Colwin, Laurie 1944- .... **CLC 5, 13, 23**
See also CA 89-92; CANR 20; DLBY 80;
MTCW

Comfort, Alex(ander) 1920-........ **CLC 7**
See also CA 1-4R; CANR 1

Comfort, Montgomery
See Campbell, (John) Ramsey

Compton-Burnett, I(vy)
1884(?)-1969 ... **CLC 1, 3, 10, 15, 34**
See also CA 1-4R; 25-28R; CANR 4;
DLB 36; MTCW

Comstock, Anthony 1844-1915 .... **TCLC 13**
See also CA 110

Conan Doyle, Arthur
See Doyle, Arthur Conan

Conde, Maryse .... **CLC 52**
See also Boucolon, Maryse

Condon, Richard (Thomas)
1915- .... **CLC 4, 6, 8, 10, 45**
See also BEST 90:3; CA 1-4R; CAAS 1;
CANR 2, 23; MTCW

Congreve, William 1670-1729 ... **LC 5; DC 2**
See also CDBLB 1660-1789; DLB 39, 84;
WLC

Connell, Evan S(helby) Jr.
1924- .... **CLC 4, 6, 45**
See also AAYA 7; CA 1-4R; CAAS 2;
CANR 2, 39; DLB 2; DLBY 81; MTCW

Connelly, Marc(us Cook)
1890-1980 .... **CLC 7**
See also CA 85-88; 102; CANR 30; DLB 7;
DLBY 80; SATA 25

Connor, Ralph .... **TCLC 31**
See also Gordon, Charles William
See also DLB 92

Conrad, Joseph
1857-1924 ...... **TCLC 1, 6, 13, 25, 43;**
SSC 9
See also CA 104; 131; CDBLB 1890-1914;
DLB 10, 34, 98; MTCW; SATA 27; WLC

Conrad, Robert Arnold
See Hart, Moss

Conroy, Pat 1945-................ **CLC 30**
See also AAYA 8; AITN 1; CA 85-88;
CANR 24; DLB 6; MTCW

Constant (de Rebecque), (Henri) Benjamin
1767-1830 .... **NCLC 6**
See also DLB 119

Conybeare, Charles Augustus
See Eliot, T(homas) S(tearns)

Cook, Michael 1933- .... **CLC 58**
See also CA 93-96; DLB 53

Cook, Robin 1940- .... **CLC 14**
See also BEST 90:2; CA 108; 111

Cook, Roy
See Silverberg, Robert

Cooke, Elizabeth 1948- .... **CLC 55**
See also CA 129

Cooke, John Esten 1830-1886..... **NCLC 5**
See also DLB 3

Cooke, John Estes
See Baum, L(yman) Frank

Cooke, M. E.
See Creasey, John

Cooke, Margaret
See Creasey, John

Cooney, Ray .... **CLC 62**

Cooper, Henry St. John
See Creasey, John

Cooper, J. California.............. **CLC 56**
See also BW; CA 125

Cooper, James Fenimore
1789-1851 .... **NCLC 1, 27**
See also CDALB 1640-1865; DLB 3;
SATA 19

Coover, Robert (Lowell)
1932- .... **CLC 3, 7, 15, 32, 46**
See also CA 45-48; CANR 3, 37; DLB 2;
DLBY 81; MTCW

Copeland, Stewart (Armstrong)
1952- .... **CLC 26**
See also The Police

Coppard, A(lfred) E(dgar)
1878-1957 .... **TCLC 5**
See also CA 114; YABC 1

Coppee, Francois 1842-1908 ...... TCLC 25

Coppola, Francis Ford 1939- .... CLC 16
See also CA 77-80; DLB 44

Corcoran, Barbara 1911- .... CLC 17
See also CA 21-24R; CAAS 2; CANR 11,
28; DLB 52; SATA 3

Cordelier, Maurice
See Giraudoux, (Hippolyte) Jean

Corman, Cid. .... CLC 9
See also Corman, Sidney
See also CAAS 2; DLB 5

Corman, Sidney 1924-
See Corman, Cid
See also CA 85-88

Cormier, Robert (Edmund)
1925- .... CLC 12, 30
See also AAYA 3; CA 1-4R; CANR 5, 23;
CDALB 1968-1988; CLR 12; DLB 52;
MAICYA; MTCW; SATA 10, 45

Corn, Alfred 1943- .... CLC 33
See also CA 104; DLB 120; DLBY 80

Cornwell, David (John Moore)
1931- .... CLC 9, 15
See also le Carre, John
See also CA 5-8R; CANR 13, 33; MTCW

Corrigan, Kevin .... CLC 55

Corso, (Nunzio) Gregory 1930- ... CLC 1, 11
See also CA 5-8R; DLB 5,16; MTCW

Cortazar, Julio
1914-1984 ..... CLC 2, 3, 5, 10, 13, 15,
33, 34; SSC 7
See also CA 21-24R; CANR 12, 32;
DLB 113; HW; MTCW

Corwin, Cecil
See Kornbluth, C(yril) M.

Cosic, Dobrica 1921- .... CLC 14
See also CA 122; 138

Costain, Thomas B(ertram)
1885-1965 .... CLC 30
See also CA 5-8R; 25-28R; DLB 9

Costantini, Humberto
1924(?)-1987 .... CLC 49
See also CA 131; 122; HW

Costello, Elvis 1955- .... CLC 21

Cotter, Joseph S. Sr.
See Cotter, Joseph Seamon Sr.

Cotter, Joseph Seamon Sr.
1861-1949 .... TCLC 28
See also BLC 1; BW; CA 124; DLB 50

Coulton, James
See Hansen, Joseph

Couperus, Louis (Marie Anne)
1863-1923 .... TCLC 15
See also CA 115

Court, Wesli
See Turco, Lewis (Putnam)

Courtenay, Bryce 1933- .... CLC 59
See also CA 138

Courtney, Robert
See Ellison, Harlan

Cousteau, Jacques-Yves 1910- ...... CLC 30
See also CA 65-68; CANR 15; MTCW;
SATA 38

Coward, Noel (Peirce)
1899-1973 .... CLC 1, 9, 29, 51
See also AITN 1; CA 17-18; 41-44R;
CANR 35; CAP 2; CDBLB 1914-1945;
DLB 10; MTCW

Cowley, Malcolm 1898-1989 .... CLC 39
See also CA 5-8R; 128; CANR 3; DLB 4,
48; DLBY 81, 89; MTCW

Cowper, William 1731-1800 .... NCLC 8
See also DLB 104, 109

Cox, William Trevor 1928- ... CLC 9, 14, 71
See also Trevor, William
See also CA 9-12R; CANR 4, 37; DLB 14;
MTCW

Cozzens, James Gould
1903-1978 .... CLC 1, 4, 11
See also CA 9-12R; 81-84; CANR 19;
CDALB 1941-1968; DLB 9; DLBD 2;
DLBY 84; MTCW

Crabbe, George 1754-1832 .... NCLC 26
See also DLB 93

Craig, A. A.
See Anderson, Poul (William)

Cram, Ralph Adams 1863-1942 .... TCLC 45

Crane, (Harold) Hart
1899-1932 .... TCLC 2, 5; PC 3
See also CA 104; 127; CDALB 1917-1929;
DLB 4, 48; MTCW; WLC

Crane, R(onald) S(almon)
1886-1967 .... CLC 27
See also CA 85-88; DLB 63

Crane, Stephen (Townley)
1871-1900 ..... TCLC 11, 17, 32; SSC 7
See also CA 109; CDALB 1865-1917;
DLB 12, 54, 78; WLC; YABC 2

Crase, Douglas 1944- .... CLC 58
See also CA 106

Craven, Margaret 1901-1980 .... CLC 17
See also CA 103

Crawford, F(rancis) Marion
1854-1909 .... TCLC 10
See also CA 107; DLB 71

Crawford, Isabella Valancy
1850-1887 .... NCLC 12
See also DLB 92

Crayon, Geoffrey
See Irving, Washington

Creasey, John 1908-1973 .... CLC 11
See also CA 5-8R; 41-44R; CANR 8;
DLB 77; MTCW

Crebillon, Claude Prosper Jolyot de (fils)
1707-1777 .... LC 1

Credo
See Creasey, John

Creeley, Robert (White)
1926- .... CLC 1, 2, 4, 8, 11, 15, 36
See also CA 1-4R; CAAS 10; CANR 23;
DLB 5, 16; MTCW

Crews, Harry (Eugene)
1935- .... CLC 6, 23, 49
See also AITN 1; CA 25-28R; CANR 20;
DLB 6; MTCW

Crichton, (John) Michael
1942- .... CLC 2, 6, 54
See also AITN 2; CA 25-28R; CANR 13;
DLBY 81; MTCW; SATA 9

Crispin, Edmund .... CLC 22
See also Montgomery, (Robert) Bruce
See also DLB 87

Cristofer, Michael 1945(?)- .... CLC 28
See also CA 110; DLB 7

Croce, Benedetto 1866-1952 ...... TCLC 37
See also CA 120

Crockett, David 1786-1836 .... NCLC 8
See also DLB 3, 11

Crockett, Davy
See Crockett, David

Croker, John Wilson 1780-1857 .. NCLC 10
See also DLB 110

Cronin, A(rchibald) J(oseph)
1896-1981 .... CLC 32
See also CA 1-4R; 102; CANR 5; SATA 25,
47

Cross, Amanda
See Heilbrun, Carolyn G(old)

Crothers, Rachel 1878(?)-1958 ..... TCLC 19
See also CA 113; DLB 7

Croves, Hal
See Traven, B.

Crowfield, Christopher
See Stowe, Harriet (Elizabeth) Beecher

Crowley, Aleister. .... TCLC 7
See also Crowley, Edward Alexander

Crowley, Edward Alexander 1875-1947
See Crowley, Aleister
See also CA 104

Crowley, John 1942- .... CLC 57
See also CA 61-64; DLBY 82; SATA 65

Crud
See Crumb, R(obert)

Crumarums
See Crumb, R(obert)

Crumb, R(obert) 1943- .... CLC 17
See also CA 106

Crumbum
See Crumb, R(obert)

Crumski
See Crumb, R(obert)

Crum the Bum
See Crumb, R(obert)

Crunk
See Crumb, R(obert)

Crustt
See Crumb, R(obert)

Cryer, Gretchen (Kiger) 1935- ...... CLC 21
See also CA 114; 123

Csath, Geza 1887-1919 .... TCLC 13
See also CA 111

Cudlip, David 1933- .... CLC 34

Cullen, Countee 1903-1946 ..... TCLC 4, 37
See also BLC 1; BW; CA 108; 124;
CDALB 1917-1929; DLB 4, 48, 51;
MTCW; SATA 18

Cum, R.
See Crumb, R(obert)

Cummings, Bruce F(rederick) 1889-1919
 See Barbellion, W. N. P.
 See also CA 123

Cummings, E(dward) E(stlin)
 1894-1962 ..... **CLC 1, 3, 8, 12, 15, 68;**
  PC 5
 See also CA 73-76; CANR 31;
  CDALB 1929-1941; DLB 4, 48; MTCW;
  WLC 2

Cunha, Euclides (Rodrigues Pimenta) da
 1866-1909 .... **TCLC 24**
 See also CA 123

Cunningham, E. V.
 See Fast, Howard (Melvin)

Cunningham, J(ames) V(incent)
 1911-1985 .... **CLC 3, 31**
 See also CA 1-4R; 115; CANR 1; DLB 5

Cunningham, Julia (Woolfolk)
 1916- .... **CLC 12**
 See also CA 9-12R; CANR 4, 19, 36;
  MAICYA; SAAS 2; SATA 1, 26

Cunningham, Michael 1952- ...... **CLC 34**
 See also CA 136

Cunninghame Graham, R(obert) B(ontine)
 1852-1936 .... **TCLC 19**
 See also Graham, R(obert) B(ontine)
  Cunninghame
 See also CA 119; DLB 98

Currie, Ellen 19th cent. (?)-........ **CLC 44**

Curtin, Philip
 See Lowndes, Marie Adelaide (Belloc)

Curtis, Price
 See Ellison, Harlan

Czaczkes, Shmuel Yosef
 See Agnon, S(hmuel) Y(osef Halevi)

D. P.
 See Wells, H(erbert) G(eorge)

Dabrowska, Maria (Szumska)
 1889-1965 .... **CLC 15**
 See also CA 106

Dabydeen, David 1955- .... **CLC 34**
 See also BW; CA 125

Dacey, Philip 1939- .... **CLC 51**
 See also CA 37-40R; CANR 14, 32;
  DLB 105

Dagerman, Stig (Halvard)
 1923-1954 .... **TCLC 17**
 See also CA 117

Dahl, Roald 1916-1990........ **CLC 1, 6, 18**
 See also CA 1-4R; 133; CANR 6, 32, 37;
  CLR 1, 7; MAICYA; MTCW; SATA 1,
  26; SATO 65

Dahlberg, Edward 1900-1977... **CLC 1, 7, 14**
 See also CA 9-12R; 69-72; CANR 31;
  DLB 48; MTCW

Dale, Colin.................... **TCLC 18**
 See also Lawrence, T(homas) E(dward)

Dale, George E.
 See Asimov, Isaac

Daly, Elizabeth 1878-1967........ **CLC 52**
 See also CA 23-24; 25-28R; CAP 2

Daly, Maureen 1921- .... **CLC 17**
 See also AAYA 5; CANR 37; MAICYA;
  SAAS 1; SATA 2

Daniels, Brett
 See Adler, Renata

Dannay, Frederic 1905-1982 .... **CLC 11**
 See also Queen, Ellery
 See also CA 1-4R; 107; CANR 1, 39;
  MTCW

D'Annunzio, Gabriele
 1863-1938 .... **TCLC 6, 40**
 See also CA 104

d'Antibes, Germain
 See Simenon, Georges (Jacques Christian)

Danvers, Dennis 1947-............ **CLC 70**

Danziger, Paula 1944- .... **CLC 21**
 See also AAYA 4; CA 112; 115; CANR 37;
  CLR 20; MAICYA; SATA 30, 36, 63

Dario, Ruben..................... **TCLC 4**
 See also Sarmiento, Felix Ruben Garcia

Darley, George 1795-1846 .... **NCLC 2**
 See also DLB 96

Daryush, Elizabeth 1887-1977.... **CLC 6, 19**
 See also CA 49-52; CANR 3; DLB 20

Daudet, (Louis Marie) Alphonse
 1840-1897 .... **NCLC 1**

Daumal, Rene 1908-1944........ **TCLC 14**
 See also CA 114

Davenport, Guy (Mattison Jr.)
 1927-.................. **CLC 6, 14, 38**
 See also CA 33-36R; CANR 23

Davidson, Avram 1923-
 See Queen, Ellery
 See also CA 101; CANR 26; DLB 8

Davidson, Donald (Grady)
 1893-1968 .... **CLC 2, 13, 19**
 See also CA 5-8R; 25-28R; CANR 4;
  DLB 45

Davidson, Hugh
 See Hamilton, Edmond

Davidson, John 1857-1909....... **TCLC 24**
 See also CA 118; DLB 19

Davidson, Sara 1943-............. **CLC 9**
 See also CA 81-84

Davie, Donald (Alfred)
 1922-................ **CLC 5, 8, 10, 31**
 See also CA 1-4R; CAAS 3; CANR 1;
  DLB 27; MTCW

Davies, Ray(mond Douglas) 1944- .. **CLC 21**
 See also CA 116

Davies, Rhys 1903-1978.......... **CLC 23**
 See also CA 9-12R; 81-84; CANR 4

Davies, (William) Robertson
 1913- .... **CLC 2, 7, 13, 25, 42**
 See also BEST 89:2; CA 33-36R; CANR 17;
  DLB 68; MTCW; WLC

Davies, W(illiam) H(enry)
 1871-1940 .... **TCLC 5**
 See also CA 104; DLB 19

Davies, Walter C.
 See Kornbluth, C(yril) M.

Davis, B. Lynch
 See Bioy Casares, Adolfo; Borges, Jorge
  Luis

Davis, Gordon
 See Hunt, E(verette) Howard Jr.

Davis, Harold Lenoir 1896-1960.... **CLC 49**
 See also CA 89-92; DLB 9

Davis, Rebecca (Blaine) Harding
 1831-1910 .... **TCLC 6**
 See also CA 104; DLB 74

Davis, Richard Harding
 1864-1916 .... **TCLC 24**
 See also CA 114; DLB 12, 23, 78, 79

Davison, Frank Dalby 1893-1970 ... **CLC 15**
 See also CA 116

Davison, Lawrence H.
 See Lawrence, D(avid) H(erbert Richards)

Davison, Peter 1928- .... **CLC 28**
 See also CA 9-12R; CAAS 4; CANR 3;
  DLB 5

Davys, Mary 1674-1732............. **LC 1**
 See also DLB 39

Dawson, Fielding 1930- .... **CLC 6**
 See also CA 85-88

Day, Clarence (Shepard Jr.)
 1874-1935 .... **TCLC 25**
 See also CA 108; DLB 11

Day, Thomas 1748-1789............. **LC 1**
 See also DLB 39; YABC 1

Day Lewis, C(ecil)
 1904-1972 .... **CLC 1, 6, 10**
 See also Blake, Nicholas
 See also CA 13-16; 33-36R; CANR 34;
  CAP 1; DLB 15, 20; MTCW

Dazai, Osamu .... **TCLC 11**
 See also Tsushima, Shuji

de Andrade, Carlos Drummond
 See Drummond de Andrade, Carlos

Deane, Norman
 See Creasey, John

**de Beauvoir, Simone (Lucie Ernestine Marie
  Bertrand)**
 See Beauvoir, Simone (Lucie Ernestine
  Marie Bertrand) de

de Brissac, Malcolm
 See Dickinson, Peter (Malcolm)

de Chardin, Pierre Teilhard
 See Teilhard de Chardin, (Marie Joseph)
  Pierre

Dee, John 1527-1608 .... **LC 20**

Deer, Sandra 1940-............... **CLC 45**

De Ferrari, Gabriella .... **CLC 65**

Defoe, Daniel 1660(?)-1731 .... **LC 1**
 See also CDBLB 1660-1789; DLB 39, 95,
  101; MAICYA; SATA 22; WLC

de Gourmont, Remy
 See Gourmont, Remy de

de Hartog, Jan 1914-............. **CLC 19**
 See also CA 1-4R; CANR 1

de Hostos, E. M.
 See Hostos (y Bonilla), Eugenio Maria de

de Hostos, Eugenio M.
 See Hostos (y Bonilla), Eugenio Maria de

Deighton, Len .... **CLC 4, 7, 22, 46**
 See also Deighton, Leonard Cyril
 See also AAYA 6; BEST 89:2;
  CDBLB 1960 to Present; DLB 87

Deighton, Leonard Cyril 1929-
  See Deighton, Len
  See also CA 9-12R; CANR 19, 33; MTCW

de la Mare, Walter (John)
  1873-1956 . . . . **TCLC 4**
  See also CA 110; 137; CDBLB 1914-1945;
  CLR 23; DLB 19; MAICYA; SATA 16;
  WLC

Delaney, Franey
  See O'Hara, John (Henry)

Delaney, Shelagh 1939- . . . . **CLC 29**
  See also CA 17-20R; CANR 30;
  CDBLB 1960 to Present; DLB 13;
  MTCW

Delany, Mary (Granville Pendarves)
  1700-1788 . . . . **LC 12**

Delany, Samuel R(ay Jr.)
  1942- . . . . **CLC 8, 14, 38**
  See also BLC 1; BW; CA 81-84; CANR 27;
  DLB 8, 33; MTCW

Delaporte, Theophile
  See Green, Julian (Hartridge)

De La Ramee, (Marie) Louise 1839-1908
  See Ouida
  See also SATA 20

de la Roche, Mazo 1879-1961 . . . . . . **CLC 14**
  See also CA 85-88; CANR 30; DLB 68;
  SATA 64

Delbanco, Nicholas (Franklin)
  1942- . . . . **CLC 6, 13**
  See also CA 17-20R; CAAS 2; CANR 29;
  DLB 6

del Castillo, Michel 1933- . . . . **CLC 38**
  See also CA 109

Deledda, Grazia (Cosima)
  1875(?)-1936 . . . . **TCLC 23**
  See also CA 123

Delibes, Miguel . . . . **CLC 8, 18**
  See also Delibes Setien, Miguel

Delibes Setien, Miguel 1920-
  See Delibes, Miguel
  See also CA 45-48; CANR 1, 32; HW;
  MTCW

DeLillo, Don
  1936- . . . . **CLC 8, 10, 13, 27, 39, 54**
  See also BEST 89:1; CA 81-84; CANR 21;
  DLB 6; MTCW

de Lisser, H. G.
  See De Lisser, Herbert George
  See also DLB 117

De Lisser, Herbert George
  1878-1944 . . . . **TCLC 12**
  See also de Lisser, H. G.
  See also CA 109

Deloria, Vine (Victor) Jr. 1933- . . . . **CLC 21**
  See also CA 53-56; CANR 5, 20; MTCW;
  SATA 21

Del Vecchio, John M(ichael)
  1947- . . . . **CLC 29**
  See also CA 110; DLBD 9

de Man, Paul (Adolph Michel)
  1919-1983 . . . . **CLC 55**
  See also CA 128; 111; DLB 67; MTCW

De Marinis, Rick 1934- . . . . **CLC 54**
  See also CA 57-60; CANR 9, 25

Demby, William 1922- . . . . **CLC 53**
  See also BLC 1; BW; CA 81-84; DLB 33

Demijohn, Thom
  See Disch, Thomas M(ichael)

de Montherlant, Henry (Milon)
  See Montherlant, Henry (Milon) de

de Natale, Francine
  See Malzberg, Barry N(athaniel)

Denby, Edwin (Orr) 1903-1983 . . . . . **CLC 48**
  See also CA 138; 110

Denis, Julio
  See Cortazar, Julio

Denmark, Harrison
  See Zelazny, Roger (Joseph)

Dennis, John 1658-1734 . . . . **LC 11**
  See also DLB 101

Dennis, Nigel (Forbes) 1912-1989 . . . . **CLC 8**
  See also CA 25-28R; 129; DLB 13, 15;
  MTCW

De Palma, Brian (Russell) 1940- . . . . **CLC 20**
  See also CA 109

De Quincey, Thomas 1785-1859 . . . **NCLC 4**
  See also CDBLB 1789-1832; DLB 110

Deren, Eleanora 1908(?)-1961
  See Deren, Maya
  See also CA 111

Deren, Maya . . . . **CLC 16**
  See also Deren, Eleanora

Derleth, August (William)
  1909-1971 . . . . **CLC 31**
  See also CA 1-4R; 29-32R; CANR 4;
  DLB 9; SATA 5

de Routisie, Albert
  See Aragon, Louis

Derrida, Jacques 1930- . . . . **CLC 24**
  See also CA 124; 127

Derry Down Derry
  See Lear, Edward

Dersonnes, Jacques
  See Simenon, Georges (Jacques Christian)

Desai, Anita 1937- . . . . **CLC 19, 37**
  See also CA 81-84; CANR 33; MTCW;
  SATA 63

de Saint-Luc, Jean
  See Glassco, John

de Saint Roman, Arnaud
  See Aragon, Louis

Descartes, Rene 1596-1650 . . . . **LC 20**

De Sica, Vittorio 1901(?)-1974 . . . . . **CLC 20**
  See also CA 117

Desnos, Robert 1900-1945 . . . . **TCLC 22**
  See also CA 121

Destouches, Louis-Ferdinand
  1894-1961 . . . . **CLC 9, 15**
  See also Celine, Louis-Ferdinand
  See also CA 85-88; CANR 28; MTCW

Deutsch, Babette 1895-1982 . . . . **CLC 18**
  See also CA 1-4R; 108; CANR 4; DLB 45;
  SATA 1, 33

Devenant, William 1606-1649 . . . . **LC 13**

Devkota, Laxmiprasad
  1909-1959 . . . . **TCLC 23**
  See also CA 123

De Voto, Bernard (Augustine)
  1897-1955 . . . . **TCLC 29**
  See also CA 113; DLB 9

De Vries, Peter
  1910- . . . . **CLC 1, 2, 3, 7, 10, 28, 46**
  See also CA 17-20R; DLB 6; DLBY 82;
  MTCW

Dexter, Pete 1943- . . . . **CLC 34, 55**
  See also BEST 89:2; CA 127; 131; MTCW

Diamano, Silmang
  See Senghor, Leopold Sedar

Diamond, Neil 1941- . . . . **CLC 30**
  See also CA 108

di Bassetto, Corno
  See Shaw, George Bernard

Dick, Philip K(indred)
  1928-1982 . . . . **CLC 10, 30, 72**
  See also CA 49-52; 106; CANR 2, 16;
  DLB 8; MTCW

Dickens, Charles (John Huffam)
  1812-1870 . . . . **NCLC 3, 8, 18, 26**
  See also CDBLB 1832-1890; DLB 21, 55,
  70; MAICYA; SATA 15

Dickey, James (Lafayette)
  1923- . . . . **CLC 1, 2, 4, 7, 10, 15, 47**
  See also AITN 1, 2; CA 9-12R; CABS 2;
  CANR 10; CDALB 1968-1988; DLB 5;
  DLBD 7; DLBY 82; MTCW

Dickey, William 1928- . . . . **CLC 3, 28**
  See also CA 9-12R; CANR 24; DLB 5

Dickinson, Charles 1951- . . . . **CLC 49**
  See also CA 128

Dickinson, Emily (Elizabeth)
  1830-1886 . . . . **NCLC 21; PC 1**
  See also CDALB 1865-1917; DLB 1;
  SATA 29; WLC

Dickinson, Peter (Malcolm)
  1927- . . . . **CLC 12, 35**
  See also AAYA 9; CA 41-44R; CANR 31;
  DLB 87; MAICYA; SATA 5, 62

Dickson, Carr
  See Carr, John Dickson

Dickson, Carter
  See Carr, John Dickson

Didion, Joan 1934- . . . . . **CLC 1, 3, 8, 14, 32**
  See also AITN 1; CA 5-8R; CANR 14;
  CDALB 1968-1988; DLB 2; DLBY 81,
  86; MTCW

Dietrich, Robert
  See Hunt, E(verette) Howard Jr.

Dillard, Annie 1945- . . . . **CLC 9, 60**
  See also AAYA 6; CA 49-52; CANR 3;
  DLBY 80; MTCW; SATA 10

Dillard, R(ichard) H(enry) W(ilde)
  1937- . . . . **CLC 5**
  See also CA 21-24R; CAAS 7; CANR 10;
  DLB 5

Dillon, Eilis 1920- . . . . **CLC 17**
  See also CA 9-12R; CAAS 3; CANR 4, 38;
  CLR 26; MAICYA; SATA 2

Dimont, Penelope
  See Mortimer, Penelope (Ruth)

Dinesen, Isak . . . . **CLC 10, 29; SSC 7**
  See also Blixen, Karen (Christentze
  Dinesen)

Ding Ling. . . . . CLC 68
See also Chiang Pin-chin

Disch, Thomas M(ichael) 1940-. . . CLC 7, 36
See also CA 21-24R; CAAS 4; CANR 17,
36; CLR 18; DLB 8; MAICYA; MTCW;
SATA 54

Disch, Tom
See Disch, Thomas M(ichael)

d'Isly, Georges
See Simenon, Georges (Jacques Christian)

Disraeli, Benjamin 1804-1881 . . . . . NCLC 2
See also DLB 21, 55

Ditcum, Steve
See Crumb, R(obert)

Dixon, Paige
See Corcoran, Barbara

Dixon, Stephen 1936-. . . . . CLC 52
See also CA 89-92; CANR 17

Doblin, Alfred . . . . TCLC 13
See also Doeblin, Alfred

Dobrolyubov, Nikolai Alexandrovich
1836-1861 . . . . NCLC 5

Dobyns, Stephen 1941-. . . . . CLC 37
See also CA 45-48; CANR 2, 18

Doctorow, E(dgar) L(aurence)
1931- . . . . . CLC 6, 11, 15, 18, 37, 44, 65
See also AITN 2; BEST 89:3; CA 45-48;
CANR 2, 33; CDALB 1968-1988; DLB 2,
28; DLBY 80; MTCW

Dodgson, Charles Lutwidge 1832-1898
See Carroll, Lewis
See also CLR 2; MAICYA; YABC 2

Doeblin, Alfred 1878-1957. . . . . TCLC 13
See also Doblin, Alfred
See also CA 110; DLB 66

Doerr, Harriet 1910- . . . . CLC 34
See also CA 117; 122

Domecq, H(onorio) Bustos
See Bioy Casares, Adolfo; Borges, Jorge
Luis

Domini, Rey
See Lorde, Audre (Geraldine)

Dominique
See Proust,
(Valentin-Louis-George-Eugene-)Marcel

Don, A
See Stephen, Leslie

Donaldson, Stephen R. 1947-. . . . . . CLC 46
See also CA 89-92; CANR 13

Donleavy, J(ames) P(atrick)
1926- . . . . CLC 1, 4, 6, 10, 45
See also AITN 2; CA 9-12R; CANR 24;
DLB 6; MTCW

Donne, John 1572-1631 . . . . LC 10; PC 1
See also CDBLB Before 1660; DLB 121;
WLC

Donnell, David 1939(?)- . . . . CLC 34

Donoso (Yanez), Jose
1924- . . . . CLC 4, 8, 11, 32
See also CA 81-84; CANR 32; DLB 113;
HW; MTCW

Donovan, John 1928-1992 . . . . CLC 35
See also CA 97-100; 137; CLR 3;
MAICYA; SATA 29

Don Roberto
See Cunninghame Graham, R(obert)
B(ontine)

Doolittle, Hilda
1886-1961 . . . CLC 3, 8, 14, 31, 34; PC 5
See also H. D.
See also CA 97-100; CANR 35; DLB 4, 45;
MTCW; WLC

Dorfman, Ariel 1942-. . . . . CLC 48
See also CA 124; 130; HW

Dorn, Edward (Merton) 1929-. . . CLC 10, 18
See also CA 93-96; DLB 5

Dorsan, Luc
See Simenon, Georges (Jacques Christian)

Dorsange, Jean
See Simenon, Georges (Jacques Christian)

Dos Passos, John (Roderigo)
1896-1970 . . . CLC 1, 4, 8, 11, 15, 25, 34
See also CA 1-4R; 29-32R; CANR 3;
CDALB 1929-1941; DLB 4, 9; DLBD 1;
MTCW; WLC

Dossage, Jean
See Simenon, Georges (Jacques Christian)

Dostoevsky, Fedor Mikhailovich
1821-1881 . . . . NCLC 2, 7, 21, 33; SSC 2
See also WLC

Doughty, Charles M(ontagu)
1843-1926 . . . . TCLC 27
See also CA 115; DLB 19, 57

Douglas, Gavin 1475(?)-1522. . . . . . . LC 20

Douglas, Keith 1920-1944 . . . . TCLC 40
See also DLB 27

Douglas, Leonard
See Bradbury, Ray (Douglas)

Douglas, Michael
See Crichton, (John) Michael

Douglass, Frederick 1817(?)-1895. . NCLC 7
See also BLC 1; CDALB 1640-1865;
DLB 1, 43, 50, 79; SATA 29; WLC

Dourado, (Waldomiro Freitas) Autran
1926-. CLC 23, 60
See also CA 25-28R; CANR 34

Dourado, Waldomiro Autran
See Dourado, (Waldomiro Freitas) Autran

Dove, Rita (Frances) 1952- . . . . CLC 50
See also BW; CA 109; CANR 27; DLB 120

Dowell, Coleman 1925-1985. . . . . . . CLC 60
See also CA 25-28R; 117; CANR 10

Dowson, Ernest Christopher
1867-1900 . . . . TCLC 4
See also CA 105; DLB 19

Doyle, A. Conan
See Doyle, Arthur Conan

Doyle, Arthur Conan 1859-1930 . . . . TCLC 7
See also CA 104; 122; CDBLB 1890-1914;
DLB 18, 70; MTCW; SATA 24; WLC

Doyle, Conan
See Doyle, Arthur Conan

Doyle, John
See Graves, Robert (von Ranke)

Doyle, Sir A. Conan
See Doyle, Arthur Conan

Doyle, Sir Arthur Conan
See Doyle, Arthur Conan

Dr. A
See Asimov, Isaac; Silverstein, Alvin

Drabble, Margaret
1939- . . . . CLC 2, 3, 5, 8, 10, 22, 53
See also CA 13-16R; CANR 18, 35;
CDBLB 1960 to Present; DLB 14;
MTCW; SATA 48

Drapier, M. B.
See Swift, Jonathan

Drayham, James
See Mencken, H(enry) L(ouis)

Drayton, Michael 1563-1631. . . . . LC 8

Dreadstone, Carl
See Campbell, (John) Ramsey

Dreiser, Theodore (Herman Albert)
1871-1945 . . . . TCLC 10, 18, 35
See also CA 106; 132; CDALB 1865-1917;
DLB 9, 12, 102; DLBD 1; MTCW; WLC

Drexler, Rosalyn 1926- . . . . CLC 2, 6
See also CA 81-84

Dreyer, Carl Theodor 1889-1968. . . . CLC 16
See also CA 116

Drieu la Rochelle, Pierre(-Eugene)
1893-1945 . . . . TCLC 21
See also CA 117; DLB 72

Drop Shot
See Cable, George Washington

Droste-Hulshoff, Annette Freiin von
1797-1848 . . . . NCLC 3

Drummond, Walter
See Silverberg, Robert

Drummond, William Henry
1854-1907 . . . . TCLC 25
See also DLB 92

Drummond de Andrade, Carlos
1902-1987 . . . . CLC 18
See also Andrade, Carlos Drummond de
See also CA 132; 123

Drury, Allen (Stuart) 1918-. . . . . . . CLC 37
See also CA 57-60; CANR 18

Dryden, John 1631-1700 . . . . LC 3

Duberman, Martin 1930-. . . . . CLC 8
See also CA 1-4R; CANR 2

Dubie, Norman (Evans) 1945-. . . . . . CLC 36
See also CA 69-72; CANR 12; DLB 120

Du Bois, W(illiam) E(dward) B(urghardt)
1868-1963 . . . . CLC 1, 2, 13, 64
See also BLC 1; BW; CA 85-88; CANR 34;
CDALB 1865-1917; DLB 47, 50, 91;
MTCW; SATA 42; WLC

Dubus, Andre 1936-. . . . . CLC 13, 36
See also CA 21-24R; CANR 17

Duca Minimo
See D'Annunzio, Gabriele

Duclos, Charles Pinot 1704-1772 . . . . . LC 1

Dudek, Louis 1918- . . . . CLC 11, 19
See also CA 45-48; CAAS 14; CANR 1;
DLB 88

Duerrenmatt, Friedrich
1921-1990 . . . . . . CLC 1, 4, 8, 11, 15, 43
See also Durrenmatt, Friedrich
See also CA 17-20R; CANR 33; DLB 69;
MTCW

Duffy, Bruce 19th cent. (?)-. . . . . . . CLC 50

Duffy, Maureen 1933- . . . . **CLC 37**
See also CA 25-28R; CANR 33; DLB 14;
MTCW

Dugan, Alan 1923- . . . . **CLC 2, 6**
See also CA 81-84; DLB 5

du Gard, Roger Martin
See Martin du Gard, Roger

Duhamel, Georges 1884-1966 . . . . **CLC 8**
See also CA 81-84; 25-28R; CANR 35;
DLB 65; MTCW

Dujardin, Edouard (Emile Louis)
1861-1949 . . . . **TCLC 13**
See also CA 109

Dumas, Alexandre (Davy de la Pailleterie)
1802-1870 . . . . **NCLC 11**
See also DLB 119; SATA 18; WLC

Dumas, Alexandre
1824-1895 . . . . **NCLC 9; DC 1**

Dumas, Claudine
See Malzberg, Barry N(athaniel)

Dumas, Henry L. 1934-1968 . . . . . **CLC 6, 62**
See also BW; CA 85-88; DLB 41

du Maurier, Daphne
1907-1989 . . . . **CLC 6, 11, 59**
See also CA 5-8R; 128; CANR 6; MTCW;
SATA 27, 60

Dunbar, Paul Laurence
1872-1906 . . . . **TCLC 2, 12; PC 5; SSC 8**
See also BLC 1; BW; CA 104; 124;
CDALB 1865-1917; DLB 50, 54, 78;
SATA 34; WLC

Dunbar, William 1460(?)-1530(?) . . . . **LC 20**

Duncan, Lois 1934- . . . . **CLC 26**
See also AAYA 4; CA 1-4R; CANR 2, 23,
36; MAICYA; SAAS 2; SATA 1, 36

Duncan, Robert (Edward)
1919-1988 . . . **CLC 1, 2, 4, 7, 15, 41, 55;
PC 2**
See also CA 9-12R; 124; CANR 28; DLB 5,
16; MTCW

Dunlap, William 1766-1839 . . . . **NCLC 2**
See also DLB 30, 37, 59

Dunn, Douglas (Eaglesham)
1942- . . . . **CLC 6, 40**
See also CA 45-48; CANR 2, 33; DLB 40;
MTCW

Dunn, Katherine (Karen) 1945- . . . . . **CLC 71**
See also CA 33-36R

Dunn, Stephen 1939- . . . . **CLC 36**
See also CA 33-36R; CANR 12; DLB 105

Dunne, Finley Peter 1867-1936 . . . . **TCLC 28**
See also CA 108; DLB 11, 23

Dunne, John Gregory 1932- . . . . **CLC 28**
See also CA 25-28R; CANR 14; DLBY 80

**Dunsany, Edward John Moreton Drax
Plunkett** 1878-1957
See Dunsany, Lord; Lord Dunsany
See also CA 104; DLB 10

Dunsany, Lord . . . . **TCLC 2**
See also Dunsany, Edward John Moreton
Drax Plunkett
See also DLB 77

du Perry, Jean
See Simenon, Georges (Jacques Christian)

Durang, Christopher (Ferdinand)
1949- . . . . **CLC 27, 38**
See also CA 105

Duras, Marguerite
1914- . . . . . . **CLC 3, 6, 11, 20, 34, 40, 68**
See also CA 25-28R; DLB 83; MTCW

Durban, (Rosa) Pam 1947- . . . . **CLC 39**
See also CA 123

Durcan, Paul 1944- . . . . **CLC 43, 70**
See also CA 134

Durrell, Lawrence (George)
1912-1990 . . . . **CLC 1, 4, 6, 8, 13, 27, 41**
See also CA 9-12R; 132;
CDBLB 1945-1960; DLB 15, 27;
DLBY 90; MTCW

Durrenmatt, Friedrich
. . . . **CLC 1, 4, 8, 11, 15, 43**
See also Duerrenmatt, Friedrich
See also DLB 69

Dutt, Toru 1856-1877 . . . . **NCLC 29**

Dwight, Timothy 1752-1817 . . . . . **NCLC 13**
See also DLB 37

Dworkin, Andrea 1946- . . . . **CLC 43**
See also CA 77-80; CANR 16, 39; MTCW

Dylan, Bob 1941- . . . . **CLC 3, 4, 6, 12**
See also CA 41-44R; DLB 16

Eagleton, Terence (Francis) 1943-
See Eagleton, Terry
See also CA 57-60; CANR 7, 23; MTCW

Eagleton, Terry . . . . **CLC 63**
See also Eagleton, Terence (Francis)

East, Michael
See West, Morris L(anglo)

Eastaway, Edward
See Thomas, (Philip) Edward

Eastlake, William (Derry) 1917- . . . . . **CLC 8**
See also CA 5-8R; CAAS 1; CANR 5;
DLB 6

Eberhart, Richard (Ghormley)
1904- . . . . **CLC 3, 11, 19, 56**
See also CA 1-4R; CANR 2;
CDALB 1941-1968; DLB 48; MTCW

Eberstadt, Fernanda 1960- . . . . **CLC 39**
See also CA 136

Echegaray (y Eizaguirre), Jose (Maria Waldo)
1832-1916 . . . . **TCLC 4**
See also CA 104; CANR 32; HW; MTCW

Echeverria, (Jose) Esteban (Antonino)
1805-1851 . . . . **NCLC 18**

Echo
See Proust,
(Valentin-Louis-George-Eugene-)Marcel

Eckert, Allan W. 1931- . . . . **CLC 17**
See also CA 13-16R; CANR 14; SATA 27,
29

Eckhart, Meister 1260(?)-1328(?) . . **CMLC 9**
See also DLB 115

Eckmar, F. R.
See de Hartog, Jan

Eco, Umberto 1932- . . . . **CLC 28, 60**
See also BEST 90:1; CA 77-80; CANR 12,
33; MTCW

Eddison, E(ric) R(ucker)
1882-1945 . . . . **TCLC 15**
See also CA 109

Edel, (Joseph) Leon 1907- . . . . . . **CLC 29, 34**
See also CA 1-4R; CANR 1, 22; DLB 103

Eden, Emily 1797-1869 . . . . **NCLC 10**

Edgar, David 1948- . . . . **CLC 42**
See also CA 57-60; CANR 12; DLB 13;
MTCW

Edgerton, Clyde (Carlyle) 1944- . . . . **CLC 39**
See also CA 118; 134

Edgeworth, Maria 1767-1849 . . . . . . **NCLC 1**
See also DLB 116; SATA 21

Edmonds, Paul
See Kuttner, Henry

Edmonds, Walter D(umaux) 1903- . . **CLC 35**
See also CA 5-8R; CANR 2; DLB 9;
MAICYA; SAAS 4; SATA 1, 27

Edmondson, Wallace
See Ellison, Harlan

Edson, Russell . . . . **CLC 13**
See also CA 33-36R

Edwards, G(erald) B(asil)
1899-1976 . . . . **CLC 25**
See also CA 110

Edwards, Gus 1939- . . . . **CLC 43**
See also CA 108

Edwards, Jonathan 1703-1758 . . . . **LC 7**
See also DLB 24

Efron, Marina Ivanovna Tsvetaeva
See Tsvetaeva (Efron), Marina (Ivanovna)

Ehle, John (Marsden Jr.) 1925- . . . . **CLC 27**
See also CA 9-12R

Ehrenbourg, Ilya (Grigoryevich)
See Ehrenburg, Ilya (Grigoryevich)

Ehrenburg, Ilya (Grigoryevich)
1891-1967 . . . . **CLC 18, 34, 62**
See also CA 102; 25-28R

Ehrenburg, Ilyo (Grigoryevich)
See Ehrenburg, Ilya (Grigoryevich)

Eich, Guenter 1907-1972 . . . . **CLC 15**
See also CA 111; 93-96; DLB 69

Eichendorff, Joseph Freiherr von
1788-1857 . . . . **NCLC 8**
See also DLB 90

Eigner, Larry . . . . **CLC 9**
See also Eigner, Laurence (Joel)
See also DLB 5

Eigner, Laurence (Joel) 1927-
See Eigner, Larry
See also CA 9-12R; CANR 6

Eiseley, Loren Corey 1907-1977 . . . . . **CLC 7**
See also AAYA 5; CA 1-4R; 73-76;
CANR 6

Eisenstadt, Jill 1963- . . . . **CLC 50**

Eisner, Simon
See Kornbluth, C(yril) M.

Ekeloef, (Bengt) Gunnar
1907-1968 . . . . **CLC 27**
See also Ekelof, (Bengt) Gunnar
See also CA 123; 25-28R

Ekelof, (Bengt) Gunnar . . . . **CLC 27**
See also Ekeloef, (Bengt) Gunnar

Ekwensi, C. O. D.
See Ekwensi, Cyprian (Odiatu Duaka)

Ekwensi, Cyprian (Odiatu Duaka)
1921- . . . . CLC 4
See also BLC 1; BW; CA 29-32R;
CANR 18; DLB 117; MTCW; SATA 66

Elaine . . . . TCLC 18
See also Leverson, Ada

El Crummo
See Crumb, R(obert)

Elia
See Lamb, Charles

Eliade, Mircea 1907-1986 . . . . CLC 19
See also CA 65-68; 119; CANR 30; MTCW

Eliot, A. D.
See Jewett, (Theodora) Sarah Orne

Eliot, Alice
See Jewett, (Theodora) Sarah Orne

Eliot, Dan
See Silverberg, Robert

Eliot, George 1819-1880 . . . . NCLC 4, 13, 23
See also CDBLB 1832-1890; DLB 21, 35,
55; WLC

Eliot, John 1604-1690 . . . . LC 5
See also DLB 24

Eliot, T(homas) S(tearns)
1888-1965 . . . . CLC 1, 2, 3, 6, 9, 10, 13,
15, 24, 34, 41, 55, 57; PC 5
See also CA 5-8R; 25-28R;
CDALB 1929-1941; DLB 7, 10, 45, 63;
MTCW; WLC 2

Elizabeth 1866-1941 . . . . TCLC 41

Elkin, Stanley L(awrence)
1930- . . . . CLC 4, 6, 9, 14, 27, 51
See also CA 9-12R; CANR 8; DLB 2, 28;
DLBY 80; MTCW

Elledge, Scott . . . . CLC 34

Elliott, Don
See Silverberg, Robert

Elliott, George P(aul) 1918-1980 . . . . . CLC 2
See also CA 1-4R; 97-100; CANR 2

Elliott, Janice 1931- . . . . CLC 47
See also CA 13-16R; CANR 8, 29; DLB 14

Elliott, Sumner Locke 1917-1991 . . . CLC 38
See also CA 5-8R; 134; CANR 2, 21

Elliott, William
See Bradbury, Ray (Douglas)

Ellis, A. E. . . . . CLC 7

Ellis, Alice Thomas . . . . CLC 40
See also Haycraft, Anna

Ellis, Bret Easton 1964- . . . . CLC 39, 71
See also AAYA 2; CA 118; 123

Ellis, (Henry) Havelock
1859-1939 . . . . TCLC 14
See also CA 109

Ellis, Landon
See Ellison, Harlan

Ellis, Trey 1962- . . . . CLC 55

Ellison, Harlan 1934- . . . . CLC 1, 13, 42
See also CA 5-8R; CANR 5; DLB 8;
MTCW

Ellison, Ralph (Waldo)
1914- . . . . CLC 1, 3, 11, 54
See also BLC 1; BW; CA 9-12R; CANR 24;
CDALB 1941-1968; DLB 2, 76; MTCW;
WLC

Ellmann, Lucy (Elizabeth) 1956- . . . . CLC 61
See also CA 128

Ellmann, Richard (David)
1918-1987 . . . . CLC 50
See also BEST 89:2; CA 1-4R; 122;
CANR 2, 28; DLB 103; DLBY 87;
MTCW

Elman, Richard 1934- . . . . CLC 19
See also CA 17-20R; CAAS 3

Elron
See Hubbard, L(afayette) Ron(ald)

Eluard, Paul . . . . TCLC 7, 41
See also Grindel, Eugene

Elyot, Sir Thomas 1490(?)-1546 . . . . . LC 11

Elytis, Odysseus 1911- . . . . CLC 15, 49
See also CA 102; MTCW

Emecheta, (Florence Onye) Buchi
1944- . . . . CLC 14, 48
See also BLC 2; BW; CA 81-84; CANR 27;
DLB 117; MTCW; SATA 66

Emerson, Ralph Waldo
1803-1882 . . . . NCLC 1
See also CDALB 1640-1865; DLB 1, 59, 73;
WLC

Eminescu, Mihail 1850-1889 . . . . . NCLC 33

Empson, William
1906-1984 . . . . CLC 3, 8, 19, 33, 34
See also CA 17-20R; 112; CANR 31;
DLB 20; MTCW

Enchi Fumiko (Ueda) 1905-1986 . . . . CLC 31
See also CA 129; 121

Ende, Michael (Andreas Helmuth)
1929- . . . . CLC 31
See also CA 118; 124; CANR 36; CLR 14;
DLB 75; MAICYA; SATA 42, 61

Endo, Shusaku 1923- . . . . . CLC 7, 14, 19, 54
See also CA 29-32R; CANR 21; MTCW

Engel, Marian 1933-1985 . . . . CLC 36
See also CA 25-28R; CANR 12; DLB 53

Engelhardt, Frederick
See Hubbard, L(afayette) Ron(ald)

Enright, D(ennis) J(oseph)
1920- . . . . CLC 4, 8, 31
See also CA 1-4R; CANR 1; DLB 27;
SATA 25

Enzensberger, Hans Magnus
1929- . . . . CLC 43
See also CA 116; 119

Ephron, Nora 1941- . . . . CLC 17, 31
See also AITN 2; CA 65-68; CANR 12, 39

Epsilon
See Betjeman, John

Epstein, Daniel Mark 1948- . . . . CLC 7
See also CA 49-52; CANR 2

Epstein, Jacob 1956- . . . . CLC 19
See also CA 114

Epstein, Joseph 1937- . . . . CLC 39
See also CA 112; 119

Epstein, Leslie 1938- . . . . CLC 27
See also CA 73-76; CAAS 12; CANR 23

Equiano, Olaudah 1745(?)-1797 . . . . . . LC 16
See also BLC 2; DLB 37, 50

Erasmus, Desiderius 1469(?)-1536 . . . . LC 16

Erdman, Paul E(mil) 1932- . . . . CLC 25
See also AITN 1; CA 61-64; CANR 13

Erdrich, Louise 1954- . . . . CLC 39, 54
See also BEST 89:1; CA 114; MTCW

Erenburg, Ilya (Grigoryevich)
See Ehrenburg, Ilya (Grigoryevich)

Erickson, Stephen Michael 1950-
See Erickson, Steve
See also CA 129

Erickson, Steve . . . . CLC 64
See also Erickson, Stephen Michael

Ericson, Walter
See Fast, Howard (Melvin)

Ericson, Walter
See Fast, Howard (Melvin)

Eriksson, Buntel
See Bergman, (Ernst) Ingmar

Eschenbach, Wolfram von
See Wolfram von Eschenbach

Eseki, Bruno
See Mphahlele, Ezekiel

Esenin, Sergei (Alexandrovich)
1895-1925 . . . . TCLC 4
See also CA 104

Eshleman, Clayton 1935- . . . . CLC 7
See also CA 33-36R; CAAS 6; DLB 5

Espriella, Don Manuel Alvarez
See Southey, Robert

Espriu, Salvador 1913-1985 . . . . CLC 9
See also CA 115

Esse, James
See Stephens, James

Esterbrook, Tom
See Hubbard, L(afayette) Ron(ald)

Estleman, Loren D. 1952- . . . . CLC 48
See also CA 85-88; CANR 27; MTCW

Evans, Mary Ann
See Eliot, George

Evarts, Esther
See Benson, Sally

Everett, Percival
See Everett, Percival L.

Everett, Percival L. 1956- . . . . CLC 57
See also CA 129

Everson, R(onald) G(ilmour)
1903- . . . . CLC 27
See also CA 17-20R; DLB 88

Everson, William (Oliver)
1912- . . . . CLC 1, 5, 14
See also CA 9-12R; CANR 20; DLB 5, 16;
MTCW

Evtushenko, Evgenii Aleksandrovich
See Yevtushenko, Yevgeny (Alexandrovich)

Ewart, Gavin (Buchanan)
1916- . . . . CLC 13, 46
See also CA 89-92; CANR 17; DLB 40;
MTCW

Ewers, Hanns Heinz   1871-1943 . . . **TCLC 12**
See also CA 109

Ewing, Frederick R.
See Sturgeon, Theodore (Hamilton)

Exley, Frederick (Earl)   1929- . . . . **CLC 6, 11**
See also AITN 2; CA 81-84; 138; DLBY 81

Eynhardt, Guillermo
See Quiroga, Horacio (Sylvestre)

Ezekiel, Nissim   1924- . . . . **CLC 61**
See also CA 61-64

Ezekiel, Tish O'Dowd   1943- . . . . **CLC 34**
See also CA 129

Fagen, Donald   1948- . . . . **CLC 26**

Fainzilberg, Ilya Arnoldovich   1897-1937
See Ilf, Ilya
See also CA 120

Fair, Ronald L.   1932- . . . . **CLC 18**
See also BW; CA 69-72; CANR 25; DLB 33

Fairbairns, Zoe (Ann)   1948- . . . . **CLC 32**
See also CA 103; CANR 21

Falco, Gian
See Papini, Giovanni

Falconer, James
See Kirkup, James

Falconer, Kenneth
See Kornbluth, C(yril) M.

Falkland, Samuel
See Heijermans, Herman

Fallaci, Oriana   1930- . . . . **CLC 11**
See also CA 77-80; CANR 15; MTCW

Faludy, George   1913- . . . . **CLC 42**
See also CA 21-24R

Faludy, Gyoergy
See Faludy, George

Fanshawe, Ann . . . . **LC 11**

Fante, John (Thomas)   1911-1983 . . . **CLC 60**
See also CA 69-72; 109; CANR 23;
DLBY 83

Farah, Nuruddin   1945- . . . . **CLC 53**
See also BLC 2; CA 106

Fargue, Leon-Paul   1876(?)-1947 . . . **TCLC 11**
See also CA 109

Farigoule, Louis
See Romains, Jules

Farina, Richard   1936(?)-1966 . . . . **CLC 9**
See also CA 81-84; 25-28R

Farley, Walter (Lorimer)
1915-1989 . . . . **CLC 17**
See also CA 17-20R; CANR 8, 29; DLB 22;
MAICYA; SATA 2, 43

Farmer, Philip Jose   1918- . . . . **CLC 1, 19**
See also CA 1-4R; CANR 4, 35; DLB 8;
MTCW

Farrell, J(ames) G(ordon)
1935-1979 . . . . **CLC 6**
See also CA 73-76; 89-92; CANR 36;
DLB 14; MTCW

Farrell, James T(homas)
1904-1979 . . . . **CLC 1, 4, 8, 11, 66**
See also CA 5-8R; 89-92; CANR 9; DLB 4,
9, 86; DLBD 2; MTCW

Farren, Richard J.
See Betjeman, John

Farren, Richard M.
See Betjeman, John

Fassbinder, Rainer Werner
1946-1982 . . . . **CLC 20**
See also CA 93-96; 106; CANR 31

Fast, Howard (Melvin)   1914- . . . . . . **CLC 23**
See also CA 1-4R; CANR 1, 33; DLB 9;
SATA 7

Faulcon, Robert
See Holdstock, Robert P.

Faulkner, William (Cuthbert)
1897-1962 . . . . **CLC 1, 3, 6, 8, 9, 11, 14,
18, 28, 52, 68; SSC 1**
See also AAYA 7; CA 81-84; CANR 33;
CDALB 1929-1941; DLB 9, 11, 44, 102;
DLBD 2; DLBY 86; MTCW; WLC

Fauset, Jessie Redmon
1884(?)-1961 . . . . **CLC 19, 54**
See also BLC 2; BW; CA 109; DLB 51

Faust, Irvin   1924- . . . . **CLC 8**
See also CA 33-36R; CANR 28; DLB 2, 28;
DLBY 80

Fawkes, Guy
See Benchley, Robert (Charles)

Fearing, Kenneth (Flexner)
1902-1961 . . . . **CLC 51**
See also CA 93-96; DLB 9

Fecamps, Elise
See Creasey, John

Federman, Raymond   1928- . . . . . . **CLC 6, 47**
See also CA 17-20R; CAAS 8; CANR 10;
DLBY 80

Federspiel, J(uerg) F.   1931- . . . . **CLC 42**

Feiffer, Jules (Ralph)   1929- . . . . **CLC 2, 8, 64**
See also AAYA 3; CA 17-20R; CANR 30;
DLB 7, 44; MTCW; SATA 8, 61

Feige, Hermann Albert Otto Maximilian
See Traven, B.

Fei-Kan, Li
See Li Fei-kan

Feinberg, David B.   1956- . . . . **CLC 59**
See also CA 135

Feinstein, Elaine   1930- . . . . **CLC 36**
See also CA 69-72; CAAS 1; CANR 31;
DLB 14, 40; MTCW

Feldman, Irving (Mordecai)   1928- . . . . **CLC 7**
See also CA 1-4R; CANR 1

Fellini, Federico   1920- . . . . **CLC 16**
See also CA 65-68; CANR 33

Felsen, Henry Gregor   1916- . . . . **CLC 17**
See also CA 1-4R; CANR 1; SAAS 2;
SATA 1

Fenton, James Martin   1949- . . . . **CLC 32**
See also CA 102; DLB 40

Ferber, Edna   1887-1968 . . . . **CLC 18**
See also AITN 1; CA 5-8R; 25-28R; DLB 9,
28, 86; MTCW; SATA 7

Ferguson, Helen
See Kavan, Anna

Ferguson, Samuel   1810-1886 . . . . . **NCLC 33**
See also DLB 32

Ferling, Lawrence
See Ferlinghetti, Lawrence (Monsanto)

Ferlinghetti, Lawrence (Monsanto)
1919(?)- . . . . **CLC 2, 6, 10, 27; PC 1**
See also CA 5-8R; CANR 3;
CDALB 1941-1968; DLB 5, 16; MTCW

Fernandez, Vicente Garcia Huidobro
See Huidobro Fernandez, Vicente Garcia

Ferrer, Gabriel (Francisco Victor) Miro
See Miro (Ferrer), Gabriel (Francisco
Victor)

Ferrier, Susan (Edmonstone)
1782-1854 . . . . **NCLC 8**
See also DLB 116

Ferrigno, Robert . . . . **CLC 65**

Feuchtwanger, Lion   1884-1958 . . . . . **TCLC 3**
See also CA 104; DLB 66

Feydeau, Georges (Leon Jules Marie)
1862-1921 . . . . **TCLC 22**
See also CA 113

Ficino, Marsilio   1433-1499 . . . . **LC 12**

Fiedler, Leslie A(aron)
1917- . . . . **CLC 4, 13, 24**
See also CA 9-12R; CANR 7; DLB 28, 67;
MTCW

Field, Andrew   1938- . . . . **CLC 44**
See also CA 97-100; CANR 25

Field, Eugene   1850-1895 . . . . **NCLC 3**
See also DLB 23, 42; MAICYA; SATA 16

Field, Gans T.
See Wellman, Manly Wade

Field, Michael . . . . **TCLC 43**

Field, Peter
See Hobson, Laura Z(ametkin)

Fielding, Henry   1707-1754 . . . . **LC 1**
See also CDBLB 1660-1789; DLB 39, 84,
101; WLC

Fielding, Sarah   1710-1768 . . . . **LC 1**
See also DLB 39

Fierstein, Harvey (Forbes)   1954- . . . **CLC 33**
See also CA 123; 129

Figes, Eva   1932- . . . . **CLC 31**
See also CA 53-56; CANR 4; DLB 14

Finch, Robert (Duer Claydon)
1900- . . . . **CLC 18**
See also CA 57-60; CANR 9, 24; DLB 88

Findley, Timothy   1930- . . . . **CLC 27**
See also CA 25-28R; CANR 12; DLB 53

Fink, William
See Mencken, H(enry) L(ouis)

Firbank, Louis   1942-
See Reed, Lou
See also CA 117

Firbank, (Arthur Annesley) Ronald
1886-1926 . . . . **TCLC 1**
See also CA 104; DLB 36

Fisher, Roy   1930- . . . . **CLC 25**
See also CA 81-84; CAAS 10; CANR 16;
DLB 40

Fisher, Rudolph   1897-1934 . . . . **TCLC 11**
See also BLC 2; BW; CA 107; 124; DLB 51,
102

Fisher, Vardis (Alvero)   1895-1968 . . . . **CLC 7**
See also CA 5-8R; 25-28R; DLB 9

Fiske, Tarleton
See Bloch, Robert (Albert)

Fitch, Clarke
See Sinclair, Upton (Beall)

Fitch, John IV
See Cormier, Robert (Edmund)

Fitgerald, Penelope 1916- .... **CLC 61**

Fitzgerald, Captain Hugh
See Baum, L(yman) Frank

FitzGerald, Edward 1809-1883 .... **NCLC 9**
See also DLB 32

Fitzgerald, F(rancis) Scott (Key)
1896-1940 .... **TCLC 1, 6, 14, 28; SSC 6**
See also AITN 1; CA 110; 123;
CDALB 1917-1929; DLB 4, 9, 86;
DLBD 1; DLBY 81; MTCW; WLC

Fitzgerald, Penelope 1916-...... **CLC 19, 51**
See also CA 85-88; CAAS 10; DLB 14

FitzGerald, Robert D(avid)
1902-1987 .... **CLC 19**
See also CA 17-20R

Fitzgerald, Robert (Stuart)
1910-1985 .... **CLC 39**
See also CA 1-4R; 114; CANR 1; DLBY 80

Flanagan, Thomas (James Bonner)
1923-.................... **CLC 25, 52**
See also CA 108; DLBY 80; MTCW

Flaubert, Gustave
1821-1880 .... **NCLC 2, 10, 19**
See also DLB 119; WLC

Flecker, (Herman) James Elroy
1884-1915 .... **TCLC 43**
See also CA 109; DLB 10, 19

Fleming, Ian (Lancaster)
1908-1964 .... **CLC 3, 30**
See also CA 5-8R; CDBLB 1945-1960;
DLB 87; MTCW; SATA 9

Fleming, Thomas (James) 1927- .... **CLC 37**
See also CA 5-8R; CANR 10; SATA 8

Fletcher, John Gould 1886-1950 ... **TCLC 35**
See also CA 107; DLB 4, 45

Fleur, Paul
See Pohl, Frederik

Flying Officer X
See Bates, H(erbert) E(rnest)

Fo, Dario 1926-................. **CLC 32**
See also CA 116; 128; MTCW

Fogarty, Jonathan Titulescu Esq.
See Farrell, James T(homas)

Folke, Will
See Bloch, Robert (Albert)

Follett, Ken(neth Martin) 1949- .... **CLC 18**
See also AAYA 6; BEST 89:4; CA 81-84;
CANR 13, 33; DLB 87; DLBY 81;
MTCW

Fontane, Theodor 1819-1898 ..... **NCLC 26**

Foote, Horton 1916-.............. **CLC 51**
See also CA 73-76; CANR 34; DLB 26

Forbes, Esther 1891-1967......... **CLC 12**
See also CA 13-14; 25-28R; CAP 1;
CLR 27; DLB 22; MAICYA; SATA 2

Forche, Carolyn (Louise) 1950-..... **CLC 25**
See also CA 109; 117; DLB 5

Ford, Elbur
See Hibbert, Eleanor Burford

Ford, Ford Madox
1873-1939 .... **TCLC 1, 15, 39**
See also CA 104; 132; CDBLB 1914-1945;
DLB 34, 98; MTCW

Ford, John 1895-1973.............. **CLC 16**
See also CA 45-48

Ford, Richard 1944-.............. **CLC 46**
See also CA 69-72; CANR 11

Ford, Webster
See Masters, Edgar Lee

Foreman, Richard 1937-........... **CLC 50**
See also CA 65-68; CANR 32

Forester, C(ecil) S(cott)
1899-1966 .... **CLC 35**
See also CA 73-76; 25-28R; SATA 13

Forez
See Mauriac, Francois (Charles)

Forman, James Douglas 1932-..... **CLC 21**
See also CA 9-12R; CANR 4, 19;
MAICYA; SATA 8, 70

Fornes, Maria Irene 1930-...... **CLC 39, 61**
See also CA 25-28R; CANR 28; DLB 7;
HW; MTCW

Forrest, Leon 1937- .... **CLC 4**
See also BW; CA 89-92; CAAS 7;
CANR 25; DLB 33

Forster, E(dward) M(organ)
1879-1970 .... **CLC 1, 2, 3, 4, 9, 10, 13,**
15, 22, 45
See also AAYA 2; CA 13-14; 25-28R;
CAP 1; CDBLB 1914-1945; DLB 34, 98;
MTCW; SATA 57; WLC

Forster, John 1812-1876 .... **NCLC 11**

Forsyth, Frederick 1938-...... **CLC 2, 5, 36**
See also BEST 89:4; CA 85-88; CANR 38;
DLB 87; MTCW

Forten, Charlotte L. .... **TCLC 16**
See also Grimke, Charlotte L(ottie) Forten
See also BLC 2; DLB 50

Foscolo, Ugo 1778-1827.......... **NCLC 8**

Fosse, Bob .... **CLC 20**
See also Fosse, Robert Louis

Fosse, Robert Louis 1927-1987
See Fosse, Bob
See also CA 110; 123

Foster, Stephen Collins
1826-1864 .... **NCLC 26**

Foucault, Michel
1926-1984 .... **CLC 31, 34, 69**
See also CA 105; 113; CANR 34; MTCW

Fouque, Friedrich Heinrich Karl) de la Motte
1777-1843 .... **NCLC 2**
See also DLB 90

Fournier, Henri Alban 1886-1914
See Alain-Fournier
See also CA 104

Fournier, Pierre 1916-............ **CLC 11**
See also Gascar, Pierre
See also CA 89-92; CANR 16

Fowles, John
1926- .... **CLC 1, 2, 3, 4, 6, 9, 10, 15, 33**
See also CA 5-8R; CANR 25; CDBLB 1960
to Present; DLB 14; MTCW; SATA 22

Fox, Paula 1923-................. **CLC 2, 8**
See also AAYA 3; CA 73-76; CANR 20,
36; CLR 1; DLB 52; MAICYA; MTCW;
SATA 17, 60

Fox, William Price (Jr.) 1926- ..... **CLC 22**
See also CA 17-20R; CANR 11; DLB 2;
DLBY 81

Foxe, John 1516(?)-1587 .... **LC 14**

Frame, Janet .... **CLC 2, 3, 6, 22, 66**
See also Clutha, Janet Paterson Frame

France, Anatole.................... **TCLC 9**
See also Thibault, Jacques Anatole Francois

Francis, Claude 19th cent. (?)- ..... **CLC 50**

Francis, Dick 1920- .... **CLC 2, 22, 42**
See also AAYA 5; BEST 89:3; CA 5-8R;
CANR 9; CDBLB 1960 to Present;
DLB 87; MTCW

Francis, Robert (Churchill)
1901-1987 .... **CLC 15**
See also CA 1-4R; 123; CANR 1

Frank, Anne(lies Marie)
1929-1945 .... **TCLC 17**
See also CA 113; 133; MTCW; SATA 42;
WLC

Frank, Elizabeth 1945-........... **CLC 39**
See also CA 121; 126

Franklin, Benjamin
See Hasek, Jaroslav (Matej Frantisek)

Franklin, (Stella Maraia Sarah) Miles
1879-1954 .... **TCLC 7**
See also CA 104

Fraser, Antonia (Pakenham)
1932- .... **CLC 32**
See also CA 85-88; MTCW; SATA 32

Fraser, George MacDonald 1925-.... **CLC 7**
See also CA 45-48; CANR 2

Fraser, Sylvia 1935-.............. **CLC 64**
See also CA 45-48; CANR 1, 16

Frayn, Michael 1933-...... **CLC 3, 7, 31, 47**
See also CA 5-8R; CANR 30; DLB 13, 14;
MTCW

Fraze, Candida (Merrill) 1945-..... **CLC 50**
See also CA 126

Frazer, J(ames) G(eorge)
1854-1941 .... **TCLC 32**
See also CA 118

Frazer, Robert Caine
See Creasey, John

Frazer, Sir James George
See Frazer, J(ames) G(eorge)

Frazier, Ian 1951-................ **CLC 46**
See also CA 130

Frederic, Harold 1856-1898...... **NCLC 10**
See also DLB 12, 23

Frederick the Great 1712-1786 ...... **LC 14**

Fredro, Aleksander 1793-1876..... **NCLC 8**

Freeling, Nicolas 1927- .... **CLC 38**
See also CA 49-52; CAAS 12; CANR 1, 17;
DLB 87

Freeman, Douglas Southall
1886-1953 .... **TCLC 11**
See also CA 109; DLB 17

Freeman, Judith 1946-........... **CLC 55**

Freeman, Mary Eleanor Wilkins
1852-1930 . . . . TCLC 9; SSC 1
See also CA 106; DLB 12, 78

Freeman, R(ichard) Austin
1862-1943 . . . . TCLC 21
See also CA 113; DLB 70

French, Marilyn 1929- . . . . . . CLC 10, 18, 60
See also CA 69-72; CANR 3, 31; MTCW

French, Paul
See Asimov, Isaac

Freneau, Philip Morin 1752-1832 . . NCLC 1
See also DLB 37, 43

Friedman, B(ernard) H(arper)
1926- . . . . CLC 7
See also CA 1-4R; CANR 3

Friedman, Bruce Jay 1930- . . . . CLC 3, 5, 56
See also CA 9-12R; CANR 25; DLB 2, 28

Friel, Brian 1929- . . . . CLC 5, 42, 59
See also CA 21-24R; CANR 33; DLB 13;
MTCW

Friis-Baastad, Babbis Ellinor
1921-1970 . . . . CLC 12
See also CA 17-20R; 134; SATA 7

Frisch, Max (Rudolf)
1911-1991 . . . . . CLC 3, 9, 14, 18, 32, 44
See also CA 85-88; 134; CANR 32;
DLB 69; MTCW

Fromentin, Eugene (Samuel Auguste)
1820-1876 . . . . NCLC 10

Frost, Robert (Lee)
1874-1963 . . . CLC 1, 3, 4, 9, 10, 13, 15,
26, 34, 44; PC 1
See also CA 89-92; CANR 33;
CDALB 1917-1929; DLB 54; DLBD 7;
MTCW; SATA 14; WLC

Froy, Herald
See Waterhouse, Keith (Spencer)

Fry, Christopher 1907- . . . . CLC 2, 10, 14
See also CA 17-20R; CANR 9, 30; DLB 13;
MTCW; SATA 66

Frye, (Herman) Northrop
1912-1991 . . . . CLC 24, 70
See also CA 5-8R; 133; CANR 8, 37;
DLB 67, 68; MTCW

Fuchs, Daniel 1909- . . . . CLC 8, 22
See also CA 81-84; CAAS 5; DLB 9, 26, 28

Fuchs, Daniel 1934- . . . . CLC 34
See also CA 37-40R; CANR 14

Fuentes, Carlos
1928- . . . . . . CLC 3, 8, 10, 13, 22, 41, 60
See also AAYA 4; AITN 2; CA 69-72;
CANR 10, 32; DLB 113; HW; MTCW;
WLC

Fuentes, Gregorio Lopez y
See Lopez y Fuentes, Gregorio

Fugard, (Harold) Athol
1932- . . . . CLC 5, 9, 14, 25, 40
See also CA 85-88; CANR 32; MTCW

Fugard, Sheila 1932- . . . . CLC 48
See also CA 125

Fuller, Charles (H. Jr.)
1939- . . . . CLC 25; DC 1
See also BLC 2; BW; CA 108; 112; DLB 38;
MTCW

Fuller, John (Leopold) 1937- . . . . CLC 62
See also CA 21-24R; CANR 9; DLB 40

Fuller, Margaret . . . . NCLC 5
See also Ossoli, Sarah Margaret (Fuller
marchesa d')

Fuller, Roy (Broadbent)
1912-1991 . . . . CLC 4, 28
See also CA 5-8R; 135; CAAS 10; DLB 15,
20

Fulton, Alice 1952- . . . . CLC 52
See also CA 116

Furphy, Joseph 1843-1912 . . . . TCLC 25

Futabatei, Shimei 1864-1909 . . . . . . TCLC 44

Futrelle, Jacques 1875-1912 . . . . . . TCLC 19
See also CA 113

G. B. S.
See Shaw, George Bernard

Gaboriau, Emile 1835-1873 . . . . . . NCLC 14

Gadda, Carlo Emilio 1893-1973 . . . . CLC 11
See also CA 89-92

Gaddis, William
1922- . . . . CLC 1, 3, 6, 8, 10, 19, 43
See also CA 17-20R; CANR 21; DLB 2;
MTCW

Gaines, Ernest J(ames)
1933- . . . . CLC 3, 11, 18
See also AITN 1; BLC 2; BW; CA 9-12R;
CANR 6, 24; CDALB 1968-1988; DLB 2,
33; DLBY 80; MTCW

Gaitskill, Mary 1954- . . . . CLC 69
See also CA 128

Galdos, Benito Perez
See Perez Galdos, Benito

Gale, Zona 1874-1938 . . . . TCLC 7
See also CA 105; DLB 9, 78

Galeano, Eduardo (Hughes) 1940- . . . CLC 72
See also CA 29-32R; CANR 13, 32; HW

Galiano, Juan Valera y Alcala
See Valera y Alcala-Galiano, Juan

Gallagher, Tess 1943- . . . . CLC 18, 63
See also CA 106; DLB 120

Gallant, Mavis
1922- . . . . CLC 7, 18, 38; SSC 5
See also CA 69-72; CANR 29; DLB 53;
MTCW

Gallant, Roy A(rthur) 1924- . . . . CLC 17
See also CA 5-8R; CANR 4, 29; MAICYA;
SATA 4, 68

Gallico, Paul (William) 1897-1976 . . . CLC 2
See also AITN 1; CA 5-8R; 69-72;
CANR 23; DLB 9; MAICYA; SATA 13

Gallup, Ralph
See Whitemore, Hugh (John)

Galsworthy, John 1867-1933 . . . . TCLC 1, 45
See also CA 104; CDBLB 1890-1914;
DLB 10, 34, 98; WLC 2

Galt, John 1779-1839 . . . . NCLC 1
See also DLB 99, 116

Galvin, James 1951- . . . . CLC 38
See also CA 108; CANR 26

Gamboa, Federico 1864-1939 . . . . . . TCLC 36

Gann, Ernest Kellogg 1910-1991 . . . . CLC 23
See also AITN 1; CA 1-4R; 136; CANR 1

Garcia Lorca, Federico
1898-1936 . . . . . TCLC 1, 7; DC 2; PC 3
See also CA 104; 131; DLB 108; HW;
MTCW; WLC

Garcia Marquez, Gabriel (Jose)
1928- . . . CLC 2, 3, 8, 10, 15, 27, 47, 55;
SSC 8
See also Marquez, Gabriel (Jose) Garcia
See also AAYA 3; BEST 89:1, 90:4;
CA 33-36R; CANR 10, 28; DLB 113;
HW; MTCW; WLC

Gard, Janice
See Latham, Jean Lee

Gard, Roger Martin du
See Martin du Gard, Roger

Gardam, Jane 1928- . . . . CLC 43
See also CA 49-52; CANR 2, 18, 33;
CLR 12; DLB 14; MAICYA; MTCW;
SAAS 9; SATA 28, 39

Gardner, Herb . . . . CLC 44

Gardner, John (Champlin) Jr.
1933-1982 . . . . CLC 2, 3, 5, 7, 8, 10, 18,
28, 34; SSC 7
See also AITN 1; CA 65-68; 107;
CANR 33; DLB 2; DLBY 82; MTCW;
SATA 31, 40

Gardner, John (Edmund) 1926- . . . . . CLC 30
See also CA 103; CANR 15; MTCW

Gardner, Noel
See Kuttner, Henry

Gardons, S. S.
See Snodgrass, William D(e Witt)

Garfield, Leon 1921- . . . . CLC 12
See also AAYA 8; CA 17-20R; CANR 38;
CLR 21; MAICYA; SATA 1, 32

Garland, (Hannibal) Hamlin
1860-1940 . . . . TCLC 3
See also CA 104; DLB 12, 71, 78

Garneau, (Hector de) Saint-Denys
1912-1943 . . . . TCLC 13
See also CA 111; DLB 88

Garner, Alan 1934- . . . . CLC 17
See also CA 73-76; CANR 15; CLR 20;
MAICYA; MTCW; SATA 18, 69

Garner, Hugh 1913-1979 . . . . CLC 13
See also CA 69-72; CANR 31; DLB 68

Garnett, David 1892-1981 . . . . CLC 3
See also CA 5-8R; 103; CANR 17; DLB 34

Garos, Stephanie
See Katz, Steve

Garrett, George (Palmer)
1929- . . . . CLC 3, 11, 51
See also CA 1-4R; CAAS 5; CANR 1;
DLB 2, 5; DLBY 83

Garrick, David 1717-1779 . . . . LC 15
See also DLB 84

Garrigue, Jean 1914-1972 . . . . CLC 2, 8
See also CA 5-8R; 37-40R; CANR 20

Garrison, Frederick
See Sinclair, Upton (Beall)

Garth, Will
See Hamilton, Edmond; Kuttner, Henry

Garvey, Marcus (Moziah Jr.)
1887-1940 . . . . TCLC 41
See also BLC 2; BW; CA 120; 124

Gary, Romain . . . . CLC 25
See also Kacew, Romain
See also DLB 83

Gascar, Pierre . . . . CLC 11
See also Fournier, Pierre

Gascoyne, David (Emery) 1916- . . . . CLC 45
See also CA 65-68; CANR 10, 28; DLB 20;
MTCW

Gaskell, Elizabeth Cleghorn
1810-1865 . . . . NCLC 5
See also CDBLB 1832-1890; DLB 21

Gass, William H(oward)
1924- . . . . CLC 1, 2, 8, 11, 15, 39
See also CA 17-20R; CANR 30; DLB 2;
MTCW

Gasset, Jose Ortega y
See Ortega y Gasset, Jose

Gautier, Theophile 1811-1872 . . . . . NCLC 1
See also DLB 119

Gawsworth, John
See Bates, H(erbert) E(rnest)

Gaye, Marvin (Penze) 1939-1984 . . . CLC 26
See also CA 112

Gebler, Carlo (Ernest) 1954- . . . . CLC 39
See also CA 119; 133

Gee, Maggie (Mary) 1948- . . . . CLC 57
See also CA 130

Gee, Maurice (Gough) 1931- . . . . CLC 29
See also CA 97-100; SATA 46

Gelbart, Larry (Simon) 1923- . . . CLC 21, 61
See also CA 73-76

Gelber, Jack 1932- . . . . CLC 1, 6, 14
See also CA 1-4R; CANR 2; DLB 7

Gellhorn, Martha Ellis 1908- . . . CLC 14, 60
See also CA 77-80; DLBY 82

Genet, Jean
1910-1986 . . . CLC 1, 2, 5, 10, 14, 44, 46
See also CA 13-16R; CANR 18; DLB 72;
DLBY 86; MTCW

Gent, Peter 1942- . . . . CLC 29
See also AITN 1; CA 89-92; DLBY 82

George, Jean Craighead 1919- . . . . . . CLC 35
See also AAYA 8; CA 5-8R; CANR 25;
CLR 1; DLB 52; MAICYA; SATA 2, 68

George, Stefan (Anton)
1868-1933 . . . . TCLC 2, 14
See also CA 104

Georges, Georges Martin
See Simenon, Georges (Jacques Christian)

Gerhardi, William Alexander
See Gerhardie, William Alexander

Gerhardie, William Alexander
1895-1977 . . . . CLC 5
See also CA 25-28R; 73-76; CANR 18;
DLB 36

Gerstler, Amy 1956- . . . . CLC 70

Gertler, T. . . . . CLC 34
See also CA 116; 121

Ghelderode, Michel de
1898-1962 . . . . CLC 6, 11
See also CA 85-88

Ghiselin, Brewster 1903- . . . . CLC 23
See also CA 13-16R; CAAS 10; CANR 13

Ghose, Zulfikar 1935- . . . . CLC 42
See also CA 65-68

Ghosh, Amitav 1956- . . . . CLC 44

Giacosa, Giuseppe 1847-1906 . . . . . . TCLC 7
See also CA 104

Gibb, Lee
See Waterhouse, Keith (Spencer)

Gibbon, Lewis Grassic . . . . TCLC 4
See also Mitchell, James Leslie

Gibbons, Kaye 1960- . . . . CLC 50

Gibran, Kahlil 1883-1931 . . . . TCLC 1, 9
See also CA 104

Gibson, William (Ford) 1948- . . . CLC 39, 63
See also CA 126; 133

Gibson, William 1914- . . . . CLC 23
See also CA 9-12R; CANR 9; DLB 7;
SATA 66

Gide, Andre (Paul Guillaume)
1869-1951 . . . . TCLC 5, 12, 36
See also CA 104; 124; DLB 65; MTCW;
WLC

Gifford, Barry (Colby) 1946- . . . . CLC 34
See also CA 65-68; CANR 9, 30

Gilbert, W(illiam) S(chwenck)
1836-1911 . . . . TCLC 3
See also CA 104; SATA 36

Gilbreth, Frank B. Jr. 1911- . . . . CLC 17
See also CA 9-12R; SATA 2

Gilchrist, Ellen 1935- . . . . CLC 34, 48
See also CA 113; 116; MTCW

Giles, Molly 1942- . . . . CLC 39
See also CA 126

Gill, Patrick
See Creasey, John

Gilliam, Terry (Vance) 1940- . . . . CLC 21
See also Monty Python
See also CA 108; 113; CANR 35

Gillian, Jerry
See Gilliam, Terry (Vance)

Gilliatt, Penelope (Ann Douglass)
1932- . . . . CLC 2, 10, 13, 53
See also AITN 2; CA 13-16R; DLB 14

Gilman, Charlotte (Anna) Perkins (Stetson)
1860-1935 . . . . TCLC 9, 37
See also CA 106

Gilmour, David 1944- . . . . CLC 35
See also Pink Floyd
See also CA 138

Gilpin, William 1724-1804 . . . . NCLC 30

Gilray, J. D.
See Mencken, H(enry) L(ouis)

Gilroy, Frank D(aniel) 1925- . . . . CLC 2
See also CA 81-84; CANR 32; DLB 7

Ginsberg, Allen
1926- . . . . . CLC 1, 2, 3, 4, 6, 13, 36, 69;
PC 4
See also AITN 1; CA 1-4R; CANR 2;
CDALB 1941-1968; DLB 5, 16; MTCW;
WLC 3

Ginzburg, Natalia
1916-1991 . . . . CLC 5, 11, 54, 70
See also CA 85-88; 135; CANR 33; MTCW

Giono, Jean 1895-1970 . . . . CLC 4, 11
See also CA 45-48; 29-32R; CANR 2, 35;
DLB 72; MTCW

Giovanni, Nikki 1943- . . . . . CLC 2, 4, 19, 64
See also AITN 1; BLC 2; BW; CA 29-32R;
CAAS 6; CANR 18; CLR 6; DLB 5, 41;
MAICYA; MTCW; SATA 24

Giovene, Andrea 1904- . . . . CLC 7
See also CA 85-88

Gippius, Zinaida (Nikolayevna) 1869-1945
See Hippius, Zinaida
See also CA 106

Giraudoux, (Hippolyte) Jean
1882-1944 . . . . TCLC 2, 7
See also CA 104; DLB 65

Gironella, Jose Maria 1917- . . . . CLC 11
See also CA 101

Gissing, George (Robert)
1857-1903 . . . . TCLC 3, 24, 47
See also CA 105; DLB 18

Giurlani, Aldo
See Palazzeschi, Aldo

Gladkov, Fyodor (Vasilyevich)
1883-1958 . . . . TCLC 27

Glanville, Brian (Lester) 1931- . . . . . . CLC 6
See also CA 5-8R; CAAS 9; CANR 3;
DLB 15; SATA 42

Glasgow, Ellen (Anderson Gholson)
1873(?)-1945 . . . . TCLC 2, 7
See also CA 104; DLB 9, 12

Glassco, John 1909-1981 . . . . CLC 9
See also CA 13-16R; 102; CANR 15;
DLB 68

Glasscock, Amnesia
See Steinbeck, John (Ernst)

Glasser, Ronald J. 1940(?)- . . . . CLC 37

Glassman, Joyce
See Johnson, Joyce

Glendinning, Victoria 1937- . . . . CLC 50
See also CA 120; 127

Glissant, Edouard 1928- . . . . CLC 10, 68

Gloag, Julian 1930- . . . . CLC 40
See also AITN 1; CA 65-68; CANR 10

Gluck, Louise 1943- . . . . CLC 7, 22, 44
See also Glueck, Louise
See also CA 33-36R; DLB 5

Glueck, Louise . . . . CLC 7, 22
See also Gluck, Louise
See also DLB 5

Gobineau, Joseph Arthur (Comte) de
1816-1882 . . . . NCLC 17

Godard, Jean-Luc 1930- . . . . CLC 20
See also CA 93-96

Godden, (Margaret) Rumer 1907- . . . CLC 53
See also AAYA 6; CA 5-8R; CANR 4, 27,
36; CLR 20; MAICYA; SAAS 12;
SATA 3, 36

Godoy Alcayaga, Lucila 1889-1957
See Mistral, Gabriela
See also CA 104; 131; HW; MTCW

Godwin, Gail (Kathleen)
1937- . . . . CLC 5, 8, 22, 31, 69
See also CA 29-32R; CANR 15; DLB 6;
MTCW

Godwin, William 1756-1836...... **NCLC 14**
See also CDBLB 1789-1832; DLB 39, 104

Goethe, Johann Wolfgang von
1749-1832 .... **NCLC 4, 22, 34; PC 5**
See also DLB 94; WLC 3

Gogarty, Oliver St. John
1878-1957 .... **TCLC 15**
See also CA 109; DLB 15, 19

Gogol, Nikolai (Vasilyevich)
1809-1852 ..... **NCLC 5, 15, 31; DC 1;**
SSC 4
See also WLC

Gold, Herbert 1924-....... **CLC 4, 7, 14, 42**
See also CA 9-12R; CANR 17; DLB 2;
DLBY 81

Goldbarth, Albert 1948-......... **CLC 5, 38**
See also CA 53-56; CANR 6; DLB 120

Goldberg, Anatol 1910-1982 .... **CLC 34**
See also CA 131; 117

Goldemberg, Isaac 1945-.......... **CLC 52**
See also CA 69-72; CAAS 12; CANR 11,
32; HW

Golden Silver
See Storm, Hyemeyohsts

Golding, William (Gerald)
1911-..... **CLC 1, 2, 3, 8, 10, 17, 27, 58**
See also AAYA 5; CA 5-8R; CANR 13, 33;
CDBLB 1945-1960; DLB 15, 100;
MTCW; WLC

Goldman, Emma 1869-1940...... **TCLC 13**
See also CA 110

Goldman, William (W.) 1931-.... **CLC 1, 48**
See also CA 9-12R; CANR 29; DLB 44

Goldmann, Lucien 1913-1970 ...... **CLC 24**
See also CA 25-28; CAP 2

Goldoni, Carlo 1707-1793 .... **LC 4**

Goldsberry, Steven 1949-......... **CLC 34**
See also CA 131

Goldsmith, Oliver 1728(?)-1774....... **LC 2**

Goldsmith, Peter
See Priestley, J(ohn) B(oynton)

Gombrowicz, Witold
1904-1969 .... **CLC 4, 7, 11, 49**
See also CA 19-20; 25-28R; CAP 2

Gomez de la Serna, Ramon
1888-1963 .... **CLC 9**
See also CA 116; HW

Goncharov, Ivan Alexandrovich
1812-1891 .... **NCLC 1**

Goncourt, Edmond (Louis Antoine Huot) de
1822-1896 .... **NCLC 7**

Goncourt, Jules (Alfred Huot) de
1830-1870 .... **NCLC 7**

Gontier, Fernande 19th cent. (?)- ... **CLC 50**

Goodman, Paul 1911-1972.... **CLC 1, 2, 4, 7**
See also CA 19-20; 37-40R; CANR 34;
CAP 2; MTCW

Gordimer, Nadine
1923-.... **CLC 3, 5, 7, 10, 18, 33, 51, 70**
See also CA 5-8R; CANR 3, 28; MTCW

Gordon, Adam Lindsay
1833-1870 .... **NCLC 21**

Gordon, Caroline
1895-1981 .... **CLC 6, 13, 29**
See also CA 11-12; 103; CANR 36; CAP 1;
DLB 4, 9, 102; DLBY 81; MTCW

Gordon, Charles William 1860-1937
See Connor, Ralph
See also CA 109

Gordon, Mary (Catherine)
1949-.................. **CLC 13, 22**
See also CA 102; DLB 6; DLBY 81;
MTCW

Gordon, Sol 1923-................ **CLC 26**
See also CA 53-56; CANR 4; SATA 11

Gordone, Charles 1925-.......... **CLC 1, 4**
See also BW; CA 93-96; DLB 7; MTCW

Gorenko, Anna Andreevna
See Akhmatova, Anna

Gorky, Maxim................... TCLC 8
See also Peshkov, Alexei Maximovich
See also WLC

Goryan, Sirak
See Saroyan, William

Gosse, Edmund (William)
1849-1928 .... **TCLC 28**
See also CA 117; DLB 57

Gotlieb, Phyllis Fay (Bloom)
1926-.................. **CLC 18**
See also CA 13-16R; CANR 7; DLB 88

Gottesman, S. D.
See Kornbluth, C(yril) M.; Pohl, Frederik

Gottschalk, Laura Riding
See Jackson, Laura (Riding)

Gould, Lois .... **CLC 4, 10**
See also CA 77-80; CANR 29; MTCW

Gourmont, Remy de 1858-1915.... **TCLC 17**
See also CA 109

Govier, Katherine 1948-......... **CLC 51**
See also CA 101; CANR 18

Goyen, (Charles) William
1915-1983 .... **CLC 5, 8, 14, 40**
See also AITN 2; CA 5-8R; 110; CANR 6;
DLB 2; DLBY 83

Goytisolo, Juan 1931- .... **CLC 5, 10, 23**
See also CA 85-88; CANR 32; HW; MTCW

Gozzi, (Conte) Carlo 1720-1806 .. **NCLC 23**

Grabbe, Christian Dietrich
1801-1836 .... **NCLC 2**

Grace, Patricia 1937-............. **CLC 56**

Gracian y Morales, Baltasar
1601-1658 .... **LC 15**

Gracq, Julien................ **CLC 11, 48**
See also Poirier, Louis
See also DLB 83

Grade, Chaim 1910-1982 .... **CLC 10**
See also CA 93-96; 107

Graduate of Oxford, A
See Ruskin, John

Graham, John
See Phillips, David Graham

Graham, Jorie 1951-.............. **CLC 48**
See also CA 111; DLB 120

Graham, R(obert) B(ontine) Cunninghame
See Cunninghame Graham, R(obert)
B(ontine)
See also DLB 98

Graham, Robert
See Haldeman, Joe (William)

Graham, Tom
See Lewis, (Harry) Sinclair

Graham, W(illiam) S(ydney)
1918-1986 .... **CLC 29**
See also CA 73-76; 118; DLB 20

Graham, Winston (Mawdsley)
1910-...................... **CLC 23**
See also CA 49-52; CANR 2, 22; DLB 77

Granville-Barker, Harley
1877-1946 .... **TCLC 2**
See also Barker, Harley Granville
See also CA 104

Grass, Guenter (Wilhelm)
1927- .. **CLC 1, 2, 4, 6, 11, 15, 22, 32, 49**
See also CA 13-16R; CANR 20; DLB 75;
MTCW; WLC

Gratton, Thomas
See Hulme, T(homas) E(rnest)

Grau, Shirley Ann 1929- .... **CLC 4, 9**
See also CA 89-92; CANR 22; DLB 2;
MTCW

Gravel, Fern
See Hall, James Norman

Graver, Elizabeth 1964-........... **CLC 70**
See also CA 135

Graves, Richard Perceval 1945- .... **CLC 44**
See also CA 65-68; CANR 9, 26

Graves, Robert (von Ranke)
1895-1985 ... **CLC 1, 2, 6, 11, 39, 44, 45**
See also CA 5-8R; 117; CANR 5, 36;
CDBLB 1914-1945; DLB 20, 100;
DLBY 85; MTCW; SATA 45

Gray, Alasdair (James) 1934- ...... **CLC 41**
See also CA 126; MTCW

Gray, Amlin 1946-................ **CLC 29**
See also CA 138

Gray, Francine du Plessix 1930-.... **CLC 22**
See also BEST 90:3; CA 61-64; CAAS 2;
CANR 11, 33; MTCW

Gray, John (Henry) 1866-1934 .... **TCLC 19**
See also CA 119

Gray, Simon (James Holliday)
1936-................... **CLC 9, 14, 36**
See also AITN 1; CA 21-24R; CAAS 3;
CANR 32; DLB 13; MTCW

Gray, Spalding 1941-.............. **CLC 49**
See also CA 128

Gray, Thomas 1716-1771....... **LC 4; PC 2**
See also CDBLB 1660-1789; DLB 109;
WLC

Grayson, David
See Baker, Ray Stannard

Grayson, Richard (A.) 1951-....... **CLC 38**
See also CA 85-88; CANR 14, 31

Greeley, Andrew M(oran) 1928-.... **CLC 28**
See also CA 5-8R; CAAS 7; CANR 7;
MTCW

Green, Brian
See Card, Orson Scott

Green, Hannah . . . . CLC 3
See also CA 73-76

Green, Hannah
See Greenberg, Joanne (Goldenberg)

Green, Henry. . . . . CLC 2, 13
See also Yorke, Henry Vincent
See also DLB 15

Green, Julian (Hartridge)
1900- . . . . CLC 3, 11
See also CA 21-24R; CANR 33; DLB 4, 72;
MTCW

Green, Julien
See Green, Julian (Hartridge)

Green, Paul (Eliot) 1894-1981 . . . . . . CLC 25
See also AITN 1; CA 5-8R; 103; CANR 3;
DLB 7, 9; DLBY 81

Greenberg, Ivan 1908-1973
See Rahv, Philip
See also CA 85-88

Greenberg, Joanne (Goldenberg)
1932- . . . . CLC 7, 30
See also CA 5-8R; CANR 14, 32; SATA 25

Greenberg, Richard 1959(?)- . . . . CLC 57
See also CA 138

Greene, Bette 1934- . . . . CLC 30
See also AAYA 7; CA 53-56; CANR 4;
CLR 2; MAICYA; SATA 8

Greene, Gael . . . . CLC 8
See also CA 13-16R; CANR 10

Greene, Graham (Henry)
1904-1991 . . . CLC 1, 3, 6, 9, 14, 18, 27,
37, 70, 72
See also AITN 2; CA 13-16R; 133;
CANR 35; CDBLB 1945-1960; DLB 13,
15, 77, 100; DLBY 91; MTCW;
SATA 20; WLC

Greer, Richard
See Silverberg, Robert

Greer, Richard
See Silverberg, Robert

Gregor, Arthur 1923- . . . . CLC 9
See also CA 25-28R; CAAS 10; CANR 11;
SATA 36

Gregor, Lee
See Pohl, Frederik

Gregory, Isabella Augusta (Persse)
1852-1932 . . . . TCLC 1
See also CA 104; DLB 10

Gregory, J. Dennis
See Williams, John A(lfred)

Grendon, Stephen
See Derleth, August (William)

Grenville, Kate 1950- . . . . CLC 61
See also CA 118

Grenville, Pelham
See Wodehouse, P(elham) G(renville)

Greve, Felix Paul (Berthold Friedrich)
1879-1948
See Grove, Frederick Philip
See also CA 104

Grey, Zane 1872-1939 . . . . TCLC 6
See also CA 104; 132; DLB 9; MTCW

Grieg, (Johan) Nordahl (Brun)
1902-1943 . . . . TCLC 10
See also CA 107

Grieve, C(hristopher) M(urray)
1892-1978 . . . . CLC 11, 19
See also MacDiarmid, Hugh
See also CA 5-8R; 85-88; CANR 33;
MTCW

Griffin, Gerald 1803-1840 . . . . NCLC 7

Griffin, John Howard 1920-1980. . . . CLC 68
See also AITN 1; CA 1-4R; 101; CANR 2

Griffin, Peter . . . . CLC 39

Griffiths, Trevor 1935- . . . . CLC 13, 52
See also CA 97-100; DLB 13

Grigson, Geoffrey (Edward Harvey)
1905-1985 . . . . CLC 7, 39
See also CA 25-28R; 118; CANR 20, 33;
DLB 27; MTCW

Grillparzer, Franz 1791-1872 . . . . . . NCLC 1

Grimble, Reverend Charles James
See Eliot, T(homas) S(tearns)

Grimke, Charlotte L(ottie) Forten
1837(?)-1914
See Forten, Charlotte L.
See also BW; CA 117; 124

Grimm, Jacob Ludwig Karl
1785-1863 . . . . NCLC 3
See also DLB 90; MAICYA; SATA 22

Grimm, Wilhelm Karl 1786-1859 . . NCLC 3
See also DLB 90; MAICYA; SATA 22

Grimmelshausen, Johann Jakob Christoffel
von 1621-1676 . . . . LC 6

Grindel, Eugene 1895-1952
See Eluard, Paul
See also CA 104

Grossman, David . . . . CLC 67
See also CA 138

Grossman, Vasily (Semenovich)
1905-1964 . . . . CLC 41
See also CA 124; 130; MTCW

Grove, Frederick Philip . . . . TCLC 4
See also Greve, Felix Paul (Berthold
Friedrich)
See also DLB 92

Grubb
See Crumb, R(obert)

Grumbach, Doris (Isaac)
1918- . . . . CLC 13, 22, 64
See also CA 5-8R; CAAS 2; CANR 9

Grundtvig, Nicolai Frederik Severin
1783-1872 . . . . NCLC 1

Grunge
See Crumb, R(obert)

Grunwald, Lisa 1959- . . . . CLC 44
See also CA 120

Guare, John 1938- . . . . CLC 8, 14, 29, 67
See also CA 73-76; CANR 21; DLB 7;
MTCW

Gudjonsson, Halldor Kiljan 1902-
See Laxness, Halldor
See also CA 103

Guenter, Erich
See Eich, Guenter

Guest, Barbara 1920- . . . . CLC 34
See also CA 25-28R; CANR 11; DLB 5

Guest, Judith (Ann) 1936- . . . . CLC 8, 30
See also AAYA 7; CA 77-80; CANR 15;
MTCW

Guild, Nicholas M. 1944- . . . . CLC 33
See also CA 93-96

Guillemin, Jacques
See Sartre, Jean-Paul

Guillen, Jorge 1893-1984. . . . . CLC 11
See also CA 89-92; 112; DLB 108; HW

Guillen (y Batista), Nicolas (Cristobal)
1902-1989 . . . . CLC 48
See also BLC 2; BW; CA 116; 125; 129;
HW

Guillevic, (Eugene) 1907- . . . . CLC 33
See also CA 93-96

Guillois
See Desnos, Robert

Guiney, Louise Imogen
1861-1920 . . . . TCLC 41
See also DLB 54

Guiraldes, Ricardo (Guillermo)
1886-1927 . . . . TCLC 39
See also CA 131; HW; MTCW

Gunn, Bill . . . . CLC 5
See also Gunn, William Harrison
See also DLB 38

Gunn, Thom(son William)
1929- . . . . CLC 3, 6, 18, 32
See also CA 17-20R; CANR 9, 33;
CDBLB 1960 to Present; DLB 27;
MTCW

Gunn, William Harrison 1934(?)-1989
See Gunn, Bill
See also AITN 1; BW; CA 13-16R; 128;
CANR 12, 25

Gunnars, Kristjana 1948- . . . . CLC 69
See also CA 113; DLB 60

Gurganus, Allan 1947- . . . . CLC 70
See also BEST 90:1; CA 135

Gurney, A(lbert) R(amsdell) Jr.
1930- . . . . CLC 32, 50, 54
See also CA 77-80; CANR 32

Gurney, Ivor (Bertie) 1890-1937 . . . TCLC 33

Gurney, Peter
See Gurney, A(lbert) R(amsdell) Jr.

Gustafson, Ralph (Barker) 1909- . . . . CLC 36
See also CA 21-24R; CANR 8; DLB 88

Gut, Gom
See Simenon, Georges (Jacques Christian)

Guthrie, A(lfred) B(ertram) Jr.
1901-1991 . . . . CLC 23
See also CA 57-60; 134; CANR 24; DLB 6;
SATA 62; SATO 67

Guthrie, Isobel
See Grieve, C(hristopher) M(urray)

Guthrie, Woodrow Wilson 1912-1967
See Guthrie, Woody
See also CA 113; 93-96

Guthrie, Woody. . . . . CLC 35
See also Guthrie, Woodrow Wilson

Guy, Rosa (Cuthbert) 1928- . . . . CLC 26
See also AAYA 4; BW; CA 17-20R;
CANR 14, 34; CLR 13; DLB 33;
MAICYA; SATA 14, 62

Gwendolyn
See Bennett, (Enoch) Arnold

H. D. . . . . CLC 3, 8, 14, 31, 34; PC 5
See also Doolittle, Hilda

Haavikko, Paavo Juhani
1931- . . . . CLC 18, 34
See also CA 106

Habbema, Koos
See Heijermans, Herman

Hacker, Marilyn 1942- . . . . CLC 5, 9, 23, 72
See also CA 77-80; DLB 120

Haggard, H(enry) Rider
1856-1925 . . . . TCLC 11
See also CA 108; DLB 70; SATA 16

Haig, Fenil
See Ford, Ford Madox

Haig-Brown, Roderick (Langmere)
1908-1976 . . . . CLC 21
See also CA 5-8R; 69-72; CANR 4, 38;
DLB 88; MAICYA; SATA 12

Hailey, Arthur 1920- . . . . CLC 5
See also AITN 2; BEST 90:3; CA 1-4R;
CANR 2, 36; DLB 88; DLBY 82; MTCW

Hailey, Elizabeth Forsythe 1938- . . . CLC 40
See also CA 93-96; CAAS 1; CANR 15

Haines, John (Meade) 1924- . . . . CLC 58
See also CA 17-20R; CANR 13, 34; DLB 5

Haldeman, Joe (William) 1943- . . . . . CLC 61
See also CA 53-56; CANR 6; DLB 8

Haley, Alex(ander Murray Palmer)
1921-1992 . . . . CLC 8, 12
See also BLC 2; BW; CA 77-80; 136;
DLB 38; MTCW

Haliburton, Thomas Chandler
1796-1865 . . . . NCLC 15
See also DLB 11, 99

Hall, Donald (Andrew Jr.)
1928- . . . . CLC 1, 13, 37, 59
See also CA 5-8R; CAAS 7; CANR 2;
DLB 5; SATA 23

Hall, Frederic Sauser
See Sauser-Hall, Frederic

Hall, James
See Kuttner, Henry

Hall, James Norman 1887-1951 . . . TCLC 23
See also CA 123; SATA 21

Hall, (Marguerite) Radclyffe
1886(?)-1943 . . . . TCLC 12
See also CA 110

Hall, Rodney 1935- . . . . CLC 51
See also CA 109

Halliday, Michael
See Creasey, John

Halpern, Daniel 1945- . . . . CLC 14
See also CA 33-36R

Hamburger, Michael (Peter Leopold)
1924- . . . . CLC 5, 14
See also CA 5-8R; CAAS 4; CANR 2;
DLB 27

Hamill, Pete 1935- . . . . CLC 10
See also CA 25-28R; CANR 18

Hamilton, Clive
See Lewis, C(live) S(taples)

Hamilton, Edmond 1904-1977 . . . . CLC 1
See also CA 1-4R; CANR 3; DLB 8

Hamilton, Eugene (Jacob) Lee
See Lee-Hamilton, Eugene (Jacob)

Hamilton, Franklin
See Silverberg, Robert

Hamilton, Gail
See Corcoran, Barbara

Hamilton, Mollie
See Kaye, M(ary) M(argaret)

Hamilton, (Anthony Walter) Patrick
1904-1962 . . . . CLC 51
See also CA 113; DLB 10

Hamilton, Virginia 1936- . . . . CLC 26
See also AAYA 2; BW; CA 25-28R;
CANR 20, 37; CLR 1, 11; DLB 33, 52;
MAICYA; MTCW; SATA 4, 56

Hammett, (Samuel) Dashiell
1894-1961 . . . . CLC 3, 5, 10, 19, 47
See also AITN 1; CA 81-84;
CDALB 1929-1941; DLBD 6; MTCW

Hammon, Jupiter 1711(?)-1800(?) . . NCLC 5
See also BLC 2; DLB 31, 50

Hammond, Keith
See Kuttner, Henry

Hamner, Earl (Henry) Jr. 1923- . . . . CLC 12
See also AITN 2; CA 73-76; DLB 6

Hampton, Christopher (James)
1946- . . . . CLC 4
See also CA 25-28R; DLB 13; MTCW

Hamsun, Knut . . . . TCLC 2, 14
See also Pedersen, Knut

Handke, Peter 1942- . . CLC 5, 8, 10, 15, 38
See also CA 77-80; CANR 33; DLB 85;
MTCW

Hanley, James 1901-1985 . . . CLC 3, 5, 8, 13
See also CA 73-76; 117; CANR 36; MTCW

Hannah, Barry 1942- . . . . CLC 23, 38
See also CA 108; 110; DLB 6; MTCW

Hannon, Ezra
See Hunter, Evan

Hansberry, Lorraine (Vivian)
1930-1965 . . . . CLC 17, 62; DC 2
See also BLC 2; BW; CA 109; 25-28R;
CABS 3; CDALB 1941-1968; DLB 7, 38;
MTCW

Hansen, Joseph 1923- . . . . CLC 38
See also CA 29-32R; CANR 16

Hansen, Martin A. 1909-1955 . . . . . TCLC 32

Hanson, Kenneth O(stlin) 1922- . . . . CLC 13
See also CA 53-56; CANR 7

Hardwick, Elizabeth 1916- . . . . CLC 13
See also CA 5-8R; CANR 3, 32; DLB 6;
MTCW

Hardy, Thomas
1840-1928 . . . TCLC 4, 10, 18, 32; SSC 2
See also CA 104; 123; CDBLB 1890-1914;
DLB 18, 19; MTCW; WLC

Hare, David 1947- . . . . CLC 29, 58
See also CA 97-100; CANR 39; DLB 13;
MTCW

Harford, Henry
See Hudson, W(illiam) H(enry)

Hargrave, Leonie
See Disch, Thomas M(ichael)

Harlan, Louis R(udolph) 1922- . . . . . CLC 34
See also CA 21-24R; CANR 25

Harling, Robert 1951(?)- . . . . CLC 53

Harmon, William (Ruth) 1938- . . . . . CLC 38
See also CA 33-36R; CANR 14, 32, 35;
SATA 65

Harper, F. E. W.
See Harper, Frances Ellen Watkins

Harper, Frances E. W.
See Harper, Frances Ellen Watkins

Harper, Frances E. Watkins
See Harper, Frances Ellen Watkins

Harper, Frances Ellen
See Harper, Frances Ellen Watkins

Harper, Frances Ellen Watkins
1825-1911 . . . . TCLC 14
See also BLC 2; BW; CA 111; 125; DLB 50

Harper, Michael S(teven) 1938- . . CLC 7, 22
See also BW; CA 33-36R; CANR 24;
DLB 41

Harper, Mrs. F. E. W.
See Harper, Frances Ellen Watkins

Harris, Christie (Lucy) Irwin
1907- . . . . CLC 12
See also CA 5-8R; CANR 6; DLB 88;
MAICYA; SAAS 10; SATA 6

Harris, Frank 1856(?)-1931 . . . . TCLC 24
See also CA 109

Harris, George Washington
1814-1869 . . . . NCLC 23
See also DLB 3, 11

Harris, Joel Chandler 1848-1908 . . . TCLC 2
See also CA 104; 137; DLB 11, 23, 42, 78,
91; MAICYA; YABC 1

Harris, John (Wyndham Parkes Lucas)
Beynon 1903-1969 . . . . CLC 19
See also CA 102; 89-92

Harris, MacDonald
See Heiney, Donald (William)

Harris, Mark 1922- . . . . CLC 19
See also CA 5-8R; CAAS 3; CANR 2;
DLB 2; DLBY 80

Harris, (Theodore) Wilson 1921- . . . . CLC 25
See also BW; CA 65-68; CAAS 16;
CANR 11, 27; DLB 117; MTCW

Harrison, Elizabeth Cavanna 1909-
See Cavanna, Betty
See also CA 9-12R; CANR 6, 27

Harrison, Harry (Max) 1925- . . . . CLC 42
See also CA 1-4R; CANR 5, 21; DLB 8;
SATA 4

Harrison, James (Thomas) 1937-
See Harrison, Jim
See also CA 13-16R; CANR 8

Harrison, Jim . . . . CLC 6, 14, 33, 66
See also Harrison, James (Thomas)
See also DLBY 82

Harrison, Kathryn 1961- . . . . CLC 70

Harrison, Tony 1937- . . . . CLC 43
See also CA 65-68; DLB 40; MTCW

Harriss, Will(ard Irvin) 1922- . . . . . . CLC 34
See also CA 111

Harson, Sley
See Ellison, Harlan

Hart, Ellis
See Ellison, Harlan

Hart, Josephine 1942(?)- .... **CLC 70**
See also CA 138

Hart, Moss 1904-1961 .... **CLC 66**
See also CA 109; 89-92; DLB 7

Harte, (Francis) Bret(t)
1836(?)-1902 .... **TCLC 1, 25; SSC 8**
See also CA 104; CDALB 1865-1917;
DLB 12, 64, 74, 79; SATA 26; WLC

Hartley, L(eslie) P(oles)
1895-1972 .... **CLC 2, 22**
See also CA 45-48; 37-40R; CANR 33;
DLB 15; MTCW

Hartman, Geoffrey H. 1929- .... **CLC 27**
See also CA 117; 125; DLB 67

Haruf, Kent 19th cent. (?)- .... **CLC 34**

Harwood, Ronald 1934- .... **CLC 32**
See also CA 1-4R; CANR 4; DLB 13

Hasek, Jaroslav (Matej Frantisek)
1883-1923 .... **TCLC 4**
See also CA 104; 129; MTCW

Hass, Robert 1941- .... **CLC 18, 39**
See also CA 111; CANR 30; DLB 105

Hastings, Hudson
See Kuttner, Henry

Hastings, Selina .... **CLC 44**

Hatteras, Amelia
See Mencken, H(enry) L(ouis)

Hatteras, Owen .... **TCLC 18**
See also Nathan, George Jean

Hatteras, Owen
See Mencken, H(enry) L(ouis)

Hauptmann, Gerhart (Johann Robert)
1862-1946 .... **TCLC 4**
See also CA 104; DLB 66, 118

Havel, Vaclav 1936- .... **CLC 25, 58, 65**
See also CA 104; CANR 36; MTCW

Haviaras, Stratis .... **CLC 33**
See also Chaviaras, Strates

Hawes, Stephen 1475(?)-1523(?) ..... **LC 17**

Hawkes, John (Clendennin Burne Jr.)
1925- ...... **CLC 1, 2, 3, 4, 7, 9, 14, 15,
27, 49**
See also CA 1-4R; CANR 2; DLB 2, 7;
DLBY 80; MTCW

Hawking, S. W.
See Hawking, Stephen W(illiam)

Hawking, Stephen W(illiam)
1942- .... **CLC 63**
See also BEST 89:1; CA 126; 129

Hawthorne, Julian 1846-1934 ..... **TCLC 25**

Hawthorne, Nathaniel
1804-1864 ... **NCLC 2, 10, 17, 23; SSC 3**
See also CDALB 1640-1865; DLB 1, 74;
WLC; YABC 2

Hayaseca y Eizaguirre, Jorge
See Echegaray (y Eizaguirre), Jose (Maria
Waldo)

Hayashi Fumiko 1904-1951 .... **TCLC 27**

Haycraft, Anna
See Ellis, Alice Thomas
See also CA 122

Hayden, Robert E(arl)
1913-1980 .... **CLC 5, 9, 14, 37**
See also BLC 2; BW; CA 69-72; 97-100;
CABS 2; CANR 24; CDALB 1941-1968;
DLB 5, 76; MTCW; SATA 19, 26

Hayford, J(oseph) E(phraim) Casely
See Casely-Hayford, J(oseph) E(phraim)

Hayman, Ronald 1932- .... **CLC 44**
See also CA 25-28R; CANR 18

Haywood, Eliza (Fowler)
1693(?)-1756 .... **LC 1**

Hazlitt, William 1778-1830 ...... **NCLC 29**
See also DLB 110

Hazzard, Shirley 1931- .... **CLC 18**
See also CA 9-12R; CANR 4; DLBY 82;
MTCW

Head, Bessie 1937-1986 .... **CLC 25, 67**
See also BLC 2; BW; CA 29-32R; 119;
CANR 25; DLB 117; MTCW

Headon, (Nicky) Topper 1956(?)- ... **CLC 30**
See also The Clash

Heaney, Seamus (Justin)
1939- .... **CLC 5, 7, 14, 25, 37**
See also CA 85-88; CANR 25;
CDBLB 1960 to Present; DLB 40;
MTCW

Hearn, (Patricio) Lafcadio (Tessima Carlos)
1850-1904 .... **TCLC 9**
See also CA 105; DLB 12, 78

Hearne, Vicki 1946- .... **CLC 56**

Hearon, Shelby 1931- .... **CLC 63**
See also AITN 2; CA 25-28R; CANR 18

Heat-Moon, William Least .... **CLC 29**
See also Trogdon, William (Lewis)
See also AAYA 9

Hebert, Anne 1916- .... **CLC 4, 13, 29**
See also CA 85-88; DLB 68; MTCW

Hecht, Anthony (Evan)
1923- .... **CLC 8, 13, 19**
See also CA 9-12R; CANR 6; DLB 5

Hecht, Ben 1894-1964 .... **CLC 8**
See also CA 85-88; DLB 7, 9, 25, 26, 28, 86

Hedayat, Sadeq 1903-1951 .... **TCLC 21**
See also CA 120

Heidegger, Martin 1889-1976 ...... **CLC 24**
See also CA 81-84; 65-68; CANR 34;
MTCW

Heidenstam, (Carl Gustaf) Verner von
1859-1940 .... **TCLC 5**
See also CA 104

Heifner, Jack 1946- .... **CLC 11**
See also CA 105

Heijermans, Herman 1864-1924 ... **TCLC 24**
See also CA 123

Heilbrun, Carolyn G(old) 1926- ..... **CLC 25**
See also CA 45-48; CANR 1, 28

Heine, Heinrich 1797-1856 .... **NCLC 4**
See also DLB 90

Heinemann, Larry (Curtiss) 1944- .. **CLC 50**
See also CA 110; CANR 31; DLBD 9

Heiney, Donald (William) 1921- ..... **CLC 9**
See also CA 1-4R; CANR 3

Heinlein, Robert A(nson)
1907-1988 ...... **CLC 1, 3, 8, 14, 26, 55**
See also CA 1-4R; 125; CANR 1, 20;
DLB 8; MAICYA; MTCW; SATA 9, 56,
69

Helforth, John
See Doolittle, Hilda

Hellenhofferu, Vojtech Kapristian z
See Hasek, Jaroslav (Matej Frantisek)

Heller, Joseph
1923- .... **CLC 1, 3, 5, 8, 11, 36, 63**
See also AITN 1; CA 5-8R; CABS 1;
CANR 8; DLB 2, 28; DLBY 80; MTCW;
WLC

Hellman, Lillian (Florence)
1906-1984 ..... **CLC 2, 4, 8, 14, 18, 34,
44, 52; DC 1**
See also AITN 1, 2; CA 13-16R; 112;
CANR 33; DLB 7; DLBY 84; MTCW

Helprin, Mark 1947- ..... **CLC 7, 10, 22, 32**
See also CA 81-84; DLBY 85; MTCW

Helyar, Jane Penelope Josephine 1933-
See Poole, Josephine
See also CA 21-24R; CANR 10, 26

Hemans, Felicia 1793-1835 ...... **NCLC 29**
See also DLB 96

Hemingway, Ernest (Miller)
1899-1961 ... **CLC 1, 3, 6, 8, 10, 13, 19,
30, 34, 39, 41, 44, 50, 61; SSC 1**
See also CA 77-80; CANR 34;
CDALB 1917-1929; DLB 4, 9, 102;
DLBD 1; DLBY 81, 87; MTCW; WLC

Hempel, Amy 1951- .... **CLC 39**
See also CA 118; 137

Henderson, F. C.
See Mencken, H(enry) L(ouis)

Henderson, Sylvia
See Ashton-Warner, Sylvia (Constance)

Henley, Beth .... **CLC 23**
See also Henley, Elizabeth Becker
See also CABS 3; DLBY 86

Henley, Elizabeth Becker 1952-
See Henley, Beth
See also CA 107; CANR 32; MTCW

Henley, William Ernest
1849-1903 .... **TCLC 8**
See also CA 105; DLB 19

Hennissart, Martha
See Lathen, Emma
See also CA 85-88

Henry, O. .... **TCLC 1, 19; SSC 5**
See also Porter, William Sydney
See also WLC

Henryson, Robert 1430(?)-1506(?).... **LC 20**

Henry VIII 1491-1547 .... **LC 10**

Henschke, Alfred
See Klabund

Hentoff, Nat(han Irving) 1925- ..... **CLC 26**
See also AAYA 4; CA 1-4R; CAAS 6;
CANR 5, 25; CLR 1; MAICYA;
SATA 27, 42, 69

Heppenstall, (John) Rayner
1911-1981 . . . . **CLC 10**
See also CA 1-4R; 103; CANR 29

Herbert, Frank (Patrick)
1920-1986 . . . . **CLC 12, 23, 35, 44**
See also CA 53-56; 118; CANR 5; DLB 8;
MTCW; SATA 9, 37, 47

Herbert, George 1593-1633 . . . . **PC 4**
See also CDBLB Before 1660

Herbert, Zbigniew 1924- . . . . **CLC 9, 43**
See also CA 89-92; CANR 36; MTCW

Herbst, Josephine (Frey)
1897-1969 . . . . **CLC 34**
See also CA 5-8R; 25-28R; DLB 9

Hergesheimer, Joseph
1880-1954 . . . . **TCLC 11**
See also CA 109; DLB 102, 9

Herlihy, James Leo 1927- . . . . **CLC 6**
See also CA 1-4R; CANR 2

Hermogenes fl. c. 175- . . . . **CMLC 6**

Hernandez, Jose 1834-1886 . . . . . . **NCLC 17**

Herrick, Robert 1591-1674 . . . . **LC 13**

Herriot, James . . . . **CLC 12**
See also Wight, James Alfred
See also AAYA 1

Herrmann, Dorothy 1941- . . . . **CLC 44**
See also CA 107

Herrmann, Taffy
See Herrmann, Dorothy

Hersey, John (Richard)
1914- . . . . **CLC 1, 2, 7, 9, 40**
See also CA 17-20R; CANR 33; DLB 6;
MTCW; SATA 25

Herzen, Aleksandr Ivanovich
1812-1870 . . . . **NCLC 10**

Herzl, Theodor 1860-1904 . . . . **TCLC 36**

Herzog, Werner 1942- . . . . **CLC 16**
See also CA 89-92

Hesiod c. 8th cent. B.C.- . . . . **CMLC 5**

Hesse, Hermann
1877-1962 . . . **CLC 1, 2, 3, 6, 11, 17, 25,
69; SSC 9**
See also CA 17-18; CAP 2; DLB 66;
MTCW; SATA 50; WLC

Hewes, Cady
See De Voto, Bernard (Augustine)

Heyen, William 1940- . . . . **CLC 13, 18**
See also CA 33-36R; CAAS 9; DLB 5

Heyerdahl, Thor 1914- . . . . **CLC 26**
See also CA 5-8R; CANR 5, 22; MTCW;
SATA 2, 52

Heym, Georg (Theodor Franz Arthur)
1887-1912 . . . . **TCLC 9**
See also CA 106

Heym, Stefan 1913- . . . . **CLC 41**
See also CA 9-12R; CANR 4; DLB 69

Heyse, Paul (Johann Ludwig von)
1830-1914 . . . . **TCLC 8**
See also CA 104

Hibbert, Eleanor Burford 1906- . . . . . **CLC 7**
See also BEST 90:4; CA 17-20R; CANR 9,
28; SATA 2

Higgins, George V(incent)
1939- . . . . **CLC 4, 7, 10, 18**
See also CA 77-80; CAAS 5; CANR 17;
DLB 2; DLBY 81; MTCW

Higginson, Thomas Wentworth
1823-1911 . . . . **TCLC 36**
See also DLB 1, 64

Highet, Helen
See MacInnes, Helen (Clark)

Highsmith, (Mary) Patricia
1921- . . . . **CLC 2, 4, 14, 42**
See also CA 1-4R; CANR 1, 20; MTCW

Highwater, Jamake (Mamake)
1942(?)- . . . . **CLC 12**
See also AAYA 7; CA 65-68; CAAS 7;
CANR 10, 34; CLR 17; DLB 52;
DLBY 85; MAICYA; SATA 30, 32, 69

Hijuelos, Oscar 1951- . . . . **CLC 65**
See also BEST 90:1; CA 123; HW

Hikmet, Nazim 1902-1963 . . . . **CLC 40**
See also CA 93-96

Hildesheimer, Wolfgang
1916-1991 . . . . **CLC 49**
See also CA 101; 135; DLB 69

Hill, Geoffrey (William)
1932- . . . . **CLC 5, 8, 18, 45**
See also CA 81-84; CANR 21;
CDBLB 1960 to Present; DLB 40;
MTCW

Hill, George Roy 1921- . . . . **CLC 26**
See also CA 110; 122

Hill, Susan (Elizabeth) 1942- . . . . **CLC 4**
See also CA 33-36R; CANR 29; DLB 14;
MTCW

Hillerman, Tony 1925- . . . . **CLC 62**
See also AAYA 6; BEST 89:1; CA 29-32R;
CANR 21; SATA 6

Hilliard, Noel (Harvey) 1929- . . . . . . **CLC 15**
See also CA 9-12R; CANR 7

Hillis, Rick 1956- . . . . **CLC 66**
See also CA 134

Hilton, James 1900-1954 . . . . **TCLC 21**
See also CA 108; DLB 34, 77; SATA 34

Himes, Chester (Bomar)
1909-1984 . . . . **CLC 2, 4, 7, 18, 58**
See also BLC 2; BW; CA 25-28R; 114;
CANR 22; DLB 2, 76; MTCW

Hinde, Thomas . . . . **CLC 6, 11**
See also Chitty, Thomas Willes

Hindin, Nathan
See Bloch, Robert (Albert)

Hine, (William) Daryl 1936- . . . . **CLC 15**
See also CA 1-4R; CAAS 15; CANR 1, 20;
DLB 60

Hinkson, Katharine Tynan
See Tynan, Katharine

Hinton, S(usan) E(loise) 1950- . . . . . **CLC 30**
See also AAYA 2; CA 81-84; CANR 32;
CLR 3, 23; MAICYA; MTCW;
SATA 19, 58

Hippius, Zinaida . . . . **TCLC 9**
See also Gippius, Zinaida (Nikolayevna)

Hiraoka, Kimitake 1925-1970
See Mishima, Yukio
See also CA 97-100; 29-32R; MTCW

Hirsch, Edward 1950- . . . . **CLC 31, 50**
See also CA 104; CANR 20; DLB 120

Hitchcock, Alfred (Joseph)
1899-1980 . . . . **CLC 16**
See also CA 97-100; SATA 24, 27

Hoagland, Edward 1932- . . . . **CLC 28**
See also CA 1-4R; CANR 2, 31; DLB 6;
SATA 51

Hoban, Russell (Conwell) 1925- . . **CLC 7, 25**
See also CA 5-8R; CANR 23, 37; CLR 3;
DLB 52; MAICYA; MTCW; SATA 1, 40

Hobbs, Perry
See Blackmur, R(ichard) P(almer)

Hobson, Laura Z(ametkin)
1900-1986 . . . . **CLC 7, 25**
See also CA 17-20R; 118; DLB 28;
SATA 52

Hochhuth, Rolf 1931- . . . . **CLC 4, 11, 18**
See also CA 5-8R; CANR 33; MTCW

Hochman, Sandra 1936- . . . . **CLC 3, 8**
See also CA 5-8R; DLB 5

Hochwaelder, Fritz 1911-1986 . . . . . . **CLC 36**
See also Hochwalder, Fritz
See also CA 29-32R; 120; MTCW

Hochwalder, Fritz . . . . **CLC 36**
See also Hochwaelder, Fritz

Hocking, Mary (Eunice) 1921- . . . . . **CLC 13**
See also CA 101; CANR 18

Hodgins, Jack 1938- . . . . **CLC 23**
See also CA 93-96; DLB 60

Hodgson, William Hope
1877(?)-1918 . . . . **TCLC 13**
See also CA 111; DLB 70

Hoffman, Alice 1952- . . . . **CLC 51**
See also CA 77-80; CANR 34; MTCW

Hoffman, Daniel (Gerard)
1923- . . . . **CLC 6, 13, 23**
See also CA 1-4R; CANR 4; DLB 5

Hoffman, Stanley 1944- . . . . **CLC 5**
See also CA 77-80

Hoffman, William M(oses) 1939- . . . **CLC 40**
See also CA 57-60; CANR 11

Hoffmann, E(rnst) T(heodor) A(madeus)
1776-1822 . . . . **NCLC 2**
See also DLB 90; SATA 27

Hofmann, Gert 1931- . . . . **CLC 54**
See also CA 128

Hofmannsthal, Hugo von
1874-1929 . . . . **TCLC 11**
See also CA 106; DLB 81, 118

Hogarth, Charles
See Creasey, John

Hogg, James 1770-1835 . . . . **NCLC 4**
See also DLB 93, 116

Holbach, Paul Henri Thiry Baron
1723-1789 . . . . **LC 14**

Holberg, Ludvig 1684-1754 . . . . **LC 6**

Holden, Ursula 1921- . . . . **CLC 18**
See also CA 101; CAAS 8; CANR 22

Holderlin, (Johann Christian) Friedrich
1770-1843 . . . . **NCLC 16; PC 4**

Holdstock, Robert
See Holdstock, Robert P.

Holdstock, Robert P.   1948-....... **CLC 39**
See also CA 131

Holland, Isabelle   1920- .... **CLC 21**
See also CA 21-24R; CANR 10, 25;
MAICYA; SATA 8, 70

Holland, Marcus
See Caldwell, (Janet Miriam) Taylor
(Holland)

Hollander, John   1929-...... **CLC 2, 5, 8, 14**
See also CA 1-4R; CANR 1; DLB 5;
SATA 13

Hollander, Paul
See Silverberg, Robert

Holleran, Andrew   1943(?)-........ **CLC 38**

Hollinghurst, Alan   1954-.......... **CLC 55**
See also CA 114

Hollis, Jim
See Summers, Hollis (Spurgeon Jr.)

Holmes, John
See Souster, (Holmes) Raymond

Holmes, John Clellon   1926-1988.... **CLC 56**
See also CA 9-12R; 125; CANR 4; DLB 16

Holmes, Oliver Wendell
1809-1894 .... **NCLC 14**
See also CDALB 1640-1865; DLB 1;
SATA 34

Holmes, Raymond
See Souster, (Holmes) Raymond

Holt, Victoria
See Hibbert, Eleanor Burford

Holub, Miroslav   1923-............. **CLC 4**
See also CA 21-24R; CANR 10

Homer   c. 8th cent. B.C.-......... **CMLC 1**

Honig, Edwin   1919-............... **CLC 33**
See also CA 5-8R; CAAS 8; CANR 4;
DLB 5

Hood, Hugh (John Blagdon)
1928-................... **CLC 15, 28**
See also CA 49-52; CANR 1, 33; DLB 53

Hood, Thomas   1799-1845........ **NCLC 16**
See also DLB 96

Hooker, (Peter) Jeremy   1941-...... **CLC 43**
See also CA 77-80; CANR 22; DLB 40

Hope, A(lec) D(erwent)   1907-.... **CLC 3, 51**
See also CA 21-24R; CANR 33; MTCW

Hope, Brian
See Creasey, John

Hope, Christopher (David Tully)
1944-..................... **CLC 52**
See also CA 106; SATA 62

Hopkins, Gerard Manley
1844-1889 .... **NCLC 17**
See also CDBLB 1890-1914; DLB 35, 57;
WLC

Hopkins, John (Richard)   1931-...... **CLC 4**
See also CA 85-88

Hopkins, Pauline Elizabeth
1859-1930 .... **TCLC 28**
See also BLC 2; DLB 50

Horatio
See Proust,
(Valentin-Louis-George-Eugene-)Marcel

Horgan, Paul   1903- .... **CLC 9, 53**
See also CA 13-16R; CANR 9, 35;
DLB 102; DLBY 85; MTCW; SATA 13

Horn, Peter
See Kuttner, Henry

Horovitz, Israel   1939- .... **CLC 56**
See also CA 33-36R; DLB 7

Horvath, Odon von
See Horvath, Oedoen von
See also DLB 85

Horvath, Oedoen von   1901-1938... **TCLC 45**
See also Horvath, Odon von
See also CA 118

Horwitz, Julius   1920-1986........ **CLC 14**
See also CA 9-12R; 119; CANR 12

Hospital, Janette Turner   1942-..... **CLC 42**
See also CA 108

Hostos, E. M. de
See Hostos (y Bonilla), Eugenio Maria de

Hostos, Eugenio M. de
See Hostos (y Bonilla), Eugenio Maria de

Hostos, Eugenio Maria
See Hostos (y Bonilla), Eugenio Maria de

Hostos (y Bonilla), Eugenio Maria de
1839-1903 .... **TCLC 24**
See also CA 123; 131; HW

Houdini
See Lovecraft, H(oward) P(hillips)

Hougan, Carolyn   19th cent. (?)- .... **CLC 34**

Household, Geoffrey (Edward West)
1900-1988 .... **CLC 11**
See also CA 77-80; 126; DLB 87; SATA 14, 59

Housman, A(lfred) E(dward)
1859-1936 .... **TCLC 1, 10; PC 2**
See also CA 104; 125; DLB 19; MTCW

Housman, Laurence   1865-1959 ..... **TCLC 7**
See also CA 106; DLB 10; SATA 25

Howard, Elizabeth Jane   1923- ... **CLC 7, 29**
See also CA 5-8R; CANR 8

Howard, Maureen   1930- ..... **CLC 5, 14, 46**
See also CA 53-56; CANR 31; DLBY 83;
MTCW

Howard, Richard   1929- ...... **CLC 7, 10, 47**
See also AITN 1; CA 85-88; CANR 25;
DLB 5

Howard, Robert Ervin   1906-1936... **TCLC 8**
See also CA 105

Howard, Warren F.
See Pohl, Frederik

Howe, Fanny   1940- .... **CLC 47**
See also CA 117; SATA 52

Howe, Julia Ward   1819-1910 ..... **TCLC 21**
See also CA 117; DLB 1

Howe, Susan   1937-............... **CLC 72**
See also DLB 120

Howe, Tina   1937-............... **CLC 48**
See also CA 109

Howell, James   1594(?)-1666 .... **LC 13**

Howells, W. D.
See Howells, William Dean

Howells, William D.
See Howells, William Dean

Howells, William Dean
1837-1920 .... **TCLC 41, 7, 17**
See also CA 104; 134; CDALB 1865-1917;
DLB 12, 64, 74, 79

Howes, Barbara   1914-............ **CLC 15**
See also CA 9-12R; CAAS 3; SATA 5

Hrabal, Bohumil   1914-........ **CLC 13, 67**
See also CA 106; CAAS 12

Hsun, Lu .... **TCLC 3**
See also Shu-Jen, Chou

Hubbard, L(afayette) Ron(ald)
1911-1986 .... **CLC 43**
See also CA 77-80; 118; CANR 22

Huch, Ricarda (Octavia)
1864-1947 .... **TCLC 13**
See also CA 111; DLB 66

Huddle, David   1942- .... **CLC 49**
See also CA 57-60

Hudson, Jeffery
See Crichton, (John) Michael

Hudson, W(illiam) H(enry)
1841-1922 .... **TCLC 29**
See also CA 115; DLB 98; SATA 35

Hueffer, Ford Madox
See Ford, Ford Madox

Hughart, Barry .... **CLC 39**
See also CA 137

Hughes, Colin
See Creasey, John

Hughes, David (John)   1930- .... **CLC 48**
See also CA 116; 129; DLB 14

Hughes, (James) Langston
1902-1967 .... **CLC 1, 5, 10, 15, 35, 44;
PC 1; SSC 6**
See also BLC 2; BW; CA 1-4R; 25-28R;
CANR 1, 34; CDALB 1929-1941;
CLR 17; DLB 4, 7, 48, 51, 86; MAICYA;
MTCW; SATA 4, 33; WLC

Hughes, Richard (Arthur Warren)
1900-1976 .... **CLC 1, 11**
See also CA 5-8R; 65-68; CANR 4;
DLB 15; MTCW; SATA 8, 25

Hughes, Ted   1930- ..... **CLC 2, 4, 9, 14, 37**
See also CA 1-4R; CANR 1, 33; CLR 3;
DLB 40; MAICYA; MTCW; SATA 27, 49

Hugo, Richard F(ranklin)
1923-1982 .... **CLC 6, 18, 32**
See also CA 49-52; 108; CANR 3; DLB 5

Hugo, Victor (Marie)
1802-1885 .... **NCLC 3, 10, 21**
See also DLB 119; SATA 47; WLC

Huidobro, Vicente
See Huidobro Fernandez, Vicente Garcia

Huidobro Fernandez, Vicente Garcia
1893-1948 .... **TCLC 31**
See also CA 131; HW

Hulme, Keri   1947- .... **CLC 39**
See also CA 125

Hulme, T(homas) E(rnest)
1883-1917 .... **TCLC 21**
See also CA 117; DLB 19

Hume, David   1711-1776............. **LC 7**
See also DLB 104

Humphrey, William   1924- . . . . **CLC 45**
　See also CA 77-80; DLB 6

Humphreys, Emyr Owen   1919- . . . . . **CLC 47**
　See also CA 5-8R; CANR 3, 24; DLB 15

Humphreys, Josephine   1945- . . . . **CLC 34, 57**
　See also CA 121; 127

Hungerford, Pixie
　See Brinsmead, H(esba) F(ay)

Hunt, E(verette) Howard Jr.   1918- . . . **CLC 3**
　See also AITN 1; CA 45-48; CANR 2

Hunt, Kyle
　See Creasey, John

Hunt, (James Henry) Leigh
　1784-1859 . . . . **NCLC 1**

Hunt, Marsha   1946- . . . . **CLC 70**

Hunter, E. Waldo
　See Sturgeon, Theodore (Hamilton)

Hunter, Evan   1926- . . . . **CLC 11, 31**
　See also CA 5-8R; CANR 5, 38; DLBY 82;
　MTCW; SATA 25

Hunter, Kristin (Eggleston)   1931- . . . **CLC 35**
　See also AITN 1; BW; CA 13-16R;
　CANR 13; CLR 3; DLB 33; MAICYA;
　SAAS 10; SATA 12

Hunter, Mollie   1922- . . . . **CLC 21**
　See also McIlwraith, Maureen Mollie
　Hunter
　See also CANR 37; CLR 25; MAICYA;
　SAAS 7; SATA 54

Hunter, Robert   (?)-1734 . . . . **LC 7**

Hurston, Zora Neale
　1903-1960 . . . . **CLC 7, 30, 61; SSC 4**
　See also BLC 2; BW; CA 85-88; DLB 51,
　86; MTCW

Huston, John (Marcellus)
　1906-1987 . . . . **CLC 20**
　See also CA 73-76; 123; CANR 34; DLB 26

Hutten, Ulrich von   1488-1523 . . . . **LC 16**

Huxley, Aldous (Leonard)
　1894-1963 . . **CLC 1, 3, 4, 5, 8, 11, 18, 35**
　See also CA 85-88; CDBLB 1914-1945;
　DLB 36, 100; MTCW; SATA 63; WLC

Huysmans, Charles Marie Georges
　1848-1907
　See Huysmans, Joris-Karl
　See also CA 104

Huysmans, Joris-Karl . . . . **TCLC 7**
　See also Huysmans, Charles Marie Georges

Hwang, David Henry   1957- . . . . **CLC 55**
　See also CA 127; 132

Hyde, Anthony   1946- . . . . **CLC 42**
　See also CA 136

Hyde, Margaret O(ldroyd)   1917- . . . **CLC 21**
　See also CA 1-4R; CANR 1, 36; CLR 23;
　MAICYA; SAAS 8; SATA 1, 42

Hynes, James   1956(?)- . . . . **CLC 65**

Ian, Janis   1951- . . . . **CLC 21**
　See also CA 105

Ibanez, Vicente Blasco
　See Blasco Ibanez, Vicente

Ibarguengoitia, Jorge   1928-1983 . . . . **CLC 37**
　See also CA 124; 113; HW

Ibsen, Henrik (Johan)
　1828-1906 . . . . . **TCLC 2, 8, 16, 37; DC 2**
　See also CA 104; WLC

Ibuse Masuji   1898- . . . . **CLC 22**
　See also CA 127

Ichikawa, Kon   1915- . . . . **CLC 20**
　See also CA 121

Idle, Eric   1943- . . . . **CLC 21**
　See also Monty Python
　See also CA 116; CANR 35

Ignatow, David   1914- . . . . . . **CLC 4, 7, 14, 40**
　See also CA 9-12R; CAAS 3; CANR 31;
　DLB 5

Ihimaera, Witi   1944- . . . . **CLC 46**
　See also CA 77-80

Ilf, Ilya . . . . **TCLC 21**
　See also Fainzilberg, Ilya Arnoldovich

Immermann, Karl (Lebrecht)
　1796-1840 . . . . **NCLC 4**

Inclan, Ramon (Maria) del Valle
　See Valle-Inclan, Ramon (Maria) del

Infante, G(uillermo) Cabrera
　See Cabrera Infante, G(uillermo)

Ingalls, Rachel (Holmes)   1940- . . . . . **CLC 42**
　See also CA 123; 127

Ingamells, Rex   1913-1955 . . . . **TCLC 35**

Inge, William Motter
　1913-1973 . . . . **CLC 1, 8, 19**
　See also CA 9-12R; CDALB 1941-1968;
　DLB 7; MTCW

Ingram, Willis J.
　See Harris, Mark

Innaurato, Albert (F.)   1948(?)- . . **CLC 21, 60**
　See also CA 115; 122

Innes, Michael
　See Stewart, J(ohn) I(nnes) M(ackintosh)

Ionesco, Eugene
　1912- . . . . **CLC 1, 4, 6, 9, 11, 15, 41**
　See also CA 9-12R; MTCW; SATA 7; WLC

Iqbal, Muhammad   1873-1938 . . . . . **TCLC 28**

Irland, David
　See Green, Julian (Hartridge)

Iron, Ralph
　See Schreiner, Olive (Emilie Albertina)

Irving, John (Winslow)
　1942- . . . . **CLC 13, 23, 38**
　See also AAYA 8; BEST 89:3; CA 25-28R;
　CANR 28; DLB 6; DLBY 82; MTCW

Irving, Washington
　1783-1859 . . . . **NCLC 2, 19; SSC 2**
　See also CDALB 1640-1865; DLB 3, 11, 30,
　59, 73, 74; WLC; YABC 2

Irwin, P. K.
　See Page, P(atricia) K(athleen)

Isaacs, Susan   1943- . . . . **CLC 32**
　See also BEST 89:1; CA 89-92; CANR 20;
　MTCW

Isherwood, Christopher (William Bradshaw)
　1904-1986 . . . . **CLC 1, 9, 11, 14, 44**
　See also CA 13-16R; 117; CANR 35;
　DLB 15; DLBY 86; MTCW

Ishiguro, Kazuo   1954- . . . . . . **CLC 27, 56, 59**
　See also BEST 90:2; CA 120; MTCW

Ishikawa Takuboku
　1886(?)-1912 . . . . **TCLC 15**
　See also CA 113

Iskander, Fazil   1929- . . . . **CLC 47**
　See also CA 102

Ivan IV   1530-1584 . . . . **LC 17**

Ivanov, Vyacheslav Ivanovich
　1866-1949 . . . . **TCLC 33**
　See also CA 122

Ivask, Ivar Vidrik   1927- . . . . **CLC 14**
　See also CA 37-40R; CANR 24

Jackson, Daniel
　See Wingrove, David (John)

Jackson, Jesse   1908-1983 . . . . **CLC 12**
　See also BW; CA 25-28R; 109; CANR 27;
　CLR 28; MAICYA; SATA 2, 29, 48

Jackson, Laura (Riding)   1901-1991 . . **CLC 7**
　See also Riding, Laura
　See also CA 65-68; 135; CANR 28; DLB 48

Jackson, Sam
　See Trumbo, Dalton

Jackson, Sara
　See Wingrove, David (John)

Jackson, Shirley
　1919-1965 . . . . **CLC 11, 60; SSC 9**
　See also AAYA 9; CA 1-4R; 25-28R;
　CANR 4; CDALB 1941-1968; DLB 6;
　SATA 2; WLC

Jacob, (Cyprien-)Max   1876-1944 . . . **TCLC 6**
　See also CA 104

Jacobs, Jim   1942- . . . . **CLC 12**
　See also CA 97-100

Jacobs, W(illiam) W(ymark)
　1863-1943 . . . . **TCLC 22**
　See also CA 121

Jacobsen, Jens Peter   1847-1885 . . **NCLC 34**

Jacobsen, Josephine   1908- . . . . **CLC 48**
　See also CA 33-36R; CANR 23

Jacobson, Dan   1929- . . . . **CLC 4, 14**
　See also CA 1-4R; CANR 2, 25; DLB 14;
　MTCW

Jacqueline
　See Carpentier (y Valmont), Alejo

Jagger, Mick   1944- . . . . **CLC 17**

Jakes, John (William)   1932- . . . . **CLC 29**
　See also BEST 89:4; CA 57-60; CANR 10;
　DLBY 83; MTCW; SATA 62

James, Andrew
　See Kirkup, James

James, C(yril) L(ionel) R(obert)
　1901-1989 . . . . **CLC 33**
　See also BW; CA 117; 125; 128; MTCW

James, Daniel (Lewis)   1911-1988
　See Santiago, Danny
　See also CA 125

James, Dynely
　See Mayne, William (James Carter)

James, Henry
　1843-1916 . . . . . **TCLC 2, 11, 24, 40, 47;
　　　　　　　　　　　　　　　　　SSC 8**
　See also CA 104; 132; CDALB 1865-1917;
　DLB 12, 71, 74; MTCW; WLC

James, Montague (Rhodes)
1862-1936 .... TCLC 6
See also CA 104

James, P. D. .... CLC 18, 46
See also White, Phyllis Dorothy James
See also BEST 90:2; CDBLB 1960 to
Present; DLB 87

James, Philip
See Moorcock, Michael (John)

James, William 1842-1910..... TCLC 15, 32
See also CA 109

James I 1394-1437 .... LC 20

Jami, Nur al-Din 'Abd al-Rahman
1414-1492 .... LC 9

Jandl, Ernst 1925- .... CLC 34

Janowitz, Tama 1957- .... CLC 43
See also CA 106

Jarrell, Randall
1914-1965 .... CLC 1, 2, 6, 9, 13, 49
See also CA 5-8R; 25-28R; CABS 2;
CANR 6, 34; CDALB 1941-1968; CLR 6;
DLB 48, 52; MAICYA; MTCW; SATA 7

Jarry, Alfred 1873-1907........ TCLC 2, 14
See also CA 104

Jarvis, E. K.
See Bloch, Robert (Albert); Ellison, Harlan;
Silverberg, Robert

Jeake, Samuel Jr.
See Aiken, Conrad (Potter)

Jean Paul 1763-1825 .... NCLC 7

Jeffers, (John) Robinson
1887-1962 .... CLC 2, 3, 11, 15, 54
See also CA 85-88; CANR 35;
CDALB 1917-1929; DLB 45; MTCW;
WLC

Jefferson, Janet
See Mencken, H(enry) L(ouis)

Jefferson, Thomas 1743-1826 .... NCLC 11
See also CDALB 1640-1865; DLB 31

Jeffrey, Francis 1773-1850....... NCLC 33

Jelakowitch, Ivan
See Heijermans, Herman

Jellicoe, (Patricia) Ann 1927- ...... CLC 27
See also CA 85-88; DLB 13

Jen, Gish .... CLC 70
See also Jen, Lillian

Jen, Lillian 1956(?)-
See Jen, Gish
See also CA 135

Jenkins, (John) Robin 1912- .... CLC 52
See also CA 1-4R; CANR 1; DLB 14

Jennings, Elizabeth (Joan)
1926- .... CLC 5, 14
See also CA 61-64; CAAS 5; CANR 8, 39;
DLB 27; MTCW; SATA 66

Jennings, Waylon 1937-........... CLC 21

Jensen, Johannes V. 1873-1950.... TCLC 41

Jensen, Laura (Linnea) 1948- ...... CLC 37
See also CA 103

Jerome, Jerome K(lapka)
1859-1927 .... TCLC 23
See also CA 119; DLB 10, 34

Jerrold, Douglas William
1803-1857 .... NCLC 2

Jewett, (Theodora) Sarah Orne
1849-1909 .... TCLC 1, 22; SSC 6
See also CA 108; 127; DLB 12, 74;
SATA 15

Jewsbury, Geraldine (Endsor)
1812-1880 .... NCLC 22
See also DLB 21

Jhabvala, Ruth Prawer
1927- .... CLC 4, 8, 29
See also CA 1-4R; CANR 2, 29; MTCW

Jiles, Paulette 1943-........... CLC 13, 58
See also CA 101

Jimenez (Mantecon), Juan Ramon
1881-1958 .... TCLC 4
See also CA 104; 131; HW; MTCW

Jimenez, Ramon
See Jimenez (Mantecon), Juan Ramon

Jimenez Mantecon, Juan
See Jimenez (Mantecon), Juan Ramon

Joel, Billy .... CLC 26
See also Joel, William Martin

Joel, William Martin 1949-
See Joel, Billy
See also CA 108

John of the Cross, St. 1542-1591 .... LC 18

Johnson, B(ryan) S(tanley William)
1933-1973 .... CLC 6, 9
See also CA 9-12R; 53-56; CANR 9;
DLB 14, 40

Johnson, Charles (Richard)
1948- .... CLC 7, 51, 65
See also BLC 2; BW; CA 116; DLB 33

Johnson, Denis 1949-............. CLC 52
See also CA 117; 121; DLB 120

Johnson, Diane (Lain)
1934- .... CLC 5, 13, 48
See also CA 41-44R; CANR 17; DLBY 80;
MTCW

Johnson, Eyvind (Olof Verner)
1900-1976 .... CLC 14
See also CA 73-76; 69-72; CANR 34

Johnson, J. R.
See James, C(yril) L(ionel) R(obert)

Johnson, James Weldon
1871-1938 .... TCLC 3, 19
See also BLC 2; BW; CA 104; 125;
CDALB 1917-1929; DLB 51; MTCW;
SATA 31

Johnson, Joyce 1935-............ CLC 58
See also CA 125; 129

Johnson, Lionel (Pigot)
1867-1902 .... TCLC 19
See also CA 117; DLB 19

Johnson, Mel
See Malzberg, Barry N(athaniel)

Johnson, Pamela Hansford
1912-1981 .... CLC 1, 7, 27
See also CA 1-4R; 104; CANR 2, 28;
DLB 15; MTCW

Johnson, Samuel 1709-1784........ LC 15

Johnson, Uwe
1934-1984 .... CLC 5, 10, 15, 40
See also CA 1-4R; 112; CANR 1, 39;
DLB 75; MTCW

Johnston, George (Benson) 1913- ... CLC 51
See also CA 1-4R; CANR 5, 20; DLB 88

Johnston, Jennifer 1930-........... CLC 7
See also CA 85-88; DLB 14

Jolley, (Monica) Elizabeth 1923- ... CLC 46
See also CA 127; CAAS 13

Jones, Arthur Llewellyn 1863-1947
See Machen, Arthur
See also CA 104

Jones, D(ouglas) G(ordon) 1929-.... CLC 10
See also CA 29-32R; CANR 13; DLB 53

Jones, David (Michael)
1895-1974 .... CLC 2, 4, 7, 13, 42
See also CA 9-12R; 53-56; CANR 28;
CDBLB 1945-1960; DLB 20, 100; MTCW

Jones, David Robert 1947-
See Bowie, David
See also CA 103

Jones, Diana Wynne 1934- .... CLC 26
See also CA 49-52; CANR 4, 26; CLR 23;
MAICYA; SAAS 7; SATA 9, 70

Jones, Gayl 1949-............... CLC 6, 9
See also BLC 2; BW; CA 77-80; CANR 27;
DLB 33; MTCW

Jones, James 1921-1977.... CLC 1, 3, 10, 39
See also AITN 1, 2; CA 1-4R; 69-72;
CANR 6; DLB 2; MTCW

Jones, John J.
See Lovecraft, H(oward) P(hillips)

Jones, LeRoi .... CLC 1, 2, 3, 5, 10, 14
See also Baraka, Amiri

Jones, Louis B. .... CLC 65

Jones, Madison (Percy Jr.) 1925-.... CLC 4
See also CA 13-16R; CAAS 11; CANR 7

Jones, Mervyn 1922-.......... CLC 10, 52
See also CA 45-48; CAAS 5; CANR 1;
MTCW

Jones, Mick 1956(?)-............. CLC 30
See also The Clash

Jones, Nettie (Pearl) 1941- .... CLC 34
See also CA 137

Jones, Preston 1936-1979 .... CLC 10
See also CA 73-76; 89-92; DLB 7

Jones, Robert F(rancis) 1934-....... CLC 7
See also CA 49-52; CANR 2

Jones, Rod 1953- .... CLC 50
See also CA 128

Jones, Terence Graham Parry
1942- .... CLC 21
See also Jones, Terry; Monty Python
See also CA 112; 116; CANR 35; SATA 51

Jones, Terry
See Jones, Terence Graham Parry
See also SATA 67

Jong, Erica 1942-.......... CLC 4, 6, 8, 18
See also AITN 1; BEST 90:2; CA 73-76;
CANR 26; DLB 2, 5, 28; MTCW

Jonson, Ben(jamin) 1572(?)-1637...... LC 6
See also CDBLB Before 1660; DLB 62, 121;
WLC

Jordan, June 1936-.......... CLC 5, 11, 23
See also AAYA 2; BW; CA 33-36R;
CANR 25; CLR 10; DLB 38; MAICYA;
MTCW; SATA 4

Jordan, Pat(rick M.) 1941-........ CLC 37
See also CA 33-36R

Jorgensen, Ivar
See Ellison, Harlan

Jorgenson, Ivar
See Silverberg, Robert

Josipovici, Gabriel 1940-........ CLC 6, 43
See also CA 37-40R; CAAS 8; DLB 14

Joubert, Joseph 1754-1824 .... NCLC 9

Jouve, Pierre Jean 1887-1976...... CLC 47
See also CA 65-68

Joyce, James (Augustine Aloysius)
1882-1941 .... TCLC 3, 8, 16, 35; SSC 3
See also CA 104; 126; CDBLB 1914-1945;
DLB 10, 19, 36; MTCW; WLC

Jozsef, Attila 1905-1937......... TCLC 22
See also CA 116

Juana Ines de la Cruz 1651(?)-1695 ... LC 5

Judd, Cyril
See Kornbluth, C(yril) M.; Pohl, Frederik

Julian of Norwich 1342(?)-1416(?) .... LC 6

Just, Ward (Swift) 1935-........ CLC 4, 27
See also CA 25-28R; CANR 32

Justice, Donald (Rodney) 1925- .. CLC 6, 19
See also CA 5-8R; CANR 26; DLBY 83

Juvenal c. 55-c. 127 .... CMLC 8

Juvenis
See Bourne, Randolph S(illiman)

Kacew, Romain 1914-1980
See Gary, Romain
See also CA 108; 102

Kadare, Ismail 1936- .... CLC 52

Kadohata, Cynthia................. CLC 59

Kafka, Franz
1883-1924 ...... TCLC 2, 6, 13, 29, 47;
SSC 5
See also CA 105; 126; DLB 81; MTCW;
WLC

Kahn, Roger 1927-............... CLC 30
See also CA 25-28R; SATA 37

Kain, Saul
See Sassoon, Siegfried (Lorraine)

Kaiser, Georg 1878-1945 .... TCLC 9
See also CA 106

Kaletski, Alexander 1946- .... CLC 39
See also CA 118

Kalidasa fl. c. 400- .... CMLC 9

Kallman, Chester (Simon)
1921-1975 .... CLC 2
See also CA 45-48; 53-56; CANR 3

Kaminsky, Melvin 1926-
See Brooks, Mel
See also CA 65-68; CANR 16

Kaminsky, Stuart M(elvin) 1934- ... CLC 59
See also CA 73-76; CANR 29

Kane, Paul
See Simon, Paul

Kane, Wilson
See Bloch, Robert (Albert)

Kanin, Garson 1912-............. CLC 22
See also AITN 1; CA 5-8R; CANR 7;
DLB 7

Kaniuk, Yoram 1930-............ CLC 19
See also CA 134

Kant, Immanuel 1724-1804 ...... NCLC 27
See also DLB 94

Kantor, MacKinlay 1904-1977 ...... CLC 7
See also CA 61-64; 73-76; DLB 9, 102

Kaplan, David Michael 1946- ...... CLC 50

Kaplan, James 1951- .... CLC 59
See also CA 135

Karageorge, Michael
See Anderson, Poul (William)

Karamzin, Nikolai Mikhailovich
1766-1826 .... NCLC 3

Karapanou, Margarita 1946-....... CLC 13
See also CA 101

Karinthy, Frigyes 1887-1938...... TCLC 47

Karl, Frederick R(obert) 1927-..... CLC 34
See also CA 5-8R; CANR 3

Kastel, Warren
See Silverberg, Robert

Kataev, Evgeny Petrovich 1903-1942
See Petrov, Evgeny
See also CA 120

Kataphusin
See Ruskin, John

Katz, Steve 1935-............... CLC 47
See also CA 25-28R; CAAS 14; CANR 12;
DLBY 83

Kauffman, Janet 1945-........... CLC 42
See also CA 117; DLBY 86

Kaufman, Bob (Garnell)
1925-1986 .... CLC 49
See also BW; CA 41-44R; 118; CANR 22;
DLB 16, 41

Kaufman, George S. 1889-1961..... CLC 38
See also CA 108; 93-96; DLB 7

Kaufman, Sue .... CLC 3, 8
See also Barondess, Sue K(aufman)

Kavafis, Konstantinos Petrou 1863-1933
See Cavafy, C(onstantine) P(eter)
See also CA 104

Kavan, Anna 1901-1968 .... CLC 5, 13
See also CA 5-8R; CANR 6; MTCW

Kavanagh, Dan
See Barnes, Julian

Kavanagh, Patrick (Joseph)
1904-1967 .... CLC 22
See also CA 123; 25-28R; DLB 15, 20;
MTCW

Kawabata, Yasunari
1899-1972 .... CLC 2, 5, 9, 18
See also CA 93-96; 33-36R

Kaye, M(ary) M(argaret) 1909-..... CLC 28
See also CA 89-92; CANR 24; MTCW;
SATA 62

Kaye, Mollie
See Kaye, M(ary) M(argaret)

Kaye-Smith, Sheila 1887-1956..... TCLC 20
See also CA 118; DLB 36

Kaymor, Patrice Maguilene
See Senghor, Leopold Sedar

Kazan, Elia 1909-........... CLC 6, 16, 63
See also CA 21-24R; CANR 32

Kazantzakis, Nikos
1883(?)-1957 .... TCLC 2, 5, 33
See also CA 105; 132; MTCW

Kazin, Alfred 1915- .... CLC 34, 38
See also CA 1-4R; CAAS 7; CANR 1;
DLB 67

Keane, Mary Nesta (Skrine) 1904-
See Keane, Molly
See also CA 108; 114

Keane, Molly.................... CLC 31
See also Keane, Mary Nesta (Skrine)

Keates, Jonathan 19th cent. (?)- .... CLC 34

Keaton, Buster 1895-1966 .... CLC 20

Keats, John 1795-1821...... NCLC 8; PC 1
See also CDBLB 1789-1832; DLB 96, 110;
WLC

Keene, Donald 1922- .... CLC 34
See also CA 1-4R; CANR 5

Keillor, Garrison .... CLC 40
See also Keillor, Gary (Edward)
See also AAYA 2; BEST 89:3; DLBY 87;
SATA 58

Keillor, Gary (Edward) 1942-
See Keillor, Garrison
See also CA 111; 117; CANR 36; MTCW

Keith, Michael
See Hubbard, L(afayette) Ron(ald)

Kell, Joseph
See Wilson, John (Anthony) Burgess

Keller, Gottfried 1819-1890...... NCLC 2

Kellerman, Jonathan 1949- .... CLC 44
See also BEST 90:1; CA 106; CANR 29

Kelley, William Melvin 1937-...... CLC 22
See also BW; CA 77-80; CANR 27; DLB 33

Kellogg, Marjorie 1922-............ CLC 2
See also CA 81-84

Kellow, Kathleen
See Hibbert, Eleanor Burford

Kelly, M(ilton) T(erry) 1947-....... CLC 55
See also CA 97-100; CANR 19

Kelman, James 1946-............. CLC 58

Kemal, Yashar 1923- .... CLC 14, 29
See also CA 89-92

Kemble, Fanny 1809-1893 .... NCLC 18
See also DLB 32

Kemelman, Harry 1908-............ CLC 2
See also AITN 1; CA 9-12R; CANR 6;
DLB 28

Kempe, Margery 1373(?)-1440(?) ..... LC 6

Kempis, Thomas a 1380-1471 .... LC 11

Kendall, Henry 1839-1882...... NCLC 12

Keneally, Thomas (Michael)
1935- ...... CLC 5, 8, 10, 14, 19, 27, 43
See also CA 85-88; CANR 10; MTCW

Kennedy, Adrienne (Lita) 1931- .... CLC 66
See also BLC 2; BW; CA 103; CABS 3;
CANR 26; DLB 38

Kennedy, John Pendleton
1795-1870 . . . . NCLC **2**
See also DLB 3

Kennedy, Joseph Charles 1929- . . . . . . CLC **8**
See also Kennedy, X. J.
See also CA 1-4R; CANR 4, 30; SATA 14

Kennedy, William 1928- . . . CLC **6, 28, 34, 53**
See also AAYA 1; CA 85-88; CANR 14,
31; DLBY 85; MTCW; SATA 57

Kennedy, X. J. . . . . CLC **42**
See also Kennedy, Joseph Charles
See also CAAS 9; CLR 27; DLB 5

Kent, Kelvin
See Kuttner, Henry

Kenton, Maxwell
See Southern, Terry

Kenyon, Robert O.
See Kuttner, Henry

Kerouac, Jack . . . . . CLC **1, 2, 3, 5, 14, 29, 61**
See also Kerouac, Jean-Louis Lebris de
See also CDALB 1941-1968; DLB 2, 16;
DLBD 3

Kerouac, Jean-Louis Lebris de 1922-1969
See Kerouac, Jack
See also AITN 1; CA 5-8R; 25-28R;
CANR 26; MTCW; WLC

Kerr, Jean 1923- . . . . CLC **22**
See also CA 5-8R; CANR 7

Kerr, M. E. . . . . CLC **12, 35**
See also Meaker, Marijane (Agnes)
See also AAYA 2; SAAS 1

Kerr, Robert . . . . CLC **55**

Kerrigan, (Thomas) Anthony
1918- . . . . CLC **4, 6**
See also CA 49-52; CAAS 11; CANR 4

Kerry, Lois
See Duncan, Lois

Kesey, Ken (Elton)
1935- . . . . CLC **1, 3, 6, 11, 46, 64**
See also CA 1-4R; CANR 22, 38;
CDALB 1968-1988; DLB 2, 16; MTCW;
SATA 66; WLC

Kesselring, Joseph (Otto)
1902-1967 . . . . CLC **45**

Kessler, Jascha (Frederick) 1929- . . . . CLC **4**
See also CA 17-20R; CANR 8

Kettelkamp, Larry (Dale) 1933- . . . . CLC **12**
See also CA 29-32R; CANR 16; SAAS 3;
SATA 2

Kherdian, David 1931- . . . . CLC **6, 9**
See also CA 21-24R; CAAS 2; CANR 39;
CLR 24; MAICYA; SATA 16

Khlebnikov, Velimir . . . . TCLC **20**
See also Khlebnikov, Viktor Vladimirovich

Khlebnikov, Viktor Vladimirovich 1885-1922
See Khlebnikov, Velimir
See also CA 117

Khodasevich, Vladislav (Felitsianovich)
1886-1939 . . . . TCLC **15**
See also CA 115

Kielland, Alexander Lange
1849-1906 . . . . TCLC **5**
See also CA 104

Kiely, Benedict 1919- . . . . CLC **23, 43**
See also CA 1-4R; CANR 2; DLB 15

Kienzle, William X(avier) 1928- . . . . CLC **25**
See also CA 93-96; CAAS 1; CANR 9, 31;
MTCW

Kierkegaard, Soeren 1813-1855 . . . NCLC **34**

Kierkegaard, Soren 1813-1855 . . . . NCLC **34**

Killens, John Oliver 1916-1987 . . . . . CLC **10**
See also BW; CA 77-80; 123; CAAS 2;
CANR 26; DLB 33

Killigrew, Anne 1660-1685 . . . . LC **4**

Kim
See Simenon, Georges (Jacques Christian)

Kincaid, Jamaica 1949- . . . . CLC **43, 68**
See also BLC 2; BW; CA 125

King, Francis (Henry) 1923- . . . . . CLC **8, 53**
See also CA 1-4R; CANR 1, 33; DLB 15;
MTCW

King, Stephen (Edwin)
1947- . . . . CLC **12, 26, 37, 61**
See also AAYA 1; BEST 90:1; CA 61-64;
CANR 1, 30; DLBY 80; MTCW;
SATA 9, 55

King, Steve
See King, Stephen (Edwin)

Kingman, Lee . . . . CLC **17**
See also Natti, (Mary) Lee
See also SAAS 3; SATA 1, 67

Kingsley, Charles 1819-1875 . . . . . NCLC **35**
See also DLB 21, 32; YABC 2

Kingsley, Sidney 1906- . . . . CLC **44**
See also CA 85-88; DLB 7

Kingsolver, Barbara 1955- . . . . CLC **55**
See also CA 129; 134

Kingston, Maxine (Ting Ting) Hong
1940- . . . . CLC **12, 19, 58**
See also AAYA 8; CA 69-72; CANR 13,
38; DLBY 80; MTCW; SATA 53

Kinnell, Galway
1927- . . . . CLC **1, 2, 3, 5, 13, 29**
See also CA 9-12R; CANR 10, 34; DLB 5;
DLBY 87; MTCW

Kinsella, Thomas 1928- . . . . CLC **4, 19**
See also CA 17-20R; CANR 15; DLB 27;
MTCW

Kinsella, W(illiam) P(atrick)
1935- . . . . CLC **27, 43**
See also AAYA 7; CA 97-100; CAAS 7;
CANR 21, 35; MTCW

Kipling, (Joseph) Rudyard
1865-1936 . . . . TCLC **8, 17; PC 3; SSC 5**
See also CA 105; 120; CANR 33;
CDBLB 1890-1914; DLB 19, 34;
MAICYA; MTCW; WLC; YABC 2

Kirkup, James 1918- . . . . CLC **1**
See also CA 1-4R; CAAS 4; CANR 2;
DLB 27; SATA 12

Kirkwood, James 1930(?)-1989 . . . . . . CLC **9**
See also AITN 2; CA 1-4R; 128; CANR 6

Kis, Danilo 1935-1989 . . . . CLC **57**
See also CA 109; 118; 129; MTCW

Kivi, Aleksis 1834-1872 . . . . NCLC **30**

Kizer, Carolyn (Ashley) 1925- . . . CLC **15, 39**
See also CA 65-68; CAAS 5; CANR 24;
DLB 5

Klabund 1890-1928 . . . . TCLC **44**
See also DLB 66

Klappert, Peter 1942- . . . . CLC **57**
See also CA 33-36R; DLB 5

Klein, A(braham) M(oses)
1909-1972 . . . . CLC **19**
See also CA 101; 37-40R; DLB 68

Klein, Norma 1938-1989 . . . . CLC **30**
See also AAYA 2; CA 41-44R; 128;
CANR 15, 37; CLR 2, 19; MAICYA;
SAAS 1; SATA 7, 57

Klein, T(heodore) E(ibon) D(onald)
1947- . . . . CLC **34**
See also CA 119

Kleist, Heinrich von 1777-1811 . . . . NCLC **2**
See also DLB 90

Klima, Ivan 1931- . . . . CLC **56**
See also CA 25-28R; CANR 17

Klimentov, Andrei Platonovich 1899-1951
See Platonov, Andrei
See also CA 108

Klinger, Friedrich Maximilian von
1752-1831 . . . . NCLC **1**
See also DLB 94

Klopstock, Friedrich Gottlieb
1724-1803 . . . . NCLC **11**
See also DLB 97

Knebel, Fletcher 1911- . . . . CLC **14**
See also AITN 1; CA 1-4R; CAAS 3;
CANR 1, 36; SATA 36

Knickerbocker, Diedrich
See Irving, Washington

Knight, Etheridge 1931-1991 . . . . CLC **40**
See also BLC 2; BW; CA 21-24R; 133;
CANR 23; DLB 41

Knight, Sarah Kemble 1666-1727 . . . . . LC **7**
See also DLB 24

Knowles, John 1926- . . . . . . CLC **1, 4, 10, 26**
See also CA 17-20R; CDALB 1968-1988;
DLB 6; MTCW; SATA 8

Knox, Calvin M.
See Silverberg, Robert

Knye, Cassandra
See Disch, Thomas M(ichael)

Koch, C(hristopher) J(ohn) 1932- . . . CLC **42**
See also CA 127

Koch, Christopher
See Koch, C(hristopher) J(ohn)

Koch, Kenneth 1925- . . . . CLC **5, 8, 44**
See also CA 1-4R; CANR 6, 36; DLB 5;
SATA 65

Kochanowski, Jan 1530-1584 . . . . LC **10**

Kock, Charles Paul de
1794-1871 . . . . NCLC **16**

Koda Shigeyuki 1867-1947
See Rohan, Koda
See also CA 121

Koestler, Arthur
1905-1983 . . . . CLC **1, 3, 6, 8, 15, 33**
See also CA 1-4R; 109; CANR 1, 33;
CDBLB 1945-1960; DLBY 83; MTCW

Kohout, Pavel 1928- . . . . CLC **13**
See also CA 45-48; CANR 3

Koizumi, Yakumo
See Hearn, (Patricio) Lafcadio (Tessima Carlos)

Kolmar, Gertrud 1894-1943 . . . . . . **TCLC 40**

Konrad, George
See Konrad, Gyoergy

Konrad, Gyoergy 1933- . . . . **CLC 4, 10**
See also CA 85-88

Konwicki, Tadeusz 1926- . . . . . **CLC 8, 28, 54**
See also CA 101; CAAS 9; CANR 39;
MTCW

Kopit, Arthur (Lee) 1937- . . . . **CLC 1, 18, 33**
See also AITN 1; CA 81-84; CABS 3;
DLB 7; MTCW

Kops, Bernard 1926- . . . . **CLC 4**
See also CA 5-8R; DLB 13

Kornbluth, C(yril) M. 1923-1958. . . . **TCLC 8**
See also CA 105; DLB 8

Korolenko, V. G.
See Korolenko, Vladimir Galaktionovich

Korolenko, Vladimir
See Korolenko, Vladimir Galaktionovich

Korolenko, Vladimir G.
See Korolenko, Vladimir Galaktionovich

Korolenko, Vladimir Galaktionovich
1853-1921 . . . . **TCLC 22**
See also CA 121

Kosinski, Jerzy (Nikodem)
1933-1991 . . . **CLC 1, 2, 3, 6, 10, 15, 53,
70**
See also CA 17-20R; 134; CANR 9; DLB 2;
DLBY 82; MTCW

Kostelanetz, Richard (Cory) 1940- . . **CLC 28**
See also CA 13-16R; CAAS 8; CANR 38

Kostrowitzki, Wilhelm Apollinaris de
1880-1918
See Apollinaire, Guillaume
See also CA 104

Kotlowitz, Robert 1924- . . . . **CLC 4**
See also CA 33-36R; CANR 36

Kotzebue, August (Friedrich Ferdinand) von
1761-1819 . . . . **NCLC 25**
See also DLB 94

Kotzwinkle, William 1938- . . . **CLC 5, 14, 35**
See also CA 45-48; CANR 3; CLR 6;
MAICYA; SATA 24, 70

Kozol, Jonathan 1936- . . . . **CLC 17**
See also CA 61-64; CANR 16

Kozoll, Michael 1940(?)- . . . . **CLC 35**

Kramer, Kathryn 19th cent. (?)- . . . . **CLC 34**

Kramer, Larry 1935- . . . . **CLC 42**
See also CA 124; 126

Krasicki, Ignacy 1735-1801 . . . . **NCLC 8**

Krasinski, Zygmunt 1812-1859 . . . . **NCLC 4**

Kraus, Karl 1874-1936. . . . . **TCLC 5**
See also CA 104; DLB 118

Kreve (Mickevicius), Vincas
1882-1954 . . . . **TCLC 27**

Kristofferson, Kris 1936- . . . . **CLC 26**
See also CA 104

Krizanc, John 1956- . . . . **CLC 57**

Krleza, Miroslav 1893-1981. . . . . **CLC 8**
See also CA 97-100; 105

Kroetsch, Robert 1927- . . . . . . **CLC 5, 23, 57**
See also CA 17-20R; CANR 8, 38; DLB 53;
MTCW

Kroetz, Franz
See Kroetz, Franz Xaver

Kroetz, Franz Xaver 1946- . . . . **CLC 41**
See also CA 130

Kropotkin, Peter (Aleksieevich)
1842-1921 . . . . **TCLC 36**
See also CA 119

Krotkov, Yuri 1917- . . . . **CLC 19**
See also CA 102

Krumb
See Crumb, R(obert)

Krumgold, Joseph (Quincy)
1908-1980 . . . . **CLC 12**
See also CA 9-12R; 101; CANR 7;
MAICYA; SATA 1, 23, 48

Krumwitz
See Crumb, R(obert)

Krutch, Joseph Wood 1893-1970. . . . **CLC 24**
See also CA 1-4R; 25-28R; CANR 4;
DLB 63

Krutzch, Gus
See Eliot, T(homas) S(tearns)

Krylov, Ivan Andreevich
1768(?)-1844 . . . . **NCLC 1**

Kubin, Alfred 1877-1959 . . . . **TCLC 23**
See also CA 112; DLB 81

Kubrick, Stanley 1928- . . . . **CLC 16**
See also CA 81-84; CANR 33; DLB 26

Kumin, Maxine (Winokur)
1925- . . . . **CLC 5, 13, 28**
See also AITN 2; CA 1-4R; CAAS 8;
CANR 1, 21; DLB 5; MTCW; SATA 12

Kundera, Milan
1929- . . . . **CLC 4, 9, 19, 32, 68**
See also AAYA 2; CA 85-88; CANR 19;
MTCW

Kunitz, Stanley (Jasspon)
1905- . . . . **CLC 6, 11, 14**
See also CA 41-44R; CANR 26; DLB 48;
MTCW

Kunze, Reiner 1933- . . . . **CLC 10**
See also CA 93-96; DLB 75

Kuprin, Aleksandr Ivanovich
1870-1938 . . . . **TCLC 5**
See also CA 104

Kureishi, Hanif 1954- . . . . **CLC 64**

Kurosawa, Akira 1910- . . . . **CLC 16**
See also CA 101

Kuttner, Henry 1915-1958. . . . . **TCLC 10**
See also CA 107; DLB 8

Kuzma, Greg 1944- . . . . **CLC 7**
See also CA 33-36R

Kuzmin, Mikhail 1872(?)-1936 . . . . **TCLC 40**

Kyprianos, Iossif
See Samarakis, Antonis

La Bruyere, Jean de 1645-1696 . . . . . . **LC 17**

**Laclos, Pierre Ambroise Francois Choderlos
de** 1741-1803 . . . . **NCLC 4**

Lacolere, Francois
See Aragon, Louis

Lacolere, Francois
See Aragon, Louis

La Colere, Francois
See Aragon, Louis

La Colere, Francois
See Aragon, Louis

La Deshabilleuse
See Simenon, Georges (Jacques Christian)

Lady Gregory
See Gregory, Isabella Augusta (Persse)

Lady of Quality, A
See Bagnold, Enid

**La Fayette, Marie (Madelaine Pioche de la
Vergne Comtes** 1634-1693 . . . . **LC 2**

Lafayette, Rene
See Hubbard, L(afayette) Ron(ald)

Laforgue, Jules 1860-1887. . . . . **NCLC 5**

Lagerkvist, Paer (Fabian)
1891-1974 . . . . **CLC 7, 10, 13, 54**
See also CA 85-88; 49-52; MTCW

Lagerkvist, Par
See Lagerkvist, Paer (Fabian)

Lagerloef, Selma (Ottiliana Lovisa)
1858-1940 . . . . **TCLC 4, 36**
See also Lagerlof, Selma (Ottiliana Lovisa)
See also CA 108; CLR 7; SATA 15

Lagerlof, Selma (Ottiliana Lovisa)
See Lagerloef, Selma (Ottiliana Lovisa)
See also CLR 7; SATA 15

La Guma, (Justin) Alex(ander)
1925-1985 . . . . **CLC 19**
See also BW; CA 49-52; 118; CANR 25;
DLB 117; MTCW

Laidlaw, A. K.
See Grieve, C(hristopher) M(urray)

Lainez, Manuel Mujica
See Mujica Lainez, Manuel
See also HW

Lamartine, Alphonse (Marie Louis Prat) de
1790-1869 . . . . **NCLC 11**

Lamb, Charles 1775-1834. . . . . **NCLC 10**
See also CDBLB 1789-1832; DLB 93, 107;
SATA 17; WLC

Lamming, George (William)
1927- . . . . **CLC 2, 4, 66**
See also BLC 2; BW; CA 85-88; CANR 26;
MTCW

L'Amour, Louis (Dearborn)
1908-1988 . . . . **CLC 25, 55**
See also AITN 2; BEST 89:2; CA 1-4R;
125; CANR 3, 25; DLBY 80; MTCW

Lampedusa, Giuseppe (Tomasi) di . . . **TCLC 13**
See also Tomasi di Lampedusa, Giuseppe

Lampman, Archibald 1861-1899 . . **NCLC 25**
See also DLB 92

Lancaster, Bruce 1896-1963. . . . . . . **CLC 36**
See also CA 9-10; CAP 1; SATA 9

Landau, Mark Alexandrovich
See Aldanov, Mark (Alexandrovich)

Landau-Aldanov, Mark Alexandrovich
See Aldanov, Mark (Alexandrovich)

Landis, John 1950- . . . . **CLC 26**
See also CA 112; 122

Landolfi, Tommaso 1908-1979... **CLC 11, 49**
See also CA 127; 117

Landon, Letitia Elizabeth
1802-1838 .... **NCLC 15**
See also DLB 96

Landor, Walter Savage
1775-1864 .... **NCLC 14**
See also DLB 93, 107

Landwirth, Heinz 1927-
See Lind, Jakov
See also CA 9-12R; CANR 7

Lane, Patrick 1939- .... **CLC 25**
See also CA 97-100; DLB 53

Lang, Andrew 1844-1912 .... **TCLC 16**
See also CA 114; 137; DLB 98; MAICYA;
SATA 16

Lang, Fritz 1890-1976 .... **CLC 20**
See also CA 77-80; 69-72; CANR 30

Lange, John
See Crichton, (John) Michael

Langer, Elinor 1939- .... **CLC 34**
See also CA 121

Langland, William 1330(?)-1400(?) ... **LC 19**

Langstaff, Launcelot
See Irving, Washington

Lanier, Sidney 1842-1881 .... **NCLC 6**
See also DLB 64; MAICYA; SATA 18

Lanyer, Aemilia 1569-1645 .... **LC 10**

Lao Tzu .... **CMLC 7**

Lapine, James (Elliot) 1949- .... **CLC 39**
See also CA 123; 130

Larbaud, Valery (Nicolas)
1881-1957 .... **TCLC 9**
See also CA 106

Lardner, Ring
See Lardner, Ring(gold) W(ilmer)

Lardner, Ring W. Jr.
See Lardner, Ring(gold) W(ilmer)

Lardner, Ring(gold) W(ilmer)
1885-1933 .... **TCLC 2, 14**
See also CA 104; 131; CDALB 1917-1929;
DLB 11, 25, 86; MTCW

Laredo, Betty
See Codrescu, Andrei

Larkin, Maia
See Wojciechowska, Maia (Teresa)

Larkin, Philip (Arthur)
1922-1985 ... **CLC 3, 5, 8, 9, 13, 18, 33,**
39, 64
See also CA 5-8R; 117; CANR 24;
CDBLB 1960 to Present; DLB 27;
MTCW

Larra (y Sanchez de Castro), Mariano Jose de
1809-1837 .... **NCLC 17**

Larsen, Eric 1941- .... **CLC 55**
See also CA 132

Larsen, Nella 1891-1964 .... **CLC 37**
See also BLC 2; BW; CA 125; DLB 51

Larson, Charles R(aymond) 1938-... **CLC 31**
See also CA 53-56; CANR 4

Latham, Jean Lee 1902-.......... **CLC 12**
See also AITN 1; CA 5-8R; CANR 7;
MAICYA; SATA 2, 68

Latham, Mavis
See Clark, Mavis Thorpe

Lathen, Emma .... **CLC 2**
See also Hennissart, Martha; Latsis, Mary
J(ane)

Lathrop, Francis
See Leiber, Fritz (Reuter Jr.)

Latsis, Mary J(ane)
See Lathen, Emma
See also CA 85-88

Lattimore, Richmond (Alexander)
1906-1984 .... **CLC 3**
See also CA 1-4R; 112; CANR 1

Laughlin, James 1914-............ **CLC 49**
See also CA 21-24R; CANR 9; DLB 48

Laurence, (Jean) Margaret (Wemyss)
1926-1987 .. **CLC 3, 6, 13, 50, 62; SSC 7**
See also CA 5-8R; 121; CANR 33; DLB 53;
MTCW; SATA 50

Laurent, Antoine 1952- .... **CLC 50**

Lauscher, Hermann
See Hesse, Hermann

Lautreamont, Comte de
1846-1870 .... **NCLC 12**

Laverty, Donald
See Blish, James (Benjamin)

Lavin, Mary 1912-...... **CLC 4, 18; SSC 4**
See also CA 9-12R; CANR 33; DLB 15;
MTCW

Lavond, Paul Dennis
See Kornbluth, C(yril) M.; Pohl, Frederik

Lawler, Raymond Evenor 1922- .... **CLC 58**
See also CA 103

Lawrence, D(avid) H(erbert Richards)
1885-1930 .... **TCLC 2, 9, 16, 33; SSC 4**
See also CA 104; 121; CDBLB 1914-1945;
DLB 10, 19, 36, 98; MTCW; WLC

Lawrence, T(homas) E(dward)
1888-1935 .... **TCLC 18**
See also Dale, Colin
See also CA 115

Lawrence Of Arabia
See Lawrence, T(homas) E(dward)

Lawson, Henry (Archibald Hertzberg)
1867-1922 .... **TCLC 27**
See also CA 120

Laxness, Halldor.................. CLC 25
See also Gudjonsson, Halldor Kiljan

Laye, Camara 1928-1980 .... **CLC 4, 38**
See also BLC 2; BW; CA 85-88; 97-100;
CANR 25; MTCW

Layton, Irving (Peter) 1912-..... **CLC 2, 15**
See also CA 1-4R; CANR 2, 33; DLB 88;
MTCW

Lazarus, Emma 1849-1887........ **NCLC 8**

Lazarus, Felix
See Cable, George Washington

Lea, Joan
See Neufeld, John (Arthur)

Leacock, Stephen (Butler)
1869-1944 .... **TCLC 2**
See also CA 104; DLB 92

Lear, Edward 1812-1888 .... **NCLC 3**
See also CLR 1; DLB 32; MAICYA;
SATA 18

Lear, Norman (Milton) 1922- ...... **CLC 12**
See also CA 73-76

Leavis, F(rank) R(aymond)
1895-1978 .... **CLC 24**
See also CA 21-24R; 77-80; MTCW

Leavitt, David 1961-.............. **CLC 34**
See also CA 116; 122

Lebowitz, Fran(ces Ann)
1951(?)- .... **CLC 11, 36**
See also CA 81-84; CANR 14; MTCW

le Carre, John .... **CLC 3, 5, 9, 15, 28**
See also Cornwell, David (John Moore)
See also BEST 89:4; CDBLB 1960 to
Present; DLB 87

Le Clezio, J(ean) M(arie) G(ustave)
1940- .... **CLC 31**
See also CA 116; 128; DLB 83

Leconte de Lisle, Charles-Marie-Rene
1818-1894 .... **NCLC 29**

Le Coq, Monsieur
See Simenon, Georges (Jacques Christian)

Leduc, Violette 1907-1972........ **CLC 22**
See also CA 13-14; 33-36R; CAP 1

Ledwidge, Francis 1887(?)-1917 ... **TCLC 23**
See also CA 123; DLB 20

Lee, Andrea 1953- .... **CLC 36**
See also BLC 2; BW; CA 125

Lee, Andrew
See Auchincloss, Louis (Stanton)

Lee, Don L........................ CLC 2
See also Madhubuti, Haki R.

Lee, George W(ashington)
1894-1976 .... **CLC 52**
See also BLC 2; BW; CA 125; DLB 51

Lee, (Nelle) Harper 1926-...... **CLC 12, 60**
See also CA 13-16R; CDALB 1941-1968;
DLB 6; MTCW; SATA 11; WLC

Lee, Julian
See Latham, Jean Lee

Lee, Lawrence 1903- .... **CLC 34**
See also CA 25-28R

Lee, Manfred B(ennington)
1905-1971 .... **CLC 11**
See also Queen, Ellery
See also CA 1-4R; 29-32R; CANR 2

Lee, Stan 1922-.................. **CLC 17**
See also AAYA 5; CA 108; 111

Lee, Tanith 1947-................ **CLC 46**
See also CA 37-40R; SATA 8

Lee, Vernon.................... TCLC 5
See also Paget, Violet
See also DLB 57

Lee, William
See Burroughs, William S(eward)

Lee, Willy
See Burroughs, William S(eward)

Lee-Hamilton, Eugene (Jacob)
1845-1907 .... **TCLC 22**
See also CA 117

Leet, Judith 1935- .... **CLC 11**

Le Fanu, Joseph Sheridan
1814-1873 .... NCLC 9
See also DLB 21, 70

Leffland, Ella 1931- .... CLC 19
See also CA 29-32R; CANR 35; DLBY 84;
SATA 65

Leger, (Marie-Rene) Alexis Saint-Leger
1887-1975 .... CLC 11
See also Perse, St.-John
See also CA 13-16R; 61-64; MTCW

Leger, Saintleger
See Leger, (Marie-Rene) Alexis Saint-Leger

Le Guin, Ursula K(roeber)
1929- .... CLC 8, 13, 22, 45, 71
See also AAYA 9; AITN 1; CA 21-24R;
CANR 9, 32; CDALB 1968-1988; CLR 3,
28; DLB 8, 52; MAICYA; MTCW;
SATA 4, 52

Lehmann, Rosamond (Nina)
1901-1990 .... CLC 5
See also CA 77-80; 131; CANR 8; DLB 15

Leiber, Fritz (Reuter Jr.) 1910- .... CLC 25
See also CA 45-48; CANR 2; DLB 8;
MTCW; SATA 45

Leimbach, Martha 1963-
See Leimbach, Marti
See also CA 130

Leimbach, Marti .... CLC 65
See also Leimbach, Martha

Leino, Eino .... TCLC 24
See also Loennbohm, Armas Eino Leopold

Leiris, Michel (Julien) 1901-1990 ... CLC 61
See also CA 119; 128; 132

Leithauser, Brad 1953- .... CLC 27
See also CA 107; CANR 27; DLB 120

Lelchuk, Alan 1938- .... CLC 5
See also CA 45-48; CANR 1

Lem, Stanislaw 1921- .... CLC 8, 15, 40
See also CA 105; CAAS 1; CANR 32;
MTCW

Lemann, Nancy 1956-.............. CLC 39
See also CA 118; 136

Lemonnier, (Antoine Louis) Camille
1844-1913 .... TCLC 22
See also CA 121

Lenau, Nikolaus 1802-1850 ...... NCLC 16

L'Engle, Madeleine (Camp Franklin)
1918- .... CLC 12
See also AAYA 1; AITN 2; CA 1-4R;
CANR 3, 21, 39; CLR 1, 14; DLB 52;
MAICYA; MTCW; SATA 1, 27

Lengyel, Jozsef 1896-1975.......... CLC 7
See also CA 85-88; 57-60

Lennon, John (Ono)
1940-1980 .... CLC 12, 35
See also CA 102

Lennox, Charlotte Ramsay
1729(?)-1804 .... NCLC 23
See also DLB 39

Lentricchia, Frank (Jr.) 1940-...... CLC 34
See also CA 25-28R; CANR 19

Lenz, Siegfried 1926- .... CLC 27
See also CA 89-92; DLB 75

Leonard, Elmore (John Jr.)
1925- .... CLC 28, 34, 71
See also AITN 1; BEST 89:1, 90:4;
CA 81-84; CANR 12, 28; MTCW

Leonard, Hugh
See Byrne, John Keyes
See also DLB 13

**Leopardi, (Conte) Giacomo (Talegardo
Francesco di Sales Save**
1798-1837 .... NCLC 22

Le Reveler
See Artaud, Antonin

Lerman, Eleanor 1952-............. CLC 9
See also CA 85-88

Lerman, Rhoda 1936-............. CLC 56
See also CA 49-52

Lermontov, Mikhail Yuryevich
1814-1841 .... NCLC 5

Leroux, Gaston 1868-1927........ TCLC 25
See also CA 108; 136; SATA 65

Lesage, Alain-Rene 1668-1747........ LC 2

Leskov, Nikolai (Semyonovich)
1831-1895 .... NCLC 25

Lessing, Doris (May)
1919- .... CLC 1, 2, 3, 6, 10, 15, 22, 40;
SSC 6
See also CA 9-12R; CAAS 14; CANR 33;
CDBLB 1960 to Present; DLB 15;
DLBY 85; MTCW

Lessing, Gotthold Ephraim
1729-1781 .... LC 8
See also DLB 97

Lester, Richard 1932-............. CLC 20

Lever, Charles (James)
1806-1872 .... NCLC 23
See also DLB 21

Leverson, Ada 1865(?)-1936(?) .... TCLC 18
See also Elaine
See also CA 117

Levertov, Denise
1923- ...... CLC 1, 2, 3, 5, 8, 15, 28, 66
See also CA 1-4R; CANR 3, 29; DLB 5;
MTCW

Levi, Peter (Chad Tigar) 1931-..... CLC 41
See also CA 5-8R; CANR 34; DLB 40

Levi, Primo 1919-1987........ CLC 37, 50
See also CA 13-16R; 122; CANR 12, 33;
MTCW

Levin, Ira 1929- .... CLC 3, 6
See also CA 21-24R; CANR 17; MTCW;
SATA 66

Levin, Meyer 1905-1981 .... CLC 7
See also AITN 1; CA 9-12R; 104;
CANR 15; DLB 9, 28; DLBY 81;
SATA 21, 27

Levine, Norman 1924- .... CLC 54
See also CA 73-76; CANR 14; DLB 88

Levine, Philip 1928-.. CLC 2, 4, 5, 9, 14, 33
See also CA 9-12R; CANR 9, 37; DLB 5

Levinson, Deirdre 1931-........... CLC 49
See also CA 73-76

Levi-Strauss, Claude 1908- .... CLC 38
See also CA 1-4R; CANR 6, 32; MTCW

Levitin, Sonia (Wolff) 1934- .... CLC 17
See also CA 29-32R; CANR 14, 32;
MAICYA; SAAS 2; SATA 4, 68

Levon, O. U.
See Kesey, Ken (Elton)

Lewes, George Henry
1817-1878 .... NCLC 25
See also DLB 55

Lewis, Alun 1915-1944............ TCLC 3
See also CA 104; DLB 20

Lewis, C. Day
See Day Lewis, C(ecil)

Lewis, C(live) S(taples)
1898-1963 .... CLC 1, 3, 6, 14, 27
See also AAYA 3; CA 81-84; CANR 33;
CDBLB 1945-1960; CLR 3, 27; DLB 15,
100; MAICYA; MTCW; SATA 13; WLC

Lewis, Janet 1899-.............. CLC 41
See also Winters, Janet Lewis
See also CA 9-12R; CANR 29; CAP 1;
DLBY 87

Lewis, Matthew Gregory
1775-1818 .... NCLC 11
See also DLB 39

Lewis, (Harry) Sinclair
1885-1951 .... TCLC 4, 13, 23, 39
See also CA 104; 133; CDALB 1917-1929;
DLB 9, 102; DLBD 1; MTCW; WLC

Lewis, (Percy) Wyndham
1884(?)-1957 .... TCLC 2, 9
See also CA 104; DLB 15

Lewisohn, Ludwig 1883-1955...... TCLC 19
See also CA 107; DLB 4, 9, 28, 102

Lezama Lima, Jose 1910-1976 ... CLC 4, 10
See also CA 77-80; DLB 113; HW

L'Heureux, John (Clarke) 1934-.... CLC 52
See also CA 13-16R; CANR 23

Liddell, C. H.
See Kuttner, Henry

Lie, Jonas (Lauritz Idemil)
1833-1908(?) .... TCLC 5
See also CA 115

Lieber, Joel 1937-1971............. CLC 6
See also CA 73-76; 29-32R

Lieber, Stanley Martin
See Lee, Stan

Lieberman, Laurence (James)
1935- .... CLC 4, 36
See also CA 17-20R; CANR 8, 36

Lieksman, Anders
See Haavikko, Paavo Juhani

Li Fei-kan 1904-................. CLC 18
See also CA 105

Lifton, Robert Jay 1926-.......... CLC 67
See also CA 17-20R; CANR 27; SATA 66

Lightfoot, Gordon 1938-.......... CLC 26
See also CA 109

Ligotti, Thomas 1953- .... CLC 44
See also CA 123

Liliencron, (Friedrich Adolf Axel) Detlev von
1844-1909 .... TCLC 18
See also CA 117

Lima, Jose Lezama
See Lezama Lima, Jose

Lima Barreto, Afonso Henrique de
1881-1922 .... TCLC **23**
See also CA 117

Limonov, Eduard................ CLC **67**

Lin, Frank
See Atherton, Gertrude (Franklin Horn)

Lincoln, Abraham 1809-1865..... NCLC **18**

Lind, Jakov .... CLC **1, 2, 4, 27**
See also Landwirth, Heinz
See also CAAS 4

Lindsay, David 1878-1945 .... TCLC **15**
See also CA 113

Lindsay, (Nicholas) Vachel
1879-1931 .... TCLC **17**
See also CA 114; 135; CDALB 1865-1917;
DLB 54; SATA 40; WLC

Linke-Poot
See Doeblin, Alfred

Linney, Romulus 1930- .... CLC **51**
See also CA 1-4R

Li Po 701-763 .... CMLC **2**

Lipsius, Justus 1547-1606 .... LC **16**

Lipsyte, Robert (Michael) 1938-.... CLC **21**
See also AAYA 7; CA 17-20R; CANR 8;
CLR 23; MAICYA; SATA 5, 68

Lish, Gordon (Jay) 1934-.......... CLC **45**
See also CA 113; 117

Lispector, Clarice 1925-1977...... CLC **43**
See also CA 116; DLB 113

Littell, Robert 1935(?)- .... CLC **42**
See also CA 109; 112

Littlewit, Humphrey Gent.
See Lovecraft, H(oward) P(hillips)

Litwos
See Sienkiewicz, Henryk (Adam Alexander
Pius)

Liu E 1857-1909................ TCLC **15**
See also CA 115

Lively, Penelope (Margaret)
1933- .... CLC **32, 50**
See also CA 41-44R; CANR 29; CLR 7;
DLB 14; MAICYA; MTCW; SATA 7, 60

Livesay, Dorothy (Kathleen)
1909- .... CLC **4, 15**
See also AITN 2; CA 25-28R; CAAS 8;
CANR 36; DLB 68; MTCW

Lizardi, Jose Joaquin Fernandez de
1776-1827 .... NCLC **30**

Llewellyn, Richard .... CLC **7**
See also Llewellyn Lloyd, Richard Dafydd
Vivian
See also DLB 15

Llewellyn Lloyd, Richard Dafydd Vivian
1906-1983
See Llewellyn, Richard
See also CA 53-56; 111; CANR 7;
SATA 11, 37

Llosa, (Jorge) Mario (Pedro) Vargas
See Vargas Llosa, (Jorge) Mario (Pedro)

Lloyd Webber, Andrew 1948-
See Webber, Andrew Lloyd
See also AAYA 1; CA 116; SATA 56

Locke, Alain (Le Roy)
1886-1954 .... TCLC **43**
See also BW; CA 106; 124; DLB 51

Locke, John 1632-1704 .... LC **7**
See also DLB 101

Locke-Elliott, Sumner
See Elliott, Sumner Locke

Lockhart, John Gibson
1794-1854 .... NCLC **6**
See also DLB 110, 116

Lodge, David (John) 1935-........ CLC **36**
See also BEST 90:1; CA 17-20R; CANR 19;
DLB 14; MTCW

Loennbohm, Armas Eino Leopold 1878-1926
See Leino, Eino
See also CA 123

Loewinsohn, Ron(ald William)
1937- .... CLC **52**
See also CA 25-28R

Logan, Jake
See Smith, Martin Cruz

Logan, John (Burton) 1923-1987..... CLC **5**
See also CA 77-80; 124; DLB 5

Lo Kuan-chung 1330(?)-1400(?)...... LC **12**

Lombard, Nap
See Johnson, Pamela Hansford

London, Jack........ TCLC **9, 15, 39; SSC 4**
See also London, John Griffith
See also AITN 2; CDALB 1865-1917;
DLB 8, 12, 78; SATA 18; WLC

London, John Griffith 1876-1916
See London, Jack
See also CA 110; 119; MAICYA; MTCW

Long, Emmett
See Leonard, Elmore (John Jr.)

Longbaugh, Harry
See Goldman, William (W.)

Longfellow, Henry Wadsworth
1807-1882 .... NCLC **2**
See also CDALB 1640-1865; DLB 1, 59;
SATA 19

Longley, Michael 1939-.......... CLC **29**
See also CA 102; DLB 40

Longus fl. c. 2nd cent. - .... CMLC **7**

Longway, A. Hugh
See Lang, Andrew

Lopate, Phillip 1943- .... CLC **29**
See also CA 97-100; DLBY 80

Lopez Portillo (y Pacheco), Jose
1920- .... CLC **46**
See also CA 129; HW

Lopez y Fuentes, Gregorio
1897(?)-1966 .... CLC **32**
See also CA 131; HW

Lorca, Federico Garcia
See Garcia Lorca, Federico

Lord, Bette Bao 1938- .... CLC **23**
See also BEST 90:3; CA 107; SATA 58

Lord Auch
See Bataille, Georges

Lord Byron
See Byron, George Gordon (Noel)

Lord Dunsany .... TCLC **2**
See also Dunsany, Edward John Moreton
Drax Plunkett

Lorde, Audre (Geraldine)
1934- .... CLC **18, 71**
See also BLC 2; BW; CA 25-28R;
CANR 16, 26; DLB 41; MTCW

Lorenzo, Heberto Padilla
See Padilla (Lorenzo), Heberto

Loris
See Hofmannsthal, Hugo von

Loti, Pierre .... TCLC **11**
See also Viaud, (Louis Marie) Julien

Louie, David Wong 1954- .... CLC **70**

Louis, Father M.
See Merton, Thomas

Lovecraft, H(oward) P(hillips)
1890-1937 .... TCLC **4, 22; SSC 3**
See also CA 104; 133; MTCW

Lovelace, Earl 1935-............. CLC **51**
See also CA 77-80; MTCW

Lowell, Amy 1874-1925 .... TCLC **1, 8**
See also CA 104; DLB 54

Lowell, James Russell 1819-1891.. NCLC **2**
See also CDALB 1640-1865; DLB 1, 11, 64,
79

Lowell, Robert (Traill Spence Jr.)
1917-1977 ... CLC **1, 2, 3, 4, 5, 8, 9, 11,
15, 37; PC 3**
See also CA 9-12R; 73-76; CABS 2;
CANR 26; DLB 5; MTCW; WLC

Lowndes, Marie Adelaide (Belloc)
1868-1947 .... TCLC **12**
See also CA 107; DLB 70

Lowry, (Clarence) Malcolm
1909-1957 .... TCLC **6, 40**
See also CA 105; 131; CDBLB 1945-1960;
DLB 15; MTCW

Lowry, Mina Gertrude 1882-1966
See Loy, Mina
See also CA 113

Loxsmith, John
See Brunner, John (Kilian Houston)

Loy, Mina .... CLC **28**
See also Lowry, Mina Gertrude
See also DLB 4, 54

Loyson-Bridet
See Schwob, (Mayer Andre) Marcel

Lucas, Craig 1951-............... CLC **64**
See also CA 137

Lucas, George 1944-.............. CLC **16**
See also AAYA 1; CA 77-80; CANR 30;
SATA 56

Lucas, Hans
See Godard, Jean-Luc

Lucas, Victoria
See Plath, Sylvia

Ludlam, Charles 1943-1987 ..... CLC **46, 50**
See also CA 85-88; 122

Ludlum, Robert 1927- .... CLC **22, 43**
See also BEST 89:1; 90:3; CA 33-36R;
CANR 25; DLBY 82; MTCW

Ludwig, Ken..................... CLC **60**

Ludwig, Otto 1813-1865.......... NCLC **4**

Lugones, Leopoldo 1874-1938 . . . . . **TCLC 15**
See also CA 116; 131; HW

Lu Hsun 1881-1936 . . . . **TCLC 3**

Lukacs, George . . . . **CLC 24**
See also Lukacs, Gyorgy (Szegeny von)

Lukacs, Gyorgy (Szegeny von) 1885-1971
See Lukacs, George
See also CA 101; 29-32R

Luke, Peter (Ambrose Cyprian)
1919- . . . . **CLC 38**
See also CA 81-84; DLB 13

Lunar, Dennis
See Mungo, Raymond

Lurie, Alison 1926- . . . . **CLC 4, 5, 18, 39**
See also CA 1-4R; CANR 2, 17; DLB 2;
MTCW; SATA 46

Lustig, Arnost 1926- . . . . **CLC 56**
See also AAYA 3; CA 69-72; SATA 56

Luther, Martin 1483-1546 . . . . **LC 9**

Luzi, Mario 1914- . . . . **CLC 13**
See also CA 61-64; CANR 9

Lynch, B. Suarez
See Bioy Casares, Adolfo; Borges, Jorge
Luis

Lynch, David (K.) 1946- . . . . **CLC 66**
See also CA 124; 129

Lynch, James
See Andreyev, Leonid (Nikolaevich)

Lynch Davis, B.
See Bioy Casares, Adolfo; Borges, Jorge
Luis

Lyndsay, SirDavid 1490-1555 . . . . **LC 20**

Lynn, Kenneth S(chuyler) 1923- . . . **CLC 50**
See also CA 1-4R; CANR 3, 27

Lynx
See West, Rebecca

Lyons, Marcus
See Blish, James (Benjamin)

Lyre, Pinchbeck
See Sassoon, Siegfried (Lorraine)

Lytle, Andrew (Nelson) 1902- . . . . . . **CLC 22**
See also CA 9-12R; DLB 6

Lyttelton, George 1709-1773 . . . . **LC 10**

Maas, Peter 1929- . . . . **CLC 29**
See also CA 93-96

Macaulay, Rose 1881-1958 . . . . . **TCLC 7, 44**
See also CA 104; DLB 36

MaCauley, Stephen 19th cent. (?)- . . **CLC 50**

MacBeth, George (Mann)
1932-1992 . . . . **CLC 2, 5, 9**
See also CA 25-28R; 136; DLB 40; MTCW;
SATA 4; SATO 70

MacCaig, Norman (Alexander)
1910- . . . . **CLC 36**
See also CA 9-12R; CANR 3, 34; DLB 27

MacCarthy, (Sir Charles Otto) Desmond
1877-1952 . . . . **TCLC 36**

MacDiarmid, Hugh . . . . . **CLC 2, 4, 11, 19, 63**
See also Grieve, C(hristopher) M(urray)
See also CDBLB 1945-1960; DLB 20

MacDonald, Anson
See Heinlein, Robert A(nson)

Macdonald, Cynthia 1928- . . . . . . **CLC 13, 19**
See also CA 49-52; CANR 4; DLB 105

MacDonald, George 1824-1905 . . . . . **TCLC 9**
See also CA 106; 137; DLB 18; MAICYA;
SATA 33

Macdonald, John
See Millar, Kenneth

MacDonald, John D(ann)
1916-1986 . . . . **CLC 3, 27, 44**
See also CA 1-4R; 121; CANR 1, 19;
DLB 8; DLBY 86; MTCW

Macdonald, John Ross
See Millar, Kenneth

Macdonald, Ross . . . . . **CLC 1, 2, 3, 14, 34, 41**
See also Millar, Kenneth
See also DLBD 6

MacDougal, John
See Blish, James (Benjamin)

MacEwen, Gwendolyn (Margaret)
1941-1987 . . . . **CLC 13, 55**
See also CA 9-12R; 124; CANR 7, 22;
DLB 53; SATA 50, 55

Machado (y Ruiz), Antonio
1875-1939 . . . . **TCLC 3**
See also CA 104; DLB 108

Machado de Assis, Joaquim Maria
1839-1908 . . . . **TCLC 10**
See also BLC 2; CA 107

Machen, Arthur . . . . **TCLC 4**
See also Jones, Arthur Llewellyn
See also DLB 36

Machiavelli, Niccolo 1469-1527 . . . . . . **LC 8**

MacInnes, Colin 1914-1976 . . . . . . **CLC 4, 23**
See also CA 69-72; 65-68; CANR 21;
DLB 14; MTCW

MacInnes, Helen (Clark)
1907-1985 . . . . **CLC 27, 39**
See also CA 1-4R; 117; CANR 1, 28;
DLB 87; MTCW; SATA 22, 44

Mackenzie, Compton (Edward Montague)
1883-1972 . . . . **CLC 18**
See also CA 21-22; 37-40R; CAP 2;
DLB 34, 100

Mackintosh, Elizabeth 1896(?)-1952
See Tey, Josephine
See also CA 110

MacLaren, James
See Grieve, C(hristopher) M(urray)

Mac Laverty, Bernard 1942- . . . . **CLC 31**
See also CA 116; 118

MacLean, Alistair (Stuart)
1922-1987 . . . . **CLC 3, 13, 50, 63**
See also CA 57-60; 121; CANR 28; MTCW;
SATA 23, 50

MacLeish, Archibald
1892-1982 . . . . **CLC 3, 8, 14, 68**
See also CA 9-12R; 106; CANR 33; DLB 4,
7, 45; DLBY 82; MTCW

MacLennan, (John) Hugh
1907- . . . . **CLC 2, 14**
See also CA 5-8R; CANR 33; DLB 68;
MTCW

MacLeod, Alistair 1936- . . . . **CLC 56**
See also CA 123; DLB 60

MacNeice, (Frederick) Louis
1907-1963 . . . . **CLC 1, 4, 10, 53**
See also CA 85-88; DLB 10, 20; MTCW

MacNeill, Dand
See Fraser, George MacDonald

Macpherson, (Jean) Jay 1931- . . . . . . **CLC 14**
See also CA 5-8R; DLB 53

MacShane, Frank 1927- . . . . **CLC 39**
See also CA 9-12R; CANR 3, 33; DLB 111

Macumber, Mari
See Sandoz, Mari(e Susette)

Madach, Imre 1823-1864 . . . . **NCLC 19**

Madden, (Jerry) David 1933- . . . . **CLC 5, 15**
See also CA 1-4R; CAAS 3; CANR 4;
DLB 6; MTCW

Maddern, Al(an)
See Ellison, Harlan

Madhubuti, Haki R. 1942- . . . . **CLC 6; PC 5**
See also Lee, Don L.
See also BLC 2; BW; CA 73-76; CANR 24;
DLB 5, 41; DLBD 8

Madow, Pauline (Reichberg) . . . . **CLC 1**
See also CA 9-12R

Maepenn, Hugh
See Kuttner, Henry

Maepenn, K. H.
See Kuttner, Henry

Maeterlinck, Maurice 1862-1949 . . . **TCLC 3**
See also CA 104; 136; SATA 66

Maginn, William 1794-1842 . . . . . . **NCLC 8**
See also DLB 110

Mahapatra, Jayanta 1928- . . . . **CLC 33**
See also CA 73-76; CAAS 9; CANR 15, 33

Mahfouz, Naguib (Abdel Aziz Al-Sabilgi)
1911(?)-
See Mahfuz, Najib
See also BEST 89:2; CA 128; MTCW

Mahfuz, Najib . . . . **CLC 52, 55**
See also Mahfouz, Naguib (Abdel Aziz
Al-Sabilgi)
See also DLBY 88

Mahon, Derek 1941- . . . . **CLC 27**
See also CA 113; 128; DLB 40

Mailer, Norman
1923- . . . . . . **CLC 1, 2, 3, 4, 5, 8, 11, 14,
28, 39**
See also AITN 2; CA 9-12R; CABS 1;
CANR 28; CDALB 1968-1988; DLB 2,
16, 28; DLBD 3; DLBY 80, 83; MTCW

Maillet, Antonine 1929- . . . . **CLC 54**
See also CA 115; 120; DLB 60

Mais, Roger 1905-1955 . . . . **TCLC 8**
See also BW; CA 105; 124; MTCW

Maitland, Sara (Louise) 1950- . . . . . . **CLC 49**
See also CA 69-72; CANR 13

Major, Clarence 1936- . . . . **CLC 3, 19, 48**
See also BLC 2; BW; CA 21-24R; CAAS 6;
CANR 13, 25; DLB 33

Major, Kevin (Gerald) 1949- . . . . **CLC 26**
See also CA 97-100; CANR 21, 38;
CLR 11; DLB 60; MAICYA; SATA 32

Maki, James
See Ozu, Yasujiro

Malabaila, Damiano
See Levi, Primo

Malamud, Bernard
1914-1986 . . . . . **CLC 1, 2, 3, 5, 8, 9, 11,
18, 27, 44**
See also CA 5-8R; 118; CABS 1; CANR 28;
CDALB 1941-1968; DLB 2, 28;
DLBY 80, 86; MTCW; WLC

Malcolm, Dan
See Silverberg, Robert

Malherbe, Francois de 1555-1628 . . . . . **LC 5**

Mallarme, Stephane
1842-1898 . . . . **NCLC 4; PC 4**

Mallet-Joris, Francoise 1930- . . . . . . **CLC 11**
See also CA 65-68; CANR 17; DLB 83

Malley, Ern
See McAuley, James Phillip

Mallowan, Agatha Christie
See Christie, Agatha (Mary Clarissa)

Maloff, Saul 1922- . . . . **CLC 5**
See also CA 33-36R

Malone, Louis
See MacNeice, (Frederick) Louis

Malone, Michael (Christopher)
1942- . . . . **CLC 43**
See also CA 77-80; CANR 14, 32

Malory, (Sir) Thomas
1410(?)-1471(?) . . . . **LC 11**
See also CDBLB Before 1660; SATA 33, 59

Malouf, (George Joseph) David
1934- . . . . **CLC 28**
See also CA 124

Malraux, (Georges-)Andre
1901-1976 . . . . . . **CLC 1, 4, 9, 13, 15, 57**
See also CA 21-22; 69-72; CANR 34;
CAP 2; DLB 72; MTCW

Malzberg, Barry N(athaniel) 1939-. . . **CLC 7**
See also CA 61-64; CAAS 4; CANR 16;
DLB 8

Mamet, David (Alan)
1947- . . . . **CLC 9, 15, 34, 46**
See also AAYA 3; CA 81-84; CABS 3;
CANR 15; DLB 7; MTCW

Mamoulian, Rouben (Zachary)
1897-1987 . . . . **CLC 16**
See also CA 25-28R; 124

Mandelstam, Osip (Emilievich)
1891(?)-1938(?) . . . . **TCLC 2, 6**
See also CA 104

Mander, (Mary) Jane 1877-1949. . . **TCLC 31**

Mandiargues, Andre Pieyre de. . . . . . **CLC 41**
See also Pieyre de Mandiargues, Andre
See also DLB 83

Mandrake, Ethel Belle
See Thurman, Wallace (Henry)

Mangan, James Clarence
1803-1849 . . . . **NCLC 27**

Maniere, J.-E.
See Giraudoux, (Hippolyte) Jean

Manley, (Mary) Delariviere
1672(?)-1724 . . . . **LC 1**
See also DLB 39, 80

Mann, Abel
See Creasey, John

Mann, (Luiz) Heinrich 1871-1950. . . **TCLC 9**
See also CA 106; DLB 66

Mann, (Paul) Thomas
1875-1955 . . . **TCLC 2, 8, 14, 21, 35, 44;
SSC 5**
See also CA 104; 128; DLB 66; MTCW;
WLC

Manning, Frederic 1887(?)-1935 . . . **TCLC 25**
See also CA 124

Manning, Olivia 1915-1980 . . . . . . **CLC 5, 19**
See also CA 5-8R; 101; CANR 29; MTCW

Mano, D. Keith 1942- . . . . **CLC 2, 10**
See also CA 25-28R; CAAS 6; CANR 26;
DLB 6

Mansfield, Katherine. . . **TCLC 2, 8, 39; SSC 9**
See also Beauchamp, Kathleen Mansfield
See also WLC

Manso, Peter 1940- . . . . **CLC 39**
See also CA 29-32R

Mantecon, Juan Jimenez
See Jimenez (Mantecon), Juan Ramon

Manton, Peter
See Creasey, John

Man Without a Spleen, A
See Chekhov, Anton (Pavlovich)

Manzoni, Alessandro 1785-1873 . . **NCLC 29**

Mapu, Abraham (ben Jekutiel)
1808-1867 . . . . **NCLC 18**

Mara, Sally
See Queneau, Raymond

Marat, Jean Paul 1743-1793. . . . . **LC 10**

Marcel, Gabriel Honore
1889-1973 . . . . **CLC 15**
See also CA 102; 45-48; MTCW

Marchbanks, Samuel
See Davies, (William) Robertson

Marchi, Giacomo
See Bassani, Giorgio

Marie de France c. 12th cent. -. . . . **CMLC 8**

Marie de l'Incarnation 1599-1672. . . . **LC 10**

Mariner, Scott
See Pohl, Frederik

Marinetti, Filippo Tommaso
1876-1944 . . . . **TCLC 10**
See also CA 107; DLB 114

Marivaux, Pierre Carlet de Chamblain de
1688-1763 . . . . **LC 4**

Markandaya, Kamala . . . . **CLC 8, 38**
See also Taylor, Kamala (Purnaiya)

Markfield, Wallace 1926-. . . . . **CLC 8**
See also CA 69-72; CAAS 3; DLB 2, 28

Markham, Edwin 1852-1940 . . . . . . **TCLC 47**
See also DLB 54

Markham, Robert
See Amis, Kingsley (William)

Marks, J
See Highwater, Jamake (Mamake)

Marks-Highwater, J
See Highwater, Jamake (Mamake)

Markson, David M(errill) 1927- . . . . **CLC 67**
See also CA 49-52; CANR 1

Marley, Bob. . . . . **CLC 17**
See also Marley, Robert Nesta

Marley, Robert Nesta 1945-1981
See Marley, Bob
See also CA 107; 103

Marlowe, Christopher 1564-1593 . . . . . **DC 1**
See also CDBLB Before 1660; DLB 62;
WLC

Marmontel, Jean-Francois
1723-1799 . . . . **LC 2**

Marquand, John P(hillips)
1893-1960 . . . . **CLC 2, 10**
See also CA 85-88; DLB 9, 102

Marquez, Gabriel (Jose) Garcia. . . . . **CLC 68**
See also Garcia Marquez, Gabriel (Jose)

Marquis, Don(ald Robert Perry)
1878-1937 . . . . **TCLC 7**
See also CA 104; DLB 11, 25

Marric, J. J.
See Creasey, John

Marrow, Bernard
See Moore, Brian

Marryat, Frederick 1792-1848 . . . . **NCLC 3**
See also DLB 21

Marsden, James
See Creasey, John

Marsh, (Edith) Ngaio
1899-1982 . . . . **CLC 7, 53**
See also CA 9-12R; CANR 6; DLB 77;
MTCW

Marshall, Garry 1934-. . . . . **CLC 17**
See also AAYA 3; CA 111; SATA 60

Marshall, Paule 1929- . . **CLC 27, 72; SSC 3**
See also BLC 3; BW; CA 77-80; CANR 25;
DLB 33; MTCW

Marsten, Richard
See Hunter, Evan

Martha, Henry
See Harris, Mark

Martin, Ken
See Hubbard, L(afayette) Ron(ald)

Martin, Richard
See Creasey, John

Martin, Steve 1945-. . . . . **CLC 30**
See also CA 97-100; CANR 30; MTCW

Martin, Webber
See Silverberg, Robert

Martin du Gard, Roger
1881-1958 . . . . **TCLC 24**
See also CA 118; DLB 65

Martineau, Harriet 1802-1876. . . . **NCLC 26**
See also DLB 21, 55; YABC 2

Martines, Julia
See O'Faolain, Julia

Martinez, Jacinto Benavente y
See Benavente (y Martinez), Jacinto

Martinez Ruiz, Jose 1873-1967
See Azorin; Ruiz, Jose Martinez
See also CA 93-96; HW

Martinez Sierra, Gregorio
1881-1947 . . . . **TCLC 6**
See also CA 115

Martinez Sierra, Maria (de la O'LeJarraga)
1874-1974 . . . . **TCLC 6**
See also CA 115

Martinsen, Martin
See Follett, Ken(neth Martin)

Martinson, Harry (Edmund)
1904-1978 .... CLC 14
See also CA 77-80; CANR 34

Marut, Ret
See Traven, B.

Marut, Robert
See Traven, B.

Marvell, Andrew 1621-1678......... LC 4
See also CDBLB 1660-1789; WLC

Marx, Karl (Heinrich)
1818-1883 .... NCLC 17

Masaoka Shiki.................. TCLC 18
See also Masaoka Tsunenori

Masaoka Tsunenori 1867-1902
See Masaoka Shiki
See also CA 117

Masefield, John (Edward)
1878-1967 .... CLC 11, 47
See also CA 19-20; 25-28R; CANR 33;
CAP 2; CDBLB 1890-1914; DLB 10;
MTCW; SATA 19

Maso, Carole 19th cent. (?)- .... CLC 44

Mason, Bobbie Ann
1940- .... CLC 28, 43; SSC 4
See also AAYA 5; CA 53-56; CANR 11,
31; DLBY 87; MTCW

Mason, Ernst
See Pohl, Frederik

Mason, Lee W.
See Malzberg, Barry N(athaniel)

Mason, Nick 1945-.............. CLC 35
See also Pink Floyd

Mason, Tally
See Derleth, August (William)

Mass, William
See Gibson, William

Masters, Edgar Lee
1868-1950 .... TCLC 2, 25; PC 1
See also CA 104; 133; CDALB 1865-1917;
DLB 54; MTCW

Masters, Hilary 1928- .... CLC 48
See also CA 25-28R; CANR 13

Mastrosimone, William
19th cent. (?)- .... CLC 36

Mathe, Albert
See Camus, Albert

Matheson, Richard Burton 1926- ... CLC 37
See also CA 97-100; DLB 8, 44

Mathews, Harry 1930-......... CLC 6, 52
See also CA 21-24R; CAAS 6; CANR 18

Mathias, Roland (Glyn) 1915-...... CLC 45
See also CA 97-100; CANR 19; DLB 27

Matsuo Basho 1644-1694........... PC 3

Mattheson, Rodney
See Creasey, John

Matthews, Greg 1949- .... CLC 45
See also CA 135

Matthews, William 1942-......... CLC 40
See also CA 29-32R; CANR 12; DLB 5

Matthias, John (Edward) 1941-...... CLC 9
See also CA 33-36R

Matthiessen, Peter
1927- .... CLC 5, 7, 11, 32, 64
See also AAYA 6; BEST 90:4; CA 9-12R;
CANR 21; DLB 6; MTCW; SATA 27

Maturin, Charles Robert
1780(?)-1824 .... NCLC 6

Matute (Ausejo), Ana Maria
1925- .... CLC 11
See also CA 89-92; MTCW

Maugham, W. S.
See Maugham, W(illiam) Somerset

Maugham, W(illiam) Somerset
1874-1965 .... CLC 1, 11, 15, 67; SSC 8
See also CA 5-8R; 25-28R;
CDBLB 1914-1945; DLB 10, 36, 77, 100;
MTCW; SATA 54; WLC

Maugham, William Somerset
See Maugham, W(illiam) Somerset

Maupassant, (Henri Rene Albert) Guy de
1850-1893 .... NCLC 1; SSC 1
See also WLC

Maurhut, Richard
See Traven, B.

Mauriac, Claude 1914-............. CLC 9
See also CA 89-92; DLB 83

Mauriac, Francois (Charles)
1885-1970 .... CLC 4, 9, 56
See also CA 25-28; CAP 2; DLB 65;
MTCW

Mavor, Osborne Henry 1888-1951
See Bridie, James
See also CA 104

Maxwell, William (Keepers Jr.)
1908- .... CLC 19
See also CA 93-96; DLBY 80

May, Elaine 1932- .... CLC 16
See also CA 124; DLB 44

Mayakovski, Vladimir (Vladimirovich)
1893-1930 .... TCLC 4, 18
See also CA 104

Mayhew, Henry 1812-1887 ...... NCLC 31
See also DLB 18, 55

Maynard, Joyce 1953-............ CLC 23
See also CA 111; 129

Mayne, William (James Carter)
1928- .... CLC 12
See also CA 9-12R; CANR 37; CLR 25;
MAICYA; SAAS 11; SATA 6, 68

Mayo, Jim
See L'Amour, Louis (Dearborn)

Maysles, Albert 1926- .... CLC 16
See also CA 29-32R

Maysles, David 1932-............. CLC 16

Mazer, Norma Fox 1931- .... CLC 26
See also AAYA 5; CA 69-72; CANR 12,
32; CLR 23; MAICYA; SAAS 1;
SATA 24, 67

Mazzini, Guiseppe 1805-1872 .... NCLC 34

Mazzini, Guiseppe 1805-1872 .... NCLC 34

McAuley, James Phillip
1917-1976 .... CLC 45
See also CA 97-100

McBain, Ed
See Hunter, Evan

McBrien, William Augustine
1930- .... CLC 44
See also CA 107

McCaffrey, Anne (Inez) 1926-...... CLC 17
See also AAYA 6; AITN 2; BEST 89:2;
CA 25-28R; CANR 15, 35; DLB 8;
MAICYA; MTCW; SAAS 11; SATA 8,
70

McCann, Arthur
See Campbell, John W(ood Jr.)

McCann, Edson
See Pohl, Frederik

McCarthy, Cormac 1933-........ CLC 4, 57
See also CA 13-16R; CANR 10; DLB 6

McCarthy, Mary (Therese)
1912-1989 ... CLC 1, 3, 5, 14, 24, 39, 59
See also CA 5-8R; 129; CANR 16; DLB 2;
DLBY 81; MTCW

McCartney, (James) Paul
1942- .... CLC 12, 35

McCauley, Stephen 19th cent. (?)- ... CLC 50

McClure, Michael (Thomas)
1932- .... CLC 6, 10
See also CA 21-24R; CANR 17; DLB 16

McCorkle, Jill (Collins) 1958-...... CLC 51
See also CA 121; DLBY 87

McCourt, James 1941-............ CLC 5
See also CA 57-60

McCoy, Horace (Stanley)
1897-1955 .... TCLC 28
See also CA 108; DLB 9

McCrae, John 1872-1918........ TCLC 12
See also CA 109; DLB 92

McCreigh, James
See Pohl, Frederik

McCullers, (Lula) Carson (Smith)
1917-1967 .. CLC 1, 4, 10, 12, 48; SSC 9
See also CA 5-8R; 25-28R; CABS 1, 3;
CANR 18; CDALB 1941-1968; DLB 2, 7;
MTCW; SATA 27; WLC

McCulloch, John Tyler
See Burroughs, Edgar Rice

McCullough, Colleen 1938(?)-...... CLC 27
See also CA 81-84; CANR 17; MTCW

McElroy, Joseph 1930- .... CLC 5, 47
See also CA 17-20R

McEwan, Ian (Russell) 1948- ... CLC 13, 66
See also BEST 90:4; CA 61-64; CANR 14;
DLB 14; MTCW

McFadden, David 1940-.......... CLC 48
See also CA 104; DLB 60

McFarland, Dennis 1950- .... CLC 65

McGahern, John 1934-........ CLC 5, 9, 48
See also CA 17-20R; CANR 29; DLB 14;
MTCW

McGinley, Patrick (Anthony)
1937- .... CLC 41
See also CA 120; 127

McGinley, Phyllis 1905-1978 ...... CLC 14
See also CA 9-12R; 77-80; CANR 19;
DLB 11, 48; SATA 2, 24, 44

McGinniss, Joe 1942-............. CLC 32
See also AITN 2; BEST 89:2; CA 25-28R;
CANR 26

McGivern, Maureen Daly
See Daly, Maureen

McGrath, Patrick 1950-.......... CLC 55
See also CA 136

McGrath, Thomas (Matthew)
1916-1990 .... CLC 28, 59
See also CA 9-12R; 132; CANR 6, 33;
MTCW; SATA 41; SATO 66

McGuane, Thomas (Francis III)
1939- .... CLC 3, 7, 18, 45
See also AITN 2; CA 49-52; CANR 5, 24;
DLB 2; DLBY 80; MTCW

McGuckian, Medbh 1950-......... CLC 48
See also DLB 40

McHale, Tom 1942(?)-1982....... CLC 3, 5
See also AITN 1; CA 77-80; 106

McIlvanney, William 1936-........ CLC 42
See also CA 25-28R; DLB 14

McIlwraith, Maureen Mollie Hunter
See Hunter, Mollie
See also SATA 2

McInerney, Jay 1955- .... CLC 34
See also CA 116; 123

McIntyre, Vonda N(eel) 1948- ..... CLC 18
See also CA 81-84; CANR 17, 34; MTCW

McKay, Claude .... TCLC 7, 41; PC 2
See also McKay, Festus Claudius
See also BLC 3; DLB 4, 45, 51, 117

McKay, Festus Claudius 1889-1948
See McKay, Claude
See also BW; CA 104; 124; MTCW; WLC

McKuen, Rod 1933-............. CLC 1, 3
See also AITN 1; CA 41-44R

McLoughlin, R. B.
See Mencken, H(enry) L(ouis)

McLuhan, (Herbert) Marshall
1911-1980 .... CLC 37
See also CA 9-12R; 102; CANR 12, 34;
DLB 88; MTCW

McMillan, Terry 1951- .... CLC 50, 61

McMurtry, Larry (Jeff)
1936- .... CLC 2, 3, 7, 11, 27, 44
See also AITN 2; BEST 89:2; CA 5-8R;
CANR 19; CDALB 1968-1988; DLB 2;
DLBY 80, 87; MTCW

McNally, Terrence 1939-...... CLC 4, 7, 41
See also CA 45-48; CANR 2; DLB 7

McNamer, Deirdre 1950-.......... CLC 70

McNeile, Herman Cyril 1888-1937
See Sapper
See also DLB 77

McPhee, John (Angus) 1931- ...... CLC 36
See also BEST 90:1; CA 65-68; CANR 20;
MTCW

McPherson, James Alan 1943- ..... CLC 19
See also BW; CA 25-28R; CANR 24;
DLB 38; MTCW

McPherson, William (Alexander)
1933- .... CLC 34
See also CA 69-72; CANR 28

McSweeney, Kerry .... CLC 34

Mead, Margaret 1901-1978....... CLC 37
See also AITN 1; CA 1-4R; 81-84;
CANR 4; MTCW; SATA 20

Meaker, Marijane (Agnes) 1927-
See Kerr, M. E.
See also CA 107; CANR 37; MAICYA;
MTCW; SATA 20, 61

Medoff, Mark (Howard) 1940- ... CLC 6, 23
See also AITN 1; CA 53-56; CANR 5;
DLB 7

Meged, Aharon
See Megged, Aharon

Meged, Aron
See Megged, Aharon

Megged, Aharon 1920-............. CLC 9
See also CA 49-52; CAAS 13; CANR 1

Mehta, Ved (Parkash) 1934-....... CLC 37
See also CA 1-4R; CANR 2, 23; MTCW

Melanter
See Blackmore, R(ichard) D(oddridge)

Melikow, Loris
See Hofmannsthal, Hugo von

Melmoth, Sebastian
See Wilde, Oscar (Fingal O'Flahertie Wills)

Meltzer, Milton 1915-............ CLC 26
See also AAYA 8; CA 13-16R; CANR 38;
CLR 13; DLB 61; MAICYA; SAAS 1;
SATA 1, 50

Melville, Herman
1819-1891 ...... NCLC 3, 12, 29; SSC 1
See also CDALB 1640-1865; DLB 3, 74;
SATA 59; WLC

Menander c. 342B.C.-c. 292B.C.... CMLC 9

Mencken, H(enry) L(ouis)
1880-1956 .... TCLC 13
See also CA 105; 125; CDALB 1917-1929;
DLB 11, 29, 63; MTCW

Mercer, David 1928-1980.......... CLC 5
See also CA 9-12R; 102; CANR 23;
DLB 13; MTCW

Merchant, Paul
See Ellison, Harlan

Meredith, George 1828-1909 ... TCLC 17, 43
See also CA 117; CDBLB 1832-1890;
DLB 18, 35, 57

Meredith, William (Morris)
1919- .... CLC 4, 13, 22, 55
See also CA 9-12R; CAAS 14; CANR 6;
DLB 5

Merezhkovsky, Dmitry Sergeyevich
1865-1941 .... TCLC 29

Merimee, Prosper
1803-1870 .... NCLC 6; SSC 7
See also DLB 119

Merkin, Daphne 1954-............ CLC 44
See also CA 123

Merlin, Arthur
See Blish, James (Benjamin)

Merrill, James (Ingram)
1926- .... CLC 2, 3, 6, 8, 13, 18, 34
See also CA 13-16R; CANR 10; DLB 5;
DLBY 85; MTCW

Merriman, Alex
See Silverberg, Robert

Merritt, E. B.
See Waddington, Miriam
See also CANR 30

Merton, Thomas
1915-1968 .... CLC 1, 3, 11, 34
See also CA 5-8R; 25-28R; CANR 22;
DLB 48; DLBY 81; MTCW

Merwin, W(illiam) S(tanley)
1927- ...... CLC 1, 2, 3, 5, 8, 13, 18, 45
See also CA 13-16R; CANR 15; DLB 5;
MTCW

Metcalf, John 1938-............... CLC 37
See also CA 113; DLB 60

Metcalf, Suzanne
See Baum, L(yman) Frank

Mew, Charlotte (Mary)
1870-1928 .... TCLC 8
See also CA 105; DLB 19

Mewshaw, Michael 1943-.......... CLC 9
See also CA 53-56; CANR 7; DLBY 80

Meyer, June
See Jordan, June

Meyer-Meyrink, Gustav 1868-1932
See Meyrink, Gustav
See also CA 117

Meyers, Jeffrey 1939- .... CLC 39
See also CA 73-76; DLB 111

Meynell, Alice (Christina Gertrude Thompson)
1847-1922 .... TCLC 6
See also CA 104; DLB 19, 98

Meyrink, Gustav .... TCLC 21
See also Meyer-Meyrink, Gustav
See also DLB 81

Michaels, Leonard 1933-........ CLC 6, 25
See also CA 61-64; CANR 21; MTCW

Michaux, Henri 1899-1984 ...... CLC 8, 19
See also CA 85-88; 114

Michelangelo 1475-1564............ LC 12

Michelet, Jules 1798-1874....... NCLC 31

Michener, James A(lbert)
1907(?)- .... CLC 1, 5, 11, 29, 60
See also AITN 1; BEST 90:1; CA 5-8R;
CANR 21; DLB 6; MTCW

Mickiewicz, Adam 1798-1855 ..... NCLC 3

Middleton, Christopher 1926- ...... CLC 13
See also CA 13-16R; CANR 29; DLB 40

Middleton, Stanley 1919-........ CLC 7, 38
See also CA 25-28R; CANR 21; DLB 14

Migueis, Jose Rodrigues 1901-..... CLC 10

Mikszath, Kalman 1847-1910 ..... TCLC 31

Miles, Josephine
1911-1985 .... CLC 1, 2, 14, 34, 39
See also CA 1-4R; 116; CANR 2; DLB 48

Militant
See Sandburg, Carl (August)

Mill, John Stuart 1806-1873 ..... NCLC 11
See also CDBLB 1832-1890; DLB 55

Millar, Kenneth 1915-1983 .... CLC 14
See also Macdonald, Ross
See also CA 9-12R; 110; CANR 16; DLB 2;
DLBD 6; DLBY 83; MTCW

Millay, E. Vincent
See Millay, Edna St. Vincent

Millay, Edna St. Vincent
1892-1950 .... TCLC 4
See also CA 104; 130; CDALB 1917-1929;
DLB 45; MTCW

Miller, Arthur
1915- . . . . . . **CLC 1, 2, 6, 10, 15, 26, 47;**
DC 1
See also AITN 1; CA 1-4R; CABS 3;
CANR 2, 30; CDALB 1941-1968; DLB 7;
MTCW; WLC

Miller, Henry (Valentine)
1891-1980 . . . . . . **CLC 1, 2, 4, 9, 14, 43**
See also CA 9-12R; 97-100; CANR 33;
CDALB 1929-1941; DLB 4, 9; DLBY 80;
MTCW; WLC

Miller, Jason 1939(?)- . . . . **CLC 2**
See also AITN 1; CA 73-76; DLB 7

Miller, Sue 19th cent. (?)- . . . . **CLC 44**
See also BEST 90:3

Miller, Walter M(ichael Jr.)
1923- . . . . **CLC 4, 30**
See also CA 85-88; DLB 8

Millett, Kate 1934- . . . . **CLC 67**
See also AITN 1; CA 73-76; CANR 32;
MTCW

Millhauser, Steven 1943- . . . . **CLC 21, 54**
See also CA 110; 111; DLB 2

Millin, Sarah Gertrude 1889-1968 . . **CLC 49**
See also CA 102; 93-96

Milne, A(lan) A(lexander)
1882-1956 . . . . **TCLC 6**
See also CA 104; 133; CLR 1, 26; DLB 10,
77, 100; MAICYA; MTCW; YABC 1

Milner, Ron(ald) 1938- . . . . **CLC 56**
See also AITN 1; BLC 3; BW; CA 73-76;
CANR 24; DLB 38; MTCW

Milosz, Czeslaw
1911- . . . . **CLC 5, 11, 22, 31, 56**
See also CA 81-84; CANR 23; MTCW

Milton, John 1608-1674 . . . . **LC 9**
See also CDBLB 1660-1789; WLC

Minehaha, Cornelius
See Wedekind, (Benjamin) Frank(lin)

Miner, Valerie 1947- . . . . **CLC 40**
See also CA 97-100

Minimo, Duca
See D'Annunzio, Gabriele

Minot, Susan 1956- . . . . **CLC 44**
See also CA 134

Minus, Ed 1938- . . . . **CLC 39**

Miranda, Javier
See Bioy Casares, Adolfo

Miro (Ferrer), Gabriel (Francisco Victor)
1879-1930 . . . . **TCLC 5**
See also CA 104

Mishima, Yukio
. . . . . . **CLC 2, 4, 6, 9, 27; DC 1; SSC 4**
See also Hiraoka, Kimitake

Mistral, Gabriela. . . . . **TCLC 2**
See also Godoy Alcayaga, Lucila

Mistry, Rohinton 1952- . . . . **CLC 71**

Mitchell, Clyde
See Ellison, Harlan; Silverberg, Robert

Mitchell, James Leslie 1901-1935
See Gibbon, Lewis Grassic
See also CA 104; DLB 15

Mitchell, Joni 1943- . . . . **CLC 12**
See also CA 112

Mitchell, Margaret (Munnerlyn)
1900-1949 . . . . **TCLC 11**
See also CA 109; 125; DLB 9; MTCW

Mitchell, Peggy
See Mitchell, Margaret (Munnerlyn)

Mitchell, S(ilas) Weir 1829-1914 . . **TCLC 36**

Mitchell, W(illiam) O(rmond)
1914- . . . . **CLC 25**
See also CA 77-80; CANR 15; DLB 88

Mitford, Mary Russell 1787-1855 . . **NCLC 4**
See also DLB 110, 116

Mitford, Nancy 1904-1973 . . . . **CLC 44**
See also CA 9-12R

Miyamoto, Yuriko 1899-1951 . . . . . **TCLC 37**

Mo, Timothy (Peter) 1950(?)- . . . . . . **CLC 46**
See also CA 117; MTCW

Modarressi, Taghi (M.) 1931- . . . . . . **CLC 44**
See also CA 121; 134

Modiano, Patrick (Jean) 1945- . . . . . **CLC 18**
See also CA 85-88; CANR 17; DLB 83

Moerck, Paal
See Roelvaag, O(le) E(dvart)

Mofolo, Thomas (Mokopu)
1875(?)-1948 . . . . **TCLC 22**
See also BLC 3; CA 121

Mohr, Nicholasa 1935- . . . . **CLC 12**
See also AAYA 8; CA 49-52; CANR 1, 32;
CLR 22; HW; SAAS 8; SATA 8

Mojtabai, A(nn) G(race)
1938- . . . . **CLC 5, 9, 15, 29**
See also CA 85-88

Moliere 1622-1673 . . . . **LC 10**
See also WLC

Molin, Charles
See Mayne, William (James Carter)

Molnar, Ferenc 1878-1952 . . . . **TCLC 20**
See also CA 109

Momaday, N(avarre) Scott
1934- . . . . **CLC 2, 19**
See also CA 25-28R; CANR 14, 34;
MTCW; SATA 30, 48

Monroe, Harriet 1860-1936 . . . . . . **TCLC 12**
See also CA 109; DLB 54, 91

Monroe, Lyle
See Heinlein, Robert A(nson)

Montagu, Elizabeth 1917- . . . . **NCLC 7**
See also CA 9-12R

Montagu, Mary (Pierrepont) Wortley
1689-1762 . . . . **LC 9**
See also DLB 95, 101

Montague, John (Patrick)
1929- . . . . **CLC 13, 46**
See also CA 9-12R; CANR 9; DLB 40;
MTCW

Montaigne, Michel (Eyquem) de
1533-1592 . . . . **LC 8**
See also WLC

Montale, Eugenio 1896-1981 . . . **CLC 7, 9, 18**
See also CA 17-20R; 104; CANR 30;
DLB 114; MTCW

Montesquieu, Charles-Louis de Secondat
1689-1755 . . . . **LC 7**

Montgomery, (Robert) Bruce 1921-1978
See Crispin, Edmund
See also CA 104

Montgomery, Marion H. Jr. 1925- . . . **CLC 7**
See also AITN 1; CA 1-4R; CANR 3;
DLB 6

Montgomery, Max
See Davenport, Guy (Mattison Jr.)

Montherlant, Henry (Milon) de
1896-1972 . . . . **CLC 8, 19**
See also CA 85-88; 37-40R; DLB 72;
MTCW

Monty Python . . . . **CLC 21**
See also Chapman, Graham; Cleese, John
(Marwood); Gilliam, Terry (Vance); Idle,
Eric; Jones, Terence Graham Parry; Palin,
Michael (Edward)
See also AAYA 7

Moodie, Susanna (Strickland)
1803-1885 . . . . **NCLC 14**
See also DLB 99

Mooney, Edward 1951- . . . . **CLC 25**
See also CA 130

Mooney, Ted
See Mooney, Edward

Moorcock, Michael (John)
1939- . . . . **CLC 5, 27, 58**
See also CA 45-48; CAAS 5; CANR 2, 17,
38; DLB 14; MTCW

Moore, Brian
1921- . . . . **CLC 1, 3, 5, 7, 8, 19, 32**
See also CA 1-4R; CANR 1, 25; MTCW

Moore, Edward
See Muir, Edwin

Moore, George Augustus
1852-1933 . . . . **TCLC 7**
See also CA 104; DLB 10, 18, 57

Moore, Lorrie . . . . **CLC 39, 45, 68**
See also Moore, Marie Lorena

Moore, Marianne (Craig)
1887-1972 . . . **CLC 1, 2, 4, 8, 10, 13, 19,**
47; PC 4
See also CA 1-4R; 33-36R; CANR 3;
CDALB 1929-1941; DLB 45; DLBD 7;
MTCW; SATA 20

Moore, Marie Lorena 1957-
See Moore, Lorrie
See also CA 116; CANR 39

Moore, Thomas 1779-1852 . . . . **NCLC 6**
See also DLB 96

Morand, Paul 1888-1976 . . . . **CLC 41**
See also CA 69-72; DLB 65

Morante, Elsa 1918-1985 . . . . **CLC 8, 47**
See also CA 85-88; 117; CANR 35; MTCW

Moravia, Alberto . . . . **CLC 2, 7, 11, 27, 46**
See also Pincherle, Alberto

More, Hannah 1745-1833 . . . . **NCLC 27**
See also DLB 107, 109, 116

More, Henry 1614-1687 . . . . **LC 9**

More, Sir Thomas 1478-1535 . . . . **LC 10**

Moreas, Jean . . . . **TCLC 18**
See also Papadiamantopoulos, Johannes

Morgan, Berry 1919- . . . . **CLC 6**
See also CA 49-52; DLB 6

Morgan, Claire
See Highsmith, (Mary) Patricia

Morgan, Edwin (George) 1920- ..... **CLC 31**
See also CA 5-8R; CANR 3; DLB 27

Morgan, (George) Frederick
1922- .... **CLC 23**
See also CA 17-20R; CANR 21

Morgan, Harriet
See Mencken, H(enry) L(ouis)

Morgan, Jane
See Cooper, James Fenimore

Morgan, Janet 1945- .... **CLC 39**
See also CA 65-68

Morgan, Lady 1776(?)-1859...... **NCLC 29**
See also DLB 116

Morgan, Robin 1941-.............. **CLC 2**
See also CA 69-72; CANR 29; MTCW

Morgan, Scott
See Kuttner, Henry

Morgan, Seth 1949(?)-1990........ **CLC 65**
See also CA 132

Morgenstern, Christian
1871-1914 .... **TCLC 8**
See also CA 105

Morgenstern, S.
See Goldman, William (W.)

Moricz, Zsigmond 1879-1942 ..... **TCLC 33**

Morike, Eduard (Friedrich)
1804-1875 .... **NCLC 10**

Mori Ogai .... **TCLC 14**
See also Mori Rintaro

Mori Rintaro 1862-1922
See Mori Ogai
See also CA 110

Moritz, Karl Philipp 1756-1793 ...... **LC 2**
See also DLB 94

Morren, Theophil
See Hofmannsthal, Hugo von

Morris, Julian
See West, Morris L(anglo)

Morris, Steveland Judkins 1950(?)-
See Wonder, Stevie
See also CA 111

Morris, William 1834-1896 .... **NCLC 4**
See also CDBLB 1832-1890; DLB 18, 35, 57

Morris, Wright 1910- ... **CLC 1, 3, 7, 18, 37**
See also CA 9-12R; CANR 21; DLB 2;
DLBY 81; MTCW

Morrison, Chloe Anthony Wofford
See Morrison, Toni

Morrison, James Douglas 1943-1971
See Morrison, Jim
See also CA 73-76

Morrison, Jim .... **CLC 17**
See also Morrison, James Douglas

Morrison, Toni 1931-..... **CLC 4, 10, 22, 55**
See also AAYA 1; BLC 3; BW; CA 29-32R;
CANR 27; CDALB 1968-1988; DLB 6,
33; DLBY 81; MTCW; SATA 57

Morrison, Van 1945- .... **CLC 21**
See also CA 116

Mortimer, John (Clifford)
1923- .... **CLC 28, 43**
See also CA 13-16R; CANR 21;
CDBLB 1960 to Present; DLB 13;
MTCW

Mortimer, Penelope (Ruth) 1918-.... **CLC 5**
See also CA 57-60

Morton, Anthony
See Creasey, John

Mosher, Howard Frank .... **CLC 62**

Mosley, Nicholas 1923-........ **CLC 43, 70**
See also CA 69-72; DLB 14

Moss, Howard
1922-1987 .... **CLC 7, 14, 45, 50**
See also CA 1-4R; 123; CANR 1; DLB 5

Motion, Andrew 1952-............ **CLC 47**
See also DLB 40

Motley, Willard (Francis)
1912-1965 .... **CLC 18**
See also BW; CA 117; 106; DLB 76

Mott, Michael (Charles Alston)
1930- .... **CLC 15, 34**
See also CA 5-8R; CAAS 7; CANR 7, 29

Mowat, Farley (McGill) 1921- ..... **CLC 26**
See also AAYA 1; CA 1-4R; CANR 4, 24;
CLR 20; DLB 68; MAICYA; MTCW;
SATA 3, 55

Mphahlele, Es'kia
See Mphahlele, Ezekiel

Mphahlele, Ezekiel 1919-......... **CLC 25**
See also BLC 3; BW; CA 81-84; CANR 26

Mqhayi, S(amuel) E(dward) K(rune Loliwe)
1875-1945 .... **TCLC 25**
See also BLC 3

Mr. Martin
See Burroughs, William S(eward)

Mrozek, Slawomir 1930-........ **CLC 3, 13**
See also CA 13-16R; CAAS 10; CANR 29;
MTCW

Mrs. Belloc-Lowndes
See Lowndes, Marie Adelaide (Belloc)

Mtwa, Percy 19th cent. (?)-........ **CLC 47**

Mueller, Lisel 1924-............. **CLC 13, 51**
See also CA 93-96; DLB 105

Muir, Edwin 1887-1959 .... **TCLC 2**
See also CA 104; DLB 20, 100

Muir, John 1838-1914 .... **TCLC 28**

Mujica Lainez, Manuel
1910-1984 .... **CLC 31**
See also Lainez, Manuel Mujica
See also CA 81-84; 112; CANR 32; HW

Mukherjee, Bharati 1940-......... **CLC 53**
See also BEST 89:2; CA 107; DLB 60;
MTCW

Muldoon, Paul 1951-.......... **CLC 32, 72**
See also CA 113; 129; DLB 40

Mulisch, Harry 1927-............. **CLC 42**
See also CA 9-12R; CANR 6, 26

Mull, Martin 1943-............... **CLC 17**
See also CA 105

Munford, Robert 1737(?)-1783 .... **LC 5**
See also DLB 31

Mungo, Raymond 1946-........... **CLC 72**
See also CA 49-52; CANR 2

Munro, Alice
1931- .... **CLC 6, 10, 19, 50; SSC 3**
See also AITN 2; CA 33-36R; CANR 33;
DLB 53; MTCW; SATA 29

Munro, H(ector) H(ugh) 1870-1916
See Saki
See also CA 104; 130; CDBLB 1890-1914;
DLB 34; MTCW; WLC

Murasaki, Lady .... **CMLC 1**

Murdoch, (Jean) Iris
1919- ...... **CLC 1, 2, 3, 4, 6, 8, 11, 15,
22, 31, 51**
See also CA 13-16R; CANR 8;
CDBLB 1960 to Present; DLB 14;
MTCW

Murphy, Richard 1927-........... **CLC 41**
See also CA 29-32R; DLB 40

Murphy, Sylvia 1937-............. **CLC 34**
See also CA 121

Murphy, Thomas (Bernard) 1935-... **CLC 51**
See also CA 101

Murray, Les(lie) A(llan) 1938- ..... **CLC 40**
See also CA 21-24R; CANR 11, 27

Murry, J. Middleton
See Murry, John Middleton

Murry, John Middleton
1889-1957 .... **TCLC 16**
See also CA 118

Musgrave, Susan 1951- .... **CLC 13, 54**
See also CA 69-72

Musil, Robert (Edler von)
1880-1942 .... **TCLC 12**
See also CA 109; DLB 81

Musset, (Louis Charles) Alfred de
1810-1857 .... **NCLC 7**

My Brother's Brother
See Chekhov, Anton (Pavlovich)

Myers, Walter Dean 1937- .... **CLC 35**
See also AAYA 4; BLC 3; BW; CA 33-36R;
CANR 20; CLR 4, 16; DLB 33;
MAICYA; SAAS 2; SATA 27, 41, 70, 71

Myers, Walter M.
See Myers, Walter Dean

Myles, Symon
See Follett, Ken(neth Martin)

Nabokov, Vladimir (Vladimirovich)
1899-1977 .... **CLC 1, 2, 3, 6, 8, 11, 15,
23, 44, 46, 64**
See also CA 5-8R; 69-72; CANR 20;
CDALB 1941-1968; DLB 2; DLBD 3;
DLBY 80, 91; MTCW; WLC

Nagy, Laszlo 1925-1978........... **CLC 7**
See also CA 129; 112

Naipaul, Shiva(dhar Srinivasa)
1945-1985 .... **CLC 32, 39**
See also CA 110; 112; 116; CANR 33;
DLBY 85; MTCW

Naipaul, V(idiadhar) S(urajprasad)
1932- .... **CLC 4, 7, 9, 13, 18, 37**
See also CA 1-4R; CANR 1, 33;
CDBLB 1960 to Present; DLBY 85;
MTCW

Nakos, Lilika 1899(?)-............ **CLC 29**

Narayan, R(asipuram) K(rishnaswami)
1906- . . . . **CLC 7, 28, 47**
See also CA 81-84; CANR 33; MTCW;
SATA 62

Nash, (Frediric) Ogden 1902-1971 . . **CLC 23**
See also CA 13-14; 29-32R; CANR 34;
CAP 1; DLB 11; MAICYA; MTCW;
SATA 2, 46

Nathan, Daniel
See Dannay, Frederic

Nathan, George Jean 1882-1958 . . . **TCLC 18**
See also Hatteras, Owen
See also CA 114

Natsume, Kinnosuke 1867-1916
See Natsume, Soseki
See also CA 104

Natsume, Soseki . . . . **TCLC 2, 10**
See also Natsume, Kinnosuke

Natti, (Mary) Lee 1919-
See Kingman, Lee
See also CA 5-8R; CANR 2

Naylor, Gloria 1950- . . . . **CLC 28, 52**
See also AAYA 6; BLC 3; BW; CA 107;
CANR 27; MTCW

Neihardt, John Gneisenau
1881-1973 . . . . **CLC 32**
See also CA 13-14; CAP 1; DLB 9, 54

Nekrasov, Nikolai Alekseevich
1821-1878 . . . . **NCLC 11**

Nelligan, Emile 1879-1941 . . . . **TCLC 14**
See also CA 114; DLB 92

Nelson, Willie 1933- . . . . **CLC 17**
See also CA 107

Nemerov, Howard (Stanley)
1920-1991 . . . . **CLC 2, 6, 9, 36**
See also CA 1-4R; 134; CABS 2; CANR 1,
27; DLB 6; DLBY 83; MTCW

Neruda, Pablo
1904-1973 . . . . **CLC 1, 2, 5, 7, 9, 28, 62;**
PC 4
See also CA 19-20; 45-48; CAP 2; HW;
MTCW; WLC

Nerval, Gerard de 1808-1855 . . . . . . **NCLC 1**

Nervo, (Jose) Amado (Ruiz de)
1870-1919 . . . . **TCLC 11**
See also CA 109; 131; HW

Nessi, Pio Baroja y
See Baroja (y Nessi), Pio

Neufeld, John (Arthur) 1938- . . . . . . **CLC 17**
See also CA 25-28R; CANR 11, 37;
MAICYA; SAAS 3; SATA 6

Neville, Emily Cheney 1919- . . . . **CLC 12**
See also CA 5-8R; CANR 3, 37; MAICYA;
SAAS 2; SATA 1

Newbound, Bernard Slade 1930-
See Slade, Bernard
See also CA 81-84

Newby, P(ercy) H(oward)
1918- . . . . **CLC 2, 13**
See also CA 5-8R; CANR 32; DLB 15;
MTCW

Newlove, Donald 1928- . . . . **CLC 6**
See also CA 29-32R; CANR 25

Newlove, John (Herbert) 1938- . . . . . **CLC 14**
See also CA 21-24R; CANR 9, 25

Newman, Charles 1938- . . . . **CLC 2, 8**
See also CA 21-24R

Newman, Edwin (Harold) 1919- . . . . **CLC 14**
See also AITN 1; CA 69-72; CANR 5

Newton, Suzanne 1936- . . . . **CLC 35**
See also CA 41-44R; CANR 14; SATA 5

Nexo, Martin Andersen
1869-1954 . . . . **TCLC 43**

Nezval, Vitezslav 1900-1958 . . . . . . **TCLC 44**
See also CA 123

Ngema, Mbongeni 1955- . . . . **CLC 57**

Ngugi, James T(hiong'o) . . . . **CLC 3, 7, 13**
See also Ngugi wa Thiong'o

Ngugi wa Thiong'o 1938- . . . . **CLC 36**
See also Ngugi, James T(hiong'o)
See also BLC 3; BW; CA 81-84; CANR 27;
MTCW

Nichol, B(arrie) P(hillip)
1944-1988 . . . . **CLC 18**
See also CA 53-56; DLB 53; SATA 66

Nichols, John (Treadwell) 1940- . . . . **CLC 38**
See also CA 9-12R; CAAS 2; CANR 6;
DLBY 82

Nichols, Peter (Richard)
1927- . . . . **CLC 5, 36, 65**
See also CA 104; CANR 33; DLB 13;
MTCW

Nicolas, F. R. E.
See Freeling, Nicolas

Niedecker, Lorine 1903-1970 . . . . **CLC 10, 42**
See also CA 25-28; CAP 2; DLB 48

Nietzsche, Friedrich (Wilhelm)
1844-1900 . . . . **TCLC 10, 18**
See also CA 107; 121

Nievo, Ippolito 1831-1861 . . . . **NCLC 22**

Nightingale, Anne Redmon 1943-
See Redmon, Anne
See also CA 103

Nik.T.O.
See Annensky, Innokenty Fyodorovich

Nin, Anais
1903-1977 . . . . . **CLC 1, 4, 8, 11, 14, 60;**
SSC 10
See also AITN 2; CA 13-16R; 69-72;
CANR 22; DLB 2, 4; MTCW

Nissenson, Hugh 1933- . . . . **CLC 4, 9**
See also CA 17-20R; CANR 27; DLB 28

Niven, Larry . . . . **CLC 8**
See also Niven, Laurence Van Cott
See also DLB 8

Niven, Laurence Van Cott 1938-
See Niven, Larry
See also CA 21-24R; CAAS 12; CANR 14;
MTCW

Nixon, Agnes Eckhardt 1927- . . . . . . **CLC 21**
See also CA 110

Nizan, Paul 1905-1940 . . . . **TCLC 40**
See also DLB 72

Nkosi, Lewis 1936- . . . . **CLC 45**
See also BLC 3; BW; CA 65-68; CANR 27

Nodier, (Jean) Charles (Emmanuel)
1780-1844 . . . . **NCLC 19**
See also DLB 119

Nolan, Christopher 1965- . . . . **CLC 58**
See also CA 111

Norden, Charles
See Durrell, Lawrence (George)

Nordhoff, Charles (Bernard)
1887-1947 . . . . **TCLC 23**
See also CA 108; DLB 9; SATA 23

Norman, Marsha 1947- . . . . **CLC 28**
See also CA 105; CABS 3; DLBY 84

Norris, Benjamin Franklin Jr.
1870-1902 . . . . **TCLC 24**
See also Norris, Frank
See also CA 110

Norris, Frank
See Norris, Benjamin Franklin Jr.
See also CDALB 1865-1917; DLB 12, 71

Norris, Leslie 1921- . . . . **CLC 14**
See also CA 11-12; CANR 14; CAP 1;
DLB 27

North, Andrew
See Norton, Andre

North, Captain George
See Stevenson, Robert Louis (Balfour)

North, Milou
See Erdrich, Louise

Northrup, B. A.
See Hubbard, L(afayette) Ron(ald)

North Staffs
See Hulme, T(homas) E(rnest)

Norton, Alice Mary
See Norton, Andre
See also MAICYA; SATA 1, 43

Norton, Andre 1912- . . . . **CLC 12**
See also Norton, Alice Mary
See also CA 1-4R; CANR 2, 31; DLB 8, 52;
MTCW

Norway, Nevil Shute 1899-1960
See Shute, Nevil
See also CA 102; 93-96

Norwid, Cyprian Kamil
1821-1883 . . . . **NCLC 17**

Nosille, Nabrah
See Ellison, Harlan

Nossack, Hans Erich 1901-1978 . . . . . **CLC 6**
See also CA 93-96; 85-88; DLB 69

Nosu, Chuji
See Ozu, Yasujiro

Nova, Craig 1945- . . . . **CLC 7, 31**
See also CA 45-48; CANR 2

Novak, Joseph
See Kosinski, Jerzy (Nikodem)

Novalis 1772-1801 . . . . **NCLC 13**
See also DLB 90

Nowlan, Alden (Albert) 1933-1983 . . **CLC 15**
See also CA 9-12R; CANR 5; DLB 53

Noyes, Alfred 1880-1958 . . . . **TCLC 7**
See also CA 104; DLB 20

Nunn, Kem 19th cent. (?)- . . . . **CLC 34**

Nye, Robert 1939- . . . . **CLC 13, 42**
See also CA 33-36R; CANR 29; DLB 14;
MTCW; SATA 6

Nyro, Laura 1947- . . . . **CLC 17**

Oates, Joyce Carol
1938- . . . . . **CLC 1, 2, 3, 6, 9, 11, 15, 19,
33, 52; SSC 6**
See also AITN 1; BEST 89:2; CA 5-8R;
CANR 25; CDALB 1968-1988; DLB 2, 5;
DLBY 81; MTCW; WLC

O'Brien, E. G.
See Clarke, Arthur C(harles)

O'Brien, Edna
1936- . . . **CLC 3, 5, 8, 13, 36, 65; SSC 10**
See also CA 1-4R; CANR 6; CDBLB 1960
to Present; DLB 14; MTCW

O'Brien, Fitz-James 1828-1862. . . **NCLC 21**
See also DLB 74

O'Brien, Flann. . . . . . . **CLC 1, 4, 5, 7, 10, 47**
See also O Nuallain, Brian

O'Brien, Richard 1942- . . . . **CLC 17**
See also CA 124

O'Brien, Tim 1946-. . . . . **CLC 7, 19, 40**
See also CA 85-88; DLBD 9; DLBY 80

Obstfelder, Sigbjoern 1866-1900. . . **TCLC 23**
See also CA 123

O'Casey, Sean
1880-1964 . . . . **CLC 1, 5, 9, 11, 15**
See also CA 89-92; CDBLB 1914-1945;
DLB 10; MTCW

O'Cathasaigh, Sean
See O'Casey, Sean

Ochs, Phil 1940-1976. . . . . **CLC 17**
See also CA 65-68

O'Connor, Edwin (Greene)
1918-1968 . . . . **CLC 14**
See also CA 93-96; 25-28R

O'Connor, (Mary) Flannery
1925-1964 . . . **CLC 1, 2, 3, 6, 10, 13, 15,
21, 66; SSC 1**
See also AAYA 7; CA 1-4R; CANR 3;
CDALB 1941-1968; DLB 2; DLBY 80;
MTCW; WLC

O'Connor, Frank. . . . . **CLC 23; SSC 5**
See also O'Donovan, Michael John

O'Dell, Scott 1898-1989. . . . . **CLC 30**
See also AAYA 3; CA 61-64; 129;
CANR 12, 30; CLR 1, 16; DLB 52;
MAICYA; SATA 12, 60

Odets, Clifford 1906-1963 . . . . **CLC 2, 28**
See also CA 85-88; DLB 7, 26; MTCW

O'Donnell, K. M.
See Malzberg, Barry N(athaniel)

O'Donnell, Lawrence
See Kuttner, Henry

O'Donovan, Michael John
1903-1966 . . . . **CLC 14**
See also O'Connor, Frank
See also CA 93-96

Oe, Kenzaburo 1935- . . . . **CLC 10, 36**
See also CA 97-100; CANR 36; MTCW

O'Faolain, Julia 1932- . . . . **CLC 6, 19, 47**
See also CA 81-84; CAAS 2; CANR 12;
DLB 14; MTCW

O'Faolain, Sean
1900-1991 . . . . **CLC 1, 7, 14, 32, 70**
See also CA 61-64; 134; CANR 12;
DLB 15; MTCW

O'Flaherty, Liam
1896-1984 . . . . **CLC 5, 34; SSC 6**
See also CA 101; 113; CANR 35; DLB 36;
DLBY 84; MTCW

Ogilvy, Gavin
See Barrie, J(ames) M(atthew)

O'Grady, Standish James
1846-1928 . . . . **TCLC 5**
See also CA 104

O'Grady, Timothy 1951- . . . . **CLC 59**
See also CA 138

O'Hara, Frank 1926-1966 . . . . . **CLC 2, 5, 13**
See also CA 9-12R; 25-28R; CANR 33;
DLB 5, 16; MTCW

O'Hara, John (Henry)
1905-1970 . . . . **CLC 1, 2, 3, 6, 11, 42**
See also CA 5-8R; 25-28R; CANR 31;
CDALB 1929-1941; DLB 9, 86; DLBD 2;
MTCW

O Hehir, Diana 1922- . . . . **CLC 41**
See also CA 93-96

Okigbo, Christopher (Ifenayichukwu)
1932-1967 . . . . **CLC 25**
See also BLC 3; BW; CA 77-80; MTCW

Olds, Sharon 1942-. . . . . **CLC 32, 39**
See also CA 101; CANR 18; DLB 120

Oldstyle, Jonathan
See Irving, Washington

Olesha, Yuri (Karlovich)
1899-1960 . . . . **CLC 8**
See also CA 85-88

Oliphant, Margaret (Oliphant Wilson)
1828-1897 . . . . **NCLC 11**
See also DLB 18

Oliver, Mary 1935-. . . . . **CLC 19, 34**
See also CA 21-24R; CANR 9; DLB 5

Olivier, Laurence (Kerr)
1907-1989 . . . . **CLC 20**
See also CA 111; 129

Olsen, Tillie 1913- . . . . **CLC 4, 13**
See also CA 1-4R; CANR 1; DLB 28;
DLBY 80; MTCW

Olson, Charles (John)
1910-1970 . . . . . **CLC 1, 2, 5, 6, 9, 11, 29**
See also CA 13-16; 25-28R; CABS 2;
CANR 35; CAP 1; DLB 5, 16; MTCW

Olson, Toby 1937- . . . . **CLC 28**
See also CA 65-68; CANR 9, 31

Olyesha, Yuri
See Olesha, Yuri (Karlovich)

Ondaatje, Michael 1943- . . . . **CLC 14, 29, 51**
See also CA 77-80; DLB 60

Oneal, Elizabeth 1934-
See Oneal, Zibby
See also CA 106; CANR 28; MAICYA;
SATA 30

Oneal, Zibby . . . . **CLC 30**
See also Oneal, Elizabeth
See also AAYA 5; CLR 13

O'Neill, Eugene (Gladstone)
1888-1953 . . . . **TCLC 1, 6, 27**
See also AITN 1; CA 110; 132;
CDALB 1929-1941; DLB 7; MTCW;
WLC

Onetti, Juan Carlos 1909- . . . . **CLC 7, 10**
See also CA 85-88; CANR 32; DLB 113;
HW; MTCW

O Nuallain, Brian 1911-1966
See O'Brien, Flann
See also CA 21-22; 25-28R; CAP 2

Oppen, George 1908-1984 . . . . **CLC 7, 13, 34**
See also CA 13-16R; 113; CANR 8; DLB 5

Oppenheim, E(dward) Phillips
1866-1946 . . . . **TCLC 45**
See also CA 111; DLB 70

Orlovitz, Gil 1918-1973. . . . . **CLC 22**
See also CA 77-80; 45-48; DLB 2, 5

Ortega y Gasset, Jose 1883-1955 . . . **TCLC 9**
See also CA 106; 130; HW; MTCW

Ortiz, Simon J(oseph) 1941- . . . . **CLC 45**
See also CA 134; DLB 120

Orton, Joe . . . . **CLC 4, 13, 43**
See also Orton, John Kingsley
See also CDBLB 1960 to Present; DLB 13

Orton, John Kingsley 1933-1967
See Orton, Joe
See also CA 85-88; CANR 35; MTCW

Orwell, George . . . . **TCLC 2, 6, 15, 31**
See also Blair, Eric (Arthur)
See also CDBLB 1945-1960; DLB 15, 98;
WLC

Osborne, David
See Silverberg, Robert

Osborne, George
See Silverberg, Robert

Osborne, John (James)
1929- . . . . **CLC 1, 2, 5, 11, 45**
See also CA 13-16R; CANR 21;
CDBLB 1945-1960; DLB 13; MTCW;
WLC

Osborne, Lawrence 1958- . . . . **CLC 50**

Oshima, Nagisa 1932- . . . . **CLC 20**
See also CA 116; 121

Oskison, John M(ilton)
1874-1947 . . . . **TCLC 35**

Ossoli, Sarah Margaret (Fuller marchesa d')
1810-1850
See Fuller, Margaret
See also SATA 25

Ostrovsky, Alexander
1823-1886 . . . . **NCLC 30**

Otero, Blas de 1916- . . . . **CLC 11**
See also CA 89-92

Otto, Whitney 1955-. . . . . **CLC 70**

Ouida . . . . **TCLC 43**
See also De La Ramee, (Marie) Louise
See also DLB 18

Ousmane, Sembene 1923- . . . . **CLC 66**
See also BLC 3; BW; CA 117; 125; MTCW

Ovid 43B.C.-18th cent. (?). . . **CMLC 7; PC 2**

Owen, Wilfred 1893-1918 . . . . . . **TCLC 5, 27**
See also CA 104; CDBLB 1914-1945;
DLB 20; WLC

Owens, Rochelle 1936-. . . . . **CLC 8**
See also CA 17-20R; CAAS 2; CANR 39

Oz, Amos 1939- . . . **CLC 5, 8, 11, 27, 33, 54**
See also CA 53-56; CANR 27; MTCW

Ozick, Cynthia 1928-...... **CLC 3, 7, 28, 62**
See also BEST 90:1; CA 17-20R; CANR 23;
DLB 28; DLBY 82; MTCW

Ozu, Yasujiro 1903-1963.........**CLC 16**
See also CA 112

Pacheco, C.
See Pessoa, Fernando (Antonio Nogueira)

Pa Chin
See Li Fei-kan

Pack, Robert 1929-...............**CLC 13**
See also CA 1-4R; CANR 3; DLB 5

Padgett, Lewis
See Kuttner, Henry

Padilla (Lorenzo), Heberto 1932-...**CLC 38**
See also AITN 1; CA 123; 131; HW

Page, Jimmy 1944-...............**CLC 12**

Page, Louise 1955-...............**CLC 40**

Page, P(atricia) K(athleen)
1916-.....................**CLC 7, 18**
See also CA 53-56; CANR 4, 22; DLB 68;
MTCW

Paget, Violet 1856-1935
See Lee, Vernon
See also CA 104

Paget-Lowe, Henry
See Lovecraft, H(oward) P(hillips)

Paglia, Camille 1947-.............**CLC 68**

Pakenham, Antonia
See Fraser, Antonia (Pakenham)

Palamas, Kostes 1859-1943........**TCLC 5**
See also CA 105

Palazzeschi, Aldo 1885-1974.......**CLC 11**
See also CA 89-92; 53-56; DLB 114

Paley, Grace 1922-....**CLC 4, 6, 37; SSC 8**
See also CA 25-28R; CANR 13; DLB 28;
MTCW

Palin, Michael (Edward) 1943-.....**CLC 21**
See also Monty Python
See also CA 107; CANR 35; SATA 67

Palliser, Charles 1947-............**CLC 65**
See also CA 136

Palma, Ricardo 1833-1919........**TCLC 29**

Pancake, Breece Dexter 1952-1979
See Pancake, Breece D'J
See also CA 123; 109

Pancake, Breece D'J...............**CLC 29**
See also Pancake, Breece Dexter

Papadiamantis, Alexandros
1851-1911................**TCLC 29**

Papadiamantopoulos, Johannes 1856-1910
See Moreas, Jean
See also CA 117

Papini, Giovanni 1881-1956.......**TCLC 22**
See also CA 121

Paracelsus 1493-1541..............**LC 14**

Parasol, Peter
See Stevens, Wallace

Parfenie, Maria
See Codrescu, Andrei

Parini, Jay (Lee) 1948-..........**CLC 54**
See also CA 97-100; CAAS 16; CANR 32

Park, Jordan
See Kornbluth, C(yril) M.; Pohl, Frederik

Parker, Bert
See Ellison, Harlan

Parker, Dorothy (Rothschild)
1893-1967........**CLC 15, 68; SSC 2**
See also CA 19-20; 25-28R; CAP 2;
DLB 11, 45, 86; MTCW

Parker, Robert B(rown) 1932-.....**CLC 27**
See also BEST 89:4; CA 49-52; CANR 1,
26; MTCW

Parkes, Lucas
See Harris, John (Wyndham Parkes Lucas)
Beynon

Parkin, Frank 1940-..............**CLC 43**

Parkman, Francis Jr. 1823-1893..**NCLC 12**
See also DLB 1, 30

Parks, Gordon (Alexander Buchanan)
1912-.....................**CLC 1, 16**
See also AITN 2; BLC 3; BW; CA 41-44R;
CANR 26; DLB 33; SATA 8

Parnell, Thomas 1679-1718.........**LC 3**
See also DLB 94

Parra, Nicanor 1914-..............**CLC 2**
See also CA 85-88; CANR 32; HW; MTCW

Parson Lot
See Kingsley, Charles

Partridge, Anthony
See Oppenheim, E(dward) Phillips

Pascoli, Giovanni 1855-1912......**TCLC 45**

Pasolini, Pier Paolo
1922-1975...............**CLC 20, 37**
See also CA 93-96; 61-64; MTCW

Pasquini
See Silone, Ignazio

Pastan, Linda (Olenik) 1932-......**CLC 27**
See also CA 61-64; CANR 18; DLB 5

Pasternak, Boris (Leonidovich)
1890-1960..........**CLC 7, 10, 18, 63**
See also CA 127; 116; MTCW; WLC

Patchen, Kenneth 1911-1972...**CLC 1, 2, 18**
See also CA 1-4R; 33-36R; CANR 3, 35;
DLB 16, 48; MTCW

Pater, Walter (Horatio)
1839-1894..................**NCLC 7**
See also CDBLB 1832-1890; DLB 57

Paterson, A(ndrew) B(arton)
1864-1941..................**TCLC 32**

Paterson, Katherine (Womeldorf)
1932-.....................**CLC 12, 30**
See also AAYA 1; CA 21-24R; CANR 28;
CLR 7; DLB 52; MAICYA; MTCW;
SATA 13, 53

Patmore, Coventry Kersey Dighton
1823-1896..................**NCLC 9**
See also DLB 35, 98

Paton, Alan (Stewart)
1903-1988..........**CLC 4, 10, 25, 55**
See also CA 13-16; 125; CANR 22; CAP 1;
MTCW; SATA 11, 56; WLC

Paton Walsh, Gillian 1939-
See Walsh, Jill Paton
See also CANR 38; MAICYA; SAAS 3;
SATA 4

Paulding, James Kirke 1778-1860..**NCLC 2**
See also DLB 3, 59, 74

Paulin, Thomas Neilson 1949-
See Paulin, Tom
See also CA 123; 128

Paulin, Tom......................**CLC 37**
See also Paulin, Thomas Neilson
See also DLB 40

Paustovsky, Konstantin (Georgievich)
1892-1968...................**CLC 40**
See also CA 93-96; 25-28R

Pavese, Cesare 1908-1950.........**TCLC 3**
See also CA 104

Pavic, Milorad 1929-.............**CLC 60**
See also CA 136

Payne, Alan
See Jakes, John (William)

Paz, Gil
See Lugones, Leopoldo

Paz, Octavio
1914-......**CLC 3, 4, 6, 10, 19, 51, 65;
PC 1**
See also CA 73-76; CANR 32; DLBY 90;
HW; MTCW; WLC

Peacock, Molly 1947-.............**CLC 60**
See also CA 103; DLB 120

Peacock, Thomas Love
1785-1866.................**NCLC 22**
See also DLB 96, 116

Peake, Mervyn 1911-1968.......**CLC 7, 54**
See also CA 5-8R; 25-28R; CANR 3;
DLB 15; MTCW; SATA 23

Pearce, Philippa.................**CLC 21**
See also Christie, (Ann) Philippa
See also CLR 9; MAICYA; SATA 1, 67

Pearl, Eric
See Elman, Richard

Pearson, T(homas) R(eid) 1956-....**CLC 39**
See also CA 120; 130

Peck, John 1941-.................**CLC 3**
See also CA 49-52; CANR 3

Peck, Richard (Wayne) 1934-......**CLC 21**
See also AAYA 1; CA 85-88; CANR 19,
38; MAICYA; SAAS 2; SATA 18, 55

Peck, Robert Newton 1928-........**CLC 17**
See also AAYA 3; CA 81-84; CANR 31;
MAICYA; SAAS 1; SATA 21, 62

Peckinpah, (David) Sam(uel)
1925-1984...................**CLC 20**
See also CA 109; 114

Pedersen, Knut 1859-1952
See Hamsun, Knut
See also CA 104; 119; MTCW

Peeslake, Gaffer
See Durrell, Lawrence (George)

Peguy, Charles Pierre
1873-1914.................**TCLC 10**
See also CA 107

Pena, Ramon del Valle y
See Valle-Inclan, Ramon (Maria) del

Pendennis, Arthur Esquir
See Thackeray, William Makepeace

Pepys, Samuel 1633-1703..........**LC 11**
See also CDBLB 1660-1789; DLB 101;
WLC

Percy, Walker
    1916-1990 . . . **CLC 2, 3, 6, 8, 14, 18, 47,**
                                              65
    See also CA 1-4R; 131; CANR 1, 23;
    DLB 2; DLBY 80, 90; MTCW

Perec, Georges   1936-1982 . . . . **CLC 56**
    See also DLB 83

Pereda (y Sanchez de Porrua), Jose Maria de
    1833-1906 . . . . **TCLC 16**
    See also CA 117

Pereda y Porrua, Jose Maria de
    See Pereda (y Sanchez de Porrua), Jose
    Maria de

Peregoy, George Weems
    See Mencken, H(enry) L(ouis)

Perelman, S(idney) J(oseph)
    1904-1979 . . . **CLC 3, 5, 9, 15, 23, 44, 49**
    See also AITN 1, 2; CA 73-76; 89-92;
    CANR 18; DLB 11, 44; MTCW

Peret, Benjamin   1899-1959 . . . . **TCLC 20**
    See also CA 117

Peretz, Isaac Loeb   1851(?)-1915 . . . **TCLC 16**
    See also CA 109

Peretz, Yitzhok Leibush
    See Peretz, Isaac Loeb

Perez Galdos, Benito   1843-1920 . . . **TCLC 27**
    See also CA 125; HW

Perrault, Charles   1628-1703 . . . . **LC 2**
    See also MAICYA; SATA 25

Perry, Brighton
    See Sherwood, Robert E(mmet)

Perse, Saint-John
    See Leger, (Marie-Rene) Alexis Saint-Leger

Perse, St.-John . . . . **CLC 4, 11, 46**
    See also Leger, (Marie-Rene) Alexis
    Saint-Leger

Peseenz, Tulio F.
    See Lopez y Fuentes, Gregorio

Pesetsky, Bette   1932- . . . . **CLC 28**
    See also CA 133

Peshkov, Alexei Maximovich   1868-1936
    See Gorky, Maxim
    See also CA 105

Pessoa, Fernando (Antonio Nogueira)
    1888-1935 . . . . **TCLC 27**
    See also CA 125

Peterkin, Julia Mood   1880-1961 . . . . **CLC 31**
    See also CA 102; DLB 9

Peters, Joan K.   1945- . . . . **CLC 39**

Peters, Robert L(ouis)   1924- . . . . **CLC 7**
    See also CA 13-16R; CAAS 8; DLB 105

Petofi, Sandor   1823-1849 . . . . **NCLC 21**

Petrakis, Harry Mark   1923- . . . . **CLC 3**
    See also CA 9-12R; CANR 4, 30

Petrov, Evgeny . . . . **TCLC 21**
    See also Kataev, Evgeny Petrovich

Petry, Ann (Lane)   1908- . . . . . . **CLC 1, 7, 18**
    See also BW; CA 5-8R; CAAS 6; CANR 4;
    CLR 12; DLB 76; MAICYA; MTCW;
    SATA 5

Petursson, Halligrimur   1614-1674 . . . . **LC 8**

Philipson, Morris H.   1926- . . . . **CLC 53**
    See also CA 1-4R; CANR 4

Phillips, David Graham
    1867-1911 . . . . **TCLC 44**
    See also CA 108; DLB 9, 12

Phillips, Jack
    See Sandburg, Carl (August)

Phillips, Jayne Anne   1952- . . . . . **CLC 15, 33**
    See also CA 101; CANR 24; DLBY 80;
    MTCW

Phillips, Richard
    See Dick, Philip K(indred)

Phillips, Robert (Schaeffer)   1938- . . . **CLC 28**
    See also CA 17-20R; CAAS 13; CANR 8;
    DLB 105

Phillips, Ward
    See Lovecraft, H(oward) P(hillips)

Piccolo, Lucio   1901-1969 . . . . **CLC 13**
    See also CA 97-100; DLB 114

Pickthall, Marjorie L(owry) C(hristie)
    1883-1922 . . . . **TCLC 21**
    See also CA 107; DLB 92

Pico della Mirandola, Giovanni
    1463-1494 . . . . **LC 15**

Piercy, Marge
    1936- . . . . **CLC 3, 6, 14, 18, 27, 62**
    See also CA 21-24R; CAAS 1; CANR 13;
    DLB 120; MTCW

Piers, Robert
    See Anthony, Piers

Pieyre de Mandiargues, Andre   1909-1991
    See Mandiargues, Andre Pieyre de
    See also CA 103; 136; CANR 22

Pilnyak, Boris . . . . **TCLC 23**
    See also Vogau, Boris Andreyevich

Pincherle, Alberto   1907-1990 . . . **CLC 11, 18**
    See also Moravia, Alberto
    See also CA 25-28R; 132; CANR 33;
    MTCW

Pineda, Cecile   1942- . . . . **CLC 39**
    See also CA 118

Pinero, Arthur Wing   1855-1934 . . . **TCLC 32**
    See also CA 110; DLB 10

Pinero, Miguel (Antonio Gomez)
    1946-1988 . . . . **CLC 4, 55**
    See also CA 61-64; 125; CANR 29; HW

Pinget, Robert   1919- . . . . **CLC 7, 13, 37**
    See also CA 85-88; DLB 83

Pink Floyd . . . . **CLC 35**
    See also Barrett, (Roger) Syd; Gilmour,
    David; Mason, Nick; Waters, Roger;
    Wright, Rick

Pinkney, Edward   1802-1828 . . . . . **NCLC 31**

Pinkwater, Daniel Manus   1941- . . . . **CLC 35**
    See also Pinkwater, Manus
    See also AAYA 1; CA 29-32R; CANR 12,
    38; CLR 4; MAICYA; SAAS 3; SATA 46

Pinkwater, Manus
    See Pinkwater, Daniel Manus
    See also SATA 8

Pinsky, Robert   1940- . . . . **CLC 9, 19, 38**
    See also CA 29-32R; CAAS 4; DLBY 82

Pinta, Harold
    See Pinter, Harold

Pinter, Harold
    1930- . . . . . **CLC 1, 3, 6, 9, 11, 15, 27, 58**
    See also CA 5-8R; CANR 33; CDBLB 1960
    to Present; DLB 13; MTCW; WLC

Pirandello, Luigi   1867-1936 . . . . . **TCLC 4, 29**
    See also CA 104; WLC

Pirsig, Robert M(aynard)   1928- . . . **CLC 4, 6**
    See also CA 53-56; MTCW; SATA 39

Pisarev, Dmitry Ivanovich
    1840-1868 . . . . **NCLC 25**

Pix, Mary (Griffith)   1666-1709 . . . . **LC 8**
    See also DLB 80

Plaidy, Jean
    See Hibbert, Eleanor Burford

Plant, Robert   1948- . . . . **CLC 12**

Plante, David (Robert)
    1940- . . . . **CLC 7, 23, 38**
    See also CA 37-40R; CANR 12, 36;
    DLBY 83; MTCW

Plath, Sylvia
    1932-1963 . . . . **CLC 1, 2, 3, 5, 9, 11, 14,
                                17, 50, 51, 62; PC 1**
    See also CA 19-20; CANR 34; CAP 2;
    CDALB 1941-1968; DLB 5, 6; MTCW;
    WLC

Plato   428(?)B.C.-348(?)B.C. . . . . **CMLC 8**

Platonov, Andrei . . . . **TCLC 14**
    See also Klimentov, Andrei Platonovich

Platt, Kin   1911- . . . . **CLC 26**
    See also CA 17-20R; CANR 11; SATA 21

Plick et Plock
    See Simenon, Georges (Jacques Christian)

Plimpton, George (Ames)   1927- . . . . . **CLC 36**
    See also AITN 1; CA 21-24R; CANR 32;
    MTCW; SATA 10

Plomer, William Charles Franklin
    1903-1973 . . . . **CLC 4, 8**
    See also CA 21-22; CANR 34; CAP 2;
    DLB 20; MTCW; SATA 24

Plowman, Piers
    See Kavanagh, Patrick (Joseph)

Plum, J.
    See Wodehouse, P(elham) G(renville)

Plumly, Stanley (Ross)   1939- . . . . . . **CLC 33**
    See also CA 108; 110; DLB 5

Poe, Edgar Allan
    1809-1849 . . . **NCLC 1, 16; PC 1; SSC 1**
    See also CDALB 1640-1865; DLB 3, 59, 73,
    74; SATA 23; WLC

Poet of Titchfield Street, The
    See Pound, Ezra (Weston Loomis)

Pohl, Frederik   1919- . . . . **CLC 18**
    See also CA 61-64; CAAS 1; CANR 11, 37;
    DLB 8; MTCW; SATA 24

Poirier, Louis   1910-
    See Gracq, Julien
    See also CA 122; 126

Poitier, Sidney   1927- . . . . **CLC 26**
    See also BW; CA 117

Polanski, Roman   1933- . . . . **CLC 16**
    See also CA 77-80

Poliakoff, Stephen   1952- . . . . **CLC 38**
    See also CA 106; DLB 13

Police . . . . CLC 26
  See also Copeland, Stewart (Armstrong);
  Summers, Andrew James; Sumner,
  Gordon Matthew

Pollitt, Katha 1949- . . . . CLC 28
  See also CA 120; 122; MTCW

Pollock, Sharon 1936- . . . . CLC 50
  See also DLB 60

Pomerance, Bernard 1940- . . . . CLC 13
  See also CA 101

Ponge, Francis (Jean Gaston Alfred)
  1899-1988 . . . . CLC 6, 18
  See also CA 85-88; 126

Pontoppidan, Henrik 1857-1943 . . . TCLC 29

Poole, Josephine . . . . CLC 17
  See also Helyar, Jane Penelope Josephine
  See also SAAS 2; SATA 5

Popa, Vasko 1922- . . . . CLC 19
  See also CA 112

Pope, Alexander 1688-1744 . . . . LC 3
  See also CDBLB 1660-1789; DLB 95, 101;
  WLC

Porter, Connie 1960- . . . . CLC 70

Porter, Gene(va Grace) Stratton
  1863(?)-1924 . . . . TCLC 21
  See also CA 112

Porter, Katherine Anne
  1890-1980 . . . . . CLC 1, 3, 7, 10, 13, 15,
                        27; SSC 4
  See also AITN 2; CA 1-4R; 101; CANR 1;
  DLB 4, 9, 102; DLBY 80; MTCW;
  SATA 23, 39

Porter, Peter (Neville Frederick)
  1929- . . . . CLC 5, 13, 33
  See also CA 85-88; DLB 40

Porter, William Sydney 1862-1910
  See Henry, O.
  See also CA 104; 131; CDALB 1865-1917;
  DLB 12, 78, 79; MTCW; YABC 2

Portillo (y Pacheco), Jose Lopez
  See Lopez Portillo (y Pacheco), Jose

Post, Melville Davisson
  1869-1930 . . . . TCLC 39
  See also CA 110

Potok, Chaim 1929- . . . . CLC 2, 7, 14, 26
  See also AITN 1, 2; CA 17-20R; CANR 19,
  35; DLB 28; MTCW; SATA 33

Potter, Beatrice
  See Webb, (Martha) Beatrice (Potter)
  See also MAICYA

Potter, Dennis (Christopher George)
  1935- . . . . CLC 58
  See also CA 107; CANR 33; MTCW

Pound, Ezra (Weston Loomis)
  1885-1972 . . . . . CLC 1, 2, 3, 4, 5, 7, 10,
                      13, 18, 34, 48, 50; PC 4
  See also CA 5-8R; 37-40R;
  CDALB 1917-1929; DLB 4, 45, 63;
  MTCW; WLC

Povod, Reinaldo 1959- . . . . CLC 44
  See also CA 136

Powell, Anthony (Dymoke)
  1905- . . . . CLC 1, 3, 7, 9, 10, 31
  See also CA 1-4R; CANR 1, 32;
  CDBLB 1945-1960; DLB 15; MTCW

Powell, Dawn 1897-1965 . . . . CLC 66
  See also CA 5-8R

Powell, Padgett 1952- . . . . CLC 34
  See also CA 126

Powers, J(ames) F(arl)
  1917- . . . . CLC 1, 4, 8, 57; SSC 4
  See also CA 1-4R; CANR 2; MTCW

Powers, John J(ames) 1945-
  See Powers, John R.
  See also CA 69-72

Powers, John R. . . . . CLC 66
  See also Powers, John J(ames)

Pownall, David 1938- . . . . CLC 10
  See also CA 89-92; DLB 14

Powys, John Cowper
  1872-1963 . . . . CLC 7, 9, 15, 46
  See also CA 85-88; DLB 15; MTCW

Powys, T(heodore) F(rancis)
  1875-1953 . . . . TCLC 9
  See also CA 106; DLB 36

Prager, Emily 1952- . . . . CLC 56

Pratt, Edwin John 1883-1964 . . . . . . CLC 19
  See also CA 93-96; DLB 92

Premchand . . . . TCLC 21
  See also Srivastava, Dhanpat Rai

Preussler, Otfried 1923- . . . . CLC 17
  See also CA 77-80; SATA 24

Prevert, Jacques (Henri Marie)
  1900-1977 . . . . CLC 15
  See also CA 77-80; 69-72; CANR 29;
  MTCW; SATA 30

Prevost, Abbe (Antoine Francois)
  1697-1763 . . . . LC 1

Price, (Edward) Reynolds
  1933- . . . . CLC 3, 6, 13, 43, 50, 63
  See also CA 1-4R; CANR 1, 37; DLB 2

Price, Richard 1949- . . . . CLC 6, 12
  See also CA 49-52; CANR 3; DLBY 81

Prichard, Katharine Susannah
  1883-1969 . . . . CLC 46
  See also CA 11-12; CANR 33; CAP 1;
  MTCW; SATA 66

Priestley, J(ohn) B(oynton)
  1894-1984 . . . . CLC 2, 5, 9, 34
  See also CA 9-12R; 113; CANR 33;
  CDBLB 1914-1945; DLB 10, 34, 77, 100;
  DLBY 84; MTCW

Prince, F(rank) T(empleton) 1912- . . CLC 22
  See also CA 101; DLB 20

Prince 1958(?)- . . . . CLC 35

Prince Kropotkin
  See Kropotkin, Peter (Alekseevich)

Prior, Matthew 1664-1721 . . . . LC 4
  See also DLB 95

Pritchard, William H(arrison)
  1932- . . . . CLC 34
  See also CA 65-68; CANR 23; DLB 111

Pritchett, V(ictor) S(awdon)
  1900- . . . . CLC 5, 13, 15, 41
  See also CA 61-64; CANR 31; DLB 15;
  MTCW

Private 19022
  See Manning, Frederic

Probst, Mark 1925- . . . . CLC 59
  See also CA 130

Prokosch, Frederic 1908-1989 . . . . CLC 4, 48
  See also CA 73-76; 128; DLB 48

Prophet, The
  See Dreiser, Theodore (Herman Albert)

Prose, Francine 1947- . . . . CLC 45
  See also CA 109; 112

Proudhon
  See Cunha, Euclides (Rodrigues Pimenta) da

Proust,
  (Valentin-Louis-George-Eugene-)Marcel
  1871-1922 . . . . TCLC 7, 13, 33
  See also CA 104; 120; DLB 65; MTCW;
  WLC

Prowler, Harley
  See Masters, Edgar Lee

Pryor, Richard (Franklin Lenox Thomas)
  1940- . . . . CLC 26
  See also CA 122

Przybyszewski, Stanislaw
  1868-1927 . . . . TCLC 36
  See also DLB 66

Pteleon
  See Grieve, C(hristopher) M(urray)

Puckett, Lute
  See Masters, Edgar Lee

Puig, Manuel
  1932-1990 . . . . CLC 3, 5, 10, 28, 65
  See also CA 45-48; CANR 2, 32; DLB 113;
  HW; MTCW

Purdy, A(lfred) W(ellington)
  1918- . . . . CLC 3, 6, 14, 50
  See also Purdy, Al
  See also CA 81-84

Purdy, Al
  See Purdy, A(lfred) W(ellington)
  See also DLB 88

Purdy, James (Amos)
  1923- . . . . CLC 2, 4, 10, 28, 52
  See also CA 33-36R; CAAS 1; CANR 19;
  DLB 2; MTCW

Pure, Simon
  See Swinnerton, Frank Arthur

Pushkin, Alexander (Sergeyevich)
  1799-1837 . . . . NCLC 3, 27
  See also SATA 61; WLC

P'u Sung-ling 1640-1715 . . . . LC 3

Putnam, Arthur Lee
  See Alger, Horatio Jr.

Puzo, Mario 1920- . . . . CLC 1, 2, 6, 36
  See also CA 65-68; CANR 4; DLB 6;
  MTCW

Pym, Barbara (Mary Crampton)
  1913-1980 . . . . CLC 13, 19, 37
  See also CA 13-14; 97-100; CANR 13, 34;
  CAP 1; DLB 14; DLBY 87; MTCW

Pynchon, Thomas (Ruggles Jr.)
  1937- . . CLC 2, 3, 6, 9, 11, 18, 33, 62, 72
  See also BEST 90:2; CA 17-20R; CANR 22;
  DLB 2; MTCW; WLC

Qian Zhongshu
  See Ch'ien Chung-shu

Qroll
  See Dagerman, Stig (Halvard)

Quarrington, Paul (Lewis) 1953-.... **CLC 65**
See also CA 129

Quasimodo, Salvatore 1901-1968 ... **CLC 10**
See also CA 13-16; 25-28R; CAP 1;
DLB 114; MTCW

Queen, Ellery................... **CLC 3, 11**
See also Dannay, Frederic; Davidson,
Avram; Lee, Manfred B(ennington);
Sturgeon, Theodore (Hamilton); Vance,
John Holbrook

Queen, Ellery Jr.
See Dannay, Frederic; Lee, Manfred
B(ennington)

Queneau, Raymond
1903-1976 .... **CLC 2, 5, 10, 42**
See also CA 77-80; 69-72; CANR 32;
DLB 72; MTCW

Quin, Ann (Marie) 1936-1973 ...... **CLC 6**
See also CA 9-12R; 45-48; DLB 14

Quinn, Martin
See Smith, Martin Cruz

Quinn, Simon
See Smith, Martin Cruz

Quiroga, Horacio (Sylvestre)
1878-1937 .... **TCLC 20**
See also CA 117; 131; HW; MTCW

Quoirez, Francoise 1935-.......... **CLC 9**
See also Sagan, Francoise
See also CA 49-52; CANR 6, 39; MTCW

Raabe, Wilhelm 1831-1910 .... **TCLC 45**

Rabe, David (William) 1940-... **CLC 4, 8, 33**
See also CA 85-88; CABS 3; DLB 7

Rabelais, Francois 1483-1553 .... **LC 5**
See also WLC

Rabinovitch, Sholem 1859-1916
See Aleichem, Sholom
See also CA 104

Radcliffe, Ann (Ward) 1764-1823 .. **NCLC 6**
See also DLB 39

Radiguet, Raymond 1903-1923 .... **TCLC 29**
See also DLB 65

Radnoti, Miklos 1909-1944 .... **TCLC 16**
See also CA 118

Rado, James 1939-.............. **CLC 17**
See also CA 105

Radvanyi, Netty 1900-1983
See Seghers, Anna
See also CA 85-88; 110

Raeburn, John (Hay) 1941-........ **CLC 34**
See also CA 57-60

Ragni, Gerome 1942-1991 .... **CLC 17**
See also CA 105; 134

Rahv, Philip..................... **CLC 24**
See also Greenberg, Ivan

Raine, Craig 1944-.............. **CLC 32**
See also CA 108; CANR 29; DLB 40

Raine, Kathleen (Jessie) 1908- ... **CLC 7, 45**
See also CA 85-88; DLB 20; MTCW

Rainis, Janis 1865-1929 .... **TCLC 29**

Rakosi, Carl..................... **CLC 47**
See also Rawley, Callman
See also CAAS 5

Raleigh, Richard
See Lovecraft, H(oward) P(hillips)

Rallentando, H. P.
See Sayers, Dorothy L(eigh)

Ramal, Walter
See de la Mare, Walter (John)

Ramon, Juan
See Jimenez (Mantecon), Juan Ramon

Ramos, Graciliano 1892-1953 ..... **TCLC 32**

Rampersad, Arnold 1941-......... **CLC 44**
See also CA 127; 133; DLB 111

Rampling, Anne
See Rice, Anne

Ramuz, Charles-Ferdinand
1878-1947 .... **TCLC 33**

Rand, Ayn 1905-1982....... **CLC 3, 30, 44**
See also CA 13-16R; 105; CANR 27;
MTCW; WLC

Randall, Dudley (Felker) 1914-...... **CLC 1**
See also BLC 3; BW; CA 25-28R;
CANR 23; DLB 41

Randall, Robert
See Silverberg, Robert

Ranger, Ken
See Creasey, John

Ransom, John Crowe
1888-1974 .... **CLC 2, 4, 5, 11, 24**
See also CA 5-8R; 49-52; CANR 6, 34;
DLB 45, 63; MTCW

Rao, Raja 1909- .... **CLC 25, 56**
See also CA 73-76; MTCW

Raphael, Frederic (Michael)
1931- .... **CLC 2, 14**
See also CA 1-4R; CANR 1; DLB 14

Ratcliffe, James P.
See Mencken, H(enry) L(ouis)

Rathbone, Julian 1935- .... **CLC 41**
See also CA 101; CANR 34

Rattigan, Terence (Mervyn)
1911-1977 .... **CLC 7**
See also CA 85-88; 73-76;
CDBLB 1945-1960; DLB 13; MTCW

Ratushinskaya, Irina 1954- .... **CLC 54**
See also CA 129

Raven, Simon (Arthur Noel)
1927- .... **CLC 14**
See also CA 81-84

Rawley, Callman 1903-
See Rakosi, Carl
See also CA 21-24R; CANR 12, 32

Rawlings, Marjorie Kinnan
1896-1953 .... **TCLC 4**
See also CA 104; 137; DLB 9, 22, 102;
MAICYA; YABC 1

Ray, Satyajit 1921-.............. **CLC 16**
See also CA 114; 137

Read, Herbert Edward 1893-1968.... **CLC 4**
See also CA 85-88; 25-28R; DLB 20

Read, Piers Paul 1941- ...... **CLC 4, 10, 25**
See also CA 21-24R; CANR 38; DLB 14;
SATA 21

Reade, Charles 1814-1884 .... **NCLC 2**
See also DLB 21

Reade, Hamish
See Gray, Simon (James Holliday)

Reading, Peter 1946-.............. **CLC 47**
See also CA 103; DLB 40

Reaney, James 1926-.............. **CLC 13**
See also CA 41-44R; CAAS 15; DLB 68;
SATA 43

Rebreanu, Liviu 1885-1944 .... **TCLC 28**

Rechy, John (Francisco)
1934-................. **CLC 1, 7, 14, 18**
See also CA 5-8R; CAAS 4; CANR 6, 32;
DLBY 82; HW

Redcam, Tom 1870-1933 .... **TCLC 25**

Reddin, Keith.................... **CLC 67**

Redgrove, Peter (William)
1932-.................... **CLC 6, 41**
See also CA 1-4R; CANR 3, 39; DLB 40

Redmon, Anne.................... **CLC 22**
See also Nightingale, Anne Redmon
See also DLBY 86

Reed, Eliot
See Ambler, Eric

Reed, Ishmael
1938-........ **CLC 2, 3, 5, 6, 13, 32, 60**
See also BLC 3; BW; CA 21-24R;
CANR 25; DLB 2, 5, 33; DLBD 8;
MTCW

Reed, John (Silas) 1887-1920 ...... **TCLC 9**
See also CA 106

Reed, Lou....................... **CLC 21**
See also Firbank, Louis

Reeve, Clara 1729-1807 .... **NCLC 19**
See also DLB 39

Reid, Christopher 1949-........... **CLC 33**
See also DLB 40

Reid, Desmond
See Moorcock, Michael (John)

Reid Banks, Lynne 1929-
See Banks, Lynne Reid
See also CA 1-4R; CANR 6, 22, 38;
CLR 24; MAICYA; SATA 22

Reilly, William K.
See Creasey, John

Reiner, Max
See Caldwell, (Janet Miriam) Taylor
(Holland)

Reis, Ricardo
See Pessoa, Fernando (Antonio Nogueira)

Remarque, Erich Maria
1898-1970 .... **CLC 21**
See also CA 77-80; 29-32R; DLB 56;
MTCW

Remizov, A.
See Remizov, Aleksei (Mikhailovich)

Remizov, A. M.
See Remizov, Aleksei (Mikhailovich)

Remizov, Aleksei (Mikhailovich)
1877-1957 .... **TCLC 27**
See also CA 125; 133

Renan, Joseph Ernest
1823-1892 .... **NCLC 26**

Renard, Jules 1864-1910 .... **TCLC 17**
See also CA 117

Renault, Mary.............. **CLC 3, 11, 17**
See also Challans, Mary
See also DLBY 83

Rendell, Ruth (Barbara) 1930- .. **CLC 28, 48**
  See also Vine, Barbara
  See also CA 109; CANR 32; DLB 87;
  MTCW

Renoir, Jean 1894-1979 . . . . **CLC 20**
  See also CA 129; 85-88

Resnais, Alain 1922- . . . . **CLC 16**

Reverdy, Pierre 1889-1960 . . . . **CLC 53**
  See also CA 97-100; 89-92

Rexroth, Kenneth
   1905-1982 . . . . . . **CLC 1, 2, 6, 11, 22, 49**
  See also CA 5-8R; 107; CANR 14, 34;
  CDALB 1941-1968; DLB 16, 48;
  DLBY 82; MTCW

Reyes, Alfonso 1889-1959 . . . . **TCLC 33**
  See also CA 131; HW

Reyes y Basoalto, Ricardo Eliecer Neftali
  See Neruda, Pablo

Reymont, Wladyslaw (Stanislaw)
   1868(?)-1925 . . . . **TCLC 5**
  See also CA 104

Reynolds, Jonathan 1942- . . . . **CLC 6, 38**
  See also CA 65-68; CANR 28

Reynolds, Joshua 1723-1792 . . . . **LC 15**
  See also DLB 104

Reynolds, Michael Shane 1937- . . . . **CLC 44**
  See also CA 65-68; CANR 9

Reznikoff, Charles 1894-1976 . . . . **CLC 9**
  See also CA 33-36; 61-64; CAP 2; DLB 28,
  45

Rezzori (d'Arezzo), Gregor von
   1914- . . . . **CLC 25**
  See also CA 122; 136

Rhine, Richard
  See Silverstein, Alvin

Rhys, Jean
   1890(?)-1979 . . . . **CLC 2, 4, 6, 14, 19, 51**
  See also CA 25-28R; 85-88; CANR 35;
  CDBLB 1945-1960; DLB 36, 117; MTCW

Ribeiro, Darcy 1922- . . . . **CLC 34**
  See also CA 33-36R

Ribeiro, Joao Ubaldo (Osorio Pimentel)
   1941- . . . . **CLC 10, 67**
  See also CA 81-84

Ribman, Ronald (Burt) 1932- . . . . **CLC 7**
  See also CA 21-24R

Ricci, Nino 1959- . . . . **CLC 70**
  See also CA 137

Rice, Anne 1941- . . . . **CLC 41**
  See also AAYA 9; BEST 89:2; CA 65-68;
  CANR 12, 36

Rice, Elmer (Leopold)
   1892-1967 . . . . **CLC 7, 49**
  See also CA 21-22; 25-28R; CAP 2; DLB 4,
  7; MTCW

Rice, Tim 1944- . . . . **CLC 21**
  See also CA 103

Rich, Adrienne (Cecile)
   1929- . . . . . **CLC 3, 6, 7, 11, 18, 36; PC 5**
  See also CA 9-12R; CANR 20; DLB 5, 67;
  MTCW

Rich, Barbara
  See Graves, Robert (von Ranke)

Rich, Robert
  See Trumbo, Dalton

Richards, David Adams 1950- . . . . . . **CLC 59**
  See also CA 93-96; DLB 53

Richards, I(vor) A(rmstrong)
   1893-1979 . . . . **CLC 14, 24**
  See also CA 41-44R; 89-92; CANR 34;
  DLB 27

Richardson, Anne
  See Roiphe, Anne Richardson

Richardson, Dorothy Miller
   1873-1957 . . . . **TCLC 3**
  See also CA 104; DLB 36

Richardson, Ethel Florence (Lindesay)
   1870-1946
  See Richardson, Henry Handel
  See also CA 105

Richardson, Henry Handel . . . . **TCLC 4**
  See also Richardson, Ethel Florence
  (Lindesay)

Richardson, Samuel 1689-1761 . . . . **LC 1**
  See also CDBLB 1660-1789; DLB 39; WLC

Richler, Mordecai
   1931- . . . . **CLC 3, 5, 9, 13, 18, 46, 70**
  See also AITN 1; CA 65-68; CANR 31;
  CLR 17; DLB 53; MAICYA; MTCW;
  SATA 27, 44

Richter, Conrad (Michael)
   1890-1968 . . . . **CLC 30**
  See also CA 5-8R; 25-28R; CANR 23;
  DLB 9; MTCW; SATA 3

Riddell, J. H. 1832-1906 . . . . **TCLC 40**

Riding, Laura . . . . **CLC 3, 7**
  See also Jackson, Laura (Riding)

Riefenstahl, Berta Helene Amalia 1902-
  See Riefenstahl, Leni
  See also CA 108

Riefenstahl, Leni . . . . **CLC 16**
  See also Riefenstahl, Berta Helene Amalia

Riffe, Ernest
  See Bergman, (Ernst) Ingmar

Riley, Tex
  See Creasey, John

Rilke, Rainer Maria
   1875-1926 . . . . **TCLC 1, 6, 19; PC 2**
  See also CA 104; 132; DLB 81; MTCW

Rimbaud, (Jean Nicolas) Arthur
   1854-1891 . . . . **NCLC 4, 35; PC 3**
  See also WLC

Ringmaster, The
  See Mencken, H(enry) L(ouis)

Ringwood, Gwen(dolyn Margaret) Pharis
   1910-1984 . . . . **CLC 48**
  See also CA 112; DLB 88

Rio, Michel 19th cent. (?)- . . . . **CLC 43**

Ritsos, Giannes
  See Ritsos, Yannis

Ritsos, Yannis 1909-1990 . . . . . **CLC 6, 13, 31**
  See also CA 77-80; 133; CANR 39; MTCW

Ritter, Erika 1948(?)- . . . . **CLC 52**

Rivera, Jose Eustasio 1889-1928 . . . **TCLC 35**
  See also HW

Rivers, Conrad Kent 1933-1968 . . . . . . **CLC 1**
  See also BW; CA 85-88; DLB 41

Rivers, Elfrida
  See Bradley, Marion Zimmer

Riverside, John
  See Heinlein, Robert A(nson)

Rizal, Jose 1861-1896. . . . . **NCLC 27**

Roa Bastos, Augusto (Antonio)
   1917- . . . . **CLC 45**
  See also CA 131; DLB 113; HW

Robbe-Grillet, Alain
   1922- . . . . . . **CLC 1, 2, 4, 6, 8, 10, 14, 43**
  See also CA 9-12R; CANR 33; DLB 83;
  MTCW

Robbins, Harold 1916- . . . . **CLC 5**
  See also CA 73-76; CANR 26; MTCW

Robbins, Thomas Eugene 1936-
  See Robbins, Tom
  See also CA 81-84; CANR 29; MTCW

Robbins, Tom . . . . **CLC 9, 32, 64**
  See also Robbins, Thomas Eugene
  See also BEST 90:3; DLBY 80

Robbins, Trina 1938- . . . . **CLC 21**
  See also CA 128

Roberts, Charles G(eorge) D(ouglas)
   1860-1943 . . . . **TCLC 8**
  See also CA 105; DLB 92; SATA 29

Roberts, Kate 1891-1985 . . . . **CLC 15**
  See also CA 107; 116

Roberts, Keith (John Kingston)
   1935- . . . . **CLC 14**
  See also CA 25-28R

Roberts, Kenneth (Lewis)
   1885-1957 . . . . **TCLC 23**
  See also CA 109; DLB 9

Roberts, Michele (B.) 1949- . . . . **CLC 48**
  See also CA 115

Robertson, Ellis
  See Ellison, Harlan; Silverberg, Robert

Robertson, Thomas William
   1829-1871 . . . . **NCLC 35**

Robertson, Thomas William
   1829-1871 . . . . **NCLC 35**

Robinson, Edwin Arlington
   1869-1935 . . . . **TCLC 5; PC 1**
  See also CA 104; 133; CDALB 1865-1917;
  DLB 54; MTCW

Robinson, Henry Crabb
   1775-1867 . . . . **NCLC 15**
  See also DLB 107

Robinson, Jill 1936- . . . . **CLC 10**
  See also CA 102

Robinson, Kim Stanley 1952- . . . . . . **CLC 34**
  See also CA 126

Robinson, Lloyd
  See Silverberg, Robert

Robinson, Marilynne 1944- . . . . **CLC 25**
  See also CA 116

Robinson, Smokey . . . . **CLC 21**
  See also Robinson, William Jr.

Robinson, William Jr. 1940-
  See Robinson, Smokey
  See also CA 116

Robison, Mary 1949- . . . . **CLC 42**
  See also CA 113; 116

Roddenberry, Eugene Wesley 1921-1991
See Roddenberry, Gene
See also CA 110; 135; CANR 37; SATA 45

Roddenberry, Gene . . . . **CLC 17**
See also Roddenberry, Eugene Wesley
See also AAYA 5; SATO 69

Rodgers, Mary 1931- . . . . **CLC 12**
See also CA 49-52; CANR 8; CLR 20;
MAICYA; SATA 8

Rodgers, W(illiam) R(obert)
1909-1969 . . . . **CLC 7**
See also CA 85-88; DLB 20

Rodman, Eric
See Silverberg, Robert

Rodman, Howard 1920(?)-1985 . . . . . **CLC 65**
See also CA 118

Rodman, Maia
See Wojciechowska, Maia (Teresa)

Rodriguez, Claudio 1934- . . . . **CLC 10**

Roelvaag, O(le) E(dvart)
1876-1931 . . . . **TCLC 17**
See also CA 117; DLB 9

Roethke, Theodore (Huebner)
1908-1963 . . . . . . **CLC 1, 3, 8, 11, 19, 46**
See also CA 81-84; CABS 2;
CDALB 1941-1968; DLB 5; MTCW

Rogers, Thomas Hunton 1927- . . . . . **CLC 57**
See also CA 89-92

Rogers, Will(iam Penn Adair)
1879-1935 . . . . **TCLC 8**
See also CA 105; DLB 11

Rogin, Gilbert 1929- . . . . **CLC 18**
See also CA 65-68; CANR 15

Rohan, Koda . . . . **TCLC 22**
See also Koda Shigeyuki

Rohmer, Eric . . . . **CLC 16**
See also Scherer, Jean-Marie Maurice

Rohmer, Sax . . . . **TCLC 28**
See also Ward, Arthur Henry Sarsfield
See also DLB 70

Roiphe, Anne Richardson 1935- . . . **CLC 3, 9**
See also CA 89-92; DLBY 80

Rolfe, Frederick (William Serafino Austin
Lewis Mary) 1860-1913 . . . . . . **TCLC 12**
See also CA 107; DLB 34

Rolland, Romain 1866-1944 . . . . **TCLC 23**
See also CA 118; DLB 65

Rolvaag, O(le) E(dvart)
See Roelvaag, O(le) E(dvart)

Romain Arnaud, Saint
See Aragon, Louis

Romains, Jules 1885-1972 . . . . **CLC 7**
See also CA 85-88; CANR 34; DLB 65;
MTCW

Romero, Jose Ruben 1890-1952 . . . **TCLC 14**
See also CA 114; 131; HW

Ronsard, Pierre de 1524-1585 . . . . **LC 6**

Rooke, Leon 1934- . . . . **CLC 25, 34**
See also CA 25-28R; CANR 23

Roper, William 1498-1578 . . . . **LC 10**

Roquelaure, A. N.
See Rice, Anne

Rosa, Joao Guimaraes 1908-1967 . . . **CLC 23**
See also CA 89-92; DLB 113

Rosen, Richard (Dean) 1949- . . . . **CLC 39**
See also CA 77-80

Rosenberg, Isaac 1890-1918 . . . . . . **TCLC 12**
See also CA 107; DLB 20

Rosenblatt, Joe . . . . **CLC 15**
See also Rosenblatt, Joseph

Rosenblatt, Joseph 1933-
See Rosenblatt, Joe
See also CA 89-92

Rosenfeld, Samuel 1896-1963
See Tzara, Tristan
See also CA 89-92

Rosenthal, M(acha) L(ouis) 1917- . . . **CLC 28**
See also CA 1-4R; CAAS 6; CANR 4;
DLB 5; SATA 59

Ross, Barnaby
See Dannay, Frederic

Ross, Bernard L.
See Follett, Ken(neth Martin)

Ross, J. H.
See Lawrence, T(homas) E(dward)

Ross, (James) Sinclair 1908- . . . . **CLC 13**
See also CA 73-76; DLB 88

Rossetti, Christina (Georgina)
1830-1894 . . . . **NCLC 2**
See also DLB 35; MAICYA; SATA 20;
WLC

Rossetti, Dante Gabriel
1828-1882 . . . . **NCLC 4**
See also CDBLB 1832-1890; DLB 35; WLC

Rossner, Judith (Perelman)
1935- . . . . **CLC 6, 9, 29**
See also AITN 2; BEST 90:3; CA 17-20R;
CANR 18; DLB 6; MTCW

Rostand, Edmond (Eugene Alexis)
1868-1918 . . . . **TCLC 6, 37**
See also CA 104; 126; MTCW

Roth, Henry 1906- . . . . **CLC 2, 6, 11**
See also CA 11-12; CANR 38; CAP 1;
DLB 28; MTCW

Roth, Joseph 1894-1939 . . . . **TCLC 33**
See also DLB 85

Roth, Philip (Milton)
1933- . . . . . . **CLC 1, 2, 3, 4, 6, 9, 15, 22,**
31, 47, 66
See also BEST 90:3; CA 1-4R; CANR 1, 22,
36; CDALB 1968-1988; DLB 2, 28;
DLBY 82; MTCW; WLC

Rothenberg, Jerome 1931- . . . . **CLC 6, 57**
See also CA 45-48; CANR 1; DLB 5

Roumain, Jacques (Jean Baptiste)
1907-1944 . . . . **TCLC 19**
See also BLC 3; BW; CA 117; 125

Rourke, Constance (Mayfield)
1885-1941 . . . . **TCLC 12**
See also CA 107; YABC 1

Rousseau, Jean-Baptiste 1671-1741 . . . **LC 9**

Rousseau, Jean-Jacques 1712-1778 . . . **LC 14**
See also WLC

Roussel, Raymond 1877-1933 . . . . . **TCLC 20**
See also CA 117

Rovit, Earl (Herbert) 1927- . . . . **CLC 7**
See also CA 5-8R; CANR 12

Rowe, Nicholas 1674-1718 . . . . **LC 8**
See also DLB 84

Rowley, Ames Dorrance
See Lovecraft, H(oward) P(hillips)

Rowson, Susanna Haswell
1762(?)-1824 . . . . **NCLC 5**
See also DLB 37

Roy, Gabrielle 1909-1983 . . . . **CLC 10, 14**
See also CA 53-56; 110; CANR 5; DLB 68;
MTCW

Rozewicz, Tadeusz 1921- . . . . **CLC 9, 23**
See also CA 108; CANR 36; MTCW

Ruark, Gibbons 1941- . . . . **CLC 3**
See also CA 33-36R; CANR 14, 31;
DLB 120

Rubens, Bernice (Ruth) 1923- . . . **CLC 19, 31**
See also CA 25-28R; CANR 33; DLB 14;
MTCW

Rudkin, (James) David 1936- . . . . . . **CLC 14**
See also CA 89-92; DLB 13

Rudnik, Raphael 1933- . . . . **CLC 7**
See also CA 29-32R

Ruffian, M.
See Hasek, Jaroslav (Matej Frantisek)

Ruiz, Jose Martinez . . . . **CLC 11**
See also Martinez Ruiz, Jose

Rukeyser, Muriel
1913-1980 . . . . **CLC 6, 10, 15, 27**
See also CA 5-8R; 93-96; CANR 26;
DLB 48; MTCW; SATA 22

Rule, Jane (Vance) 1931- . . . . **CLC 27**
See also CA 25-28R; CANR 12; DLB 60

Rulfo, Juan 1918-1986 . . . . **CLC 8**
See also CA 85-88; 118; CANR 26;
DLB 113; HW; MTCW

Runyon, (Alfred) Damon
1884(?)-1946 . . . . **TCLC 10**
See also CA 107; DLB 11, 86

Rush, Norman 1933- . . . . **CLC 44**
See also CA 121; 126

Rushdie, (Ahmed) Salman
1947- . . . . **CLC 23, 31, 55**
See also BEST 89:3; CA 108; 111;
CANR 33; MTCW

Rushforth, Peter (Scott) 1945- . . . . . **CLC 19**
See also CA 101

Ruskin, John 1819-1900 . . . . **TCLC 20**
See also CA 114; 129; CDBLB 1832-1890;
DLB 55; SATA 24

Russ, Joanna 1937- . . . . **CLC 15**
See also CA 25-28R; CANR 11, 31; DLB 8;
MTCW

Russell, George William 1867-1935
See A. E.
See also CA 104; CDBLB 1890-1914

Russell, (Henry) Ken(neth Alfred)
1927- . . . . **CLC 16**
See also CA 105

Russell, Willy 1947- . . . . **CLC 60**

Rutherford, Mark . . . . **TCLC 25**
See also White, William Hale
See also DLB 18

Ruyslinck, Ward
  See Belser, Reimond Karel Maria de

Ryan, Cornelius (John) 1920-1974 . . . **CLC 7**
  See also CA 69-72; 53-56; CANR 38

Ryan, Michael 1946- . . . . **CLC 65**
  See also CA 49-52; DLBY 82

Rybakov, Anatoli (Naumovich)
  1911- . . . . **CLC 23, 53**
  See also CA 126; 135

Ryder, Jonathan
  See Ludlum, Robert

Ryga, George 1932-1987 . . . . **CLC 14**
  See also CA 101; 124; DLB 60

S. S.
  See Sassoon, Siegfried (Lorraine)

Saba, Umberto 1883-1957 . . . . **TCLC 33**
  See also DLB 114

Sabatini, Rafael 1875-1950 . . . . **TCLC 47**

Sabato, Ernesto (R.) 1911- . . . . . . **CLC 10, 23**
  See also CA 97-100; CANR 32; HW;
  MTCW

Sacastru, Martin
  See Bioy Casares, Adolfo

Sacher-Masoch, Leopold von
  1836(?)-1895 . . . . **NCLC 31**

Sachs, Marilyn (Stickle) 1927- . . . . . **CLC 35**
  See also AAYA 2; CA 17-20R; CANR 13;
  CLR 2; MAICYA; SAAS 2; SATA 3, 68

Sachs, Nelly 1891-1970 . . . . **CLC 14**
  See also CA 17-18; 25-28R; CAP 2

Sackler, Howard (Oliver)
  1929-1982 . . . . **CLC 14**
  See also CA 61-64; 108; CANR 30; DLB 7

Sacks, Oliver (Wolf) 1933- . . . . **CLC 67**
  See also CA 53-56; CANR 28; MTCW

Sade, Donatien Alphonse Francois Comte
  1740-1814 . . . . **NCLC 3**

Sadoff, Ira 1945- . . . . **CLC 9**
  See also CA 53-56; CANR 5, 21; DLB 120

Saetone
  See Camus, Albert

Safire, William 1929- . . . . **CLC 10**
  See also CA 17-20R; CANR 31

Sagan, Carl (Edward) 1934- . . . . **CLC 30**
  See also AAYA 2; CA 25-28R; CANR 11,
  36; MTCW; SATA 58

Sagan, Francoise . . . . **CLC 3, 6, 9, 17, 36**
  See also Quoirez, Francoise
  See also DLB 83

Sahgal, Nayantara (Pandit) 1927- . . . **CLC 41**
  See also CA 9-12R; CANR 11

Saint, H(arry) F. 1941- . . . . **CLC 50**
  See also CA 127

St. Aubin de Teran, Lisa 1953-
  See Teran, Lisa St. Aubin de
  See also CA 118; 126

Sainte-Beuve, Charles Augustin
  1804-1869 . . . . **NCLC 5**

**Saint-Exupery, Antoine (Jean Baptiste Marie
Roger) de** 1900-1944 . . . . **TCLC 2**
  See also CA 108; 132; CLR 10; DLB 72;
  MAICYA; MTCW; SATA 20; WLC

St. John, David
  See Hunt, E(verette) Howard Jr.

Saint-John Perse
  See Leger, (Marie-Rene) Alexis Saint-Leger

Saintsbury, George (Edward Bateman)
  1845-1933 . . . . **TCLC 31**
  See also DLB 57

Sait Faik . . . . **TCLC 23**
  See also Abasiyanik, Sait Faik

Saki . . . . **TCLC 3**
  See also Munro, H(ector) H(ugh)

Salama, Hannu 1936- . . . . **CLC 18**

Salamanca, J(ack) R(ichard)
  1922- . . . . **CLC 4, 15**
  See also CA 25-28R

Sale, J. Kirkpatrick
  See Sale, Kirkpatrick

Sale, Kirkpatrick 1937- . . . . **CLC 68**
  See also CA 13-16R; CANR 10

Salinas (y Serrano), Pedro
  1891(?)-1951 . . . . **TCLC 17**
  See also CA 117

Salinger, J(erome) D(avid)
  1919- . . . . **CLC 1, 3, 8, 12, 55, 56; SSC 2**
  See also AAYA 2; CA 5-8R; CANR 39;
  CDALB 1941-1968; CLR 18; DLB 2, 102;
  MAICYA; MTCW; SATA 67; WLC

Salisbury, John
  See Caute, David

Salter, James 1925- . . . . **CLC 7, 52, 59**
  See also CA 73-76

Saltus, Edgar (Everton)
  1855-1921 . . . . **TCLC 8**
  See also CA 105

Saltykov, Mikhail Evgrafovich
  1826-1889 . . . . **NCLC 16**

Samarakis, Antonis 1919- . . . . **CLC 5**
  See also CA 25-28R; CAAS 16; CANR 36

Sanchez, Florencio 1875-1910 . . . . . **TCLC 37**
  See also HW

Sanchez, Luis Rafael 1936- . . . . **CLC 23**
  See also CA 128; HW

Sanchez, Sonia 1934- . . . . **CLC 5**
  See also BLC 3; BW; CA 33-36R;
  CANR 24; CLR 18; DLB 41; DLBD 8;
  MAICYA; MTCW; SATA 22

Sand, George 1804-1876 . . . . **NCLC 2**
  See also DLB 119; WLC

Sandburg, Carl (August)
  1878-1967 . . . **CLC 1, 4, 10, 15, 35; PC 2**
  See also CA 5-8R; 25-28R; CANR 35;
  CDALB 1865-1917; DLB 17, 54;
  MAICYA; MTCW; SATA 8; WLC

Sandburg, Charles
  See Sandburg, Carl (August)

Sandburg, Charles A.
  See Sandburg, Carl (August)

Sanders, (James) Ed(ward) 1939- . . . **CLC 53**
  See also CA 13-16R; CANR 13; DLB 16

Sanders, Lawrence 1920- . . . . **CLC 41**
  See also BEST 89:4; CA 81-84; CANR 33;
  MTCW

Sanders, Noah
  See Blount, Roy (Alton) Jr.

Sanders, Winston P.
  See Anderson, Poul (William)

Sandoz, Mari(e Susette)
  1896-1966 . . . . **CLC 28**
  See also CA 1-4R; 25-28R; CANR 17;
  DLB 9; MTCW; SATA 5

Saner, Reg(inald Anthony) 1931- . . . . **CLC 9**
  See also CA 65-68

Sannazaro, Jacopo 1456(?)-1530 . . . . . . **LC 8**

Sansom, William 1912-1976 . . . . **CLC 2, 6**
  See also CA 5-8R; 65-68; MTCW

Santayana, George 1863-1952 . . . . . **TCLC 40**
  See also CA 115; DLB 54, 71

Santiago, Danny . . . . **CLC 33**
  See also James, Daniel (Lewis)

Santmyer, Helen Hooven
  1895-1986 . . . . **CLC 33**
  See also CA 1-4R; 118; CANR 15, 33;
  DLBY 84; MTCW

Santos, Bienvenido N(uqui) 1911- . . . **CLC 22**
  See also CA 101; CANR 19

Sapper . . . . **TCLC 44**
  See also McNeile, Herman Cyril

Sappho fl. 6th cent. B.C.- . . . . **CMLC 3; PC 5**

Sarduy, Severo 1937- . . . . **CLC 6**
  See also CA 89-92; DLB 113; HW

Sargeson, Frank 1903-1982 . . . . **CLC 31**
  See also CA 25-28R; 106; CANR 38

Sarmiento, Felix Ruben Garcia 1867-1916
  See Dario, Ruben
  See also CA 104

Saroyan, William
  1908-1981 . . . . . **CLC 1, 8, 10, 29, 34, 56**
  See also CA 5-8R; 103; CANR 30; DLB 7,
  9, 86; DLBY 81; MTCW; SATA 23, 24;
  WLC

Sarraute, Nathalie
  1900- . . . . **CLC 1, 2, 4, 8, 10, 31**
  See also CA 9-12R; CANR 23; DLB 83;
  MTCW

Sarton, (Eleanor) May
  1912- . . . . **CLC 4, 14, 49**
  See also CA 1-4R; CANR 1, 34; DLB 48;
  DLBY 81; MTCW; SATA 36

Sartre, Jean-Paul
  1905-1980 . . . **CLC 1, 4, 7, 9, 13, 18, 24,
                      44, 50, 52**
  See also CA 9-12R; 97-100; CANR 21;
  DLB 72; MTCW; WLC

Sassoon, Siegfried (Lorraine)
  1886-1967 . . . . **CLC 36**
  See also CA 104; 25-28R; CANR 36;
  DLB 20; MTCW

Satterfield, Charles
  See Pohl, Frederik

Saul, John (W. III) 1942- . . . . **CLC 46**
  See also BEST 90:4; CA 81-84; CANR 16

Saunders, Caleb
  See Heinlein, Robert A(nson)

Saura (Atares), Carlos 1932- . . . . **CLC 20**
  See also CA 114; 131; HW

Sauser-Hall, Frederic 1887-1961 . . . . **CLC 18**
  See also CA 102; 93-96; CANR 36; MTCW

Savage, Catharine
See Brosman, Catharine Savage

Savage, Thomas 1915- . . . . **CLC 40**
See also CA 126; 132; CAAS 15

Savan, Glenn . . . . **CLC 50**

Saven, Glenn 19th cent. (?)- . . . . **CLC 50**

Sayers, Dorothy L(eigh)
1893-1957 . . . . **TCLC 2, 15**
See also CA 104; 119; CDBLB 1914-1945;
DLB 10, 36, 77, 100; MTCW

Sayers, Valerie 1952- . . . . **CLC 50**
See also CA 134

Sayles, John Thomas 1950- . . . **CLC 7, 10, 14**
See also CA 57-60; DLB 44

Scammell, Michael . . . . **CLC 34**

Scannell, Vernon 1922- . . . . **CLC 49**
See also CA 5-8R; CANR 8, 24; DLB 27;
SATA 59

Scarlett, Susan
See Streatfeild, (Mary) Noel

Schaeffer, Susan Fromberg
1941- . . . . **CLC 6, 11, 22**
See also CA 49-52; CANR 18; DLB 28;
MTCW; SATA 22

Schary, Jill
See Robinson, Jill

Schell, Jonathan 1943- . . . . **CLC 35**
See also CA 73-76; CANR 12

Schelling, Friedrich Wilhelm Joseph von
1775-1854 . . . . **NCLC 30**
See also DLB 90

Scherer, Jean-Marie Maurice 1920-
See Rohmer, Eric
See also CA 110

Schevill, James (Erwin) 1920- . . . . **CLC 7**
See also CA 5-8R; CAAS 12

Schisgal, Murray (Joseph) 1926- . . . . . **CLC 6**
See also CA 21-24R

Schlee, Ann 1934- . . . . **CLC 35**
See also CA 101; CANR 29; SATA 36, 44

Schlegel, August Wilhelm von
1767-1845 . . . . **NCLC 15**
See also DLB 94

Schlegel, Johann Elias (von)
1719(?)-1749 . . . . **LC 5**

Schmidt, Arno (Otto) 1914-1979 . . . . **CLC 56**
See also CA 128; 109; DLB 69

Schmitz, Aron Hector 1861-1928
See Svevo, Italo
See also CA 104; 122; MTCW

Schnackenberg, Gjertrud 1953- . . . . . **CLC 40**
See also CA 116; DLB 120

Schneider, Leonard Alfred 1925-1966
See Bruce, Lenny
See also CA 89-92

Schnitzler, Arthur 1862-1931 . . . . . . **TCLC 4**
See also CA 104; DLB 81, 118

Schor, Sandra (M.) 1932(?)-1990 . . . **CLC 65**
See also CA 132

Schorer, Mark 1908-1977 . . . . **CLC 9**
See also CA 5-8R; 73-76; CANR 7;
DLB 103

Schrader, Paul Joseph 1946- . . . . **CLC 26**
See also CA 37-40R; DLB 44

Schreiner, Olive (Emilie Albertina)
1855-1920 . . . . **TCLC 9**
See also CA 105; DLB 18

Schulberg, Budd (Wilson)
1914- . . . . **CLC 7, 48**
See also CA 25-28R; CANR 19; DLB 6, 26,
28; DLBY 81

Schulz, Bruno 1892-1942 . . . . **TCLC 5**
See also CA 115; 123

Schulz, Charles M(onroe) 1922- . . . . **CLC 12**
See also CA 9-12R; CANR 6; SATA 10

Schuyler, James Marcus
1923-1991 . . . . **CLC 5, 23**
See also CA 101; 134; DLB 5

Schwartz, Delmore (David)
1913-1966 . . . . **CLC 2, 4, 10, 45**
See also CA 17-18; 25-28R; CANR 35;
CAP 2; DLB 28, 48; MTCW

Schwartz, Ernst
See Ozu, Yasujiro

Schwartz, John Burnham 1965- . . . . **CLC 59**
See also CA 132

Schwartz, Lynne Sharon 1939- . . . . . **CLC 31**
See also CA 103

Schwartz, Muriel A.
See Eliot, T(homas) S(tearns)

Schwarz-Bart, Andre 1928- . . . . **CLC 2, 4**
See also CA 89-92

Schwarz-Bart, Simone 1938- . . . . **CLC 7**
See also CA 97-100

Schwob, (Mayer Andre) Marcel
1867-1905 . . . . **TCLC 20**
See also CA 117

Sciascia, Leonardo
1921-1989 . . . . **CLC 8, 9, 41**
See also CA 85-88; 130; CANR 35; MTCW

Scoppettone, Sandra 1936- . . . . **CLC 26**
See also CA 5-8R; SATA 9

Scorsese, Martin 1942- . . . . **CLC 20**
See also CA 110; 114

Scotland, Jay
See Jakes, John (William)

Scott, Duncan Campbell
1862-1947 . . . . **TCLC 6**
See also CA 104; DLB 92

Scott, Evelyn 1893-1963 . . . . **CLC 43**
See also CA 104; 112; DLB 9, 48

Scott, F(rancis) R(eginald)
1899-1985 . . . . **CLC 22**
See also CA 101; 114; DLB 88

Scott, Frank
See Scott, F(rancis) R(eginald)

Scott, Joanna 1960- . . . . **CLC 50**
See also CA 126

Scott, Paul (Mark) 1920-1978 . . . . **CLC 9, 60**
See also CA 81-84; 77-80; CANR 33;
DLB 14; MTCW

Scott, Walter 1771-1832 . . . . **NCLC 15**
See also CDBLB 1789-1832; DLB 93, 107,
116; WLC; YABC 2

Scribe, (Augustin) Eugene
1791-1861 . . . . **NCLC 16**

Scrum, R.
See Crumb, R(obert)

Scudery, Madeleine de 1607-1701 . . . . . **LC 2**

Scum
See Crumb, R(obert)

Scumbag, Little Bobby
See Crumb, R(obert)

Seabrook, John
See Hubbard, L(afayette) Ron(ald)

Sealy, I. Allan 1951- . . . . **CLC 55**

Search, Alexander
See Pessoa, Fernando (Antonio Nogueira)

Sebastian, Lee
See Silverberg, Robert

Sebastian Owl
See Thompson, Hunter S(tockton)

Sebestyen, Ouida 1924- . . . . **CLC 30**
See also AAYA 8; CA 107; CLR 17;
MAICYA; SAAS 10; SATA 39

Sedges, John
See Buck, Pearl S(ydenstricker)

Sedgwick, Catharine Maria
1789-1867 . . . . **NCLC 19**
See also DLB 1, 74

Seelye, John 1931- . . . . **CLC 7**

Seferiades, Giorgos Stylianou 1900-1971
See Seferis, George
See also CA 5-8R; 33-36R; CANR 5, 36;
MTCW

Seferis, George . . . . **CLC 5, 11**
See also Seferiades, Giorgos Stylianou

Segal, Erich (Wolf) 1937- . . . . **CLC 3, 10**
See also BEST 89:1; CA 25-28R; CANR 20,
36; DLBY 86; MTCW

Seger, Bob 1945- . . . . **CLC 35**

Seghers, Anna . . . . **CLC 7**
See also Radvanyi, Netty
See also DLB 69

Seidel, Frederick (Lewis) 1936- . . . . . **CLC 18**
See also CA 13-16R; CANR 8; DLBY 84

Seifert, Jaroslav 1901-1986 . . . . . **CLC 34, 44**
See also CA 127; MTCW

Sei Shonagon c. 966-1017(?) . . . . . . **CMLC 6**

Selby, Hubert Jr. 1928- . . . . **CLC 1, 2, 4, 8**
See also CA 13-16R; CANR 33; DLB 2

Sembene, Ousmane
See Ousmane, Sembene

Senancour, Etienne Pivert de
1770-1846 . . . . **NCLC 16**
See also DLB 119

Sender, Ramon (Jose) 1902-1982 . . . . **CLC 8**
See also CA 5-8R; 105; CANR 8; HW;
MTCW

Seneca, Lucius Annaeus
4B.C.-65 . . . . **CMLC 6**

Senghor, Leopold Sedar 1906- . . . . . . **CLC 54**
See also BLC 3; BW; CA 116; 125; MTCW

Serling, (Edward) Rod(man)
1924-1975 . . . . **CLC 30**
See also AITN 1; CA 65-68; 57-60; DLB 26

Serna, Ramon Gomez de la
See Gomez de la Serna, Ramon

Serpieres
See Guillevic, (Eugene)

Service, Robert
See Service, Robert W(illiam)
See also DLB 92

Service, Robert W(illiam)
1874(?)-1958 . . . . TCLC 15
See also Service, Robert
See also CA 115; SATA 20; WLC

Seth, Vikram 1952- . . . . CLC 43
See also CA 121; 127; DLB 120

Seton, Cynthia Propper
1926-1982 . . . . CLC 27
See also CA 5-8R; 108; CANR 7

Seton, Ernest (Evan) Thompson
1860-1946 . . . . TCLC 31
See also CA 109; DLB 92; SATA 18

Seton-Thompson, Ernest
See Seton, Ernest (Evan) Thompson

Settle, Mary Lee 1918- . . . . CLC 19, 61
See also CA 89-92; CAAS 1; DLB 6

Seuphor, Michel
See Arp, Jean

**Sevine, Marquise de Marie de
Rabutin-Chantal** 1626-1696 . . . . . LC 11

**Sevine, Marquise de Marie de
Rabutin-Chantal** 1626-1696 . . . . . LC 11

Sexton, Anne (Harvey)
1928-1974 . . . CLC 2, 4, 6, 8, 10, 15, 53;
PC 2
See also CA 1-4R; 53-56; CABS 2;
CANR 3, 36; CDALB 1941-1968; DLB 5;
MTCW; SATA 10; WLC

Shaara, Michael (Joseph Jr.)
1929-1988 . . . . CLC 15
See also AITN 1; CA 102; DLBY 83

Shackleton, C. C.
See Aldiss, Brian W(ilson)

Shacochis, Bob . . . . CLC 39
See also Shacochis, Robert G.

Shacochis, Robert G. 1951-
See Shacochis, Bob
See also CA 119; 124

Shaffer, Anthony (Joshua) 1926- . . . . CLC 19
See also CA 110; 116; DLB 13

Shaffer, Peter (Levin)
1926- . . . . CLC 5, 14, 18, 37, 60
See also CA 25-28R; CANR 25;
CDBLB 1960 to Present; DLB 13;
MTCW

Shakey, Bernard
See Young, Neil

Shalamov, Varlam (Tikhonovich)
1907(?)-1982 . . . . CLC 18
See also CA 129; 105

Shamlu, Ahmad 1925- . . . . CLC 10

Shammas, Anton 1951- . . . . CLC 55

Shange, Ntozake 1948- . . . . CLC 8, 25, 38
See also AAYA 9; BLC 3; BW 2; CA 85-88;
CABS 3; CANR 27; DLB 38; MTCW

Shapcott, Thomas William 1935- . . . CLC 38
See also CA 69-72

Shapiro, Karl (Jay) 1913- . . CLC 4, 8, 15, 53
See also CA 1-4R; CAAS 6; CANR 1, 36;
DLB 48; MTCW

Sharp, William 1855-1905 . . . . TCLC 39

Sharpe, Thomas Ridley 1928-
See Sharpe, Tom
See also CA 114; 122

Sharpe, Tom . . . . CLC 36
See also Sharpe, Thomas Ridley
See also DLB 14

Shaw, Bernard . . . . TCLC 45
See also Shaw, George Bernard

Shaw, G. Bernard
See Shaw, George Bernard

Shaw, George Bernard
1856-1950 . . . . TCLC 3, 9, 21
See also Shaw, Bernard
See also CA 104; 128; CDBLB 1914-1945;
DLB 10, 57; MTCW; WLC

Shaw, Henry Wheeler
1818-1885 . . . . NCLC 15
See also DLB 11

Shaw, Irwin 1913-1984 . . . . CLC 7, 23, 34
See also AITN 1; CA 13-16R; 112;
CANR 21; CDALB 1941-1968; DLB 6,
102; DLBY 84; MTCW

Shaw, Robert 1927-1978 . . . . CLC 5
See also AITN 1; CA 1-4R; 81-84;
CANR 4; DLB 13, 14

Shaw, T. E.
See Lawrence, T(homas) E(dward)

Shawn, Wallace 1943- . . . . CLC 41
See also CA 112

Sheed, Wilfrid (John Joseph)
1930- . . . . CLC 2, 4, 10, 53
See also CA 65-68; CANR 30; DLB 6;
MTCW

Sheldon, Alice Hastings Bradley
1915(?)-1987
See Tiptree, James Jr.
See also CA 108; 122; CANR 34; MTCW

Sheldon, John
See Bloch, Robert (Albert)

Shelley, Mary Wollstonecraft (Godwin)
1797-1851 . . . . NCLC 14
See also CDBLB 1789-1832; DLB 110, 116;
SATA 29; WLC

Shelley, Percy Bysshe
1792-1822 . . . . NCLC 18
See also CDBLB 1789-1832; DLB 96, 110;
WLC

Shepard, Jim 1956- . . . . CLC 36
See also CA 137

Shepard, Lucius 19th cent. (?)- . . . . . CLC 34
See also CA 128

Shepard, Sam
1943- . . . . CLC 4, 6, 17, 34, 41, 44
See also AAYA 1; CA 69-72; CABS 3;
CANR 22; DLB 7; MTCW

Shepherd, Michael
See Ludlum, Robert

Sherburne, Zoa (Morin) 1912- . . . . . . CLC 30
See also CA 1-4R; CANR 3, 37; MAICYA;
SATA 3

Sheridan, Frances 1724-1766 . . . . LC 7
See also DLB 39, 84

Sheridan, Richard Brinsley
1751-1816 . . . . NCLC 5; DC 1
See also CDBLB 1660-1789; DLB 89; WLC

Sherman, Jonathan Marc . . . . CLC 55

Sherman, Martin 1941(?)- . . . . CLC 19
See also CA 116; 123

Sherwin, Judith Johnson 1936- . . . CLC 7, 15
See also CA 25-28R; CANR 34

Sherwood, Robert E(mmet)
1896-1955 . . . . TCLC 3
See also CA 104; DLB 7, 26

Shiel, M(atthew) P(hipps)
1865-1947 . . . . TCLC 8
See also CA 106

Shiga, Naoya 1883-1971 . . . . CLC 33
See also CA 101; 33-36R

Shimazaki Haruki 1872-1943
See Shimazaki Toson
See also CA 105; 134

Shimazaki Toson . . . . TCLC 5
See also Shimazaki Haruki

Sholokhov, Mikhail (Aleksandrovich)
1905-1984 . . . . CLC 7, 15
See also CA 101; 112; MTCW; SATA 36

Shone, Patric
See Hanley, James

Shreve, Susan Richards 1939- . . . . . . CLC 23
See also CA 49-52; CAAS 5; CANR 5, 38;
MAICYA; SATA 41, 46

Shue, Larry 1946-1985 . . . . CLC 52
See also CA 117

Shu-Jen, Chou 1881-1936
See Hsun, Lu
See also CA 104

Shulman, Alix Kates 1932- . . . . CLC 2, 10
See also CA 29-32R; SATA 7

Shuster, Joe 1914- . . . . CLC 21

Shute, Nevil . . . . CLC 30
See also Norway, Nevil Shute

Shuttle, Penelope (Diane) 1947- . . . . . CLC 7
See also CA 93-96; CANR 39; DLB 14, 40

Sidney, Mary 1561-1621 . . . . LC 19

Sidney, Sir Philip 1554-1586 . . . . LC 19
See also CDBLB Before 1660

Siegel, Jerome 1914- . . . . CLC 21
See also CA 116

Siegel, Jerry
See Siegel, Jerome

Sienkiewicz, Henryk (Adam Alexander Pius)
1846-1916 . . . . TCLC 3
See also CA 104; 134

Sierra, Gregorio Martinez
See Martinez Sierra, Gregorio

Sierra, Maria (de la O'LeJarraga) Martinez
See Martinez Sierra, Maria (de la
O'LeJarraga)

Sigal, Clancy 1926- . . . . CLC 7
See also CA 1-4R

Sigourney, Lydia Howard (Huntley)
1791-1865 . . . . NCLC 21
See also DLB 1, 42, 73

Siguenza y Gongora, Carlos de
1645-1700 . . . . **LC 8**

Sigurjonsson, Johann 1880-1919 . . . **TCLC 27**

Sikelianos, Angelos 1884-1951 . . . . **TCLC 39**

Silkin, Jon 1930- . . . . **CLC 2, 6, 43**
See also CA 5-8R; CAAS 5; DLB 27

Silko, Leslie Marmon 1948- . . . . **CLC 23**
See also CA 115; 122

Sillanpaa, Frans Eemil 1888-1964 . . . **CLC 19**
See also CA 129; 93-96; MTCW

Sillitoe, Alan
1928- . . . . **CLC 1, 3, 6, 10, 19, 57**
See also AITN 1; CA 9-12R; CAAS 2;
CANR 8, 26; CDBLB 1960 to Present;
DLB 14; MTCW; SATA 61

Silone, Ignazio 1900-1978 . . . . **CLC 4**
See also CA 25-28; 81-84; CANR 34;
CAP 2; MTCW

Silver, Joan Micklin 1935- . . . . **CLC 20**
See also CA 114; 121

Silverberg, Robert 1935- . . . . **CLC 7**
See also CA 1-4R; CAAS 3; CANR 1, 20,
36; DLB 8; MAICYA; MTCW; SATA 13

Silverstein, Alvin 1933- . . . . **CLC 17**
See also CA 49-52; CANR 2; CLR 25;
MAICYA; SATA 8, 69

Silverstein, Virginia B(arbara Opshelor)
1937- . . . . **CLC 17**
See also CA 49-52; CANR 2; CLR 25;
MAICYA; SATA 8, 69

Sim, Georges
See Simenon, Georges (Jacques Christian)

Simak, Clifford D(onald)
1904-1988 . . . . **CLC 1, 55**
See also CA 1-4R; 125; CANR 1, 35;
DLB 8; MTCW; SATA 56

Simenon, Georges (Jacques Christian)
1903-1989 . . . . **CLC 1, 2, 3, 8, 18, 47**
See also CA 85-88; 129; CANR 35;
DLB 72; DLBY 89; MTCW

Simic, Charles 1938- . . . **CLC 6, 9, 22, 49, 68**
See also CA 29-32R; CAAS 4; CANR 12,
33; DLB 105

Simmons, Charles (Paul) 1924- . . . . . **CLC 57**
See also CA 89-92

Simmons, Dan . . . . **CLC 44**
See also CA 138

Simmons, James (Stewart Alexander)
1933- . . . . **CLC 43**
See also CA 105; DLB 40

Simms, William Gilmore
1806-1870 . . . . **NCLC 3**
See also DLB 3, 30, 59, 73

Simon, Carly 1945- . . . . **CLC 26**
See also CA 105

Simon, Claude 1913- . . . . **CLC 4, 9, 15, 39**
See also CA 89-92; CANR 33; DLB 83;
MTCW

Simon, (Marvin) Neil
1927- . . . . **CLC 6, 11, 31, 39, 70**
See also AITN 1; CA 21-24R; CANR 26;
DLB 7; MTCW

Simon, Paul 1942(?)- . . . . **CLC 17**
See also CA 116

Simonon, Paul 1956(?)- . . . . **CLC 30**
See also The Clash

Simpson, Harriette
See Arnow, Harriette (Louisa) Simpson

Simpson, Louis (Aston Marantz)
1923- . . . . **CLC 4, 7, 9, 32**
See also CA 1-4R; CAAS 4; CANR 1;
DLB 5; MTCW

Simpson, Mona (Elizabeth) 1957- . . . **CLC 44**
See also CA 122; 135

Simpson, N(orman) F(rederick)
1919- . . . . **CLC 29**
See also CA 13-16R; DLB 13

Sinclair, Andrew (Annandale)
1935- . . . . **CLC 2, 14**
See also CA 9-12R; CAAS 5; CANR 14, 38;
DLB 14; MTCW

Sinclair, Emil
See Hesse, Hermann

Sinclair, Mary Amelia St. Clair 1865(?)-1946
See Sinclair, May
See also CA 104

Sinclair, May . . . . **TCLC 3, 11**
See also Sinclair, Mary Amelia St. Clair
See also DLB 36

Sinclair, Upton (Beall)
1878-1968 . . . . **CLC 1, 11, 15, 63**
See also CA 5-8R; 25-28R; CANR 7;
CDALB 1929-1941; DLB 9; MTCW;
SATA 9; WLC

Singer, Isaac
See Singer, Isaac Bashevis

Singer, Isaac Bashevis
1904-1991 . . . **CLC 1, 3, 6, 9, 11, 15, 23,
38, 69; SSC 3**
See also AITN 1, 2; CA 1-4R; 134;
CANR 1, 39; CDALB 1941-1968; CLR 1;
DLB 6, 28, 52; DLBY 91; MAICYA;
MTCW; SATA 3, 27; SATO 68; WLC

Singer, Israel Joshua 1893-1944 . . . **TCLC 33**

Singh, Khushwant 1915- . . . . **CLC 11**
See also CA 9-12R; CAAS 9; CANR 6

Sinjohn, John
See Galsworthy, John

Sinyavsky, Andrei (Donatevich)
1925- . . . . **CLC 8**
See also CA 85-88

Sirin, V.
See Nabokov, Vladimir (Vladimirovich)

Sissman, L(ouis) E(dward)
1928-1976 . . . . **CLC 9, 18**
See also CA 21-24R; 65-68; CANR 13;
DLB 5

Sisson, C(harles) H(ubert) 1914- . . . . . **CLC 8**
See also CA 1-4R; CAAS 3; CANR 3;
DLB 27

Sitwell, Dame Edith
1887-1964 . . . . **CLC 2, 9, 67; PC 3**
See also CA 9-12R; CANR 35;
CDBLB 1945-1960; DLB 20; MTCW

Sjoewall, Maj 1935- . . . . **CLC 7**
See also CA 65-68

Sjowall, Maj
See Sjoewall, Maj

Skelton, Robin 1925- . . . . **CLC 13**
See also AITN 2; CA 5-8R; CAAS 5;
CANR 28; DLB 27, 53

Skolimowski, Jerzy 1938- . . . . **CLC 20**
See also CA 128

Skram, Amalie (Bertha)
1847-1905 . . . . **TCLC 25**

Skvorecky, Josef (Vaclav)
1924- . . . . **CLC 15, 39, 69**
See also CA 61-64; CAAS 1; CANR 10, 34;
MTCW

Slade, Bernard . . . . **CLC 11, 46**
See also Newbound, Bernard Slade
See also CAAS 9; DLB 53

Slaughter, Carolyn 1946- . . . . **CLC 56**
See also CA 85-88

Slaughter, Frank G(ill) 1908- . . . . . . **CLC 29**
See also AITN 2; CA 5-8R; CANR 5

Slavitt, David R. 1935- . . . . **CLC 5, 14**
See also CA 21-24R; CAAS 3; DLB 5, 6

Slesinger, Tess 1905-1945 . . . . **TCLC 10**
See also CA 107; DLB 102

Slessor, Kenneth 1901-1971 . . . . **CLC 14**
See also CA 102; 89-92

Slowacki, Juliusz 1809-1849 . . . . . **NCLC 15**

Smart, Christopher 1722-1771 . . . . **LC 3**
See also DLB 109

Smart, Elizabeth 1913-1986 . . . . **CLC 54**
See also CA 81-84; 118; DLB 88

Smiley, Jane (Graves) 1949- . . . . **CLC 53**
See also CA 104; CANR 30

Smith, A(rthur) J(ames) M(arshall)
1902-1980 . . . . **CLC 15**
See also CA 1-4R; 102; CANR 4; DLB 88

Smith, Betty (Wehner) 1896-1972 . . . **CLC 19**
See also CA 5-8R; 33-36R; DLBY 82;
SATA 6

Smith, Charlotte (Turner)
1749-1806 . . . . **NCLC 23**
See also DLB 39, 109

Smith, Clark Ashton 1893-1961 . . . . **CLC 43**

Smith, Dave . . . . **CLC 22, 42**
See also Smith, David (Jeddie)
See also CAAS 7; DLB 5

Smith, David (Jeddie) 1942-
See Smith, Dave
See also CA 49-52; CANR 1

Smith, Florence Margaret
1902-1971 . . . . **CLC 8**
See also Smith, Stevie
See also CA 17-18; 29-32R; CANR 35;
CAP 2; MTCW

Smith, Iain Crichton 1928- . . . . **CLC 64**
See also CA 21-24R; DLB 40

Smith, John 1580(?)-1631 . . . . **LC 9**

Smith, Johnston
See Crane, Stephen (Townley)

Smith, Lee 1944- . . . . **CLC 25**
See also CA 114; 119; DLBY 83

Smith, Martin
See Smith, Martin Cruz

Smith, Martin Cruz 1942- . . . . **CLC 25**
See also BEST 89:4; CA 85-88; CANR 6, 23

Smith, Mary-Ann Tirone 1944-..... **CLC 39**
See also CA 118; 136

Smith, Patti 1946- .... **CLC 12**
See also CA 93-96

Smith, Pauline (Urmson)
1882-1959 .... **TCLC 25**

Smith, Rosamond
See Oates, Joyce Carol

Smith, Sheila Kaye
See Kaye-Smith, Sheila

Smith, Stevie .... **CLC 3, 8, 25, 44**
See also Smith, Florence Margaret
See also DLB 20

Smith, Wilbur A(ddison) 1933-..... **CLC 33**
See also CA 13-16R; CANR 7; MTCW

Smith, William Jay 1918- .... **CLC 6**
See also CA 5-8R; DLB 5; MAICYA;
SATA 2, 68

Smith, Woodrow Wilson
See Kuttner, Henry

Smolenskin, Peretz 1842-1885.... **NCLC 30**

Smollett, Tobias (George) 1721-1771 .. **LC 2**
See also CDBLB 1660-1789; DLB 39, 104

Snodgrass, William D(e Witt)
1926- .... **CLC 2, 6, 10, 18, 68**
See also CA 1-4R; CANR 6, 36; DLB 5;
MTCW

Snow, C(harles) P(ercy)
1905-1980 .... **CLC 1, 4, 6, 9, 13, 19**
See also CA 5-8R; 101; CANR 28;
CDBLB 1945-1960; DLB 15, 77; MTCW

Snow, Frances Compton
See Adams, Henry (Brooks)

Snyder, Gary (Sherman)
1930- .... **CLC 1, 2, 5, 9, 32**
See also CA 17-20R; CANR 30; DLB 5, 16

Snyder, Zilpha Keatley 1927-...... **CLC 17**
See also CA 9-12R; CANR 38; MAICYA;
SAAS 2; SATA 1, 28

Soares, Bernardo
See Pessoa, Fernando (Antonio Nogueira)

Sobh, A.
See Shamlu, Ahmad

Sobol, Joshua .... **CLC 60**

Soderberg, Hjalmar 1869-1941 .... **TCLC 39**

Sodergran, Edith (Irene)
See Soedergran, Edith (Irene)

Soedergran, Edith (Irene)
1892-1923 .... **TCLC 31**

Softly, Edgar
See Lovecraft, H(oward) P(hillips)

Softly, Edward
See Lovecraft, H(oward) P(hillips)

Sokolov, Raymond 1941-........... **CLC 7**
See also CA 85-88

Solo, Jay
See Ellison, Harlan

Sologub, Fyodor .... **TCLC 9**
See also Teternikov, Fyodor Kuzmich

Solomons, Ikey Esquir
See Thackeray, William Makepeace

Solomos, Dionysios 1798-1857 ... **NCLC 15**

Solwoska, Mara
See French, Marilyn

Solzhenitsyn, Aleksandr I(sayevich)
1918- ... **CLC 1, 2, 4, 7, 9, 10, 18, 26, 34**
See also AITN 1; CA 69-72; MTCW; WLC

Somers, Jane
See Lessing, Doris (May)

Sommer, Scott 1951- .... **CLC 25**
See also CA 106

Sondheim, Stephen (Joshua)
1930- .... **CLC 30, 39**
See also CA 103

Sontag, Susan 1933-... **CLC 1, 2, 10, 13, 31**
See also CA 17-20R; CANR 25; DLB 2, 67;
MTCW

Sophocles
496(?)B.C.-406(?)B.C.... **CMLC 2; DC 1**

Sorel, Julia
See Drexler, Rosalyn

Sorrentino, Gilbert
1929- .... **CLC 3, 7, 14, 22, 40**
See also CA 77-80; CANR 14, 33; DLB 5;
DLBY 80

Soto, Gary 1952-................. **CLC 32**
See also CA 119; 125; DLB 82; HW

Soupault, Philippe 1897-1990 ...... **CLC 68**
See also CA 116; 131

Souster, (Holmes) Raymond
1921- .... **CLC 5, 14**
See also CA 13-16R; CAAS 14; CANR 13,
29; DLB 88; SATA 63

Southern, Terry 1926- .... **CLC 7**
See also CA 1-4R; CANR 1; DLB 2

Southey, Robert 1774-1843 .... **NCLC 8**
See also DLB 93, 107; SATA 54

Southworth, Emma Dorothy Eliza Nevitte
1819-1899 .... **NCLC 26**

Souza, Ernest
See Scott, Evelyn

Soyinka, Wole
1934- .... **CLC 3, 5, 14, 36, 44; DC 2**
See also BLC 3; BW; CA 13-16R;
CANR 27, 39; MTCW; WLC

Spackman, W(illiam) M(ode)
1905-1990 .... **CLC 46**
See also CA 81-84; 132

Spacks, Barry 1931-................ **CLC 14**
See also CA 29-32R; CANR 33; DLB 105

Spanidou, Irini 1946- .... **CLC 44**

Spark, Muriel (Sarah)
1918- .... **CLC 2, 3, 5, 8, 13, 18, 40;
SSC 10**
See also CA 5-8R; CANR 12, 36;
CDBLB 1945-1960; DLB 15; MTCW

Spaulding, Douglas
See Bradbury, Ray (Douglas)

Spaulding, Leonard
See Bradbury, Ray (Douglas)

Spence, J. A. D.
See Eliot, T(homas) S(tearns)

Spencer, Elizabeth 1921-.......... **CLC 22**
See also CA 13-16R; CANR 32; DLB 6;
MTCW; SATA 14

Spencer, Leonard G.
See Silverberg, Robert

Spencer, Scott 1945-.............. **CLC 30**
See also CA 113; DLBY 86

Spender, Stephen (Harold)
1909- .... **CLC 1, 2, 5, 10, 41**
See also CA 9-12R; CANR 31;
CDBLB 1945-1960; DLB 20; MTCW

Spengler, Oswald (Arnold Gottfried)
1880-1936 .... **TCLC 25**
See also CA 118

Spenser, Edmund 1552(?)-1599 .... **LC 5**
See also CDBLB Before 1660; WLC

Spicer, Jack 1925-1965 ...... **CLC 8, 18, 72**
See also CA 85-88; DLB 5, 16

Spielberg, Peter 1929- .... **CLC 6**
See also CA 5-8R; CANR 4; DLBY 81

Spielberg, Steven 1947- .... **CLC 20**
See also AAYA 8; CA 77-80; CANR 32;
SATA 32

Spillane, Frank Morrison 1918-
See Spillane, Mickey
See also CA 25-28R; CANR 28; MTCW;
SATA 66

Spillane, Mickey .... **CLC 3, 13**
See also Spillane, Frank Morrison

Spinoza, Benedictus de 1632-1677 .... **LC 9**

Spinrad, Norman (Richard) 1940-... **CLC 46**
See also CA 37-40R; CANR 20; DLB 8

Spitteler, Carl (Friedrich Georg)
1845-1924 .... **TCLC 12**
See also CA 109

Spivack, Kathleen (Romola Drucker)
1938- .... **CLC 6**
See also CA 49-52

Spoto, Donald 1941-.............. **CLC 39**
See also CA 65-68; CANR 11

Springsteen, Bruce (F.) 1949- ...... **CLC 17**
See also CA 111

Spurling, Hilary 1940-............ **CLC 34**
See also CA 104; CANR 25

Squires, Radcliffe 1917-.......... **CLC 51**
See also CA 1-4R; CANR 6, 21

Srivastava, Dhanpat Rai 1880(?)-1936
See Premchand
See also CA 118

Stacy, Donald
See Pohl, Frederik

Stael, Germaine de
See Stael-Holstein, Anne Louise Germaine
Necker Baronn
See also DLB 119

**Stael-Holstein, Anne Louise Germaine Necker
Baronn** 1766-1817 .... **NCLC 3**
See also Stael, Germaine de

Stafford, Jean 1915-1979... **CLC 4, 7, 19, 68**
See also CA 1-4R; 85-88; CANR 3; DLB 2;
MTCW; SATA 22

Stafford, William (Edgar)
1914- .... **CLC 4, 7, 29**
See also CA 5-8R; CAAS 3; CANR 5, 22;
DLB 5

Staines, Trevor
See Brunner, John (Kilian Houston)

Stairs, Gordon
  See Austin, Mary (Hunter)

Stannard, Martin . . . . CLC 44

Stanton, Maura 1946- . . . . CLC 9
  See also CA 89-92; CANR 15; DLB 120

Stanton, Schuyler
  See Baum, L(yman) Frank

Stapledon, (William) Olaf
  1886-1950 . . . . TCLC 22
  See also CA 111; DLB 15

Starbuck, George (Edwin) 1931- . . . . CLC 53
  See also CA 21-24R; CANR 23

Stark, Richard
  See Westlake, Donald E(dwin)

Staunton, Schuyler
  See Baum, L(yman) Frank

Stead, Christina (Ellen)
  1902-1983 . . . . CLC 2, 5, 8, 32
  See also CA 13-16R; 109; CANR 33;
  MTCW

Steele, Richard 1672-1729 . . . . LC 18
  See also CDBLB 1660-1789; DLB 84, 101

Steele, Timothy (Reid) 1948- . . . . CLC 45
  See also CA 93-96; CANR 16; DLB 120

Steffens, (Joseph) Lincoln
  1866-1936 . . . . TCLC 20
  See also CA 117

Stegner, Wallace (Earle) 1909- . . . CLC 9, 49
  See also AITN 1; BEST 90:3; CA 1-4R;
  CAAS 9; CANR 1, 21; DLB 9; MTCW

Stein, Gertrude 1874-1946 . . . TCLC 1, 6, 28
  See also CA 104; 132; CDALB 1917-1929;
  DLB 4, 54, 86; MTCW; WLC

Steinbeck, John (Ernst)
  1902-1968 . . . CLC 1, 5, 9, 13, 21, 34, 45
  See also CA 1-4R; 25-28R; CANR 1, 35;
  CDALB 1929-1941; DLB 7, 9; DLBD 2;
  MTCW; SATA 9; WLC

Steinem, Gloria 1934- . . . . CLC 63
  See also CA 53-56; CANR 28; MTCW

Steiner, George 1929- . . . . CLC 24
  See also CA 73-76; CANR 31; DLB 67;
  MTCW; SATA 62

Steiner, Rudolf 1861-1925 . . . . TCLC 13
  See also CA 107

Stendhal 1783-1842 . . . . NCLC 23
  See also DLB 119; WLC

Stephen, Leslie 1832-1904 . . . . TCLC 23
  See also CA 123; DLB 57

Stephen, Sir Leslie
  See Stephen, Leslie

Stephen, Virginia
  See Woolf, (Adeline) Virginia

Stephens, James 1882(?)-1950 . . . . . . TCLC 4
  See also CA 104; DLB 19

Stephens, Reed
  See Donaldson, Stephen R.

Steptoe, Lydia
  See Barnes, Djuna

Sterchi, Beat 1949- . . . . CLC 65

Sterling, Brett
  See Bradbury, Ray (Douglas); Hamilton,
  Edmond

Sterling, Bruce 1954- . . . . CLC 72
  See also CA 119

Sterling, George 1869-1926 . . . . TCLC 20
  See also CA 117; DLB 54

Stern, Gerald 1925- . . . . CLC 40
  See also CA 81-84; CANR 28; DLB 105

Stern, Richard (Gustave) 1928- . . . CLC 4, 39
  See also CA 1-4R; CANR 1, 25; DLBY 87

Sternberg, Josef von 1894-1969 . . . . . CLC 20
  See also CA 81-84

Sterne, Laurence 1713-1768 . . . . LC 2
  See also CDBLB 1660-1789; DLB 39; WLC

Sternheim, (William Adolf) Carl
  1878-1942 . . . . TCLC 8
  See also CA 105; DLB 56, 118

Stevens, Mark 1951- . . . . CLC 34
  See also CA 122

Stevens, Wallace
  1879-1955 . . . . TCLC 3, 12, 45
  See also CA 104; 124; CDALB 1929-1941;
  DLB 54; MTCW; WLC

Stevenson, Anne (Katharine)
  1933- . . . . CLC 7, 33
  See also CA 17-20R; CAAS 9; CANR 9, 33;
  DLB 40; MTCW

Stevenson, Robert Louis (Balfour)
  1850-1894 . . . . NCLC 5, 14
  See also CDBLB 1890-1914; CLR 10, 11;
  DLB 18, 57; MAICYA; WLC; YABC 2

Stewart, J(ohn) I(nnes) M(ackintosh)
  1906- . . . . CLC 7, 14, 32
  See also CA 85-88; CAAS 3; MTCW

Stewart, Mary (Florence Elinor)
  1916- . . . . CLC 7, 35
  See also CA 1-4R; CANR 1; SATA 12

Stewart, Mary Rainbow
  See Stewart, Mary (Florence Elinor)

Still, James 1906- . . . . CLC 49
  See also CA 65-68; CANR 10, 26; DLB 9;
  SATA 29

Sting
  See Sumner, Gordon Matthew

Stirling, Arthur
  See Sinclair, Upton (Beall)

Stitt, Milan 1941- . . . . CLC 29
  See also CA 69-72

Stockton, Francis Richard 1834-1902
  See Stockton, Frank R.
  See also CA 108; 137; MAICYA; SATA 44

Stockton, Frank R. . . . . TCLC 47
  See also Stockton, Francis Richard
  See also DLB 42, 74; SATA 32

Stoddard, Charles
  See Kuttner, Henry

Stoker, Abraham 1847-1912
  See Stoker, Bram
  See also CA 105; SATA 29

Stoker, Bram . . . . TCLC 8
  See also Stoker, Abraham
  See also CDBLB 1890-1914; DLB 36, 70;
  WLC

Stolz, Mary (Slattery) 1920- . . . . CLC 12
  See also AAYA 8; AITN 1; CA 5-8R;
  CANR 13; MAICYA; SAAS 3;
  SATA 10, 70, 71

Stone, Irving 1903-1989 . . . . CLC 7
  See also AITN 1; CA 1-4R; 129; CAAS 3;
  CANR 1, 23; MTCW; SATA 3; SATO 64

Stone, Robert (Anthony)
  1937- . . . . CLC 5, 23, 42
  See also CA 85-88; CANR 23; MTCW

Stone, Zachary
  See Follett, Ken(neth Martin)

Stoppard, Tom
  1937- . . . CLC 1, 3, 4, 5, 8, 15, 29, 34, 63
  See also CA 81-84; CANR 39;
  CDBLB 1960 to Present; DLB 13;
  DLBY 85; MTCW; WLC

Storey, David (Malcolm)
  1933- . . . . CLC 2, 4, 5, 8
  See also CA 81-84; CANR 36; DLB 13, 14;
  MTCW

Storm, Hyemeyohsts 1935- . . . . CLC 3
  See also CA 81-84

Storm, (Hans) Theodor (Woldsen)
  1817-1888 . . . . NCLC 1

Storni, Alfonsina 1892-1938 . . . . TCLC 5
  See also CA 104; 131; HW

Stout, Rex (Todhunter) 1886-1975 . . . CLC 3
  See also AITN 2; CA 61-64

Stow, (Julian) Randolph 1935- . . CLC 23, 48
  See also CA 13-16R; CANR 33; MTCW

Stowe, Harriet (Elizabeth) Beecher
  1811-1896 . . . . NCLC 3
  See also CDALB 1865-1917; DLB 1, 12, 42,
  74; MAICYA; WLC; YABC 1

Strachey, (Giles) Lytton
  1880-1932 . . . . TCLC 12
  See also CA 110

Strand, Mark 1934- . . . . . . CLC 6, 18, 41, 71
  See also CA 21-24R; DLB 5; SATA 41

Straub, Peter (Francis) 1943- . . . . . . CLC 28
  See also BEST 89:1; CA 85-88; CANR 28;
  DLBY 84; MTCW

Strauss, Botho 1944- . . . . CLC 22

Streatfeild, (Mary) Noel
  1895(?)-1986 . . . . CLC 21
  See also CA 81-84; 120; CANR 31;
  CLR 17; MAICYA; SATA 20, 48

Stribling, T(homas) S(igismund)
  1881-1965 . . . . CLC 23
  See also CA 107; DLB 9

Strindberg, (Johan) August
  1849-1912 . . . . TCLC 1, 8, 21, 47
  See also CA 104; 135; WLC

Stringer, Arthur 1874-1950 . . . . TCLC 37
  See also DLB 92

Stringer, David
  See Roberts, Keith (John Kingston)

Strugatskii, Arkadii (Natanovich)
  1925-1991 . . . . CLC 27
  See also CA 106; 135

Strugatskii, Boris (Natanovich)
  1933- . . . . CLC 27
  See also CA 106

Strummer, Joe 1953(?)- . . . . CLC 30
  See also The Clash

Stuart, Don A.
  See Campbell, John W(ood Jr.)

Stuart, Ian
See MacLean, Alistair (Stuart)

Stuart, Jesse (Hilton)
1906-1984 . . . . **CLC 1, 8, 11, 14, 34**
See also CA 5-8R; 112; CANR 31; DLB 9, 48, 102; DLBY 84; SATA 2, 36

Sturgeon, Theodore (Hamilton)
1918-1985 . . . . **CLC 22, 39**
See also Queen, Ellery
See also CA 81-84; 116; CANR 32; DLB 8; DLBY 85; MTCW

Styron, William
1925- . . . . **CLC 1, 3, 5, 11, 15, 60**
See also BEST 90:4; CA 5-8R; CANR 6, 33; CDALB 1968-1988; DLB 2; DLBY 80; MTCW

Suarez Lynch, B.
See Borges, Jorge Luis

Suarez Lynch, B.
See Bioy Casares, Adolfo; Borges, Jorge Luis

Su Chien 1884-1918
See Su Man-shu
See also CA 123

Sudermann, Hermann 1857-1928 . . **TCLC 15**
See also CA 107; DLB 118

Sue, Eugene 1804-1857 . . . . **NCLC 1**
See also DLB 119

Sueskind, Patrick 1949- . . . . **CLC 44**

Sukenick, Ronald 1932- . . . . . **CLC 3, 4, 6, 48**
See also CA 25-28R; CAAS 8; CANR 32; DLBY 81

Suknaski, Andrew 1942- . . . . **CLC 19**
See also CA 101; DLB 53

Sullivan, Vernon
See Vian, Boris

Sully Prudhomme 1839-1907 . . . . . . **TCLC 31**

Su Man-shu . . . . **TCLC 24**
See also Su Chien

Summerforest, Ivy B.
See Kirkup, James

Summers, Andrew James 1942- . . . . . **CLC 26**
See also The Police

Summers, Andy
See Summers, Andrew James

Summers, Hollis (Spurgeon Jr.)
1916- . . . . **CLC 10**
See also CA 5-8R; CANR 3; DLB 6

Summers, (Alphonsus Joseph-Mary Augustus) Montague 1880-1948 . . . . **TCLC 16**
See also CA 118

Sumner, Gordon Matthew 1951- . . . . **CLC 26**
See also The Police

Surtees, Robert Smith
1803-1864 . . . . **NCLC 14**
See also DLB 21

Susann, Jacqueline 1921-1974 . . . . **CLC 3**
See also AITN 1; CA 65-68; 53-56; MTCW

Suskind, Patrick
See Sueskind, Patrick

Sutcliff, Rosemary 1920- . . . . **CLC 26**
See also CA 5-8R; CANR 37; CLR 1; MAICYA; SATA 6, 44

Sutro, Alfred 1863-1933 . . . . **TCLC 6**
See also CA 105; DLB 10

Sutton, Henry
See Slavitt, David R.

Svevo, Italo . . . . **TCLC 2, 35**
See also Schmitz, Aron Hector

Swados, Elizabeth 1951- . . . . **CLC 12**
See also CA 97-100

Swados, Harvey 1920-1972 . . . . **CLC 5**
See also CA 5-8R; 37-40R; CANR 6; DLB 2

Swan, Gladys 1934- . . . . **CLC 69**
See also CA 101; CANR 17, 39

Swarthout, Glendon (Fred) 1918- . . . **CLC 35**
See also CA 1-4R; CANR 1; SATA 26

Sweet, Sarah C.
See Jewett, (Theodora) Sarah Orne

Swenson, May 1919-1989 . . . . . **CLC 4, 14, 61**
See also CA 5-8R; 130; CANR 36; DLB 5; MTCW; SATA 15

Swift, Augustus
See Lovecraft, H(oward) P(hillips)

Swift, Graham 1949- . . . . **CLC 41**
See also CA 117; 122

Swift, Jonathan 1667-1745 . . . . **LC 1**
See also CDBLB 1660-1789; DLB 39, 95, 101; SATA 19; WLC

Swinburne, Algernon Charles
1837-1909 . . . . **TCLC 8, 36**
See also CA 105; CDBLB 1832-1890; DLB 35, 57; WLC

Swinfen, Ann . . . . **CLC 34**

Swinnerton, Frank Arthur
1884-1982 . . . . **CLC 31**
See also CA 108; DLB 34

Swithen, John
See King, Stephen (Edwin)

Sylvia
See Ashton-Warner, Sylvia (Constance)

Symmes, Robert Edward
See Duncan, Robert (Edward)

Symonds, John Addington
1840-1893 . . . . **NCLC 34**
See also DLB 57

Symons, Arthur 1865-1945 . . . . **TCLC 11**
See also CA 107; DLB 19, 57

Symons, Julian (Gustave)
1912- . . . . **CLC 2, 14, 32**
See also CA 49-52; CAAS 3; CANR 3, 33; DLB 87; MTCW

Synge, (Edmund) J(ohn) M(illington)
1871-1909 . . . . **TCLC 6, 37; DC 2**
See also CA 104; CDBLB 1890-1914; DLB 10, 19

Syruc, J.
See Milosz, Czeslaw

Szirtes, George 1948- . . . . **CLC 46**
See also CA 109; CANR 27

Tabori, George 1914- . . . . **CLC 19**
See also CA 49-52; CANR 4

Tagore, Rabindranath 1861-1941 . . . . **TCLC 3**
See also CA 104; 120; MTCW

Taine, Hippolyte Adolphe
1828-1893 . . . . **NCLC 15**

Talese, Gay 1932- . . . . **CLC 37**
See also AITN 1; CA 1-4R; CANR 9; MTCW

Tallent, Elizabeth (Ann) 1954- . . . . . **CLC 45**
See also CA 117

Tally, Ted 1952- . . . . **CLC 42**
See also CA 120; 124

Tamayo y Baus, Manuel
1829-1898 . . . . **NCLC 1**

Tammsaare, A(nton) H(ansen)
1878-1940 . . . . **TCLC 27**

Tan, Amy 1952- . . . . **CLC 59**
See also AAYA 9; BEST 89:3; CA 136

Tandem, Felix
See Spitteler, Carl (Friedrich Georg)

Tanizaki, Jun'ichiro
1886-1965 . . . . **CLC 8, 14, 28**
See also CA 93-96; 25-28R

Tanner, William
See Amis, Kingsley (William)

Tao Lao
See Storni, Alfonsina

Tarassoff, Lev
See Troyat, Henri

Tarbell, Ida M(inerva)
1857-1944 . . . . **TCLC 40**
See also CA 122; DLB 47

Tarkington, (Newton) Booth
1869-1946 . . . . **TCLC 9**
See also CA 110; DLB 9, 102; SATA 17

Tasso, Torquato 1544-1595 . . . . **LC 5**

Tate, (John Orley) Allen
1899-1979 . . . . **CLC 2, 4, 6, 9, 11, 14, 24**
See also CA 5-8R; 85-88; CANR 32; DLB 4, 45, 63; MTCW

Tate, Ellalice
See Hibbert, Eleanor Burford

Tate, James (Vincent) 1943- . . . **CLC 2, 6, 25**
See also CA 21-24R; CANR 29; DLB 5

Tavel, Ronald 1940- . . . . **CLC 6**
See also CA 21-24R; CANR 33

Taylor, Cecil Philip 1929-1981 . . . . . **CLC 27**
See also CA 25-28R; 105

Taylor, Edward 1642(?)-1729 . . . . **LC 11**
See also DLB 24

Taylor, Eleanor Ross 1920- . . . . **CLC 5**
See also CA 81-84

Taylor, Elizabeth 1912-1975 . . . **CLC 2, 4, 29**
See also CA 13-16R; CANR 9; MTCW; SATA 13

Taylor, Henry (Splawn) 1942- . . . . . . **CLC 44**
See also CA 33-36R; CAAS 7; CANR 31; DLB 5

Taylor, Kamala (Purnaiya) 1924-
See Markandaya, Kamala
See also CA 77-80

Taylor, Mildred D. . . . . **CLC 21**
See also BW; CA 85-88; CANR 25; CLR 9; DLB 52; MAICYA; SAAS 5; SATA 15, 70

Taylor, Peter (Hillsman)
1917- ..... **CLC 1, 4, 18, 37, 44, 50, 71; SSC 10**
See also CA 13-16R; CANR 9; DLBY 81; MTCW

Taylor, Robert Lewis 1912-........ **CLC 14**
See also CA 1-4R; CANR 3; SATA 10

Tchekhov, Anton
See Chekhov, Anton (Pavlovich)

Teasdale, Sara 1884-1933......... **TCLC 4**
See also CA 104; DLB 45; SATA 32

Tegner, Esaias 1782-1846........ **NCLC 2**

Teilhard de Chardin, (Marie Joseph) Pierre
1881-1955 .... **TCLC 9**
See also CA 105

Temple, Ann
See Mortimer, Penelope (Ruth)

Tennant, Emma (Christina)
1937- .... **CLC 13, 52**
See also CA 65-68; CAAS 9; CANR 10, 38; DLB 14

Tenneshaw, S. M.
See Silverberg, Robert

Tennyson, Alfred 1809-1892 ..... **NCLC 30**
See also CDBLB 1832-1890; DLB 32; WLC

Teran, Lisa St. Aubin de .... **CLC 36**
See also St. Aubin de Teran, Lisa

Teresa de Jesus, St. 1515-1582 ...... **LC 18**

Terkel, Louis 1912-
See Terkel, Studs
See also CA 57-60; CANR 18; MTCW

Terkel, Studs .... **CLC 38**
See also Terkel, Louis
See also AITN 1

Terry, C. V.
See Slaughter, Frank G(ill)

Terry, Megan 1932- .... **CLC 19**
See also CA 77-80; CABS 3; DLB 7

Tertz, Abram
See Sinyavsky, Andrei (Donatevich)

Tesich, Steve 1943(?)-........... **CLC 40, 69**
See also CA 105; DLBY 83

Teternikov, Fyodor Kuzmich 1863-1927
See Sologub, Fyodor
See also CA 104

Tevis, Walter 1928-1984 .... **CLC 42**
See also CA 113

Tey, Josephine .... **TCLC 14**
See also Mackintosh, Elizabeth
See also DLB 77

Thackeray, William Makepeace
1811-1863 .... **NCLC 5, 14, 22**
See also CDBLB 1832-1890; DLB 21, 55; SATA 23; WLC

Thakura, Ravindranatha
See Tagore, Rabindranath

Tharoor, Shashi 1956- .... **CLC 70**

Thelwell, Michael Miles 1939- ..... **CLC 22**
See also CA 101

Theobald, Lewis Jr.
See Lovecraft, H(oward) P(hillips)

The Prophet
See Dreiser, Theodore (Herman Albert)

Theroux, Alexander (Louis)
1939- .... **CLC 2, 25**
See also CA 85-88; CANR 20

Theroux, Paul (Edward)
1941-........ **CLC 5, 8, 11, 15, 28, 46**
See also BEST 89:4; CA 33-36R; CANR 20; DLB 2; MTCW; SATA 44

Thesen, Sharon 1946-............. **CLC 56**

Thevenin, Denis
See Duhamel, Georges

Thibault, Jacques Anatole Francois
1844-1924
See France, Anatole
See also CA 106; 127; MTCW

Thiele, Colin (Milton) 1920- .... **CLC 17**
See also CA 29-32R; CANR 12, 28; CLR 27; MAICYA; SAAS 2; SATA 14

Thomas, Audrey (Callahan)
1935- .... **CLC 7, 13, 37**
See also AITN 2; CA 21-24R; CANR 36; DLB 60; MTCW

Thomas, D(onald) M(ichael)
1935- .... **CLC 13, 22, 31**
See also CA 61-64; CAAS 11; CANR 17; CDBLB 1960 to Present; DLB 40; MTCW

Thomas, Dylan (Marlais)
1914-1953 .... **TCLC 1, 8, 45; PC 2; SSC 3**
See also CA 104; 120; CDBLB 1945-1960; DLB 13, 20; MTCW; SATA 60; WLC

Thomas, (Philip) Edward
1878-1917 .... **TCLC 10**
See also CA 106; DLB 19

Thomas, Joyce Carol 1938-........ **CLC 35**
See also BW; CA 113; 116; CLR 19; DLB 33; MAICYA; MTCW; SAAS 7; SATA 40

Thomas, Lewis 1913- .... **CLC 35**
See also CA 85-88; CANR 38; MTCW

Thomas, Paul
See Mann, (Paul) Thomas

Thomas, Piri 1928-................ **CLC 17**
See also CA 73-76; HW

Thomas, R(onald) S(tuart)
1913- .... **CLC 6, 13, 48**
See also CA 89-92; CAAS 4; CANR 30; CDBLB 1960 to Present; DLB 27; MTCW

Thomas, Ross (Elmore) 1926-...... **CLC 39**
See also CA 33-36R; CANR 22

Thompson, Francis Clegg
See Mencken, H(enry) L(ouis)

Thompson, Francis Joseph
1859-1907 .... **TCLC 4**
See also CA 104; CDBLB 1890-1914; DLB 19

Thompson, Hunter S(tockton)
1939- .... **CLC 9, 17, 40**
See also BEST 89:1; CA 17-20R; CANR 23; MTCW

Thompson, Jim 1906-1976........ **CLC 69**

Thompson, Judith .... **CLC 39**

Thomson, James 1700-1748........ **LC 16**

Thomson, James 1834-1882...... **NCLC 18**

Thoreau, Henry David
1817-1862 .... **NCLC 7, 21**
See also CDALB 1640-1865; DLB 1; WLC

Thornton, Hall
See Silverberg, Robert

Thurber, James (Grover)
1894-1961 .... **CLC 5, 11, 25; SSC 1**
See also CA 73-76; CANR 17, 39; CDALB 1929-1941; DLB 4, 11, 22, 102; MAICYA; MTCW; SATA 13

Thurman, Wallace (Henry)
1902-1934 .... **TCLC 6**
See also BLC 3; BW; CA 104; 124; DLB 51

Ticheburn, Cheviot
See Ainsworth, William Harrison

Tieck, (Johann) Ludwig
1773-1853 .... **NCLC 5**
See also DLB 90

Tiger, Derry
See Ellison, Harlan

Tilghman, Christopher 1948(?)-..... **CLC 65**

Tillinghast, Richard (Williford)
1940- .... **CLC 29**
See also CA 29-32R; CANR 26

Timrod, Henry 1828-1867 .... **NCLC 25**
See also DLB 3

Tindall, Gillian 1938-.............. **CLC 7**
See also CA 21-24R; CANR 11

Tiptree, James Jr............... **CLC 48, 50**
See also Sheldon, Alice Hastings Bradley
See also DLB 8

Titmarsh, Michael Angelo
See Thackeray, William Makepeace

Tocqueville, Alexis (Charles Henri Maurice Clerel Comte) 1805-1859..... **NCLC 7**

Tolkien, J(ohn) R(onald) R(euel)
1892-1973 .... **CLC 1, 2, 3, 8, 12, 38**
See also AITN 1; CA 17-18; 45-48; CANR 36; CAP 2; CDBLB 1914-1945; DLB 15; MAICYA; MTCW; SATA 2, 24, 32; WLC

Toller, Ernst 1893-1939.......... **TCLC 10**
See also CA 107

Tolson, M. B.
See Tolson, Melvin B(eaunorus)

Tolson, Melvin B(eaunorus)
1898(?)-1966 .... **CLC 36**
See also BLC 3; BW; CA 124; 89-92; DLB 48, 76

Tolstoi, Aleksei Nikolaevich
See Tolstoy, Alexey Nikolaevich

Tolstoy, Alexey Nikolaevich
1882-1945 .... **TCLC 18**
See also CA 107

Tolstoy, Count Leo
See Tolstoy, Leo (Nikolaevich)

Tolstoy, Leo (Nikolaevich)
1828-1910 ..... **TCLC 4, 11, 17, 28, 44; SSC 9**
See also CA 104; 123; SATA 26; WLC

Tomasi di Lampedusa, Giuseppe 1896-1957
See Lampedusa, Giuseppe (Tomasi) di
See also CA 111

Tomlin, Lily..................... **CLC 17**
See also Tomlin, Mary Jean

Tomlin, Mary Jean 1939(?)-
See Tomlin, Lily
See also CA 117

Tomlinson, (Alfred) Charles
1927- .... **CLC 2, 4, 6, 13, 45**
See also CA 5-8R; CANR 33; DLB 40

Tonson, Jacob
See Bennett, (Enoch) Arnold

Toole, John Kennedy
1937-1969 .... **CLC 19, 64**
See also CA 104; DLBY 81

Toomer, Jean
1894-1967 ..... **CLC 1, 4, 13, 22; SSC 1**
See also BLC 3; BW; CA 85-88;
CDALB 1917-1929; DLB 45, 51; MTCW

Torley, Luke
See Blish, James (Benjamin)

Tornimparte, Alessandra
See Ginzburg, Natalia

Torre, Raoul della
See Mencken, H(enry) L(ouis)

Torrey, E(dwin) Fuller 1937-........ **CLC 34**
See also CA 119

Torsvan, Ben Traven
See Traven, B.

Torsvan, Benno Traven
See Traven, B.

Torsvan, Berick Traven
See Traven, B.

Torsvan, Berwick Traven
See Traven, B.

Torsvan, Bruno Traven
See Traven, B.

Torsvan, Traven
See Traven, B.

Tournier, Michel (Edouard)
1924- .... **CLC 6, 23, 36**
See also CA 49-52; CANR 3, 36; DLB 83;
MTCW; SATA 23

Tournimparte, Alessandra
See Ginzburg, Natalia

Towers, Ivar
See Kornbluth, C(yril) M.

Townsend, Sue 1946- .... **CLC 61**
See also CA 119; 127; MTCW; SATA 48,
55

Townshend, Peter (Dennis Blandford)
1945- .... **CLC 17, 42**
See also CA 107

Tozzi, Federigo 1883-1920........ **TCLC 31**

Traill, Catharine Parr
1802-1899 .... **NCLC 31**
See also DLB 99

Trakl, Georg 1887-1914.......... **TCLC 5**
See also CA 104

Transtroemer, Tomas (Goesta)
1931- .... **CLC 52, 65**
See also CA 117; 129

Transtromer, Tomas Gosta
See Transtroemer, Tomas (Goesta)

Traven, B. (?)-1969............. **CLC 8, 11**
See also CA 19-20; 25-28R; CAP 2; DLB 9,
56; MTCW

Treitel, Jonathan 1959- .... **CLC 70**

Tremain, Rose 1943-.............. **CLC 42**
See also CA 97-100; DLB 14

Tremblay, Michel 1942-.......... **CLC 29**
See also CA 116; 128; DLB 60; MTCW

Trevanian (a pseudonym) 1930(?)-... **CLC 29**
See also CA 108

Trevor, Glen
See Hilton, James

Trevor, William
1928- .... **CLC 7, 9, 14, 25, 71**
See also Cox, William Trevor
See also DLB 14

Trifonov, Yuri (Valentinovich)
1925-1981 .... **CLC 45**
See also CA 126; 103; MTCW

Trilling, Lionel 1905-1975 .... **CLC 9, 11, 24**
See also CA 9-12R; 61-64; CANR 10;
DLB 28, 63; MTCW

Trimball, W. H.
See Mencken, H(enry) L(ouis)

Tristan
See Gomez de la Serna, Ramon

Tristram
See Housman, A(lfred) E(dward)

Trogdon, William (Lewis) 1939-
See Heat-Moon, William Least
See also CA 115; 119

Trollope, Anthony 1815-1882 .. **NCLC 6, 33**
See also CDBLB 1832-1890; DLB 21, 57;
SATA 22; WLC

Trollope, Frances 1779-1863 ..... **NCLC 30**
See also DLB 21

Trotsky, Leon 1879-1940........ **TCLC 22**
See also CA 118

Trotter (Cockburn), Catharine
1679-1749 .... **LC 8**
See also DLB 84

Trout, Kilgore
See Farmer, Philip Jose

Trow, George W. S. 1943-......... **CLC 52**
See also CA 126

Troyat, Henri 1911-.............. **CLC 23**
See also CA 45-48; CANR 2, 33; MTCW

Trudeau, G(arretson) B(eekman) 1948-
See Trudeau, Garry B.
See also CA 81-84; CANR 31; SATA 35

Trudeau, Garry B.................. **CLC 12**
See also Trudeau, G(arretson) B(eekman)
See also AITN 2

Truffaut, Francois 1932-1984....... **CLC 20**
See also CA 81-84; 113; CANR 34

Trumbo, Dalton 1905-1976 .... **CLC 19**
See also CA 21-24R; 69-72; CANR 10;
DLB 26

Trumbull, John 1750-1831....... **NCLC 30**
See also DLB 31

Trundlett, Helen B.
See Eliot, T(homas) S(tearns)

Tryon, Thomas 1926-1991 .... **CLC 3, 11**
See also AITN 1; CA 29-32R; 135;
CANR 32; MTCW

Tryon, Tom
See Tryon, Thomas

Ts'ao Hsueh-ch'in 1715(?)-1763....... **LC 1**

Tsushima, Shuji 1909-1948
See Dazai, Osamu
See also CA 107

Tsvetaeva (Efron), Marina (Ivanovna)
1892-1941 .... **TCLC 7, 35**
See also CA 104; 128; MTCW

Tuck, Lily 1938-................. **CLC 70**

Tunis, John R(oberts) 1889-1975 ... **CLC 12**
See also CA 61-64; DLB 22; MAICYA;
SATA 30, 37

Tuohy, Frank..................... **CLC 37**
See also Tuohy, John Francis
See also DLB 14

Tuohy, John Francis 1925-
See Tuohy, Frank
See also CA 5-8R; CANR 3

Turco, Lewis (Putnam) 1934- ... **CLC 11, 63**
See also CA 13-16R; CANR 24; DLBY 84

Turgenev, Ivan
1818-1883 .... **NCLC 21; SSC 7**
See also WLC

Turner, Frederick 1943-........... **CLC 48**
See also CA 73-76; CAAS 10; CANR 12,
30; DLB 40

Tusan, Stan 1936-................ **CLC 22**
See also CA 105

Tutuola, Amos 1920- .... **CLC 5, 14, 29**
See also BLC 3; BW; CA 9-12R; CANR 27;
MTCW

Twain, Mark ..... **TCLC 6, 12, 19, 36; SSC 6**
See also Clemens, Samuel Langhorne
See also DLB 11, 12, 23, 64, 74; WLC

Tyler, Anne
1941- .... **CLC 7, 11, 18, 28, 44, 59**
See also BEST 89:1; CA 9-12R; CANR 11,
33; DLB 6; DLBY 82; MTCW; SATA 7

Tyler, Royall 1757-1826.......... **NCLC 3**
See also DLB 37

Tynan, Katharine 1861-1931 .... **TCLC 3**
See also CA 104

Tytell, John 1939- .... **CLC 50**
See also CA 29-32R

Tyutchev, Fyodor 1803-1873 ..... **NCLC 34**

Tyutchev, Fyodor 1803-1873 ..... **NCLC 34**

Tzara, Tristan .... **CLC 47**
See also Rosenfeld, Samuel

Uhry, Alfred 1936-.............. **CLC 55**
See also CA 127; 133

Ulf, Haerved
See Strindberg, (Johan) August

Ulf, Harved
See Strindberg, (Johan) August

Unamuno (y Jugo), Miguel de
1864-1936 .... **TCLC 2, 9**
See also CA 104; 131; DLB 108; HW;
MTCW

Undercliffe, Errol
See Campbell, (John) Ramsey

Underwood, Miles
See Glassco, John

Undset, Sigrid 1882-1949.......... **TCLC 3**
See also CA 104; 129; MTCW; WLC

Ungaretti, Giuseppe
1888-1970 . . . . CLC 7, 11, 15
See also CA 19-20; 25-28R; CAP 2;
DLB 114

Unger, Douglas 1952- . . . . CLC 34
See also CA 130

Updike, John (Hoyer)
1932- . . . . . . CLC 1, 2, 3, 5, 7, 9, 13, 15,
23, 34, 43, 70
See also CA 1-4R; CABS 1; CANR 4, 33;
CDALB 1968-1988; DLB 2, 5; DLBD 3;
DLBY 80, 82; MTCW; WLC

Upshaw, Margaret Mitchell
See Mitchell, Margaret (Munnerlyn)

Upton, Mark
See Sanders, Lawrence

Urdang, Constance (Henriette)
1922- . . . . CLC 47
See also CA 21-24R; CANR 9, 24

Uris, Leon (Marcus) 1924- . . . . CLC 7, 32
See also AITN 1, 2; BEST 89:2; CA 1-4R;
CANR 1; MTCW; SATA 49

Urmuz
See Codrescu, Andrei

USAitzer, Hilma 1930- . . . . CLC 17
See also CA 65-68; CANR 18; SATA 31

Ustinov, Peter (Alexander) 1921- . . . . CLC 1
See also AITN 1; CA 13-16R; CANR 25;
DLB 13

V
See Chekhov, Anton (Pavlovich)

Vaculik, Ludvik 1926- . . . . CLC 7
See also CA 53-56

Valenzuela, Luisa 1938- . . . . CLC 31
See also CA 101; CANR 32; DLB 113; HW

Valera y Alcala-Galiano, Juan
1824-1905 . . . . TCLC 10
See also CA 106

Valery, (Ambroise) Paul (Toussaint Jules)
1871-1945 . . . . TCLC 4, 15
See also CA 104; 122; MTCW

Valle-Inclan, Ramon (Maria) del
1866-1936 . . . . TCLC 5
See also CA 106

Vallejo, Antonio Buero
See Buero Vallejo, Antonio

Vallejo, Cesar (Abraham)
1892-1938 . . . . TCLC 3
See also CA 105; HW

Valle Y Pena, Ramon del
See Valle-Inclan, Ramon (Maria) del

Van Ash, Cay 1918- . . . . CLC 34

Van Campen, Karl
See Campbell, John W(ood Jr.)

Vance, Gerald
See Silverberg, Robert

Vance, Jack . . . . CLC 35
See also Vance, John Holbrook
See also DLB 8

Vance, John Holbrook 1916-
See Queen, Ellery; Vance, Jack
See also CA 29-32R; CANR 17; MTCW

Van Den Bogarde, Derek Jules Gaspard Ulric
Niven 1921-
See Bogarde, Dirk
See also CA 77-80

Vandenburgh, Jane . . . . CLC 59

Vanderhaeghe, Guy 1951- . . . . CLC 41
See also CA 113

van der Post, Laurens (Jan) 1906- . . . CLC 5
See also CA 5-8R; CANR 35

van de Wetering, Janwillem 1931- . . CLC 47
See also CA 49-52; CANR 4

Van Dine, S. S. . . . . TCLC 23
See also Wright, Willard Huntington

Van Doren, Carl (Clinton)
1885-1950 . . . . TCLC 18
See also CA 111

Van Doren, Mark 1894-1972 . . . . . CLC 6, 10
See also CA 1-4R; 37-40R; CANR 3;
DLB 45; MTCW

Van Druten, John (William)
1901-1957 . . . . TCLC 2
See also CA 104; DLB 10

Van Duyn, Mona (Jane)
1921- . . . . CLC 3, 7, 63
See also CA 9-12R; CANR 7, 38; DLB 5

Van Dyne, Edith
See Baum, L(yman) Frank

van Itallie, Jean-Claude 1936- . . . . CLC 3
See also CA 45-48; CAAS 2; CANR 1;
DLB 7

Van Peebles, Melvin 1932- . . . . . . CLC 2, 20
See also BW; CA 85-88; CANR 27

Vansittart, Peter 1920- . . . . CLC 42
See also CA 1-4R; CANR 3

Van Vechten, Carl 1880-1964 . . . . . . CLC 33
See also CA 89-92; DLB 4, 9, 51

Van Vogt, A(lfred) E(lton) 1912- . . . . . CLC 1
See also CA 21-24R; CANR 28; DLB 8;
SATA 14

Vara, Madeleine
See Jackson, Laura (Riding)

Varda, Agnes 1928- . . . . CLC 16
See also CA 116; 122

Vargas Llosa, (Jorge) Mario (Pedro)
1936- . . . . CLC 3, 6, 9, 10, 15, 31, 42
See also CA 73-76; CANR 18, 32; HW;
MTCW

Vasiliu, Gheorghe 1881-1957
See Bacovia, George
See also CA 123

Vassa, Gustavus
See Equiano, Olaudah

Vassilikos, Vassilis 1933- . . . . CLC 4, 8
See also CA 81-84

Vaughn, Stephanie . . . . CLC 62

Vazov, Ivan (Minchov)
1850-1921 . . . . TCLC 25
See also CA 121

Veblen, Thorstein (Bunde)
1857-1929 . . . . TCLC 31
See also CA 115

Venison, Alfred
See Pound, Ezra (Weston Loomis)

Verdi, Marie de
See Mencken, H(enry) L(ouis)

Verdu, Matilde
See Cela, Camilo Jose

Verga, Giovanni (Carmelo)
1840-1922 . . . . TCLC 3
See also CA 104; 123

Vergil 70B.C.-19B.C. . . . . CMLC 9

Verhaeren, Emile (Adolphe Gustave)
1855-1916 . . . . TCLC 12
See also CA 109

Verlaine, Paul (Marie)
1844-1896 . . . . NCLC 2; PC 2

Verne, Jules (Gabriel) 1828-1905 . . . TCLC 6
See also CA 110; 131; MAICYA; SATA 21

Very, Jones 1813-1880 . . . . NCLC 9
See also DLB 1

Vesaas, Tarjei 1897-1970 . . . . CLC 48
See also CA 29-32R

Vialis, Gaston
See Simenon, Georges (Jacques Christian)

Vian, Boris 1920-1959 . . . . TCLC 9
See also CA 106; DLB 72

Viaud, (Louis Marie) Julien 1850-1923
See Loti, Pierre
See also CA 107

Vicar, Henry
See Felsen, Henry Gregor

Vicker, Angus
See Felsen, Henry Gregor

Vidal, Gore
1925- . . . . . CLC 2, 4, 6, 8, 10, 22, 33, 72
See also AITN 1; BEST 90:2; CA 5-8R;
CANR 13; DLB 6; MTCW

Viereck, Peter (Robert Edwin)
1916- . . . . CLC 4
See also CA 1-4R; CANR 1; DLB 5

Vigny, Alfred (Victor) de
1797-1863 . . . . NCLC 7
See also DLB 119

Vilakazi, Benedict Wallet
1906-1947 . . . . TCLC 37

Villiers de l'Isle Adam, Jean Marie Mathias
Philippe Auguste Comte
1838-1889 . . . . NCLC 3

Vincent, Gabrielle . . . . CLC 13
See also CA 126; CLR 13; MAICYA;
SATA 61

Vinci, Leonardo da 1452-1519 . . . . . . LC 12

Vine, Barbara . . . . CLC 50
See also Rendell, Ruth (Barbara)
See also BEST 90:4

Vinge, Joan D(ennison) 1948- . . . . . . CLC 30
See also CA 93-96; SATA 36

Violis, G.
See Simenon, Georges (Jacques Christian)

Visconti, Luchino 1906-1976 . . . . CLC 16
See also CA 81-84; 65-68; CANR 39

Vittorini, Elio 1908-1966 . . . . . . CLC 6, 9, 14
See also CA 133; 25-28R

Vizinczey, Stephen 1933- . . . . CLC 40
See also CA 128

Vliet, R(ussell) G(ordon)
1929-1984 .... **CLC 22**
See also CA 37-40R; 112; CANR 18

Vogau, Boris Andreyevich 1894-1937(?)
See Pilnyak, Boris
See also CA 123

Voigt, Cynthia 1942- .... **CLC 30**
See also AAYA 3; CA 106; CANR 18, 37;
CLR 13; MAICYA; SATA 33, 48

Voigt, Ellen Bryant 1943- .... **CLC 54**
See also CA 69-72; CANR 11, 29; DLB 120

Voinovich, Vladimir (Nikolaevich)
1932- .... **CLC 10, 49**
See also CA 81-84; CAAS 12; CANR 33;
MTCW

Voltaire 1694-1778 .... **LC 14**
See also WLC

von Daeniken, Erich 1935- .... **CLC 30**
See also von Daniken, Erich
See also AITN 1; CA 37-40R; CANR 17

von Daniken, Erich .... **CLC 30**
See also von Daeniken, Erich

von Heidenstam, (Carl Gustaf) Verner
See Heidenstam, (Carl Gustaf) Verner von

von Heyse, Paul (Johann Ludwig)
See Heyse, Paul (Johann Ludwig von)

von Hofmannsthal, Hugo
See Hofmannsthal, Hugo von

von Horvath, Odon
See Horvath, Oedoen von

von Horvath, Oedoen
See Horvath, Oedoen von

von Liliencron, (Friedrich Adolf Axel) Detlev
See Liliencron, (Friedrich Adolf Axel)
Detlev von

Vonnegut, Kurt Jr.
1922- ...... **CLC 1, 2, 3, 4, 5, 8, 12, 22,**
40, 60; SSC 8
See also AAYA 6; AITN 1; BEST 90:4;
CA 1-4R; CANR 1, 25;
CDALB 1968-1988; DLB 2, 8; DLBD 3;
DLBY 80; MTCW; WLC

Von Rachen, Kurt
See Hubbard, L(afayette) Ron(ald)

von Rezzori (d'Arezzo), Gregor
See Rezzori (d'Arezzo), Gregor von

von Sternberg, Josef
See Sternberg, Josef von

Vorster, Gordon 1924- .... **CLC 34**
See also CA 133

Vosce, Trudie
See Ozick, Cynthia

Voznesensky, Andrei (Andreievich)
1933- .... **CLC 1, 15, 57**
See also CA 89-92; CANR 37; MTCW

Waddington, Miriam 1917- .... **CLC 28**
See also Merritt, E. B.
See also CA 21-24R; CANR 12, 30;
DLB 68

Wagman, Fredrica 1937- .... **CLC 7**
See also CA 97-100

Wagner, Richard 1813-1883 .... **NCLC 9**

Wagner-Martin, Linda 1936- .... **CLC 50**

Wagoner, David (Russell)
1926- .... **CLC 3, 5, 15**
See also CA 1-4R; CAAS 3; CANR 2;
DLB 5; SATA 14

Wah, Fred(erick James) 1939- ...... **CLC 44**
See also CA 107; DLB 60

Wahloo, Per 1926-1975 .... **CLC 7**
See also CA 61-64

Wahloo, Peter
See Wahloo, Per

Wain, John (Barrington)
1925- .... **CLC 2, 11, 15, 46**
See also CA 5-8R; CAAS 4; CANR 23;
CDBLB 1960 to Present; DLB 15, 27;
MTCW

Wajda, Andrzej 1926- .... **CLC 16**
See also CA 102

Wakefield, Dan 1932- .... **CLC 7**
See also CA 21-24R; CAAS 7

Wakoski, Diane
1937- .... **CLC 2, 4, 7, 9, 11, 40**
See also CA 13-16R; CAAS 1; CANR 9;
DLB 5

Wakoski-Sherbell, Diane
See Wakoski, Diane

Walcott, Derek (Alton)
1930- .... **CLC 2, 4, 9, 14, 25, 42, 67**
See also BLC 3; BW; CA 89-92; CANR 26;
DLB 117; DLBY 81; MTCW

Waldman, Anne 1945- .... **CLC 7**
See also CA 37-40R; CANR 34; DLB 16

Waldo, E. Hunter
See Sturgeon, Theodore (Hamilton)

Waldo, Edward Hamilton
See Sturgeon, Theodore (Hamilton)

Walker, Alice (Malsenior)
1944- ...... **CLC 5, 6, 9, 19, 27, 46, 58;**
SSC 5
See also AAYA 3; BEST 89:4; BLC 3; BW;
CA 37-40R; CANR 9, 27;
CDALB 1968-1988; DLB 6, 33; MTCW;
SATA 31

Walker, David Harry 1911- .... **CLC 14**
See also CA 1-4R; 137; CANR 1; SATA 8,
71

Walker, Edward Joseph 1934-
See Walker, Ted
See also CA 21-24R; CANR 12, 28

Walker, George F. 1947- .... **CLC 44, 61**
See also CA 103; CANR 21; DLB 60

Walker, Joseph A. 1935- .... **CLC 19**
See also BW; CA 89-92; CANR 26; DLB 38

Walker, Margaret (Abigail)
1915- .... **CLC 1, 6**
See also BLC 3; BW; CA 73-76; CANR 26;
DLB 76; MTCW

Walker, Ted .... **CLC 13**
See also Walker, Edward Joseph
See also DLB 40

Wallace, David Foster 1962- .... **CLC 50**
See also CA 132

Wallace, Dexter
See Masters, Edgar Lee

Wallace, Irving 1916-1990 .... **CLC 7, 13**
See also AITN 1; CA 1-4R; 132; CAAS 1;
CANR 1, 27; MTCW

Wallant, Edward Lewis
1926-1962 .... **CLC 5, 10**
See also CA 1-4R; CANR 22; DLB 2, 28;
MTCW

Walpole, Horace 1717-1797 .... **LC 2**
See also DLB 39, 104

Walpole, Hugh (Seymour)
1884-1941 .... **TCLC 5**
See also CA 104; DLB 34

Walser, Martin 1927- .... **CLC 27**
See also CA 57-60; CANR 8; DLB 75

Walser, Robert 1878-1956 .... **TCLC 18**
See also CA 118; DLB 66

Walsh, Jill Paton .... **CLC 35**
See also Paton Walsh, Gillian
See also CLR 2; SAAS 3

Walter, Villiam Christian
See Andersen, Hans Christian

Wambaugh, Joseph (Aloysius Jr.)
1937- .... **CLC 3, 18**
See also AITN 1; BEST 89:3; CA 33-36R;
DLB 6; DLBY 83; MTCW

Ward, Arthur Henry Sarsfield 1883-1959
See Rohmer, Sax
See also CA 108

Ward, Douglas Turner 1930- .... **CLC 19**
See also BW; CA 81-84; CANR 27; DLB 7,
38

Warhol, Andy 1928(?)-1987 .... **CLC 20**
See also BEST 89:4; CA 89-92; 121;
CANR 34

Warner, Francis (Robert le Plastrier)
1937- .... **CLC 14**
See also CA 53-56; CANR 11

Warner, Marina 1946- .... **CLC 59**
See also CA 65-68; CANR 21

Warner, Rex (Ernest) 1905-1986. ... **CLC 45**
See also CA 89-92; 119; DLB 15

Warner, Susan (Bogert)
1819-1885 .... **NCLC 31**
See also DLB 3, 42

Warner, Sylvia (Constance) Ashton
See Ashton-Warner, Sylvia (Constance)

Warner, Sylvia Townsend
1893-1978 .... **CLC 7, 19**
See also CA 61-64; 77-80; CANR 16;
DLB 34; MTCW

Warren, Mercy Otis 1728-1814. ... **NCLC 13**
See also DLB 31

Warren, Robert Penn
1905-1989 ... **CLC 1, 4, 6, 8, 10, 13, 18,**
39, 53, 59; SSC 4
See also AITN 1; CA 13-16R; 129;
CANR 10; CDALB 1968-1988; DLB 2,
48; DLBY 80, 89; MTCW; SATA 46, 63;
WLC

Warshofsky, Isaac
See Singer, Isaac Bashevis

Warton, Thomas 1728-1790 .... **LC 15**
See also DLB 104, 109

Waruk, Kona
See Harris, (Theodore) Wilson

Warung, Price 1855-1911......... **TCLC 45**

Warwick, Jarvis
See Garner, Hugh

Washington, Alex
See Harris, Mark

Washington, Booker T(aliaferro)
1856-1915 .... **TCLC 10**
See also BLC 3; BW; CA 114; 125;
SATA 28

Wassermann, (Karl) Jakob
1873-1934 .... **TCLC 6**
See also CA 104; DLB 66

Wasserstein, Wendy 1950-...... **CLC 32, 59**
See also CA 121; 129; CABS 3

Waterhouse, Keith (Spencer)
1929- .... **CLC 47**
See also CA 5-8R; CANR 38; DLB 13, 15;
MTCW

Waters, Roger 1944-.............. **CLC 35**
See also Pink Floyd

Watkins, Frances Ellen
See Harper, Frances Ellen Watkins

Watkins, Gerrold
See Malzberg, Barry N(athaniel)

Watkins, Paul 1964-.............. **CLC 55**
See also CA 132

Watkins, Vernon Phillips
1906-1967 .... **CLC 43**
See also CA 9-10; 25-28R; CAP 1; DLB 20

Watson, Irving S.
See Mencken, H(enry) L(ouis)

Watson, John H.
See Farmer, Philip Jose

Watson, Richard F.
See Silverberg, Robert

Waugh, Auberon (Alexander) 1939- .. **CLC 7**
See also CA 45-48; CANR 6, 22; DLB 14

Waugh, Evelyn (Arthur St. John)
1903-1966 ... **CLC 1, 3, 8, 13, 19, 27, 44**
See also CA 85-88; 25-28R; CANR 22;
CDBLB 1914-1945; DLB 15; MTCW;
WLC

Waugh, Harriet 1944- .... **CLC 6**
See also CA 85-88; CANR 22

Ways, C. R.
See Blount, Roy (Alton) Jr.

Waystaff, Simon
See Swift, Jonathan

Webb, (Martha) Beatrice (Potter)
1858-1943 .... **TCLC 22**
See also Potter, Beatrice
See also CA 117

Webb, Charles (Richard) 1939-...... **CLC 7**
See also CA 25-28R

Webb, James H(enry) Jr. 1946- .... **CLC 22**
See also CA 81-84

Webb, Mary (Gladys Meredith)
1881-1927 .... **TCLC 24**
See also CA 123; DLB 34

Webb, Mrs. Sidney
See Webb, (Martha) Beatrice (Potter)

Webb, Phyllis 1927-.............. **CLC 18**
See also CA 104; CANR 23; DLB 53

Webb, Sidney (James)
1859-1947 .... **TCLC 22**
See also CA 117

Webber, Andrew Lloyd............. **CLC 21**
See also Lloyd Webber, Andrew

Weber, Lenora Mattingly
1895-1971 .... **CLC 12**
See also CA 19-20; 29-32R; CAP 1;
SATA 2, 26

Webster, John 1579(?)-1634(?) .... **DC 2**
See also CDBLB Before 1660; DLB 58;
WLC

Webster, Noah 1758-1843 .... **NCLC 30**

Wedekind, (Benjamin) Frank(lin)
1864-1918 .... **TCLC 7**
See also CA 104; DLB 118

Weidman, Jerome 1913-............ **CLC 7**
See also AITN 2; CA 1-4R; CANR 1;
DLB 28

Weil, Simone (Adolphine)
1909-1943 .... **TCLC 23**
See also CA 117

Weinstein, Nathan
See West, Nathanael

Weinstein, Nathan von Wallenstein
See West, Nathanael

Weir, Peter (Lindsay) 1944- .... **CLC 20**
See also CA 113; 123

Weiss, Peter (Ulrich)
1916-1982 .... **CLC 3, 15, 51**
See also CA 45-48; 106; CANR 3; DLB 69

Weiss, Theodore (Russell)
1916- .... **CLC 3, 8, 14**
See also CA 9-12R; CAAS 2; DLB 5

Welch, (Maurice) Denton
1915-1948 .... **TCLC 22**
See also CA 121

Welch, James 1940-......... **CLC 6, 14, 52**
See also CA 85-88

Weldon, Fay
1933(?)-....... **CLC 6, 9, 11, 19, 36, 59**
See also CA 21-24R; CANR 16;
CDBLB 1960 to Present; DLB 14;
MTCW

Wellek, Rene 1903- .... **CLC 28**
See also CA 5-8R; CAAS 7; CANR 8;
DLB 63

Weller, Michael 1942-......... **CLC 10, 53**
See also CA 85-88

Weller, Paul 1958-............... **CLC 26**

Wellershoff, Dieter 1925-.......... **CLC 46**
See also CA 89-92; CANR 16, 37

Welles, (George) Orson
1915-1985 .... **CLC 20**
See also CA 93-96; 117

Wellman, Mac 1945- .... **CLC 65**

Wellman, Manly Wade 1903-1986 .. **CLC 49**
See also CA 1-4R; 118; CANR 6, 16;
SATA 6, 47

Wells, Carolyn 1869(?)-1942 ...... **TCLC 35**
See also CA 113; DLB 11

Wells, H(erbert) G(eorge)
1866-1946 ...... **TCLC 6, 12, 19; SSC 6**
See also CA 110; 121; CDBLB 1914-1945;
DLB 34, 70; MTCW; SATA 20; WLC

Wells, Rosemary 1943-............ **CLC 12**
See also CA 85-88; CLR 16; MAICYA;
SAAS 1; SATA 18, 69

Welty, Eudora
1909- .... **CLC 1, 2, 5, 14, 22, 33; SSC 1**
See also CA 9-12R; CABS 1; CANR 32;
CDALB 1941-1968; DLB 2, 102;
DLBY 87; MTCW; WLC

Wen I-to 1899-1946 .... **TCLC 28**

Wentworth, Robert
See Hamilton, Edmond

Werfel, Franz (V.) 1890-1945 ..... **TCLC 8**
See also CA 104; DLB 81

Wergeland, Henrik Arnold
1808-1845 .... **NCLC 5**

Wersba, Barbara 1932-............ **CLC 30**
See also AAYA 2; CA 29-32R; CANR 16,
38; CLR 3; DLB 52; MAICYA; SAAS 2;
SATA 1, 58

Wertmueller, Lina 1928- .... **CLC 16**
See also CA 97-100; CANR 39

Wescott, Glenway 1901-1987....... **CLC 13**
See also CA 13-16R; 121; CANR 23;
DLB 4, 9, 102

Wesker, Arnold 1932- .... **CLC 3, 5, 42**
See also CA 1-4R; CAAS 7; CANR 1, 33;
CDBLB 1960 to Present; DLB 13;
MTCW

Wesley, Richard (Errol) 1945-....... **CLC 7**
See also BW; CA 57-60; DLB 38

Wessel, Johan Herman 1742-1785 .... **LC 7**

West, Anthony (Panther)
1914-1987 .... **CLC 50**
See also CA 45-48; 124; CANR 3, 19;
DLB 15

West, C. P.
See Wodehouse, P(elham) G(renville)

West, (Mary) Jessamyn
1902-1984 .... **CLC 7, 17**
See also CA 9-12R; 112; CANR 27; DLB 6;
DLBY 84; MTCW; SATA 37

West, Morris L(anglo) 1916-..... **CLC 6, 33**
See also CA 5-8R; CANR 24; MTCW

West, Nathanael
1903-1940 .... **TCLC 1, 14, 44**
See also CA 104; 125; CDALB 1929-1941;
DLB 4, 9, 28; MTCW

West, Paul 1930- .... **CLC 7, 14**
See also CA 13-16R; CAAS 7; CANR 22;
DLB 14

West, Rebecca 1892-1983 .. **CLC 7, 9, 31, 50**
See also CA 5-8R; 109; CANR 19; DLB 36;
DLBY 83; MTCW

Westall, Robert (Atkinson) 1929-.... **CLC 17**
See also CA 69-72; CANR 18; CLR 13;
MAICYA; SAAS 2; SATA 23, 69

Westlake, Donald E(dwin)
1933- .... **CLC 7, 33**
See also CA 17-20R; CAAS 13; CANR 16

Westmacott, Mary
See Christie, Agatha (Mary Clarissa)

Weston, Allen
See Norton, Andre

Wetcheek, J. L.
See Feuchtwanger, Lion

Wetering, Janwillem van de
See van de Wetering, Janwillem

Wetherell, Elizabeth
See Warner, Susan (Bogert)

Whalen, Philip 1923- . . . . **CLC 6, 29**
See also CA 9-12R; CANR 5, 39; DLB 16

Wharton, Edith (Newbold Jones)
1862-1937 . . . . **TCLC 3, 9, 27; SSC 6**
See also CA 104; 132; CDALB 1865-1917;
DLB 4, 9, 12, 78; MTCW; WLC

Wharton, James
See Mencken, H(enry) L(ouis)

Wharton, William (a pseudonym)
. . . . **CLC 18, 37**
See also CA 93-96; DLBY 80

Wheatley (Peters), Phillis
1754(?)-1784 . . . . **LC 3; PC 3**
See also BLC 3; CDALB 1640-1865;
DLB 31, 50; WLC

Wheelock, John Hall 1886-1978 . . . . **CLC 14**
See also CA 13-16R; 77-80; CANR 14;
DLB 45

White, E(lwyn) B(rooks)
1899-1985 . . . . **CLC 10, 34, 39**
See also AITN 2; CA 13-16R; 116;
CANR 16, 37; CLR 1, 21; DLB 11, 22;
MAICYA; MTCW; SATA 2, 29, 44

White, Edmund (Valentine III)
1940- . . . . **CLC 27**
See also AAYA 7; CA 45-48; CANR 3, 19,
36; MTCW

White, Patrick (Victor Martindale)
1912-1990 . . **CLC 3, 4, 5, 7, 9, 18, 65, 69**
See also CA 81-84; 132; MTCW

White, Phyllis Dorothy James 1920-
See James, P. D.
See also CA 21-24R; CANR 17; MTCW

White, T(erence) H(anbury)
1906-1964 . . . . **CLC 30**
See also CA 73-76; CANR 37; MAICYA;
SATA 12

White, Terence de Vere 1912- . . . . . . **CLC 49**
See also CA 49-52; CANR 3

White, Walter
See White, Walter F(rancis)
See also BLC 3

White, Walter F(rancis)
1893-1955 . . . . **TCLC 15**
See also White, Walter
See also CA 115; 124; DLB 51

White, William Hale 1831-1913
See Rutherford, Mark
See also CA 121

Whitehead, E(dward) A(nthony)
1933- . . . . **CLC 5**
See also CA 65-68

Whitemore, Hugh (John) 1936- . . . . . **CLC 37**
See also CA 132

Whitman, Sarah Helen (Power)
1803-1878 . . . . **NCLC 19**
See also DLB 1

Whitman, Walt(er)
1819-1892 . . . . **NCLC 4, 31; PC 3**
See also CDALB 1640-1865; DLB 3, 64;
SATA 20; WLC

Whitney, Phyllis A(yame) 1903- . . . . **CLC 42**
See also AITN 2; BEST 90:3; CA 1-4R;
CANR 3, 25, 38; MAICYA; SATA 1, 30

Whittemore, (Edward) Reed (Jr.)
1919- . . . . **CLC 4**
See also CA 9-12R; CAAS 8; CANR 4;
DLB 5

Whittier, John Greenleaf
1807-1892 . . . . **NCLC 8**
See also CDALB 1640-1865; DLB 1

Whittlebot, Hernia
See Coward, Noel (Peirce)

Wicker, Thomas Grey 1926-
See Wicker, Tom
See also CA 65-68; CANR 21

Wicker, Tom . . . . **CLC 7**
See also Wicker, Thomas Grey

Wideman, John Edgar
1941- . . . . **CLC 5, 34, 36, 67**
See also BLC 3; BW; CA 85-88; CANR 14;
DLB 33

Wiebe, Rudy (H.) 1934- . . . . . . **CLC 6, 11, 14**
See also CA 37-40R; DLB 60

Wieland, Christoph Martin
1733-1813 . . . . **NCLC 17**
See also DLB 97

Wieners, John 1934- . . . . **CLC 7**
See also CA 13-16R; DLB 16

Wiesel, Elie(zer) 1928- . . . . . **CLC 3, 5, 11, 37**
See also AAYA 7; AITN 1; CA 5-8R;
CAAS 4; CANR 8; DLB 83; DLBY 87;
MTCW; SATA 56

Wiggins, Marianne 1947- . . . . **CLC 57**
See also BEST 89:3; CA 130

Wight, James Alfred 1916-
See Herriot, James
See also CA 77-80; SATA 44, 55

Wilbur, Richard (Purdy)
1921- . . . . **CLC 3, 6, 9, 14, 53**
See also CA 1-4R; CABS 2; CANR 2, 29;
DLB 5; MTCW; SATA 9

Wild, Peter 1940- . . . . **CLC 14**
See also CA 37-40R; DLB 5

Wilde, Oscar (Fingal O'Flahertie Wills)
1854(?)-1900 . . . . **TCLC 1, 8, 23, 41**
See also CA 104; 119; CDBLB 1890-1914;
DLB 10, 19, 34, 57; SATA 24; WLC

Wilder, Billy . . . . **CLC 20**
See also Wilder, Samuel
See also DLB 26

Wilder, Samuel 1906-
See Wilder, Billy
See also CA 89-92

Wilder, Thornton (Niven)
1897-1975 . . . . . **CLC 1, 5, 6, 10, 15, 35;
DC 1**
See also AITN 2; CA 13-16R; 61-64;
DLB 4, 7, 9; MTCW; WLC

Wiley, Richard 1944- . . . . **CLC 44**
See also CA 121; 129

Wilhelm, Kate . . . . **CLC 7**
See also Wilhelm, Katie Gertrude
See also CAAS 5; DLB 8

Wilhelm, Katie Gertrude 1928-
See Wilhelm, Kate
See also CA 37-40R; CANR 17, 36; MTCW

Wilkins, Mary
See Freeman, Mary Eleanor Wilkins

Willard, Nancy 1936- . . . . **CLC 7, 37**
See also CA 89-92; CANR 10, 39; CLR 5;
DLB 5, 52; MAICYA; MTCW;
SATA 30, 37, 71

Williams, C(harles) K(enneth)
1936- . . . . **CLC 33, 56**
See also CA 37-40R; DLB 5

Williams, Charles
See Collier, James L(incoln)

Williams, Charles (Walter Stansby)
1886-1945 . . . . **TCLC 1, 11**
See also CA 104; DLB 100

Williams, (George) Emlyn
1905-1987 . . . . **CLC 15**
See also CA 104; 123; CANR 36; DLB 10,
77; MTCW

Williams, Hugo 1942- . . . . **CLC 42**
See also CA 17-20R; DLB 40

Williams, J. Walker
See Wodehouse, P(elham) G(renville)

Williams, John A(lfred) 1925- . . . . **CLC 5, 13**
See also BLC 3; BW; CA 53-56; CAAS 3;
CANR 6, 26; DLB 2, 33

Williams, Jonathan (Chamberlain)
1929- . . . . **CLC 13**
See also CA 9-12R; CAAS 12; CANR 8;
DLB 5

Williams, Joy 1944- . . . . **CLC 31**
See also CA 41-44R; CANR 22

Williams, Norman 1952- . . . . **CLC 39**
See also CA 118

Williams, Tennessee
1911-1983 . . . . **CLC 1, 2, 5, 7, 8, 11, 15,
19, 30, 39, 45, 71**
See also AITN 1, 2; CA 5-8R; 108;
CABS 3; CANR 31; CDALB 1941-1968;
DLB 7; DLBD 4; DLBY 83; MTCW;
WLC

Williams, Thomas (Alonzo)
1926-1990 . . . . **CLC 14**
See also CA 1-4R; 132; CANR 2

Williams, William C.
See Williams, William Carlos

Williams, William Carlos
1883-1963 . . . **CLC 1, 2, 5, 9, 13, 22, 42,
67**
See also CA 89-92; CANR 34;
CDALB 1917-1929; DLB 4, 16, 54, 86;
MTCW

Williamson, David Keith 1942- . . . . . **CLC 56**
See also CA 103

Williamson, Jack . . . . **CLC 29**
See also Williamson, John Stewart
See also CAAS 8; DLB 8

Williamson, John Stewart 1908-
See Williamson, Jack
See also CA 17-20R; CANR 23

Willie, Frederick
See Lovecraft, H(oward) P(hillips)

Willingham, Calder (Baynard Jr.)
1922- . . . . **CLC 5, 51**
See also CA 5-8R; CANR 3; DLB 2, 44;
MTCW

Willis, Charles
See Clarke, Arthur C(harles)

Willy
See Colette, (Sidonie-Gabrielle)

Willy, Colette
See Colette, (Sidonie-Gabrielle)

Wilson, A(ndrew) N(orman) 1950- . . **CLC 33**
See also CA 112; 122; DLB 14

Wilson, Angus (Frank Johnstone)
1913-1991 . . . . **CLC 2, 3, 5, 25, 34**
See also CA 5-8R; 134; CANR 21; DLB 15;
MTCW

Wilson, August
1945- . . . . **CLC 39, 50, 63; DC 2**
See also BLC 3; BW; CA 115; 122; MTCW

Wilson, Brian 1942- . . . . **CLC 12**

Wilson, Colin 1931- . . . . **CLC 3, 14**
See also CA 1-4R; CAAS 5; CANR 1, 22,
33; DLB 14; MTCW

Wilson, Dirk
See Pohl, Frederik

Wilson, Edmund
1895-1972 . . . . **CLC 1, 2, 3, 8, 24**
See also CA 1-4R; 37-40R; CANR 1;
DLB 63; MTCW

Wilson, Ethel Davis (Bryant)
1888(?)-1980 . . . . **CLC 13**
See also CA 102; DLB 68; MTCW

Wilson, John (Anthony) Burgess
1917- . . . . **CLC 8, 10, 13**
See also Burgess, Anthony
See also CA 1-4R; CANR 2; MTCW

Wilson, John 1785-1854 . . . . **NCLC 5**

Wilson, Lanford 1937- . . . . **CLC 7, 14, 36**
See also CA 17-20R; CABS 3; DLB 7

Wilson, Robert M. 1944- . . . . **CLC 7, 9**
See also CA 49-52; CANR 2; MTCW

Wilson, Robert McLiam 1964- . . . . . **CLC 59**
See also CA 132

Wilson, Sloan 1920- . . . . **CLC 32**
See also CA 1-4R; CANR 1

Wilson, Snoo 1948- . . . . **CLC 33**
See also CA 69-72

Wilson, William S(mith) 1932- . . . . . **CLC 49**
See also CA 81-84

Winchilsea, Anne (Kingsmill) Finch Counte
1661-1720 . . . . **LC 3**

Windham, Basil
See Wodehouse, P(elham) G(renville)

Wingrove, David (John) 1954- . . . . . . **CLC 68**
See also CA 133

Winters, Janet Lewis . . . . **CLC 41**
See also Lewis, Janet
See also DLBY 87

Winters, (Arthur) Yvor
1900-1968 . . . . **CLC 4, 8, 32**
See also CA 11-12; 25-28R; CAP 1;
DLB 48; MTCW

Winterson, Jeanette 1959- . . . . **CLC 64**
See also CA 136

Wiseman, Frederick 1930- . . . . **CLC 20**

Wister, Owen 1860-1938 . . . . **TCLC 21**
See also CA 108; DLB 9, 78; SATA 62

Witkacy
See Witkiewicz, Stanislaw Ignacy

Witkiewicz, Stanislaw Ignacy
1885-1939 . . . . **TCLC 8**
See also CA 105

Wittig, Monique 1935(?)- . . . . **CLC 22**
See also CA 116; 135; DLB 83

Wittlin, Jozef 1896-1976 . . . . **CLC 25**
See also CA 49-52; 65-68; CANR 3

Wodehouse, P(elham) G(renville)
1881-1975 . . . **CLC 1, 2, 5, 10, 22; SSC 2**
See also AITN 2; CA 45-48; 57-60;
CANR 3, 33; CDBLB 1914-1945;
DLB 34; MTCW; SATA 22

Woiwode, L.
See Woiwode, Larry (Alfred)

Woiwode, Larry (Alfred) 1941- . . . **CLC 6, 10**
See also CA 73-76; CANR 16; DLB 6

Wojciechowska, Maia (Teresa)
1927- . . . . **CLC 26**
See also AAYA 8; CA 9-12R; CANR 4;
CLR 1; MAICYA; SAAS 1; SATA 1, 28

Wolf, Christa 1929- . . . . **CLC 14, 29, 58**
See also CA 85-88; DLB 75; MTCW

Wolfe, Gene (Rodman) 1931- . . . . **CLC 25**
See also CA 57-60; CAAS 9; CANR 6, 32;
DLB 8

Wolfe, George C. 1954- . . . . **CLC 49**

Wolfe, Thomas (Clayton)
1900-1938 . . . . **TCLC 4, 13, 29**
See also CA 104; 132; CDALB 1929-1941;
DLB 9, 102; DLBD 2; DLBY 85;
MTCW; WLC

Wolfe, Thomas Kennerly Jr. 1930-
See Wolfe, Tom
See also CA 13-16R; CANR 9, 33; MTCW

Wolfe, Tom . . . . **CLC 1, 2, 9, 15, 35, 51**
See also Wolfe, Thomas Kennerly Jr.
See also AAYA 8; AITN 2; BEST 89:1

Wolff, Geoffrey (Ansell) 1937- . . . . . **CLC 41**
See also CA 29-32R; CANR 29

Wolff, Sonia
See Levitin, Sonia (Wolff)

Wolff, Tobias (Jonathan Ansell)
1945- . . . . **CLC 39, 64**
See also BEST 90:2; CA 114; 117

Wolfram von Eschenbach
c. 1170-c. 1220 . . . . **CMLC 5**

Wollstonecraft, Mary 1759-1797 . . . . . **LC 5**
See also CDBLB 1789-1832; DLB 39, 104

Wonder, Stevie . . . . **CLC 12**
See also Morris, Steveland Judkins

Wong, Jade Snow 1922- . . . . **CLC 17**
See also CA 109

Woodcott, Keith
See Brunner, John (Kilian Houston)

Woodruff, Robert W.
See Mencken, H(enry) L(ouis)

Woolf, (Adeline) Virginia
1882-1941 . . . . **TCLC 1, 5, 20, 43; SSC 7**
See also CA 104; 130; CDBLB 1914-1945;
DLB 36, 100; MTCW; WLC

Woollcott, Alexander (Humphreys)
1887-1943 . . . . **TCLC 5**
See also CA 105; DLB 29

Wordsworth, Dorothy
1771-1855 . . . . **NCLC 25**
See also DLB 107

Wordsworth, William
1770-1850 . . . . **NCLC 12; PC 4**
See also CDBLB 1789-1832; DLB 93, 107;
WLC

Wouk, Herman 1915- . . . . **CLC 1, 9, 38**
See also CA 5-8R; CANR 6, 33; DLBY 82;
MTCW

Wright, Charles (Penzel Jr.)
1935- . . . . **CLC 6, 13, 28**
See also CA 29-32R; CAAS 7; CANR 23,
36; DLBY 82; MTCW

Wright, Charles Stevenson 1932- . . . **CLC 49**
See also BLC 3; BW; CA 9-12R; CANR 26;
DLB 33

Wright, Jack R.
See Harris, Mark

Wright, James (Arlington)
1927-1980 . . . . **CLC 3, 5, 10, 28**
See also AITN 2; CA 49-52; 97-100;
CANR 4, 34; DLB 5; MTCW

Wright, Judith (Arandell)
1915- . . . . **CLC 11, 53**
See also CA 13-16R; CANR 31; MTCW;
SATA 14

Wright, L(aurali) R. . . . . **CLC 44**
See also CA 138

Wright, Richard B(ruce) 1937- . . . . . . **CLC 6**
See also CA 85-88; DLB 53

Wright, Richard (Nathaniel)
1908-1960 . . . **CLC 1, 3, 4, 9, 14, 21, 48;
SSC 2**
See also AAYA 5; BLC 3; BW; CA 108;
CDALB 1929-1941; DLB 76, 102;
DLBD 2; MTCW; WLC

Wright, Rick 1945- . . . . **CLC 35**
See also Pink Floyd

Wright, Rowland
See Wells, Carolyn

Wright, Stephen 1946- . . . . **CLC 33**

Wright, Willard Huntington 1888-1939
See Van Dine, S. S.
See also CA 115

Wright, William 1930- . . . . **CLC 44**
See also CA 53-56; CANR 7, 23

Wu Ch'eng-en 1500(?)-1582(?) . . . . **LC 7**

Wu Ching-tzu 1701-1754 . . . . **LC 2**

Wurlitzer, Rudolph 1938(?)- . . . **CLC 2, 4, 15**
See also CA 85-88

Wycherley, William 1641-1715 . . . . **LC 8**
See also CDBLB 1660-1789; DLB 80

Wylie, Elinor (Morton Hoyt)
1885-1928 . . . . **TCLC 8**
See also CA 105; DLB 9, 45

Wylie, Philip (Gordon) 1902-1971 . . . **CLC 43**
See also CA 21-22; 33-36R; CAP 2; DLB 9

Wyndham, John
See Harris, John (Wyndham Parkes Lucas)
Beynon

Wyss, Johann David Von
1743-1818 . . . . **NCLC 10**
See also MAICYA; SATA 27, 29

Yakumo Koizumi
See Hearn, (Patricio) Lafcadio (Tessima
Carlos)

Yanez, Jose Donoso
See Donoso (Yanez), Jose

Yanovsky, Basile S.
See Yanovsky, V(assily) S(emenovich)

Yanovsky, V(assily) S(emenovich)
1906-1989 . . . . **CLC 2, 18**
See also CA 97-100; 129

Yates, Richard 1926- . . . . **CLC 7, 8, 23**
See also CA 5-8R; CANR 10; DLB 2;
DLBY 81

Yeats, W. B.
See Yeats, William Butler

Yeats, William Butler
1865-1939 . . . . **TCLC 1, 11, 18, 31**
See also CA 104; 127; CDBLB 1890-1914;
DLB 10, 19, 98; MTCW; WLC

Yehoshua, Abraham B. 1936- . . . **CLC 13, 31**
See also CA 33-36R

Yep, Laurence Michael 1948- . . . . . . **CLC 35**
See also AAYA 5; CA 49-52; CANR 1;
CLR 3, 17; DLB 52; MAICYA; SATA 7,
69

Yerby, Frank G(arvin)
1916-1991 . . . . **CLC 1, 7, 22**
See also BLC 3; BW; CA 9-12R; 136;
CANR 16; DLB 76; MTCW

Yesenin, Sergei Alexandrovich
See Esenin, Sergei (Alexandrovich)

Yevtushenko, Yevgeny (Alexandrovich)
1933- . . . . **CLC 1, 3, 13, 26, 51**
See also CA 81-84; CANR 33; MTCW

Yezierska, Anzia 1885(?)-1970 . . . . . **CLC 46**
See also CA 126; 89-92; DLB 28; MTCW

Yglesias, Helen 1915- . . . . **CLC 7, 22**
See also CA 37-40R; CANR 15; MTCW

Yokomitsu Riichi 1898-1947 . . . . . **TCLC 47**

York, Jeremy
See Creasey, John

York, Simon
See Heinlein, Robert A(nson)

Yorke, Henry Vincent 1905-1974 . . . **CLC 13**
See also Green, Henry
See also CA 85-88; 49-52

Young, Al(bert James) 1939- . . . . **CLC 19**
See also BLC 3; BW; CA 29-32R;
CANR 26; DLB 33

Young, Andrew (John) 1885-1971 . . . . **CLC 5**
See also CA 5-8R; CANR 7, 29

Young, Collier
See Bloch, Robert (Albert)

Young, Edward 1683-1765 . . . . **LC 3**
See also DLB 95

Young, Neil 1945- . . . . **CLC 17**
See also CA 110

Yourcenar, Marguerite
1903-1987 . . . . **CLC 19, 38, 50**
See also CA 69-72; CANR 23; DLB 72;
DLBY 88; MTCW

Yurick, Sol 1925- . . . . **CLC 6**
See also CA 13-16R; CANR 25

Zamiatin, Yevgenii
See Zamyatin, Evgeny Ivanovich

Zamyatin, Evgeny Ivanovich
1884-1937 . . . . **TCLC 8, 37**
See also CA 105

Zangwill, Israel 1864-1926. . . . . . . **TCLC 16**
See also CA 109; DLB 10

Zappa, Francis Vincent Jr. 1940-
See Zappa, Frank
See also CA 108

Zappa, Frank . . . . **CLC 17**
See also Zappa, Francis Vincent Jr.

Zaturenska, Marya 1902-1982. . . . **CLC 6, 11**
See also CA 13-16R; 105; CANR 22

Zelazny, Roger (Joseph) 1937- . . . . . **CLC 21**
See also AAYA 7; CA 21-24R; CANR 26;
DLB 8; MTCW; SATA 39, 57

Zhdanov, Andrei A(lexandrovich)
1896-1948 . . . . **TCLC 18**
See also CA 117

Zhukovsky, Vasily 1783-1852 . . . . **NCLC 35**

Ziegenhagen, Eric . . . . **CLC 55**

Zimmer, Jill Schary
See Robinson, Jill

Zimmerman, Robert
See Dylan, Bob

Zindel, Paul 1936- . . . . **CLC 6, 26**
See also AAYA 2; CA 73-76; CANR 31;
CLR 3; DLB 7, 52; MAICYA; MTCW;
SATA 16, 58

Zinov'Ev, A. A.
See Zinoviev, Alexander (Aleksandrovich)

Zinoviev, Alexander (Aleksandrovich)
1922- . . . . **CLC 19**
See also CA 116; 133; CAAS 10

Zoilus
See Lovecraft, H(oward) P(hillips)

Zola, Emile 1840-1902 . . . **TCLC 1, 6, 21, 41**
See also CA 104; WLC

Zoline, Pamela 1941- . . . . **CLC 62**

Zorrilla y Moral, Jose 1817-1893 . . **NCLC 6**

Zoshchenko, Mikhail (Mikhailovich)
1895-1958 . . . . **TCLC 15**
See also CA 115

Zuckmayer, Carl 1896-1977. . . . . . . **CLC 18**
See also CA 69-72; DLB 56

Zuk, Georges
See Skelton, Robin

Zukofsky, Louis
1904-1978 . . . . **CLC 1, 2, 4, 7, 11, 18**
See also CA 9-12R; 77-80; CANR 39;
DLB 5; MTCW

Zweig, Paul 1935-1984 . . . . **CLC 34, 42**
See also CA 85-88; 113

Zweig, Stefan 1881-1942 . . . . **TCLC 17**
See also CA 112; DLB 81, 118

Literary Criticism Series
Cumulative Topic Index

This index lists all topic entries in the Gale Literary Criticism Series *Contemporary Literary Criticism, Literature Criticism from 1400 to 1800, Nineteenth-Century Literature Criticism,* and *Twentieth-Century Literary Criticism.*

Age of Johnson LC 15: 1-87
Johnson's London, 3-15
aesthetics of neoclassicism, 15-36
"age of prose and reason," 36-45
clubmen and bluestockings, 45-56
printing technology, 56-62
periodicals: "a map of busy life,"
62-74
transition, 74-86

American Civil War in Literature
NCLC 32: 1-109
overviews, 2-20
regional perspectives, 20-54
fiction popular during the war, 54-79
the historical novel, 79-108

American Frontier in Literature
NCLC 28: 1-103
definitions, 2-12
development, 12-17
nonfiction writing about the frontier,
17-30
frontier fiction, 30-45
frontier protagonists, 45-66
portrayals of Native Americans,
66-86
feminist readings, 86-98
twentieth-century reaction against
frontier literature, 98-100

**American Popular Song, Golden Age
of** TCLC 42: 1-49
background and major figures, 2-34
the lyrics of popular songs, 34-47

American Western Literature TCLC
46: 1-100
definition and development of
American Western literature, 2-7
characteristics of the Western novel,
8-23
Westerns as history and fiction,
23-34
critical reception of American
Western literature, 34-41
the Western hero, 41-73
women in Western fiction, 73-91
later Western fiction, 91-99

Arthurian Revival NCLC 36: 1-77
overviews, 2-12
Tennyson and his influence, 12-43
other leading figures, 43-73
the Arthurian legend in the visual
arts, 73-6

**Beat Generation, Literature of
the** TCLC 42: 50-102
overviews, 51-9
the Beat generation as a social
phenomenon, 59-62
development, 62-5
Beat literature, 66-96
influence, 97-100

**Bildungsroman in Nineteenth-Century
Literature** NCLC 20: 92-168
surveys, 93-113
in Germany, 113-40
in England, 140-56
female *Bildungsroman,* 156-67

Bloomsbury Group TCLC 34: 1-73
history and major figures, 2-13
definitions, 13-17
influences, 17-27
thought, 27-40
prose, 40-52
and literary criticism, 52-4
political ideals, 54-61
response to, 61-71

**Bly, Robert, *Iron John: A Book about
Men* and Men's Work** CLC 70:414-62

The Book of J CLC 65: 289-311

Businessman in American Literature
TCLC 26: 1-48
portrayal of the businessman, 1-32
themes and techniques in business
fiction, 32-47

Celtic Twilight
See **Irish Literary Renaissance**

Civic Critics, Russian NCLC 20: 402-
46
principal figures and background,
402-09
and Russian Nihilism, 410-16
aesthetic and critical views, 416-45

**Columbus, Christopher, Books on the
Quincentennial of His Arrival in the
New World** CLC 70: 329-60

**Czechoslovakian Literature of the
Twentieth Century** TCLC 42: 103-96
through World War II, 104-35
de-Stalinization, The Prague Spring,
and contemporary literature, 135-
72
Slovak literature, 172-85
Czech science fiction, 185-93

Dadaism TCLC 46: 101-71
background and major figures, 102-
16
definitions, 116-26
manifestos and commentary by
Dadaists, 126-40
theater and film, 140-58
nature and characteristics of Dadaist
writing, 158-70

Darwinism and Literature NCLC 32:
110-206
background, 110-31
direct responses to Darwin, 131-71
collateral effects of Darwinism, 171-
205

de Man, Paul, Wartime Journalism of
CLC 55: 382-424

Detective Fiction, Nineteenth-Century
NCLC 36: 78-148
origins of the genre, 79-100
history of nineteenth-century

detective fiction, 101-33
significance of nineteenth-century
  detective fiction, 133-46

Detective Fiction, Twentieth-Century
TCLC 38: 1-96
  genesis and history of the detective
    story, 3-22
  defining detective fiction, 22-32
  evolution and varieties, 32-77
  the appeal of detective fiction, 77-90

Eliot, T. S., Centenary of Birth   CLC
55: 345-75

English Caroline Literature   LC 13:
221-307
  background, 222-41
  evolution and varieties, 241-62
  the Cavalier mode, 262-75
  court and society, 275-91
  politics and religion, 291-306

**English Decadent Literature of the
1890s**   NCLC 28: 104-200
  fin de siècle: the Decadent period,
    105-19
  definitions, 120-37
  major figures: "the tragic
    generation," 137-50
  French literature and English
    literary Decadence, 150-57
  themes, 157-61
  poetry, 161-82
  periodicals, 182-96

English Essay, Rise of the
LC 18: 238-308
  definitions and origins, 239-54
  influences on the essay, 254-69
  historical background, 269-78
  the essay in the seventeenth century,
    279-93
  the essay in the eighteenth century,
    293-307

English Romantic Poetry   NCLC 28:
201-327
  overviews and reputation, 202-37
  major subjects and themes, 237-67
  forms of Romantic poetry, 267-78
  politics, society, and Romantic
    poetry, 278-99
  philosophy, religion, and Romantic
    poetry, 299-324

European Romanticism   NCLC 36:
149-284
  definitions, 149-77

origins of the movement, 177-82
Romantic theory, 182-200
themes and techniques, 200-23
Romanticism in Germany, 223-39
Romanticism in France, 240-61
Romanticism in Italy, 261-64
Romanticism in Spain, 264-68
impact and legacy, 268-82

Existentialism and Literature   TCLC
42: 197-268
  overviews and definitions, 198-209
  history and influences, 209-19
  Existentialism critiqued and
    defended, 220-35
  philosophical and religious
    perspectives, 235-41
  Existentialist fiction and drama, 241-
    67

Feminist Criticism in 1990   CLC 65:
312-60

Fifteenth-Century English Literature
LC 17: 248-334
  background, 249-72
  poetry, 272-315
  drama, 315-23
  prose, 323-33

Film and Literature   TCLC 38: 97-226
  overviews, 97-119
  film and theater, 119-34
  film and the novel, 134-45
  the art of the screenplay, 145-66
  genre literature/genre film, 167-79
  the writer and the film industry,
    179-90
  authors on film adaptations of their
    works, 190-200
  fiction into film: comparative essays
    200-23

French Enlightenment   LC 14: 81-145
  the question of definition, 82-9
  Le siècle des lumières, 89-94
  women and the salons, 94-105
  censorship, 105-15
  the philosophy of reason, 115-31
  influence and legacy, 131-44

Futurism, Italian   TCLC 42: 269-354
  principles and formative influences,
    271-79
  manifestos, 279-88
  literature, 288-303
  theater, 303-19
  art, 320-30
  music, 330-36

architecture, 336-39
and politics, 339-46
reputation and significance, 346-51

Gaelic Revival
See **Irish Literary Renaissance**

**Gates, Henry Louis, Jr., and African-
American Literary Criticism**   CLC 65:
361-405

German Exile Literature   TCLC 30:
1-58
  the writer and the Nazi state, 1-10
  definition of, 10-14
  life in exile, 14-32
  surveys, 32-50
  Austrian literature in exile, 50-2
  German publishing in the United
    States, 52-7

German Expressionism   TCLC 34: 74-
160
  history and major figures, 76-85
  aesthetic theories, 85-109
  drama, 109-26
  poetry, 126-38
  film, 138-42
  painting, 142-47
  music, 147-53
  and politics, 153-58

***Glasnost* and Contemporary Soviet
Literature**   CLC 59: 355-97

Gothic Novel   NCLC 28: 328-402
  development and major works, 328-
    34
  definitions, 334-50
  themes and techniques, 350-78
  in America, 378-85
  in Scotland, 385-91
  influence and legacy, 391-400

Harlem Renaissance   TCLC 26: 49-125
  principal issues and figures, 50-67
  the literature and its audience, 67-74
  theme and technique in poetry,
    fiction, and drama, 74-115
  and American society, 115-21
  achievement and influence, 121-22

**Havel, Václav, Playwright and
President**   CLC 65: 406-63

Holocaust, Literature of the TCLC
42: 355-450
   historical overview, 357-61
   critical overview, 361-70
   diaries and memoirs, 370-95
   novels and short stories, 395-425
   poetry, 425-41
   drama, 441-48

**Hungarian Literature of the Twentieth
Century** TCLC 26: 126-88
   surveys of, 126-47
   Nyugat and early twentieth-century
      literature, 147-56
   mid-century literature, 156-68
   and politics, 168-78
   since the 1956 revolt, 178-87

Italian Futurism
   See **Futurism, Italian**

Italian Humanism LC 12: 205-77
   origins and early development, 206-
      18
   revival of classical letters, 218-23
   humanism and other philosophies,
      224-39
   humanisms and humanists, 239-46
   the plastic arts, 246-57
   achievement and significance, 258-76

Irish Literary Renaissance TCLC 46:
172-287
   overview, 173-83
   development and major figures, 184-
      202
   influence of Irish folklore and
      mythology, 202-22
   Irish poetry, 222-34
   Irish drama and the Abbey Theatre,
      234-56
   Irish fiction, 256-86

**Muckraking Movement in American
Journalism** TCLC 34: 161-242
   development, principles, and major
      figures, 162-70
   publications, 170-79
   social and political ideas, 179-86
   targets, 186-208
   fiction, 208-19
   decline, 219-29
   impact and accomplishments, 229-40

**Multiculturalism in Literature and
Education** CLC 70: 361-413

Natural School, Russian NCLC 24:
205-40
   history and characteristics, 205-25
   contemporary criticism, 225-40

Naturalism NCLC 36: 285-382
   definitions and theories, 286-305
   critical debates on Naturalism, 305-
      16
   Naturalism in theater, 316-32
   European Naturalism, 332-61
   American Naturalism, 361-72
   the legacy of Naturalism, 372-81

New Criticism TCLC 34: 243-318
   development and ideas, 244-70
   debate and defense, 270-99
   influence and legacy, 299-315

Newgate Novel NCLC 24: 166-204
   development of Newgate literature,
      166-73
   Newgate Calendar, 173-77
   Newgate fiction, 177-95
   Newgate drama, 195-204

**New York Intellectuals and *Partisan
Review*** TCLC 30: 117-98
   development and major figures, 118-
      28
   influence of Judaism, 128-39
   Partisan Review, 139-57
   literary philosophy and practice,
      157-75
   political philosophy, 175-87
   achievement and significance, 187-97

**Nigerian Literature of the Twentieth
Century** TCLC 30: 199-265
   surveys of, 199-227
   English language and African life,
      227-45
   politics and the Nigerian writer, 245-
      54
   Nigerian writers and society, 255-62

Northern Humanism LC 16: 281-356
   background, 282-305
   precursor of the Reformation, 305-14
   the Brethren of the Common Life,
      the Devotio Moderna, and
      education, 314-40
   the impact of printing, 340-56

**Nuclear Literature: Writings and
Criticism in the Nuclear Age** TCLC
46: 288-390
   overviews, 290-301
   fiction, 301-35
   poetry, 335-38
   nuclear war in Russo-Japanese
      literature, 338-55
   nuclear war and women writers,
      355-67
   the nuclear referent and literary
      criticism, 367-88

**Opium and the Nineteenth-Century
Literary Imagination** NCLC 20: 250-
301
   original sources, 250-62
   historical background, 262-71
   and literary society, 271-79
   and literary creativity, 279-300

Periodicals, Nineteenth-Century British
NCLC 24: 100-65
   overviews, 100-30
   in the Romantic Age, 130-41
   in the Victorian era, 142-54
   and the reviewer, 154-64

Pre-Raphaelite Movement NCLC 20:
302-401
   overview, 302-04
   genesis, 304-12
   Germ and *Oxford and Cambridge
      Magazine,* 312-20
   Robert Buchanan and the "Fleshly
      School of Poetry," 320-31
   satires and parodies, 331-34
   surveys, 334-51
   aesthetics, 351-75
   sister arts of poetry and painting,
      375-94
   influence, 394-99

Psychoanalysis and Literature TCLC
38: 227-338
   overviews, 227-46
   Freud on literature, 246-51
   psychoanalytic views of the literary
      process, 251-61
   psychoanalytic theories of response
      to literature, 261-88
   psychoanalysis and literary criticism,
      288-312
   psychoanalysis as literature/literature
      as psychoanalysis, 313-34

Robin Hood, Legend of LC 19: 205-58
   origins and development of the
      Robin Hood legend, 206-20
   representations of Robin Hood, 220-
      44
   Robin Hood as hero, 244-56

**Rushdie, Salman, *Satanic Verses*
Controversy** CLC 55: 214-63; 59: 404-
56

Russian Nihilism NCLC 28: 403-47
   definitions and overviews, 404-17
   women and Nihilism, 417-27
   literature as reform: the Civic
      Critics, 427-33
   Nihilism and the Russian novel:
      Turgenev and Dostoevsky, 433-47

Topic Index

Russian Thaw TCLC 26: 189-247
  literary history of the period, 190-
    206
  theoretical debate of socialist
    realism, 206-11
  Novy Mir, 211-17
  Literary Moscow, 217-24
  Pasternak, *Zhivago,* and the Nobel
    Prize, 224-27
  poetry of liberation, 228-31
  Brodsky trial and the end of the
    Thaw, 231-36
  achievement and influence, 236-46

**Salinger, J. D., Controversy
Surrounding** *In Search of J. D.
Salinger* CLC 55: 325-44

Science Fiction, Nineteenth-Century
NCLC 24: 241-306
  background, 242-50
  definitions of the genre, 251-56
  representative works and writers,
    256-75
  themes and conventions, 276-305

Scottish Chaucerians LC 20: 363-412

Sherlock Holmes Centenary TCLC
26: 248-310
  Doyle's life and the composition of
    the Holmes stories, 248-59
  life and character of Holmes, 259-78
  method, 278-79
  Holmes and the Victorian world,
    279-92
  Sherlockian scholarship, 292-301
  Doyle and the development of the
    detective story, 301-07
  Holmes's continuing popularity, 307-
    09

Slave Narratives, American NCLC 20:
1-91
  background, 2-9
  overviews, 9-24
  contemporary responses, 24-7
  language, theme, and technique,
    27-70
  historical authenticity, 70-5
  antecedents, 75-83
  role in development of Black
    American literature, 83-8

Spanish Civil War Literature TCLC
26: 311-85
  topics in, 312-33
  British and American literature, 333-
    59
  French literature, 359-62

Spanish literature, 362-73
German literature, 373-75
political idealism and war literature,
    375-83

Spasmodic School of Poetry NCLC
24: 307-52
  history and major figures, 307-21
  the Spasmodics on poetry, 321-27
  Firmilian and critical disfavor, 327-
    39
  theme and technique, 339-47
  influence, 347-51

**Steinbeck, John, Fiftieth Anniversary
of** *The Grapes of Wrath* CLC 59: 311-
54

**Supernatural Fiction in the Nineteenth
Century** NCLC 32: 207-87
  major figures and influences, 208-35
  the Victorian ghost story, 236-54
  the influence of science and
    occultism, 254-66
  supernatural fiction and society, 266-
    86

Supernatural Fiction, Modern TCLC
30: 59-116
  evolution and varieties, 60-74
  "decline" of the ghost story, 74-86
  as a literary genre, 86-92
  technique, 92-101
  nature and appeal, 101-15

Surrealism TCLC 30: 334-406
  history and formative influences,
    335-43
  manifestos, 343-54
  philosophic, aesthetic, and political
    principles, 354-75
  poetry, 375-81
  novel, 381-86
  drama, 386-92
  film, 392-98
  painting and sculpture, 398-403
  achievement, 403-05

Symbolism, Russian TCLC 30: 266-
333
  doctrines and major figures, 267-92
  theories, 293-98
  and French Symbolism, 298-310
  themes in poetry, 310-14
  theater, 314-20
  and the fine arts, 320-32

Symbolist Movement, French NCLC
20: 169-249
  background and characteristics, 170-
    86

principles, 186-91
attacked and defended, 191-97
influences and predecessors, 197-211
and Decadence, 211-16
theater, 216-26
prose, 226-33
decline and influence, 233-47

Theater of the Absurd TCLC 38: 339-
415
  "The Theater of the Absurd," 340-
    47
  major plays and playwrights, 347-58
  and the concept of the absurd, 358-
    86
  theatrical techniques, 386-94
  predecessors of, 394-402
  influence of, 402-13

Tin Pan Alley
  See **American Popular Song, Golden
  Age of**

Transcendentalism, American NCLC
24: 1-99
  overviews, 3-23
  contemporary documents, 23-41
  theological aspects of, 42-52
  and social issues, 52-74
  literature of, 74-96

**Travel Writing in the Twentieth
Century** TCLC 30: 407-56
  conventions and traditions, 407-27
  and fiction writing, 427-43
  comparative essays on travel writers,
    443-54

Ulysses **and the Process of Textual
Reconstruction** TCLC 26: 386-416
  evaluations of the new *Ulysses,* 386-
    94
  editorial principles and procedures,
    394-401
  theoretical issues, 401-16

Utopian Literature, Nineteenth-Century
NCLC 24: 353-473
  definitions, 354-74
  overviews, 374-88
  theory, 388-408
  communities, 409-26
  fiction, 426-53
  women and fiction, 454-71

Vampire in Literature TCLC 46: 391-
454
  origins and evolution, 392-412

social and psychological perspectives,
413-44
vampire fiction and science fiction,
445-53

Victorian Novel   NCLC 32: 288-454
development and major
characteristics, 290-310
themes and techniques, 310-58
social criticism in the Victorian
novel, 359-97
urban and rural life in the Victorian
novel, 397-406
women in the Victorian novel, 406-
25
Mudie's Circulating Library, 425-34
the late-Victorian novel, 434-51

World War I Literature   TCLC 34:
392-486
overview, 393-403
English, 403-27
German, 427-50
American, 450-66
French, 466-74
and modern history, 474-82

Yellow Journalism   NCLC 36: 383-456
overviews, 384-96
major figures, 396-413
the role of reporters, 413-28
the Spanish-American War, 428-48
Yellow Journalism and society, 448-
54

Young Playwrights Festival
1988—CLC 55: 376-81
1989—CLC 59: 398-403
1990—CLC 65: 444-48

Topic Index

TCLC Cumulative Nationality Index

AMERICAN

Adams, Henry **4**
Agee, James **1, 19**
Anderson, Maxwell **2**
Anderson, Sherwood **1, 10, 24**
Atherton, Gertrude **2**
Austin, Mary **25**
Baker, Ray Stannard **47**
Barry, Philip **11**
Baum, L. Frank **7**
Beard, Charles A. **15**
Belasco, David **3**
Bell, James Madison **43**
Benchley, Robert **1**
Benét, Stephen Vincent **7**
Benét, William Rose **28**
Bierce, Ambrose **1, 7, 44**
Black Elk **33**
Bodenheim, Maxwell **44**
Bourne, Randolph S. **16**
Bradford, Gamaliel **36**
Bromfield, Louis **11**
Burroughs, Edgar Rice **2, 32**
Cabell, James Branch **6**
Cable, George Washington **4**
Cather, Willa **1, 11, 31**
Chambers, Robert W. **41**
Chandler, Raymond **1, 7**
Chapman, John Jay **7**
Chesnutt, Charles Waddell **5, 39**
Chopin, Kate **5, 14**
Comstock, Anthony **13**
Cotter, Joseph Seamon, Sr. **28**
Cram, Ralph Adams **45**
Crane, Hart **2, 5**
Crane, Stephen **11, 17, 32**
Crawford, F. Marion **10**
Crothers, Rachel **19**
Cullen, Countee **4, 37**

Davis, Rebecca Harding **6**
Davis, Richard Harding **24**
Day, Clarence **25**
DeVoto, Bernard **29**
Dreiser, Theodore **10, 18, 35**
Dunbar, Paul Laurence **2, 12**
Dunne, Finley Peter **28**
Fisher, Rudolph **11**
Fitzgerald, F. Scott **1, 6, 14, 28**
Flecker, James Elroy **43**
Fletcher, John Gould **35**
Forten, Charlotte L. **16**
Freeman, Douglas Southall **11**
Freeman, Mary Wilkins **9**
Futrelle, Jacques **19**
Gale, Zona **7**
Garland, Hamlin **3**
Gilman, Charlotte Perkins **9, 37**
Glasgow, Ellen **2, 7**
Goldman, Emma **13**
Grey, Zane **6**
Guiney, Louise Imogen **41**
Hall, James Norman **23**
Harper, Frances Ellen Watkins **14**
Harris, Joel Chandler **2**
Harte, Bret **1, 25**
Hawthorne, Julian **25**
Hearn, Lafcadio **9**
Henry, O. **1, 19**
Hergesheimer, Joseph **11**
Higginson, Thomas Wentworth **36**
Hopkins, Pauline Elizabeth **28**
Howard, Robert E. **8**
Howe, Julia Ward **21**
Howells, William Dean **7, 17, 41**
James, Henry **2, 11, 24, 40, 47**
James, William **15, 32**
Jewett, Sarah Orne **1, 22**
Johnson, James Weldon **3, 19**

Kornbluth, C. M. **8**
Kuttner, Henry **10**
Lardner, Ring **2, 14**
Lewis, Sinclair **4, 13, 23, 39**
Lewisohn, Ludwig **19**
Lindsay, Vachel **17**
Locke, Alain **43**
London, Jack **9, 15, 39**
Lovecraft, H. P. **4, 22**
Lowell, Amy **1, 8**
Markham, Edwin **47**
Marquis, Don **7**
Masters, Edgar Lee **2, 25**
McCoy, Horace **28**
McKay, Claude **7, 41**
Mencken, H. L. **13**
Millay, Edna St. Vincent **4**
Mitchell, Margaret **11**
Mitchell, S. Weir **36**
Monroe, Harriet **12**
Muir, John **28**
Nathan, George Jean **18**
Nordhoff, Charles **23**
Norris, Frank **24**
O'Neill, Eugene **1, 6, 27**
Oskison, John M. **35**
Phillips, David Graham **44**
Porter, Gene Stratton **21**
Post, Melville **39**
Rawlings, Marjorie Kinnan **4**
Reed, John **9**
Roberts, Kenneth **23**
Robinson, Edwin Arlington **5**
Rogers, Will **8**
Rölvaag, O. E. **17**
Rourke, Constance **12**
Runyon, Damon **10**
Saltus, Edgar **8**
Santayana, George **40**

Sherwood, Robert E.   3
Slesinger, Tess   10
Steffens, Lincoln   20
Stein, Gertrude   1, 6, 28
Sterling, George   20
Stevens, Wallace   3, 12, 45
Stockton, Frank R.   47
Tarbell, Ida   40
Tarkington, Booth   9
Teasdale, Sara   4
Thurman, Wallace   6
Twain, Mark   6, 12, 19, 36
Van Dine, S. S.   23
Van Doren, Carl   18
Veblen, Thorstein   31
Washington, Booker T.   10
Wells, Carolyn   35
West, Nathanael   1, 14, 44
Wharton, Edith   3, 9, 27
White, Walter   15
Wister, Owen   21
Wolfe, Thomas   4, 13, 29
Woollcott, Alexander   5
Wylie, Elinor   8

ARGENTINE
Arlt, Roberto   29
Güiraldes, Ricardo   39
Lugones, Leopoldo   15
Storni, Alfonsina   5

AUSTRALIAN
Brennan, Christopher John   17
Franklin, Miles   7
Furphy, Joseph   25
Ingamells, Rex   35
Lawson, Henry   27
Paterson, A. B.   32
Richardson, Henry Handel   4
Warung, Price   45

AUSTRIAN
Broch, Hermann   20
Hofmannsthal, Hugo von   11
Kafka, Franz   2, 6, 13, 29, 47
Kraus, Karl   5
Kubin, Alfred   23
Meyrink, Gustav   21
Musil, Robert   12
Roth, Joseph   33
Schnitzler, Arthur   4
Steiner, Rudolf   13
Trakl, Georg   5
Werfel, Franz   8
Zweig, Stefan   17

BELGIAN
Bosschère, Jean de   19
Lemonnier, Camille   22
Maeterlinck, Maurice   3
Van Ostaijen, Paul   33
Verhaeren, Émile   12

BRAZILIAN
Andrade, Mário de   43
Cunha, Euclides da   24
Lima Barreto   23
Machado de Assis, Joaquim Maria   10
Ramos, Graciliano   32

BULGARIAN
Vazov, Ivan   25

CANADIAN
Campbell, Wilfred   9
Carman, Bliss   7
Carr, Emily   32
Connor, Ralph   31
Drummond, William Henry   25
Garneau, Hector Saint- Denys   13
Grove, Frederick Philip   4
Leacock, Stephen   2
McCrae, John   12
Nelligan, Emile   14
Pickthall, Marjorie   21
Roberts, Charles G. D.   8
Scott, Duncan Campbell   6
Service, Robert W.   15
Seton, Ernest Thompson   31
Stringer, Arthur   37

CHILEAN
Huidobro, Vicente   31
Mistral, Gabriela   2

CHINESE
Liu E   15
Lu Hsün   3
Su Man-shu   24
Wen I-to   28

COLOMBIAN
Rivera, Jose Eustasio   35

CZECHOSLOVAKIAN
Čapek, Karel   6, 37
Czechoslovakian Literature of the Twentieth
   Century   42
Hašek, Jaroslav   4
Nezval, Vítězslav   44

DANISH
Brandes, Georg   10
Hansen, Martin A.   32
Jensen, Johannes V.   41
Nexo, Martin Andersen   43
Pontopiddan, Henrik   29

DUTCH
Couperus, Louis   15
Frank, Anne   17
Heijermans, Herman   24

ENGLISH
Barbellion, W. N. P.   24
Baring, Maurice   8
Beerbohm, Max   1, 24
Belloc, Hilaire   7, 18
Bennett, Arnold   5, 20
Benson, E. F.   27
Benson, Stella   17
Bentley, E. C.   12
Besant, Annie   9
Blackmore, R. D.   27
Blackwood, Algernon   5
Bridges, Robert   1
Brooke, Rupert   2, 7
Butler, Samuel   1, 33
Chesterton, G. K.   1, 6
Conrad, Joseph   1, 6, 13, 25, 43
Coppard, A. E.   5
Crowley, Aleister   7
De la Mare, Walter   4
Doughty, Charles   27
Douglas, Keith   40

Dowson, Ernest   4
Doyle, Arthur Conan   7, 26
Eddison, E. R.   15
Elizabeth   41
Ellis, Havelock   14
Field, Michael   43
Firbank, Ronald   1
Ford, Ford Madox   1, 15, 39
Freeman, R. Austin   21
Galsworthy, John   1, 45
Gilbert, W. S.   3
Gissing, George   3, 24, 47
Gosse, Edmund   28
Granville-Barker, Harley   2
Gray, John   19
Gurney, Ivor   33
Haggard, H. Rider   11
Hall, Radclyffe   12
Hardy, Thomas   4, 10, 18, 32
Henley, William Ernest   8
Hilton, James   21
Hodgson, William Hope   13
Housman, A. E.   1, 10
Housman, Laurence   7
Hudson, W. H.   29
Hulme, T. E.   21
Jacobs, W. W.   22
James, M. R.   6
Jerome, Jerome K.   23
Johnson, Lionel   19
Kaye-Smith, Sheila   20
Kipling, Rudyard   8, 17
Lawrence, D. H.   2, 9, 16, 33
Lawrence, T. E.   18
Lee, Vernon   5
Lee-Hamilton, Eugene   22
Leverson, Ada   18
Lewis, Wyndham   2, 9
Lindsay, David   15
Lowndes, Marie Belloc   12
Lowry, Malcolm   6, 40
Macaulay, Rose   7, 44
MacCarthy, Desmond   36
Manning, Frederic   25
Meredith, George   17, 43
Mew, Charlotte   8
Meynell, Alice   6
Milne, A. A.   6
Murry, John Middleton   16
Noyes, Alfred   7
Oppenheim, E. Phillips   45
Orwell, George   2, 6, 15, 31
Ouida   43
Owen, Wilfred   5, 27
Pinero, Arthur Wing   32
Powys, T. F.   9
Richardson, Dorothy   3
Rohmer, Sax   28
Rolfe, Frederick   12
Rosenberg, Isaac   12
Ruskin, John   20
Rutherford, Mark   25
Sabatini, Rafael   47
Saintsbury, George   31
Saki   3
Sapper   44
Sayers, Dorothy L.   2, 15
Shiel, M. P.   8
Sinclair, May   3, 11
Stapledon, Olaf   22
Stephen, Leslie   23
Strachey, Lytton   12

Summers, Montague 16
Sutro, Alfred 6
Swinburne, Algernon Charles 8, 36
Symons, Arthur 11
Thomas, Edward 10
Thompson, Francis 4
Van Druten, John 2
Walpole, Hugh 5
Warung, Price 45
Webb, Beatrice 22
Webb, Mary 24
Webb, Sidney 22
Welch, Denton 22
Wells, H. G. 6, 12, 19
Williams, Charles 1, 11
Woolf, Virginia 1, 5, 20, 43
Zangwill, Israel 16

ESTONIAN
Tammsaare, A. H. 27

FINNISH
Leino, Eino 24
Södergran, Edith 31

FRENCH
Alain 41
Alain-Fournier 6
Apollinaire, Guillaume 3, 8
Artaud, Antonin 3, 36
Barbusse, Henri 5
Barrès, Maurice 47
Bergson, Henri 32
Bernanos, Georges 3
Bloy, Léon 22
Bourget, Paul 12
Claudel, Paul 2, 10
Colette 1, 5, 16
Coppée, François 25
Daumal, René 14
Desnos, Robert 22
Drieu La Rochelle, Pierre 21
Dujardin, Edouard 13
Eluard, Paul 7, 41
Fargue, Léon-Paul 11
Feydeau, Georges 22
France, Anatole 9
Gide, André 5, 12, 36
Giraudoux, Jean 2, 7
Gourmont, Remy de 17
Huysmans, Joris-Karl 7
Jacob, Max 6
Jarry, Alfred 2, 14
Larbaud, Valéry 9
Leroux, Gaston 25
Loti, Pierre 11
Martin du Gard, Roger 24
Moréas, Jean 18
Nizan, Paul 40
Péguy, Charles 10
Péret, Benjamin 20
Proust, Marcel 7, 13, 33
Radiguet, Raymond 29
Renard, Jules 17
Rolland, Romain 23
Rostand, Edmond 6, 37
Roussel, Raymond 20
Saint-Exupéry, Antoine de 2
Schwob, Marcel 20
Sully Prudhomme 31
Teilhard de Chardin, Pierre 9
Valéry, Paul 4, 15

Verne, Jules 6
Vian, Boris 9
Weil, Simone 23
Zola, Emile 1, 6, 21, 41

GERMAN
Auerbach, Erich 43
Benjamin, Walter 39
Benn, Gottfried 3
Borchert, Wolfgang 5
Brecht, Bertolt 1, 6, 13, 35
Döblin, Alfred 13
Ewers, Hanns Heinz 12
Feuchtwanger, Lion 3
George, Stefan 2, 14
Hauptmann, Gerhart 4
Heym, Georg 9
Heyse, Paul 8
Huch, Ricarda 13
Kaiser, Georg 9
Klabund 44
Kolmar, Gertrud 40
Liliencron, Detlev von 18
Mann, Heinrich 9
Mann, Thomas 2, 8, 14, 21, 35, 44
Morgenstern, Christian 8
Nietzsche, Friedrich 10, 18
Raabe, Wilhelm 45
Rilke, Rainer Maria 1, 6, 19
Spengler, Oswald 25
Sternheim, Carl 8
Sudermann, Hermann 15
Toller, Ernst 10
Wassermann, Jakob 6
Wedekind, Frank 7

GHANIAN
Casely-Hayford, J. E. 24

GREEK
Cavafy, C. P. 2, 7
Kazantzakis, Nikos 2, 5, 33
Palamas, Kostes 5
Papadiamantis, Alexandros 29
Sikelianos, Angelos 39

HAITIAN
Roumain, Jacques 19

HUNGARIAN
Ady, Endre 11
Babits, Mihály 14
Csáth, Géza 13
Herzl, Theodor 36
Horváth, Ödön von 45
Hungarian Literature of the Twentieth
  Century 26
József, Attila 22
Karinthy, Frigyes 47
Mikszáth, Kálmán 31
Molnár, Ferenc 20
Móricz, Zsigmond 33
Radnóti, Miklós 16

ICELANDIC
Sigurjónsson, Jóhann 27

INDIAN
Chatterji, Saratchandra 13
Iqbal, Muhammad 28
Premchand 21
Tagore, Rabindranath 3

INDONESIAN
Anwar, Chairil 22

IRANIAN
Hedayat, Sadeq 21

IRISH
A. E. 3, 10
Cary, Joyce 1, 29
Dunsany, Lord 2
Gogarty, Oliver St. John 15
Gregory, Lady 1
Harris, Frank 24
Joyce, James 3, 8, 16, 26, 35
Ledwidge, Francis 23
Moore, George 7
O'Grady, Standish 5
Riddell, Mrs. J. H. 40
Shaw, Bernard 3, 9, 21, 45
Stephens, James 4
Stoker, Bram 8
Synge, J. M. 6, 37
Tynan, Katharine 3
Wilde, Oscar 1, 8, 23, 41
Yeats, William Butler 1, 11, 18, 31

ITALIAN
Betti, Ugo 5
Brancati, Vitaliano 12
Campana, Dino 20
Carducci, Giosuè 32
Croce, Benedetto 37
D'Annunzio, Gabriele 6, 40
Deledda, Grazia 23
Giacosa, Giuseppe 7
Lampedusa, Giuseppe Tomasi di 13
Marinetti, F. T. 10
Papini, Giovanni 22
Pascoli, Giovanni 45
Pavese, Cesare 3
Pirandello, Luigi 4, 29
Saba, Umberto 33
Svevo, Italo 2, 35
Tozzi, Federigo 31
Verga, Giovanni 3

JAMAICAN
De Lisser, H. G. 12
Garvey, Marcus 41
Mais, Roger 8
Redcam, Tom 25

JAPANESE
Akutagawa Ryūnosuke 16
Dazai Osamu 11
Futabatei Shimei 44
Hayashi Fumiko 27
Ishikawa Takuboku 15
Masaoka Shiki 18
Miyamoto Yuriko 37
Mori Ōgai 14
Natsume, Sōseki 2, 10
Rohan, Kōda 22
Shimazaki, Tōson 5
Yokomitsu Riichi 47

LATVIAN
Rainis, Janis 29

LEBANESE
Gibran, Kahlil 1, 9

Nationality Index

LESOTHAN
Mofolo, Thomas 22

LITHUANIAN
Krévé, Vincas 27

MEXICAN
Azuela, Mariano 3
Gamboa, Frederico 36
Nervo, Amado 11
Reyes, Alfonso 33
Romero, José Rubén 14

NATIVE AMERICAN
See American

NEPALI
Devkota, Laxmiprasad 23

NEW ZEALAND
Mander, Jane 31
Mansfield, Katherine 2, 8, 39

NICARAGUAN
Darío, Rubén 4

NIGERIAN
Nigerian Literature of the Twentieth
Century 30

NORWEGIAN
Bjørnson, Bjørnstjerne 7, 37
Grieg, Nordhal 10
Hamsun, Knut 2, 14
Ibsen, Henrik 2, 8, 16, 37
Kielland, Alexander 5
Lie, Jonas 5
Obstfelder, Sigbjørn 23
Skram, Amalie 25
Undset, Sigrid 3

PAKISTANI
Iqbal, Muhammad 28

PERUVIAN
Palma, Ricardo 29
Vallejo, César 3

POLISH
Asch, Sholem 3
Borowski, Tadeusz 9
Peretz, Isaac Leib 16
Przybyszewski, Stanisław 36
Reymont, Władysław Stanisław 5
Schulz, Bruno 5
Sienkiewitz, Henryk 3
Singer, Israel Joshua 33
Witkiewicz, Stanisław Ignacy 8

PORTUGUESE
Pessoa, Fernando 27

PUERTO RICAN
Hostos, Eugenio María de 24

RUMANIAN
Bacovia, George 24
Rebreanu, Liviu 28

RUSSIAN
Aldanov, Mark 23
Andreyev, Leonid 3

Annensky, Innokenty 14
Artsybashev, Mikhail 31
Babel, Isaak 2, 13
Balmont, Konstantin Dmitriyevich 11
Bely, Andrey 7
Blok, Aleksandr 5
Bryusov, Valery 10
Bulgakov, Mikhail 2, 16
Bunin, Ivan 6
Chekhov, Anton 3, 10, 31
Esenin, Sergei 4
Gladkov, Fyodor 27
Gorky, Maxim 8
Hippius, Zinaida 9
Ilf, Ilya 21
Ivanov, Vyacheslav 33
Khlebnikov, Velimir 20
Khodasevich, Vladislav 15
Korolenko, Vladimir 22
Kropotkin, Peter 36
Kuprin, Aleksandr 5
Kuzmin, Mikhail 40
Mandelstam, Osip 2, 6
Mayakovsky, Vladimir 4, 18
Merezhkovsky, Dmitri 29
Petrov, Evgeny 21
Pilnyak, Boris 23
Platonov, Andrei 14
Remizov, Alexey 27
Sologub, Fyodor 9
Tolstoy, Alexey Nikolayevich 18
Tolstoy, Leo 4, 11, 17, 28, 44
Trotsky, Leon 22
Tsvetaeva, Marina 7, 35
Zamyatin, Yevgeny Ivanovich 8, 37
Zhdanov, Andrei 18
Zoshchenko, Mikhail 15

SCOTTISH
Barrie, J. M. 2
Bridie, James 3
Brown, George Douglas 28
Buchan, John 41
Davidson, John 24
Frazer, James 32
Gibbon, Lewis Grassic 4
Graham, R. B. Cunninghame 19
Lang, Andrew 16
MacDonald, George 9
Muir, Edwin 2
Sharp. William 39
Tey, Josephine 14

SOUTH AFRICAN
Campbell, Roy 5
Mqhayi, S. E. K. 25
Schreiner, Olive 9
Smith, Pauline 25
Vilakazi, Benedict Wallet 37

SPANISH
Alas, Leopoldo 29
Barea, Arturo 14
Baroja, Pío 8
Benavente, Jacinto 3
Blasco Ibáñez, Vicente 12
Echegaray, José 4
García Lorca, Federico 1, 7
Jiménez, Juan Ramón 4
Machado, Antonio 3
Martínez Sierra, Gregorio 6
Miró, Gabriel 5

Ortega y Gasset, José 9
Pereda, José María de 16
Pérez, Galdós, Benito 27
Salinas, Pedro 17
Unamuno, Miguel de 2, 9
Valera, Juan 10
Valle-Inclán, Ramón del 5

SWEDISH
Dagerman, Stig 17
Heidenstam, Verner von 5
Lagerlöf, Selma 4, 36
Soderberg, Hjalmar 39
Strindberg, August 1, 8, 21, 47

SWISS
Ramuz, Charles-Ferdinand 33
Spitteler, Carl 12
Walser, Robert 18

TURKISH
Sait Faik 23

UKRAINIAN
Bialik, Chaim Nachman 25
Sholom Aleichem 1, 35

URUGUAYAN
Quiroga, Horacio 20
Sánchez, Florencio 37

WELSH
Davies, W. H. 5
Lewis, Alun 3
Machen, Arthur 4
Thomas, Dylan 1, 8, 45

ISBN 0-8103-7972-4

90000